NINETY THIRD EDITION
SINCE 1912

WHO'S WHO IN BASEBALL 2008

Official Lifetime Records Of Major League Players

D1096989

Editor
Pete Palmer

Associate Editor
Stuart Shea

Managing Editor
Rory S. Slifkin

EDITOR'S NOTE: *Denotes League Leader throughout the publication.

BATTERS

ABREU, BOB KELLY (BOBBY)
Born, Maracay, Venezuela, March 11, 1974.
Bats Left. Throws Right. Height, 6 feet. Weight, 210 pounds.

Year	Club	Lea	Pos	G	AB	R	H	2B	3B	HR	RBI	SB	Avg
1991 Astros	Gulf Coast	OF-SS	56	183	21	55	7	3	0	20	10	.301
1992 Asheville	So. Atl.	OF	135	480	81	140	21	4	8	48	15	.292
1993 Osceola	Fla. St.	OF	129	474	62	134	21	17	5	55	10	.283
1994 Jackson	Texas	OF	118	400	61	121	25	9	16	73	12	.303
1995 Tucson	P.C.	OF-2B	114	415	72	126	24	17	10	75	16	.304
1996 Tucson	P.C.	OF	132	484	86	138	14	16	13	68	24	.285
1996 Houston	N.L.	OF	15	22	1	5	1	0	0	1	0	.227
1997 Jackson	Texas	OF	3	12	2	2	1	0	0	0	0	.167
1997 New Orleans	A.A.	OF	47	194	25	52	9	4	2	22	7	.268
1997 Houston a-b-c	N.L.	OF	59	188	22	47	10	2	3	26	7	.250
1998 Philadelphia	N.L.	OF	151	497	68	155	29	6	17	74	19	.312
1999 Philadelphia	N.L.	OF	152	546	118	183	35	*11	20	93	27	.335
2000 Philadelphia	N.L.	OF	154	576	103	182	42	10	25	79	28	.316
2001 Philadelphia	N.L.	OF	*162	588	118	170	48	4	31	110	36	.289
2002 Philadelphia	N.L.	OF	157	572	102	176	*50	6	20	85	31	.308
2003 Philadelphia	N.L.	OF	158	577	99	173	35	1	20	101	22	.300
2004 Philadelphia	N.L.	OF	159	574	118	173	47	1	30	105	40	.301
2005 Philadelphia	N.L.	OF	*162	588	104	168	37	1	24	102	31	.286
2006 Philadelphia	N.L.	OF	98	339	61	94	25	2	8	65	20	.277
2006 New York d	A.L.	OF	58	209	37	69	16	0	7	42	10	.330
2007 New York	A.L.	OF	158	605	123	171	40	5	16	101	25	.283
Major League Totals		12 Yrs.	1643	5881	1074	1766	415	49	221	984	296	.300
Division Series												
1997 Houston	N.L.	PH	3	3	0	1	0	0	0	0	1	.333
2006 New York	A.L.	OF	4	15	2	5	1	0	0	4	0	.333
2007 New York	A.L.	OF	4	15	1	4	1	0	1	2	1	.267
Division Series Totals			11	33	3	10	2	0	1	6	2	.303

a On disabled list from May 25 to July 1, 1997.
b Selected in expansion draft by Tampa Bay Devil Rays, November 18, 1997.
c Traded to Philadelphia Phillies for infielder Kevin Stocker, November 19, 1997.
d Traded to New York Yankees with pitcher Cory Lidle for infielder C.J. Henry, pitcher Matt Smith, catcher Jesus Sanchez and pitcher Carlos Monasterios, July 30, 2006.

ABREU, ETANISLAO TONI (TONY)
Born, Puerta Plata, Puerto Rico, November 13, 1984.
Bats Both. Throws Right. Height, 5 feet, 11 inches. Weight, 200 pounds.

Year	Club	Lea	Pos	G	AB	R	H	2B	3B	HR	RBI	SB	Avg
2003 Vero Beach	Fla.St.	2B	3	10	0	0	0	0	0	0	0	.000
2003 Dodgers	Gulf Coast	2B-SS	44	163	30	48	7	5	0	20	9	.294
2004 Vero Beach	Fla.St.	SS	11	43	8	18	3	1	0	3	4	.419
2004 Columbus	So.Atl.	2B-SS	104	358	50	108	21	8	8	54	16	.302
2005 Jacksonville	Southern	2B-SS	24	96	10	24	3	2	0	9	0	.250
2006 Jacksonville	Southern	2B-SS	118	457	66	131	24	3	6	55	8	.287
2007 Las Vegas	P.C.	2B-SS-3B	54	234	48	83	22	5	2	18	5	.355
2007 Los Angeles	N.L.	3B-2B-SS	59	166	19	45	14	1	2	17	0	.271

ALFONZO, ELIEZER JESUS
Born, Puerto La Cruz, Venezuela, February 7, 1979.
Bats Right. Throws Right. Height, 6 feet. Weight, 225 pounds.

Year	Club	Lea	Pos	G	AB	R	H	2B	3B	HR	RBI	SB	Avg
1996 St. Louis	Dominican	C	24	80	6	26	5	1	1	16	2	.325
1997 Johnson Cty	Appal.	C	38	120	15	33	11	1	2	15	0	.275
1998 New Jersey	N.Y.-Penn.	C	48	175	16	43	4	1	2	19	1	.246
1999 New Jersey	N.Y.-Penn.	C	46	178	14	58	12	2	3	28	3	.326
2000 Beloit	Midwest	C	60	221	22	59	10	0	5	27	2	.267
2000 Peoria a	Midwest	C	49	175	28	54	16	0	5	21	2	.309
2001 Beloit	Midwest	C	106	397	52	110	28	2	14	48	0	.277
2002 High Desert	Calif.	C	12	43	7	15	2	0	2	9	0	.349

2

Year	Club	Lea	Pos	G	AB	R	H	2B	3B	HR	RBI	SB	Avg
2002 Huntsville b	Southern	C-1B	69	244	23	63	15	1	7	38	2	.258
2003 St. Paul (Ind) c	Northern	C	68	253	46	76	15	1	9	46	0	.300
2004 Jupiter	Fla.St.	C-1B-3B	105	399	51	112	12	2	18	70	6	.281
2004 Carolina d-e	Southern	DH	4	4	0	0	0	0	0	0	0	.000
2005 San Jose	Calif.	C	53	196	35	70	16	0	13	45	1	.357
2005 Norwich	Eastern	C	49	176	30	55	9	0	9	31	1	.313
2005 Fresno	P.C.	C	4	14	3	4	1	0	1	3	0	.286
2006 Connecticut	Eastern	C-1B	20	65	8	18	3	0	0	7	1	.277
2006 Fresno	P.C.	C	24	74	5	14	0	1	2	6	0	.189
2006 San Francisco	N.L.	C	87	286	27	76	17	2	12	39	1	.266
2007 Azl Giants.........	Arizona	C	5	13	2	6	0	0	0	5	0	.462
2007 Fresno	P.C	C	18	64	9	19	6	0	3	10	0	.297
2007 San Francisco f	N.L.	C	26	64	5	16	2	1	1	6	0	.250
Major League Totals		2 Yrs.	113	350	32	92	19	3	13	45	1	.263

a Sent by St. Louis Cardinals to Milwaukee Brewers with pitcher Matt Parker to complete trade for Fernando Vina, June 13, 2000.
b Filed for free agency October 15, 2002. Signed with Chicago Cubs organization, November 24, 2002.
c Released by Chicago Cubs, March 29, 2003. Signed with independent St. Paul (Northern), May 2003.
d Signed with Florida Marlins organization, January 9,2004.
e Filed for free agency, October 15, 2004. Signed with San Francisco Giants organization, December 16, 2004.
f On disabled list from June 9 to August 22, 2007.

ALOU, MOISES ROJAS

Born, Atlanta, Georgia, July 3, 1966.
Bats Right. Throws Right. Height, 6 feet, 3 inches. Weight, 225 pounds.

Year	Club	Lea	Pos	G	AB	R	H	2B	3B	HR	RBI	SB	Avg
1986 Watertown	N.Y.-Penn.	OF	69	254	30	60	9	*8	6	35	14	.236
1987 Macon a	So. Atl.	OF	4	8	1	1	0	0	0	0	0	.125
1987 Watertown	N.Y.-Penn.	OF	39	117	20	25	6	2	4	18	6	.214
1988 Augusta	So. Atl.	OF	105	358	58	112	23	5	7	62	24	.313
1989 Salem	Carolina	OF	86	321	50	97	29	2	14	53	12	.302
1989 Harrisburg	Eastern	OF	54	205	36	60	5	2	3	19	8	.293
1990 Buff.-Indianap.	A.A.	OF	90	326	44	86	5	6	5	37	13	.264
1990 Harrisburg	Eastern	OF	36	132	19	39	12	2	3	22	7	.295
1990 Pitts.-Montreal b	N.L.	OF	16	20	4	4	0	1	0	0	0	.200
1991 Montreal c	N.L.		INJURED—Did Not Play									
1992 Montreal d	N.L.	OF	115	341	53	96	28	2	9	56	16	.282
1993 Montreal	N.L.	OF	136	482	70	138	29	6	18	85	17	.286
1994 Montreal..........	N.L.	OF	107	422	81	143	31	5	22	78	7	.339
1995 Montreal f	N.L.	OF	93	344	48	94	22	0	14	58	4	.273
1996 Montreal g-h	N.L.	OF	143	540	87	152	28	2	21	96	9	.281
1997 Florida i	N.L.	OF	150	538	88	157	29	5	23	115	9	.292
1998 Houston	N.L.	OF	159	584	104	182	34	5	38	124	11	.312
1999 Houston j	N.L.		INJURED—Did Not Play									
2000 Houston k	N.L.	OF	126	454	82	161	28	2	30	114	3	.355
2001 Houston l-m	N.L.	OF	136	513	79	170	31	1	27	108	5	.331
2002 Daytona	Fla.St.	OF	2	8	0	5	1	0	0	2	0	.625
2002 Chicago n...........	N.L.	OF	132	484	50	133	23	1	15	61	8	.275
2003 Chicago	N.L.	OF	151	565	83	158	35	1	22	91	3	.280
2004 Chicago o.........	N.L.	OF	155	601	106	176	36	3	39	106	3	.293
2005 San Francisco p	N.L.	OF	123	427	67	137	21	3	19	63	5	.321
2006 San Francisco q-r ...	N.L.	OF	98	345	52	104	25	1	22	74	2	.301
2007 Mets...........	Gulf Coast	OF	5	15	2	5	1	0	1	3	0	.333
2007 Brooklyn........	N.Y.-Penn.	OF	1	4	0	1	0	0	0	1	0	.250
2007 New York s...........	N.L.	OF	87	328	51	112	19	1	13	49	3	.341
Major League Totals		16 Yrs.	1927	6988	1105	2117	419	39	332	1278	105	.303
Division Series													
1997 Florida	N.L.	OF	3	14	1	3	1	0	0	1	0	.214
1998 Houston............	N.L.	OF	4	16	0	3	0	0	0	0	0	.188
2001 Houston............	N.L.	OF	3	12	0	2	1	0	0	1	0	.167
2003 Chicago	N.L.	OF	5	20	3	10	1	0	0	3	1	.500
Division Series Totals			15	62	4	18	3	0	0	5	1	.290
Championship Series													
1997 Florida	N.L.	OF	5	15	0	1	1	0	0	5	0	.067
2003 Chicago	N.L.	OF	7	29	4	9	1	0	2	5	0	.310
Championship Series Totals			12	44	4	10	2	0	2	10	0	.227
World Series Record													
1997 Florida	N.L.	OF	7	28	6	9	2	0	3	9	1	.321

a On disabled list from March 31 to April 18, 1987.
b Traded to Montreal Expos organization to complete August 8 trade in which Pittsburgh Pirates acquired pitcher Zane Smith for pitcher Scott Ruskin, shortstop Willie Greene and player to be named, August 16, 1990.
c On disabled list from March 19 to end of 1991 season.
d On disabled list from July 7 to July 27, 1992.
e On disabled list from September 18 to end of 1993 season.
f On disabled list from August 19 to September 5 and September 11 to October 2, 1995.
g On disabled list from July 8 to July 23, 1996.
h Signed as free agent with Florida Marlins, December 12, 1996.
i Traded to Houston Astros for pitcher Oscar Henriquez, pitcher Manuel Barrios and player to be named later, November 11, 1997. Florida Marlins received pitcher Mark Johnson on December 16, 1997.
j On disabled list from April 3 to October 4, 1999.
k On disabled list from April 27 to May 13, 2000.
l On disabled list from March 29 to April 16, 2001.
m Filed for free agency, November 5, 2001. Signed with Chicago Cubs, December 19, 2001.
n On disabled list from March 31 to April 15, 2002.
o Filed for free agency, November 1, 2004. Signed with San Francisco Giants, December 27, 2004.
p On disabled list from April 7 to April 22 and August 3 to August 19, 2005.
q On disabled list from May 6 to June 6 and June 18 to July 6, 2006.
r Filed for free agency, October 29, 2006. Signed with New York Mets, November 20, 2006.
s On disabled list from May 13 to July 27, 2007.

AMEZAGA (DELGADO), ALFREDO

Born, Ciudad Obregon, Mexico, January 16, 1978.
Bats Both. Throws Right. Height, 5 feet, 10 inches. Weight, 165 pounds.

Year	Club	Lea	Pos	G	AB	R	H	2B	3B	HR	RBI	SB	Avg
1999 Boise	Northwest		2B-SS	48	205	52	66	6	4	2	29	14	.322
1999 Butte	Pioneer		2B-SS	8	34	11	10	2	0	0	5	6	.294
2000 Lake Elsinore	Calif.		2B-SS	108	420	90	117	13	4	4	44	73	.279
2001 Salt Lake	P.C.		SS	49	200	28	50	5	4	1	16	9	.250
2001 Arkansas	Texas		SS	70	285	50	89	10	5	4	21	24	.312
2002 Salt Lake	P.C.		SS-2B	128	518	77	130	25	7	6	51	23	.251
2002 Anaheim	A.L.		SS	12	13	3	7	2	0	0	2	1	.538
2003 Salt Lake	P.C.		SS-2B	75	317	55	110	20	5	3	45	14	.347
2003 Anaheim	A.L.		SS-3B	37	105	15	22	3	2	2	7	2	.210
2004 Salt Lake	P.C.		SS	32	135	15	35	5	2	2	14	7	.259
2004 Anaheim a	A.L.		SS-3B-2B	73	93	12	15	2	0	2	11	3	.161
2005 Indianapolis	Int.		SS-2B-OF-3B	64	185	28	63	12	2	1	12	14	.341
2005 Colorado-Pitt. b-c	N.L.		3B-SS	5	6	2	1	0	0	0	0	1	.167
2006 Florida	N.L.		OF-2B-SS-3B	132	334	42	87	9	3	3	19	20	.260
2007 Florida	N.L.		OF-SS-3B-2B	133	400	46	105	14	9	2	30	13	.262
Major League Totals		6 Yrs.		392	951	120	237	30	14	9	69	40	.249
Division Series													
2004 Anaheim	A.L.		2B	2	2	0	0	0	0	0	0	0	.000

a Claimed on waivers by Colorado Rockies, December 17, 2004.
b Claimed on waivers by Pittsburgh Pirates, April 20, 2005.
c Filed for free agency, October 15, 2005. Signed with Florida Marlins, November 22, 2005.

ANDERSON, GARRET JOSEPH

Born, Los Angeles, California, June 30, 1972.
Bats Left. Throws Left. Height, 6 feet, 3 inches. Weight, 225 pounds.

Year	Club	Lea	Pos	G	AB	R	H	2B	3B	HR	RBI	SB	Avg
1990 Mesa Angels	Arizona		OF	32	127	5	27	2	0	0	14	3	.213
1990 Boise	Northwest		OF	25	83	11	21	3	1	1	8	0	.253
1991 Quad City	Midwest		OF	105	392	40	102	22	2	2	42	5	.260
1992 Palm Springs	California		OF	81	322	46	104	15	2	1	62	1	.323
1992 Midland	Texas		OF	39	146	16	40	5	0	2	19	2	.274
1993 Vancouver	P.C.		OF-1B	124	467	57	137	34	4	4	71	3	.293
1994 Vancouver	P.C.		OF-1B	123	505	75	162	42	6	12	102	3	.321
1994 California	A.L.		OF	5	13	0	5	0	0	0	1	0	.385
1995 Vancouver	P.C.		OF	14	61	9	19	7	0	0	12	0	.311
1995 California	A.L.		OF	106	374	50	120	19	1	16	69	6	.321
1996 California	A.L.		OF	150	607	79	173	33	2	12	72	7	.285
1997 Anaheim	A.L.		OF	154	624	76	189	36	3	8	92	10	.303
1998 Anaheim	A.L.		OF	156	622	62	183	41	7	15	79	8	.294
1999 Anaheim	A.L.		OF	157	620	88	188	36	2	21	80	3	.303
2000 Anaheim	A.L.		OF	159	647	92	185	40	3	35	117	7	.286
2001 Anaheim	A.L.		OF	161	672	83	194	39	2	28	123	13	.289
2002 Anaheim	A.L.		OF	158	638	93	195	*56	3	29	123	6	.306

4

Year	Club	Lea	Pos	G	AB	R	H	2B	3B	HR	RBI	SB	Avg
2003 Anaheim	A.L.	OF	159	638	80	201	*49	4	29	116	6	.315	
2004 Rancho Cucamonga	Calif.	OF	3	9	1	4	0	0	1	1	0	.444	
2004 Anaheim a	A.L.	OF	112	442	57	133	20	1	14	75	2	.301	
2005 Los Angeles	A.L.	OF	142	575	68	163	34	1	17	96	1	.283	
2006 Los Angeles	A.L.	OF	141	543	63	152	28	2	17	85	1	.280	
2007 Rancho Cucamonga	Calif.	OF	6	18	3	4	1	0	0	2	0	.222	
2007 Los Angeles b	A.L.	OF	108	417	67	124	31	1	16	80	1	.297	
Major League Totals		14 Yrs.	1868	7432	958	2205	462	32	257	1208	71	.297	
Division Series													
2002 Anaheim	A.L.	OF	4	18	5	7	2	0	1	4	0	.389	
2004 Anaheim	A.L.	OF	3	13	1	2	0	0	0	0	0	.154	
2005 Los Angeles	A.L.	OF	5	19	2	5	0	1	2	7	0	.263	
2007 Los Angeles	A.L.	OF	3	9	0	2	1	0	0	0	0	.222	
Division Series Totals			15	59	8	16	3	1	3	11	0	.271	
Championship Series													
2002 Anaheim	A.L.	OF	5	20	3	5	1	0	1	3	0	.250	
2005 Los Angeles	A.L.	OF	5	17	2	3	0	0	1	2	0	.176	
Championship Series Totals			10	37	5	8	1	0	2	5	0	.216	
World Series Record													
2002 Anaheim	A.L.	OF	7	32	3	9	1	0	0	6	0	.281	

a On disabled list from April 22 to June 10, 2004.
b On disabled list from April 28 to June 3 and June 17 to July 3, 2007.

ANDERSON, MARLON ORDELL

Born, Montgomery, Alabama, January 6, 1974.
Bats Left. Throws Right. Height, 5 feet, 11 inches. Weight, 200 pounds.

Year	Club	Lea	Pos	G	AB	R	H	2B	3B	HR	RBI	SB	Avg
1995 Batavia a	N.Y.-Penn.	2B	74	312	52	92	13	4	3	40	22	.295	
1996 Clearwater	Fla.St.	2B	60	257	37	70	10	3	2	22	26	.272	
1996 Reading	Eastern	2B	75	314	38	86	14	3	3	28	17	.274	
1997 Reading	Eastern	2B	137	553	88	147	18	6	10	62	27	.266	
1998 Scranton-W.B.	Int.	2B	136	575	104	176	32	14	16	86	24	.306	
1998 Philadelphia	N.L.	2B	17	43	4	14	3	0	1	4	2	.326	
1999 Philadelphia	N.L.	2B	129	452	48	114	26	4	5	54	13	.252	
2000 Scranton-W.B.	Int.	2B	103	397	57	121	18	8	8	53	24	.305	
2000 Philadelphia	N.L.	2B	41	162	10	37	8	1	1	15	2	.228	
2001 Philadelphia	N.L.	2B	147	522	69	153	30	2	11	61	8	.293	
2002 Philadelphia b-c	N.L.	2B	145	539	64	139	30	6	8	48	5	.258	
2003 Tampa Bay d	A.L.	2B-OF	145	482	59	130	27	3	6	67	19	.270	
2004 St. Louis e	N.L.	2B-OF-1B	113	253	31	60	12	0	8	28	6	.237	
2005 New York f	N.L.	1B-OF-2B	123	235	31	62	9	0	7	19	6	.264	
2006 Washington-L.A. g	N.L.	2B-OF-1B	134	279	43	83	16	4	12	38	4	.297	
2007 Las Vegas	P.C.	OF-2B-1B	11	29	6	7	2	1	1	11	2	.241	
2007 New Orleans	P.C.	OF-2B	6	23	1	4	1	0	0	1	0	.174	
2007 Los Angeles-New York h-i-j	N.L.	OF-1B-2B	66	95	17	28	7	0	3	27	4	.295	
Major League Totals		10 Yrs.	1060	3062	376	820	168	20	62	361	69	.268	
Division Series													
2004 St. Louis	N.L.	PH	3	3	0	0	0	0	0	0	0	.000	
2006 Los Angeles	N.L.	OF	3	13	2	4	1	0	0	1	0	.308	
Division Series Totals			6	16	2	4	1	0	0	1	0	.250	
Championship Series													
2004 St. Louis	N.L.	2B	5	3	1	1	1	0	0	0	0	.333	
World Series Record													
2004 St. Louis	N.L.	2B-DH	4	6	0	1	1	0	0	0	0	.167	

a Drafted by Philadelphia Phillies with choice received for St. Louis Cardinals signing of Danny Jackson, June 1, 1995.
b Not offered 2003 contract, December 21, 2002.
c Signed with Tampa Bay Devil Rays, January 16, 2003.
d Not offered contract, December 21, 2003. Signed with St. Louis Cardinals, January 9, 2004.
e Released by St. Louis Cardinals, November 19, 2004. Signed with New York Mets organization, December 23, 2004.
f Filed for free agency, October 27, 2005. Signed with Washington Nationals, November 18, 2005.
g Traded to Los Angeles Dodgers for pitcher Jhonny Nunez, August 31, 2006.
h On disabled list from May 5 to June 18, 2007.
i Released by Los Angeles Dodgers, July 11, 2007. Signed with New York Mets organization, July 12, 2007.
j Filed for free agency, October 29, 2007, re-signed with New York Mets, November 9, 2007.

ATKINS, GARRETT BERNARD

Born, Orange, California, December 12, 1979.
Bats Right. Throws Right. Height, 6 feet, 3 inches. Weight, 215 pounds.

Year Club	Lea	Pos	G	AB	R	H	2B	3B	HR	RBI	SB	Avg
2000 Portland	Northwest	1B-3B	69	251	34	76	12	0	7	47	2	.303
2001 Salem	Carolina	1B-3B	135	465	70	151	43	5	5	67	6	.325
2002 Carolina	Southern	3B-1B	128	510	71	138	27	3	12	61	6	.271
2003 Colorado Springs	P.C.	3B-1B	118	439	80	140	30	1	13	67	2	.319
2003 Colorado	N.L.	3B	25	69	6	11	2	0	0	4	0	.159
2004 Colorado Springs	P.C.	3B-1B	122	445	88	163	43	3	15	94	0	.366
2004 Colorado	N.L.	3B-1B-OF	15	28	3	10	2	0	1	8	0	.357
2005 Colorado Springs	P.C.	3B	5	21	4	7	1	0	1	3	0	.333
2005 Colorado a	N.L.	3B	138	519	62	149	31	1	13	89	0	.287
2006 Colorado	N.L.	3B-1B	157	602	117	198	48	1	29	120	4	.329
2007 Colorado	N.L.	3B-1B	157	605	83	182	35	1	25	111	3	.301
Major League Totals	5 Yrs.		492	1823	271	550	118	3	68	332	7	.302
Division Series												
2007 Colorado	N.L.	3B	3	13	3	3	2	0	0	1	0	.231
Championship Series												
2007 Colorado	N.L.	3B	4	14	0	2	0	0	0	0	0	.143
World Series Record												
2007 Colorado	N.L.	3B	4	13	3	2	1	0	1	2	0	.154

a On disabled list from April 3 to April 26, 2005.

AURILIA, RICHARD SANTO (RICH)

Born, Brooklyn, New York, September 2, 1971.
Bats Right. Throws Right. Height, 6 feet. Weight, 190 pounds.

Year Club	Lea	Pos	G	AB	R	H	2B	3B	HR	RBI	SB	Avg
1992 Butte	Pioneer	SS	59	202	37	68	11	3	3	30	13	.337
1993 Charlotte	Fla. St.	SS	122	440	80	136	16	5	5	56	15	.309
1994 Tulsa	Texas	SS	129	458	67	107	18	6	12	57	10	.234
1995 Shreveport	Texas	SS	64	226	29	74	17	1	4	42	10	.327
1995 Phoenix	P.C.	SS	71	258	42	72	12	0	5	34	2	.279
1995 San Francisco	N.L.	SS	9	19	4	9	3	0	2	4	1	.474
1996 Phoenix	P.C.	SS-2B	7	30	9	13	7	0	0	4	1	.433
1996 San Francisco a	N.L.	SS-2B	105	318	27	76	7	1	3	26	4	.239
1997 Phoenix	P.C.	SS	8	34	9	10	2	0	1	5	2	.294
1997 San Francisco	N.L.	SS	46	102	16	28	8	0	5	19	1	.275
1998 San Francisco b	N.L.	SS	122	413	54	110	27	2	9	49	3	.266
1999 San Francisco	N.L.	SS	152	558	68	157	23	1	22	80	2	.281
2000 San Francisco	N.L.	SS	141	509	67	138	24	2	20	79	1	.271
2001 San Francisco	N.L.	SS	156	636	114	*206	37	5	37	97	1	.324
2002 San Francisco c	N.L.	SS	133	538	76	138	35	2	15	61	1	.257
2003 San Francisco d-e	N.L.	SS	129	505	65	140	26	1	13	58	2	.277
2004 Seattle	A.L.	SS	73	261	27	63	13	0	4	28	1	.241
2004 San Diego f-g	N.L.	3B-2B-SS-1B	51	138	22	35	8	2	2	16	0	.254
2005 Louisville	Int.	SS	1	3	2	1	1	0	0	1	0	.333
2005 Cincinnati h-i	N.L.	2B-SS-3B	114	426	61	120	23	2	14	68	2	.282
2006 Cincinnati j-k	N.L.	3B-1B-SS-2B	122	440	61	132	25	1	23	70	3	.300
2007 Fresno	P.C.	1B-3B-SS	2	6	1	2	0	0	0	2	0	.333
2007 San Francisco l	N.L.	1B-3B-SS-2B	99	329	40	83	19	2	5	33	0	.252
Major League Totals	13 Yrs.		1452	5192	702	1435	278	21	174	688	22	.276
Division Series												
2000 San Francisco	N.L.	SS	4	15	0	2	1	0	0	0	0	.133
2002 San Francisco	N.L.	SS	5	21	4	5	1	0	2	7	0	.238
2003 San Francisco	N.L.	SS	4	15	4	2	1	0	0	1	0	.133
Division Series Totals			13	51	8	9	3	0	2	8	0	.176
Championship Series												
2002 San Francisco	N.L.	SS	5	15	4	5	1	0	2	5	0	.333
World Series Record												
2002 San Francisco	N.L.	SS	7	32	5	8	2	0	2	5	0	.250

a On disabled list from September 24 to September 30, 1996.
b On disabled list from July 4 to July 20, 1998.
c On disabled list from May 20 to June 4, 2002.
d On disabled list from August 4 to August 19, 2003.
e Filed for free agency, October 27, 2003. Signed with Seattle Mariners, January 8, 2004.
f Traded to San Diego Padres for player to be named later, July 19, 2004.
g Filed for free agency, October 28, 2004. Signed with Cincinnati Reds organization, January 24, 2005.
h On disabled list from May 11 to May 29, 2005.

i Filed for free agency, November 2, 2005, re-signed with Cincinnati Reds, January 9, 2006.
j On disabled list from May 4 to May 19, 2006.
k Filed for free agency, October 31, 2006. Signed with San Francisco Giants, December 4, 2006.
l On disabled list from June 17 to July 2 and August 2 to August 17, 2007.

AUSMUS, BRADLEY DAVID (BRAD)

Born, New Haven, Connecticut, April 14, 1969.
Bats Right. Throws Right. Height, 5 feet, 11 inches. Weight, 190 pounds.

Year	Club	Lea	Pos	G	AB	R	H	2B	3B	HR	RBI	SB	Avg
1988	Oneonta	N.Y.-Penn.	C	2	4	0	1	0	0	0	0	0	.250
1988	Sarasota Yankees	Gulf C.	C	43	133	22	34	2	0	0	15	5	.256
1989	Oneonta	N.Y.-Penn.	C-3B	52	165	29	43	6	0	1	18	6	.261
1990	Prince William	Carolina	C	107	364	46	86	12	2	0	27	2	.236
1991	Prince William	Carolina	C	63	230	28	70	14	3	2	30	17	.304
1991	Albany	Eastern	C	67	229	36	61	9	2	1	29	14	.266
1992	Albany	Eastern	C	5	18	0	3	0	1	0	1	2	.167
1992	Columbus a	Int.	C-OF	111	364	48	88	14	3	2	35	19	.242
1993	Colorado Springs b	P.C.	C-OF	76	241	31	65	10	4	2	33	10	.270
1993	San Diego	N.L.	C	49	160	18	41	8	1	5	12	2	.256
1994	San Diego	N.L.	C-1B	101	327	45	82	12	1	7	24	5	.251
1995	San Diego	N.L.	C-1B	103	328	44	96	16	4	5	34	16	.293
1996	San Diego	N.L.	C	50	149	16	27	4	0	1	13	1	.181
1996	Detroit d	A.L.	C	75	226	30	56	12	0	4	22	3	.248
1997	Houston	N.L.	C	130	425	45	113	25	1	4	44	14	.266
1998	Houston e	N.L.	C	128	412	62	111	10	4	6	45	10	.269
1999	Detroit	A.L.	C	127	458	62	126	25	6	9	54	12	.275
2000	Detroit f	A.L.	C-1-2-3B	150	523	75	139	25	3	7	51	11	.266
2001	Houston	N.L.	C	128	422	45	98	23	4	5	34	4	.232
2002	Houston	N.L.	C	130	447	57	115	19	3	6	50	2	.257
2003	Houston g	N.L.	C	143	450	43	103	12	2	4	47	5	.229
2004	Houston	N.L.	C	129	403	38	100	14	1	5	31	2	.248
2005	Houston h	N.L.	C-2B-SS	134	387	35	100	19	0	3	47	5	.258
2006	Houston	N.L.	C-2B-1B	139	439	37	101	16	1	2	39	3	.230
2007	Houston i	N.L.	C-1B-3B-2B	117	349	38	82	16	3	3	25	6	.235
Major League Totals		15 Yrs.		1833	5905	690	1490	256	34	76	572	101	.252
Division Series													
1997	Houston	N.L.	C	2	5	1	2	1	0	0	2	0	.400
1998	Houston	N.L.	C	4	9	0	2	0	0	0	0	0	.222
2001	Houston	N.L.	C	3	8	1	2	0	0	1	2	0	.250
2004	Houston	N.L.	C	5	9	3	3	0	0	1	1	0	.333
2005	Houston	N.L.	C-1B	4	18	3	4	1	0	1	1	0	.222
Division Series Totals				18	49	8	13	2	0	3	6	0	.265
Championship Series													
2004	Houston	N.L.	C	7	19	0	2	0	0	0	0	0	.105
2005	Houston	N.L.	C	6	22	3	7	2	0	0	1	1	.318
Championship Series Totals				13	41	3	9	2	0	0	1	1	.220
World Series Record													
2005	Houston	N.L.	C	4	16	1	4	1	0	0	0	0	.250

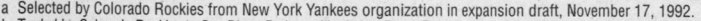

a Selected by Colorado Rockies from New York Yankees organization in expansion draft, November 17, 1992.
b Traded by Colorado Rockies to San Diego Padres with pitcher Doug Bochtler and player to be named for pitchers Greg W. Harris and Bruce Hurst, July 26; San Diego Padres acquired pitcher Andy Ashby to complete trade, July 28, 1993.
c Traded to Detroit Tigers with infielder Andujar Cedeno for catcher John Flaherty and infielder Chris Gomez, June 18, 1996.
d Traded to Houston Astros with pitcher C.J. Nitkowski, pitcher Jose Lima, pitcher Trever Miller and infielder Daryle Ward for outfielder Brian Hunter, infielder Orlando Miller, pitcher Todd Jones and pitcher Doug Brocail, December 10, 1996.
e Traded to Detroit Tigers with pitcher C.J. Nitkowski for pitcher Dean Crow, pitcher Mark Persails, pitcher Brian Powell, catcher Paul Bako and infielder Carlos Villalobos, January 14, 1999.
f Traded to Houston Astros with pitcher Doug Brocail and pitcher Nelson Cruz for pitcher Chris Holt, outfielder Roger Cedeno and catcher Mitch Meluskey, December 11, 2000.
g Filed for free agency, October 27, 2003, re-signed with Houston Astros, November 19, 2003.
h Filed for free agency, November 1, 2005, re-signed with Houston Astros, December 13, 2005.
i Filed for free agency, October 29, 2007, re-signed with Houston Astros, November 2, 2007.

AYBAR, ERICK JOHAN

Born, Bani, Dominican Republic, January 14, 1984.
Bats Both. Throws Right. Height, 5 feet, 10 inches. Weight, 170 pounds.

Year	Club	Lea	Pos	G	AB	R	H	2B	3B	HR	RBI	SB	Avg
2002	Provo	Pioneer	SS	67	273	64	89	15	6	4	29	15	.326
2003	Cedar Rapids	Midwest	SS	125	496	83	153	30	10	6	57	32	.308

Year	Club	Lea	Pos	G	AB	R	H	2B	3B	HR	RBI	SB	Avg
2004 Rancho Cucamonga	Calif.	SS-2B	136	573	102	189	25	11	14	65	51	.330
2005 Arkansas	Texas	SS	134	535	101	162	29	10	9	54	49	.303
2006 Salt Lake	P.C.	SS	81	339	63	96	20	3	6	45	32	.283
2006 Los Angeles	A.L.	SS-2B	34	40	5	10	1	1	0	2	1	.250
2007 Rancho Cucamonga	Calif.	SS	2	5	3	2	0	0	0	0	3	.400
2007 Salt Lake	P.C.	SS-2B	3	12	2	4	0	0	0	2	2	.333
2007 Los Angeles a	A.L.	2B-SS-OF-3B	79	194	18	46	5	1	1	19	4	.237
Major League Totals		2 Yrs.	113	234	23	56	6	2	1	21	5	.239
Division Series												
2007 Los Angeles	A.L.	OF	1	1	0	0	0	0	0	0	0	.000

a On disabled list from July 2 to August 6 and August 20 to September 5, 2007.

BAKER, JEFFREY GLEN (JEFF)

Born, Bad Kissingen, West Germany, June 21, 1981.
Bats Right. Throws Right. Height, 6 feet, 2 inches. Weight, 210 pounds.

Year	Club	Lea	Pos	G	AB	R	H	2B	3B	HR	RBI	SB	Avg
2003 Asheville	So.Atl.	3B	70	263	44	76	17	0	11	44	4	.289
2004 Visalia	Calif.	3B-SS	73	271	60	88	23	1	11	64	1	.325
2004 Tulsa	Texas	3B	24	91	10	27	5	1	4	20	1	.297
2005 Colorado	N.L.	3B	12	38	6	8	4	0	1	4	0	.211
2005 Colorado Springs	P.C.	3B	61	228	40	69	16	1	10	41	3	.303
2006 Colorado Springs	P.C.	OF-3B	128	482	71	147	30	4	20	108	7	.305
2006 Colorado	N.L.	OF-1B	18	57	13	21	7	2	5	21	2	.368
2007 Colorado Springs	P.C.	1B-OF	7	26	3	6	1	0	1	2	0	.231
2007 Colorado a	N.L.	1B-OF-3B	85	144	17	32	2	2	4	12	0	.222
Major League Totals		3 Yrs.	115	239	36	61	13	4	10	37	2	.255
Division Series												
2007 Colorado	N.L.	PH	1	1	0	1	0	0	0	1	0	1.000
Championship Series												
2007 Colorado	N.L.	PH	2	2	0	1	0	0	0	0	0	.500
World Series Record												
2007 Colorado	N.L.	PH	1	1	0	0	0	0	0	0	0	.000

a On disabled list from August 12 to September 1, 2007.

BAKO, GABOR PAUL (PAUL)

Born, Lafayette, Louisiana, June 20, 1972.
Bats Left. Throws Right. Height, 6 feet, 2 inches. Weight, 205 pounds.

Year	Club	Lea	Pos	G	AB	R	H	2B	3B	HR	RBI	SB	Avg
1993 Billings	Pioneer	C-1B	57	194	34	61	11	0	4	30	5	.314
1994 Winston-Sal	Carolina	C	90	289	29	59	9	1	3	26	2	.204
1995 Winston-Sal	Carolina	C	82	249	29	71	11	2	7	27	3	.285
1996 Chattanooga	Southern	C	110	360	53	106	27	0	8	48	1	.294
1997 Indianapolis a	A.A.	C	104	321	34	78	14	1	8	43	0	.243
1998 Toledo	Int.	C	13	48	5	14	3	1	1	6	0	.292
1998 Detroit	A.L.	C	96	305	23	83	12	1	3	30	1	.272
1999 New Orleans	P.C.	C	12	47	2	9	3	1	1	4	0	.191
1999 Houston b	N.L.	C	73	215	16	55	14	1	2	17	1	.256
2000 Houston-Florida-Atlanta c-d	N.L.	C-1B	81	221	18	50	10	1	2	20	0	.226
2001 Atlanta	N.L.	C	61	137	19	29	10	1	2	15	1	.212
2002 Milwaukee e-f-g	N.L.	C	87	234	24	55	8	1	4	20	0	.235
2003 Chicago	N.L.	C	70	188	19	43	13	3	0	17	0	.229
2004 Chicago	N.L.	C	49	138	13	28	8	0	1	10	1	.203
2005 Los Angeles h-i-j	N.L.	C	13	40	1	10	2	0	0	4	0	.250
2006 Wichita	Texas	C	3	12	3	2	0	0	0	2	0	.167
2006 Kansas City k-l	A.L.	C	56	153	7	32	3	0	0	10	0	.209
2007 Baltimore m	A.L.	C	60	156	13	32	3	1	1	8	0	.205
Major League Totals		10 Yrs.	646	1787	153	417	83	9	15	151	4	.233
Division Series												
2000 Atlanta	N.L.	C	2	1	0	0	0	0	0	0	0	.000
2001 Atlanta	N.L.	C	3	7	1	2	1	0	1	3	0	.286
2003 Chicago	N.L.	C	3	4	0	0	0	0	0	1	0	.000
Division Series Totals			8	12	1	2	1	0	1	4	0	.167
Championship Series												
2001 Atlanta	N.L.	C	3	3	0	0	0	0	0	0	0	.000
2003 Chicago	N.L.	C	6	16	4	4	1	0	0	1	0	.250
Championship Series Totals			9	19	4	4	1	0	0	1	0	.211

a Traded to Detroit Tigers by Cincinnati Reds with pitcher Donne Wall for outfielder Melvin Nieves, November 11, 1997.
b Traded to Houston Astros with pitcher Dean Crow, pitcher Mark Persails, pitcher Brian Powell and infielder Carlos Villalobos for pitcher C.J. Nitkowski and catcher Brad Ausmus, January 14, 1999.
c Traded to Florida Marlins for player to be named later, April 11, 2000. Houston Astros received cash to complete trade, October 10, 2000.
d Claimed on waivers by Atlanta Braves, July 21, 2000.
e On disabled list from June 9 to June 24, 2002.
f Traded to Milwaukee Brewers with pitcher Jose Cabrera for catcher Henry Blanco, March 19, 2002.
g Traded to Chicago Cubs for player to be named later, November 26, 2002. Milwaukee Brewers received infielder Ryan Gipp to complete trade, December 16, 2002.
h Filed for free agency, October 29, 2004. Signed with Los Angeles Dodgers, January 13, 2005.
i On disabled list from May 27 to October 28, 2005.
j Filed for free agency, October 31, 2005. Signed with Kansas City Royals, December 16, 2005.
k On disabled list from July 2 to August 2, 2006.
l Filed for free agency, October 30, 2006. Signed with Baltimore Orioles, December 6, 2006.
m Filed for free agency, October 30, 2007.

BALDELLI, ROCCO DANIEL

Born, Woonsocket, Rhode Island, September 25, 1981.
Bats Right. Throws Right. Height, 6 feet, 4 inches. Weight, 200 pounds.

Year	Club	Lea	Pos	G	AB	R	H	2B	3B	HR	RBI	SB	Avg
2000 Princeton	Appal.	OF-3B	60	232	33	50	9	2	3	25	11	.216
2001 Charleston-Sc	So.Atl.	OF	113	406	58	101	23	6	8	55	25	.249
2002 Bakersfield	California	OF	77	312	63	104	19	1	14	51	21	.333
2002 Orlando	Southern	OF	17	70	10	26	3	1	2	13	3	.371
2002 Durham	Int.	OF	23	96	13	28	6	1	3	7	2	.292
2003 Tampa Bay	A.L.	OF	156	637	89	184	32	8	11	78	27	.289
2004 Tampa Bay a	A.L.	OF	136	518	79	145	27	3	16	74	17	.280
2005 Tampa Bay b				INJURED—Did Not Play									
2006 Durham	Int.	OF	12	47	7	19	5	0	0	4	0	.404
2006 Tampa Bay c	A.L.	OF	92	364	59	110	24	6	16	57	10	.302
2007 Vero Beach	Fla.St.	DH	2	5	1	0	0	0	0	0	0	.000
2007 Durham	Int.	OF	2	8	2	1	0	0	1	1	0	.125
2007 Tampa Bay d	A.L.	OF	35	137	16	28	6	0	5	12	4	.204
Major League Totals		4 Yrs.	419	1656	243	467	89	17	48	221	58	.282

a On disabled list from August 14 to September 1, 2004.
b On disabled list from March 25 to November 4, 2005.
c On disabled list from March 24 to June 7, 2006.
d On disabled list from May 16 to November 12, 2007.

BARD, JOSHUA DAVID (JOSH)

Born, Ithaca, New York, March 30, 1978.
Bats Both. Throws Right. Height, 6 feet, 3 inches. Weight, 210 pounds.

Year	Club	Lea	Pos	G	AB	R	H	2B	3B	HR	RBI	SB	Avg
2000 Salem	Carolina	C	93	309	40	88	17	0	2	25	3	.285
2000 Colorado Springs	P.C.	C	4	17	0	4	0	0	0	1	0	.235
2001 Akron	Eastern	C	51	194	26	54	11	0	4	25	0	.278
2001 Buffalo	Int.	DH	1	4	0	0	0	0	0	0	0	.000
2001 Mahoning Valley	N.Y.-Penn.	C	13	44	7	12	4	0	2	8	0	.273
2001 Carolina a	Southern	C	35	124	14	32	13	0	1	24	0	.258
2002 Buffalo	Int.	C	94	344	36	102	26	2	6	53	0	.297
2002 Cleveland	A.L.	C	24	90	9	20	5	0	3	12	0	.222
2003 Cleveland	A.L.	C	91	303	25	74	13	1	8	36	0	.244
2003 Buffalo	Int.	C	35	115	14	38	7	0	5	21	1	.330
2004 Akron	Eastern	C	10	30	5	5	1	0	0	5	0	.167
2004 Buffalo	Int.	C	40	156	25	41	10	0	4	18	0	.263
2004 Cleveland b	A.L.	C	7	19	5	8	2	0	1	4	0	.421
2005 Cleveland	A.L.	C	34	83	6	16	4	0	1	9	0	.193
2006 Boston	A.L.	C	7	18	2	5	1	0	0	0	0	.278
2006 San Diego c-d	N.L.	C	93	231	28	78	19	0	9	40	1	.338
2007 San Diego e	N.L.	C	118	389	42	111	27	2	5	51	0	.285
Major League Totals		6 Yrs.	374	1133	117	312	71	3	27	152	1	.275
Division Series													
2006 San Diego	N.L.	C	3	7	0	1	0	0	0	0	0	.143

a Traded to Cleveland Indians with outfielder Jody Gerut for outfielder Jacob Cruz, June 1, 2001.
b On disabled list from March 28 to July 5, 2004.

c Traded to Boston Red Sox with outfielder Coco Crisp and pitcher David Riske for infielder Andy Marte, catcher Kelly Shoppach and pitcher Guillermo Mota, January 27, 2006.
d Traded to San Diego Padres with pitcher Cla Meredith for catcher Doug Mirabelli, May 1, 2006.
e On disabled list from April 12 to April 27, 2007.

BARFIELD, JOSHUA LAROY (JOSH)
Born, Barquisimeto, Venezuela, December 17, 1982.
Bats Right. Throws Right. Height, 6 feet. Weight, 190 pounds.

Year	Club	Lea	Pos	G	AB	R	H	2B	3B	HR	RBI	SB	Avg
2001	Idaho Falls	Pioneer	2B-SS	66	277	51	86	15	4	4	53	12	.310
2002	Lake Elsinore	Calif.	2B	6	23	2	2	0	0	0	4	0	.087
2002	Fort Wayne	Midwest	2B-OF	129	536	73	164	22	3	8	57	26	.306
2003	Lake Elsinore	Calif.	2B	135	549	99	185	46	6	16	128	16	.337
2004	Mobile	Southern	2B	138	521	79	129	28	3	18	90	4	.248
2005	Portland	P.C.	2B	137	516	74	160	25	1	15	72	20	.310
2006	San Diego a	N.L.	2B	150	539	72	151	32	3	13	58	21	.280
2007	Cleveland	A.L.	2B	130	420	53	102	19	3	3	50	14	.243
Major League Totals		2 Yrs.	280	959	125	253	51	6	16	108	35	.264
Division Series													
2006	San Diego	N.L.	2B	4	8	0	2	1	0	0	0	0	.250
Championship Series													
2007	Cleveland	A.L.	PH	1	0	0	0	0	0	0	0	1	.000

a Traded to Cleveland Indians for infielder Kevin Kouzmanoff and pitcher Andrew Brown, November 8, 2006.

BARMES, CLINT HAROLD
Born, Vincennes, Indiana, March 6, 1979.
Bats Right. Throws Right. Height, 6 feet. Weight, 210 pounds.

Year	Club	Lea	Pos	G	AB	R	H	2B	3B	HR	RBI	SB	Avg
2000	Portland	Northwest	SS-OF	45	181	37	51	6	4	2	16	12	.282
2000	Asheville	So.Atl.	2B-SS-3B-OF	19	81	11	14	4	0	0	4	4	.173
2001	Salem	Carolina	SS	38	121	17	30	3	3	0	9	4	.248
2001	Asheville	So.Atl.	SS	74	285	40	74	14	1	5	24	21	.260
2002	Carolina	Southern	SS	103	438	62	119	23	2	15	60	15	.272
2003	Colorado Springs	P.C.	SS-2B	136	493	63	136	35	1	7	54	12	.276
2003	Colorado	N.L.	SS	12	25	2	8	2	0	0	2	0	.320
2004	Colorado Springs	P.C.	SS-2B	125	533	104	175	42	2	16	51	20	.328
2004	Colorado	N.L.	2B-SS	20	71	14	20	3	1	2	10	0	.282
2005	Tulsa	Texas	SS	8	34	6	11	1	0	0	0	1	.324
2005	Colorado a	N.L.	SS	81	350	55	101	19	1	10	46	6	.289
2006	Colorado	N.L.	SS-2B	131	478	57	105	26	4	7	56	5	.220
2007	Colorado Springs	P.C.	SS-OF-2B-3B	108	428	68	128	20	6	11	44	8	.299
2007	Colorado	N.L.	SS-2B-OF-3B	27	37	5	8	3	0	0	1	0	.216
Major League Totals		5 Yrs.	271	961	133	242	53	6	19	115	11	.252

a On disabled list from June 6 to September 2, 2005.

BARRETT, MICHAEL PATRICK
Born, Atlanta, Georgia, October 22, 1976.
Bats Right. Throws Right. Height, 6 feet, 3 inches. Weight, 210 pounds.

Year	Club	Lea	Pos	G	AB	R	H	2B	3B	HR	RBI	SB	Avg
1995	Expos	Gulf Coast	SS-3B	50	183	22	57	13	4	0	19	7	.311
1995	Vermont	N.Y.-Penn.	DH-SS	3	10	0	1	0	0	0	1	0	.100
1996	Delmarva	So.Atl.	C-3B	129	474	57	113	29	4	4	62	5	.238
1997	Wst Plm Bch	Fla.St.	C	119	423	52	120	30	0	8	61	7	.284
1998	Harrisburg	Eastern	C-3B	120	453	78	145	32	2	19	87	7	.320
1998	Montreal	N.L.	C-3B	8	23	3	7	2	0	1	2	0	.304
1999	Ottawa	Int.	3B	2	7	1	3	0	0	0	2	0	.429
1999	Montreal a	N.L.	3B-C-SS	126	433	53	127	32	3	8	52	0	.293
2000	Ottawa	Int.	3B	31	120	21	43	7	0	2	19	1	.358
2000	Montreal	N.L.	3B-C	89	271	28	58	15	1	1	22	0	.214
2001	Montreal	N.L.	C	132	472	42	118	33	2	6	38	2	.250
2002	Montreal	N.L.	C-1B	117	376	41	99	20	1	12	49	6	.263
2003	Edmonton	P.C.	C	2	6	2	2	1	0	0	0	1	.333
2003	Montreal b-c-d-e	N.L.	C	70	226	33	47	9	2	10	30	0	.208
2004	Chicago	N.L.	C	134	456	55	131	32	6	16	65	1	.287
2005	Chicago	N.L.	C	133	424	48	117	32	3	16	61	0	.276
2006	Chicago f	N.L.	C	107	375	54	115	25	3	16	53	0	.307

Year	Club	Lea	Pos	G	AB	R	H	2B	3B	HR	RBI	SB	Avg
2007 Portland.............P.C.			C	3	11	2	2	1	0	0	1	0	.182
2007 Chicago-San Diego g-h-i:. N.L.			*C	101	344	29	84	17	0	9	41	2	.244
Major League Totals............		10 Yrs.		1017	3400	386	903	217	21	95	413	11	.266

a On disabled list from June 23 to July 11, 1999.
b On disabled list from July 27 to September 10, 2003.
c Traded to Oakland Athletics for player to be named later, December 15, 2003. Oakland Athletics received catcher Damian Miller to complete trade, December 21, 2003.
d Traded to Chicago Cubs for player to be named later, December 16, 2003. Montreal Expos received pitcher Brett Price to complete trade, December 19, 2003.
e Not offered contract, December 21, 2003, re-signed with Chicago Cubs, December 21, 2003.
f On disabled list from September 3 to October 2, 2006.
g Traded to San Diego Padres for catcher Rob Bowen and outfielder Kyler Burke, June 20, 2007.
h On disabled list from August 11 to September 1, 2007.
i Filed for free agency, October 29, 2007. Accepted arbitration to return to San Diego, December 7, 2007.

BARTLETT, JASON ALAN

Born, Mountain View, California, October 30, 1979.
Bats Right. Throws Right. Height, 6 feet. Weight, 180 pounds.

Year	Club	Lea	Pos	G	AB	R	H	2B	3B	HR	RBI	SB	Avg
2001 Eugene........	Northwest		SS	68	267	49	80	12	4	3	37	12	.300
2002 Lake Elsinore.....	California		SS	75	308	57	77	14	4	1	33	24	.250
2002 Fort Myers a........	Fla.St.	SS-3B-2B		39	145	24	38	7	0	2	9	11	.262
2003 New Britain........	Eastern		SS	139	548	96	162	31	8	8	48	41	.296
2004 Rochester.............	Int.	SS-2B		67	269	54	89	15	7	3	29	7	.331
2004 Twins..........	Gulf Coast		SS	5	14	1	5	1	0	0	1	0	.357
2004 Minnesota..........	A.L.	SS-2B		8	12	2	1	0	0	0	1	2	.083
2005 Rochester.............	Int.		SS	61	229	41	76	10	2	5	33	2	.332
2005 Minnesota...........	A.L.		SS	74	224	33	54	10	1	3	16	4	.241
2006 Rochester.............	Int.		SS	58	235	42	72	23	3	1	20	6	.306
2006 Minnesota...........	A.L.		SS	99	333	44	103	18	2	2	32	10	.309
2007 Minnesota a........	A.L.		SS	140	510	75	135	20	7	5	43	23	.265
Major League Totals............		4 Yrs.		321	1079	154	293	48	10	10	92	39	.272
Division Series													
2006 Minnesota...........	A.L.		SS	3	11	0	3	1	0	0	0	0	.273

a Traded by San Diego Padres to Minnesota Twins for outfielder Brian Buchanan, July 12, 2002.

BATISTA, LEOCADIO FRANCISCO (TONY)

Born, Puerto Plata, Dominican Republic, December 9, 1973.
Bats Right. Throws Right. Height, 6 feet. Weight, 190 pounds.

Year	Club	Lea	Pos	G	AB	R	H	2B	3B	HR	RBI	SB	Avg
1991 Oakland....	Dominican		2B	46	166	16	31	5	1	2	15	4	.187
1992 Athletics.......	Arizona	2B-SS-OF		45	167	32	41	6	2	0	22	1	.246
1993 Athletics.......	Arizona	3B-2B-SS		24	104	21	34	6	2	2	17	6	.327
1993 Tacoma..........	P.C.		SS	4	12	1	2	1	0	0	1	0	.167
1994 Modesto.........	Calif.	SS-2B		119	466	91	131	26	3	17	68	7	.281
1995 Huntsville.....	Southern	SS-2B		120	419	55	107	23	1	16	61	7	.255
1996 Edmonton........	P.C.		SS	57	205	33	66	17	4	8	40	2	.322
1996 Oakland..........	A.L.	2B-3B-SS		74	238	38	71	10	2	6	25	7	.298
1997 Edmonton........	P.C.		SS	33	124	25	39	10	1	3	21	2	.315
1997 Oakland a-b.......	A.L.	SS-3B-2B		68	188	22	38	10	1	4	18	2	.202
1998 Arizona...........	N.L.	2B-SS-3B		106	293	46	80	16	1	18	41	1	.273
1999 Arizona..........	N.L.		SS	44	144	16	37	5	0	5	21	2	.257
1999 Toronto c.........	A.L.		SS	98	375	61	107	25	1	26	79	2	.285
2000 Toronto...........	A.L.		3B	154	620	96	163	32	2	41	114	5	.263
2001 Toronto-Baltimore d	A.L.	3B-SS		156	579	70	138	27	6	25	87	5	.238
2002 Baltimore.........	A.L.		3B	161	615	90	150	36	1	31	87	5	.244
2003 Baltimore e.......	A.L.		3B	161	631	76	148	20	1	26	99	4	.235
2004 Montreal..........	N.L.		3B	157	606	76	146	30	2	32	110	14	.241
2005 Fukuoka f-g.	Japan Pac.		3B	135	559	78	147	29	1	27	90	3	.263
2006 Minnesota h.......	A.L.		3B	50	178	24	42	12	0	5	21	0	.236
2007 Columbus.........	Int.		3B	30	107	14	31	7	1	6	22	1	.290
2007 Washington i......	N.L.	1B-3B		80	101	10	26	3	0	2	16	0	.257
Major League Totals............		11 Yrs.		1309	4568	625	1146	226	17	221	718	47	.251

a On disabled list from August 27 to September 12, 1997.
b Selected in expansion draft by Arizona Diamondbacks, November 18, 1997.
c Traded to Toronto Blue Jays with pitcher John Frascatore for pitcher Dan Plesac, June 12, 1999.

d Claimed on waivers by Baltimore Orioles, June 25, 2001.
e Filed for free agency, October 30, 2003. Signed with Montreal Expos, December 26, 2003.
f Filed for free agency, November 4, 2004. Signed with Fukuoka Hawks, January 6, 2005.
g Signed with Minnesota Twins, December 15, 2005.
h Released by Minnesota Twins, June 19, 2006. Signed with Washington Nationals organization, February 14, 2007.
i Filed for free agency, October 15, 2007.

BAUTISTA, JOSE ANTONIO

Born, Santo Domingo, Dominican Republic, October 19, 1980.
Bats Right. Throws Right. Height, 6 feet. Weight, 190 pounds.

Year	Club	Lea	Pos	G	AB	R	H	2B	3B	HR	RBI	SB	Avg
2001	Williamsport	N.Y.-Penn.	3B-OF	62	220	43	63	10	3	5	30	8	.286
2002	Hickory	So.Atl.	3B-SS	129	438	72	132	26	3	14	57	3	.301
2003	Lynchburg	Carolina	3B-2B	51	165	28	40	14	2	4	20	1	.242
2003	Pirates a	Gulf Coast	3B	7	23	5	8	1	0	1	3	0	.348
2004	Pittsburgh	N.L.	OF	23	40	1	8	2	0	0	0	0	.200
2004	Balt.-Tam. Bay-K.C. b-c-d-e.	A.L.	3B-OF	41	48	5	10	1	0	0	2	0	.208
2005	Altoona	Eastern	3B	117	445	63	126	27	1	23	90	7	.283
2005	Indianapolis	Int.	3B	13	51	6	13	3	0	1	4	1	.255
2005	Pittsburgh	N.L.	3B	11	28	3	4	1	0	0	1	1	.143
2006	Indianapolis	Int.	3B-OF-2B	29	101	12	28	9	0	2	9	2	.277
2006	Pittsburgh	N.L.	OF-3B-2B	117	400	58	94	20	3	16	51	2	.235
2007	Pirates	Gulf Coast	3B	2	8	1	3	2	0	0	1	0	.375
2007	Pittsburgh f	N.L.	3B-OF	142	532	75	135	36	2	15	63	6	.254
Major League Totals		4 Yrs.		334	1048	142	251	60	5	31	117	9	.240

a Selected by Baltimore Orioles from Pittsburgh in Rule V draft, December 15, 2003.
b Claimed on waivers by Tampa Bay Devil Rays, June 3, 2004.
c Sold to Kansas City Royals, June 28, 2004.
d Traded to New York Mets for catcher Justin Huber, July 30, 2004.
e Traded to Pittsburgh Pirates with infielder Ty Wigginton and pitcher Matt Peterson for pitcher Kris Benson and infielder Jeff Keppinger, July 30, 2004.
f On disabled list from July 15 to August 1, 2007.

BAY, JASON RAYMOND

Born, Trail, British Columbia, Canada, September 20, 1978.
Bats Right. Throws Right. Height, 6 feet, 2 inches. Weight, 205 pounds.

Year	Club	Lea	Pos	G	AB	R	H	2B	3B	HR	RBI	SB	Avg
2000	Vermont	N.Y.-Penn.	OF	35	135	17	41	5	0	2	12	17	.304
2001	Jupiter	Fla.St.	OF-2B	38	123	12	24	4	1	1	10	10	.195
2001	Clinton	Midwest	OF	87	318	67	115	20	4	13	61	15	.362
2002	St. Lucie	Fla.St.	OF	69	261	48	71	12	2	9	54	22	.272
2002	Binghamton	Eastern	OF	34	107	17	31	4	2	4	19	13	.290
2002	Mobile a-b	Southern	OF	23	81	16	25	5	2	4	12	4	.309
2003	Portland	P.C.	OF	91	307	64	93	11	1	20	59	23	.303
2003	San Diego-Pittsburgh c-d-e.	N.L.	OF	30	87	15	25	7	1	4	14	3	.287
2004	Nashville	P.C.	OF	4	10	3	4	2	0	1	3	0	.400
2004	Pittsburgh f-g.	N.L.	OF	120	411	61	116	24	4	26	82	4	.282
2005	Pittsburgh	N.L.	OF	*162	599	110	183	44	6	32	101	21	.306
2006	Pittsburgh	N.L.	OF	159	570	101	163	29	3	35	109	11	.286
2007	Pittsburgh	N.L.	OF	145	538	78	133	25	2	21	84	4	.247
Major League Totals		5 Yrs.		616	2205	365	620	129	16	118	390	43	.281

a Traded by Montreal Expos to New York Mets with pitcher Jim Serrano for infielder Lou Collier, March 26, 2002.
b Traded to San Diego Padres with pitcher Bobby M. Jones and pitcher Josh Reynolds for pitcher Jason Middlebrook and pitcher Steve Reed, July 31, 2002.
c On disabled list from May 26 to July 8, 2003.
d Traded to Pittsburgh Pirates with pitcher Oliver Perez and player to be named later for outfielder Brian Giles, August 26, 2003.
e Pittsburgh Pirates received pitcher Cory Stewart to complete trade, October 2, 2003.
f On disabled list from March 26 to May 7, 2004.
g Selected Rookie of the Year in National League for 2004.

BELLIARD, RONALD (RONNIE)

Born, Bronx, New York, April 7, 1975.
Bats Right. Throws Right. Height, 5 feet, 8 inches. Weight,180 pounds.

Year	Club	Lea	Pos	G	AB	R	H	2B	3B	HR	RBI	SB	Avg
1994 Brewers	Arizona		2B-3B-SS	39	143	32	42	7	3	0	27	7	.294
1995 Beloit	Midwest		2B-3B	130	461	76	137	28	5	13	76	16	.297
1996 El Paso	Texas		2B	109	416	73	116	20	8	3	57	26	.279
1997 Tucson	P.C.		2B-SS	118	443	80	125	35	4	4	55	10	.282
1998 Louisville	Int.		2B-SS	133	507	114	163	36	7	14	73	32	.321
1998 Milwaukee	N.L.		2B	8	5	0	1	0	0	0	0	0	.20
1999 Louisville	Int.		2B	29	108	14	26	4	0	1	8	12	.241
1999 Milwaukee	N.L.		2B-3B-SS	124	457	60	135	29	4	8	58	4	.295
2000 Milwaukee	N.L.		2B	152	571	83	150	30	9	8	54	7	.263
2001 Milwaukee a	N.L.		2B	101	364	69	96	30	3	11	36	5	.264
2002 Milwaukee b	N.L.		2B-3B	104	289	30	61	13	0	3	26	2	.211
2003 Colorado Springs	P.C.		2B	6	19	2	5	1	0	0	0	0	.263
2003 Colorado c-d	N.L.		2B	116	447	73	124	31	2	8	50	7	.277
2004 Cleveland	A.L.		2B	152	599	78	169	48	1	12	70	3	.282
2005 Cleveland	A.L.		2B	145	536	71	152	36	1	17	78	2	.284
2006 Cleveland	A.L.		2B-3B	93	350	43	102	21	0	8	44	2	.291
2006 St. Louis e-f	N.L.		2B	54	194	20	46	9	1	5	23	0	.237
2007 Washington	N.L.	2B-1B-SS-3B	147	511	57	148	35	1	11	58	3	.290
Major League Totals			10 Yrs.	1196	4323	585	1184	282	22	91	497	35	.274
Division Series													
2006 St. Louis	N.L.		2B	4	13	2	6	1	0	0	2	1	.462
Championship Series													
2006 St. Louis	N.L.		2B	7	25	0	6	0	0	0	2	1	.240
World Series Record													
2006 St. Louis	N.L.		2B	3	12	0	0	0	0	0	0	0	.000

a On disabled list from August 9 to September 30, 2001.
b Not offered 2003 contract, December 21, 2002. Signed with Colorado Rockies organization, January 17, 2003
c On disabled list from June 2 to June 23, 2003.
d Waived by Colorado Rockies, November 20, 2003. Signed with Cleveland Indians, December 26, 2003.
e Traded to St. Louis Cardinals for infielder Hector Luna, July 30, 2006.
f Filed for free agency, October 30, 2006. Signed with Washington Nationals organization, February 19, 2007.

BELTRAN, CARLOS IVAN

Born, Manati, Puerto Rico, April 24, 1977.
Bats Both. Throws Right. Height, 6 feet. Weight,200 pounds.

Year	Club	Lea	Pos	G	AB	R	H	2B	3B	HR	RBI	SB	Avg
1995 Royals	Gulf Coast		OF	52	180	29	50	9	0	0	23	5	.278
1996 Lansing	Midwest		OF	11	42	3	6	2	0	0	0	1	.143
1996 Spokane	Northwest		OF	59	215	29	58	8	3	7	29	10	.270
1997 Wilmington	Carolina		OF	120	419	57	96	15	4	11	46	17	.229
1998 Wilmington	Carolina		OF	52	192	32	53	14	0	5	32	11	.276
1998 Wichita	Texas		OF	47	182	50	64	13	3	14	44	7	.352
1998 Kansas City	A.L.		OF	14	58	12	16	5	3	0	7	3	.276
1999 Kansas City a	A.L.		OF	156	663	112	194	27	7	22	108	27	.293
2000 GC Royals	Gulf Coast		PH	1	4	3	2	1	0	1	1	0	.500
2000 Wilmington	Carolina		OF	3	13	2	4	0	1	2	6	0	.308
2000 Omaha	P.C.		OF	5	18	4	6	1	0	2	2	1	.333
2000 Kansas City b	A.L.		OF	98	372	49	92	15	4	7	44	13	.247
2001 Kansas City	A.L.		OF	155	617	106	189	32	12	24	101	31	.306
2002 Kansas City	A.L.		OF	*162	637	114	174	44	7	29	105	35	.273
2003 Wichita	Texas		OF	3	9	3	3	2	0	0	1	1	.333
2003 Kansas City c	A.L.		OF	141	521	102	160	14	10	26	100	41	.307
2004 Kansas City	A.L.		OF	69	266	51	74	19	2	15	51	14	.278
2004 Houston d-e	N.L.		OF	90	333	70	86	17	7	23	53	28	.258
2005 New York	N.L.		OF	151	582	83	155	34	2	16	78	17	.266
2006 New York	N.L.		OF	140	510	127	140	38	1	41	116	18	.275
2007 New York f	N.L.		OF	144	554	93	153	33	3	33	112	23	.276
Major League Totals			10 Yrs.	1320	5113	919	1433	278	58	236	875	250	.280
Division Series													
2004 Houston	N.L.		OF	5	22	9	10	2	0	4	9	2	.455
2006 New York	N.L.		OF	3	9	2	2	0	0	0	1	1	.222
Division Series Totals				8	31	11	12	2	0	4	10	3	.387
Championship Series													
2004 Houston	N.L.		OF	7	24	12	10	1	0	4	5	4	.417

Year	Club	Lea	Pos	G	AB	R	H	2B	3B	HR	RBI	SB	Avg
2006 New York .... N.L.		OF	7	27	8	8	1	0	3	4	1	.296
Championship Series Totals.......			14	51	20	18	2	0	7	9	5	.353

a Selected Rookie of the Year in American League for 1999.
b On disabled list from July 4 to September 3, 2000.
c On disabled list from March 21 to April 18, 2003.
d Traded to Houston Astros for pitcher Octavio Dotel and catcher John Buck, June 24, 2004.
e Filed for free agency, October 28, 2004. Signed with New York Mets, January 11, 2005.
f On disabled list from July 25 to August 10, 2007.

BELTRE, ADRIAN

Born, Santo Domingo, Dominican Republic, April 7, 1979.
Bats Right. Throws Right. Height, 5 feet, 11 inches. Weight, 220 pounds.

Year	Club	Lea	Pos	G	AB	R	H	2B	3B	HR	RBI	SB	Avg
1995 La-S.Doming .....Dominican		3B	62	218	56	67	15	3	8	40	2	.307
1996 Savannah .... So.Atl.		3B-2B	68	244	48	75	14	3	16	59	4	.307
1996 San Berndno a .... California		3B	63	238	40	62	13	1	10	40	3	.261
1997 Vero Beach......... Fla.St.		3B-OF	123	435	95	138	24	2	26	104	25	.317
1998 San Antonio .... Texas		3B	64	246	49	79	21	2	13	56	20	.321
1998 Los Angeles .... N.L.		3B-SS	77	195	18	42	9	0	7	22	3	.215
1999 Los Angeles .... N.L.		3B	152	538	84	148	27	5	15	67	18	.275
2000 Los Angeles b .... N.L.		3B-SS	138	510	71	148	30	2	20	85	12	.290
2001 Vero Beach .... Fla.St.		3B	3	9	0	4	1	0	0	1	0	.444
2001 Las Vegas............. P.C.		3B	2	5	2	3	1	0	1	2	0	.600
2001 Los Angeles c......... N.L.		3B-SS	126	475	59	126	22	4	13	60	13	.265
2002 Los Angeles .... N.L.		3B	159	587	70	151	26	5	21	75	7	.257
2003 Los Angeles .... N.L.		3B-SS	158	559	50	134	30	2	23	80	2	.240
2004 Los Angeles d .... N.L.		3B-SS	156	598	104	200	32	0	*48	121	7	.334
2005 Seattle .... A.L.		3B	156	603	69	154	36	1	19	87	3	.255
2006 Seattle .... A.L.		3B-2B	156	620	88	166	39	4	25	89	11	.268
2007 Seattle .... A.L.		3B	149	595	87	164	41	2	26	99	14	.276
Major League Totals			10 Yrs.	1427	5280	700	1433	292	25	217	785	90	.271
Division Series												
2004 Los Angeles .... N.L.		3B	4	15	1	4	0	0	0	1	0	.267

a On disabled list from June 25 to July 2, 1996.
b On disabled list from May 28 to June 16, 2000.
c On disabled list from March 23 to May 12, 2001.
d Filed for free agency, October 29, 2004. Signed with Seattle Mariners, December 17, 2004.

BERKMAN, WILLIAM LANCE (LANCE)

Born, Waco, Texas, February 10, 1976.
Bats Both. Throws Left. Height, 6 feet, 1 inch. Weight, 220 pounds.

Year	Club	Lea	Pos	G	AB	R	H	2B	3B	HR	RBI	SB	Avg
1997 Kissimmee .... Fla.St.		OF	53	184	31	54	10	0	12	35	2	.293
1998 Jackson .... Texas		OF	122	425	82	130	34	0	24	89	6	.306
1998 New Orleans......... P.C.		OF	17	59	14	16	4	0	6	13	0	.271
1999 New Orleans.......... P.C.		OF	64	226	42	73	20	0	8	49	7	.323
1999 Houston a .... N.L.		OF-1B	34	93	10	22	2	0	4	15	5	.237
2000 New Orleans......... P.C.		OF	31	112	18	37	4	2	6	27	4	.330
2000 Houston............. N.L.		OF-1B	114	353	76	105	28	1	21	67	6	.297
2001 Houston .... N.L.		OF	156	577	110	191	*55	5	34	126	7	.331
2002 Houston .... N.L.		OF	158	578	106	169	35	2	42	*128	8	.292
2003 Houston .... N.L.		OF	153	538	110	155	35	6	25	93	5	.288
2004 Houston .... N.L.		OF-1B	160	544	104	172	40	3	30	106	9	.316
2005 Round Rock .... P.C.		OF	4	14	2	4	1	0	0	1	0	.286
2005 Houston b .... N.L.		1B-OF	132	468	76	137	34	1	24	82	4	.293
2006 Houston .... N.L.		1B-OF	152	536	95	169	29	0	45	136	3	.315
2007 Houston .... N.L.		1B-OF	153	561	95	156	24	2	34	102	7	.278
Major League Totals			9 Yrs.	1212	4248	782	1276	282	20	259	855	54	.300
Division Series												
2001 Houston .... N.L.		OF	3	12	0	2	0	0	0	0	0	.167
2004 Houston .... N.L.		OF	5	22	5	9	1	0	1	3	0	.409
2005 Houston .... N.L.		1B-OF	4	14	4	5	1	0	1	5	0	.357
Division Series Totals			12	48	9	16	2	0	2	8	0	.333
Championship Series												
2004 Houston .... N.L.		OF	7	24	7	7	2	0	3	9	1	.292
2005 Houston .... N.L.		1B-OF	6	21	2	6	2	0	1	3	0	.286

14

Year	Club	Lea	Pos	G	AB	R	H	2B	3B	HR	RBI	SB	Avg
Championship Series Totals				13	45	9	13	4	0	4	12	1	.289
World Series Record													
2005 Houston..............	N.L.		OF-1B	4	13	0	5	2	0	0	6	1	.385

a On disabled list from April 13 to May 14, 1999.
b On disabled list from March 25 to May 6, 2005.

BETANCOURT, YUNIESKY (PEREZ)

Born, Santa Clara, Cuba, January 31, 1982.
Bats Right. Throws Right. Height, 5 feet, 10 inches. Weight, 190 pounds.

Year	Club	Lea	Pos	G	AB	R	H	2B	3B	HR	RBI	SB	Avg
2005 San Antonio	Texas	SS-2B	52	227	25	62	10	3	5	20	12	.273
2005 Tacoma	P.C.	SS-2B	49	183	13	54	9	6	2	30	7	.295
2005 Seattle a.............	A.L.	SS-2B	60	211	24	54	11	5	1	15	1	.256
2006 Seattle	A.L.	SS	157	558	68	161	28	6	8	47	11	.289
2007 Seattle	A.L.	SS	155	536	72	155	38	2	9	67	5	.289
Major League Totals	3 Yrs.	372	1305	164	370	77	13	18	129	17	.284

a Played in Cuba 2000-2004. Signed with Seattle Mariners, January 26, 2005.

BETEMIT, WILSON

Born, Santo Domingo, Dominican Republic, November 2, 1981.
Bats Both. Throws Right. Height, 6 feet, 3 inches. Weight, 230 pounds.

Year	Club	Lea	Pos	G	AB	R	H	2B	3B	HR	RBI	SB	Avg
1997 Braves ......Gulf Coast		SS	32	113	12	24	6	1	0	15	0	.212
1998 Braves ......Gulf Coast		SS	51	173	23	38	8	4	5	16	6	.220
1999 Danville ....Appal.		SS	67	259	39	83	18	2	5	53	6	.320
2000 Jamestown ...N.Y.-Penn.		SS	69	269	54	89	15	2	5	37	3	.331
2001 Myrtle Beach .. Carolina		SS	84	318	38	88	20	1	7	43	8	.277
2001 Greenville.....Southern		SS	47	183	22	65	14	0	5	19	6	.355
2001 Atlanta...........N.L.		SS	8	3	1	0	0	0	0	0	1	.000
2002 Braves ......Gulf Coast		SS	7	19	2	5	4	0	0	2	1	.263
2002 Richmond ....Int.		SS	93	343	43	84	17	1	8	34	8	.245
2003 Richmond ....Int.		3B-SS	127	478	55	125	23	13	8	65	8	.262
2004 Richmond ....Int.		3B-SS	105	356	48	99	24	2	13	59	3	.278
2004 Atlanta..........N.L.		3B-SS	22	47	2	8	0	0	0	3	0	.170
2005 Atlanta..........N.L.		3B-SS-2B	115	246	36	75	12	4	4	20	1	.305
2006 Atlanta-Los Angeles a ..N.L.		3B-SS-2B	143	373	49	98	23	0	18	53	3	.263
2007 Los Angeles.......N.L.		3B-SS-2B-OF	84	156	22	36	8	0	10	26	0	.231
2007 New York b........A.L.		1B-3B-SS-2B	37	84	11	19	4	0	4	24	0	.226
Major League Totals	5 Yrs.	409	909	121	236	47	4	36	126	5	.260
Division Series												
2004 Atlanta...........N.L.		PH	1	0	0	0	0	0	0	0	0	.000
2005 Atlanta...........N.L.		PH	2	2	0	1	0	0	0	0	0	.500
2006 Los Angeles.......N.L.		3B	3	8	3	4	1	0	1	1	0	.500
Division Series Totals			6	10	3	5	1	0	1	1	0	.500

a Traded to Los Angeles Dodgers for pitcher Danys Baez, infielder Willy Aybar and cash, July 28, 2006.
b Traded to New York Yankees for pitcher Scott Proctor, July 31, 2007.

BIGGIO, CRAIG ALAN

Born, Smithtown, New York, December 14, 1965.
Bats Right. Throws Right. Height, 5 feet, 11 inches. Weight, 185 pounds.

Year	Club	Lea	Pos	G	AB	R	H	2B	3B	HR	RBI	SB	Avg
1987 Asheville........	So. Atl.	C	64	216	59	81	17	2	9	49	31	.375
1988 Tucson...............	P.C.	C	77	281	60	90	21	4	3	39	19	.320
1988 Houston.............	N.L.	C	50	123	14	26	6	1	3	5	6	.211
1989 Houston.............	N.L.	C-OF	134	443	64	114	21	2	13	60	21	.257
1990 Houston.............	N.L.	C-OF	150	555	53	153	24	2	4	42	25	.276
1991 Houston.............	N.L.	C-2B-OF	149	546	79	161	23	4	4	46	19	.295
1992 Houston.............	N.L.	2B	*162	613	96	170	32	3	6	39	38	.277
1993 Houston.............	N.L.	2B	155	610	98	175	41	5	21	64	15	.287
1994 Houston.............	N.L.	2B	114	437	88	139	*44	5	6	56	*39	.318
1995 Houston a-b..........	N.L.	2B	141	553	*123	167	30	2	22	77	33	.302
1996 Houston.............	N.L.	2B	*162	605	113	174	24	4	15	75	25	.288
1997 Houston.............	N.L.	2B	*162	619	*146	191	37	8	22	81	47	.309
1998 Houston.............	N.L.	2B	160	646	123	210	*51	2	20	88	50	.325
1999 Houston.............	N.L.	2B-OF	160	639	123	188	*56	0	16	73	28	.294

15

Year	Club	Lea	Pos	G	AB	R	H	2B	3B	HR	RBI	SB	Avg
2000 Houston c	N.L.	2B	101	377	67	101	13	5	8	35	12	.268
2001 Houston	N.L.	2B	155	617	118	180	35	3	20	70	7	.292
2002 Houston	N.L.	2B-OF	145	577	96	146	36	3	15	58	16	.253
2003 Houston	N.L.	OF	153	628	102	166	44	2	15	62	8	.264
2004 Houston	N.L.	OF	156	633	100	178	47	0	24	63	7	.281
2005 Houston	N.L.	2B	155	590	94	156	40	1	26	69	11	.264
2006 Houston	N.L.	2B	145	548	79	135	33	0	21	62	3	.246
2007 Houston d	N.L.	2B-C	141	517	68	130	31	3	10	50	4	.251
Major League Totals		20 Yrs.	2850	10876	1844	3060	668	55	291	1175	414	.281
Division Series												
1997 Houston	N.L.	2B	3	12	0	1	0	0	0	0	0	.083
1998 Houston	N.L.	2B	4	11	3	2	1	0	0	1	0	.182
1999 Houston	N.L.	2B	4	19	1	2	0	0	0	0	0	.105
2001 Houston	N.L.	2B	3	12	0	2	0	0	0	0	0	.167
2004 Houston	N.L.	OF	5	20	5	8	2	0	1	4	1	.400
2005 Houston	N.L.	2B	4	19	6	6	4	0	0	1	1	.316
Division Series Totals			23	93	15	21	7	0	1	6	2	.226
Championship Series												
2004 Houston	N.L.	OF	7	32	3	6	1	0	1	1	0	.188
2005 Houston	N.L.	2B	6	24	2	8	0	0	0	3	0	.333
Championship Series Totals			13	56	5	14	1	0	1	4	0	.250
World Series Record												
2005 Houston	N.L.	2B	4	18	3	4	1	0	0	1	0	.222

a Filed for free agency, November 12, 1995.
b Re-signed with Houston Astros, December 14, 1995.
c On disabled list from August 2 to November 5, 2000.
d Announced plans to retire at the end of the season, July 24, 2007.

BLAKE, WILLIAM CASEY (CASEY)

Born, Des Moines, Iowa, August 23, 1973.
Bats Right. Throws Right. Height, 6 feet, 2 inches. Weight, 210 pounds.

Year	Club	Lea	Pos	G	AB	R	H	2B	3B	HR	RBI	SB	Avg
1996 Hagerstown	So.Atl.	3B-1B-OF	48	172	29	43	13	1	2	18	5	.250
1997 Dunedin	Fla.St.	3B-SS	129	449	56	107	21	0	7	39	19	.238
1998 Dunedin	Fla.St.	3B	88	340	62	119	28	3	11	65	9	.350
1998 Knoxville	Southern	3B	45	172	41	64	15	4	7	38	10	.372
1999 Syracuse	Int.	3B	110	387	69	95	16	2	22	75	9	.245
1999 St. Catharines	N.Y.-Penn.	3B	1	3	0	2	0	0	0	0	0	.667
1999 Toronto	A.L.	3B	14	39	6	10	2	0	1	1	0	.256
2000 Syracuse	Int.	3B-SS	30	106	10	23	6	1	2	7	0	.217
2000 Salt Lake	P.C.	3B-SS-1B	80	293	59	93	22	2	12	52	7	.317
2000 Minnesota a-b ...	A.L.	3B-1B	7	16	1	3	2	0	0	1	0	.188
2001 Edmonton	P.C.	3B-1B-2B-SS	94	375	64	116	24	6	10	49	14	.309
2001 Minn.-Baltimore c-d	A.L.	1B-3B	19	37	3	9	1	0	1	4	3	.243
2002 Edmonton	P.C.	3B-2B-1B-OF	126	482	87	149	25	3	19	58	24	.309
2002 Minnesota e	A.L.	3B-1B	9	20	2	4	1	0	0	1	0	.200
2003 Cleveland	A.L.	3B-1B	152	557	80	143	35	0	17	67	7	.257
2004 Cleveland	A.L.	3B-1B	152	587	93	159	36	3	28	88	5	.271
2005 Cleveland	A.L.	OF-3B-1B	147	523	72	126	32	1	23	58	4	.241
2006 Lake County	So.Atl.	OF	1	2	1	1	0	0	1	2	0	.500
2006 Akron	Eastern	OF	1	3	0	1	1	0	0	1	0	.333
2006 Cleveland f	A.L.	OF-1B	109	401	63	113	20	1	19	68	6	.282
2007 Cleveland	A.L.	3B-1B-OF	156	588	81	159	36	4	18	78	4	.270
Major League Totals		9 Yrs.	765	2768	401	726	165	9	107	366	29	.262
Division Series												
2007 Cleveland	A.L.	3B	4	17	1	2	1	0	0	2	0	.118
Championship Series												
2007 Cleveland	A.L.	3B	7	26	4	9	2	0	1	2	0	.346

a Claimed on waivers from Toronto Blue Jays by Minnesota Twins, May 23, 2000.
b On disabled list from June 28 to July 7, 2000.
c Claimed on waivers by Baltimore Orioles, September 21, 2001.
d Claimed on waivers by Minnesota Twins, October 12, 2001.
e Filed for free agency, October 14, 2002. Signed with Cleveland Indians, December 18, 2002.
f On disabled list from June 14 to July 13 and August 6 to August 25, 2006.

BLALOCK, HANK JOE

Born, San Diego, California, November 21, 1980.
Bats Left. Throws Right. Height, 6 feet, 1 inch. Weight, 200 pounds.

Year	Club	Lea	Pos	G	AB	R	H	2B	3B	HR	RBI	SB	Avg
1999 Rangers	Gulf Coast		3B	51	191	34	69	17	6	3	38	3	.361
1999 Savannah	So.Atl.		3B	6	25	3	6	1	0	1	2	0	.240
2000 Savannah	So.Atl.		3B	139	512	66	153	32	2	10	77	31	.299
2001 Charlotte	Fla.St.		3B	63	237	46	90	19	1	7	47	7	.380
2001 Tulsa	Texas		3B	68	272	50	89	18	4	11	61	3	.327
2002 Oklahoma	P.C.		3B-2B	95	387	63	119	32	1	8	62	2	.307
2002 Texas	A.L.		3B	49	147	16	31	8	0	3	17	0	.211
2003 Texas	A.L.		3B-2B	143	567	89	170	33	3	29	90	2	.300
2004 Texas	A.L.		3B	159	624	107	172	38	3	32	110	2	.276
2005 Texas	A.L.		3B	161	647	80	170	34	0	25	92	1	.263
2006 Texas	A.L.		3B	152	591	76	157	26	3	16	89	1	.266
2007 Texas a	A.L.		3B	58	208	32	61	16	3	10	33	4	.293
Major League Totals			6 Yrs.	722	2784	400	761	155	12	115	431	10	.273

a On disabled list from May 17 to September 1, 2007.

BLOOMQUIST, WILLIAM PAUL (WILLIE)

Born, Bremerton, Washington, November 27, 1977.
Bats Right. Throws Right. Height, 5 feet, 11 inches. Weight, 195 pounds.

Year	Club	Lea	Pos	G	AB	R	H	2B	3B	HR	RBI	SB	Avg
1999 Everett	Northwest		2B	41	178	35	51	10	3	2	27	17	.287
2000 Lancaster	California		2B-SS	64	256	63	97	19	6	2	51	22	.379
2000 Tacoma a	P.C.		2B	51	191	17	43	5	1	1	23	5	.225
2001 San Antonio	Texas		SS-2B	123	491	59	125	23	2	0	28	34	.255
2002 Tacoma	P.C.		OF-2B-3B-SS	104	337	47	91	14	3	6	47	20	.270
2002 Seattle b	A.L.		OF-2B	12	33	11	15	4	0	0	7	3	.455
2003 Seattle	A.L.		3B-SS-OF	89	196	30	49	7	2	1	14	4	.250
2004 Tacoma	P.C.		SS-OF	3	12	2	5	0	0	1	3	1	.417
2004 Seattle c	A.L.		3B-SS-1B-OF	93	188	27	46	10	0	2	18	13	.245
2005 Seattle d	A.L.		2B-SS-OF-3B	82	249	27	64	15	2	0	22	14	.257
2006 Seattle	A.L.		OF-SS-2B-3B	102	251	36	62	6	2	1	15	16	.247
2007 Seattle	A.L.		OF-2B-3B-SS	91	173	28	48	3	0	2	13	7	.277
Major League Totals			6 Yrs.	469	1090	159	284	45	6	6	89	57	.261

a On disabled list from August 6 to September 29, 2000.
b On disabled list from April 22 to May 3 and June 6 to 18, 2002.
c On disabled list from May 2 to May 21, 2004.
d On disabled list from August 30 to October 31, 2005.

BLUM, GEOFFREY E. (GEOFF)

Born, Redwood City, California, April 26, 1973.
Bats Both. Throws Right. Height, 6 feet, 3 inches. Weight, 205 pounds.

Year	Club	Lea	Pos	G	AB	R	H	2B	3B	HR	RBI	SB	Avg
1994 Vermont	N.Y.-Penn.		SS	63	241	48	83	15	1	3	38	5	.344
1995 Wst Plm Bch	Fla.St.		2B-SS-3B	125	457	54	120	20	2	1	62	6	.263
1996 Harrisburg	Eastern		2B-SS-1B-OF	120	396	47	95	22	2	1	41	6	.240
1997 Ottawa	Int.		2B-SS-3B	118	407	59	101	21	2	3	35	14	.248
1998 Ottawa	Int.		2B-SS	8	23	1	4	0	0	0	1	0	.174
1998 Expos	Gulf Coast		2B	5	18	0	3	1	1	0	1	0	.167
1998 Jupiter	Fla.St.		2B-3B-SS	17	58	13	16	6	0	0	5	1	.276
1998 Harrisburg	Eastern		3B-SS-2B	39	139	25	43	12	3	6	21	2	.309
1999 Ottawa	Int.		SS	77	268	43	71	14	1	10	37	6	.265
1999 Montreal a	N.L.		SS-2B	45	133	21	32	7	2	8	18	1	.241
2000 Montreal	N.L.		3B-SS-2B-1B	124	343	40	97	20	2	11	45	1	.283
2001 Montreal	N.L.		3B-OF-2B-1B	148	453	57	107	25	0	9	50	9	.236
2002 Houston b	N.L.		3B-OF-SS-1B	130	368	45	104	20	4	10	52	2	.283
2003 Houston c	N.L.		3B-2B-SS-1B	123	420	51	110	19	0	10	52	0	.262
2004 Tampa Bay d	A.L.		3B-2B-OF-1B	112	339	38	73	21	0	8	35	2	.215
2005 Lake Elsinore	California		3B-OF	2	8	3	2	0	0	2	5	0	.250
2005 San Diego	N.L.		3B-2B-SS-1B	78	224	26	54	13	1	5	22	3	.241
2005 Chicago e-f-g	A.L.		1B-3B-SS-2B	31	95	6	19	2	1	1	3	0	.200
2006 San Diego h	N.L.		SS-3B-1B-2B	109	276	27	70	17	1	4	34	0	.254
2007 San Diego i	N.L.		2B-3B-SS-OF	122	330	34	83	21	1	5	33	0	.252
Major League Totals			9 Yrs.	1022	2981	345	749	165	12	71	344	18	.251
Division Series													
2005 Chicago	A.L.		1B	1	1	0	0	0	0	0	0	0	.000

17

Year	Club	Lea	Pos	G	AB	R	H	2B	3B	HR	RBI	SB	Avg
2006 San Diego .......N.L. •	SS-3B	4	8	0	1	1	0	0	1	0	.125
Division Series Totals			5	9	0	1	1	0	0	1	0	.111
World Series Record												
2005 Chicago .........A.L.	2B	1	1	1	1	0	0	1	1	0	1.000

a On disabled list from May 21 to June 15, 1999.
b Traded to Houston Astros for infielder Chris Truby, March 12, 2002.
c Traded to Tampa Bay Devil Rays for pitcher Brandon Backe, December 14, 2003.
d Released by Tampa Bay Devil Rays, November 19, 2004. Signed with San Diego Padres, December 8, 2004.
e On disabled list from April 30 to May 18, 2005.
f Traded to Chicago White Sox for pitcher Ryan Meaux, July 31, 2005.
g Filed for free agency, October 31, 2005. Signed with San Diego Padres, November 16, 2005.
h Filed for free agency, October 28, 2006, re-signed with San Diego Padres, December 1, 2006.
i Filed for free agency, October 30, 2007. Signed with Houston Astros, November 20, 2007.

BONDS, BARRY LAMAR

Born, Riverside, California, July 24, 1964.
Bats Left. Throws Left. Height, 6 feet, 2 inches. Weight, 230 pounds.

Year	Club	Lea	Pos	G	AB	R	H	2B	3B	HR	RBI	SB	Avg
1985 Prince William ..... Carolina	OF	71	254	49	76	16	4	13	37	15	.299
1986 Pittsburgh .... N.L.	OF	113	413	72	92	26	3	16	48	36	.223
1986 Hawaii .... P.C.	OF	44	148	30	46	7	2	7	37	16	.311
1987 Pittsburgh .... N.L.	OF	150	551	99	144	34	9	25	59	32	.261
1988 Pittsburgh .... N.L.	OF	144	538	97	152	30	5	24	58	17	.283
1989 Pittsburgh .... N.L.	OF	159	580	96	144	34	6	19	58	32	.248
1990 Pittsburgh a .... N.L.	OF	151	519	104	156	32	3	33	114	52	.301
1991 Pittsburgh .... N.L.	OF	153	510	95	149	28	5	25	116	43	.292
1992 Pittsburgh b-c-d ...... N.L.	OF	140	473	*109	147	36	5	34	103	39	.311
1993 San Francisco e ...... N.L.	OF	159	539	129	181	38	4	*46	*123	29	.336
1994 San Francisco .... N.L.	OF	112	391	89	122	18	1	37	81	29	.312
1995 San Francisco .... N.L.	OF	*144	506	109	149	30	7	33	104	31	.294
1996 San Francisco .... N.L.	OF	158	517	122	159	27	3	42	129	40	.308
1997 San Francisco .... N.L.	OF	159	532	123	155	26	5	40	101	37	.291
1998 San Francisco .... N.L.	OF	156	552	120	167	44	7	37	122	28	.303
1999 San Francisco f ...... N.L.	OF	102	355	91	93	20	2	34	83	15	.262
2000 San Francisco .... N.L.	OF	143	480	129	147	28	4	49	106	11	.306
2001 San Francisco g ...... N.L.	OF	153	476	129	156	32	2	*73	137	13	.328
2002 San Francisco h ...... N.L.	OF	143	403	117	149	31	2	46	110	9	*.370
2003 San Francisco i ...... N.L.	OF	130	390	111	133	22	1	45	90	7	.341
2004 San Francisco j ...... N.L.	OF	147	373	129	135	27	3	45	101	6	*.362
2005 San Francisco k ...... N.L.	OF	14	42	8	12	1	0	5	10	0	.286
2006 San Francisco l ...... N.L.	OF	130	367	74	99	23	0	26	77	3	.270
2007 San Francisco m ...... N.L.	OF	126	340	75	94	14	0	28	66	5	.276
Major League Totals	22 Yrs.	2986	9847	2227	2935	601	77	762	1996	514	.298
Division Series											
1997 San Francisco .... N.L.	OF	3	12	0	3	2	0	0	2	1	.250
2000 San Francisco .... N.L.	OF	4	17	2	3	1	1	0	1	1	.176
2002 San Francisco .... N.L.	OF	5	17	5	5	0	0	3	4	0	.294
2003 San Francisco .... N.L.	OF	4	9	3	2	1	0	0	2	1	.222
Division Series Totals			16	55	10	13	4	1	3	9	3	.236
Championship Series											
1990 Pittsburgh .... N.L.	OF	6	18	4	3	0	0	0	1	2	.167
1991 Pittsburgh .... N.L.	OF	7	27	1	4	1	0	0	0	3	.148
1992 Pittsburgh .... N.L.	OF	7	23	5	6	1	0	1	2	1	.261
2002 San Francisco .... N.L.	OF	5	11	5	3	0	1	1	6	0	.273
Championship Series Totals			25	79	15	16	2	1	2	9	6	.203
World Series Record											
2002 San Francisco .... N.L.	OF	7	17	8	8	2	0	4	6	0	.471

a Selected Most Valuable Player in National League for 1990.
b On disabled list from June 15 to July 3, 1992.
c Selected Most Valuable Player in National League for 1992.
d Filed for free agency, October 26. Signed with San Francisco Giants, December 6, 1992.
e Selected Most Valuable Player in National League for 1993.
f On disabled list from April 18 to June 9, 1999.
g Filed for free agency, November 5, 2001, re-signed with San Francisco Giants, December 19, 2001.
h Selected Most Valuable Player in National League for 2002.
i Selected Most Valuable Player in National League for 2003.
j Selected Most Valuable Player in National League for 2004.
k On disabled list from March 25 to September 12, 2005.
l Filed for free agency, October 28, 2006, re-signed with San Francisco Giants, December 8, 2006.
m Filed for free agency, October 29, 2007.
n Barry Bonds broke Henry Aaron's all-time homer run record with his 756th homer on August 7, 2007

BOONE, AARON JOHN

Born, LaMesa, California, March 9, 1973.
Bats Right. Throws Right. Height, 6 feet, 2 inches. Weight, 200 pounds.

Year	Club	Lea	Pos	G	AB	R	H	2B	3B	HR	RBI	SB	Avg
1994	Billings	Pioneer	3B-1B-SS	67	256	48	70	15	5	7	55	6	.273
1995	Chattanooga	Southern	3B	23	66	6	15	3	0	0	3	2	.227
1995	Winston-Sal	Carolina	3B	108	395	61	103	19	1	14	50	11	.261
1996	Chattanooga	Southern	3B-SS	136	548	86	158	44	7	17	95	21	.288
1997	Indianapolis	A.A.	3B-SS-2B	131	476	79	138	30	4	22	75	12	.290
1997	Cincinnati	N.L.	3B-2B	16	49	5	12	1	0	0	5	1	.245
1998	Indianapolis	Int.	3B-2B-SS	87	332	56	80	18	1	7	38	17	.241
1998	Cincinnati	N.L.	3B-2B-SS	58	181	24	51	13	2	2	28	6	.282
1999	Indianapolis	Int.	3B	11	41	6	14	2	1	0	7	2	.341
1999	Cincinnati	N.L.	3B-SS	139	472	56	132	26	5	14	72	17	.280
2000	Cincinnati a	N.L.	3B-SS	84	291	44	83	18	0	12	43	6	.285
2001	Louisville	Int.	3B	1	4	0	1	0	0	0	0	0	.250
2001	Cincinnati b	N.L.	3B	103	381	54	112	26	2	14	62	6	.294
2002	Cincinnati	N.L.	3B-SS	*162	606	83	146	38	2	26	87	32	.241
2003	Cincinnati	N.L.	3B-2B-SS	106	403	61	110	19	3	18	65	15	.273
2003	New York c	A.L.	3B	54	189	31	48	13	0	6	31	8	.254
2004	Cleveland d-e	A.L.					INJURED—Did Not Play						
2005	Cleveland	A.L.	3B	143	511	61	124	19	1	16	60	9	.243
2006	Cleveland f	A.L.	3B-2B	104	354	50	89	19	1	7	46	5	.251
2007	Jupiter	Fla.St.	1B	1	3	1	0	0	0	0	1	0	.000
2007	Florida g-h	N.L.	1B-3B	69	189	27	54	11	0	5	28	2	.286
Major League Totals		10 Yrs.	1038	3626	496	961	203	16	120	527	107	.265	

Division Series													
2003	New York	A.L.	3B	4	15	1	3	1	0	0	0	1	.200
Championship Series													
2003	New York	A.L.	3B	7	17	2	3	0	0	1	2	1	.176
World Series Record													
2003	New York	A.L.	3B	6	21	1	3	0	0	1	2	0	.143

a On disabled list from July 10 to October 3, 2000.
b On disabled list from May 15 to June 15 and August 15 to September 1 and September 24 to October 11, 2001.
c Traded to New York Yankees for pitcher Brandon Claussen, pitcher Charlie Manning and cash, July 31, 2003.
d Released by New York Yankees, March 1, 2004. Signed with Cleveland Indians, June 26, 2004.
e On disabled list from June 26 to November 15, 2004.
f Filed for free agency, October 30, 2006. Signed with Florida Marlins, December 29, 2006.
g On disabled list from June 25 to October 30, 2007.
h Filed for free agency, October 30, 2007. Signed with Washington Nationals, December 6, 2007.

BORCHARD, JOSEPH EDWARD (JOE)

Born, Los Angeles, California, November 25, 1978.
Bats Both. Throws Right. Height, 6 feet, 5 inches. Weight, 230 pounds.

Year	Club	Lea	Pos	G	AB	R	H	2B	3B	HR	RBI	SB	Avg
2000	White Sox	Arizona	OF	7	29	3	12	4	0	0	8	0	.414
2000	Winston-Salem	Carolina	OF	14	52	7	15	3	0	2	7	0	.288
2000	Birmingham	Southern	OF	6	22	3	5	0	1	0	3	0	.227
2001	Birmingham	Southern	OF	133	515	95	152	27	1	27	98	5	.295
2002	Winston-Salem	Carolina	OF	2	3	1	0	0	0	0	0	0	.000
2002	Charlotte	Int.	OF	117	438	62	119	35	2	20	59	2	.272
2002	Chicago	A.L.	OF	16	36	5	8	0	0	2	5	0	.222
2003	Charlotte	Int.	OF	114	435	62	110	20	2	13	53	2	.253
2003	Chicago	A.L.	OF	16	49	5	9	1	0	1	5	0	.184
2004	Charlotte	Int.	OF	82	301	44	80	21	0	16	48	4	.266
2004	Chicago	A.L.	OF	63	201	26	35	4	1	9	20	1	.174
2005	Charlotte	Int.	OF	134	494	69	130	20	0	29	67	6	.263
2005	Chicago	A.L.	OF	7	12	0	5	2	0	0	0	0	.417
2006	Seattle	A.L.	OF	6	9	3	2	0	0	0	0	0	.222
2006	Florida a-b	N.L.	OF-1B	108	230	30	53	7	1	10	28	0	.230
2007	Albuquerque	P.C.	OF	22	76	19	27	3	0	8	28	1	.355
2007	Florida	N.L.	OF	85	179	20	35	9	0	4	19	4	.196
Major League Totals		6 Yrs.	301	716	89	147	23	2	26	77	5	.205	

a Traded to Seattle Mariners for pitcher Matt Thornton, March 20, 2006.
b Claimed on waivers by Florida Marlins, May 4, 2006.

BOTTS, JASON CARL
Born, Paso Robles, California, July 26, 1980.
Bats Both. Throws Right. Height, 6 feet, 6 inches. Weight, 250 pounds.

Year	Club	Lea	Pos	G	AB	R	H	2B	3B	HR	RBI	SB	Avg
2000 Rangers	Gulf Coast	1B	48	163	36	52	12	0	6	34	4	.319
2001 Charlotte	Fla.St.	OF	4	12	1	2	1	0	0	0	0	.167
2001 Savannah	So.Atl.	1B-OF	114	392	63	121	24	2	9	50	13	.309
2002 Charlotte	Fla.St.	OF-1B	116	401	67	102	22	5	9	54	7	.254
2003 Stockton	Calif.	1B	76	283	58	89	14	2	9	61	12	.314
2003 Frisco	Texas	OF-1B	55	194	26	51	11	1	4	27	6	.263
2004 Frisco	Texas	1B	133	481	85	141	25	3	24	92	7	.293
2005 Oklahoma	P.C.	OF	133	510	93	146	31	7	25	102	2	.286
2005 Texas	A.L.	OF	10	27	4	8	0	0	0	3	0	.296
2006 Texas	A.L.	DH-OF	20	50	8	11	4	0	1	6	0	.220
2006 Rangers	Arizona	OF	3	12	1	3	2	0	0	1	0	.250
2006 Frisco	Texas	OF	5	16	3	2	0	0	0	2	0	.125
2006 Oklahoma	P.C.	OF-1B	63	220	43	68	19	1	13	39	6	.309
2007 Oklahoma	P.C.	OF	102	369	69	118	36	4	13	78	0	.320
2007 Texas	A.L.	OF	48	167	19	40	8	1	2	14	1	.240
Major League Totals			3 Yrs.	78	244	31	59	12	1	3	23	1	.242

BOURN, MICHAEL RAY
Born, Houston, Texas, December 27, 1982.
Bats Left. Throws Right. Height, 5 feet, 11 inches. Weight, 180 pounds.

Year	Club	Lea	Pos	G	AB	R	H	2B	3B	HR	RBI	SB	Avg
2003 Batavia	N.Y.-Penn.	OF	35	125	12	35	0	1	0	4	23	.280
2004 Lakewood	So.Atl.	OF	109	413	92	130	20	14	5	53	58	.315
2005 Reading	Eastern	OF	135	544	80	146	18	8	6	44	38	.268
2006 Reading	Eastern	OF	80	318	62	87	5	6	4	26	30	.274
2006 Scranton-WB	Int.	OF	38	152	34	43	5	7	1	15	15	.283
2006 Philadelphia	N.L.	OF	17	8	2	1	0	0	0	0	1	.125
2007 Philadelphia a-b	N.L.	OF	105	119	29	33	3	3	1	6	18	.277
Major League Totals			2 Yrs.	122	127	31	34	3	3	1	6	19	.268
Division Series													
2007 Philadelphia	N.L.	PH	2	1	0	0	0	0	0	0	0	.000

a On disabled list from July 31 to September 10, 2007.
b Traded to Houston Astros with pitcher Geoff Geary and infielder Mike Costanzo for infielder Eric Bruntlett and pitcher Brad Lidge, November 12, 2007.

BOWEN, ROBERT MC CLURE (ROB)
Born, Bedford, Texas, February 24, 1981.
Bats Both. Throws Right. Height, 6 feet, 3 inches. Weight, 225 pounds.

Year	Club	Lea	Pos	G	AB	R	H	2B	3B	HR	RBI	SB	Avg
1999 Twins	Gulf Coast	C	29	77	10	20	4	0	0	11	2	.260
2000 Elizabethton	Appal.	C	21	73	17	21	3	0	4	19	0	.288
2001 Quad Cities	Midwest	C	106	385	47	98	18	2	18	70	4	.255
2002 Fort Myers	Fla.St.	C-1B	100	342	52	63	12	1	10	49	1	.184
2002 Quad Cities	Midwest	C	5	21	1	4	1	0	0	0	0	.190
2003 New Britain	Eastern	C	42	134	17	41	13	0	1	16	0	.306
2003 Rochester	Int.	C	30	105	14	27	7	0	6	17	0	.257
2003 Minnesota	A.L.	C	7	10	0	1	0	0	0	1	0	.100
2004 Minnesota	A.L.	C	17	27	1	3	0	0	1	2	0	.111
2004 New Britain	Eastern	C	77	249	28	49	10	0	9	24	3	.197
2005 Rochester	Int.	C	87	262	38	70	13	2	6	25	0	.267
2006 Lake Elsinore	Calif.	C	2	7	0	1	0	0	0	0	0	.143
2006 San Diego a-b-c	N.L.	C-1B	94	94	22	23	5	0	3	13	0	.245
2007 Chicago-San Diego	N.L.	C	40	113	15	24	9	0	2	13	1	.212
2007 Oakland d-e	A.L.	C	21	43	6	12	1	0	2	5	0	.279
Major League Totals			4 Yrs.	179	287	44	63	15	0	8	34	1	.220
Division Series													
2006 San Diego	N.L.	C	1	1	0	1	0	0	0	0	0	1.000

a Claimed on waivers by Detroit Tigers, March 29, 2006.
b Claimed on waivers by San Diego Padres, April 3, 2006.
c On disabled list from May 12 to May 28, 2006.
d Traded to Chicago Cubs with outfielder Kyler Burke for catcher Michael Barrett, June 20, 2007.
e Traded to Oakland Athletics with pitcher Jerry Blevins for catcher Jason Kendall and cash, July 17, 2007.

BRADLEY, MILTON OBELLE

Born, Harbor City, Florida, April 15, 1978.
Bats Both. Throws Right. Height, 6 feet. Weight, 225 pounds.

Year	Club	Lea	Pos	G	AB	R	H	2B	3B	HR	RBI	SB	Avg
1996	Expos	Gulf Coast	OF	32	112	18	27	7	1	1	12	7	.241
1997	Expos	Gulf Coast	OF	9	25	6	5	2	0	1	2	2	.200
1997	Vermont	N.Y.-Penn.	OF	50	200	29	60	7	5	3	30	7	.300
1998	Jupiter	Fla.St.	OF	67	261	55	75	14	1	5	34	17	.287
1998	Cape Fear	So.Atl.	OF	75	281	54	85	21	4	6	50	13	.302
1999	Harrisburg	Eastern	OF	86	346	62	114	22	5	12	50	14	.329
2000	Ottawa	Int.	OF	88	342	58	104	20	1	6	29	10	.304
2000	Montreal	N.L.	OF	42	154	20	34	8	1	2	15	2	.221
2001	Montreal	N.L.	OF	67	220	19	49	16	3	1	19	7	.223
2001	Ottawa	Int.	OF	35	136	21	37	7	2	2	13	14	.272
2001	Buffalo	Int.	OF	30	114	18	29	3	0	5	15	9	.254
2001	Cleveland a	A.L.	OF	10	18	3	4	1	0	0	0	1	.222
2002	Buffalo	Int.	OF	6	23	3	6	0	0	0	3	2	.261
2002	Akron	Eastern	OF	3	11	1	3	1	0	0	1	0	.273
2002	Cleveland b	A.L.	OF	98	325	48	81	18	3	9	38	6	.249
2003	Cleveland c	A.L.	OF	101	377	61	121	34	2	10	56	17	.321
2004	Los Angeles d-e	N.L.	OF	141	516	72	138	24	0	19	67	15	.267
2005	Las Vegas	P.C.	OF	5	13	2	4	0	0	0	1	1	.308
2005	Los Angeles f-g	N.L.	OF	75	283	49	82	14	1	13	38	6	.290
2006	Stockton	Calif.	OF	2	7	1	1	0	0	0	0	0	.143
2006	Sacramento	P.C.	OF	6	24	3	5	0	0	2	6	1	.208
2006	Oakland h	A.L.	OF	96	351	53	97	14	2	14	52	10	.276
2007	Sacramento	P.C.	OF	2	5	1	0	0	0	0	0	0	.000
2007	Oakland	A.L.	OF	19	65	6	19	4	0	2	7	2	.292
2007	San Diego i-j-k-l	N.L.	OF	42	144	31	45	5	1	11	30	3	.313
Major League Totals			8 Yrs.	691	2453	362	670	138	13	81	322	69	.273
Division Series													
2004	Los Angeles	N.L.	OF	4	11	1	3	1	0	1	1	2	.273
2006	Oakland	A.L.	OF	3	13	1	1	0	0	1	2	0	.077
Division Series Totals				7	24	2	4	1	0	2	3	2	.167
Championship Series													
2006	Oakland	A.L.	OF	4	18	4	9	2	0	2	5	0	.500

a Traded to Cleveland Indians for pitcher Zach Day, July 31, 2001.
b On disabled list from May 2 to June 4 and August 12 to August 30, 2002.
c On disabled list from April 23 to May 8 and August 10 to October 3, 2003.
d Traded to Los Angeles Dodgers for outfielder Franklin Gutierrez and player to be named later, April 4, 2004.
e Cleveland Indians received pitcher Andrew Brown to complete trade, May 19, 2004.
f On disabled list from May 30 to July 23 and August 23 to October 28, 2005.
g Traded to Oakland Athletics with infielder Antonio Perez for outfielder Andre Ethier, December 13, 2005.
h On disabled list from April 27 to June 6 and June 15 to July 14, 2006.
i On disabled list from April 23 to May 11 and May 15 to May 30 and June 3 to June 20, 2007.
j Traded to San Diego Padres for pitcher Andrew Brown, June 29, 2007.
k On disabled list from June 21 to July 7, 2007.
l Filed for free agency, October 29, 2007. Signed with Texas Rangers, December 12, 2007.

BRANYAN, RUSSELL OLES

Born, Warner Robins, Georgia, December 19, 1975.
Bats Left. Throws Right. Height, 6 feet, 3 inches. Weight, 195 pounds.

Year	Club	Lea	Pos	G	AB	R	H	2B	3B	HR	RBI	SB	Avg
1994	Burlington	Appal.	3B	55	171	21	36	10	0	5	13	4	.211
1995	Columbus	So.Atl.	3B	76	277	46	71	8	6	19	55	1	.256
1996	Columbus	So.Atl.	3B	130	482	102	129	20	4	40	106	7	.268
1997	Kinston	Carolina	3B	83	297	59	86	26	2	27	75	3	.290
1997	Akron	Eastern	3B	41	137	26	32	4	0	12	30	0	.234
1998	Akron	Eastern	3B	43	163	35	48	11	3	16	46	1	.294
1998	Cleveland a	A.L.	3B	1	4	0	0	0	0	0	0	0	.000
1999	Buffalo	Int.	3B	109	395	51	82	11	1	30	67	8	.208
1999	Cleveland	A.L.	3B	11	38	4	8	2	0	1	6	0	.211
2000	Buffalo	Int.	3B-OF	64	229	46	56	9	2	21	60	1	.245
2000	Cleveland	A.L.	OF-3B	67	193	32	46	7	2	16	38	0	.238
2001	Cleveland	A.L.	3B-OF	113	315	48	73	16	2	20	54	1	.232
2002	Cleveland	A.L.	OF-3B	50	161	16	33	4	0	8	17	1	.205
2002	Cincinnati b	N.L.	OF-1B-3B	84	217	34	53	9	1	16	39	3	.244
2003	Louisville	Int.	OF-1B-3B	14	49	5	16	5	0	1	3	0	.327
2003	Cincinnati c-d	N.L.	3B-OF-1B	74	176	22	38	12	0	9	26	0	.216
2004	Richmond	Int.	OF	11	28	5	5	0	0	1	4	1	.179

Year	Club	Lea	Pos	G	AB	R	H	2B	3B	HR	RBI	SB	Avg
2004 Buffalo	Int.	1B-3B-OF	82	313	58	90	16	2	25	75	5	.288
2004 Milwaukee e-f-g	N.L.	3B-1B	51	158	21	37	11	1	11	27	1	.234
2005 Nashville	.P.C.	OF-3B	6	17	4	5	4	0	1	3	0	.294
2005 Milwaukee h-i.........	N.L.	3B-1B-OF	85	202	23	52	11	0	12	31	1	.257
2006 Tampa Bay	A.L.	OF-3B-1B	64	169	23	34	10	0	12	27	2	.201
2006 San Diego j-k-l	N.L.	3B	27	72	14	21	1	0	6	9	0	.292
2007 Buffalo	Int.	DH	1	4	0	0	0	0	0	0	0	.000
2007 S.D.-Phil.-St. Louis m-n-o-p	N.L.	3B-OF-1B	89	163	22	32	5	1	10	26	1	.196
Major League Totals	10 Yrs.		716	1868	259	427	88	7	121	300	10	.229
Division Series													
2001 Cleveland	A.L.	OF	2	3	1	1	0	0	0	0	0	.333
2006 San Diego	N.L.	3B	4	13	1	3	1	1	0	3	0	.231
Division Series Totals			6	16	2	4	1	1	0	3	0	.250

a On disabled list from April 23 to May 11 and May 16 to August 15, 1998.
b Traded to Cincinnati Reds for infielder Ben Broussard, June 7, 2002.
c On disabled list from March 18 to May 29, 2003.
d On disabled list from August 13 to August 28, 2003.
e Not offered contract, December 21, 2003. Signed with Atlanta Braves organization, January 21, 2004.
f Traded to Cleveland Indians for pitcher Scott Sturkie, April 26, 2004.
g On disabled list from June 2 to July 4, 2005.
h Sold to Milwaukee Brewers, July 26, 2005.
i Designated for assignment by Milwaukee Brewers, January 9, 2006.
j Released by Milwaukee Brewers, January 17, 2006. Signed with Tampa Bay Devil Rays organization, January 31, 2006.
k Traded to San Diego Padres for pitcher Evan Meek and player to be named later, August 24, 2006.
l Tampa Bay Devil Rays received pitcher Dale Thayer to complete trade, September 15, 2006.
m Released by San Diego Padres, July 28, 2007. Signed with Cleveland Indians organization, August 7, 2007.
n Sold to Philadelphia Phillies, August 9, 2007.
o Traded to St. Louis Cardinals for player to be named later, August 31, 2007.
p Filed for free agency, October 30, 2007.

BRAUN, RYAN JOSEPH

Born, Mission Hills, California, November 17, 1983.
Bats Right. Throws Right. Height, 6 feet, 2 inches. Weight, 200 pounds.

Year	Club	Lea	Pos	G	AB	R	H	2B	3B	HR	RBI	SB	Avg
2005 Helena	Pioneer	3B	10	41	6	14	2	1	2	10	2	.341
2005 West Tenn	So.Atl.	3B	37	152	21	54	16	2	8	35	2	.355
2006 Brevard County	Fla.St.	3B	59	226	34	62	12	2	7	37	14	.274
2006 Huntsville	Southern	3B	59	231	42	70	19	1	15	40	12	.303
2007 Nashville	.P.C.	3B	34	117	28	40	12	0	10	22	4	.342
2007 Milwaukee a..........	N.L.	3B	113	451	91	146	26	6	34	97	15	.324

a Selected Rookie of the Year in National League for 2007.

BROUSSARD, BENJAMIN ISAAC (BEN)

Born, Beaumont, Texas, September 24, 1976.
Bats Left. Throws Right. Height, 6 feet, 2 inches. Weight, 220 pounds.

Year	Club	Lea	Pos	G	AB	R	H	2B	3B	HR	RBI	SB	Avg
1999 Clinton	Midwest	1B	5	20	8	11	4	1	2	6	0	.550
1999 Billings...........	Pioneer	OF	38	145	39	59	11	2	14	48	1	.407
1999 Chattanooga......	Southern	OF	34	127	26	27	5	0	8	21	1	.213
2000 Chattanooga a	Southern	OF-1B	87	286	64	73	8	4	14	51	15	.255
2001 Mudville........	California	1B	30	102	14	25	5	0	5	21	0	.245
2001 Chattanooga b	Southern	1B-OF	100	353	81	113	27	0	23	69	10	.320
2002 Louisville	Int.	1B	57	187	31	51	14	1	11	30	4	.273
2002 Buffalo	Int.	OF-1B	42	153	30	37	8	0	5	21	0	.242
2002 Cleveland c..........	A.L.	OF-1B	39	112	10	27	4	0	4	9	0	.241
2003 Buffalo	Int.	1B	32	120	17	30	2	1	3	15	3	.250
2003 Cleveland d	A.L.	1B	116	386	53	96	21	3	16	55	5	.249
2004 Cleveland	A.L.	1B	139	418	57	115	28	5	17	82	4	.275
2005 Cleveland	A.L.	1B	142	466	59	119	30	5	19	68	2	.255
2006 Cleveland-Seattle e-f ...	A.L.	1B	144	432	61	125	21	0	21	63	2	.289
2007 Seattle g.............	A.L.	1B-OF	99	240	27	66	10	0	7	29	2	.275
Major League Totals	6 Yrs.		679	2054	267	548	114	13	84	306	15	.267

a On disabled list from May 10 to June 26, 2000.
b On disabled list from May 22 to 29, 2001.
c Traded by Cincinnati Reds to Cleveland Indians for infielder Russell Branyan, June 7, 2002.

d On disabled list from March 21 to April 6, 2003.
e Traded to Seattle Mariners with cash for outfielder Shin-Soo Choo and player to be named later, July 27, 2006.
f Cleveland Indians received pitcher Shawn Nottingham to complete trade, August 24, 2006.
g Traded to Texas Rangers for infielder Tug Hulett, December 12, 2007.

BROWN, EMIL QUINCY

Born, Chicago, Illinois, December 29, 1974.
Bats Right. Throws Right. Height, 6 feet, 2 inches. Weight, 210 pounds.

Year	Club	Lea	Pos	G	AB	R	H	2B	3B	HR	RBI	SB	Avg
1994 Athletics	Arizona	OF	32	86	13	19	1	1	3	12	5	.221
1995 W Michigan	Midwest	OF	124	459	63	115	17	3	3	67	35	.251
1996 Athletics	Arizona	OF	4	15	5	4	3	0	0	2	1	.267
1996 Modesto a-b	California	OF	57	211	50	64	10	1	10	47	13	.303
1997 Pittsburgh	N.L.	OF	66	95	16	17	2	1	2	6	5	.179
1998 Carolina	Southern	OF	123	466	89	154	31	2	14	67	24	.330
1998 Pittsburgh	N.L.	OF	13	39	2	10	1	0	0	3	0	.256
1999 Nashville	P.C.	OF	110	430	97	132	20	5	18	60	16	.307
1999 Pittsburgh c	N.L.	OF	6	14	0	2	1	0	0	0	0	.143
2000 Nashville	P.C.	OF	70	237	44	74	20	1	5	25	26	.312
2000 Pittsburgh d	N.L.	OF	50	119	13	26	5	0	3	16	3	.218
2001 Portland	P.C.	OF	22	78	10	25	8	2	3	8	3	.321
2001 Pittsburgh-San Diego e	N.L.	OF	74	137	21	26	4	1	3	13	12	.190
2002 Durham f-g	Int.	OF	116	422	58	120	24	3	12	58	10	.284
2003 Louisville	Int.	OF	97	369	58	109	20	3	12	63	18	.295
2004 Campeche	Mexican	OF	28	101	23	32	8	0	8	24	0	.317
2004 Memphis	P.C.	OF	19	57	7	16	3	0	0	4	1	.281
2004 New Orleans h-i-j-k	P.C.	OF	26	92	12	31	10	1	2	17	4	.337
2005 Kansas City	A.L.	OF	150	545	75	156	31	5	17	86	10	.286
2006 Kansas City	A.L.	OF	147	527	77	151	41	2	15	81	6	.287
2007 Kansas City l	A.L.	OF	113	366	44	94	13	1	6	62	12	.257
Major League Totals		8 Yrs.	619	1842	248	482	98	10	46	267	48	.262

a On disabled list from April 10 to July 1, 1996.
b Selected by Pittsburgh Pirates from Oakland A's in Rule V draft, December 9, 1996.
c On disabled list from April 24 to May 2, 1999.
d On disabled list from June 19 to July 3, 2000.
e Traded to San Diego Padres for pitcher Shawn Camp, July 10, 2001.
f Filed for free agency, October 15, 2001. Signed with Tampa Bay Devil Rays organization, January 9, 2002.
g Filed for free agency, October 15, 2002. Signed with Cincinnati Reds organization, December 10, 2002.
h Filed for free agency, October 15, 2003. Signed with St. Louis Cardinals organization, January 18, 2004.
i Released by St. Louis Cardinals organization, May 2, 2004. Signed with Campeche, Mexico, May 2004.
j Signed with Houston Astros organization, August 17, 2004.
k Filed for free agency, October 15, 2004. Signed with Kansas City Royals organization, December 15, 2004.
l Not offered contract, December 12, 2007. Signed with Oakland Athletics, January 11, 2008.

BRUNTLETT, ERIC KEVIN

Born, Lafayette, Indiana, March 29, 1978.
Bats Right. Throws Right. Height, 6 feet. Weight, 190 pounds.

Year	Club	Lea	Pos	G	AB	R	H	2B	3B	HR	RBI	SB	Avg
2000 Martinsville	Appal.	SS-OF	50	172	40	47	11	4	1	21	14	.273
2001 New Orleans	P.C.	SS	5	16	3	2	0	0	0	1	0	.125
2001 Round Rock	Texas	SS	123	503	84	134	23	3	3	40	23	.266
2002 New Orleans	P.C.	SS-2B	68	68	9	14	3	0	0	1	1	.206
2002 Round Rock	Texas	SS-2B	116	464	81	123	21	2	2	48	35	.265
2003 New Orleans	P.C.	SS-2B-OF	84	324	48	84	10	0	2	27	9	.259
2003 Houston	N.L.	SS-2B-OF-3B	31	54	3	14	3	0	1	4	0	.259
2004 Houston	N.L.	SS-2B-OF	45	52	14	13	2	0	4	8	4	.250
2004 New Orleans	P.C.	SS-OF-2B	86	332	50	83	12	4	6	37	14	.250
2005 Houston	N.L.	2B-OF-SS-3B	91	109	19	24	5	2	4	14	7	.220
2006 Round Rock	P.C.	OF-SS-2B-3B	22	73	11	16	3	1	1	7	3	.219
2006 Houston	N.L.	2B-SS-OF-3B	73	119	11	33	8	0	0	10	3	.277
2007 Round Rock	P.C.	OF-3B-2B-1B	61	227	31	63	10	4	1	21	13	.278
2007 Houston a	N.L.	SS-OF-3B	80	138	16	34	5	0	0	14	6	.246
Major League Totals		5 Yrs.	320	472	63	118	23	2	9	50	20	.250
Division Series													
2004 Houston	N.L.	SS	2	1	0	0	0	0	0	0	0	.000
2005 Houston	N.L.	OF-2B-SS	3	6	1	1	0	0	0	0	1	.167
Division Series Totals			5	7	1	1	0	0	0	0	1	.143

Year	Club	Lea	Pos	G	AB	R	H	2B	3B	HR	RBI	SB	Avg
Championship Series													
2004 Houston		N.L.	SS	4	2	0	0	0	0	0	0	0	.000
2005 Houston		N.L.	2B-SS	5	1	0	0	0	0	0	0	0	.000
Championship Series Totals ..				9	3	0	0	0	0	0	0	0	.000
World Series Record													
2005 Houston		N.L.	OF-2B	2	0	0	0	0	0	0	0	0	.000

a Traded to Philadelphia Phillies with pitcher Brad Lidge for pitcher Geoff Geary, outfielder Michael Bourn and infielder Mike Costanzo, November 12, 2007.

BUCK, JOHNATHAN RICHARD (JOHN)
Born, Kemmerer, Wyoming, July 7, 1980.
Bats Right. Throws Right. Height, 6 feet, 3 inches. Weight, 220 pounds.

Year	Club	Lea	Pos	G	AB	R	H	2B	3B	HR	RBI	SB	Avg
1998 Astros	Gulf Coast		C	36	126	24	36	9	0	3	15	2	.286
1999 Auburn	N.Y.-Penn.		C	63	233	36	57	17	0	3	29	7	.245
1999 Michigan	Midwest		C	4	10	.1	1	1	0	0	0	0	.100
2000 Michigan	Midwest		C	109	390	57	110	33	0	10	71	2	.282
2001 Lexington	So.Atl.		C	122	443	72	122	24	1	22	73	4	.275
2002 Round Rock	Texas		C	120	448	48	118	29	3	12	89	2	.263
2003 New Orleans	P.C.		C	78	274	32	70	18	2	2	39	1	.255
2004 New Orleans	P.C.		C	65	227	31	68	11	0	12	35	0	.300
2004 Kansas City a	A.L.		C	71	238	36	56	9	0	12	30	1	.235
2005 Kansas City	A.L.		C	118	401	40	97	21	1	12	47	2	.242
2006 Kansas City	A.L.		C	114	371	37	91	21	1	11	50	0	.245
2007 Kansas City	A.L.		C	113	347	41	77	18	0	18	48	0	.222
Major League Totals		4 Yrs.		416	1357	154	321	69	2	53	175	3	.237

a Traded by Houston Astros to Kansas City Royals with pitcher Octavio Dotel for outfielder Carlos Beltran, June 24, 2004.

BUCK, TRAVIS GEORGE
Born, Richland, Washington, November 18, 1983.
Bats Left. Throws Right. Height, 6 feet, 2 inches. Weight, 225 pounds.

Year	Club	Lea	Pos	G	AB	R	H	2B	3B	HR	RBI	SB	Avg
2006 Stockton	Calif.		OF	34	126	24	44	17	3	3	26	2	.349
2006 Midland	Texas		OF	50	212	32	64	22	1	4	22	9	.302
2007 Sacramento	P.C.		OF	2	7	0	1	0	1	0	1	0	.143
2007 Oakland a	A.L.		OF	82	285	41	82	22	5	7	34	4	.288

a On disabled list from June 28 to July 14 and August 18 to October 8, 2007.

BURKE, CHRISTOPHER ALLEN (CHRIS)
Born, Louisville, Kentucky, March 11, 1980.
Bats Right. Throws Right. Height, 5 feet, 11 inches. Weight, 180 pounds.

Year	Club	Lea	Pos	G	AB	R	H	2B	3B	HR	RBI	SB	Avg
2001 Michigan	Midwest		SS	56	233	47	70	11	6	3	17	21	.300
2002 Round Rock	Texas		2B-SS	136	481	66	127	19	8	3	37	16	.264
2003 Round Rock	Texas		2B-SS-OF	137	549	88	165	23	8	3	41	34	.301
2004 New Orleans	P.C.		2B	123	483	93	152	33	6	16	52	37	.315
2004 Houston	N.L.		2B	17	17	2	1	0	0	0	0	0	.059
2005 Round Rock	P.C.		2B-OF	22	90	15	28	6	2	2	11	9	.311
2005 Houston	N.L.		OF-2B	108	318	49	79	19	2	5	26	11	.248
2006 Round Rock	P.C.		2B-OF	2	8	2	4	1	0	1	2	1	.500
2006 Houston a	N.L.		2B-OF-SS	123	366	58	101	23	1	9	40	11	.276
2007 Round Rock	P.C.		2B-OF	18	66	14	16	1	0	2	7	5	.242
2007 Houston b	N.L.		2B-OF-SS	111	319	39	73	19	2	6	28	9	.229
Major League Totals		4 Yrs.		359	1020	148	254	61	5	20	94	31	.249
Division Series													
2005 Houston		N.L.	OF	3	3	1	2	1	0	1	1	0	.667
Championship Series													
2005 Houston		N.L.	OF	6	20	5	6	0	1	1	3	0	.300
World Series Record													
2005 Houston		N.L.	OF-2B	4	5	1	0	0	0	0	0	2	.000

a On disabled list from May 7 to May 22, 2006.

b Traded to Arizona Diamondbacks with pitcher Chad Qualls and pitcher Juan Gutierrez for pitcher Jose Valverde, December 14, 2007.

BURKE, JAMES EUGENE (JAMIE)

Born, Roseburg, Oregon, September 24, 1971.
Bats Right. Throws Right. Height, 6 feet. Weight, 195 pounds.

Year	Club	Lea	Pos	G	AB	R	H	2B	3B	HR	RBI	SB	Avg
1993	Boise	Northwest	3B	66	226	32	68	11	1	1	30	2	.301
1994	Cedar Rapds	Midwest	1B-3B	127	469	57	124	24	1	1	47	6	.264
1995	Lk Elsinore	Calif.	3B-1B	106	365	47	100	15	6	2	56	6	.274
1996	Midland	Texas	3B-OF-C-1B	45	144	24	46	8	2	2	16	1	.319
1996	Vancouver	P.C.	3B-OF	41	156	12	39	5	0	1	14	2	.250
1997	Midland	Texas	3B-C-OF-1B	116	428	77	141	44	3	6	72	2	.329
1997	Vancouver	P.C.	C-3B	8	27	4	8	1	0	0	3	0	.296
1998	Vancouver	P.C.	C-3B-1B	61	162	16	35	6	0	2	14	0	.216
1998	Midland	Texas	3B	12	41	7	10	1	0	0	4	0	.244
1999	Edmonton	P.C.	3B-C-1B-2B	46	149	29	50	9	0	3	16	0	.336
2000	Edmonton	P.C.	3B-C-2B	75	263	25	63	12	0	0	17	1	.240
2001	Salt Lake	P.C.	C-3B-1B-OF	61	215	25	47	10	3	0	27	1	.219
2001	Anaheim	A.L.	C-1B	9	5	1	1	0	0	0	0	0	.200
2002	Salt Lake	P.C.	C-3B-1B	88	316	47	96	12	4	8	44	1	.304
2003	Charlotte	Int.	C-1B-3B	94	323	47	104	13	0	6	50	1	.322
2003	Chicago a	A.L.	C-1B	6	8	0	3	0	0	0	2	0	.375
2004	Charlotte	Int.	C	37	134	12	31	6	0	2	12	0	.231
2004	Chicago	A.L.	C-1B-3B-OF	57	120	22	40	9	0	0	15	0	.333
2005	Chicago	A.L.	1B	1	1	0	0	0	0	0	0	0	.000
2005	Charlotte b	Int.	C-3B-2B-1B	102	358	50	95	22	1	10	53	1	.265
2006	Oklahoma	P.C.	C-3B-1B	102	370	46	103	21	1	10	49	0	.278
2007	Seattle c	A.L.	C	50	113	19	34	8	0	1	12	0	.301
Major League Totals		5 Yrs.		123	247	42	78	17	0	1	29	0	.316

a Filed for free agency, October 15, 2002. Signed with Chicago White Sox organization, January 27, 2003.
b Filed for free agency, October 5, 2005. Signed with Texas Rangers organization, November 3, 2005.
c Filed for free agency, November 1, 2006. Signed with Seattle Mariners organization, January 25, 2007.

BURRELL, PATRICK BRIAN (PAT)

Born, Eureka Springs, Arkansas, October 10, 1976.
Bats Right. Throws Right. Height, 6 feet, 4 inches. Weight, 235 pounds.

Year	Club	Lea	Pos	G	AB	R	H	2B	3B	HR	RBI	SB	Avg
1998	Clearwater	Fla.St.	1B	37	132	29	40	7	1	7	30	2	.303
1999	Scranton-WB	Int.	1B	9	33	4	5	0	0	1	4	0	.152
1999	Reading	Eastern	1B	117	417	84	139	28	6	28	90	3	.333
2000	Scranton-WB	Int.	OF	40	143	31	42	15	1	4	25	1	.294
2000	Philadelphia	N.L.	1B-OF	111	408	57	106	27	1	18	79	0	.260
2001	Philadelphia	N.L.	OF	155	539	70	139	29	2	27	89	2	.258
2002	Philadelphia	N.L.	OF	157	586	96	165	39	2	37	116	1	.282
2003	Philadelphia	N.L.	OF	146	522	57	109	31	4	21	64	0	.209
2004	Reading	Eastern	OF	4	15	2	3	0	0	2	4	0	.200
2004	Philadelphia a	N.L.	OF	127	448	66	115	17	0	24	84	2	.257
2005	Philadelphia	N.L.	OF	154	562	78	158	27	1	32	117	0	.281
2006	Philadelphia	N.L.	OF	144	462	80	119	24	1	29	95	0	.258
2007	Philadelphia	N.L.	OF	155	472	77	121	26	0	30	97	0	.256
Major League Totals		8 Yrs.		1149	3999	581	1032	220	11	218	741	5	.258
Division Series													
2007	Philadelphia	N.L.	OF	3	11	1	2	0	0	1	1	0	.182

a On disabled list from August 4 to September 3, 2004.

BUTLER, BILLY RAY

Born, Orange Park, Florida, April 18, 1986.
Bats Right. Throws Right. Height, 6 feet, 1 inch. Weight, 240 pounds.

Year	Club	Lea	Pos	G	AB	R	H	2B	3B	HR	RBI	SB	Avg
2004	Idaho Falls	Pioneer	3B	72	260	74	97	22	3	10	68	5	.373
2005	High Desert	Calif.	3B-OF	92	379	70	132	30	2	25	91	0	.348
2005	Wichita	Texas	OF	29	112	14	35	9	0	5	19	0	.313
2006	Wichita	Texas	OF	119	477	82	158	33	1	15	96	1	.331
2007	Omaha	P.C.	OF-1B	57	203	40	59	10	1	13	46	1	.291
2007	Kansas City	A.L.	DH-1B-OF	92	329	38	96	23	2	8	52	0	.292

BYNUM, FREDDIE LEE
Born, Wilson, North Carolina, March 15, 1980.
Bats Left. Throws Right. Height, 6 feet, 1 inch. Weight, 185 pounds.

Year	Club	Lea	Pos	G	AB	R	H	2B	3B	HR	RBI	SB	Avg
2000 Vancouver	...	Northwest	SS-OF	72	281	52	72	10	1	1	26	22	.256
2001 Modesto	....	Calif.	SS-2B-3B	120	440	59	115	19	7	2	46	28	.261
2002 Visalia	....	Calif.	2B	135	539	83	165	26	5	3	56	41	.306
2003 Midland	....	Texas	2B-SS-3B	132	510	84	134	18	9	5	58	22	.263
2004 Sacramento	....	P.C.	OF-SS-3B-2B	66	258	42	73	11	2	2	26	21	.283
2004 Midland	....	Texas	OF-2B	65	265	38	71	13	4	1	22	18	.268
2005 Sacramento	....	P.C.	OF-SS-2B	102	378	56	105	16	9	2	40	23	.278
2005 Oakland	....	A.L.	2B-OF	7	7	0	2	1	0	0	1	0	.286
2006 Iowa	....	P.C.	2B-OF-SS	6	22	3	5	0	0	0	3	0	.227
2006 Chicago a-b-c-d	....	N.L.	OF-2B	71	136	20	35	5	5	4	12	8	.257
2007 Delmarva	....	So.Atl.	OF	1	1	0	0	0	0	0	0	1	.000
2007 Frederick	.....	Carolina	2B-OF-SS	5	17	3	4	0	1	0	2	0	.235
2007 Bowie	....	Eastern	SS	1	3	0	0	0	0	0	0	0	.000
2007 Baltimore e	....	A.L.	OF-SS-2B	70	96	21	25	8	2	2	11	8	.260
Major League Totals	....	3 Yrs.		148	239	41	62	14	7	6	24	16	.259

a Traded to Texas Rangers with pitcher John Rheinecker for pitcher Juan Dominguez, March 31, 2006.
b Traded to Chicago Cubs for pitcher John Koronka, March 31, 2006.
c On disabled list from June 25 to August 21, 2006.
d Traded to Baltimore Orioles for player to be named later, December 6, 2006. Chicago Cubs received pitcher Kevin Hart to complete trade, December 7, 2006.
e On disabled list from July 7 to August 20, 2007.

BYRD, MARLON JERRARD
Born, Boynton Beach, Florida, August 30, 1977.
Bats Right. Throws Right. Height, 6 feet. Weight, 235 pounds.

Year	Club	Lea	Pos	G	AB	R	H	2B	3B	HR	RBI	SB	Avg
1999 Batavia	....	N.Y.-Penn.	OF	65	239	39	70	7	6	13	49	8	.293
2000 Piedmont	....	So.Atl.	OF	133	515	104	159	29	13	17	93	41	.309
2001 Reading	....	Eastern	OF	137	510	108	161	22	8	28	89	32	.316
2002 Scranton-WB	....	Int.	OF	136	538	103	160	37	7	15	63	15	.297
2002 Philadelphia	....	N.L.	OF	10	35	2	8	2	0	1	1	0	.229
2003 Scranton-WB	....	Int.	OF	1	4	1	3	1	0	0	0	0	.750
2003 Reading	....	Eastern	OF	3	16	3	5	0	0	1	3	0	.313
2003 Philadelphia a	....	N.L.	OF	135	495	86	150	28	4	7	45	11	.303
2004 Scranton/WB	....	Int.	OF	37	152	13	40	11	1	2	17	2	.263
2004 Philadelphia	....	N.L.	OF	106	346	48	79	13	2	5	33	2	.228
2005 New Orleans	....	P.C.	OF	21	81	19	33	6	0	5	11	4	.407
2005 Scranton/WB	....	Int.	OF	5	19	4	7	1	0	3	5	0	.368
2005 Washington-Philadelphia b-c		N.L.	OF	79	229	20	61	15	2	2	26	5	.266
2006 New Orleans	....	P.C.	OF	46	155	20	42	9	0	7	29	3	.271
2006 Washington d	......	N.L.	OF	78	197	28	44	8	1	5	18	3	.223
2007 Oklahoma	....	P.C.	OF	44	176	29	63	15	2	6	32	3	.358
2007 Texas	....	A.L.	OF	109	414	60	127	17	8	10	70	5	.307
Major League Totals	....	6 Yrs.		517	1716	244	469	83	17	30	193	26	.273

a On disabled list from April 14 to April 29, 2003.
b On disabled list from March 29 to May 3, 2005.
c Traded to Washington Nationals for outfielder Endy Chavez, May 14, 2005.
d Filed for free agency, October 2, 2006. Signed with Texas Rangers, December 8, 2006.

BYRNES, ERIC JAMES
Born, Redwood City, California, February 16, 1976.
Bats Right. Throws Right. Height, 6 feet, 2 inches. Weight, 210 pounds.

Year	Club	Lea	Pos	G	AB	R	H	2B	3B	HR	RBI	SB	Avg
1998 Sou Oregon	.....	Northwest	OF	42	169	36	53	10	2	7	31	6	.314
1998 Visalia	....	California	OF	29	108	26	46	9	2	4	21	11	.426
1999 Modesto	....	California	OF	95	365	86	123	28	1	6	66	28	.337
1999 Midland	....	Texas	OF	43	164	25	39	14	0	1	22	6	.238
2000 Midland	....	Texas	OF	67	259	49	78	25	2	5	37	21	.301
2000 Oakland	....	A.L.	OF	10	10	5	3	0	0	0	0	2	.300
2000 Sacramento	....	P.C.	OF	67	243	55	81	23	1	9	47	12	.333
2001 Sacramento	....	P.C.	OF	100	415	81	120	23	2	20	51	25	.289
2001 Oakland	....	A.L.	OF	19	38	9	9	1	0	3	5	1	.237
2002 Sacramento	....	P.C.	OF	31	119	16	31	7	0	4	16	5	.261
2002 Oakland	....	A.L.	OF	90	94	24	23	4	2	3	11	3	.245

Year	Club	Lea	Pos	G	AB	R	H	2B	3B	HR	RBI	SB	Avg
2003 Oakland	A.L.	OF	121	414	64	109	27	9	12	51	10	.263
2004 Oakland a	A.L.	OF	143	569	91	161	39	3	20	73	17	.283
2005 Colorado	N.L.	OF	15	53	2	10	2	0	0	5	2	.189
2005 Oakland-Baltimore b-c ..	A.L.	OF	111	359	47	83	22	3	10	35	5	.231
2006 Arizona..............	N.L.	OF	143	562	82	150	37	3	26	79	25	.267
2007 Arizona..............	N.L.	OF	160	626	103	179	30	8	21	83	50	.286
Major League Totals	8 Yrs.		812	2725	427	727	162	28	95	342	115	.267
Division Series												
2001 Oakland	A.L.	DH	2	2	0	0	0	0	0	0	0	.000
2002 Oakland	A.L.	OF	2	1	0	0	0	0	0	0	0	.000
2003 Oakland	A.L.	OF	5	13	2	6	1	0	0	2	1	.462
2007 Arizona..............	N.L.	OF	3	12	1	3	0	1	1	3	1	.250
Division Series Totals			12	28	3	9	1	1	1	5	2	.321
Championship Series												
2007 Arizona..............	N.L.	OF	4	17	0	3	1	0	0	2	0	.176

a Traded to Colorado Rockies with infielder Omar Quintanilla for pitcher Jay Witasick and pitcher Joe Kennedy, July 13, 2005.
b Traded to Baltimore Orioles for outfielder Larry Bigbie, July 30, 2005.
c Not offered contract, December 21, 2005. Signed with Arizona Diamondbacks, December 30, 2005.

CABRERA, ASDRUBAL JOSE

Born, Puerto La Cruz, Venezuela, November 13, 1985.
Bats Both. Throws Right. Height, 6 feet. Weight, 170 pounds.

Year	Club	Lea	Pos	G	AB	R	H	2B	3B	HR	RBI	SB	Avg
2004 Everett	Northwest	SS-2B-3B	63	239	44	65	16	3	5	41	7	.272
2005 Inland Empire.....	Calif.	SS	55	225	31	64	15	6	1	26	3	.284
2005 Wisconsin ...	Midwest	2B-SS-3B	51	192	26	61	12	3	4	30	2	.318
2005 Tacoma	P.C.	SS	6	23	4	5	0	1	0	3	0	.217
2006 Buffalo	Int.	SS	52	190	26	50	11	0	1	14	5	.263
2006 Tacoma a	P.C.	SS	60	203	27	48	12	2	3	22	7	.236
2007 Akron	Eastern	SS-2B	96	368	78	114	23	3	8	54	23	.310
2007 Buffalo	Int.	SS-2B	9	38	6	12	3	0	0	3	2	.316
2007 Cleveland	A.L.	2B-SS-3B	45	159	30	45	9	2	3	22	0	.283
Division Series												
2007 Cleveland	A.L.	2B	4	17	3	3	0	0	1	2	0	.176
Championship Series												
2007 Cleveland	A.L.	2B	7	29	2	7	0	0	0	4	0	.241

a Traded to Cleveland Indians by Seattle Mariners for outfielder Eduardo Perez, June 30, 2006.

CABRERA, JOSE MIGUEL (MIGUEL)

Born, Maracay, Venezuela, April 18, 1983.
Bats Right. Throws Right. Height, 6 feet, 2 inches. Weight, 210 pounds.

Year	Club	Lea	Pos	G	AB	R	H	2B	3B	HR	RBI	SB	Avg
2000 Marlins.........	Gulf Coast	SS	57	219	38	57	10	2	2	22	1	.260
2000 Utica.............	N.Y.-Penn	SS	8	32	3	8	2	0	0	6	0	.250
2001 Kane County......	Midwest	SS	110	422	61	134	19	4	7	66	3	.318
2002 Jupiter	Fla.St.	3B	124	478	77	134	43	1	9	75	10	.274
2003 Carolina	Southern	3B-OF	69	266	46	97	29	3	10	59	9	.365
2003 Florida	N.L.	OF-3B	87	314	39	84	21	3	12	62	0	.268
2004 Florida	N.L.	OF	160	603	101	177	31	1	33	112	5	.294
2005 Florida	N.L.	OF-3B	158	613	106	198	43	2	33	116	1	.323
2006 Florida	N.L.	3B	158	576	112	195	50	2	26	114	9	.339
2007 Florida a.............	N.L.	3B	157	588	91	188	38	2	34	119	2	.320
Major League Totals	5 Yrs.		720	2694	449	842	183	10	138	523	17	.313
Division Series												
2003 Florida	N.L.	3B	4	14	1	4	2	0	0	3	0	.286
Championship Series												
2003 Florida	N.L.	OF-3B-SS	7	30	9	10	0	0	3	6	0	.333
World Series Record												
2003 Florida	N.L.	OF	6	24	1	4	0	0	1	3	0	.167

a Traded to Detroit Tigers with pitcher Dontrelle Willis for pitcher Burke Badenhop, pitcher Eulogio De La Cruz, pitcher Andrew Miller, catcher Mike Rabelo and outfielder Cameron Maybin, December 5, 2007.

CABRERA, MELKY

Born, Santo Domingo, Dominican Republic, August 11, 1984.
Bats Both. Throws Left. Height, 5 feet, 11 inches. Weight, 170 pounds.

Year	Club	Lea	Pos	G	AB	R	H	2B	3B	HR	RBI	SB	Avg
2003	Staten Island	N.Y.-Penn.	OF	67	279	34	79	10	2	2	31	13	.283
2004	Tampa	Fla.St.	OF	85	333	48	96	20	3	8	51	3	.288
2004	Battle .... Midwest		OF	42	171	35	57	16	3	0	16	7	.333
2005	New York	A.L.	OF	6	19	1	4	0	0	0	0	0	.211
2005	Columbus............	Int.	OF	26	101	15	25	3	0	3	17	2	.248
2005	Trenton........... Eastern		OF	106	426	57	117	22	3	10	60	11	.275
2006	Columbus............	Int.	OF	31	122	19	47	6	2	4	24	3	.385
2006	New York	A.L.	OF	130	460	75	129	26	2	7	50	12	.280
2007	New York	A.L.	OF	150	545	66	149	24	8	8	73	13	.273
Major League Totals			3 Yrs.	286	1024	142	282	50	10	15	123	25	.275
Division Series													
2006	New York	A.L.	OF	2	3	0	0	0	0	0	0	0	.000
2007	New York	A.L.	OF	4	16	2	3	0	0	1	2	0	.188
Division Series Totals				6	19	2	3	0	0	1	2	0	.158

CABRERA, ORLANDO LUIS

Born, Cartagena, Colombia, November 2, 1974.
Bats Right. Throws Right. Height, 5 feet, 9 inches. Weight, 180 pounds.

Year	Club	Lea	Pos	G	AB	R	H	2B	3B	HR	RBI	SB	Avg
1994	Expos.......... Gulf Coast		2B-SS-OF	22	73	13	23	4	1	0	11	6	.315
1995	Wst Plm Bch	Fla. St.	SS	3	5	0	1	0	0	0	0	0	.200
1995	Vermont........ N.Y.-Penn.		2B-SS	65	248	37	70	12	5	3	33	15	.282
1996	Delmarva	So. Atl.	SS-2B	134	512	86	129	28	4	14	65	51	.252
1997	Wst Plm Bch	Fla. St.	SS-2B	69	279	56	77	19	2	5	26	32	.276
1997	Harrisburg .... Eastern		SS-2B	35	133	34	41	13	2	5	20	7	.308
1997	Ottawa	Int.	SS-2B	31	122	17	32	5	2	2	14	8	.262
1997	Montreal.............	N.L.	SS-2B	16	18	4	4	0	0	0	2	1	.222
1998	Ottawa	Int.	SS-2B	66	272	31	63	9	4	0	26	19	.232
1998	Montreal.............	N.L.	SS-2B	79	261	44	73	16	5	3	22	6	.280
1999	Montreal a	N.L.	SS	104	382	48	97	23	5	8	39	2	.254
2000	Ottawa	Int.	SS	2	6	1	4	0	0	0	0	1	.667
2000	Montreal b	N.L.	SS-2B	125	422	47	100	25	1	13	55	4	.237
2001	Montreal.............	N.L.	SS	*162	626	64	173	41	6	14	96	19	.276
2002	Montreal.............	N.L.	SS	153	563	64	148	43	1	7	56	25	.263
2003	Montreal.............	N.L.	SS	*162	626	95	186	47	2	17	80	24	.297
2004	Montreal.............	N.L.	SS	103	390	41	96	19	2	4	31	12	.246
2004	Boston c-d-e	A.L.	SS	58	228	33	67	19	1	6	31	4	.294
2005	Los Angeles f	A.L.	SS	141	540	70	139	28	3	8	57	21	.257
2006	Los Angeles	A.L.	SS	153	607	95	171	45	1	9	72	27	.282
2007	Los Angeles g	A.L.	SS	155	638	101	192	35	1	8	86	20	.301
Major League Totals			11 Yrs.	1411	5301	706	1446	341	28	97	627	165	.273
Division Series													
2004	Boston	A.L.	SS	3	13	1	2	1	0	0	3	0	.154
2005	Los Angeles	A.L.	SS	5	21	3	5	2	0	0	3	0	.238
2007	Los Angeles	A.L.	SS	3	12	0	3	1	0	0	1	0	.250
Division Series Totals				11	46	4	10	4	0	0	7	0	.217
Championship Series													
2004	Boston	A.L.	SS	7	29	5	11	2	0	0	5	1	.379
2005	Los Angeles	A.L.	SS	5	20	1	4	1	0	1	3	0	.200
Championship Series Totals				12	49	6	15	3	0	1	8	1	.306
World Series Record													
2004	Boston	A.L.	SS	4	17	3	4	1	0	0	3	0	.235

a On disabled list from August 9 to October 13, 1999.

b On disabled list from July 15 to August 14, 2000.

c Traded to Chicago Cubs for infielder Alex Gonzalez, infielder Brendan Harris and pitcher Francis Beltran, July 31, 2004.

d Traded to Boston Red Sox with infielder Doug Mientkiewicz for infielder Nomar Garciaparra and outfielder Matt Murton, July 31, 2004.

e Filed for free agency, November 1, 2004. Signed with Anaheim Angels, December 20, 2004.

f On disabled list from June 27 to July 16, 2005.

g Traded to Chicago White Sox for pitcher Jon Garland, November 19, 2007.

CAIRO, MIGUEL JESUS

Born, Anaco, Venezuela, May 4, 1974.
Bats Right. Throws Right. Height, 6 feet, 1 inch. Weight, 210 pounds.

Year	Club	Lea	Pos	G	AB	R	H	2B	3B	HR	RBI	SB	Avg
1992 Dodgers	Gulf Coast		SS-3B	21	76	10	23	5	2	0	9	1	.303
1992 Vero Beach	Fla. St.		2B-SS	36	125	7	28	0	0	0	7	5	.224
1993 Vero Beach	Fla. St.		2B-SS-3B	90	346	50	109	10	1	1	23	23	.315
1994 Bakersfield	California		2B-SS	133	533	76	155	23	4	2	48	44	.291
1995 San Antonio a-b	Texas		2B-SS	107	435	53	121	20	1	1	41	33	.278
1996 Syracuse	Int.		2B-3B-SS	120	465	71	129	14	4	3	48	27	.277
1996 Toronto c	A.L.		2B	9	27	5	6	2	0	0	1	0	.222
1997 Iowa	A.A.		2B-SS	135	569	82	159	35	4	5	46	40	.279
1997 Chicago d	N.L.		2B-SS	16	29	7	7	1	0	0	1	0	.241
1998 Tampa Bay	A.L.		2B	150	515	49	138	26	5	5	46	19	.268
1999 St.Petersburg	Fla.St.		2B	3	13	2	5	0	0	0	0	1	.385
1999 Orlando	Southern		2B	3	13	1	5	2	0	0	1	0	.385
1999 Tampa Bay e	A.L.		2B	120	465	61	137	15	5	3	36	22	.295
2000 Tampa Bay d	A.L.		2B	119	375	49	98	18	2	1	34	28	.261
2001 Iowa	P.C.		2B-SS-3B	34	123	22	37	7	1	3	14	3	.301
2001 Chicago-St. Louis e-f	N.L.		3B-2B-OF-SS	93	156	25	46	8	1	3	16	2	.295
2002 St. Louis	N.L.		OF-2B-3B-SS	108	184	28	46	9	2	2	23	1	.250
2003 Memphis	P.C.		2B	3	13	2	3	1	0	0	0	0	.231
2003 St. Louis g-h	N.L.		2B-OF-3B-SS	92	261	41	64	15	2	5	32	4	.245
2004 New York i	A.L.		2B-3B-SS-1B	122	360	48	105	17	5	6	42	11	.292
2005 Mets	Gulf Coast		2B	3	13	3	4	1	0	0	0	0	.308
2005 St. Lucie	Fla.St.		DH	1	4	0	1	0	0	0	0	0	.250
2005 New York j-k	N.L.		2B-1B-3B-OF	100	327	31	82	18	0	2	19	13	.251
2006 New York l-m	A.L.		2B-1B-SS-3B	81	222	28	53	12	3	0	30	13	.239
2007 Memphis	P.C.		3B-SS-OF-1B	9	31	8	9	2	0	0	3	2	.290
2007 New York	A.L.		1B-SS-3B-2B	54	107	12	27	7	0	0	10	8	.252
2007 St. Louis n-o	N.L.		3B-2B-1B-OF	28	67	8	17	2	2	0	5	2	.254
Major League Totals		12 Yrs.		1092	3095	392	826	150	27	27	295	123	.267
Division Series													
2001 St. Louis	N.L.		OF	3	5	0	1	0	0	0	0	1	.200
2002 St. Louis	N.L.		3B	2	4	2	4	1	0	0	3	0	1.000
2004 New York	A.L.		2B	4	14	3	3	1	0	0	1	0	.214
Division Series Totals				9	23	5	8	2	0	0	4	1	.348
Championship Series													
2002 St. Louis	N.L.		3B	3	13	2	5	0	0	1	2	0	.385
2004 New York	A.L.		2B	7	25	4	7	3	0	0	0	1	.280
Championship Series Totals				10	38	6	12	3	0	1	2	1	.316

a Traded to Seattle Mariners with infielder Willie Otanez for third baseman Mike Blowers, November 29, 1995.
b Traded to Toronto Blue Jays with pitcher Bill Risley for pitchers Edwin Hurtado and Paul Menhart, December 18, 1995.
c On disabled list, May 27 to June 5, 1996.
d Selected in expansion draft by Tampa Bay Devil Rays, November 18, 1997.
e On disabled list from April 24 to May 17 and July 26 to August 11, 1999.
d Released by Tampa Bay Devil Rays, November 27, 2000. Signed by Oakland A's organization, January 8, 2001.
e Traded to Chicago Cubs for infielder Eric Hinske, March 28, 2001.
f Claimed on waivers by St. Louis Cardinals, August 10, 2001.
g On disabled list from June 19 to July 29, 2003.
h Filed for free agency, October 26, 2003. Signed with New York Yankees, December 19, 2003.
i Filed for free agency, October 28, 2004. Signed with New York Mets, January 10, 2005.
j On disabled list from June 15 to July 2, 2005.
k Filed for free agency, October 28, 2005. Signed with New York Yankees, January 5, 2006.
l On disabled list from August 6 to September 11, 2006.
m Filed for free agency, October 28, 2006, re-signed with New York Yankees, January 6, 2007.
n Released by New York Yankees, August 15, 2007. Signed with St. Louis Cardinals organization, August 19, 2007.
o Filed for free agency, October 29, 2007. Signed with Seattle Mariners, January 8, 2008

CAMERON, MICHAEL TERRANCE (MIKE)

Born, La Grange, Georgia, January 8, 1973.
Bats Right. Throws Right. Height, 6 feet, 2 inches. Weight, 200 pounds.

Year	Club	Lea	Pos	G	AB	R	H	2B	3B	HR	RBI	SB	Avg
1991 White Sox	Gulf Coast		OF	44	136	20	30	3	0	0	11	13	.221
1992 Utica	N.Y.-Penn.		OF	28	87	15	24	1	4	2	12	3	.276
1992 South Bend	Midwest		OF	35	114	19	26	8	1	1	9	2	.228
1993 South Bend	Midwest		OF	122	411	52	98	14	5	0	30	19	.238
1994 Pr William	Carolina		OF	131	468	86	116	15	17	6	48	22	.248

Year	Club	Lea	Pos	G	AB	R	H	2B	3B	HR	RBI	SB	Avg
1995 Birmingham	Southern	OF	107	350	64	87	20	5	11	60	21	.249
1995 Chicago	A.L.	OF	28	38	4	7	2	0	1	2	0	.184
1996 Birmingham	Southern	OF	123	473	120	142	34	12	28	77	39	.300
1996 Chicago	A.L.	OF	11	11	1	1	0	0	0	0	0	.091
1997 Nashville	A.A.	OF	30	120	21	33	7	3	6	17	4	.275
1997 Chicago	A.L.	OF	116	379	63	98	18	3	14	55	23	.259
1998 Chicago a	A.L.	OF	141	396	53	83	16	5	8	43	27	.210
1999 Cincinnati	N.L.	OF	146	542	93	139	34	9	21	66	38	.256
2000 Seattle b	A.L.	OF	155	543	96	145	28	4	19	78	24	.267
2001 Seattle	A.L.	OF	150	540	99	144	30	5	25	110	34	.267
2002 Seattle	A.L.	OF	158	545	84	130	26	5	25	80	31	.239
2003 Seattle c	A.L.	OF	147	534	74	135	31	5	18	76	17	.253
2004 New York	N.L.	OF	140	493	76	114	30	1	30	76	22	.231
2005 St. Lucie	Fla.St.	OF	4	10	3	3	2	0	0	0	0	.300
2005 Norfolk	Int.	OF	2	7	2	2	0	1	0	2	0	.286
2005 New York d-e	N.L.	OF	76	308	47	84	23	2	12	39	13	.273
2006 Lake Elsinore	Calif.	OF	2	6	1	2	1	0	0	1	0	.333
2006 San Diego f	N.L.	OF	141	552	88	148	34	9	22	83	25	.268
2007 San Diego g	N.L.	OF	151	571	88	138	33	6	21	78	18	.242
Major League Totals	13 Yrs.		1560	5452	866	1366	305	54	216	786	272	.251
Division Series												
2000 Seattle	A.L.	OF	3	12	2	3	0	0	0	2	1	.250
2001 Seattle	A.L.	OF	5	18	2	4	3	0	1	3	0	.222
2006 San Diego	N.L.	OF	4	14	1	2	1	0	0	1	1	.143
Division Series Totals			12	44	5	9	4	0	1	6	2	.205
Championship Series												
2000 Seattle	A.L.	OF	6	18	3	2	0	0	0	1	1	.111
2001 Seattle	A.L.	OF	5	17	3	3	2	0	0	0	0	.176
Championship Series Totals			11	35	6	5	2	0	0	1	1	.143

a Traded to Cincinnati Reds for infielder Paul Konerko, November 11, 1998.
b Traded to Seattle Mariners with pitcher Brett Tomko, infielder Antonio Perez and pitcher Jake Meyer for outfielder Ken Griffey, February 10, 2000.
c Filed for free agency, October 27, 2003. Signed with New York Mets, December 14, 2003.
d On disabled list from April 1 to May 5 and August 12 to October 31, 2005.
e Traded to San Diego Padres for infielder Xavier Nady, November 18, 2005.
f On disabled list from March 31 to April 23, 2006.
g Filed for free agency, October 31, 2007. Signed with Milwaukee Brewers, January 14, 2008.

CANO (MERCEDES), ROBINSON JOSE

Born, San Pedro de Macoris, Dominican Republic, October 22, 1982.
Bats Left. Throws Right. Height, 6 feet. Weight, 190 pounds.

Year	Club	Lea	Pos	G	AB	R	H	2B	3B	HR	RBI	SB	Avg
2001 Yankees	Gulf Coast	2B-SS-3B	57	200	37	46	14	2	3	34	11	.230
2001 Staten Island	N.Y.-Penn.	3B-SS	2	8	0	2	0	0	0	2	0	.250
2002 Staten Island	N.Y.-Penn.	2B-SS	22	87	11	24	5	1	1	15	6	.276
2002 Greensboro	So.Atl.	SS-2B	113	474	67	131	20	9	14	66	2	.276
2003 Trenton	Eastern	2B-SS-C	46	164	21	46	9	1	1	13	0	.280
2003 Tampa	Fla.St.	2B	90	366	50	101	16	3	5	50	1	.276
2004 Trenton	Eastern	2B-3B	74	292	43	88	20	8	7	44	2	.301
2004 Columbus	Int.	2B	61	216	22	56	9	2	6	30	0	.259
2005 Columbus	Int.	2B-3B	24	108	19	36	8	3	4	24	0	.333
2005 New York	A.L.	2B	132	522	78	155	34	4	14	62	1	.297
2006 Yankees	Gulf Coast	DH	1	5	0	2	0	0	0	1	0	.400
2006 Trenton	Eastern	2B	3	10	1	5	2	0	0	2	0	.500
2006 New York a	A.L.	2B	122	482	62	165	41	1	15	78	5	.342
2007 New York	A.L.	2B	160	617	93	189	41	7	19	97	4	.306
Major League Totals	3 Yrs.		414	1621	233	509	116	12	48	237	10	.314
Division Series												
2005 New York	A.L.	2B	5	19	3	5	3	0	0	5	0	.263
2006 New York	A.L.	2B	4	15	0	2	0	0	0	0	0	.133
2007 New York	A.L.	2B	4	15	3	5	1	0	2	3	0	.333
Division Series Totals			13	49	6	12	4	0	2	8	0	.245

a On disabled list from June 26 to August 8, 2006.

CARROLL, JAMEY BLAKE

Born, Evansville, Indiana, February 18, 1974.
Bats Right. Throws Right. Height, 5 feet, 9 inches. Weight, 170 pounds.

Year	Club	Lea	Pos	G	AB	R	H	2B	3B	HR	RBI	SB	Avg
1996	Vermont	N.Y.-Penn.	SS-2B-3B	54	203	40	56	6	1	0	17	16	.276
1997	Wst Plm Bch	Fla.St.	SS-2B-3B	121	407	56	99	19	1	0	38	17	.243
1998	Jupiter	Fla.St.	2B-SS	55	222	40	58	5	0	0	14	11	.261
1998	Harrisburg	Eastern	2B-SS	75	261	43	66	11	3	0	20	11	.253
1999	Harrisburg	Eastern	2B	141	561	78	164	34	5	5	63	21	.292
2000	Harrisburg	Eastern	3B-SS-2B	45	169	23	49	5	3	0	18	8	.290
2000	Ottawa	Int.	2B-3B-SS	91	349	53	97	17	2	2	23	6	.278
2001	Ottawa	Int.	2B-SS-3B	83	267	26	64	8	2	0	16	5	.240
2002	Harrisburg	Eastern	2B	3	9	1	4	0	0	0	1	0	.444
2002	Ottawa	Int.	3B-SS-2B	117	421	57	118	19	2	8	49	6	.280
2002	Montreal	N.L.	3B-SS-2B	16	71	16	22	5	3	1	6	1	.310
2003	Montreal	N.L.	3B-SS-2B	105	227	31	59	10	1	1	10	5	.260
2004	Montreal	N.L.	2B-3B-SS-OF	102	218	36	63	14	2	0	16	5	.289
2005	Washington	N.L.	2B-SS-3B	113	303	44	76	8	1	0	22	3	.251
2006	Colorado a	N.L.	2B-SS-3B	136	463	84	139	23	5	5	36	10	.300
2007	Colorado b	N.L.	3B-SS-OF	108	227	45	51	9	1	2	22	6	.225
Major League Totals			6 Yrs.	580	1509	256	410	69	13	9	112	30	.272
Division Series													
2007	Colorado	N.L.	2B	1	0	0	0	0	0	0	0	0	.000
Championship Series													
2007	Colorado	N.L.	3B	2	1	0	0	0	0	0	0	0	.000
World Series Record													
2007	Colorado	N.L.	2B	1	1	0	0	0	0	0	0	0	.000

a Sold to Colorado Rockies, February 11, 2006.
b Traded to Cleveland Indians for player to be named later, December 8, 2007.

CASEY, SEAN THOMAS

Born, Willingboro, New Jersey, July 2, 1974.
Bats Left. Throws Right. Height, 6 feet, 4 inches. Weight, 235 pounds.

Year	Club	Lea	Pos	G	AB	R	H	2B	3B	HR	RBI	SB	Avg
1995	Watertown	N.Y.-Penn.	1B	55	207	26	68	18	0	2	37	3	.329
1996	Kinston	Carolina	1B	92	344	62	114	31	3	12	57	1	.331
1997	Akron	Eastern	1B	62	241	38	93	19	1	10	66	0	.386
1997	Buffalo	A.A.	DH-1B	20	72	12	26	7	0	5	18	0	.361
1997	Cleveland a	A.L.	1B	6	10	1	2	0	0	0	1	0	.200
1998	Indianapolis	Int.	1B	27	95	14	31	8	1	1	13	0	.326
1998	Cincinnati b-c	N.L.	1B	96	302	44	82	21	1	7	52	1	.272
1999	Cincinnati	N.L.	1B	151	594	103	197	42	3	25	99	0	.332
2000	Cincinnati d	N.L.	1B	133	480	69	151	33	2	20	85	1	.315
2001	Cincinnati	N.L.	1B	145	533	69	165	40	0	13	89	3	.310
2002	Louisville	Int.	DH	2	8	2	4	0	0	1	3	0	.500
2002	Cincinnati e	N.L.	1B	120	425	56	111	25	0	6	42	2	.261
2003	Cincinnati	N.L.	1B	147	573	71	167	19	3	14	80	4	.291
2004	Cincinnati f	N.L.	1B	146	571	101	185	44	2	24	99	2	.324
2005	Cincinnati g	N.L.	1B	137	529	75	165	32	0	9	58	2	.312
2006	Altoona	Eastern	1B	3	11	1	3	0	0	1	2	0	.273
2006	Pittsburgh	N.L.	1B	59	213	30	63	15	0	3	29	0	.296
2006	Detroit h-i-j	A.L.	1B	53	184	17	45	7	0	5	30	0	.245
2007	Detroit k	A.L.	1B	143	453	40	134	30	1	4	54	2	.296
Major League Totals			11 Yrs.	1336	4867	676	1467	308	12	130	718	17	.301
Division Series													
2006	Detroit	A.L.	1B	4	17	1	6	3	0	0	4	0	.353
Championship Series													
2006	Detroit	A.L.	1B	1	3	0	1	0	0	0	0	0	.333
World Series Record													
2006	Detroit	A.L.	1B-DH	5	17	2	9	2	0	2	5	0	.529

a On disabled list from April 4 to June 8, 1997.
b Traded to Cincinnati Reds for pitcher Dave Burba, March 30, 1998.
c On disabled list from April 3 to May 5, 1998.
d On disabled list from April 2 to April 18, 2000.
e On disabled list from July 23 to August 9 and September 10 to September 30, 2002.
f On disabled list from June 28 to July 14, 2004.
g Traded to Pittsburgh Pirates for pitcher Dave Williams, December 8, 2005.
h On disabled list from April 15 to May 29, 2006.
i Traded to Detroit Tigers for pitcher Brian Rogers, July 31, 2006.
j Filed for free agency, October 31, 2006, re-signed with Detroit Tigers, November 16, 2006.
k Filed for free agency, October 29, 2007.

CASTILLO (RONDON), JOSE

Born, Las Mercedes, Venezuela, March 19, 1981.
Bats Right. Throws Right. Height, 6 feet. Weight, 210 pounds.

Year Club	Lea	Pos	G	AB	R	H	2B	3B	HR	RBI	SB	Avg
1998 Montalban . . . Venzuelan		SS	55	179	31	52	9	1	1	13	23	.291
1999 Pirates	Gulf Coast	SS-2B	47	173	27	46	9	0	4	30	8	.266
2000 Hickory.	So.Atl.	SS	125	529	95	158	32	8	16	72	16	.299
2001 Lynchburg	Carolina	SS	125	485	57	119	20	7	7	49	23	.245
2002 Lynchburg	Carolina	SS	134	503	82	151	25	2	16	81	27	.300
2003 Altoona.	Eastern	2B-SS	126	498	68	143	24	6	5	66	19	.287
2004 Pittsburgh . . . . .N.L.		2B-SS	129	383	44	98	15	2	8	39	3	.256
2005 Indianapolis	Int.	2B	4	13	2	5	1	0	2	2	0	.385
2005 Pittsburgh a . . . . . . .N.L.		2B	101	370	49	99	16	3	11	53	2	.268
2006 Pittsburgh . . . . .N.L.		2B	148	518	54	131	25	0	14	65	6	.253
2007 Pittsburgh b . . . . . .N.L.		3B-2B-SS-OF	87	221	18	54	18	1	0	24	0	.244
Major League Totals	4 Yrs.		465	1492	165	382	74	6	33	181	11	.256

a On disabled list from April 7 to May 5 and August 23 to October 3, 2005.
b Released by Pittsburgh Pirates, December 6, 2007. Signed with Florida Marlins, December 24, 2007.

CASTILLO, LUIS ANTONIO

Born, San Pedro de Macoris, Dominican Republic, September 12, 1975.
Bats Both. Throws Right. Height, 5 feet, 11 inches. Weight, 190 pounds.

Year Club	Lea	Pos	G	AB	R	H	2B	3B	HR	RBI	SB	Avg
1993 Florida	Dominican	2B	69	266	48	75	7	1	4	31	9	.282
1994 Marlins.	Gulf Coast	2B-SS	57	216	49	57	8	0	0	16	31	.264
1995 Kane County.	Midwest	2B	89	340	71	111	4	4	0	23	41	.326
1996 Portland	Eastern	2B	109	420	83	133	15	7	1	35	51	.317
1996 Florida	N.L.	2B	41	164	26	43	2	1	1	8	17	.262
1997 Florida	N.L.	2B	75	263	27	63	8	0	0	8	16	.240
1997 Charlotte	Int.	2B	37	130	25	46	5	0	0	5	8	.354
1998 Charlotte	Int.	2B	100	381	74	109	11	2	0	15	41	.286
1998 Florida	N.L.	2B	44	153	21	31	3	2	1	10	3	.203
1999 Florida	N.L.	2B	128	487	76	147	23	4	0	28	50	.302
2000 Calgary.	P.C.	2B	4	13	4	4	1	1	0	0	1	.308
2000 Florida a	N.L.	2B	136	539	101	180	17	3	2	17	*62	.334
2001 Florida	N.L.	2B	134	537	76	141	16	10	2	45	33	.263
2002 Florida b	N.L.	2B	146	606	86	185	18	5	2	39	48	.305
2003 Florida b	N.L.	2B	152	595	99	187	19	6	6	39	21	.314
2004 Florida	N.L.	2B	150	564	91	164	12	7	2	47	21	.291
2005 Florida c	N.L.	2B	122	439	72	132	12	4	4	30	10	.301
2006 Minnesota	A.L.	2B	142	584	84	173	22	6	3	49	25	.296
2007 Minnesota	A.L.	2B	85	349	54	106	11	3	0	18	9	.304
2007 New York d-e	N.L.	2B	50	199	37	59	8	2	1	20	10	.296
Major League Totals	12 Yrs.		1405	5479	850	1611	171	53	24	358	325	.294
Division Series												
2003 Florida	N.L.	2B	4	17	2	5	3	0	0	1	0	.294
2006 Minnesota	A.L.	2B	3	11	0	3	0	0	0	0	0	.273
Division Series Totals			7	28	2	8	3	0	0	1	0	.286
Championship Series												
2003 Florida	N.L.	2B	7	28	3	6	1	0	0	2	2	.214
World Series Record												
2003 Florida	N.L.	2B	6	26	1	4	0	0	0	1	1	.154

a On disabled list from April 16 to May 5, 2000.
b Filed for free agency, November 6, 2003, re-signed with Florida Marlins, December 2, 2003.
c Traded to Minnesota Twins for pitcher Travis Bowyer and pitcher Scott Tyler, December 2, 2005.
d Traded to New York Mets for catcher Drew Butera and outfielder Dustin Martin, July 30, 2007.
e Filed for free agency, October 29, 2007, re-signed with New York Mets, November 19, 2007.

CATALANOTTO, FRANK JOHN

Born, Smithtown, New York, April 27, 1974.
Bats Left. Throws Right. Height, 6 feet. Weight, 195 pounds.

Year Club	Lea	Pos	G	AB	R	H	2B	3B	HR	RBI	SB	Avg
1992 Bristol	Appal.	2B-1B	21	50	6	10	2	0	0	4	0	.200
1993 Bristol	Appal.	2B	55	199	37	61	9	5	3	22	3	.307
1994 Fayettevlle	So. Atl.	2B	119	458	72	149	24	8	3	56	4	.325
1995 Jacksnville	Southern	2B	134	491	66	111	19	5	8	48	13	.226
1996 Jacksnville	Southern	2B	132	497	105	148	34	6	17	67	15	.298

Year	Club	Lea	Pos	G	AB	R	H	2B	3B	HR	RBI	SB	Avg
1997 Toledo	Int.		2B-3B-OF	134	500	75	150	32	3	16	68	12	.300
1997 Detroit	A.L.		2B	13	26	2	8	2	0	0	3	0	.308
1998 Toledo	Int.		1B-2B	28	105	20	35	6	3	4	28	0	.333
1998 Detroit	A.L.		2B-1B-3B	89	213	23	60	13	2	6	25	3	.282
1999 Detroit a	A.L.		1B-2B-3B	100	286	41	79	19	0	11	35	3	.276
2000 Oklahoma.........	P.C.		2B	3	11	2	3	0	0	0	1	0	.273
2000 Texas b..........	A.L.		2B-1B-OF	103	282	55	82	13	2	10	42	6	.291
2001 Texas	A.L.		OF-2B-3B-1B	133	463	77	153	31	5	11	54	15	.330
2002 Tulsa	Texas		1B-2B-OF	4	16	1	2	0	1	0	3	0	.125
2002 Texas c-d	A.L.		OF-2B-1B	68	212	42	57	16	6	3	23	9	.269
2003 Toronto	A.L.		OF-1B	133	489	83	146	34	6	13	59	2	.299
2004 Toronto e	A.L.		OF	75	249	27	73	19	1	1	26	1	.293
2005 Toronto	A.L.		OF	130	419	56	126	29	5	8	59	1	.301
2006 Toronto f	A.L.		OF	128	437	56	131	36	2	7	56	1	.300
2007 Frisco	Texas		DH	1	4	1	0	0	0	0	0	0	.000
2007 Oklahoma........	P.C.		DH	4	13	5	5	2	0	0	0	0	.385
2007 Texas g...........	A.L.		OF-1B	103	331	52	86	20	4	11	44	2	.260
Major League Totals			11 Yrs.	1075	3407	514	1001	232	33	81	426	42	.294

a Traded to Texas Rangers with pitcher Justin Thompson, pitcher Francisco Cordero, pitcher Alan Webb, outfielder Gabe Kapler and catcher Bill Haselman for outfielder Juan Gonzalez, pitcher Danny Patterson and catcher Greg Zaun, November 2, 1999.
b On disabled list from April 22 to May 14, 2000.
c On disabled list from May 11 to June 28 and August 17 to November 19, 2002.
d Not offered 2003 contract, December 20, 2002. Signed with Toronto Blue Jays, December 30, 2002.
e On disabled list from May 20 to June 8 and from June 18 to July 20 and from August 21 to October 29, 2004.
f Filed for free agency, October 28, 2006. Signed with Texas Rangers, November 21, 2006.
g On disabled list from April 30 to May 21, 2007.

CHAVEZ, ENDY DE JESUS

Born, Valencia, Venezuela, February 7, 1978.
Bats Left. Throws Left. Height, 6 feet. Weight, 165 pounds.

Year	Club	Lea	Pos	G	AB	R	H	2B	3B	HR	RBI	SB	Avg
1996 N.Y. Mets	Dominican		OF	48	164	42	58	11	1	7	29	3	.354
1997 Mets..........	Gulf Coast		OF	33	119	26	33	6	3	0	15	1	.277
1997 Kingsport	Appal.		OF	19	73	16	22	4	0	0	4	5	.301
1998 Kingsport...........	Appal.		OF	33	114	26	33	8	4	0	16	10	.289
1999 St. Lucie..........	Fla.St.		OF	45	183	33	57	8	3	2	18	9	.311
1999 Columbia	So.Atl.		OF	73	253	40	64	8	1	0	15	20	.253
2000 St. Lucie..........	Fla.St.		OF	111	433	84	129	20	2	1	43	38	.298
2001 Wichita.............	Texas		OF	43	168	27	50	6	1	1	13	11	.298
2001 Kansas City	A.L.		OF	29	77	4	16	2	0	0	5	0	.208
2001 Omaha a-b............	P.C.		OF	23	104	18	35	6	0	0	4	4	.337
2002 Ottawa	Int.		OF	103	405	67	139	28	5	4	41	21	.343
2002 Montreal c-d	N.L.		OF	36	125	20	37	8	5	1	9	3	.296
2003 Montreal...........	N.L.		OF	141	483	66	121	25	5	5	47	18	.251
2004 Edmonton	P.C.		OF	14	61	9	21	3	2	0	7	5	.344
2004 Montreal.............	N.L.		OF	132	502	65	139	20	6	5	34	32	.277
2005 New Orleans.........	P.C.		OF	23	87	11	22	4	0	1	4	6	.253
2005 Wash.-Philadelphia e-f	N.L.		OF	98	116	19	25	4	3	0	11	2	.216
2006 New York	N.L.		OF	133	353	48	108	22	5	4	42	12	.306
2007 Mets..........	Gulf Coast		OF	2	8	2	5	0	0	0	4	0	.625
2007 St. Lucie.............	Fla.St.		OF	4	16	3	8	1	0	0	2	0	.500
2007 Binghamton	Eastern		OF	1	3	0	0	0	0	0	0	0	.000
2007 New York g...........	N.L.		OF	71	150	20	43	7	2	1	17	5	.287
Major League Totals			7 Yrs.	640	1806	242	489	88	26	16	165	72	.271
Division Series													
2006 New York	N.L.		OF	3	8	1	3	0	0	0	0	0	.375
Championship Series													
2006 New York	N.L.		OF	7	27	1	5	2	0	0	0	0	.185

a Traded by New York Mets to Kansas City Royals for outfielder Michael Curry, March 30, 2001.
b Claimed on waivers by Detroit Tigers, December 20, 2001.
c Claimed on waivers by New York Mets, February 1, 2002.
d Claimed on waivers by Montreal Expos, February 22, 2002.
e Traded to Philadelphia Phillies for outfielder Marlon Byrd, May 14, 2005.
f Not offered contract, December 21, 2005. Signed with New York Mets, December 23, 2005.
g On disabled list from June 7 to August 28, 2007.

CHAVEZ, ERIC CESAR
Born, Los Angeles, California, December 7, 1977.
Bats Left. Throws Right. Height, 6 feet, 1 inch. Weight,210 pounds.

Year Club	Lea	Pos	G	AB	R	H	2B	3B	HR	RBI	SB	Avg
1997 Visalia	California	3B	134	520	67	141	30	3	18	100	13	.271
1998 Huntsville.	Southern	3B	88	335	66	110	27	1	22	86	12	.328
1998 Edmonton	.P.C.	3B	47	194	38	63	18	0	11	40	2	.325
1998 Oakland	A.L.	3B	16	45	6	14	4	1	0	6	1	.311
1999 Oakland a	A.L.	3B-SS	115	356	47	88	21	2	13	50	1	.247
2000 Oakland	A.L.	3B-SS	153	501	89	139	23	4	26	86	2	.277
2001 Oakland	A.L.	3B-1B-SS	151	552	91	159	43	0	32	114	8	.288
2002 Oakland	A.L.	3B-OF	153	585	87	161	31	3	34	109	8	.275
2003 Oakland	A.L.	3B	156	588	94	166	39	5	29	101	8	.282
2004 Sacramento	.P.C.	3B	3	13	2	4	1	0	0	0	0	.308
2004 Oakland b	A.L.	3B-OF	125	475	87	131	20	0	29	77	6	.276
2005 Oakland	A.L.	3B	160	625	92	168	40	1	27	101	6	.269
2006 Oakland	A.L.	3B	137	485	74	117	24	2	22	72	3	.241
2007 Oakland c	A.L.	3B	90	341	43	82	21	2	15	46	4	.240
Major League Totals	10 Yrs.		1256	4553	710	1225	266	20	227	762	47	.269
Division Series												
2000 Oakland	A.L.	3B	5	21	4	7	3	0	0	4	0	.333
2001 Oakland	A.L.	3B	5	21	0	3	1	0	0	0	0	.143
2002 Oakland	A.L.	3B	5	21	3	8	0	0	1	5	0	.381
2003 Oakland	A.L.	3B	5	22	1	1	1	0	0	0	1	.045
2006 Oakland	A.L.	3B	3	10	2	2	1	0	1	1	0	.200
Division Series Totals			23	95	10	21	6	0	2	10	1	.221
Championship Series												
2006 Oakland	A.L.	3B	4	13	1	3	1	0	1	2	0	.231

a On disabled list from August 21 to September 19, 1999.
b On disabled list from June 2 to July 9, 2004.
c On disabled list from July 27 to October 8, 2007.

CHURCH, RYAN MATTHEW
Born, Santa Barbara, California, October 14, 1978.
Bats Left. Throws Left. Height, 6 feet, 1 inch. Weight, 220 pounds.

Year Club	Lea	Pos	G	AB	R	H	2B	3B	HR	RBI	SB	Avg
2000 Mahoning Valley. .	N.Y.-Penn.	OF	73	272	51	81	16	5	10	65	11	.298
2001 Kinston.	Carolina	OF	24	83	16	20	7	0	5	15	1	.241
2001 Columbus.	So.Atl.	OF	101	363	64	104	23	3	17	76	4	.287
2002 Kinston.	Carolina	OF	53	181	30	59	12	1	10	30	4	.326
2002 Akron	Eastern	OF	71	291	39	86	17	4	12	51	1	.296
2003 Akron	Eastern	OF	99	371	47	97	17	3	13	52	4	.261
2004 Edmonton	.P.C.	OF	98	347	74	120	29	8	17	79	0	.346
2004 Montreal a	N.L.	OF	30	63	6	11	1	0	1	6	0	.175
2005 Harrisburg	Eastern	OF	4	18	2	5	1	0	0	0	0	.278
2005 Washington b	N.L.	OF	102	268	41	77	15	3	9	42	3	.287
2006 Harrisburg	Eastern	OF	5	19	3	4	0	0	2	3	1	.211
2006 New Orleans.	.P.C.	OF	53	175	29	43	6	0	7	29	5	.246
2006 Washington	N.L.	OF	71	196	22	54	17	1	10	35	6	.276
2007 Washington c	N.L.	OF	144	470	57	128	43	1	15	70	3	.272
Major League Totals	4 Yrs.		347	997	126	270	76	5	35	153	12	.271

a Traded by Cleveland Indians to Montreal Expos with infielder Maicer Izturis for pitcher Scott Stewart, January 5, 2004.
b On disabled list from June 23 to July 13 and August 25 to September 9, 2005.
c Traded to New York Mets with catcher Brian Schneider for outfielder Lastings Milledge, November 30, 2007.

CINTRON, ALEXANDER (ALEX)
Born, Humacao, Puerto Rico, December 17, 1978.
Bats Both. Throws Right. Height, 6 feet, 1 inch. Weight, 205 pounds.

Year Club	Lea	Pos	G	AB	R	H	2B	3B	HR	RBI	SB	Avg
1997 Diamondbcks . . .	Arizona	SS	43	152	23	30	6	1	0	20	1	.197
1997 Lethbridge	Pioneer	SS	1	3	0	1	0	0	0	0	0	.333
1998 Lethbridge	Pioneer	SS-2B	67	258	41	68	11	4	3	34	8	.264
1999 High Desert . .	California	SS	128	499	78	153	25	4	3	64	15	.307
2000 El Paso	Texas	SS	125	522	83	157	30	6	4	59	9	.301
2001 Tucson	.P.C.	SS-2B	107	425	53	124	24	3	3	35	9	.292
2001 Arizona a	.N.L.	SS	8	7	0	2	0	1	0	0	0	.286
2002 Tucson	.P.C.	SS-2B	85	351	53	113	22	3	4	26	9	.322

34

Year	Club	Lea	Pos	G	AB	R	H	2B	3B	HR	RBI	SB	Avg
2002 Arizona............N.L.			2B-3B-SS	38	75	11	16	6	0	0	4	0	.213
2003 Tucson...........P.C.			SS-2B	26	107	21	42	11	2	2	21	1	.393
2003 Arizona...........N.L.			SS-3B-2B	117	448	70	142	26	6	13	51	2	.317
2004 Arizona...........N.L.			SS-2B-3B	154	564	56	148	31	7	4	49	3	.262
2005 Arizona...........N.L.			SS-3B-2B	122	330	36	90	19	2	8	48	1	.273
2006 Chicago b.........A.L.			SS-2B-3B	91	288	35	82	10	3	5	41	10	.285
2007 Chicago c.........A.L.			3B-SS-2B	68	185	23	45	7	1	2	19	2	.243
Major League Totals...........		7 Yrs.		598	1897	231	525	99	20	32	212	18	.277
Division Series													
2002 Arizona...........N.L.			3B	2	0	0	0	0	0	0	0	0	.000

a On disabled list from April 30 to May 8, 2001.
b Traded to Chicago White Sox for pitcher Jeff Bajenaru, March 8, 2006.
c Released by Chicago White Sox, November 28, 2007.

CIRILLO, JEFFREY HOWARD (JEFF)
Born, Pasadena, California, September 23, 1969.
Bats Right. Throws Right. Height, 6 feet, 1 inch. Weight, 205 pounds.

Year	Club	Lea	Pos	G	AB	R	H	2B	3B	HR	RBI	SB	Avg
1991 Helena........Pioneer			3B-OF	70	286	60	100	16	2	10	51	3	.350
1992 Stockton.....California			3B	7	27	2	6	1	0	0	5	0	.222
1992 Beloit........Midwest			3B-2B	126	444	65	135	27	3	9	71	21	.304
1993 El Paso.........Texas			2B-3B	67	249	53	85	16	2	9	41	2	.341
1993 New Orleans.......A.A.			3B-2B-SS	58	215	31	63	13	2	3	32	2	.293
1994 New Orleans.......A.A.			3B-2B-SS	61	236	45	73	18	2	10	46	4	.309
1994 Milwaukee........A.L.			3B-2B	39	126	17	30	9	0	3	12	0	.238
1995 Milwaukee........A.L.			3B-2B-1B-SS	125	328	57	91	19	4	9	39	7	.277
1996 Milwaukee........A.L.			3B-1B-2B	158	566	101	184	46	5	15	83	4	.325
1997 Milwaukee........A.L.			3B	154	580	74	167	46	2	10	82	4	.288
1998 Milwaukee........N.L.			3B-1B	156	604	97	194	31	1	14	68	10	.321
1999 Milwaukee a......N.L.			3B	157	607	98	198	35	1	15	88	7	.326
2000 Colorado.........N.L.			3B	157	598	111	195	53	2	11	115	3	.326
2001 Colorado.........N.L.			3B	138	528	72	165	26	4	17	83	12	.313
2001 Colorado Springs b-cP.C.			3B	1	4	2	3	1	0	0	3	0	.750
2002 Seattle..........A.L.			3B-1B	146	485	51	121	20	0	6	54	8	.249
2003 Mariners......Arizona			3B-C	6	24	2	7	0	0	0	0	0	.292
2003 Inland Empire. California			3B	5	15	1	3	1	0	0	1	0	.200
2003 Tacoma...........P.C.			3B	5	17	7	6	3	0	2	6	0	.353
2003 Seattle d.........A.L.			3B	87	258	24	53	11	0	2	23	1	.205
2004 Portland.........P.C.			3B-1B-2B-SS	7	23	3	8	3	0	0	2	1	.348
2004 San Diego e-f-g....N.L.			3B-1B-2B-OF	33	75	12	16	3	0	1	7	0	.213
2005 Nashville.........P.C.			3B	9	29	2	7	1	0	0	6	0	.241
2005 Milwaukee h-i-j....N.L.			3B-2B-1B	77	185	29	52	15	0	4	23	4	.281
2006 Milwaukee k......N.L.			3B-1B-2B-SS	112	263	33	84	16	0	3	23	1	.319
2007 Fort Myers.......Fla.St.			3B	1	3	0	0	0	0	0	0	0	.000
2007 Minnesota........A.L.			DH-3B-1B	50	153	18	40	9	2	2	21	2	.261
2007 Arizona l-m-n.....N.L.			3B-1B-2B-P	28	40	6	8	4	0	0	6	0	.200
Major League Totals...........		14 Yrs.		1617	5396	800	1598	343	21	112	727	63	.296
Division Series													
2007 Arizona..........N.L.			PH	1	1	0	0	0	0	0	0	0	.000
Championship Series													
2007 Arizona..........N.L.			2B	3	5	0	2	0	0	0	0	0	.400

a Traded to Colorado Rockies with pitcher Scott Karl for catcher Henry Blanco, pitcher Jamey Wright and pitcher Justin Miller, December 13, 1999.
b On disabled list from April 27 to May 13, 2001.
c Traded to Seattle Mariners for pitcher Dennis Stark, pitcher Brian Fuentes and pitcher Jose Paniagua, December 15, 2001.
d On disabled list from July 24 to August 19, 2003.
e Traded to San Diego Padres with pitcher Brian Sweeney and cash for pitcher Kevin Jarvis, catcher Wiki Gonzalez, infielder Dave Hansen and outfielder Vince Faison, January 6, 2004.
f On disabled list from April 2 to May 11, 2004.
g Released by San Diego Padres, August 4, 2004.
h Signed with Milwaukee Brewers organization, February 4, 2005.
i On disabled list from June 25 to September 1, 2005.
j Filed for free agency, November 4, 2005, re-signed with Milwaukee Brewers, November 21, 2005.
k Filed for free agency, October 29, 2006. Signed with Minnesota Twins, November 13, 2006.
l On disabled list from April 8 to May 1, 2007.
m Claimed on waivers by Arizona Diamondbacks, August 3, 2007.
n Filed for free agency, October 29, 2007.

CLARK, ANTHONY CHRISTOPHER (TONY)

Born, Newton, Kansas, June 15, 1972.
Bats Both. Throws Right. Height, 6 feet, 7 inches. Weight, 245 pounds.

Year	Club	Lea	Pos	G	AB	R	H	2B	3B	HR	RBI	SB	Avg
1990	Bristol	Appal.	OF	25	73	2	12	2	0	1	8	0	.164
1991	Niagara Falls a	N.Y.-Penn.		INJURED—Did Not Play									
1992	Niagara Falls b	N.Y.-Penn.	OF	27	85	12	26	9	0	5	17	1	.306
1993	Lakeland c	Fla. St.	OF	36	117	14	31	4	14	1	22	0	.265
1994	Trenton	Eastern	1B	107	394	50	110	25	0	21	86	0	.279
1994	Toledo	Int.	1B	25	92	10	24	4	0	2	13	2	.261
1995	Toledo	Int.	1B	110	405	50	98	17	2	14	63	0	.242
1995	Detroit	A.L.	1B	27	101	10	24	5	1	3	11	0	.238
1996	Toledo	Int.	1B	55	194	42	58	7	1	14	36	1	.299
1996	Detroit	A.L.	1B	100	376	56	94	14	0	27	72	0	.250
1997	Detroit	A.L.	1B	159	580	105	160	28	3	32	117	1	.276
1998	Detroit	A.L.	1B	157	602	84	175	37	0	34	103	3	.291
1999	Toledo	Int.	1B	1	3	0	0	0	0	0	0	0	.000
1999	Detroit d.	A.L.	1B	143	536	74	150	29	0	31	99	2	.280
2000	Toledo	Int.	1B	6	22	1	2	1	0	1	2	0	.091
2000	Detroit e	A.L.	1B	60	208	32	57	14	0	13	37	0	.274
2001	Detroit f	A.L.	1B	126	428	67	123	29	3	16	75	0	.287
2002	Boston g	A.L.	1B	90	275	25	57	12	1	3	29	0	.207
2003	St. Lucie	Fla.St.	1B	1	4	0	1	0	0	0	0	0	.250
2003	New York h.	N.L.	1B-OF	125	254	29	59	13	0	16	43	0	.232
2004	New York i	A.L.	1B	106	253	37	56	12	0	16	49	0	.221
2005	Arizona	N.L.	1B	130	349	47	106	22	2	30	87	0	.304
2006	Tucson	P.C.	1B	2	6	2	2	0	0	1	1	0	.333
2006	Arizona j.	N.L.	1B	79	132	13	26	4	0	6	16	0	.197
2007	Arizona k	N.L.	1B	113	221	31	55	5	1	17	51	0	.249
Major League Totals		13 Yrs.		1415	4315	610	1142	224	11	244	789	6	.265
Division Series													
2004	New York	A.L.	1B	1	1	0	0	0	0	0	0	0	.000
2007	Arizona	N.L.	1B	3	6	0	0	0	0	0	0	0	.000
Division Series Totals				4	7	0	0	0	0	0	0	0	.000
Championship Series													
2004	New York	A.L.	1B	5	21	0	3	1	0	0	1	0	.143
2007	Arizona	N.L.	1B	3	9	0	2	1	0	0	0	0	.222
Championship Series Totals				8	30	0	5	2	0	0	1	0	.167

a On disabled list from May 30 to June 17; transferred to temporary inactive list from June 17 to end of 1991 season.
b On temporary inactive list from August 17 to end of 1992 season.
c On disabled list from August 24 to end of 1993 season.
d On disabled list from May 26 to June 10, 1999.
e On disabled list from May 13 to June 11 and July 15 to August 31 and September 17 to November 6, 2000.
f Claimed on waivers by Boston Red Sox, November 20, 2001.
g Filed for free agency, October 30, 2002. Signed with New York Mets organization, February 20, 2003.
h Filed for free agency, October 27, 2003. Signed with New York Yankees, January 12, 2004.
i Filed for free agency, October 29, 2004. Signed with Arizona Diamondbacks, January 24, 2005.
j On disabled list from July 17 to August 25, 2006.
k Filed for free agency, October 30, 2007.

CLARK, BRADY WILLIAM

Born, Portland, Oregon, April 18, 1973.
Bats Right. Throws Right. Height, 6 feet, 2 inches. Weight, 205 pounds.

Year	Club	Lea	Pos	G	AB	R	H	2B	3B	HR	RBI	SB	Avg
1997	Burlington a	Midwest	OF	126	459	108	149	29	7	11	63	31	.325
1998	Chattanooga	Southern	OF	64	222	41	60	13	1	2	16	12	.270
1999	Chattanooga	Southern	OF	138	506	103	165	37	4	17	75	25	.326
2000	Louisville	Int.	OF	132	487	90	148	41	6	16	79	12	.304
2000	Cincinnati	N.L.	OF	11	11	1	3	1	0	0	2	0	.273
2001	Louisville	Int.	OF	49	167	24	44	5	1	2	18	6	.263
2001	Cincinnati	N.L.	OF	89	129	22	34	3	0	6	18	4	.264
2002	Louisville	Int.	OF-3B	25	109	17	33	7	0	1	17	0	.303
2002	Cincinnati-New York b	N.L.	OF	61	78	9	15	4	0	0	10	1	.192
2003	Indianapolis	Int.	OF	9	34	4	9	3	0	0	3	1	.265
2003	Milwaukee c-d	N.L.	OF	128	315	33	86	21	1	6	40	13	.273
2004	Milwaukee	N.L.	OF	138	353	41	99	18	1	7	46	15	.280
2005	Milwaukee e	N.L.	OF	145	599	94	183	31	1	13	53	10	.306
2006	Milwaukee	N.L.	OF	138	415	51	109	14	2	4	29	3	.263
2007	Portland	P.C.	OF	14	59	12	20	6	0	0	8	1	.339
2007	Pawtucket	Int.	OF	5	19	2	5	2	0	1	3	0	.263

Year	Club	Lea	Pos	G	AB	R	H	2B	3B	HR	RBI	SB	Avg
2007 L.A.-San Diego f-g-h-i		N.L.	OF	68	107	13	28	5	2	0	11	1	.262
Major League Totals		8 Yrs.	778	2007	264	557	97	7	36	209	47	.278

a Released by Cincinnati Reds, January 13, 1996, re-signed with Reds, February 15, 1997.
b Sent to New York Mets to complete trade for pitcher Shawn Estes, September 9, 2002.
c Claimed on waivers by Milwaukee Brewers, January 21, 2003.
d On disabled list from March 21 to April 15, 2003.
e On disabled list from August 11 to August 26, 2005.
f Traded to Los Angeles Dodgers for pitcher Elmer Dessens, March 26, 2007.
g Released by Los Angeles Dodgers, June 10, 2007. Signed with Boston Red Sox organization, July 26, 2007.
h Released by Boston Red Sox, August 6, 2007. Signed with San Diego Padres organization, August 16, 2007.
i Released by San Diego Padres, October 4, 2007.

CLAYTON, ROYCE SPENCER
Born, Burbank, California, January 2, 1970.
Bats Right. Throws Right. Height, 6 feet. Weight, 200 pounds.

Year	Club	Lea	Pos	G	AB	R	H	2B	3B	HR	RBI	SB	Avg
1988 Everett	Northwest	SS	60	212	35	55	4	0	3	29	10	.259
1989 Clinton	Midwest	SS	104	385	39	91	13	3	0	24	28	.236
1989 San Jose	California	SS	28	92	5	11	2	0	0	4	10	.120
1990 San Jose	California	SS	123	460	80	123	15	10	7	71	33	.267
1991 Shreveport	Texas	SS	126	485	84	136	22	8	5	68	36	.280
1991 San Francisco	N.L.	SS	9	26	0	3	1	0	0	2	0	.115
1992 Phoenix	P.C.	SS	48	192	30	46	6	2	3	18	15	.240
1992 San Francisco	N.L.	SS-3B	98	321	31	72	7	4	4	24	8	.224
1993 San Francisco	N.L.	SS	153	549	54	155	21	5	6	70	11	.282
1994 San Francisco	N.L.	SS	108	385	38	91	14	6	3	30	23	.236
1995 San Francisco a	N.L.	SS	138	509	56	124	29	3	5	58	24	.244
1996 St. Louis	N.L.	SS	129	491	64	136	20	4	6	35	33	.277
1997 St. Louis	N.L.	SS	154	576	75	153	39	5	9	61	30	.266
1998 St. Louis b	N.L.	SS	90	355	59	83	19	1	4	29	19	.234
1998 Texas c-d-e	A.L.	SS	52	186	30	53	12	1	5	24	5	.285
1999 Oklahoma	P.C.	SS	2	7	1	1	0	0	0	1	0	.143
1999 Texas f	A.L.	SS	133	465	69	134	21	5	14	52	8	.288
2000 Texas g	A.L.	SS	148	513	70	124	21	5	14	54	11	.242
2001 Chicago	A.L.	SS	135	433	62	114	21	4	9	60	10	.263
2002 Chicago h	A.L.	SS	112	342	51	86	14	2	7	35	5	.251
2003 Milwaukee i	N.L.	SS	146	483	49	110	16	1	11	39	5	.228
2004 Colorado j	N.L.	SS	146	574	95	160	36	4	8	54	13	.279
2005 Arizona k	N.L.	SS	143	522	59	141	28	4	2	44	13	.270
2006 Washington-Cincinnati l-m	N.L.	SS	137	454	49	117	30	1	2	40	14	.258
2007 Pawtucket	Int.	SS	7	28	2	4	3	0	0	3	0	.143
2007 Toronto-Boston n-o	A.L.	SS-3B	77	195	24	48	14	0	1	12	2	.246
Major League Totals		17 Yrs.	2108	7379	935	1904	363	55	110	723	231	.258

Division Series

Year	Club	Lea	Pos	G	AB	R	H	2B	3B	HR	RBI	SB	Avg
1996 St. Louis	N.L.	SS	2	6	1	2	0	0	0	0	0	.333
1998 Texas	A.L.	SS	3	9	0	2	0	0	0	0	0	.22
1999 Texas	A.L.	SS	3	10	0	0	0	0	0	0	0	.000
Division Series Totals			8	25	1	4	0	0	0	0	0	.160

Championship Series

Year	Club	Lea	Pos	G	AB	R	H	2B	3B	HR	RBI	SB	Avg
1996 St. Louis	N.L.	SS	5	20	4	7	0	0	0	1	1	.350

a Traded from San Francisco Giants to St. Louis Cardinals for pitchers Allen Watson, Rich DeLucia, and Doug Creek, December 14, 1995.
b On disabled list from June 24 to July 9, 1998.
c Traded to Texas Rangers with pitcher Todd Stottlemyre for pitcher Darren Oliver, infielder Fernando Tatis and player to be named later, July 31, 1998.
d St. Louis Cardinals received infielder Mark Little to complete trade, August 9, 1998.
e Filed for free agency, October 23, 1998, re-signed with Texas Rangers, November 30, 1998.
f On disabled list from May 1 to May 21, 1999.
g Traded to Chicago White Sox for pitcher Aaron Myette and pitcher Brian Schmack, December 14, 2000.
h Released by Chicago White Sox, September 8, 2002. Signed with Milwaukee Brewers, December 11, 2002.
i Filed for free agency, October 27, 2003. Signed with Colorado Rockies organization, January 5, 2004.
j Filed for free agency, October 28, 2004. Signed with Arizona Diamondbacks, December 14, 2004.
k Filed for free agency, October 27, 2005. Signed with Washington Nationals organization, January 31, 2006.
l Traded to Cincinnati Reds with pitcher Gary Majewski, pitcher Bill Bray, infielder Brendan Harris and pitcher Daryl Thompson for outfielder Austin Kearns, infielder Felipe Lopez and pitcher Ryan Wagner, July 13, 2006.
m Filed for free agency, October 28, 2006. Signed with Toronto Blue Jays, November 29, 2006.
n Released by Toronto Blue Jays, August 7, 2007. Signed with Boston Red Sox organization, August 23, 2007.
o Filed for free agency, November 7, 2007.

CONINE, JEFFREY GUY (JEFF)

Born, Tacoma, Washington, June 27, 1966.
Bats Right. Throws Right. Height, 6 feet, 1 inch. Weight, 225 pounds.

Year Club	Lea	Pos	G	AB	R	H	2B	3B	HR	RBI	SB	Avg
1988 Baseball City	Fla. St.	1B-3B	118	415	63	112	23	9	10	59	26	.272
1989 Baseball City	Fla. St.	1B	113	425	89	116	12	7	14	60	32	.273
1990 Memphis	Southern	1B-3B	137	487	89	156	37	8	15	95	21	.320
1990 Kansas City	A.L.	1B	9	20	3	5	2	0	0	2	0	.250
1991 Omaha a	A.A.	1B-OF	51	171	23	44	9	1	3	15	0	.257
1992 Omaha	A.A.	1B-OF	110	397	69	120	24	5	20	72	4	.302
1992 Kansas City b	A.L.	OF-1B	28	91	10	23	5	2	0	9	0	.253
1993 Florida	N.L.	OF-1B	*162	595	75	174	24	3	12	79	2	.292
1994 Florida	N.L.	OF-1B	115	451	60	144	27	6	18	82	1	.319
1995 Florida	N.L.	OF-1B	133	483	72	146	26	2	25	105	2	.302
1996 Florida	N.L.	OF-1B	157	597	84	175	32	2	26	95	1	.293
1997 Florida c	N.L.	1B-OF	151	405	46	98	13	1	17	61	2	.242
1998 Omaha	P.C.	OF	2	9	0	0	0	0	0	0	0	.000
1998 Kansas City d	A.L.	OF-1B	93	309	30	79	26	0	8	43	3	.256
1999 Baltimore e-f	A.L.	1B-OF-3B	139	444	54	129	31	1	13	75	0	.291
2000 Baltimore	A.L.	3B-1B-OF	119	409	53	116	20	2	13	46	4	.284
2001 Baltimore	A.L.	1B-OF-3B	139	524	75	163	23	2	14	97	12	.311
2002 Baltimore g	A.L.	1B-OF	116	451	44	123	26	4	15	63	8	.273
2003 Baltimore	A.L.	1B-OF-3B	124	493	75	143	33	3	15	80	5	.290
2003 Florida h	N.L.	OF	25	84	13	20	3	0	5	15	0	.238
2004 Florida	N.L.	OF-1B	140	521	55	146	35	1	14	83	5	.280
2005 Florida i	N.L.	OF-1B	131	335	42	102	20	2	3	33	2	.304
2006 Baltimore	A.L.	1B-OF-3B	114	389	43	103	20	3	9	49	3	.265
2006 Philadelphia j-k-l	N.L.	OF	28	100	11	28	6	1	1	17	0	.280
2007 Cincinnati-New York m	N.L.	1B-OF-3B	101	256	25	65	13	1	6	37	4	.254
Major League Totals	17 Yrs.	2024	6957	870	1982	385	36	214	1071	54	.285
Division Series												
1997 Florida	N.L.	1B	3	11	3	4	1	0	0	0	0	.364
2003 Florida	N.L.	OF	4	15	2	4	0	0	0	2	0	.267
Division Series Totals			7	26	5	8	1	0	0	2	0	.308
Championship Series												
1997 Florida	N.L.	1B	6	18	1	2	0	0	0	1	0	.111
2003 Florida	N.L.	OF	7	24	4	11	1	1	1	3	0	.458
Championship Series Totals			13	42	5	13	1	1	1	4	0	.310
World Series Record												
1997 Florida	N.L.	1B	6	13	1	3	0	0	0	2	0	.231
2003 Florida	N.L.	OF	6	21	4	7	1	0	0	0	0	.333
World Series Totals			12	34	5	10	1	0	0	2	0	.294

a On disabled list from June 28 to end of 1991 season.
b Selected by Florida Marlins in expansion draft, November 17, 1992.
c Traded to Kansas City Royals for pitcher Blaine Mull, November 21, 1997.
d On disabled list from March 31 to May 5 and July 27 to August 19, 1998.
e Traded to Baltimore Orioles for pitcher Chris Fussell, April 2, 1999.
f Filed for free agency, November 5, 1999, re-signed with Baltimore Orioles, December 16, 1999.
g On disabled list from June 15 to August 7, 2002.
h Traded to Florida Marlins for pitcher Danny Bautista and Pitcher Don Levinski, August 31, 2003.
i Filed for free agency, November 4, 2005. Signed with Baltimore Orioles, January 4, 2006.
j Traded to Philadelphia Phillies for player to be named later, August 27, 2006.
k Baltimore Orioles received infielder Angel Chavez to complete trade, August 30, 2006.
l Traded to Cincinnati Reds for outfielder Javon Moran and infielder Brad Key, December 21, 2006.
m Traded to New York Mets for infielder Jose Castro and outfielder Sean Henry, August 20, 2007.

CORA, JOSE ALEXANDER (ALEX)

Born, Caguas, Puerto Rico, October 18, 1975.
Bats Left. Throws Right. Height, 6 feet. Weight, 200 pounds.

Year Club	Lea	Pos	G	AB	R	H	2B	3B	HR	RBI	SB	Avg
1996 Vero Beach	Fla.St.	SS-OF	61	214	26	55	5	4	0	26	5	.257
1997 San Antonio	Texas	SS	127	448	52	105	20	4	3	48	12	.234
1998 Albuquerque	P.C.	SS-2B	81	299	42	79	16	6	5	45	10	.264
1998 Los Angeles	N.L.	SS-2B	29	33	1	4	0	1	0	0	0	.121
1999 Albuquerque	P.C.	SS	80	302	51	93	11	7	4	37	9	.308
1999 Los Angeles a	N.L.	SS-2B	11	30	2	5	1	0	0	3	0	.167
2000 Albuquerque	P.C.	SS	30	110	18	41	8	3	0	20	5	.373
2000 Los Angeles	N.L.	SS-2B	109	353	39	84	18	6	4	32	4	.238
2001 Los Angeles	N.L.	SS-2B	134	405	38	88	18	3	4	29	0	.217

Year	Club	Lea	Pos	G	AB	R	H	2B	3B	HR	RBI	SB	Avg
2002 Los Angeles	N.L.		SS-2B	115	258	37	75	14	4	5	28	7	.291
2003 Los Angeles	N.L.		2B-SS	148	477	39	119	24	3	4	34	4	.249
2004 Los Angeles b	N.L.		2B	138	405	47	107	9	4	10	47	3	.264
2005 Cleveland-Boston c	A.L.		2B-SS-3B-OF	96	250	25	58	8	4	3	24	7	.232
2006 Boston d	A.L.		SS-2B-3B	96	235	31	56	7	2	1	18	6	.238
2007 Boston	A.L.		2B-SS-1B	83	207	30	51	10	5	3	18	1	.246
Major League Totals			10 Yrs.	959	2653	289	647	109	32	34	233	32	.244
Division Series													
2004 Los Angeles	N.L.		2B	4	15	1	2	0	1	0	1	0	.133
2005 Boston	A.L.		SS	1	0	0	0	0	0	0	0	0	.000
Division Series Totals				5	15	1	2	0	1	0	1	0	.133
Championship Series													
2007 Boston	A.L.		2B-SS	2	0	0	0	0	0	0	0	0	.000
World Series Record													
2007 Boston	A.L.		2B-SS	2	0	0	0	0	0	0	0	0	.000

a On disabled list from March 25 to June 27, 1999.
b Not offered contract, December 21, 2004. Signed with Cleveland Indians, January 18, 2005.
c Traded to Boston Red Sox for infielder Ramon Vazquez, July 7, 2005.
d Filed for free agency, October 31, 2006, re-signed with Boston Red Sox, November 17, 2006.

COUNSELL, CRAIG JOHN

Born, South Bend, Indiana, August 21, 1970.
Bats Left. Throws Right. Height, 6 feet. Weight, 185 pounds.

Year	Club	Lea	Pos	G	AB	R	H	2B	3B	HR	RBI	SB	Avg
1992 Bend	Northwest		2B-SS	18	61	11	15	6	1	0	8	1	.246
1993 Central Val	California		SS	131	471	79	132	26	3	5	59	14	.280
1994 New Haven	Eastern		SS-2B	83	300	47	84	20	1	5	37	4	.280
1995 Colo Sprngs	P.C.		SS	118	399	60	112	22	6	5	53	10	.281
1995 Colorado	N.L.		SS	3	1	0	0	0	0	0	0	0	.000
1996 Colo Sprngs	P.C.		2B-3B-SS	25	75	17	18	3	0	2	10	4	.240
1997 Colo Sprngs	P.C.		2B-SS	96	376	77	126	31	6	5	63	12	.335
1997 Colorado-Florida a	N.L.		2B	52	164	20	49	9	2	1	16	1	.299
1998 Florida b	N.L.		2B	107	335	43	84	19	5	4	40	3	.251
1999 Florida-Los Angeles c-d	N.L.		2B-SS	87	174	24	38	7	0	0	11	1	.218
2000 Tucson	P.C.		2B	50	198	45	69	14	3	3	27	4	.348
2000 Arizona e	N.L.		2B-3B-SS	67	152	23	48	8	1	2	11	3	.316
2001 Arizona	N.L.		SS-2B-3B-1B	141	458	76	126	22	3	4	38	6	.275
2002 Arizona e	N.L.		3B-SS-2B	112	436	63	123	22	1	2	51	7	.282
2003 Tucson	P.C.		2B-SS-3B	5	23	8	10	2	0	0	2	0	.435
2003 Arizona f-g	N.L.		3B-SS-2B-1B	89	303	40	71	6	3	3	21	11	.234
2004 Milwaukee h	N.L.		SS-3B	140	473	59	114	19	5	2	23	17	.241
2005 Arizona	N.L.		2B-SS	150	578	85	148	34	4	9	42	26	.256
2006 Lancaster	Calif.		DH	1	3	1	3	1	0	0	0	0	1.000
2006 Tucson	P.C.		DH	2	11	2	2	0	0	0	0	0	.182
2006 Arizona i-j	N.L.		SS-3B-2B	105	372	56	95	14	4	4	30	15	.255
2007 Milwaukee	N.L.		3B-SS-2B	122	282	31	62	12	2	3	24	4	.220
Major League Totals			12 Yrs.	1175	3728	520	958	172	30	34	307	94	.257
Division Series													
1997 Florida	N.L.		2B	3	5	0	2	1	0	0	1	0	.400
2001 Arizona	N.L.		2B	5	16	2	3	0	0	1	3	0	.187
Division Series Totals				8	21	2	5	1	0	1	4	0	.238
Championship Series													
1997 Florida	N.L.		2B	5	14	0	6	0	0	0	2	0	.429
2001 Arizona	N.L.		2B-SS	5	21	5	8	3	0	0	4	1	.381
Championship Series Totals				10	35	5	14	3	0	0	6	1	.400
World Series Record													
1997 Florida	N.L.		2B	7	22	4	4	1	0	0	2	1	.182
2001 Arizona	N.L.		2B	6	24	1	2	0	0	1	1	0	.083
World Series Totals				13	46	5	6	1	0	1	3	1	.130

a Traded to Florida Marlins for pitcher Mark Hutton, July 27, 1997.
b On disabled list from August 4 to September 28, 1998.
c Traded to Los Angeles Dodgers for player to be named later, June 15, 1999.
   Florida Marlins received pitcher Ryan Moskau to complete trade, July 15, 1999.
d Released by Los Angeles Dodgers, March 17, 2000. Signed with Arizona Diamondbacks organization, March 20, 2000.
e On disabled list from August 9 to October 14, 2002.
f On disabled list from May 7 to July 7, 2003.

g Traded to Milwaukee Brewers with infielder Junior Spivey, infielder Lyle Overbay, catcher Chad Moeller, pitcher Chris Capuano and pitcher Jorge DeRosa for infielder Richie Sexson, pitcher Shane Nance and player to be named later. Arizona Diamondbacks received outfielder Gary Varner to complete trade, December 15, 2003.
h Filed for free agency, October 29, 2004. Signed with Arizona Diamondbacks December 15, 2004.
i On disabled list from July 15 to August 22, 2006.
j Filed for free agency, October 30, 2006. Signed with Milwaukee Brewers, November 29, 2006.

CRAWFORD, CARL DEMONTE
Born, Houston, Texas, August 5, 1981.
Bats Left. Throws Left. Height, 6 feet, 2 inches. Weight, 220 pounds.

Year Club	Lea	Pos	G	AB	R	H	2B	3B	HR	RBI	SB	Avg
1999 Princeton .... .Appal.		OF	60	260	62	83	14	4	0	25	17	.319
2000 Charleston-Sc ...... So.Atl.		OF	135	564	99	.170	21	11	6	57	55	.301
2001 Orlando .... Southern		OF	132	537	64	147	24	3	4	51	36	.274
2002 Durham .... Int.		OF	85	353	59	105	17	9	7	52	26	.297
2002 Tampa Bay .... A.L.		OF	63	259	23	67	11	6	2	30	9	.259
2003 Tampa Bay .... A.L.		OF	151	630	80	177	18	9	5	54	*55	.281
2004 Tampa Bay .... A.L.		OF	152	626	104	185	26	*19	11	55	*59	.296
2005 Tampa Bay .... A.L.		OF	156	644	101	194	33	*15	15	81	46	.301
2006 Tampa Bay .... A.L.		OF	151	600	89	183	20	*16	18	77	*58	.305
2007 Tampa Bay .... A.L.		OF	143	584	93	184	37	9	11	80	*50	.315
Major League Totals	6 Yrs.	816	3343	490	990	145	74	62	377	277	.296	

CREDE, JOSEPH (JOE)
Born, Jefferson City, Missouri, April 26, 1978.
Bats Right. Throws Right. Height, 6 feet, 2 inches. Weight, 220 pounds.

Year Club	Lea	Pos	G	AB	R	H	2B	3B	HR	RBI	SB	Avg
1996 White Sox ...... Gulf Coast		3B	56	221	30	66	17	1	4	32	1	.299
1997 Hickory. .... So.Atl.		3B	113	402	45	109	25	0	5	62	3	.271
1998 Winston-Sal ...... Carolina		3B	137	492	92	155	32	3	20	88	9	.315
1999 Birmingham a .... Southern		3B	74	291	37	73	14	1	4	42	2	.251
2000 Birmingham ...... Southern		3B	138	533	84	163	35	0	21	94	3	.306
2000 Chicago .... A.L.		3B	7	14	2	5	1	0	0	3	0	.357
2001 Charlotte .... Int.		3B	124	463	67	128	34	1	17	65	2	.276
2001 Chicago .... A.L.		3B	17	50	1	11	1	1	0	7	1	.220
2002 Charlotte .... Int.		3B	95	359	57	112	21	0	24	65	0	.312
2002 Chicago .... A.L.		3B	53	200	28	57	10	0	12	35	0	.285
2003 Chicago .... A.L.		3B	151	536	68	140	31	2	19	75	1	.261
2004 Chicago .... A.L.		3B	144	490	67	117	25	0	21	69	1	.239
2005 Chicago b .... A.L.		3B-SS	132	432	54	109	21	0	22	62	1	.252
2006 Chicago .... A.L.		3B	150	544	76	154	31	0	30	94	0	.283
2007 Chicago c .... A.L.		3B	47	167	13	36	5	0	4	22	0	.216
Major League Totals	8 Yrs.	701	2433	309	629	125	3	108	367	4	.259	
Division Series												
2005 Chicago .... A.L.		3B	3	9	2	1	0	0	0	1	0	.111
Championship Series												
2005 Chicago .... A.L.		3B	5	19	2	7	4	0	2	7	0	.368
World Series Record												
2005 Chicago .... A.L.		3B	4	17	2	5	1	0	2	3	0	.294

a On disabled list from July 2 to September 30, 1999.
b On disabled list from August 26 to September 10, 2005.
c On disabled list from June 5 to October 26, 2007.

CRISP, COVELLI LOYCE (COCO)
Born, Los Angeles, California, November 1, 1979.
Bats Both. Throws Right. Height, 6 feet. Weight, 180 pounds.

Year Club	Lea	Pos	G	AB	R	H	2B	3B	HR	RBI	SB	Avg
1999 Johnson City .... .Appal.		2B	65	229	55	59	5	4	3	22	27	.258
2000 New Jersey ..... N.Y.-Penn.		OF-2B	36	134	18	32	5	0	0	14	25	.239
2000 Peoria. .... Midwest		OF	27	98	14	27	9	0	0	7	7	.276
2001 Potomac. .... Carolina		OF	139	530	80	162	23	3	11	47	39	.306
2002 New Haven .... Eastern		OF	89	355	61	107	16	1	9	47	26	.301
2002 Akron .... Eastern		OF	7	32	9	13	1	0	1	4	4	.406
2002 Buffalo .... Int.		OF	4	21	3	5	1	0	0	2	1	.238
2002 Cleveland a .... A.L.		OF	32	127	16	33	9	2	1	9	4	.260
2003 Buffalo .... Int.		OF	56	225	42	81	19	6	1	24	20	.360
2003 Cleveland .... A.L.		OF	99	414	55	110	15	6	3	27	15	.266

Year	Club	Lea	Pos	G	AB	R	H	2B	3B	HR	RBI	SB	Avg
2004	Cleveland	A.L.	OF	139	491	78	146	24	2	15	71	20	.297
2005	Cleveland b	A.L.	OF	145	594	86	178	42	4	16	69	15	.300
2006	Pawtucket	Int.	OF	1	3	0	1	0	0	0	2	0	.333
2006	Boston c-d	A.L.	OF	105	413	58	109	22	2	8	36	22	.264
2007	Boston	A.L.	OF	145	526	85	141	28	7	6	60	28	.268
Major League Totals			6 Yrs.	665	2565	378	717	140	23	49	272	104	.280
Division Series													
2007	Boston	A.L.	OF	3	10	0	2	0	0	0	2	1	.200
Championship Series													
2007	Boston	A.L.	OF	7	21	2	3	1	0	0	0	1	.143
World Series Record													
2007	Boston	A.L.	OF	3	2	1	1	0	0	0	0	0	.500

a Sent to Cleveland Indians as player to be named later for pitcher Chuck Finley, August 6, 2002.
b On disabled list from May 18 to June 2, 2005.
c Traded to Boston Red Sox with pitcher David Riske and catcher Josh Bard for infielder Andy Marte, catcher Kelly Shoppach and pitcher Guillermo Mota, January 27, 2006.
d On disabled list from April 9 to May 28, 2006.

CROSBY, ROBERT EDWARD (BOBBY)

Born, Lakewood, California, January 12, 1980.
Bats Right. Throws Right. Height, 6 feet, 3 inches. Weight, 215 pounds.

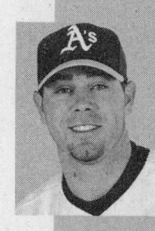

Year	Club	Lea	Pos	G	AB	R	H	2B	3B	HR	RBI	SB	Avg
2001	Modesto	California	SS	11	38	7	15	5	0	1	3	0	.395
2002	Modesto	California	SS	73	280	47	86	17	2	2	38	5	.307
2002	Midland	Texas	SS	59	228	31	64	16	0	7	31	9	.281
2003	Sacramento	P.C.	SS	127	465	86	143	32	6	22	90	24	.308
2003	Oakland	A.L.	SS	11	12	1	0	0	0	0	0	0	.000
2004	Oakland a	A.L.	SS	151	545	70	130	34	1	22	64	7	.239
2005	Stockton	California	SS	3	9	1	3	1	0	0	1	0	.333
2005	Sacramento	P.C.	SS	3	12	0	1	0	0	0	1	0	.083
2005	Oakland b	A.L.	SS	84	333	66	92	25	4	9	38	0	.276
2006	Oakland c	A.L.	SS	96	358	42	82	12	0	9	40	8	.229
2007	Oakland d	A.L.	SS	93	349	40	79	16	0	8	31	10	.226
Major League Totals			5 Yrs.	435	1597	219	383	87	5	48	173	25	.240

a Selected Rookie of the Year in American League for 2004.
b On disabled list from April 5 to May 30 and August 28 to September 19, 2005.
c On disabled list from July 31 to August 18 and August 22 to October 25, 2006.
d On disabled list from July 15 to October 8, 2007.

CRUZ, JOSE L.

Born, Arroyo, Puerto Rico, April 19, 1974.
Bats Both. Throws Right. Height, 6 feet. Weight, 210 pounds.

Year	Club	Lea	Pos	G	AB	R	H	2B	3B	HR	RBI	SB	Avg
1995	Everett	Northwest	OF	3	11	6	5	0	0	0	2	1	.455
1995	Riverside	California	OF	35	144	34	37	7	1	7	29	3	.257
1996	Lancaster	California	OF	53	203	38	66	17	1	6	43	7	.325
1996	Port City	Southern	OF	47	181	39	51	10	2	3	31	5	.282
1996	Tacoma	P.C.	OF	22	76	15	18	1	2	6	15	1	.237
1997	Tacoma	P.C.	OF	50	190	33	51	16	2	6	30	3	.268
1997	Seattle-Toronto a	A.L.	OF	104	395	59	98	19	1	26	68	7	.248
1998	Syracuse	Int.	OF	40	141	29	42	14	1	7	23	8	.298
1998	Toronto	A.L.	OF	105	352	55	89	14	3	11	42	11	.253
1999	Syracuse	Int.	OF	31	103	17	19	3	1	3	14	5	.184
1999	Toronto b	A.L.	OF	106	349	63	84	19	3	14	45	14	.241
2000	Toronto	A.L.	OF	*162	603	91	146	32	5	31	76	15	.242
2001	Toronto c	A.L.	OF	146	577	92	158	38	4	34	88	32	.274
2002	Toronto d-e	A.L.	OF	124	466	64	114	26	5	18	70	7	.245
2003	San Francisco f	N.L.	OF	158	539	90	135	26	1	20	68	5	.250
2004	Tampa Bay	A.L.	OF	153	545	76	132	25	8	21	78	11	.242
2005	Tucson	P.C.	OF	1	3	1	1	1	0	0	1	0	.333
2005	Boston	A.L.	OF	4	12	0	3	1	0	0	0	0	.250
2005	Arizona-Los Angeles g-h-i-j	N.L.	OF	111	358	46	90	23	2	18	50	0	.251
2006	Los Angeles k	N.L.	OF	86	223	34	52	16	1	5	17	5	.233
2007	Scranton-WB	Int.	OF	16	62	12	17	4	0	1	7	3	.274
2007	San Diego l-m	N.L.	OF	91	256	37	60	12	3	6	21	6	.234
Major League Totals			11 Yrs.	1350	4675	707	1161	251	36	204	623	113	.248
Division Series													
2003	San Francisco	N.L.	OF	4	11	0	0	0	0	0	1	0	.000

a Traded to Toronto Blue Jays for pitchers Mike Timlin and Paul Spoljaric, July 31, 1997.
b On disabled list from June 24 to July 9, 1999.
c On disabled list from May 6 to May 21, 2001.
d On disabled list from August 10 to September 15, 2002.
e Not offered 2003 contract, December 20, 2002. Signed with San Francisco Giants, January 28, 2003.
f Filed for free agency, October 30, 2003. Signed with Tampa Bay Devil Rays, December 16, 2003.
g Traded to Arizona Diamondbacks for pitcher Casey Fossum, February 6, 2005.
h On disabled list from April 10 to May 9, 2005.
i Traded to Boston Red Sox for infielder Kenny Perez and pitcher Kyle Bono, July 30, 2005.
j Traded to Los Angeles Dodgers for player to be named later, August 9, 2005.
k Released by Los Angeles Dodgers, August 5, 2006.
l Released by San Diego Padres, July 31, 2007. Signed with New York Yankees organization, August 18, 2007.
m Filed for free agency, October 31, 2007. Signed with Houston Astros organization, November 28, 2007.

CRUZ, NELSON RAMON

Born, Monte Cristi, Dominican Republic, July 1, 1980.
Bats Right. Throws Right. Height, 6 feet, 3 inches. Weight, 175 pounds.

Year Club	Lea	Pos	G	AB	R	H	2B	3B	HR	RBI	SB	Avg
1998 Ny Mets . . . . Dominican	OF	30	70	10	19	0	0	1	13	6	.271
2001 Athletics a . . . . Arizona	OF	23	88	11	22	3	1	3	16	6	.250
2002 Vancouver . . . . . . Northwest	OF	63	214	23	59	14	0	4	25	12	.276
2003 Kane County . . . . . Midwest	OF	119	470	65	112	26	2	20	85	10	.238
2004 Modesto . . . . Calif.	OF	66	261	54	90	27	1	11	52	8	.345
2004 Sacramento . . . . .P.C.	OF	4	13	4	3	1	0	1	2	0	.231
2004 Midland b . . . . Texas	OF	67	262	51	82	14	2	14	46	8	.313
2005 Huntsville . . . . Southern	OF	68	248	45	76	19	0	16	54	10	.306
2005 Nashville . . . . .P.C.	OF	60	208	33	56	13	0	11	27	9	.269
2005 Milwaukee . . . . N.L.	OF	8	5	1	1	1	0	0	0	0	.200
2006 Nashville . . . . .P.C.	OF	104	371	68	112	22	1	20	73	17	.302
2006 Texas c . . . . A.L.	OF	41	130	15	29	3	0	6	22	1	.223
2007 Oklahoma . . . . .P.C.	OF	44	162	32	57	9	1	15	45	1	.352
2007 Texas . . . . A.L.	OF	96	307	35	72	15	2	9	34	2	.235
Major League Totals . . . . 3 Yrs.	145	442	51	102	19	2	15	56	3	.231	

a Traded to Oakland Athletics for infielder Jorge Velandia, August 30, 2000.
b Traded to Milwaukee Brewers with pitcher Justin Lehr for infielder Keith Ginter, December 15, 2004.
c Traded to Texas Rangers with outfielder Carlos Lee for pitcher Francisco Cordero, outfielder Kevin Mench, outfielder Laynce Nix and pitcher Julian Cordero, July 28, 2006.

CUDDYER, MICHAEL BRENT

Born, Norfolk, Virginia, March 27, 1979.
Bats Right. Throws Right. Height, 6 feet, 2 inches. Weight, 220 pounds.

Year Club	Lea	Pos	G	AB	R	H	2B	3B	HR	RBI	SB	Avg
1998 Fort Wayne . . . . Midwest	SS-2B	129	497	82	137	37	7	12	81	16	.276
1999 Fort Myers . . . . . . Fla.St.	3B	130	466	87	139	24	4	16	82	14	.298
2000 New Britain . . . . Eastern	3B	138	490	72	129	30	8	6	61	5	.263
2001 New Britain . . . . Eastern	3B-1B-OF	141	509	95	153	36	3	30	87	5	.301
2001 Minnesota . . . . A.L.	1B-3B	8	18	1	4	2	0	0	1	1	.222
2002 Edmonton . . . . .P.C.	OF-1B-3B	86	330	70	102	16	9	20	53	12	.309
2002 Minnesota . . . . A.L.	OF-3B-1B	41	112	12	29	7	0	4	13	2	.259
2003 Twins . . . . Gulf Coast	OF	2	5	1	4	0	0	1	3	0	.800
2003 Rochester. . . . . Int.	OF-2B-3B-1B	53	186	25	57	17	0	3	34	5	.306
2003 Minnesota . . . . A.L.	OF-3B-1B-2B	35	102	14	25	1	3	4	8	1	.245
2004 Minnesota . . . . A.L.	2B-3B-OF-1B	115	339	49	89	22	1	12	45	5	.263
2005 Rochester . . . . Int.	3B-1B	3	9	1	1	0	0	0	0	2	.111
2005 Minnesota a . . . . A.L.	3B-OF-2B-1B	126	422	55	111	25	3	12	42	3	.263
2006 Minnesota . . . . A.L.	OF-1B	150	557	102	158	41	5	24	109	6	.284
2007 Minnesota b . . . . A.L.	OF-1B	144	547	87	151	28	5	16	81	5	.276
Major League Totals . . . . 7 Yrs.	619	2097	320	567	126	17	72	299	23	.270	
Division Series											
2002 Minnesota . . . . A.L.	OF	5	13	1	5	1	0	0	1	0	.385
2003 Minnesota . . . . A.L.	PH	1	4	0	1	0	0	0	1	0	.250
2004 Minnesota . . . . A.L.	2B-1B	4	15	1	7	0	0	0	2	0	.467
2006 Minnesota . . . . A.L.	OF	3	12	2	3	0	1	1	1	0	.250
Division Series Totals		13	44	4	16	1	1	1	5	0	.364
Championship Series											
2002 Minnesota . . . . A.L.	OF	3	5	0	1	0	0	0	0	0	.200

a On disabled list from June 30 to July 17, 2005.
b On disabled list from July 19 to August 3, 2007.

CUST, JOHN JOSEPH (JACK)

Born, Flemington, New Jersey, January 16, 1979.
Bats Left. Throws Right. Height, 6 feet, 2 inches. Weight, 205 pounds.

Year	Club	Lea	Pos	G	AB	R	H	2B	3B	HR	RBI	SB	Avg
1997	Diamondbcks	Arizona	OF	35	121	26	37	11	1	3	33	2	.306
1998	South Bend	Midwest	1B	16	62	5	15	3	0	0	4	0	.242
1998	Lethbridge	Pioneer	OF-1B	73	223	75	77	20	2	11	56	15	.345
1999	High Desert	Calif.	OF	125	455	107	152	42	3	32	112	1	.334
2000	El Paso	Texas	OF	129	447	100	131	32	6	20	75	12	.293
2001	Tucson	P.C.	OF	135	442	81	123	24	2	27	79	6	.278
2001	Arizona	N.L.	OF	3	2	0	1	0	0	0	0	0	.500
2002	Colorado Springs	P.C.	OF	105	359	74	95	24	0	23	55	6	.265
2002	Colorado a	N.L.	OF	35	65	8	11	2	0	1	8	0	.169
2003	Ottawa	Int.	OF	97	333	55	95	18	1	9	58	5	.285
2003	Baltimore b	A.L.	DH-OF	27	73	7	19	7	0	4	11	0	.260
2004	Baltimore	A.L.	DH	1	1	0	0	0	0	0	0	0	.000
2004	Ottawa c	Int.	OF	102	344	55	81	15	1	17	55	4	.235
2005	Sacramento d	P.C.	OF	134	479	95	123	28	1	19	75	2	.257
2006	Portland	P.C.	OF	138	441	97	129	23	0	30	77	0	.293
2006	San Diego	N.L.	OF	4	3	1	1	0	0	0	0	0	.333
2007	Portland	P.C.	OF	25	80	17	24	7	0	9	20	0	.300
2007	Oakland e	A.L.	OF	124	395	61	101	18	1	26	82	0	.256
Major League Totals			6 Yrs.	194	539	77	133	27	1	31	101	0	.247

a Traded to Colorado Rockies with catcher JD Closser for pitcher Mike Myers, January 7, 2002.
b Traded to Baltimore Orioles for outfielder Chris Richard and cash, March 11, 2003.
c Filed for free agency, October 27, 2004. Signed by Oakland Athletics organization, November 19, 2004.
d Filed for free agency, October 28, 2005. Signed by San Diego Padres organization, December 6, 2005.
e Traded to Oakland Athletics for player to be named later, May 3, 2007.

DAMON, JOHNNY DAVID

Born, Fort Riley, Kansas, November 5, 1973.
Bats Left. Throws Left. Height, 6 feet, 2 inches. Weight, 205 pounds.

Year	Club	Lea	Pos	G	AB	R	H	2B	3B	HR	RBI	SB	Avg
1992	Royals	Gulf Coast	OF	50	192	58	67	12	9	4	24	23	.349
1992	Baseball City	Fla. St.	OF	1	1	0	0	0	0	0	0	0	.000
1993	Rockford	Midwest	OF	127	511	82	148	25	13	5	50	59	.290
1994	Wilmington	Carolina	OF	119	472	96	149	25	13	6	75	44	.316
1995	Wichita	Texas	OF	111	423	83	145	15	9	16	54	26	.343
1995	Kansas City	A.L.	OF	47	188	32	53	11	5	3	23	7	.282
1996	Kansas City	A.L.	OF	145	517	61	140	22	5	6	50	25	.271
1997	Kansas City	A.L.	OF	146	472	70	130	12	8	8	48	16	.275
1998	Kansas City	A.L.	OF	161	642	104	178	30	10	18	66	26	.277
1999	Kansas City	A.L.	OF	145	583	101	179	39	9	14	77	36	.307
2000	Kansas City a	A.L.	OF	159	655	*136	214	42	10	16	88	*46	.327
2001	Oakland b	A.L.	OF	155	644	108	165	34	4	9	49	27	.256
2002	Boston	A.L.	OF	154	623	118	178	34	*11	14	63	31	.286
2003	Boston	A.L.	OF	145	608	103	166	32	6	12	*67	30	.273
2004	Boston	A.L.	OF	150	621	123	189	35	6	20	94	19	.304
2005	Boston c	A.L.	OF	148	624	117	197	35	6	10	75	18	.316
2006	New York	A.L.	OF-1B	149	593	115	169	35	5	24	80	25	.285
2007	New York	A.L.	OF-1B	141	533	93	144	27	2	12	63	27	.270
Major League Totals			13 Yrs.	1845	7303	1281	2102	388	87	166	843	333	.288
Division Series													
2001	Oakland	A.L.	OF	5	22	3	9	2	1	0	0	2	.409
2003	Boston	A.L.	OF	5	19	2	6	2	0	1	3	2	.316
2004	Boston	A.L.	OF	3	15	4	7	1	0	0	0	3	.467
2005	Boston	A.L.	OF	3	13	2	3	1	0	0	0	0	.231
2006	New York	A.L.	OF	4	17	3	4	0	0	1	3	0	.235
2007	New York	A.L.	OF	4	18	2	5	0	0	2	5	0	.278
Division Series Totals				24	104	16	34	6	1	4	11	7	.327
Championship Series													
2003	Boston	A.L.	OF	5	20	1	4	1	0	0	1	1	.200
2004	Boston	A.L.	OF	7	35	5	6	0	0	2	7	2	.171
Championship Series Totals				12	55	6	10	1	0	2	8	3	.182
World Series Record													
2004	Boston	A.L.	OF	4	21	4	6	2	1	1	2	0	.286

a Traded to Oakland Athletics with infielder Mark Ellis for pitcher Roberto Hernandez, catcher A.J. Hinch, outfielder Angel Berroa and cash, January 8, 2001.
b Filed for free agency, November 5, 2001. Signed with Boston Red Sox, December 21, 2001.
c Filed for free agency, October 28, 2005. Signed with New York Yankees, December 23, 2005.

DAVIS, RAJAI LAVAE
Born, Norwich, Connecticut, October 19, 1980.
Bats Right. Throws Right. Height, 5 feet, 11 inches. Weight, 195 pounds.

Year	Club	Lea	Pos	G	AB	R	H	2B	3B	HR	RBI	SB	Avg
2001 Pirates	Gulf Coast	OF	26	84	19	22	1	0	0	4	11	.262
2001 Williamsport	N.Y.-Penn.	OF-2B	6	12	1	1	0	0	0	0	0	.083
2002 Pirates	Gulf Coast	OF	58	224	38	86	16	5	4	35	24	.384
2002 Williamsport	N.Y.-Penn.	OF	1	4	0	0	0	0	0	0	0	.000
2002 Hickory	So.Atl.	OF	6	14	4	6	0	0	0	3	2	.429
2003 Hickory	So.Atl.	OF	125	478	84	146	21	7	6	54	40	.305
2004 Lynchburg	Carolina	OF	127	509	91	160	27	7	5	38	57	.314
2005 Altoona	Eastern	OF	123	499	82	140	22	5	4	34	45	.281
2006 Indianapolis	Int.	OF	100	385	53	109	17	1	2	21	45	.283
2006 Pittsburgh	N.L.	OF	20	14	1	2	1	0	0	0	1	.143
2007 Indianapolis	Int.	OF	53	211	31	67	12	4	4	30	27	.318
2007 Pittsburgh-San Francisco a	N.L.	OF	75	190	32	53	11	2	1	9	22	.279
Major League Totals		2 Yrs.	95	204	33	55	12	2	1	9	23	.270

a Traded to San Francisco Giants with player to be named later for pitcher Matt Morris, July 31, 2007. San Francisco Giants received pitcher Steve MacFarland to complete trade, August 27, 2007.

DE JESUS, DAVID CHRISTOPHER
Born, Brooklyn, New York, December 20, 1979.
Bats Left. Throws Left. Height, 6 feet. Weight, 170 pounds.

Year	Club	Lea	Pos	G	AB	R	H	2B	3B	HR	RBI	SB	Avg
2002 Wilmington	Carolina	OF	87	334	69	99	22	6	4	41	15	.296
2002 Wichita a	Texas	OF	25	79	7	20	5	2	2	15	3	.253
2003 Wichita	Texas	OF	17	71	14	24	4	0	2	10	1	.338
2003 Omaha	P.C.	OF	59	215	49	64	16	3	5	23	8	.298
2003 Kansas City	A.L.	OF	12	7	0	2	0	1	0	0	0	.286
2004 Omaha	P.C.	OF	50	197	38	62	14	4	6	16	7	.315
2004 Kansas City	A.L.	OF	96	363	58	104	15	3	7	39	8	.287
2005 Kansas City	A.L.	OF	122	461	69	135	31	6	9	56	5	.293
2006 Omaha	P.C.	OF	3	13	0	5	0	0	0	2	0	.385
2006 Kansas City b	A.L.	OF	119	491	83	145	36	7	8	56	6	.295
2007 Kansas City	A.L.	OF	157	605	101	157	29	9	7	58	10	.260
Major League Totals		5 Yrs.	506	1927	311	543	111	26	31	209	29	.282

a On minor league disabled list from June 19 to September 17, 2001.
b On disabled list from April 19 to May 29, 2006.

DELGADO (HERNANDEZ), CARLOS JUAN
Born, Aguadilla, Puerto Rico, June 25, 1972.
Bats Left. Throws Right. Height, 6 feet, 3 inches. Weight, 240 pounds.

Year	Club	Lea	Pos	G	AB	R	H	2B	3B	HR	RBI	SB	Avg
1989 St. Catharines	N.Y.-Penn.	DH-C	31	89	9	16	5	0	0	11	0	.180
1990 St. Catharines	N.Y.-Penn.	C	67	228	30	64	13	0	6	39	2	.281
1991 Myrtle Beach	So. Atl.	C	132	441	72	126	18	2	18	70	9	.286
1991 Syracuse	Int.	C	1	3	0	0	0	0	0	0	0	.000
1992 Dunedin	Fla. St.	C	133	485	83	*157	*30	2	*30	*100	2	.324
1993 Knoxville	Southern	C	140	468	91	142	28	0	*25	*102	10	.303
1993 Toronto	A.L.	C	2	1	0	0	0	0	0	0	0	.000
1994 Toronto	A.L.	OF-C	43	130	17	28	2	0	9	24	1	.215
1994 Syracuse	Int.	DH-C-1B	85	307	52	98	11	0	19	58	1	.319
1995 Syracuse	Int.	1B-OF	91	333	59	106	23	4	22	74	0	.318
1995 Toronto	A.L.	OF-1B	37	91	7	15	3	0	3	11	0	.165
1996 Toronto	A.L.	DH-1B	138	488	68	132	28	2	25	92	0	.270
1997 Toronto	A.L.	1B	153	519	79	136	42	3	30	91	0	.262
1998 Dunedin	Fla.St.	1B	4	16	4	5	1	0	2	7	0	.313
1998 Syracuse	Int.	1B	2	7	4	4	2	0	1	6	0	.571
1998 Toronto a	A.L.	1B	142	530	94	155	43	1	38	115	3	.292
1999 Toronto	A.L.	1B	152	573	113	156	39	0	44	134	1	.272
2000 Toronto	A.L.	1B	*162	569	115	196	*57	1	41	137	0	.344
2001 Toronto b	A.L.	1B	*162	574	102	160	31	1	39	102	3	.279
2002 Toronto	A.L.	1B	143	505	103	140	34	2	33	108	1	.277
2003 Toronto	A.L.	1B	161	570	117	172	38	1	42	*145	0	.302
2004 Dunedin	Fla.St.	1B	2	8	1	2	0	0	1	2	0	.250
2004 Syracuse	Int.	1B	2	9	2	5	2	0	1	4	0	.556
2004 Toronto c-d	A.L.	1B	128	458	74	123	26	0	32	99	0	.269
2005 Florida e-f-g	N.L.	1B	144	521	81	157	41	3	33	115	0	.301
2006 New York	N.L.	1B	144	524	89	139	30	2	38	114	0	.265

Year	Club	Lea	Pos	G	AB	R	H	2B	3B	HR	RBI	SB	Avg
2007 New York		N.L.	1B	139	538	71	139	30	0	24	87	4	.258
Major League Totals		15 Yrs.		1850	6591	1130	1848	444	16	431	1374	13	.280
Division Series													
2006 New York		N.L.	1B	3	14	3	6	0	0	1	2	0	.429
Championship Series													
2006 New York		N.L.	1B	7	23	5	7	3	0	3	9	0	.304

a On disabled list from March 31 to April 24, 1998.
b On disabled list from August 9 to August 25, 2002.
c On disabled list from May 30 to July 6, 2004.
d Filed for free agency, October 28, 2004. Signed with Florida Marlins, January 26, 2005.
e Signed with Florida Marlins, January 27, 2005.
f On disabled list from July 28 to August 13, 2005.
g Traded to New York Mets with cash for infielder Mike Jacobs, pitcher Yusmeiro Petit and infielder Grant Psomas, November 23, 2005.

DELLUCCI, DAVID MICHAEL

Born, Baton Rouge, Louisiana, October 31, 1973.
Bats Left. Throws Left. Height, 5 feet, 11 inches. Weight, 195 pounds.

Year	Club	Lea	Pos	G	AB	R	H	2B	3B	HR	RBI	SB	Avg
1995 Bluefield		Appal.	OF	20	69	11	23	5	1	2	12	3	.333
1995 Frederick		Carolina	OF	28	96	16	27	3	0	1	10	1	.281
1996 Frederick		Carolina	OF	59	185	33	60	11	1	4	28	5	.324
1996 Bowie		Eastern	OF	66	251	27	73	14	1	2	33	2	.291
1997 Bowie		Eastern	OF	107	385	71	126	29	3	20	55	11	.327
1997 Baltimore a		A.L.	OF	17	27	3	6	1	0	1	3	0	.222
1998 Tucson		P.C.	OF	17	72	17	22	4	3	1	11	4	.306
1998 Arizona		N.L.	OF	124	416	43	108	19	12	5	51	3	.260
1999 Arizona b		N.L.	OF	63	109	27	43	7	1	1	15	2	.394
2000 Arizona		N.L.	OF	34	50	2	15	3	0	0	2	0	.300
2000 Tucson		P.C.	OF	33	122	16	28	6	3	3	17	4	.230
2000 Diamondbacks		Arizona	OF	2	6	0	2	1	0	0	2	0	.333
2000 South Bend c		Midwest	OF	2	5	3	1	1	0	0	1	0	.200
2001 Arizona		N.L.	OF	115	217	28	60	10	2	10	40	2	.276
2002 Tucson		P.C.	OF	4	15	2	2	1	0	0	1	0	.133
2002 Arizona d		N.L.	OF	97	229	34	56	11	2	7	29	2	.245
2003 Arizona e		N.L.	OF	70	165	18	40	11	3	2	19	9	.242
2003 New York f-g-h		A.L.	OF	21	51	8	9	1	0	1	4	3	.176
2004 Texas i		A.L.	OF	107	331	59	80	13	1	17	61	9	.242
2005 Texas		A.L.	DH-OF	128	435	97	109	17	5	29	65	5	.251
2006 Philadelphia j-k		N.L.	OF	132	264	41	77	14	5	13	39	1	.292
2007 Cleveland l		A.L.	OF	56	178	25	41	11	2	4	20	2	.230
Major League Totals		11 Yrs.		964	2472	385	644	118	33	90	348	38	.261
Division Series													
2001 Arizona		N.L.	PH	2	0	0	0	0	0	0	0	0	.000
2002 Arizona		N.L.	OF	3	7	1	2	0	0	1	2	0	.286
2003 New York		A.L.	PH	1	0	0	0	0	0	0	0	0	.000
Division Series Totals				6	7	1	2	0	0	1	2	0	.286
Championship Series													
2001 Arizona		N.L.	PH	2	2	1	1	0	0	0	0	0	.500
2003 New York		A.L.	OF	3	3	2	1	0	0	0	0	1	.333
Championship Series Totals				5	5	3	2	0	0	0	0	1	.400
World Series Record													
2001 Arizona		N.L.	OF	2	2	0	1	0	0	0	0	0	.500
2003 New York		A.L.	OF	4	2	1	0	0	0	0	0	0	.000
World Series Totals				6	4	1	1	0	0	0	0	0	.250

a Selected in expansion draft by Arizona Diamondbacks, November 18, 1997.
b On disabled list from July 25 to November 18, 1999.
c On disabled list from May 8 to July 26, 2000.
d On disabled list from May 2 to May 24, 2002.
e On disabled list from June 2 to June 17, 2003.
f Traded to New York Yankees with pitcher Bret Prinz and catcher Jon-Mark Sprowl for outfielder Raul Mondesi, July 29, 2003.
g On disabled list from August 28 to September 27, 2003.
h Not offered contract, December 21, 2003. Signed with Texas Rangers, December 29, 2003.
i Filed for free agency, November 1, 2004, re-signed with Texas Rangers, December 20, 2004.
j Traded to Philadelphia Phillies for pitcher Robinson Tejeda and outfielder Jake Blalock, April 1, 2006.
k Filed for free agency, November 2, 2006. Signed with Cleveland Indians, December 6, 2006.
l On disabled list from June 20 to September 6, 2007.

DE ROSA, MARK THOMAS
Born, Passaic, New Jersey, February 26, 1975.
Bats Right. Throws Right. Height, 6 feet, 1 inch. Weight, 185 pounds.

Year	Club	Lea	Pos	G	AB	R	H	2B	3B	HR	RBI	SB	Avg
1996	Eugene	Northwest	SS	70	255	43	66	13	1	2	28	3	.259
1997	Durham	Carolina	SS	92	346	51	93	11	3	8	37	6	.269
1998	Greenville	Southern	SS	125	461	67	123	26	2	8	49	7	.267
1998	Atlanta	N.L.	SS	5	3	2	1	0	0	0	0	0	.333
1999	Richmond	Int.	SS	105	364	41	99	16	2	1	40	7	.272
1999	Atlanta	N.L.	SS	7	8	0	0	0	0	0	0	0	.000
2000	Richmond	Int.	SS-2B-3B	101	370	62	108	22	3	3	35	13	.292
2000	Atlanta	N.L.	SS	22	13	9	4	1	0	0	3	0	.308
2001	Richmond	Int.	SS-3B-2B	49	186	31	55	18	0	2	17	7	.296
2001	Atlanta	N.L.	SS-2B-3B-OF	66	164	27	47	8	0	3	20	2	.287
2002	Myrtle Beach	Car.	2B	2	7	0	0	0	0	0	0	0	.000
2002	Richmond	Int.	2B-SS	16	55	9	14	3	0	0	6	2	.255
2002	Atlanta a	N.L.	2B-SS-OF-3B	72	212	24	63	9	2	5	23	2	.297
2003	Atlanta	N.L.	2B-3B-SS-OF	103	266	40	70	14	0	6	22	1	.263
2004	Atlanta b	N.L.	3B-SS-2B-OF	118	309	33	74	16	0	3	31	1	.239
2005	Texas	A.L.	OF-2B-SS-3B	66	148	26	36	5	0	8	20	1	.243
2006	Oklahoma	P.C.	2B-3B	3	12	2	6	1	0	0	0	0	.500
2006	Texas c-d	A.L.	OF-3B-2B-SS	136	520	78	154	40	2	13	74	4	.296
2007	Chicago	N.L.	2B-3B-OF-1B	149	502	64	147	28	3	10	72	1	.293
Major League Totals		10 Yrs.		744	2145	303	596	121	7	48	265	12	.278
Division Series													
2001	Atlanta	N.L.	SS	1	1	0	1	0	0	0	0	0	1.000
2002	Atlanta	N.L.	2B	4	7	2	3	1	1	0	3	0	.429
2003	Atlanta	N.L.	2B-3B	4	7	1	3	2	0	0	2	0	.429
2007	Chicago	N.L.	2B	3	9	2	3	0	0	0	0	0	.333
Division Series Totals				12	24	5	10	3	1	0	5	0	.417
Championship Series													
2001	Atlanta	N.L.	SS	4	4	0	0	0	0	0	0	0	.000

a On disabled list from May 18 to July 17, 2002.
b Not offered contract, December 20, 2004. Signed with Texas Rangers organization, January 19, 2005.
c On disabled list from April 15 to April 30, 2006.
d Filed for free agency, October 28, 2006. Signed with Chicago Cubs, November 15, 2006.

DIAZ, MATTHEW EDWARD (MATT)
Born, Portland, Oregon, March 3, 1978.
Bats Right. Throws Right. Height, 6 feet, 1 inch. Weight, 205 pounds.

Year	Club	Lea	Pos	G	AB	R	H	2B	3B	HR	RBI	SB	Avg
1999	Hudson Valley	N.Y.-Penn.	OF	54	208	22	51	15	2	1	20	6	.245
2000	St. Petersburg	Fla.St.	OF	106	392	37	106	21	3	6	53	2	.270
2001	Bakersfield	Calif.	OF	131	524	79	172	40	2	17	81	11	.328
2002	Orlando	Southern	OF-1B	122	449	71	123	28	1	10	50	31	.274
2003	Orlando	Southern	OF	60	227	32	87	21	0	5	41	9	.383
2003	Durham	Int.	OF	67	253	35	83	18	3	8	45	6	.328
2003	Tampa Bay	A.L.	OF	4	9	2	1	0	0	0	0	0	.111
2004	Durham	Int.	OF	134	503	81	167	47	5	21	93	15	.332
2004	Tampa Bay	A.L.	OF	10	21	3	4	1	1	1	3	0	.190
2005	Royals	Arizona	OF	3	13	2	6	2	0	0	2	0	.462
2005	Wichita	Texas	OF	7	26	6	7	0	0	1	6	1	.269
2005	Omaha	P.C.	OF	65	259	48	96	22	4	14	56	10	.371
2005	Kansas City a-b-c	A.L.	OF	34	89	7	25	4	2	1	9	0	.281
2006	Atlanta	N.L.	OF	124	297	37	97	15	4	7	32	5	.327
2007	Atlanta	N.L.	OF-1B	135	358	44	121	21	0	12	45	4	.338
Major League Totals		5 Yrs.		307	774	93	248	41	7	21	89	9	.320

a Released by Tampa Bay Devil Rays, February 18, 2005. Signed with Kansas City Royals organization, February 24, 2005.
b On disabled list from June 11 to July 18, 2005.
c Traded to Atlanta Braves for pitcher Ricardo Rodriguez, December 20, 2005.

DILLON, JOSEPH WILLIAM (JOE)
Born, Modesto, California, August 2, 1975.
Bats Right. Throws Right. Height, 6 feet, 2 inches. Weight, 200 pounds.

Year	Club	Lea	Pos	G	AB	R	H	2B	3B	HR	RBI	SB	Avg
1997	Spokane	Northwest	DH	19	70	6	15	3	0	2	6	1	.214
1998	Lansing	Midwest	1B-3B	73	268	37	70	17	2	15	43	9	.261

Year	Club	Lea	Pos	G	AB	R	H	2B	3B	HR	RBI	SB	Avg
1999	Wilmington . . .	Carolina	3B	134	503	73	133	31	2	16	90	9	.264
2000	Omaha	P.C.	3B	45	149	19	42	11	2	1	11	1	.282
2000	Wichita.	Texas	3B	62	220	35	70	16	2	10	43	0	.318
2001	Wichita a	Texas	1B-3B-2B-SS	101	369	62	106	19	3	15	59	4	.287
2002	New Britain	Eastern	3B-1B	103	344	47	90	20	2	9	50	3	.262
2002	Edmonton	P.C.	3B	6	18	5	3	1	0	0	0	1	.167
2003	. . . .			Did Not Play									
2004	Albuquerque.	P.C.	3B-OF-2B-1B	108	403	96	131	33	7	30	86	12	.325
2004	Carolina b.	Southern	3B	33	117	26	40	13	0	9	31	3	.342
2005	Albuquerque.	P.C.	3B-OF-2B	98	350	80	126	21	1	24	72	11	.360
2005	Florida c	N.L.	2B-OF-3B-1B	27	36	6	6	1	0	1	1	0	.167
2006	Yomuri	Japan Cent.	2B	31	87	9	17	3	1	2	7	0	.195
2007	Nashville	P.C.	3B-OF-1B-2B	94	319	69	101	28	2	20	73	6	.317
2007	Milwaukee d-e	N.L.	OF-1B-2B-3B	39	76	12	26	8	2	0	10	0	.342
Major League Totals			2 Yrs.	66	112	18	32	9	2	1	11	0	.286

a Selected by Minnesota Twins from Kansas City Royals in Rule V minor league draft, December 13, 2001.
b Filed for free agency, October 15, 2003. Signed with Florida Marlins organization, March 16, 2004.
c Not offered contract by Florida Marlins, December 21, 2005. Signed with Yomuri Giants, December 21, 2005.
d Signed with Florida Marlins organization, January 4, 2007.
e Released by Florida Marlins, March 23, 2007. Signed with Milwaukee Brewers organization, April 1, 2007.

DOBBS, GREGORY STUART (GREG)
Born, Los Angeles, California, July 2, 1978.
Bats Left. Throws Right. Height, 6 feet, 1 inch. Weight, 205 pounds.

Year	Club	Lea	Pos	G	AB	R	H	2B	3B	HR	RBI	SB	Avg
2001	San Bernardino . . .	Calif.	OF	3	13	2	5	1	0	1	3	0	.385
2001	Everett	Northwest	1B-OF-3B	65	249	37	80	17	2	6	41	5	.321
2002	Wisconsin	Midwest	3B	86	320	43	88	16	2	10	48	13	.275
2002	San Antonio	Texas	OF-1B	27	96	13	35	2	0	5	15	1	.365
2003	San Antonio	Texas	3B	2	6	0	2	2	0	0	0	0	.333
2004	San Antonio	Texas	3B	51	203	25	66	14	4	5	34	5	.325
2004	Tacoma	P.C.	3B	67	255	28	69	9	2	8	31	4	.271
2004	Seattle	A.L.	3B	18	53	4	12	1	0	1	9	0	.226
2005	Tacoma	P.C.	1B-3B-OF	50	190	27	61	9	0	3	22	5	.321
2005	Seattle	A.L.	DH-1B-OF	59	142	8	35	7	1	1	20	1	.246
2006	Tacoma	P.C.	3B-1B-OF	99	379	60	119	19	3	9	55	14	.314
2006	Seattle	A.L.	1B-OF-3B	23	27	4	10	3	1	0	3	0	.370
2007	Philadelphia a	N.L.	3B-OF-1B-2B	142	324	45	88	20	4	10	55	3	.272
Major League Totals			4 Yrs.	242	546	61	145	31	6	12	87	4	.266
Division Series													
2007	Philadelphia	N.L.	3B	3	3	0	0	0	0	0	0	0	.000

a Claimed by Philadelphia Phillies on waivers, January 16, 2007.

DOUMIT, RYAN MATTHEW
Born, Moses Lake, Washington, April 3, 1981.
Bats Both. Throws Right. Height, 6 feet. Weight, 200 pounds.

Year	Club	Lea	Pos	G	AB	R	H	2B	3B	HR	RBI	SB	Avg
1999	Pirates	Gulf Coast	C	29	85	17	24	5	0	1	7	4	.282
2000	Williamsport.	N.Y.-Penn.	C	66	246	25	77	15	5	2	40	2	.313
2001	Altoona.	Eastern	C	2	4	0	1	0	0	0	2	0	.250
2001	Pirates	Gulf Coast	C	7	17	2	4	2	0	0	3	0	.235
2001	Hickory.	So.Atl.	C	39	148	14	40	6	0	2	14	2	.270
2002	Hickory.	So.Atl.	C	68	258	46	83	14	1	6	47	3	.322
2003	Lynchburg	Carolina	C	127	458	75	126	38	1	11	77	4	.275
2004	Altoona.	Eastern	C	67	221	31	58	20	0	10	34	0	.262
2005	Indianapolis	Int.	C-OF	51	165	41	57	11	0	12	35	1	.345
2005	Pittsburgh	N.L.	C-OF	75	231	25	59	13	1	6	35	2	.255
2006	Pirates	Gulf Coast	C-1B	5	14	1	0	0	0	0	0	0	.000
2006	Altoona.	Eastern	C-1B	4	15	4	5	3	0	0	4	0	.333
2006	Indianapolis	Int.	C	6	22	3	7	1	1	0	7	0	.318
2006	Pittsburgh a	N.L.	1B-C	61	149	15	31	9	0	6	17	0	.208
2007	Indianapolis	Int.	C	16	53	15	22	4	0	4	20	0	.415
2007	Pittsburgh b	N.L.	OF-C-1B	83	252	33	69	19	2	9	32	1	.274
Major League Totals			3 Yrs.	219	632	73	159	41	3	21	84	3	.252

a On disabled list from April 12 to May 3 and June 5 to August 23, 2006.
b On disabled list from August 13 to September 8 and September 9 to November 13, 2007.

DREW, DAVID JONATHAN (J.D.)

Born, Tallahassee, Florida, November 20, 1975.
Bats Left. Throws Right. Height, 6 feet, 1 inch. Weight, 200 pounds.

Year	Club	Lea	Pos	G	AB	R	H	2B	3B	HR	RBI	SB	Avg
1997 St. Paul	....	Northern	OF	44	170	51	58	6	1	18	50	5	.341
1998 St. Paul	....	Northern	OF	30	114	27	44	11	2	9	33	8	.386
1998 Arkansas	....	Texas	OF	19	67	18	22	3	1	5	11	2	.328
1998 Memphis	....	P.C.	OF	26	79	15	25	8	1	2	13	1	.316
1998 St. Louis	....	N.L.	OF	14	36	9	15	3	1	5	13	0	.417
1999 St. Louis a	....	N.L.	OF	104	368	72	89	16	6	13	39	19	.242
2000 St. Louis b		N.L.	OF	135	407	73	120	17	2	18	57	17	.295
2001 Peoria	....	Midwest	OF	3	11	3	6	2	0	0	0	0	.545
2001 St. Louis c	....	N.L.	OF	109	375	80	121	18	5	27	73	13	.323
2002 St. Louis d		N.L.	OF	135	424	61	107	19	1	18	56	8	.252
2003 Palm Beach	....	Fla.St.	OF	8	19	4	7	0	0	1	3	0	.368
2003 St. Louis e-f	....	N.L.	OF	100	287	60	83	13	3	15	42	2	.289
2004 Atlanta g		N.L.	OF	145	518	118	158	28	8	31	93	12	.305
2005 Los Angeles h	....	N.L.	OF	72	252	48	72	12	1	15	36	1	.286
2006 Los Angeles i	....	N.L.	OF	146	494	84	140	34	6	20	100	2	.283
2007 Boston		A.L.	OF	140	466	84	126	30	4	11	64	4	.270
Major League Totals	....	10 Yrs.		1100	3627	689	1031	190	37	173	573	78	.284
Division Series													
2000 St. Louis	....	N.L.	OF	2	6	1	1	0	0	0	0	2	.167
2001 St. Louis	....	N.L.	OF	5	13	1	2	0	0	1	2	0	.154
2002 St. Louis	....	N.L.	OF	2	9	1	2	0	0	1	1	0	.222
2004 Atlanta	....	N.L.	OF	5	20	1	4	0	0	0	1	1	.200
2006 Los Angeles		N.L.	OF	3	13	1	2	0	0	0	0	0	.154
2007 Boston	....	A.L.	OF	3	11	1	2	0	0	0	3	0	.182
Division Series Totals	....			20	72	6	13	0	0	2	7	3	.181
Championship Series													
2000 St. Louis	....	N.L.	OF	5	12	2	4	1	0	0	1	0	.333
2002 St. Louis	....	N.L.	OF	5	13	1	5	0	0	1	1	0	.385
2007 Boston	....	A.L.	OF	7	25	5	9	1	0	1	6	0	.360
Championship Series Totals	......			17	50	8	18	2	0	2	8	0	.360
World Series Record													
2007 Boston	....	A.L.	OF	4	15	1	5	2	0	0	2	0	.333

a On disabled list from May 16 to June 17, 1999.
b On disabled list from July 8 to July 26, 2000.
c On disabled list from June 18 to July 31, 2001.
d On disabled list from June 28 to July 13, 2002.
e On disabled list from March 21 to April 20 and August 9 to September 1, 2003.
f Traded to Atlanta Braves with catcher Eli Marrero for pitcher Jason Marquis, pitcher Ray King and pitcher Adam Wainwright, December 13, 2003.
g Filed for free agency, October 28, 2004. Signed with Los Angeles Dodgers, December 23, 2004.
h On disabled list from July 4 to October 7, 2005.
i Filed for free agency, November 10, 2006. Signed with Boston Red Sox, December 5, 2006.

DREW, STEPHEN ORIS

Born, Hahira, Georgia, March 16, 1983.
Bats Left. Throws Right. Height, 6 feet, 1 inch. Weight, 185 pounds.

Year	Club	Lea	Pos	G	AB	R	H	2B	3B	HR	RBI	SB	Avg
2005 Tennessee	....	Southern	SS	27	101	11	22	5	0	4	13	2	.218
2006 Tucson	....	P.C.	SS	83	342	55	97	16	3	13	51	3	.284
2006 Arizona	....	N.L.	SS	59	209	27	66	13	7	5	23	2	.316
2007 Arizona	....	N.L.	SS	150	543	60	129	28	4	12	60	9	.238
Major League Totals	....	2 Yrs.		209	752	87	195	41	11	17	83	11	.259
Division Series													
2007 Arizona	....	N.L.	SS	3	14	4	7	1	1	2	4	1	.500
Championship Series													
2007 Arizona	....	N.L.	SS	4	17	2	5	0	0	0	0	0	.294

DUFFY, CHRISTOPHER ELLIS (CHRIS)

Born, Brattleboro, Vermont, April 20, 1980.
Bats Left. Throws Left. Height, 5 feet, 9 inches. Weight, 190 pounds.

Year	Club	Lea	Pos	G	AB	R	H	2B	3B	HR	RBI	SB	Avg
2001 Williamsport	.....	N.Y.-Penn.	OF	64	221	50	70	12	4	1	24	30	.317
2002 Lynchburg	....	Carolina	OF	132	539	85	162	27	5	10	52	22	.301

Year	Club	Lea	Pos	G	AB	R	H	2B	3B	HR	RBI	SB	Avg
2003 Altoona.............	Eastern	OF	137	494	84	135	23	6	1	42	34	.273	
2004 Altoona.............	Eastern	OF	113	453	84	140	23	6	8	41	32	.309	
2005 Indianapolis	Int.	OF	78	308	55	95	13	7	7	31	17	.308	
2005 Pittsburgh a.........	N.L.	OF	39	126	22	43	4	2	1	9	2	.341	
2006 Indianapolis	Int.	OF	26	106	18	37	7	2	2	19	13	.349	
2006 Pittsburgh	N.L.	OF	84	314	46	80	14	3	2	18	26	.255	
2007 Pirates	Gulf Coast	OF	4	13	1	4	1	0	0	1	0	.308	
2007 Pittsburgh b.........	N.L.	OF	70	241	31	60	11	3	3	22	13	.249	
Major League Totals		3 Yrs.	193	681	99	183	29	8	6	49	41	.269	

a On disabled list from August 26 to October 3, 2005.
b On disabled list from June 29 to November 13, 2007.

DUNCAN, CHRISTOPHER EDWARD (CHRIS)
Born, Tucson, Arizona, May 5, 1981.
Bats Left. Throws Right. Height, 6 feet, 5 inches. Weight, 210 pounds.

Year	Club	Lea	Pos	G	AB	R	H	2B	3B	HR	RBI	SB	Avg
1999 Johnson City	Appal.	1B	55	201	23	43	8	1	6	34	3	.214	
1999 Piedmont	So.Atl.	3B-SS	73	276	41	60	15	3	11	40	15	.217	
2000 Clearwater	Fla.St.	OF	107	390	49	103	25	3	8	47	13	.264	
2000 Peoria...........	Midwest	1B	122	450	52	115	34	0	8	57	1	.256	
2001 Potomac.........	Carolina	1B	49	168	12	30	6	0	3	16	4	.179	
2001 Peoria...........	Midwest	1B	80	297	44	91	23	2	13	59	13	.306	
2002 Peoria...........	Midwest	1B	129	487	58	132	25	4	16	75	5	.271	
2003 Palm Beach	Fla.St.	1B	121	425	26	108	20	0	2	42	4	.254	
2003 Tennessee	Southern	OF	10	25	1	5	1	0	1	3	0	.200	
2004 Tennessee	Southern	1B-OF	120	387	57	112	23	0	16	65	8	.289	
2005 Memphis	P.C.	1B-OF	128	431	57	114	21	2	21	73	1	.265	
2005 St. Louis..........	N.L.	1B-OF	9	10	2	2	1	0	1	3	0	.200	
2006 Memphis	P.C.	OF	52	181	23	49	11	0	7	31	1	.271	
2006 St. Louis..........	N.L.	OF-1B	90	280	60	82	11	3	22	43	0	.293	
2007 St. Louis..........	N.L.	OF-1B	127	375	51	97	20	0	21	70	2	.259	
Major League Totals		3 Yrs.	226	665	113	181	32	3	44	116	2	.272	
Division Series													
2006 St. Louis..........	N.L.	OF	2	6	1	1	0	0	0	0	0	.167	
Championship Series													
2006 St. Louis..........	N.L.	OF	5	8	1	1	0	0	1	1	0	.125	
World Series Record													
2006 St. Louis..........	N.L.	OF-DH	3	8	1	1	1	0	0	1	0	.125	

DUNCAN, DAVID SHELLEY (SHELLEY)
Born, Tucson, Arizona, September 29, 1979.
Bats Right. Throws Right. Height, 6 feet, 5 inches. Weight, 215 pounds.

Year	Club	Lea	Pos	G	AB	R	H	2B	3B	HR	RBI	SB	Avg
2001 Staten Island	N.Y.-Penn.	DH	70	273	43	67	17	2	8	39	5	.245	
2002 Greensboro	So.Atl.	OF	101	356	58	95	23	2	14	56	15	.267	
2003 Tampa	Fla.St.	OF	91	330	42	87	19	2	8	47	5	.264	
2004 Tampa	Fla.St.	1B-OF	123	424	65	105	27	1	19	78	6	.248	
2005 Trenton............	Eastern	1B	142	537	86	129	28	2	34	92	3	.240	
2006 Trenton............	Eastern	1B-OF	92	351	47	90	24	0	19	61	3	.256	
2006 Columbus..........	Int.	OF	12	43	1	8	1	0	1	4	0	.186	
2007 Scranton-WB	Int.	OF-1B	91	336	58	99	18	1	25	79	2	.295	
2007 New York	A.L.	DH-OF-1B	34	74	16	19	1	0	7	17	0	.257	
Division Series													
2007 New York	A.L.	1B	3	4	1	2	0	0	0	0	0	.500	

DUNN, ADAM TROY
Born, Houston, Texas, November 9, 1979.
Bats Left. Throws Right. Height, 6 feet, 6 inches. Weight, 275 pounds.

Year	Club	Lea	Pos	G	AB	R	H	2B	3B	HR	RBI	SB	Avg
1998 Billings...........	Pioneer	OF	34	125	26	36	3	1	4	13	4	.288	
1999 Rockford	Midwest	OF	92	313	62	96	16	2	11	44	21	.307	
2000 Dayton	Midwest	OF	122	420	101	118	29	1	16	79	24	.281	
2001 Chattanooga......	Southern	OF	39	140	30	48	9	0	12	31	6	.343	
2001 Louisville	Int.	OF	55	210	44	69	13	0	20	53	5	.329	
2001 Cincinnati..........	N.L.	OF	66	244	54	64	18	1	19	43	4	.262	
2002 Cincinnati..........	N.L.	OF-1B	158	535	84	133	28	2	26	71	19	.249	

Year	Club	Lea	Pos	G	AB	R	H	2B	3B	HR	RBI	SB	Avg
2003 Cincinnati a	N.L.	OF-1B	116	.381	70	82	12	1	27	57	8	.215
2004 Cincinnati	N.L.	OF-1B	161	568	105	151	34	0	46	102	6	.266
2005 Cincinnati	N.L.	OF-1B	160	543	107	134	35	2	40	101	4	.247
2006 Cincinnati	N.L.	OF-1B	160	561	99	131	24	0	40	92	7	.234
2007 Cincinnati	N.L.	OF	152	522	101	138	27	2	40	106	9	.264
Major League Totals		7 Yrs.	973	3354	620	833	178	8	238	572	57	.248

a On disabled list from August 16 to October 2, 2003.

DURHAM, RAY

Born, Charlotte, North Carolina, November 30, 1971.
Bats Both. Throws Right. Height, 5 feet, 8 inches. Weight, 190 pounds.

Year	Club	Lea	Pos	G	AB	R	H	2B	3B	HR	RBI	SB	Avg
1990 White Sox	Gulf C.	2B	35	116	18	32	3	3	0	13	23	.276
1991 White Sox	Gulf C.	2B	6	23	3	7	1	0	0	4	5	.304
1991 Utica	N.Y.-Penn.	2B	39	142	29	36	2	7	0	17	12	.254
1992 White Sox	Gulf C.	DH	5	13	3	7	2	0	0	2	1	.538
1992 Sarasota a	Fla. St.	2B	57	202	37	55	6	3	0	7	28	.272
1993 Birmingham	Southern	2B	137	528	83	143	22	10	3	37	39	.271
1994 Nashville	A.A.	2B	133	527	89	156	33	*12	16	66	34	.296
1995 Chicago	A.L.	2B	125	471	68	121	27	6	7	51	18	.257
1996 Chicago	A.L.	2B	156	557	79	153	33	5	10	65	30	.275
1997 Chicago	A.L.	2B	155	634	106	172	27	5	11	53	33	.271
1998 Chicago	A.L.	2B	158	635	126	181	35	8	19	67	36	.285
1999 Chicago	A.L.	2B	153	612	109	181	30	8	13	60	34	.296
2000 Chicago	A.L.	2B	151	614	121	172	35	9	17	75	25	.280
2001 Chicago	A.L.	2B	152	611	104	163	42	10	20	65	23	.267
2002 Chicago-Oakland b-c	A.L.	2B	150	564	114	163	34	6	15	70	26	.289
2003 San Francisco d	N.L.	2B	110	410	61	117	30	5	8	33	7	.285
2004 San Jose	California	2B	1	3	0	1	0	0	0	0	0	.333
2004 Fresno	P.C.	2B	5	14	4	8	0	1	1	5	0	.571
2004 San Francisco e	N.L.	2B	120	471	95	133	28	8	17	65	10	.282
2005 San Francisco	N.L.	2B-OF	142	497	67	144	33	0	12	62	6	.290
2006 San Francisco f-g	N.L.	2B	137	498	79	146	30	7	26	93	7	.293
2007 San Francisco	N.L.	2B	138	464	56	101	21	2	11	71	.10	.218
Major League Totals		13 Yrs.	1847	7038	1185	1947	405	79	186	830	265	.277
Division Series												
2000 Chicago	A.L.	2B	3	10	2	2	1	0	1	1	0	.200
2002 Oakland	A.L.	DH	5	21	7	7	3	0	2	2	1	.333
2003 San Francisco	N.L.	2B	4	17	2	4	0	0	0	0	0	.235
Division Series Totals			12	48	11	13	4	0	3	3	1	.271

a On disabled list from June 16 to July 9, 1992.
b Traded to Oakland Athletics for pitcher Jon Adkins, July 25, 2002.
c Filed for free agency, November 1, 2002. Signed with San Francisco Giants, December 7, 2002.
d On disabled list from May 11 to May 26 and August 7 to September 1, 2003.
e On disabled list from April 28 to May 13 and from May 23 to June 15, 2004.
f On disabled list from April 27 to May 12, 2006.
g Filed for free agency, October 30, 2006, re-signed with San Francisco Giants, December 1, 2006.

DYE, JERMAINE TERRELL

Born, Oakland, California, January 28, 1974.
Bats Right. Throws Right. Height, 6 feet, 5 inches. Weight, 235 pounds.

Year	Club	Lea	Pos	G	AB	R	H	2B	3B	HR	RBI	SB	Avg
1993 Braves	Gulf Coast	OF-3B	31	124	17	43	14	0	0	27	5	.347
1993 Danville	Appal.	OF	25	94	6	26	6	1	2	12	4	.277
1994 Macon	So.Atl.	OF	135	506	73	151	41	1	15	98	19	.298
1995 Greenville	Southern	OF	104	403	50	115	26	4	15	71	4	.285
1996 Richmond	Int.	OF	36	142	25	33	7	1	6	19	3	.232
1996 Atlanta	N.L.	OF	98	292	32	82	16	0	12	37	1	.281
1997 Omaha	A.A.	OF	39	144	21	44	6	0	10	25	0	.306
1997 Kansas City a-b	A.L.	OF	75	263	26	62	14	0	7	22	2	.236
1998 Omaha	P.C.	OF-1B	41	157	29	47	6	0	12	35	7	.299
1998 Kansas City c	A.L.	OF	60	214	24	50	5	1	5	23	2	.234
1999 Kansas City	A.L.	OF	158	608	96	179	44	8	27	119	2	.294
2000 Kansas City	A.L.	OF	157	601	107	193	41	2	33	118	0	.321
2001 Kansas City-Oakland d	A.L.	OF	158	599	91	169	31	1	26	106	9	.282
2002 Sacramento	P.C.	DH	4	16	3	3	2	0	0	1	0	.188
2002 Modesto	California	OF	2	8	1	4	3	0	0	2	0	.500

Year	Club	Lea	Pos	G	AB	R	H	2B	3B	HR	RBI	SB	Avg
2002 Oakland e	A.L.		OF	131	488	74	123	27	1	24	86	2	.252
2003 Sacramento	P.C.		OF	13	49	9	14	2	0	2	9	0	.286
2003 Oakland f	A.L.		OF	65	221	28	38	6	0	4	20	1	.172
2004 Oakland g	A.L.		OF	137	532	87	141	29	4	23	80	4	.265
2005 Chicago	A.L.	OF-1B-SS	145	529	74	145	29	2	3†	86	11	.274
2006 Chicago	A.L.		OF	146	539	103	170	27	3	44	120	7	.315
2007 Chicago	A.L.		OF	138	508	68	129	34	0	28	78	2	.254
Major League Totals	12 Yrs.	1468	5394	810	1481	303	22	264	895	43	.275
Division Series													
1996 Atlanta	N.L.		OF	3	11	1	2	0	0	1	1	1	.182
2001 Oakland	A.L.		OF	4	13	0	3	2	0	0	0	0	.231
2002 Oakland	A.L.		OF	5	20	3	8	2	0	1	1	0	.400
2003 Oakland	A.L.		OF	4	13	2	3	0	0	1	3	0	.231
2005 Chicago	A.L.		OF	3	10	1	2	0	0	0	0	0	.200
Division Series Totals				19	67	7	18	4	0	3	5	1	.269
Championship Series													
1996 Atlanta	N.L.		OF	7	28	2	6	1	0	0	4	0	.214
2005 Chicago	A.L.		OF	5	19	3	5	2	0	0	3	1	.263
Championship Series Totals				12	47	5	11	3	0	0	7	1	.234
World Series Record													
1996 Atlanta	N.L.		OF	5	17	0	2	0	0	0	1	0	.118
2005 Chicago	A.L.		OF	4	16	3	7	1	0	1	3	0	.438
World Series Totals				9	33	3	9	1	0	1	4	0	.273

a Traded to Kansas City Royals with pitcher Jamie Walker for infielder Keith Lockhart and outfielder Michael Tucker, March 27, 1997.
b On disabled list from April 17 to May 3 and July 3 to August 13, 1997.
c On disabled list from March 31 to May 8 and September 1 to September 28, 1998.
d Traded to Oakland Athletics for infielder Neifi Perez, July 25, 2001.
e On disabled list from March 22 to April 26, 2002.
f On disabled list from April 25 to May 30 and July 7 to September 1, 2003.
g Filed for free agency, October 28, 2004. Signed with Chicago White Sox, December 9, 2004.

EASLEY, JACINTO DAMION (DAMION)

Born, New York, New York, November 11, 1969.
Bats Right. Throws Right. Height, 5 feet, 11 inches. Weight, 190 pounds.

Year	Club	Lea	Pos	G	AB	R	H	2B	3B	HR	RBI	SB	Avg
1989 Bend	Northwest		SS	36	131	34	39	5	1	4	21	9	.298
1990 Quad City	Midwest		SS	103	365	59	100	19	3	10	56	25	.274
1991 Midland	Texas		SS	127	452	73	115	24	5	6	57	23	.254
1992 Edmonton	P.C.		SS-3B	108	429	61	124	18	3	3	44	26	.289
1992 California	A.L.		3B-SS	47	151	14	39	5	0	1	12	9	.258
1993 California	A.L.		2B-3B	73	230	33	72	13	2	2	22	6	.313
1994 California	A.L.		3B-2B	88	316	41	68	16	1	6	30	4	.215
1995 California	A.L.		2B-SS	114	357	35	77	14	2	4	35	5	.216
1996 Midland	Texas		3B-SS	4	14	1	6	2	0	0	2	1	.429
1996 Vancouver	P.C.		SS-2B-3B	12	48	13	15	2	1	2	8	4	.313
1996 California-Detroit a-b	A.L.		SS-2B-3B-OF	49	112	14	30	2	0	4	17	3	.268
1997 Detroit	A.L.		2B-SS	151	527	97	139	37	3	22	72	28	.264
1998 Detroit	A.L.		2B-SS	151	594	84	161	38	2	27	100	15	.271
1999 Detroit	A.L.		2B-SS	151	549	83	146	30	1	20	65	11	.266
2000 Detroit	A.L.		2B	126	464	76	120	27	2	14	58	13	.259
2000 Toledo c	Int.		2B	4	13	3	3	1	0	1	4	0	.231
2001 Detroit	A.L.		2B	154	585	77	146	27	7	11	65	10	.250
2002 Detroit	A.L.		2B	85	304	29	68	14	1	8	30	1	.224
2002 Toledo d	Int.		2B	8	26	5	3	1	0	0	0	0	.115
2003 Tampa Bay e-f	A.L.		3D-2D	36	107	8	20	3	1	1	7	0	.187
2004 Florida g	N.L.	2B-1B-SS-3B	98	223	26	53	20	1	9	43	4	.238
2005 Florida h	N.L.		2B-SS-3B	102	267	37	64	19	1	9	30	4	.240
2006 Arizona i	N.L.		SS-3B-2B-1B	90	189	24	44	6	1	9	28	1	.233
2007 New York j-k	N.L.	2B-OF-1B-3B	76	193	24	54	6	0	10	26	0	.280
Major League Totals	16 Yrs.	1593	5168	702	1301	277	25	157	640	114	.252

a On disabled list from April 1 to May 10, 1996.
b Traded to Detroit Tigers for pitcher Greg Gohr, July 31, 1996.
c On disabled list from April 10 to April 24 and May 9 to June 1, 2000.
d On disabled list from April 17 to June 1, 2002.
e Released by Detroit Tigers, March 28, 2003. Signed with Tampa Bay Devil Rays, April 2, 2003.
f Released by Tampa Bay Devil Rays, June 4, 2003. Signed with Florida Marlins, December 19, 2003.

g Filed for free agency, October 28, 2004, re-signed with Florida Marlins, November 22, 2004.
h Filed for free agency, October 28, 2005. Signed with Arizona Diamondbacks, December 12, 2005.
i Filed for free agency, October 30, 2006. Signed with New York Mets, November 17, 2006.
j On disabled list from August 19 to October 29, 2007.
k Filed for free agency, October 29, 2007, re-signed with New York Mets, November 6, 2007.

ECKSTEIN, DAVID MARK
Born, Sanford, Florida, January 20, 1975.
Bats Right. Throws Right. Height, 5 feet, 7 inches. Weight, 165 pounds.

Year Club	Lea	Pos	G	AB	R	H	2B	3B	HR	RBI	SB	Avg
1997 Lowell	N.Y.-Penn.	2B	68	249	43	75	11	4	4	39	21	.301
1998 Sarasota	Fla.St.	2B-SS	135	503	99	154	29	4	3	58	45	.306
1999 Trenton	Eastern	2B	131	483	109	151	22	5	6	52	32	.313
2000 Pawtucket	Int.	2B-SS	119	422	77	104	20	0	1	31	11	.246
2000 Edmonton a	P.C.	2B	15	52	17	18	8	0	3	8	5	.346
2001 Anaheim	A.L.	SS-2B	153	582	82	166	26	2	4	41	29	.285
2002 Anaheim	A.L.	SS	152	608	107	178	22	6	8	63	21	.293
2003 Anaheim b	A.L.	SS	120	452	59	114	22	1	3	31	16	.252
2004 Anaheim c	A.L.	SS	142	566	92	156	24	1	2	35	16	.276
2005 St. Louis	N.L.	SS	158	630	90	185	26	7	8	61	11	.294
2006 St. Louis d	N.L.	SS	123	500	68	146	18	1	2	23	7	.292
2007 St. Louis e-f	N.L.	SS	117	434	58	134	23	0	3	31	10	.309
Major League Totals	7 Yrs.		965	3772	556	1079	161	18	30	285	110	.286
Division Series												
2002 Anaheim	A.L.	SS	4	18	2	5	0	0	0	1	1	.278
2004 Anaheim	A.L.	SS	3	12	2	4	0	0	0	0	0	.333
2005 St. Louis	N.L.	SS	3	13	3	5	0	0	1	4	0	.385
2006 St. Louis	N.L.	SS	4	15	1	2	0	0	0	1	1	.133
Division Series Totals			14	58	8	16	0	0	1	6	2	.276
Championship Series												
2002 Anaheim	A.L.	SS	5	21	1	6	0	0	0	2	0	.286
2005 St. Louis	N.L.	SS	6	20	5	4	0	0	0	2	1	.200
2006 St. Louis	N.L.	SS	7	26	3	6	1	0	1	1	3	.231
Championship Series Totals			18	67	9	16	1	0	1	5	4	.239
World Series Record												
2002 Anaheim	A.L.	SS	7	29	6	9	0	0	0	3	1	.310
2006 St. Louis	N.L.	SS	5	22	3	8	3	0	0	4	0	.364
World Series Totals			12	51	9	17	3	0	0	7	1	.333

a Claimed on waivers by Anaheim Angels from Boston Red Sox, August 16, 2000.
b On disabled list from August 18 to September 9, 2003.
c Not offered contract, December 20, 2004. Signed with St. Louis Cardinals, December 23, 2004.
d On disabled list from August 19 to September 15, 2006.
e On disabled list from June 14 to July 13, 2007.
f Filed for free agency, October 29, 2007. Signed with Texas Rangers, December 14, 2007.

EDMONDS, JAMES PATRICK (JIM)
Born, Fullerton, California, June 27, 1970.
Bats Left. Throws Left. Height, 6 feet, 1 inch. Weight, 210 pounds.

Year Club	Lea	Pos	G	AB	R	H	2B	3B	HR	RBI	SB	Avg
1988 Bend	Northwest	OF	35	122	23	27	4	0	0	13	4	.221
1989 Quad City a	Midwest	OF	31	92	11	24	4	0	1	4	1	.261
1990 Palm Springs	California	OF	91	314	36	92	18	6	3	56	5	.293
1991 Palm Springs b-c	California	OF-1B-P	60	187	28	55	15	1	2	27	2	.294
1992 Midland	Texas	OF	70	246	42	77	15	2	8	32	3	.313
1992 Edmonton	P.C.	OF	50	194	37	58	15	2	6	36	3	.299
1993 Vancouver d	P.C.	OF	95	356	59	112	28	4	9	74	6	.315
1993 California	A.L.	OF	18	61	5	15	4	1	0	4	0	.246
1994 California	A.L.	OF-1B	94	289	35	79	13	1	5	37	4	.273
1995 California	A.L.	OF	141	558	120	162	30	4	33	107	1	.290
1996 Lk Elsinore e	California	OF	5	15	4	6	2	0	1	4	0	.400
1996 California	A.L.	OF	114	431	73	131	28	3	27	66	4	.304
1997 Anaheim f	A.L.	OF-1B	133	502	82	146	27	0	26	80	5	.291
1998 Anaheim	A.L.	OF	154	599	115	184	42	1	25	91	7	.307
1999 Lake Elsinore	California	DH	5	19	4	8	2	0	0	3	2	.421
1999 Anaheim g	A.L.	OF-1B	55	204	34	51	17	2	5	23	5	.250
2000 St. Louis	N.L.	OF-1B	152	525	129	155	25	0	42	108	10	.295
2001 St. Louis	N.L.	OF-1B	150	500	95	152	38	1	30	110	5	.304

52

Year	Club	Lea	Pos	G	AB	R	H	2B	3B	HR	RBI	SB	Avg
2002 St. Louis i...........	N.L.	OF	144	476	96	148	31	2	28	83	4	.311
2003 St. Louis............	N.L.	OF	137	447	89	123	32	2	39	89	1	.275
2004 St. Louis............	N.L.	OF-1B	153	498	102	150	38	3	42	111	8	.301
2005 St. Louis............	N.L.	OF	142	467	88	123	37	1	29	89	5	.263
2006 St. Louis j...........	N.L.	OF-1B	110	350	52	90	18	0	19	70	4	.257
2007 St. Louis k-l.........	N.L.	OF-1B	117	365	39	92	15	2	12	53	0	.252
Major League Totals		15 Yrs.	1814	6272	1154	1801	395	23	362	1121	63	.287
Division Series												
2000 St. Louis............	N.L.	OF	3	14	5	8	4	0	2	7	1	.571
2001 St. Louis............	N.L.	OF	5	17	3	4	1	0	2	3	0	.235
2002 St. Louis............	N.L.	OF	3	11	1	3	0	0	1	2	0	.273
2004 St. Louis............	N.L.	OF	4	15	1	4	0	0	1	2	0	.267
2005 St. Louis............	N.L.	OF	3	11	5	4	2	0	1	1	0	.364
2006 St. Louis............	N.L.	OF	4	13	2	4	0	0	0	2	0	.308
Division Series Totals			22	81	17	27	7	0	7	17	1	.333
Championship Series												
2000 St. Louis............	N.L.	OF	5	22	1	5	1	0	1	5	0	.227
2002 St. Louis............	N.L.	OF	5	20	2	8	2	0	1	4	0	.400
2004 St. Louis............	N.L.	OF	7	24	2	7	2	0	2	7	0	.292
2005 St. Louis............	N.L.	OF	6	19	2	4	1	0	0	0	1	.211
2006 St. Louis............	N.L.	OF	7	22	5	5	0	0	2	4	0	.227
Championship Series Totals			30	107	12	29	6	0	6	20	1	.271
World Series Record												
2004 St. Louis............	N.L.	OF	4	15	2	1	0	0	0	0	0	.067
2006 St. Louis............	N.L.	OF	5	17	1	4	2	0	0	4	0	.235
World Series Totals............			9	32	3	5	2	0	0	4	0	.156

a On disabled list from June 19 to end of 1989 season.
b Record of 0-0 in one game as pitcher.
c On disabled list from April 10 to May 7 and July 23 to end of 1991 season.
d On disabled list from June 29 to July 19, 1993.
e On disabled list from May 26 to June 10 and June 12 to July 18, 1996.
f On disabled list from July 31 to August 16, 1997.
g On disabled list from March 30 to August 2, 1999.
h Traded to St. Louis Cardinals for pitcher Kent Bottenfield and infielder Adam Kennedy, March 23, 2000.
i On disabled list from June 1 to June 16, 2002.
j Filed for free agency, November 2, 2006, re-signed with St. Louis Cardinals, November 10, 2006.
k On disabled list from June 16 to July 19, 2007.
l Traded to San Diego Padres for infielder David Freese, December 15, 2007.

ELLIS, MARK WILLIAM

Born, Rapid City, South Dakota, June 6, 1977.
Bats Right. Throws Right. Height, 5 feet, 11 inches. Weight, 195 pounds.

Year	Club	Lea	Pos	G	AB	R	H	2B	3B	HR	RBI	SB	Avg
1999 Spokane.....Northwest			SS	71	281	67	92	14	0	7	47	21	.327
2000 Wilmington ... Carolina			SS-2B	132	484	83	146	27	4	6	62	25	.302
2000 Wichita........ Texas			2B	7	22	4	7	1	0	0	4	1	.318
2001 Sacramento a......P.C.			SS	132	472	71	129	38	4	10	53	21	.273
2002 Sacramento .......P.C.			SS	21	84	14	25	10	1	0	5	4	.298
2002 Oakland .........A.L.			2B-SS-3B	98	345	58	94	16	4	6	35	4	.272
2003 Oakland .........A.L.			2B	154	553	78	137	31	5	9	52	6	.248
2004 Oakland b........A.L.			INJURED—Did Not Play										
2005 Oakland .........A.L.			2B-SS-1B	122	434	76	137	21	5	13	52	1	.316
2006 Oakland .......P.C.			2B	4	12	1	2	0	0	0	2	0	.167
2006 Oakland c........A.L.			2B-1B	124	441	64	110	25	1	11	52	4	.249
2007 Oakland .........A.L.			2B	150	583	84	161	33	3	19	76	9	.276
Major League Totals		5 Yrs.	648	2356	360	639	126	18	58	267	24	.271
Division Series												
2002 Oakland .........A.L.			2B	5	19	1	7	2	0	1	4	0	.368
2003 Oakland .........A.L.			2B	5	17	2	2	0	0	0	0	0	.118
2006 Oakland .........A.L.			2B	2	7	0	2	0	0	0	0	0	.286
Division Series Totals			12	43	3	11	2	0	1	4	0	.256

a Traded to Oakland Athletics by Kansas City Royals with outfielder Johnny Damon and player to be named later for pitcher Roberto Hernandez, catcher A.J. Hinch, infielder Angel Berroa and cash, January 8, 2001.
b On disabled list from March 26 to October 20,2004
c On disabled list from June 1 to June 30, 2006.

ELLISON, JASON JEROME
Born, Quincy, California, April 4, 1978.
Bats Right. Throws Right. Height, 5 feet, 10 inches. Weight, 180 pounds.

Year	Club	Lea	Pos	G	AB	R	H	2B	3B	HR	RBI	SB	Avg
2000 Salem-Keizer	....	Northwest	OF	74	300	67	90	15	2	0	28	13	.300
2001 Hagerstown	....	So.Atl.	OF	130	494	95	144	38	3	8	55	19	.291
2002 San Jose	....	California	OF	81	322	40	87	13	0	5	40	9	.270
2002 Fresno	....	P.C.	OF	49	196	31	61	8	1	3	8	16	.311
2003 Fresno	....	P.C.	OF	119	461	74	136	22	4	6	39	21	.295
2003 San Francisco	....	N.L.	OF	7	10	1	1	0	0	0	0	0	.100
2004 Fresno	....	P.C.	OF	125	505	90	159	32	7	9	40	27	.315
2004 San Francisco	....	N.L.	OF	13	4	4	2	0	0	1	3	2	.500
2005 Fresno	....	P.C.	OF	8	38	5	9	2	0	0	3	0	.237
2005 San Francisco	....	N.L.	OF	131	352	49	93	18	2	4	24	14	.264
2006 Fresno	....	P.C.	OF	46	192	41	78	18	2	1	18	7	.406
2006 San Francisco	....	N.L.	OF	84	81	14	18	5	1	2	4	2	.222
2007 Seattle a	....	A.L.	OF	63	46	9	13	0	0	0	0	3	.283
2007 Cincinnati b-c	....	N.L.	OF	37	48	7	9	1	0	1	2	1	.188
Major League Totals	....	5 Yrs.		335	541	84	136	24	3	8	33	22	.251

a Traded to Seattle Mariners for pitcher Travis Blackley, April 1, 2007.
b Claimed on waivers by Cincinnati Reds, August 8, 2007.
c Filed for free agency, October 11, 2007.

ELLSBURY, JACOBY MCCABE
Born, Madras, Oregon, September 11, 1983.
Bats Left. Throws Left. Height, 6 feet, 1 inch. Weight, 185 pounds.

Year	Club	Lea	Pos	G	AB	R	H	2B	3B	HR	RBI	SB	Avg
2005 Lowell	....	N.Y.-Penn.	OF	35	139	28	44	3	5	1	19	23	.317
2006 Wilmington	....	Carolina	OF	61	244	35	73	7	5	4	32	25	.299
2006 Portland	....	Eastern	OF	50	198	29	61	10	3	3	19	16	.308
2007 Portland	....	Eastern	OF	17	73	16	33	10	2	0	13	8	.452
2007 Pawtucket	....	Int.	OF	87	363	66	108	14	5	2	28	33	.298
2007 Boston	....	A.L.	OF	33	116	20	41	7	1	3	18	9	.353
Division Series													
2007 Boston	....	A.L.	OF	2	1	1	0	0	0	0	0	0	.000
Championship Series													
2007 Boston	....	A.L.	OF	5	8	3	2	0	0	0	1	1	.250
World Series Record													
2007 Boston	....	A.L.	OF	4	16	4	7	4	0	0	3	1	.438

ENCARNACION, EDWIN ELPIDIO
Born, LaRomana, Dominican Republic, January 7, 1983.
Bats Right. Throws Right. Height, 6 feet, 1 inch. Weight, 195 pounds.

Year	Club	Lea	Pos	G	AB	R	H	2B	3B	HR	RBI	SB	Avg
2000 Rangers	....	Gulf Coast	3B	51	177	31	55	6	3	0	36	3	.311
2001 Dayton	....	Midwest	3B	9	37	2	6	2	0	1	6	0	.162
2001 Billings	....	Pioneer	3B	52	211	27	55	8	2	5	26	8	.261
2001 Savannah a	....	So.Atl.	3B	45	170	23	52	9	2	4	25	3	.306
2002 Dayton	....	Midwest	3B-SS	136	517	80	146	32	4	17	73	25	.282
2003 Potomac	....	Carolina	3B	58	215	40	69	15	1	6	29	7	.321
2003 Chattanooga	......	Southern	3B-SS	67	254	40	69	13	1	5	36	8	.272
2004 Chattanooga	......	Southern	3B	120	469	73	132	35	1	13	76	17	.281
2005 Louisville	....	Int.	3B	78	290	44	91	23	0	15	54	7	.314
2005 Cincinnati	....	N.L.	3B	69	211	25	49	16	0	9	31	3	.232
2006 Louisville	....	Int.	3B-1B	10	36	6	11	3	0	1	1	0	.306
2006 Cincinnati b	....	N.L.	3B-1B	117	406	60	112	33	1	15	72	6	.276
2007 Louisville	....	Int.	3B	11	46	12	19	3	0	3	7	1	.413
2007 Cincinnati	....	N.L.	3B	139	502	66	145	25	1	16	76	8	.289
Major League Totals	....	3 Yrs.		325	1119	151	306	74	2	40	179	17	.273

a Traded by Texas Rangers to Cincinnati Reds with outfielder Ruben Mateo for pitcher Rob Bell, June 15, 2001.
b On disabled list from June 7 to July 6, 2006.

ENCARNACION, JUAN DE DIOS

Born, Las Matas de Faran, Dominican Republic, March 8, 1976.
Bats Right. Throws Right. Height, 6 feet, 3 inches. Weight, 215 pounds.

Year Club	Lea	Pos	G	AB	R	H	2B	3B	HR	RBI	SB	Avg
1994 Fayetteville	So. Atl.	OF	24	83	6	16	1	1	1	4	1	.193
1994 Bristol	Appal.	OF	54	197	16	49	7	1	4	31	9	.249
1994 Lakeland	Fla. St.	OF	3	6	1	2	0	0	0	0	0	.333
1995 Fayetteville	So. Atl.	OF	124	457	62	129	31	7	16	72	5	.282
1996 Lakeland	Fla. St.	OF	131	499	54	120	31	2	15	58	11	.240
1997 Jacksonville	Southern	OF	131	493	91	159	31	4	26	90	17	.323
1997 Detroit	A.L.	OF	11	33	3	7	1	1	1	5	3	.212
1998 Lakeland	Fla.St.	OF	4	16	4	4	0	1	0	4	4	.250
1998 Toledo	Int.	OF	92	356	55	102	17	3	8	41	24	.287
1998 Detroit a	A.L.	OF	40	164	30	54	9	4	7	21	7	.329
1999 Detroit	A.L.	OF	132	509	62	130	30	6	19	74	33	.255
2000 Detroit	A.L.	OF	141	547	75	158	25	6	14	72	16	.289
2001 Detroit b	A.L.	OF	120	417	52	101	19	7	12	52	9	.242
2002 Cincinnati-Florida c	N.L.	OF	152	584	77	158	22	5	24	85	21	.271
2003 Florida d	N.L.	OF	156	601	80	162	37	6	19	94	19	.270
2004 Los Angeles-Florida e-f	N.L.	OF	135	484	63	114	30	2	16	62	5	.236
2005 Florida g	N.L.	OF	141	506	59	145	27	3	16	76	6	.287
2006 St. Louis	N.L.	OF	153	557	74	155	25	5	19	79	6	.278
2007 Springfield	Texas	OF	15	58	5	9	4	0	0	4	1	.155
2007 St. Louis h	N.L.	OF	78	283	43	80	17	1	9	47	2	.283
Major League Totals	11 Yrs.		1259	4685	618	1264	242	46	156	667	127	.270
Division Series												
2003 Florida	N.L.	OF	4	15	1	2	0	0	1	1	0	.133
2006 St. Louis	N.L.	OF	4	14	1	4	0	1	0	2	0	.286
Division Series Totals			8	29	2	6	0	1	1	3	0	.207
Championship Series												
2003 Florida	N.L.	OF	5	12	1	3	1	0	1	1	0	.250
2006 St. Louis	N.L.	OF	6	22	1	4	0	1	0	2	0	.182
Championship Series Totals			11	34	2	7	1	1	1	3	0	.206
World Series Record												
2003 Florida	N.L.	OF	6	11	1	2	0	0	0	1	0	.182
2006 St. Louis	N.L.	OF	3	8	0	0	0	0	0	1	0	.000
World Series Totals			9	19	1	2	0	0	0	2	0	.105

a On disabled list from March 31 to April 29, 1998.
b Traded to Cincinnati Reds with pitcher Luis Pineda for infielder Dmitri Young, December 11, 2001.
c Traded to Florida Marlins with infielder Wilton Guerrero and pitcher Ryan Snare for pitcher Ryan Dempster, July 11, 2002.
d Traded to Los Angeles Dodgers for player to be named later, December 13, 2003. Florida Marlins received outfielder Travis Ezi to complete trade, December 15, 2003.
e On disabled list from July 4 to July 19, 2004.
f Traded to Florida Marlins with catcher Paul LoDuca and pitcher Guillermo Mota for pitcher Brad Penny, pitcher Bill Murphy and infielder Hee Seop Choi, July 30, 2004.
g Filed for free agency, October 27, 2005. Signed with St. Louis Cardinals, December 23, 2005.
h On disabled list from March 23 to May 13 and September 4 to November 2, 2007.

ENSBERG, MORGAN PAUL

Born, Redondo Beach, California, August 26, 1975.
Bats Right. Throws Right. Height, 6 feet, 2 inches. Weight, 220 pounds.

Year Club	Lea	Pos	G	AB	R	H	2B	3B	HR	RBI	SB	Avg
1998 Auburn	N.Y.-Penn.	3B-SS	59	196	39	45	10	1	5	31	15	.230
1999 Kissimmee	Fla.St.	3B	123	427	72	102	25	2	15	69	17	.239
2000 Round Rock	Texas	3B	137	483	95	145	34	0	28	90	9	.300
2000 Houston	N.L.	3B	4	7	0	2	0	0	0	0	0	.286
2001 New Orleans a	P.C.	3B-SS	87	316	65	98	20	0	23	61	6	.310
2002 Houston	N.L.	3B	49	132	14	32	7	2	3	19	2	.242
2002 New Orleans	P.C.	3B-1B	83	292	50	84	12	3	7	37	9	.288
2003 Houston	N.L.	3B	127	385	69	112	15	1	25	60	7	.291
2004 Houston	N.L.	3B-SS	131	411	51	113	20	3	10	66	6	.275
2005 Houston	N.L.	3B	150	526	86	149	30	3	36	101	6	.283
2006 Round Rock	P.C.	3B	3	12	2	6	2	0	2	7	0	.500
2006 Houston b	N.L.	3B	127	387	67	91	17	1	23	58	1	.235
2007 Houston-San Diego c-d	N.L.	3B-1B	115	282	47	65	13	0	12	39	0	.230
Major League Totals	7 Yrs.		703	2130	334	564	102	10	109	343	22	.265
Division Series												
2004 Houston	N.L.	3B	5	19	1	7	2	0	0	5	0	.368

Year Club	Lea	Pos	G	AB	R	H	2B	3B	HR	RBI	SB	Avg
2005 Houston . . . . N.L.		3B	4	18	2	5	2	0	0	7	0	.278
Division Series Totals			9	37	3	12	4	0	0	12	0	.324
Championship Series												
2004 Houston . . . . N.L.		3B	7	22	2	3	0	0	1	2	0	.136
2005 Houston . . . . N.L.		3B	6	21	1	5	1	0	0	2	0	.238
Championship Series Totals			13	43	3	8	1	0	1	4	0	.186
World Series Record												
2005 Houston . . . . N.L.		3B	4	18	2	2	0	0	1	2	0	.111

a On disabled list from June 22 to August 10, 2001.
b On disabled list from July 10 to August 1, 2006.
c Traded to San Diego Padres with cash for player to be named later, July 31, 2007.
d Not offered contract, December 12, 2007.

ERSTAD, DARIN CHARLES
Born, Jamestown, North Dakota, June 4, 1974.
Bats Left. Throws Left. Height, 6 feet, 2 inches. Weight, 215 pounds.

Year Club	Lea	Pos	G	AB	R	H	2B	3B	HR	RBI	SB	Avg
1995 Angels . . . . Arizona		OF	4	18	2	10	1	0	0	1	1	.556
1995 Lk Elsinore . . . . . . California		OF	25	113	24	41	7	3	5	24	3	.363
1996 Vancouver . . . . P.C.		OF-1B	85	351	63	107	22	5	6	41	11	.305
1996 California . . . . A.L.		OF	57	208	34	59	5	1	4	20	3	.284
1997 Anaheim . . . . A.L.		1B-OF	139	539	99	161	34	4	16	77	23	.299
1998 Anaheim a . . . . A.L.		OF-1B	133	537	84	159	39	3	19	82	20	.296
1999 Anaheim b . . . . A.L.		1B-OF	142	585	84	148	22	5	13	53	13	.253
2000 Anaheim . . . . A.L.		OF-1B	157	*676	121	*240	39	6	25	100	28	.355
2001 Anaheim . . . . A.L.		OF-1B	157	631	89	163	35	1	9	63	24	.258
2002 Anaheim . . . . A.L.		OF-1B	150	625	99	177	28	4	10	73	23	.283
2003 Salt Lake . . . . P.C.		OF	7	27	6	11	0	0	0	4	1	.407
2003 Anaheim c . . . . A.L.		OF	67	258	35	65	7	1	4	17	9	.252
2004 Salt Lake . . . . P.C.		1B	4	16	2	2	0	0	0	3	0	.125
2004 Anaheim d . . . . A.L.		1B	125	495	79	146	29	1	7	69	16	.295
2005 Los Angeles . . . . A.L.		1B	153	609	86	166	33	3	7	66	10	.273
2006 Rancho Cucamonga . . . . Calif.		1B	7	14	4	3	0	0	0	0	0	.214
2006 Salt Lake . . . . P.C.		OF	7	30	0	3	0	0	0	3	1	.100
2006 Los Angeles e-f . . . . A.L.		OF-1B	40	95	8	21	8	1	0	5	1	.221
2007 Charlotte . . . . Int.		OF-1B	12	47	3	6	0	0	0	2	0	.128
2007 Chicago g-h . . . . A.L.		OF-1B	87	310	33	77	13	1	4	32	7	.248
Major League Totals		12 Yrs.	1407	5568	851	1582	292	31	118	657	177	.284
Division Series												
2002 Anaheim . . . . A.L.		OF	4	19	4	8	2	0	0	2	1	.421
2004 Anaheim . . . . A.L.		1B	3	10	2	5	1	0	1	2	0	.500
2005 Los Angeles . . . . A.L.		1B	5	20	1	6	2	0	0	3	0	.300
Division Series Totals			12	49	7	19	5	0	1	7	1	.388
Championship Series												
2002 Anaheim . . . . A.L.		OF	5	22	4	8	0	0	1	2	1	.364
2005 Los Angeles . . . . A.L.		1B	5	17	1	4	1	0	0	0	1	.235
Championship Series Totals			10	39	5	12	1	0	1	2	2	.308
World Series Record												
2002 Anaheim . . . . A.L.		OF	7	30	6	9	3	0	1	3	1	.300

a On disabled list from August 4 to August 19, 1998.
b On disabled list from August 11 to August 26, 1999.
c On disabled list from April 20 to June 9 and August 7 to October 6, 2003.
d On disabled list from May 9 to June 14, 2004.
e On disabled list from May 1 to June 12 and June 18 to September 1, 2006.
f Filed for free agency, October 28, 2006. Signed with Chicago White Sox, January 25, 2007.
g On disabled list from June 1 to June 22 and June 23 to July 31, 2007.
h Filed for free agency, October 31, 2007. Signed with Houston Astros, December 28, 2007.

ESCOBAR, YUNEL
Born, Havana, Cuba, November 2, 1982.
Bats Right. Throws Right. Height, 6 feet, 2 inches. Weight, 200 pounds.

Year Club	Lea	Pos	G	AB	R	H	2B	3B	HR	RBI	SB	Avg
2005 Danville . . . . Appal.		SS	8	30	9	12	2	1	2	8	0	.400
2005 Rome . . . . So.Atl.		SS	48	198	30	62	13	3	4	19	0	.313
2006 Mississippi . . . . Southern		SS-3B-2B	121	428	55	113	21	4	2	45	7	.264
2007 Richmond . . . . Int.		SS	46	180	20	60	10	3	2	29	7	.333
2007 Atlanta . . . . N.L.		SS-3B-2B	94	319	54	104	25	0	5	28	5	.326

ESTRADA, JOHNNY PULADO

Born, Hayward, California, June 27, 1976.
Bats Both. Throws Right. Height, 5 feet, 11 inches. Weight, 215 pounds.

Year	Club	Lea	Pos	G	AB	R	H	2B	3B	HR	RBI	SB	Avg
1997	Batavia	N.Y.-Penn.	C-1B	58	223	28	70	17	2	6	43	0	.314
1998	Piedmont	So.Atl.	C	77	303	33	94	14	2	7	44	0	.310
1998	Clearwater	Fla.St.	C	37	117	8	26	8	0	0	13	0	.222
1999	Clearwater	Fla.St.	C	98	346	35	96	15	0	9	52	1	.277
2000	Reading	Eastern	C	95	356	42	105	18	0	12	42	1	.295
2001	Scranton-WB	Int.	C	32	131	13	38	13	0	0	16	0	.290
2001	Philadelphia	N.L.	C	89	298	26	68	15	0	8	37	0	.228
2002	Scranton-WB	Int.	C	118	434	49	121	27	0	11	67	1	.279
2002	Philadelphia a	N.L.	C	10	17	0	2	1	0	0	2	0	.118
2003	Richmond	Int.	C	106	354	40	116	29	0	10	66	0	.328
2003	Atlanta	N.L.	C	16	36	2	11	0	0	0	2	0	.306
2004	Atlanta	N.L.	C	134	462	56	145	34	0	9	76	0	.314
2005	Atlanta b-c	N.L.	C	105	357	31	93	26	0	4	39	0	.261
2006	Arizona d	N.L.	C	115	414	43	125	26	0	11	71	0	.302
2007	Milwaukee e-f	N.L.	C	120	442	40	123	25	0	10	54	0	.278
Major League Totals		7 Yrs.		589	2026	198	567	129	0	42	281	0	.280
Division Series													
2004	Atlanta	N.L.	C	5	17	3	6	0	0	2	4	0	.353
2005	Atlanta	N.L.	C	1	4	0	1	0	0	0	1	0	.250
Division Series Totals				6	21	3	7	0	0	2	5	0	.333

a Traded to Atlanta Braves for pitcher Kevin Millwood, December 20, 2002.
b On disabled list from August 6 to August 22, 2005.
c Traded to Arizona Diamondbacks for pitcher Lance Cormier and pitcher Oscar Villarreal, December 7, 2005.
d Traded to Milwaukee Brewers with pitcher Greg Aquino and pitcher Claudio Vargas for pitcher Doug Davis, pitcher Dana Eveland and outfielder David Krynzel, November 25, 2006.
e Traded to New York Mets for pitcher Guillermo Mota, November 20, 2007.
f Not offered contract, December 12, 2007.

ETHIER, ANDRE EVERETT

Born, Phoenix, Arizona, April 10, 1982.
Bats Left. Throws Left. Height, 6 feet, 1 inch. Weight, 210 pounds.

Year	Club	Lea	Pos	G	AB	R	H	2B	3B	HR	RBI	SB	Avg
2003	Kane County	Midwest	OF	40	162	23	44	10	0	0	11	2	.272
2003	Vancouver	Northwest	OF	10	41	7	16	4	1	1	7	2	.390
2004	Modesto	Calif.	OF	99	419	72	131	23	5	7	53	2	.313
2005	Sacramento	P.C.	OF	4	15	0	4	1	0	0	2	0	.267
2005	Midland a	Texas	OF	131	505	104	161	30	3	18	80	1	.319
2006	Las Vegas	P.C.	OF	25	86	15	30	4	3	1	12	2	.349
2006	Los Angeles	N.L.	OF	126	396	50	122	20	7	11	55	5	.308
2007	Los Angeles	N.L.	OF	153	447	50	127	32	2	13	64	0	.284
Major League Totals		2 Yrs.		279	843	100	249	52	9	24	119	5	.295
Division Series													
2006	Los Angeles	N.L.	OF	2	1	0	0	0	0	0	0	0	.000

a Traded by Oakland Athletics to Los Angeles for outfielder Milton Bradley and infielder Antonio Perez, December 13, 2005.

EVERETT, JEFFREY ADAM (ADAM)

Born, Austell, Georgia, February 2, 1977.
Bats Right. Throws Right. Height, 6 feet. Weight, 170 pounds.

Year	Club	Lea	Pos	G	AB	R	H	2B	3B	HR	RBI	SB	Avg
1998	Lowell	N.Y.-Penn.	SS	21	71	11	21	6	2	0	9	2	.296
1999	Trenton a	Eastern	SS	98	338	56	89	11	0	10	44	21	.263
2000	New Orleans	P.C.	SS	126	453	82	111	25	2	5	37	13	.245
2001	New Orleans	P.C.	SS	114	441	69	110	20	8	5	40	24	.249
2001	Houston	N.L.	SS	9	3	1	0	0	0	0	0	1	.000
2002	Houston	N.L.	SS	40	88	11	17	3	0	0	4	3	.193
2002	New Orleans	P.C.	SS	88	345	51	95	16	7	2	25	12	.275
2003	New Orleans	P.C.	SS-2B	25	100	23	25	6	1	1	9	3	.250
2003	Houston	N.L.	SS	128	387	51	99	18	3	8	51	8	.256
2004	Houston b	N.L.	SS	104	384	66	105	15	2	8	31	13	.273
2005	Houston	N.L.	SS	152	549	58	136	27	4	11	54	21	.248
2006	Houston	N.L.	SS	150	514	52	123	28	6	6	59	9	.239
2007	Houston c-d	N.L.	SS	66	220	18	51	11	1	2	15	4	.232
Major League Totals		7 Yrs.		649	2145	257	531	102	14	35	214	59	.248

Year	Club	Lea	Pos	G	AB	R	H	2B	3B	HR	RBI	SB	Avg
	Division Series												
2004 Houston		N.L.	SS	2	0	0	0	0	0	0	0	0	.000
2005 Houston		N.L.	SS	4	14	1	3	0	0	0	1	0	.214
Division Series Totals				6	14	1	3	0	0	0	1	0	.214
	Championship Series												
2004 Houston		N.L.	SS	3	1	0	0	0	0	0	0	0	.000
2005 Houston		N.L.	SS	6	23	2	7	1	1	0	2	0	.304
Championship Series Totals				9	24	2	7	1	1	0	2	0	.292
	World Series Record												
2005 Houston		N.L.	SS	4	15	2	1	0	0	0	0	0	.067

a Traded by Boston Red Sox to Houston Astros for outfielder Carl Everett, December 15, 1999.
b On disabled list from August 7 to September 29, 2004.
c On disabled list from June 15 to September 17, 2007.
d Not offered contract, December 12, 2007. Signed with Minnesota Twins, December 13, 2007.

FELIZ, PEDRO JULIO

Born, Azua, Dominican Republic, April 27, 1975.
Bats Right. Throws Right. Height, 6 feet, 1 inch. Weight, 210 pounds.

Year	Club	Lea	Pos	G	AB	R	H	2B	3B	HR	RBI	SB	Avg
1994 Giants	Arizona		3B	38	119	7	23	0	0	0	3	2	.193
1995 Bellingham	Northwest		3B-1B	43	113	14	31	2	1	0	16	1	.274
1996 Burlington	Midwest		3B-1B	93	321	36	85	12	2	5	36	5	.265
1997 Bakersfield	California		3B	135	515	59	140	25	4	14	56	5	.272
1998 Shreveport	Texas		3B	100	364	39	96	23	2	12	50	0	.264
1998 Fresno		P.C.	3B	3	7	1	3	1	0	1	3	0	.429
1999 Shreveport	Texas		3B	131	491	52	124	24	6	13	77	4	.253
2000 Fresno		P.C.	3B	128	503	85	150	34	2	33	105	1	.298
2000 San Francisco		N.L.	3B	8	7	1	2	0	0	0	0	0	.286
2001 San Francisco		N.L.	3B	94	220	23	50	9	1	7	22	2	.227
2002 San Francisco		N.L.	3B-SS-OF	67	146	14	37	4	1	2	13	0	.253
2003 San Francisco		N.L.	3B-OF-1B	95	235	31	58	9	3	16	48	2	.247
2004 San Francisco		N.L.	1B-3B-SS-OF	144	503	72	139	33	3	22	84	5	.276
2005 San Francisco		N.L.	3B-OF-1B	156	569	69	142	30	4	20	81	0	.250
2006 San Francisco a	N.L.		3B-OF-SS	160	603	75	147	35	5	22	98	1	.244
2007 San Francisco b	N.L.		3B-1B-OF-C	150	557	61	141	28	2	20	72	2	.253
Major League Totals		8 Yrs.		874	2840	346	716	148	19	109	418	12	.252
	Division Series												
2002 San Francisco		N.L.	PH	1	1	0	0	0	0	0	0	0	.000
2003 San Francisco		N.L.	PH	3	3	1	2	0	1	0	1	0	.667
Division Series Totals				4	4	1	2	0	1	0	1	0	.500
	Championship Series												
2002 San Francisco		N.L.	PH	1	1	0	0	0	0	0	0	0	.000
	World Series Record												
2002 San Francisco		N.L.	DH	3	5	0	0	0	0	0	0	0	.000

a Filed for free agency, November 1, 2006, re-signed with San Francisco Giants, December 4, 2006.
b Filed for free agency, October 29, 2007.

FICK, ROBERT CHARLES JOHN (ROB)

Born, Torrance, California, March 15, 1974.
Bats Left. Throws Right. Height, 6 feet, 1 inch. Weight, 205 pounds.

Year	Club	Lea	Pos	G	AB	R	H	2B	3B	HR	RBI	SB	Avg
1996 Jamestown	N.Y.-Penn.		C	43	133	18	33	6	0	1	14	3	.248
1997 W Michigan	Midwest		1B-C-3B	122	463	100	158	50	3	16	90	13	.341
1998 Jacksnville	Southern		C-1B-OF	130	515	101	164	47	6	18	114	8	.318
1998 Detroit		A.L.	C-1B	7	22	6	8	1	0	3	7	1	.364
1999 West Michigan	Midwest		1B	3	11	2	3	0	0	0	0	1	.273
1999 Toledo		Int.	1B	14	48	11	15	0	1	2	8	1	.313
1999 GC Tigers	Gulf Coast		1B	3	9	2	3	1	0	0	2	1	.333
1999 Detroit a		A.L.	C	15	41	6	9	0	0	3	10	1	.220
2000 Toledo		Int.	1B	17	68	5	10	5	0	1	7	1	.147
2000 Detroit b		A.L.	1B-C	66	163	18	41	7	2	3	22	2	.252
2001 Detroit		A.L.	C-1B-OF	124	401	62	109	21	2	19	61	0	.272
2002 Detroit c		A.L.	OF	148	556	66	150	36	2	17	63	0	.270
2003 Atlanta d-e		N.L.	1B	126	409	52	110	26	1	11	80	1	.269
2004 Tampa Bay		A.L.	DH-OF-1B-C	76	214	12	43	5	2	6	26	0	.201
2004 Portland		P.C.	1B-C	12	50	8	19	4	0	2	6	1	.380
2004 San Diego f-g	N.L.		1B	13	12	2	2	0	0	0	0	0	.167

Year	Club	Lea	Pos	G	AB	R	H	2B	3B	HR	RBI	SB	Avg
2005 Portland.........P.C.			1B-C	10	32	5	12	1	0	3	11	1	.375
2005 San Diego h......N.L.			1B-C-OF-3B	93	230	25	61	10	2	3	30	0	.265
2006 Harrisburg.....Eastern			C-1B-OF	16	57	11	16	1	0	1	4	2	.281
2006 New Orleans......P.C.			1B-OF	2	7	0	1	0	0	0	0	1	.143
2006 Washington i-j....N.L.			C-1B-OF	60	128	14	34	4	0	2	9	1	.266
2007 Washington k....N.L.			1B-OF	118	197	24	46	6	1	2	16	0	.234
Major League Totals...........			10 Yrs.	846	2373	287	613	116	12	69	324	6	.258
Division Series													
2003 Atlanta..........N.L.			1B	4	11	0	0	0	0	0	0	0	.000
2005 San Diego........N.L.			1B	2	5	0	1	0	0	0	0	0	.200
Division Series Totals.......				6	16	0	1	0	0	0	0	0	.063

a On disabled list from March 31 to September 7, 1999.
b On disabled list from July 6 to August 31, 2000.
c Not offered 2003 contract, December 20, 2002. Signed with Atlanta Braves, January 6, 2003.
d On disabled list from April 13 to April 29, 2003.
e Waived by Atlanta Braves, November 7, 2003. Signed with Tampa Bay Devil Rays, January 8, 2004.
f Released by Tampa Bay Devil Rays, August 13, 2004. Signed with San Diego Padres organization, August 15, 2004.
g Filed for free agency, November 1, 2004. Signed with San Diego Padres organization, February 23, 2005.
h Filed for free agency, October 28, 2005. Signed with Washington Nationals, December 13, 2005.
i On disabled list from March 24 to May 13 and August 1 to August 25, 2006.
j Filed for free agency, October 30, 2006. re-signed with Washington Nationals organization, December 20, 2006.
k Filed for free agency, October 29, 2007. Signed with San Diego Padres organization, December 19, 2007.

FIELDER, PRINCE SEMIEN
Born, Ontario, California, May 9, 1984.
Bats Left. Throws Right. Height, 6 feet. Weight, 260 pounds.

Year	Club	Lea	Pos	G	AB	R	H	2B	3B	HR	RBI	SB	Avg
2002 Beloit...........Midwest			1B	32	112	15	27	7	0	3	11	0	.241
2002 Ogden...........Pioneer			1B	41	146	35	57	12	0	10	40	3	.390
2003 Beloit...........Midwest			1B	137	502	81	157	22	2	27	112	2	.313
2004 Huntsville......Southern			1B-OF	136	497	70	135	29	1	23	78	11	.272
2005 Nashville..........P.C.			1B	103	378	68	110	21	0	28	86	8	.291
2005 Milwaukee..........N.L.			1B	39	59	2	17	4	0	2	10	0	.288
2006 Milwaukee..........N.L.			1B	157	569	82	154	35	1	28	81	7	.271
2007 Milwaukee..........N.L.			1B	158	573	109	165	35	2	*50	119	2	.288
Major League Totals...........			3 Yrs.	354	1201	193	336	74	3	80	210	9	.280

FIELDS, JOSHUA DEAN (JOSH)
Born, Ada, Oklahoma, December 14, 1982.
Bats Right. Throws Right. Height, 6 feet, 1 inch. Weight, 215 pounds.

Year	Club	Lea	Pos	G	AB	R	H	2B	3B	HR	RBI	SB	Avg
2004 Winston-Salem....Carolina			3B	66	256	36	73	12	4	7	39	0	.285
2005 Birmingham......Southern			3B-1B	134	477	76	120	27	0	16	79	7	.252
2006 Charlotte............Int.			3B	124	462	85	141	32	4	19	70	28	.305
2006 Chicago.............A.L.			3B-OF	11	20	4	3	2	0	1	2	0	.150
2007 Charlotte............Int.			3B-SS	56	205	28	58	14	0	10	37	8	.283
2007 Chicago.............A.L.			3B-OF	100	373	54	91	17	1	23	67	1	.244
Major League Totals...........			2 Yrs.	111	393	58	94	19	1	24	69	1	.239

FIGGINS, DESMOND DECHONE (CHONE)
Born, Leary, Georgia, January 22, 1978.
Bats Both. Throws Right. Height, 5 feet, 7 inches. Weight, 180 pounds.

Year	Club	Lea	Pos	G	AB	R	H	2B	3B	HR	RBI	SB	Avg
1997 Rockies.......Arizona			SS	54	214	41	60	5	6	1	23	30	.280
1998 Portland.....Northwest			SS	69	269	41	76	9	3	1	26	25	.283
1999 Salem........Carolina			SS	123	444	65	106	12	3	0	22	27	.239
2000 Salem........Carolina			2B	134	522	92	145	26	14	3	48	37	.278
2001 Carolina......Southern			2B-SS	86	332	41	73	14	5	2	25	27	.220
2001 Arkansas a.....Texas			2B-SS-3B	39	138	21	37	12	2	0	12	7	.268
2002 Salt Lake.........P.C.			2B-SS	125	511	100	156	25	18	7	62	39	.305
2002 Anaheim.........A.L.			2B	15	12	6	2	1	0	0	1	2	.167
2003 Salt Lake.........P.C.			2B-SS-OF-3B	68	285	55	89	14	15	4	30	16	.312
2003 Anaheim.........A.L.			OF-2B-SS	71	240	34	71	9	4	0	27	13	.296
2004 Anaheim.........A.L.			3B-OF-2B-SS	148	577	83	171	22	17	5	60	34	.296

Year Club Lea	Pos	G	AB	R	H	2B	3B	HR	RBI	SB	Avg
2005 Los Angeles ......A.L.	OF-3B-2B-SS	158	642	113	186	25	10	8	57	*62	.290
2006 Los Angeles ......A.L.	OF-3B-2B-SS	155	604	93	161	23	8	9	62	52	.267
2007 Salt Lake .........P.C.	3B	4	14	3	5	1	0	0	1	0	.357
2007 Los Angeles b .....A.L.	3B-OF-2B	115	442	81	146	24	6	3	58	41	.330
Major League Totals	6 Yrs.	662	2517	410	737	104	45	25	265	204	.293
Division Series											
2002 Anaheim..........A.L.	DH	1	0	1	0	0	0	0	0	1	.000
2004 Anaheim..........A.L.	2B-3B	3	14	0	2	0	0	0	0	1	.143
2005 Los Angeles ......A.L.	3B-OF	5	21	2	3	1	1	0	2	0	.143
2007 Los Angeles ......A.L.	OF	3	13	1	3	2	0	0	1	0	.231
Division Series Totals		12	48	4	8	3	1	0	3	2	.167
Championship Series											
2002 Anaheim..........A.L.	PH	3	1	2	1	0	0	0	0	0	1.000
2005 Los Angeles ......A.L.	3B-OF	5	17	1	2	1	0	0	1	1	.118
Championship Series Totals ..		8	18	3	3	1	0	0	1	1	.167
World Series Record											
2002 Anaheim...........A.L.	PH	2	0	1	0	0	0	0	0	0	.000

a Traded by Colorado Rockies to Anaheim Angels for outfielder Kimera Bartee, July 13, 2001.
b On disabled list from March 23 to April 30, 2007.

FLORES, JESUS MIGUEL

Born, Carupano, Venezuela, October 26, 1984.
Bats Right. Throws Right. Height, 6 feet, 1 inch. Weight, 185 pounds.

Year Club Lea	Pos	G	AB	R	H	2B	3B	HR	RBI	SB	Avg
2004 Mets.......... Gulf Coast	C	45	141	16	45	12	3	4	25	1	.319
2004 Brooklyn........ N.Y.-Penn.	C	3	6	1	2	0	0	1	3	0	.333
2005 Hagerstown .... So.Atl.	C	82	319	34	69	18	0	7	42	2	.216
2006 St. Lucie a ....Fla.St.	C	120	429	66	114	32	0	21	70	2	.266
2007 Washington .... N.L.	C	79	180	21	44	9	0	4	25	0	.244

a Selected by Washington Nationals from New York Mets in Rule V draft, December 7, 2006.

FLOYD, CORNELIUS CLIFFORD (CLIFF)

Born, Chicago, Illinois, December 5, 1972.
Bats Left. Throws Left. Height, 6 feet, 4 inches. Weight, 230 pounds.

Year Club Lea	Pos	G	AB	R	H	2B	3B	HR	RBI	SB	Avg
1991 Bradenton Expos .... Gulf C.	1B	56	214	35	56	9	3	6	30	13	.262
1992 Albany .... So. Atl.	OF-1B	134	516	83	157	24	*16	16	*97	32	.304
1992 West Palm Beach.... Fla. St.	OF	1	4	0	0	0	0	0	1	0	.000
1993 Harrisburg ....Eastern	1B-OF	101	380	82	125	17	4	*26	*101	31	.329
1993 Ottawa ....Int.	1B	32	125	12	30	2	2	2	18	2	.240
1993 Montreal...........N.L.	1B	10	31	3	7	0	0	1	2	0	.226
1994 Montreal...........N.L.	1B-OF	100	334	43	94	19	4	4	41	10	.281
1995 Montreal a .........N.L.	1B-OF	29	69	6	9	1	0	1	8	3	.130
1996 Ottawa ....Int.	OF-3B	20	76	7	23	3	1	1	8	2	.303
1996 Montreal...........N.L.	OF-1B	117	227	29	55	15	4	6	26	7	.242
1997 Charlotte ....Int.	OF-1B	39	131	27	48	10	0	9	33	7	.366
1997 Florida b-c ..........N.L.	OF-1B	61	137	23	32	9	1	6	19	6	.234
1998 Florida .............N.L.	OF	153	588	85	166	45	3	22	90	27	.282
1999 Calgary .............P.C.	OF	9	31	6	12	1	0	3	8	0	.387
1999 Florida d............N.L.	OF	69	251	37	76	19	1	11	49	5	.303
2000 Florida e............N.L.	OF	121	420	75	126	30	0	22	91	24	.300
2001 Florida .............N.L.	OF	149	555	123	176	44	4	31	103	18	.317
2002 Florida-Montreal f ... N.L.	OF	99	349	56	96	22	0	21	61	11	.275
2002 Boston g-h...........N.L.	OF	47	171	30	54	21	0	7	18	4	.316
2003 New York j ..........N.L.	OF	108	365	57	106	25	2	18	68	3	.290
2004 St. Lucie...........Fla.St.	OF	1	4	2	2	0	0	0	1	0	.500
2004 New York j ..........N.L.	OF	113	396	55	103	26	0	18	63	11	.260
2005 New York ...........N.L.	OF	150	550	85	150	22	2	34	98	12	.273
2006 Mets.......... Gulf Coast	OF	2	6	2	3	0	0	1	4	0	.500
2006 Brooklyn....... N.Y.-Penn.	OF	1	2	0	0	0	0	0	0	0	.000
2006 St. Lucie...........Fla.St.	OF	3	10	2	4	0	0	2	4	0	.400
2006 New York k-l.........N.L.	OF	97	332	45	81	19	1	11	44	6	.244
2007 Chicago m ..........N.L.	OF	108	282	40	80	10	1	9	45	0	.284
Major League Totals		15 Yrs. 1531	5057	792	1411	327	23	222	826	147	.279
Division Series											
2006 New York ...........N.L.	OF	3	9	3	4	0	0	1	2	0	.444

Year	Club	Lea	Pos	G	AB	R	H	2B	3B	HR	RBI	SB	Avg
2007 Chicago	N.L.	OF	2	5	0	0	0	0	0	0	0	0	.000
Division Series Totals			5	14	3	4	0	0	1	2	0	.286
Championship Series												
2006 New York	N.L.	OF	3	3	0	0	0	0	0	0	0	.000
World Series Record												
1997 Florida	N.L.	DH	4	2	1	0	0	0	0	0	0	.000

a On disabled list from May 16 to September 11, 1995.
b Traded to Florida Marlins for pitcher Dustin Hermanson and outfielder Joe Orsulak, March 26, 1997.
c On disabled list from May 9 to May 24 and June 21 to September 1, 1997.
d On disabled list from March 30 to April 27 and June 20 to September 7, 1999.
e On disabled list from July 29 to August 28, 2000.
f Traded to Montreal Expos with infielder Wilton Guerrero and cash for pitcher Carl Pavano, pitcher Graeme Lloyd, infielder Mike Mordecai and pitcher Justin Wayne, July 11, 2002.
g Traded to Boston Red Sox for pitcher Sun-Woo Kim, pitcher Seung Song and player to be named later, July 30, 2002.
h Filed for free agency, October 28, 2002. Signed with New York Mets, December 20, 2002.
i On disabled list from August 19 to November 6, 2003.
j On disabled list from April 12 to May 13, 2004.
k On disabled list from June 7 to June 30 and August 9 to September 2, 2006.
l Filed for free agency, October 28, 2006. Signed with Chicago Cubs, January 24, 2007.
m Filed for free agency, October 31, 2007. Signed with Tampa Bay Devil Rays, December 14, 2007.

FONTENOT, MICHAEL EUGENE (MIKE)

Born, Slidell, Louisiana, June 9, 1980.
Bats Left. Throws Right. Height, 5 feet, 8 inches. Weight, 165 pounds.

Year	Club	Lea	Pos	G	AB	R	H	2B	3B	HR	RBI	SB	Avg
2002 Frederick	Carolina	2B	122	481	61	127	16	4	8	53	13	.264
2003 Bowie	Eastern	2B	126	449	63	146	24	5	12	66	16	.325
2004 Ottawa	Int.	2B	136	524	73	146	30	10	8	49	14	.279
2005 Iowa...........	P.C.	2B-3B-SS-OF	111	379	60	103	22	10	6	39	3	.272
2005 Chicago a	N.L.	DH	7	2	4	0	0	0	0	0	0	.000
2006 Iowa...........	P.C.	2B-3B-SS	111	362	54	107	28	2	8	36	5	.296
2007 Iowa...........	P.C.	SS-2B-3B-OF	55	211	46	71	17	4	6	34	3	.336
2007 Chicago	N.L.	2B-SS	86	234	32	65	12	4	3	29	5	.278
Major League Totals		2 Yrs.	93	236	36	65	12	4	3	29	5	.275
Division Series												
2007 Chicago	N.L.	PH	2	2	0	0	0	0	0	0	0	.000

a Traded to Chicago Cubs by Baltimore Orioles with infielder Jerry Hairston and pitcher Dave Crouthers for outfielder Sammy Sosa, February 2, 2005.

FRANCOEUR, JEFFREY BRADEN (JEFF)

Born, Atlanta, Georgia, January 8, 1984.
Bats Right. Throws Right. Height, 6 feet, 4 inches. Weight, 220 pounds.

Year	Club	Lea	Pos	G	AB	R	H	2B	3B	HR	RBI	SB	Avg
2002 Danville	Appal.	OF	38	147	31	48	12	1	8	31	8	.327
2003 Rome	So.Atl.	OF	134	524	78	147	26	9	14	68	14	.281
2004 Myrtle Beach	Carolina	OF	88	334	56	98	26	0	15	52	10	.293
2004 Greenville........	Southern	OF	18	76	8	15	2	0	3	9	1	.197
2005 Mississippi.......	Southern	OF	84	335	40	92	28	2	13	62	13	.275
2005 Atlanta	N.L.	OF	70	257	41	77	20	1	14	45	3	.300
2006 Atlanta	N.L.	OF	*162	651	83	169	24	6	29	103	1	.260
2007 Atlanta	N.L.	OF	*162	642	84	188	40	0	19	105	5	.293
Major League Totals		3 Yrs.	394	1550	208	434	84	7	62	253	9	.280
Division Series												
2005 Atlanta	N.L.	OF	4	17	2	4	1	1	0	1	0	.235

FRANDSEN, KEVIN VINCENT

Born, San Jose, California, May 24, 1982.
Bats Right. Throws Right. Height, 6 feet. Weight, 175 pounds.

Year	Club	Lea	Pos	G	AB	R	H	2B	3B	HR	RBI	SB	Avg
2004 Salem-Keizer .	Northwest	2B-SS	25	98	22	29	5	0	3	14	0	.296
2005 San Jose	Calif.	2B-SS	75	291	57	102	22	3	2	40	13	.351
2005 Norwich	Eastern	2B-SS-3B	33	129	22	37	8	0	2	20	7	.287
2005 Fresno	P.C.	2B	20	94	18	33	10	1	2	16	1	.351
2006 Fresno	P.C.	2B-3B-SS	71	293	46	89	25	3	3	30	7	.304

Year Club Lea	Pos	G	AB	R	H	2B	3B	HR	RBI	SB	Avg
2006 San Jose .... Calif.	SS	2	7	1	3	0	0	0	1	0	.429
2006 San Francisco a ... N.L.	2B-SS	41	93	12	20	4	0	2	7	0	.215
2007 Fresno .... P.C.	2B-SS-3B	19	67	13	27	5	0	1	7	4	.403
2007 San Francisco ..... N.L.	2B-SS-OF-3B	109	264	26	71	12	1	5	31	4	.269
Major League Totals	2 Yrs. 150	357	38	91	16	1	7	38	4	.255	

a On disabled list from August 18 to September 2, 2006.

FREEL, RYAN PAUL
Born, Jacksonville, Florida, March 8, 1976.
Bats Right. Throws Right. Height, 5 feet, 10 inches. Weight, 180 pounds.

Year Club Lea	Pos	G	AB	R	H	2B	3B	HR	RBI	SB	Avg
1995 St.Cathrnes ..N.Y.-Penn.	2B	65	243	30	68	10	5	3	29	12	.280
1996 Dunedin .... Fla.St.	2B-3B	104	381	64	97	23	3	4	41	19	.255
1997 Knoxville ..... Southern	SS	33	94	18	19	1	1	0	4	5	.202
1997 Dunedin .... Fla.St.	SS-OF-2B	61	181	42	51	8	2	3	17	24	.282
1998 Knoxville ..... Southern	OF-2B-SS	66	252	47	72	17	3	4	36	18	.286
1998 Syracuse .... Int.	OF-2B	37	118	19	27	4	0	2	12	9	.229
1999 Syracuse .... Int.	OF	20	77	15	23	3	2	1	11	10	.299
1999 Knoxville ..... Southern	OF	11	46	9	13	5	1	1	9	4	.283
2000 Dunedin .... Fla.St.	OF	4	18	7	9	1	0	3	6	0	.500
2000 Syracuse .... Int.	2B-OF-3B-SS	80	283	62	81	14	5	10	30	30	.286
2000 Tennessee ... Southern	OF-2B	12	44	11	13	3	1	0	8	2	.295
2001 Toronto .... A.L.	2B-OF	9	22	1	6	1	0	0	3	2	.273
2001 Syracuse a .... Int.	OF-2B-3B-SS	85	319	60	83	21	3	5	33	22	.260
2002 Durham b .... Int.	2B-OF	119	448	65	117	27	4	8	48	37	.261
2003 Louisville .... Int.	2B-OF-3B	54	215	38	59	11	1	3	12	25	.274
2003 Cincinnati c .......N.L.	OF-2B-3B	43	137	23	39	6	1	4	12	9	.285
2004 Cincinnati ........N.L.	OF-3B-2B	143	505	74	140	21	8	3	28	37	.277
2005 Chattanooga.. .Southern	2B-OF-3B	5	17	3	3	0	0	0	1	0	.176
2005 Cincinnati d .......N.L.	OF-2B-3B	103	369	69	100	19	3	4	21	36	.271
2006 Cincinnati ........N.L.	OF-2B-3B	132	454	67	123	30	2	8	27	37	.271
2007 Louisville .... Int.	OF-3B	8	33	6	11	2	0	0	3	2	.333
2007 Cincinnati e .......N.L.	OF-3B-2B	75	277	44	68	13	3	3	16	15	.245
Major League Totals	6 Yrs. 505	1764	278	476	90	17	22	107	136	.270	

a Filed for free agency, October 19, 2001. Signed with Tampa Bay Devil Rays organization, November 8, 2001.
b Filed for free agency, October 15, 2002. Signed with Cincinnati Reds organization, November 19, 2002.
c On disabled list from May 29 to July 4, 2003.
d On disabled list from June 19 to July 20 and August 16 to September 5, 2005.
e On disabled list from May 29 to July 3 and August 3 to November 2, 2007.

FURCAL, RAFAEL
Born, Loma de Cabrera, Dominican Republic, August 24, 1977.
Bats Both. Throws Right. Height, 5 feet, 8 inches. Weight, 195 pounds.

Year Club Lea	Pos	G	AB	R	H	2B	3B	HR	RBI	SB	Avg
1997 Braves .... Gulf Coast	2B-OF	50	190	31	49	5	4	1	9	15	.258
1998 Danville ....Appal.	2B	66	268	56	88	15	4	0	23	60	.328
1999 Myrtle Beach ...... Carolina	SS	43	184	32	54	9	3	0	12	23	.293
1999 Macon .... So.Atl.	SS	83	335	73	113	15	1	1	29	73	.337
2000 Greenville........ Southern	SS	3	10	1	2	0	0	1	3	0	.200
2000 Atlanta a-b .... N.L.	SS-2B	131	455	87	134	20	4	4	37	40	.295
2001 Atlanta c............ N.L.	SS	79	324	39	89	19	0	4	30	22	.275
2002 Atlanta .... N.L.	SS-2B	154	636	95	175	31	8	8	47	27	.275
2003 Atlanta .... N.L.	SS	156	664	130	194	35	*10	15	61	25	.292
2004 Atlanta d............. N.L.	SS-2B	143	563	103	157	24	5	14	59	29	.279
2005 Atlanta d............. N.L.	SS	154	616	100	175	31	11	12	58	46	.284
2006 Los Angeles .... N.L.	SS	159	654	113	196	32	9	15	63	37	.300
2007 Inland Empire........Calif.	SS	2	6	0	1	0	0	0	0	1	.167
2007 Los Angeles e........ N.L.	SS	138	581	87	157	23	4	6	47	25	.270
Major League Totals	8 Yrs. 1114	4493	754	1277	215	51	78	402	251	.284	
Division Series											
2000 Atlanta .... N.L.	SS	3	11	2	1	0	0	0	0	1	.091
2002 Atlanta .... N.L.	SS	5	24	2	6	1	1	0	2	1	.250
2003 Atlanta .... N.L.	SS	5	19	3	4	0	0	0	1	1	.211
2004 Atlanta .... N.L.	SS	5	21	5	8	0	1	2	4	3	.381
2005 Atlanta .... N.L.	SS	4	20	1	3	0	0	0	0	3	.150
2006 Los Angeles .... N.L.	SS	3	11	1	2	0	0	0	1	2	.182
Division Series Totals		25	106	14	24	1	2	2	7	11	.226

a On disabled list from June 13 to June 28, 2000.
b Selected Rookie of the Year in National League for 2000.
c On disabled list from July 7 to November 6, 2001.
d Filed for free agency, October 31, 2005. Signed with Los Angeles Dodgers, December 7, 2005.
e On disabled list from March 23 to April 13, 2007.

GARCIAPARRA, ANTHONY NOMAR (NOMAR)

Born, Whittier, Calif., July 23, 1973.
Bats Right. Throws Right. Height, 6 feet. Weight, 190 pounds.

Year	Club	Lea	Pos	G	AB	R	H	2B	3B	HR	RBI	SB	Avg
1994 Sarasota	Fla.St.	SS	28	105	20	31	8	1	1	16	5	.295
1995 Trenton	Eastern	SS	125	513	77	137	20	8	8	47	35	.267
1996 Red Sox	Gulf Coast	SS	5	14	4	4	2	1	0	5	0	.286
1996 Pawtucket	Int.	SS	43	172	40	59	15	2	16	46	3	.343
1996 Boston	A.L.	SS-2B	24	87	11	21	2	3	4	16	5	.241
1997 Boston a	A.L.	SS	153	*684	122	*209	44*	*11	30	98	22	.306
1998 Boston b	A.L.	SS	143	604	111	195	37	8	35	122	12	.323
1999 Boston	A.L.	SS	135	532	103	190	42	4	27	104	14	*.357
2000 Boston c	A.L.	SS	140	529	104	197	51	.3	21	96	5	*.372
2001 Pawtucket	Int.	SS	4	16	3	7	2	0	1	4	0	.438
2001 Boston d	A.L.	SS	21	83	13	24	3	0	4	8	0	.289
2002 Boston	A.L.	SS	156	635	101	197	56	5	24	120	5	.310
2003 Boston	A.L.	SS	156	658	120	198	37	13	28	105	19	.301
2004 Pawtucket	Int.	SS	6	21	1	5	1	0	1	3	0	.238
2004 Boston	A.L.	SS	38	156	24	50	7	3	5	21	2	.321
2004 Chicago e-f-g	N.L.	SS	43	165	28	49	14	0	4	20	2	.297
2005 Cubs	Arizona	SS	2	5	0	1	0	0	0	0	0	.200
2005 Peoria	Midwest	SS	2	5	1	1	0	0	0	2	0	.200
2005 West Tenn	Southern	SS	4	13	2	3	0	0	0	0	0	.231
2005 Chicago h-i	N.L.	3B-SS	62	230	28	65	12	0	9	30	0	.283
2006 Las Vegas	P.C.	1B	2	8	3	4	2	0	0	1	0	.500
2006 Los Angeles j-k	N.L.	1B	122	469	82	142	31	2	20	93	3	.303
2007 Los Angeles l	N.L.	1B-3B	121	431	39	122	17	0	7	59	3	.283
Major League Totals		12 Yrs.	1314	5263	886	1659	353	52	218	892	92	.315

Division Series

Year	Club	Lea	Pos	G	AB	R	H	2B	3B	HR	RBI	SB	Avg
1998 Boston	A.L.	SS	4	15	4	5	1	0	3	11	0	.333
1999 Boston	A.L.	SS	4	12	6	5	2	0	2	4	0	.417
2003 Boston	A.L.	SS	5	20	2	6	1	0	0	0	1	.300
2006 Los Angeles	N.L.	1B	3	9	0	2	1	0	0	2	0	.222
Division Series Totals			16	56	12	18	5	0	5	17	1	.321

Championship Series

Year	Club	Lea	Pos	G	AB	R	H	2B	3B	HR	RBI	SB	Avg
1999 Boston	A.L.	SS	5	20	2	8	2	0	2	5	1	.400
2003 Boston	A.L.	SS	7	29	2	7	0	1	0	1	0	.241
Championship Series Totals			12	49	4	15	2	1	2	6	1	.306

a Selected Rookie of the Year in American League for 1997.
b On disabled list from May 9 to May 28, 1998.
c On disabled list from May 12 to May 26, 2000.
d On disabled list from March 21 to July 29 and August 27 to November 7, 2001.
e On disabled list from March 26 to June 9, 2004.
f Traded to Chicago Cubs with outfielder Matt Murton for infielder Orlando Cabrera and infielder Doug Mientkiewicz, July 31, 2004.
g Filed for free agency, October 29, 2004, re-signed with Chicago Cubs, December 7, 2004.
h On disabled list from April 21 to August 5, 2005.
i Filed for free agency, October 28, 2005. Signed with the Los Angeles Dodgers December 19, 2005.
j On disabled list from April 3 to April 22 and July 30 to August 9, 2006.
k Filed for free agency, October 28, 2006, re-signed with Los Angeles Dodgers, November 20, 2006.
l On disabled list from August 14 to September 4, 2007.

GARKO, RYAN F.

Born, Pittsburgh, Pennsylvania, January 2, 1981.
Bats Right. Throws Right. Height, 6 feet, 2 inches. Weight, 225 pounds.

Year	Club	Lea	Pos	G	AB	R	H	2B	3B	HR	RBI	SB	Avg
2003 Mahoning Valley	N.Y.-Penn.	C	45	165	23	45	8	1	4	16	1	.273
2004 Kinston	Carolina	1B-C	65	238	44	78	17	1	16	57	4	.328
2004 Akron	Eastern	C-1B	43	172	29	57	15	0	6	38	1	.331
2004 Buffalo	Int.	1B-C	5	20	2	7	1	0	0	4	0	.350
2005 Buffalo	Int.	1B-C	127	452	75	137	25	3	19	77	1	.303
2005 Cleveland	A.L.	DH	1	1	0	0	0	0	0	0	0	.000

Year	Club	Lea	Pos	G	AB	R	H	2B	3B	HR	RBI	SB	Avg
2006 Buffalo	Int.	1B-C	103	364	43	90	18	0	15	59	4	.247
2006 Cleveland	A.L.	1B	50	185	28	54	12	0	7	45	0	.292
2007 Cleveland	A.L.	1B	138	484	62	140	29	1	21	61	0	.289
Major League Totals	3 Yrs.		189	670	90	194	41	1	28	106	0	.290
Division Series												
2007 Cleveland	A.L.	1B	3	11	3	4	0	0	1	3	0	.364
Championship Series												
2007 Cleveland	A.L.	1B	6	24	4	7	2	1	0	2	0	.292

GATHRIGHT, JOEY RENARD

Born, Hattiesburg, Mississippi, April 22, 1981.
Bats Left. Throws Right. Height, 5 feet, 10 inches. Weight, 170 pounds.

Year	Club	Lea	Pos	G	AB	R	H	2B	3B	HR	RBI	SB	Avg
2002 Charleston-SC	So.Atl.	OF	59	208	30	55	1	0	0	14	22	.264
2003 Bakersfield	California	OF	89	340	65	110	6	3	0	23	57	.324
2003 Orlando	Southern	OF	22	85	12	32	1	0	0	5	12	.376
2004 Montgomery	Southern	OF	32	126	23	43	5	1	0	8	10	.341
2004 Durham	Int.	OF	60	236	34	77	9	1	0	8	33	.326
2004 Tampa Bay	A.L.	OF	19	52	11	13	0	0	0	1	6	.250
2005 Durham	Int.	OF	58	226	46	69	10	5	1	18	31	.305
2005 Tampa Bay	A.L.	OF	76	203	29	56	7	3	0	13	20	.276
2006 Durham	Int.	OF	10	31	5	8	2	0	0	1	6	.258
2006 Tampa Bay-Kansas City a.	A.L.	OF	134	383	59	91	12	3	1	41	22	.238
2007 Omaha..............	P.C.	OF	60	223	44	76	10	4	0	25	25	.341
2007 Kansas City	A.L.	OF	74	228	28	70	8	0	0	19	9	.307
Major League Totals	4 Yrs.		303	866	127	230	27	6	1	74	57	.266

a Traded to Kansas City Royals with infielder Fernando Cortez for pitcher J.P. Howell, June 20, 2006.

GERMAN, ESTEBAN (GURIDI)

Born, Haina, Dominican Republic, January 26, 1978.
Bats Right. Throws Right. Height, 5 feet, 10 inches. Weight, 180 pounds.

Year	Club	Lea	Pos	G	AB	R	H	2B	3B	HR	RBI	SB	Avg
1997 Oaklnd-East .	Dominican	2B	69	249	69	79	17	1	2	29	58	.317
1998 Athletics.......	Arizona	2B	55	202	52	62	3	10	2	28	40	.307
1998 Oaklnd West.	Dominican	2B	10	32	9	10	1	1	0	4	1	.313
1999 Modesto........	Calif.	2B	128	501	107	156	16	12	4	52	40	.311
2000 Visalia	Calif.	2B-SS	109	428	82	113	14	10	2	35	78	.264
2000 Midland	Texas	2B	24	75	13	16	1	0	1	6	5	.213
2001 Sacramento	P.C.	2B	38	150	40	56	8	0	4	14	17	.373
2001 Midland	Texas	2B	92	335	79	95	20	3	6	30	31	.284
2002 Sacramento	P.C.	2B	121	458	72	126	16	4	2	43	26	.275
2002 Oakland	A.L.	2B	9	35	4	7	0	0	0	0	1	.200
2003 Sacramento	P.C.	2B	115	467	86	143	20	8	3	51	32	.306
2003 Oakland	A.L.	2B	5	4	0	1	0	0	0	1	0	.250
2004 Oakland	A.L.	3B-2B	31	60	9	15	1	1	0	7	0	.250
2004 Sacramento a-b	P.C.	2B-SS	55	231	33	76	8	4	2	29	18	.329
2005 Oklahoma.........	P.C.	3B-SS-2B-OF	117	489	103	153	27	6	5	68	43	.313
2005 Texas c.........	A.L.	2B-3B	5	4	3	3	1	0	0	1	2	.750
2006 Kansas City	A.L.	2B-OF-3B	106	279	44	91	18	5	3	34	7	.326
2007 Kansas City	A.L.	2B-3B-OF-SS	121	348	49	92	15	6	4	37	11	.264
Major League Totals	6 Yrs.		277	730	109	209	35	12	7	80	21	.286

a On disabled list from July 4 to July 31, 2004.

b Filed for free agency, October 15, 2004. Signed with Texas Rangers organization, November 19, 2004.

c Traded to Kansas City Royals for pitcher Fabio Castro, December 8, 2005.

GIAMBI, JASON GILBERT

Born, West Covina, California, January 8, 1971.
Bats Left. Throws Right. Height, 6 feet, 3 inches. Weight, 230 pounds.

Year	Club	Lea	Pos	G	AB	R	H	2B	3B	HR	RBI	SB	Avg
1992 South Oregon....	Northwest	3B	13	41	9	13	3	0	3	13	1	.317
1993 Modesto........	California	3B	89	313	72	91	16	2	12	60	2	.291
1994 Huntsville........	Southern	3B-1B	56	193	31	43	9	0	6	30	0	.223
1994 Tacoma	P.C.	3B-1B-SS	52	176	28	56	20	0	4	38	1	.318
1995 Edmonton	P.C.	3B-1B	55	190	34	65	26	1	3	41	0	.342
1995 Oakland	A.L.	3B-1B	54	176	27	45	7	0	6	25	2	.256

Year	Club	Lea	Pos	G	AB	R	H	2B	3B	HR	RBI	SB	Avg
1996 Oakland		A.L.	1B-OF-3B	140	536	84	156	40	1	20	79	0	.291
1997 Oakland		A.L.	OF-1B	142	519	66	152	41	2	20	81	0	.293
1998 Oakland		A.L.	1B	153	562	92	166	28	0	27	110	2	.295
1999 Oakland		A.L.	1B-3B	158	575	115	181	36	1	33	123	1	.315
2000 Oakland a		A.L.	1B	152	510	108	170	29	1	43	137	2	.333
2001 Oakland b		A.L.	1B	154	520	109	178	*47	2	38	120	2	.342
2002 New York		A.L.	1B	155	560	120	176	34	1	41	122	2	.314
2003 New York		A.L.	1B	156	535	97	134	25	0	41	107	2	.250
2004 Tampa		Fla.St.	1B	2	6	0	1	0	0	0	0	0	.167
2004 New York c		A.L.	1B	80	264	33	55	9	0	12	40	0	.208
2005 New York		A.L.	1B	139	417	74	113	14	0	32	87	0	.271
2006 New York		A.L.	DH-1B	139	446	92	113	25	0	37	113	2	.253
2007 Tampa		Fla.St.	DH	5	13	0	4	1	0	0	1	0	.308
2007 Scranton-WB		Int.	1B	4	9	1	1	0	0	1	1	0	.111
2007 New York d		A.L.	DH-1B	83	254	31	60	8	0	14	39	1	.236
Major League Totals		13 Yrs.		1705	5874	1048	1699	343	8	364	1183	16	.289
Division Series													
2000 Oakland		A.L.	1B	5	14	2	4	0	0	0	1	1	.286
2001 Oakland		A.L.	1B	5	17	2	6	0	0	1	4	0	.353
2002 New York		A.L.	1B-DH	4	14	5	5	0	0	1	3	0	.357
2003 New York		A.L.	DH	4	16	1	4	2	0	0	2	0	.250
2005 New York		A.L.	1B-DH	5	19	1	8	3	0	0	2	0	.421
2006 New York		A.L.	DH-1B	3	8	1	1	0	0	1	2	1	.125
2007 New York		A.L.	1B	3	4	0	1	0	0	0	0	0	.250
Division Series Totals				29	92	12	29	5	0	3	14	2	.315
Championship Series													
2003 New York		A.L.	DH	7	26	4	6	0	0	0	3	0	.231
World Series Record													
2003 New York		A.L.	1B	6	17	2	4	1	0	1	1	0	.235

a Selected Most Valuable Player in American League for 2000.
b Filed for free agency, November 5, 2001. Signed with New York Yankees, December 13, 2001.
c On disabled list from May 22 to June 6 and from July 26 to September 14, 2004.
d On disabled list from May 31 to August 7, 2007.

GIBBONS, JAY JONATHAN
Born, Rochester, Michigan, March 2, 1977.
Bats Left. Throws Left. Height, 6 feet. Weight, 205 pounds.

Year	Club	Lea	Pos	G	AB	R	H	2B	3B	HR	RBI	SB	Avg
1998 Medicine Hat		Pioneer	DH-1B	73	290	66	115	29	1	19	98	2	.397
1999 Dunedin		Fla.St.	1B	60	212	34	66	14	0	9	39	2	.311
1999 Hagerstown		So.Atl.	DH	71	292	53	89	20	2	16	69	3	.305
2000 Tennessee		Southern	1B-OF	132	474	85	152	38	1	19	75	3	.321
2001 Baltimore b		A.L.	OF-1B	73	225	27	53	10	0	15	36	0	.236
2002 Baltimore		A.L.	OF-1B	136	490	71	121	29	1	28	69	1	.247
2003 Baltimore		A.L.	OF-1B	160	625	80	173	39	2	23	100	0	.277
2004 Frederick		Carolina	OF	3	11	2	2	1	0	1	5	0	.182
2004 Bowie		Eastern	OF	5	15	3	1	0	0	0	1	0	.067
2004 Baltimore c		A.L.	OF-1B	97	346	36	85	14	1	10	47	1	.246
2005 Baltimore		A.L.	OF-1B	139	488	72	135	33	3	26	79	0	.277
2006 Frederick		Carolina	DH	2	8	1	0	0	0	0	0	0	.000
2006 Bowie		Eastern	DH	3	10	2	4	2	0	0	0	0	.400
2006 Baltimore d		A.L.	DH-OF	90	343	34	95	23	0	13	46	0	.277
2007 Baltimore e		A.L.	OF	84	270	28	62	14	0	6	28	0	.230
Major League Totals		7 Yrs.		779	2787	348	724	162	7	121	405	2	.260

a Selected by Baltimore Orioles from Toronto Blue Jays in Rule V draft, December 11, 2000.
b On disabled list from August 5 to November 19, 2001.
c On disabled list from May 26 to June 14 and June 15 to August 10, 2004.
d On disabled list from May 27 to June 12 and June 14 to July 29, 2006.
e On disabled list from August 13 to October 23, 2007.

GILES, BRIAN STEPHEN
Born, El Cajon, California, January 20, 1971.
Bats Left. Throws Left. Height, 5 feet, 10 inches. Weight, 205 pounds.

Year	Club	Lea	Pos	G	AB	R	H	2B	3B	HR	RBI	SB	Avg
1989 Burlington		Appal.	OF	36	129	18	40	7	0	0	20	6	.310
1990 Watertown		N.Y.-Penn.	OF	70	246	44	71	15	2	1	23	11	.289
1991 Kinston		Carolina	OF	125	394	71	122	14	0	4	47	19	.310

Year	Club	Lea	Pos	G	AB	R	H	2B	3B	HR	RBI	SB	Avg
1992 Canton-Akrn.	Eastern	OF	23	74	6	16	4	0	0	3	3	.216
1992 Kinston.	Carolina	OF	42	140	28	37	5	1	3	18	3	.264
1993 Canton-Akrn.	Eastern	OF	123	425	64	139	17	6	8	64	18	.327
1994 Charlotte	Int.	OF	128	434	74	136	18	3	16	58	8	.313
1995 Buffalo	A.A.	OF	123	413	67	128	18	8	15	67	7	.310
1995 Cleveland	A.L.	OF	6	9	6	5	0	0	1	3	0	.556
1996 Buffalo	A.A.	OF	83	318	65	100	17	6	20	64	1	.314
1996 Cleveland	A.L.	DH-OF	51	121	26	43	14	1	5	27	3	.355
1997 Cleveland	A.L.	OF	130	377	62	101	15	3	17	61	13	.268
1998 Buffalo	Int.	OF	13	46	5	11	2	0	2	7	0	.239
1998 Cleveland a-b	A.L.	OF	112	350	56	94	19	0	16	66	10	.269
1999 Pittsburgh	N.L.	OF	141	521	109	164	33	3	39	115	6	.315
2000 Pittsburgh	N.L.	OF	156	559	111	176	37	7	35	123	6	.315
2001 Pittsburgh	N.L.	OF	160	576	116	178	37	7	37	95	13	.309
2002 Pittsburgh	N.L.	OF	153	497	95	148	37	5	38	103	15	.298
2003 Pittsburgh-San Diego c-d-e	N.L.	OF	134	492	93	147	34	6	20	88	4	.299
2004 San Diego	N.L.	OF	159	609	97	173	33	7	23	94	10	.284
2005 San Diego f	N.L.	OF	158	545	92	164	38	8	15	83	13	.301
2006 San Diego	N.L.	OF	158	604	87	159	37	1	14	83	9	.263
2007 Lake Elsinore	Calif.	OF	3	10	2	4	0	0	1	3	0	.400
2007 San Diego g	N.L.	OF	121	483	72	131	27	2	13	51	4	.271
Major League Totals		13 Yrs.	1639	5743	1022	1683	361	50	273	992	106	.293
Division Series												
1996 Cleveland	A.L.	PH	1	1	0	0	0	0	0	0	0	.000
1997 Cleveland	A.L.	OF	3	7	0	1	0	0	0	0	0	.143
1998 Cleveland	A.L.	OF-DH	3	10	1	2	1	0	0	0	0	.200
2005 San Diego	N.L.	OF	3	13	0	3	0	0	0	1	1	.231
2006 San Diego	N.L.	OF	4	14	1	4	1	0	0	1	0	.286
Division Series Totals			14	45	2	10	2	0	0	2	1	.222
Championship Series												
1997 Cleveland	A.L.	OF	6	16	1	3	3	0	0	0	0	.188
1998 Cleveland	A.L.	OF	4	12	0	1	0	0	0	0	0	.083
Championship Series Totals			10	28	1	4	3	0	0	0	0	.143
World Series Record												
1997 Cleveland	A.L.	OF	5	4	1	2	1	0	0	2	0	.400

a On disabled list from June 1 to July 7, 1998.
b Traded to Pittsburgh Pirates for pitcher Ricardo Rincon, November 18, 1998.
c On disabled list from April 11 to May 7, 2003.
d Traded to San Diego Padres for pitcher Oliver Perez, outfielder Jason Bay and player to be named later, August 26, 2003.
e Pittsburgh Pirates received pitcher Cory Stewart to complete trade, October 2, 2003.
f Filed for free agency, October 27, 2005, re-signed with San Diego Padres, December 1, 2005.
g On disabled list from May 20 to June 28, 2007.

GILES, MARCUS WILLIAM

Born, San Diego, California, May 18, 1978.
Bats Right. Throws Right. Height, 5 feet, 8 inches. Weight, 175 pounds.

Year	Club	Lea	Pos	G	AB	R	H	2B	3B	HR	RBI	SB	Avg
1997 Danville	Appal.	2B	55	207	53	72	13	3	8	45	5	.348
1998 Macon	So.Atl.	2B	135	505	111	166	38	3	37	108	12	.329
1999 Myrtle Beach	Carolina	2B	126	497	80	162	40	7	13	73	9	.326
2000 Greenville	Southern	2B	132	458	73	133	28	2	17	62	25	.290
2001 Richmond	Int.	2B-SS-3B-OF	67	252	48	84	19	1	6	44	13	.333
2001 Atlanta	N.L.	2B	68	244	36	64	10	2	9	31	2	.262
2002 Richmond	Int.	2B-3B	31	115	25	37	6	0	3	16	3	.322
2002 Atlanta a	N.L.	2B-3B	68	213	27	49	10	1	8	23	1	.230
2003 Atlanta	N.L.	2B	145	551	101	174	49	2	21	69	14	.316
2004 Rome	So.Atl.	DH	2	2	0	0	0	0	0	0	0	.000
2004 Myrtle Beach	Carolina	2B	4	13	1	1	1	0	0	2	0	.077
2004 Atlanta b	N.L.	2B	102	379	61	118	22	2	8	48	17	.311
2005 Atlanta	N.L.	2B-3B	152	577	104	168	45	4	15	63	16	.291
2006 Atlanta c	N.L.	2B	141	550	87	144	32	2	11	60	10	.262
2007 San Diego d-e	N.L.	2B	116	420	52	96	19	3	4	39	10	.229
Major League Totals		7 Yrs.	792	2934	468	813	187	16	76	333	70	.277
Division Series												
2001 Atlanta	N.L.	2B	3	12	2	3	1	0	0	1	0	.250
2002 Atlanta	N.L.	PH	3	2	0	1	0	0	0	0	0	.500
2003 Atlanta	N.L.	2B	5	14	3	5	0	0	1	3	0	.357

Year Club	Lea	Pos	G	AB	R	H	2B	3B	HR	RBI	SB	Avg
2004 Atlanta	N.L.	2B	5	24	1	3	0	0	0	1	1	.125
2005 Atlanta	N.L.	2B	4	20	5	4	1	0	0	0	0	.200
Division Series Totals			20	72	11	16	2	0	1	5	1	.222
Championship Series												
2001 Atlanta	N.L.	2B	5	20	4	4	1	0	1	1	0	.200

a On disabled list from May 29 to July 16, 2002.
b On disabled list from May 16 to July 15, 2004.
c Not offered contract, December 12, 2006. Signed with San Diego Padres, December 20, 2006.
d On disabled list from August 25 to September 9, 2007.
e Waived by San Diego Padres, October 26, 2007. Signed with Colorado Rockies organization, January 8, 2008.

GLAUS, TROY TARZANA

Born, Tarzana, California, August 3, 1976.
Bats Right. Throws Right. Height, 6 feet, 5 inches. Weight, 240 pounds.

Year Club	Lea	Pos	G	AB	R	H	2B	3B	HR	RBI	SB	Avg
1998 Midland	Texas	3B	50	188	51	58	11	2	19	51	4	.309
1998 Vancouver	P.C.	3B	59	219	33	67	16	0	16	42	3	.306
1998 Anaheim	A.L.	3B	48	165	19	36	9	0	1	23	1	.218
1999 Anaheim	A.L.	3B	154	551	85	132	29	0	29	79	5	.240
2000 Anaheim	A.L.	3B-SS	159	563	120	160	37	1	*47	102	14	.284
2001 Anaheim	A.L.	3B-SS	161	588	100	147	38	2	41	108	10	.250
2002 Anaheim	A.L.	3B-SS	156	569	99	142	24	1	30	111	10	.250
2003 Rancho Cucamonga	Calif.	DH	2	6	1	2	0	0	0	1	0	.333
2003 Anaheim a		3B	91	319	53	79	17	2	16	50	7	.248
2004 Rancho Cucamonga	Calif.	DH	5	15	4	3	0	0	2	4	0	.200
2004 Anaheim b-c.	A.L.	DH-3B	58	207	47	52	11	1	18	42	2	.251
2005 Arizona d	N.L.	3B	149	538	78	139	29	1	37	97	4	.258
2006 Toronto	A.L.	3B-SS	153	540	105	136	27	0	38	104	3	.252
2007 Toronto e-f	A.L.	3B	115	385	60	101	19	1	20	62	0	.262
Major League Totals	10 Yrs.	1244	4425	766	1124	240	9	277	778	56		.254
Division Series												
2002 Anaheim	A.L.	3B	4	16	4	5	0	0	3	3	0	.313
2004 Anaheim	A.L.	DH	3	11	3	4	2	0	2	3	0	.364
Division Series Totals			7	27	7	9	2	0	5	6	0	.333
Championship Series												
2002 Anaheim	A.L.	3B	5	19	4	6	0	1	1	2	0	.316
World Series Record												
2002 Anaheim	A.L.	3B	7	26	7	10	3	0	3	8	0	.385

a On disabled list from July 22 to October 6, 2003.
b On disabled list from May 12 to August 29, 2004.
c Filed for free agency, October 28, 2004. Signed with Arizona Diamondbacks, December 9, 2004.
d Traded to Toronto Blue Jays with infielder Sergio Santos for infielder Orlando Hudson and pitcher Miguel Batista, December 27, 2005.
e On disabled list from April 13 to April 28 and September 14 to November 13, 2007.
f Traded to St. Louis Cardinals for infielder Scott Rolen, January 14, 2008.

GLOAD, ROSS PETER

Born, Brooklyn, New York, April 5, 1976.
Bats Left. Throws Left. Height, 6 feet, 1 inches. Weight, 190 pounds.

Year Club	Lea	Pos	G	AB	R	H	2B	3B	HR	RBI	SB	Avg
1997 Utica	N.Y.-Penn.	1B	68	245	28	64	15	2	3	43	1	.261
1998 Kane County	Midwest	1B	132	501	77	157	41	3	12	92	7	.313
1999 Brevard County	Fla.St.	1B	133	490	80	146	26	3	10	74	3	.298
2000 Portland	Eastern	OF-1B	100	401	60	114	28	4	16	65	4	.284
2000 Iowa	P.C.	OF	28	104	24	42	10	2	14	39	1	.404
2000 Chicago a	N.L.	OF-1B	18	31	4	6	0	1	1	3	0	.194
2001 Iowa b	P.C.	1B	133	475	70	141	32	10	15	93	9	.297
2002 Colorado Springs	P.C.	1B-OF	104	442	69	139	28	6	16	71	9	.314
2002 Colorado c-d	N.L.	1B-OF	26	31	4	8	1	0	1	4	0	.258
2003 Charlotte e	Int.	1B-OF	133	508	72	160	40	6	18	70	6	.315
2004 Chicago	A.L.	1B-OF	110	234	28	75	16	0	7	44	0	.321
2005 Charlotte	Int.	1B-OF	60	236	45	86	22	1	15	45	0	.364
2005 Chicago f	A.L.	1B-OF	28	42	2	7	2	0	0	5	0	.167
2006 Chicago g	A.L.	1B-OF	77	156	22	51	8	2	3	18	6	.327
2007 Omaha	P.C.	DH	1	4	1	2	0	0	1	1	0	.500
2007 Kansas City h	A.L.	1B-OF	102	320	37	92	22	3	7	51	2	.287
Major League Totals	6 Yrs.	361	814	97	239	49	6	19	125	8		.294

a Traded to Chicago Cubs with pitcher David Noyce for outfielder Henry Rodriguez and cash, July 31, 2000.
b Claimed on waivers by Colorado Rockies, September 12, 2001.
c Traded to New York Mets with pitcher Craig House and outfielder Alex Ochoa for outfielder Benny Agbayani and infielder Todd Zeile, January 21, 2002.
d Sold to Colorado Rockies, January 26, 2002.
e Traded to Chicago White Sox for pitcher Wade Parrish, March 31, 2003.
f On disabled list from April 25 to July 17, 2005.
g Traded to Kansas City Royals for pitcher Andy Sisco, December 16, 2006.
h On disabled list from May 14 to June 30, 2007.

GOMES, JONNY JOHNSON

Born, Petaluma, California, November 22, 1980.
Bats Right. Throws Right. Height, 6 feet, 1 inch. Weight, 205 pounds.

Year	Club	Lea	Pos	G	AB	R	H	2B	3B	HR	RBI	SB	Avg
2001	Princeton	Appal.	OF	62	206	58	60	11	2	16	44	15	.291
2002	Bakersfield	California	OF	133	446	102	123	24	9	30	72	15	.276
2003	Orlando	Southern	OF	120	442	68	110	28	3	17	56	23	.249
2003	Durham	Int.	OF	5	19	2	6	2	1	0	1	0	.316
2003	Tampa Bay	A.L.	DH	8	15	1	2	1	0	0	0	0	.133
2004	Durham	Int.	OF	114	389	73	100	27	1	26	78	8	.257
2004	Tampa Bay	A.L.	DH	5	14	0	1	0	0	0	1	0	.071
2005	Durham	Int.	OF	45	162	34	52	13	0	14	46	7	.321
2005	Tampa Bay	A.L.	OF	101	348	61	98	13	6	21	54	9	.282
2006	Tampa Bay a	A.L.	DH-OF	117	385	53	83	21	1	20	59	1	.216
2007	Durham	Int.	OF	13	43	6	13	2	0	1	7	4	.302
2007	Tampa Bay	A.L.	OF	107	348	48	85	20	2	17	49	12	.244
Major League Totals		5 Yrs.		338	1110	163	269	55	9	58	163	22	.242

a On disabled list from August 22 to October 2, 2006.

GOMEZ, CHRISTOPHER CORY (CHRIS)

Born, Los Angeles, California, June 16, 1971.
Bats Right. Throws Right. Height, 6 feet, 1 inch. Weight, 195 pounds.

Year	Club	Lea	Pos	G	AB	R	H	2B	3B	HR	RBI	SB	Avg
1992	London	Eastern	SS-3B	64	220	20	59	13	2	1	19	1	.268
1993	Toledo	Int.	SS	87	277	29	68	12	2	0	20	6	.245
1993	Detroit	A.L.	SS-2B	46	128	11	32	7	1	0	11	2	.250
1994	Detroit	A.L.	SS-2B	84	296	32	76	19	0	8	53	5	.257
1995	Detroit	A.L.	SS-2B	123	431	49	96	20	2	11	50	4	.223
1996	Detroit	A.L.	SS	48	128	21	31	5	0	1	16	1	.242
1996	San Diego a	N.L.	SS	89	328	32	86	16	1	3	29	2	.262
1997	San Diego	N.L.	SS	150	522	62	132	19	2	5	54	5	.253
1998	San Diego	N.L.	SS	145	449	55	120	32	3	4	39	1	.267
1999	San Diego	N.L.	SS	76	234	20	59	8	1	1	15	1	.252
1999	Las Vegas b	P.C.	SS	10	27	3	9	1	0	0	4	0	.333
2000	San Diego c	N.L.	SS-2B	33	54	4	12	0	0	0	3	0	.222
2001	San Diego	N.L.	SS-2B	40	112	6	21	3	0	0	7	1	.188
2001	Portland	P.C.	SS-2B	11	40	5	12	3	0	1	5	1	.300
2001	Durham	Int.	SS	23	93	16	28	5	1	4	17	1	.301
2001	Tampa Bay d-e	A.L.	SS	58	189	31	57	16	0	8	36	3	.302
2002	Tampa Bay	A.L.	SS	130	461	51	122	31	3	10	46	1	.265
2003	Minnesota f-g	A.L.	2B-3B-SS	58	175	14	44	9	3	1	15	2	.251
2004	Toronto h-i-j	A.L.	SS-1B-3B-2B	109	341	41	96	11	1	3	37	3	.282
2005	Baltimore	A.L.	1B-2B-3B-SS	89	219	27	61	11	0	1	18	2	.279
2006	Bowie	Eastern	SS-3B	4	16	4	4	1	0	0	1	0	.250
2006	Aberdeen	N.Y.-Penn.	3B	1	3	0	1	0	0	0	1	0	.333
2006	Baltimore k-l	A.L.	1B-2B-3B-SS	55	132	14	45	7	0	2	17	1	.341
2007	Baltimore-Cleveland m-n	A.L.	1B-3B-2B-SS	92	222	21	66	12	1	1	21	1	.297
Major League Totals		15 Yrs.		1425	4421	491	1156	226	18	59	467	35	.261
Division Series													
1996	San Diego	N.L.	SS	3	12	0	2	0	0	0	1	0	.167
1998	San Diego	N.L.	SS	4	11	1	3	0	0	0	0	0	.273
2003	Minnesota	A.L.	2B	1	0	0	0	0	0	0	0	0	.000
Division Series Totals				8	23	1	5	0	0	0	1	0	.217
Championship Series													
1998	San Diego	N.L.	SS	6	20	2	3	1	0	0	0	0	.150
2007	Cleveland	A.L.	PH	1	1	0	0	0	0	0	0	0	.000
Championship Series Totals				7	21	2	3	1	0	0	0	0	.143

Year Club	Lea	Pos	G	AB	R	H	2B	3B	HR	RBI	SB	Avg
World Series Record												
1998 San Diego .......N.L.		SS	4	11	2	4	0	1	0	0	0	.364

a Traded to San Diego Padres with catcher John Flaherty for catcher Brad Ausmus and infielder Andujar Cedeno, June 18, 1996.
b On disabled list from June 2 to July 31, 1999.
c On disabled list from June 22 to October 12, 2000.
d Waived by San Diego Padres, June 22, 2001. Signed with Tampa Bay Devil Rays organization, June 27, 2001.
e Filed for free agency, November 5, 2001, re-signed with Tampa Bay Devil Rays, December 7, 2001.
f Released by Tampa Bay Devil Rays, September 30, 2002. Signed with Minnesota Twins organization, January 2, 2003.
g On disabled list from June 7 to July 5, 2003.
h Filed for free agency, October 28, 2003. Signed with Toronto Blue Jays, January 7, 2004.
i Filed for free agency, October 28, 2004. Signed with Baltimore Orioles organization, December 8, 2004.
j Selected by Philadelphia Phillies in Rule V minor league draft, December 14, 2004. Sold to Baltimore Orioles, December 20, 2004.
k On disabled list from May 11 to July 11, 2006.
l Filed for free agency, October 31, 2006, re-signed with Baltimore Orioles, December 18, 2006.
m Claimed on waivers by Cleveland Indians, August 9, 2007.
n Filed for free agency, October 30, 2007. Signed with Pittsburgh Pirates, December 12, 2007.

GONZALEZ, ADRIAN

Born, San Diego, California, May 8, 1982.
Bats Left. Throws Left. Height, 6 feet, 2 inches. Weight, 220 pounds.

Year Club	Lea	Pos	G	AB	R	H	2B	3B	HR	RBI	SB	Avg
2000 Marlins.........	Gulf Coast	1B	53	193	24	57	10	1	0	30	0	.295
2000 Utica..........	N.Y.-Penn.	1B	8	29	7	9	3	0	0	3	0	.310
2001 Kane County.......	Midwest	1B	127	516	86	161	37	1	17	103	5	.312
2002 Portland..........	Eastern	1B	138	508	70	135	34	1	17	96	6	.266
2003 Albuquerque.........	.P.C.	1B	39	139	17	30	5	1	1	18	1	.216
2003 Carolina.........	Southern	1B	36	137	15	42	9	1	1	16	1	.307
2003 Frisco a	Texas	1B	45	173	16	49	6	2	3	17	0	.283
2004 Oklahoma.........P.C.		1B	123	457	61	139	28	3	12	88	1	.304
2004 Texas	A.L.	1B	16	42	7	10	3	0	1	7	0	.238
2005 Oklahoma.........P.C.		1B	84	328	61	111	17	1	18	65	0	.338
2005 Texas	A.L.	DH-1B-OF	43	150	17	34	7	1	6	17	0	.227
2006 San Diego b	N.L.	1B	156	570	83	173	38	1	24	82	0	.304
2007 San Diego	N.L.	1B	161	646	101	182	46	3	30	100	0	.282
Major League Totals	4 Yrs.		376	1408	208	399	94	5	61	206	0	.283
Division Series												
2006 San Diego	N.L.	1B	4	14	2	5	0	0	0	0	0	.357

a Traded to Texas Rangers with pitcher Ryan Snare and outfielder Will Smith for pitcher Ugueth Urbina, July 11, 2003.
b Traded to San Diego Padres with pitcher Chris Young and outfielder Termel Sledge for pitcher Adam Eaton, pitcher Akinori Otsuka and catcher Billy Killian, January 4, 2006.

GONZALEZ, ALEXANDER (ALEX)

Born, Cagua, Venezuela, February 15, 1977.
Bats Right. Throws Right. Height, 6 feet. Weight, 200 pounds.

Year Club	Lea	Pos	G	AB	R	H	2B	3B	HR	RBI	SB	Avg
1994 Florida ....Dominican		SS	66	282	39	67	9	5	4	39	5	.238
1995 Brevard Cty ....Fla.St.		SS	17	59	6	12	2	1	0	8	1	.203
1995 Marlins.........	Gulf Coast	SS	53	187	30	55	7	4	2	30	11	.294
1996 Marlins.........	Gulf Coast	SS	10	41	6	16	3	0	0	6	1	.390
1996 Kane County.......	Midwest	SS	4	10	2	2	0	0	0	0	0	.200
1996 Portland..........	Eastern	SS	11	34	4	8	0	1	0	1	0	.235
1997 Portland..........	Eastern	SS	133	449	69	114	16	4	19	65	4	.254
1998 Charlotte ....Int.		SS	108	422	71	117	20	10	10	51	4	.277
1998 Florida	N.L.	SS	25	86	11	13	2	0	3	7	0	.151
1999 Florida	N.L.	SS	136	560	81	155	28	8	14	59	3	.277
2000 Brevard County ......Fla.St.		SS	4	17	1	2	0	0	0	2	1	.118
2000 Florida a.............	N.L.	SS	109	385	35	77	17	4	7	42	7	.200
2001 Florida	N.L.	SS	145	515	57	129	36	1	9	48	2	.250
2002 Florida b.............	N.L.	SS	42	151	15	34	7	1	2	18	3	.225
2002 Marlins.........	Gulf Coast	SS	5	12	0	2	1	0	0	1	0	.167
2003 Florida	N.L.	SS	150	528	52	135	33	6	18	77	0	.256
2004 Florida	N.L.	SS	159	561	67	130	30	3	23	79	3	.232
2005 Florida c.............	N.L.	SS	130	435	45	115	30	0	5	45	5	.264
2006 Pawtucket ....Int.		SS	1	3	0	1	0	0	0	0	0	.333

Year	Club	Lea	Pos	G	AB	R	H	2B	3B	HR	RBI	SB	Avg
2006 Boston d-e		A.L.	SS	111	388	48	99	24	2	9	50	1	.255
2007 Cincinnati		N.L.	SS	110	393	55	107	27	1	16	55	0	.272
Major League Totals		10 Yrs.	1117	4002	466	994	234	26	106	480	24	.248	
Division Series													
2003 Florida		N.L.	SS	4	16	2	1	0	0	0	0	0	.063
Championship Series													
2003 Florida		N.L.	SS	7	24	1	3	2	0	0	4	0	.125
World Series Record													
2003 Florida		N.L.	SS	6	22	3	6	2	0	1	2	0	.273

a On disabled list from July 28 to August 31, 2000.
b On disabled list from May 19 to November 6, 2002.
c Filed for free agency, October 27, 2005. Signed with Boston Red Sox, February 6, 2006.
d On disabled list from August 19 to September 3, 2006.
e Filed for free agency, October 30, 2006. Signed with Cincinnati Reds, November 20, 2006.

GONZALEZ, ANGEL MANUEL (ANDY)
Born, Rio Piedras, Puerto Rico, December 15, 1981.
Bats Right. Throws Right. Height, 6 feet, 2 inches. Weight, 190 pounds.

Year	Club	Lea	Pos	G	AB	R	H	2B	3B	HR	RBI	SB	Avg
2001 White Sox	Arizona		SS-1B	48	189	33	61	18	1	5	30	13	.323
2002 Bristol	Appal.		SS	66	254	48	71	17	0	1	45	5	.280
2003 Kannapolis	So.Atl.		SS-3B	123	429	58	99	17	1	1	39	22	.231
2004 Winston-Salem	Carolina		3B-SS-2B	83	318	61	81	19	1	8	31	3	.255
2004 Kannapolis	So.Atl.		SS-2B-3B	12	48	6	13	1	0	1	3	1	.271
2004 Birmingham	Southern		SS-3B	36	112	19	19	3	0	3	8	1	.170
2005 Birmingham	Southern		SS-2B-3B	123	434	50	119	19	2	4	63	6	.274
2006 Charlotte	Int.		2B-3B-OF-SS	116	402	48	109	27	0	6	51	16	.271
2007 Charlotte	Int.		2B-SS-OF	35	124	15	30	7	1	3	17	6	.242
2007 Chicago a	A.L.		OF-3B-1B-2B	67	189	17	35	6	0	2	11	1	.185

a Not offered contract, December 12, 2007. Signed with Cleveland Indians organization, December 21, 2007.

GONZALEZ, LUIS EMILIO
Born, Tampa, Florida, September 3, 1967.
Bats Left. Throws Right. Height, 6 feet, 2 inches. Weight, 180 pounds.

Year	Club	Lea	Pos	G	AB	R	H	2B	3B	HR	RBI	SB	Avg
1988 Asheville	So. Atl.		3B	31	115	13	29	7	1	2	14	2	.252
1988 Auburn	N.Y.-Penn.		3B	39	157	32	49	10	3	5	27	2	.312
1989 Osceola a	Fla. St.		DH	86	287	46	82	16	7	6	38	2	.286
1990 Columbus	Southern		1B-3B	138	495	86	131	30	6	*24	89	27	.265
1990 Houston		N.L.	3B-1B	12	21	1	4	2	0	0	0	0	.190
1991 Houston b		N.L.	OF	137	473	51	120	28	9	13	69	10	.254
1992 Tucson		P.C.	OF	13	44	11	19	4	2	1	9	4	.432
1992 Houston c		N.L.	OF	122	387	40	94	19	3	10	55	7	.243
1993 Houston		N.L.	OF	154	540	82	162	34	3	15	72	20	.300
1994 Houston		N.L.	OF	112	392	57	107	29	4	8	67	15	.273
1995 Houston-Chicago d-e		N.L.	OF	133	471	69	130	29	8	13	69	6	.276
1996 Chicago f-g		N.L.	OF-1B	146	483	70	131	30	4	15	79	9	.271
1997 Houston h-i		N.L.	OF-1B	152	550	78	142	31	2	10	68	10	.258
1998 Detroit j		A.L.	OF	154	547	84	146	35	5	23	71	12	.267
1999 Arizona		N.L.	OF	153	614	112	*206	45	4	26	111	9	.336
2000 Arizona		N.L.	OF	*162	618	106	192	47	2	31	114	2	.311
2001 Arizona		N.L.	OF	*162	609	128	198	36	7	57	142	1	.325
2002 Arizona		N.L.	OF	148	524	90	151	19	3	28	103	9	.288
2003 Arizona		N.L.	OF	156	579	92	176	46	4	26	104	5	.304
2004 Arizona k		N.L.	OF	105	379	69	98	28	5	17	48	2	.259
2005 Arizona		N.L.	OF	155	579	90	157	37	0	24	79	4	.271
2006 Arizona l		N.L.	OF	153	586	93	159	52	2	15	73	0	.271
2007 Los Angeles m		N.L.	OF	139	464	70	129	23	2	15	68	6	.278
Major League Totals		18 Yrs.	2455	8816	1382	2502	570	67	346	1392	127	.284	
Division Series													
1997 Houston		N.L.	OF	3	12	0	4	0	0	0	0	0	.333
1999 Arizona		N.L.	OF	4	10	3	2	1	0	1	2	0	.200
2001 Arizona		N.L.	OF	5	19	1	5	0	0	1	1	0	.263
Division Series Totals				12	41	4	11	1	0	2	3	0	.268
Championship Series													
2001 Arizona		N.L.	OF	5	19	4	4	0	0	1	4	0	.211
World Series Record													
2001 Arizona		N.L.	OF	7	27	4	7	2	0	1	5	0	.259

70

a On disabled list from May 26 to July 5, 1989.
b On disabled list from August 29 to September 13, 1991.
c On disabled list from July 21 to August 5, 1992.
d Traded to Chicago Cubs with catcher Scott Servais for catcher Rick Wilkins, June 28, 1995.
e Was not offered contract by Chicago Cubs, December 20, 1995, re-signed with Chicago Cubs for 1996.
f Filed for free agency, October 28, 1996.
g Signed with Houston Astros, December 19, 1996.
h Filed for free agency, October 28, 1997.
i Signed with Detroit Tigers, December 9, 1997.
j Traded to Arizona Diamondbacks for outfielder Karim Garcia, December 28, 1998.
k On disabled list from August 2 to October 4, 2003.
l Filed for free agency, October 28, 2006. Signed with Los Angeles Dodgers, December 12, 2006.
m Filed for free agency, October 31, 2007.

GORDON, ALEX JONATHAN

Born, Lincoln, Nebraska, February 10, 1984.
Bats Left. Throws Right. Height, 6 feet, 1 inch. Weight, 220 pounds.

Year	Club	Lea	Pos	G	AB	R	H	2B	3B	HR	RBI	SB	Avg
2006 Wichita	Texas		3B-1B	130	486	111	158	39	1	29	101	22	.325
2007 Kansas City	A.L.		3B-1B-SS	151	543	60	134	36	4	15	60	14	.247

GOTAY, RUBEN BRUCE

Born, Rio Piedras, Puerto Rico, December 25, 1982.
Bats Both. Throws Right. Height, 5 feet, 11 inches. Weight, 160 pounds.

Year	Club	Lea	Pos	G	AB	R	H	2B	3B	HR	RBI	SB	Avg
2001 Royals	Gulf Coast		2B-3B	52	184	29	58	15	1	3	19	5	.315
2002 Burlington	Midwest		2B-3B	133	509	87	145	42	9	9	83	5	.285
2003 Wilmington	Carolina		2B	134	502	68	131	31	2	9	72	8	.261
2004 Wichita	Texas		2B	106	405	71	117	22	6	9	68	9	.289
2004 Kansas City	A.L.		2B	44	152	17	41	7	3	1	16	0	.270
2005 Kansas City	A.L.		2B	86	282	32	64	14	2	5	29	2	.227
2005 Wichita	Texas		2B	28	110	22	27	8	0	3	15	0	.245
2006 Norfolk	Int.		2B-3B-SS	42	154	19	41	12	1	3	21	4	.266
2006 Omaha a	P.C.		2B	87	337	45	89	16	2	9	43	7	.264
2007 New Orleans	P.C.		2B-SS-3B	23	82	12	21	7	1	2	13	1	.256
2007 New York	N.L.		2B-SS-3B	98	190	25	56	12	0	4	24	3	.295
Major League Totals			3 Yrs.	228	624	74	161	33	5	10	69	5	.258

a Traded to New York Mets for infielder Jeff Keppinger, July 19, 2006.

GRAFFANINO, ANTHONY JOSEPH (TONY)

Born, Amityville, New York, June 6, 1972.
Bats Right. Throws Right. Height, 6 feet, 1 inch. Weight, 190 pounds.

Year	Club	Lea	Pos	G	AB	R	H	2B	3B	HR	RBI	SB	Avg
1990 Pulaski	Appal.		SS	42	131	23	27	5	1	0	11	6	.206
1991 Idaho Falls	Pioneer		SS	66	274	53	95	16	4	4	56	19	.347
1992 Macon	So.Atl.		2B	112	400	50	96	15	5	10	31	9	.240
1993 Durham	Carolina		2B-SS	123	459	78	126	30	5	15	69	24	.275
1994 Greenville	Southern		2B	124	440	66	132	28	3	7	52	29	.300
1995 Richmond a	Int.		2B	50	179	20	34	6	0	4	17	2	.190
1996 Richmond	Int.		2B	96	353	57	100	29	2	7	33	11	.283
1996 Atlanta	N.L.		2B	22	46	7	8	1	1	0	2	0	.174
1997 Atlanta	N.L.		2B-3B-SS-1B	104	186	33	48	9	1	8	20	6	.258
1998 Atlanta	N.L.		2B-SS-3B	105	289	32	61	14	1	5	22	1	.211
1999 Durham	Int.		2B	87	345	66	108	25	6	9	58	16	.313
1999 Tampa Bay b	A.L.		2B-SS-3B	39	130	20	41	9	4	2	19	3	.315
2000 Durham	Int.		SS	10	35	9	10	3	0	2	6	2	.286
2000 Tampa Bay-Chicago c	A.L.		2B-SS-3B	70	168	33	46	6	1	2	17	7	.274
2001 Chicago	A.L.		3B-2B-SS-OF	74	145	23	44	9	0	2	15	4	.303
2002 Chicago d	A.L.		3B-2B-SS	70	229	35	60	12	4	6	31	2	.262
2003 Chicago e	A.L.		SS-2B-3B-1B	90	250	51	65	15	3	7	23	8	.260
2004 Omaha	P.C.		2B	4	14	2	3	0	0	1	2	0	.214
2004 Kansas City f	A.L.		2B	75	278	37	73	11	0	3	26	10	.263
2005 Kansas City-Boston g-h	A.L.		2B-1B-3B-SS	110	379	68	117	17	3	7	38	7	.309
2006 Kansas City	A.L.		3B-1B-2B-SS	69	220	34	59	16	0	5	32	3	.268
2006 Milwaukee i-j-k	N.L.		2B-SS	60	236	34	66	17	3	2	27	2	.280
2007 Milwaukee l-m	N.L.		2B-3B-1B-OF	86	231	34	55	8	0	9	30	0	.238
Major League Totals			12 Yrs.	974	2787	441	743	144	21	58	302	53	.267

Year	Club	Lea	Pos	G	AB	R	H	2B	3B	HR	RBI	SB	Avg
Division Series													
1997 Atlanta		N.L.	2B	3	3	0	0	0	0	0	0	0	.000
1998 Atlanta		N.L.	PH	1	0	0	0	0	0	0	0	0	.000
2000 Chicago		A.L.	3B	1	0	0	0	0	0	0	0	0	.000
2005 Boston		A.L.	2B	3	12	0	3	2	0	0	0	0	.250
Division Series Totals				8	15	0	3	2	0	0	0	0	.200
Championship Series													
1997 Atlanta		N.L.	2B	3	8	1	2	1	0	0	0	0	.250
1998 Atlanta		N.L.	2B	4	3	2	1	1	0	0	1	0	.333
Championship Series Totals				7	11	3	3	2	0	0	1	0	.273

a On disabled list from July 3 to September 1, 1995.
b Released by Atlanta Braves, March 31, 1999. Signed with Tampa Bay Devil Rays organization, April 9, 1999.
c Traded to Chicago White Sox for pitcher Tanyon Sturtze, May 31, 2000.
d On disabled list from August 26 to September 30, 2002.
e Filed for free agency, October 27, 2003. Signed with Kansas City Royals, December 14, 2003.
f On disabled list from May 1 to May 28 and from August 1 to November 1, 2004.
g Traded to Boston Red Sox for outfielder Chip Ambres and pitcher Juan Cedeno, July 19, 2005.
h Filed for free agency, October 28, 2005. Accepted arbitration to be to return to Boston Red Sox, December 19, 2005.
i Claimed on waivers by Kansas City Royals, March 28, 2006.
j Traded to Milwaukee Brewers for pitcher Jorge De La Rosa, July 25, 2006.
k Filed for free agency, October 29, 2006. Accepted arbitration to return to Milwaukee, December 7, 2006.
l On disabled list from August 9 to October 9, 2007.
m Filed for free agency, October 30, 2007.

GRANDERSON, CURTIS
Born, Blue Island, Illinois, March 16, 1981.
Bats Left. Throws Right. Height, 6 feet, 1 inch. Weight, 185 pounds.

Year	Club	Lea	Pos	G	AB	R	H	2B	3B	HR	RBI	SB	Avg
2002 Oneonta	N.Y.-Penn.		OF	52	212	45	73	15	4	3	34	9	.344
2003 Lakeland	Fla.St.		OF	127	476	71	136	29	10	11	51	10	.286
2004 Erie	Eastern		OF	123	462	89	139	19	8	21	94	14	.301
2004 Detroit	A.L.		OF	9	25	2	6	1	1	0	0	0	.240
2005 Toledo	Int.		OF	111	445	79	129	29	13	15	65	22	.290
2005 Detroit	A.L.		OF	47	162	18	44	6	3	8	20	1	.272
2006 Detroit	A.L.		OF	159	596	90	155	31	9	19	68	8	.260
2007 Detroit	A.L.		OF	158	612	122	185	38	*23	23	74	26	.302
Major League Totals			4 Yrs.	373	1395	232	390	76	36	50	162	35	.280
Division Series													
2006 Detroit	A.L.		OF	4	17	3	5	0	1	2	5	1	.294
Championship Series													
2006 Detroit	A.L.		OF	4	15	4	5	2	0	1	2	1	.333
World Series Record													
2006 Detroit	A.L.		OF	5	21	1	2	1	0	0	0	0	.095

GREEN, SHAWN DAVID
Born, Des Plaines, Illinois, November 10, 1972.
Bats Left. Throws Left. Height, 6 feet, 4 inches. Weight, 210 pounds.

Year	Club	Lea	Pos	G	AB	R	H	2B	3B	HR	RBI	SB	Avg
1992 Dunedin	Fla. St.		OF	114	417	44	114	21	3	1	49	22	.273
1993 Knoxville	Southern		OF	99	360	40	102	14	2	4	34	4	.283
1993 Toronto	A.L.		OF	3	6	0	0	0	0	0	0	0	.000
1994 Syracuse	Int.		OF	109	433	82	149	27	3	13	61	19	*.344
1994 Toronto	A.L.		OF	14	33	1	3	1	0	0	1	1	.091
1995 Toronto	A.L.		OF	121	379	52	109	31	4	15	54	1	.288
1996 Toronto	A.L.		OF	132	422	52	118	32	3	11	45	5	.280
1997 Toronto	A.L.		OF	135	429	57	123	22	4	16	53	14	.287
1998 Toronto	A.L.		OF	158	630	106	175	33	4	35	100	35	.278
1999 Toronto a	A.L.		OF	153	614	134	190	*45	0	42	123	20	.309
2000 Los Angeles	N.L.		OF	*162	610	98	164	44	4	24	99	24	.269
2001 Los Angeles	N.L.		OF-1B	161	619	121	184	31	4	49	125	20	.297
2002 Los Angeles	N.L.		OF	158	582	110	166	31	1	42	114	8	.285
2003 Los Angeles	N.L.		OF	160	611	84	171	49	2	19	85	6	.280
2004 Los Angeles b	N.L.		1B-OF	157	590	92	157	28	1	28	86	5	.266
2005 Arizona	N.L.		OF	158	581	87	166	37	4	22	73	8	.286
2006 Arizona-New York c	N.L.		OF-1B	149	530	73	147	31	3	15	66	4	.277
2007 New York d-e	N.L.		OF-1B	130	446	62	130	30	1	10	46	11	.291
Major League Totals			15 Yrs.	1951	7082	1129	2003	445	35	328	1070	162	.283

72

Year	Club	Lea	Pos	G	AB	R	H	2B	3B	HR	RBI	SB	Avg
Division Series													
2004 Los Angeles	N.L.		1B	4	16	3	4	0	0	3	3	0	.250
2006 New York	N.L.		OF	2	9	1	3	2	0	0	2	0	.333
Division Series Totals				6	25	4	7	2	0	3	5	0	.280
Championship Series													
2006 New York	N.L.		OF	7	23	2	7	1	0	0	2	1	.304

a Traded to Los Angeles Dodgers with infielder Jorge Nunez for outfielder Raul Mondesi and pitcher Pedro Borbon, November 8, 1999.
b Traded to Arizona Diamondbacks for catcher Dioner Navarro, pitcher Danny Muegge, pitcher Beltran Perez and pitcher William Juarez, January 11, 2005.
c Traded to New York Mets for pitcher Evan MacLane, August 22, 2006.
d On disabled list from May 26 to June 11, 2007.
e Filed for free agency, October 29, 2007.

GREENE, KHALIL TABIT

Born, Butler, Pennsylvania, October 21, 1979.
Bats Right. Throws Right. Height, 5 feet, 11 inches. Weight, 195 pounds.

Year	Club	Lea	Pos	G	AB	R	H	2B	3B	HR	RBI	SB	Avg
2002 Eugene	Northwest		SS	10	37	5	10	1	0	0	6	0	.270
2002 Lake Elsinore	California		SS-2B-3B	46	183	33	58	9	1	9	32	0	.317
2003 Mobile	Southern		SS	59	229	20	63	17	2	3	20	2	.275
2003 Portland	P.C.		SS	76	319	42	92	19	0	10	47	5	.288
2003 San Diego	N.L.		SS	20	65	8	14	4	1	2	6	0	.215
2004 San Diego	N.L.		SS	139	484	67	132	31	4	15	65	4	.273
2005 Lake Elsinore	California		SS	4	12	4	6	1	0	0	3	0	.500
2005 San Diego a	N.L.		SS	121	436	51	109	30	2	15	70	5	.250
2006 San Diego b	N.L.		SS	121	412	56	101	26	2	15	55	5	.245
2007 San Diego	N.L.		SS	153	611	89	155	44	3	27	97	4	.254
Major League Totals			5 Yrs.	554	2008	271	511	135	12	74	293	18	.254
Division Series													
2005 San Diego	N.L.		SS	3	10	2	4	2	0	0	1	0	.400
2006 San Diego	N.L.		SS	3	4	0	0	0	0	0	0	0	.000
Division Series Totals				6	14	2	4	2	0	0	1	0	.286

a On disabled list from April 17 to May 9 and August 15 to August 30, 2005.
b On disabled list from August 18 to September 3, 2006.

GRIFFEY, GEORGE KENNETH, JR. (KEN)

Born, Donora, Pennsylvania, November 21, 1969.
Bats Left. Throws Left. Height, 6 feet, 3 inches. Weight, 220 pounds.

Year	Club	Lea	Pos	G	AB	R	H	2B	3B	HR	RBI	SB	Avg
1987 Bellingham	Northwest		OF	54	182	43	57	9	1	14	40	13	.313
1988 San Bernardino a	California		OF	58	219	50	74	13	3	11	42	32	.338
1988 Vermont	Eastern		OF	17	61	10	17	5	1	2	10	4	.279
1989 Seattle b	A.L.		OF	127	455	61	120	23	0	16	61	16	.264
1990 Seattle	A.L.		OF	155	597	91	179	28	7	22	80	16	.300
1991 Seattle	A.L.		OF	154	548	76	179	42	1	22	100	18	.327
1992 Seattle c	A.L.		OF	142	565	83	174	39	4	27	103	10	.308
1993 Seattle	A.L.		OF-1B	156	582	113	180	38	3	45	109	17	.309
1994 Seattle	A.L.		OF	111	433	94	140	24	4	*40	90	11	.323
1995 Tacoma	P.C.		DH	1	3	0	0	0	0	0	0	0	.000
1995 Seattle d	A.L.		OF	72	260	52	67	7	0	17	42	4	.258
1996 Seattle e	A.L.		OF	140	545	*125	165	26	2	49	140	16	.303
1997 Seattle f	A.L.		OF	157	608	*125	185	34	3	*56	*147	15	.304
1998 Seattle	A.L.		OF-1B	161	633	120	180	33	3	*56	146	20	.284
1999 Seattle	A.L.		OF	160	606	123	173	26	3	*48	134	24	.285
2000 Cincinnati g	N.L.		OF	145	520	100	141	22	3	40	118	6	.271
2001 Cincinnati h	N.L.		OF	111	364	57	104	20	2	22	65	2	.286
2002 Cincinnati i	N.L.		OF	70	197	17	52	8	0	8	23	1	.264
2003 Cincinnati j	N.L.		OF	53	166	34	41	12	1	13	26	1	.247
2004 Cincinnati k	N.L.		OF	83	300	49	76	18	0	20	60	1	.253
2005 Cincinnati	N.L.		OF	128	491	85	148	30	0	35	92	0	.301
2006 Cincinnati l	N.L.		OF	109	428	62	108	19	0	27	72	0	.252
2007 Cincinnati	N.L.		OF	144	528	78	146	24	1	30	93	6	.277
Major League Totals			19 Yrs.	2378	8826	1545	2558	473	37	593	1701	184	.290
Division Series													
1995 Seattle	A.L.		OF	5	23	9	9	0	0	5	7	1	.391

Year	Club	Lea	Pos	G	AB	R	H	2B	3B	HR	RBI	SB	Avg
1997 Seattle	A.L.	OF	4	15	0	2	0	0	0	2	2	.133
Division Series Totals			9	38	9	11	0	0	5	9 *	3	.289
Championship Series												
1995 Seattle	A.L.	OF	6	21	2	7	2	0	1	2	2	.333

a On disabled list from June 9 to August 15, 1988.
b On disabled list from July 24 to August 20, 1989.
c On disabled list from June 9 to June 25, 1992.
d On disabled list from May 27 to August 15, 1995.
e On disabled list from June 20 to July 13, 1996.
f Selected Most Valuable Player in American League for 1997.
g Traded to Cincinnati Reds for pitcher Brett Tomko, outfielder Mike Cameron, infielder Antonio Perez and pitcher Jake Meyer, February 10, 2000.
h On disabled list from April 29 to June 15, 2001.
i On disabled list from April 8 to May 24 and June 24 to July 22, 2002.
j On disabled list from April 6 to May 13 and July 18 to November 5, 2003.
k On disabled list from July 11 to August 3 and from August 12 to November 2, 2004.
l On disabled list from April 13 to May 11, 2006.

GROSS, GABRIEL JORDAN (GABE)

Born, Baltimore, Maryland, October 21, 1979.
Bats Left. Throws Right. Height, 6 feet, 3 inches. Weight, 210 pounds.

Year	Club	Lea	Pos	G	AB	R	H	2B	3B	HR	RBI	SB	Avg
2001 Dunedin	.Fla.St.	OF	35	126	23	38	9	2	4	15	4	.302
2001 Tennessee	Southern	OF	11	41	8	10	1	0	3	11	0	.244
2002 Tennessee	Southern	OF	112	403	57	96	17	5	10	54	8	.238
2003 New Haven	.Eastern	OF	84	310	52	99	23	3	7	51	3	.319
2003 Syracuse	Int.	OF	53	182	22	48	16	2	5	23	1	.264
2004 Syracuse	Int.	OF	103	377	52	111	29	2	9	54	4	.294
2004 Toronto	A.L.	OF	44	129	18	27	4	0	3	16	2	.209
2005 Syracuse	Int.	OF	102	390	64	116	29	4	6	46	14	.297
2005 Toronto a	A.L.	OF	40	92	11	23	4	1	1	7	1	.250
2006 Milwaukee	N.L.	OF	117	208	42	57	15	0	9	38	1	.274
2007 Nashville	.P.C.	OF	20	76	13	27	3	2	4	10	2	.355
2007 Milwaukee	N.L.	OF	93	183	28	43	12	2	7	24	3	.235
Major League Totals		4 Yrs.	294	612	99	150	35	3	20	85	7	.245

a Traded to Milwaukee Brewers with pitcher Dave Bush and pitcher Zach Jackson for infielder Lyle Overbay and pitcher Ty Taubenheim, December 7, 2005.

GRUDZIELANEK, MARK JAMES

Born, Milwaukee, Wisconsin, June 30, 1970.
Bats Right. Throws Right. Height, 6 feet, 1 inch. Weight, 190 pounds.

Year	Club	Lea	Pos	G	AB	R	H	2B	3B	HR	RBI	SB	Avg
1991 Jamestown......	N.Y.-Penn.	SS	72	275	44	72	9	3	2	32	14	.262
1992 Rockford	Midwest	SS	128	496	64	122	12	5	5	54	25	.246
1993 West Palm Beach...	. Fla. St.	2B-SS-OF	86	300	41	80	11	6	1	34	17	.267
1994 Harrisburg	.Eastern	SS-3B	122	488	92	157	37	3	11	66	32	.322
1995 Ottawa	Int.	SS	49	181	26	54	9	1	1	22	12	.298
1995 Montreal.............	N.L.	SS-3B-2B	78	269	27	66	12	2	1	20	8	.245
1996 Montreal.............	N.L.	SS	153	657	99	201	34	4	6	49	33	.306
1997 Montreal.............	N.L.	SS	156	*649	76	177	*54	3	4	51	25	.273
1998 Montreal-Los Angeles a .	N.L.	SS	156	589	62	160	21	1	10	62	18	.272
1999 San Bernardino ...	California	SS	4	16	2	4	0	0	0	0	0	.250
1999 Los Angeles b	N.L.	SS	123	488	72	159	23	5	7	46	6	.326
2000 Los Angeles	N.L.	2B-SS	148	617	101	172	35	6	7	49	12	.279
2001 Los Angeles c	N.L.	2B	133	539	83	146	21	3	13	55	4	.271
2002 Los Angeles d	N.L.	2B	150	536	56	145	23	0	9	50	4	.271
2003 Iowa.................	.P.C.	2B	2	10	1	5	0	0	0	1	0	.500
2003 Chicago e-f..........	N.L.	2B	121	481	73	151	38	1	3	38	6	.314
2004 Iowa.................	.P.C.	2B	8	28	6	7	3	0	2	4	0	.250
2004 Chicago g-h...........	N.L.	2B	81	257	32	79	12	1	6	23	1	.307
2005 St. Louis i...........	N.L.	2B	137	528	64	155	30	3	8	59	8	.294
2006 Kansas City	A.L.	2B-SS	134	548	85	163	32	4	7	52	3	.297
2007 Kansas City j	A.L.	2B-SS	116	453	70	137	32	3	6	51	1	.302
Major League Totals		13 Yrs.	1686	6611	900	1911	367	36	87	605	129	.289
Division Series												
2003 Chicago	N.L.	2B	5	20	2	3	0	0	0	0	0	.150
2005 St. Louis.............	N.L.	2B	3	13	2	2	0	0	0	0	0	.154

Year	Club	Lea	Pos	G	AB	R	H	2B	3B	HR	RBI	SB	Avg
Division Series Totals				8	33	4	5	0	0	0	0	0	.152
Championship Series													
2003 Chicago	N.L.		2B	7	30	2	6	1	1	0	3	0	.200
2005 St. Louis.............	N.L.		2B	6	22	2	5	0	0	0	2	0	.227
Championship Series Totals				13	52	4	11	1	1	0	5	0	.212

a Traded to Los Angeles Dodgers with outfielder Hiram Bocachica and pitcher Carlos Perez for infielder Wilton Guerrero, outfielder Peter Bergeron, pitcher Ted Lilly and infielder Jonathan Tucker, July 31, 1998

b On disabled list from June 3 to July 6, 1999.

c On disabled list from June 12 to June 28, 2001.

d Traded to Chicago Cubs with infielder Eric Karros for catcher Todd Hundley and outfielder Chad Hermansen, December 4, 2002.

e On disabled list from August 3 to September 2, 2003.

f Filed for free agency, October 29, 2003, re-signed with Chicago Cubs, December 7, 2003.

g On disabled list from April 10 to June 19, 2004.

h Filed for free agency, October 28, 2004. Signed with St. Louis Cardinals, January 5, 2005.

i Filed for free agency, October 27, 2005. Signed with Kansas City Royals, December 16, 2005.

j On disabled list from June 13 to July 5, 2007.

GUERRERO, VLADIMIR NIZAO

Born, Nizao, Dominican Republic, February 9, 1976.
Bats Right. Throws Right. Height, 6 feet, 3 inches. Weight, 235 pounds.

Year	Club	Lea	Pos	G	AB	R	H	2B	3B	HR	RBI	SB	Avg
1994 Montreal.............	DSL			25	92	34	39	11	0	12	35	5	.424
1994 Expos..........	Gulf Coast		OF	37	137	24	43	13	3	5	25	0	.314
1995 Albany	So.Atl.		OF	110	421	77	140	21	10	16	63	12	.333
1996 Wst Plm Bch	Fla.St.		OF	20	80	16	29	8	0	5	18	2	.363
1996 Harrisburg	Eastern		OF	118	417	84	150	32	8	19	78	17	.360
1996 Montreal.............	N.L.		OF	9	27	2	5	0	0	1	1	0	.185
1997 Wst. Plm. Bch	Fla. St.		OF	3	10	0	4	2	0	0	2	1	.400
1997 Montreal a	N.L.		OF	90	325	44	98	22	2	11	40	3	.302
1998 Montreal.............	N.L.		OF	159	623	108	202	37	7	38	109	11	.324
1999 Montreal.............	N.L.		OF	160	610	102	193	37	5	42	131	14	.316
2000 Montreal.............	N.L.		OF	154	571	101	197	28	11	44	123	9	.345
2001 Montreal.............	N.L.		OF	159	599	107	184	45	4	34	108	37	.307
2002 Montreal.............	N.L.		OF	161	614	106	*206	37	2	39	111	40	.336
2003 Brevard County	Fla.St.		OF	3	6	2	3	0	0	1	1	0	.500
2003 Montreal b-c	N.L.		OF	112	394	71	130	20	3	25	79	9	.330
2004 Anaheim d	A.L.		OF	156	612	*124	206	39	2	39	126	15	.337
2005 Los Angeles e........	A.L.		OF	141	520	95	165	29	2	32	108	13	.317
2006 Los Angeles.........	A.L.		OF	156	607	92	200	34	1	33	116	15	.329
2007 Los Angeles.........	A.L.		OF	150	574	89	186	45	1	27	125	2	.324
Major League Totals		12 Yrs.	1607	6076	1041	1972	373	40	365	1177	168	.325	
Division Series													
2004 Anaheim.............	A.L.		OF	3	12	1	2	0	0	1	6	0	.167
2005 Los Angeles.........	A.L.		OF	5	18	5	6	0	0	0	0	1	.333
2007 Los Angeles.........	A.L.		OF-DH	3	10	0	2	0	0	0	0	0	.200
Division Series Totals				11	40	6	10	0	0	1	6	1	.250
Championship Series													
2005 Los Angeles.........	A.L.		OF-DH	5	20	0	1	0	0	0	1	0	.050

a On disabled list from April 1 to May 2 and June 6 to June 21 and July 12 to July 27, 1997.

b On disabled list from June 5 to July 21, 2003.

c Filed for free agency, October 27, 2003. Signed with Anaheim Angels, January 12, 2004.

d Selected Most Valuable Player in American League for 2004.

e On disabled list from May 21 to June 10, 2005.

GUILLEN, CARLOS ALFONSO

Born, Maracay, Venezuela, September 30, 1975.
Bats Both. Throws Right. Height, 6 feet, 1 inch. Weight, 215 pounds.

Year	Club	Lea	Pos	G	AB	R	H	2B	3B	HR	RBI	SB	Avg
1993 Houston a ....Domincan			SS	18	56	12	14	4	2	0	8	0	.250
1994				INJURED—Did Not Play									
1995 Astros .... Gulf Coast			DH	30	105	17	31	4	2	2	15	17	.295
1996 Quad City b .... Midwest			SS	29	112	23	37	7	1	3	17	13	.330
1997 Jackson .... Texas			SS	115	390	47	99	16	1	10	39	6	.254
1997 New Orleans .... A.A.			SS	3	13	3	4	1	0	0	0	0	.308
1998 New Orleans.......... P.C.			SS	100	374	67	109	18	4	12	51	3	.291

Year Club	Lea	Pos	G	AB	R	H	2B	3B	HR	RBI	SB	Avg
1998 Tacoma .............P.C.		2B	24	92	8	21	1	1	1	4	1	.228
1998 Seattle c-d .... A.L.		2B	10	39	9	13	1	1	0	5	2	.333
1999 Seattle e .... A.L.		SS-2B	5	19	2	3	0	0	1	3	0	.158
2000 Tacoma .............P.C.		3B	24	87	19	26	4	1	2	11	4	.299
2000 Seattle f .... A.L.		3B-SS	90	288	45	74	15	2	7	42	1	.257
2001 Seattle .... A.L.		SS	140	456	72	118	21	4	5	53	4	.259
2002 Seattle .... A.L.		SS	134	475	73	124	24	6	9	56	4	.261
2003 Tacoma .............P.C.		3B	4	14	2	5	1	0	2	4	0	.357
2003 Seattle g-h .... A.L.		SS-3B	109	388	63	107	19	3	7	52	4	.276
2004 Detroit .... A.L.		SS	136	522	97	166	37	10	20	97	12	.318
2004 Anaheim .... A.L.		OF	148	565	88	166	28	3	27	104	5	.294
2005 Detroit i .... A.L.		SS	87	334	48	107	15	4	5	23	2	.320
2006 Detroit .... A.L.		SS-1B	153	543	100	174	41	5	19	85	20	.320
2007 Detroit .... A.L.		SS-1B	151	564	86	167	35	9	21	102	13	.296
Major League Totals			10 Yrs.	1015	3628	595	1053	208	44	94	518	62	.290
Division Series												
2000 Seattle .... A.L.		PH	1	1	0	1	0	0	0	1	0	1.000
2006 Detroit .... A.L.		SS	4	14	3	8	3	0	1	2	0	.571
Division Series Totals			5	15	3	9	3	0	1	3	0	.600
Championship Series												
2000 Seattle .... A.L.		3B	2	5	1	1	0	0	1	2	0	.200
2001 Seattle .... A.L.		SS	3	8	1	2	0	0	0	0	0	.250
2006 Detroit .... A.L.		1B-SS	4	16	1	3	1	0	0	0	0	.188
Championship Series Totals			9	29	3	6	1	0	1	2	0	.207
World Series Record												
2006 Detroit .... A.L.		SS-1B	5	17	2	6	1	1	0	2	1	.353

a On disabled list from June 1 to September 12, 1994.
b On disabled list from May 21 to September 11, 1996.
c Traded by Houston Astros to Seattle Mariners with pitcher Freddy Garcia and player to be named later for pitcher Randy Johnson, July 31, 1998.
d Seattle Mariners received pitcher John Halama to complete trade, October 1, 1998.
e On disabled list from April 11 to November 12, 1999.
f On disabled list from April 13 to April 27, 2000.
g On disabled list from July 29 to August 23, 2003.
h Traded to Detroit Tigers for infielder Ramon Santiago and infielder Juan Gonzalez, January 8, 2004.
i On disabled list from June 8 to June 26 and August 11 to September 23, 2005.

GUILLEN, JOSE MANUEL

Born, San Cristobal, Dominican Republic, May 17, 1976.
Bats Right. Throws Right. Height, 5 feet, 11 inches. Weight, 195 pounds.

Year Club	Lea	Pos	G	AB	R	H	2B	3B	HR	RBI	SB	Avg
1993 Pittsburgh ...... Dominican		OF	63	234	39	53	3	4	11	31	10	.226
1994 Pirates .... Gulf Coast		OF	30	110	17	29	4	1	4	11	2	.264
1995 Erie .... N.Y.-Penn.		OF	66	258	41	81	17	1	12	46	1	.314
1995 Augusta .... So.Atl.		OF	10	34	6	8	1	1	2	6	0	.235
1996 Lynchburg .... Carolina		OF	136	528	78	170	30	0	21	94	24	.322
1997 Pittsburgh .... N.L.		OF	143	498	58	133	20	5	14	70	1	.267
1998 Pittsburgh .... N.L.		OF	153	573	60	153	38	2	14	84	3	.267
1999 Pittsburgh .... N.L.		OF	40	120	18	32	6	0	1	18	1	.267
1999 Nashville .............P.C.		OF	35	132	28	44	10	0	5	22	0	.333
1999 Durham .... Int.		OF	9	34	8	13	1	0	3	12	0	.382
1999 Tampa Bay a-b .... A.L.		OF	47	168	24	41	10	0	2	13	0	.244
2000 Tampa Bay .... Int.		OF	19	78	20	33	8	2	9	31	0	.423
2000 Tampa Bay c .... A.L.		OF	105	316	40	80	16	5	10	41	3	.253
2001 Durham .... Int.		OF	33	119	18	35	9	0	7	29	0	.294
2001 Tampa Bay d-e-f .... A.L.		OF	41	135	14	37	5	0	3	11	2	.274
2002 Colorado Springs .......P.C.		OF	5	17	2	7	3	0	0	5	0	.412
2002 Louisville .... Int.		OF	8	29	4	9	4	0	2	8	0	.310
2002 Arizona-Cincinnati g .... N.L.		OF	85	240	25	57	7	0	8	31	4	.237
2003 Louisville .... Int.		OF	4	15	4	5	1	0	0	3	1	.333
2003 Cincinnati .... N.L.		OF	91	315	52	106	21	1	23	63	1	.337
2003 Oakland h-i .... A.L.		OF	45	170	25	45	7	1	8	23	0	.265
2004 Anaheim j .... A.L.		OF	148	565	88	166	28	3	27	104	5	.294
2005 Washington .... N.L.		OF	148	551	81	156	32	2	24	76	1	.283
2006 Potomac .... Carolina		OF	3	6	2	3	0	0	2	3	0	.500
2006 Washington k-l .... N.L.		OF	69	241	28	52	15	1	9	40	1	.216
2007 Seattle m .... A.L.		OF	153	593	84	172	28	2	23	99	5	.290
Major League Totals			11 Yrs.	1268	4485	597	1230	233	22	166	673	27	.274

Year	Club	Lea	Pos	G	AB	R	H	2B	3B	HR	RBI	SB	Avg
Division Series													
2003 Oakland	A.L.		OF	4	11	1	5	1	0	0	1	0	.455

a Traded to Tampa Bay Devil Rays with pitcher Jeff Sparks for catcher Joe Oliver and catcher Humberto Cota, July 23, 1999.
b On disabled list from July 23 to 30, 1999.
c On disabled list from March 28 to April 11, 2000.
d On disabled list from May 18 to June 24 and June 25 to July 30, 2001.
e On disabled list from August 7 to 24, 2001.
f Released by Tampa Bay Devil Rays, November 27, 2001. Signed with Arizona Diamondbacks, December 12, 2001.
g Released by Arizona Diamondbacks, July 22, 2002. Signed with Cincinnati Reds organization, July 26, 2002.
h Traded to Oakland Athletics for pitcher Aaron Harang, pitcher Joe Valentine and pitcher Jeff Bruksch, July 30, 2003.
i Filed for free agency, October 30, 2003. Signed with Anaheim Angels, December 19, 2003.
j Traded to Washington Nationals for outfielder Juan Rivera and infielder Maicer Izturis, November 19, 2004.
k On disabled list from May 26 to June 10 and July 19 to October 9, 2006.
l Filed for free agency, October 29, 2006. Signed with Seattle Mariners, December 4, 2006.
m Filed for free agency, November 12, 2007. Signed with Kansas City Royals, December 6, 2007.

GUTIERREZ, FRANKLIN RAFAEL

Born, Caracas, Venezuela, February 21, 1983.
Bats Right. Throws Right. Height, 6 feet, 2 inches. Weight, 180 pounds.

Year	Club	Lea	Pos	G	AB	R	H	2B	3B	HR	RBI	SB	Avg
2001 Dodgers........	Gulf Coast	OF	56	234	38	63	16	0	4	30	9	.269
2002 Las Vegas.............	P.C.	OF	2	10	2	3	2	0	0	2	0	.300
2002 South Bend	So.Atl.	OF	92	361	61	102	18	4	12	45	13	.283
2003 Vero Beach.........	Fla.St.	OF	110	425	65	120	28	5	20	68	17	.282
2003 Jacksonville	Southern	OF	18	67	12	21	3	2	4	12	3	.313
2004 Akron	Eastern	OF	70	262	38	79	24	2	5	35	6	.302
2004 Buffalo a.............	Int.	DH	7	27	4	4	1	0	1	3	0	.148
2005 Akron	Eastern	OF	95	383	70	100	25	2	11	42	14	.261
2005 Buffalo	Int.	OF	19	67	10	17	6	2	0	7	2	.254
2005 Cleveland	A.L.	OF	7	1	2	0	0	0	0	0	0	.000
2006 Buffalo	Int.	OF	90	349	63	97	27	0	9	38	13	.278
2006 Cleveland	A.L.	OF	43	136	21	37	9	0	1	8	0	.272
2007 Buffalo	Int.	OF	30	129	29	44	7	0	4	16	7	.341
2007 Cleveland b	A.L.	OF	100	271	41	72	13	2	13	36	8	.266
Major League Totals	3 Yrs.	150	408	64	109	22	2	14	44	8	.267		
Division Series													
2007 Cleveland	A.L.	OF	4	10	2	2	0	0	0	0	0	.200
Championship Series													
2007 Cleveland	A.L.	OF	6	19	3	4	0	0	1	4	0	.211

a Traded to Cleveland Indians with player to be named later for outfielder Milton Bradley, April 4, 2004. Cleveland Indians received pitcher Andrew Brown to complete trade, May 19, 2004.
b On disabled list from March 23 to April 13, 2007.

GUZMAN, CRISTIAN

Born, Santo Domingo, Dominican Republic, March 21, 1978.
Bats Both. Throws Right. Height, 6 feet. Weight, 195 pounds.

Year	Club	Lea	Pos	G	AB	R	H	2B	3B	HR	RBI	SB	Avg
1995 Yankees	Dominican	SS	46	160	24	43	6	5	3	20	11	.269
1996 Yankees	Gulf Coast	SS	42	170	37	50	8	2	1	21	7	.294
1997 Tampa	Fla.St.	SS	4	14	4	4	0	0	0	1	0	.286
1997 Greensboro	So.Atl.	SS	124	495	68	135	21	4	4	52	23	.273
1998 New Britain a	Eastern	SS	140	566	68	157	29	5	1	40	23	.277
1999 Minnesota b.........	A.L.	SS	131	420	47	95	12	3	1	26	9	.226
2000 Minnesota	A.L.	SS	156	631	89	156	25	*20	8	54	28	.247
2001 Twins	Gulf Coast	SS	5	16	4	4	1	0	0	0	0	.250
2001 Minnesota c..........	A.L.	SS	118	493	80	149	28	*14	10	51	25	.302
2002 Minnesota	A.L.	SS	148	623	80	170	31	6	9	59	12	.273
2003 Minnesota	A.L.	SS	143	534	78	143	15	*14	3	53	18	.268
2004 Minnesota d..........	A.L.	SS	145	576	84	158	31	4	8	46	10	.274
2005 Washington	N.L.	SS	142	456	39	100	19	6	4	31	7	.219
2006 Washington e.........	N.L.			INJURED — Did Not Play									
2007 Washington f.........	N.L.	SS	46	174	31	57	6	6	2	14	2	.328
Major League Totals	8 Yrs.	1029	3907	528	1028	167	73	45	334	111	.263		
Division Series													
2002 Minnesota	A.L.	SS	5	21	5	6	2	0	1	2	2	.286

Year	Club	Lea	Pos	G	AB	R	H	2B	3B	HR	RBI	SB	Avg
2003 Minnesota	A.L.		SS	4	13	1	2	0	0	0	0	0	.154
2004 Minnesota	A.L.		SS	4	15	2	5	0	0	0	0	1	.333
Division Series Totals				13	49	8	13	2	0	1	2	3	.265
Championship Series													
2002 Minnesota	A.L.		SS	5	18	1	3	1	0	0	0	0	.167

a Traded by New York Yankees to Minnesota Twins with pitcher Eric Milton, pitcher Danny Mota, outfielder Brian Buchanan and cash for infielder Chuck Knoblauch, February 6, 1998.
b On disabled list from May 27 to June 11, 1999.
c On disabled list from July 13 to August 17, 2001.
d Filed for free agency, October 29, 2004. Signed with Washington Nationals, November 16, 2004.
e On disabled list from March 24 to October 9, 2006.
f On disabled list from April 3 to May 7 and June 25 to September 21, 2007.

GWYNN, ANTHONY KEITH JR. (TONY)
Born, Long Beach, California, October 4, 1982.
Bats Left. Throws Right. Height, 6 feet. Weight, 185 pounds.

Year	Club	Lea	Pos	G	AB	R	H	2B	3B	HR	RBI	SB	Avg
2003 Beloit	Midwest		OF	61	236	35	66	8	0	1	33	14	.280
2004 Huntsville........	Southern		OF	138	534	74	130	20	5	2	37	35	.243
2005 Huntsville........	Southern		OF	133	509	83	138	21	5	1	41	34	.271
2006 Nashville........	.P.C.		OF	112	447	73	134	21	5	4	42	30	.300
2006 Milwaukee	N.L.		OF	32	77	5	20	2	1	0	4	3	.260
2007 Nashville	.P.C.		OF	32	126	19	36	3	3	0	13	4	.286
2007 Milwaukee	N.L.		OF	69	123	13	32	3	2	0	10	8	.260
Major League Totals	2 Yrs.			101	200	18	52	5	3	0	14	11	.260

HAFNER, TRAVIS LEE
Born, Jamestown, North Dakota, June 3, 1977.
Bats Left. Throws Right. Height, 6 feet, 3 inches. Weight, 240 pounds.

Year	Club	Lea	Pos	G	AB	R	H	2B	3B	HR	RBI	SB	Avg
1997 Rangers	Gulf Coast		1B-OF	55	189	38	54	14	0	5	24	7	.286
1998 Savannah..........	So.Atl.		1B-3B-OF	123	405	62	96	15	4	16	84	7	.237
1999 Savannah..........	So.Atl.		1B	134	480	94	140	30	4	28	111	5	.292
2000 Charlotte a	Fla.St.		1B-3B	122	436	90	151	34	1	22	109	0	.346
2001 Tulsa b	Texas		1B	88	323	59	91	25	0	20	74	3	.282
2002 Oklahoma.............	.P.C.		1B	110	401	79	137	22	1	21	77	2	.342
2002 Texas c.............	A.L.		DH-1B	23	62	6	15	4	1	1	6	0	.242
2003 Buffalo	Int.		1B	29	100	15	27	4	0	2	10	2	.270
2003 Cleveland d	A.L.		DH-1B	91	291	35	74	19	3	14	40	2	.254
2004 Cleveland	A.L.		DH-1B	140	482	96	150	41	3	28	109	3	.311
2005 Akron.............	Eastern		DH	3	9	0	0	0	0	0	0	0	.000
2005 Cleveland e...........	A.L.		DH-1B	137	486	94	148	42	0	33	108	0	.305
2006 Cleveland	A.L.		DH-1B	129	454	100	140	31	1	42	117	0	.308
2007 Cleveland	A.L.		DH-1B	152	545	80	145	25	2	24	100	1	.266
Major League Totals	6 Yrs.			672	2320	411	672	162	10	142	480	6	.290
Division Series													
2007 Cleveland	A.L.		DH	4	16	4	4	0	0	1	2	0	.250
Championship Series													
2007 Cleveland	A.L.		DH	7	27	2	4	1	0	1	2	0	.148

a On disabled list from August 6 to 22, 2000.
b On disabled list from April 5 to May 11, 2001.
c Traded to Cleveland Indians with pitcher Aaron Myette for catcher Einar Diaz and pitcher Ryan Drese, December 6, 2002.
d On disabled list from May 10 to May 26, 2003.
e On disabled list from July 17 to August 4, 2005.

HAIRSTON, JERRY WAYNE JR.
Born, Naperville, Illinois, May 29, 1976.
Bats Right. Throws Right. Height, 5 feet, 10 inches. Weight, 185 pounds.

Year	Club	Lea	Pos	G	AB	R	H	2B	3B	HR	RBI	SB	Avg
1997 Bluefield........	Appal.		SS	59	221	44	73	13	4	2	36	13	.330
1998 Frederick	Carolina		SS-2B	80	293	56	83	22	3	5	33	13	.283
1998 Bowie.........	Eastern		2B-SS	55	221	42	72	12	3	5	37	6	.326
1998 Baltimore	A.L.		2B	6	7	2	0	0	0	0	0	0	.000
1999 Rochester.........	Int.		2B	107	413	65	120	24	5	7	48	19	.291
1999 Baltimore	A.L.		2B	50	175	26	47	12	1	4	17	9	.269

78

Year Club	Lea	Pos	G	AB	R	H	2B	3B	HR	RBI	SB	Avg
2000 Rochester.........	Int.	2B-SS	58	201	43	59	15	1	4	21	6	.294
2000 Orioles......Gulf Coast		2B	4	10	3	3	2	0	0	3	4	.300
2000 Frederick.....	Carolina	2B	2	8	1	3	2	0	0	1	0	.375
2000 Baltimore a.......	A.L.	2B	49	180	27	46	5	0	5	19	8	.256
2001 Baltimore.........	A.L.	2B	159	532	63	124	25	5	8	47	29	.233
2002 Baltimore.........	A.L.	2B	122	426	55	114	25	3	5	32	21	.268
2003 Aberdeen....	N.Y.-Penn.	2B	2	3	2	1	0	0	0	0	1	.333
2003 Bowie.........	Eastern	2B	6	20	4	6	1	0	1	2	0	.300
2003 Baltimore b.......	A.L.	2B	58	218	25	59	12	2	2	21	14	.271
2004 Bowie.........	Eastern	2B	5	13	4	2	1	0	0	2	2	.154
2004 Baltimore c.......	A.L.	OF-2B-3B	86	287	43	87	19	1	2	24	13	.303
2005 Iowa.............	P.C.	2B-OF	5	22	3	7	0	1	0	2	3	.318
2005 Chicago d-e.......	N.L.	OF-2B-SS	114	380	51*	99	25	2	4	30	8	.261
2006 Chicago..........	N.L.	2B-OF-1B	38	82	8	17	3	0	0	4	3	.207
2006 Texas f-g.........	A.L.	OF-2B-SS-3B	63	88	17	18	3	1	0	6	2	.205
2007 Frisco........	Texas	DH	3	12	2	2	1	0	1	2	0	.167
2007 Oklahoma........	P.C.	SS-OF	4	15	2	2	0	0	1	1	0	.133
2007 Texas h-i.......	A.L.	OF-2B-3B-SS	73	159	22	30	7	0	3	16	5	.189
Major League Totals	10 Yrs.		818	2534	339	641	136	15	33	216	112	.253

a On disabled list from May 16 to July 4, 2000.
b On disabled list from May 21 to September 4, 2003.
c On disabled list from March 31 to May 11 and from August 18 to November 3, 2004.
d Traded to Chicago Cubs with infielder Mike Fontenot and pitcher Dave Crouthers for outfielder Sammy Sosa, February 2, 2005.
e On disabled list from August 4 to August 19, 2005.
f Traded to Texas Rangers for infielder Phil Nevin, May 31, 2006.
g Filed for free agency, October 13, 2006. re-signed with Texas Rangers organization, January 5, 2007.
h On disabled list from May 17 to June 5 and August 8 to August 29, 2007.
i Filed for free agency, October 30, 2007.

HAIRSTON, SCOTT ALEXANDER

Born, Fort Worth, Texas, May 25, 1980.
Bats Right. Throws Right. Height, 6 feet. Weight, 190 pounds.

Year Club	Lea	Pos	G	AB	R	H	2B	3B	HR	RBI	SB	Avg
2001 Missoula	Pioneer	2B	74	291	81	101	16	6	14	65	2	.347
2002 Lancaster...........	Calif.	2B-3B	18	79	20	32	11	1	6	26	1	.405
2002 South Bend	Midwest	2B-3B	109	394	79	131	35	4	16	72	9	.332
2003 Tucson.............	P.C.	DH	1	0	0	0	0	0	0	1	0	.000
2003 El Paso...........	Texas	2B	88	337	53	93	21	7	10	47	6	.276
2004 Tucson.............	P.C.	2B-OF	28	115	29	36	8	3	5	20	0	.313
2004 Arizona............	N.L.	2D-OF	101	339	39	84	15	6	13	29	3	.248
2005 Arizona..........	N.L.	OF	15	20	0	2	1	0	0	0	0	.100
2005 Tucson a..........	P.C.	OF-2B	58	209	45	65	8	3	16	40	3	.311
2006 Tucson...........	P.C.	OF	98	381	83	123	22	1	26	81	3	.323
2006 Arizona b.......	N.L.	OF	9	15	2	6	2	0	0	2	0	.400
2007 Arizona-San Diego c-d ..	N.L.	OF	107	263	37	64	18	2	11	36	2	.243
Major League Totals	4 Yrs.		232	637	78	156	36	8	24	67	5	.245

a On disabled list from September 2 to November 14, 2005.
b On disabled list from June 20 to July 29, 2006.
c Traded to San Diego Padres for pitcher Leo Rosales, July 27, 2007.
d On disabled list from August 10 to September 8, 2007.

HALL, WILLIAM (BILL)

Born, Tupelo, Mississippi, December 28, 1979.
Bats Right. Throws Right. Height, 6 feet. Weight, 210 pounds.

Year Club	Lea	Pos	G	AB	R	H	2B	3B	HR	RBI	SB	Avg
1998 Helena	Pioneer	SS	29	85	11	15	3	0	0	5	5	.176
1999 Ogden	Pioneer	SS	69	280	41	81	15	2	6	31	19	.289
2000 Beloit	Midwest	SS	130	470	57	123	30	6	3	41	10	.262
2001 High Desert ..	California	SS	89	346	61	105	21	6	15	51	18	.303
2001 Huntsville.....	Southern	SS	41	160	14	41	8	1	3	14	5	.256
2002 Indianapolis ...	Int.	SS	134	465	35	106	20	1	4	31	17	.228
2002 Milwaukee	N.L.	SS-3B	19	36	3	7	1	1	1	5	0	.194
2003 Indianapolis	Int.	2B-SS-OF	89	354	57	100	25	2	5	32	10	.282
2003 Milwaukee	N.L.	2B-SS-3B	52	142	23	37	9	2	5	20	1	.261
2004 Milwaukee	N.L.	2B-SS-3B	126	390	43	93	20	3	9	53	12	.238
2005 Milwaukee	N.L.	SS-3B-2B	146	501	69	146	39	6	17	62	18	.291

79

Year	Club	Lea	Pos	G	AB	R	H	2B	3B	HR	RBI	SB	Avg
2006 Milwaukee	........N.L.	SS-3B-OF-2B	148	537	101	145	39	4	35	85	8	.270
2007 Azl Brewers	....Arizona	OF	2	6	0	1	0	0	0	2	0	.167
2007 Milwaukee a	.......N.L.	OF	136	452	59	115	35	0	14	63	4	.254
Major League Totals	6 Yrs.	627	2058	298	543	143	16	81	288	43	.264		

a On disabled list from July 6 to July 25, 2007.

HAMILTON, JOSHUA HOLT (JOSH)
Born, Raleigh, North Carolina, May 21, 1981.
Bats Left. Throws Left. Height, 6 feet, 4 inches. Weight, 235 pounds.

Year	Club	Lea	Pos	G	AB	R	H	2B	3B	HR	RBI	SB	Avg
1999 Princeton	..........Appal.	OF	56	236	49	82	20	4	10	48	17	.347
1999 Hudson Valley	... N.Y.-Penn.	OF	16	72	7	14	3	0	0	7	1	.194
2000 Charleston-SC	...... So.Atl.	OF	96	391	62	118	23	3	13	61	14	.302
2001 Charleston-SC	...... So.Atl.	OF	4	11	3	4	1	0	1	2	0	.364
2001 Orlando	.... Southern	OF	23	89	5	16	5	0	0	4	2	.180
2003	....					Did Not Play							
2002 Bakersfield	..........Calif.	OF	56	211	32	64	14	1	9	44	10	.303
2006 Hudson Valley a	.. N.Y.-Penn.	OF	15	50	7	13	3	1	0	5	0	.260
2007 Louisville	.... Int.	OF	11	40	9	14	1	0	4	8	3	.350
2007 Cincinnati b-c	.... N.L.	OF	90	298	52	87	17	2	19	47	3	.292

a Selected by Chicago Cubs from Tampa Bay Devil Rays in Rule V draft, December 7,2006. Sold to Cincinnati Reds, December 7, 2006.

b On disabled list from May 19 to June 4 and July 8 to August 12, 2007.

c Traded to Texas Rangers for pitcher Edinson Volquez and pitcher Danny Herrera, December 21, 2007.

HARDY, JAMES JERRY (J.J.)
Born, Tucson, Arizona, August 19, 1982.
Bats Right. Throws Right. Height, 6 feet, 2 inches. Weight, 190 pounds.

Year	Club	Lea	Pos	G	AB	R	H	2B	3B	HR	RBI	SB	Avg
2001 Brewers	..........Arizona	SS	5	20	6	5	2	1	0	1	0	.250
2001 Ogden	..........Pioneer	SS	35	125	20	31	5	0	2	15	1	.248
2002 High Desert	...... California	SS	84	335	53	98	19	1	6	48	9	.293
2002 Huntsville	.... Southern	SS	38	145	14	33	7	0	1	13	1	.228
2003 Huntsville	.... Southern	SS	114	416	67	116	26	0	12	62	6	.279
2004 Indianapolis	...........Int.	SS	26	101	17	28	10	0	4	20	0	.277
2005 Milwaukee	.... N.L.	SS	124	372	46	92	22	1	9	50	0	.247
2006 Milwaukee a	.... N.L.	SS	35	128	13	31	5	0	5	14	1	.242
2007 Milwaukee	.... N.L.	SS	151	592	89	164	30	1	26	80	2	.277
Major League Totals	3 Yrs.	310	1092	148	287	57	2	40	144	3	.263		

a On disabled list from May 17 to October 31, 2006.

HARRIS, BRENDAN MICHAEL
Born, Albany, New York, August 26, 1980.
Bats Right. Throws Right. Height, 6 feet, 1 inch. Weight, 200 pounds.

Year	Club	Lea	Pos	G	AB	R	H	2B	3B	HR	RBI	SB	Avg
2001 Lansing	...... Midwest	2B-3B-SS	32	113	25	31	5	1	4	22	5	.274
2002 Daytona	...... Fla.St.	3B-2B	110	425	82	140	35	6	13	54	16	.329
2002 West Tenn	....Southern	3B-2B	13	53	8	17	4	1	2	11	1	.321
2003 West Tenn	....Southern	3B-2B-SS	120	435	56	122	34	7	5	52	6	.280
2004 Iowa	..............P.C.	2B-SS-3B	69	254	48	79	21	1	11	35	0	.311
2004 Edmonton	........P.C.	3B	33	123	20	35	6	0	6	24	0	.285
2004 Chicago-Montreal a	.N.L.	2B-3B	23	59	4	10	3	0	1	3	0	.169
2005 Washington	.......N.L.	2B-3B	4	9	1	3	1	0	1	3	0	.333
2005 New Orleans	......P.C.	2B-3B-OF	127	470	67	127	22	4	13	81	9	.270
2006 Louisville	.... Int.	3B-2B-SS	43	148	22	48	14	1	5	28	2	.324
2006 New Orleans	......P.C.	3B-SS-2B-1B	59	219	37	62	14	0	5	32	3	.283
2006 Washington-Cincinnati b	N.L.	2B-SS-3B	25	42	5	10	2	0	1	3	0	.238
2007 Tampa Bay c-d	.....A.L.	SS-2B-3B	137	521	72	149	35	3	12	59	4	.286
Major League Totals	4 Yrs.	189	631	82	172	41	3	15	68	4	.273		

a Traded to Montreal Expos with infielder Alex Gonzalez and pitcher Francis Beltran for infielder Orlando Cabrera, July 31, 2004.

b Traded to Cincinnati Reds with pitcher Gary Majewski, pitcher Bill Bray, infielder Royce Clayton and pitcher Daryl Thompson for outfielder Austin Kearns, infielder Felipe Lopez and pitcher Ryan Wagner, July 13, 2006.

c Traded to Tampa Bay Devil Rays for player to be named later, January 2, 2007.

d Traded to Minnesota Twins with outfielder Jason Pridie and outfielder Delmon Young for infielder Jason Bartlett, pitcher Matt Garza and pitcher Eduardo Morlan, November 28, 2007.

HARRIS, WILLIAM CHARLES (WILLIE)

Born, Cairo, Georgia, June 22, 1978.
Bats Left. Throws Right. Height, 5 feet, 9 inches. Weight, 175 pounds.

Year	Club	Lea	Pos	G	AB	R	H	2B	3B	HR	RBI	SB	Avg
1999	Bluefield	Appal.	2B	5	22	3	6	1	0	0	3	1	.273
1999	Delmarva	So.Atl.	2B-OF	66	272	42	72	13	3	2	32	17	.265
2000	Delmarva	So.Atl.	2B-OF-SS	133	474	106	130	27	10	6	60	38	.274
2001	Bowie	Eastern	2B-OF	133	525	83	160	27	4	9	49	54	.305
2001	Baltimore	A.L.	OF	9	24	3	3	1	0	0	0	0	.125
2002	Charlotte	Int.	2B-OF	89	360	54	102	16	5	5	33	32	.283
2002	Chicago a	A.L.	2B-OF	49	163	14	38	4	0	2	12	8	.233
2003	Charlotte	Int.	2B-OF	28	100	22	38	6	1	6	13	9	.380
2003	Chicago b	A.L.	OF-2B	79	137	19	28	3	1	0	5	12	.204
2004	Chicago	A.L.	2B-OF	129	409	68	107	15	2	2	27	19	.262
2005	Charlotte	Int.	2B	28	109	21	29	11	1	1	10	10	.266
2005	Chicago	A.L.	2B-SS	56	121	17	31	2	1	1	8	10	.256
2006	Boston c-d	A.L.	OF-2B	47	45	17	7	2	0	0	1	6	.156
2006	Pawtucket	Int.	OF-2B	60	218	32	48	6	1	8	17	11	.220
2007	Richmond	Int.	3B-2B-OF	17	58	17	21	7	2	1	7	7	.362
2007	Atlanta e	N.L.	OF-3B	117	344	56	93	20	8	2	32	17	.270
Major League Totals			7 Yrs.	486	1243	194	307	47	12	7	85	72	.247
Division Series													
2005	Chicago	A.L.	2B	1	1	0	1	0	0	0	1	0	1.000
World Series Record													
2005	Chicago	A.L.	2B	2	1	1	1	0	0	0	0	1	1.000

a Traded to Chicago White Sox for outfielder Chris Singleton, January 29, 2002.
b On disabled list from May 22 to June 16, 2003.
c Not offered contract, December 21, 2005. Signed with Boston Red Sox organization, January 19, 2006.
d Filed for free agency, October 2, 2006. Signed with Atlanta Braves organization, December 9, 2006.
e Released by Atlanta Braves, December 12, 2007. Signed with Washington Nationals, December 13, 2007.

HART, JON COREY (COREY)

Born, Bowling Green, Kentucky, March 24, 1982.
Bats Right. Throws Right. Height, 6 feet, 6 inches. Weight, 215 pounds.

Year	Club	Lea	Pos	G	AB	R	H	2B	3B	HR	RBI	SB	Avg
2000	Ogden	Pioneer	1B	57	216	32	62	9	1	2	30	6	.287
2001	Ogden	Pioneer	1B-OF	69	262	53	89	18	1	11	62	14	.340
2002	High Desert	Calif.	3B-1B	100	393	76	113	26	10	22	84	24	.288
2002	Huntsville	Southern	3B-1B	28	94	16	25	3	0	2	15	3	.266
2003	Huntsville	Southern	3B-OF	130	493	70	149	40	1	13	94	25	.302
2004	Indianapolis	Int.	OF-1B	121	440	68	124	29	8	15	67	17	.282
2004	Milwaukee	N.L.	DH	1	1	0	0	0	0	0	0	0	.000
2005	Milwaukee	N.L.	OF	21	57	9	11	2	1	2	7	2	.193
2005	Nashville	P.C.	OF-1B	113	429	85	132	29	9	17	69	31	.308
2006	Milwaukee	N.L.	OF-1B	87	237	32	67	13	2	9	33	5	.283
2007	Milwaukee	N.L.	OF	140	505	86	149	33	9	24	81	23	.295
Major League Totals			4 Yrs.	249	800	127	227	48	12	35	121	30	.284

HATTEBERG, SCOTT ALLEN

Born, Salem, Oregon, December 14, 1969.
Bats Left. Throws Right. Height, 6 feet, 1 inch. Weight, 210 pounds.

Year	Club	Lea	Pos	G	AB	R	H	2B	3B	HR	RBI	SB	Avg
1991	Winter Havn	Fla. St.	C	56	191	21	53	7	3	1	25	1	.277
1991	Lynchburg	Carolina	C	8	25	4	5	1	0	0	2	0	.200
1992	New Britain	Eastern	C-1B	103	297	28	69	13	2	1	30	1	.232
1993	New Britain	Eastern	C	68	227	35	63	10	2	7	28	1	.278
1993	Pawtucket	Int.	C	18	53	6	10	0	0	1	2	0	.189
1994	New Britain	Eastern	C	20	68	6	18	4	1	1	9	0	.265
1994	Pawtucket	Int.	C	78	238	26	56	14	0	7	19	2	.235
1995	Pawtucket	Int.	C	85	251	36	68	15	1	7	27	2	.271
1995	Boston	A.L.	C	2	2	1	1	0	0	0	0	0	.500
1996	Pawtucket	Int.	C	90	287	52	77	16	0	12	49	1	.268
1996	Boston	A.L.	C	10	11	3	2	1	0	0	0	0	.182
1997	Boston	A.L.	C	114	350	46	97	23	1	10	44	0	.277
1998	Boston	A.L.	C	112	359	46	99	23	1	12	43	0	.276
1999	Sarasota	Fla.St.	C	1	1	0	1	0	0	0	1	0	1.000
1999	Pawtucket	Int.	C	10	34	3	6	2	0	0	4	0	.176
1999	GC Red Sox	Gulf Coast	C	6	15	4	6	2	0	1	6	0	.400

Year Club	Lea	Pos	G	AB	R	H	2B	3B	HR	RBI	SB	Avg
1999 Boston a.	A.L.	C	30	80	12	22	5	0	1	11	0	.275
2000 Boston	A.L.	C-3B	92	230	21	61	15	0	8	36	0	.265
2001 Boston b-c	A.L.	C	94	278	34	68	19	0	3	25	1	.245
2002 Oakland	A.L.	1B	136	492	58	138	22	4	15	61	0	.280
2003 Oakland	A.L.	1B	147	541	63	137	34	0	12	61	0	.253
2004 Oakland	A.L.	1B	152	550	87	156	30	0	15	82	0	.284
2005 Oakland d	A.L.	DH-1B	134	464	52	119	19	0	7	59	0	.256
2006 Cincinnati	N.L.	1B	141	456	62	132	28	0	13	51	2	.289
2007 Cincinnati	N.L.	1B	116	361	50	112	27	1	10	47	0	.310
Major League Totals	13 Yrs.		1280	4174	535	1144	246	7	106	520	3	.274
Division Series												
1998 Boston	A.L.	C	3	9	0	1	0	0	0	0	0	.111
1999 Boston	A.L.	C	1	1	1	1	0	0	0	1	0	1.000
2002 Oakland	A.L.	1B	5	14	5	7	2	0	1	3	0	.500
2003 Oakland	A.L.	1B	5	17	3	3	0	0	0	0	0	.176
Division Series Totals			14	41	9	12	2	0	1	4	0	.293
Championship Series												
1999 Boston	A.L.	C	3	1	0	0	0	0	0	0	0	.000

a On disabled list from April 16 to May 7 and May 17 to August 16, 1999.
b Traded to Colorado Rockies for infielder Pokey Reese, December 18, 2001.
c Not offered contract, December 21, 2001. Signed with Oakland Athletics, December 30, 2001.
d Filed for free agency, November 1, 2005. Signed with Cincinnati Reds, February 12, 2006.

HAWPE, BRADLEY BONTE (BRAD)

Born, Fort Worth, Texas, June 22, 1979.
Bats Left. Throws Left. Height, 6 feet, 3 inches. Weight, 205 pounds.

Year Club	Lea	Pos	G	AB	R	H	2B	3B	HR	RBI	SB	Avg
2000 Portland	Northwest	OF-1B	62	205	38	59	19	2	7	29	2	.288
2001 Asheville	So.Atl.	OF-1B	111	393	78	105	22	3	22	72	7	.267
2002 Salem	Carolina	1B	122	450	87	156	38	2	22	97	1	.347
2003 Tulsa	Texas	OF-1B	93	346	52	96	27	0	17	68	1	.277
2004 Colorado Springs	P.C.	OF	92	345	62	111	19	1	31	86	3	.322
2004 Colorado	N.L.	OF	42	105	12	26	3	2	3	9	1	.248
2005 Colorado Springs	P.C.	OF	7	28	7	13	3	0	3	11	0	.464
2005 Colorado a	N.L.	OF	101	305	38	80	10	3	9	47	2	.262
2006 Colorado	N.L.	OF	150	499	67	146	33	6	22	84	5	.293
2007 Colorado	N.L.	OF	152	516	80	150	33	4	29	116	0	.291
Major League Totals	4 Yrs.		445	1425	197	402	79	15	63	256	8	.282
Division Series												
2007 Colorado	N.L.	OF	3	11	1	3	0	0	0	0	0	.273
Championship Series												
2007 Colorado	N.L.	OF	4	12	2	4	0	0	0	2	0	.333
World Series Record												
2007 Colorado	N.L.	OF	4	16	1	4	0	1	1	2	0	.250

a On disabled list from July 12 to September 2, 2005.

HAYNES, NATHAN RAYMOND QUINN

Born, Oakland, California, September 7, 1979.
Bats Left. Throws Left. Height, 5 feet, 9 inches. Weight, 180 pounds.

Year Club	Lea	Pos	G	AB	R	H	2B	3B	HR	RBI	SB	Avg
1997 Athletics	Arizona	OF	17	54	8	15	1	0	0	6	5	.278
1997 Sou Oregon	Northwest	OF	24	82	18	23	1	1	0	9	19	.280
1998 Modesto	Calif.	OF	125	507	89	128	13	7	1	41	42	.252
1999 Visalia a	Calif.	OF	35	145	28	45	7	1	1	14	12	.310
1999 Lake Elsinore	Calif.	OF	26	110	19	36	5	5	1	15	10	.327
1999 Erie	Eastern	OF	5	19	3	3	1	0	0	0	0	.158
2000 Erie	Eastern	OF	118	457	56	116	16	4	6	43	37	.254
2001 Arkansas	Texas	OF	79	316	49	98	11	5	5	23	33	.310
2002 Rancho Cucamonga	Calif.	OF	11	50	6	14	0	0	0	2	6	.280
2002 Salt Lake	P.C.	OF	67	283	37	80	14	6	2	12	10	.283
2003 Salt Lake	P.C.	OF	28	120	16	26	3	3	1	7	6	.217
2003 Arkansas b	Texas	OF	91	372	59	110	16	10	5	42	27	.296
2004 Fresno	P.C.	OF	1	4	1	1	0	1	0	0	1	.250
2005 Giants c	Arizona	OF	7	16	4	4	1	2	0	1	3	.250
2006 Gary	Northern	OF	31	114	24	30	4	1	5	17	8	.263
2006 Salt Lake	P.C.	OF	16	57	7	13	1	2	1	11	3	.228

Year	Club	Lea	Pos	G	AB	R	H	2B	3B	HR	RBI	SB	Avg
2006 Arkansas d	Texas	OF	52	207	38	58	14	3	2	19	18	.280
2007 Salt Lake	P.C.	OF	44	171	33	66	9	6	4	32	14	.386
2007 Los Angeles	A.L.	OF	40	45	10	12	0	1	0	1	1	.267
Division Series													
2007 Los Angeles	A.L.	PH	1	1	0	0	0	0	0	0	0	.000

a Traded to Anaheim Angels by Oakland Athletics with pitcher Elvin Nina and outfielder Jeff DaVanon for pitcher Omar Olivares and infielder Randy Velarde, July 29, 1999.

b Filed for free agency, October 15, 2003. Signed with San Francisco Giants organization, December 19, 2003.

c Filed for free agency, October 28, 2005. Signed with Gary, Northern (Independent). Signed with Los Angeles Angels organization, June 22, 2006.

d Filed for free agency, October 15, 2006, re-signed with Los Angeles Angels organization, January 4, 2007.

HELMS, WESLEY RAY (WES)
Born, Gastonia, North Carolina, May 12, 1976.
Bats Right. Throws Right. Height, 6 feet, 4 inches. Weight, 230 pounds.

Year	Club	Lea	Pos	G	AB	R	H	2B	3B	HR	RBI	SB	Avg
1994 Braves	Gulf Coast	3B	56	184	22	49	15	1	4	29	6	.266
1995 Macon	So.Atl.	3B	136	539	89	149	32	1	11	85	2	.276
1996 Durham	Carolina	3B	67	258	40	83	19	2	13	54	1	.322
1996 Greenville	Southern	3B	64	231	24	59	13	2	4	22	2	.255
1997 Richmond	Int.	3B	32	110	11	21	4	0	3	15	1	.191
1997 Greenville	Southern	3B	86	314	50	93	14	1	11	44	3	.296
1998 Richmond	Int.	3B	125	451	56	124	27	1	13	75	6	.275
1998 Atlanta	N.L.	3B	7	13	2	4	1	0	1	2	0	.308
1999 Braves	Gulf Coast	DH	9	33	1	15	2	0	0	10	0	.455
1999 Greenville a-b	Southern	1B	30	113	15	34	6	0	8	26	1	.301
2000 Richmond	Int.	3B	136	539	74	155	27	7	20	88	0	.288
2000 Atlanta	N.L.	3B	6	5	0	1	0	0	0	0	0	.200
2001 Atlanta	N.L.	1B-3B-OF	100	216	28	48	10	3	10	36	1	.222
2002 Atlanta c-d	N.L.	1B-3B-OF	85	210	20	51	16	0	6	22	1	.243
2003 Indianapolis	Int.	3B	2	5	0	2	0	0	0	0	0	.400
2003 Milwaukee e	N.L.	3B	134	476	56	124	21	0	23	67	0	.261
2004 Indianapolis	Int.	3B	6	19	4	6	1	0	0	1	0	.316
2004 Milwaukee f	N.L.	3B-1B	92	274	24	72	13	1	4	28	0	.263
2005 Milwaukee g	N.L.	3B-1B	95	168	18	50	13	1	4	24	0	.298
2006 Florida h	N.L.	1B-3B-OF	140	240	30	79	19	5	10	47	0	.329
2007 Philadelphia	N.L.	3B-1B	112	280	21	69	19	0	5	39	0	.246
Major League Totals		9 Yrs.	771	1882	199	498	112	10	63	265	2	.265
Division Series													
2002 Atlanta	N.L.	1B	1	0	0	0	0	0	0	0	0	.000
2007 Philadelphia	N.L.	3B	2	2	1	0	0	0	0	0	0	.000
Division Series Totals			3	2	1	0	0	0	0	0	0	.000

a On Atlanta disabled list from April 3 to July 15 and September 4 to November 1, 1999.

b On Greenville disabled list from August 15 to September 4, 1999.

c On disabled list from August 10 to September 10, 2002.

d Traded to Milwaukee Brewers with pitcher John Foster for pitcher Ray King, December 16, 2002.

e On disabled list from August 6 to August 22, 2003.

f On disabled list from May 19 to June 28, 2004.

g Filed for free agency, October 27, 2005. Signed with Florida Marlins, December 30, 2005.

h Filed for free agency, October 28, 2006. Signed with Philadelphia Phillies, November 17, 2006.

HELTON, TODD LYNN
Born, Knoxville, Tennessee, August 20, 1973.
Bats Left. Throws Left. Height, 6 feet, 2 inches. Weight, 210 pounds.

Year	Club	Lea	Pos	G	AB	R	H	2B	3B	HR	RBI	SB	Avg
1995 Asheville	So. Atl.	1B	54	201	24	51	11	1	1	15	1	.254
1996 New Haven	Eastern	1B	93	319	46	106	24	2	7	51	2	.332
1996 Colo Sprngs	P.C.	1B-OF	21	71	13	25	4	1	2	13	0	.352
1997 Colo Sprngs	P.C.	1B-OF	99	392	87	138	31	2	16	88	3	.352
1997 Colorado	N.L.	OF-1B	35	93	13	26	2	1	5	11	0	.280
1998 Colorado	N.L.	1B	152	530	78	167	37	1	25	97	3	.315
1999 Colorado	N.L.	1B	159	578	114	185	39	5	35	113	7	.320
2000 Colorado	N.L.	1B	160	580	138	*216	*59	2	42	*147	5	*.372
2001 Colorado	N.L.	1B	159	587	132	197	54	2	49	146	7	.336
2002 Colorado	N.L.	1B	156	553	107	182	39	4	30	109	5	.329
2003 Colorado	N.L.	1B	160	583	135	209	49	5	33	117	0	.358
2004 Colorado	N.L.	1B	154	547	115	190	49	2	32	96	3	.347

Year	Club	Lea	Pos	G	AB	R	H	2B	3B	HR	RBI	SB	Avg
2005	Colo Sprngs	P.C.	2B	2	5	1	3	2	0	0	1	0	.600
2005	Colorado a	N.L.	1B	144	509	92	163	45	2	20	79	3	.320
2006	Colorado Springs	P.C.	1B	2	6	0	2	0	0	0	0	0	.333
2006	Colorado b	N.L.	1B	145	546	94	165	40	5	15	81	3	.302
2007	Colorado	N.L.	1B	154	557	86	178	42	2	17	91	0	.320
Major League Totals			11 Yrs.	1578	5663	1104	1878	455	31	303	1087	36	.332
Division Series													
2007	Colorado	N.L.	1B	3	12	1	1	0	1	0	0	0	.083
Championship Series													
2007	Colorado	N.L.	1B	4	14	3	3	0	0	0	1	0	.214
World Series Record													
2007	Colorado	N.L.	1B	4	15	2	5	2	0	0	1	0	.333

a On disabled list from July 26 to August 10, 2005.
b On disabled list from April 20 to May 5, 2006.

HERMIDA, JEREMY RYAN

Born, Atlanta, Georgia, January 30, 1984.
Bats Left. Throws Right. Height, 6 feet, 3 inches. Weight, 210 pounds.

Year	Club	Lea	Pos	G	AB	R	H	2B	3B	HR	RBI	SB	Avg
2002	Marlins	Gulf Coast	OF	38	134	15	30	7	3	0	14	5	.224
2002	Jamestown	N.Y.-Penn.	OF	13	47	8	15	2	1	0	7	1	.319
2003	Albuquerque	P.C.	OF	1	3	0	0	0	0	0	0	0	.000
2003	Greensboro	So.Atl.	OF	133	468	73	133	23	5	6	49	28	.284
2004	Jupiter	Fla.St.	OF	91	340	53	101	17	1	10	50	10	.297
2005	Carolina	Southern	OF	118	386	77	113	29	2	18	63	23	.293
2005	Florida	N.L.	OF	23	41	9	12	2	0	4	11	2	.293
2006	Jupiter	Fla.St.	OF	6	17	3	3	1	0	0	2	0	.176
2006	Florida a	N.L.	OF	99	307	37	77	19	1	5	28	4	.251
2007	Jupiter	Fla.St.	OF	3	12	4	4	0	1	2	5	0	.333
2007	Albuquerque	P.C.	OF	2	5	0	1	0	0	0	2	0	.200
2007	Florida b	N.L.	OF	123	429	54	127	32	1	18	63	3	.296
Major League Totals			3 Yrs.	245	777	100	216	53	2	27	102	9	.278

a On disabled list from April 12 to May 22, 2006.
b On disabled list from March 23 to May 14, 2007.

HERNANDEZ (MARIN), RAMON JOSE

Born, Caracas, Venezuela, May 20, 1976.
Bats Right. Throws Right. Height, 6 feet. Weight, 225 pounds.

Year	Club	Lea	Pos	G	AB	R	H	2B	3B	HR	RBI	SB	Avg
1994	Oakland	Dominican	C	42	134	24	33	2	0	2	18	1	.246
1995	Athletics	Arizona	C-1B-3B	48	143	37	52	9	6	4	37	6	.364
1996	W Michigan	Midwest	C-1B	123	447	62	114	26	2	12	68	2	.255
1997	Visalia	California	C-1B	86	332	57	120	21	2	15	85	2	.361
1997	Huntsville	Southern	C-1B-3B	44	161	27	31	3	0	4	24	0	.193
1998	Huntsville	Southern	DH-C-1B	127	479	83	142	24	1	15	98	4	.296
1999	Vancouver	P.C.	C	77	291	38	76	11	3	13	55	1	.261
1999	Oakland a	A.L.	C	40	136	13	38	7	0	3	21	1	.279
2000	Oakland	A.L.	C	143	419	52	101	19	0	14	62	1	.241
2001	Oakland	A.L.	C-1B	136	453	55	115	25	0	15	60	1	.254
2002	Oakland b	A.L.	C	136	403	51	94	20	0	7	42	0	.233
2003	Oakland	A.L.	C	140	483	70	132	24	1	21	78	0	.273
2004	Portland	P.C.	C	7	19	2	6	1	0	0	6	0	.316
2004	San Diego c	N.L.	C	111	384	45	106	23	0	18	63	1	.276
2005	San Diego d-e	N.L.	C	99	369	36	107	19	2	12	58	1	.290
2006	Indians	Gulf Coast	OF	47	164	22	42	4	0	0	13	16	.256
2006	Baltimore	A.L.	C-1B	144	501	66	138	29	2	23	91	1	.275
2007	Aberdeen	N.Y.-Penn.	C	2	4	2	2	1	0	0	0	1	.500
2007	Frederick	Carolina	C	2	6	0	2	1	0	0	0	0	.333
2007	Baltimore f	A.L.	C-1B	106	364	40	94	18	0	9	62	1	.258
Major League Totals			9 Yrs.	1055	3512	428	925	184	5	122	537	7	.263
Division Series													
2000	Oakland	A.L.	C	5	16	3	6	2	0	0	3	0	.375
2001	Oakland	A.L.	C	5	10	0	0	0	0	0	0	0	.000
2002	Oakland	A.L.	C	5	17	0	1	0	0	0	0	0	.059
2003	Oakland	A.L.	C	4	15	1	3	0	0	0	2	0	.200
2005	San Diego	N.L.	C	3	11	2	5	0	0	1	1	0	.455
Division Series Totals				22	69	6	15	2	0	1	6	0	.217

a On disabled list from July 26 to August 27, 1999.
b Traded to San Diego Padres with outfielder Terrence Long for outfielder Mark Kotsay, November 26, 2003.
c On disabled list from June 21 to July 26, 2004.
d On disabled list from June 18 to July and July 25 to September 2, 2005.
e Filed for free agency, October 27, 2005. Signed with Baltimore Orioles, December 13, 2005.
f On disabled list from March 31 to April 26 and June 7 to June 22, 2007.

HILL, AARON WALTER

Born, Visalia, California, March 21, 1982.
Bats Right. Throws Right. Height, 5 feet, 11 inches. Weight, 195 pounds.

Year	Club	Lea	Pos	G	AB	R	H	2B	3B	HR	RBI	SB	Avg
2003	Dunedin	Fla.St.	SS	32	119	26	34	7	0	0	11	1	.286
2003	Auburn	N.Y.-Penn.	SS	33	122	22	44	4	0	4	34	1	.361
2004	New Hampshire	Eastern	SS	135	479	78	134	26	2	11	80	3	.280
2005	Syracuse	Int.	SS	38	156	22	47	11	0	5	18	2	.301
2005	Toronto	A.L.	3B-2B-SS	105	361	49	99	25	3	3	40	2	.274
2006	Toronto	A.L.	2B-SS	155	546	70	159	28	3	6	50	5	.291
2007	Toronto	A.L.	2B	160	608	87	177	47	2	17	78	4	.291
Major League Totals			3 Yrs.	420	1515	206	435	100	8	26	168	11	.287

HILLENBRAND, SHEA MATTHEW

Born, Mesa, Arizona, July 27, 1975.
Bats Right. Throws Right. Height, 6 feet, 1 inch. Weight, 210 pounds.

Year	Club	Lea	Pos	G	AB	R	H	2B	3B	HR	RBI	SB	AVG
1996	Lowell	N.Y.-Penn.	1B-SS-3B	72	279	33	88	18	2	2	38	4	.315
1997	Michigan	Midwest	DH-1B-3B	64	224	28	65	13	3	3	39	1	.290
1997	Sarasota	Fla.St.	3B-1B	57	220	25	65	12	0	2	28	9	.295
1998	Michigan	Midwest	C-1B-3B	129	498	80	174	33	4	19	93	13	.349
1999	Trenton a-b.	Eastern	C	69	282	41	73	15	0	7	36	6	.259
2000	Trenton	Eastern	1B-3B	135	529	77	171	35	3	11	79	3	.323
2001	Boston	A.L.	3B-1B	139	468	52	123	20	2	12	49	3	.263
2002	Boston	A.L.	3B	156	634	94	186	43	4	18	83	4	.293
2003	Boston	A.L.	3B-1B	49	185	20	56	17	0	3	38	1	.303
2003	Tucson	P.C.	1B-3B	3	10	0	3	1	0	0	1	0	.300
2003	Arizona c-d.	N.L.	1B-3B	85	330	40	88	18	1	17	59	0	.267
2004	Arizona e	N.L.	1B-3B	148	562	68	174	36	3	15	80	2	.310
2005	Toronto	A.L.	1B-3B	152	594	91	173	36	2	18	82	5	.291
2006	Toronto	A.L.	DH-1B-3B	81	296	40	89	15	1	12	39	1	.301
2006	San Francisco f-g	N.L.	1B-3B	60	234	33	58	12	0	9	29	0	.248
2007	Las Vegas	P.C.	1B-3B	3	13	3	7	1	0	1	4	0	.538
2007	Portland	P.C.	3B	9	34	2	5	1	0	0	1	0	.147
2007	Los Angeles	A.L.	DH-1B	53	197	19	50	5	0	3	22	0	.254
2007	Los Angeles h-i-j	N.L.	3B-1B	20	70	6	17	0	2	1	9	0	.243
Major League Totals			7 Yrs.	943	3570	463	1014	202	15	108	490	16	.284

a On Trenton disabled list from July 5 to August 31, 1999.
b On Boston disabled list from August 31 to October 5, 1999.
c Traded to Arizona Diamondbacks for pitcher Byung-Hyun Kim, May 29, 2003.
d On disabled list from June 9 to June 29, 2003.
e Traded to Toronto Blue Jays for pitcher Adam Peterson, January 12, 2005.
f Traded to San Francisco Giants with pitcher Vinnie Chulk for pitcher Jeremy Accardo, July 21, 2006.
g Filed for free agency, October 38, 2006. Signed with Los Angeles Angels, December 26, 2006.
h Released by Los Angeles Angels, July 9, 2007. Signed with San Diego Padres organization, July 27, 2007.
i Released by San Diego Padres, August 7, 2007. Signed with Los Angeles Dodgers organization, August 11, 2007.
j Filed for free agency, October 12, 2007.

HINSKE, ERIC SCOTT

Born, Menasha, Wisconsin, August 5, 1977.
Bats Left. Throws Right. Height, 6 feet, 2 inches. Weight, 235 pounds.

Year	Club	Lea	Pos	G	AB	R	H	2B	3B	HR	RBI	SB	Avg
1998	Williamsprt.	N.Y.-Penn.	1B	68	248	46	74	20	0	9	57	19	.298
1998	Rockford	Midwest	1B-OF	6	20	8	9	4	0	1	4	1	.450
1999	Daytona	Fla.St.	3B	130	445	76	132	28	6	19	79	16	.297
1999	Iowa	P.C.	1B	4	15	3	4	0	1	1	2	0	.267
2000	West Tenn	Southern	3B-1B-OF	131	436	76	113	21	9	20	73	14	.259
2001	Sacramento a-b-c	P.C.	3B-2B	121	436	71	123	27	1	25	79	20	.282
2002	Toronto d	A.L.	3B	151	566	99	158	38	2	24	84	13	.279
2003	Syracuse	Int.	3B	2	8	2	4	1	0	1	2	0	.500

Year	Club	Lea	Pos	G	AB	R	H	2B	3B	HR	RBI	SB	Avg
2003 Toronto e	. . . . A.L.		3B	124	449	74	109	45	3	12	63	12	.243
2004 Toronto	. . . . A.L.		3B	155	570	66	140	23	3	15	69	12	.246
2005 Toronto	. . . . A.L.		1B	147	477	79	125	31	2	15	68	8	.262
2006 Toronto-Boston f	. . . . . . A.L.		OF-1B-3B	109	277	43	75	17	2	13	34	2	.271
2007 Boston g	. . . . A.L.		1B-OF	84	186	25	38	12	3	6	21	3	.204
Major League Totals	. . . .		6 Yrs.	770	2525	386	645	166	15	85	339	50	.255
Division Series													
2007 Boston	. . . . A.L.		PH	1	1	0	0	0	0	0	0	0	.000
Championship Series													
2007 Boston	. . . . A.L.		PH	1	0	1	0	0	0	0	0	0	.000
World Series Record													
2007 Boston	. . . . A.L.		PH	1	1	0	0	0	0	0	0	0	.000

a Traded by Chicago Cubs to Oakland A's for infielder Miguel Cairo, March 28, 2001.
b On disabled list from May 1 to 12, 2001.
c Traded by Oakland A's to Toronto Blue Jays with pitcher Justin Miller for pitcher Billy Koch, December 7, 2001.
d Selected Rookie of the Year in American League for 2002.
e On disabled list from May 2 to June 26, 2003.
f Traded to Boston Red Sox for player to be named later, August 17, 2006.
g Filed for free agency, October 30, 2007.

HOLLIDAY, MATTHEW THOMAS (MATT)
Born, Stillwater, Oklahoma, January 15, 1980.
Bats Right. Throws Right. Height, 6 feet, 4 inches. Weight, 235 pounds.

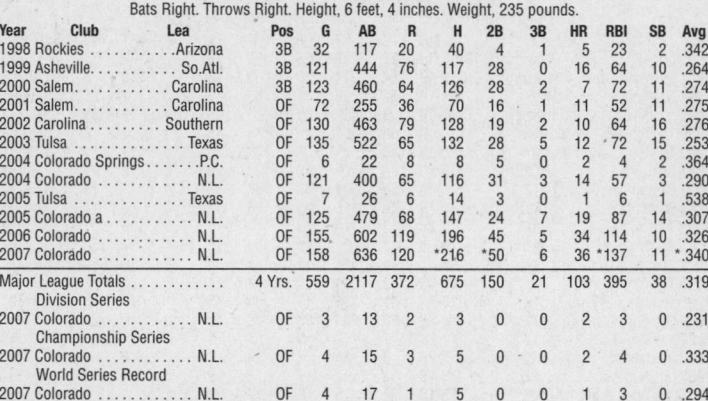

Year	Club	Lea	Pos	G	AB	R	H	2B	3B	HR	RBI	SB	Avg
1998 Rockies	. . . . .Arizona		3B	32	117	20	40	4	1	5	23	2	.342
1999 Asheville	. . . . So.Atl.		3B	121	444	76	117	28	0	16	64	10	.264
2000 Salem	. . . . Carolina		3B	123	460	64	126	28	2	7	72	11	.274
2001 Salem	. . . . Carolina		OF	72	255	36	70	16	1	11	52	11	.275
2002 Carolina	. . . . Southern		OF	130	463	79	128	19	2	10	64	16	.276
2003 Tulsa	. . . . Texas		OF	135	522	65	132	28	5	12	72	15	.253
2004 Colorado Springs	. . . . . . .P.C.		OF	6	22	8	8	5	0	2	4	2	.364
2004 Colorado	. . . . N.L.		OF	121	400	65	116	31	3	14	57	3	.290
2005 Tulsa	. . . . Texas		OF	7	26	6	14	3	0	1	6	1	.538
2005 Colorado a	. . . . N.L.		OF	125	479	68	147	24	7	19	87	14	.307
2006 Colorado	. . . . N.L.		OF	155	602	119	196	45	5	34	114	10	.326
2007 Colorado	. . . . N.L.		OF	158	636	120	*216	*50	6	36	*137	11	*.340
Major League Totals	. . . .		4 Yrs.	559	2117	372	675	150	21	103	395	38	.319
Division Series													
2007 Colorado	. . . . N.L.		OF	3	13	2	3	0	0	2	3	0	.231
Championship Series													
2007 Colorado	. . . . N.L.		OF	4	15	3	5	0	0	2	4	0	.333
World Series Record													
2007 Colorado	. . . . N.L.		OF	4	17	1	5	0	0	1	3	0	.294

a On disabled list from June 9 to July 19, 2005.

HOPPER, NORRIS STEPHEN
Born, Shelby, North Carolina, March 24, 1979.
Bats Right. Throws Right. Height, 5 feet, 10 inches. Weight, 200 pounds.

Year	Club	Lea	Pos	G	AB	R	H	2B	3B	HR	RBI	SB	Avg
1998 Royals	. . . . Gulf Coast		2B-SS	40	133	19	41	2	1	0	11	11	.308
1999 Royals	. . . . Gulf Coast		2B	46	179	33	46	3	2	0	13	22	.257
1999 Charleston-WV	. . . . . . So.Atl.		2B	5	22	3	11	0	2	0	2	1	.500
2000 Charleston-WV	. . . . . . So.Atl.		OF-2B	116	454	70	127	20	6	0	29	24	.280
2001 Wilmington	. . . . Carolina		OF-2B	110	389	38	96	6	2	1	38	16	.247
2002 Wilmington	. . . . Carolina		OF	125	514	78	140	12	3	1	46	22	.272
2003 Wichita	. . . . Texas		OF-2B	115	424	56	127	14	2	0	40	24	.300
2004 Wichita	. . . . Texas		OF-2B	98	363	48	101	5	3	0	40	17	.278
2005 Chattanooga a	. . . . . . Southern		OF-2B	116	451	70	140	15	4	1	37	25	.310
2006 Chattanooga	. . . . . . Southern		OF-2B	13	46	7	13	2	1	0	10	3	.283
2006 Louisville	. . . . Int.		OF-2B	98	383	47	133	11	3	0	26	25	.347
2006 Cincinnati	. . . . N.L.		OF	21	39	6	14	1	0	1	5	2	.359
2007 Sarasota	. . . . .Fla.St.		OF	4	17	1	5	0	0	0	2	0	.294
2007 Louisville	. . . . Int.		OF	4	15	2	4	0	0	0	1	2	.267
2007 Cincinnati b	. . . . N.L.		OF	121	307	51	101	14	2	0	14	14	.329
Major League Totals	. . . .		2 Yrs.	142	346	57	115	15	2	1	19	16	.332

a Filed for free agency, October 15, 2004. Signed with Cincinnati Reds organization, January 10, 2005.
b On disabled list from March 23 to April 18, 2007.

HOWARD, RYAN JAMES

Born, St. Louis, Missouri, November 19, 1979.
Bats Left. Throws Left. Height, 6 feet, 4 inches. Weight, 250 pounds.

Year	Club	Lea	Pos	G	AB	R	H	2B	3B	HR	RBI	SB	Avg
2001 Batavia	N.Y.-Penn.	1B	48	169	26	46	7	3	6	35	0	.272
2002 Lakewood	So.Atl.	1B	135	493	56	138	20	6	19	87	5	.280
2003 Clearwater	Fla.St.	1B	130	490	67	149	32	1	23	82	0	.304
2004 Reading	Eastern	1B	102	374	73	111	18	1	37	102	1	.297
2004 Scranton/W.B.	Int.	1B	29	111	21	30	10	0	9	29	0	.270
2004 Philadelphia	N.L.	1B	19	39	5	11	5	0	2	5	0	.282
2005 Scranton/WB	Int.	1B	61	210	38	78	19	0	16	54	0	.371
2005 Philadelphia a	N.L.	1B	88	312	52	90	17	2	22	63	0	.288
2006 Philadelphia b	N.L.	1B	159	581	104	182	25	1	*58	*149	0	.313
2007 Lakewood	So.Atl.	1B	2	6	1	2	1	0	1	4	0	.333
2007 Philadelphia c	N.L.	1B	144	529	94	142	26	0	47	136	1	.268
Major League Totals		4 Yrs.	410	1461	255	425	73	3	129	353	1	.291
Division Series												
2007 Philadelphia	N.L.	1B	3	12	1	3	0	0	1	1	0	.250

a Selected Rookie of the Year in National League for 2005.
b Selected Most Valuable Player in National League for 2006.
c On disabled list from May 10 to May 25, 2007.

HUDSON, ORLANDO THILL

Born, Darlington, South Carolina, December 12, 1977.
Bats Both. Throws Right. Height, 6 feet. Weight, 185 pounds.

Year	Club	Lea	Pos	G	AB	R	H	2B	3B	HR	RBI	SB	Avg
1998 Medicine Hat	Pioneer	2B	65	242	50	71	18	1	8	42	6	.293
1999 Hagerstown	So.Atl.	3B	132	513	66	137	36	6	7	74	8	.267
2000 Dunedin	Fla.St.	3B-2B-SS	96	358	54	102	16	2	7	48	9	.285
2000 Tennessee	Southern	3B	39	134	17	32	4	3	2	15	3	.239
2001 Syracuse	Int.	2B-3B	55	194	31	59	14	3	4	27	11	.304
2001 Tennessee	Southern	2B-3B	84	306	51	94	22	8	4	52	8	.307
2002 Syracuse	Int.	2B	100	417	63	127	27	3	10	37	8	.305
2002 Toronto	A.L.	2B	54	192	20	53	10	5	4	23	0	.276
2003 Toronto	A.L.	2B	142	474	54	127	21	6	9	57	5	.268
2004 Toronto a	A.L.	2B	135	489	73	132	32	7	12	58	7	.270
2005 Toronto b	A.L.	2B	131	461	62	125	25	5	10	63	7	.271
2006 Arizona	N.L.	2B	157	579	87	166	34	9	15	67	9	.287
2007 Arizona	N.L.	2B	139	517	69	152	28	9	10	63	10	.294
Major League Totals		6 Yrs.	758	2712	365	755	150	41	60	331	38	.278

a On disabled list from May 24 to June 16, 2004.
b Traded to Arizona Diamondbacks with pitcher Miguel Batista for infielder Troy Glaus and infielder Sergio Santos, December 27, 2005.

HUFF, AUBREY LEWIS

Born, Marion, Ohio, December 20, 1976.
Bats Left. Throws Right. Height, 6 feet, 4 inches. Weight, 230 pounds.

Year	Club	Lea	Pos	G	AB	R	H	2B	3B	HR	RBI	SB	Avg
1998 Chston-Sc	So.Atl.	3B	69	265	38	85	19	1	13	54	3	.321
1999 Orlando	Southern	3B	133	491	85	148	40	3	22	78	2	.301
2000 Durham	Int.	3B	108	408	73	129	36	3	20	76	2	.316
2000 Tampa Bay	A.L.	3B	39	122	12	35	7	0	4	14	0	.287
2001 Durham	Int.	3B	17	66	14	19	6	0	3	10	0	.288
2001 Tampa Bay	A.L.	3B-1B	111	411	42	102	25	1	8	45	1	.248
2002 Durham	Int.	1B	32	126	18	41	9	0	3	20	0	.325
2002 Tampa Bay	A.L.	DH-1B-3B	113	454	67	142	25	0	23	59	4	.313
2003 Tampa Bay	A.L.	OF-1B-3B	162	636	91	198	47	3	34	107	2	.311
2004 Tampa Bay	A.L.	3B-1B-OF	157	600	92	178	27	2	29	104	5	.297
2005 Tampa Bay	A.L.	OF-1B-3B	154	575	70	150	26	2	22	92	8	.261
2006 Visalia	Calif.	3B	2	8	2	2	1	0	0	1	0	.250
2006 Tampa Bay	A.L.	3B	63	230	26	65	15	1	8	28	0	.283
2006 Houston a-b-c	N.L.	OF-3B-1B	68	224	31	56	10	1	13	38	0	.250
2007 Baltimore	A.L.	DH-1B-3B	151	550	68	154	34	5	15	72	1	.280
Major League Totals		8 Yrs.	1018	3802	499	1080	216	15	156	559	21	.284

a On disabled list from April 12 to May 5, 2006.
b Traded to Houston Astros with cash for pitcher Mitch Talbot and infielder Ben Zobrist, July 12, 2006.
c Filed for free agency, October 28, 2006. Signed with Baltimore Orioles, December 30, 2006.

HUNTER, TORII KEDAR

Born, Pine Bluff, Arkansas, July 18, 1975.
Bats Right. Throws Right. Height, 6 feet, 2 inches. Weight, 215 pounds.

Year	Club	Lea	Pos	G	AB	R	H	2B	3B	HR	RBI	SB	Avg
1993 Twins	Gulf Coast	OF	28	100	6	19	3	0	0	8	4	.190
1994 Fort Wayne	Midwest	OF	91	335	57	98	17	1	10	50	8	.293
1995 Fort Myers	Fla.St.	OF	113	391	64	96	15	2	7	36	7	.246
1996 Ft. Myers	Fla.St.	OF	4	16	1	3	0	0	0	1	1	.188
1996 New Britain	Eastern	OF	99	342	49	90	20	3	7	33	7	.263
1997 New Britain	Eastern	OF	127	471	57	109	22	2	8	56	8	.231
1997 Minnesota	A.L.	OF	1	0	0	0	0	0	0	0	0	.000
1998 New Britain	Eastern	OF	82	308	42	87	24	3	6	32	11	.282
1998 Salt Lake	P.C.	OF	26	92	15	31	7	0	4	20	2	.337
1998 Minnesota	A.L.	OF	6	17	0	4	1	0	0	2	0	.235
1999 Minnesota	A.L.	OF	135	384	52	98	17	2	9	35	10	.255
2000 Salt Lake	P.C.	OF	55	209	58	77	17	2	18	61	11	.368
2000 Minnesota	A.L.	OF	99	336	44	94	14	7	5	44	4	.280
2001 Minnesota a	A.L.	OF	148	564	82	147	32	5	27	92	9	.261
2002 Minnesota	A.L.	OF	148	561	89	162	37	4	29	94	23	.289
2003 Minnesota	A.L.	OF	154	581	83	145	31	4	26	102	6	.250
2004 Minnesota b	A.L.	OF	138	520	79	141	37	0	23	81	21	.271
2005 Minnesota c	A.L.	OF	98	372	63	100	24	1	14	56	23	.269
2006 Minnesota d	A.L.	OF	147	557	86	155	21	2	31	98	12	.278
2007 Minnesota e	A.L.	OF	160	600	94	172	45	1	28	107	18	.287
Major League Totals		11 Yrs.	1234	4492	672	1218	259	26	192	711	126	.271
Division Series												
2002 Minnesota	A.L.	OF	5	20	4	6	4	0	0	2	0	.300
2003 Minnesota	A.L.	OF	4	14	3	6	0	1	1	2	0	.429
2004 Minnesota	A.L.	OF	4	17	5	6	1	0	1	2	2	.353
2006 Minnesota	A.L.	OF	3	11	1	3	1	0	1	2	0	.273
Division Series Totals			16	62	13	21	6	1	3	8	2	.339
Championship Series												
2002 Minnesota	A.L.	OF	5	18	2	3	2	0	0	0	0	.167

a On disabled list from April 6 to April 21, 2001.
b On disabled list from April 7 to April 25, 2004.
c On disabled list from July 30 to October 6, 2005.
d On disabled list from July 16 to July 31, 2006.
e Filed for free agency, October 29, 2007. Signed with Los Angeles Angels, November 21, 2007.

IANNETTA, CHRISTOPHER DOMENIC (CHRIS)

Born, Providence, Rhode Island, April 8, 1983.
Bats Right. Throws Right. Height, 5 feet, 11 inches. Weight, 195 pounds.

Year	Club	Lea	Pos	G	AB	R	H	2B	3B	HR	RBI	SB	Avg
2004 Asheville	So.Atl.	C	36	121	23	38	5	1	5	17	0	.314
2005 Tulsa	Texas	C	19	60	7	14	3	1	2	11	0	.233
2006 Tulsa	Texas	C	44	156	38	50	10	2	11	26	1	.321
2006 Colorado Springs	P.C.	C	47	151	23	53	11	2	3	22	0	.351
2006 Colorado	N.L.	C	21	77	12	20	4	0	2	10	0	.260
2007 Colorado Springs	P.C.	C	16	54	8	16	3	0	1	7	0	.296
2007 Colorado	N.L.	C	67	197	22	43	8	3	4	27	0	.218
Major League Totals		2 Yrs.	88	274	34	63	12	3	6	37	0	.230

IBANEZ, RAUL JAVIER

Born, New York, New York, June 2, 1972.
Bats Left. Throws Right. Height, 6 feet, 2 inches. Weight, 220 pounds.

Year	Club	Lea	Pos	G	AB	R	H	2B	3B	HR	RBI	SB	Avg
1992 Mariners	Arizona	DH-1B-C-OF	33	120	25	37	8	2	1	16	1	.308
1993 Appleton	Midwest	DH-1B-OF-C	52	157	26	43	9	0	5	21	0	.274
1993 Bellingham	Northwest	C	43	134	16	38	5	2	0	15	0	.284
1994 Appleton	Midwest	DH-C-1B-OF	91	327	55	102	30	3	7	59	10	.312
1995 Riverside	California	C-1B	95	361	59	120	23	9	20	108	4	.332
1996 Port City	Southern	OF-1B-C	19	76	12	28	8	1	1	13	3	.368
1996 Seattle	A.L.	DH	4	5	0	0	0	0	0	0	0	.000
1996 Tacoma	P.C.	OF-1B	111	405	59	115	20	3	11	47	7	.284
1997 Tacoma	P.C.	OF	111	438	84	133	30	5	15	84	7	.304
1997 Seattle	A.L.	OF	11	26	3	4	0	1	1	4	0	.154
1998 Tacoma	P.C.	OF	52	190	24	41	8	1	6	25	1	.216
1998 Seattle	A.L.	OF-1B	37	98	12	25	7	1	2	12	0	.255

Year	Club	Lea	Pos	G	AB	R	H	2B	3B	HR	RBI	SB	Avg
1999 Tacoma	....	P.C.	OF	8	31	6	11	1	0	3	5	1	.355
1999 Seattle a	....	A.L.	OF-1B-C	87	209	23	54	7	0	9	27	5	.258
2000 Tacoma	....	P.C.	OF	10	40	3	10	4	0	0	6	0	.250
2000 Seattle b-c	....	A.L.	OF-1B	92	140	21	32	8	0	2	15	2	.229
2001 Omaha	....	P.C.	OF-SS	8	27	3	4	1	0	2	5	0	.148
2001 Kansas City d	.....	A.L.	OF-1B-3B	104	279	44	78	11	5	13	54	0	.280
2002 Kansas City	......	A.L.	OF-1B	137	497	70	146	37	6	24	103	5	.294
2003 Kansas City d	.....	A.L.	OF-1B	157	608	95	179	33	5	18	90	8	.294
2004 Tacoma	....	P.C.	OF	4	17	2	4	1	0	0	1	0	.235
2004 Seattle e	....	A.L.	OF-1B	123	481	67	146	31	1	16	62	1	.304
2005 Seattle	....	A.L.	DH-OF-1B	*162	614	92	172	32	2	20	89	9	.280
2006 Seattle	....	A.L.	OF	159	626	103	181	33	5	33	123	2	.289
2007 Seattle	....	A.L.	OF	149	573	80	167	35	5	21	105	0	.291
Major League Totals	....		12 Yrs.	1222	4156	610	1184	234	31	159	684	32	.285
Division Series													
2000 Seattle	....	A.L.	OF	3	8	2	3	0	0	0	0	0	.375
Championship Series													
2000 Seattle	....	A.L.	OF	6	9	0	0	0	0	0	0	0	.000

a On disabled list from May 18 to June 3, 1999.
b On disabled list from August 7 to August 21, 2000.
c Not offered contract, December 21, 2000. Signed with Kansas City Royals organization, January 13, 2001.
d Filed for free agency, October 27, 2003. Signed with Seattle Mariners, November 19, 2003.
e On disabled list from June 3 to July 10, 2004.

IGUCHI, TADAHITO

Born, Tokyo, Japan, December 4, 1974.
Bats Right. Throws Right. Height, 5 feet, 10 inches. Weight, 200 pounds.

Year	Club	Lea	Pos	G	AB	R	H	2B	3B	HR	RBI	SB	Avg
1997 Fukuoka	....	Japan Pac.	SS	76	217	31	44	6	3	8	23	3	.203
1998 Fukuoka	....	Japan Pac.	SS	135	421	58	93	18	4	21	66	12	.221
1999 Fukuoka	....	Japan Pac.	SS	116	370	38	83	15	1	14	47	14	.224
2000 Fukuoka	....	Japan Pac.	SS	54	162	21	40	9	2	7	23	5	.247
2001 Fukuoka	....	Japan Pac.	2B	140	552	104	144	26	1	30	97	44	.261
2002 Fukuoka	....	Japan Pac.	2B	114	428	64	111	14	1	18	53	21	.259
2003 Fukuoka	....	Japan Pac.	2B	135	515	112	175	37	1	27	109	42	.340
2004 Fukuoka	....	Japan Pac.	2B	124	510	96	170	34	2	24	89	18	.333
2005 Chicago a	....	A.L.	2B	135	511	74	142	25	6	15	71	15	.278
2006 Chicago	....	A.L.	2B	138	555	97	156	24	0	18	67	11	.281
2007 Chicago	....	A.L.	2B	90	327	45	82	17	4	6	31	8	.251
2007 Philadelphia b-c	....	N.L.	2B	45	138	22	42	10	0	3	12	6	.304
Major League Totals	....		3 Yrs.	408	1531	238	422	76	10	42	181	40	.276
Division Series													
2005 Chicago	....	A.L.	2B	3	12	1	3	0	0	1	4	0	.250
2007 Philadelphia	....	N.L.	PH	3	1	0	0	0	0	0	0	0	.000
Division Series Totals	....			6	13	1	3	0	0	1	4	0	.231
Championship Series													
2005 Chicago	....	A.L.	2B	5	17	4	3	1	0	0	0	0	.176
World Series Record													
2005 Chicago	....	A.L.	2B	4	18	2	3	0	0	0	1	0	.167

a Signed with Chicago White Sox, January 27, 2005.
b Traded to Philadelphia Phillies for pitcher Michael Dubee, July 27, 2007.
c Released by Philadelphia Phillies, November 15, 2007. Signed with San Diego Padres, December 18, 2007.

INFANTE, OMAR RAFAEL

Born, Puerto La Cruz, Venezuela, December 26, 1981.
Bats Right. Throws Right. Height, 6 feet. Weight, 180 pounds.

Year	Club	Lea	Pos	G	AB	R	H	2B	3B	HR	RBI	SB	Avg
1999 Tigers	....	Gulf Coast	SS	21	75	9	20	0	0	0	4	4	.267
2000 Lakeland	....	Fla.St.	SS	79	259	35	71	11	0	2	24	11	.274
2000 West Michigan	.	Midwest	SS-2B	12	48	7	11	0	0	0	5	1	.229
2001 Erie	....	Eastern	SS	132	540	86	163	21	4	2	62	27	.302
2002 Toledo	....	Int.	SS	120	436	49	117	16	8	4	51	19	.268
2002 Detroit	....	A.L.	SS-2B	18	72	4	24	3	0	1	6	0	.333
2003 Toledo	....	Int.	SS	64	224	28	50	10	0	2	18	22	.223
2003 Detroit	....	A.L.	SS-3B-2B	69	221	24	49	6	1	0	8	6	.222
2004 Detroit	....	A.L.	2B-SS-3B-OF	142	503	69	133	27	9	16	55	13	.264
2005 Detroit	....	A.L.	2B-SS	121	406	36	90	28	2	9	43	8	.222

Year	Club	Lea	Pos	G	AB	R	H	2B	3B	HR	RBI	SB	Avg
2006 Detroit .... A.L.			2B-SS-3B	78	224	35	62	11	4	4	25	3	.277
2007 Toledo .... Int.			SS-2B	10	38	3	14	2	0	0	4	1	.368
2007 Detroit a-b .... A.L.			2B-OF-SS-3B	66	166	24	45	6	1	2	17	4	.271
Major League Totals	6 Yrs.	494	1592	192	403	81	17	32	154	34	.253		
Championship Series													
2006 Detroit .... A.L.			DH	1	2	0	1	0	0	0	0	1	.500
World Series Record													
2006 Detroit .... A.L.			PH	1	1	0	0	0	0	0	0	0	.000

a Traded to Chicago Cubs for outfielder Jacque Jones, November 12, 2007.
b Traded to Atlanta Braves with pitcher Will Ohman for pitcher Jose Ascanio, December 4, 2007.

INGE, CHARLES BRANDON (BRANDON)

Born, Lynchburg, Virginia, May 19, 1977.
Bats Both. Throws Right. Height, 5 feet, 11 inches. Weight, 190 pounds.

Year	Club	Lea	Pos	G	AB	R	H	2B	3B	HR	RBI	SB	Avg
1998 Jamestown...... N.Y.-Penn.			C	51	191	24	44	10	1	8	29	8	.230
1999 West Michigan..... Midwest			C	100	352	54	86	25	2	9	46	15	.244
2000 Toledo .... Int.			C	55	190	24	42	9	3	5	20	2	.221
2000 Jacksonville ...... Southern			C-OF	78	298	39	77	25	1	6	53	10	.258
2001 Tigers......... Gulf Coast			C	3	10	1	1	0	0	1	2	0	.100
2001 West Michigan..... Midwest			C	4	16	3	3	1	0	0	2	0	.188
2001 Toledo .... Int.			C	27	90	11	26	11	1	2	15	1	.289
2001 Detroit a........... A.L.			C	79	189	13	34	11	0	0	15	1	.180
2002 Toledo .... Int.			C	21	65	10	17	2	4	3	13	1	.262
2002 Detroit b............. A.L.			C	95	321	27	65	15	3	7	24	1	.202
2003 Toledo .... Int.			C	39	142	15	39	9	0	5	15	3	.275
2003 Detroit .... A.L.			C	104	330	32	67	15	3	8	30	4	.203
2004 Detroit c............. A.L.			3B-C-OF	131	408	43	117	15	7	13	64	5	.287
2005 Detroit .... A.L.			3B-OF	160	616	75	161	31	9	16	72	7	.261
2006 Detroit .... A.L.			3B	159	542	83	137	29	2	27	83	7	.253
2007 Detroit .... A.L.			3B	151	508	64	120	25	2	14	71	9	.236
Major League Totals	7 Yrs.	879	2914	337	701	141	26	85	359	34	.241		
Division Series													
2006 Detroit .... A.L.			3B	4	15	1	2	0	0	0	0	0	.133
Championship Series													
2006 Detroit .... A.L.			3B	4	12	3	4	1	0	1	3	0	.333
World Series Record													
2006 Detroit .... A.L.			3B	5	17	0	6	2	0	0	1	0	.353

a On disabled list from June 25 to August 6, 2001.
b On disabled list from May 12 to May 27, 2002.
c On disabled list from June 26 to July 15, 2004.

IWAMURA, AKINORI

Born, Ehime, Japan, February 9, 1979.
Bats Left. Throws Right. Height, 5 feet, 9 inches. Weight, 175 pounds.

Year	Club	Lea	Pos	G	AB	R	H	2B	3B	HR	RBI	SB	Avg
1998 Yakult......... Japan Pac.			3B	1	3	0	0	0	0	0	0	0	.000
1999 Yakult......... Japan Pac.			3B	83	252	28	74	11	4	11	35	7	.341
2000 Yakult......... Japan Pac.			3B	130	436	67	121	13	9	18	66	13	.342
2001 Yakult......... Japan Pac.			3B	136	520	79	149	24	4	18	81	15	.329
2002 Yakult......... Japan Pac.			3B	140	510	79	163	35	2	23	71	5	.390
2003 Yakult......... Japan Pac.			3B	60	232	43	61	6	2	12	35	5	.328
2004 Yakult......... Japan Pac.			3B	138	533	99	160	19	0	44	103	8	.383
2005 Yakult......... Japan Pac.			3B	144	548	83	175	31	4	30	102	6	.388
2006 Yakult a........ Japan Pac.			3B	145	546	84	170	27	2	32	77	8	.389
2007 Tampa Bay b .... A.L.			3B-2B	123	491	82	140	21	10	7	34	12	.285

a Signed with Tampa Bay Devil Rays, December 15, 2006.
b On disabled list from April 24 to May 28, 2007.

IZTURIS, CESAR DAVID

Born, Barquisimeto, Venezuela, February 10, 1980.
Bats Both. Throws Right. Height, 5 feet, 9 inches. Weight, 175 pounds.

Year	Club	Lea	Pos	G	AB	R	H	2B	3B	HR	RBI	SB	Avg
1997 St.Cathrnes ...... N.Y.-Penn.			2B-SS	70	231	32	44	3	0	1	11	6	.190
1998 Hagerstown .... So.Atl.			SS-2B-3B	130	413	56	108	13	1	1	38	20	.262
1999 Dunedin .... Fla.St.			SS-2B-3B	131	536	77	165	28	12	3	77	32	.308

Year	Club	Lea	Pos	G	AB	R	H	2B	3B	HR	RBI	SB	Avg
2000 Syracuse	Int.	SS	132	435	54	95	16	5	0	27	21	.218
2001 Syracuse	Int.	SS-2B	87	342	32	100	16	3	2	35	24	.292
2001 Toronto a	A.L.	2B-SS	46	134	19	36	6	2	2	9	8	.269
2002 Los Angeles	N.L.	SS-2B	135	439	43	102	24	2	1	31	7	.232
2003 Los Angeles	N.L.	SS	158	558	47	140	21	6	1	40	10	.251
2004 Los Angeles	N.L.	SS	159	670	90	193	32	9	4	62	25	.288
2005 Los Angeles b	N.L.	SS	106	444	48	114	19	2	2	31	8	.257
2006 Las Vegas.............	P.C.	SS-2B	15	59	9	16	3	0	0	3	0	.271
2006 Los Angeles-Chicago c-d-e .	N.L.	3B-SS-2B	54	192	14	47	9	1	1	18	1	.245
2007 Chicago-Pittsburgh f-g .	N.L.	SS-3B	110	314	31	81	14	2	0	16	3	.258
Major League Totals		7 Yrs.	768	2751	292	713	125	24	11	207	62	.259
Division Series												
2004 Los Angeles	N.L.	SS	4	17	1	3	1	0	0	0	0	.176

a Traded to Los Angeles Dodgers with pitcher Paul Quantrill for pitcher Luke Prokopec and pitcher Chad Ricketts, December 13, 2001.
b On disabled list from June 30 to July 15 and August 23 to October 7, 2005.
c On disabled list from March 28 to June 20, 2006.
d Traded to Chicago Cubs for pitcher Greg Maddux, July 31, 2006.
e On disabled list from August 22 to September 6, 2006.
f Traded to Pittsburgh Pirates with cash for player to be named later, July 19, 2007.
g Filed for free agency, November 12, 2007. Signed with St. Louis Cardinals, November 30, 2007.

IZTURIS, MAICER

Born, Barquisimeto, Venezuela, September 12, 1980.
Bats Both. Throws Right. Height, 5 feet, 8 inches. Weight, 160 pounds.

Year	Club	Lea	Pos	G	AB	R	H	2B	3B	HR	RBI	SB	Avg
1998 Burlington	Appal.	SS	55	217	33	63	8	2	2	33	16	.290
1999 Columbus.......	So.Atl.	SS	57	220	46	66	5	3	4	23	14	.300
2000 Columbus.......	So.Atl.	SS	10	29	4	8	1	0	0	1	0	.276
2001 Kinston.......	Carolina	2B	114	433	47	104	16	6	1	39	32	.240
2002 Kinston......	Carolina	2B	58	233	28	61	13	1	1	30	24	.262
2002 Akron.........	Eastern	2B	67	253	34	70	12	7	0	32	8	.277
2003 Akron.........	Eastern	2B-SS-OF	54	218	31	61	11	5	1	20	14	.280
2003 Buffalo	Int.	SS-2B	85	301	43	79	16	4	2	29	14	.262
2004 Edmonton	P.C.	SS-2B	99	376	65	127	19	2	3	36	14	.338
2004 Montreal a-b	N.L.	SS-2B	32	107	10	22	5	2	1	4	4	.206
2005 Salt Lake	P.C.	SS-3B-2B	10	31	10	14	4	0	0	2	4	.452
2005 Los Angeles c.....	A.L.	3B-SS-2B-OF	77	191	18	47	8	4	1	15	9	.246
2006 Salt Lake	P.C.	SS-3B-2B	9	36	5	11	5	1	0	5	1	.306
2006 Los Angeles d	A.L.	3B-SS-2B	104	352	64	103	21	3	5	44	14	.293
2007 Rancho Cucamonga	Calif.	3B	7	22	5	7	1	0	0	3	0	.318
2007 Salt Lake	P.C.	2B-SS	5	17	3	6	1	0	0	0	0	.353
2007 Los Angeles e......	A.L.	3B-2B-SS	102	336	47	97	17	2	6	51	7	.289
Major League Totals		4 Yrs.	315	986	139	269	51	11	13	114	34	.273
Division Series												
2007 Los Angeles	A.L.	3B	3	12	1	4	2	0	0	0	2	.333
Championship Series												
2005 Los Angeles	A.L.	SS	1	0	0	0	0	0	0	0	0	.000

a Traded by Cleveland Indians to Montreal Expos with outfielder Ryan Church for pitcher Scott Stewart, January 5, 2004.
b Traded to Anaheim Angels with outfielder Juan Rivera for outfielder Jose Guillen, November 19, 2004.
c On disabled list from April 26 to June 18, 2005.
d On disabled list from April 24 to June 9, 2006.
e On disabled list from April 30 to May 15 and May 21 to July 3, 2007.

JACKSON, CONOR SIMS

Born, Austin, Texas, May 7, 1982.
Bats Right. Throws Right. Height, 6 feet, 2 inches. Weight, 225 pounds.

Year	Club	Lea	Pos	G	AB	R	H	2B	3B	HR	RBI	SB	Avg
2003 Yakima.........	Northwest	OF	68	257	44	82	35	1	6	60	3	.319
2004 Lancaster.............	Calif.	OF	67	258	64	89	19	2	11	54	4	.345
2004 El Paso.............	Texas	OF-3B	60	226	33	68	13	2	6	37	3	.301
2005 Tucson.............	P.C.	1B-OF	93	333	66	118	38	2	8	73	3	.354
2005 Arizona.............	N.L.	1B-OF	40	85	8	17	3	0	2	8	0	.200
2006 Arizona.............	N.L.	1B	140	485	75	141	26	1	15	79	1	.291
2007 Arizona.............	N.L.	1B-3B-OF	130	415	56	118	29	1	15	60	2	.284
Major League Totals		3 Yrs.	310	985	139	276	58	2	32	147	3	.280

Year	Club	Lea	Pos	G	AB	R	H	2B	3B	HR	RBI	SB	Avg
Division Series													
2007 Arizona..............		N.L.	1B	3	8	0	1	1	0	0	1	0	.125
Championship Series													
2007 Arizona..............		N.L.	1B	3	9	1	3	0	0	0	1	0	.333

JACOBS, MICHAEL JAMES (MIKE)
Born, Chula Vista, California, October 30, 1980.
Bats Left. Throws Right. Height, 6 feet, 2 inches. Weight, 200 pounds.

Year	Club	Lea	Pos	G	AB	R	H	2B	3B	HR	RBI	SB	Avg
1999 Mets..........	Gulf Coast		C-1B	44	147	18	49	12	0	4	30	2	.333
2000 Kingsport..........	Appal.		C	59	204	28	55	15	4	7	40	6	.270
2000 Columbia..........	So.Atl.		C	18	56	1	12	5	0	0	8	1	.214
2001 Brooklyn........	N.Y.-Penn.		C	19	66	12	19	5	0	1	15	1	.288
2001 Columbia..........	So.Atl.		C	46	180	18	50	13	0	2	26	0	.278
2002 St. Lucie............	Fla.St.		C-1B	118	467	62	117	26	1	11	64	2	.251
2003 Binghamton........	Eastern		C-1B	119	407	56	134	36	1	17	81	0	.329
2004 Norfolk..............	Int.		C-1B-SS	27	96	8	17	3	0	2	6	0	.177
2005 Binghamton........	Eastern		1B-C-OF	117	433	66	139	37	2	25	93	1	.321
2005 New York a........		N.L.	1B	30	100	19	31	7	0	11	23	0	.310
2006 Florida..............		N.L.	1B	136	469	54	123	37	1	20	77	3	.262
2007 Jupiter............	Fla.St.		1B	3	12	2	2	0	0	1	3	0	.167
2007 Carolina........	Southern		1B	4	10	1	3	0	0	1	2	0	.300
2007 Florida b...........		N.L.	1B	114	426	57	113	27	2	17	54	1	.265
Major League Totals............		3 Yrs.	280	995	130	267	71	3	48	154	4	.268	

a Traded to Florida Marlins with pitcher Yusmeiro Petit and infielder Grant Psomas for infielder Carlos Delgado and cash, November 23, 2005.

b On disabled list from May 14 to June 23, 2007.

JENKINS, GEOFFREY SCOTT (GEOFF)
Born, Olympia, Washington, July 21, 1974.
Bats Left. Throws Right. Height, 6 feet, 1 inch. Weight, 210 pounds.

Year	Club	Lea	Pos	G	AB	R	H	2B	3B	HR	RBI	SB	Avg
1995 Helena..........	Pioneer		OF	7	28	2	9	0	1	0	9	0	.321
1995 Stockton........	California		OF	13	47	13	12	2	0	3	12	2	.255
1995 El Paso.............	Texas		OF	22	79	12	22	4	2	1	13	3	.278
1996 El Paso.............	Texas		DH	22	77	17	22	5	4	1	11	1	.286
1996 Stockton a.......	California		DH-OF	37	138	27	48	8	4	3	25	3	.348
1997 Tucson b.............	P.C.		OF-SS	93	347	44	82	24	3	10	56	0	.236
1998 Louisville.........	Int.		OF	55	215	38	71	10	4	7	52	1	.330
1998 Milwaukee...........		N.L.	OF	84	262	33	60	12	1	9	28	1	.229
1999 Milwaukee...........		N.L.	OF	135	447	70	140	43	3	21	82	5	.313
2000 Milwaukee c...........		N.L.	OF	135	512	100	155	36	4	34	94	11	.303
2001 Beloit...........	Midwest		OF	1	3	1	1	1	0	0	1	0	.333
2001 Milwaukee d...........		N.L.	OF	105	397	60	105	21	1	20	63	4	.264
2002 Milwaukee e...........		N.L.	OF	67	243	35	59	17	1	10	29	1	.243
2003 Huntsville........	Southern		OF	6	20	6	5	0	0	2	3	1	.250
2003 Milwaukee f...........		N.L.	OF	124	487	81	144	30	2	28	95	0	.296
2004 Milwaukee...........		N.L.	OF	157	617	88	163	36	6	27	93	3	.264
2005 Milwaukee...........		N.L.	OF	148	538	87	157	42	1	25	86	0	.292
2006 Milwaukee...........		N.L.	OF	147	484	62	131	26	1	17	70	4	.271
2007 Milwaukee g...........		N.L.	OF	132	420	45	107	24	2	21	64	2	.255
Major League Totals............		10 Yrs.	1234	4407	661	1221	287	22	212	704	31	.277	

a On disabled list from May 8 to July 13, 1996.

b On disabled list from July 4 to August 11, 1997.

c On disabled list from May 6 to May 28, 2000.

d On disabled list from May 2 to May 19 and July 29 to August 28, 2001.

e On disabled list from June 18 to September 30, 2002.

f On disabled list from March 21 to April 9 and August 29 to September 29, 2003.

g Filed for free agency, October 30, 2007. Signed with Philadelphia Phillies, December 20, 2007.

JETER, DEREK SANDERSON

Born, Pequannock, New Jersey, June 26, 1974.
Bats Right. Throws Right. Height, 6 feet, 3 inches. Weight, 195 pounds.

Year	Club	Lea	Pos	G	AB	R	H	2B	3B	HR	RBI	SB	Avg
1992 Tampa Yankees	.....	Gulf C.	SS	47	173	19	35	10	0	3	25	2	.202
1992 Greensboro	....	So. Atl.	SS	11	37	4	9	0	0	1	4	0	.243
1993 Greensboro	....	So. Atl.	SS	128	515	85	152	14	11	5	71	18	.295
1994 Tampa	....	Fla. St.	SS	69	292	61	96	13	8	0	39	28	.329
1994 Albany	......	Eastern	SS	34	122	17	46	7	2	2	13	12	.377
1994 Columbus	..., ...	Int.	SS	35	126	25	44	7	1	3	16	10	.349
1995 Columbus	....	Int.	SS	123	486	96	154	27	9	2	45	20	.317
1995 New York	....	A.L.	SS	15	48	5	12	4	1	0	7	0	.250
1996 New York a	....	A.L.	SS	157	582	104	183	25	6	10	78	14	.314
1997 New York	....	A.L.	SS	159	654	116	190	31	7	10	70	23	.291
1998 Columbus	....	Int.	SS	1	5	2	2	2	0	0	0	0	.400
1998 New York b	....	A.L.	SS	149	626	*127	203	25	8	19	84	30	.324
1999 New York	....	A.L.	SS	158	627	134	219	37	9	24	102	19	.349
2000 Tampa	....	Fla.St.	SS	1	3	2	2	1	0	0	0	0	.667
2000 New York c	....	A.L.	SS	148	593	119	201	31	4	15	73	22	.339
2001 New York d	....	A.L.	SS	150	614	110	191	35	3	21	74	27	.311
2002 New York	....	A.L.	SS	157	644	124	191	26	0	18	75	32	.297
2003 Trenton	....	Eastern	SS	5	18	2	8	1	1	0	5	0	.444
2003 New York e	....	A.L.	SS	119	482	87	156	25	3	10	52	11	.324
2004 New York	....	A.L.	SS	154	643	111	188	44	1	23	78	23	.292
2005 New York	....	A.L.	SS	159	654	122	202	25	5	19	70	14	.309
2006 New York	....	A.L.	SS	154	623	118	214	39	3	14	97	34	.343
2007 New York	....	A.L.	SS	156	639	102	206	39	4	12	73	15	.322
Major League Totals			**13 Yrs.**	**1835**	**7429**	**1379**	**2356**	**386**	**54**	**195**	**933**	**264**	**.317**

Division Series

Year	Club	Lea	Pos	G	AB	R	H	2B	3B	HR	RBI	SB	Avg
1996 New York	....	A.L.	SS	4	17	2	7	1	0	0	1	0	.412
1997 New York	....	A.L.	SS	5	21	6	7	1	0	2	2	1	.333
1998 New York	....	A.L.	SS	3	9	0	1	0	0	0	0	0	.111
1999 New York	....	A.L.	SS	3	11	3	5	1	1	0	0	0	.455
2000 New York	....	A.L.	SS	5	19	1	4	0	0	0	2	0	.211
2001 New York	....	A.L.	SS	5	18	2	8	1	0	0	1	0	.444
2002 New York	....	A.L.	SS	4	16	6	8	0	0	2	3	0	.500
2003 New York	....	A.L.	SS	4	14	2	6	0	0	1	1	1	.429
2004 New York	....	A.L.	SS	4	19	3	6	1	0	1	4	1	.316
2005 New York	....	A.L.	SS	5	21	4	7	0	0	2	5	1	.333
2006 New York	....	A.L.	SS	4	16	4	8	4	0	1	1	0	.500
2007 New York	....	A.L.	SS	4	17	0	3	0	0	0	1	0	.176
Division Series Totals				**50**	**198**	**33**	**70**	**9**	**1**	**9**	**21**	**4**	**.354**

Championship Series

Year	Club	Lea	Pos	G	AB	R	H	2B	3B	HR	RBI	SB	Avg
1996 New York	....	A.L.	SS	5	24	5	10	2	0	1	1	2	.417
1998 New York	....	A.L.	SS	6	25	3	5	1	1	0	2	3	.200
1999 New York	....	A.L.	SS	5	20	3	7	1	0	1	3	0	.350
2000 New York	....	A.L.	SS	6	22	6	7	0	0	2	5	1	.318
2001 New York	....	A.L.	SS	5	17	0	2	0	0	0	2	0	.118
2003 New York	....	A.L.	SS	7	30	3	7	2	0	1	2	1	.233
2004 New York	....	A.L.	SS	7	30	5	6	1	0	0	5	1	.200
Championship Series Totals				**41**	**168**	**25**	**44**	**7**	**1**	**5**	**20**	**8**	**.262**

World Series

Year	Club	Lea	Pos	G	AB	R	H	2B	3B	HR	RBI	SB	Avg
1996 New York	....	A.L.	SS	6	20	5	5	0	0	0	1	1	.250
1998 New York	....	A.L.	SS	4	17	4	6	0	0	0	1	0	.353
1999 New York	....	A.L.	SS	4	17	4	6	1	0	0	1	3	.353
2000 New York	....	A.L.	SS	5	22	6	9	2	1	2	2	0	.409
2001 New York	....	A.L.	SS	7	27	3	4	0	0	1	1	0	.148
2003 New York	....	A.L.	SS	6	26	5	9	3	0	0	2	0	.346
World Series Totals				**32**	**129**	**27**	**39**	**6**	**1**	**3**	**8**	**4**	**.302**

a Selected Rookie of the Year in American League for 1996.
b On disabled list from June 4 to June 19, 1998.
c On disabled list from May 12 to May 26, 2000.
d On disabled list from March 23 to April 7, 2001.
e On disabled list from April 1 to May 13, 2003.

JIMENEZ, D'ANGELO

Born, Santo Domingo, Dominican Republic, December 21, 1977.
Bats Both. Throws Right. Height, 6 feet. Weight, 160 pounds.

Year	Club	Lea	Pos	G	AB	R	H	2B	3B	HR	RBI	SB	Avg
1995 Yankees	Gulf Coast	SS	57	214	41	60	14	8	2	28	6	.280
1996 Greensboro	So.Atl.	SS	138	537	68	131	25	5	6	48	15	.244
1997 Columbus	Int.	SS	2	7	1	1	0	0	0	1	0	.143
1997 Tampa	Fla.St.	SS	94	352	52	99	14	6	6	48	8	.281
1998 Norwich	Eastern	SS	40	152	21	41	6	2	2	21	5	.270
1998 Columbus	Int.	SS-2B	91	344	55	88	19	4	8	51	6	.256
1999 Columbus	Int.	SS-3B-2B	126	526	97	172	32	5	15	88	26	.327
1999 New York	A.L.	3B-2B	7	20	3	8	2	0	0	4	0	.400
2000 Tampa	Fla.St.	SS-2B	12	41	8	8	1	1	1	2	0	.195
2000 Yankees	Gulf Coast	2B-SS	4	10	2	1	0	0	0	0	0	.100
2000 Columbus	Int.	2B-3B-SS	21	73	11	17	3	1	1	5	2	.233
2001 Columbus	Int.	2B-SS-3B	56	214	33	56	11	1	5	19	5	.262
2001 San Diego a	N.L.	SS	86	308	45	85	19	0	3	33	2	.276
2002 San Diego b	N.L.	2B-3B-P	87	321	39	77	11	4	3	33	4	.240
2002 Charlotte	Int.	SS	42	157	24	44	11	1	6	18	6	.280
2002 Chicago	A.L.	2B-SS-3B	27	108	22	31	4	3	1	11	2	.287
2003 Chicago	A.L.	2B-3B	73	271	35	69	11	5	7	26	4	.255
2003 Cincinnati c	N.L.	2B-3B	73	290	34	84	13	2	7	31	7	.290
2004 Cincinnati	N.L.	2B-SS	152	563	76	152	28	3	12	67	13	.270
2005 Cincinnati	N.L.	2B	35	105	14	24	7	0	0	5	2	.229
2005 Chattanooga d	Southern	SS-2B	90	327	55	91	20	0	9	45	16	.278
2006 Sacramento	P.C.	2B-SS	35	125	30	38	8	1	4	23	2	.304
2006 Texas-Oakland e	A.L.	2B-3B-SS	28	71	8	13	3	0	1	8	0	.183
2007 Columbus	Int.	SS-3B-2B	50	171	28	63	13	2	7	25	2	.368
2007 Washington f-g	N.L.	SS-2B-3B	73	102	14	25	7	0	2	10	2	.245
Major League Totals		8 Yrs.	641	2159	290	568	105	17	36	228	36	.263
Division Series												
2006 Oakland	A.L.	2B	2	4	0	0	0	0	0	0	0	.000
Championship Series												
2006 Oakland	A.L.	2B	4	12	0	2	0	0	0	0	0	.167

a Traded to San Diego Padres for pitcher Jay Witasick, June 23, 2001.
b Traded to Chicago White Sox for pitcher Alex Fernandez and catcher Humberto Quintero, July 12, 2002.
c Traded to Cincinnati Reds for pitcher Scott Dunn, July 6, 2003.
d Filed for free agency, October 5, 2005. Signed with Texas Rangers organization, December 16, 2005.
e Released by Texas Rangers, June 14, 2006. Signed with Oakland Athletics organization, June 23, 2006.
f Released by Oakland Athletics, October 23, 2006. Signed with Washington Nationals organization, January 18, 2007.
g Filed for free agency, October 27, 2007. Signed with St. Louis Cardinals organization, December 18, 2007.

JOHJIMA, KENJI

Born, Nagasaki, Japan, June 8, 1976.
Bats Right. Throws Right. Height, 6 feet. Weight, 200 pounds.

Year	Club	Lea	Pos	G	AB	R	H	2B	3B	HR	RBI	SB	Avg
1995 Fukuoka	Japan Pac.	C	12	12	2	2	0	0	0	1	0	.167
1996 Fukuoka	Japan Pac.	C	17	58	5	14	2	0	4	9	1	.241
1997 Fukuoka	Japan Pac.	C	120	432	49	133	24	2	15	68	6	.308
1998 Fukuoka	Japan Pac.	C	122	395	53	99	19	0	16	58	5	.251
1999 Fukuoka	Japan Pac.	C	135	493	65	151	33	1	17	77	6	.306
2000 Fukuoka	Japan Pac.	C	84	303	38	94	22	2	9	50	10	.310
2001 Fukuoka	Japan Pac.	C	140	534	63	138	18	0	31	95	9	.258
2002 Fukuoka	Japan Pac.	C	115	416	60	122	18	0	25	74	8	.293
2003 Fukuoka	Japan Pac.	C	140	551	101	182	39	2	34	119	9	.330
2004 Fukuoka	Japan Pac.	C	116	426	91	144	25	1	36	91	6	.338
2005 Fukuoka a	Japan Pac.	C	116	411	70	127	22	4	24	57	3	.309
2006 Seattle	A.L.	C	144	506	61	147	25	1	18	76	3	.291
2007 Seattle	A.L.	C	135	485	52	139	29	0	14	61	0	.287
Major League Totals		2 Yrs.	279	991	113	286	54	1	32	137	3	.289

a Signed with Seattle Mariners, November 21, 2005.

JOHNSON, DANIEL RYAN (DAN)

Born, Coon Rapids, Minnesota, August 10, 1979.
Bats Left. Throws Right. Height, 6 feet, 2 inches. Weight, 225 pounds.

Year	Club	Lea	Pos	G	AB	R	H	2B	3B	HR	RBI	SB	Avg
2001 Vancouver	Northwest	1B	69	247	36	70	15	2	11	41	0	.283
2002 Modesto	California	1B	126	426	56	125	23	1	21	85	4	.293

Year	Club	Lea	Pos	G	AB	R	H	2B	3B	HR	RBI	SB	Avg
2003 Sacramento	P.C.	1B	1	4	0	1	1	0	0	0	0	0	.250
2003 Midland	Texas	1B-OF	139	538	90	156	26	4	27	114	7	.290
2004 Sacramento	P.C.	1B-OF	142	535	95	160	29	5	29	111	0	.299
2005 Sacramento	P.C.	1B-OF	47	182	36	59	17	0	8	41	0	.324
2005 Oakland	A.L.	1B	109	375	54	103	21	0	15	58	0	.275
2006 Sacramento	P.C.	1B-3B	46	172	34	54	13	1	7	44	0	.314
2006 Oakland	A.L.	1B	91	286	30	67	13	1	9	37	0	.234
2007 Sacramento	P.C.	1B	2	5	1	3	0	0	1	3	0	.600
2007 Oakland a	A.L.	1B	117	416	53	98	20	1	18	62	0	.236
Major League Totals		3 Yrs.	317	1077	137	268	54	2	42	157	0	.249	

a On disabled list from March 27 to April 25, 2007.

JOHNSON, KELLY ANDREW
Born, Austin, Texas, February 22, 1982.
Bats Left. Throws Right. Height, 6 feet, 1 inch. Weight, 205 pounds.

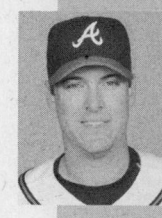

Year	Club	Lea	Pos	G	AB	R	H	2B	3B	HR	RBI	SB	Avg
2000 Braves	Gulf Coast	SS-3B	53	193	27	52	12	3	4	29	6	.269
2001 Macon	So.Atl.	SS	124	415	75	120	22	1	23	66	25	.289
2002 Myrtle Beach	Carolina	SS-3B	126	482	62	123	21	5	12	49	12	.255
2003 Braves	Gulf Coast	SS	6	26	10	10	1	1	1	3	1	.385
2003 Greenville	Southern	SS	98	334	46	92	22	5	6	45	10	.275
2004 Greenville	Southern	OF-3B-2B	135	479	70	135	35	3	16	50	9	.282
2005 Richmond	Int.	OF-3B-SS	44	155	35	48	12	3	8	22	7	.310
2005 Atlanta	N.L.	OF	87	290	46	70	12	3	9	40	2	.241
2006 Richmond	Int.	OF	10	39	3	13	4	0	1	7	1	.333
2006 Rome a	So.Atl.	OF	5	19	5	9	2	1	1	3	2	.474
2007 Atlanta	N.L.	2B	147	521	91	144	26	10	16	68	9	.276
Major League Totals		2 Yrs.	234	811	137	214	38	13	25	108	11	.264	
Division Series													
2005 Atlanta	N.L.	PH	4	2	0	0	0	0	0	0	0	.000

a On disabled list from March 24 to November 1, 2006.

JOHNSON, NICHOLAS ROBERT (NICK)
Born, Sacramento, California, September 19, 1978.
Bats Left. Throws Left. Height, 6 feet, 3 inches. Weight, 224 pounds.

Year	Club	Lea	Pos	G	AB	R	H	2B	3B	HR	RBI	SB	Avg
1996 Yankees	Gulf Coast	1B	47	157	31	45	11	1	2	33	0	.287
1997 Greensboro	So.Atl.	1B	127	433	77	118	23	1	16	75	16	.273
1998 Tampa	Fla.St.	1B	92	303	69	96	14	1	17	58	1	.317
1999 Norwich	Eastern	1B	132	420	114	145	33	5	14	87	8	.345
2000				INJURED—Did Not Play									
2001 Columbus a	Int.	1B	110	359	68	92	20	0	18	49	9	.256
2001 New York	A.L.	1B	23	67	6	13	2	0	2	8	0	.194
2002 Columbus	Int.	1B	3	11	1	1	0	0	0	0	0	.091
2002 New York b	A.L.	1B-OF	129	378	56	92	15	0	15	58	1	.243
2003 Trenton	Eastern	1B	4	12	3	5	1	0	0	1	0	.417
2003 Columbus	Int.	1B	3	10	1	5	2	0	1	3	0	.500
2003 New York c-d	A.L.	1B	96	324	60	92	19	0	14	47	5	.284
2004 Brevard County	Fla.St.	1B	6	21	3	4	0	0	1	5	0	.190
2004 Edmonton	P.C.	1B	3	9	2	2	1	0	0	0	0	.222
2004 Montreal e	N.L.	1B	73	251	35	63	16	0	7	33	6	.251
2005 New Orleans	P.C.	1B	3	6	0	0	0	0	0	0	0	.000
2005 Washington f	N.L.	1B	131	453	66	131	35	3	15	74	3	.289
2006 Washington	N.L.	1B	147	500	100	145	46	0	23	77	10	.290
2007 Washington g	N.L.			INJURED—Did Not Play									
Major League Totals		6 Yrs.	599	1973	323	536	133	3	76	297	25	.272	
Division Series													
2002 New York	A.L.	DH-1B	3	11	1	2	0	0	0	1	0	.182
2003 New York	A.L.	1B	4	13	2	1	1	0	0	2	0	.077
Division Series Totals			7	24	3	3	1	0	0	3	0	.125	
Championship Series													
2003 New York	A.L.	1B	7	26	4	6	1	0	1	3	0	.231
World Series Record													
2003 New York	A.L.	1B	6	17	3	5	1	0	0	0	0	.294

a On disabled list from March 25 to November 12, 2000.
b On disabled list from August 9 to September 3, 2002.

c On disabled list from May 16 to July 25, 2003.
d Traded to Montreal Expos with outfielder Juan Rivera and pitcher Randy Choate for pitcher Javier Vazquez, December 4, 2003.
e On disabled list from March 31 to May 28 and from August 21 to November 1, 2004.
f On disabled list from June 27 to July 26, 2005.
g On disabled list from March 28 to October 17, 2007.

JOHNSON, REED CAMERON

Born, Riverside, California, December 8, 1976.
Bats Right. Throws Right. Height, 5 feet, 10 inches. Weight, 180 pounds.

Year	Club	Lea	Pos	G	AB	R	H	2B	3B	HR	RBI	SB	Avg
1999 St. Catharines	N.Y.-Penn.	OF	60	189	24	44	8	2	2	23	5	.233
2000 Dunedin	Fla.St.	OF	36	133	26	42	9	2	4	28	3	.316
2000 Hagerstown	So.Atl.	OF	95	324	66	94	24	5	8	70	14	.290
2001 Tennessee	Southern	OF	136	554	104	174	29	4	13	74	42	.314
2002 Dunedin	Fla.St.	OF	8	33	7	9	3	0	0	6	0	.273
2002 Syracuse	Int.	OF	44	159	27	37	8	3	2	10	1	.233
2003 Syracuse	Int.	OF	26	101	14	33	4	1	2	16	3	.327
2003 Toronto	A.L.	OF	114	412	79	121	21	2	10	52	5	.294
2004 Toronto	A.L.	OF	141	537	68	145	25	2	10	61	6	.270
2005 Toronto	A.L.	OF	142	398	55	107	21	6	8	58	5	.269
2006 Toronto	A.L.	OF	134	461	86	147	34	2	12	49	8	.319
2007 Dunedin	Fla.St.	OF	4	12	1	4	1	0	1	1	0	.333
2007 Syracuse	Int.	OF	2	8	1	3	0	0	0	1	0	.375
2007 Toronto a	A.L.	OF	79	275	31	65	13	2	2	14	4	.236
Major League Totals		5 Yrs.	610	2083	319	585	114	14	42	234	28	.281

a On disabled list from April 12 to July 6, 2007.

JONES, ANDRUW RUDOLF

Born, Willemstad, Curacao, Netherlands Antilles, April 23, 1977.
Bats Right. Throws Right. Height, 6 feet, 1 inch. Weight, 210 pounds.

Year	Club	Lea	Pos	G	AB	R	H	2B	3B	HR	RBI	SB	Avg
1994 Braves	Gulf Coast	OF	27	95	22	21	5	1	2	10	5	.221
1994 Danville	Appal.	OF	36	143	20	48	9	2	1	16	16	.336
1995 Macon	So.Atl.	OF	139	537	104	149	41	5	25	100	56	.277
1996 Durham	Carolina	OF	66	243	65	76	14	3	17	43	16	.313
1996 Greenville	Southern	OF	38	157	39	58	10	1	12	37	12	.369
1996 Richmond	Int.	OF	12	45	11	17	3	1	5	12	2	.378
1996 Atlanta	N.L.	OF	31	106	11	23	7	1	5	13	3	.217
1997 Atlanta	N.L.	OF	153	399	60	92	18	1	18	70	20	.231
1998 Atlanta	N.L.	OF	159	582	89	158	33	8	31	90	27	.271
1999 Atlanta	N.L.	OF	162	592	97	163	35	5	26	84	24	.275
2000 Atlanta	N.L.	OF	161	*656	122	199	36	6	36	104	21	.303
2001 Atlanta	N.L.	OF	161	625	104	157	25	2	34	104	11	.251
2002 Atlanta	N.L.	OF	154	560	91	148	34	0	35	94	8	.264
2003 Atlanta	N.L.	OF	156	595	101	165	28	2	36	116	4	.277
2004 Atlanta	N.L.	OF	154	570	85	149	34	4	29	91	6	.261
2005 Atlanta	N.L.	OF	160	586	95	154	24	3	*51	*128	5	.263
2006 Atlanta	N.L.	OF	156	565	107	148	29	0	41	129	4	.262
2007 Atlanta a	N.L.	OF	154	572	83	127	27	2	26	94	5	.222
Major League Totals		12 Yrs.	1761	6408	1045	1683	330	34	368	1117	138	.263
Division Series													
1996 Atlanta	N.L.	OF	3	0	0	0	0	0	0	0	0	.000
1997 Atlanta	N.L.	OF	3	5	1	0	0	0	0	1	0	.000
1998 Atlanta	N.L.	OF	3	9	2	0	0	0	0	1	2	.000
1999 Atlanta	N.L.	OF	4	18	1	4	1	0	0	2	0	.222
2000 Atlanta	N.L.	OF	3	9	3	1	0	0	1	1	0	.111
2001 Atlanta	N.L.	OF	3	12	2	6	0	0	1	1	0	.500
2002 Atlanta	N.L.	OF	5	19	4	6	1	0	0	2	0	.316
2003 Atlanta	N.L.	OF	5	17	1	1	0	0	0	1	0	.059
2004 Atlanta	N.L.	OF	5	19	4	10	2	0	2	5	1	.526
2005 Atlanta	N.L.	OF	4	17	5	8	3	0	1	5	0	.471
Division Series Totals			38	125	23	36	7	0	5	19	3	.288
Championship Series													
1996 Atlanta	N.L.	OF	5	9	5	2	0	0	1	3	0	.222
1997 Atlanta	N.L.	OF	5	9	0	4	0	0	0	1	0	.444
1998 Atlanta	N.L.	OF	6	22	3	6	0	0	1	2	1	.273

Year	Club	Lea	Pos	G	AB	R	H	2B	3B	HR	RBI	SB	Avg
1999 Atlanta		N.L.	OF	6	23	5	5	0	0	0	0	1	0	.217
2001 Atlanta		N.L.	OF	5	17	4	3	0	0	1	1	0	.176
Championship Series Totals				27	80	15	20	0	0	3	8	1	.250
World Series													
1996 Atlanta		N.L.	OF	6	20	4	8	1	0	2	6	1	.400
1999 Atlanta		N.L.	OF	4	13	1	1	0	0	0	0	0	.077
World Series Totals				10	33	5	9	1	0	2	6	1	.27

a Filed for free agency, October 31, 2007. Signed with Los Angeles Dodgers, December 12, 2007.

JONES, JACQUE DEWAYNE

Born, San Diego, California, April 25, 1975.
Bats Left. Throws Left. Height, 5 feet, 10 inches. Weight, 200 pounds.

Year	Club	Lea	Pos	G	AB	R	H	2B	3B	HR	RBI	SB	Avg
1996 Ft. Myers		Fla.St.	OF	1	3	0	2	1	0	0	1	0	.667
1997 Ft. Myers		Fla.St.	OF	131	539	84	160	33	6	15	82	24	.297
1998 New Britain		Eastern	OF	134	518	78	155	39	3	21	85	18	.299
1999 Salt Lake		P.C.	OF	52	198	32	59	13	2	4	26	9	.298
1999 Minnesota		A.L.	OF	95	322	54	93	24	2	9	44	3	.289
2000 Minnesota		A.L.	OF	154	523	66	149	26	5	19	76	7	.285
2001 Minnesota		A.L.	OF	149	475	57	131	25	0	14	49	12	.276
2002 Minnesota		A.L.	OF	149	577	96	173	37	2	27	85	6	.300
2003 Minnesota a		A.L.	OF	136	517	76	157	33	1	16	69	13	.304
2004 Minnesota		A.L.	OF	151	555	69	141	22	1	24	80	13	.254
2005 Minnesota b		A.L.	OF	142	523	74	130	22	4	23	73	13	.249
2006 Chicago		N.L.	OF	149	533	73	152	31	1	27	81	9	.285
2007 Chicago c		N.L.	OF	135	453	52	129	33	2	5	66	6	.285
Major League Totals		9 Yrs.	1260	4478	617	1255	253	18	164	623	82	.280	
Division Series													
2002 Minnesota		A.L.	OF	5	20	3	5	3	0	0	1	0	.250
2003 Minnesota		A.L.	OF	4	16	0	2	0	0	0	0	0	.125
2004 Minnesota		A.L.	OF	4	20	3	6	1	0	2	2	0	.300
2007 Chicago		N.L.	OF	3	9	1	2	1	0	0	0	0	.222
Division Series Totals				16	65	7	15	5	0	2	3	0	.231
Championship Series													
2002 Minnesota		A.L.	OF	5	20	0	2	1	0	0	2	0	.100

a On disabled list from July 1 to July 17, 2003.
b Filed for free agency, October 28, 2005. Signed with Chicago Cubs, December 20, 2005.
c Traded to Detroit Tigers for infielder Omar Infante, November 12, 2007.

JONES, LARRY WAYNE (CHIPPER)

Born, Deland, Florida, April 24, 1972.
Bats Both. Throws Right. Height, 6 feet, 4 inches. Weight, 230 pounds.

Year	Club	Lea	Pos	G	AB	R	H	2B	3B	HR	RBI	SB	Avg
1990 Bradenton Braves		Gulf C.	SS	44	140	20	32	1	1	1	18	5	.229
1991 Macon		So. Atl.	SS	136	473	*104	154	24	11	15	98	40	.326
1992 Durham		Carolina	SS	70	264	43	73	22	1	4	31	10	.277
1992 Greenville		Southern	SS	67	266	43	92	17	11	9	42	14	.346
1993 Richmond		Int.	SS	139	536	97	174	31	12	13	89	23	.325
1993 Atlanta		N.L.	SS	8	3	2	2	1	0	0	0	0	.667
1994 Atlanta a		N.L.		INJURED—Did Not Play									
1995 Atlanta		N.L.	3B-OF	140	524	87	139	22	3	23	86	8	.265
1996 Atlanta b		N.L.	3B-SS-OF	157	598	114	185	32	5	30	110	14	.309
1997 Atlanta		N.L.	3B-OF	157	597	100	176	41	3	21	111	20	.295
1998 Atlanta		N.L.	3B	160	601	123	188	29	5	34	107	16	.313
1999 Atlanta c		N.L.	3B-SS	157	567	116	181	41	1	45	110	25	.319
2000 Atlanta		N.L.	3B-SS	156	579	118	180	38	1	36	111	14	.311
2001 Atlanta		N.L.	3B-OF	159	572	113	189	33	5	38	102	9	.330
2002 Atlanta		N.L.	OF	158	548	90	179	35	1	26	100	8	.327
2003 Atlanta		N.L.	OF	153	555	103	169	33	2	27	106	2	.305
2004 Rome		So.Atl.	OF	1	4	0	0	0	0	0	0	0	.000
2004 Atlanta d		N.L.	3B-OF	137	472	69	117	20	1	30	96	2	.248
2005 Rome		So.Atl.	3B	3	6	1	3	0	0	0	2	0	.500
2005 Atlanta e		N.L.	3B	109	358	66	106	30	0	21	72	5	.296
2006 Mississippi		Southern	3B	2	6	1	1	0	0	0	0	0	.167
2006 Atlanta f		N.L.	3B	110	411	87	133	28	3	26	86	6	.324
2007 Atlanta g		N.L.	3B-SS	134	513	108	173	42	4	29	102	5	.337
Major League Totals		14 Yrs.	1895	6898	1296	2117	425	34	386	1299	134	.307	

97

Year	Club	Lea	Pos	G	AB	R	H	2B	3B	HR	RBI	SB	Avg
Division Series													
1995 Atlanta	N.L.	3B	4	18	4	7	2	0	2	4	0	.389
1996 Atlanta	N.L.	3B	3	9	2	2	0	0	1	2	1	.222
1997 Atlanta	N.L.	3B	3	8	3	4	0	0	1	2	1	.500
1998 Atlanta	N.L.	3B	3	10	2	2	0	0	0	1	0	.200
1999 Atlanta	N.L.	3B	4	13	2	3	0	0	0	1	0	.231
2000 Atlanta	N.L.	3B	3	12	2	4	1	0	0	1	0	.333
2001 Atlanta	N.L.	3B	3	9	2	4	0	0	2	5	0	.444
2002 Atlanta	N.L.	OF	5	17	3	5	0	0	0	2	0	.294
2003 Atlanta	N.L.	OF	5	18	3	3	0	0	2	6	0	.167
2004 Atlanta	N.L.	3B	5	20	4	4	0	0	0	0	0	.200
2005 Atlanta	N.L.	3B	4	17	3	3	2	0	1	2	0	.176
Division Series Totals			42	151	30	41	5	0	9	26	2	.272
Championship Series													
1995 Atlanta	N.L.	3B	4	16	3	7	0	0	1	3	1	.438
1996 Atlanta	N.L.	3B	7	25	6	11	2	0	0	4	1	.440
1997 Atlanta	N.L.	3B	6	24	5	7	1	0	2	4	0	.292
1998 Atlanta	N.L.	3B	6	24	2	5	1	0	0	1	0	.208
1999 Atlanta	N.L.	3B	6	19	3	5	2	0	0	1	3	.263
2001 Atlanta	N.L.	3B	5	19	1	5	1	0	0	2	0	.263
Championship Series Totals			34	127	20	40	7	0	3	15	5	.315
World Series Record													
1995 Atlanta	N.L.	3B	6	21	3	6	3	0	0	1	0	.286
1996 Atlanta	N.L.	3B-SS	6	21	3	6	3	0	0	3	1	.286
1999 Atlanta	N.L.	3B	4	13	2	3	0	0	1	2	0	.231
World Series Totals			16	55	8	15	6	0	1	6	1	.273

a On disabled list from March 20 to end of 1994 season.
b On disabled list from April 1 to April 6, 1996.
c Selected Most Valuable Player in National League for 1999.
d On disabled list from April 19 to May 8, 2004.
e On disabled list from June 6 to July 18, 2005.
f On disabled list from April 10 to April 25 and July 30 to August 13 and September 4 to September 19, 2006.
g On disabled list from May 24 to June 13, 2007.

KATA, MATTHEW JOHN (MATT)
Born, Avon Lake, Ohio, March 14, 1978.
Bats Both. Throws Right. Height, 6 feet, 1 inch. Weight, 180 pounds.

Year	Club	Lea	Pos	G	AB	R	H	2B	3B	HR	RBI	SB	Avg
1999 South Bend	Midwest	SS	78	318	40	83	14	5	3	33	5	.261
2000 South Bend	Midwest	SS-2B-OF	133	521	82	133	22	9	6	59	38	.255
2001 Lancaster	Calif.	2B-SS	119	494	80	146	19	6	10	54	30	.296
2001 El Paso	Texas	2B	4	16	4	7	2	0	0	4	0	.438
2002 El Paso	Texas	2B-SS-3B	136	578	95	172	33	9	11	57	12	.298
2003 Tucson	P.C.	2B-SS	48	201	31	58	13	5	3	25	2	.289
2003 Arizona	N.L.	2B-3B-SS	78	288	42	74	16	5	7	29	3	.257
2004 Arizona a	N.L.	2B-3B-SS	42	162	17	40	9	2	2	13	4	.247
2005 Tucson	P.C.	2B-OF-SS-3B	46	200	25	62	10	3	3	28	5	.310
2005 Scranton-WB	Int.	2B-SS-OF-3B	24	96	10	30	5	1	0	4	2	.313
2005 Arizona-Philadelphia b	N.L.	2B-SS-OF	40	37	7	7	2	1	0	0	0	.189
2006 Louisville c-d	Int.	OF-2B-3B-SS	113	331	45	87	20	4	9	34	4	.263
2007 Indianapolis	Int.	2B-3B	19	72	12	20	5	1	2	5	2	.278
2007 Texas	A.L.	OF-3B-SS-1B	31	70	12	13	2	0	2	6	1	.186
2007 Pittsburgh e-f	N.L.	2B-3B-SS-OF	47	88	9	22	7	1	1	10	0	.250
Major League Totals		4 Yrs.	238	645	87	156	36	9	12	58	8	.242

a On disabled list from May 30 to October 4, 2004.
b Traded to Philadelphia Phillies for pitcher Tim Worrell and cash, July 21, 2005.
c Claimed on waivers by Cincinnati Reds, March 15, 2006.
d Filed for free agency, November 1, 2006. Signed with Texas Rangers organization, November 8, 2006.
e Filed for free agency, June 12, 2007. Signed with Pittsburgh Pirates organization, June 18, 2007.
f Filed for free agency, October 25, 2007. Signed with Colorado Rockies organization, December 21, 2007.

KEARNS, AUSTIN RYAN
Born, Lexington, Kentucky, May 20, 1980.
Bats Right. Throws Right. Height, 6 feet, 3 inches. Weight, 235 pounds.

Year	Club	Lea	Pos	G	AB	R	H	2B	3B	HR	RBI	SB	Avg
1998 Billings	Pioneer	OF-3B	30	108	17	34	9	0	1	14	1	.315
1999 Rockford	Midwest	OF	124	426	72	110	36	5	13	48	21	.258

Year Club	Lea	Pos	G	AB	R	H	2B	3B	HR	RBI	SB	Avg
2000 Dayton	Midwest	OF	136	484	110	148	37	2	27	104	18	.306
2001 Reds.	Gulf Coast	OF	6	17	2	3	2	0	0	4	0	.176
2001 Chattanooga a	Southern	OF	59	205	30	55	11	2	6	36	7	.268
2002 Chattanooga.	Southern	OF	12	41	10	11	2	0	5	13	1	.268
2002 Louisville	Int.	OF	1	4	3	3	2	0	0	2	0	.750
2002 Cincinnati b	N.L.	OF	107	372	66	117	24	3	13	56	6	.315
2003 Chattanooga.	Southern	OF	3	5	2	1	0	0	0	1	0	.200
2003 Cincinnati c	N.L.	OF	82	292	39	77	11	0	15	58	5	.264
2004 Louisville	Int.	OF	25	83	19	28	7	1	2	15	3	.337
2004 Cincinnati d	N.L.	OF	64	217	28	50	10	2	9	32	2	.230
2005 Louisville	Int.	OF	28	111	24	38	15	1	7	21	0	.342
2005 Cincinnati.	N.L.	OF	112	387	62	93	26	1	18	67	0	.240
2006 Cincinnati-Washington e .	N.L.	OF	150	537	86	142	33	2	24	86	9	.264
2007 Washington	N.L.	OF	161	587	84	156	35	1	16	74	2	.266
Major League Totals	6 Yrs.		676	2392	365	635	139	9	95	373	24	.265

a On disabled list from May 27 to August 13, 2001.
b On disabled list from August 27 to September 30, 2002.
c On disabled list from July 9 to November 5, 2003.
d On disabled list from April 27 to May 19 and from June 2 to August 24, 2004.
e Traded to Washington Nationals with infielder Felipe Lopez and pitcher Ryan Wagner for pitcher Gary Majewski, pitcher Bill Bray, infielder Royce Clayton, infielder Brendan Harris and pitcher Daryl Thompson, July 13, 2006.

KEMP, MATTHEW RYAN (MATT)

Born, Midwest City, Oklahoma, September 23, 1984.
Bats Right. Throws Right. Height, 6 feet, 2 inches. Weight, 230 pounds.

Year Club	Lea	Pos	G	AB	R	H	2B	3B	HR	RBI	SB	Avg
2003 Dodgers	Gulf Coast	OF	42	159	11	43	5	2	1	17	2	.270
2004 Vero Beach	Fla.St.	OF	11	37	5	13	5	0	1	9	2	.351
2004 Columbus.	So.Atl.	OF	112	423	67	122	22	8	17	66	8	.288
2006 Jacksonville	Southern	OF	48	199	38	65	15	2	7	34	11	.327
2006 Las Vegas	P.C.	OF	44	182	37	67	14	6	3	36	14	.368
2006 Los Angeles	N.L.	OF	52	154	30	39	7	1	7	23	6	.253
2007 Las Vegas	P.C.	OF	39	161	32	53	16	3	4	20	9	.329
2007 Los Angeles a	N.L.	OF	98	292	47	100	12	5	10	42	10	.342
Major League Totals	2 Yrs.		150	446	77	139	19	6	17	65	16	.312

a On disabled list from April 10 to April 27, 2007.

KENDALL, JASON DANIEL

Born, San Diego, California, June 26, 1974.
Bats Right. Throws Right. Height, 6 feet. Weight, 205 pounds.

Year Club	Lea	Pos	G	AB	R	H	2B	3B	HR	RBI	SB	Avg
1992 Pirates	Gulf Coast	C	33	111	7	29	2	0	0	10	2	.261
1993 Augusta	So.Atl.	C	102	366	43	101	17	4	1	40	8	.276
1994 Salem.	Carolina	C	101	371	68	118	19	2	7	66	14	.318
1994 Carolina	Southern	C	13	47	6	11	2	0	0	6	0	.234
1995 Carolina	Southern	C	117	429	87	140	26	1	8	71	10	.326
1996 Pittsburgh	N.L.	C	130	414	54	124	23	5	3	42	5	.300
1997 Pittsburgh	N.L.	C	144	486	71	143	36	4	8	49	18	.294
1998 Pittsburgh	N.L.	C	149	535	95	175	36	3	12	75	26	.327
1999 Pittsburgh a	N.L.	C	78	280	61	93	20	3	8	41	22	.332
2000 Pittsburgh	N.L.	C	152	579	112	185	33	6	14	58	22	.320
2001 Pittsburgh	N.L.	C-OF	157	606	84	161	22	2	10	53	13	.266
2002 Pittsburgh	N.L.	C	145	545	59	154	25	3	3	44	15	.283
2003 Pittsburgh	N.L.	C	150	587	84	191	29	3	6	58	8	.325
2004 Pittsburgh b	N.L.	C	147	574	86	183	32	0	3	51	11	.319
2005 Oakland	A.L.	C	150	601	70	163	28	1	0	53	8	.271
2006 Oakland	A.L.	C	143	552	76	163	23	0	1	50	11	.295
2007 Oakland	A.L.	C-OF	80	292	24	66	10	0	2	22	3	.226
2007 Chicago c-d	N.L.	C	57	174	21	47	10	1	1	19	0	.270
Major League Totals	12 Yrs.		1682	6225	897	1848	327	31	71	615	162	.297
Division Series												
2006 Oakland	A.L.	C	3	14	1	3	1	0	0	1	0	.214
2007 Chicago	N.L.	C	1	4	0	1	0	0	0	1	0	.250
Division Series Totals			4	18	1	4	1	0	0	2	0	.222
Championship Series												
2006 Oakland	A.L.	C	4	17	0	5	0	0	0	0	0	.294

a On disabled list from July 5 to November 17, 1999.
b Traded to Oakland Athletics with cash for pitcher Mark Redman and pitcher Arthur Rhodes, November 25, 2004.
c Traded to Chicago Cubs with cash for pitcher Jerry Blevins and catcher Rob Bowen, July 17, 2007.
d Filed for free agency, October 30, 2007. Signed with Milwaukee Brewers, November 28, 2007.

KENDRICK, HOWARD JOSEPH (HOWIE)
Born, Jacksonville, Florida, July 12, 1983.
Bats Right. Throws Right. Height, 5 feet, 10 inches. Weight, 195 pounds.

Year	Club	Lea	Pos	G	AB	R	H	2B	3B	HR	RBI	SB	Avg
2002	Angels	Arizona	2B	42	157	24	50	6	4	0	13	12	.318
2003	Provo	Pioneer	2B	63	234	65	86	20	3	3	36	8	.368
2004	Angels	Arizona	2B	3	12	1	3	1	0	0	0	2	.250
2004	Cedar Rapids	Midwest	2B	75	313	66	115	24	6	10	49	15	.367
2005	Rancho Cucamonga	Calif.	2B	63	279	69	107	23	6	12	47	13	.384
2005	Arkansas	Texas	2B	46	190	35	65	20	2	7	42	12	.342
2006	Salt Lake	P.C.	2B-3B	69	290	57	107	25	6	13	62	11	.369
2006	Los Angeles	A.L.	1B-2B-3B	72	267	25	76	21	1	4	30	6	.285
2007	Rancho Cucamonga	Calif.	DH	1	4	0	1	0	0	0	0	0	.250
2007	Salt Lake	P.C.	2B	13	50	9	15	1	0	3	11	1	.300
2007	Los Angeles a	A.L.	2B	88	338	55	109	24	2	5	39	5	.322
Major League Totals		2 Yrs.		160	605	80	185	45	3	9	69	11	.306
Division Series													
2007	Los Angeles	A.L.	2B	3	10	0	2	0	0	0	1	2	.200

a On disabled list from April 18 to May 23 and July 8 to August 20, 2007.

KENNEDY, ADAM THOMAS
Born, Riverside, California, January 10, 1976.
Bats Left. Throws Right. Height, 6 feet. Weight, 185 pounds.

Year	Club	Lea	Pos	G	AB	R	H	2B	3B	HR	RBI	SB	Avg
1997	New Jersey	N.Y.-Penn.	SS	29	114	20	39	6	3	0	19	9	.342
1997	Pr William	Carolina	SS	35	154	24	48	9	3	1	27	4	.312
1998	Pr William	Carolina	2B-SS	17	69	9	18	6	0	0	7	5	.261
1998	Arkansas	Texas	SS-2B	52	205	35	57	11	2	6	24	6	.278
1998	Memphis	P.C.	SS-2B	74	305	36	93	22	7	4	41	15	.305
1999	Memphis	P.C.	2B	91	367	69	120	22	4	10	63	20	.327
1999	St. Louis	N.L.	2B	33	102	12	26	10	1	1	16	0	.255
2000	Anaheim a	A.L.	2B	156	598	82	159	33	11	9	72	22	.266
2001	Rancho Cucamonga	Calif.	2B	3	8	3	3	2	0	0	1	3	.375
2001	Anaheim b	A.L.	2B	137	478	48	129	25	3	6	40	12	.270
2002	Anaheim	A.L.	2B-OF	144	474	65	148	32	6	7	52	17	.312
2003	Rancho Cucamonga	Calif.	2B	3	11	3	3	1	0	1	1	0	.273
2003	Anaheim c	A.L.	2B	143	449	71	121	17	1	13	49	22	.269
2004	Anaheim	A.L.	2B	144	468	70	130	20	5	10	48	15	.278
2005	Rancho Cucamonga	Calif.	2B	2	5	1	2	0	0	0	1	1	.400
2005	Salt Lake	P.C.	2B	4	17	4	7	1	0	0	4	2	.412
2005	Los Angeles d	A.L.	2B	129	416	49	125	23	0	2	37	19	.300
2006	Los Angeles e	A.L.	2B	139	451	50	123	26	6	4	55	16	.273
2007	St. Louis f	N.L.	2B-SS-OF	87	279	27	61	9	1	3	18	6	.219
Major League Totals		9 Yrs.		1112	3715	474	1022	195	34	55	387	129	.275
Division Series													
2002	Anaheim	A.L.	2B	4	8	4	4	1	0	1	3	1	.500
2005	Los Angeles	A.L.	2B	5	17	0	4	0	1	0	2	0	.235
Division Series Totals				9	25	4	8	1	1	1	5	1	.320
Championship Series													
2002	Anaheim	A.L.	2B	4	14	5	5	0	0	3	5	0	.357
2005	Los Angeles	A.L.	2B	5	14	3	4	0	0	0	1	0	.286
Championship Series Totals				9	28	8	9	0	0	3	6	0	.321
World Series Record													
2002	Anaheim	A.L.	2B	7	25	1	7	2	0	0	2	0	.280

a Traded to Anaheim Angels with pitcher Kent Bottenfield for outfielder Jim Edmonds, March 23, 2000.
b On disabled list from March 23 to April 13, 2001.
c On disabled list from April 7 to April 22, 2003.
d On disabled list from March 25 to May 2, 2005.
e Filed for free agency, October 29, 2006. Signed with St. Louis Cardinals, November 28, 2006.
f On disabled list from August 12 to November 2, 2007.

KENT, JEFFREY FRANKLIN (JEFF)

Born, Bellflower, California, March 7, 1968.
Bats Right. Throws Right. Height, 6 feet, 1 inch. Weight, 210 pounds.

Year	Club	Lea	Pos	G	AB	R	H	2B	3B	HR	RBI	SB	Avg
1989 St. Catharines....	N.Y.-Penn.	3B-SS	73	268	34	60	14	1	*13	37	5	.224
1990 Dunedin...........	Fla. St.	2B	132	447	72	124	32	2	16	60	17	.277
1991 Knoxville	Southern	2B	139	445	68	114	34	1	12	61	25	.256
1992 Toronto a	A.L.	3B-2B-1B	65	192	36	46	13	1	8	35	2	.240
1992 New York	N.L.	2B-3B-SS	37	113	16	27	8	1	3	15	0	.239
1993 New York	N.L.	2B-3B-SS	140	496	65	134	24	0	21	80	4	.270
1994 New York	N.L.	2B	107	415	53	121	24	5	14	68	1	.292
1995 New York b.........	N.L.	2B	125	472	65	131	22	3	20	65	3	.278
1996 New York c........	N.L.	3B	89	335	45	97	20	1	9	39	4	.290
1996 Cleveland d	A.L.	1B-2B-3B	39	102	16	27	7	0	3	16	2	.265
1997 San Francisco	N.L.	2B-1B	155	580	90	145	38	2	29	121	11	.250
1998 San Francisco e	N.L.	2B-1B	137	526	94	156	37	3	31	128	9	.297
1999 San Francisco f	N.L.	2B-1B	138	511	86	148	40	2	23	101	13	.290
2000 San Francisco g	N.L.	2B-1B	159	587	114	196	41	7	33	125	12	.334
2001 San Francisco	N.L.	2B-1B	159	607	84	181	49	6	22	106	7	.298
2002 San Francisco h-i......	N.L.	2B-1B	152	623	102	195	42	2	37	108	5	.313
2003 Round Rock........	Texas	2B	3	10	1	3	0	0	1	6	0	.300
2003 Houston j...........	N.L.	2B	130	505	77	150	39	1	22	93	6	.297
2004 Houston k	N.L.	2B	145	540	96	156	34	8	27	107	7	.289
2005 Los Angeles	N.L.	2B-1B	149	553	100	160	36	0	29	105	6	.289
2006 Los Angeles l	N.L.	2B-1B	115	407	61	119	27	3	14	68	1	.292
2007 Los Angeles	N.L.	2B	136	494	78	149	36	1	20	79	1	.302
Major League Totals	16 Yrs.		2177	8058	1278	2338	537	46	365	1459	94	.290
Division Series												
1996 Cleveland	A.L.	2B-1B-3B	4	8	2	1	1	0	0	0	0	.125
1997 San Francisco	N.L.	2B-1B	3	10	2	3	0	0	2	2	0	.300
2000 San Francisco	N.L.	2B-1B	4	16	3	6	1	0	0	1	1	.375
2002 San Francisco	N.L.	2B	5	19	1	5	2	0	0	1	0	.263
2004 Houston	N.L.	2B	5	22	3	5	3	0	0	3	0	.227
2006 Los Angeles	N.L.	2B-1B	3	13	2	8	1	0	1	2	0	.615
Division Series Totals			24	88	13	28	8	0	3	9	1	.318
Championship Series												
2002 San Francisco	N.L.	2B	5	19	3	5	0	0	0	0	0	.263
2004 Houston	N.L.	2B	7	25	3	6	2	0	3	7	0	.240
Championship Series Totals			12	44	6	11	2	0	3	7	0	.250
World Series Record												
2002 San Francisco	N.L.	2B	7	29	6	8	1	0	3	7	0	.276

a Traded to New York Mets with player to be named for pitcher David Cone, August 27, 1992. New York acquired outfielder Ryan Thompson to complete trade, September 1, 1992.
b On disabled list from July 6 to July 21, 1995.
c Traded to Cleveland Indians with infielder Jose Vizcaino for infielder Carlos Baerga and infielder Alvaro Espinoza, July 29, 1996.
d Traded to San Francisco Giants with pitcher Julian Taverez, infielder Jose Vizcaino and player to be named later for infielder Matt Williams and player to be named later, November 13, 1996. San Francisco Giants received pitcher Joe Roa and Cleveland Indians received outfielder Trenidad Hubbard to complete trade, December 16, 1996.
e On disabled list from June 10 to July 10, 1998.
f. On disabled list from August 3 to August 21, 1999.
g Selected Most Valuable Player in National League for 2000.
h On disabled list from March 21 to April 6, 2002.
i Filed for free agency, October 29, 2002. Signed with Houston Astros, December 18, 2002.
j On disabled list from June 25 to July 16, 2003.
k Filed for free agency, November 1, 2004. Signed with Los Angeles Dodgers, December 9, 2004.
l On disabled list from May 28 to June 13 and July 18 to August 7, 2006.

KEPPINGER, JEFFREY SCOTT (JEFF)

Born, Miami, Florida, April 21, 1980.
Bats Right. Throws Right. Height, 6 feet. Weight, 180 pounds.

Year	Club	Lea	Pos	G	AB	R	H	2B	3B	HR	RBI	SB	Avg
2002 Hickory.........	So.Atl.	2B	126	478	75	132	23	4	10	73	6	.276
2003 Lynchburg	Carolina	2B-3B-1B	92	342	55	111	21	2	3	51	3	.325
2004 Altoona........	Eastern	2B	82	323	45	108	17	2	1	33	10	.334
2004 Binghamton...	Eastern	2B-3B	14	47	14	17	3	1	0	5	2	.362
2004 Norfolk..........	Int.	2B	6	19	1	6	1	0	0	2	0	.316
2004 New York a.......	N.L.	2B	33	116	9	33	2	0	3	9	2	.284
2005 Norfolk b	Int.	2B-3B-SS	64	255	40	86	15	3	3	29	5	.337
2006 Norfolk..........	Int.	2B-OF-3B	87	323	36	97	13	0	2	26	0	.300

Year	Club	Lea	Pos	G	AB	R	H	2B	3B	HR	RBI	SB	Avg
2006 Omaha............	P.C.	2B-3B-1B-SS	32	127	21	45	6	1	2	17	0	.354
2006 Kansas City c.....	A.L.	3B-1B-2B-OF	22	60	11	16	2	0	2	8	0	.267
2007 Sarasota........	Fla.St.	3B-2B	3	12	1	4	2	0	0	1	0	.333
2007 Louisville.........	Int.	3B-2B-OF-1B	57	228	31	84	15	1	2	18	1	.368
2007 Cincinnati d-e.....	N.L.	SS-3B-2B-OF	67	241	39	80	16	2	5	32	2	.332
Major League Totals		3 Yrs.	122	417	59	129	20	2	10	49	4	.309

a Traded to New York Mets with pitcher Kris Benson for infielder Ty Wigginton, pitcher Matt Peterson and infielder Jose Bautista, July 30, 2004.

b On disabled list from September 9 to October 31, 2005.

c Traded to Kansas City Royals for infielder Ruben Gotay, July 19, 2006.

d Traded to Cincinnati Reds for pitcher Russ Haltiwanger, January 11, 2007.

e On disabled list from March 23 to April 22, 2007.

KINSLER, IAN MICHAEL

Born, Tucson, Arkansas, June 22, 1982.
Bats Right. Throws Right. Height, 6 feet. Weight, 200 pounds.

Year	Club	Lea	Pos	G	AB	R	H	2B	3B	HR	RBI	SB	Avg
2003 Spokane.....	Northwest	SS	51	188	32	52	10	6	1	15	11	.277
2004 Clinton.......	Midwest	SS	60	227	52	91	30	1	11	53	16	.401
2004 Frisco..........	Texas	SS	71	277	51	83	21	1	9	46	7	.300
2005 Oklahoma........	P.C.	2B-SS-3B	131	530	102	145	28	2	23	94	19	.274
2006 Oklahoma........	P.C.	2B	10	39	7	10	3	0	2	6	1	.256
2006 Texas a...........	A.L.	2B	120	423	65	121	27	1	14	55	11	.286
2007 Oklahoma........	P.C.	2B	3	13	1	5	0	0	0	3	2	.385
2007 Texas b...........	A.L.	2B	130	483	96	127	22	2	20	61	23	.263
Major League Totals		2 Yrs.	250	906	161	248	49	3	34	116	34	.274

a On disabled list from April 12 to May 25, 2006.

b On disabled list from July 2 to July 31, 2007.

KLESKO, RYAN ANTHONY

Born, Westminster, California, June 12, 1971.
Bats Left. Throws Left. Height, 6 feet, 3 inches. Weight, 220 pounds.

Year	Club	Lea	Pos	G	AB	R	H	2B	3B	HR	RBI	SB	Avg
1989 Bradenton Braves....	Gulf C.	1B	17	57	14	23	5	4	1	16	4	.404
1989 Sumter............	So. Atl.	1B	25	90	17	26	6	0	1	12	1	.289
1990 Sumter............	So. Atl.	1B	63	231	41	85	15	1	10	38	13	.368
1990 Durham	Carolina	1B	77	292	40	80	16	1	7	47	10	.274
1991 Greenville........	Southern	1B	126	419	64	122	22	3	14	67	14	.291
1992 Richmond	Int.	1B	123	418	63	105	22	2	17	59	3	.251
1992 Atlanta	N.L.	1B	13	14	0	0	0	0	0	1	0	.000
1993 Richmond	Int.	1B-OF	98	343	59	94	14	2	22	74	4	.274
1993 Atlanta	N.L.	1B-OF	22	17	3	6	1	0	2	5	0	.353
1994 Atlanta	N.L.	OF-1B	92	245	42	68	13	3	17	47	1	.278
1995 Greenville........	Southern	OF	4	13	1	3	0	0	1	4	0	.231
1995 Atlanta a.............	N.L.	OF-1B	107	329	48	102	25	2	23	70	5	.310
1996 Atlanta	N.L.	OF-1B	153	528	90	149	21	4	34	93	6	.282
1997 Atlanta	N.L.	OF-1B	143	467	67	122	23	6	24	84	4	.261
1998 Atlanta	N.L.	OF-1B	129	427	69	117	29	1	18	70	5	.274
1999 Atlanta b.............	N.L.	1B-OF	133	404	55	120	28	2	21	80	5	.297
2000 San Diego	N.L.	1B-OF	145	494	88	140	33	2	26	92	23	.283
2001 San Diego	N.L.	1B	146	538	105	154	34	6	30	113	23	.286
2002 San Diego	N.L.	1B-OF	146	540	90	162	39	1	29	95	6	.300
2003 San Diego c..........	N.L.	1B	121	397	47	100	18	0	21	67	2	.252
2004 San Diego d..........	N.L.	OF-1B	127	402	58	117	32	2	9	66	3	.291
2005 San Diego	N.L.	OF-1B	137	443	61	110	19	1	18	58	3	.248
2006 Lake Elsinore	Calif.	1B	8	22	2	6	2	0	0	1	0	.273
2006 San Diego e-f.........	N.L.	DH	6	4	0	3	1	0	0	2	0	.750
2007 San Francisco g.......	N.L.	1B-OF	116	362	51	94	27	3	6	44	5	.260
Major League Totals		16 Yrs.	1736	5611	874	1564	343	33	278	987	91	.279
Division Series												
1995 Atlanta	N.L.	OF	4	15	5	7	1	0	0	1	0	.467
1996 Atlanta	N.L.	OF	3	8	1	1	0	0	1	1	1	.125
1997 Atlanta	N.L.	OF	3	8	2	2	1	0	1	1	0	.250
1998 Atlanta	N.L.	OF	3	11	1	3	0	0	1	4	0	.173
1999 Atlanta	N.L.	1B	4	12	3	4	0	0	0	1	0	.333
2005 San Diego	N.L.	OF	3	10	1	2	0	0	0	0	0	.200

Year	Club	Lea	Pos	G	AB	R	H	2B	3B	HR	RBI	SB	Avg
2006 San Diego	N.L.	PH	3	3	0	2	1	0	0	0	0	.667
Division Series Totals			23	67	13	21	3	0	3	8	1	.313
Championship Series												
1995 Atlanta	N.L.	OF	4	7	0	0	0	0	0	0	0	.000
1996 Atlanta	N.L.	OF	6	16	1	4	0	0	1	3	0	.250
1997 Atlanta	N.L.	OF	5	17	2	4	0	0	2	4	0	.235
1998 Atlanta	N.L.	OF	5	12	2	1	0	0	0	1	0	.083
1999 Atlanta	N.L.	1B	4	8	1	1	0	0	1	1	0	.125
Championship Series Totals			24	60	6	10	0	0	4	9	0	.167
World Series Record												
1995 Atlanta	N.L.	OF-DH	6	16	4	5	0	0	3	4	0	.313
1996 Atlanta	N.L.	1B-DH	5	10	2	1	0	0	0	1	0	.100
1999 Atlanta	N.L.	1B	4	12	0	2	0	0	0	0	0	.167
World Series Totals.............			15	38	6	8	0	0	3	5	0	.211

a On disabled list from May 3 to May 18, 1995.
b Traded to San Diego Padres with infielder Bret Boone and pitcher Jason Shiell for infielder Wally Joyner, infielder Quilvio Veras and outfielder Reggie Sanders, December 22, 1999.
c On disabled list from September 1 to September 29, 2003.
d On disabled list from May 27 to June 16, 2004.
e On disabled list from March 26 to September 20, 2006.
f Filed for free agency, November 1, 2006. Signed with San Francisco Giants, December 19, 2006.
g Filed for free agency, November 1, 2007.

KONERKO, PAUL HENRY

Born, Providence, Rhode Island, March 5, 1976.
Bats Right. Throws Right. Height, 6 feet, 2 inches. Weight, 220 pounds.

Year	Club	Lea	Pos	G	AB	R	H	2B	3B	HR	RBI	SB	Avg
1994 Yakima........	Northwest	C	67	257	25	74	15	2	6	58	1	.288
1995 San Berndno	California	C	118	448	77	124	21	1	19	77	3	.277
1996 San Antonio	Texas	1B	133	470	78	141	23	2	29	86	1	.300
1996 Albuquerque..........	P.C.	1B	4	14	2	6	0	0	1	2	0	.429
1997 Albuquerque..........	P.C.	3B-1B-2B	130	483	97	156	31	1	37	127	2	.323
1997 Los Angeles	N.L.	1B-3B	6	7	0	1	0	0	0	0	0	.143
1998 Albuquerque.:........	P.C.	OF-1B-3B	24	87	16	33	10	0	6	26	0	.379
1998 Indianapolis	Int.	3B	39	150	25	49	8	0	8	39	1	.327
1998 Los Angeles-Cinc. a-b ..	N.L.	1B-3B-OF	75	217	21	47	4	0	7	29	0	.217
1999 Chicago	A.L.	1B-3B	142	513	71	151	31	4	24	81	1	.294
2000 Chicago	A.L.	1B-3B	143	524	84	156	31	1	21	97	1	.298
2001 Chicago	A.L.	1B	156	582	92	164	35	0	32	99	1	.282
2002 Chicago	A.L.	1B	151	570	81	173	30	0	27	104	0	.304
2003 Chicago	A.L.	1B	137	444	49	104	19	0	18	65	0	.234
2004 Chicago	A.L.	1B	155	563	84	156	22	0	41	117	1	.277
2005 Chicago c.............	A.L.	1B	158	575	98	163	24	0	40	100	0	.283
2006 Chicago	A.L.	1B	152	566	97	177	30	0	35	113	1	.313
2007 Chicago	A.L.	1B	151	549	71	142	34	0	31	90	0	.259
Major League Totals	11 Yrs.		1426	5110	748	1434	260	5	276	895	5	.281
Division Series												
2000 Chicago	A.L.	1B	3	9	1	0	0	0	0	0	0	.000
2005 Chicago	A.L.	1B	3	12	3	3	0	0	2	4	0	.250
Division Series Totals			6	21	4	3	0	0	2	4	0	.143
Championship Series												
2005 Chicago	A.L.	1B	5	21	2	6	1	0	2	7	0	.286
World Series Record												
2005 Chicago	A.L.	1B	4	16	1	4	1	0	1	4	0	.250

a Traded to Cincinnati Reds with pitcher Dennis Reyes for pitcher Jeff Shaw, July 4, 1998.
b Traded to Chicago White Sox for outfielder Mike Cameron, November 11, 1998.
c Filed for free agency, October 27, 2005, re-signed with Chicago White Sox, November 30, 2005.

KOTCHMAN, CASEY JOHN

Born, St. Petersburg, Florida, February 22, 1983.
Bats Left. Throws Left. Height, 6 feet, 3 inches. Weight, 215 pounds.

Year	Club	Lea	Pos	G	AB	R	H	2B	3B	HR	RBI	SB	Avg
2001 Angels	Arizona	1B	4	15	5	9	1	0	1	5	0	.600
2001 Provo.............	Pioneer	1B	7	22	6	11	3	0	0	7	0	.500
2002 Cedar Rapids	Midwest	1B	81	288	42	81	30	1	5	50	2	.281
2003 Angels	Arizona	1B	7	27	5	9	1	0	2	6	0	.333

Year Club Lea	Pos	G	AB	R	H	2B	3B	HR	RBI	SB	Avg
2003 Rancho Cucamonga....Calif.	1B	57	206	42	72	12	0	8	28	2	.350
2004 Arkansas ....Texas	1B	28	114	19	42	11	0	3	18	0	.368
2004 Anaheim.............A.L.	1B	38	116	7	26	6	0	0	15	3	.224
2004 Salt Lake............P.C.	1B	49	199	32	74	22	0	5	38	0	.372
2005 Salt Lake............P.C.	1B	94	363	62	105	23	1	10	58	0	.289
2005 Los Angeles..........A.L.	1B	47	126	16	35	5	0	7	22	1	.278
2006 Salt Lake............P.C.	1B	3	7	0	0	0	0	0	1	0	.000
2006 Los Angeles a........A.L.	1B	29	79	6	12	2	0	1	6	0	.152
2007 Los Angeles..........A.L.	1B	137	443	64	131	37	3	11	68	2	.296
Major League Totals	4 Yrs.	251	764	93	204	50	3	19	111	6	.267
Division Series											
2004 Anaheim.............A.L.	PH	2	1	0	0	0	0	0	0	0	.000
2005 Los Angeles..........A.L.	PH	2	2	0	0	0	0	0	0	0	.000
2007 Los Angeles..........A.L.	1B	2	5	1	0	0	0	0	0	0	.000
Division Series Totals		6	8	1	0	0	0	0	0	0	.000
Championship Series											
2005 Los Angeles..........A.L.	DH	2	7	0	2	1	0	0	1	0	.286

a On disabled list from May 9 to October 2, 2006.

KOTSAY, MARK STEVEN
Born, Whittier, California, December 2, 1975.
Bats Left. Throws Left. Height, 6 feet. Weight, 205 pounds.

Year Club Lea	Pos	G	AB	R	H	2B	3B	HR	RBI	SB	Avg
1996 Kane County.......Midwest	OF	17	60	16	17	5	0	2	8	3	.283
1997 Florida ..............N.L.	OF	14	52	5	10	1	1	0	4	3	.192
1997 Portland ....Eastern	OF	114	438	103	134	27	2	20	77	17	.306
1998 Florida ..............N.L.	OF-1B	154	578	72	161	25	7	11	68	10	.279
1999 Florida ..............N.L.	OF-1B	148	495	57	134	23	9	8	50	7	.271
2000 Florida ..............N.L.	OF-1B	152	530	87	158	31	5	12	57	19	.298
2001 San Diego a ..........N.L.	OF	119	406	67	118	29	1	10	58	13	.291
2002 San Diego b ..........N.L.	OF	153	578	82	169	27	7	17	61	11	.292
2003 San Diego c-d ........N.L.	OF	128	482	64	128	28	4	7	38	6	.266
2004 Oakland .............A.L.	OF	148	606	78	190	37	3	15	63	8	.314
2005 Oakland .............A.L.	OF	139	582	75	163	35	1	15	82	5	.280
2006 Oakland .............A.L.	OF-1B	129	502	57	138	29	3	7	59	6	.275
2007 Sacramento ..........P.C.	OF	10	37	2	10	1	0	0	2	2	.270
2007 Oakland e-f...........A.L.	OF	56	206	20	44	14	0	1	20	1	.214
Major League Totals	11 Yrs.	1340	5017	664	1413	279	41	103	560	89	.282
Division Series											
2006 Oakland .............A.L.	OF	3	14	2	2	0	0	1	2	0	.143
Championship Series											
2006 Oakland .............A.L.	OF	4	16	3	4	2	0	0	0	0	.250

a On disabled list from April 16 to May 1, 2001.
b Traded to San Diego Padres with outfielder Cesar Crespo for pitcher Matt Clement, pitcher Omar Ortiz and outfielder Eric Owens, March 28, 2001.
c On disabled list from May 19 to June 5, 2003.
d Traded to Oakland Athletics for catcher Ramon Hernandez and outfielder Terrence Long, November 26, 2003.
e On disabled list from March 23 to June 1 and August 15 to October 8, 2007.
f Traded to Atlanta Braves, for pitcher Joey Devine, pitcher Jamie Richmond and cash, January 14, 2008.

KOUZMANOFF, KEVIN
Born, Newport Beach, California, July 25, 1981.
Bats Right. Throws Right. Height, 6 feet, 1 inch. Weight, 210 pounds.

Year Club Lea	Pos	G	AB	R	H	2B	3B	HR	RBI	SB	Avg
2003 Mahoning Valley..N.Y.-Penn.	3B	54	206	31	56	8	1	8	33	2	.272
2004 Akron.............Eastern	3B	7	24	3	5	1	1	1	6	0	.208
2004 Lake County........So.Atl.	3B	123	473	74	156	35	5	16	87	5	.330
2005 Kinston..........Carolina	3B	68	254	47	86	20	4	12	58	3	.339
2005 Mahoning Valley..N.Y.-Penn.	3B	3	7	0	1	0	0	0	0	0	.143
2006 Akron.............Eastern	3B	67	244	46	95	19	1	15	55	2	.389
2006 Buffalo ....Int.	3B-1B	27	102	22	36	9	0	7	20	2	.353
2006 Cleveland a..........A.L.	DH-3B	16	56	4	12	2	0	3	11	0	.214
2007 San Diego ..........N.L.	3B	145	484	57	133	30	2	18	74	1	.275
Major League Totals	2 Yrs.	161	540	61	145	32	2	21	85	1	.269

a Traded to San Diego Padres with pitcher Andrew Brown for infielder Josh Barfield, November 8, 2006.

KUBEL, JASON JAMES

Born, Belle Fourche, South Dakota, May 25, 1982.
Bats Left. Throws Right. Height, 5 feet, 11 inches. Weight, 200 pounds.

Year	Club	Lea	Pos	G	AB	R	H	2B	3B	HR	RBI	SB	Avg
2000 Twins	Gulf Coast	OF	23	78	17	22	3	2	0	13	0	.282
2001 Twins	Gulf Coast	OF	37	124	14	41	10	4	1	30	3	.331
2002 Quad Cities	Midwest	OF	115	424	60	136	26	4	17	69	3	.321
2003 Fort Myers	Fla.St.	OF	116	420	56	125	20	4	5	82	4	.298
2004 New Britain	Eastern	OF	37	138	25	52	14	4	6	29	0	.377
2004 Rochester	Int.	OF	90	350	71	120	28	0	16	71	16	.343
2004 Minnesota	A.L.	OF	23	60	10	18	2	0	2	7	1	.300
2005 Minnesota a	A.L.	INJURED—Did Not Play										
2006 Rochester	Int.	OF	30	120	18	34	7	2	4	22	2	.283
2006 Minnesota	A.L.	OF	73	220	23	53	8	0	8	26	2	.241
2007 Minnesota	A.L.	OF	128	418	49	114	31	2	13	65	5	.273
Major League Totals		3 Yrs.	224	698	82	185	41	2	23	98	8	.265

Division Series

Year	Club	Lea	Pos	G	AB	R	H	2B	3B	HR	RBI	SB	Avg
2004 Minnesota	A.L.	DH	2	7	0	1	1	0	0	0	0	.143

a On disabled list from March 15 to October 14, 2005.

LAIRD, GERALD LEE

Born, Westminster, California, November 13, 1979.
Bats Right. Throws Right. Height, 6 feet, 1 inch. Weight, 225 pounds.

Year	Club	Lea	Pos	G	AB	R	H	2B	3B	HR	RBI	SB	Avg
1999 Southern Oregon	Northwest	C	60	228	45	65	7	2	2	39	10	.285
2000 Athletics	Arizona	C	14	50	10	15	2	1	0	9	2	.300
2000 Visalia	Calif.	C	33	103	14	25	3	0	0	13	7	.243
2001 Modesto	Calif.	C-OF-1B-2B	119	443	71	113	13	5	5	46	10	.255
2002 Tulsa a	Texas	C-OF	123	442	70	122	21	4	11	67	8	.276
2003 Oklahoma	P.C.	C	99	338	50	88	20	5	9	42	9	.260
2003 Texas	A.L.	C	19	44	9	12	2	1	1	4	0	.273
2004 Texas	A.L.	C	49	147	20	33	6	0	1	16	0	.224
2004 Oklahoma b	P.C.	C	6	22	2	4	2	0	0	2	1	.182
2005 Rangers	Arizona	C	8	26	4	5	2	2	0	3	1	.192
2005 Oklahoma	P.C.	C	75	281	51	87	12	4	17	55	12	.310
2005 Texas	A.L.	C-OF	13	40	7	9	2	0	1	4	0	.225
2006 Texas	A.L.	C-OF	78	243	46	72	20	1	7	22	3	.296
2007 Texas	A.L.	C-OF	120	407	48	91	18	3	9	47	6	.224
Major League Totals		5 Yrs.	279	881	130	217	48	5	19	93	9	.246

a Traded to Texas Rangers with pitcher Mario Ramos, outfielder Ryan Ludwick and infielder Jason Hart for pitcher Mike Venafro and outfielder Carlos Pena, January 14, 2002.
b On disabled list from May 21 to July 23, 2004.

LAMB, MICHAEL ROBERT (MIKE)

Born, West Covina, California, August 9, 1975.
Bats Left. Throws Right. Height, 6 feet, 1 inch. Weight, 190 pounds.

Year	Club	Lea	Pos	G	AB	R	H	2B	3B	HR	RBI	SB	Avg
1997 Pulaski	Appal.	3B	60	233	59	78	19	3	9	47	7	.335
1998 Charlotte	Fla.St.	3B-1B	135	536	83	162	35	3	9	93	18	.302
1999 Tulsa	Texas	3B-C	137	544	98	176	51	5	21	100	4	.324
1999 Oklahoma	P.C.	3B	2	2	0	1	0	0	0	0	0	.500
2000 Oklahoma	P.C.	3B	14	55	8	14	5	1	2	5	2	.255
2000 Texas	A.L.	3B	138	493	65	137	25	2	6	47	0	.278
2001 Oklahoma	P.C.	3B	69	273	35	81	19	3	8	40	0	.297
2001 Texas	A.L.	3B	76	284	42	87	18	0	4	35	2	.306
2002 Oklahoma	P.C.	C-3B	6	28	3	11	1	0	0	4	0	.393
2002 Texas	A.L.	1B-OF-3B	115	314	54	89	13	0	9	33	0	.283
2003 Texas	A.L.	1B-OF-3B	28	38	3	5	0	0	0	2	1	.132
2003 Oklahoma	P.C.	3B-1B	73	274	45	79	19	4	9	46	1	.288
2004 Houston a	N.L.	3B-1B-2B	112	278	38	80	14	3	14	58	1	.288
2005 Houston	N.L.	1B-OF-3B	125	322	41	76	13	5	12	53	1	.236
2006 Houston	N.L.	3B-2B	126	381	70	117	22	3	12	45	2	.307
2007 Houston b	N.L.	3B-1B-OF	124	311	45	90	14	2	11	40	0	.289
Major League Totals		8 Yrs.	844	2421	358	681	119	15	68	313	7	.281

Division Series

Year	Club	Lea	Pos	G	AB	R	H	2B	3B	HR	RBI	SB	Avg
2004 Houston	N.L.	PH	4	3	0	0	0	0	0	1	0	.000
2005 Houston	N.L.	1B	2	6	1	3	0	0	1	1	0	.500

Year	Club	Lea	Pos	G	AB	R	H	2B	3B	HR	RBI	SB	Avg
Division Series Totals				6	9	1	3	0	0	1	2	0	.333
Championship Series													
2004 Houston..........N.L.			3B	2	5	2	2	0	0	2	2	0	.400
2005 Houston..........N.L.			1B	4	16	3	3	1	0	1	2	0	.188
Championship Series Totals ..				6	21	5	5	1	0	3	4	0	.238
World Series Record													
2005 Houston..........N.L.			1B	4	10	1	2	1	0	1	1	0	.200

a Traded to Houston Astros for pitcher Juan DeLeon, March 25, 2004.
b Filed for free agency, October 29, 2007. Signed with Minnesota Twins, December 14, 2007.

LANE, JASON DEAN

Born, Santa Rosa, California, December 22, 1976.
Bats Right. Throws Left. Height, 6 feet, 2 inches. Weight, 220 pounds.

Year	Club	Lea	Pos	G	AB	R	H	2B	3B	HR	RBI	SB	Avg
1999 Auburn.........	N.Y.-Penn.		1B	74	283	46	79	18	5	13	59	6	.279
2000 Michigan	Midwest		OF-1B	133	511	98	153	38	0	23	104	20	.299
2001 Round Rock.........	Texas		OF	137	526	103	166	36	2	38	124	14	.316
2002 New Orleans............	P.C.		OF-1B	111	426	65	116	36	2	15	83	13	.272
2002 Houston.............	N.L.		OF	44	69	12	20	3	1	4	10	1	.290
2003 New Orleans..........	P.C.		OF-1B	71	248	37	74	17	0	7	39	2	.298
2003 Houston.............	N.L.		OF	18	27	5	8	2	0	4	10	0	.296
2004 Houston.............	N.L.		OF-1B	107	136	21	37	10	2	4	19	1	.272
2005 Houston.............	N.L.		OF	145	517	65	138	34	4	26	78	6	.267
2006 Round Rock..........	P.C.		OF	12	46	7	12	2	0	1	11	1	.261
2006 Houston.............	N.L.		OF-1B	112	288	44	58	10	0	15	45	1	.201
2007 Round Rock..........	P.C.		OF-1B	50	185	37	59	15	0	9	41	2	.319
2007 Houston-San Diego a-b	N.L.		OF	71	171	18	30	5	0	8	27	1	.175
Major League Totals		6 Yrs.		497	1208	165	291	64	7	61	189	10	.241
Division Series													
2004 Houston.............	N.L.		OF	5	5	2	3	0	0	1	2	0	.600
2005 Houston.............	N.L.		OF	4	17	1	4	1	0	0	3	0	.235
Division Series Totals				9	22	3	7	1	0	1	5	0	.318
Championship Series													
2004 Houston.............	N.L.		OF	2	1	0	0	0	0	0	0	0	.000
2005 Houston.............	N.L.		OF	6	21	3	5	0	0	2	3	0	.238
Championship Series Totals				8	22	3	5	0	0	2	3	0	.227
World Series Record													
2005 Houston.............	N.L.		OF	4	18	1	4	1	0	1	2	1	.222

a Sold to San Diego Padres, September 24, 2007.
b Not offered contract, December 12, 2007. Signed with New York Yankees organization, January 10, 2008.

LANGERHANS, RYAN DAVID

Born, San Antonio, Texas, February 20, 1980.
Bats Left. Throws Left. Height, 6 feet, 3 inches. Weight, 205 pounds.

Year	Club	Lea	Pos	G	AB	R	H	2B	3B	HR	RBI	SB	Avg
1998 Braves	Gulf Coast		OF	43	148	15	41	10	4	2	19	2	.277
1999 Macon	So.Atl.		OF	121	448	66	120	30	1	9	49	19	.268
2000 Myrtle Beach	Carolina		OF	116	392	55	83	14	7	6	37	25	.212
2001 Myrtle Beach	Carolina		OF	125	450	66	129	30	3	7	48	22	.287
2002 Greenville........	Southern		OF	109	391	57	98	23	2	9	62	10	.251
2002 Atlanta..............	N.L.		OF	1	1	0	0	0	0	0	0	0	.000
2003 Greenville..........	Southern		OF	94	336	42	85	23	2	6	38	10	.253
2003 Richmond	Int.		OF	38	132	13	37	10	2	4	11	2	.280
2003 Atlanta	N.L.		OF	16	15	2	4	0	0	0	0	0	.267
2004 Richmond	Int.		OF	135	456	103	136	34	3	20	72	5	.298
2005 Atlanta	N.L.		OF	128	326	48	87	22	3	8	42	0	.267
2006 Atlanta	N.L.		OF	131	315	46	76	16	3	7	28	1	.241
2007 Columbus............	Int.		OF	14	51	11	14	3	0	1	2	1	.275
2007 Atlanta-Washington	N.L.		OF	123	206	27	35	7	2	6	23	3	.170
2007 Oakland a-b	A.L.		OF	2	4	0	0	0	0	0	0	0	.000
Major League Totals		5 Yrs.		401	867	123	202	45	8	21	93	4	.233
Division Series													
2005 Atlanta	N.L.		OF	4	12	1	4	1	0	0	0	1	.333

a Traded to Oakland Athletics for player to be named later, April 29, 2007.
b Traded to Washington Nationals for outfielder Chis Snelling, May 2, 2007.

LA ROCHE, DAVID ADAM (ADAM)

Born, Orange Co., California, November 6, 1979.
Bats Left. Throws Left. Height, 6 feet, 3 inches. Weight, 180 pounds.

Year	Club	Lea	Pos	G	AB	R	H	2B	3B	HR	RBI	SB	Avg
2000 Danville	Appal.	1B	56	201	38	62	13	3	7	45	4	.308
2001 Myrtle Beach	Carolina	1B-OF	126	471	49	118	31	0	7	47	10	.251
2002 Myrtle Beach	Carolina	1B	69	250	30	84	17	0	9	53	0	.336
2002 Greenville	Southern	1B	45	173	17	50	9	0	4	19	1	.289
2003 Greenville	Southern	1B	61	219	42	62	12	1	12	37	1	.283
2003 Richmond	Int.	1B	72	264	33	78	21	0	8	35	1	.295
2004 Richmond	Int.	1B	4	11	1	2	0	0	1	2	0	.182
2004 Atlanta a	N.L.	1B	110	324	45	90	27	1	13	45	0	.278
2005 Atlanta	N.L.	1B	141	451	53	117	28	0	20	78	0	.259
2006 Atlanta b	N.L.	1B	149	492	89	140	38	1	32	90	0	.285
2007 Pittsburgh	N.L.	1B	152	563	71	153	42	0	21	88	1	.272
Major League Totals		4 Yrs.	552	1830	258	500	135	2	86	301	1	.273
Division Series												
2004 Atlanta	N.L.	1B	5	17	1	4	1	0	1	4	0	.235
2005 Atlanta	N.L.	1B	3	8	2	4	1	0	1	6	0	.500
Division Series Totals				8	25	3	8	2	0	2	10	0	.320

a On disabled list from May 29 to July 2, 2004.
b Traded to Pittsburgh Pirates with outfielder Jamie Romak for pitcher Mike Gonzalez and infielder Brent Lillibridge, January 17, 2007.

LA RUE, MICHAEL JASON (JASON)

Born, Houston, Texas, March 19, 1974.
Bats Right. Throws Right. Height, 5 feet, 11 inches. Weight, 200 pounds.

Year	Club	Lea	Pos	G	AB	R	H	2B	3B	HR	RBI	SB	Avg
1995 Billings	Pioneer	C	58	183	35	50	8	1	5	31	3	.273
1996 Chston-W.V. a	So.Atl.	C-1B	37	123	17	26	8	0	2	14	3	.211
1997 Chston-W.V.	So.Atl.	C-1B-3B	132	473	78	149	50	3	8	81	14	.315
1998 Indianapols	Int.	C	15	51	5	12	4	0	0	5	0	.235
1998 Chattanooga	Southern	C-3B-1B	105	386	71	141	39	8	14	82	4	.365
1999 Indianapolis	Int.	C	70	263	42	66	12	2	12	37	0	.251
1999 Cincinnati	N.L.	C	36	90	12	19	7	0	3	10	4	.211
2000 Louisville	Int.	C	82	307	54	78	22	1	14	48	3	.254
2000 Cincinnati	N.L.	C	31	98	12	23	3	0	5	12	0	.235
2001 Cincinnati	N.L.	C-3B-OF-1B	121	364	39	86	21	2	12	43	3	.236
2002 Cincinnati b	N.L.	C	113	353	42	88	17	1	12	52	1	.249
2003 Cincinnati	N.L.	C-1B-OF	118	379	52	87	23	1	16	50	3	.230
2004 Louisville	Int.	C	3	10	3	1	0	0	1	4	0	.100
2004 Cincinnati c	N.L.	C-OF	114	390	46	98	24	2	14	55	0	.251
2005 Cincinnati	N.L.	C-OF	110	361	38	94	27	0	14	60	0	.260
2006 Sarasota	Fla.St.	C	3	12	1	2	0	0	0	1	0	.167
2006 Louisville	Int.	C	2	8	1	2	1	0	0	0	0	.250
2006 Cincinnati d-e	N.L.	C	72	191	22	37	5	0	8	21	1	.194
2007 Omaha	P.C.	C	4	12	2	1	1	0	0	0	0	.083
2007 Kansas City f-g	A.L.	C-3B	66	169	14	25	9	0	4	13	1	.148
Major League Totals		9 Yrs.	781	2395	277	557	136	6	88	316	13	.233

a On disabled list from June 30 to September 13, 1996.
b On disabled list from September 23 to September 30, 2002.
c On disabled list from April 29 to May 14, 2004.
d On disabled list from March 26 to April 18, 2006.
e Traded to Kansas City Royals for player to be named later, November 20, 2006.
f On disabled list from May 11 to May 26, 2007.
g Filed for free agency, October 29, 2007. Signed with St. Louis Cardinals, November 13, 2007.

LEE, CARLOS

Born, Aguadúlce, Panama, June 20, 1976.
Bats Right. Throws Right. Height, 6 feet, 2 inches. Weight, 240 pounds.

Year	Club	Lea	Pos	G	AB	R	H	2B	3B	HR	RBI	SB	Avg
1994 White Sox	Gulf Coast	3B	29	56	6	7	1	0	0	1	0	.125
1995 Hickory	So.Atl.	3B-SS	63	218	18	54	9	1	4	30	1	.248
1995 Bristol	Appal.	3B-1B	67	269	43	93	17	1	7	45	17	.346
1996 Hickory	So.Atl.	3B-1B	119	480	65	150	23	6	8	70	18	.313
1997 Winston-Sal	Carolina	3B	139	546	81	173	50	4	17	82	11	.317
1998 Birmingham	Southern	3B	138	549	77	166	33	2	21	106	11	.302
1999 Charlotte	Int.	3B	25	94	16	33	5	0	4	20	2	.351

Year Club	Lea	Pos	G	AB	R	H	2B	3B	HR	RBI	SB	Avg
1999 Chicago	A.L.	OF-1B	127	492	66	144	32	2	16	84	4	.293
2000 Chicago	A.L.	OF	152	572	107	172	29	2	24	92	13	.301
2001 Chicago	A.L.	OF	150	558	75	150	33	3	24	84	17	.269
2002 Chicago	A.L.	OF	140	492	82	130	26	2	26	80	1	.264
2003 Chicago	A.L.	OF	158	623	100	181	35	1	31	113	18	.291
2004 Chicago a	A.L.	OF	153	591	103	180	37	0	31	99	11	.305
2005 Milwaukee	N.L.	OF	*162	618	85	164	41	0	32	114	13	.265
2006 Milwaukee	N.L.	OF	102	388	60	111	18	0	28	81	12	.286
2006 Texas b-c	A.L.	OF	59	236	42	76	19	1	9	35	7	.322
2007 Houston	N.L.	OF	*162	627	93	190	43	1	32	119	10	.303
Major League Totals		9 Yrs.	1365	5197	813	1498	313	12	253	901	106	.288
Division Series												
2000 Chicago	A.L.	OF	3	11	0	1	1	0	0	1	0	.091

a Traded to Milwaukee Brewers for outfielder Scott Podsednik, pitcher Luis Vizcaino and player to be named later, December 13, 2004. Chicago White Sox received infielder Travis Hinton to complete trade, January 10, 2005.

b Traded to Texas Rangers with outfielder Nelson Cruz for pitcher Francisco Cordero, outfielder Kevin Mench, outfielder Laynce Nix and pitcher Julian Cordero, July 28, 2006.

c Filed for free agency, October 30, 2006. Signed with Houston Astros, November 24, 2006.

LEE, DERREK LEON
Born, Sacramento, California, September 6, 1975.
Bats Right. Throws Right. Height, 6 feet, 5 inches. Weight, 245 pounds.

Year Club	Lea	Pos	G	AB	R	H	2B	3B	HR	RBI	SB	Avg
1993 Padres	Arizona	1B	15	52	11	17	1	1	2	5	4	.327
1993 Rancho Cucamonga	Calif.	1B	20	73	13	20	5	1	1	10	0	.274
1994 Rancho Cucamonga	Calif.	3B-1B	126	442	66	118	19	2	8	53	18	.267
1995 Rancho Cucamonga	Calif.	1B	128	502	82	151	25	2	23	95	14	.301
1995 Memphis	Southern	1B	2	9	0	1	0	0	0	1	0	.111
1996 Memphis	Southern	1B-3B	134	500	98	140	39	2	34	104	13	.280
1997 Las Vegas	P.C.	1B	124	468	85	152	29	2	13	64	17	.325
1997 San Diego a	N.L.	1B	22	54	9	14	3	0	1	4	0	.259
1998 Florida	N.L.	1B	141	454	62	106	29	1	17	74	5	.233
1999 Calgary	P.C.	1B	89	339	60	96	20	1	19	73	3	.283
1999 Florida	N.L.	1B	70	218	21	45	9	1	5	20	2	.206
2000 Florida	N.L.	1B	158	477	70	134	18	3	28	70	0	.281
2001 Florida	N.L.	1B	158	561	83	158	37	4	21	75	4	.282
2002 Florida	N.L.	1B	*162	581	95	157	35	7	27	86	19	.270
2003 Florida b	N.L.	1B	155	539	91	146	31	2	31	92	21	.271
2004 Chicago	N.L.	1B	161	605	90	168	39	1	32	98	12	.278
2005 Chicago	N.L.	1B	158	594	120	*199	*50	3	46	107	15	*.335
2006 Iowa	P.C.	1B	1	4	0	1	0	0	0	1	0	.250
2006 Chicago c	N.L.	1B	50	175	30	50	9	0	8	30	8	.286
2007 Chicago	N.L.	1B	150	567	91	180	43	1	22	82	6	.317
Major League Totals		11 Yrs.	1385	4825	762	1357	303	23	238	738	92	.281
Division Series												
2003 Florida	N.L.	1B	4	16	2	4	1	0	0	2	1	.250
2007 Chicago	N.L.	1B	3	12	1	4	0	0	0	0	0	.333
Division Series Totals			7	28	3	8	1	0	0	2	1	.286
Championship Series												
2003 Florida	N.L.	1B	7	32	2	6	2	0	1	4	1	.188
World Series Record												
2003 Florida	N.L.	1B	6	24	2	5	0	0	0	2	0	.208

a Traded to Florida Marlins with pitcher Rafael Medina and pitcher Steve Hoff for pitcher Kevin Brown, December 15, 1997.

b Traded to Chicago Cubs for infielder Hee Seop Choi and player to be named later, November 25, 2003. Florida Marlins received pitcher Mike Nannini to complete trade, December 15, 2003.

c On disabled list from April 20 to June 25 and July 24 to August 28, 2006.

LEWIS, FREDERICK DESHAUN (FRED)
Born, Hattiesburg, Mississippi, December 9, 1980.
Bats Left. Throws Right. Height, 6 feet, 2 inches. Weight, 190 pounds.

Year Club	Lea	Pos	G	AB	R	H	2B	3B	HR	RBI	SB	Avg
2002 Salem-Keizer	Northwest	OF	58	239	43	77	9	3	1	23	9	.322
2003 Hagerstown	So.Atl.	OF	114	420	61	105	17	8	1	27	30	.250
2004 San Jose	Calif.	OF	115	439	88	132	20	11	8	57	33	.301
2004 Fresno	P.C.	OF	6	23	3	7	1	0	1	2	1	.304
2005 Norwich	Eastern	OF	137	512	79	140	28	7	7	47	30	.273

Year	Club	Lea	Pos	G	AB	R	H	2B	3B	HR	RBI	SB	Avg
2006 Fresno		P.C.	OF	120	439	85	121	20	11	12	56	18	.276
2006 San Francisco		N.L.	OF	13	11	5	5	1	0	0	2	0	.455
2007 Fresno		P.C.	OF	42	171	31	50	8	6	8	32	9	.292
2007 San Francisco a		N.L.	OF	58	157	34	45	6	2	3	19	5	.287
Major League Totals			2 Yrs.	71	168	39	50	7	2	3	21	5	.298

a On disabled list from June 9 to June 30, 2007.

LIND, ADAM ALAN

Born, Anderson, Indiana, July 17, 1983.
Bats Left. Throws Left. Height, 6 feet, 2 inches. Weight, 195 pounds.

Year	Club	Lea	Pos	G	AB	R	H	2B	3B	HR	RBI	SB	Avg
2004 Auburn	N.Y.-Penn.		OF	70	266	43	82	23	0	7	50	1	.308
2005 Dunedin	Fla.St.		OF	126	392	64	123	28	4	12	84	2	.313
2006 New Hampshire	Eastern		OF	91	348	43	108	24	0	19	71	2	.310
2006 Syracuse	Int.		OF	34	109	20	43	7	0	5	18	1	.394
2006 Toronto	A.L.		DH-OF	18	60	8	22	8	0	2	8	0	.367
2007 Syracuse	Int.		OF	46	174	20	52	8	2	6	28	0	.299
2007 Toronto	A.L.		OF	89	290	34	69	14	0	11	46	1	.238
Major League Totals			2 Yrs.	107	350	42	91	22	0	13	54	1	.260

LINDEN, TODD ANTHONY

Born, Edmonds, Washington, June 30, 1980.
Bats Both. Throws Right. Height, 6 feet, 3 inches. Weight, 220 pounds.

Year	Club	Lea	Pos	G	AB	R	H	2B	3B	HR	RBI	SB	Avg
2002 Fresno		P.C.	OF	29	100	18	25	2	1	3	10	2	.250
2002 Shreveport		Texas	OF	111	392	64	123	26	2	12	52	9	.314
2003 Fresno		P.C.	OF	125	471	75	131	24	3	11	56	14	.278
2003 San Francisco		N.L.	OF	18	38	2	8	1	0	1	6	0	.211
2004 Fresno		P.C.	OF	130	489	93	127	28	2	23	75	8	.260
2004 San Francisco		N.L.	OF	16	32	6	5	1	0	0	1	0	.156
2005 Fresno		P.C.	OF	95	340	81	109	25	4	30	80	6	.321
2005 San Francisco		N.L.	OF	60	171	20	37	8	0	4	13	3	.216
2006 Fresno		P.C.	OF	52	187	31	52	11	3	5	23	5	.278
2006 San Francisco		N.L.	OF	61	77	15	21	4	2	2	5	1	.273
2007 Albuquerque		P.C.	OF	14	48	10	18	3	1	1	10	0	.375
2007 San Francisco-Florida a-b		N.L.	OF	115	184	21	45	8	1	1	11	4	.245
Major League Totals			5 Yrs.	270	502	64	116	22	3	8	36	8	.231

a Claimed on waivers by Florida Marlins, May 18, 2007.
b Filed for free agency, October 13, 2007. Signed with Oakland Athletics organization, November 21, 2007.

LO DUCA, PAUL ANTHONY

Born, Brooklyn, New York, April 12, 1972.
Bats Right. Throws Right. Height, 5 feet, 10 inches. Weight, 193 pounds.

Year	Club	Lea	Pos	G	AB	R	H	2B	3B	HR	RBI	SB	Avg
1993 Vero Beach		Fla.St.	C	39	134	17	42	6	0	0	13	0	.313
1994 Bakersfield	California		1B-C	123	455	65	141	32	1	6	68	16	.310
1995 San Antonio		Texas	C-1B-3B	61	199	27	49	8	0	1	8	5	.246
1996 Vero Beach		Fla.St.	C-1B-3B	124	439	54	134	22	0	3	66	8	.305
1997 San Antonio		Texas	C-1B	105	385	63	126	28	2	7	69	16	.327
1998 Albuquerque		P.C.	C-1B-3B	126	451	69	144	30	3	8	58	19	.319
1998 Los Angeles		N.L.	C	6	14	2	4	1	0	0	1	0	.286
1999 Los Angeles		N.L.	C	36	95	11	22	1	0	3	11	1	.232
1999 Albuquerque a		P.C.	C	26	76	17	28	9	0	1	8	1	.368
2000 Albuquerque		P.C.	C-OF-1B-3B	78	279	47	98	27	3	4	54	8	.351
2000 Los Angeles		N.L.	C-OF-3B	34	65	6	16	2	0	2	8	0	.246
2001 Las Vegas		P.C.	C-1B	3	9	3	3	2	0	0	3	0	.333
2001 Los Angeles b		N.L.	C-1B-OF	125	460	71	147	28	0	25	90	2	.320
2002 Los Angeles		N.L.	C-1B-OF	149	580	74	163	38	1	10	64	3	.281
2003 Los Angeles		N.L.	C-1B-OF	147	568	64	155	34	2	7	52	0	.273
2004 Los Angeles-Florida c	N.L.		C-OF-1B	143	535	68	153	29	2	13	80	4	.286
2005 Florida d-e		N.L.	C	132	445	45	126	23	1	6	57	4	.283
2006 New York		N.L.	C	124	512	80	163	39	1	5	49	3	.318
2007 Brooklyn		N.Y.-Penn.	C	2	5	1	2	0	0	1	2	0	.400
2007 Binghamton	Eastern		C	1	3	0	1	0	0	0	0	0	.333
2007 New York f-g		N.L.	C	119	445	46	121	18	1	9	54	2	.272
Major League Totals			10 Yrs.	1015	3719	467	1070	213	8	80	466	19	.288

109

Year	Club	Lea	Pos	G	AB	R	H	2B	3B	HR	RBI	SB	Avg
	Division Series												
2006 New York	....	N.L.	C	3	11	2	5	1	0	0	3	0	.455
	Championship Series												
2006 New York	....	N.L.	C	7	29	3	6	1	0	0	3	0	.207

a On disabled list from June 4 to July 20, 1999.
b On disabled list from April 29 to May 21, 2001.
c Traded to Florida Marlins with outfielder Juan Encarnacion and pitcher Guillermo Mota for pitcher Brad Penny, pitcher Bill Murphy and infielder Hee Seop Choi, July 30, 2004.
d Traded to New York Mets two players to be named later, December 5, 2005.
e Florida Marlins received pitcher Gaby Hernandez and outfielder Dante Brinkley to complete trade, December 9, 2005.
f On disabled list from August 12 to August 27, 2007.
g Filed for free agency, October 29, 2007. Signed with Washington Nationals, December 11, 2007.

LOFTON, KENNETH (KENNY)

Born, East Chicago, Indiana, May 31, 1967.
Bats Left. Throws Left. Height, 5 feet, 11-Inches. Weight, 190 pounds.

Year	Club	Lea	Pos	G	AB	R	H	2B	3B	HR	RBI	SB	Avg
1988 Auburn	.... N.Y.-Penn.		OF	48	187	23	40	6	1	1	14	26	.214
1989 Auburn	.... N.Y.-Penn.		OF	34	110	21	29	3	1	0	8	26	.264
1989 Asheville	.... So. Atl.		OF	22	82	14	27	2	0	1	9	14	.329
1990 Osceola	.... Fla. St.		OF	124	481	98	*159	15	5	2	35	62	.331
1991 Tucson	.... P.C.		OF	130	545	93	*168	19	*17	2	50	40	.308
1991 Houston a	.... N.L.		OF	20	74	9	15	1	0	0	0	2	.203
1992 Cleveland	.... A.L.		OF	148	576	96	164	15	8	5	42	*66	.285
1993 Cleveland	.... A.L.		OF	148	569	116	185	28	8	1	42	*70	.325
1994 Cleveland	.... A.L.		OF	112	459	105	*160	32	9	12	57	*60	.349
1995 Cleveland b	.... A.L.		OF	118	481	93	149	22	*13	7	53	*54	.310
1996 Cleveland	.... A.L.		OF	154	*662	132	210	35	4	14	67	75	.317
1997 Atlanta c-d-e-f	.... N.L.		OF	122	493	90	164	20	6	5	48	27	.333
1998 Cleveland	.... A.L.		OF	154	600	101	169	31	6	12	64	54	.282
1999 Cleveland g	.... A.L.		OF	120	465	110	140	28	6	7	39	25	.301
2000 Cleveland h	.... A.L.		OF	137	543	107	151	23	5	15	73	30	.278
2001 Cleveland i-j	.... A.L.		OF	133	517	91	135	21	4	14	66	16	.261
2002 Chicago	.... A.L.		OF	93	352	68	91	20	6	8	42	22	.259
2002 San Francisco k-l	...... N.L.		OF	46	180	30	48	10	3	3	9	7	.267
2003 Pittsburgh-Chicago m-n-o N.L.			OF	140	547	97	162	32	8	12	46	30	.296
2004 Tampa	.... Fla.St.		OF	1	4	1	1	0	0	0	0	0	.250
2004 Trenton	.... Eastern		OF	4	14	0	3	1	0	0	2	0	.214
2004 New York p-q	.... A.L.		OF	83	276	51	76	10	7	3	18	7	.275
2005 Philadelphia r-s	...... N.L.		OF	110	367	67	123	15	5	2	36	22	.335
2006 Los Angeles t-u	.... N.L.		OF	129	469	79	141	15	12	3	41	32	.301
2007 Texas-Cleveland v-w. ... A.L.			OF	136	490	86	145	25	6	7	38	23	.296
Major League Totals	....		17 Yrs.	2103	8120	1528	2428	383	116	130	781	622	.299
	Division Series												
1995 Cleveland	.... A.L.		OF	3	13	1	2	0	0	0	0	0	.154
1996 Cleveland	.... A.L.		OF	4	18	3	3	0	0	0	1	5	.167
1997 Atlanta	.... N.L.		OF	3	13	2	2	1	0	0	0	0	.154
1998 Cleveland	.... A.L.		OF	4	16	5	6	1	0	2	4	2	.475
1999 Cleveland	.... A.L.		OF	5	16	5	2	1	0	0	1	2	.125
2001 Cleveland	.... A.L.		OF	5	19	2	2	0	0	1	3	0	.105
2002 San Francisco	.... N.L.		OF	5	20	5	7	1	0	0	2	1	.350
2003 Chicago	.... N.L.		OF	5	21	3	6	1	0	0	1	3	.286
2004 New York	.... A.L.		DH	1	4	0	1	0	0	0	1	0	.250
2006 Los Angeles	.... N.L.		OF	3	13	0	1	0	0	0	0	0	.077
2007 Cleveland	.... A.L.		OF	4	16	2	6	1	0	0	4	1	.375
Division Series Totals	....			42	169	28	38	6	0	3	17	14	.225
	Championship Series												
1995 Cleveland	.... A.L.		OF	6	24	4	11	0	2	0	3	5	.458
1997 Atlanta	.... N.L.		OF	6	27	3	5	0	1	0	1	1	.185
1998 Cleveland	.... A.L.		OF	6	27	2	5	1	0	1	3	1	.185
2002 San Francisco	.... N.L.		OF	5	21	4	5	0	0	1	2	1	.238
2003 Chicago	.... N.L.		OF	7	31	8	10	1	0	0	2	1	.323
2004 New York	.... A.L.		DH	3	10	1	3	0	0	1	2	1	.300
2007 Cleveland	.... A.L.		OF	7	27	2	6	2	0	1	2	1	.222
Championship Series Totals	......			40	167	24	45	4	3	4	15	11	.269
	World Series Record												
1995 Cleveland	.... A.L.		OF	6	25	6	5	1	0	0	0	6	.200

Year	Club	Lea	Pos	G	AB	R	H	2B	3B	HR	RBI	SB	Avg
2002 San Francisco	N.L.	OF	7	31	7	9	1	1	0	2	3	.290
World Series Totals			13	56	13	14	2	1	0	2	9	.250

a Traded to Cleveland Indians with infielder Dave Rohde for pitcher Willie Blair and catcher Ed Taubensee, December 10, 1991.
b On disabled list from July 17 to August 1, 1995.
c Traded to Atlanta Braves with pitcher Alan Embree for outfielder Marquis Grissom and outfielder David Justice, March 25, 1997.
d On disabled list from June 18 to July 5 and July 6 to July 28, 1997.
e Filed for free agency, October 28, 1997.
f Signed as free agent with Cleveland Indians, December 8, 1997.
g On disabled list from July 28 to August 14 and August 17 to September 1, 1999.
h On disabled list from April 27 to May 11, 2000.
i On disabled list from May 16 to June 1, 2001.
j Filed for free agency, November 5, 2001. Signed with Chicago White Sox, February 1, 2002.
k Traded to San Francisco Giants for pitcher Felix Diaz and pitcher Ryan Meaux, July 28, 2002.
l Filed for free agency, November 1, 2002. Signed with Pittsburgh Pirates, March 14, 2003.
m Traded to Chicago Cubs with infielder Aramis Ramirez for infielder Jose Hernandez, pitcher Matt Bruback and player to be named later, July 22, 2003.
n Pittsburgh Pirates received infielder Bobby Hill to complete trade, August 15, 2003.
o Filed for free agency, October 30, 2003. Signed with New York Yankees, December 23, 2003.
p On disabled list from April 17 to May 2 and from May 28 to June 12, 2004.
q Traded to Philadelphia Phillies for pitcher Felix Rodriguez, December 3, 2004.
r On disabled list from May 3 to May 20, 2005.
s Filed for free agency, November 2, 2005. Signed with Los Angeles Dodgers, December 20, 2005.
t On disabled list from March 30 to April 14, 2006.
u Filed for free agency, November 2, 2006. Signed with Texas Rangers, December 12, 2006.
v Traded to Cleveland Indians for catcher Max Ramirez, July 27, 2007.
w Filed for free agency, October 30, 2007.

LOGAN, EXAVIER PRENTE (NOOK)

Born, Natchez, Mississippi, November 28, 1979.
Bats Both. Throws Right. Height, 6 feet, 2 inches. Weight, 180 pounds.

Year	Club	Lea	Pos	G	AB	R	H	2B	3B	HR	RBI	SB	Avg
2000 Lakeland	Fla.St.	SS	11	42	4	14	1	0	0	3	2	.333
2000 Tigers	Gulf Coast	SS	43	136	29	38	2	2	0	14	20	.279
2001 West Michigan	Midwest	OF	128	522	82	137	19	8	1	27	67	.262
2002 Lakeland	Fla.St.	OF	124	506	75	136	14	7	2	26	55	.269
2003 Erie	Eastern	OF	136	514	71	129	16	7	4	38	37	.251
2004 Toledo	Int.	OF	105	426	67	112	14	9	2	27	38	.263
2004 Detroit	A.L.	OF	47	133	12	37	5	2	0	10	8	.278
2005 Detroit	A.L.	OF	129	322	47	83	12	5	1	17	23	.258
2006 Erie	Eastern	OF	20	77	14	19	2	1	0	2	9	.247
2006 Toledo	Int.	OF	19	65	9	12	2	1	0	4	3	.185
2006 Washington a	N.L.	OF	27	90	13	27	3	1	1	8	2	.300
2007 Washington b-c	N.L.	OF	118	325	39	86	18	4	0	21	23	.265
Major League Totals	4 Yrs.	321	870	111	233	38	12	2	56	56	.268

a Traded to Washington Nationals for player to be named later, September 1, 2006.
b On disabled list from April 3 to May 7, 2007.
c Not offered contract, December 12, 2007.

LONEY, JAMES ANTHONY

Born, Houston, Texas, May 7, 1984.
Bats Left. Throws Left. Height, 6 feet, 3 inches. Weight, 220 pounds.

Year	Club	Lea	Pos	G	AB	R	H	2B	3B	HR	RBI	SB	Avg
2002 Vero Beach	Fla.St.	1B	17	67	6	20	6	0	0	5	0	.299
2002 Great Falls	Pioneer	1B	47	170	33	63	22	3	5	30	5	.371
2003 Vero Beach	Fla.St.	1B-OF	125	468	64	129	31	3	7	46	9	.276
2004 Jacksonville	Southern	1B	104	395	39	94	19	2	4	35	6	.238
2005 Jacksonville	Southern	1B-OF	138	504	74	143	31	2	11	65	1	.284
2006 Las Vegas	P.C.	1B-OF	98	366	64	139	33	2	8	67	9	.380
2006 Los Angeles	N.L.	1B-OF	48	102	20	29	6	5	4	18	1	.284
2007 Las Vegas	P.C.	1B-OF	58	233	28	65	19	1	1	32	2	.279
2007 Los Angeles	N.L.	1B-OF	96	344	41	114	18	4	15	67	0	.331
Major League Totals	2 Yrs.	144	446	61	143	24	9	19	85	1	.321
Division Series												
2006 Los Angeles	N.L.	1B	1	4	0	3	0	0	0	3	0	.750

LOPEZ, FELIPE

Born, Bayamon, Puerto Rico, May 12, 1980.
Bats Both. Throws Right. Height, 6 feet, 1 Inch. Weight, 185 pounds.

Year Club	Lea	Pos	G	AB	R	H	2B	3B	HR	RBI	SB	Avg
1998 St.Cathrnes	.N.Y.-Penn.	SS	19	83	14	31	5	2	1	11	4	.373
1998 Dunedin	Fla.St.	SS	4	13	3	5	0	1	1	1	0	.385
1999 Hagerstown	.So.Atl.	SS	134	537	87	149	27	4	14	80	21	.277
2000 Tennessee	.Southern	SS	127	463	52	119	18	4	9	41	12	.257
2001 Tennessee	.Southern	SS-2B	19	72	12	16	2	1	2	4	4	.222
2001 Syracuse	Int.	SS-2B-3B	89	358	65	100	19	7	16	44	13	.279
2001 Toronto	.A.L.	3B-SS	49	177	21	46	5	4	5	23	4	.260
2002 Toronto	.A.L.	SS-3B	85	282	35	64	15	3	8	34	5	.227
2002 Syracuse a	Int.	SS	43	173	35	55	11	2	3	16	13	.318
2003 Cincinnati	.N.L.	SS-3B-2B	59	197	28	42	7	2	2	13	8	.213
2003 Louisville	Int.	SS-2B	35	143	22	40	11	0	2	18	2	.280
2004 Louisville	Int.	SS-2B-3B	75	293	50	80	11	3	9	44	2	.273
2004 Cincinnati	.N.L.	SS-3B-2B	79	264	35	64	18	2	7	31	1	.242
2005 Cincinnati	.N.L.	SS-2B-3B	148	580	97	169	34	5	23	85	15	.291
2006 Cincinnati-Wash. b	.N.L.	SS	156	617	98	169	27	3	11	52	44	.274
2007 Washington	.N.L.	SS-2B	154	603	70	148	25	6	9	50	24	.245
Major League Totals		7 Yrs.	730	2720	384	702	131	25	65	288	101	.258

a Traded by Toronto Blue Jays to Cincinnati Reds in four team deal. Cincinnati sent pitcher Elmer Dessens to Arizona Diamondbacks, who sent infield Eurbiel Durazo to Oakland A's, who sent pitcher Jamie Arnold to Toronto Blue Jays, December 15, 2002.

b Traded to Washington Nationals with outfielder Austin Kearns and pitcher Ryan Wagner for pitcher Gary Majewski, pitcher Bill Bray, infielder Royce Clayton, infielder Brendan Harris and pitcher Daryl Thompson, July 13, 2006.

LOPEZ, JOSE CELESTINO

Born, Barcelona, Venezuela, November 24, 1983.
Bats Right. Throws Right. Height, 6 feet. Weight, 200 pounds.

Year Club	Lea	Pos	G	AB	R	H	2B	3B	HR	RBI	SB	Avg
2001 Everett	Northwest	SS-2B	70	289	42	74	15	0	2	20	13	.256
2002 San Bernardino	Calif.	SS-2B	123	522	82	169	39	5	8	60	31	.324
2003 San Antonio	Texas	SS-2B-3B	132	538	82	139	35	2	13	69	18	.258
2004 Tacoma	P.C.	SS-3B-2B	74	275	40	81	19	0	13	39	5	.295
2004 Mariners	Arizona	3B-SS-2B	4	12	3	2	1	0	0	1	1	.167
2004 Seattle	.A.L.	SS-3B	57	207	28	48	13	0	5	22	0	.232
2005 Tacoma	P.C.	2B	44	182	29	58	19	0	5	31	2	.319
2005 Seattle	.A.L.	2B-3B	54	190	18	47	19	0	2	25	4	.247
2006 Seattle	.A.L.	2B	151	603	78	170	28	8	10	79	5	.282
2007 Seattle	.A.L.	2B-3B	149	524	58	132	17	2	11	62	2	.252
Major League Totals		4 Yrs.	411	1524	182	397	77	10	28	188	11	.260

LORETTA, MARK DAVID

Born, Santa Monica, California, August 14, 1971.
Bats Right. Throws Right. Height, 6 feet. Weight, 185 pounds.

Year Club	Lea	Pos	G	AB	R	H	2B	3B	HR	RBI	SB	Avg
1993 Helena	Pioneer	SS	6	28	5	9	1	0	1	8	0	.321
1993 Stockton	California	SS-3B	53	201	36	73	4	1	4	31	8	.363
1994 El Paso	Texas	SS-P	77	302	50	95	13	6	0	38	8	.315
1994 New Orleans	.A.A.	SS-2B	43	138	16	29	7	0	1	14	2	.210
1995 New Orleans	.A.A.	SS-3B-2B	127	479	48	137	22	5	7	79	8	.286
1995 Milwaukee	.A.L.	SS	19	50	13	13	3	0	1	3	1	.260
1996 New Orleans	.A.A.	SS	19	71	10	18	5	1	0	11	1	.254
1996 Milwaukee	.A.L.	2B-3B-SS	73	154	20	43	3	0	1	13	2	.279
1997 Milwaukee	.A.L.	2B-SS-1B-3B	132	418	56	120	17	5	5	47	5	.287
1998 Milwaukee	.N.L.	1B-SS-3B-2B	140	434	55	137	29	0	6	54	9	.316
1999 Milwaukee	.N.L.	SS-1B-2B-3B	153	587	93	170	34	5	5	67	4	.290
2000 Indianapolis	Int.	SS	10	25	6	6	1	0	0	5	0	.240
2000 Milwaukee a	.N.L.	SS-2B	91	352	49	99	21	1	7	40	0	.281
2001 Indianapolis	Int.	SS-2B-3B	8	31	4	3	0	0	0	1	0	.097
2001 Milwaukee b	.N.L.	2B-3B-SS-P	102	384	40	111	14	2	2	29	1	.289
2002 Milwaukee-Houston c-d-e	N.L.	3B-SS-2B-1B	107	283	33	86	18	0	4	27	1	.304
2003 San Diego	N.L.	2B-SS	154	589	74	185	28	4	13	72	5	.314
2004 San Diego	.N.L.	2B	154	620	108	208	47	2	16	76	5	.335
2005 Portland	P.C.	2B	3	10	0	1	0	0	0	0	0	.100
2005 San Diego f-g	.N.L.	2B-3B	105	404	54	113	16	1	3	38	8	.280

Year	Club	Lea	Pos	G	AB	R	H	2B	3B	HR	RBI	SB	Avg
2006 Boston h	A.L.		2B-1B	155	635	75	181	33	0	5	59	4	.285
2007 Houston i	N.L.		SS-2B-1B-3B	133	460	52	132	23	2	4	41	1	.287
Major League Totals		13 Yrs.		1518	5370	722	1598	286	22	72	566	46	.298
Division Series													
2005 San Diego	N.L.		2B	3	15	0	4	0	0	0	2	0	.267

a On disabled list from June 3 to August 17, 2000.
b On disabled list from March 27 to May 19, 2001.
c Traded to Houston Astros with cash for two players to be named later, August 31, 2002.
d Milwaukee Brewers received pitcher Wayne Franklin to complete trade, September 3, 2002.
e Filed for free agency, October 28, 2002. Signed with San Diego Padres, December 16, 2002.
f On disabled list from May 19 to July 18, 2005.
g Traded to Boston Red Sox for catcher Doug Mirabelli, December 7, 2005.
h Filed for free agency, October 30, 2006. Signed with Houston Astros, January 4, 2007.
i Filed for free agency, October 29, 2007. Accepted arbitration to return to Houston, December 7, 2007.

LOWELL, MICHAEL AVERETT (MIKE)

Born, San Juan, Puerto Rico, February 24, 1974.
Bats Right. Throws Right. Height, 6 feet, 3 inches. Weight, 210 pounds.

Year	Club	Lea	Pos	G	AB	R	H	2B	3B	HR	RBI	SB	Avg
1995 Oneonta	N.Y.-Penn.		3B	72	281	36	73	18	0	1	27	3	.260
1996 Greensboro	So.Atl.		3B-SS-P	113	433	58	122	33	0	8	64	10	.282
1996 Tampa	Fla.St.		3B	24	78	8	22	5	0	0	11	1	.282
1997 Norwich	Eastern		3D-SS	78	285	60	98	17	0	15	47	2	.344
1997 Columbus	Int.		3B-SS	57	210	36	58	13	1	15	45	2	.276
1998 Columbus	Int.		3B-1B-SS	126	510	79	155	34	3	26	99	4	.304
1998 New York	A.L.		3B	8	15	1	4	0	0	0	0	0	.267
1999 Calgary	P.C.		3B	24	83	11	26	3	0	2	9	0	.313
1999 Florida a-b	N.L.		3B	97	308	32	78	15	0	12	47	0	.253
2000 Florida c	N.L.		3B	140	508	73	137	38	0	22	91	4	.270
2001 Florida	N.L.		3B	146	551	65	156	37	0	18	100	1	.283
2002 Florida	N.L.		3B	160	597	88	165	44	0	24	92	4	.276
2003 Florida d	N.L.		3B	130	492	76	136	27	1	32	105	3	.276
2004 Florida	N.L.		3B	158	598	87	175	44	1	27	85	5	.293
2005 Florida e	N.L.		3B-2B	150	500	56	118	36	1	8	58	4	.236
2006 Boston	A.L.		3B	153	573	79	163	47	1	20	80	2	.284
2007 Boston f	A.L.		3B	154	589	79	191	37	2	21	120	3	.324
Major League Totals		10 Yrs.		1296	4731	636	1323	325	6	184	778	26	.280
Division Series													
2003 Florida	N.L.		3B	2	3	0	0	0	0	0	0	0	.000
2007 Florida	N.L.		3B	3	9	1	3	2	0	0	3	0	.333
Division Series Totals				5	12	1	3	2	0	0	3	0	.250
Championship Series													
2003 Florida	N.L.		3B	7	20	5	4	0	0	2	3	0	.200
2007 Boston	A.L.		3B	7	27	3	9	2	0	1	8	0	.333
Championship Series Totals				14	47	8	13	2	0	3	11	0	.277
World Series Record													
2003 Florida	N.L.		3B	6	23	1	5	1	0	0	2	0	.217
2007 Boston	A.L.		3B	4	15	6	6	3	0	1	4	1	.400
World Series Totals				10	38	7	11	4	0	1	6	1	.289

a Traded to Florida Marlins for pitcher Ed Yarnall, pitcher Mark Johnson and pitcher Todd Noel, February 1, 1999.
b On disabled list from March 26 to May 29, 1999.
c On disabled list from May 13 to May 28, 2000.
d On disabled list from August 31 to September 28, 2003.
e Traded to Boston Red Sox with pitcher Josh Beckett and pitcher Guillermo Mota for infielder Hanley Ramirez, pitcher Anibal Sanchez and pitcher Jesus Delgado, November 24, 2005.
f Filed for free agency, November 6, 2007, re-signed with Boston Red Sox, November 20, 2007.

LUDWICK, RYAN ANDREW

Born, Satellite Beach, Florida, July 13, 1978.
Bats Right. Throws Left. Height, 6 feet, 3 inches. Weight, 203 pounds.

Year	Club	Lea	Pos	G	AB	R	H	2B	3B	HR	RBI	SB	Avg
1999 Modesto	Calif.		OF	43	171	28	47	11	3	4	34	2	.275
2000 Modesto	Calif.		OF	129	493	86	130	26	3	29	102	10	.264
2001 Sacramento	P.C.		OF	17	57	10	13	3	0	1	7	2	.228
2001 Midland	Texas		OF	119	443	82	119	23	3	25	96	9	.269

Year	Club	Lea	Pos	G	AB	R	H	2B	3B	HR	RBI	SB	Avg
2002	Oklahoma............	P.C.	OF	78	305	62	87	27	4	15	52	2	.285
2002	Texas a.............	A.L.	OF	23	81	10	19	6	0	1	9	2	.235
2003	Oklahoma............	P.C.	OF	81	317	51	96	24	3	17	63	1	.303
2003	Texas-Cleveland b-c....	A.L.	OF	47	162	17	40	8	1	7	26	2	.247
2004	Akron.............	Eastern	OF	8	26	4	7	2	0	1	5	0	.269
2004	Buffalo..............	Int.	OF	44	166	25	45	15	0	8	30	0	.271
2004	Cleveland d..........	A.L.	OF	15	50	3	11	2	0	2	4	0	.220
2005	Cleveland...........	A.L.	OF	19	41	8	9	0	0	4	5	0	.220
2005	Buffalo..............	Int.	OF	54	188	27	36	10	2	4	16	0	.191
2006	Toledo e-f............	Int.	OF	134	508	81	135	34	2	28	80	2	.266
2007	Memphis............	P.C.	OF	29	106	27	36	8	0	8	36	1	.340
2007	St. Louis...........	N.L.	OF	120	303	42	81	22	0	14	52	4	.267
Major League Totals		5 Yrs.		224	637	80	160	38	1	28	96	8	.251

a Traded to Texas Rangers by Oakland Athletics with pitcher Mario Ramos, infielder Jason Hart and catcher Gerald Laird for pitcher Mike Venafro and outfielder Carlos Pena, January 14, 2002.
b On disabled list from September 9 to October 28, 2003.
c Traded to Cleveland Indians for outfielder Shane Spencer and pitcher Ricardo Rodriguez, July 18, 2003.
d On disabled list from April 2 to July 5, 2004.
e Filed for free agency, October 28, 2005. Signed with Detroit Tigers organization, January 4, 2006.
f Filed for free agency, October 15, 2006. Signed with St. Louis Cardinals organization, December 1, 2006.

LUGO, JULIO CESAR

Born, Barahona, Dominican Republic, November 16, 1975.
Bats Right. Throws Right. Height, 6 feet, 1 Inch. Weight, 175 pounds.

Year	Club	Lea	Pos	G	AB	R	H	2B	3B	HR	RBI	SB	Avg
1995	Auburn......	N.Y.-Penn.	2B-SS-OF	59	230	36	67	6	3	1	16	17	.291
1996	Quad City....	Midwest	SS-2B-3B	101	393	60	116	18	2	10	50	24	.295
1997	Kissimmee......	Fla.St.	SS-2B-3B	125	505	89	135	22	14	7	61	35	.267
1998	Kissimmee......	Fla.St.	SS	128	509	81	154	20	14	7	62	51	.303
1999	Jackson a.......	Texas	SS	116	445	77	142	24	5	10	42	25	.319
2000	New Orleans.......	P.C.	2B	24	101	22	33	4	1	3	12	12	.327
2000	Houston..........	N.L.	SS-2B-OF	116	420	78	119	22	5	10	40	22	.283
2001	Houston..........	N.L.	SS-OF-2B	140	513	93	135	20	3	10	37	12	.263
2002	Houston b	N.L.	SS	88	322	45	84	15	1	8	35	9	.261
2003	Houston..........	N.L.	SS	22	65	6	16	3	0	0	2	2	.246
2003	Tampa Bay c.......	A.L.	SS	117	433	58	119	13	4	15	53	10	.275
2004	Tampa Bay	A.L.	SS-2B	157	581	83	160	41	4	7	75	21	.275
2005	Tampa Bay	A.L.	SS	158	616	89	182	36	6	6	57	39	.295
2006	Tampa Bay d	A.L.	SS	73	289	53	89	17	1	12	27	18	.308
2006	Los Angeles e-f	N.L.	2B-3B-SS-OF	49	146	16	32	5	1	0	10	6	.219
2007	Boston...........	A.L.	SS	147	570	71	135	36	2	8	73	33	.237
Major League Totals		8 Yrs.		1067	3955	592	1071	208	27	76	409	172	.271
Division Series													
2001	Houston..........	N.L.	SS	3	8	1	0	0	0	0	0	0	.000
2006	Los Angeles.......	N.L.	2B-3B	2	4	0	1	1	0	0	0	0	.250
2007	Boston...........	A.L.	SS	3	10	2	3	0	0	0	0	1	.300
Division Series Totals				8	22	3	4	1	0	0	0	1	.182
Championship Series													
2007	Boston...........	A.L.	SS	7	25	3	5	2	0	0	2	0	.200
World Series Record													
2007	Boston...........	A.L.	SS	4	13	2	5	1	0	0	1	0	.385

a On disabled list from July 21 to 29, 1999.
b On disabled list from August 13 to September 30, 2002.
c Released by Houston Astros, May 13, 2003. Signed with Tampa Bay Devil Rays, May 15, 2003.
d On disabled list from April 4 to May 5, 2006.
e Traded to Los Angeles Dodgers for infielder Joel Guzman and outfielder Sergio Pedroza, July 31, 2006.
f Filed for free agency, October 28, 2006. Signed with Boston Red Sox, December 13, 2006.

MACKOWIAK, ROBERT WILLIAM (ROB)

Born, Oak Lawn, Illinois, June 20, 1976.
Bats Left. Throws Right. Height, 6 feet. Weight, 200 pounds,

Year	Club	Lea	Pos	G	AB	R	H	2B	3B	HR	RBI	SB	Avg
1996	Pirates	Gulf Coast	OF-SS	27	86	8	23	6	1	0	14	3	.267
1997	Erie.........	N.Y.-Penn.	OF-3B-2B	61	203	26	58	14	2	1	25	1	.286
1998	Augusta......	So.Atl.	OF-3B	25	70	16	17	4	0	1	8	4	.243
1998	Lynchburg	Carolina	3B-2B-SS-OF	86	292	30	80	24	6	3	31	6	.274
1999	Lynchburg	Carolina	2B	74	263	51	80	7	4	7	30	9	.304

Year	Club	Lea	Pos	G	AB	R	H	2B	3B	HR	RBI	SB	Avg
1999 Altoona	Eastern		2B	53	195	21	51	15	3	3	27	0	.262
2000 Altoona	Eastern		2B-OF-3B-SS	134	526	82	156	33	4	13	87	18	.297
2001 Nashville	P.C.		OF-2B-3B	32	118	14	31	5	0	4	14	1	.263
2001 Pittsburgh a	N.L.		OF-2B-3B-1B	83	214	30	57	15	2	4	21	4	.266
2002 Pittsburgh	N.L.		OF-3B-2B	136	385	57	94	22	0	16	48	9	.244
2003 Nashville	P.C.		1B-3B-2B-OF	59	217	21	50	11	1	2	23	7	.230
2003 Pittsburgh	N.L.		OF-3B-2B	77	174	20	47	4	4	6	19	6	.270
2004 Pittsburgh	N.L.		OF-3B-1B	155	491	65	121	22	6	17	75	13	.246
2005 Pittsburgh b			3B-OF-2B-1B	142	463	57	126	21	3	9	58	8	.272
2006 Chicago	A.L.		OF-3B	112	255	31	74	12	1	5	23	5	.290
2007 Chicago	A.L.		OF-1B-3B	85	237	34	66	11	2	6	36	3	.278
2007 San Diego c-d	N.L.		OF	28	56	6	11	3	0	0	2	1	.196
Major League Totals			7 Yrs.	818	2275	300	596	110	18	63	282	49	.262

a On disabled list from July 20 to August 18, 2001.
b Traded to Chicago White Sox for pitcher Damaso Marte, December 13, 2005.
c Traded to San Diego Padres for pitcher Jon Link, July 31, 2007.
d Filed for free agency, November 2, 2007. Signed with Washington Nationals, December 13, 2007.

MARKAKIS, NICHOLAS WILLIAM (NICK)

Born, Woodstock, Georgia, November 17, 1983.
Bats Left. Throws Left. Height, 6 feet, 2 inches. Weight, 195 pounds.

Year	Club	Lea	Pos	G	AB	R	H	2B	3B	HR	RBI	SB	Avg
2003 Aberdeen	N.Y.-Penn.		OF	59	205	22	58	14	3	1	28	13	.283
2004 Delmarva	So.Atl.		OF	96	355	57	106	22	3	11	64	12	.299
2005 Frederick	Carolina		OF	91	350	59	105	25	1	12	62	2	.300
2005 Bowie	Eastern		OF	33	124	19	42	16	2	3	30	0	.339
2006 Baltimore	A.L.		OF	147	491	72	143	25	2	16	62	2	.291
2007 Baltimore	A.L.		OF	161	637	97	191	43	3	23	112	18	.300
Major League Totals			2 Yrs.	308	1128	169	334	68	5	39	174	20	.296

MARTIN, RUSSELL NATHAN

Born, East York, Ontario, Canada, February 15, 1983.
Bats Right. Throws Right. Height, 5 feet, 10 inches. Weight, 210 pounds.

Year	Club	Lea	Pos	G	AB	R	H	2B	3B	HR	RBI	SB	Avg
2002 Dodgers	Gulf Coast		3B-SS	41	126	22	36	3	3	0	10	7	.286
2003 Ogden	Pioneer		C	52	188	25	51	13	0	6	36	3	.271
2003 South Bend	So.Atl.		C-OF-3B	25	98	15	28	4	1	3	14	5	.286
2004 Vero Beach	Fla.St.		C	122	416	74	104	24	1	15	64	9	.250
2005 Jacksonville	Southern		C-OF	129	409	83	127	17	1	9	61	15	.311
2006 Las Vegas	P.C.		C	23	74	14	22	9	0	0	9	0	.297
2006 Los Angeles	N.L.		C	121	415	65	117	26	4	10	65	10	.282
2007 Los Angeles	N.L.		C	151	540	87	158	32	3	19	87	21	.293
Major League Totals			2 Yrs.	272	955	152	275	58	7	29	152	31	.288
Division Series													
2006 Los Angeles	N.L.		C	3	12	2	4	0	0	0	0	0	.333

MARTINEZ, RAMON E.

Born, Philadelphia, Pennsylvania, October 10, 1972.
Bats Right. Throws Right. Height, 6 feet. Weight, 190 pounds.

Year	Club	Lea	Pos	G	AB	R	H	2B	3B	HR	RBI	SB	Avg
1993 Royals	Gulf Coast		2B-OF	37	97	16	23	5	0	0	9	3	.237
1993 Wilmington	Carolina		2B-SS	24	75	8	19	4	0	0	6	1	.253
1994 Rockford	Midwest		2B	6	18	3	5	0	0	0	3	1	.278
1994 Wilmington	Carolina		2B	90	325	40	87	13	2	2	35	6	.268
1995 Wichita	Texas		2B-SS	103	393	58	108	20	2	3	51	11	.275
1996 Omaha	A.A.		2B	85	320	35	81	12	3	6	41	3	.253
1996 Wichita a	Texas		2B	26	93	16	32	4	1	1	8	4	.344
1997 Phoenix	P.C.		2B-SS	18	57	6	16	2	0	1	7	1	.281
1997 Shreveport	Texas		SS	105	404	72	129	32	4	5	54	4	.319
1998 Fresno	P.C.		2B-SS	98	364	58	114	21	2	14	59	0	.313
1998 San Francisco	N.L.		2B	19	19	4	6	1	0	0	0	0	.316
1999 San Francisco	N.L.		2B-SS-3B	61	144	21	38	6	0	5	19	1	.264
1999 Fresno	P.C.		SS-3B	29	114	13	37	7	1	2	17	2	.325
2000 San Francisco	N.L.		SS-2B-1B-3B	88	189	30	57	13	2	6	25	3	.302
2001 San Francisco	N.L.		3B-2B-SS	128	391	48	99	18	3	5	37	1	.253

Year	Club	Lea	Pos	G	AB	R	H	2B	3B	HR	RBI	SB	Avg
2002 San Francisco b	....N.L.		SS-2B-1B-OF	.72	181	26	49	10	2	4	25	2	.271
2003 Chicago c	........N.L.		2B-3B-SS-1B	108	293	30	83	16	1	3	34	0	.283
2004 Chicago d	........N.L.		SS-3B-2B	102	260	22	64	15	1	3	30	1	.246
2005 Toledo	..........Int.		SS-2B	3	15	4	11	0	0	0	1	0	.733
2005 Detroit	.........A.L.		SS-2B-1B-3B	19	56	4	15	1	0	0	5	0	.268
2005 Philadelphia e-f-g-h	.N.L.		1B-3B-SS-2B	33	56	7	16	2	0	1	9	0	.286
2006 Los Angeles i-j	....N.L.		2B-3B-SS-1B	82	176	20	49	7	1	2	24	0	.278
2007 Las Vegas	.........P.C.		2B-3B-SS	6	14	6	5	1	0	0	2	0	.357
2007 Los Angeles k-l	....N.L.		2B-3B-SS-1B	67	129	10	25	4	0	0	27	1	.194
Major League Totals	....	10 Yrs.		779	1894	222	501	93	10	29	235	9	.265
Division Series													
2000 San Francisco	.....N.L.		2B-SS	2	6	0	2	0	0	0	0	0	.333
2002 San Francisco	.....N.L.		PH	1	0	0	0	0	0	0	0	0	.000
2003 Chicago	..........N.L.		SS	2	4	0	0	0	0	0	0	0	.000
2006 Los Angeles	.......N.L.		PH	3	3	0	1	1	0	0	1	0	.333
Division Series Totals	....			8	13	0	3	1	0	0	1	0	.231
Championship Series													
2002 San Francisco	.....N.L.		SS	2	1	0	0	0	0	0	1	0	.000
2003 Chicago	..........N.L.		SS-2B	4	4	0	0	0	0	0	0	0	.000
Championship Series Totals	..			6	5	0	0	0	0	0	1	0	.000
World Series Record													
2002 San Francisco	....N.L.		PH	2	2	0	0	0	0	0	0	0	.000

a Sent by Kansas City Royals to San Francisco Giants to complete trade in which Royals received pitcher Jamie Brewington, December 9, 1996.

b On disabled list from June 1 to June 16, 2002.

c Not offered contract, December 20, 2002. Signed with Chicago Cubs, January 2, 2003.

d On disabled list from September 18 to October 3, 2004.

e Filed for free agency, October 28, 2004. Signed with Detroit Tigers, January 5, 2005.

f On disabled list from April 9 to April 29, 2005.

g Traded to Philadelphia Phillies with pitcher Ugueth Urbina for infielder Placido Polanco, June 8, 2005.

h Filed for free agency, October 27, 2005.

i Signed with Los Angeles Dodgers organization, February 2, 2006.

j Filed for free agency, October 28, 2006, re-signed with Los Angeles Dodgers, November 8, 2006.

k On disabled list from June 4 to July 8, 2007.

l Filed for free agency, October 31, 2007.

MARTINEZ, VICTOR JESUS
Born, Ciudad Bolivar, Venezuela, December 23, 1978.
Bats Both. Throws Right. Height, 6 feet, 2 inches. Weight, 195 pounds.

Year	Club	Lea	Pos	G	AB	R	H	2B	3B	HR	RBI	SB	Avg
1997 Maracay-1	.......Venzuelan	C	53	122	21	42	12	0	0	26	6	.344
1998 Guacara-2	.......Venzuelan	C	55	160	28	43	13	0	1	27	8	.269
1999 Mahoning Valley..	N.Y.-Penn.	C	64	235	37	65	9	0	4	36	0	.277
2000 Kinston	..........Carolina	C	26	83	9	18	7	0	0	8	1	.217
2000 Columbus a	.... So.Atl.	C	21	70	11	26	9	1	2	12	0	.371
2001 Kinston	..........Carolina	C	114	420	59	138	33	2	10	57	3	.329
2002 Akron	.............Eastern	C	121	443	84	149	40	0	22	85	3	.336
2002 Cleveland	.............A.L.	C	12	32	2	9	1	0	1	5	0	.281
2003 Buffalo	...............Int.	C-1B	73	274	42	90	19	0	7	45	3	.328
2003 Akron	.............Eastern	C	3	12	1	4	2	0	0	2	0	.333
2003 Cleveland b	..........A.L.	C	49	159	15	46	4	0	1	16	1	.289
2004 Cleveland	............A.L.	C	141	520	77	147	38	1	23	108	0	.283
2005 Cleveland	.............A.L.	C	147	547	73	167	33	0	20	80	0	.305
2006 Cleveland	............A.L.	C-1B	153	572	82	181	37	0	16	93	0	.316
2007 Cleveland	............A.L.	C-1B	147	562	78	169	40	0	25	114	0	.301
Major League Totals	....	6 Yrs.	649	2392	327	719	153	1	86	416	1	.301
Division Series												
2007 Cleveland	..:........A.L.	C-1B	4	17	2	6	1	0	1	4	0	.353
Championship Series												
2007 Cleveland	............A.L.	C-1B	7	27	4	8	1	0	1	3	0	.296

a On minor league disabled list from May 25 to July 19, 2000.

b On disabled list from August 9 to September 2, 2003.

MATSUI, HIDEKI (GODZILLA)

Born: Ishikawa, Japan June 12, 1974
Bats Left, Throws Right, Height 6 feet two inches, Weight 230 pounds

Year	Club	Lea	Pos	G	AB	R	H	2B	3B	HR	RBI	SB	Avg
1993 Yomiuri Giants....	Japan Cent.	OF	57	184	27	41	9	0	11	27	1	.223
1994 Yomiuri Giants....	Japan Cent.	OF	130	503	70	148	23	4	20	66	6	.294
1995 Yomiuri Giants....	Japan Cent.	OF	131	501	76	142	31	1	22	80	9	.283
1996 Yomiuri Giants....	Japan Cent.	OF	130	487	97	153	34	1	38	99	7	.314
1997 Yomiuri Giants....	Japan Cent.	OF	135	484	93	144	18	0	37	103	9	.298
1998 Yomiuri Giants....	Japan Cent.	OF	135	487	103	142	24	3	34	100	3	.292
1999 Yomiuri Giants....	Japan Cent.	OF	135	471	100	143	24	2	42	95	0	.304
2000 Yomiuri Giants....	Japan Cent.	OF	135	474	116	150	32	1	42	108	5	.316
2001 Yomiuri Giants....	Japan Cent.	OF	140	481	107	160	23	3	36	104	3	.333
2002 Yomiuri Giants a ..	Japan Cent.	OF	140	500	112	167	27	1	50	107	3	.334
Japan Central Totals	10 years	1268	4572	901	1390	245	16	332	889	46	.304
2003 New York	A.L.	OF	*163	623	82	179	42	.1	16	106	2	.287
2004 New York	A.L.	OF	*162	584	109	174	34	2	31	108	3	.298
2005 New York	A.L.	OF	*162	629	108	192	45	3	23	116	2	.305
2006 New York b..........	A.L.	OF	51	172	32	52	9	0	8	29	1	.302
2007 Tampa	Fla.St.	OF	2	6	1	2	0	0	0	0	0	.333
2007 New York c..........	A.L.	OF	143	547	100	156	28	4	25	103	4	.285
Major League Totals	5 Yrs.	681	2555	431	753	158	10	103	462	12	.295
Division Series												
2003 New York	A.L.	OF	4	15	2	4	1	0	1	3	0	.267
2004 New York	A.L.	OF	4	17	3	7	1	0	1	3	0	.412
2005 New York	A.L.	OF	5	20	4	4	1	0	1	1	0	.200
2006 New York	A.L.	OF-DH	4	16	1	4	1	0	0	1	0	.250
2007 New York	A.L.	DH	4	11	4	2	0	0	0	0	0	.182
Division Series Totals			21	79	14	21	4	0	3	8	0	.266
Championship Series												
2003 New York	A.L.	OF	7	26	3	8	3	0	0	4	0	.308
2004 New York	A.L.	OF	7	34	9	14	6	1	2	10	0	.412
Championship Series Totals			14	60	12	22	9	1	2	14	0	.367
World Series Record												
2003 New York	A.L.	OF	6	23	1	6	0	0	1	4	0	.261

a Reached agreement with New York Yankees on three year contract, December 19, 2002.
b On disabled list from May 12 to September 12, 2006.
c On disabled list from April 8 to April 23, 2007.

MATSUI, KAZUO

Born, Osaka, Japan, October 23, 1975.
Bats Both. Throws Right. Height, 5 feet, 10 inches. Weight, 185 pounds.

Year	Club	Lea	Pos	G	AB	R	H	2B	3B	HR	RBI	SB	Avg
1995 Seibu	Japan Pac.	SS	69	204	25	45	9	1	2	15	21	.221
1996 Seibu	Japan Pac.	SS	130	473	51	134	22	5	1	29	50	.283
1997 Seibu	Japan Pac.	SS	135	645	91	178	23	13	7	63	62	.276
1998 Seibu	Japan Pac.	SS	135	641	92	179	38	5	9	58	43	.279
1999 Seibu	Japan Pac.	SS	135	609	87	178	29	4	15	67	32	.292
2000 Seibu	Japan Pac.	SS	135	611	99	177	40	11	23	90	26	.290
2001 Seibu	Japan Pac.	SS	140	613	94	170	28	2	24	76	26	.277
2002 Seibu	Japan Pac.	SS	140	651	119	193	46	6	36	87	33	.296
2003 Seibu a........	Japan Pac.	SS	140	587	104	179	36	4	33	84	13	.305
2004 New York b..........	N.L.	SS-2B	114	460	65	125	32	2	7	44	14	.272
2005 Mets...........	Gulf Coast	2B	3	9	3	4	0	0	1	3	0	.444
2005 Binghamton	Eastern	2B	3	9	4	4	1	0	0	0	2	.444
2005 New York c..........	N.L.	2B	87	267	31	68	9	4	3	24	6	.255
2006 St. Lucie.......	Fla.St.	2B	2	7	1	2	0	0	0	0	0	.286
2006 Colorado Springs.......	P.C.	SS-2B	31	115	26	32	4	0	3	16	3	.278
2006 Norfolk..........	Int.	2B	4	12	2	4	2	0	0	1	0	.333
2006 New York-Colorado d-e-f.	N.L.	2B-SS	70	243	32	65	12	3	3	26	10	.267
2007 Colorado Springs.......	P.C.	2B	2	6	1	3	0	0	0	0	1	.500
2007 Colorado g-h	N.L.	2B	104	410	84	118	24	6	4	37	32	.288
Major League Totals	4 Yrs.	375	1380	212	376	77	15	17	131	62	.272
Division Series												
2007 Colorado	N.L.	2B	3	12	2	5	1	2	1	6	0	.417
Championship Series												
2007 Colorado	N.L.	2B	4	17	2	4	0	0	0	2	1	.235
World Series Record												
2007 Colorado	N.L.	2B	4	17	1	5	1	0	0	0	1	.294

MATTHEWS, GARY NATHANIEL, JR.

Born, San Francisco, California, August 25, 1974.
Bats Both. Throws Right. Height, 6 feet, 3 inches. Weight, 225 pounds.

Year Club	Lea	Pos	G	AB	R	H	2B	3B	HR	RBI	SB	Avg
1994 Spokane	Northwest	OF-2B	52	191	23	40	6	1	0	18	3	.209
1995 Clinton	Midwest	OF	128	421	57	100	18	4	2	40	28	.238
1996 Rancho Cuca	California	OF	123	435	65	118	21	11	7	54	7	.271
1997 Rancho Cuca	California	OF	69	268	66	81	15	4	8	40	10	.302
1997 Mobile	Southern	OF	28	90	14	22	4	1	2	12	3	.244
1998 Mobile	Southern	OF	72	254	62	78	15	4	7	51	11	.307
1999 Las Vegas	P.C.	OF	121	422	57	108	22	3	9	52	17	.256
1999 San Diego	N.L.	OF	23	36	4	8	0	0	0	7	2	.222
2000 Iowa	P.C.	OF	60	211	27	51	11	3	5	22	6	.242
2000 Chicago a	N.L.	OF	80	158	24	30	1	2	4	14	3	.190
2001 Chicago-Pittsburgh b-c	N.L.	OF	152	405	63	92	15	2	14	44	8	.227
2002 New York	N.L.	PH	2	1	0	0	0	0	0	0	0	.000
2002 Baltimore d-e	A.L.	OF	109	344	54	95	25	3	7	58	15	.276
2003 Baltimore	A.L.	OF	41	162	21	33	12	1	2	20	0	.204
2003 San Diego f	N.L.	OF	103	306	50	83	19	1	4	22	12	.271
2004 Oklahoma	P.C.	OF	38	145	33	47	9	4	9	36	4	.324
2004 Texas g-h	A.L.	OF	87	280	37	77	17	1	11	36	5	.275
2005 Frisco	Texas	OF	1	5	0	2	0	0	0	1	0	.400
2005 Texas i	A.L.	OF	131	475	72	121	25	5	17	55	9	.255
2006 Oklahoma	P.C.	OF	6	21	10	9	2	0	0	1	2	.429
2006 Texas j-k	A.L.	OF	147	620	102	194	44	6	19	79	10	.313
2007 Los Angeles	A.L.	OF	140	516	79	130	26	3	18	72	18	.252
Major League Totals		9 Yrs.	1015	3303	506	863	184	24	96	387	82	.261

MAUER, JOSEPH PATRICK (JOE)

Born, St. Paul, Minnesota, April 19, 1983.
Bats Left. Throws Right. Height, 6 feet, 4 inches. Weight, 220 pounds.

Year Club	Lea	Pos	G	AB	R	H	2B	3B	HR	RBI	SB	Avg
2001 Elizabethton	Appal.	C	32	110	14	44	6	2	0	14	4	.400
2002 Quad Cities	Midwest	C-1B	110	411	58	124	23	1	4	62	0	.302
2003 Fort Myers	Fla.St.	C-1B	62	233	25	78	13	1	1	44	3	.335
2003 New Britain	Eastern	C	73	276	48	94	17	1	4	41	0	.341
2004 Fort Myers	Fla.St.	C	2	6	0	4	0	0	0	2	0	.667
2004 Rochester	Int.	C	5	19	1	6	3	0	0	2	0	.316
2004 Minnesota a	A.L.	C	35	107	18	33	8	1	6	17	1	.308
2005 Minnesota	A.L.	C	131	489	61	144	26	2	9	55	13	.294
2006 Minnesota	A.L.	C	140	521	86	181	36	4	13	84	8	.347
2007 Fort Myers	Fla.St.	C	1	3	0	0	0	0	0	0	0	.000
2007 Minnesota b	A.L.	C	109	406	62	119	27	3	7	60	7	.293
Major League Totals		4 Yrs.	415	1523	227	477	97	10	35	216	29	.313
Division Series												
2006 Minnesota	A.L.	C	3	11	0	2	0	0	0	0	0	.182

MAYBIN, CAMERON KEITH

Born, Asheville, North Carolina, April 4, 1987.
Bats Right. Throws Right. Height, 6 feet, 4 inches. Weight, 205 pounds.

Year	Club	Lea	Pos	G	AB	R	H	2B	3B	HR	RBI	SB	Avg
2006 West Michigan	Midwest	OF	101	385	59	117	20	6	9	69	27	.304
2007 Tigers	Gulf Coast	OF	2	7	1	4	0	0	0	1	0	.571
2007 Lakeland	Fla.St.	OF	83	296	58	90	14	5	10	44	25	.304
2007 Erie	Eastern	OF	6	20	9	8	1	0	4	8	0	.400
2007 Detroit a	A.L.	OF	24	49	8	7	3	0	1	2	5	.143

a Traded to Florida Marlins with pitcher Burke Badenhop, pitcher Eulogio De La Cruz, pitcher Andrew Miller and catcher Mike Rabelo for pitcher Dontrelle Willis and infielder Miguel Cabrera, December 5, 2007.

MC CANN, BRIAN MICHAEL

Born, Athens, Georgia, February 20, 1984.
Bats Left. Throws Right. Height, 6 feet, 3 inches. Weight, 210 pounds.

Year	Club	Lea	Pos	G	AB	R	H	2B	3B	HR	RBI	SB	Avg
2002 Braves	Gulf Coast	C	29	100	9	22	5	0	2	11	0	.220
2003 Rome	So.Atl.	C	115	424	40	123	31	3	12	71	7	.290
2004 Myrtle Beach	Carolina	C	111	385	45	107	35	0	16	66	2	.278
2005 Mississippi	Southern	C	48	166	27	44	13	2	6	26	2	.265
2005 Atlanta	N.L.	C	59	180	20	50	7	0	5	23	1	.278
2006 Rome	So.Atl.	DH	2	7	0	2	0	0	0	0	0	.286
2006 Atlanta a	N.L.	C	130	442	61	147	34	0	24	93	2	.333
2007 Atlanta	N.L.	C	139	504	51	136	38	0	18	92	0	.270
Major League Totals		3 Yrs.	328	1126	132	333	79	0	47	208	3	.296
Division Series												
2005 Atlanta	N.L.	C	3	16	2	3	0	0	2	5	0	.188

a On disabled list from May 24 to June 9, 2006.

MC DONALD, JOHN JOSEPH

Born, New London, Connecticut, September 24, 1974.
Bats Right. Throws Right. Height, 5 feet, 11 inches. Weight, 175 pounds.

Year	Club	Lea	Pos	G	AB	R	H	2B	3B	HR	RBI	SB	Avg
1996 Watertown	N.Y.-Penn.	SS	75	278	48	75	11	0	2	26	11	.270
1997 Kinston	Carolina	SS	130	541	77	140	27	3	5	53	6	.259
1998 Akron	Eastern	SS	132	514	68	118	18	2	2	43	17	.230
1999 Akron	Eastern	SS	55	226	31	67	12	0	1	26	7	.296
1999 Buffalo	Int.	SS	66	237	30	75	12	1	0	25	6	.316
1999 Cleveland	A.L.	2B-SS	18	21	2	7	0	0	0	0	0	.333
2000 Buffalo	Int.	SS-2B	75	286	37	77	17	2	1	36	4	.269
2000 Mahoning Valley	N.Y.-Penn.	SS	5	17	0	2	1	0	0	1	0	.118
2000 Cleveland	A.L.	SS-2B	9	9	0	4	0	0	0	0	0	.444
2000 Kinston a	Carolina	SS	1	3	0	1	0	0	0	0	0	.333
2001 Buffalo	Int.	SS-2B-3B	116	410	52	100	17	1	2	33	17	.244
2001 Cleveland b	A.L.	SS-2B-3B	17	22	1	2	1	0	0	0	0	.091
2002 Cleveland	A.L.	2B-SS-3B	93	264	35	66	11	3	1	12	3	.250
2003 Lake County	So.Atl.	SS	1	3	0	0	0	0	0	0	0	.000
2003 Mahoning Valley	N.Y.-Penn.	SS	1	2	1	0	0	0	0	0	0	.000
2003 Cleveland c	A.L.	2B-SS-3B	82	214	21	46	9	1	1	14	3	.215
2004 Cleveland d	A.L.	SS-2B-3B	66	93	17	19	5	1	2	7	0	.204
2005 Toronto-Detroit e-f	A.L.	SS-2B-3B	68	166	18	46	6	1	0	16	6	.277
2006 Toronto g	A.L.	SS-2B-3B	104	260	35	58	7	3	3	23	7	.223
2007 Toronto	A.L.	SS-3B	123	327	32	82	20	2	1	31	7	.251
Major League Totals		9 Yrs.	580	1376	161	330	59	11	8	103	26	.240

a On disabled list from April 27 to May 9 and May 10 to June 22, 2000.
b On disabled list from May 10 to 17, 2001.
c On disabled list from June 30 to July 17 and August 27 to October 3, 2003.
d Traded to Toronto Blue Jays for player to be named later, December 2, 2004.
e Sold to Detroit Tigers, July 22, 2005.
f Sold to Toronto Blue Jays, November 10, 2005.
g On disabled list from May 28 to June 12, 2006.

MC LOUTH, NATHAN RICHARD (NATE)
Born, Muskegon, Michigan, October 28, 1981.
Bats Left. Throws Right. Height, 5 feet, 11 inches. Weight, 185 pounds.

Year	Club	Lea	Pos	G	AB	R	H	2B	3B	HR	RBI	SB	Avg
2001 Hickory	So.Atl.	OF-2B	96	351	59	100	17	5	12	54	21	.285
2002 Lynchburg	Carolina	OF	114	393	58	96	23	4	9	46	20	.244
2003 Lynchburg	Carolina	OF	117	440	85	132	27	2	6	33	40	.300
2004 Altoona	Eastern	OF	133	515	93	166	40	4	8	73	31	.322
2005 Indianapolis	Int.	OF	110	397	64	118	20	3	5	39	34	.297
2005 Pittsburgh	N.L.	OF	41	109	20	28	6	0	5	12	2	.257
2006 Pittsburgh a	N.L.	OF	106	270	50	63	16	2	7	16	10	.233
2007 Pittsburgh	N.L.	OF	137	329	62	85	21	3	13	38	22	.258
Major League Totals	3 Yrs.	284	708	132	176	43	5	25	66	34	.249

a On disabled list from August 12 to October 3, 2006.

MC PHERSON, DALLAS LYLE
Born, Greensboro, North Carolina, July 23, 1980.
Bats Left. Throws Right. Height, 6 feet, 4 inches. Weight, 230 pounds.

Year	Club	Lea	Pos	G	AB	R	H	2B	3B	HR	RBI	SB	Avg
2001 Provo	Pioneer	3B-1B	31	124	30	49	11	0	5	29	1	.395
2002 Cedar Rapids	Midwest	3B	132	499	71	138	24	3	15	88	30	.277
2003 Rancho Cucamonga	Calif.	3B	77	292	65	90	21	6	18	59	12	.308
2003 Arkansas	Texas	3B	28	102	22	32	9	1	5	27	4	.314
2004 Arkansas	Texas	3B	68	262	53	84	17	6	20	69	6	.321
2004 Salt Lake	P.C.	3B-OF	67	259	54	81	19	8	20	57	6	.313
2004 Anaheim	A.L.	3B	16	40	5	9	1	0	3	6	1	.225
2005 Angels	Arizona	3B	3	9	1	2	1	1	0	2	0	.222
2005 Rancho Cucamonga	Calif.	3B	5	16	3	7	2	0	2	5	1	.438
2005 Salt Lake	P.C.	3B	14	54	8	15	1	2	6	19	1	.278
2005 Los Angeles a	A.L.	3B	61	205	29	50	14	2	8	26	3	.244
2006 Salt Lake	P.C.	3B-1B	56	208	35	52	11	5	17	45	3	.250
2006 Los Angeles b	A.L.	3B-1B	40	115	16	30	4	0	7	13	1	.261
2007 Los Angeles c-d	A.L.				INJURED—Did Not Play								
Major League Totals	3 Yrs.	117	360	50	89	19	2	18	45	5	.247
Division Series												
2004 Anaheim	A.L.	3B	3	9	0	1	0	0	0	1	0	.111

a On disabled list from July 8 to October 31, 2005.
b On disabled list from June 22 to September 1, 2006.
c On disabled list from March 23 to November 13, 2007.
d Not offered contract, December 12, 2007.

MENCH, KEVIN FORD
Born, Wilmington, Delaware, January 7, 1978.
Bats Right. Throws Right. Height, 6 feet. Weight, 225 pounds.

Year	Club	Lea	Pos	G	AB	R	H	2B	3B	HR	RBI	SB	Avg
1999 Pulaski	Appal.	OF	65	260	63	94	22	1	16	60	12	.362
1999 Savannah a	So.Atl.	OF	6	23	4	7	1	1	2	8	0	.304
2000 Charlotte	Fla.St.	OF	132	491	118	164	39	9	27	121	19	.334
2001 Tulsa b	Texas	OF	120	475	78	126	34	2	26	83	4	.265
2002 Oklahoma	P.C.	OF	26	98	17	21	8	0	6	15	0	.214
2002 Texas	A.L.	OF	110	366	52	95	20	2	15	60	1	.260
2003 Frisco	Texas	OF	3	11	1	1	0	0	0	0	0	.091
2003 Oklahoma	P.C.	OF	29	105	16	28	8	0	4	21	2	.267
2003 Texas c	A.L.	OF	38	125	15	40	12	0	2	11	1	.320
2004 Frisco	Texas	OF	4	16	3	5	0	0	1	1	0	.313
2004 Texas d	A.L.	OF	125	438	69	122	30	3	26	71	0	.279
2005 Texas	A.L.	OF	150	557	71	147	33	3	25	73	4	.264
2006 Texas	A.L.	OF	87	320	36	91	18	1	12	50	1	.284
2006 Milwaukee d	N.L.	OF	40	126	9	29	6	1	1	18	0	.230
2007 Milwaukee e	N.L.	OF	101	288	39	77	20	3	8	37	3	.267
Major League Totals	6 Yrs.	651	2220	291	601	139	13	89	320	10	.271

a Drafted by Texas Rangers with choice received for Arizona Diamondbacks signing of pitcher Todd Stottlemyre, June 2, 1999.
b On disabled list from June 10 to 30, 2001.
c On disabled list from March 21 to April 17 and July 9 to November 14, 2003.
d Traded to Milwaukee Brewers with pitcher Francisco Cordero, outfielder Laynce Nix and pitcher Julian Cordero for outfielder Carlos Lee and outfielder Nelson Cruz, July 28, 2006.
e Not offered contract, December 12, 2007.

MICHAELS, JASON DREW

Born, Tampa, Florida, May 4, 1976.
Bats Right. Throws Right. Height, 6 feet. Weight, 205 pounds.

Year Club	Lea	Pos	G	AB	R	H	2B	3B	HR	RBI	SB	Avg
1998 Batavia	N.Y.-Penn.	OF	67	235	45	63	14	3	11	49	4	.268
1999 Clearwater	Fla.St.	OF	122	452	91	138	31	6	14	65	10	.305
2000 Reading	Eastern	OF	113	437	71	129	30	4	10	74	7	.295
2001 Scranton-WB	Int.	OF	109	418	58	109	19	3	17	69	11	.261
2001 Philadelphia a	N.L.	OF	6	6	0	1	0	0	0	1	0	.167
2002 Scranton-WB	Int.	OF	9	32	3	9	2	0	0	7	1	.281
2002 Philadelphia	N.L.	OF-3B	81	105	16	28	10	3	2	11	1	.267
2003 Clearwater	Fla.St.	OF	4	14	1	0	0	0	0	0	0	.000
2003 Philadelphia b	N.L.	OF	76	109	20	36	11	0	5	17	0	.330
2004 Philadelphia	N.L.	OF	115	299	44	82	12	0	10	40	2	.274
2005 Philadelphia	N.L.	OF	105	289	54	88	16	2	4	31	3	.304
2006 Buffalo	Int.	OF	2	7	1	3	0	0	1	1	0	.429
2006 Cleveland c-d	A.L.	OF	123	494	77	132	32	1	9	55	9	.267
2007 Cleveland	A.L.	OF	105	267	43	72	11	1	7	39	3	.270
Major League Totals		7 Yrs.	611	1569	254	439	92	7	37	194	18	.280
Division Series												
2007 Cleveland	A.L.	OF	1	1	0	1	1	0	0	0	0	1.000
Championship Series												
2007 Cleveland	A.L.	PH	1	0	1	0	0	0	0	0	0	.000

a On disabled list from May 1 to 10, 2001.
b On disabled list from March 21 to April 14, 2003.
c Traded to Cleveland Indians for pitcher Arthur Rhodes, January 27, 2006.
d On disabled list from June 16 to July 4, 2006.

MIENTKIEWICZ, DOUGLAS (DOUG)

Born, Toledo, Ohio, June 19, 1974.
Bats Left. Throws Right. Height, 6 feet, 2 inches. Weight, 205 pounds.

Year Club	Lea	Pos	G	AB	R	H	2B	3B	HR	RBI	SB	Avg
1995 Fort Myers	Fla.St.	1B	38	110	9	27	6	1	1	15	2	.245
1996 Ft. Myers	Fla.St.	1B-C	133	492	69	143	36	4	5	79	12	.291
1997 New Britain	Eastern	1B-OF	132	467	87	119	28	2	15	61	21	.255
1998 New Britain	Eastern	1B-OF	139	502	96	162	45	0	16	88	11	.323
1998 Minnesota	A.L.	1B	8	25	1	5	1	0	0	2	1	.200
1999 Minnesota	A.L.	1B	118	327	34	75	21	3	2	32	1	.229
2000 Salt Lake	P.C.	1B-3B-2B-OF	130	485	96	162	32	3	18	96	9	.334
2000 Minnesota	A.L.	1B	3	14	0	6	0	0	0	4	0	.429
2001 Minnesota	A.L.	1B	151	543	77	166	39	1	15	74	2	.306
2002 Minnesota	A.L.	1B	143	467	60	122	29	1	10	64	1	.261
2003 Minnesota	A.L.	1B-OF-2B-3B	142	487	67	146	38	1	11	65	4	.300
2004 Minn.-Boston a-b-c	A.L.	1B-2B	127	391	47	93	24	1	6	35	2	.238
2005 Mets	Gulf Coast	1B	4	10	2	5	1	0	1	5	0	.500
2005 St. Lucie	Fla.St.	1B	8	27	3	7	4	0	0	2	0	.259
2005 New York d-e-f	N.L.	1B	87	275	36	66	13	0	11	29	0	.240
2006 Kansas City g-h	A.L.	1B	91	314	37	89	24	2	4	43	3	.283
2007 Tampa	Fla.St.	1B	5	14	4	6	3	0	0	8	0	.429
2007 Scranton-WB	Int.	1B	5	21	5	8	3	0	1	7	0	.381
2007 New York i-j	A.L.	1B	72	166	26	46	12	0	5	24	0	.277
Major League Totals		10 Yrs.	942	3009	385	814	201	9	64	372	14	.271
Division Series												
2002 Minnesota	A.L.	1B	5	20	3	5	0	0	2	4	0	.250
2003 Minnesota	A.L.	1B	4	15	0	2	0	0	0	0	0	.133
2004 Boston	A.L.	1B	3	4	0	2	0	0	0	1	0	.500
2007 New York	A.L.	1B	4	6	0	0	0	0	0	0	0	.000*
Division Series Totals			16	45	3	9	0	0	2	5	0	.200
Championship Series												
2002 Minnesota	A.L.	1B	5	18	1	5	1	0	0	2	0	.278
2004 Boston	A.L.	1B	4	4	0	2	1	0	0	0	0	.500
Championship Series Totals			9	22	1	7	2	0	0	2	0	.318
World Series Record												
2004 Boston	A.L.	1B	4	1	0	0	0	0	0	0	0	.000

a On disabled list from July 7 to July 23, 2004.
b Traded to Chicago Cubs for pitcher Justin Jones, July 31, 2004.
c Traded to Boston Red Sox with infielder Orlando Cabrera for infielder Nomar Garciaparra and outfielder Matt Murton, July 31, 2004.
d Traded to New York Mets for infielder Ian Bladergroen, January 26, 2005.

e On disabled list from June 26 to July 16 and August 4 to September 2, 2005.
f Filed for free agency, November 1, 2005. Signed with Kansas City Royals, December 16, 2005.
g On disabled list from July 31 to October 28, 2006.
h Filed for free agency, October 28, 2006. Signed with New York Yankees, January 5, 2007.
i On disabled list from June 3 to September 1, 2007.
j Filed for free agency, October 29, 2007.

MILES, AARON WADE

Born, Pittsburg, California, December 15, 1976.
Bats Both. Throws Right. Height, 5 feet, 8 inches. Weight, 175 pounds.

Year	Club	Lea	Pos	G	AB	R	H	2B	3B	HR	RBI	SB	Avg
1995 Astros	......	Gulf Coast	SS-2B	47	171	32	44	9	3	0	18	9	.257
1996 Astros	......	Gulf Coast	2B	55	214	48	63	3	2	0	15	14	.294
1997 Quad City	....	Midwest	2B	97	370	55	97	13	2	1	35	18	.262
1998 Quad City	....	Midwest	2B-3B-OF	108	369	42	90	22	6	2	37	28	.244
1999 Michigan	.....	Midwest	2B	112	470	72	149	28	8	10	71	17	.317
2000 Kissimmee a	....	Fla.St.	2B	75	295	40	86	20	1	2	36	11	.292
2001 Birmingham b	.Southern		3B-2B	84	343	53	89	16	3	8	42	3	.259
2002 Birmingham c	.Southern		2B-3B	138	531	67	171	39	1	9	68	25	.322
2003 Charlotte	....	Int.	2B-3B	133	546	80	166	34	5	11	50	8	.304
2003 Chicago d	....	A.L.	2B	8	12	3	4	3	0	0	2	0	.333
2004 Colorado Springs	...	P.C.	2B	12	54	8	18	3	0	0	8	2	.333
2004 Colorado	....	N.L.	2B	134	522	75	153	15	3	6	47	12	.293
2005 Colorado Springs	...	P.C.	2B	8	32	6	7	0	1	0	1	1	.219
2005 Colorado e-f	......	N.L.	2B-SS	99	324	37	91	12	3	2	28	4	.281
2006 St. Louis	....	N.L.	2B-SS-3B	135	426	48	112	20	5	2	30	2	.263
2007 St. Louis g	....	N.L.	2B-SS-3B-P	133	414	55	120	16	1	2	32	2	.290
Major League Totals	....		5 Yrs.	509	1698	218	480	66	12	12	139	20	.283
Division Series													
2006 St. Louis	....	N.L.	2B	2	2	0	1	0	0	0	0	0	.500
Championship Series													
2006 St. Louis	....	N.L.	2B	3	3	0	2	0	1	0	0	0	.667
World Series Record													
2006 St. Louis	....	N.L.	2B	2	6	2	1	0	0	0	0	1	.167

a Selected by Chicago White Sox organization from Houston Astros organization in Rule V draft, December 11, 2000.
b Filed for free agency, October 15, 2001, re-signed with Chicago White Sox, November 16, 2001.
c Filed for free agency, October 15, 2002, re-signed with Chicago White Sox, October 25, 2002.
d Traded to Colorado Rockies for infielder Juan Uribe, December 2, 2003.
e On disabled list from May 26 to June 28, 2005.
f Traded to St. Louis Cardinals with outfielder Larry Bigbie for pitcher Ray King, December 7, 2005.
g Not offered contract, December 12, 2007, re-signed with St. Louis Cardinals organization, January 4, 2008.

MILLAR, KEVIN CHARLES

Born, Los Angeles, California, September 24, 1971.
Bats Right. Throws Right. Height, 6 feet. Weight, 215 pounds.

Year	Club	Lea	Pos	G	AB	R	H	2B	3B	HR	RBI	SB	Avg
1993 St. Paul	......	Northern	3B-2B	63	227	33	59	11	1	5	30	2	.260
1994 Kane County	...	Midwest	1B	135	477	75	144	35	2	19	93	3	.302
1995 Brevard Cty	.....	Fla.St.	1B	129	459	53	132	32	2	13	68	4	.288
1996 Portland	....	Eastern	1B-3B	130	472	69	150	32	0	18	86	6	.318
1997 Portland a	......	Eastern	1B-3B	135	511	94	175	34	2	32	131	2	.342
1998 Charlotte	....	Int.	3B-1B	14	46	14	15	3	0	4	15	1	.326
1998 Florida	....	N.L.	3B	2	2	1	1	0	0	0	0	0	.500
1999 Calgary	....	P.C.	OF	36	143	24	43	11	1	7	26	2	.301
1999 Florida	....	N.L.	1B-3B-OF	105	351	48	100	17	4	9	67	1	.285
2000 Florida	....	N.L.	1B-OF-3B	123	259	36	67	14	3	14	42	0	.259
2001 Florida	....	N.L.	OF-1B-3B	144	449	62	141	39	5	20	85	0	.314
2002 Portland	....	Eastern	OF	3	12	1	1	0	0	1	3	0	.083
2002 Florida b-c	......	N.L.	OF-1B-3B	126	438	58	134	41	0	16	57	0	.306
2003 Boston d	....	A.L.	1B-OF	148	544	83	150	30	1	25	96	3	.276
2004 Boston	....	A.L.	OF-1B	150	508	74	151	36	0	18	74	1	.297
2005 Boston e	....	A.L.	1B-OF	134	449	57	122	28	1	9	50	0	.272
2006 Baltimore f	......	A.L.	1B	132	430	64	117	26	0	15	64	1	.272
2007 Baltimore	....	A.L.	1B-OF	140	476	63	121	26	1	17	63	1	.254
Major League Totals	....		10 Yrs.	1204	3906	546	1104	257	15	143	598	7	.283
Division Series													
2003 Boston	....	A.L.	1B	5	21	0	5	0	0	0	0	0	.238
2004 Boston	....	A.L.	1B	3	10	2	3	0	0	1	4	0	.300

Year	Club	Lea	Pos	G	AB	R	H	2B	3B	HR	RBI	SB	Avg
2005 Boston.........,A.L.			1B	2	3	0	1	1	0	0	1	0	.333
Division Series Totals				10	34	2	9	1	0	1	5	0	.265
Championship Series													
2003 Boston...........A.L.			1B	7	29	3	7	0	0	1	3	0	.241
2004 Boston.....\.....A.L.			1B	7	24	4	6	3	0	0	2	0	.250
Championship Series Totals ..				14	53	7	13	3	0	1	5	0	.245
World Series Record													
2004 Boston...........A.L.			1B	4	8	2	1	1	0	0	0	0	.125

a Filed for free agency, December 19, 1997, re-signed with Florida Marlins, December 21, 1997.
b On disabled list from April 29 to May 28, 2002.
c Sold to Chunichi Dragons, January 8, 2003.
d Sale to Japan voided and sold to Boston Red Sox, February 15, 2003.
e Filed for free agency, October 27, 2005. Signed with Baltimore Orioles, January 13, 2006.
f Filed for free agency, October 31, 2006, re-signed with Baltimore Orioles, December 2, 2006.

MILLEDGE, LASTINGS DARNELL

Born, Bradenton, Florida, April 5, 1985.
Bats Right. Throws Right. Height, 6 feet, 1 inch. Weight, 185 pounds.

Year	Club	Lea	Pos	G	AB	R	H	2B	3B	HR	RBI	SB	Avg
2003 Kingsport..........Appal.			DH	7	26	4	6	2	0	0	2	5	.231
2004 St. Lucie............Fla.St.			OF	22	81	6	19	6	2	2	8	3	.235
2004 Capital City........So.Atl.			OF	65	262	66	89	22	1	13	58	23	.340
2005 Binghamton.......Eastern			OF	48	193	33	65	17	0	4	24	11	.337
2005 St. Lucie............Fla.St.			OF	62	232	48	70	15	0	4	22	18	.302
2006 Norfolk.............Int.			OF	84	307	52	85	21	4	7	36	13	.277
2006 New York...........N.L.			OF	56	166	14	40	7	2	4	22	1	.241
2007 Mets..........Gulf Coast			OF	2	7	1	1	1	0	0	0	0	.143
2007 St. Lucie............Fla.St.			OF	1	4	2	1	0	0	0	0	0	.250
2007 Binghamton.......Eastern			OF	5	23	7	10	1	1	3	8	1	.435
2007 New Orleans.........P.C.			OF	11	39	9	13	1	0	1	5	5	.333
2007 New York a..........N.L.			OF	59	184	27	50	9	1	7	29	4	.272
Major League Totals			2 Yrs.	115	350	41	90	16	3	11	51	4	.257

a Traded to Washington Nationals for outfielder Ryan Church and catcher Brian Schneider, November 30, 2007.

MIRABELLI, DOUGLAS (DOUG)

Born, Kingman, Arizona, October 18, 1970.
Bats Right. Throws Right. Height, 6 feet, 1 inch. Weight, 220 pounds.

Year	Club	Lea	Pos	G	AB	R	H	2B	3B	HR	RBI	SB	Avg
1992 San Jose ....Calif.			C	53	177	30	41	11	1	0	21	1	.232
1993 San Jose ....Calif.			C	113	371	58	100	19	2	1	48	0	.270
1994 Shreveport.........Texas			C-1B	85	255	23	56	8	0	4	24	3	.220
1995 Phoenix.............P.C.			C	23	66	3	11	0	1	0	7	1	.167
1995 Shreveport a ....Texas			C-1B	40	126	14	38	13	0	0	16	1	.302
1996 Phoenix.............P.C.			C	14	47	10	14	7	0	0	7	0	.298
1996 Shreveport..........Texas			C-1B	115	380	60	112	23	0	21	70	0	.295
1996 San Francisco ........N.L.			C	9	18	2	4	1	0	0	1	0	.222
1997 Phoenix.............P.C.			C	100	332	49	88	23	2	8	48	1	.265
1997 San Francisco ........N.L.			C	6	7	0	1	0	0	0	0	0	.143
1998 Fresno...............P.C.			C	85	265	45	69	12	2	13	53	2	.260
1998 San Francisco ........N.L.			C	10	17	2	4	2	0	1	4	0	.235
1999 Fresno...............P.C.			C-1B	86	320	63	100	24	1	14	51	8	.313
1999 San Francisco ........N.L.			C	33	87	10	22	6	0	1	10	0	.253
2000 San Francisco ........N.L.			C	82	230	23	53	10	2	6	28	1	.230
2001 Texas-Boston b-c .....A.L.			C	77	190	20	43	10	0	11	29	0	.226
2002 Boston..............A.L.			C	57	151	17	34	7	0	7	25	0	.225
2003 Boston..............A.L.			C-1B	62	163	23	42	13	0	6	18	0	.258
2004 Boston d ............A.L.			C	59	160	27	45	12	0	9	32	0	.281
2005 Boston e-f ...........A.L.			C	50	136	16	31	7	0	6	18	2	.228
2006 San Diego ...........N.L.			C	14	22	1	4	1	0	0	0	0	.182
2006 Boston g-h ..........A.L.			C	59	161	12	31	6	0	6	25	0	.193
2007 Boston i-j ...........A.L.			C	48	114	9	23	3	0	5	16	0	.202
Major League Totals			12 Yrs.	566	1456	162	337	78	2	58	206	3	.231
Division Series													
2000 San Francisco ........N.L.			C	2	2	0	0	0	0	0	0	0	.000
2003 Boston..............A.L.			C	2	4	2	2	1	0	0	0	0	.500
2005 Boston..............A.L.			C	1	2	0	0	0	0	0	0	0	.000
Division Series Totals				5	8	2	2	1	0	0	0	0	.250

Year	Club	Lea	Pos	G	AB	R	H	2B	3B	HR	RBI	SB	Avg
Championship Series													
2003 Boston	A.L.		C	3	7	0	2	0	0	0	0	0	.286
2004 Boston	A.L.		C	1	1	0	0	0	0	0	0	0	.000
2007 Boston	A.L.		C	1	2	0	0	0	0	0	0	0	.000
Championship Series Totals				5	10	0	2	0	0	0	0	0	.200
World Series Record													
2004 Boston	A.L.		C	1	3	1	1	0	0	0	0	0	.333

a On disabled list from May 16 to 23, 1995.
b Sold to Texas Rangers, March 27, 2001.
c Traded to Boston Red Sox for pitcher Justin Duchscherer, June 12, 2001.
d Filed for free agency, November 1, 2004, re-signed with Boston Red Sox, November 29, 2004.
e On disabled list from May 19 to June 12, 2005.
f Traded to San Diego Padres for infielder Mark Loretta, December 7, 2005.
g Traded to Boston Red Sox for pitcher Cla Meredith and catcher Josh Bard, May 1, 2006.
h Filed for free agency, October 28, 2006, re-signed with Boston Red Sox, December 15, 2006.
i On disabled list from August 17 to September 1, 2007.
j Filed for free agency, November 1, 2007, re-signed with Boston Red Sox, January 11, 2008.

MOLINA, BENJAMIN JOSE (BENGIE)
Born, Rio Piedras, Puerto Rico, July 20, 1974.
Bats Right. Throws Right. Height, 5 feet, 11 inches. Weight, 225 pounds.

Year	Club	Lea	Pos	G	AB	R	H	2B	3B	HR	RBI	SB	Avg
1993 Angels	Arizona	DH-C	27	80	9	21	6	2	0	10	0	.262
1994 Cedar Rapds	Midwest	C	48	171	14	48	8	0	3	16	1	.281
1995 Vancouver	P.C.	C	1	2	0	0	0	0	0	0	0	.000
1995 Cedar Rapds	Midwest	C	39	133	15	39	9	0	4	17	1	.293
1995 Lk Elsinore	California	C	27	96	21	37	7	2	2	12	0	.385
1996 Midland	Texas	C	108	365	45	100	21	2	8	54	0	.274
1997 Lk Elsinore	California	C	36	149	18	42	10	2	4	33	0	.282
1997 Midland	Texas	DH-C	29	106	18	35	8	0	6	30	0	.330
1998 Midland	Texas	C	41	154	28	55	8	0	9	39	0	.357
1998 Vancouver	P.C.	C	49	184	13	54	9	1	1	22	1	.293
1998 Anaheim a	A.L.	C	2	1	0	0	0	0	0	0	0	.000
1999 Edmonton	P.C.	C	65	241	28	69	16	0	7	41	1	.286
1999 Anaheim b	A.L.	C	31	101	8	26	5	0	1	10	0	.257
2000 Anaheim	A.L.	C	130	473	59	133	20	2	14	71	1	.281
2001 Salt Lake	P.C.	C	5	18	2	5	1	0	0	3	0	.278
2001 Rancho Cucamonga	Calif.	C	3	11	1	6	1	0	0	2	0	.545
2001 Anaheim c	A.L.	C	96	325	31	85	11	0	6	40	0	.262
2002 Rancho Cucamonga	Calif.	C	1	2	0	1	0	0	0	0	0	.500
2002 Anaheim d	A.L.	C	122	428	34	105	18	0	5	47	0	.245
2003 Anaheim e	A.L.	C	119	409	37	115	24	0	14	71	1	.281
2004 Anaheim f	A.L.	C	97	337	36	93	13	0	10	54	0	.276
2005 Los Angeles g-h	A.L.	C	119	410	45	121	17	0	15	69	0	.295
2006 Toronto i	A.L.	C	117	433	44	123	20	1	19	57	1	.284
2007 San Francisco	N.L.	C	134	497	38	137	19	1	19	81	0	.276
Major League Totals		10 Yrs.	967	3414	332	938	147	4	103	500	3	.275
Division Series												
2002 Anaheim	A.L.	C	4	15	0	4	2	0	0	2	0	.267
2004 Anaheim	A.L.	C	3	6	0	1	0	0	0	0	0	.167
2005 Los Angeles	A.L.	C	5	18	5	8	0	0	3	5	0	.444
Division Series Totals			12	39	5	13	2	0	3	7	0	.333
Championship Series												
2002 Anaheim	A.L.	C	5	14	0	3	0	1	0	2	0	.214
2005 Los Angeles	A.L.	C-DH	5	17	0	2	0	0	0	1	0	.118
Championship Series Totals			10	31	0	5	0	1	0	3	0	.161
World Series Record												
2002 Anaheim	A.L.	C	7	21	2	6	2	0	0	2	0	.286

a On disabled list from May 13 to 22, 1998.
b On disabled list from June 4 to 14, 1999.
c On disabled list from May 5 to June 27, 2001.
d On disabled list from July 17 to August 1, 2002.
e On disabled list from September 4 to October 6, 2003.
f On disabled list from June 4 to June 19 and from August 1 to August 17, 2004.
g On disabled list from April 18 to May 13, 2005.
h Filed for free agency, October 27, 2005. Signed with Toronto Blue Jays, February 28, 2006.
i Filed for free agency, November 31, 2006, re-signed with San Francisco Giants, December 6, 2006.

MOLINA (MATTA), JOSE BENJAMIN

Born, Bayamon, Puerto Rico, June 3, 1975.
Bats Right. Throws Right. Height, 6 feet, 2 inch. Weight, 245 pounds.

Year	Club	Lea	Pos	G	AB	R	H	2B	3B	HR	RBI	SB	Avg
1993 Cubs	Gulf Coast	C-1B	33	78	5	17	2	0	0	4	3	.218
1993 Daytona	Fla.St.	C	3	7	0	1	0	0	0	1	0	.143
1994 Peoria	Midwest	C	78	253	31	58	13	1	1	33	4	.229
1995 Daytona	Fla.St.	C	82	233	27	55	9	1	1	19	1	.236
1996 Rockford	Midwest	C	96	305	35	69	10	1	2	27	2	.226
1997 Iowa	A.A.	C	1	3	0	1	0	0	0	0	0	.333
1997 Daytona	Fla.St.	C	55	179	17	45	9	1	0	23	4	.251
1997 Orlando	Southern	C	37	99	10	17	3	0	1	15	0	.172
1998 West Tenn	Southern	C-1B	109	320	33	71	10	1	2	28	1	.222
1999 West Tenn	Southern	C	14	35	2	6	3	0	0	5	0	.171
1999 Iowa	P.C.	C	74	240	24	63	11	1	4	26	0	.262
1999 Chicago	N.L.	C	10	19	3	5	1	0	0	1	0	.263
2000 Iowa	P.C.	C-1B	76	248	22	58	9	0	1	17	1	.234
2001 Salt Lake	P.C.	C	61	213	29	64	11	1	5	31	1	.300
2001 Anaheim a-b	A.L.	C	15	37	8	10	3	0	2	4	0	.270
2002 Salt Lake	P.C.	C	79	290	30	89	14	2	4	43	0	.307
2002 Anaheim	A.L.	C	29	70	5	19	3	0	0	5	0	.271
2003 Anaheim	A.L.	C	53	114	12	21	4	0	0	6	0	.184
2004 Anaheim	A.L.	C-1B	73	203	26	53	10	2	3	25	4	.261
2005 Los Angeles	A.L.	C-1B	75	184	14	42	4	0	6	25	2	.228
2006 Los Angeles	A.L.	C-1B	78	225	18	54	17	0	4	22	1	.240
2007 Los Angeles-New York c-d	A.L.	C	69	191	18	49	13	0	1	19	2	.257
Major League Totals		8 Yrs.	402	1043	104	253	55	2	16	107	9	.243
Division Series													
2004 Anaheim	A.L.	C	2	3	2	1	0	0	0	0	0	.333
2005 Los Angeles	A.L.	C	1	1	1	1	0	0	0	1	0	1.000
Division Series Totals			3	4	3	2	0	0	0	1	0	.500
Championship Series													
2002 Anaheim	A.L.	C	3	1	0	0	0	0	0	0	0	.000
2005 Los Angeles	A.L.	C	1	3	0	1	0	0	0	0	0	.333
Championship Series Totals			4	4	0	1	0	0	0	0	0	.250
World Series Record													
2002 Anaheim	A.L.	C	3	0	0	0	0	0	0	0	0	.000

a Released by Chicago Cubs November 27, 2000. Signed with Anaheim Angels organization, January 15, 2001.
b On disabled list from May 21 to July 2, 2001.
c Traded to New York Yankees for pitcher Jeff Kennard, July 21, 2007.
d Filed for free agency, October 30, 2007, re-signed with New York Yankees, December 3, 2007.

MOLINA, YADIER B.

Born, Bayamon, Puerto Rico, July 13, 1982.
Bats Right. Throws Right. Height, 5 feet, 11 inches. Weight, 225 pounds.

Year	Club	Lea	Pos	G	AB	R	H	2B	3B	HR	RBI	SB	Avg
2001 Johnson City	Appal.	C	44	158	18	41	11	0	4	18	1	.259
2002 Peoria	Midwest	C	112	393	39	110	20	0	7	50	2	.280
2003 Tennessee	Southern	C	104	364	32	100	13	1	2	51	0	.275
2004 Memphis	P.C.	C	37	129	19	39	6	0	1	14	0	.302
2004 St. Louis	N.L.	C	51	135	12	36	6	0	2	15	0	.267
2005 St. Louis a	N.L.	C-1B	114	385	36	97	15	1	8	49	2	.252
2006 St. Louis	N.L.	C-1B	129	417	29	90	26	0	6	49	1	.216
2007 St. Louis b	N.L.	C-1B	111	353	30	97	15	0	6	40	1	.275
Major League Totals		4 Yrs.	405	1290	107	320	62	1	22	153	4	.248
Division Series													
2005 St. Louis	N.L.	C	3	13	1	3	0	0	0	3	0	.231
2006 St. Louis	N.L.	C	4	13	0	4	1	0	0	1	0	.308
Division Series Totals			7	26	1	7	1	0	0	4	0	.269
Championship Series													
2004 St. Louis	N.L.	C	1	4	0	1	0	0	0	0	0	.250
2005 St. Louis	N.L.	C	6	22	1	7	3	0	0	0	0	.318
2006 St. Louis	N.L.	C	7	23	2	8	1	0	2	6	0	.348
Championship Series Totals			14	49	3	16	4	0	2	6	0	.327
World Series Record													
2004 St. Louis	N.L.	C	3	3	0	0	0	0	0	0	0	.000
2006 St. Louis	N.L.	C	5	17	3	7	2	0	0	1	0	.412
World Series Totals			8	20	3	7	2	0	0	1	0	.350

MONROE, CRAIG KEYSTONE

Born, Texarkana, Texas, February 27, 1977.
Bats Right. Throws Right. Height, 6 feet, 1 inch. Weight, 205 pounds.

Year Club	Lea	Pos	G	AB	R	H	2B	3B	HR	RBI	SB	Avg
1995 Rangers . . . . Gulf Coast		OF	54	193	22	48	6	2	0	33	13	.249
1996 Chston-Sc . . . . So.Atl.		OF	49	153	11	23	11	1	0	9	2	.150
1996 Hudson Val. . . . . . N.Y.-Penn.		OF	67	268	53	74	16	6	5	29	21	.276
1997 Charlotte . . . . Fla.St.		OF	92	328	54	77	23	1	7	41	24	.235
1998 Charlotte . . . . Fla.St.		OF	132	472	73	114	26	7	17	76	50	.242
1999 Charlotte . . . . Fla.St.		OF	130	480	77	125	21	1	17	81	40	.260
1999 Oklahoma. . . . . P.C.		OF	6	16	2	4	1	0	0	1	0	.250
2000 Tulsa . . . . Texas		OF	120	464	89	131	34	5	20	89	12	.282
2001 Oklahoma. . . . . P.C.		OF	114	410	60	115	25	5	20	75	10	.280
2001 Texas . . . . A.L.		OF	27	52	8	11	1	0	2	5	2	.212
2002 Toledo . . . . Int.		OF	99	358	61	115	30	4	10	49	7	.321
2002 Detroit a. . . . . A.L.		OF	13	25	3	3	1	0	1	1	0	.120
2003 Toledo . . . . Int.		OF	14	47	14	19	4	1	2	6	1	.404
2003 Detroit . . . . A.L.		OF	128	425	51	102	18	1	23	70	4	.240
2004 Toledo . . . . Int.		OF	6	25	4	8	4	0	2	6	0	.320
2004 Detroit b. . . . . A.L.		OF	128	447	65	131	27	3	18	72	3	.293
2005 Detroit . . . . A.L.		OF	157	567	69	157	30	3	20	89	8	.277
2006 Detroit . . . . A.L.		OF	147	541	89	138	35	2	28	92	2	.255
2007 Detroit . . . . A.L.		OF	99	343	47	76	19	0	11	55	0	.222
2007 Chicago c-d . . . . N.L.		OF	23	49	6	10	4	0	1	4	0	.204
Major League Totals	7 Yrs.		722	2449	338	628	135	9	104	388	19	.256
Division Series												
2006 Detroit . . . . A.L.		OF	4	16	3	3	1	0	2	3	0	.188
Championship Series												
2006 Detroit . . . . A.L.		OF	4	14	5	6	2	0	1	4	0	.429
World Series Record												
2006 Detroit . . . . A.L.		OF	5	20	3	3	1	0	2	2	0	.150

a Claimed on waivers by Detroit Tigers, February 1, 2002
b On disabled list from July 21 to August 7, 2004.
c Traded to Chicago Cubs for player to be named later, August 23, 2007. Detroit Tigers received pitcher Clay Rapada
   to complete trade, August 30, 2007.
e Traded to Minnesota Twins for player to be named later, November 13, 2007.

MONTERO, MIGUEL ANGEL

Born, Caracas, Venezuela, July 9, 1983.
Bats Left. Throws Right. Height, 5 feet, 11 inches. Weight, 195 pounds.

Year Club	Lea	Pos	G	AB	R	H	2B	3B	HR	RBI	SB	Avg
2002 Missoula . . . . Pioneer		C-3B-1B	50	152	21	40	10	1	3	14	2	.263
2003 Missoula . . . . Pioneer		C	59	196	24	59	10	2	4	32	2	.301
2004 South Bend . . . . Midwest		C-1B-SS	115	403	47	106	22	2	11	59	8	.263
2005 Lancaster . . . . Calif.		C-1B	85	355	73	124	24	1	24	82	1	.349
2005 Tennessee . . . . Southern		C-1B	30	108	13	27	1	2	2	13	1	.250
2006 Tennessee . . . . Southern		C	81	289	24	78	18	0	10	46	0	.270
2006 Tucson. . . . . P.C.		C	36	134	21	43	5	0	7	29	1	.321
2006 Arizona. . . . . N.L.		C	6	16	0	4	1	0	0	3	0	.250
2007 Arizona. . . . . N.L.		C	84	214	30	48	7	0	10	37	0	.224
Major League Totals	2 Yrs.		90	230	30	52	8	0	10	40	0	.226
Division Series												
2007 Arizona. . . . . N.L.		C	1	2	1	0	0	0	0	0	0	.000
Championship Series												
2007 Arizona. . . . . N.L.		C	3	5	0	2	0	0	0	0	0	.400

MORA, MELVIN

Born, Agua Negra, Venezuela, February 2, 1972.
Bats Right. Throws Right. Height, 5 feet, 11 inches. Weight, 200 pounds.

Year Club	Lea	Pos	G	AB	R	H	2B	3B	HR	RBI	SB	Avg
1992 Astros . . . . . . Gulf Coast		OF-2B-3B	49	144	28	32	3	0	0	8	16	.222
1993 Asheville. . . . . So.Atl.		2B-OF-3B	108	365	66	104	22	2	2	31	20	.285
1994 Osceola . . . . Fla.St.		OF-3B-2B	118	425	57	120	29	4	8	46	24	.282
1995 Jackson . . . . Texas		OF-2B-3B	123	467	63	139	32	0	3	45	22	.298

Year	Club	Lea	Pos	G	AB	R	H	2B	3B	HR	RBI	SB	Avg
1995 Tucson	P.C.	OF	2	5	3	3	0	1	0	1	1	.600
1996 Tucson	P.C.	3B-OF-2B	62	228	35	64	11	2	3	26	3	.281
1996 Jackson	Texas	OF-2B-SS-3B	70	255	36	73	6	1	5	23	4	.286
1997 New Orleans	A.A.	OF-3B-2B-SS	119	370	55	95	15	3	2	38	7	.257
1998 St. Lucie	Fla.St.	2B-SS-OF	17	55	5	15	0	0	0	8	1	.273
1998 Norfolk a	Int.	3B-OF-2B	11	28	5	5	1	0	0	2	0	.179
1999 Norfolk	Int.	SS	82	304	55	92	17	2	8	36	18	.303
1999 New York b	N.L.	OF-2B-3B-SS	66	31	6	5	0	0	0	1	2	.161
2000 Norfolk	Int.	OF	8	27	7	9	2	0	0	7	2	.333
2000 New York	N.L.	SS-OF-2B-3B	79	215	35	56	13	2	6	30	7	.260
2000 Baltimore c	A.L.	SS-2B	53	199	25	58	9	3	2	17	5	.291
2001 Baltimore	A.L.	OF-SS-2B	128	436	49	109	28	0	7	48	11	.250
2002 Baltimore	A.L.	OF-SS-2B	149	557	86	130	30	4	19	64	16	.233
2003 Bowie	Eastern	OF	6	21	3	6	0	0	2	5	0	.286
2003 Baltimore d	A.L.	OF-SS-2B-1B	96	344	68	109	17	1	15	48	6	.317
2004 Baltimore e	A.L.	3B-SS	140	550	111	187	41	0	27	104	11	.340
2005 Baltimore	A.L.	3B	149	593	86	168	30	1	27	88	7	.283
2006 Baltimore	A.L.	3B-2B	155	624	96	171	25	0	16	83	11	.274
2007 Orioles	Gulf Coast	DH	2	7	1	2	1	0	0	1	0	.286
2007 Baltimore f	A.L.	3B	126	467	67	128	23	1	14	58	9	.274
Major League Totals	9 Yrs.		1141	4016	629	1121	216	12	133	541	85	.279
Division Series													
1999 New York	N.L.	OF	3	1	1	0	0	0	0	0	0	.000
Championship Series													
1999 New York	N.L.	OF	6	14	3	6	0	0	1	2	2	.429

a Filed for free agency from Houston Astros, October 17, 1997. Signed with New York Mets, July 24, 1998.
b Filed for free agency, October 16, 1998, re-signed with New York Mets, February 2, 1999.
c Traded to Baltimore Orioles with infielder Mike Kinkade, pitcher Pat Gorman and pitcher Leslie Brea for infielder Mike Bordick, July 28, 2000.
d On disabled list from August 1 to September 2, 2003.
e On disabled list from July 3 to July 18, 2004.
f On disabled list from July 13 to August 5, 2007.

MORNEAU, JUSTIN ERNEST GEORGE

Born, New Westminster, British Columbia, Canada, May 15, 1981.
Bats Left. Throws Right. Height, 6 feet, 4 inches. Weight, 225 pounds.

Year	Club	Lea	Pos	G	AB	R	H	2B	3B	HR	RBI	SB	Avg
1999 Twins	Gulf Coast	DH	17	53	3	16	5	0	0	9	0	.302
2000 Twins	Gulf Coast	1B-C-OF	52	194	47	78	21	0	10	58	3	.402
2000 Elizabethton	Appal.	C	6	23	4	5	0	0	1	3	0	.217
2001 Quad Cities	Midwest	1B	64	236	50	84	17	2	12	53	0	.356
2001 Fort Myers	Fla.St.	1B	53	197	25	58	10	3	4	40	0	.294
2001 New Britain	Eastern	1B	10	38	3	6	1	0	0	4	0	.158
2002 New Britain	Eastern	1B	126	494	72	147	31	4	16	80	7	.298
2003 New Britain	Eastern	1B	20	79	14	26	3	1	6	13	0	.329
2003 Rochester	Int.	1B	71	265	39	71	11	1	16	42	0	.268
2003 Minnesota	A.L.	DH-1B	40	106	14	24	4	0	4	16	0	.226
2004 Rochester	Int.	1B	72	288	51	88	23	0	22	63	1	.306
2004 Minnesota	A.L.	1B	74	280	39	76	17	0	19	58	0	.271
2005 Minnesota a	A.L.	1B	141	490	62	117	23	4	22	79	0	.239
2006 Minnesota b	A.L.	1B	157	592	97	190	37	4	34	130	3	.321
2007 Minnesota	A.L.	1B	157	590	84	160	31	3	31	111	1	.271
Major League Totals	5 Yrs.		569	2058	296	567	112	8	110	394	4	.276
Division Series													
2004 Minnesota	A.L.	1B	4	17	1	4	2	0	0	2	0	.235
2006 Minnesota	A.L.	1B	3	12	3	5	1	0	2	2	0	.417
Division Series Totals				7	29	4	9	3	0	2	4	0	.310

a On disabled list from April 7 to April 22, 2005.
b Selected Most Valuable Player in American League for 2006.

MURPHY, DAVID MATTHEW

Born, Houston, Texas, October 18, 1981.
Bats Left. Throws Left. Height, 6 feet, 4 inches. Weight, 190 pounds.

Year	Club	Lea	Pos	G	AB	R	H	2B	3B	HR	RBI	SB	Avg
2003 Sarasota	Fla.St.	OF	45	153	18	37	5	1	1	18	6	.242
2003 Lowell	N.Y.-Penn.	OF	21	78	13	27	4	0	0	13	4	.346
2004 Sarasota	Fla.St.	OF	73	272	35	71	11	0	4	38	3	.261

Year	Club	Lea	Pos	G	AB	R	H	2B	3B	HR	RBI	SB	Avg
2004 Red Sox	Gulf Coast	OF	5	18	3	5	1	0	0	1	1	.278
2005 Portland	Eastern	OF	135	484	71	133	25	4	14	75	13	.275
2006 Portland	Eastern	OF	42	172	22	47	17	1	3	25	4	.273
2006 Pawtucket	Int.	OF	84	318	45	85	23	5	8	44	3	.267
2006 Boston	A.L.	OF	20	22	4	5	1	0	1	2	0	.227
2007 Oklahoma	P.C.	OF	2	7	0	2	0	0	0	0	0	.286
2007 Pawtucket	Int.	OF	100	400	50	112	20	5	9	47	8	.280
2007 Boston-Texas a	A.L.	OF	46	105	17	36	12	2	2	14	0	.343
Major League Totals		2 Yrs.	66	127	21	41	13	2	3	16	0	.323	

a Traded to Texas Rangers with pitcher Kason Gabbard and outfielder Engle Beltre for pitcher Eric Gagne, July 31, 2007.

MURTON, MATTHEW HENRY (MATT)
Born, Fort Lauderdale, Florida, October 3, 1981.
Bats Right. Throws Right. Height, 6 feet, 1 inch. Weight, 220 pounds.

Year	Club	Lea	Pos	G	AB	R	H	2B	3B	HR	RBI	SB	Avg
2003 Lowell	N.Y.-Penn.	OF	53	189	30	54	11	2	2	29	9	.286
2004 Daytona	Fla.St.	OF	24	79	13	20	1	1	2	8	2	.253
2004 Sarasota a	Fla.St.	OF	102	376	60	113	16	4	11	55	5	.301
2005 West Tenn	Southern	OF	78	313	46	107	17	4	8	46	18	.342
2005 Iowa	P.C.	OF	9	34	4	12	2	0	1	3	0	.353
2005 Chicago	N.L.	OF	51	140	19	45	3	2	7	14	2	.321
2006 Chicago	N.L.	OF	144	455	70	135	22	3	13	62	5	.297
2007 Iowa	P.C.	OF	39	151	30	50	16	1	6	27	1	.331
2007 Chicago	N.L.	OF	94	235	35	66	13	0	8	22	1	.281
Major League Totals		3 Yrs.	289	830	124	246	38	5	28	98	8	.296	
Division Series													
2007 Chicago	N.L.	OF	1	4	1	1	0	0	0	0	0	.250

a Traded by Boston Red Sox to Chicago Cubs with infielder Nomar Garciaparra for infielder Orlando Cabrera and infielder Doug Mientkiewicz, July 31, 2004.

NADY, XAVIER CLIFFORD
Born, Salinas, California, November 14, 1978.
Bats Right. Throws Right. Height, 6 feet, 2 inches. Weight, 205 pounds.

Year	Club	Lea	Pos	G	AB	R	H	2B	3B	HR	RBI	SB	Avg
2000 San Diego	N.L.	PH	1	1	1	1	0	0	0	0	0	1.000
2001 Lake Elsinore	California	1B	137	524	96	158	38	1	26	100	6	.302
2002 Lake Elsinore	California	OF	45	169	41	47	6	3	13	37	2	.278
2002 Portland	P.C.	OF	85	315	46	89	12	1	10	43	0	.283
2003 Portland	P.C.	OF	37	136	19	36	7	0	7	23	0	.265
2003 San Diego	N.L.	OF	110	371	50	99	17	1	9	39	6	.267
2004 Portland	P.C.	OF-1B	74	291	52	96	19	1	22	70	3	.330
2004 San Diego	N.L.	OF	34	77	7	19	4	0	3	9	0	.247
2005 San Diego a	N.L.	OF-1B-3B	124	326	40	85	15	2	13	43	2	.261
2006 Norfolk	Int.	OF	3	11	2	4	1	0	0	3	0	.364
2006 New York-Pittsburgh b-c	N.L.	OF-1B	130	468	57	131	28	1	17	63	3	.280
2007 Pittsburgh	N.L.	OF	125	431	55	120	23	1	20	72	3	.278
Major League Totals		6 Yrs.	524	1674	210	455	87	5	62	226	14	.272	
Division Series													
2005 San Diego	N.L.	1B	2	3	0	1	0	0	0	2	0	.333

a Traded to New York Mets for outfielder Mike Cameron, November 18, 2005.

b On disabled list from May 30 to June 18, 2006.

c Traded to Pittsburgh Pirates for pitcher Oliver Perez and pitcher Roberto Hernandez, July 31, 2006.

NAPOLI, MICHAEL ANTHONY (MIKE)
Born, Hollywood, Florida, October 31, 1981.
Bats Right. Throws Right. Height, 6 feet. Weight, 205 pounds.

Year	Club	Lea	Pos	G	AB	R	H	2B	3B	HR	RBI	SB	Avg
2000 Butte	Pioneer	1B-C	10	26	3	6	2	0	0	3	1	.231
2001 Rancho Cucamonga	Calif.	C	7	20	3	4	0	0	1	4	0	.200
2001 Cedar Rapids	Midwest	C-1B	43	155	23	36	10	1	5	18	3	.232
2002 Cedar Rapids	Midwest	C-1B-3B	106	362	57	91	19	1	10	50	6	.251
2003 Rancho Cucamonga	Calif.	C-1B	47	165	28	44	10	1	4	26	5	.267
2004 Rancho Cucamonga	Calif.	C-1B-3B	132	482	94	136	29	4	29	118	9	.282
2005 Arkansas	Texas	C-1B	131	439	96	104	22	2	31	99	12	.237

Year	Club	Lea	Pos	G	AB	R	H	2B	3B	HR	RBI	SB	Avg
2006 Salt Lake	.............P.C.	C-1B	21	78	12	19	6	0	3	10	1	.244
2006 Los Angeles	..........A.L.	C	99	268	47	61	13	0	16	42	2	.228
2007 Los Angeles a.	.........A.L.	C	75	219	40	54	11	1	10	34	5	.247
Major League Totals	....		2 Yrs.	174	487	87	115	24	1	26	76	7	.236
Division Series													
2007 Los Angeles	..........A.L.	C	3	6	0	1	0	0	0	0	0	.167

a On disabled list from July 2 to July 18 and July 28 to September 1, 2007.

NAVARRO, DIONER FAVIAU

Born, Caracas, Venezuela, February 9, 1984.
Bats Both. Throws Right. Height, 5 feet, 10 inches. Weight, 215 pounds.

Year	Club	Lea	Pos	G	AB	R	H	2B	3B	HR	RBI	SB	Avg
2001 Yankees	....	Gulf Coast	C	43	143	27	40	10	1	2	22	6	.280
2002 Tampa	.............Fla.St.	C	1	2	1	1	0	0	0	0	0	.500
2002 Greensboro	........So.Atl.	C	92	328	41	78	12	2	8	36	1	.238
2003 Trenton.	...........Eastern	C	58	208	28	71	15	0	4	37	2	.341
2003 Tampa	.............Fla.St.	C	52	197	28	59	16	4	3	28	1	.299
2004 Trenton.	...........Eastern	C	70	255	32	69	14	1	3	29	1	.271
2004 Columbus.	............Int.	C	40	136	18	34	8	2	1	16	1	.250
2004 New York	..........A.L.	C	5	7	2	3	0	0	0	1	0	.429
2005 Las Vegas.	.............P.C.	C	75	241	31	64	12	0	6	29	2	.266
2005 Los Angeles a-b	..........N.L.	C	50	176	21	48	9	0	3	14	0	.273
2006 Las Vegas.	.............P.C.	C	11	40	3	7	2	0	0	2	1	.175
2006 Los Angeles c.	........N.L.	C	25	75	5	21	2	0	2	8	1	.280
2006 Tampa Bay d	........A.L.	C	56	193	23	47	7	0	4	20	1	.244
2007 Tampa Bay	..........A.L.	C	119	388	46	88	19	2	9	44	3	.227
Major League Totals	....		4 Yrs.	255	839	97	207	37	2	18	87	5	.247

a Traded to Arizona Diamondbacks with pitcher Javier Vazquez, pitcher Brad Halsey and cash for pitcher Randy Johnson, January 11, 2005.

b Traded to Los Angeles Dodgers with pitcher Danny Muegge, pitcher Beltran Perez and pitcher William Juarez for outfielder Shawn Green, January 11, 2005.

c On disabled list from May 5 to June 15, 2006.

d Traded to Tampa Bay Devil Rays with pitcher Jae Seo and player to be named later for pitcher Mark Hendrickson, catcher Toby Hall and cash, June 27, 2006.

NIXON, CHRISTOPHER TROTMAN (TROT)

Born, Durham, North Carolina, April 11, 1974.
Bats Left. Throws Left. Height, 6 feet, 2 inch. Weight, 210 pounds.

Year	Club	Lea	Pos	G	AB	R	H	2B	3B	HR	RBI	SB	Avg
1994 Lynchburg	....	Carolina	OF	71	264	33	65	12	0	12	43	10	.246
1995 Sarasota.	...........Fla.St.	OF	73	264	43	80	11	4	5	39	7	.303
1995 Trenton.	...........Eastern	OF	25	94	9	15	3	1	2	8	2	.160
1996 Trenton.	...........Eastern	OF	123	438	55	110	14	4	11	63	7	.251
1996 Boston	.............A.L.	OF	2	4	2	2	1	0	0	0	1	.500
1997 Pawtucket	.......Int.	OF	130	475	80	116	18	3	20	61	11	.244
1998 Pawtucket	.............Int.	OF-1B	135	509	97	158	26	4	23	74	26	.310
1998 Boston	.............A.L.	OF	13	27	3	7	1	0	0	0	0	.259
1999 Boston	.............A.L.	OF	124	381	67	103	22	5	15	52	3	.270
2000 Red Sox	....	Gulf Coast	OF	3	10	3	4	0	0	1	5	0	.400
2000 Boston a.	.............A.L.	OF	123	427	66	118	27	8	12	60	8	.276
2001 Boston	.............A.L.	OF	148	535	100	150	31	4	27	88	7	.280
2002 Boston	.............A.L.	OF	152	532	81	136	36	3	24	94	4	.256
2003 Boston	.............A.L.	OF	134	441	81	135	24	6	28	87	4	.306
2004 Sarasota.	...........Fla.St.	OF	1	3	1	2	1	0	0	1	0	.667
2004 Pawtucket	.............Int.	OF	6	21	2	7	1	0	0	2	0	.333
2004 Boston b	.............A.L.	OF	48	149	24	47	9	1	6	23	0	.315
2005 Pawtucket	.............Int.	C	2	6	3	3	0	0	1	2	0	.500
2005 Boston c.	.............A.L.	OF	124	408	64	112	29	1	13	67	2	.275
2006 Pawtucket	.............Int.	OF	3	12	2	2	1	0	0	0	0	.167
2006 Boston d-e	.............A.L.	OF	114	381	59	102	24	0	8	52	0	.268
2007 Cleveland f	...........A.L.	OF	99	307	30	77	17	0	3	31	0	.251
Major League Totals	....		11 Yrs.	1081	3592	577	989	221	28	136	554	29	.275
Division Series													
1998 Boston	.............A.L.	OF	2	3	0	1	0	0	0	0	0	.333
1999 Boston	.............A.L.	OF	5	14	5	3	3	0	0	6	0	.214
2003 Boston	.............A.L.	OF	4	10	1	2	0	0	1	2	0	.200
2004 Boston	.............A.L.	OF	2	8	0	2	0	0	0	2	0	.250

Year Club	Lea	Pos	G	AB	R	H	2B	3B	HR	RBI	SB	Avg
2005 Boston	A.L.	OF	3	11	1	3	0	0	0	1	0	.273
2007 Cleveland	A.L.	OF	1	4	1	2	1	0	1	2	0	.500
Division Series Totals			17	50	8	13	4	0	2	13	0	.260
Championship Series												
1999 Boston	A.L.	OF	4	14	2	4	2	0	0	0	0	.286
2003 Boston	A.L.	OF	7	24	3	8	1	0	3	5	1	.333
2004 Boston	A.L.	OF	7	29	4	6	1	0	1	3	0	.207
2007 Cleveland	A.L.	OF	3	7	0	3	0	0	0	1	0	.429
Championship Series Totals			21	74	9	21	4	0	4	9	1	.284
World Series Record												
2004 Boston	A.L.	OF	4	14	1	5	3	0	0	3	0	.357

a On disabled list from June 24 to July 24, 2000.
b On disabled list from March 31 to June 16 and from July 25 to September 7, 2004.
c On disabled list from July 27 to August 23, 2005.
d On disabled list from July 31 to September 3, 2006.
e Filed for free agency, October 29, 2006. Signed with Cleveland Indians, January 19, 2007.
f Filed for free agency, October 29, 2007.

NORTON, GREGORY BLAKEMOOR (GREG)

Born, San Leandro, California, July 6, 1972.
Bats Both. Throws Right. Height, 6 feet, 1 inch. Weight, 205 pounds.

Year Club	Lea	Pos	G	AB	R	H	2B	3B	HR	RBI	SB	Avg
1993 White Sox . . . Gulf Coast		3B	3	9	1	2	0	0	0	2	0	.222
1993 Hickory. . . . . So.Atl.		3B-SS	71	254	36	62	12	2	4	36	0	.244
1994 South Bend . . . Midwest		3B	127	477	73	137	22	2	6	64	5	.287
1995 Birmingham . . . Southern		3B	133	469	65	117	23	2	6	60	19	.249
1996 Birmingham . . . Southern		SS	76	287	40	81	14	3	8	44	5	.282
1996 Nashville . . . . A.A.		SS-3B	43	164	28	47	14	2	7	26	2	.287
1996 Chicago . . . . A.L.		3B	11	23	4	5	0	0	2	3	0	.217
1997 Nashville . . . . A.A.		3B-SS-2B	114	414	82	114	27	1	26	76	3	.275
1997 Chicago . . . . A.L.		3B	18	34	5	9	2	2	0	1	0	.265
1998 Chicago . . . . A.L.		1B-3B-2B	105	299	38	71	17	2	9	36	3	.237
1999 Chicago . . . . A.L.		3B-1B	132	436	62	111	26	0	16	50	4	.255
2000 Chicago . . . . A.L.		3B-1B	71	201	25	49	6	1	6	28	1	.244
2000 Charlotte . . . . Int.		3B-1B-SS	29	97	18	28	4	0	5	17	1	.289
2001 Colorado a . . . . N.L.		OF-3B-1B	117	225	30	60	13	2	13	40	1	.267
2002 Colorado Springs . . . P.C.		1B-3B	3	12	2	1	0	0	0	0	0	.083
2002 Colorado b . . . . N.L.		3B-1B-OF	113	168	19	37	8	1	7	37	2	.220
2003 Colorado . . . . N.L.		3B-1B-OF	114	179	19	47	15	0	6	31	2	.263
2004 Detroit . . . . A.L.		3B-1B-OF	41	86	9	15	1	0	2	2	0	.174
2004 Toledo c-d-e . . . . Int.		3B-1B	53	184	26	38	6	1	4	16	1	.207
2005 Charlotte f . . . . Int.		3B-1B	90	330	57	94	19	1	17	56	0	.285
2006 Durham . . . . Int.		1B	3	9	0	1	0	0	0	1	0	.111
2006 Tampa Bay g . . . . . . A.L.		OF-1B	98	294	47	87	15	0	17	45	1	.296
2007 Montgomery . . . . . Southern		1B	7	25	2	7	2	0	0	4	0	.280
2007 Tampa Bay h-i . . . . . A.L.		DH-OF-1B	75	202	25	49	9	0	4	23	1	.243
Major League Totals	11 Yrs.		895	2147	283	540	112	8	82	296	15	.252

a Not offered contract, December 21, 2000. Signed with Colorado Rockies, January 5, 2001.
b On disabled list from June 30 to July 18, 2002.
c Filed for free agency, October 28, 2003. Signed with Detroit Tigers organization, January 14, 2004.
d On disabled list from June 18 to July 25, 2004.
e Filed for free agency, October 4, 2004. Signed with Colorado Rockies organization, December 21, 2004.
f Released by Colorado Rockies, March 29, 2005. Signed with Chicago White Sox organization, April 24, 2005.
g Filed for free agency, October 15, 2005. Signed with Tampa Bay Devil Rays organization, January 11, 2006.
h On disabled list from March 31 to May 17, 2007.
i Filed for free agency, November 9, 2007.

NUNEZ (ADAMES), ABRAHAM ORLANDO

Born, Santo Domingo, Dominican Republic, March 16, 1976.
Bats Both. Throws Right. Height, 5 feet, 11 inches. Weight, 190 pounds.

Year Club	Lea	Pos	G	AB	R	H	2B	3B	HR	RBI	SB	Avg
1994 Toronto #2 . . . Dominican		2B	59	188	31	47	5	0	0	15	22	.250
1995 Toronto . . . . . Dominican		2B	54	186	49	56	10	3	4	25	24	.301
1996 St.Cathrnes a-bN.Y.-Penn.		SS-2B	75	297	43	83	6	4	3	26	37	.279
1997 Lynchburg . . . . Carolina		SS	78	304	45	79	9	4	3	32	29	.260
1997 Carolina . . . . . Southern		SS	47	198	31	65	6	1	1	14	10	.328

Year	Club	Lea	Pos	G	AB	R	H	2B	3B	HR	RBI	SB	Avg
1997	Pittsburgh	N.L.	SS-2B	19	40	3	9	2	2	0	6	1	.225
1998	Lynchburg	Carolina	SS-2B	5	18	2	4	1	0	0	2	1	.222
1998	Nashville	P.C.	SS	94	366	50	91	12	3	3	32	16	.249
1998	Pittsburgh	N.L.	SS	24	52	6	10	2	0	1	2	4	.192
1999	Pittsburgh	N.L.	SS-2B	90	259	25	57	8	0	0	17	9	.220
1999	Nashville	P.C.	SS	15	58	12	18	0	0	0	3	1	.310
2000	Nashville	P.C.	SS-2B	90	351	49	97	11	1	3	29	20	.276
2000	Pittsburgh	N.L.	SS-2B	40	91	10	20	1	0	1	8	0	.220
2001	Pittsburgh	N.L.	2B-SS-3B-OF	115	301	30	79	11	4	1	21	8	.262
2002	Nashville	P.C.	SS-2B-OF	5	18	3	4	0	0	0	0	4	.222
2002	Pittsburgh	N.L.	2B-SS	112	253	28	59	14	1	2	15	3	.233
2003	Pittsburgh	N.L.	2B-SS-3B	118	311	37	77	8	7	4	35	9	.248
2004	Pittsburgh c	N.L.	2B-SS-3B-P	112	182	17	43	9	0	2	13	1	.236
2005	St. Louis d	N.L.	3B-2B-SS	139	421	64	120	13	2	5	44	0	.285
2006	Philadelphia	N.L.	3B-2B-SS	123	322	42	68	10	2	2	32	1	.211
2007	Philadelphia e	N.L.	3B-SS-2B	136	252	24	59	10	1	0	16	2	.234
Major League Totals			11 Yrs.	1028	2484	286	601	88	19	18	209	38	.242
Division Series													
2005	St. Louis	N.L.	3B	3	11	3	4	1	0	0	0	1	.364
2007	Philadelphia	N.L.	3B	3	2	0	0	0	0	0	0	0	.000
Division Series Totals				6	13	3	4	1	0	0	0	1	.308
Championship Series													
2005	St. Louis	N.L.	3B	4	13	1	5	0	0	0	0	0	.385

a Pittsburgh Pirates traded outfielder Brandon Cromer, pitcher Jose Silva and pitcher Jose Pett to Toronto Blue Jays for outfielder Orlando Merced, infielder Carlos Garcia and pitcher Dan Plesac, November 14, 1996.

b Sent to Pittsburgh Pirates with pitcher Mike Halperin and catcher Craig Wilson to complete trade, December 11, 1996.

c Released by Pittsburgh Pirates, November 29, 2004. Signed with St. Louis Cardinals organization, December 25, 2004.

d Filed for free agency, October 27, 2005. Signed with Philadelphia Phillies, November 29, 2005.

e Filed for free agency, October 29, 2007.

OLIVO (PENA), MIGUEL EDUARDO

Born, Villa Vasquez, Dominican Republic, July 15, 1978.
Bats Right. Throws Right. Height, 6 feet. Weight, 220 pounds.

Year	Club	Lea	Pos	G	AB	R	H	2B	3B	HR	RBI	SB	Avg
1997	Oakland-East	Dominican	C	63	221	37	60	11	4	6	57	6	.271
1998	Athletics	Arizona	C-OF	46	164	30	51	11	3	2	23	2	.311
1999	Modesto	California	C	73	243	46	74	13	6	9	42	4	.305
2000	Modesto	California	C	58	227	40	64	11	5	5	35	5	.282
2000	Midland a-b-c	Texas	C	19	59	8	14	2	0	1	9	0	.237
2001	Birmingham d	Southern	C	93	316	45	82	23	1	14	55	6	.259
2002	Birmingham	Southern	C	106	359	51	110	24	10	6	49	29	.306
2002	Chicago e	A.L.	C	6	19	2	4	1	0	1	5	0	.211
2003	Chicago	A.L.	C	114	317	37	75	19	1	6	27	6	.237
2004	Everett	Northwest	C	2	6	0	0	0	0	0	0	0	.000
2004	Chicago-Seattle f-g	A.L.	C	96	301	46	70	15	4	13	40	7	.233
2005	Tacoma	P.C.	C	24	90	13	21	4	1	3	21	8	.233
2005	Seattle	A.L.	C	54	152	14	23	4	0	5	18	1	.151
2005	San Diego h	N.L.	C	37	115	16	35	7	1	4	16	6	.304
2006	Florida i	N.L.	C-1B	127	430	52	113	22	3	16	58	2	.263
2007	Florida j	N.L.	C	122	452	43	107	20	4	16	60	3	.237
Major League Totals			6 Yrs.	556	1786	210	427	88	13	61	224	25	.239
Division Series													
2005	San Diego	N.L.	PH	1	1	0	0	0	0	0	0	0	.000

a On disabled list from August 8 to September 29, 2000.

b Chicago White Sox traded pitcher Chad Bradford to Oakland Athletics for player to be named later, December 7, 2000.

c Sent by Oakland Athletics to Chicago White Sox to complete trade, December 12, 2000.

d On disabled list from April 22 to May 2, 2001.

e On disabled list from June 4 to July 15, 2002.

f Traded to Seattle Mariners with outfielder Jeremy Reed and infielder Michael Morse for pitcher Freddy Garcia, catcher Ben Davis and cash, June 27, 2004.

g On disabled list from June 30 to July 15, 2004.

h Traded to San Diego Padres for catcher Miguel Ojeda and pitcher Nathaniel Mateo, July 31, 2005.

i Filed for free agency, December 21, 2005. Signed with Florida Marlins, January 3, 2006.

j Not offered contract, December 12, 2007. Signed with Kansas City Royals, December 27, 2007.

ORDONEZ, MAGGLIO
Born, Caracas, Venezuela, January 28, 1974.
Bats Right. Throws Right. Height, 6 feet. Weight, 215 pounds.

Year	Club	Lea	Pos	G	AB	R	H	2B	3B	HR	RBI	SB	Avg
1993	Hickory	So. Atl.	OF	84	273	32	59	14	4	3	20	5	.216
1994	Hickory	So. Atl.	OF	132	490	86	144	24	5	11	69	16	.294
1995	Pr William	Carolina	OF	131	487	61	116	24	2	12	65	11	.238
1996	Birmingham	Southern	OF	130	479	66	126	41	0	18	67	9	.263
1997	Nashville	A.A.	OF	135	523	65	172	29	3	14	90	14	.329
1997	Chicago	A.L.	OF	21	69	12	22	6	0	4	11	1	.319
1998	Chicago	A.L.	OF	145	535	70	151	25	2	14	65	9	.282
1999	Chicago	A.L.	OF	157	624	100	188	34	3	30	117	13	.301
2000	Chicago	A.L.	OF	153	588	102	185	34	3	32	126	18	.315
2001	Chicago	A.L.	OF	160	593	97	181	40	1	31	113	25	.305
2002	Chicago	A.L.	OF	153	590	116	189	47	1	38	135	7	.320
2003	Chicago	A.L.	OF	160	606	95	192	46	3	29	99	9	.317
2004	Chicago a-b	A.L.	OF	52	202	32	59	8	2	9	37	0	.292
2005	Toledo	Int.	OF	4	14	3	3	1	0	1	2	0	.214
2005	Detroit c	A.L.	OF	82	305	38	92	17	0	8	46	0	.302
2006	Detroit	A.L.	OF	155	593	82	177	32	1	24	104	1	.298
2007	Detroit	A.L.	OF	157	595	117	216	*54	0	28	139	4	*.363
Major League Totals		11 Yrs.		1395	5300	861	1652	343	16	247	992	87	.312
Division Series													
2000	Chicago	A.L.	OF	3	11	0	2	0	1	0	1	1	.182
2006	Detroit	A.L.	OF	4	15	3	4	1	0	1	2	0	.267
Division Series Totals				7	26	3	6	1	1	1	3	1	.231
Championship Series													
2006	Detroit	A.L.	OF	4	17	3	4	0	0	2	6	0	.235
World Series Record													
2006	Detroit	A.L.	OF	5	19	2	2	0	0	0	0	0	.105

a On disabled list from May 26 to July 8 and from July 22 to October 12, 2004.
b Filed for free agency, October 28, 2004. Signed with Detroit Tigers organization, February 7, 2005.
c On disabled list from April 13 to July 1, 2005.

ORTIZ (ARIAS), DAVID AMERICO (BIG PAPI)
Born, Santo Domingo, Dominican Republic, November 18, 1975.
Bats Left. Throws Left. Height, 6 feet, 4 inches. Weight, 230 pounds.

Year	Club	Lea	Pos	G	AB	R	H	2B	3B	HR	RBI	SB	Avg
1993	Seattle	Dominican	1B	61	201	37	53	17	1	7	31	1	.264
1994	Mariners	Arizona	1B	53	167	14	41	10	1	2	20	1	.246
1995	Mariners	Arizona	1B	48	184	30	61	18	4	4	37	2	.332
1996	Wisconsin a	Midwest	1B	129	485	89	156	34	2	18	93	3	.322
1997	Salt Lake	P.C.	1B	10	42	5	9	1	0	4	10	0	.214
1997	New Britain	Eastern	DH-1B	69	258	40	83	22	2	14	56	2	.322
1997	Ft. Myers	Fla.St.	1B	61	239	45	79	15	0	13	58	2	.331
1997	Minnesota	A.L.	1B	15	49	10	16	3	0	1	6	0	.327
1998	Salt Lake	P.C.	1B	11	37	5	9	3	0	2	6	0	.243
1998	Minnesota b	A.L.	1B	86	278	47	77	20	0	9	46	1	.277
1999	Salt Lake	P.C.	1B	130	476	85	150	35	3	30	110	2	.315
1999	Minnesota	A.L.	1B	10	20	1	0	0	0	0	0	0	.000
2000	Minnesota	A.L.	DH-1B	130	415	59	117	36	1	10	63	1	.282
2001	Twins	Gulf Coast	DH	4	10	3	4	0	0	0	1	1	.400
2001	Fort Myers	Fla.St.	1B	1	3	0	0	0	0	0	0	0	.000
2001	New Britain	Eastern	1B	9	37	3	9	4	0	0	1	0	.243
2001	Minnesota c	A.L.	DH-1B	89	303	46	71	17	1	18	48	1	.234
2002	Minnesota d-e	A.L.	DH-1B	125	412	52	112	32	1	20	75	1	.272
2003	Boston	A.L.	DH-1B	128	448	79	129	39	2	31	101	0	.288
2004	Boston	A.L.	DH-1B	150	582	94	175	47	3	41	139	0	.301
2005	Boston	A.L.	DH-1B	159	601	119	180	40	1	47	*148	1	.300
2006	Boston	A.L.	DH-1B	151	558	115	160	29	2	*54	*137	1	.287
2007	Boston	A.L.	DH-1B	149	549	116	182	52	1	35	117	3	.332
Major League Totals		11 Yrs.		1192	4215	738	1219	315	12	266	880	9	.289
Division Series													
2002	Minnesota	A.L.	DH	4	13	0	3	2	0	0	2	0	.231
2003	Boston	A.L.	DH	5	21	0	2	1	0	0	2	0	.095
2004	Boston	A.L.	DH	3	11	4	6	2	0	1	4	0	.545
2005	Boston	A.L.	DH	3	12	2	4	2	0	1	1	0	.333
2007	Boston	A.L.	DH	3	7	5	5	0	0	2	3	0	.714
Division Series Totals				18	64	11	20	7	0	4	12	0	.313

Year	Club	Lea	Pos	G	AB	R	H	2B	3B	HR	RBI	SB	Avg
	Championship Series												
2002 Minnesota	A.L.		DH	5	16	0	5	1	0	0	2	0	.313
2003 Boston	A.L.		DH	7	26	4	7	1	0	2	6	0	.269
2004 Boston	A.L.		DH	7	31	6	12	0	1	3	11	0	.387
2007 Boston	A.L.		DH	7	24	7	7	3	0	1	3	0	.292
Championship Series Totals				26	97	17	31	5	1	6	22	0	.320
	World Series Record												
2004 Boston	A.L.		1B-DH	4	13	3	4	1	0	1	4	0	.308
2007 Boston	A.L.		1B-DH	4	15	4	5	3	0	0	4	0	.333
World Series Totals.............				8	28	7	9	4	0	1	8	0	.321

a Sent to Minnesota Twins by Seattle Mariners to complete trade for infielder Dave Hollins, September 13, 1996.
b On disabled list from May 10 to July 9, 1998.
c On disabled list from May 5 to July 21, 2001.
d On disabled list from April 20 to May 13, 2002.
e Released by Minnesota Twins, December 16, 2002. Signed with Boston Red Sox, January 22, 2003.

ORTMEIER, DANIEL DAVID (DAN)
Born, Chattanooga, Tennessee, May 11, 1981.
Bats Both. Throws Left. Height, 6 feet, 4 inches. Weight, 220 pounds.

Year	Club	Lea	Pos	G	AB	R	H	2B	3B	HR	RBI	SB	Avg
2002 Salem-Keizer	Northwest		OF	49	195	32	57	9	1	5	31	3	.292
2003 San Jose	Calif.		OF	115	408	62	124	32	6	8	56	13	.304
2004 Norwich	Eastern		OF	106	377	55	95	23	6	10	48	18	.252
2005 Norwich	Eastern		OF	135	503	85	138	23	6	20	79	35	.274
2005 San Francisco	N.L.		OF	15	22	1	3	0	0	0	1	1	.136
2006 San Francisco	N.L.		OF	9	12	0	3	1	0	0	2	0	.250
2006 Connecticut	Eastern		OF	47	167	17	42	9	1	2	11	7	.251
2006 Fresno	P.C.		OF	68	262	37	64	14	3	6	33	8	.244
2007 Fresno	P.C.		OF-1B	79	305	39	80	19	1	10	54	16	.262
2007 San Francisco	N.L.		OF-1B	62	157	20	45	7	4	6	16	2	.287
Major League Totals	3 Yrs.			86	191	21	51	8	4	6	19	3	.267

OVERBAY, LYLE STEFAN
Born, Centralia, Washington, January 28, 1977.
Bats Left. Throws Left. Height, 6 feet, 2 inches. Weight, 235 pounds.

Year	Club	Lea	Pos	G	AB	R	H	2B	3B	HR	RBI	SB	Avg
1999 Missoula	Pioneer		1B	75	306	66	105	25	7	12	101	10	.343
2000 South Bend	Midwest		1B	71	259	47	86	19	3	6	47	9	.332
2000 El Paso	Texas		1B	62	244	43	86	16	2	8	49	3	.352
2001 El Paso	Texas		1B-OF	138	532	82	187	49	3	13	100	5	.352
2001 Arizona..............	N.L.		PH	2	2	0	1	0	0	0	0	0	.500
2002 Tucson	P.C.		1B	134	525	83	180	40	0	19	109	4	.343
2002 Arizona..............	N.L.		PH	10	10	0	1	0	0	0	1	0	.100
2003 Tucson	P.C.		1B	35	119	24	34	11	0	4	16	0	.286
2003 Arizona	N.L.		1B	86	254	23	70	20	0	4	28	1	.276
2004 Milwaukee	N.L.		1B	159	579	83	174	*53	1	16	87	2	.301
2005 Milwaukee b..........	N.L.		1B	158	537	80	148	34	1	19	72	1	.276
2006 Toronto	A.L.		1B	157	581	82	181	46	1	22	92	5	.312
2007 New Hampshire	Eastern		1B	4	15	2	4	1	0	1	5	0	.267
2007 Toronto c	A.L.		1B	122	425	49	102	30	2	10	44	2	.240
Major League Totals	7 Yrs.			694	2388	317	677	183	5	71	324	11	.284

a Traded to Milwaukee Brewers with infielder Junior Spivey, infielder Craig Counsell, catcher Chad Moeller, pitcher Chris Capuano and pitcher Jorge DeRosa for infielder Richie Sexson, pitcher Shane Nance and player to be named later, December 1, 2003. Arizona Diamondbacks received outfielder Gary Varner to complete trade, December 15, 2003.
b Traded to Toronto Blue Jays with pitcher Ty Taubenheim for pitcher Dave Bush, outfielder Gabe Gross and pitcher Zach Jackson, December 7, 2005.
c On disabled list from June 4 to July 12, 2007.

OWENS, JERRY LEE
Born, Hollywood, California, February 16, 1981.
Bats Left. Throws Left. Height, 6 feet, 3 inches. Weight, 195 pounds.

Year	Club	Lea	Pos	G	AB	R	H	2B	3B	HR	RBI	SB	Avg
2003 Vermont........	N.Y.-Penn.		OF	2	8	0	1	0	0	0	0	1	.125
2004 Savannah..........	So.Atl.		OF	108	418	69	122	17	2	1	37	30	.292
2005 Birmingham a	Southern		OF	130	522	99	173	21	6	2	52	38	.331

133

Year Club	Lea	Pos	G	AB	R	H	2B	3B	HR	RBI	SB	Avg
2006 Charlotte	Int.	OF	112	439	75	115	15	5	4	48	40	.262
2006 Chicago b............	A.L.	OF	12	9	4	3	1	0	0	0	1	.333
2007 Charlotte	Int.	OF	59	232	39	66	10	0	3	21	23	.284
2007 Chicago	A.L.	OF	93	356	44	95	9	2	1	17	32	.267
Major League Totals	2 Yrs.	105	365	48	98	10	2	1	17	33	.268	

a Traded to Chicago White Sox by Washington Nationals for outfielder Alex Escobar, February 13, 2005.
b On disabled list from August 26 to September 10, 2006.

PAGAN, ANGEL ANTHONY
Born, Rio Piedras, Puerto Rico, July 2, 1981.
Bats Both. Throws Right. Height, 6 feet, 1 inch. Weight, 180 pounds.

Year Club	Lea	Pos	G	AB	R	H	2B	3B	HR	RBI	SB	Avg
2000 Kingsport	Appal.	OF	19	72	13	26	5	1	0	8	6	.361
2001 Brooklyn........	N.Y.-Penn.	OF	62	238	46	75	10	2	0	15	30	.315
2001 Columbia	So.Atl.	OF	15	57	4	17	1	1	0	5	3	.298
2002 St. Lucie	Fla.St.	OF	16	67	12	23	2	1	1	7	10	.343
2002 Columbia	So.Atl.	OF	108	458	79	128	14	5	1	36	52	.279
2003 St. Lucie...........	Fla.St.	OF	113	441	64	110	15	5	1	33	35	.249
2004 Binghamton	Eastern	OF	112	448	71	129	25	8	4	63	29	.288
2004 Norfolk.............	Int.	OF	12	45	13	13	3	3	0	1	4	.289
2005 Norfolk.............	Int.	OF	129	516	69	140	20	10	8	40	27	.271
2006 Cubs.............	Arizona	OF	3	9	1	1	0	0	0	0	1	.111
2006 Iowa................	P.C.	OF	4	15	2	4	1	0	0	0	1	.267
2006 Chicago a-b	N.L.	OF	77	170	28	42	6	2	5	18	4	.247
2007 Iowa................	P.C.	OF	33	116	18	29	4	3	3	9	6	.250
2007 Chicago c-d	N.L.	OF	71	148	21	39	10	2	4	21	4	.264
Major League Totals	2 Yrs.	148	318	49	81	16	4	9	39	8	.255	

a Sold to Chicago by New York Mets, January 25, 2006.
b On disabled list from April 16 to June 30, 2006.
c On disabled list from August 8 to November 1, 2007.
d Traded to New York Mets for pitcher Ryan Meyers and outfielder Corey Coles, January 5, 2008.

PALMEIRO, ORLANDO
Born, Hoboken, New Jersey, January 19, 1969.
Bats Left. Throws Left. Height, 5 feet, 11 inches. Weight, 185 pounds.

Year Club	Lea	Pos	G	AB	R	H	2B	3B	HR	RBI	SB	Avg
1995 Vancouver	P.C.	OF	107	398	66	122	21	4	0	47	16	.307
1995 California	A.L.	OF	15	20	3	7	0	0	0	1	0	.350
1996 Vancouver	P.C.	OF	62	245	40	75	13	4	0	33	7	.306
1996 California	A.L.	OF	50	87	6	25	6	1	0	6	0	.287
1997 Anaheim a	A.L.	OF	74	134	19	29	2	2	0	8	2	.216
1998 Vancouver	P.C.	OF	43	140	21	42	13	3	1	29	3	.300
1998 Anaheim..........	A.L.	OF	75	165	28	53	7	2	0	21	5	.321
1999 Anaheim..........	A.L.	OF	109	317	46	88	12	1	1	23	5	.278
2000 Anaheim..........	A.L.	OF	108	243	38	73	20	2	0	25	4	.300
2001 Anaheim..........	A.L.	OF	104	230	29	56	10	1	2	23	6	.243
2002 Anaheim b	A.L.	OF	110	263	35	79	12	1	0	31	7	.300
2003 St. Louis c	N.L.	OF	141	317	37	86	13	1	3	33	3	.271
2004 Houston d	N.L.	OF	102	133	19	32	5	0	3	12	2	.241
2005 Houston e	N.L.	OF	114	204	22	58	17	2	3	20	3	.284
2006 Houston	N.L.	OF	103	119	12	30	6	1	0	17	0	.252
2007 Houston f...........	N.L.	OF	101	103	12	24	3	0	0	6	0	.233
Major League Totals	13 Yrs.	1206	2335	306	640	113	14	12	226	37	.274	
Division Series												
2004 Houston	N.L.	OF	5	4	0	1	0	0	0	0	0	.250
2005 Houston	N.L.	OF	4	7	0	1	0	0	0	3	0	.143
Division Series Totals			9	11	0	2	0	0	0	3	0	.182
Championship Series												
2002 Anaheim.............	A.L.	OF	2	2	0	0	0	0	0	0	0	.000
2004 Houston	N.L.	OF	7	6	0	2	1	0	0	0	0	.333
2005 Houston	N.L.	PH	4	3	0	1	0	0	0	0	0	.333
Championship Series Totals			13	11	0	3	1	0	0	0	0	.273
World Series Record												
2002 Anaheim.............	A.L.	PH	4	4	1	1	1	0	0	0	0	.250
2005 Houston	N.L.	OF	2	2	0	0	0	0	0	0	0	.000
World Series Totals			6	6	1	1	1	0	0	0	0	.167

b Filed for free agency, October 30, 2002. Signed with St. Louis Cardinals, February 1, 2003.
c Filed for free agency, October 26, 2003. Signed with Houston Astros, January 15, 2004.
d. Filed for free agency, November 5, 2004, re-signed with Houston Astros, December 7, 2004.
e Filed for free agency, November 9, 2005, re-signed with Houston Astros, December 8, 2005.
f Filed for free agency, October 29, 2007.

PATTERSON, DONALD COREY (COREY)

Born, Atlanta, Georgia, August 13, 1979.
Bats Left. Throws Right. Height, 5 feet, 9 inches. Weight, 175 pounds.

Year	Club	Lea	Pos	G	AB	R	H	2B	3B	HR	RBI	SB	Avg
1999 Lansing	Midwest	OF	112	475	94	152	35	17	20	79	33	.320
2000 West Tenn	Southern	OF	118	444	73	116	26	5	22	82	27	.261
2000 Chicago	N.L.	OF	11	42	9	7	1	0	2	2	1	.167
2001 Iowa	P.C.	OF	89	367	63	93	22	3	7	32	19	.253
2001 Chicago	N.L.	OF	59	131	26	29	3	0	4	14	4	.221
2002 Chicago	N.L.	OF	153	592	71	150	30	5	14	54	18	.253
2003 Chicago a	N.L.	OF	83	329	49	98	17	7	13	55	16	.298
2004 Chicago	N.L.	OF	157	631	91	168	33	6	24	72	32	.266
2005 Iowa	P.C.	OF	24	91	16	27	4	0	5	12	6	.297
2005 Chicago b	N.L.	OF	126	451	47	97	15	3	13	34	15	.215
2006 Baltimore	A.L.	OF	135	463	75	128	19	5	16	53	45	.276
2007 Baltimore c	A.L.	OF	132	461	65	124	26	2	8	45	37	.269
Major League Totals		8 Yrs.	856	3100	433	801	144	28	94	329	168	.258

a On disabled list from July 7 to October 31, 2003.
b Traded to Baltimore Orioles for infielder Nate Spears and pitcher Carlos Perez, January 9, 2006.
c Filed for free agency, October 31, 2007.

PAULINO, RONNY LEONEL

Born, Santo Domingo, Dominican Republic, April 21, 1981.
Bats Right. Throws Right. Height, 6 feet, 2 inches. Weight, 240 pounds.

Year	Club	Lea	Pos	G	AB	R	H	2B	3B	HR	RBI	SB	Avg
1998 Pittsburgh	Dominican	C	53	170	18	40	5	0	4	26	6	.235
1999 Pirates	Gulf Coast	C	29	83	6	21	2	4	1	13	1	.253
2000 Hickory	So.Atl.	C-1B-3B	88	301	38	87	16	2	6	39	3	.289
2001 Lynchburg	Carolina	C	103	352	30	102	16	1	6	51	4	.290
2002 Lynchburg	Carolina	C-1B	119	442	63	116	26	2	12	55	2	.262
2003 Lynchburg	Carolina	C	23	81	8	19	3	0	1	12	1	.235
2003 Altoona a	Eastern	C	46	159	19	36	6	1	6	19	0	.226
2004 Altoona	Eastern	C-1B	99	369	54	105	23	2	15	60	3	.285
2005 Altoona	Eastern	C	43	168	24	49	6	0	6	20	3	.292
2005 Indianapolis	Int.	C	77	273	49	86	18	2	13	42	3	.315
2005 Pittsburgh	N.L.	C	2	4	1	2	0	0	0	0	0	.500
2006 Indianapolis	Int.	C	8	29	2	7	3	0	0	4	1	.241
2006 Pittsburgh	N.L.	C	129	442	37	137	19	0	6	55	0	.310
2007 Pittsburgh	N.L.	C	133	457	56	120	25	0	11	55	2	.263
Major League Totals		3 Yrs.	264	903	94	259	44	0	17	110	2	.287

a Selected by Kansas City Royals from Pittsburgh Pirates in Rule V draft, December 16, 2002. Returned to
   Pittsburgh Pirates, March 13, 2003.

PAYTON, JASON LEE (JAY)

Born, Zanesville, Ohio, November 22, 1972.
Bats Right. Throws Right. Height, 5 feet, 10 inches. Weight, 205 pounds.

Year	Club	Lea	Pos	G	AB	R	H	2B	3B	HR	RBI	SB	Avg
1994 Pittsfield	N.Y.-Penn.	OF	58	219	47	80	16	2	3	37	10	.365
1994 Binghamton	Eastern	OF	8	25	3	7	1	0	0	1	1	.280
1995 Binghamton	Eastern	OF	85	357	59	123	20	3	14	54	16	.345
1995 Norfolk	Int.	OF	50	196	33	47	11	4	4	30	11	.240
1996 Mets	Gulf Coast	DH	3	13	3	5	1	0	1	2	1	.385
1996 Binghamton	Eastern	DH	4	10	0	2	0	0	0	2	0	.200
1996 St. Lucie	Fla.St.	DH	9	26	4	8	2	0	0	1	2	.308
1996 Norfolk a-b	Int.	DH-OF	55	153	30	47	6	3	6	26	10	.307
1997		INJURED—Did Not Play										
1998 St. Lucie	Fla.St.	OF	3	7	0	1	0	0	0	0	0	.143
1998 Norfolk	Int.	OF-1B	82	322	45	84	14	4	8	30	12	.261
1998 New York c	N.L.	OF	15	22	2	7	1	0	0	0	0	.318
1999 Norfolk	Int.	OF	38	144	27	56	13	2	8	35	2	.389

135

Year	Club	Lea	Pos	G	AB	R	H	2B	3B	HR	RBI	SB	Avg
1999 St. Lucie...........Fla.St.			OF	7	26	3	9	1	1	0	3	0	.346
1999 New York d-e.........N.L.			OF	13	8	1	2	1	0	0	1	1	.250
2000 New York............N.L.			OF	149	488	63	142	23	1	17	62	5	.291
2001 St. Lucie...........Fla.St.			OF	4	16	7	6	3	0	0	0	0	.375
2001 New York f..........N.L.			OF	104	361	44	92	16	1	8	34	4	.255
2002 New York-Colorado g...N.L.			OF	134	445	69	135	20	7	16	59	7	.303
2003 Colorado h..........N.L.			OF	157	600	93	181	32	5	28	89	6	.302
2004 San Diego i..........N.L.			OF	143	458	57	119	17	4	8	55	2	.260
2005 Boston-Oakland j.....A.L.			OF	124	408	62	109	16	1	18	63	0	.267
2006 Oakland k...........A.L.			OF	142	557	78	165	32	3	10	59	8	.296
2007 Norfolk.............Int.			OF	2	8	3	2	1	0	0	0	0	.250
2007 Baltimore l..........A.L.			OF	131	434	48	111	21	5	7	58	5	.256
Major League Totals ....10 Yrs.				1112	3781	517	1063	179	27	112	480	38	.281
Division Series													
2000 New York.............N.L.			OF	4	17	1	3	0	0	0	2	1	.176
2006 Oakland .............A.L.			OF	3	12	3	4	0	0	0	0	0	.333
Division Series Totals				7	29	4	7	0	0	0	2	1	.241
Championship Series													
2000 New York.............N.L.			OF	5	19	1	3	0	0	1	3	0	.158
2006 Oakland .............A.L.			OF	4	14	1	4	2	0	1	2	0	.286
Championship Series Totals				9	33	2	7	2	0	2	5	0	.212
World Series Record													
2000 New York.............N.L.			OF	5	21	3	7	0	0	1	3	0	.333

a On disabled list from April 29 to July 3, 1996.
b On disabled list from April 3 to September 1, 1997.
c On disabled list from May 27 to June 15 and June 24 to July 20, 1998.
d On disabled list from March 21 to June 8, 1999.
e On disabled list from July 10 to August 19, 1999.
f On disabled list from May 8 to June 26, 2001.
g Traded to Colorado Rockies with outfielder Robert Stratton and pitcher Mark Corey for pitcher John Thomson and outfielder Mark Little, July 31, 2002.
h Not offered contract, December 21, 2003. Signed with San Diego Padres, January 13, 2004.
i Traded to Boston Red Sox with infielder Ramon Vazquez, pitcher David Pauley and cash for outfielder Dave Roberts, December 20, 2004.
j Traded to Oakland Athletics for pitcher Chad Bradford, July 13, 2005.
k Filed for free agency, October 29, 2006. Signed with Baltimore Orioles, December 11, 2006.
l On disabled list from March 27 to April 20, 2007.

PEDROIA, DUSTIN LUIS
Born, Woodland, California, August 17, 1983.
Bats Right. Throws Right. Height, 5 feet, 9 inches. Weight, 180 pounds.

Year	Club	Lea	Pos	G	AB	R	H	2B	3B	HR	RBI	SB	Avg
2004 Sarasota........Fla.St.			SS	30	107	23	36	8	3	2	14	0	.336
2004 Augusta........So.Atl.			SS	12	50	11	20	5	0	1	5	2	.400
2005 Portland......Eastern			2B-SS	66	256	39	83	19	2	8	40	7	.324
2005 Pawtucket ....Int.			2B-SS	51	204	39	52	9	1	5	24	1	.255
2006 Pawtucket ....Int.			SS-2B-3B	111	423	55	129	30	3	5	50	1	.305
2006 Boston...........A.L.			2B-SS	31	89	5	17	4	0	2	7	0	.191
2007 Boston a..........A.L.			2B	139	520	86	165	39	1	8	50	7	.317
Major League Totals ....2 Yrs.				170	609	91	182	43	1	10	57	7	.299
Division Series													
2007 Boston...........A.L.			2B	3	13	2	2	2	0	0	1	0	.154
Championship Series													
2007 Boston...........A.L.			2B	7	29	8	10	3	0	1	5	0	.345
World Series Record													
2007 Boston...........A.L.			2B	4	18	2	5	1	0	1	4	0	.278

a Selected Rookie of the Year in American League for 2007.

PENA, CARLOS FELIPE
Born, Santo Domingo, Dominican Republic, May 17, 1978.
Bats Left. Throws Left. Height, 6 feet, 2 inches. Weight, 210 pounds.

Year	Club	Lea	Pos	G	AB	R	H	2B	3B	HR	RBI	SB	Avg
1998 Rangers ....Gulf Coast			1B	2	5	1	2	0	0	0	0	1	.400
1998 Savannah ....So.Atl.			1B-OF	30	117	22	38	14	0	6	20	3	.325
1998 Charlotte ....Fla.St.			1B	7	22	1	6	1	0	0	3	0	.273
1999 Charlotte ....Fla.St.			1B	136	501	85	128	31	8	18	103	2	.255
2000 Tulsa ....Texas			1B	138	529	117	158	36	2	28	105	12	.299

Year	Club	Lea	Pos	G	AB	R	H	2B	3B	HR	RBI	SB	Avg
2001 Oklahoma	P.C.	1B	119	431	71	124	38	3	23	74	11	.288
2001 Texas	A.L.	1B	22	62	6	16	4	1	3	12	0	.258
2002 Sacramento	P.C.	1B	44	175	30	42	10	1	10	33	3	.240
2002 Oakland-Detroit a-b	A.L.	1B	115	397	43	96	17	4	19	52	2	.242
2003 Toledo	Int.	1B	8	30	4	10	4	1	0	5	0	.333
2003 Detroit c	A.L.	1B	131	452	51	112	21	6	18	50	4	.248
2004 Detroit	A.L.	1B	142	481	89	116	22	4	27	82	7	.241
2005 Toledo	Int.	1B	71	257	43	80	17	1	12	45	3	.311
2005 Detroit	A.L.	1B	79	260	37	61	9	0	18	44	0	.235
2006 Columbus	Int.	1B	105	381	65	99	17	0	19	66	4	.260
2006 Pawtucket	Int.	1B	11	37	7	17	3	0	4	8	0	.459
2006 Boston d-e-f	A.L.	1B-OF	18	33	3	9	2	0	1	3	0	.273
2007 Tampa Bay	A.L.	1B	148	490	99	138	29	1	46	121	1	.282
Major League Totals		7 Yrs.	655	2175	328	548	104	16	132	364	14	.252

a Traded to Oakland Athletics with pitcher Mike Venafro for pitcher Mario Ramos, outfielder Ryan Ludwick, infielder Jason Hart and catcher Gerald Laird, January 14, 2002.

b Traded to Detroit Tigers with pitcher Franklyn German and player to be named later for pitcher Jeff Weaver, July 5, 2002. Detroit Tigers received pitcher Jeremy Bonderman to complete trade, August 22, 2002.

c On disabled list from June 2 to June 27, 2003.

d Released by Detroit Tigers, March 26, 2006. Signed with New York Yankees organization, April 15, 2006.

e Filed for free agency, August 16, 2006. Signed with Boston Red Sox organization, August 17, 2006.

f Filed for free agency, October 13, 2006. Signed with Tampa Bay Devil Rays organization, February 1, 2007.

PENA, TONY FRANCISCO

Born, Santiago, Dominican Republic, March 23, 1981.
Bats Right. Throws Right. Height, 6 feet, 1 inch. Weight, 180 pounds.

Year	Club	Lea	Pos	G	AB	R	H	2B	3B	HR	RBI	SB	Avg
2000 Danville	Appal.	SS-2B	55	215	22	46	5	0	2	20	6	.214
2001 Jamestown	N.Y.-Penn.	SS	72	264	26	65	12	2	0	18	8	.246
2002 Macon	So.Atl.	SS	118	405	42	101	9	5	2	36	11	.249
2003 Myrtle Beach	Carolina	SS	120	405	43	105	14	1	4	30	17	.259
2004 Greenville	Southern	SS	130	495	65	126	22	0	11	34	25	.255
2005 Richmond	Int.	SS	138	490	49	122	25	4	5	40	17	.249
2006 Richmond	Int.	SS	81	298	38	84	12	4	1	23	12	.282
2006 Atlanta	N.L.	SS-3B	40	44	12	10	2	0	1	3	0	.227
2007 Kansas City a	A.L.	SS-2B	152	509	58	136	25	7	2	47	5	.267
Major League Totals		2 Yrs.	192	553	70	146	27	7	3	50	5	.264

a Traded to Kansas City Royals for pitcher Erik Cordier, March 23, 2007.

PENA, WILY MODESTO (WILY MO)

Born, Laguna Salada, Dominican Republic, January 23, 1982.
Bats Right. Throws Right. Height, 6 feet, 3 inches. Weight, 215 pounds.

Year	Club	Lea	Pos	G	AB	R	H	2B	3B	HR	RBI	SB	Avg
1999 Yankees	Gulf Coast	OF	45	166	21	41	10	1	7	26	3	.247
2000 Greensboro	So.Atl.	OF	67	249	41	51	7	1	10	28	6	.205
2000 Staten Island	N.Y.-Penn.	OF	20	73	7	22	1	2	0	10	2	.301
2001 Dayton a	Midwest	OF	135	511	87	135	25	5	26	113	26	.264
2002 Chattanooga	Southern	OF	105	388	47	99	23	1	11	47	8	.255
2002 Cincinnati	N.L.	OF	13	18	1	4	0	0	1	1	0	.222
2003 Louisville	Int.	OF	14	51	16	19	3	0	4	14	0	.373
2003 Cincinnati b	N.L.	OF-3B	80	165	20	36	6	1	5	16	3	.218
2004 Cincinnati	N.L.	OF	110	336	45	87	10	1	26	66	5	.259
2005 Louisville	Int.	OF	7	24	1	7	1	0	1	4	0	.292
2005 Cincinnati c	N.L.	OF	99	311	42	79	17	0	19	51	2	.254
2006 Lowell	N.Y.-Penn.	OF	2	6	1	1	0	0	0	0	0	.167
2006 Pawtucket	Int.	OF-1B	12	41	8	10	1	0	2	7	0	.244
2006 Boston d-e	A.L.	OF	84	276	36	83	15	2	11	42	0	.301
2007 Boston	A.L.	OF	73	156	18	34	9	1	5	17	0	.218
2007 Washington f	N.L.	OF	37	133	24	39	4	0	8	22	2	.293
Major League Totals		6 Yrs.	496	1395	186	362	61	5	75	215	12	.259

a Traded by New York Yankees to Cincinnati Reds with cash for infielder Drew Henson and outfielder Michael Coleman, March 21, 2001.

b On disabled list from July 5 to July 30, 2003.

c On disabled list from May 3 to June 7, 2005.

d Traded to Boston Red Sox for pitcher Bronson Arroyo, March 20, 2006.

e On disabled list from May 27 to July 18, 2006.

f Traded to Washington Nationals for player to be named later and cash, August 17, 2007. Boston Red Sox received infielder Chris Carter to complete trade, August 21, 2007.

PENCE, HUNTER ANDREW
Born, Arlington, Texas, April 13, 1983.
Bats Right. Throws Right. Height, 6 feet, 4 inches. Weight, 210 pounds.

Year	Club	Lea	Pos	G	AB	R	H	2B	3B	HR	RBI	SB	Avg
2004 Tri-City	N.Y.-Penn.	OF	51	199	36	59	18	1	8	37	3	.296
2005 Lexington	So.Atl.	OF	80	302	59	102	14	3	25	60	8	.338
2005 Salem	Carolina	OF	41	151	24	46	8	1	6	30	1	.305
2006 Corpus Christi	Texas	OF	136	523	97	148	31	8	28	95	17	.283
2007 Round Rock	P.C.	OF	25	95	17	31	11	1	3	21	2	.326
2007 Houston a	N.L.	OF	108	456	57	147	30	9	17	69	11	.322

a On disabled list from July 23 to August 21, 2007.

PERALTA, JHONNY ANTONIO
Born, Santiago, Dominican Republic, May 28, 1982.
Bats Right. Throws Right. Height, 6 feet, 1 inch. Weight, 195 pounds.

Year	Club	Lea	Pos	G	AB	R	H	2B	3B	HR	RBI	SB	Avg
2001 Kinston	Carolina	SS	125	441	57	106	24	2	7	47	4	.240
2002 Akron	Eastern	SS	130	470	62	132	28	5	15	62	4	.281
2003 Buffalo	Int.	SS-3B	63	237	25	61	12	1	1	21	1	.257
2003 Cleveland	A.L.	SS-3B	77	242	24	55	10	1	4	21	1	.227
2004 Buffalo	Int.	SS-3B	138	556	109	181	44	2	15	86	8	.326
2004 Cleveland	A.L.	SS-3B	8	25	2	6	1	0	0	2	0	.240
2005 Cleveland	A.L.	SS	141	504	82	147	35	4	24	78	0	.292
2006 Cleveland	A.L.	SS	149	569	84	146	28	3	13	68	0	.257
2007 Cleveland	A.L.	SS	152	574	87	155	27	1	21	72	4	.270
Major League Totals		5 Yrs.	527	1914	279	509	101	9	62	241	5	.266
Division Series													
2007 Cleveland	A.L.	SS	4	15	2	7	3	0	0	2	1	.467
Championship Series													
2007 Cleveland	A.L.	SS	7	27	4	7	2	0	2	8	0	.259

PHELPS, JOSHUA LEE (JOSH)
Born, Anchorage, Alaska, May 12, 1978.
Bats Right. Throws Right. Height, 6 feet, 3 inches. Weight, 215 pounds.

Year	Club	Lea	Pos	G	AB	R	H	2B	3B	HR	RBI	SB	Avg
1996 Medcine Hat	Pioneer	C-OF	59	191	28	46	3	0	5	29	5	.241
1997 Hagerstown	So.Atl.	C	68	233	26	49	9	1	7	24	3	.210
1998 Hagerstown	So.Atl.	C-3B-OF	117	385	48	102	24	1	8	44	2	.265
1999 Dunedin	Fla.St.	C	110	406	72	133	27	4	20	88	6	.328
2000 Tennessee	Southern	C	56	184	23	42	9	1	9	28	1	.228
2000 Toronto	A.L.	C	1	1	0	0	0	0	0	0	0	.000
2000 Dunedin	Fla.St.	C	30	113	26	36	7	0	12	34	0	.319
2001 Tennessee	Southern	C	136	486	95	142	36	1	31	97	3	.292
2001 Toronto	A.L.	C	8	12	3	0	0	0	0	1	1	.000
2002 Syracuse	Int.	C-1B	70	257	50	75	20	1	24	64	0	.292
2002 Toronto	A.L.	DH-1B	74	265	41	82	20	1	15	58	0	.309
2003 Syracuse	Int.	DH	4	11	2	5	0	0	2	4	0	.455
2003 Toronto a	A.L.	DH-1B	119	396	57	106	18	1	20	66	1	.268
2004 Toronto-Cleveland b-c	A.L.	DH-1B	103	371	51	93	19	2	17	61	0	.251
2005 Tampa Bay	A.L.	DH-1B	47	158	21	42	10	0	5	26	0	.266
2005 Durham	Int.	1B	59	222	35	60	14	3	14	33	0	.270
2006 Toledo d-e-f	Int.	1B	126	464	60	143	26	3	24	90	6	.308
2007 New York	A.L.	1B-C	36	80	8	21	2	0	2	12	0	.262
2007 Pittsburgh g-h	N.L.	1B-C	58	77	13	27	4	2	5	19	0	.351
Major League Totals		7 Yrs.	446	1360	194	371	73	6	64	243	2	.273

a On disabled list from July 7 to July 25, 2003.

b Traded to Cleveland Indians for infielder Eric Crozier, August 3, 2004.

c Not offered contract December 21, 2004. Signed with Tampa Bay Devil Rays, December 22, 2004.

d Filed for free agency, October 3, 2005. Signed with Detroit Tigers organization, January 10, 2006.

e Filed for free agency, Ocrtober 15, 2006. Signed with Baltimore Orioles organization, November 15, 2006.

f Selected by New York Yankees in Rule V major league draft, December 7, 2006.

g Claimed on waivers by Pittsburgh Pirates, June 22, 2007.

h Released by Pittsburgh Pirates, November 20, 2007. Signed with St. Louis Cardinals organization, January 10, 2008.

PHILLIPS, BRANDON EMIL
Born, Raleigh, North Carolina, June 28, 1981.
Bats Right. Throws Right. Height, 6 feet. Weight, 195 pounds.

Year	Club	Lea	Pos	G	AB	R	H	2B	3B	HR	RBI	SB	Avg
1999 Expos	Gulf Coast	SS	47	169	23	49	11	3	1	21	12	.290

Year	Club	Lea	Pos	G	AB	R	H	2B	3B	HR	RBI	SB	Avg
2000 Cape Fear	So.Atl.	SS-2B	126	484	74	117	17	8	11	72	23	.242
2001 Harrisburg	Eastern	SS-2B-3B	67	265	35	79	19	0	7	36	13	.298
2001 Jupiter	Fla.St.	SS	55	194	36	55	12	2	4	23	17	.284
2002 Harrisburg	Eastern	SS	60	245	40	80	13	2	9	35	6	.327
2002 Ottawa	Int.	SS	10	35	1	9	4	0	1	5	0	.257
2002 Buffalo	Int.	SS-2B	55	223	30	63	14	0	8	27	8	.283
2002 Cleveland a-b	A.L.	2B	11	31	5	8	3	1	0	4	0	.258
2003 Cleveland	A.L.	2B	112	370	36	77	18	1	6	33	4	.208
2003 Buffalo	Int.	2B	43	154	14	27	7	0	3	13	7	.175
2004 Buffalo	Int.	2B-SS	135	521	83	158	34	4	8	50	14	.303
2004 Cleveland	A.L.	2B	6	22	1	4	2	0	0	1	0	.182
2005 Cleveland	A.L.	2B-SS	6	9	1	0	0	0	0	0	0	.000
2005 Buffalo	Int.	SS	112	465	79	119	24	1	15	46	7	.256
2006 Cincinnati c-d	N.L.	2B-SS	149	536	65	148	28	1	17	75	25	.276
2007 Cincinnati	N.L.	2B-SS	158	650	107	187	26	6	30	94	32	.288
Major League Totals		6 Yrs.	442	1618	215	424	77	9	53	207	61	.262

a Traded to Cleveland Indians with infielder Lee Stevens, outfielder Grady Sizemore and pitcher Cliff Lee for pitcher
   Bartolo Colon and player to be named later, June 27, 2002.
b Montreal Expos received pitcher Tim Drew to complete trade, June 28, 2002.
c Traded to Cincinnati Reds for player to be named later, April 7, 2006.
d Cleveland Indians received pitcher Jeff Stevens to complete trade, June 13, 2006.

PHILLIPS, GEORGE ANDREW (ANDY)

Born, Tuscaloosa, Alabama, April 6, 1977.
Bats Right. Throws Right. Height, 6 feet. Weight, 210 pounds.

Year	Club	Lea	Pos	G	AB	R	H	2B	3B	HR	RBI	SB	Avg
1999 Staten Island	N.Y.-Penn.	3B	64	233	35	75	11	7	7	48	3	.322
2000 Norwich	Eastern	3B	7	28	5	7	2	1	0	3	1	.250
2000 Tampa	Fla.St.	3B	127	478	66	137	33	2	13	58	2	.287
2001 Norwich	Eastern	2B	51	183	23	49	9	2	6	25	1	.268
2001 Tampa	Fla.St.	2B	75	288	43	87	17	4	11	50	2	.302
2002 Norwich	Eastern	2B	73	272	58	83	24	2	19	51	4	.305
2002 Columbus	Int.	2B-1B	51	205	32	54	11	1	9	36	0	.263
2003 Columbus	Int.	2B	17	67	7	14	4	0	2	5	0	.209
2004 Trenton	Eastern	3B-1B	10	42	8	15	2	1	4	16	3	.357
2004 Columbus	Int.	1B-2B-3B	115	434	82	137	19	6	25	84	2	.316
2004 New York	A.L.	3B	5	8	1	2	0	0	1	2	0	.250
2005 Columbus	Int.	3B-1B-2B	75	300	60	90	14	1	22	54	2	.300
2005 New York	A.L.	1B-3B-OF	27	40	7	6	4	0	1	4	0	.150
2006 New York a	A.L.	1B-3B-2B	110	246	30	59	11	3	7	29	3	.240
2007 Scranton-WB	Int.	2B	65	249	37	75	11	2	11	36	2	.301
2007 New York b-c	A.L.	1B-3B-2B	61	185	27	54	7	1	2	25	0	.292
Major League Totals		4 Yrs.	203	479	65	121	22	4	11	60	3	.253
Division Series												
2006 New York	A.L.	1B	1	1	0	0	0	0	0	0	0	.000

a On disabled list from August 18 to September 2, 2006.
b On disabled list from September 3 to October 31, 2007.
c Filed for free agency, December 7, 2007. Signed with Cincinnati Reds organization, January 4, 2008.

PIAZZA, MICHAEL JOSEPH (MIKE)

Born, Norristown, Pennsylvania, September 4, 1968.
Bats Right. Throws Right. Height, 6 feet, 3 inches. Weight, 215 pounds.

Year	Club	Lea	Pos	G	AB	R	H	2B	3B	HR	RBI	SB	Avg
1989 Salem	Northwest	C	57	198	22	53	11	0	8	25	0	.268
1990 Vero Beach	Fla. St.	C-1B	88	272	27	68	20	0	6	45	0	.250
1991 Bakersfield	California	C-1B	117	448	71	124	27	2	29	80	0	.277
1992 San Antonio	Texas	C	31	114	18	43	11	0	7	20	0	.377
1992 Albuquerque	P.C.	C-1B	94	358	54	122	22	5	16	69	1	.341
1992 Los Angeles	N.L.	C	21	69	5	16	3	0	1	7	0	.232
1993 Los Angeles a	N.L.	C-1B	149	547	81	174	24	2	35	112	3	.318
1994 Los Angeles	N.L.	C	107	405	64	129	18	0	24	92	1	.319
1995 Los Angeles b	N.L.	C	112	434	82	150	17	0	32	93	1	.346
1996 Los Angeles	N.L.	C	148	547	87	184	16	0	36	105	0	.336
1997 Los Angeles	N.L.	C	152	556	104	201	32	1	40	124	5	.362
1998 L.A.-Florida-N.Y. c-d-e	N.L.	C	151	561	88	184	38	1	32	111	1	.328
1999 New York f	N.L.	C	141	534	100	162	25	0	40	124	2	.303
2000 New York	N.L.	C	136	482	90	156	26	0	38	113	4	.324

Year Club	Lea	Pos	G	AB	R	H	2B	3B	HR	RBI	SB	Avg
2001 New York	N.L.	C	141	503	81	151	29	0	36	94	0	.300
2002 New York	N.L.	C	135	478	69	134	23	2	33	98	0	.280
2003 Norfolk..............	Int.	C-1B	5	17	2	3	0	0	1	2	0	.176
2003 New York g..........	N.L.	C-1B	68	234	37	67	13	0	11	34	0	.286
2004 St. Lucie...........	Fla.St.	1B	2	6	0	3	1	0	0	2	0	.500
2004 New York h..........	N.L.	1B-C	129	455	47	121	21	0	20	54	0	.266
2005 New York i-j.........	N.L.	C	113	398	41	100	23	0	19	62	0	.251
2006 San Diego k.........	N.L.	C	126	399	39	.113	19	1	22	68	0	.283
2007 Stockton...........	Calif.	DH	3	9	2	3	0	0	2	4	0	.333
2007 Sacramento..........	P.C.	DH	3	17	1	7	2	0	0	1	0	.412
2007 Oakland l-m.........	A.L.	DH	83	309	33	85	17	1	8	44	0	.275
Major League Totals	16 Yrs.		1912	6911	1048	2127	344	8	427	1335	17	.308
Division Series												
1995 Los Angeles	N.L.	C	3	14	1	3	1	0	1	1	0	.214
1996 Los Angeles	N.L.	C	3	10	1	3	0	0	0	2	0	.300
1999 New York	N.L.	C	2	9	0	2	0	0	0	0	0	.222
2000 New York	N.L.	C	4	14	1	3	1	0	0	0	0	.214
2006 San Diego	N.L.	C	4	10	0	1	1	0	0	0	0	.100
Division Series Totals			16	57	3	12	3	0	1	3	0	.211
Championship Series												
1999 New York	N.L.	C	6	24	1	4	0	0	1	4	0	.167
2000 New York	N.L.	C	5	17	7	7	3	0	2	4	0	.412
Championship Series Totals			11	41	8	11	3	0	3	8	0	.268
World Series Record												
2000 New York	N.L.	C-DH	5	22	3	6	2	0	2	4	0	.273

a Selected Rookie of the Year in National League for 1993.

b On disabled list from May 11 to June 4, 1995.

c Traded to Florida Marlins with infielder Todd Zeile for outfielder Gary Sheffield, outfielder Jim Eisenreich, catcher Charles Johnson, infielder Bobby Bonilla and pitcher Manuel Barrios, May 15, 1998.

d Traded to New York Mets for outfielder Preston Wilson, pitcher Ed Yarnall and player to be named later, May 22, 1998.

e Florida Marlins received pitcher Geoff Goetz to complete trade, July 3, 1998.

f On disabled list from April 10 to April 25, 1999.

g On disabled list from May 17 to August 13, 2003.

h On disabled list from August 7 to August 30, 2004.

i On disabled list from August 17 to September 10, 2005.

j Filed for free agency, October 28, 2005. Signed with San Diego Padres, January 29, 2006.

k Filed for free agency, November 2, 2006. Signed with Oakland Athletics, December 8, 2006.

l On disabled list from May 3 to July 20, 2007.

m Filed for free agency, October 30, 2007.

PIE, FELIX

Born, Laromana, Dominican Republic, February 8, 1985.
Bats Left. Throws Left. Height, 6 feet, 2 inches. Weight, 170 pounds.

Year Club	Lea	Pos	G	AB	R	H	2B	3B	HR	RBI	SB	Avg
2002 Cubs.............	Arizona	OF	55	218	42	70	16	13	4	37	17	.321
2002 Boise	Northwest	OF	2	8	1	1	1	0	0	1	0	.125
2003 Lansing	Midwest	OF	124	505	72	144	22	9	4	47	19	.285
2004 Daytona	Fla.St.	OF	105	412	79	123	17	9	8	47	31	.299
2005 West Tenn	Southern	OF	59	240	41	73	17	5	11	25	13	.304
2006 Iowa...............	P.C.	OF	141	559	78	158	33	8	15	57	17	.283
2007 Iowa...............	P.C.	OF	55	229	51	83	9	5	9	43	9	.362
2007 Chicago	N.L.	OF	87	177	26	38	9	3	2	20	8	.215
Division Series												
2007 Chicago	N.L.	PH	1	1	0	0	0	0	0	0	0	.000

PIERRE, JUAN D'VAUGHN

Born, Mobile, Alabama, August 14, 1977.
Bats Left. Throws Left. Height, 6 feet. Weight, 180 pounds.

Year Club	Lea	Pos	G	AB	R	H	2B	3B	HR	RBI	SB	Avg
1998 Portland........	Northwest	OF	64	264	55	93	9	2	0	30	38	.352
1999 Asheville...........	So.Atl.	OF	140	585	93	187	28	5	1	55	66	.320
2000 Carolina	Southern	OF	107	439	63	143	16	4	0	32	46	.326
2000 Colorado Spgs.........	P.C.	OF	4	17	3	8	0	1	0	1	1	.471
2000 Colorado	N.L.	OF	51	200	26	62	2	0	0	20	7	.310
2001 Colorado	N.L.	OF	156	617	108	202	26	11	2	55	*46	.327
2002 Colorado a.........	N.L.	OF	152	592	90	170	20	5	1	35	47	.287

Year	Club	Lea	Pos	G	AB	R	H	2B	3B	HR	RBI	SB	Avg
2003 Florida	N.L.	OF	*162	*668	100	204	28	7	1	41	*65	.305
2004 Florida	N.L.	OF	*162	*678	100	*221	22	*12	3	49	45	.326
2005 Florida b	N.L.	OF	*162	656	96	181	19	13	2	47	57	.276
2006 Chicago c	N.L.	OF	*162	*699	87	*204	32	13	3	40	58	.292
2007 Los Angeles	N.L.	OF	*162	668	96	196	24	8	0	41	64	.293
Major League Totals		8 Yrs.	1169	4778	703	1440	173	69	12	328	389	.301
Division Series												
2003 Florida	N.L.	OF	4	19	5	5	1	0	0	3	1	.263
Championship Series												
2003 Florida	N.L.	OF	7	33	5	10	1	2	0	1	1	.303
World Series Record												
2003 Florida	N.L.	OF	6	21	2	7	2	0	0	3	1	.333

a Traded to Florida Marlins with pitcher Mike Hampton for outfielder Preston Wilson, catcher Charles Johnson, pitcher Vic Darensbourg and infielder Pablo Ozuna, November 16, 2002.
b Traded to Chicago Cubs for pitcher Sergio Mitre, pitcher Ricky Nolasco and pitcher Renyel Pinto, December 7, 2005.
c Filed for free agency, October 29, 2006. Signed with Los Angeles Dodgers, November 22, 2006.

PIERZYNSKI, ANTHONY JOHN (A.J.)
Born, Bridgehampton, New York, December 30, 1976.
Bats Left. Throws Right. Height, 6 feet, 3 inches. Weight, 235 pounds.

Year	Club	Lea	Pos	G	AB	R	H	2B	3B	HR	RBI	SB	Avg
1994 Twins	Gulf Coast	C	43	152	21	44	8	1	1	19	0	.289
1995 Ft. Wayne	Midwest	C	22	84	10	26	5	1	2	14	0	.310
1995 Elizabethtn	Appal.	C-1B	56	205	29	68	13	1	7	45	0	.332
1996 Ft. Wayne	Midwest	C-OF	114	431	48	118	30	3	7	70	0	.274
1997 Ft. Myers	Fla.St.	C-1B	118	412	49	115	23	1	9	64	2	.279
1998 New Britain	Eastern	C	59	212	30	63	11	0	3	17	0	.297
1998 Salt Lake	P.C.	C	59	208	29	53	7	2	7	30	3	.255
1998 Minnesota	A.L.	C	7	10	-1	3	0	0	0	1	0	.300
1999 Salt Lake	P.C.	C	67	228	29	59	10	0	1	25	0	.259
1999 Minnesota a	A.L.	C	9	22	3	6	2	0	0	3	0	.273
2000 New Britain	Eastern	C	62	228	36	68	17	2	4	34	0	.298
2000 Salt Lake	P.C.	C	41	155	22	52	14	1	4	25	1	.335
2000 Minnesota	A.L.	C	33	88	12	27	5	1	2	11	1	.307
2001 Minnesota	A.L.	C	114	381	51	110	33	2	7	55	1	.289
2002 Minnesota	A.L.	C	130	440	54	132	31	6	6	49	1	.300
2003 Minnesota b	A.L.	C	137	487	63	152	35	3	11	74	3	.312
2004 San Francisco c	N.L.	C	131	471	45	128	28	2	11	77	0	.272
2005 Chicago	A.L.	C	128	460	61	118	21	0	18	56	0	.257
2006 Chicago	A.L.	C	140	509	65	150	24	0	16	64	1	.295
2007 Chicago	A.L.	C	136	472	54	124	24	0	14	50	1	.263
Major League Totals		10 Yrs.	965	3340	409	950	203	14	85	440	8	.284
Division Series												
2002 Minnesota	A.L.	C	5	16	4	7	0	1	1	4	0	.438
2003 Minnesota	A.L.	C	4	13	1	3	0	0	1	1	0	.231
2005 Chicago	A.L.	C	3	9	5	4	2	0	2	4	1	.444
Division Series Totals			12	38	10	14	2	1	4	9	1	.368
Championship Series												
2002 Minnesota	A.L.	C	5	16	1	4	0	0	0	2	0	.250
2005 Chicago	A.L.	C	5	18	1	3	0	0	1	2	0	.167
Championship Series Totals			10	34	2	7	0	0	1	4	0	.206
World Series Record												
2005 Chicago	A.L.	C	4	15	3	4	2	0	0	3	1	.267

a On disabled list from August 24 to September 30, 1999.
b Traded to San Francisco Giants with player to be named later for pitcher Joe Nathan, pitcher Boof Bonser and pitcher Francisco Liriano, November 14, 2003.
c Released by San Francisco Giants, December 16, 2004. Signed with Chicago White Sox, January 5, 2005.

PODSEDNIK, SCOTT ERIC
Born, West, Texas, March 18, 1976.
Bats Left. Throws Left. Height, 6 feet, 1 Inch. Weight, 190 pounds.

Year	Club	Lea	Pos	G	AB	R	H	2B	3B	HR	RBI	SB	Avg
1994 Rangers	Gulf Coast	OF	60	211	34	48	7	1	1	17	18	.227
1995 Hudson Val a	N.Y.-Penn.	OF	65	252	42	67	3	0	0	20	20	.266
1996 Brevard Cty	Fla.St.	OF	108	383	39	100	9	2	0	30	20	.261

Year	Club	Lea	Pos	G	AB	R	H	2B	3B	HR	RBI	SB	Avg
1997 Kane County b	Midwest	OF	135	531	80	147	23	4	3	49	28	.277
1998 Tulsa	Texas	OF	17	75	9	18	4	1	0	4	5	.240
1998 Charlotte	Fla.St.	OF	81	302	55	86	12	4	4	39	26	.285
1999 Rangers	Gulf Coast	OF	5	17	6	7	2	0	0	5	1	.412
1999 Tulsa	Texas	OF	37	116	10	18	4	0	0	1	6	.155
2000 Tulsa c-d	Texas	OF	49	169	20	42	7	2	2	13	19	.249
2001 Tacoma	P.C.	OF	66	269	46	78	15	4	3	30	12	.290
2001 Seattle e	A.L.	OF	5	6	1	1	0	1	0	3	0	.167
2002 Tacoma	P.C.	OF	125	438	63	122	25	6	9	61	35	.279
2002 Seattle f	A.L.	OF	14	20	2	4	0	0	1	5	0	.200
2003 Milwaukee	N.L.	OF	154	558	100	175	29	8	9	58	43	.314
2004 Milwaukee g	N.L.	OF	154	640	85	156	27	7	12	39	*70	.244
2005 Charlotte	Int.	OF	2	9	2	2	2	0	0	1	0	.222
2005 Chicago h	A.L.	OF	129	507	80	147	28	1	0	25	59	.290
2006 Chicago	A.L.	OF	139	524	86	137	27	6	3	45	40	.261
2007 Charlotte	Int.	OF	20	73	12	21	5	0	1	6	2	.288
2007 Chicago i-j	A.L.	OF	62	214	30	52	13	4	2	11	12	.243
Major League Totals	7 Yrs.	657	2469	384	672	124	27	27	186	224	.272		
Division Series													
2005 Chicago	A.L.	OF	3	11	3	3	1	0	1	4	1	.273
Championship Series													
2005 Chicago	A.L.	OF	5	17	4	5	0	1	0	0	3	.294
World Series Record													
2005 Chicago	A.L.	OF	4	21	2	6	0	2	1	2	2	.286

a Sent to Florida Marlins by Texas Rangers to complete trade for pitcher Bobby Witt, August 8, 1995.
b Selected by Texas Rangers organization in Rule V draft, December 15, 1997.
c On disabled list from April 6 to May 22, 2000.
d Filed for free agency, October 15, 2000. Signed with Seattle Mariners organization, November 7, 2000.
e On disabled list from May 4 to June 12 and August 14 to 26, 2001.
f Claimed on waivers by Milwaukee Brewers, October 11, 2002.
g Traded to Chicago White Sox with pitcher Luis Vizcaino and player to be named later for outfielder Carlos Lee, December 13, 2004. Chicago White Sox received infielder Travis Hinton to complete trade, January 10, 2005.
h On disabled list from August 13 to August 29, 2005.
i On disabled list from April 16 to June 23 and July 2 to July 24, 2007.
j Released by Chicago White Sox, November 28, 2007.

POLANCO, PLACIDO ENRIQUE

Born, Santo Domingo, Dominican Republic, October 10, 1975.
Bats Right. Throws Right. Height, 5 feet, 10 inches. Weight, 195 pounds.

Year	Club	Lea	Pos	G	AB	R	H	2B	3B	HR	RBI	SB	Avg
1994 Cardinals	Arizona	SS-2B	32	127	17	27	4	0	1	10	4	.213
1995 Peoria	Midwest	SS-2B	103	361	43	96	7	4	2	41	7	.266
1996 St. Pete	Fla.St.	2B	137	540	65	157	29	5	0	51	4	.291
1997 Arkansas	Texas	2B	129	508	71	148	16	3	2	51	19	.291
1998 Memphis	P.C.	2B-SS	70	246	36	69	19	1	1	21	6	.280
1998 St. Louis	N.L.	SS-2B	45	114	10	29	3	2	1	11	2	.254
1999 Memphis	P.C.	2B	29	120	18	33	4	1	0	10	2	.275
1999 St. Louis	N.L.	2B-3B-SS	88	220	24	61	9	3	1	19	1	.277
2000 St. Louis a	N.L.	2B-3B-SS-1B	118	323	50	102	12	3	5	39	4	.316
2001 St. Louis	N.L.	3B-SS-2B	144	564	87	173	26	4	3	38	12	.307
2002 St. Louis-Phil. b	N.L.	3B-SS-2B	147	548	75	158	32	2	9	49	5	.288
2003 Philadelphia c	N.L.	2B-3B	122	492	87	142	30	3	14	63	14	.289
2004 Reading	Eastern	2B	1	3	0	2	0	0	0	0	0	.667
2004 Scranton/W.B.	Int.	2B	1	3	1	0	0	0	0	0	0	.000
2004 Philadelphia d-e	N.L.	2B-3B	126	503	74	150	21	0	17	55	7	.298
2005 Philadelphia	N.L.	2B-3B-OF-SS	43	158	26	50	7	0	3	20	0	.316
2005 Detroit f-g	A.L.	2B-3B	86	343	58	116	20	2	6	36	4	.338
2006 Detroit h	A.L.	2B	110	461	58	136	18	1	4	52	1	.295
2007 Detroit	A.L.	2B	142	587	105	200	36	3	9	67	7	.341
Major League Totals	10 Yrs.	1171	4313	654	1317	214	23	72	449	57	.305		
Division Series													
2000 St. Louis	N.L.	3B	3	10	1	3	0	0	0	3	1	.300
2001 St. Louis	N.L.	3B	5	15	1	4	0	0	0	1	1	.267
2006 Detroit	A.L.	2B	4	17	3	7	1	0	0	2	0	.412
Division Series Totals			12	42	5	14	1	0	0	6	2	.333	
Championship Series													
2000 St. Louis	N.L.	3B	4	5	0	1	0	0	0	0	0	.200
2006 Detroit	A.L.	2B	4	17	2	9	1	0	0	2	0	.529

Year	Club	Lea	Pos	G	AB	R	H	2B	3B	HR	RBI	SB	Avg
Championship Series Totals ..				8	22	2	10	1	0	0	2	0	.455
World Series Record													
2006 Detroit .... A.L.			2B	5	17	0	0	0	0	0	0	0	.000

a On disabled list from July 1 to July 15, 2000.
b Traded to Philadelphia Phillies with pitcher Bud Smith and pitcher Mike Timlin for infielder Scott Rolen and pitcher Doug Nickle, July 29, 2002.
c On disabled list from April 16 to May 1, 2003.
d On disabled list from May 8 to June 7, 2004.
e Filed for free agency, October 29, 2004, re-signed with Philadelphia Phillies, December 19, 2004.
f Traded to Detroit Tigers for pitcher Ugueth Urbina and infielder Ramon Martinez, June 8, 2005.
g On disabled list from July 12 to July 27, 2005.
h On disabled list from August 16 to September 22, 2006.

POSADA, JORGE RAFAEL

Born, Santurce, Puerto Rico, August 17, 1971.
Bats Both. Throws Right. Height, 6 feet, 2 inches. Weight, 205 pounds

Year	Club	Lea	Pos	G	AB	R	H	2B	3B	HR	RBI	SB	Avg
1991 Oneonta .... N.Y.-Penn			2B-C	71	217	34	51	5	5	4	33	6	.235
1992 Greensboro .... So. Atl.			DH-C-3B	101	339	60	94	22	4	12	58	11	.277
1993 Pr William .... Carolina			C-3B	118	410	71	106	27	2	17	61	17	.259
1993 Albany .... Eastern			C	7	25	3	7	0	0	0	0	0	.280
1994 Columbus............ Int.			C-OF	92	313	46	75	13	3	11	48	5	.240
1995 Columbus............ Int.			C	108	368	60	94	32	5	8	51	4	.255
1995 New York .... A.L.			C	1	0	0	0	0	0	0	0	0	.000
1996 Columbus............ Int.			C-OF	106	354	76	96	22	6	11	62	3	.271
1996 New York .... A.L.			C	8	14	1	1	0	0	0	0	0	.071
1997 New York .... A.L.			C	60	188	29	47	12	0	6	25	1	.250
1998 New York .... A.L.			C-1B	111	358	56	96	23	0	17	63	0	.268
1999 New York .... A.L.			C-1B	112	379	50	93	19	2	12	57	1	.245
2000 New York .... A.L.			C-1B	151	505	92	145	35	1	28	86	2	.287
2001 New York .... A.L.			C-1B	138	484	59	134	28	1	22	95	2	.277
2002 New York .... A.L.			C	143	511	79	137	40	1	20	99	1	.268
2003 New York .... A.L.			C	142	481	83	135	24	0	30	101	2	.281
2004 New York .... A.L.			C	137	449	72	122	31	0	21	81	1	.272
2005 New York .... A.L.			C	142	474	67	124	23	0	19	71	1	.262
2006 New York .... A.L.			C-1B	143	465	65	129	27	2	23	93	3	.277
2007 New York a........... A.L.			C-1B	144	506	91	171	42	1	20	90	2	.338
Major League Totals		13 Yrs.		1432	4814	744	1334	304	8	218	861	16	.277
Division Series													
1995 New York .... A.L.			C	1	0	1	0	0	0	0	0	0	.000
1997 New York .... A.L.			C	2	2	0	0	0	0	0	0	0	.000
1998 New York .... A.L.			C	1	2	1	0	0	0	0	0	0	.000
1999 New York .... A.L.			C	1	4	0	1	1	0	0	0	0	.250
2000 New York .... A.L.			C	5	17	2	4	2	0	0	1	0	.235
2001 New York .... A.L.			C	5	18	3	8	1	0	1	2	1	.444
2002 New York .... A.L.			C	4	17	2	4	0	0	1	3	0	.235
2003 New York .... A.L.			C	4	17	1	3	1	0	0	0	0	.176
2004 New York .... A.L.			C	4	18	2	4	0	0	0	0	0	.222
2005 New York .... A.L.			C	5	13	3	3	1	0	1	2	0	.231
2006 New York .... A.L.			C	4	14	2	7	1	0	1	2	0	.500
2007 New York .... A.L.			C	4	15	1	2	1	0	0	0	0	.133
Division Series Totals				40	137	18	36	8	0	4	10	1	.263
Championship Series													
1998 New York .... A.L.			C	5	11	1	2	0	0	1	2	0	.182
1999 New York .... A.L.			C	3	10	1	1	0	0	1	2	0	.100
2000 New York .... A.L.			C	6	19	2	3	1	0	0	3	0	.158
2001 New York .... A.L.			C	5	14	4	3	1	0	0	0	0	.214
2003 New York .... A.L.			C	7	27	5	8	4	0	1	6	0	.296
2004 New York .... A.L.			C	7	27	4	7	1	0	0	2	0	.259
Championship Series Totals				33	108	17	24	7	0	3	15	0	.222
World Series Record													
1998 New York .... A.L.			C	3	9	2	3	0	0	1	2	0	.333
1999 New York .... A.L.			C	2	8	0	2	1	0	0	1	0	.250
2000 New York .... A.L.			C	5	18	2	4	1	0	0	1	0	.222
2001 New York .... A.L.			C	7	23	2	4	1	0	1	1	0	.174
2003 New York .... A.L.			C	6	19	0	3	1	0	0	1	0	.158
World Series Totals.............				23	77	6	16	4	0	2	6	1	.208

a Filed for free agency, October 29, 2007, re-signed with New York Yankees, November 29, 2007.

PUJOLS, JOSE ALBERTO (ALBERT)
Born, Santo Domingo, Dominican Republic, January 16, 1980.
Bats Right. Throws Right. Height, 6 feet, 3 inches. Weight, 225 pounds.

Year	Club	Lea	Pos	G	AB	R	H	2B	3B	HR	RBI	SB	Avg
2000 Potomac	Carolina	3B	21	81	11	23	8	1	2	10	1	.284
2000 Peoria	Midwest	3B	109	395	62	128	32	6	17	84	2	.324
2000 Memphis	P.C.	3B-OF	3	14	1	3	1	0	0	2	1	.214
2001 St. Louis a	N.L.	OF-3B-1B	161	590	112	194	47	4	37	130	1	.329
2002 St. Louis	N.L.	OF-3B-1B-SS	157	590	118	185	40	2	34	127	2	.314
2003 St. Louis	N.L.	OF-1B	157	591	*137	*212	*51	1	43	124	5	*.359
2004 St. Louis	N.L.	1B	154	592	*133	196	51	2	46	123	5	.331
2005 St. Louis b	N.L.	1B	161	591	*129	195	38	2	41	117	16	.330
2006 St. Louis c	N.L.	1B	143	535	119	177	33	1	49	137	7	.331
2007 St. Louis	N.L.	1B	158	565	99	185	38	1	32	103	2	.327
Major League Totals		7 Yrs.	1091	4054	847	1344	298	13	282	861	38	.332
Division Series													
2001 St. Louis	N.L.	1B-OF	5	18	1	2	0	0	1	2	0	.111
2002 St. Louis	N.L.	OF-1B-3B	3	10	3	3	0	1	0	3	0	.300
2004 St. Louis	N.L.	1B	4	15	4	5	0	0	2	5	0	.333
2005 St. Louis	N.L.	1B	3	9	4	5	2	0	0	2	0	.556
2006 St. Louis	N.L.	1B	4	15	3	5	1	0	1	3	0	.333
Division Series Totals			19	67	15	20	3	1	4	15	0	.299
Championship Series													
2002 St. Louis	N.L.	OF-3B-1B	5	19	2	5	1	0	1	2	0	.263
2004 St. Louis	N.L.	1B	7	28	10	14	2	0	4	9	0	.500
2005 St. Louis	N.L.	1B	6	23	3	7	0	0	2	6	0	.304
2006 St. Louis	N.L.	1B	7	22	5	7	1	0	1	1	0	.318
Championship Series Totals			25	92	20	33	4	0	8	18	0	.359
World Series Record													
2004 St. Louis	N.L.	1B	4	15	1	5	2	0	0	0	0	.333
2006 St. Louis	N.L.	1B	5	15	3	3	1	0	1	2	0	.200
World Series Totals			9	30	4	8	3	0	1	2	0	.267

a Selected Rookie of the Year in National League for 2001.
b Selected Most Valuable Player in National League for 2005.
c On disabled list from June 4 to June 22, 2006.

PUNTO, NICHOLAS PAUL (NICK)
Born, San Diego, California, November 8, 1977.
Bats Both. Throws Right. Height, 5 feet, 9 inches. Weight, 185 pounds.

Year	Club	Lea	Pos	G	AB	R	H	2B	3B	HR	RBI	SB	Avg
1998 Batavia	N.Y.-Penn.	SS-2B	72	279	51	69	9	4	1	20	19	.247
1999 Clearwater	Fla.St.	SS	106	400	65	122	18	6	1	48	16	.305
2000 Reading	Eastern	SS	121	456	77	116	15	4	5	47	33	.254
2001 Scranton-WB	Int.	SS	123	463	57	106	19	5	1	39	33	.229
2001 Philadelphia	N.L.	SS	4	5	0	2	0	0	0	0	0	.400
2002 Philadelphia	N.L.	2B-SS	9	6	0	1	0	0	0	0	0	.167
2002 Scranton-WB	Int.	SS	115	443	74	120	12	5	1	29	42	.271
2003 Philadelphia	N.L.	2B-3B-SS	64	92	14	20	2	0	1	4	2	.217
2003 Scranton/WB a	Int.	SS	25	111	19	35	7	1	0	9	7	.315
2004 Minnesota	A.L.	2B-SS-3B-OF	38	91	17	23	0	0	2	12	6	.253
2004 Quad Cities b	Midwest	SS-2B-3B	4	16	4	7	1	0	1	6	1	.438
2005 Rochester	Int.	2B	4	15	2	3	1	0	0	1	0	.200
2005 Minnesota c	A.L.	2B-SS-3B-OF	112	394	45	94	18	4	4	26	13	.239
2006 Minnesota	A.L.	3B-SS-2B-OF	135	459	73	133	21	7	1	45	17	.290
2007 Minnesota	A.L.	3B-SS-2B	150	472	53	99	18	4	1	25	16	.210
Major League Totals		7 Yrs.	512	1519	202	372	59	15	9	112	54	.245
Division Series													
2006 Minnesota	A.L.	3B	3	12	0	2	0	0	0	0	0	.167

a Traded to Minnesota Twins with pitcher Carlos Silva and player to be named later for pitcher Eric Milton, December 3, 2003.
b On disabled list from May 9 to June 30 and July 27 to October 28, 2004.
c On disabled list from June 3 to July 3, 2005.

QUENTIN, CARLOS JOSE
Born, Bellflower, California, August 28, 1982.
Bats Right. Throws Right. Height, 6 feet, 1 inch. Weight, 225 pounds.

Year	Club	Lea	Pos	G	AB	R	H	2B	3B	HR	RBI	SB	Avg
2004 Lancaster	Calif.	OF	65	242	64	75	14	1	15	51	5	.310

Year	Club	Lea	Pos	G	AB	R	H	2B	3B	HR	RBI	SB	Avg
2004 El Paso	Texas		OF	60	210	39	75	19	0	6	38	0	.357
2005 Tucson	.P.C.		OF	136	452	98	136	28	4	21	89	9	.301
2006 Tucson	.P.C.		OF	85	318	66	92	30	3	9	52	5	.289
2006 Arizona	N.L.		OF	57	166	23	42	13	3	9	32	1	.253
2007 Tucson	.P.C.		OF	33	115	30	40	12	1	4	27	0	.348
2007 Arizona a-b	N.L.		OF	81	229	29	49	16	0	5	31	2	.214
Major League Totals		2 Yrs.	138	395	52	91	29	3	14	63	3	.230	

a On disabled list from March 23 to April 16 and August 2 to September 1, 2007.
b Traded to Chicago White Sox for infielder Chris Carter, December 3, 2007.

QUINLAN, ROBB WILLIAM

Born, St.Paul, Minnesota, March 17, 1977.
Bats Right. Throws Right. Height, 6 feet, 1 inch. Weight, 200 pounds.

Year	Club	Lea	Pos	G	AB	R	H	2B	3B	HR	RBI	SB	Avg
1999 Boise	Northwest		3B-2B-1B	73	295	51	95	20	1	9	77	5	.322
2000 Lake Elsinore	Calif.		1B-OF	127	482	79	153	35	5	5	85	6	.317
2001 Arkansas	Texas		1B-OF	129	492	82	145	33	7	14	79	0	.295
2002 Salt Lake	.P.C.		OF-1B	136	528	95	176	31	13	20	112	8	.333
2003 Salt Lake	.P.C.		1B-OF	95	393	55	122	18	4	9	68	10	.310
2003 Anaheim	A.L.		1B-OF	38	94	13	27	4	2	0	4	1	.287
2004 Salt Lake	.P.C.		1B-3B-OF	27	108	15	32	9	1	2	17	1	.296
2004 Anaheim a	A.L.		3B-1B-OF	56	160	23	55	14	0	5	23	3	.344
2005 Angels	Arizona		1B-3B	4	12	3	3	2	0	0	3	1	.250
2005 Salt Lake	.P.C.		1B-3B	15	60	13	23	6	0	1	4	0	.383
2005 Los Angeles b	A.L.		3B-1B-OF	54	134	17	31	8	0	5	14	0	.231
2006 Los Angeles	A.L.		1B-3B-OF	86	234	28	75	11	1	9	32	2	.321
2007 Los Angeles	A.L.		1B-OF-3B	79	178	21	44	9	0	3	21	3	.247
Major League Totals		5 Yrs.	313	800	102	232	46	3	22	94	9	.290	
Division Series													
2005 Los Angeles	A.L.		3B	2	2	0	1	0	0	0	0	0	.500
2007 Los Angeles	A.L.		PH	1	1	0	0	0	0	0	0	0	.000
Division Series Totals				3	3	0	1	0	0	0	0	0	.333
Championship Series													
2005 Los Angeles	A.L.		3B	1	3	1	1	0	0	1	1	0	.333

a On disabled list from August 16 to October 14, 2004.
b On disabled list from July 1 to August 23, 2005.

RABURN, RYAN NEIL

Born, Tampa, Florida, April 17, 1981.
Bats Right. Throws Right. Height, 6 feet. Weight, 185 pounds.

Year	Club	Lea	Pos	G	AB	R	H	2B	3B	HR	RBI	SB	Avg
2001 Tigers	Gulf Coast		3B	19	58	4	9	2	0	1	5	2	.155
2001 Oneonta	N.Y.-Penn.		3B-2B	44	171	25	62	17	8	8	42	1	.363
2002 Tigers	Gulf Coast		3B	8	30	4	9	3	1	1	5	0	.300
2002 West Michigan	Midwest		3B	40	150	27	33	10	1	6	28	0	.220
2003 Lakeland	Fla.St.		3B	95	325	52	72	14	3	12	56	2	.222
2003 West Michigan	Midwest		3B	16	57	14	20	7	0	3	12	1	.351
2004 Lakeland	Fla.St.		2B	3	11	1	3	1	0	1	3	0	.273
2004 Erie	Eastern		2B	98	366	66	110	29	4	16	63	3	.301
2004 Detroit	A.L.		2B	12	29	4	4	1	0	0	1	1	.138
2005 Toledo	Int.		2B-OF	130	471	62	119	22	4	19	64	8	.253
2006 Toledo	Int.		OF-2B	118	451	68	124	29	4	20	79	16	.275
2007 Toledo	Int.		OF-2B	85	315	60	92	21	3	17	64	12	.292
2007 Detroit	A.L.		OF-2B-3B	49	138	28	42	12	2	4	27	3	.304
Major League Totals		2 Yrs.	61	167	32	46	13	2	4	28	4	.275	

RAMIREZ (NIN), ARAMIS

Born, Santo Domingo, Dominican Republic, June 25, 1978.
Bats Right. Throws Right. Height, 6 feet, 1 inch. Weight, 215 pounds.

Year	Club	Lea	Pos	G	AB	R	H	2B	3B	HR	RBI	SB	Avg
1995 Pittsburgh	Dominican		3B	64	214	41	63	13	0	11	54	2	.294
1996 Erie	N.Y.-Penn.		3B	61	223	37	68	14	4	9	42	0	.305
1996 Augusta	So.Atl.		3B	6	20	3	4	1	0	1	2	0	.200
1997 Lynchburg	Carolina		3B	137	482	85	134	24	2	29	114	5	.278
1998 Nashville	.P.C.		3B-SS	47	168	19	46	10	0	5	18	0	.274

Year Club	Lea	Pos	G	AB	R	H	2B	3B	HR	RBI	SB	Avg
1998 Pittsburgh a	N.L.	3B	72	251	23	59	9	1	6	24	0	.235
1999 Nashville	P.C.	3B	131	460	92	151	35	1	21	74	5	.328
1999 Pittsburgh	N.L.	3B	18	56	2	10	2	1	0	7	0	.179
2000 Nashville	P.C.	3B	44	167	28	59	12	2	4	26	2	.353
2000 Pittsburgh b	N.L.	3B	73	254	19	65	15	2	6	35	0	.256
2001 Pittsburgh	N.L.	3B	158	603	83	181	40	0	34	112	5	.300
2002 Pittsburgh	N.L.	3B	142	522	51	122	26	0	18	71	2	.234
2003 Pittsburgh-Chicago c-d	N.L.	3B	159	607	75	165	32	2	27	106	2	.272
2004 Chicago	N.L.	3B	145	547	99	174	32	1	36	103	0	.318
2005 Chicago e	N.L.	3B	123	463	72	140	30	0	31	92	0	.302
2006 Chicago f	N.L.	3B	157	594	93	173	38	4	38	119	2	.291
2007 Chicago g	N.L.	3B	132	506	72	157	35	4	26	101	0	.310
Major League Totals		10 Yrs.	1179	4403	589	1246	259	15	222	770	11	.283
Division Series												
2003 Chicago	N.L.	3B	5	18	2	5	1	0	1	3	0	.278
2007 Chicago	N.L.	3B	3	12	0	0	0	0	0	0	0	.000
Division Series Totals			8	30	2	5	1	0	1	3	0	.167
Championship Series												
2003 Chicago	N.L.	3B	7	26	4	6	0	1	3	7	0	.231

a On disabled list from August 10 to September 4, 1998.
b On disabled list from August 29 to October 1, 2000.
c Traded to Chicago Cubs with outfielder Kenny Lofton for infielder Jose Hernandez, pitcher Matt Bruback and player to be named later, July 22, 2003.
d Pittsburgh Pirates received infielder Bobby Hill to complete trade, August 15, 2003.
e On disabled list from August 25 to October 3, 2005.
f Filed for free agency, October 30, 2006, re-signed with Chicago Cubs, November 12, 2006.
g On disabled list from June 7 to June 22, 2007.

RAMIREZ, HANLEY

Born, Samana, Dominican Republic, December 23, 1983.
Bats Right. Throws Right. Height, 6 feet, 3 inches. Weight, 195 pounds.

Year Club	Lea	Pos	G	AB	R	H	2B	3B	HR	RBI	SB	Avg
2002 Red Sox	Gulf Coast	SS-2B-3B	45	164	29	56	11	3	6	26	8	.341
2002 Lowell	N.Y.-Penn.	SS	22	97	17	36	9	2	1	19	4	.371
2003 Augusta	So.Atl.	SS	111	422	69	116	24	3	8	50	36	.275
2004 Portland	Eastern	SS	32	129	26	40	7	2	5	15	12	.310
2004 Sarasota	Fla.St.	SS	62	239	33	74	8	4	1	24	12	.310
2004 Red Sox	Gulf Coast	SS-2B	6	20	5	8	0	1	0	1	1	.400
2005 Portland	Eastern	SS-2B-3B	122	465	66	126	21	7	6	52	26	.271
2005 Boston a	A.L.	SS	2	2	0	0	0	0	0	0	0	.000
2006 Florida b	N.L.	SS	158	633	119	185	46	11	17	59	51	.292
2007 Florida	N.L.	SS	154	639	125	212	48	6	29	81	51	.332
Major League Totals		3 Yrs.	314	1274	244	397	94	17	46	140	102	.312

a Traded to Florida Marlins with pitcher Anibal Sanchez and pitcher Jesus Delgado for pitcher Josh Beckett, infielder Mike Lowell and pitcher Guillermo Mota, November 24, 2005.
b Selected Rookie of the Year in National League for 2006.

RAMIREZ, MANUEL ARISTIDES (MANNY)

Born, Santo Domingo, Domininican Republic, May 30, 1972.
Bats Right. Throws Right. Height, 6 feet. Weight, 200 pounds.

Year Club	Lea	Pos	G	AB	R	H	2B	3B	HR	RBI	SB	Avg
1991 Burlington	Appal.	OF	59	215	44	70	11	4	19	63	7	.326
1992 Kinston a	Carolina	OF	81	291	52	81	18	4	13	63	1	.278
1993 Canton	Eastern	OF	89	344	67	117	32	0	17	79	2	.340
1993 Charlotte	Int.	OF	40	145	38	46	12	0	14	36	1	.317
1993 Cleveland	A.L.	DH-OF	22	53	5	9	1	0	2	5	0	.170
1994 Cleveland	A.L.	OF	91	290	51	78	22	0	17	60	4	.269
1995 Cleveland	A.L.	OF	137	484	85	149	26	1	31	107	6	.308
1996 Cleveland	A.L.	OF	152	550	94	170	45	3	33	112	8	.309
1997 Cleveland	A.L.	OF	150	561	99	184	40	0	26	88	2	.328
1998 Cleveland	A.L.	OF	150	571	108	168	35	2	45	145	5	.294
1999 Cleveland	A.L.	OF	147	522	131	174	34	3	44	*165	2	.333
2000 Akron	Eastern	PH	1	2	1	1	0	0	1	2	0	.500
2000 Buffalo	Int.	PH	5	11	5	5	1	0	3	7	0	.455
2000 Cleveland b-c	A.L.	OF	118	439	92	154	34	2	38	122	1	.351
2001 Boston	A.L.	DH-OF	142	529	93	162	33	2	41	125	0	.306

Year	Club	Lea	Pos	G	AB	R	H	2B	3B	HR	RBI	SB	Avg
2002 Pawtucket	Int.	OF	11	30	2	3	1	0	1	2	0	.100
2002 Boston d	A.L.	OF	120	436	84	152	31	0	33	107	0	*.349
2003 Boston	A.L.	OF	154	569	117	185	36	1	37	104	3	.325
2004 Boston	A.L.	OF	152	568	108	175	44	0	*43	130	2	.308
2005 Boston	A.L.	OF	152	554	112	162	30	1	45	144	1	.292
2006 Boston	A.L.	OF	130	449	79	144	27	1	35	102	0	.321
2007 Boston	A.L.	OF	133	483	84	143	33	1	20	88	0	.296

Major League Totals	15 Yrs.	1950	7058	1342	2209	471	17	490	1604	34	.313

Division Series

Year	Club	Lea	Pos	G	AB	R	H	2B	3B	HR	RBI	SB	Avg
1995 Cleveland	A.L.	OF	3	12	1	0	0	0	0	0	0	.000
1996 Cleveland	A.L.	OF	4	16	4	6	2	0	2	2	0	.375
1997 Cleveland	A.L.	OF	5	21	2	3	1	0	0	3	0	.143
1998 Cleveland	A.L.	OF	4	14	2	5	2	0	2	3	0	.357
1999 Cleveland	A.L.	OF	5	18	5	1	1	0	0	1	0	.056
2003 Boston	A.L.	OF	5	20	2	4	0	0	1	3	0	.200
2004 Boston	A.L.	OF	3	13	3	5	2	0	1	7	0	.385
2005 Boston	A.L.	OF	3	10	2	3	0	0	2	4	0	.300
2007 Boston	A.L.	OF	3	8	3	3	0	0	2	4	0	.375

Division Series Totals	35	132	24	30	8	0	10	27	0	.227

Championship Series

Year	Club	Lea	Pos	G	AB	R	H	2B	3B	HR	RBI	SB	Avg
1995 Cleveland	A.L.	OF	6	21	2	6	0	0	2	2	0	.286
1997 Cleveland	A.L.	OF	6	21	3	6	1	0	2	3	0	.286
1998 Cleveland	A.L.	OF	6	21	2	7	1	0	2	4	0	.333
2003 Boston	A.L.	OF	7	29	6	9	1	0	2	4	0	.310
2004 Boston	A.L.	OF	7	30	3	9	1	0	0	0	0	.300
2007 Boston	A.L.	OF	7	22	5	9	1	0	2	10	0	.409

Championship Series Totals	39	144	21	46	5	0	10	23	0	.319

World Series Record

Year	Club	Lea	Pos	G	AB	R	H	2B	3B	HR	RBI	SB	Avg
1995 Cleveland	A.L.	OF	6	18	2	4	0	0	1	2	1	.222
1997 Cleveland	A.L.	OF	7	26	3	4	0	0	2	6	0	.154
2004 Boston	A.L.	OF	4	17	2	7	0	0	1	4	0	.412
2007 Boston	A.L.	OF	4	16	3	4	1	0	0	2	0	.250

World Series Totals	21	77	10	19	1	0	4	14	1	.247

a On disabled list from July 10 to end of 1992 season.
b On disabled list from May 30 to July 12, 2000.
c Filed for free agency, October 27, 2000. Signed with Boston Red Sox, December 13, 2000.
d On disabled list from May 14 to June 25, 2002.

REDMAN, JULIAN JAWONN (TIKE)

Born, Tuscaloosa, Alabama, March 10, 1977.
Bats Left. Throws Left. Height, 5 feet, 11 inches. Weight, 166 pounds.

Year	Club	Lea	Pos	G	AB	R	H	2B	3B	HR	RBI	SB	Avg
1996 Pirates	Gulf Coast	OF	26	104	20	31	4	1	1	16	15	.298
1996 Erie...........	N.Y.-Penn.	OF	43	170	31	50	4	6	2	21	7	.294
1997 Lynchburg	Carolina	OF-1B	125	415	55	104	18	5	4	45	21	.251
1998 Lynchburg	Carolina	OF	131	525	70	135	26	10	6	46	36	.257
1999 Altoona.........	Eastern	OF	136	532	84	143	20	12	3	60	29	.269
2000 Nashville	P.C.	OF	121	506	62	132	24	11	4	51	24	.261
2000 Pittsburgh	N.L.	OF	9	18	2	6	1	0	1	1	1	.333
2001 Nashville	P.C.	OF	95	398	53	121	18	10	3	42	21	.304
2001 Pittsburgh	N.L.	OF	37	125	8	28	4	1	1	4	3	.224
2002 Nashville	P.C.	OF	76	311	40	84	9	4	2	20	16	.270
2003 Nashville	P.C.	OF	100	360	60	106	12	7	4	29	42	.294
2003 Pittsburgh	N.L.	OF	56	230	36	76	16	5	3	19	7	.330
2004 Pittsburgh	N.L.	OF	155	546	65	153	19	4	8	51	18	.280
2005 Pittsburgh a	N.L.	OF	135	319	33	80	12	4	2	26	4	.251
2006 Toledo	Int.	OF	79	300	30	76	15	2	1	13	12	.253
2006 Corpus Christi b-c	Texas	OF	27	103	17	32	3	0	1	6	4	.311
2007 Norfolk	Int.	OF	80	296	53	90	15	6	2	27	25	.304
2007 Baltimore d	A.L.	OF	40	132	23	42	9	2	2	16	7	.318

Major League Totals	6 Yrs.	432	1370	167	385	61	16	17	117	40	.281

a Sold to New York Mets, November 28, 2005.
b Released by New York Mets, March 31, 2006. Signed with Detroit Tigers organization, April 10, 2006.
c Released by Detroit Tigers, July 28, 2006. Signed with Houston Astros organization, August 4, 2006.
d Filed for free agency, October 15, 2006. Signed with Baltimore Orioles organization, May 14, 2007.

REDMOND, MICHAEL PATRICK (MIKE)

Born, Seattle, Washington, May 5, 1971.
Bats Right. Throws Right. Height, 6 feet, 1 inch. Weight, 185 pounds.

Year	Club	Lea	Pos	G	AB	R	H	2B	3B	HR	RBI	SB	Avg
1993	Kane County	Midwest	C	43	100	10	20	2	0	0	10	2	.200
1994	Kane County	Midwest	C	92	306	39	83	10	0	1	24	3	.271
1994	Brevard Cty	Fla.St.	C	12	42	4	11	4	0	0	2	0	.262
1995	Portland	Eastern	C-3B	105	333	37	85	11	1	3	39	2	.255
1996	Portland	Eastern	C	120	394	43	113	22	0	4	44	3	.287
1997	Charlotte	Int.	C	22	61	8	13	5	1	1	2	0	.213
1997	Marlins	Gulf Coast	DH	16	55	7	19	3	0	0	5	2	.345
1997	Brevard Cty	Fla.St.	DH-1B	5	17	2	0	0	0	0	0	0	.000
1998	Portland	Eastern	C	8	28	7	9	4	0	1	7	0	.321
1998	Charlotte	Int.	C	18	58	4	14	2	0	2	7	0	.241
1998	Florida a	N.L.	C	37	118	10	39	9	0	2	12	0	.331
1999	Florida	N.L.	C	84	242	22	73	9	0	1	27	0	.302
2000	Florida	N.L.	C	87	210	17	53	8	1	0	15	0	.252
2001	Florida	N.L.	C	48	141	19	44	4	0	4	14	0	.312
2002	Florida	N.L.	C-1B	89	256	19	78	15	0	2	28	0	.305
2003	Florida	N.L.	C-1B-3B	59	125	12	30	7	1	0	11	0	.240
2004	Florida b	N.L.	C	81	246	19	63	15	0	2	25	1	.256
2005	Minnesota	A.L.	C	45	148	17	46	9	0	1	26	0	.311
2006	Minnesota	A.L.	C	47	179	20	61	13	0	0	23	0	.341
2007	Minnesota	A.L.	C	82	272	23	80	13	0	1	38	0	.294
Major League Totals		10 Yrs.		659	1937	178	567	102	2	13	219	1	.293
Championship Series													
2003	Florida	N.L.	C	1	0	1	0	0	0	0	0	0	.000
World Series Record													
2003	Florida	N.L.	C	1	1	0	0	0	0	0	0	0	.000

a On disabled list from August 24 to September 8, 1998.
b Filed for free agency, November 2, 2004. Signed with Minnesota Twins, November 24, 2004.

RENTERIA, EDGAR ENRIQUE

Born, Barranquilla, Colombia, August 7, 1976.
Bats Right. Throws Right. Height, 6 feet, 1 inch. Weight, 200 pounds.

Year	Club	Lea	Pos	G	AB	R	H	2B	3B	HR	RBI	SB	Avg
1992	Marlins	Gulf Coast	SS	43	163	25	47	8	1	0	9	10	.288
1993	Kane County	Midwest	SS	116	384	40	78	8	0	1	35	7	.203
1994	Brevard Cty	Fla. St.	SS	128	439	46	111	15	1	0	36	6	.253
1995	Portland	Eastern	SS	135	508	70	147	15	7	5	68	30	.289
1996	Charlotte	Int.	SS	35	132	17	37	8	0	2	16	10	.280
1996	Florida a	N.L.	SS	106	431	68	133	18	3	5	31	16	.309
1997	Florida	N.L.	SS	154	617	90	171	21	3	4	52	32	.277
1998	Florida b-c	N.L.	SS	133	517	79	146	18	2	3	31	41	.282
1999	St. Louis	N.L.	SS	154	585	92	161	36	2	11	63	37	.275
2000	St. Louis	N.L.	SS	150	562	94	156	32	1	16	76	21	.278
2001	St. Louis	N.L.	SS-1B	141	493	54	128	19	3	10	57	17	.260
2002	St. Louis	N.L.	SS	152	544	77	166	36	2	11	83	22	.305
2003	St. Louis	N.L.	SS	157	587	96	194	47	1	13	100	34	.330
2004	St. Louis d	N.L.	SS	149	586	84	168	37	0	10	72	17	.287
2005	Boston e	A.L.	SS	153	623	100	172	36	4	8	70	9	.276
2006	Atlanta	N.L.	SS	149	598	100	175	40	2	14	70	17	.293
2007	Atlanta f-g	N.L.	SS	124	494	87	164	30	1	12	57	11	.332
Major League Totals		12 Yrs.		1722	6637	1021	1934	370	24	117	762	274	.291
Division Series													
1997	Florida	N.L.	SS	3	13	1	2	0	0	0	1	0	.154
2000	St. Louis	N.L.	SS	3	10	5	2	0	0	0	0	2	.200
2001	St. Louis	N.L.	SS	5	17	2	4	1	0	1	1	0	.235
2002	St. Louis	N.L.	SS	3	12	3	3	0	0	0	0	2	.250
2004	St. Louis	N.L.	SS	4	11	4	5	2	0	0	4	1	.455
2005	Boston	A.L.	SS	3	13	1	3	2	0	0	0	0	.231
Division Series Totals				21	76	16	19	5	0	1	6	5	.250
Championship Series													
1997	Florida	N.L.	SS	6	22	4	5	1	0	0	0	1	.227
2000	St. Louis	N.L.	SS	5	20	4	6	1	0	0	4	3	.300
2002	St. Louis	N.L.	SS	5	19	0	3	0	0	0	1	0	.158
2004	St. Louis	N.L.	SS	7	24	1	4	0	0	0	2	0	.167
Championship Series Totals				23	85	9	18	2	0	0	7	4	.212

Year	Club	Lea	Pos	G	AB	R	H	2B	3B	HR	RBI	SB	Avg
	World Series Record												
1997 Florida	....	N.L.	SS	7	31	3	9	2	0	0	3	0	.290
2004 St. Louis	....	N.L.	SS	4	15	2	5	3	0	0	1	0	.333
World Series Totals	....			11	46	5	14	5	0	0	4	0	.304

a On disabled list from June 24 to July 11, 1996
b On disabled list from August 25 to September 9, 1998.
c Traded to St. Louis Cardinals for infielder Pablo Ozuna, pitcher Armando Almanza and pitcher Braden Looper, December 14, 1998.
d Filed for free agency, October 29, 2004. Signed with Boston Red Sox, December 17, 2004.
e Traded to Atlanta Braves with cash for infielder Andy Marte, December 7, 2005.
f On disabled list from August 3 to August 22 and from August 23 to September 7, 2007.
g Traded to Detroit Tigers for pitcher Jair Jurrjens and outfielder Gorkys Hernandez, October 29, 2007.

REYES, JOSE BERNABE

Born, Villa Gonzalez, Dominican Republic, June 11, 1983.
Bats Both. Throws Right. Height, 6 feet. Weight, 175 pounds.

Year	Club	Lea	Pos	G	AB	R	H	2B	3B	HR	RBI	SB	Avg
2000 Kingsport	....	Appal.	SS-3B-2B-OF	49	132	22	33	3	3	0	8	10	.250
2001 Columbia	....	So.Atl.	SS	108	407	71	125	22	15	5	48	30	.307
2002 Binghamton	....	Eastern	SS	65	275	46	79	16	8	2	24	27	.287
2002 St. Lucie	......	Fla.St.	SS	69	288	58	83	10	11	6	38	31	.288
2003 Norfolk	....	Int.	SS	42	160	28	43	6	4	0	13	26	.269
2003 New York a	....	N.L.	SS	69	274	47	84	12	4	5	32	13	.307
2004 St. Lucie	....	Fla.St.	2B	6	23	3	6	2	0	0	1	2	.261
2004 Binghamton	....	Eastern	2B	4	18	2	2	0	0	0	3	3	.111
2004 New York b	....	N.L.	2B-SS	53	220	33	56	16	2	2	14	19	.255
2005 New York	....	N.L.	SS	161	*696	99	190	24	*17	7	58	*60	.273
2006 New York	....	N.L.	SS	153	647	*122	194	30	17	19	81	*64	.300
2007 New York	....	N.L.	SS	160	681	119	191	36	12	12	57	*78	.280
Major League Totals	....		5 Yrs.	596	2518	420	715	118	52	45	242	234	.284
	Division Series												
2006 New York	....	N.L.	SS	3	12	2	2	0	0	0	3	1	.167
	Championship Series												
2006 New York	....	N.L.	SS	7	32	5	9	1	1	1	2	2	.281

a On disabled list from September 1 to November 6, 2003.
b On disabled list from March 26 to June 19 and August 12 to September 24, 2004.

REYNOLDS, MARK ANDREW

Born, Pikeville, Kentucky, August 3, 1983.
Bats Right. Throws Right. Height, 6 feet, 1 inch. Weight, 200 pounds.

Year	Club	Lea	Pos	G	AB	R	H	2B	3B	HR	RBI	SB	Avg
2004 Lancaster	....	Calif.	3B-SS	4	12	1	1	0	0	0	1	0	.083
2004 South Bend	...	Midwest	3B	4	15	0	1	1	0	0	0	0	.067
2004 Yakima	......	Northwest	SS-3B-2B	64	234	58	64	19	1	12	41	5	.274
2005 South Bend	...	Midwest	SS-3B	118	434	65	110	26	4	19	76	4	.253
2006 Lancaster	....	Calif.	SS-3B-2B-1B	76	273	64	92	18	2	23	77	1	.337
2006 Tennessee	....	Southern	OF-3B-2B	30	114	23	31	7	0	8	21	0	.272
2007 Mobile	......	Southern	3B-2B	37	134	28	41	9	2	6	22	2	.306
2007 Arizona	....	N.L.	3B-2B-OF	111	366	62	102	20	4	17	62	0	.279
	Division Series												
2007 Arizona	....	N.L.	3B	3	10	2	2	0	0	1	1	0	.200
	Championship Series												
2007 Arizona	....	N.L.	3B	4	16	1	2	0	0	1	1	0	.125

RICHAR, DANNY ADAM

Born, Laromana, Dominican Republic, June 9, 1983.
Bats Left. Throws Right. Height, 6 feet. Weight, 170 pounds.

Year	Club	Lea	Pos	G	AB	R	H	2B	3B	HR	RBI	SB	Avg
2002 Lancaster	....	Calif.	SS	85	251	27	58	7	1	1	17	4	.231
2002 Yakima	......	Northwest	SS-2B	25	88	7	20	5	1	0	9	0	.227
2003 Lancaster	....	Calif.	2B-SS	123	405	51	123	19	9	1	42	6	.304
2004 Lancaster	....	Calif.	SS	96	383	51	108	13	4	6	44	22	.282
2004 El Paso	....	Texas	2B	26	82	6	17	3	0	0	5	2	.207
2005 Lancaster	....	Calif.	SS-2B-3B-OF	121	454	78	136	32	8	20	79	9	.300
2006 Tennessee	....	Southern	2B	130	480	79	140	25	5	8	42	15	.292
2007 Tucson	....	P.C.	2B-SS	166	267	40	76	20	4	8	46	4	.285
2007 Charlotte	....	Int.	2B-SS	32	133	21	46	5	4	5	15	4	.346
2007 Chicago a	....	A.L.	2B	56	187	30	43	9	3	6	15	1	.230

a Traded to Chicago White Sox by Arizona Diamondbacks for outfielder Aaron Cunningham, June 16, 2007.

RIOS, ALEXIS ISRAEL

Born, Coffee County, Alabama, February 18, 1981.
Bats Right. Throws Right. Height, 6 feet, 5 inches. Weight, 195 pounds.

Year	Club	Lea	Pos	G	AB	R	H	2B	3B	HR	RBI	SB	Avg
1999 Medicine Hat	Pioneer	OF	67	234	35	63	7	3	0	13	8	.269
2000 Hagerstown	So.Atl.	DH	22	74	5	17	3	1	0	5	2	.230
2000 Queens	N.Y.-Penn.	OF	50	206	22	55	9	2	1	25	5	.267
2001 Charleston-W.V.	So.Atl.	OF	130	480	40	126	20	9	2	58	22	.262
2002 Dunedin	Fla.St.	OF	111	456	60	139	22	8	3	61	14	.305
2003 New Haven	Eastern	OF	127	514	86	181	32	11	11	82	11	.352
2004 Syracuse	Int.	OF	46	185	14	48	10	1	3	23	2	.259
2004 Toronto	A.L.	OF	111	426	55	122	24	7	1	28	15	.286
2005 Toronto	A.L.	OF	146	481	71	126	23	6	10	59	14	.262
2006 Syracuse	Int.	OF	3	10	0	3	1	0	0	1	0	.300
2006 Toronto a	A.L.	OF	128	450	68	136	33	6	17	82	15	.302
2007 Toronto	A.L.	OF	161	643	114	191	43	7	24	85	17	.297
Major League Totals		4 Yrs.	546	2000	308	575	123	26	52	254	61	.287

a On disabled list from June 28 to July 28, 2006.

RIVERA, JUAN LUIS

Born, Guarenas, Venezuela, July 3, 1978.
Bats Right. Throws Right. Height, 6 feet, 2 inches. Weight, 225 pounds.

Year	Club	Lea	Pos	G	AB	R	H	2B	3B	HR	RBI	SB	Avg
1996 NY Yankees	Dominican	OF	10	18	0	3	0	0	0	2	0	.167
1997 Maracay-2	Venzuelan	OF	52	142	25	40	9	0	0	14	12	.282
1998 Yankees	Gulf Coast	OF	57	210	43	70	9	1	12	45	8	.333
1998 Oneonta	N.Y.-Penn.	OF	6	18	2	5	0	0	1	3	1	.278
1999 Tampa	Fla.St.	OF	109	427	50	112	20	2	14	77	5	.262
1999 Yankees	Gulf Coast	OF	5	18	7	6	0	0	1	4	0	.333
2000 Norwich	Eastern	OF	17	62	9	14	5	0	2	12	0	.226
2000 Tampa	Fla.St.	OF-1B	115	409	62	113	26	1	14	69	11	.276
2001 Norwich	Eastern	OF	77	316	50	101	18	3	14	58	5	.320
2001 Columbus	Int.	OF	55	199	39	65	11	1	14	40	4	.327
2001 New York	A.L.	OF	3	4	0	0	0	0	0	0	0	.000
2002 Columbus	Int.	OF	65	265	40	86	21	1	8	47	5	.325
2002 New York a	A.L.	OF	28	83	9	22	5	0	1	6	1	.265
2003 Columbus	Int.	OF	79	308	47	100	21	0	7	37	1	.325
2003 New York b	A.L.	OF	57	173	22	46	14	0	7	26	0	.266
2004 Montreal c	N.L.	OF	134	391	48	120	24	1	12	49	6	.307
2005 Los Angeles	A.L.	OF	106	350	46	95	17	1	15	59	1	.271
2006 Salt Lake	P.C.	OF	2	9	3	5	3	0	1	6	0	.556
2006 Los Angeles d	A.L.	OF	124	448	65	139	27	0	23	85	0	.310
2007 Rancho Cucamonga	Calif.	OF	3	10	3	4	1	0	0	2	0	.400
2007 Salt Lake	P.C.	OF	15	61	4	16	8	0	0	17	0	.262
2007 Los Angeles e	A.L.	OF	14	43	3	12	1	0	2	8	0	.279
Major League Totals		7 Yrs.	466	1492	193	434	88	2	60	233	8	.291
Division Series													
2002 New York	A.L.	OF	4	12	2	3	0	0	0	3	0	.250
2003 New York	A.L.	OF	4	12	2	4	0	0	0	0	0	.333
2005 Los Angeles	A.L.	DH	5	17	3	6	1	0	1	1	0	.353
2007 Los Angeles	A.L.	DH	2	3	0	1	0	0	0	0	0	.333
Division Series Totals			15	44	7	14	1	0	1	4	0	.318
Championship Series													
2003 New York	A.L.	OF	2	2	0	0	0	0	0	0	0	.000
2005 Los Angeles	A.L.	OF-DH	3	9	1	1	1	0	0	0	0	.111
Championship Series Totals			5	11	1	1	1	0	0	0	0	.091
World Series Record													
2003 New York	A.L.	OF	4	6	0	1	1	0	0	1	0	.167

a On disabled list from June 8 to August 19, 2002.
b Traded to Montreal Expos with infielder Nick Johnson and pitcher Randy Choate for pitcher Javier Vazquez, December 4, 2003.
c Traded to Anaheim Angels with infielder Maicer Izturis for outfielder Jose Guillen, November 19, 2004.
d On disabled list from April 17 to May 8, 2006.
e On disabled list from March 23 to September 2, 2007.

ROBERTS, BRIAN MICHAEL
Born, Durham, North Carolina, October 9, 1977.
Bats Both. Throws Right. Height, 5 feet, 9 inches. Weight, 175 pounds.

Year	Club	Lea	Pos	G	AB	R	H	2B	3B	HR	RBI	SB	Avg
1999	Delmarva a	So.Atl.	SS	47	167	22	40	12	1	0	21	17	.240
2000	Frederick	Carolina	SS	48	163	27	49	6	3	0	16	13	.301
2000	Orioles b	Gulf Coast	SS	9	29	8	9	1	2	1	3	7	.310
2001	Bowie	Eastern	2B-SS	22	81	12	24	7	0	1	7	10	.296
2001	Rochester	Int.	SS	44	161	16	43	4	1	1	12	23	.267
2001	Baltimore	A.L.	SS-2B	75	273	42	69	12	3	2	17	12	.253
2002	Rochester	Int.	2B	78	313	49	86	9	7	3	30	22	.275
2002	Baltimore	A.L.	2B	38	128	18	29	6	0	1	11	9	.227
2003	Ottawa	Int.	2B-SS	44	178	36	56	13	1	0	15	19	.315
2003	Baltimore	A.L.	2B-SS	112	460	65	124	22	4	5	41	23	.270
2004	Baltimore	A.L.	2B	159	641	107	175	*50	2	4	53	29	.273
2005	Baltimore	A.L.	2B	143	561	92	176	45	7	18	73	27	.314
2006	Bowie	Eastern	2B	2	5	0	1	0	0	0	0	0	.200
2006	Baltimore c	A.L.	2B	138	563	85	161	34	3	10	55	36	.286
2007	Baltimore	A.L.	2B	156	621	103	180	42	5	12	57	*50	.290
Major League Totals			7 Yrs.	821	3247	512	914	211	24	52	307	186	.281

a Drafted by Baltimore Orioles with choice received for Texas Rangers signing infielder Rafael Palmeiro, June 2, 1999.
b On disabled list from April 19 to July 13, 2000.
c On disabled list from April 30 to May 24, 2006.

ROBERTS, DAVID RAY (DAVE)
Born, Okinawa, Japan, May 31, 1972.
Bats Left. Throws Left. Height, 5 feet, 10 inches. Weight, 180 pounds.

Year	Club	Lea	Pos	G	AB	R	H	2B	3B	HR	RBI	SB	Avg
1994	Jamestown	N.Y.-Penn.	DH-OF	54	178	33	52	7	2	0	12	12	.292
1995	Lakeland	Fla.St.	DH-OF	92	357	67	108	10	5	3	30	30	.303
1996	Visalia	California	OF	126	482	112	131	24	7	5	37	65	.272
1996	Jacksnville a	Southern	OF	3	9	0	2	0	0	0	0	0	.222
1997	Jacksnville	Southern	DH-OF	105	415	76	123	24	2	4	41	23	.296
1998	Jacksnville	Southern	OF	69	279	71	91	14	5	5	42	21	.326
1998	Buffalo	Int.	OF	5	15	2	2	0	0	0	2	2	.133
1998	Akron b-c	Eastern	OF	56	227	49	82	10	5	7	33	28	.361
1999	Buffalo	Int.	OF	89	350	65	95	17	10	0	38	39	.271
1999	Cleveland	A.L.	OF	41	143	26	34	4	0	2	12	11	.238
2000	Buffalo	Int.	OF	120	462	93	135	16	3	13	55	39	.292
2000	Cleveland	A.L.	OF	10	10	1	2	0	0	0	0	1	.200
2001	Akron	Eastern	OF	17	64	9	13	5	0	0	2	4	.203
2001	Buffalo	Int.	OF	62	241	34	73	12	4	0	22	17	.303
2001	Cleveland d-e	A.L.	OF	15	12	3	4	1	0	0	2	0	.333
2002	Los Angeles	N.L.	OF	127	422	63	117	14	7	3	34	45	.277
2003	Ogden	Pioneer	OF	3	10	4	4	0	0	0	0	1	.400
2003	Las Vegas	P.C.	OF	2	5	2	0	0	0	0	0	0	.000
2003	Los Angeles f	N.L.	OF	107	388	56	97	6	5	2	16	40	.250
2004	Vero Beach	Fla.St.	OF	2	8	0	0	0	0	0	0	0	.000
2004	Los Angeles	N.L.	OF	68	233	45	59	4	7	2	21	33	.253
2004	Boston g-h-i	A.L.	OF	45	86	19	22	10	0	2	14	5	.256
2005	Lake Elsinore	California	OF	3	10	2	2	1	0	0	0	0	.200
2005	San Diego j	N.L.	OF	115	411	65	113	19	10	8	38	23	.275
2006	Lake Elsinore	Calif.	OF	1	3	0	1	0	0	0	0	0	.333
2006	San Diego k-l	N.L.	OF	129	499	80	146	18	13	2	44	49	.293
2007	Fresno	P.C.	OF	2	7	1	1	0	0	0	0	0	.143
2007	San Francisco m	N.L.	OF	114	396	61	103	17	9	2	23	31	.260
Major League Totals			9 Yrs.	780	2600	419	697	93	51	23	204	238	.268

Division Series

1999	Cleveland	A.L.	OF	2	3	0	0	0	0	0	0	0	.000
2004	Boston	A.L.	PH	1	0	0	0	0	0	0	0	0	.000
2005	San Diego	N.L.	OF	3	9	1	2	0	0	1	1	0	.222
2006	San Diego	N.L.	OF	4	16	1	7	0	1	0	0	1	.438
Division Series Totals				10	28	2	9	0	1	1	1	1	.321

Championship Series

2004	Boston	A.L.	PH	2	0	2	0	0	0	0	0	1	.000

a Loaned by Detroit Tigers to Oakland A's organization from March 30 to August 30, 1996.
b Traded by Detroit Tigers to Cleveland Indians with pitcher Tim Worrell for outfielder Geronimo Berroa, June 22, 1998.

c On disabled list from August 10 to 18, 1998.
d On disabled list from March 21 to June 24, 2001.
e Traded to Los Angeles Dodgers for pitcher Christian Bridenbaugh and pitcher Nial Hughes, December 21, 2001.
f On disabled list from May 17 to June 1 and July 2 to July 26, 2003.
g On disabled list from May 5 to May 28, 2004.
h Traded to Boston Red Sox for outfielder Henri Stanley, July 31, 2004.
i Traded to San Diego Padres for outfielder Jay Payton, infielder Ramon Vazquez, pitcher David Pauley and cash, December 20, 2004.
j On disabled list from March 30 to April 18, 2005.
k On disabled list from June 18 to July 5, 2006.
l Filed for free agency, October 28, 2006. Signed with San Francisco Giants, December 1, 2006.
m On disabled list from May 10 to June 9, 2007.

RODRIGUEZ, ALEXANDER EMMANUEL (ALEX)

Born, New York, New York, July 27, 1975.
Bats Right. Throws Right. Height, 6 feet, 3 inches. Weight, 225 pounds.

Year	Club	Lea	Pos	G	AB	R	H	2B	3B	HR	RBI	SB	Avg
1994	Appleton	Midwest	SS	65	248	49	79	17	6	14	55	16	.319
1994	Jacksonville	Southern	SS	17	59	7	17	4	1	1	8	2	.288
1994	Seattle	A.L.	SS	17	54	4	11	0	0	0	2	3	.204
1994	Calgary	P.C.	SS	32	119	22	37	7	4	6	21	2	.311
1995	Tacoma	P.C.	SS	54	214	37	77	12	3	15	45	2	.360
1995	Seattle	A.L.	SS	48	142	15	33	6	2	5	19	4	.232
1996	Tacoma a	P.C.	SS	2	5	0	1	0	0	0	0	0	.200
1996	Seattle	A.L.	SS	146	601	*141	215	*54	1	36	123	15	*.358
1997	Seattle b	A.L.	SS	141	587	100	176	40	3	23	84	29	.300
1998	Seattle	A.L.	SS	161	*686	123	*213	35	5	42	124	46	.310
1999	Seattle c	A.L.	SS	129	502	110	143	25	0	42	111	21	.285
2000	Seattle d-e	A.L.	SS	148	554	134	175	34	2	41	132	15	.316
2001	Texas	A.L.	SS	*162	632	*133	201	34	1	*52	135	18	.318
2002	Texas	A.L.	SS	*162	624	125	187	27	2	*57	*142	9	.300
2003	Texas	A.L.	SS	161	607	*124	181	30	6	*47	118	17	.298
2004	New York f-g	A.L.	3B-SS	155	601	112	172	24	2	36	106	28	.286
2005	New York h	A.L.	3B-SS	*162	605	*124	194	29	1	*48	130	21	.321
2006	New York	A.L.	3B	154	572	113	166	26	1	35	121	15	.290
2007	New York i	A.L.	3B	158	583	*143	183	31	0	*54	*156	24	.314
Major League Totals		14 Yrs.		1904	7350	1501	2250	395	26	518	1503	265	.306
Division Series													
1995	Seattle	A.L.	SS	1	1	1	0	0	0	0	0	0	.000
1997	Seattle	A.L.	SS	4	16	1	5	1	0	1	1	0	.313
2000	Seattle	A.L.	SS	3	13	0	4	0	0	0	2	0	.308
2004	New York	A.L.	3B	4	19	3	8	3	0	1	3	2	.421
2005	New York	A.L.	3B	5	15	2	2	1	0	0	0	1	.133
2006	New York	A.L.	3B	4	14	0	1	0	0	0	0	0	.071
2007	New York	A.L.	3B	4	15	2	4	0	0	1	1	0	.267
Division Series Totals				25	93	9	24	5	0	3	7	3	.258
Championship Series													
1995	Seattle	A.L.	PH	1	1	0	0	0	0	0	0	0	.000
2000	Seattle	A.L.	SS	6	22	4	9	2	0	2	5	1	.409
2004	New York	A.L.	3B	7	31	8	8	2	0	2	5	0	.258
Championship Series Totals				14	54	12	17	4	0	4	10	1	.315

a On disabled list from April 22 to May 7, 1996.
b On disabled list from June 12 to June 27, 1997.
c On disabled list from April 7 to May 14, 1999.
d On disabled list from July 8 to July 23, 2000.
e Filed for free agency, October 30, 2000. Signed with Texas Rangers, December 11, 2000.
f Traded to New York Yankees for infielder Alfonso Soriano and player to be named later, February 16, 2004.
g Texas Rangers received infielder Joaquin Arias to complete trade, March 23, 2004.
h Selected Most Valuable Player in American League for 2005.
j Filed for free agency, October 29, 2007, re-signed with New York Yankees, December 13, 2007.

RODRIGUEZ (TORRES), IVAN

Born, Manati, Puerto Rico, November 27, 1971.
Bats Right. Throws Right. Height, 5 feet, 9 inches. Weight, 195 pounds.

Year	Club	Lea	Pos	G	AB	R	H	2B	3B	HR	RBI	SB	Avg
1989	Gastonia	So. Atl.	C	112	386	38	92	22	1	7	42	2	.238
1990	Charlotte	Fla. St.	C	109	408	48	117	17	7	2	55	1	.287

Year	Club	Lea	Pos	G	AB	R	H	2B	3B	HR	RBI	SB	Avg
1991 Tulsa	Texas	C	50	175	16	48	7	2	3	28	1	.274
1991 Texas	A.L.	C	88	280	24	74	16	0	3	27	0	.264
1992 Texas a............	A.L.	C	123	420	39	109	16	1	8	37	0	.260
1993 Texas	A.L.	C	137	473	56	129	28	4	10	66	8	.273
1994 Texas	A.L.	C	99	363	56	108	19	1	16	57	6	.298
1995 Texas	A.L.	C	130	492	56	149	32	2	12	67	0	.303
1996 Texas	A.L.	C	153	639	116	192	47	3	19	86	5	.300
1997 Texas	A.L.	C	150	597	98	187	34	4	20	77	7	.313
1998 Texas	A.L.	C	145	579	88	186	40	4	21	91	9	.321
1999 Texas b.............	A.L.	C	144	600	116	199	29	1	35	113	25	.332
2000 Texas c.............	A.L.	C	91	363	66	126	27	4	27	83	5	.347
2001 Texas d.............	A.L.	C	111	442	70	136	24	2	25	65	10	.308
2002 Charlotte	Fla.St.	C	3	9	1	3	0	0	0	0	0	.333
2002 Texas e-f..........	A.L.	C	108	408	67	128	32	2	19	60	5	.314
2003 Florida g..........	N.L.	C	144	511	90	152	36	3	16	85	10	.297
2004 Detroit	A.L.	C	135	527	72	176	32	2	19	86	7	.334
2005 Detroit	A.L.	C	129	504	71	139	33	5	14	50	7	.276
2006 Detroit	A.L.	C-1B-2B	136	547	74	164	28	4	13	69	8	.300
2007 Detroit	A.L.	C	129	502	50	141	31	3	11	63	2	.281
Major League Totals		17 Yrs.	2152	8247	1209	2495	504	45	288	1182	114	.303

Division Series

Year	Club	Lea	Pos	G	AB	R	H	2B	3B	HR	RBI	SB	Avg
1996 Texas	A.L.	C	4	16	1	6	1	0	0	2	0	.375
1998 Texas	A.L.	C	3	10	0	1	0	0	0	1	0	.100
1999 Texas	A.L.	C	3	12	0	3	1	0	0	0	1	.250
2003 Florida	N.L.	C	4	17	3	6	1	0	1	6	0	.353
2006 Detroit	A.L.	C	4	13	3	3	1	0	0	3	0	.231
Division Series Totals			18	68	7	19	4	0	1	12	1	.279

Championship Series

Year	Club	Lea	Pos	G	AB	R	H	2B	3B	HR	RBI	SB	Avg
2003 Florida	N.L.	C	7	28	5	9	2	0	2	10	0	.321
2006 Detroit	A.L.	C	4	16	2	2	0	0	1	1	0	.125
Championship Series Totals			11	44	7	11	2	0	3	11	0	.250

World Series Record

Year	Club	Lea	Pos	G	AB	R	H	2B	3B	HR	RBI	SB	Avg
2003 Florida	N.L.	C	6	22	2	6	2	0	0	1	0	.273
2006 Detroit	A.L.	C	5	19	1	3	1	0	0	1	0	.158
World Series Totals............			11	41	3	9	3	0	0	2	0	.220

a On disabled list from June 6 to June 27, 1992.
b Selected Most Valuable Player in American League for 1999.
c On disabled list from July 25 to October 1, 2000.
d On disabled list from May 2 to May 17 and August 31 to November 19, 2001.
e On disabled list from April 17 to June 7, 2002.
f Filed for free agency, October 20, 2002. Signed with Florida Marlins, January 24, 2003
g Filed for free agency, November 2, 2003. Signed with Detroit Tigers, February 2, 2004.

RODRIGUEZ, LUIS ORLANDO
Born, San Carlos, Venezuela, June 27, 1980.
Bats Both. Throws Right. Height, 5 feet, 9 inches. Weight, 180 pounds.

Year	Club	Lea	Pos	G	AB	R	H	2B	3B	HR	RBI	SB	Avg
1997 Maracay-1 ...	Venzuelan		2B	51	107	21	33	6	1	0	12	5	.308
1998 Twins	Gulf Coast	2B-SS-3B	52	180	33	50	11	1	1	15	14	.278
1999 Quad Cities....	Midwest	2B-3B	119	434	63	117	20	0	3	50	8	.270
2000 Quad Cities....	Midwest	2B-SS-3B	106	342	35	77	11	2	0	28	4	.225
2001 Fort Myers	Fla.St.	SS-2B-3B	125	463	71	127	21	3	4	64	11	.274
2002 New Britain	Eastern	SS-2B	129	455	60	117	18	2	8	40	3	.257
2003 Rochester.......	Int.	2B-SS	131	518	65	153	35	2	1	44	6	.295
2004 Rochester........	Int.	2B-3B-SS	127	486	73	139	33	1	5	52	3	.286
2005 Rochester........	Int.	2B-3B-SS	40	138	19	42	10	0	1	17	0	.304
2005 Minnesota .......A.L.		2B-3B-SS	79	175	21	47	10	2	2	20	2	.269
2006 Minnesota a.......A.L.		3B-2B-SS-1B	59	115	11	27	4	0	2	6	0	.235
2007 Rochester........	Int.	SS	6	19	3	8	1	0	0	1	0	.421
2007 Minnesota b.......A.L.		3B-2B-1B	68	155	18	34	5	1	2	12	1	.219
Major League Totals		3 Yrs.	206	445	50	108	19	3	6	38	3	.243

a Not offered contract, December 12, 2006, re-signed with Minnesota Twins organization, December 13, 2006.
b Claimed on waivers by San Diego Padres, October 4, 2007.

ROLEN, SCOTT BRUCE
Born, Evansville, Indiana, April 4, 1975.
Bats Right. Throws Right. Height, 6 feet, 4 inches. Weight, 240 pounds.

Year	Club	Lea	Pos	G	AB	R	H	2B	3B	HR	RBI	SB	Avg
1993	Martinsville	Appal.	3B	25	80	8	25	5	0	0	12	3	.313
1994	Spartanburg	So.Atl.	3B	138	513	83	151	34	5	14	72	6	.294
1995	Clearwater	Fla.St.	3B	66	238	45	69	13	2	10	39	4	.290
1995	Reading	Eastern	3B	20	76	16	22	3	0	3	15	1	.289
1996	Reading	Eastern	3B	61	230	44	83	22	2	9	42	8	.361
1996	Scranton-WB	Int.	3B	45	168	23	46	17	0	2	19	4	.274
1996	Philadelphia	N.L.	3B	37	130	10	33	7	0	4	18	0	.254
1997	Philadelphia a	N.L.	3B	156	561	93	159	35	3	21	92	16	.283
1998	Philadelphia	N.L.	3B	160	601	120	174	45	4	31	110	14	.290
1999	Philadelphia	N.L.	3B	112	421	74	113	28	1	26	77	12	.268
2000	Philadelphia b	N.L.	3B	128	483	88	144	32	6	26	89	8	.298
2001	Philadelphia	N.L.	3B	151	554	96	160	39	1	25	107	16	.289
2002	Philadelphia-St. Louis c	N.L.	3B	155	580	89	154	29	8	31	110	8	.266
2003	St. Louis	N.L.	3B	154	559	98	160	49	1	28	104	13	.286
2004	St. Louis	N.L.	3B	142	500	109	157	32	4	34	124	4	.314
2005	St. Louis d	N.L.	3B	56	196	28	46	12	1	5	28	1	.235
2006	St. Louis	N.L.	3B	142	521	94	154	48	1	22	95	7	.296
2007	St. Louis e-f	N.L.	3B	112	392	55	104	24	2	8	58	5	.265
Major League Totals		12 Yrs.	1505	5498	954	1558	380	32	261	1012	104	.283
Division Series													
2002	St. Louis	N.L.	3B	2	7	1	3	0	0	1	2	0	.429
2004	St. Louis	N.L.	3B	4	12	1	0	0	0	0	0	0	.000
2006	St. Louis	N.L.	3B	3	11	0	1	1	0	0	0	0	.091
Division Series Totals			9	30	2	4	1	0	1	2	0	.133
Championship Series													
2004	St. Louis	N.L.	3B	7	29	6	9	2	0	3	6	0	.310
2006	St. Louis	N.L.	3B	7	21	4	5	1	0	0	0	0	.238
Championship Series Totals			14	50	10	14	3	0	3	6	0	.280
World Series Record													
2004	St. Louis	N.L.	3B	4	15	0	0	0	0	0	1	0	.000
2006	St. Louis	N.L.	3B	5	19	5	8	3	0	1	2	0	.421
World Series Totals			9	34	5	8	3	0	1	3	0	.235

a Selected Rookie of the Year in National League for 1997.
b On disabled list from May 24 to June 8, 2000.
c Traded to St. Louis Cardinals with pitcher Doug Nickle for infielder Placido Polanco, pitcher Bud Smith and pitcher Mike Timlin, July 29, 2002.
d On disabled list from May 11 to June 18 and July 22 to October 31, 2005.
e On disabled list from August 29 to November 2, 2007.
f Traded to Toronto Blue Jays for infielder Troy Glaus, January 14, 2008.

ROLLINS, JAMES CALVIN (JIMMY)
Born, Oakland, California, November 27, 1978.
Bats Both. Throws Right. Height, 5 feet, 8 inches. Weight, 170 pounds.

Year	Club	Lea	Pos	G	AB	R	H	2B	3B	HR	RBI	SB	Avg
1996	Martinsvlle	Appal.	SS	49	172	22	41	3	1	1	16	11	.238
1997	Piedmont	So.Atl.	SS	139	560	94	151	22	8	6	59	46	.270
1998	Clearwater	Fla.St.	SS	119	495	72	121	18	9	6	35	23	.244
1999	Reading	Eastern	SS	133	532	81	145	21	8	11	56	24	.273
1999	Scranton-WB	Int.	SS	4	13	0	1	1	0	0	0	1	.077
2000	Scranton-WB	Int.	SS	133	470	67	129	28	11	12	69	24	.274
2000	Philadelphia	N.L.	SS	14	53	5	17	1	1	0	5	3	.321
2001	Philadelphia	N.L.	SS	158	*656	97	180	29	*12	14	54	*46	.274
2002	Philadelphia	N.L.	SS-2B	154	*637	82	156	33	*10	11	60	31	.245
2003	Philadelphia	N.L.	SS	156	628	85	165	42	6	8	62	20	.263
2004	Philadelphia	N.L.	SS	154	657	119	190	43	*12	14	73	30	.289
2005	Philadelphia	N.L.	SS	158	677	115	196	38	11	12	54	41	.290
2006	Philadelphia	N.L.	SS	158	689	127	191	45	9	25	83	36	.277
2007	Philadelphia a	N.L.	SS	*162	*716	*139	212	38	*20	30	94	41	.296
Major League Totals		8 Yrs.	1114	4713	769	1307	269	81	114	485	248	.277
Division Series													
2007	Philadelphia	N.L.	SS	3	11	1	2	0	1	1	4	1	.182

a Selected Most Valuable Player in National League for 2007.

ROSS, CODY JOSEPH

Born, Portales, New Mexico, December 23, 1980.
Bats Right. Throws Left. Height, 5 feet, 9 inches. Weight, 205 pounds.

Year	Club	Lea	Pos	G	AB	R	H	2B	3B	HR	RBI	SB	Avg
1999 Tigers	Gulf Coast	OF	42	142	19	31	8	3	4	18	3	.218
2000 West Michigan	Midwest	OF	122	434	71	116	17	9	7	68	11	.267
2001 Lakeland	Fla.St.	OF	127	482	84	133	34	5	15	80	28	.276
2002 Erie	Eastern	OF	105	400	73	112	28	3	19	72	16	.280
2003 Toledo	Int.	OF	124	470	74	135	35	6	20	61	15	.287
2003 Detroit	A.L.	OF	6	19	1	4	1	0	1	5	0	.211
2004 Las Vegas a	P.C.	OF	60	238	44	65	17	2	14	49	2	.273
2005 Los Angeles	N.L.	OF	14	25	1	4	1	0	0	1	0	.160
2005 Las Vegas	P.C.	OF	115	393	79	105	21	4	22	63	4	.267
2006 L.A.-Cin.-Florida b-c-d-e	N.L.	OF	101	269	34	61	12	2	13	46	1	.227
2007 Jupiter	Fla.St.	OF	7	23	2	6	1	0	2	3	0	.261
2007 Florida f	N.L.	OF	66	173	35	58	19	0	12	39	2	.335
Major League Totals		4 Yrs.	187	486	71	127	33	2	26	91	3	.261

a Traded to Los Angeles Dodgers for pitcher Steve Cuyler and player to be named later, April 1, 2004.
b Traded to Cincinnati Reds for player to be named later, April 24, 2006.
c On disabled list from April 29 to May 23, 2006.
d Traded to Florida Marlins for player to be named later, May 27, 2006.
e Los Angeles Dodgers received pitcher Ben Kozlowski to complete trade, June 1, 2006.
f On disabled list from May 6 to July 19, 2007.

ROSS, DAVID WADE

Born, Bainbridge, Georgia, March 19, 1977.
Bats Right. Throws Right. Height, 6 feet, 2 inches. Weight, 225 pounds.

Year	Club	Lea	Pos	G	AB	R	H	2B	3B	HR	RBI	SB	Avg
1998 Yakima	Northwest	C	59	191	31	59	14	1	6	25	2	.309
1999 Vero Beach	Fla.St.	C-1B-OF	114	375	47	85	19	1	7	39	5	.227
2000 San Bernardino	Calif.	C	51	191	27	49	11	1	7	21	3	.257
2000 San Antonio	Texas	C	24	67	11	14	2	1	3	12	1	.209
2001 Jacksonville	Southern	C	74	246	35	65	13	1	11	45	1	.264
2002 Las Vegas	P.C.	C	92	293	48	87	16	2	15	68	1	.297
2002 Los Angeles	N.L.	C	8	10	2	2	1	0	1	2	0	.200
2003 Las Vegas	P.C.	C	24	86	12	19	4	0	5	16	0	.221
2003 Los Angeles	N.L.	C	40	124	19	32	7	0	10	18	0	.258
2004 Los Angeles	N.L.	C	70	165	13	28	3	1	5	15	0	.170
2005 Indianapolis	Int.	C	6	19	1	4	1	0	0	1	0	.211
2005 Portland	P.C.	C	6	21	3	3	1	0	0	1	0	.143
2005 Pittsburgh-San Diego a-b	N I	C	51	125	11	30	8	1	3	15	0	.240
2006 Chattanooga	Southern	C	2	6	0	2	0	0	0	2	0	.333
2006 Cincinnati c-d	N.L.	C	90	247	37	63	15	1	21	52	0	.255
2007 Louisville	Int.	C	3	9	0	2	1	0	0	0	0	.222
2007 Cincinnati e	N.L.	C	112	311	32	63	10	0	17	39	0	.203
Major League Totals		6 Yrs.	371	982	114	218	44	3	57	141	0	.222
Division Series													
2004 Los Angeles	N.L.	C	2	3	0	0	0	0	0	0	0	.000

a Sold to Pittsburgh Pirates, March 30, 2005.
b Traded to San Diego Padres for infielder J.J. Furmaniak, July 28, 2005.
c Traded to Cincinnati Reds for pitcher Bobby Basham, March 21, 2006.
d On disabled list from July 8 to July 26, 2006.
e On disabled list from August 13 to August 28, 2007.

ROWAND, AARON RYAN

Born, Portland, Oregon, August 29, 1977.
Bats Right. Throws Right. Height, 6 feet. Weight, 200 pounds.

Year	Club	Lea	Pos	G	AB	R	H	2B	3B	HR	RBI	SB	Avg
1998 Hickory a	So.Atl.	OF	60	218	42	75	13	3	5	32	7	.344
1999 Winston-Salem	Carolina	OF	133	512	96	143	37	3	24	88	15	.279
2000 Birmingham	Southern	OF	139	532	80	137	26	5	20	98	22	.258
2001 Charlotte	Int.	OF	82	329	54	97	28	0	16	48	8	.295
2001 Chicago	A.L.	OF	63	123	21	36	5	0	4	20	5	.293
2002 Chicago	A.L.	OF	126	302	41	78	16	2	7	29	0	.258
2003 Charlotte	Int.	OF	32	120	15	29	9	0	3	13	0	.242
2003 Chicago	A.L.	OF	93	157	22	45	8	0	6	24	0	.287
2004 Chicago	A.L.	OF	140	487	94	151	38	2	24	69	17	.310
2005 Chicago b	A.L.	OF	157	578	77	156	30	5	13	69	16	.270

Year	Club	Lea	Pos	G	AB	R	H	2B	3B	HR	RBI	SB	Avg
2006 Philadelphia c		N.L.	OF	109	405	59	106	24	3	12	47	10	.262
2007 Philadelphia d		N.L.	OF	161	612	105	189	45	0	27	89	6	.309
Major League Totals			7 Yrs.	849	2664	419	761	166	12	93	347	54	.286
Division Series													
2005 Chicago		A.L.	OF	3	10	3	4	2	0	0	2	1	.400
2007 Philadelphia		N.L.	OF	3	12	1	1	0	0	1	1	0	.083
Division Series Totals				6	22	4	5	2	0	1	3	1	.227
Championship Series													
2005 Chicago		A.L.	OF	5	18	3	3	3	0	0	1	0	.167
World Series Record													
2005 Chicago		A.L.	OF	4	17	2	5	1	0	0	0	0	.294

a Drafted by Chicago White Sox with choice received for Tampa Bay Devil Rays signing of outfielder Dave Martinez, June 2, 1998.
b Traded to Philadelphia Phillies with pitcher Dan Haigwood and player to be named later for infielder Jim Thome, November 25, 2005. Philadelphia Phillies received pitcher Giovany Gonzalez to complete trade, December 8, 2005.
c On disabled list from May 12 to May 27 and August 22 to October 4, 2006.
d Filed for free agency, October 29, 2007. Signed with San Francisco Giants, December 12, 2007.

RUIZ, CARLOS JOAQUIN

Born, David, Panama, January 22, 1979.
Bats Right. Throws Right. Height, 5 feet, 10 inches. Weight, 200 pounds.

Year	Club	Lea	Pos	G	AB	R	H	2B	3B	HR	RBI	SB	Avg
2000 Phillies	Gulf Coast		C	38	130	11	36	7	1	1	22	3	.277
2001 Lakewood	So.Atl.		C-OF	73	249	21	65	14	3	4	32	5	.261
2002 Clearwater	Fla.St.		C	92	342	35	73	18	3	5	32	3	.213
2003 Reading	Eastern		C-OF	52	169	22	45	6	0	2	16	1	.266
2003 Clearwater	Fla.St.		C	15	54	5	17	0	0	2	9	2	.315
2004 Reading	Eastern		C	101	349	45	99	15	2	17	50	8	.284
2005 Scranton-WB	Int.		C-1B	100	347	50	104	25	9	4	40	4	.300
2006 Scranton-WB	Int.		C	100	368	56	113	25	0	16	69	4	.307
2006 Philadelphia	N.L.		C	27	69	5	18	1	1	3	10	0	.261
2007 Philadelphia	N.L.		C	115	374	42	97	29	2	6	54	6	.259
Major League Totals			2 Yrs.	142	443	47	115	30	3	9	64	6	.260
Division Series													
2007 Philadelphia	N.L.		C	3	9	1	3	1	0	0	0	1	.333

RYAN, BRENDAN WOOD

Born, Los Angeles, California, March 26, 1982.
Bats Right. Throws Right. Height, 6 feet, 2 inches. Weight, 195 pounds.

Year	Club	Lea	Pos	G	AB	R	H	2B	3B	HR	RBI	SB	Avg
2003 New Jersey	N.Y.-Penn.		SS-3B	53	193	20	60	14	4	0	13	11	.311
2004 Peoria	Midwest		SS	105	426	72	137	21	4	2	59	30	.322
2005 Palm Beach	Fla.St.		SS	49	188	29	57	17	0	1	16	8	.303
2005 Springfield	Texas		SS	43	154	28	42	8	1	2	9	6	.273
2006 Palm Beach	Fla.St.		SS	3	14	2	6	1	0	0	1	1	.429
2006 State College	N.Y.-Penn.		SS	8	34	5	8	0	0	0	3	1	.235
2006 Memphis	P.C.		SS	7	26	4	4	0	0	1	6	1	.154
2006 Springfield	Texas		SS	10	43	6	13	1	0	0	3	1	.302
2007 Memphis	P.C.		SS	81	323	55	88	9	5	1	15	17	.272
2007 St. Louis	N.L.		SS-3B-2B	67	180	30	52	9	0	4	12	7	.289

SAENZ (SANCHEZ), OLMEDO

Born, Chitre, Panama, October 8, 1970.
Bats Right. Throws Right. Height, 5 feet, 11 Inches. Weight, 220 pounds.

Year	Club	Lea	Pos	G	AB	R	H	2B	3B	HR	RBI	SB	Avg
1991 Sarasota	Fla.St.		3B	5	19	1	2	0	1	0	2	0	.105
1991 South Bend	Midwest		3B	56	192	23	47	10	1	2	22	5	.245
1992 South Bend	Midwest		3B-1B	132	493	66	121	26	4	7	59	16	.245
1993 South Bend	Midwest		3B	13	50	3	18	4	1	0	7	1	.360
1993 Sarasota	Fla.St.		3B	33	121	13	31	9	4	0	27	3	.256
1993 Birmingham	Southern		3B	49	173	30	60	17	2	6	29	2	.347
1994 Chicago	A.L.		3B	5	14	2	2	0	1	0	0	0	.143
1994 Nashville	A.A.		3B	107	383	48	100	27	2	12	59	3	.261
1995 Nashville	A.A.		3B	111	415	60	126	26	1	13	74	0	.304

Year Club	Lea	Pos	G	AB	R	H	2B	3B	HR	RBI	SB	Avg
1996 Nashville .... A.A.		3B	134	476	86	124	29	1	18	63	4	.261
1997 White Sox ...... Gulf Coast		DH	2	1	0	1	1	0	0	0	0	1.000
1998 Calgary a-b .... P.C.		3B	124	466	89	146	29	0	29	102	3	.313
1999 Oakland .... A.L.		3B-1B	97	255	41	70	18	0	11	41	1	.275
1999 Vancouver c .... P.C.		3B	2	5	1	3	1	0	0	2	0	.600
2000 Oakland .... A.L.		DH-3B-1B	76	214	40	67	12	2	9	33	1	.313
2000 Sacramento d .... P.C.		DH	1	4	1	2	0	0	0	1	0	.500
2001 Oakland .... A.L.		DH-1B-3B	106	305	33	67	21	1	9	32	1	.220
2002 Oakland .... A.L.		1B-3B	68	156	15	43	10	1	6	18	1	.276
2003 Athletics .... Arizona		1B-3B	13	45	13	15	2	0	2	8	1	.333
2003 Modesto e ...... California		DH	1	4	0	0	0	0	0	1	0	.000
2004 Los Angeles .... N.L.		1B-3B	77	111	9	31	1	0	8	22	0	.279
2005 Los Angeles f .... N.L.		1B-3B	109	319	39	84	24	0	15	63	0	.263
2006 Los Angeles .... N.L.		1B-3B	103	179	30	53	15	0	11	48	0	.296
2007 Los Angeles g .... N.L.		1B-3B	92	110	9	21	5	0	4	18	0	.191
Major League Totals		9 Yrs.	733	1663	226	438	106	5	73	275	3	.263
Division Series												
2000 Oakland .... A.L.		DH	4	13	1	3	0	0	1	4	0	.231
2001 Oakland .... A.L.		DH	3	4	0	0	0	0	0	0	0	.000
2002 Oakland .... A.L.		1B	1	0	0	0	0	0	0	0	0	.000
2006 Los Angeles .... N.L.		PH	2	2	0	0	0	0	0	0	0	.000
Division Series Totals			10	19	1	3	0	0	1	4	0	.158

a Filed for free agency, October 17, 1997, re-signed with Chicago White Sox organization, January 25, 1998.
b Filed for free agency, October 16, 1998. Signed with Oakland Athletics organization, November 13, 1998.
c On disabled list from July 26 to August 16, 1999.
d On disabled list from August 1 to September 18, 2000.
e Filed for free agency, October 31, 2002. Signed with Los Angeles Dodgers organization, December 19, 2003.
f Filed for free agency, October 28, 2005, re-signed with Los Angeles Dodgers, December 7, 2005.
g Filed for free agency, October 12, 2007.

SALTALAMACCHIA, JARROD SCOTT

Born, West Palm Beach, Florida, May 2, 1985.
Bats Both. Throws Right. Height, 6 feet, 4 inches. Weight, 195 pounds.

Year Club	Lea	Pos	G	AB	R	H	2B	3B	HR	RBI	SB	Avg
2003 Braves .... Gulf Coast		C-3B	46	134	23	32	11	2	2	14	0	.239
2004 Rome .... So.Atl.		C	91	323	42	88	19	2	10	51	1	.272
2005 Myrtle Beach ...... Carolina		C	129	459	70	144	35	1	19	81	4	.314
2006 Mississippi .... Southern		C	92	313	30	72	18	1	9	39	0	.230
2007 Mississippi .... Southern		C	22	81	18	25	7	0	6	13	2	.309
2007 Atlanta .... N.L.		C-1B	47	141	11	40	6	0	4	12	0	.284
2007 Texas a .... A.L.		1B-C	46	167	28	42	7	1	7	21	0	.251
Major League Totals		1 Yrs.	93	308	39	82	13	1	11	33	0	.266

a Traded to Texas Rangers with infielder Elvis Andrews, pitcher Neftali Feliz, pitcher Matt Harrison and pitcher Beau James for infielder Mark Teixeira and pitcher Ron Mahay, July 31, 2007.

SANCHEZ, FREDERICK PHILLIP (FREDDY)

Born, Hollywood, California, December 21, 1977.
Bats Right. Throws Right. Height, 5 feet, 10 inches. Weight, 185 pounds.

Year Club	Lea	Pos	G	AB	R	H	2B	3B	HR	RBI	SB	Avg
2000 Lowell ...... N.Y.-Penn.		SS	34	132	24	38	13	2	1	14	2	.288
2000 Augusta .... So.Atl.		SS	30	109	17	33	7	0	0	15	4	.303
2001 Trenton .... Eastern		SS	44	178	25	58	20	0	2	19	3	.326
2001 Sarasota .... Fla.St.		SS	69	280	40	95	19	4	1	24	5	.339
2002 Trenton .... Eastern		SS-2B	80	311	60	102	23	1	3	38	19	.328
2002 Pawtucket .... Int.		SS-2B	45	183	25	55	10	1	4	28	5	.301
2002 Boston .... A.L.		2B-SS	12	16	3	3	0	0	0	2	0	.188
2003 Pawtucket .... Int.		SS-2B-3B	58	211	46	72	17	0	5	25	8	.341
2003 Boston .... A.L.		3B-SS-2B	20	34	6	8	2	0	0	2	0	.235
2003 Nashville .... P.C.		2B	1	5	1	2	1	0	0	0	0	.400
2004 Nashville .... P.C.		2B-SS	44	125	10	33	7	1	1	11	4	.264
2004 Pittsburgh b .... N.L.		SS-2B-3B	9	19	2	3	0	0	0	2	0	.158
2005 Pittsburgh .... N.L.		3B-2B-SS	132	453	54	132	26	4	5	35	2	.291
2006 Pittsburgh .... N.L.		3B-SS-2B	157	582	85	200	*53	2	6	85	3	*.344
2007 Indianapolis .... Int.		2B	1	2	1	1	1	0	0	0	0	.500
2007 Pittsburgh c .... N.L.		2B-SS	147	602	77	183	42	4	11	81	0	.304
Major League Totals		6 Yrs.	477	1706	227	529	123	10	22	207	5	.310

a Traded to Pittsburgh Pirates with pitcher Mike Gonzalez and cash for pitcher Jeff Suppan, pitcher Brandon Lyon and pitcher Anastacio Martinez, July 31, 2003.
b On disabled list from March 26 to July 9, 2004.
c On disabled list from March 23 to April 8, 2007.

SCHNEIDER, BRIAN DUNCAN
Born, Jacksonville, Florida, November 26, 1976.
Bats Left. Throws Right. Height, 6 feet, 1 inch. Weight, 195 pounds.

Year Club	Lea	Pos	G	AB	R	H	2B	3B	HR	RBI	SB	Avg
1995 Expos	Gulf Coast	C	30	97	7	22	3	0	0	4	2	.227
1996 Expos	Gulf Coast	C	52	164	26	44	5	2	0	23	2	.268
1996 Delmarva	So.Atl.	C	5	9	0	3	0	0	0	1	0	.333
1997 Cape Fear	So.Atl.	C	113	381	46	96	20	1	4	49	3	.252
1998 Cape Fear	So.Atl.	C	38	134	33	40	7	2	7	30	6	.299
1998 Jupiter	Fla.St.	C	82	302	32	82	12	1	3	30	4	.272
1999 Harrisburg	Eastern	C	121	421	48	111	19	1	17	66	2	.264
2000 Ottawa	Int.	C-1B	67	238	22	59	22	3	4	31	1	.248
2000 Montreal	N.L.	C	45	115	6	27	6	0	0	11	0	.235
2001 Ottawa	Int.	C	97	338	33	93	27	1	6	43	2	.275
2001 Montreal	N.L.	C	27	41	4	13	3	0	1	6	0	.317
2002 Montreal	N.L.	C-OF	73	207	21	57	19	2	5	29	1	.275
2003 Montreal	N.L.	C	108	335	34	77	26	1	9	46	0	.230
2004 Montreal	N.L.	C	135	436	40	112	20	3	12	49	0	.257
2005 Washington	N.L.	C	116	369	38	99	20	1	10	44	1	.268
2006 Potomac	Carolina	DH	2	9	1	2	1	0	0	1	0	.222
2006 Washington a	N.L.	C-1B	124	410	30	105	18	0	4	55	2	.256
2007 Washington b	N.L.	C-1B	129	408	33	96	21	1	6	54	0	.235
Major League Totals		8 Yrs.	757	2321	206	586	133	8	47	294	4	.252

a On disabled list from May 11 to May 26, 2006.
b Traded to New York Mets with outfielder Ryan Church for outfielder Lastings Milledge, November 30, 2007.

SCHUMAKER, JARED MICHAEL (SKIP)
Born, Torrance, California, February 3, 1980.
Bats Left. Throws Right. Height, 5 feet, 10 inches. Weight, 175 pounds.

Year Club	Lea	Pos	G	AB	R	H	2B	3B	HR	RBI	SB	Avg
2001 New Jersey	N.Y.-Penn.	OF	49	162	22	41	10	1	0	14	11	.253
2002 Potomac	Carolina	OF	136	551	71	158	22	4	2	44	26	.287
2003 Tennessee	Southern	OF	91	342	43	86	20	3	2	22	6	.251
2004 Tennessee	Southern	OF-3B	138	516	78	163	29	6	4	43	19	.316
2005 Memphis	P.C.	OF	115	443	66	127	24	3	7	34	14	.287
2005 St. Louis	N.L.	OF	27	24	9	6	1	0	0	1	1	.250
2006 Memphis	P.C.	OF	95	369	47	113	13	3	3	27	11	.306
2006 St. Louis	N.L.	OF	28	54	3	10	1	0	1	2	2	.185
2007 Memphis	P.C.	OF	59	232	34	71	16	0	7	31	2	.306
2007 St. Louis	N.L.	OF	88	177	19	59	12	2	2	19	1	.333
Major League Totals		3 Yrs.	143	255	31	75	14	2	3	22	4	.294

SCOTT, LUKE BRANDON
Born, DeLeon Springs, Florida, June 25, 1978.
Bats Left. Throws Right. Height, 6 feet. Weight, 210 pounds.

Year Club	Lea	Pos	G	AB	R	H	2B	3B	HR	RBI	SB	Avg
2001 Kinston a	Carolina		INJURED — Did Not Play									
2002 Kinston	Carolina	OF-1B	48	163	22	39	7	1	8	30	2	.239
2002 Columbus	So.Atl.	OF	49	171	28	44	15	4	7	32	9	.257
2003 Kinston	Carolina	OF	67	241	37	67	12	1	13	44	6	.278
2003 Akron	Eastern	OF	50	183	21	50	13	1	7	37	0	.273
2004 Salem	Carolina	OF	66	241	45	67	20	1	8	35	6	.278
2004 Round Rock b	Texas	OF	63	208	45	62	17	0	19	62	0	.298
2005 Round Rock	P.C.	OF	103	398	69	114	25	4	31	87	2	.286
2005 Houston	N.L.	OF	34	80	6	15	4	2	0	4	1	.188
2006 Round Rock	P.C.	OF	87	318	63	95	15	1	20	63	6	.299
2006 Houston	N.L.	OF	65	214	31	72	19	6	10	37	2	.336
2007 Houston c	N.L.	OF	132	369	49	94	28	5	18	64	3	.255
Major League Totals		3 Yrs.	231	663	86	181	51	13	28	105	6	.273
Division Series												
2005 Houston	N.L.	OF	2	2	1	0	0	0	0	0	0	.000
World Series Record												
2005 Houston	N.L.	PH	0	0	0	0	0	0	0	0	0	.000

a On disabled list from June 21 to September 14, 2001.
b Traded by Cleveland Indians to Houston Astros with outfielder Willy Taveras for pitcher Jeriome Robertston, March 31, 2004.
c Traded to Baltimore Orioles with pitcher Troy Patton, pitcher Matt Albers, pitcher Dennis Sarfate and infielder Michael Costanzo for infielder Miguel Tejada, December 12, 2007.

SCUTARO, MARCOS (MARCO)

Born, San Felipe, Venezuela, October 30, 1975.
Bats Right. Throws Right. Height, 5 feet, 10 inches. Weight, 190 pounds.

Year	Club	Lea	Pos	G	AB	R	H	2B	3B	HR	RBI	SB	Avg
1995	Cleveland . . .	Dominican	3B	66	262	71	103	18	6	0	38	32	.393
1996	Columbus.	So.Atl.	2B-SS-3B	85	315	66	79	12	3	10	45	6	.251
1997	Buffalo	A.A.	2B-3B-SS	21	57	8	15	3	0	1	6	0	.263
1997	Kinston.	Carolina	2B-3B	97	378	58	103	17	6	10	59	23	.272
1998	Buffalo	Int.	2B-3B	8	26	3	6	3	0	0	4	0	.231
1998	Akron	Eastern	2B-SS	124	462	68	146	27	6	11	62	33	.316
1999	Buffalo	Int.	2B-SS	129	462	76	126	24	2	8	51	21	.273
2000	Buffalo	Int.	2B-SS	124	425	67	117	20	5	5	54	9	.275
2000	Indianapolis a . . .	Int.	2B-SS	4	13	5	7	1	1	1	3	1	.538
2001	Indianapolis	Int.	2B-SS-3B	132	495	87	146	29	3	11	50	11	.295
2002	Norfolk.	Int.	2B-SS-OF-3B	97	354	48	113	22	6	7	28	7	.319
2002	New York b	N.L.	2B-SS-3B-OF	27	36	2	8	0	1	1	6	0	.222
2003	Norfolk.	Int.	3B-2B-SS-OF	70	244	42	76	18	3	9	32	11	.311
2003	New York c	N.L.	2B-SS	48	75	10	16	4	0	2	6	2	.213
2004	Oakland	A.L.	2B-SS-3B	137	455	50	124	32	1	7	43	0	.273
2005	Oakland	A.L.	SS-3B-OF	118	381	48	94	22	3	9	37	5	.247
2006	Oakland	A.L.	SS-2B-3B-OF	117	365	52	97	21	6	5	41	5	.266
2007	Oakland d	A.L.	SS-3B-OF	104	338	49	88	13	0	7	41	2	.260
Major League Totals				6 Yrs.	551	1650	211	427	92	11	31	174	14	.2598
Division Series													
2006	Oakland	A.L.	SS	3	12	1	4	4	0	0	6	0	.333
Championship Series													
2006	Oakland	A.L.	SS	4	15	0	1	0	0	0	0	0	.067

a Sent by Cleveland Indians to Milwaukee Brewers as player to be named later in Richie Sexson trade, August 30, 2000.
b Claimed on waivers by New York Mets, April 3, 2002.
c Claimed on waivers by Oakland Athletics, October 9, 2003.
d Traded to Toronto Blue Jays for pitcher Kristian Bell and pitcher Graham Godfrey, November 18, 2007.

SEXSON, RICHMOND LOCKWOOD (RICHIE)

Born, Portland, Oregon, December 29, 1974.
Bats Right. Throws Right. Height, 6 feet, 8 inches. Weight, 235 pounds.

Year	Club	Lea	Pos	G	AB	R	H	2B	3B	HR	RBI	SB	Avg
1993	Burlington	Appal.	1B	40	97	11	18	3	0	1	5	1	.186
1994	Columbus.	So.Atl.	1B	130	488	88	133	25	2	14	77	7	.273
1995	Kinston.	Carolina	1B	131	494	80	151	34	0	22	85	4	.306
1996	Canton-Akron.	Eastern	1B	133	518	85	143	33	3	16	76	2	.276
1997	Buffalo	A.A.	1B	115	434	57	113	20	2	31	88	5	.260
1997	Cleveland	A.L.	1B	5	11	1	3	0	0	0	0	0	.273
1998	Buffalo	Int.	OF-1B	89	344	58	102	20	1	21	74	1	.297
1998	Cleveland	A.L.	1B-OF	49	174	28	54	14	1	11	35	1	.310
1999	Cleveland . . . . : .	A.L.	1B-OF	134	479	72	122	17	7	31	116	3	.255
2000	Cleveland	A.L.	OF-1B	91	324	45	83	16	1	16	44	1	.256
2000	Milwaukee a-b	N.L.	1B	57	213	44	63	14	0	14	47	1	.296
2001	Milwaukee	N.L.	1B	158	598	94	162	24	3	45	125	2	.271
2002	Milwaukee	N.L.	1B	157	570	86	159	37	2	29	102	0	.279
2003	Milwaukee c	N.L.	1B	*162	606	97	165	28	2	45	124	2	.272
2004	Arizona d-e	N.L.	1B	23	90	20	21	4	0	9	23	0	.233
2005	Seattle	A.L.	1B	156	558	99	147	36	1	39	121	1	.263
2006	Seattle	A.L.	1B	158	591	75	156	40	0	34	107	1	.264
2007	Seattle	A.L.	1B	121	434	58	89	21	0	21	63	1	.205
Major League Totals				11 Yrs.	1271	4648	719	1224	251	17	294	907	13	.263
Division Series													
1998	Cleveland	A.L.	1B	3	2	0	0	0	0	0	0	0	.000
1999	Cleveland	A.L.	1B-OF	3	6	1	1	0	0	0	1	0	.167
Division Series Totals					6	8	1	1	0	0	0	1	0	.125
Championship Series													
1998	Cleveland	A.L.	1B	3	6	0	0	0	0	0	0	0	.000

a Traded to Milwaukee Brewers with pitcher Paul Rigdon, pitcher Kane Davis and player to be named later for pitcher Bob Wickman, pitcher Steve Woodard and pitcher Jason Bere, July 28, 2000.
b Milwaukee Brewers received infielder Marcus Scutaro to complete trade, August 30, 2000.
c Traded to Arizona Diamondbacks with pitcher Shane Nance and player to be named later for infielder Junior Spivey, infielder Craig Counsell, infielder Lyle Overbay, catcher Chad Moeller, pitcher Chris Capuano and pitcher Jorge DeRosa, December 1, 2003. Arizona Diamondbacks received outfielder Gary Varner to complete trade, December 15, 2003.
d On disabled list from April 29 to May 21 and from May 23 to November 1, 2004.
e Filed for free agency, November 1, 2004. Signed with Seattle Mariners, December 15, 2004.

SHEALY, RYAN NELSON

Born, Fort Lauderdale, Florida, August 29, 1979.
Bats Right. Throws Right. Height, 6 feet, 5 inches. Weight, 250 pounds.

Year	Club	Lea	Pos	G	AB	R	H	2B	3B	HR	RBI	SB	Avg
2002 Casper	Pioneer		1B	69	231	55	85	21	1	19	70	0	.368
2003 Visalia	Calif.		1B	93	341	70	102	31	1	14	73	0	.299
2004 Tulsa	Texas		1B	132	469	88	149	32	3	29	99	1	.318
2005 Colorado Springs	P.C.		1B-OF	108	411	85	135	30	2	26	88	4	.328
2005 Colorado	N.L.		1B	36	91	14	30	7	0	2	16	1	.330
2006 Colorado Springs	P.C.		1B	58	222	37	63	16	1	15	55	0	.284
2006 Colorado	N.L.		1B	5	9	2	2	2	0	0	1	0	.222
2006 Kansas City a-b	A.L.		1B	51	193	29	54	10	.1	7	36	1	.280
2007 Omaha	P.C.		1B	34	122	14	32	7	0	7	24	0	.262
2007 Kansas City c	A.L.		1B	52	172	18	38	6	0	3	21	0	.221
Major League Totals			3 Yrs.	144	465	63	124	25	1	12	74	2	.267

a On disabled list from March 24 to May 12, 2006.
b Traded to Kansas City Royals with pitcher Scott Dohmann for pitcher Jeremy Affeldt and pitcher Denny Bautista, July 31, 2006.
c On disabled list from May 1 to May 16 and June 26 to August 11 and August 30 to November 13, 2007.

SHEFFIELD, GARY ANTONIAN

Born, Tampa, Florida, November 18, 1968.
Bats Right. Throws Right. Height, 6 feet. Weight, 215 pounds.

Year	Club	Lea	Pos	G	AB	R	H	2B	3B	HR	RBI	SB	Avg
1986 Helena	Pioneer		SS	57	222	53	81	12	2	15	71	14	.365
1987 Stockton	California		SS	129	469	84	130	23	3	17	*103	25	.277
1988 El Paso	Texas		SS	77	296	70	93	19	3	19	65	5	.314
1988 Denver	A.A.		3B-SS	57	212	42	73	9	5	9	54	8	.344
1988 Milwaukee	A.L.		SS	24	80	12	19	1	0	4	12	3	.238
1989 Denver a	A.A.		SS	7	29	3	4	1	1	0	0	0	.138
1989 Milwaukee	A.L.		SS-3B	95	368	34	91	18	0	5	32	10	.247
1990 Milwaukee b	A.L.		3B	125	487	67	143	30	1	10	67	25	.294
1991 Milwaukee c-d	A.L.		3B	50	175	25	34	12	2	2	22	5	.194
1992 San Diego	N.L.		3B	146	557	87	184	34	3	33	100	5	*.330
1993 San Diego-Florida e-f	N.L.		3B	140	494	67	145	20	5	20	73	17	.294
1994 Portland	Eastern		OF	2	7	1	2	1	0	0	0	0	.286
1994 Florida g	N.L.		OF	87	322	61	89	16	1	27	78	12	.276
1995 Florida h	N.L.		OF	63	213	46	69	8	0	16	46	19	.324
1996 Florida	N.L.		OF	161	519	118	163	33	1	42	120	16	.314
1997 Florida i	N.L.		OF	135	444	86	111	22	1	21	71	11	.250
1998 Florida-Los Angeles j	N.L.		OF	130	437	73	132	27	2	22	85	22	.302
1999 Los Angeles	N.L.		OF	152	549	103	165	20	0	34	101	11	.301
2000 Los Angeles	N.L.		OF	141	501	105	163	24	3	43	109	4	.325
2001 Los Angeles k-l	N.L.		OF	143	515	98	160	28	2	36	100	10	.311
2002 Atlanta	N.L.		OF	135	492	82	151	26	0	25	84	12	.307
2003 Atlanta m	N.L.		OF	155	576	126	190	37	2	39	132	18	.330
2004 New York	A.L.		OF-3B	154	573	117	166	30	1	36	121	5	.290
2005 New York	A.L.		OF	154	584	104	170	27	0	34	123	10	.291
2006 Trenton	Eastern		DH	1	3	0	1	0	0	0	1	0	.333
2006 New York n-o	A.L.		OF-1B	39	151	22	45	5	0	6	25	5	.298
2007 Detroit p	A.L.		DH-OF	133	494	107	131	20	1	25	75	22	.265
Major League Totals			20 Yrs.	2362	8531	1540	2521	438	25	480	1576	242	.296

Division Series

Year	Club	Lea	Pos	G	AB	R	H	2B	3B	HR	RBI	SB	Avg
1997 Florida	N.L.		OF	3	9	2	5	1	0	1	1	1	.556
2002 Atlanta	N.L.		OF	5	16	3	1	0	0	1	1	0	.063
2003 Atlanta	N.L.		OF	4	14	0	2	0	0	0	1	0	.143
2004 New York	A.L.		OF	4	18	2	4	1	0	1	2	0	.222
2005 New York	A.L.		OF	5	21	1	6	0	0	0	2	0	.286
2006 New York	A.L.		1B	3	12	1	1	0	0	0	1	0	.083

Year	Club	Lea	Pos	G	AB	R	H	2B	3B	HR	RBI	SB	Avg
Division Series Totals				24	90	10	19	2	0	3	8	1	.211
Championship Series													
1997 Florida	N.L.		OF	6	17	6	4	0	0	1	1	0	.235
2004 New York	A.L.		OF	7	30	7	10	3	0	1	5	0	.333
Championship Series Totals				13	47	13	14	3	0	2	6	0	.298
World Series Record													
1997 Florida	N.L.		OF	7	24	4	7	1	0	1	5	0	.292

a On disabled list from July 14 to September 9, 1989.
b Suspended three games by American League for June 30 fight, August 31 to September 2, 1990.
c On disabled list from June 2 to July 3 and July 25 to end of 1991 season.
d Traded to San Diego Padres with pitcher Geoff Kellogg for pitcher Ricky Bones, infielder Jose Valentin and outfielder Matt Mieske, March 27, 1992.
e Suspended three games by National League for June 10 fight from July 9 to July 11, 1993.
f Traded to Florida Marlins with pitcher Rich Rodriguez for pitchers Trevor Hoffman, Andres Berumen and Jose Martinez, June 25, 1993.
g On disabled list from May 10 to May 25 and May 28 to June 11, 1994.
h On disabled list from June 11 to September 1, 1995.
i On disabled list from May 14 to May 29, 1997.
j Traded to Los Angeles Dodgers with outfielder Jim Eisenreich, catcher Charles Johnson, infielder Bobby Bonilla and pitcher Manuel Barrios for catcher Mike Piazza and infielder Todd Zeile, May 15, 1998.
k On disabled list from May 24 to June 8, 2001.
l Traded to Atlanta Braves for outfielder Brian Jordan, pitcher Odalis Perez and pitcher Andy Brown, January 15, 2002.
m Filed for free agency, October 27, 2003. Signed with New York Yankees, December 17, 2003.
n On disabled list from May 6 to May 23 and May 30 to September 19, 2006.
o Traded to Detroit Tigers for pitcher Humberto Sanchez, pitcher Kevin Whelan and pitcher Anthony Claggett, November 10, 2006.
p On disabled list from August 22 to September 6, 2007.

SHOPPACH, KELLY BRIAN

Born, Fort Worth, Texas, April 29, 1980.
Bats Right. Throws Right. Height, 6 feet, 1 inch. Weight, 210 pounds.

Year	Club	Lea	Pos	G	AB	R	H	2B	3B	HR	RBI	SB	Avg
2002 Sarasota........	Fla.St.		C	116	414	54	112	35	1	10	66	2	.271
2003 Portland........	Eastern		C	92	340	45	96	30	2	12	60	0	.282
2004 Pawtucket	Int.		C	113	399	62	93	25	0	22	64	0	.233
2005 Pawtucket	Int.		C	102	371	60	94	16	0	26	75	0	.253
2005 Boston	A.L.		C	9	15	1	0	0	0	0	0	0	.000
2006 Buffalo	Int.		C	21	78	11	22	8	0	4	9	0	.282
2006 Cleveland a..........	A.L.		C	41	110	7	27	6	0	3	16	0	.245
2007 Cleveland	A.L.		C	59	161	26	42	13	0	7	30	0	.261
Major League Totals			3 Yrs.	109	286	34	69	19	0	10	46	0	.241
Division Series													
2007 Cleveland	A.L.		C	1	3	1	2	2	0	0	0	0	.667
Championship Series													
2007 Cleveland	A.L.		C	1	3	0	1	0	0	0	0	0	.333

a Traded to Cleveland Indians with infielder Andy Marte and pitcher Guillermo Mota for outfielder Coco Crisp, pitcher David Riske and catcher Josh Bard, January 27, 2006.

SIZEMORE, GRADY

Born, Seattle, Washington, August 2, 1982.
Bats Left. Throws Left. Height, 6 feet, 2 inches. Weight, 200 pounds.

Year	Club	Lea	Pos	G	AB	R	H	2B	3B	HR	RBI	SB	Avg
2000 Expos..........	Gulf Coast		OF	55	205	31	60	8	3	1	14	16	.293
2001 Clinton	Midwest		OF	123	451	64	121	16	4	2	61	32	.268
2002 Kinston..........	Carolina		OF	47	172	31	59	9	3	3	20	14	.343
2002 Brevard County a	Fla.St.		OF	75	256	37	66	15	4	0	26	9	.258
2003 Akron	Eastern		OF-2B	128	496	96	151	26	11	13	78	10	.304
2004 Buffalo	Int.		OF	101	418	73	120	23	8	8	51	15	.287
2004 Cleveland	A.L.		OF	43	138	15	34	6	2	4	24	2	.246
2005 Cleveland	A.L.		OF	158	640	111	185	37	11	22	81	22	.289
2006 Cleveland	A.L.		OF	*162	655	*134	190	*53	11	28	76	22	.290
2007 Cleveland	A.L.		OF	*162	628	118	174	34	5	24	78	33	.277
Major League Totals			4 Yrs.	525	2061	378	583	130	29	78	259	79	.283
Division Series													
2007 Cleveland	A.L.		OF	4	16	3	6	0	1	1	1	1	.375
Championship Series													
2007 Cleveland	A.L.		OF	7	27	6	6	2	0	1	2	1	.222

a Traded by Montreal Expos to Cleveland Indians with infielder Lee Stevens, infielder Brandon Phillips and pitcher Cliff Lee for pitcher Bartolo Colon and player to be named later, June 27, 2002. Montreal Expos received pitcher Tim Drew to complete trade, June 28, 2002.

SLEDGE, TERRMEL

Born, Fayetteville, North Carolina, March 18, 1977.
Bats Left. Throws Left. Height, 6 feet. Weight, 185 pounds.

Year	Club	Lea	Pos	G	AB	R	H	2B	3B	HR	RBI	SB	Avg
1999 Everett	Northwest	OF	62	233	43	74	8	3	5	32	9	.318
2000 Lancaster	Calif.	OF	103	384	90	130	22	7	11	75	35	.339
2000 Wisconsin a	Midwest	OF	7	23	5	5	2	2	0	3	1	.217
2001 Harrisburg	Eastern	1B-OF	129	448	66	124	22	6	9	48	30	.277
2002 Harrisburg	Eastern	OF-1B	102	396	74	119	18	6	8	43	11	.301
2002 Ottawa	Int.	OF-1B	24	80	12	21	5	2	1	11	1	.262
2003 Edmonton	P.C.	OF-1B	131	497	95	161	26	9	22	92	13	.324
2004 Montreal	N.L.	OF-1B	133	398	45	107	20	6	15	62	3	.269
2005 Washington b-c	N.L.	OF	20	37	7	9	0	1	1	8	2	.243
2006 Portland	P.C.	OF	101	367	69	114	18	5	24	73	5	.311
2006 San Diego d	N.L.	OF	38	70	7	16	3	0	2	7	0	.229
2007 Portland	P.C.	OF	8	27	5	10	2	0	1	3	1	.370
2007 San Diego e-f	N.L.	OF	100	200	22	42	9	0	7	23	1	.210
Major League Totals			4 Yrs.	291	705	81	174	32	7	25	100	6	.247

a Sent to Montreal Expos as player to be named later for catcher Chris Widger, September 28, 2000.
b On disabled list from May 3 to November 2, 2005.
c Traded to Texas Rangers with outfielder Brad Wilkerson and pitcher Armando Galarraga for infielder Alfonso Soriano, December 13, 2005.
d Traded to San Diego Padres with pitcher Chris Young and infielder Adrian Gonzalez for pitcher Adam Eaton, pitcher Akinori Otsuka and catcher Billy Killian, January 4, 2006.
e On disabled list from June 28 to July 18, 2007.
f Sold to Hokkaido Nippon Ham Fighters, December 5, 2007.

SMITH, JASON WILLIAM

Born, Meridian, Mississippi, July 24, 1977.
Bats Left. Throws Right. Height, 6 feet, 3 inches. Weight, 195 pounds.

Year	Club	Lea	Pos	G	AB	R	H	2B	3B	HR	RBI	SB	Avg
1997 Williamsprt.	N.Y.-Penn.	SS	51	205	25	59	5	2	0	11	9	.288
1997 Rockford	Midwest	SS	9	33	4	6	0	1	0	3	1	.182
1998 Rockford	Midwest	SS	126	464	67	111	15	9	7	60	23	.239
1999 Daytona	Fla.St.	SS	39	142	22	37	5	2	5	26	9	.261
2000 West Tenn	Southern	SS	119	481	55	114	22	7	12	61	16	.237
2001 Iowa	P.C.	SS	70	240	31	56	8	6	4	15	6	.233
2001 Chicago	N.L.	SS	2	1	0	0	0	0	0	0	0	.000
2001 Durham a	Int.	SS	8	31	2	6	1	0	0	3	0	.194
2002 Tampa Bay	A.L.	3B-SS-2B	26	65	9	13	1	2	1	6	3	.200
2002 Durham	Int.	SS-3B	54	206	29	57	11	2	4	28	5	.277
2003 Durham	Int.	SS-2B-3B	130	515	76	147	20	14	15	71	14	.285
2003 Tampa Bay b	A.L.	3B	1	4	0	1	0	0	0	0	0	.250
2004 Toledo	Int.	3B	33	122	18	33	8	2	3	13	5	.270
2004 Detroit	A.L.	2B-SS-3B	61	155	20	37	7	4	5	19	1	.239
2005 Detroit	A.L.	SS-2B-3B-1B	27	58	4	11	1	2	0	2	2	.190
2005 Toledo c	Int.	1B-2B-3B-SS	55	187	24	43	11	2	6	25	8	.230
2006 Colorado	N.L.	2B-1B-3B-SS	49	99	9	26	1	0	5	13	3	.263
2006 Colorado Springs d-e	P.C.	3B-1B-SS-2B	41	141	26	41	9	5	4	23	3	.291
2007 Visalia	Calif.	3B-SS	3	9	4	4	0	0	1	5	0	.444
2007 Tucson	P.C.	SS-2B	14	54	9	17	3	1	3	10	0	.315
2007 Arizona	N.L.	SS	2	4	0	1	0	0	0	0	0	.250
2007 Toronto-K.C. f-g-h	A.L.	SS-3B-2B-1B	67	137	16	27	3	2	6	18	0	.197
Major League Totals			7 Yrs.	235	523	58	116	13	10	17	58	9	.222

a Sent to Tampa Bay Devil Rays as player to be named later for infielder Fred McGriff, August 6, 2001.
b Filed for free agency, October 16, 2003. Signed with Detroit Tigers organization, December 8, 2003.
c Filed for free agency, October 3, 2005. Signed with Colorado Rockies organization, November 30, 2005.
d Filed for free agency, October 6, 2006. Signed with Chicago Cubs organization, November 16, 2006.
e Selected by Toronto Blue Jays in Rule V major league draft, December 7, 2006.
f Claimed on waivers by Arizona Diamondbacks, May 16, 2007.
g On disabled list from May 19 to July 5, 2007.
h Claimed on waivers by Kansas City Royals, July 11, 2007.

SNYDER, CHRISTOPHER RYAN (CHRIS)

Born, Houston, Texas, February 12, 1981.
Bats Right. Throws Right. Height, 6 feet, 3 inches. Weight, 230 pounds.

Year	Club	Lea	Pos	G	AB	R	H	2B	3B	HR	RBI	SB	Avg
2002 Lancaster	California	C	60	217	32	56	16	0	9	44	0	.258
2003 Lancaster	California	C	69	245	53	77	16	2	10	53	0	.314
2003 El Paso	Texas	C	53	188	21	38	14	0	4	26	0	.202
2004 El Paso	Texas	C-1B	99	346	66	104	31	0	15	57	3	.301
2004 Arizona	N.L.	C	29	96	10	23	6	0	5	15	0	.240
2005 Arizona	N.L.	C	115	326	24	66	14	0	6	28	0	.202
2006 Arizona	N.L.	C	61	184	19	51	9	0	6	32	0	.277
2007 Arizona	N.L.	C-1B-OF	110	326	37	82	20	0	13	47	0	.252
Major League Totals		4 Yrs.	315	932	90	222	49	0	30	122	0	.238
Division Series												
2007 Arizona	N.L.	C	3	7	2	1	0	0	0	0	0	.143
Championship Series												
2007 Arizona	N.L.	C	3	12	1	4	2	0	1	3	0	.333

SORIANO, ALFONSO GUILLEARD

Born, San Pedro de Macoris, Dominican Republic, January 7, 1976.
Bats Right. Throws Right. Height, 6 feet, 1 inch. Weight, 180 pounds.

Year	Club	Lea	Pos	G	AB	R	H	2B	3B	HR	RBI	SB	Avg
1995 Hiroshima	Dominican	SS	63	227	52	83	12	3	4	55	8	.366
1996 Hiroshima	Japan East	SS	57	131	11	28	0	0	0	13	0	.214
1997 Hiroshima	Japan Cent.	SS	9	17	2	2	0	0	0	2	0	.118
1998 a						Did Not Play							
1999 Norwich	Eastern	SS	89	361	57	110	20	3	15	68	24	.305
1999 Yankees	Gulf Coast	SS	5	19	7	5	2	0	1	5	0	.263
1999 Columbus	Int.	SS	20	82	8	15	5	1	2	11	1	.183
1999 New York b	A.L.	SS	9	8	2	1	0	0	1	1	0	.125
2000 Columbus	Int.	SS-2B	111	459	90	133	32	6	12	66	14	.290
2000 New York	A.L.	3B-SS-2B	22	50	5	9	3	0	2	3	2	.180
2001 New York	A.L.	2B	158	574	77	154	34	3	18	73	43	.268
2002 New York	A.L.	2B	156	*696	*128	*209	51	2	39	102	41	.300
2003 New York	A.L.	2B	156	*682	114	198	36	5	38	91	35	.290
2004 Texas c-d	A.L.	2B	145	608	77	170	32	4	28	91	18	.280
2005 Texas e	A.L.	2B	156	637	102	171	43	2	36	104	30	.268
2006 Washington f	N.L.	OF	159	647	119	179	41	2	46	95	41	.277
2007 Chicago g	N.L.	OF-2B	135	579	97	173	42	5	33	70	19	.299
Major League Totals		9 Yrs.	1096	4481	721	1264	282	23	241	630	229	.282
Division Series												
2001 New York	A.L.	2B	5	18	2	4	0	0	0	3	2	.222
2002 New York	A.L.	2B	4	17	2	2	1	0	1	2	1	.118
2003 New York	A.L.	2B	4	19	2	7	1	0	0	4	2	.368
2007 Chicago	N.L.	OF	3	14	0	2	0	0	0	0	0	.143
Division Series Totals			16	68	6	15	2	0	1	9	5	.221
Championship Series												
2001 New York	A.L.	2B	5	15	5	6	0	0	1	2	2	.500
2003 New York	A.L.	2B	7	30	0	4	1	0	0	3	2	.133
Championship Series Totals			12	45	5	10	1	0	1	5	4	.222
World Series Record												
2001 New York	A.L.	2B	7	25	1	6	0	0	1	2	0	.240
2003 New York	A.L.	2B OF	6	22	2	5	0	0	1	2	1	.227
World Series Totals			13	47	3	11	0	0	2	4	1	.234

a Signed by New York Yankees as free agent, September 29, 1998.
b On disabled list from July 15 to August 15, 1999.
c Traded to Texas Rangers with player to be named later for infielder Alex Rodriguez, February 16, 2004.
d Texas Rangers received infielder Joaquin Arias to complete trade, March 23, 2004.
e Traded to Washington Nationals for outfielder Brad Wilkerson, outfielder Terrmel Sledge and pitcher Armando Galarraga, December 13, 2005.
f Filed for free agency, October 29, 2006. Signed with Chicago Cubs, November 20, 2006.
g On disabled list from August 6 to August 28, 2007.

SOSA, SAMUEL PERALTA (SAMMY)

Born, San Pedro de Macoris, Dominican Republic, November 12, 1968.
Bats Right. Throws Right. Height, 6 feet. Weight, 190 pounds.

Year	Club	Lea	Pos	G	AB	R	H	2B	3B	HR	RBI	SB	Avg
1986	Rangers	Gulf Coast	OF	61	229	38	63	19	1	4	28	11	.275
1987	Gastonia	So.Atl.	OF	129	519	73	145	27	4	11	59	22	.279
1988	Charlotte	Fla.St.	OF	131	507	70	116	13	12	9	51	42	.229
1989	Tulsa	Texas	OF	66	273	45	81	15	4	7	31	16	.297
1989	Okla City	A.A.	OF	10	39	2	4	2	0	0	3	4	.103
1989	Vancouver	P.C.	OF	13	49	7	18	3	0	1	5	3	.367
1989	Texas-Chicago a	A.L.	OF	58	183	27	47	8	0	4	13	7	.257
1990	Chicago	A.L.	OF	153	532	72	124	26	10	15	70	32	.233
1991	Vancouver	P.C.	OF	32	116	19	31	7	2	3	19	9	.267
1991	Chicago	A.L.	OF	116	316	39	64	10	1	10	33	13	.203
1992	Iowa	A.A.	OF	5	19	3	6	2	0	0	1	5	.316
1992	Chicago b	N.L.	OF	67	262	41	68	7	2	8	25	15	.260
1993	Chicago	N.L.	OF	159	598	92	156	25	5	33	93	36	.261
1994	Chicago	N.L.	OF	105	426	59	128	17	6	25	70	22	.300
1995	Chicago	N.L.	OF	*144	564	89	151	17	3	36	119	34	.268
1996	Chicago c	N.L.	OF	124	498	84	136	21	2	40	100	18	.273
1997	Chicago	N.L.	OF	*162	642	90	161	31	4	36	119	22	.251
1998	Chicago	N.L.	OF	159	643	*134	198	20	0	66	*158	18	.308
1999	Chicago	N.L.	OF	*162	625	114	180	24	2	63	141	7	.288
2000	Chicago	N.L.	OF	156	604	106	193	38	1	*50	138	7	.320
2001	Chicago	N.L.	OF	160	577	*146	189	34	5	64	*160	0	.328
2002	Chicago	N.L.	OF	150	556	*122	160	19	2	*49	108	2	.288
2003	Chicago d	N.L.	OF	137	517	99	144	22	0	40	103	0	.279
2004	West Tenn	Southern	DH	2	6	0	2	1	0	0	1	0	.333
2004	Chicago e	N.L.	OF	126	478	69	121	21	0	35	80	0	.253
2005	Baltimore f-g-h	A.L.	OF	102	380	39	84	15	1	14	45	1	.221
2006							Did Not Play						
2007	Texas i	A.L.	DH-OF	114	412	53	104	24	1	21	92	0	.252
Major League Totals		18 Yrs.		2354	8813	1475	2408	379	45	609	1667	234	.273
Division Series													
1998	Chicago	N.L.	OF	3	11	0	2	1	0	0	0	0	.182
2003	Chicago	N.L.	OF	5	16	1	3	1	0	0	1	1	.188
Division Series Totals				8	27	1	5	2	0	0	1	1	.185
Championship Series													
2003	Chicago	N.L.	OF	7	26	7	8	1	0	2	6	0	.308

a Traded to Chicago White Sox with pitcher Wilson Alvarez and infielder Scott Fletcher for outfielder Harold Baines and infielder Fred Manrique, July 29, 1989.
b Traded to Chicago Cubs with pitcher Ken Patterson for outfielder George Bell, March 30, 1992.
c On disabled list from August 21 to September 30, 1996.
d On disabled list from May 10 to May 30, 2003.
e On disabled list from May 16 to June 18, 2004.
f Traded to Baltimore Orioles for infielder Jerry Hairston, infielder Mike Fontenot and pitcher Dave Crouthers, February 2, 2005.
g On disabled list from May 5 to May 24 and August 26 to October 27, 2005.
h Filed for free agency, October 31, 2005. Signed with Texas Rangers organization, January 30, 2007.
i Filed for free agency, October 30, 2007.

SPIEZIO, SCOTT EDWARD

Born, Joliet, Illinois, September 21, 1972.
Bats Both. Throws Right. Height, 6 feet, 2 inches. Weight, 220 pounds.

Year	Club	Lea	Pos	G	AB	R	H	2B	3B	HR	RBI	SB	Avg
1993	Sou Oregon	Northwest	3B-1B	31	125	32	41	10	2	3	19	0	.328
1993	Modesto	Calif.	3B-1B	32	110	12	28	9	1	1	13	1	.255
1994	Modesto	Calif.	3B-2B-SS	127	453	84	127	32	5	14	68	5	.280
1995	Huntsville	Southern	3B-1B-2B	141	528	78	149	33	8	13	86	10	.282
1996	Edmonton	P.C.	3B-1B	140	523	87	137	30	4	20	91	6	.262
1996	Oakland	A.L.	3B	9	29	6	9	2	0	2	8	0	.310
1997	Sou Oregon	Northwest	2B	2	9	1	5	0	0	0	2	0	.556
1997	Oakland a	A.L.	2B-3B	147	538	58	131	28	4	14	65	9	.243
1998	Edmonton	P.C.	2B	5	13	3	3	1	0	1	4	0	.231
1998	Oakland b	A.L.	2B	114	406	54	105	19	1	9	50	1	.259
1999	Oakland	A.L.	2B-3B-1B	89	247	31	60	24	0	8	33	0	.243
1999	Vancouver	P.C.	2B-3B	28	105	27	41	7	1	6	27	0	.390
2000	Anaheim c	A.L.	DH-1B-3B-OF	123	297	47	72	11	2	17	49	1	.242
2001	Anaheim	A.L.	1B-OF-3B	139	457	57	124	29	4	13	54	5	.271

Year	Club	Lea	Pos	G	AB	R	H	2B	3B	HR	RBI	SB	Avg
2002 Anaheim	....	A.L.	1B-3B-OF-2B	153	491	80	140	34	2	12	82	6	.285
2003 Anaheim d	......	A.L.	1B-3B-OF	158	521	69	138	36	7	16	83	6	.265
2004 Inland Empire	....	Calif.	3B	2	5	0	0	0	0	0	1	0	.000
2004 Seattle e	....	A.L.	3B-1B	112	367	38	79	12	3	10	41	4	.215
2005 Tacoma	....	P.C.	1B-3B-OF	14	58	11	19	3	1	2	9	0	.328
2005 Seattle f-g	......	A.L.	3B-1B-2B	29	47	2	3	1	0	1	1	0	.064
2006 St. Louis h	......	N.L.	3B-OF-1B-2B	119	276	44	75	15	4	13	52	1	.272
2007 St. Louis i	....	N.L.	3B-OF-1B-2B	82	223	31	60	14	0	4	31	0	.269
Major League Totals	....	12 Yrs.		1274	3899	517	996	225	27	119	549	33	.255
Division Series													
2002 Anaheim	....	A.L.	1B	4	15	2	6	1	0	1	6	0	.400
2006 St. Louis	....	N.L.	3B	2	5	1	1	0	0	0	1	0	.200
Division Series Totals	....			6	20	3	7	1	0	1	7	0	.350
Championship Series													
2002 Anaheim	....	A.L.	1B	5	17	5	6	2	0	1	5	0	.353
2006 St. Louis	....	N.L.	OF-3B	6	17	3	4	1	2	0	5	0	.235
Championship Series Totals	......			11	34	8	10	3	2	1	10	0	.294
World Series Record													
2002 Anaheim	....	A.L.	1B	7	23	3	6	1	1	1	8	1	.261
2006 St. Louis	....	N.L.	DH	2	4	0	0	0	0	0	0	0	.000
World Series Totals	....			9	27	3	6	1	1	1	8	1	.222

a On disabled list from June 8 to June 25, 1997.
b On disabled list from June 15 to July 31, 1998.
c Filed for free agency, December 21, 1999. Signed with Anaheim Angels organization, January 11, 2000.
d Filed for free agency, October 28, 2003. Signed with Seattle Mariners, December 17, 2003.
e On disabled list from March 28 to April 17, 2004.
f On disabled list from April 19 to July 1, 2005.
g Released by Seattle Mariners, August 19, 2005. Signed with St. Louis Cardinals organization, February 17, 2006.
h Filed for free agency, October 30, 2006, re-signed with St. Louis Cardinals, November 16, 2006.
i On disabled list from July 14 to July 29, 2007.

SPILBORGHS, RYAN ADAM
Born, Santa Barbara, California, September 5, 1979.
Bats Right. Throws Right. Height, 6 feet, 1 inch. Weight, 190 pounds.

Year	Club	Lea	Pos	G	AB	R	H	2B	3B	HR	RBI	SB	Avg
2002 Tri-City	....	Northwest	OF	71	261	34	60	11	1	4	34	11	.230
2003 Asheville	....	So.Atl.	OF	119	434	78	122	22	2	15	61	10	.281
2004 Visalia	....	Calif.	OF-SS	125	444	59	115	26	3	8	57	8	.259
2005 Tulsa	....	Texas	OF	71	255	52	87	23	3	6	54	10	.341
2005 Colorado	....	N.L.	OF	1	4	0	2	0	0	0	1	0	.500
2005 Colorado Springs a	.....	P.C.	OF	60	227	49	77	23	5	5	30	7	.339
2006 Colorado Springs	......	P.C.	OF	68	269	50	91	20	1	5	34	8	.338
2006 Colorado	....	N.L.	OF	67	167	26	48	6	3	4	21	5	.287
2007 Colorado Springs	......	P.C.	OF-1B	34	124	25	40	7	1	5	17	4	.323
2007 Colorado	....	N.L.	OF	97	264	40	79	14	1	11	51	4	.299
Major League Totals	....	3 Yrs.		165	435	66	129	20	4	15	73	9	.297
Division Series													
2007 Colorado	....	N.L.	OF	3	8	2	2	0	0	0	0	0	.250
Championship Series													
2007 Colorado	....	N.L.	OF	2	2	1	1	0	0	0	0	0	.500
World Series Record													
2007 Colorado	....	N.L.	OF-DH	4	10	0	0	0	0	0	0	0	.000

a Not offered contract, December 21, 2005, re-signed with Colorado Rockies organization, December 22, 2005.

STAIRS, MATTHEW WADE (MATT)
Born, St. John, New Brunswick, Canada, February 27, 1969.
Bats Left. Throws Right. Height, 5 feet, 9 inches. Weight, 215 pounds.

Year	Club	Lea	Pos	G	AB	R	H	2B	3B	HR	RBI	SB	Avg
1989 Jamestown	......	N.Y.Penn.	2B-3B	14	43	8	11	1	0	1	5	1	.256
1989 West Palm Bch.	.....	Fla. St.	3B-SS-2B	36	111	12	21	3	1	1	9	0	.189
1989 Rockford	....	Midwest	3B	44	141	20	40	9	2	2	14	5	.284
1990 West Palm Bch.	....	Fla. St.	3B-SS	55	183	30	62	9	3	3	30	15	.339
1990 Jacksonville	.....	Southern	3B-OF-2B	79	280	26	71	17	0	3	34	5	.254
1991 Harrisburg	....	Eastern	2B-3B-OF	129	505	87	168	30	10	13	78	23	.333
1992 Montreal	....	N.L.	OF	13	30	2	5	2	0	0	5	0	.167
1992 Indianapolis	....	A.A.	OF	110	401	57	107	23	4	11	56	11	.267

Year	Club	Lea	Pos	G	AB	R	H	2B	3B	HR	RBI	SB	Avg
1993	Ottawa a - b	Int.	OF	34	125	18	35	4	2	3	20	4	.280
1993	Montreal	N.L.	OF	6	8	1	3	1	0	0	2	0	.375
1993	Chunichi	Japan Cent.	OF	60	132	10	33	6	0	6	23	1	.250
1994	New Britain	Eastern	OF-1B	93	317	44	98	25	2	9	61	10	.309
1995	Pawtucket	Int.	OF	75	271	40	77	17	0	13	56	3	.284
1995	Boston c	A.L.	OF	39	88	8	23	7	1	1	17	0	.261
1996	Edmonton	P.C.	DH-OF-1B	51	180	35	62	16	1	8	41	0	.344
1996	Oakland	A.L.	OF-1B	61	137	21	38	5	1	10	23	1	.277
1997	Oakland	A.L.	OF-1B	133	352	62	105	19	0	27	73	3	.298
1998	Oakland	A.L.	DH-OF-1B	149	523	88	154	33	1	26	106	8	.294
1999	Oakland	A.L.	OF-1B	146	531	94	137	26	3	38	102	2	.258
2000	Oakland d	A.L.	OF-1B	143	476	74	108	26	0	21	81	5	.227
2001	Chicago e	N.L.	1B-OF-2B	128	340	48	85	21	0	17	61	2	.250
2002	Milwaukee f-g	N.L.	OF	107	270	41	66	15	0	16	41	2	.244
2003	Nashville	P.C.	OF-1B	7	18	4	3	0	0	2	3	0	.167
2003	Pittsburgh h-i	N.L.	OF-1B	121	305	49	89	20	1	20	57	0	.292
2004	Kansas City j	A.L.	OF-1B	126	439	48	117	21	3	18	66	1	.267
2005	Kansas City	A.L.	1B-OF	127	396	55	109	26	1	13	66	1	.275
2006	K.C.-Texas-Detroit k-l-m	A.L.	DH-1B-OF	117	348	42	86	21	0	13	51	0	.247
2007	Toronto n	A.L.	OF-1B	125	357	58	103	28	1	21	64	2	.289
Major League Totals		15 Yrs.		1541	4600	691	1228	271	12	241	815	27	.267
Division Series													
1995	Boston	A.L.	PH	1	1	F0	0	0	0	0	0	0	.000
2000	Oakland	A.L.	OF	3	9	0	1	1	0	0	0	0	.111
Division Series Totals				4	10	0	1	1	0	0	0	0	.100

a Released, June 8, 1993, played in Japan, re-signed by Montreal Expos organization, December 15, 1993.
b Traded to Boston Red Sox with pitcher Pete Young for player to be named later and cash, February 18, 1994.
c Filed for free agency, October 14, 1995. Signed by Oakland Athletics organization, December 1, 1995.
d Traded to Chicago Cubs for pitcher Eric Ireland, November 20, 2000.
e Filed for free agency, November 5, 2001. Signed with Milwaukee Brewers, January 25, 2002.
f On disabled list from May 16 to June 3, 2002.
g Filed for free agency, October 28, 2002. Signed with Pittsburgh Pirates, December 15, 2002.
h On disabled list from May 19 to June 10, 2003.
i Filed for free agency, October 31, 2003. Signed with Kansas City Royals, December 9, 2003.
j On disabled list from August 7 to August 22, 2004.
k Traded to Texas Rangers for pitcher Joselo Diaz, July 31, 2006.
l Claimed on waivers by Detroit Tigers, September 15, 2006.
m Filed for free agency, October 30, 2006. Signed with Toronto Blue Jays organization, December 12, 2006.
n Filed for free agency, October 29, 2007, re-signed with Toronto Blue Jays, November 2, 2007.

STEWART, SHANNON HAROLD

Born, Cincinnati, Ohio, February 25, 1974.
Bats Right. Throws Right. Height, 5 feet, 11 inches. Weight, 210 pounds.

Year	Club	Lea	Pos	G	AB	R	H	2B	3B	HR	RBI	SB	Avg
1992	Blue Jays	Gulf Coast	OF	50	172	44	40	1	0	1	11	32	.233
1993	St. Catherines	N.Y.-Penn.	DH-OF	75	301	53	84	15	2	3	29	25	.279
1994	Hagerstown	So. Atl.	OF	56	225	39	73	10	5	4	25	15	.324
1995	Knoxville	Southern	OF	138	498	89	143	24	6	5	55	42	.287
1995	Toronto	A.L.	OF	12	38	2	8	0	0	0	1	2	.211
1996	Syracuse	Int.	OF	112	420	77	125	26	8	6	42	35	.298
1996	Toronto a	A.L.	OF	7	17	2	3	1	0	0	2	1	.176
1997	Syracuse	Int.	OF	58	208	41	72	13	1	5	24	9	.346
1997	Toronto	A.L.	OF	44	168	25	48	13	7	0	22	10	.286
1998	Toronto	A.L.	OF	144	516	90	144	29	3	12	55	51	.279
1999	Toronto	A.L.	OF	145	608	102	185	28	2	11	67	37	.304
2000	Dunedin	Fla.St.	OF	1	3	2	3	1	0	0	1	0	1.000
2000	Toronto b	A.L.	OF	136	583	107	186	43	5	21	69	20	.319
2001	Toronto	A.L.	OF	155	640	103	202	44	7	12	60	27	.316
2002	Toronto c	A.L.	OF	141	577	103	175	38	6	10	45	14	.303
2003	Syracuse	Int.	OF	1	3	0	0	0	0	0	0	0	.000
2003	Toronto-Minnesota d-e-f	A.L.	OF	136	573	90	176	44	2	13	73	4	.307
2004	Rochester	Int.	OF	3	9	3	3	1	0	0	0	0	.333
2004	Minnesota g	A.L.	OF	92	378	46	115	17	2	11	47	6	.304
2005	Minnesota	A.L.	OF	132	551	69	151	27	3	10	56	7	.274
2006	Rochester	Int.	OF	5	18	2	5	1	0	0	1	1	.278
2006	Minnesota h-i	A.L.	OF	44	174	21	51	5	1	2	21	3	.293
2007	Oakland j	A.L.	OF	146	576	79	167	22	1	12	48	11	.290
Major League Totals		13 Yrs.		1334	5399	839	1611	311	39	114	566	193	.298

Year	Club	Lea	Pos	G	AB	R	H	2B	3B	HR	RBI	SB	Avg
	Division Series												
2003	Minnesota	A.L.	OF	4	15	0	6	2	0	0	0	1	.400
2004	Minnesota	A.L.	OF-DH	4	20	1	4	0	0	0	2	0	.200
Division Series Totals				8	35	1	10	2	0	0	2	1	.286

a On disabled list May 13 to May 31, 1996.
b On disabled list from April 29 to May 13, 2000.
c On disabled list from May 1 to May 16, 2002.
d On disabled list from May 29 to June 23, 2003.
e Traded to Minnesota Twins with player to be named later for outfielder Bobby Kielty, July 16, 2003. Minnesota Twins received pitcher David Gassner to complete trade, December 17, 2003.
f Filed for free agency, October 26, 2003, re-signed with Minnesota Twins, December 8, 2003.
g On disabled list from May 18 to July 15, 2004.
h On disabled list from May 20 to June 30 and July 16 to October 9, 2006.
i Filed for free agency, October 28, 2006. Signed with Oakland Athletics, February 8, 2007.
j Filed for free agency, October 29, 2007.

SULLIVAN, CORY

Born, Tulsa, Oklahoma, August 20, 1979.
Bats Left. Throws Left. Height, 6 feet. Weight, 180 pounds.

Year	Club	Lea	Pos	G	AB	R	H	2B	3B	HR	RBI	SB	Avg
2001	Asheville	So.Atl.	OF	67	258	36	71	12	1	5	22	13	.275
2002	Salem	Carolina	OF	138	560	90	161	42	6	12	67	26	.287
2003	Tulsa	Texas	OF	135	557	81	167	34	8	5	61	17	.300
2004	Colorado a-b	N.L.			INJURED—Did Not Play								
2005	Colorado	N.L.	OF	139	378	64	111	15	4	4	30	12	.294
2006	Colorado	N.L.	OF	126	386	47	103	26	10	2	30	10	.267
2007	Colorado Springs	P.C.	OF	53	206	29	54	9	3	1	21	4	.262
2007	Colorado	N.L.	OF	72	140	19	40	6	1	2	14	2	.286
Major League Totals		3 Yrs.		337	904	130	254	47	15	8	74	24	.281
	Division Series												
2007	Colorado	N.L.	OF	3	2	0	1	0	0	0	0	0	.500
	Championship Series												
2007	Colorado	N.L.	OF	1	1	0	0	0	0	0	0	0	.000
	World Series Record												
2007	Colorado	N.L.	OF	2	3	0	1	0	0	0	0	0	.333

a On minor league disabled list from April 8 to May 17, 2004.
b On disabled list from May 17 to October 27, 2004.

SUZUKI, ICHIRO

Born, Kasugai, Japan, October 22, 1973.
Bats Left. Throws Right. Height, 5 feet, 9 inches. Weight, 170 pounds.

Year	Club	Lea	Pos	G	AB	R	H	2B	3B	HR	RBI	SB	Avg
1992	Orix	Japan Pac.	OF	40	95	9	24	5	0	0	5	3	.253
1993	Orix	Japan Pac.	OF	43	64	4	12	2	0	1	2	0	.188
1994	Orix	Japan Pac.	OF	130	546	111	210	41	5	13	54	29	.385
1995	Orix	Japan Pac.	OF	130	524	104	179	23	4	25	80	49	.342
1996	Orix	Japan Pac.	OF	130	542	104	193	24	4	16	84	35	.356
1997	Orix	Japan Pac.	OF	135	536	94	185	31	4	17	91	39	.345
1998	Orix	Japan Pac.	OF	135	506	79	181	36	3	13	71	11	.358
1999	Orix	Japan Pac.	OF	103	411	80	141	27	2	21	68	12	.343
2000	Orix a	Japan Pac.	OF	105	395	73	153	22	1	12	73	21	.387
2001	Seattle b-c	A.L.	OF	157	*692	127	*242	34	8	8	69	*56	*.350
2002	Seattle	A.L.	OF	157	647	111	208	27	8	8	51	31	.321
2003	Seattle	A.L.	OF	159	679	111	212	29	8	13	62	34	.312
2004	Seattle	A.L.	OF	161	*704	101	*262	24	5	8	60	36	*.372
2005	Seattle	A.L.	OF	*162	679	111	206	21	12	15	68	33	.303
2006	Seattle	A.L.	OF	161	*695	110	*224	20	9	9	49	45	.322
2007	Seattle	A.L.	OF	161	*678	111	*238	22	7	6	68	37	.351
Major League Totals		7 Yrs.		1118	4774	782	1592	177	57	67	427	272	.333
	Division Series												
2001	Seattle	A.L.	OF	5	20	4	12	1	0	0	2	1	.600
	Championship Series												
2001	Seattle	A.L.	OF	5	18	3	4	1	0	0	1	2	.222

a Signed by Seattle Mariners as free agent, November 18, 2000.
b Selected Rookie of the Year in American League for 2001.
c Selected Most Valuable Player in American League for 2001.

SUZUKI, KURT KIYOSHI
Born, Wailuku, Hawaii, October 4, 1983.
Bats Right. Throws Right. Height, 6 feet. Weight, 205 pounds.

Year Club	Lea	Pos	G	AB	R	H	2B	3B	HR	RBI	SB	Avg
2004 Vancouver ...... Northwest	C	46	175	27	52	10	3	3	31	0	.297
2005 Stockton............Calif.	C	114	441	85	122	26	5	12	65	5	.277
2006 Midland .... Texas	C-1B	99	376	64	107	26	1	7	55	5	.285
2007 Sacramento ..........P.C.	C	55	211	32	59	9	0	3	27	0	.280
2007 Oakland .... A.L.	C	68	213	27	53	13	0	7	39	0	.249

SWEENEY, MARK PATRICK
Born, Framingham, Massachusetts, October 26, 1969.
Bats Left. Throws Left. Height, 6 feet, 1 inch. Weight, 215 pounds.

Year Club	Lea	Pos	G	AB	R	H	2B	3B	HR	RBI	SB	Avg
1991 Boise .... Northwest	OF	70	234	45	66	10	3	4	34	9	.282
1992 Quad City........ Midwest	OF	120	424	65	115	20	5	14	76	15	.271
1993 Palm Springs ..... California	OF-1B	66	245	41	87	18	3	3	47	9	.355
1993 Midland .... Texas	OF	51	188	41	67	13	2	9	32	1	.356
1994 Midland .... Texas	OF-1B	14	50	13	15	3	0	3	18	1	.300
1994 Vancouver ...........P.C.	DH-1B-OF	103	344	59	98	12	3	8	49	3	.285
1995 Vancouver .........P.C.	OF-1B	69	226	48	78	14	2	7	59	3	.345
1995 Louisville .... A.A.	1B	22	76	15	28	8	0	2	22	2	.368
1995 St. Louis............ N.L.	1B-OF	37	77	5	21	2	0	2	13	1	.273
1996 St. Louis a .... N.L.	OF-1B	98	170	32	45	9	0	3	22	3	.265
1997 St. Louis-San Diego b .. N.L.	OF-1B	115	164	16	46	7	0	2	23	2	.280
1998 San Diego .... N.L.	OF-1B	122	192	17	45	8	3	2	15	1	.234
1999 Cincinnati .... N.L.	1B-OF	37	31	6	11	3	0	2	7	0	.355
1999 Indianapolis c......... Int.	OF	86	311	66	100	17	1	12	51	3	.322
2000 Milwaukee .... N.L.	OF-1B	71	73	9	16	6	0	1	6	0	.219
2000 Indianapolis d-e....... Int.	1B-OF	18	55	13	28	8	0	2	14	0	.509
2001 Indianapolis .... Int.	OF-1B	109	404	65	116	34	1.	6	69	3	.287
2001 Milwaukee f .... N.L.	OF-1B	48	89	9	23	3	1	3	11	2	.258
2002 San Diego .... N.L.	1B-OF	48	65	3	11	3	0	1	4	0	.169
2002 Portland g-h-i-j ........P.C.	1B	1	1	0	1	0	0	0	0	0	1.000
2003 Colorado Springs.......P.C.	OF-1B	51	165	24	49	10	1	5	35	1	.297
2003 Colorado k-l-m........ N.L.	OF-1B	67	97	13	25	9	0	2	14	0	.258
2004 Colorado n.......... N.L.	OF-1B	122	177	25	47	12	2	9	40	1	.266
2005 San Diego o........ N.L.	1B-OF	135	221	31	65	12	1	8	40	4	.294
2006 San Francisco .... N.L.	1B-OF	114	259	32	65	15	2	5	37	0	.251
2007 San Fran.-L.A. p-q-r .... N.L.	1B-OF	106	123	20	32	9	0	2	13	2	.260
Major League Totals	13 Yrs.	1120	1738	218	452	98	9	42	245	16	.260
Division Series											
1996 St. Louis............ N.L.	PH	1	1	0	1	0	0	0	0	0	1.000
1998 San Diego .... N.L.	PH	2	1	0	0	0	0	0	0	0	.000
2005 San Diego .... N.L.	1B	3	3	1	2	1	0	0	0	0	.667
Division Series Totals		6	5	1	3	1	0	0	0	0	.600
Championship Series											
1996 St. Louis............ N.L.	OF	5	4	1	0	0	0	0	0	0	.000
1998 San Diego .... N.L.	PH	3	2	1	0	0	0	0	0	0	.000
Championship Series Totals		8	6	2	0	0	0	0	0	0	.000
World Series Record											
1998 San Diego .... N.L.	PH	3	3	0	2	0	0	0	1	0	.000

a Traded by California Angels to St. Louis Cardinals with player to be named later for pitcher John Habyan, July 8, 1995. St. Louis Cardinals received infielder Rod Correia to complete trade, January 31, 1996.

b Traded to San Diego Padres with pitcher Danny Jackson and pitcher Rich Batchelor for outfielder Phil Plantier, infielder Scott Livingstone and pitcher Fernando Valenzuela, June 14, 1997.

c Traded to Cincinnati Reds with outfielder Greg Vaughn for outfielder Reggie Sanders, infielder Damian Jackson and pitcher Josh Harris, February 2, 1999.

d Traded to Milwaukee Brewers with player to be named later for outfielder Alex Ochoa, January 14, 2000. Milwaukee Brewers received pitcher Gene Altman to complete trade, May 15, 2000.

e On disabled list from March 31 to May 6 and July 18 to August 14, 2000.

f Filed for free agency, October 5, 2000, re-signed with Milwaukee Brewers, January 3, 2001.

g Traded to New York Mets with outfielder Jeromy Burnitz, pitcher Jeff D'Amico, infielder Lou Collier and cash for outfielder Alex Ochoa, pitcher Glendon Rusch and infielder Lenny Harris, January 21, 2002.

h Released by New York Mets, March 13, 2002. Signed with San Diego Padres organization, March 16, 2002.

i On disabled list from June 6 to June 26, 2002.

j Released by San Diego Padres, July 13, 2002, re-signed with San Diego Padres, August 13, 2002.

k Released by San Diego Padres, August 16, 2002. Signed with Colorado Rockies, January 21, 2003.

l Signed with Colorado Rockies organization, January 21, 2003.

m Filed for free agency, October 27, 2003. Signed with Colorado Rockies organization, January 5, 2004.
n Filed for free agency, October 28, 2004. Signed with San Diego Padres, December 22, 2004.
o Filed for free agency, October 28, 2005. Signed with San Francisco Giants, December 8, 2005.
p On disabled list from March 29 to April 13, 2007.
q Traded to Los Angeles Dodgers for player to be named later, August 9, 2007.
r Filed for free agency, October 30, 2007.

SWEENEY, MICHAEL JOHN (MIKE)

Born, Orange, California, July 22, 1973.
Bats Right. Throws Right. Height, 6 feet, 3 inches. Weight, 220 pounds.

Year	Club	Lea	Pos	G	AB	R	H	2B	3B	HR	RBI	SB	Avg
1991	Royals . . . . Gulf Coast	C-1B	38	102	8	22	3	0	1	11	1	.216
1992	Eugene . . . . Northwest	C	59	199	17	44	12	1	4	28	3	.221
1993	Eugene . . . . Northwest	C	53	175	32	42	10	2	6	29	1	.240
1994	Rockford . . . . Midwest	C	86	276	47	83	20	3	10	52	0	.301
1995	Wilmington . . . . . Carolina	C-3B	99	332	61	103	23	1	18	53	6	.310
1995	Kansas City . . . . A.L.	C	4	4	1	1	0	0	0	0	0	.250
1996	Wichita . . . . Texas	DH-C	66	235	45	75	18	1	14	51	3	.319
1996	Omaha . . . . A.A.	C	25	101	14	26	9	0	3	16	0	.257
1996	Kansas City . . . . A.L.	C	50	165	23	46	10	0	4	24	1	.279
1997	Omaha . . . . A.A.	C	40	144	22	34	8	1	10	29	0	.236
1997	Kansas City . . . . A.L.	C	84	240	30	58	8	0	7	31	3	.242
1998	Kansas City . . . . A.L.	C	92	282	32	73	18	0	8	35	2	.259
1999	Kansas City . . . . A.L.	DH-1B-C	150	575	101	185	44	2	22	102	6	.322
2000	Kansas City . . . . A.L.	1B	159	618	105	206	30	0	29	144	8	.333
2001	Kansas City . . . . A.L.	1B	147	559	97	170	46	0	29	99	10	.304
2002	Omaha . . . . P.C.	1B	3	12	2	3	1	0	1	4	0	.250
2002	Kansas City a . . . . A.L.	1B	126	471	81	160	31	1	24	86	9	.340
2003	Omaha . . . . P.C.	DH	2	8	3	2	1	0	1	1	0	.250
2003	Kansas City b . . . . A.L.	DH-1B	108	392	62	115	18	1	16	83	3	.293
2004	Kansas City c . . . . A.L.	1B	106	411	56	118	23	0	22	79	3	.287
2005	Kansas City d . . . . A.L.	DH-1B	122	470	63	141	39	0	21	83	3	.300
2006	Burlington . . . . Midwest	DH	2	7	2	1	0	0	1	1	0	.143
2006	Wichita . . . . Texas	DH	4	13	3	5	1	0	2	5	0	.385
2006	Omaha . . . . P.C.	DH	5	15	3	5	2	0	1	4	0	.333
2006	Kansas City e . . . . A.L.	DH	60	217	23	56	15	0	8	33	2	.258
2007	Omaha . . . . P.C.	DH	6	21	1	4	1	0	0	1	0	.190
2007	Kansas City f-g . . . . A.L.	DH-1B	74	265	26	69	15	1	7	38	0	.260
Major League Totals			13 Yrs.	1282	4669	700	1398	297	5	197	837	50	.299

a On disabled list from July 14 to August 13, 2002.
b On disabled list from June 21 to August 8, 2003.
c On disabled list from August 22 to October 18, 2004.
d On disabled list from June 16 to July 1, 2005.
e On disabled list from May 2 to August 8, 2006.
f On disabled list from June 18 to August 31, 2007.
g Filed for free agency, October 30, 2007.

SWISHER, NICHOLAS THOMPSON (NICK)

Born, Columbus, Ohio, January 25, 1980.
Bats Both. Throws Left. Height, 6 feet. Weight, 215 pounds.

Year	Club	Lea	Pos	G	AB	R	H	2B	3B	HR	RBI	SB	Avg
2002	Visalia . . . . California	OF	49	183	22	44	13	2	4	23	3	.240
2002	Vancouver . . . . . Northwest	OF	13	44	10	11	3	0	2	12	3	.250
2003	Modesto . . . . California	OF-1B	51	189	38	56	14	2	10	43	3	.296
2003	Midland . . . . Texas	OF-1B	76	287	36	66	24	2	5	43	0	.230
2004	Sacramento . . . . P.C.	OF-1B	125	443	109	119	28	2	29	92	3	.269
2004	Oakland . . . . A.L.	OF-1B	20	60	11	15	4	0	2	8	0	.250
2005	Sacramento . . . . P.C.	OF-1B	6	23	4	9	3	0	0	1	0	.391
2005	Oakland a . . . . A.L.	OF-1B	131	462	66	109	32	1	21	74	0	.236
2006	Oakland . . . . A.L.	1B-OF	157	556	106	141	24	2	35	95	1	.254
2007	Oakland b . . . . A.L.	OF-1B	150	539	84	141	36	1	22	78	3	.262
Major League Totals			4 Yrs.	458	1617	267	406	96	4	80	255	4	.251
Division Series													
2006	Oakland . . . . A.L.	1B	3	10	3	3	2	0	0	1	0	.300
Championship Series													
2006	Oakland . . . . A.L.	1B	4	10	0	1	0	0	0	0	0	.100

a On disabled list from May 2 to May 25, 2005.
b Traded to Chicago White Sox for pitcher Gio Gonzalez, pitcher Fautino de los Santos and outfielder Ryan Sweeney, January 3, 2008.

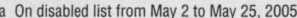

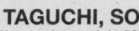

TAGUCHI, SO

Born, Hyogo, Japan, July 22, 1969.
Bats Right. Throws Right. Height, 5 feet, 10 inches. Weight, 165 pounds.

Year	Club	Lea	Pos	G	AB	R	H	2B	3B	HR	RBI	SB	Avg
1992	Orix	Japan Pac.	OF	47	123	12	33	10	0	1	7	5	.268
1993	Orix	Japan Pac.	OF	31	83	12	23	7	1	0	5	3	.277
1994	Orix	Japan Pac.	OF	108	329	55	101	17	1	6	43	10	.307
1995	Orix	Japan Pac.	OF	130	495	76	122	24	2	9	61	14	.246
1996	Orix	Japan Pac.	OF	128	509	74	142	24	1	7	44	10	.279
1997	Orix	Japan Pac.	OF	135	572	92	168	32	4	10	56	7	.294
1998	Orix	Japan Pac.	OF	132	497	85	135	26	2	9	41	8	.272
1999	Orix	Japan Pac.	OF	133	524	77	141	21	3	9	56	11	.269
2000	Orix	Japan Pac.	OF	129	509	77	142	26	6	8	49	9	.279
2001	Orix	Japan Pac.	OF	134	453	70	127	21	0	8	42	6	.280
2002	Memphis	P.C.	OF	91	304	37	75	17	0	5	36	6	.247
2002	St. Louis	N.L.	OF	19	15	4	6	0	0	0	2	1	.400
2002	New Haven a	Eastern	OF	26	107	21	33	10	0	1	15	3	.308
2003	Memphis	P.C.	OF	90	258	31	66	8	2	2	24	14	.256
2003	St. Louis	N.L.	OF-2B	43	54	9	14	3	1	3	13	0	.259
2004	Memphis	P.C.	OF	17	55	5	18	4	0	1	7	6	.327
2004	St. Louis b	N.L.	OF	109	179	26	52	10	2	3	25	6	.291
2005	St. Louis	N.L.	OF	143	396	45	114	21	2	8	53	11	.288
2006	St. Louis	N.L.	OF-2B	134	316	46	84	19	1	2	31	11	.266
2007	St. Louis c	N.L.	OF-2B	130	307	48	89	15	0	3	30	7	.290
Major League Totals		6 Yrs.		578	1267	178	359	68	6	19	154	36	.283
Division Series													
2004	St. Louis	N.L.	OF	1	0	0	0	0	0	0	0	0	.000
2005	St. Louis	N.L.	OF	3	1	0	0	0	0	0	0	0	.000
2006	St. Louis	N.L.	OF	2	1	1	1	0	0	1	1	0	1.000
Division Series Totals				6	2	1	1	0	0	1	1	0	.500
Championship Series													
2004	St. Louis	N.L.	OF	3	2	0	0	0	0	0	0	0	.000
2005	St. Louis	N.L.	OF	6	6	0	0	0	0	0	0	0	.000
2006	St. Louis	N.L.	OF	5	3	1	3	1	0	1	3	0	1.000
Championship Series Totals				14	11	1	3	1	0	1	3	0	.273
World Series Record													
2004	St. Louis	N.L.	OF	2	4	1	1	0	0	0	1	0	.250
2006	St. Louis	N.L.	OF	4	11	3	2	0	0	0	0	0	.182
World Series Totals				6	15	4	3	0	0	0	1	0	.200

a Signed by St. Louis Cardinals, January 9, 2002.
b Not offered contract, December 21, 2004, re-signed with St. Louis Cardinals, December 22, 2004.
c Released by St. Louis Cardinals, December 5, 2007. Signed with Philadelphia Phillies, December 23, 2007.

TAVERAS, WILLY

Born, Tenares, Dominican Republic, December 25, 1981.
Bats Right. Throws Right. Height, 6 feet. Weight, 160 pounds.

Year	Club	Lea	Pos	G	AB	R	H	2B	3B	HR	RBI	SB	Avg
2000	Burlington	Appal.	OF	50	190	46	50	4	3	1	16	36	.263
2001	Columbus	So.Atl.	OF	97	395	55	107	15	7	3	32	29	.271
2002	Columbus	So.Atl.	OF	85	313	68	83	14	1	4	27	54	.265
2003	Kinston	Carolina	OF	113	397	64	112	9	6	2	35	57	.282
2004	Round Rock	Texas	OF	103	409	76	137	13	1	2	27	55	.335
2004	Houston a	N.L.	OF	10	1	2	0	0	0	0	0	1	.000
2005	Houston	N.L.	OF	152	592	82	172	13	4	3	29	34	.291
2006	Houston b	N.L.	OF	149	529	83	147	19	5	1	30	33	.278
2007	Colorado Springs	P.C.	OF	4	14	0	5	0	0	0	0	1	.357
2007	Colorado c	N.L.	OF	97	372	64	119	13	2	2	24	33	.320
Major League Totals		4 Yrs.		408	1494	231	438	45	11	6	83	101	.293
Division Series													
2005	Houston	N.L.	OF	4	14	2	5	1	0	0	0	0	.357
Championship Series													
2005	Houston	N.L.	OF	6	14	1	5	0	0	0	0	0	.357
2007	Colorado	N.L.	OF	4	18	3	3	1	0	0	1	1	.167
Championship Series Totals				10	32	4	8	1	0	0	1	1	.250
World Series Record													
2005	Houston	N.L.	OF	4	15	2	5	2	1	0	0	1	.333
2007	Colorado	N.L.	OF	3	8	1	0	0	0	0	0	0	.000
World Series Totals				7	23	3	5	2	1	0	0	1	.217

a Traded by Cleveland Indians to Houston Astros with outfielder Luke Scott for pitcher Jeriome Robertson, March 31, 2004.
b Traded to Colorado Rockies with pitcher Taylor Buchholz and pitcher Jason Hirsh for pitcher Jason Jennings and pitcher Miguel Asencio, December 12, 2006.
c On disabled list from August 15 to September 1, 2007.

TEAHEN, MARK THOMAS

Born, Redlands, California, September 6, 1981.
Bats Left. Throws Right. Height, 6 feet, 3 inches. Weight, 220 pounds.

Year	Club	Lea	Pos	G	AB	R	H	2B	3B	HR	RBI	SB	Avg
2002	Modesto	California	3B	59	234	25	56	9	1	1	26	1	.239
2002	Vancouver	Northwest	3B	13	57	10	23	5	1	0	6	4	.404
2003	Modesto	California	3B	121	453	68	128	27	4	3	71	4	.283
2004	Omaha	P.C.	3B	66	246	33	69	15	1	8	31	0	.280
2004	Sacramento	P.C.	3B	20	69	9	19	8	0	0	10	0	.275
2004	Midland a	Texas	3B	53	197	31	66	15	4	6	36	0	.335
2005	Omaha	P.C.	3B	8	27	4	7	2	0	0	4	0	.259
2005	Kansas City b	A.L.	3B	130	447	60	110	29	4	7	55	7	.246
2006	Omaha	P.C.	3B	24	79	14	30	8	4	2	14	0	.380
2006	Kansas City	A.L.	3B	109	393	70	114	21	7	18	69	10	.290
2007	Kansas City c	A.L.	OF-1B	144	544	78	155	31	8	7	60	13	.285
Major League Totals			3 Yrs.	383	1384	208	379	81	19	32	184	30	.274

a Traded to Kansas City Royals with pitcher Mike Wood for outfielder Octavio Dotel and cash, June 24, 2004.
b On disabled list from April 12 to May 3, 2005.
c On disabled list from August 19 to September 3, 2007.

TEIXEIRA, MARK CHARLES

Born, Annapolis, Maryland, April 11, 1980.
Bats Both. Throws Right. Height, 6 feet, 3 inches. Weight, 220 pounds.

Year	Club	Lea	Pos	G	AB	R	H	2B	3B	HR	RBI	SB	Avg
2002	Charlotte	Fla.St.	3B	38	150	32	48	10	2	9	41	2	.320
2002	Tulsa	Texas	3B	48	171	31	54	11	3	10	28	3	.316
2003	Texas	A.L.	1B-OF-3B	146	529	66	137	29	5	26	84	1	.259
2004	Frisco	Texas	1B	1	3	0	0	0	0	0	0	0	.000
2004	Texas a	A.L.	1B-OF	145	545	101	153	34	2	38	112	4	.281
2005	Texas	A.L.	1B	*162	644	112	194	41	3	43	144	4	.301
2006	Texas	A.L.	1B	*162	628	99	177	45	1	33	110	2	.282
2007	Frisco	Texas	1B	1	2	0	0	0	0	0	0	0	.000
2007	Texas	A.L.	1B	78	286	48	85	24	1	13	49	0	.297
2007	Atlanta b-c	N.L.	1B	54	208	38	66	9	1	17	56	0	.317
Major League Totals			5 Yrs.	747	2840	464	812	182	13	170	555	11	.286

a On disabled list from April 13 to April 29, 2004.
b On disabled list from June 9 to July 13, 2007.
c Traded to Atlanta Braves with pitcher Ron Mahay for catcher Jarrod Saltalamacchia, infielder Elvis Andrews, pitcher Neftali Feliz, pitcher Matt Harrison and pitcher Beau James, July 31, 2007.

TEJADA, MIGUEL ODALIS

Born, Bani, Dominican Republic, May 25, 1976.
Bats Right. Throws Right. Height, 5 feet, 9 inches. Weight, 215 pounds.

Year	Club	Lea	Pos	G	AB	R	H	2B	3B	HR	RBI	SB	Avg
1994	Oakland	Dominican	2B	74	218	51	64	9	1	18	62	13	.294
1995	Sou. Oregon	Northwest	SS	74	269	45	66	15	5	8	44	19	.245
1996	Modesto	California	SS-3B	114	458	97	128	12	5	20	72	27	.279
1997	Huntsville	Southern	SS	128	502	85	138	20	3	22	97	15	.275
1997	Oakland	A.L.	SS	26	99	10	20	3	2	2	10	2	.202
1998	Edmonton	P.C.	SS	1	3	0	0	0	0	0	0	0	.000
1998	Huntsville	Southern	SS	15	52	9	17	6	0	2	7	1	.327
1998	Oakland a	A.L.	SS	105	365	53	85	20	1	11	45	5	.233
1999	Oakland	A.L.	SS	159	593	93	149	33	4	21	84	8	.251
2000	Oakland	A.L.	SS	160	607	105	167	32	1	30	115	6	.275
2001	Oakland	A.L.	SS	*162	622	107	166	31	3	31	113	11	.267
2002	Oakland b	A.L.	SS	*162	662	108	204	30	0	34	131	7	.308
2003	Oakland c	A.L.	SS	*162	636	98	177	42	0	27	106	10	.278
2004	Baltimore	A.L.	SS	*162	653	107	203	40	2	34	*150	4	.311
2005	Baltimore	A.L.	SS	*162	654	89	199	*50	5	26	98	5	.304
2006	Baltimore	A.L.	SS	*162	648	99	214	37	0	24	100	6	.330
2007	Frederick	Carolina	3B	1	2	1	2	0	1	1	1	0	1.000

Year	Club	Lea	Pos	G	AB	R	H	2B	3B	HR	RBI	SB	Avg
2007 Bowie............Eastern			SS	1	3	0	0	0	0	0	1	0	.000
2007 Baltimore d-e.........A.L.			SS	133	514	72	152	19	1	18	81	2	.296
Major League Totals............		11 Yrs.	1555	6053	941	1736	337	19	258	1033	66	.287
Division Series													
2000 Oakland.............A.L.			SS	5	20	5	7	2	0	0	1	1	.350
2001 Oakland.............A.L.			SS	5	21	1	6	3	0	0	1	0	.286
2002 Oakland.............A.L.			SS	5	21	3	3	1	0	1	4	0	.143
2003 Oakland.............A.L.			SS	5	23	0	2	1	0	0	2	0	.087
Division Series Totals...........				20	85	9	18	7	0	1	8	1	.212

a On disabled list from March 31 to May 20, 1998.
b Selected Most Valuable Player in American League for 2002.
c Filed for free agency, October 27, 2003. Signed with Baltimore Orioles, December 14, 2003.
d On disabled list from June 22 to July 27, 2007.
e Traded to Houston Astros for pitcher Troy Patton, outfielder Luke Scott, pitcher Matt Albers, pitcher Dennis Sarfate and infielder Michael Costanzo, December 12, 2007.

TERRERO, LUIS ENRIQUE
Born, Barahona, Barahona, Dominican Republic, May 18, 1980.
Bats Right. Throws Right. Height, 6 feet, 2 inches. Weight, 206 pounds.

Year	Club	Lea	Pos	G	AB	R	H	2B	3B	HR	RBI	SB	Avg
1998 Arizona........Dominican			OF	56	169	19	39	7	1	2	15	9	.231
1999 Missoula..........Pioneer			OF	71	272	74	78	13	7	8	40	27	.287
2000 High Desert.........Calif.			OF	19	79	10	15	3	1	0	1	5	.190
2000 Missoula ....Pioneer			OF	68	276	48	72	10	4	8	44	23	.261
2001 Lancaster...........Calif.			OF	19	71	16	32	9	1	4	11	5	.451
2001 South Bend ......Midwest			OF	24	89	4	14	2	0	1	8	3	.157
2001 Yakima........Northwest			OF	11	41	7	13	2	1	0	0	0	.317
2001 El Paso..........Texas			OF	34	147	29	44	13	3	3	8	9	.299
2002 El Paso............Texas			OF	104	360	49	103	20	6	8	54	18	.286
2003 Tucson.............P.C.			OF	118	467	83	134	20	15	3	46	23	.287
2003 Arizona.............N.L.			OF	5	4	0	1	0	0	0	0	0	.250
2004 Tucson............P.C.			OF	58	217	36	68	9	6	9	35	15	.313
2004 Arizona.............N.L.			OF	62	229	21	56	14	0	4	14	10	.245
2005 Tucson.............P.C.			OF	7	30	4	8	1	0	0	1	1	.267
2005 Arizona a.........N.L.			OF	88	161	23	37	6	1	4	20	3	.230
2006 Baltimore............A.L.			OF	27	40	4	8	1	0	1	6	0	.200
2006 Ottawa b-c..........Int.			OF	84	302	52	96	21	2	16	44	18	.318
2007 Charlotte............Int.			OF	20	65	7	15	4	0	4	9	3	.231
2007 Chicago d-e.........A.L.			OF	61	117	18	27	2	0	5	12	4	.231
Major League Totals............		5 Yrs.	243	551	66	129	23	1	14	52	17	.234

a On disabled list from June 6 to June 28, 2005.
b Released by Arizona Diamondbacks, March 30, 2006. Signed with Baltimore Orioles organization, April 12, 2006.
c Filed for free agency, October 9, 2006. Signed with Chicago White Sox, November 2, 2006.
d On disabled list from July 24 to September 1, 2007.
e Filed for free agency, October 12, 2007. Signed with Baltimore Orioles organization, January 8, 2008.

THAMES, MARCUS MARKLEY
Born, Louisville, Mississippi, March 6, 1977.
Bats Right. Throws Right. Height, 6 feet, 2 inches. Weight, 220 pounds.

Year	Club	Lea	Pos	G	AB	R	H	2B	3B	HR	RBI	SB	Avg
1997 Yankees .... Gulf Coast			OF	57	195	51	67	17	4	7	36	6	.344
1997 Greensboro .... So.Atl.			OF	4	16	2	5	1	0	0	2	1	.313
1998 Tampa.............Fla.St.			OF	122	457	62	130	18	3	11	59	13	.284
1999 Norwich..........Eastern			OF	51	182	25	41	6	2	4	26	0	.225
1999 Tampa.............Fla.St.			OF	69	266	47	65	12	4	11	38	3	.244
2000 Norwich..........Eastern			OF	131	474	72	114	30	2	15	79	1	.241
2001 Norwich..........Eastern			OF	139	520	114	167	43	4	31	97	10	.321
2002 Columbus............Int.			OF	107	386	51	80	21	3	13	45	5	.207
2002 New York............A.L.			OF	7	13	2	3	1	0	1	2	0	.231
2003 Columbus............Int.			OF	52	194	26	54	15	2	2	28	3	.278
2003 Oklahoma...........P.C.			OF	18	66	9	17	4	0	2	7	1	.258
2003 Texas a-b...........A.L.			OF	30	73	12	15	2	0	1	4	0	.205
2004 Toledo............Int.			OF	64	234	57	77	21	1	24	59	4	.329
2004 Detroit.............A.L.			OF	61	165	24	42	12	0	10	33	0	.255
2005 Toledo..............Int.			OF	73	265	53	90	18	3	22	56	4	.340
2005 Detroit.............A.L.			OF	38	107	11	21	2	0	7	16	0	.196

172

Year Club	Lea	Pos	G	AB	R	H	2B	3B	HR	RBI	SB	Avg
2006 Detroit	A.L.	OF	110	348	61	89	20	2	26	60	1	.256
2007 Toledo	Int.	1B	2	8	2	3	0	0	1	2	0	.375
2007 Detroit c	A.L.	OF-1B	86	269	37	65	15	0	18	54	2	.242
Major League Totals		6 Yrs.	332	975	147	235	52	2	63	169	3	.241
Division Series												
2006 Detroit	A.L.	DH	4	15	2	5	2	0	0	1	0	.333
Championship Series												
2006 Detroit	A.L.	DH	2	5	1	0	0	0	0	0	0	.000
World Series Record												
2006 Detroit	A.L.	OF	2	1	0	0	0	0	0	0	0	.000

a Traded to Texas Rangers for outfielder Ruben Sierra, June 6, 2003.
b Filed for free agency, October 14, 2003. Signed with Detroit Tigers organization, December 7, 2003.
c On disabled list from July 19 to August 9, 2007.

THERIOT, RYAN STEWART

Born, Baton Rouge, Louisiana, December 7, 1979.
Bats Right. Throws Right. Height, 5 feet, 11 inches. Weight, 175 pounds.

Year Club	Lea	Pos	G	AB	R	H	2B	3B	HR	RBI	SB	Avg
2001 Daytona	Fla.St.	SS	30	103	20	21	5	0	0	9	2	.204
2002 Lansing	Midwest	2B-SS	130	489	75	123	19	4	1	37	32	.252
2003 Lansing	Midwest	2B-SS	58	220	29	57	8	1	1	17	21	.259
2003 West Tenn	Southern	SS	53	178	20	42	3	0	1	9	9	.236
2004 Daytona	Fla.St.	2B-SS-3B	103	330	47	90	14	3	1	34	13	.273
2005 West Tenn	Southern	2B-SS-3B	120	448	52	136	28	4	1	53	24	.304
2005 Chicago	N.L.	2B	9	13	3	2	1	0	0	0	0	.154
2006 Iowa	P.C.	SS-2B-OF-3B	73	280	41	85	11	5	0	22	14	.304
2006 Chicago	N.L.	2B-SS-3B	53	134	34	44	11	3	0	16	13	.328
2007 Chicago	N.L.	SS-2B-3B-OF	148	537	80	143	30	2	3	45	28	.266
Major League Totals		3 Yrs.	210	684	117	189	42	5	6	61	41	.276
Division Series												
2007 Chicago	N.L.	SS	3	12	0	3	0	0	0	1	1	.250

THOMAS, FRANK EDWARD

Born, Columbus, Georgia, May 27, 1968.
Bats Right. Throws Right. Height, 6 feet, 5 inches. Weight, 275 pounds.

Year Club	Lea	Pos	G	AB	R	H	2B	3B	HR	RBI	SB	Avg
1989 Sarasota White Sox ..	Gulf C.	1B	16	48	7	16	5	0	1	11	4	.333
1989 Sarasota..........	Fla. St.	1B	55	188	27	52	9	1	4	30	0	.277
1990 Birmingham	Southern	1B	109	353	84	114	27	5	18	71	7	.323
1990 Chicago	A.L.	1B	60	191	39	63	11	3	7	31	0	.330
1991 Chicago	A.L.	1B	158	559	104	178	31	2	32	109	1	.318
1992 Chicago	A.L.	1B	160	573	108	185	*46	2	24	115	6	.323
1993 Chicago a	A.L.	1B	153	549	106	174	36	0	41	128	4	.317
1994 Chicago b	A.L.	1B	113	399	*106	141	34	1	38	101	2	.353
1995 Chicago	A.L.	1B	*145	493	102	152	27	0	40	111	3	.308
1996 Chicago c	A.L.	1B	141	527	110	184	26	0	40	134	1	.349
1997 Chicago d	A.L.	1B	146	530	110	184	35	0	35	125	1	*.347
1998 Chicago	A.L.	DH-1B	160	585	109	155	35	2	29	109	7	.265
1999 Chicago	A.L.	DH-1B	135	486	74	148	36	0	15	77	3	.305
2000 Chicago	A.L.	DH-1B	159	582	115	191	44	0	43	143	1	.328
2001 Chicago e	A.L.	DH-1B	20	68	8	15	3	0	4	10	0	.221
2002 Chicago f	A.L.	DH-1B	148	523	77	132	29	1	28	92	3	.252
2003 Chicago	A.L.	DH-1B	153	546	87	146	35	0	42	105	0	.267
2004 Chicago g	A.L.	DH-1B	74	240	53	65	16	0	18	49	0	.271
2005 Charlotte	Int.	DH	11	42	3	8	1	0	1	4	0	.190
2005 Chicago h-i........	A.L.	DH	34	105	19	23	3	0	12	26	0	.219
2006 Oakland j-k.......	A.L.	DH	137	466	77	126	11	0	39	114	0	.270
2007 Toronto l.........	A.L.	DH	155	531	63	147	30	0	26	95	0	.277
Major League Totals		18 Yrs.	2251	7953	1467	2409	488	11	513	1674	32	.303
Division Series												
2000 Chicago	A.L.	DH-1B	3	9	0	0	0	0	0	0	0	.000
2006 Oakland	A.L.	DH	3	10	3	5	1	0	2	2	0	.500
Division Series Totals			6	19	3	5	1	0	2	2	0	.263
Championship Series												
1993 Chicago	A.L.	1B	6	17	2	6	0	0	1	3	0	.353
2006 Oakland	A.L.	DH	4	13	0	0	0	0	0	0	0	.000
Championship Series Totals			10	30	2	6	0	0	1	3	0	.200

a Selected Most Valuable Player in American League for 1993.
b Selected Most Valuable Player in American League for 1994.
c On disabled list from July 8 to July 30, 1996.
d On disabled list from June 7 to June 22, 1997.
e On disabled list from April 30 to October 12, 2001.
f Filed for free agency, October 31, 2002, re-signed with Chicago White Sox, December 6, 2002.
g On disabled list from July 7 to October 12, 2004.
h On disabled list from March 25 to May 30 and July 21 to October 31, 2005.
i Filed for free agency, November 8, 2005. Signed with Oakland Athletics, January 24, 2006.
j On disabled list from June 15 to June 30, 2006.
k Filed for free agency, October 28, 2006. Signed with Toronto Blue Jays, November 17, 2006.
l On disabled list from March 31 to June 16, 2007.

THOME, JAMES HOWARD (JIM)
Born, Peoria, Illinois, August 27, 1970.
Bats Left. Throws Right. Height, 6 feet, 4 inches. Weight, 245 pounds.

Year	Club	Lea	Pos	G	AB	R	H	2B	3B	HR	RBI	SB	Avg
1989 Indians	Gulf Coast	SS-3B	55	186	22	44	5	3	0	22	6	.237
1990 Burlington	Appal.	3B	34	118	31	44	7	1	12	34	6	.373
1990 Kinston	Carolina	3B	33	117	19	36	4	1	4	16	4	.308
1991 Canton	Eastern	3B	84	294	47	99	20	2	5	45	8	.337
1991 Colorado Springs	P.C.	3B	41	151	20	43	7	3	2	28	0	.285
1991 Cleveland	A.L.	3B	27	98	7	25	4	2	1	9	1	.255
1992 Colorado Springs	P.C.	3B	12	48	11	15	4	1	2	14	0	.313
1992 Cleveland a	A.L.	3B	40	117	8	24	3	1	2	12	2	.205
1993 Charlotte	Int.	3B	115	410	85	136	21	4	25	*102	1	*.332
1993 Cleveland	A.L.	3B	47	154	28	41	11	0	7	22	2	.266
1994 Cleveland	A.L.	3B	98	321	58	86	20	1	20	52	3	.268
1995 Cleveland	A.L.	3B	137	452	92	142	29	3	25	73	4	.314
1996 Cleveland	A.L.	3B	151	505	122	157	28	5	38	116	2	.311
1997 Cleveland	A.L.	1B	147	496	104	142	25	0	40	102	1	.286
1998 Cleveland b	A.L.	1B	123	440	89	129	34	2	30	85	1	.293
1999 Cleveland	A.L.	1B	146	494	101	137	27	2	33	108	0	.277
2000 Cleveland	A.L.	1B	158	557	106	150	33	1	37	106	1	.269
2001 Cleveland	A.L.	1B	156	526	101	153	26	1	49	124	0	.291
2002 Cleveland c	A.L.	1B	147	480	101	146	19	2	52	118	1	.304
2003 Philadelphia	N.L.	1B	159	578	111	154	30	3	*47	131	0	.266
2004 Philadelphia	N.L.	1B	143	508	97	139	28	1	42	105	0	.274
2005 Clearwater	Fla.St.	DH	5	12	2	4	0	0	1	3	0	.333
2005 Philadelphia d-e	N.L.	1B	59	193	26	40	7	0	7	30	0	.207
2006 Chicago	A.L.	DH-1B	143	490	108	141	26	0	42	109	0	.288
2007 Charlotte	Int.	DH	5	14	2	3	1	0	0	5	0	.214
2007 Chicago f	A.L.	DH-1B	130	432	79	119	19	0	35	96	0	.275
Major League Totals	17 Yrs.		2011	6841	1338	1925	369	24	507	1398	18	.281
Division Series												
1995 Cleveland	A.L.	3B	3	13	1	2	0	0	1	3	0	.154
1996 Cleveland	A.L.	3B	4	10	1	3	0	0	0	0	0	.300
1997 Cleveland	A.L.	1B	5	15	1	3	0	0	0	1	0	.200
1998 Cleveland	A.L.	1B-DH	4	15	2	2	0	0	2	2	0	.133
1999 Cleveland	A.L.	1B	5	17	7	6	0	0	4	10	0	.353
2001 Cleveland	A.L.	1B	5	19	2	3	0	0	1	1	0	.158
Division Series Totals			25	89	14	19	0	0	8	17	0	.213
Championship Series												
1995 Cleveland	A.L.	3B	5	15	2	4	0	0	2	5	0	.267
1997 Cleveland	A.L.	1B	6	14	3	1	0	0	0	0	0	.071
1998 Cleveland	A.L.	1B-DH	6	23	4	7	0	0	4	8	0	.304
Championship Series Totals			17	52	9	12	0	0	6	13	0	.231
World Series Record												
1995 Cleveland	A.L.	3B	6	19	1	4	1	0	1	2	0	.211
1997 Cleveland	A.L.	1B	7	28	8	8	0	1	2	4	0	.286
World Series Totals			13	47	9	12	1	1	3	6	0	.255

a On disabled list from March 28 to May 18 and May 29 to June 15, 1992.
b On disabled list from August 8 to September 16, 1998.
c Filed for free agency, October 28, 2002. Signed with Philadelphia Phillies, December 3, 2002.
d On disabled list from May 1 to May 21 and July 1 to November 1, 2005.
e Traded to Chicago White Sox for outfielder Aaron Rowand, pitcher Dan Haigwood and player to be named later, November 25, 2005. Philadelphia Phillies received pitcher Giovany Gonzalez to complete trade, December 8, 2005.
f On disabled list from April 28 to May 20, 2007.

THORMAN, SCOTT ROBERT
Born, Cambridge, Ontario, Canada, January 6, 1982.
Bats Left. Throws Right. Height, 6 feet, 3 inches. Weight, 235 pounds.

Year	Club	Lea	Pos	G	AB	R	H	2B	3B	HR	RBI	SB	Avg
2000	Braves	Gulf Coast	3B	29	97	15	22	7	1	1	19	0	.227
2001					INJURED—Did Not Play								
2002	Macon	So.Atl.	1B	127	470	57	138	38	3	16	82	2	.294
2003	Myrtle Beach	Carolina	1B	124	445	44	108	26	2	12	56	0	.243
2004	Myrtle Beach	Carolina	1B	43	154	20	46	11	1	4	29	1	.299
2004	Greenville	Southern	1B	94	345	31	87	14	3	11	51	5	.252
2005	Richmond	Int.	1B	52	210	23	58	10	3	6	27	0	.276
2005	Mississippi	Southern	1B	90	348	49	106	21	2	15	65	2	.305
2006	Richmond	Int.	1B-OF	81	309	38	92	16	2	15	48	4	.298
2006	Atlanta	N.L.	OF-1B	55	128	13	30	11	0	5	14	1	.234
2007	Atlanta	N.L.	1B	120	287	37	62	18	0	11	36	1	.216
Major League Totals			2 Yrs.	175	415	50	92	29	0	16	50	2	.222

TORREALBA, YORVIT ADOLFO
Born, Caracas, Venezuela, July 19, 1978.
Bats Right. Throws Right. Height, 5 feet, 11 inches. Weight, 200 pounds.

Year	Club	Lea	Pos	G	AB	R	H	2B	3B	HR	RBI	SB	Avg
1995	Bellingham	Northwest	C	26	71	2	11	3	0	0	8	0	.155
1996	San Jose	California	C	2	5	0	0	0	0	0	0	0	.000
1996	Burlington	Midwest	C	1	4	0	0	0	0	0	0	0	.000
1996	Bellingham	Northwest	C	48	150	23	40	4	0	1	10	4	.267
1997	Bakersfield	California	C	119	446	52	122	15	3	4	40	4	.274
1998	San Jose	California	C	21	70	10	20	2	0	0	10	2	.286
1998	Shreveport	Texas	C	59	196	18	46	7	0	0	13	0	.235
1998	Fresno	P.C.	C	4	11	1	2	1	0	0	1	0	.182
1999	San Jose	California	C	19	73	10	23	3	0	2	14	0	.315
1999	Fresno	P.C.	C	17	63	9	16	2	0	2	10	0	.254
1999	Shreveport	Texas	C	65	217	25	53	10	1	4	19	0	.244
2000	Shreveport	Texas	C	108	398	50	114	21	1	4	32	2	.286
2001	Fresno	P.C.	C	115	394	56	108	23	3	8	36	2	.274
2001	San Francisco	N.L.	C	3	4	0	2	0	1	0	2	0	.500
2002	San Francisco	N.L.	C	53	136	17	38	10	0	2	14	0	.279
2003	San Francisco	N.L.	C-OF	66	200	22	52	10	2	4	29	1	.260
2004	San Francisco	N.L.	C	64	172	19	39	7	3	6	23	2	.227
2005	San Francisco	N.L.	C	34	93	18	21	8	0	1	7	1	.226
2005	Seattle a-b	A.L.	C	42	108	14	26	4	0	2	8	0	.241
2006	Colorado Springs	P.C.	C	10	36	0	6	2	0	0	2	0	.167
2006	Colorado c	N.L.	C	65	223	23	55	16	3	7	43	4	.247
2007	Colorado d	N.L.	C	113	396	47	101	22	1	8	47	2	.255
Major League Totals			7 Yrs.	440	1332	160	334	77	10	30	173	10	.251
Division Series													
2003	San Francisco	N.L.	C	2	3	0	0	0	0	0	1	0	.000
2007	Colorado	N.L.	C	3	10	3	5	1	0	0	3	0	.500
Division Series Totals				5	13	3	5	1	0	0	4	0	.385
Championship Series													
2007	Colorado	N.L.	C	4	15	2	3	1	0	1	4	0	.200
World Series Record													
2007	Colorado	N.L.	C	4	14	0	2	0	0	0	1	0	.143

a Traded to Seattle Mariners with pitcher Jesse Foppert for outfielder Randy Winn, July 31, 2005.
b Traded to Colorado Rockies for player to be named later, December 7, 2005. Seattle Mariners received pitcher Marcos Carvajal to complete trade, December 8, 2005.
c On disabled list from March 24 to June 2 and September 10 to November 1, 2006.
d Filed for free agency, October 31, 2007, re-signed with Colorado Rockies, November 29, 2007.

TRACY, CHAD AUSTIN
Born, Charlotte, North Carolina, May 22, 1980.
Bats Left. Throws Right. Height, 6 feet, 2 inches. Weight, 200 pounds.

Year	Club	Lea	Pos	G	AB	R	H	2B	3B	HR	RBI	SB	Avg
2001	South Bend	Midwest	3B-1B	54	215	43	73	11	0	4	36	3	.340
2001	Yakima	Northwest	3B	10	36	2	10	1	0	0	5	1	.278
2002	El Paso	Texas	3B-1B	129	514	80	177	39	5	8	74	2	.344
2003	Tucson	P.C.	3B	133	522	91	169	31	4	10	80	0	.324
2004	Tucson	P.C.	3B-OF	11	40	7	16	4	0	2	11	2	.400
2004	Arizona	N.L.	3B-1B-OF	143	481	45	137	29	3	8	53	2	.285
2005	Arizona	N.L.	1B-OF	145	503	73	155	34	4	27	72	3	.308

Year	Club	Lea	Pos	G	AB	R	H	2B	3B	HR	RBI	SB	Avg
2006 Arizona..........N.L.			3B-1B	154	597	91	168	41	0	20	80	5	.281
2007 Tucson..........P.C.			3B	3	15	3	7	2	0	1	4	0	.467
2007 Arizona a.........N.L.			3B-1B	76	227	30	60	18	2	7	35	0	.264
Major League Totals............		4 Yrs.	518	1808	239	520	122	9	62	240	10	.288

a On disabled list from May 16 to June 10 and August 13 to September 16, 2007.

TULOWITZKI, TROY TREVER
Born, Santa Clara, California, October 10, 1984.
Bats Right. Throws Right. Height, 6 feet, 3 inches. Weight, 205 pounds.

Year	Club	Lea	Pos	G	AB	R	H	2B	3B	HR	RBI	SB	Avg
2005 Modesto.............Calif.			SS	22	94	17	25	6	0	4	14	1	.266
2006 Tulsa............... Texas			SS	104	423	75	123	34	2	13	61	6	.291
2006 Colorado .... N.L.			SS	25	96	15	23	2	0	1	6	3	.240
2007 Colorado .... N.L.			SS	155	609	104	177	33	5	24	99	7	.291
Major League Totals............		2 Yrs.	180	705	119	200	35	5	25	105	10	.284

Division Series

Year	Club	Lea	Pos	G	AB	R	H	2B	3B	HR	RBI	SB	Avg
2007 Colorado ............N.L.			SS	3	12	1	2	1	0	1	2	0	.167

Championship Series

Year	Club	Lea	Pos	G	AB	R	H	2B	3B	HR	RBI	SB	Avg
2007 Colorado ..........N.L.			SS	4	16	1	3	0	0	0	0	0	.188

World Series Record

Year	Club	Lea	Pos	G	AB	R	H	2B	3B	HR	RBI	SB	Avg
2007 Colorado ....-.. N.L.			SS	4	13	1	3	2	0	0	1	0	.231

TYNER, JASON RENYT
Born, Bedford, Texas, April 23, 1977.
Bats Left. Throws Left. Height, 6 feet, 1 inch. Weight, 175 pounds.

Year	Club	Lea	Pos	G	AB	R	H	2B	3B	HR	RBI	SB	Avg
1998 St. Lucie............Fla.St.			OF	50	201	30	61	2	3	0	16	15	.303
1999 Binghamton ....Eastern			OF	129	518	91	162	19	5	0	33	49	.313
1999 Norfolk...............Int.			OF	3	8	0	0	0	0	0	0	0	.000
2000 Norfolk..............Int.			OF	84	327	54	105	5	2	0	28	33	.321
2000 New York .... N.L.			OF	13	41	3	8	2	0	0	5	1	.195
2000 Tampa Bay a..........A.L.			OF	37	83	6	20	2	0	0	8	6	.241
2001 Durham ....Int.			OF	39	157	25	49	2	1	0	12	11	.312
2001 Tampa Bay ..........A.L.			OF	105	396	51	111	8	5	0	21	31	.280
2002 Tampa Bay...........A.L.			OF	44	168	17	36	2	1	0	9	7	.214
2002 Durham ....Int.			OF	88	351	59	102	12	4	0	27	20	.291
2003 Durham ....Int.			OF	65	275	34	89	11	5	0	24	10	.324
2003 Tampa Bay b-c.......A.L.			OF	46	90	12	25	7	0	0	6	2	.278
2004 Buffalo...............Int.			OF	38	139	25	48	4	1	0	16	5	.345
2004 Richmond d-e-f ....Int.			OF	64	243	40	70	12	1	1	16	18	.288
2005 Rochester.............Int.			OF	133	524	81	150	18	2	1	36	18	.286
2005 Minnesota g..........A.L.			OF	18	56	8	18	1	1	0	5	2	.321
2006 Rochester.............Int.			OF	80	316	52	104	14	5	0	22	8	.329
2006 Minnesota ...........A.L.			OF	62	218	29	68	5	2	0	18	4	.312
2007 Minnesota h..........A.L.			OF	114	304	42	87	14	2	1	22	8	.286
Major League Totals............		7 Yrs.	439	1356	168	373	41	11	1	94	61	.275

Division Series

Year	Club	Lea	Pos	G	AB	R	H	2B	3B	HR	RBI	SB	Avg
2006 Minnesota ...........A.L.			DH	2	6	0	0	0	0	0	0	1	.000

a Traded to Tampa Bay Devil Rays with pitcher Paul Wilson for outfielder Bubba Trammell and pitcher Rick White, July 28, 2000.
b Claimed on waivers by Texas Rangers, December 8, 2003.
c Not offered contract, December 21, 2003, re-signed with Texas Rangers organization, December 24, 2003.
d Released by Texas Rangers, April 7, 2004. Signed with Atlanta Braves organization, April 26, 2004.
e Released by Atlanta Braves, July 25, 2004. Signed with Cleveland Indians organization, July 30, 2004.
f Filed for free agency, October 15, 2004. Signed with Minnesota Twins organization, November 10, 2004.
g Filed for free agency, October 11, 2005, re-signed with Minnesota Twins organization, October 14, 2005.
h Not offered contract, December 12, 2007.

UGGLA, DANIEL COOLEY (DAN)
Born, Louisville, Kentucky, March 11, 1980.
Bats Right. Throws Right. Height, 5 feet, 11 inches. Weight, 200 pounds.

Year	Club	Lea	Pos	G	AB	R	H	2B	3B	HR	RBI	SB	Avg
2001 Yakima......Northwest			2B	72	278	39	77	21	0	5	40	8	.277
2002 Lancaster........Calif.			2B-3B	54	184	21	42	7	2	3	16	3	.228
2002 South Bend ... Midwest			3B-2B	53	171	16	34	5	1	2	10	0	.199
2003 Lancaster........Calif.			3B-2B	134	534	104	155	31	7	23	90	24	.290
2004 Lancaster........Calif.			2B-3B-SS-1B	37	140	29	47	13	3	6	38	2	.336

Year	Club	Lea	Pos	G	AB	R	H	2B	3B	HR	RBI	SB	Avg
2004 El Paso	Texas	3B-OF-2B	83	295	29	76	12	2	4	30	10	.258
2005 Tennessee a	Southern	2B-3B-1B-SS	135	498	88	148	33	3	21	87	15	.297
2006 Florida	N.L.	2B	154	611	105	172	26	7	27	90	6	.282
2007 Florida	N.L.	2B	159	632	113	155	49	3	31	88	2	.245
Major League Totals		2 Yrs.	313	1243	218	327	75	10	58	178	8	.263

a Selected by Florida Marlins from Arizona Diamondbacks in Rule V draft, December 8, 2005.

UPTON, JUSTIN IRVIN

Born, Norfolk, Virginia, August 25, 1987.
Bats Right. Throws Right. Height, 6 feet, 3 inches. Weight, 205 pounds.

Year	Club	Lea	Pos	G	AB	R	H	2B	3B	HR	RBI	SB	Avg
2006 South Bend	Midwest	OF	113	438	71	115	28	1	12	66	15	.263
2007 Visalia	Calif.	OF	32	126	27	43	6	2	5	17	9	.341
2007 Mobile	Southern	OF	71	259	48	80	17	4	13	53	10	.309
2007 Arizona	N.L.	OF	43	140	17	31	8	3	2	11	2	.221
Division Series													
2007 Arizona	N.L.	OF	2	5	2	3	0	0	0	1	1	.600
Championship Series													
2007 Arizona	N.L.	OF	4	9	0	2	1	1	0	0	0	.222

UPTON, MELVIN EMANUEL (B.J.)

Born, Norfolk, Virginia, August 21, 1984.
Bats Right. Throws Right. Height, 6 feet, 3 inches. Weight, 180 pounds.

Year	Club	Lea	Pos	G	AB	R	H	2B	3B	HR	RBI	SB	Avg
2003 Charleston	So.Atl.	SS	101	384	70	116	22	6	7	46	38	.302
2003 Orlando	Southern	SS	29	105	14	29	8	0	1	16	2	.276
2004 Montgomery	Southern	SS	29	104	21	34	7	1	2	15	3	.327
2004 Durham	Int.	SS	69	264	65	82	17	1	12	36	17	.311
2004 Tampa Bay	A.L.	SS-3B-OF	45	159	19	41	8	2	4	12	4	.258
2005 Durham	Int.	SS	139	545	98	165	36	6	18	74	44	.303
2006 Durham	Int.	SS-3B	106	398	72	107	18	4	8	41	46	.269
2006 Tampa Bay	A.L.	3B	50	175	20	43	5	0	1	10	11	.246
2007 Vero Beach	Fla.St.	2B-OF	7	17	4	4	0	0	1	3	0	.235
2007 Durham	Int.	2B	2	7	1	3	0	0	1	1	0	.429
2007 Tampa Bay a	A.L.	OF-2B	129	474	86	142	25	1	24	82	22	.300
Major League Totals		3 Yrs.	224	808	125	226	38	3	29	104	37	.280

a On disabled list from June 9 to July 13, 2007.

URIBE (TENA), JUAN C.

Born, Bani, Dominican Republic, July 22, 1979.
Bats Right. Throws Right. Height, 6 feet. Weight, 220 pounds.

Year	Club	Lea	Pos	G	AB	R	H	2B	3B	HR	RBI	SB	Avg
1997 Colorado	Dominican	SS	65	234	32	63	12	0	0	29	7	.269
1998 Rockies	Arizona	SS	40	148	25	41	5	3	0	17	8	.277
1999 Asheville	So.Atl.	SS	125	430	57	115	28	3	9	46	11	.267
2000 Salem	Carolina	SS	134	485	64	124	22	7	13	65	22	.256
2001 Carolina	Southern	SS	3	13	1	3	1	0	0	1	1	.231
2001 Colo Sprngs	P.C.	SS	74	281	40	87	27	7	7	48	11	.310
2001 Colorado	N.L.	SS	72	273	32	82	15	11	8	53	3	.300
2002 Colorado	N.L.	SS	155	566	69	136	25	7	6	49	9	.240
2003 Visalia	California	2B-SS	2	9	4	5	1	0	0	1	0	.556
2003 Tulsa	Texas	2B-3B-SS-OF	5	20	3	5	2	0	1	4	0	.250
2003 Colorado a-b	N.L.	SS-2B-OF	87	316	45	80	19	3	10	33	7	.253
2004 Chicago	A.L.	2B-SS-3B	134	502	82	142	31	6	23	74	9	.283
2005 Chicago	A.L.	SS	146	481	58	121	23	3	16	71	4	.252
2006 Chicago	A.L.	SS	132	463	53	109	28	2	21	71	1	.235
2007 Chicago	A.L.	SS	150	513	55	120	18	2	20	68	1	.234
Major League Totals		7 Yrs.	876	3114	394	790	159	34	104	419	34	.254
Division Series													
2005 Chicago	A.L.	SS	3	10	4	4	1	0	1	4	0	.400
Championship Series													
2005 Chicago	A.L.	SS	5	16	1	4	1	0	0	0	0	.250
World Series Record													
2005 Chicago	A.L.	SS	4	16	2	4	3	0	0	2	1	.250

a On disabled list from March 18 to June 3, 2003.
b Traded to Chicago White Sox for infielder Aaron Miles, December 2, 2003.

UTLEY, CHASE CAMERON

Born, Pasadena, California, December 17, 1978.
Bats Left. Throws Right. Height, 6 feet, 1 inch. Weight, 185 pounds.

Year	Club	Lea	Pos	G	AB	R	H	2B	3B	HR	RBI	SB	Avg
2000	Batavia	N.Y.-Penn.	2B	40	153	21	47	13	1	2	22	5	.307
2001	Clearwater	Fla.St.	2B	122	467	65	120	25	2	16	59	19	.257
2002	Scranton/W.B.	Int.	3B	125	464	73	122	39	1	17	70	8	.263
2003	Scranton/W.B.	Int.	2B	113	431	80	139	26	2	18	77	10	.323
2003	Philadelphia	N.L.	2B	43	134	13	32	10	1	2	21	2	.239
2004	Scranton/W.B.	Int.	2B	33	123	23	35	8	1	6	25	4	.285
2004	Philadelphia	N.L.	2B-1B	94	267	36	71	11	2	13	57	4	.266
2005	Philadelphia	N.L.	2B-1B	147	543	93	158	39	6	28	105	16	.291
2006	Philadelphia	N.L.	2B-1B	160	658	*131	203	40	4	32	102	15	.309
2007	Reading	Eastern	2B	3	10	0	1	0	0	0	0	0	.100
2007	Philadelphia a	N.L.	2B-1B	132	530	104	176	48	5	22	103	9	.332
Major League Totals			5 Yrs.	576	2132	377	640	148	18	97	388	46	.300
Division Series													
2007	Philadelphia	N.L.	2B	3	11	0	2	0	0	0	0	0	.182

a On disabled list from July 27 to August 27, 2007.

VALENTIN, JOSE ANTONIO

Born, Manati, Puerto Rico, October 12, 1969.
Bats Both. Throws Right. Height, 5 feet, 10 inches. Weight, 190 pounds.

Year	Club	Lea	Pos	G	AB	R	H	2B	3B	HR	RBI	SB	Avg
1987	Spokane	Northwest	SS	70	244	52	61	8	2	2	24	8	.250
1988	Chston-SC	So.Atl.	SS	133	444	56	103	20	1	6	44	11	.232
1989	Riverside	Calif.	SS	114	381	40	74	10	5	10	41	8	.194
1989	Wichita	Texas	SS-3B	18	49	8	12	1	0	2	5	1	.245
1990	Wichita	Texas	SS	11	36	4	10	2	0	0	2	2	.278
1991	Wichita	Texas	SS	129	447	73	112	22	5	17	68	8	.251
1992	Denver	A.A.	SS	139	492	78	118	19	11	3	45	9	.240
1992	Milwaukee a	A.L.	2B-SS	4	3	1	0	0	0	0	1	0	.000
1993	New Orleans	A.A.	SS-1B	122	389	56	96	22	5	9	53	9	.247
1993	Milwaukee	A.L.	SS	19	53	10	13	1	2	1	7	1	.245
1994	Milwaukee	A.L.	SS-2B-3B	97	285	47	68	19	0	11	46	12	.239
1995	Milwaukee	A.L.	SS-3B	112	338	62	74	23	3	11	49	16	.219
1996	Milwaukee	A.L.	SS	154	552	90	143	33	7	24	95	17	.259
1997	Beloit	Midwest	SS	2	6	3	3	1	0	0	1	0	.500
1997	Milwaukee b	A.L.	SS	136	494	58	125	23	1	17	58	19	.253
1998	Milwaukee	N.L.	SS	151	428	65	96	24	0	16	49	10	.224
1999	Milwaukee	N.L.	SS	89	256	45	58	9	5	10	38	3	.227
1999	Louisville c	Int.	SS	6	20	6	5	0	0	3	3	0	.250
2000	Chicago d-e	A.L.	SS-OF	144	568	107	155	37	6	25	92	19	.273
2001	Chicago f	A.L.	3B-SS-OF	124	438	74	113	22	2	28	68	9	.258
2002	Chicago	A.L.	3B-SS	135	474	70	118	26	4	25	75	3	.249
2003	Chicago	A.L.	SS	144	503	79	119	26	2	28	74	8	.237
2004	Charlotte	Int.	SS	8	31	1	2	0	0	0	2	0	.065
2004	Chicago g-h	A.L.	SS	125	450	73	97	20	3	30	70	8	.216
2005	Las Vegas	P.C.	3B-OF-2B	12	35	8	14	3	0	2	5	1	.400
2005	Los Angeles i-j	N.L.	3B-OF-SS	56	147	17	25	4	2	2	14	3	.170
2006	New York k	N.L.	2B-OF-1B-3B	137	384	56	104	24	3	18	62	6	.271
2007	St. Lucie	Fla.St.	2B	3	8	4	1	0	0	1	4	0	.125
2007	New York l-m	N.L.	2B	51	166	18	40	11	1	3	18	2	.241
Major League Totals			16 Yrs.	1678	5539	872	1348	302	41	249	816	136	.243
Division Series													
2000	Chicago	A.L.	SS	3	10	2	3	2	0	0	1	3	.300
2006	New York	N.L.	2B	3	9	2	0	0	0	0	0	0	.000
Division Series Totals				6	19	4	3	2	0	0	1	3	.158
Championship Series													
2006	New York	N.L.	2B	7	24	0	6	2	0	0	5	0	.250

a Traded by San Diego Padres to Milwaukee Brewers with pitcher Ricky Bones and outfielder Matt Mieske for infielder Gary Sheffield and outfielder Geoff Kellogg, March 27, 1992.
b On disabled list from April 14 to May 5, 1997.
c On disabled list from April 11 to June 16, 1999.
d Traded to Chicago White Sox with pitcher Cal Eldred for pitcher John Snyder and pitcher Jaime Navarro, January 12, 2000.
e Filed for free agency, October 30, 2000, re-signed with Chicago White Sox, November 22, 2000.
f On disabled list from June 9 to June 24, 2001.
g On disabled list from April 19 to May 7, 2004.

h Filed for free agency, October 29, 2004. Signed with Los Angeles Dodgers, December 21, 2004.
i On disabled list from May 4 to July 31, 2005.
j Filed for free agency, October 27, 2005. Signed with New York Mets, December 8, 2005.
k Filed for free agency, October 29, 2006, re-signed with New York Mets, November 15, 2006.
l On disabled list from April 29 to June 7 and July 21 to November 6, 2007.
m Filed for free agency, November 6, 2007, re-signed with New York Mets organization, January 18, 2008.

VALENTIN, JOSE JAVIER (JAVIER)

Born, Manati, Puerto Rico, September 19, 1975.
Bats Both. Throws Right. Height, 5 feet, 10 inches. Weight, 210 pounds.

Year	Club	Lea	Pos	G	AB	R	H	2B	3B	HR	RBI	SB	Avg
1993 Twins	Gulf Coast		C-3B-OF	32	103	18	27	6	1	1	19	0	.262
1993 Elizabethtn	Appal.		C	9	24	3	5	1	0	0	3	0	.208
1994 Elizabethtn	Appal.		C-OF-3B	54	210	23	44	5	0	9	27	0	.210
1995 Ft. Wayne	Midwest		C-3B	112	383	59	123	26	5	19	65	0	.321
1996 Ft. Myers	Fla.St.		C-3B	87	338	34	89	26	1	7	54	1	.263
1996 New Britain	Eastern		C-3B	48	165	22	39	8	0	3	14	0	.236
1997 New Britain	Eastern		C-3B	102	370	41	90	17	0	8	50	2	.243
1997 Minnesota	A.L.		C	4	7	1	2	0	0	0	0	0	.286
1998 Minnesota	A.L.		C	55	162	11	32	7	1	3	18	0	.198
1999 Minnesota	A.L.		C	78	218	22	54	12	1	5	28	0	.248
2000 Salt Lake	P.C.		C	39	140	25	50	16	2	7	35	1	.357
2001 Edmonton	P.C.		C-3B-1B	121	431	53	121	29	2	17	71	0	.281
2002 Edmonton	P.C.		C-3B-1B	127	455	69	130	33	1	21	80	0	.286
2002 Minnesota a	A.L.		C	4	4	0	2	0	0	0	0	0	.500
2003 Tampa Bay b	A.L.		C	49	135	13	30	7	1	3	15	0	.222
2004 Cincinnati c	N.L.		C-1B	82	202	18	47	10	1	6	20	0	.233
2005 Cincinnati	N.L.		C-1B	76	221	36	62	11	0	14	50	0	.281
2006 Cincinnati	N.L.		C-1B	92	186	24	50	6	1	8	27	0	.269
2007 Cincinnati	N.L.		C-1B	97	243	19	67	21	0	2	34	0	.276
Major League Totals			9 Yrs.	537	1378	144	346	74	5	41	192	0	.251

a Traded to Milwaukee Brewers with pitcher Matt Kinney for pitcher Matt Yeatman and pitcher Gerry Oakes, November 14, 2002.
b Traded to Tampa Bay Devil Rays for outfielder Jason Conti, March 24, 2003.
c Filed for free agency, October 15, 2003. Signed with Cincinnati Reds organization, January 9, 2004.

VARITEK, JASON ANDREW

Born, Rochester, Minnesota, April 11, 1972.
Bats Both. Throws Right. Height, 6 feet, 2 inches. Weight, 230 pounds.

Year	Club	Lea	Pos	G	AB	R	H	2B	3B	HR	RBI	SB	Avg
1995 Port City	Southern		C	104	352	42	79	14	2	10	44	0	.224
1996 Port City	Southern		C-3B-OF	134	503	63	132	34	1	12	67	7	.262
1997 Tacoma	P.C.		C	87	307	54	78	13	0	15	48	0	.254
1997 Pawtucket	Int.		C	20	66	6	13	5	0	1	5	0	.197
1997 Boston a	A.L.		C	1	1	0	1	0	0	0	0	0	1.000
1998 Boston	A.L.		C	86	221	31	56	13	0	7	33	2	.253
1999 Boston	A.L.		C	144	483	70	130	39	2	20	76	1	.269
2000 Boston	A.L.		C	139	448	55	111	31	1	10	65	1	.248
2001 Boston b	A.L.		C	51	174	19	51	11	1	7	25	0	.293
2002 Boston	A.L.		C	132	467	58	124	27	1	10	61	4	.266
2003 Boston	A.L.		C	142	451	63	123	31	1	25	85	3	.273
2004 Boston c	A.L.		C	137	463	67	137	30	1	18	73	10	.296
2005 Boston	A.L.		C	133	470	70	132	30	1	22	70	2	.281
2006 Pawtucket	Int.		C	2	7	2	3	0	0	1	1	0	.429
2006 Boston d	A.L.		C	103	305	46	87	19	2	12	55	1	.238
2007 Boston	A.L.		C	131	435	57	111	15	3	17	68	1	.255
Major League Totals			11 Yrs.	1199	3978	536	1063	246	13	148	611	25	.267
Division Series													
1998 Boston	A.L.		C	1	4	0	1	0	0	0	1	0	.250
1999 Boston	A.L.		C	5	21	7	5	3	0	1	3	0	.238
2003 Boston	A.L.		C	5	14	4	4	0	0	2	2	0	.286
2004 Boston	A.L.		C	3	12	3	2	0	0	1	2	0	.167
2005 Boston	A.L.		C	3	10	1	3	0	0	0	1	0	.300
2007 Boston	A.L.		C	3	11	1	2	1	0	0	1	0	.182
Division Series Totals				20	72	16	17	4	0	4	10	0	.236
Championship Series													
1999 Boston	A.L.		C	5	20	1	4	1	1	1	1	0	.200
2003 Boston	A.L.		C	6	20	4	6	2	0	2	3	0	.300

Year Club	Lea	Pos	G	AB	R	H	2B	3B	HR	RBI	SB	Avg
2004 Boston .... A.L.		C	7	28	5	9	1	0	2	7	0	.321
2007 Boston .... A.L.		C	7	26	3	7	3	0	1	4	0	.269
Championship Series Totals			25	94	13	26	7	1	6	15	0	.277
World Series Record												
2004 Boston .... A.L.		C	4	13	2	2	0	1	0	2	0	.154
2007 Boston .... A.L.		C	4	15	2	5	1	0	0	5	0	.333
World Series Totals			8	28	4	7	1	1	0	7	0	.250

a Traded to Boston Red Sox by Seattle Mariners with pitcher Derek Lowe for pitcher Heathcliff Slocumb, July 31, 1997.

b On disabled list from June 8 to November 7, 2001.

c Filed for free agency, November 1, 2004, re-signed with Boston Red Sox, December 24, 2004.

d On disabled list from August 1 to September 3, 2006.

VAZQUEZ, RAMON LUIS
Born, Aibonito, Puerto Rico, August 21, 1976.
Bats Left. Throws Right. Height, 5 feet, 11 inches. Weight, 170 pounds.

Year Club	Lea	Pos	G	AB	R	H	2B	3B	HR	RBI	SB	Avg
1995 Mariners....... Arizona		SS-3B-2B	39	141	20	29	3	1	0	11	4	.206
1996 Everett ...... Northwest		SS	33	126	25	35	5	2	1	18	7	.278
1996 Tacoma .... P.C.		2B-SS	18	49	7	11	2	1	0	4	0	.224
1996 Wisconsin .... Midwest		3B	3	10	1	3	1	0	0	1	0	.300
1997 Wisconsin .... Midwest		SS	131	479	79	129	25	5	8	49	16	.269
1998 Lancaster .... Calif.		SS	121	468	77	129	26	4	2	72	15	.276
1999 New Haven ..... Eastern		SS-3B	127	438	58	113	27	3	5	45	8	.258
2000 New Haven ..... Eastern		SS	124	405	58	116	25	4	8	59	1	.286
2001 Tacoma .... P.C.		SS	127	466	85	140	28	1	10	79	9	.300
2001 Seattle .... A.L.		SS-2B-3B	17	35	5	8	0	0	0	4	0	.229
2002 San Diego .... N.L.		2B-SS-3B	128	423	50	116	21	5	2	32	7	.274
2003 Lake Elsinore .... Calif.		SS	5	16	3	3	0	0	1	4	0	.188
2003 San Diego b ..... N.L.		SS-3B-2B	116	422	56	110	17	4	3	30	10	.261
2004 San Diego .... N.L.		SS-2B-3B-1B	52	115	12	27	3	2	1	13	1	.235
2004 Portland c-d .... P.C.		2B-3B-SS	53	184	36	55	21	1	8	34	2	.299
2005 Buffalo .... Int.		SS-2B-3B	21	84	13	18	3	1	0	4	1	.214
2005 Boston-Cleveland e ..A.L.		SS-2B-3B	39	85	7	18	5	0	0	5	0	.212
2006 Cleveland .... A.L.		3B-2B-SS	34	67	11	14	2	0	1	8	0	.209
2006 Buffalo f .... Int.		SS-3B-1B	28	99	19	24	2	1	2	11	2	.242
2007 Oklahoma........ P.C.		SS-2B-3B	35	132	27	34	10	2	2	13	3	.258
2007 Texas .... A.L.		3B-SS-2B-1B	104	300	42	69	13	3	8	28	1	.230
Major League Totals	7 Yrs.		490	1447	183	362	61	14	15	120	19	.250
Division Series												
2001 Seattle .... A.L.		SS	1	0	0	0	0	0	0	0	0	.000

a Traded to San Diego Padres with pitcher Brett Tomko and catcher Tom Lampkin for catcher Ben Davis, pitcher Wascar Serrano and infielder Alex Arias, December 11, 2001.

b On disabled list from June 1 to July 7, 2003.

c On disabled list from May 20 to June 20, 2004.

d Traded to Boston Red Sox with outfielder Jay Payton, pitcher David Pauley and cash for outfielder Dave Roberts, December 20, 2004.

e Traded to Cleveland Indians for infielder Alex Cora, July 7, 2005.

f Filed for free agency, October 2, 2006. Signed with Texas Rangers organization, November 17, 2006.

VICTORINO, SHANE PATRICK
Born, Wailuku, Hawaii, November 30, 1980.
Bats Both. Throws Right. Height, 5 feet, 9 inches. Weight, 180 pounds.

Year Club	Lea	Pos	G	AB	R	H	2B	3B	HR	RBI	SB	Avg
1999 Great Falls .... Pioneer		OF	55	225	53	63	7	6	2	25	20	.280
2000 Yakima......... Northwest		2B-SS	61	236	32	58	7	2	2	20	21	.246
2001 Vero Beach.......... Fla.St.		OF	2	6	2	1	0	0	0	0	0	.167
2001 Wilmington ...... So.Atl.		OF	112	435	71	123	21	9	4	32	47	.283
2002 Jacksonville ...... Southern		OF	122	481	61	124	15	1	4	34	45	.258
2003 Jacksonville ..... Southern		OF	66	266	37	75	9	4	2	15	16	.282
2003 Las Vegas........... P.C.		OF	11	41	6	16	1	2	1	9	0	.390
2003 San Diego a .... N.L.		OF	36	73	8	11	2	0	0	4	7	.151
2004 Las Vegas............. P.C.		OF-2B	55	200	28	47	9	1	3	20	7	.235
2004 Jacksonville b .... Southern		OF	75	293	70	96	13	7	16	43	9	.328
2005 Scranton/WB .... Int.		OF	126	494	93	153	25	16	18	70	17	.310
2005 Philadelphia .... N.L.		OF	21	17	5	5	0	0	2	8	0	.294
2006 Philadelphia .... N.L.		OF	153	415	70	119	19	8	6	46	4	.287
2007 Lakewood.......... So.Atl.		DH	1	5	1	1	0	0	0	0	0	.200

Year	Club	Lea	Pos	G	AB	R	H	2B	3B	HR	RBI	SB	Avg
2007 Reading	. . . . Eastern	OF	2	6	0	2	0	0	0	1	1	.333
2007 Philadelphia c	. . . . N.L.	OF	131	456	78	128	23	3	12	46	37	.281
Major League Totals	. . . .	4 Yrs.	341	961	161	263	44	11	20	104	48	.274
Division Series												
2007 Philadelphia	. . . . N.L.	OF	3	9	2	2	0	0	1	1	1	.222

a Selected by San Diego Padres from Los Angeles Dodgers in Rule V draft, December 16, 2002. Returned to Los Angeles Dodgers, May 28, 2003.
b Selected by Philadelphia Phillies in Rule V draft, December 13, 2004.
c On disabled list from July 31 to August 22, 2007.

VIDRO, JOSE ANGEL
Born, Mayaguez, Puerto Rico, August 27, 1974.
Bats Both. Throws Right. Height, 5 feet, 11 inches. Weight, 195 pounds.

Year	Club	Lea	Pos	G	AB	R	H	2B	3B	HR	RBI	SB	Avg
1992 Expos	. . . . . . Gulf Coast	2B	54	200	29	66	6	2	4	31	10	.330
1993 Burlington	. . . . Midwest	2B	76	287	39	69	19	0	2	34	3	.240
1994 Wst Plm Bch	. . . Fla. St.	2B	125	465	57	124	30	2	4	49	8	.267
1995 Harrisburg	. . . . . Eastern	2B-SS-3B	64	246	33	64	16	2	4	38	3	.260
1995 Wst Plm Bch	. . Fla. St.	2B-SS-3B	44	163	20	53	15	2	3	24	0	.325
1996 Harrisburg	. . . . . Eastern	3B-2B-SS	126	452	57	117	25	3	18	82	3	.259
1997 Ottawa	. . . . Int.	3B-2B	73	279	40	90	17	0	13	47	2	.323
1997 Montreal	. . . . N.L.	3B-2B	67	169	19	42	12	1	2	17	1	.249
1998 Ottawa	. . . . Int.	2B-3B	63	235	35	68	14	2	2	32	5	.289
1998 Montreal	. . . . N.L.	2B-3B	83	205	24	45	12	0	0	18	2	.220
1999 Montreal	. . . . N.L.	2B-1B-OF-3B	140	494	67	150	45	2	12	59	0	.304
2000 Montreal	. . . . N.L.	2B	153	606	101	200	51	2	24	97	5	.330
2001 Montreal a	. . . . N.L.	2B	124	486	82	155	34	1	15	59	4	.319
2002 Montreal	. . . . N.L.	2B	152	604	103	190	43	3	19	96	2	.315
2003 Montreal	. . . . N.L.	2B	144	509	77	158	36	0	15	65	3	.310
2004 Montreal b	. . . . N.L.	2B	110	412	51	121	24	0	14	60	3	.294
2005 Potomac	. . . . . Carolina	2B	5	13	3	2	1	0	0	3	0	.154
2005 Washington c	. . . . . N.L.	2B	87	309	38	85	21	2	7	32	0	.275
2006 Potomac	. . . . . Carolina	DH	1	3	0	1	1	0	0	0	0	.333
2006 Harrisburg	. . . . Eastern	2B	3	8	0	2	0	0	0	1	0	.250
2006 Washington d-e	. . N.L.	2B-1B	126	463	52	134	26	1	7	47	1	.289
2007 Seattle	. . . . A.L.	DH-1B-2B	147	548	78	172	26	0	6	59	0	.314
Major League Totals	. . . .	11 Yrs.	1333	4805	692	1452	330	12	121	609	21	.302

a On disabled list from May 20 to June 12, 2001.
b On disabled list from August 26 to November 1, 2004.
c On disabled list from May 5 to July 5, 2005.
d On disabled list from July 18 to August 18, 2006.
e Traded to Seattle Mariners for pitcher Emiliano Fruto and outfielder Chris Snelling, December 18, 2006.

VIZQUEL, OMAR ENRIQUE
Born, Caracas, Venezuela, April 24, 1967.
Bats Both. Throws Right. Height, 5 feet, 9 inches. Weight, 175 pounds.

Year	Club	Lea	Pos	G	AB	R	H	2B	3B	HR	RBI	SB	Avg
1984 Butte a	. . . . Pioneer	SS-2B	15	45	7	14	2	0	0	4	2	.311
1985 Bellingham	. . . . . . Northwest	SS-2B	50	187	24	42	9	0	5	17	4	.225
1986 Wausau	. . . . Midwest	SS-2B	105	352	60	75	13	2	4	28	19	.213
1987 Salinas	. . . . California	SS-2B	114	407	61	107	12	8	0	38	25	.263
1988 Vermont	. . . . Eastern	SS	103	375	54	95	18	2	2	35	30	.253
1988 Calgary	. . . . P.C.	SS	33	107	10	24	2	3	1	12	2	.224
1989 Seattle	. . . . A.L.	SS	143	387	45	85	7	3	1	20	1	.220
1989 Calgary	. . . . P.C.	SS	7	28	3	6	2	0	0	3	0	.214
1990 San Bernardino	. . . California	SS	6	28	5	7	0	0	0	3	1	.250
1990 Calgary	. . . . P.C.	SS	48	150	18	35	6	2	0	8	4	.233
1990 Seattle b	. . . . A.L.	SS	81	255	19	63	3	2	2	18	4	.247
1991 Seattle	. . . . A.L.	SS-2B	142	426	42	98	16	4	1	41	7	.230
1992 Seattle c	. . . . A.L.	SS	136	483	49	142	20	4	0	21	15	.294
1992 Calgary	. . . . P.C.	SS	6	22	0	6	1	0	0	2	0	.273
1993 Seattle d	. . . . A.L.	SS	158	560	68	143	14	2	2	31	12	.255
1994 Charlotte	. . . . Int.	SS	7	26	3	7	1	0	0	1	1	.269
1994 Cleveland e	. . . . A.L.	SS	69	286	39	78	10	1	1	33	13	.273
1995 Cleveland	. . . . A.L.	SS	136	542	87	144	28	0	6	56	29	.266
1996 Cleveland	. . . . A.L.	SS	151	542	98	161	36	1	9	64	35	.297
1997 Cleveland	. . . . A.L.	SS	153	565	89	158	23	6	5	49	43	.280
1998 Cleveland	. . . . A.L.	SS	151	576	86	166	30	6	2	50	37	.288

Year	Club	Lea	Pos	G	AB	R	H	2B	3B	HR	RBI	SB	Avg
1999 Cleveland	A.L.	SS-OF	144	574	112	191	36	4	5	66	42	.333
2000 Cleveland	A.L.	SS	156	613	101	176	27	3	7	66	22	.287
2001 Cleveland	A.L.	SS	155	611	84	156	26	8	2	50	13	.255
2002 Cleveland	A.L.	SS	151	582	85	160	31	5	14	72	18	.275
2003 Lake County	So.Atl.	SS	4	14	0	1	0	0	0	0	1	.071
2003 Cleveland f	A.L.	SS	64	250	43	61	13	2	2	19	8	.244
2004 Cleveland g	A.L.	SS	148	567	82	165	28	3	7	59	19	.291
2005 San Francisco	N.L.	SS	152	568	66	154	28	4	3	45	24	.271
2006 San Francisco	N.L.	SS	153	579	88	171	22	10	4	58	24	.295
2007 San Francisco	N.L.	SS	145	513	54	126	18	3	4	51	14	.246
Major League Totals	19 Yrs.	2588	9479	1337	2598	416	71	77	869	380	.274

Division Series

Year	Club	Lea	Pos	G	AB	R	H	2B	3B	HR	RBI	SB	Avg
1995 Cleveland	A.L.	SS	3	12	2	2	1	0	0	4	1	.167
1996 Cleveland	A.L.	SS	4	14	4	6	1	0	0	2	4	.429
1997 Cleveland	A.L.	SS	5	18	3	9	0	0	0	1	4	.500
1998 Cleveland	A.L.	SS	4	15	1	1	0	0	0	0	0	.067
1999 Cleveland	A.L.	SS	5	21	3	5	1	1	0	3	0	.238
2001 Cleveland	A.L.	SS	5	22	2	9	1	1	0	6	1	.409
Division Series Totals			26	102	15	32	4	2	0	16	10	.314

Championship Series

Year	Club	Lea	Pos	G	AB	R	H	2B	3B	HR	RBI	SB	Avg
1995 Cleveland	A.L.	SS	6	23	2	2	1	0	0	2	3	.087
1997 Cleveland	A.L.	SS	6	25	1	1	0	0	0	0	0	.040
1998 Cleveland	A.L.	SS	6	25	2	11	0	1	0	0	4	.440
Championship Series Totals			18	73	5	14	1	1	0	2	7	.192

World Series Record

Year	Club	Lea	Pos	G	AB	R	H	2B	3B	HR	RBI	SB	Avg
1995 Cleveland	A.L.	SS	6	23	3	4	0	1	0	1	1	.174
1997 Cleveland	A.L.	SS	7	30	5	7	2	0	0	1	5	.233
World Series Totals			13	53	8	11	2	1	0	2	6	.208

a Batted righthanded only from 1984 through 1988 season.
b On disabled list from April 7 to May 14, 1990.
c On disabled list from April 13 to May 11, 1992.
d Traded to Cleveland Indians for shortstop Felix Fermin and first baseman Reggie Jefferson, December 20, 1993.
e On disabled list from April 23 to June 13, 1994.
f On disabled list from June 12 to August 26 and September 6 to October 28, 2003.
g Filed for free agency, October 29, 2004. Signed with San Francisco Giants, November 14, 2004.

VOTTO, JOSEPH DANIEL (JOEY)
Born, Toronto, Ontario, Canada, September 10, 1983.
Bats Left. Throws Right. Height, 6 feet, 3 inches. Weight, 220 pounds.

Year	Club	Lea	Pos	G	AB	R	H	2B	3B	HR	RBI	SB	Avg
2002 Reds	Gulf Coast	3B-C-OF	50	175	29	47	13	3	9	33	7	.269
2003 Dayton	Midwest	1B	60	195	19	45	8	0	1	20	2	.231
2003 Billings	Pioneer	1B	70	240	47	76	17	3	6	37	4	.317
2004 Potomac	Carolina	1B	24	84	11	25	7	0	5	20	1	.298
2004 Dayton	Midwest	1B	111	391	60	118	26	2	14	73	9	.302
2005 Sarasota	Fla.St.	1B	124	464	64	119	23	2	17	83	4	.256
2006 Chattanooga	Southern	1B	136	508	85	162	46	2	22	77	24	.319
2007 Louisville	Int.	1B-OF	133	496	74	146	21	2	22	92	17	.294
2007 Cincinnati	N.L.	1B-OF	24	84	11	27	7	0	4	17	1	.321

WARD, DARYLE LAMAR
Born, Lynwood, California, June 27, 1975.
Bats Left. Throws Left. Height, 6 feet, 2 inches. Weight, 240 pounds.

Year	Club	Lea	Pos	G	AB	R	H	2B	3B	HR	RBI	SB	Avg
1994 Bristol	Appal.	1B	48	161	17	43	6	0	5	30	4	.267
1995 Fayetteville	So.Atl.	1B	137	524	75	149	32	0	14	106	1	.284
1996 Toledo	Int.	1B	6	23	1	4	0	0	0	1	0	.174
1996 Lakeland a	Fla.St.	1B	128	464	65	135	29	4	10	68	1	.291
1997 Jackson	Texas	1B	114	422	72	139	25	0	19	90	4	.329
1997 New Orleans	A.A.	1B	14	48	4	18	1	0	2	8	0	.375
1998 Houston	N.L.	PH	4	3	1	1	0	0	0	0	0	.333
1998 New Orleans	P.C.	OF-1B	116	463	78	141	31	1	23	96	2	.305
1999 New Orleans	P.C.	1B-OF	61	241	56	85	15	1	28	65	1	.353
1999 Houston	N.L.	OF-1B	64	150	11	41	6	0	8	30	0	.273
2000 Houston	N.L.	OF-1B	119	264	36	68	10	2	20	47	0	.258

Year	Club	Lea	Pos	G	AB	R	H	2B	3B	HR	RBI	SB	Avg
2001 Houston	N.L.	OF-1B	95	213	21	56	15	0	9	39	0	.263	
2002 Houston	N.L.	OF	136	453	41	125	31	0	12	72	1	.276	
2003 Jacksonville	Southern	1B-OF	4	16	0	2	0	0	0	1	0	.125	
2003 Los Angeles	N.L.	1B-OF	52	109	6	20	1	0	0	9	0	.183	
2003 Las Vegas b-c-d	P.C.	1B	34	128	16	38	9	0	4	24	0	.297	
2004 Nashville	P.C.	1B-OF	28	96	14	27	7	0	7	17	0	.281	
2004 Pittsburgh e	N.L.	1B-OF	79	293	39	73	17	2	15	57	0	.249	
2005 Pittsburgh f	N.L.	1B	133	407	46	106	21	1	12	63	0	.260	
2006 Washington-Atlanta g-h	N.L.	OF-1B	98	130	17	40	10	0	7	26	0	.308	
2007 Iowa	P.C.	1B	4	13	0	1	1	0	0	1	0	.077	
2007 Chicago i	N.L.	1B-OF	79	110	16	36	13	0	3	19	0	.327	
Major League Totals			10 Yrs.	859	2132	234	566	124	5	86	362	1	.265
Division Series													
1999 Houston	N.L.	OF	3	7	1	1	0	0	1	1	0	.143	
2001 Houston	N.L.	PH	2	2	1	1	0	0	1	2	0	.500	
2007 Chicago	N.L.	PH	3	2	0	1	1	0	0	2	0	.500	
Division Series Totals			8	11	2	3	1	0	2	5	0	.273	

a Traded by Detroit Tigers to Houston Astros with catcher Brad Ausmus, pitcher C.J. Nitkowski, pitcher Jose Lima and pitcher Trever Miller for outfielder Brian Hunter, infielder Orlando Miller, pitcher Todd Jones and pitcher Doug Brocail, December 10, 1996.
b Traded to Los Angeles Dodgers for infielder Ruddy Lugo, January 28, 2003.
c On disabled list from May 29 to June 17, 2003.
d Filed for free agency, September 30, 2003. Signed with Pittsburgh Pirates organization, December 10, 2003.
e On disabled list from June 26 to August 15, 2004.
f Filed for free agency, October 27, 2005. Signed with Washington Nationals organization, January 27, 2006.
g Traded to Atlanta Braves for pitcher Luis Atilano, August 31, 2006.
h Filed for free agency, October 28, 2006. Signed with Chicago Cubs, December 15, 2006.
i On disabled list from June 3 to June 18 and July 20 to August 12, 2007.

WEEKS, RICKIE DARNELL

Born, Altamonte Springs, Florida, September 13, 1982.
Bats Right. Throws Right. Height, 6 feet. Weight, 205 pounds.

Year	Club	Lea	Pos	G	AB	R	H	2B	3B	HR	RBI	SB	Avg
2003 Brewers	Arizona	DH	1	4	0	2	0	0	0	4	1	.500	
2003 Beloit	Midwest	2B	20	63	13	22	8	1	1	16	2	.349	
2003 Milwaukee	N.L.	2B	7	12	1	2	1	0	0	0	0	.167	
2004 Huntsville	Southern	2B	133	479	67	124	35	6	8	42	11	.259	
2005 Nashville	P.C.	2B	55	203	43	65	14	9	12	48	10	.320	
2005 Milwaukee	N.L.	2B	96	360	56	86	13	2	13	42	15	.239	
2006 Milwaukee a	N.L.	2B	95	359	73	100	15	3	8	34	19	.279	
2007 Nashville	P.C.	2B	6	22	5	10	3	1	0	3	1	.455	
2007 Milwaukee b	N.L.	2B	118	409	87	96	21	6	16	36	25	.235	
Major League Totals			4 Yrs.	316	1140	217	284	50	11	37	112	59	.249

a On disabled list from July 29 to October 31, 2006.
b On disabled list from May 30 to June 18, 2007.

WELLS, VERNON M.

Born, Shreveport, Louisiana, December 8, 1978.
Bats Right. Throws Right. Height, 6 feet, 1 inch. Weight, 225 pounds.

Year	Club	Lea	Pos	G	AB	R	H	2B	3B	HR	RBI	SB	Avg
1997 St.Catherines	N.Y.-Penn.	OF	66	264	52	81	20	1	10	31	8	.307	
1998 Hagerstown	So.Atl.	OF	134	509	86	145	35	2	11	65	13	.285	
1999 Dunedin	Fla.St.	OF	70	265	43	91	16	2	11	43	13	.343	
1999 Knoxville	Southern	OF	26	106	18	36	6	2	3	17	6	.340	
1999 Syracuse	Int.	OF	33	129	20	40	8	1	4	21	5	.310	
1999 Toronto	A.L.	OF	24	88	8	23	5	0	1	8	1	.261	
2000 Syracuse	Int.	OF	127	493	76	120	31	7	16	66	23	.243	
2000 Toronto	A.L.	OF	3	2	0	0	0	0	0	0	0	.000	
2001 Syracuse	Int.	OF	107	413	57	116	27	4	12	52	15	.281	
2001 Toronto a	A.L.	OF	30	96	14	30	8	0	1	6	5	.313	
2002 Toronto	A.L.	OF	159	608	87	167	34	4	23	100	9	.275	
2003 Toronto	A.L.	OF	161	678	118	*215	*49	5	33	117	4	.317	
2004 Toronto b	A.L.	OF	134	536	82	146	34	2	23	67	9	.272	
2005 Toronto	A.L.	OF	156	620	78	167	30	3	28	97	8	.269	
2006 Toronto	A.L.	OF	154	611	91	185	40	5	32	106	17	.303	
2007 Toronto c	A.L.	OF	149	584	85	143	36	4	16	80	10	.245	
Major League Totals			9 Yrs.	970	3823	563	1076	236	23	157	581	63	.281

a On disabled list from April 14 to 24, 2001.
b On disabled list from June 16 to July 16, 2004.
c On disabled list from September 22 to November 13, 2007.

WERTH, JAYSON RICHARD GOWAN
Born, Springfield, Illinois, May 20, 1979.
Bats Right. Throws Right. Height, 6 feet, 5 inches. Weight, 220 pounds.

Year Club	Lea	Pos	G	AB	R	H	2B	3B	HR	RBI	SB	Avg
1997 Orioles .... Gulf Coast	C-1B-OF	32	88	16	26	6	0	1	8	7	.295
1998 Delmarva .... So.Atl.	C	120	408	71	108	20	3	8	53	21	.265
1998 Bowie............. Eastern	C	5	19	2	3	2	0	0	1	1	.158
1999 Frederick .... Carolina	C	66	236	41	72	10	1	3	30	16	.305
1999 Bowie............ Eastern	C-OF	35	121	18	33	5	1	1	11	7	.273
2000 Frederick .... Carolina	C	24	83	16	23	3	0	2	18	5	.277
2000 Bowie a .... Eastern	C-OF	85	276	47	63	16	2	5	26	9	.228
2001 Dunedin .... Fla.St.	C	21	70	9	14	3	0	2	14	1	.200
2001 Tennessee .... Southern	C-1B	104	369	51	105	23	1	18	69	12	.285
2002 Syracuse .... Int.	OF-C	127	443	65	114	25	2	18	82	24	.257
2002 Toronto .... A.L.	OF	15	46	4	12	2	1	0	6	1	.261
2003 Dunedin .... Fla.St.	OF	18	62	10	23	5	0	4	18	1	.371
2003 Toronto .... A.L.	OF	26	48	7	10	4	0	2	10	1	.208
2003 Syracuse b .... Int.	OF	64	236	37	56	19	1	9	34	11	.237
2004 Los Angeles .... N.L.	OF	89	290	56	76	11	3	16	47	4	.262
2004 Las Vegas c-d .... P.C.	OF	14	51	13	21	2	1	5	20	2	.412
2005 Las Vegas.......... P.C.	OF	15	49	9	18	0	0	3	10	6	.367
2005 Los Angeles e........ N.L.	OF	102	337	46	79	22	2	7	43	11	.234
2006 Los Angeles f-g .... N.L.					INJURED—Did Not Play						
2007 Clearwater .... Fla.St.	OF	4	13	3	1	0	0	0	0	0	.077
2007 Philadelphia h .... N.L.	OF-1B	94	255	43	76	11	3	8	49	7	.298
Major League Totals	5 Yrs.	326	976	156	253	50	9	33	155	24	.259
Division Series												
2004 Los Angeles .... N.L.	OF	4	14	3	4	1	0	2	3	0	.286
2007 Philadelphia .... N.L.	OF	2	3	0	0	0	0	0	0	0	.000
Division Series Totals		6	17	3	4	1	0	2	3	0	.235

a Traded to Toronto Blue Jays by Baltimore Orioles for pitcher John Bale, December 11, 2000.
b On disabled list from March 21 to April 11, 2003.
c On disabled list from April 6 to June 4, 2004.
d Traded to Los Angeles Dodgers for pitcher Jason Frasor, March 30, 2004.
e On disabled list from March 25 to May 25 and from July 27 to August 11, 2005.
f On disabled list from April 1 to November 2, 2006.
g Not offered contract, December 12, 2006. Signed with Philadelphia Phillies, December 19, 2006.
h On disabled list from June 29 to August 1, 2007.

WIGGINTON, TY ALLEN (TY)
Born, San Diego, California, October 11, 1977.
Bats Right. Throws Right. Height, 6 feet. Weight, 225 pounds.

Year Club	Lea	Pos	G	AB	R	H	2B	3B	HR	RBI	SB	Avg
1998 Pittsfield..... N.Y.-Penn.	2B-3B-OF	70	272	39	65	14	4	8	29	11	.239
1999 St. Lucie........ Fla.St.	2B	123	456	69	133	23	5	21	73	9	.292
2000 Binghamton.... Eastern	2B-3B	122	453	64	129	27	3	20	77	5	.285
2001 Binghamton.... Eastern	2B-3B	8	28	5	8	3	0	0	0	1	.286
2001 St. Lucie....... Fla.St.	2B	3	9	1	3	1	0	0	1	0	.333
2001 Norfolk........... Int.	3B-2B-1B-OF	78	260	29	65	12	0	7	24	3	.250
2002 Norfolk........... Int.	3B-2B-OF-1B	104	383	49	115	26	3	6	48	5	.300
2002 New York.......... N.L.	3B-1B-2B-OF	46	116	18	35	8	0	6	18	2	.302
2003 New York......... N.L.	3B	156	573	73	146	36	6	11	71	12	.255
2004 St. Lucie......... Fla.St.	3B	2	8	1	3	0	0	0	0	0	.375
2004 N.Y.-Pittsburgh a-b .N.L.	3B-2B-1B	144	494	63	129	30	2	17	66	7	.261
2005 Indianapolis .... Int.	3B-1B-2B	72	280	53	82	18	0	14	52	8	.293
2005 Pittsburgh c....... N.L.	3B-1B-2B	57	155	20	40	9	1	7	25	0	.258
2006 Durham .... Int.	1B	2	8	2	3	2	0	1	2	0	.375
2006 Tampa Bay d ...... A.L.	1B-2B-3B-OF	122	444	55	122	25	1	24	79	4	.275
2007 Tampa Bay .... A.L.	2B-3B-1B	98	378	47	104	21	0	16	49	1	.275
2007 Houston e .... N.L.	3B-OF-1B	50	169	24	48	12	0	6	18	2	.284
Major League Totals	6 Yrs.	673	2329	300	624	141	10	87	326	28	.268

a On disabled list from April 21 to May 7, 2004.
b Traded to Pittsburgh Pirates with pitcher Matt Peterson and infielder Jose Bautista for pitcher Kris Benson and infielder Jeff Keppinger, July 30, 2004.

c Released by Pittsburgh Pirates, December 8, 2005. Signed with Tampa Bay Devil Rays, January 10, 2006.
d On disabled list from July 31 to September 1, 2006.
e Traded to Houston Astros for pitcher Dan Wheeler, July 28, 2007.

WILKERSON, STEPHEN BRADLEY (BRAD)

Born, Owensboro, Kentucky, June 1, 1977.
Bats Left. Throws Left. Height, 6 feet. Weight, 205 pounds.

Year	Club	Lea	Pos	G	AB	R	H	2B	3B	HR	RBI	SB	Avg
1999 Harrisburg a	Eastern	OF	138	422	66	99	21	3	8	49	3	.235
2000 Harrisburg	Eastern	OF-1B	66	229	53	77	36	2	6	44	8	.336
2000 Ottawa	Int.	OF	63	212	40	53	11	1	12	35	5	.250
2001 Jupiter	Fla.St.	DH	6	26	3	6	3	0	0	1	0	.231
2001 Ottawa	Int.	OF	69	233	43	63	10	0	12	48	12	.270
2001 Montreal b	N.L.	OF	47	117	11	24	7	2	1	5	2	.205
2002 Montreal	N.L.	OF-1B	153	507	92	135	27	8	20	59	7	.266
2003 Montreal	N.L.	OF-1B	146	504	78	135	34	4	19	77	13	.268
2004 Montreal	N.L.	1B-OF	160	572	112	146	39	2	32	67	13	.255
2005 Washington c	N.L.	OF-1B	148	565	76	140	42	7	11	57	8	.248
2006 Texas d	A.L.	OF	95	320	56	71	15	2	15	44	3	.222
2007 Frisco	Texas	OF	3	10	3	2	1	0	0	0	0	.200
2007 Texas e-f	A.L.	1B-OF	119	338	54	79	17	1	20	62	4	.234
Major League Totals			7 Yrs.	868	2923	479	730	181	26	118	371	50	.250

a Drafted by Montreal Expos with choice received for Toronto Blue Jays signing of catcher Darrin Fletcher, June 2, 1998.
b On disabled list from April 5 to May 5, 2001.
c Traded to Texas Rangers with outfielder Terrmel Sledge and pitcher Armando Galarraga for infielder Alfonso Soriano, December 13, 2005.
d On disabled list from August 10 to November 8, 2006.
e On disabled list from May 16 to June 9, 2007.
f Filed for free agency, October 31, 2007.

WILLINGHAM, JOSHUA DAVID (JOSH)

Born, Florence, Alabama, February 17, 1979.
Bats Right. Throws Right. Height, 6 feet, 1 inch. Weight, 200 pounds.

Year	Club	Lea	Pos	G	AB	R	H	2B	3B	HR	RBI	SB	Avg
2000 Utica	N.Y.-Penn.	OF-2B-3B-SS	65	205	37	54	16	0	6	29	9	.263
2001 Kane County	Midwest	3B-OF-2B	97	320	57	83	20	2	7	36	24	.259
2002 Jupiter	Fla.St.	1B-3B-OF	107	376	72	103	21	4	17	69	18	.274
2003 Jupiter	Fla.St.	C-1B-OF-3B	59	193	46	51	17	1	12	34	9	.264
2003 Marlins	Gulf Coast	DH	2	7	3	3	1	0	1	3	0	.429
2003 Carolina	Southern	1B-C-3B-OF	22	67	15	20	2	1	5	14	0	.299
2004 Carolina	Southern	C-1B-OF-3B	112	338	81	95	24	0	24	76	6	.281
2004 Florida	N.L.	C-OF	12	25	2	5	0	0	1	1	0	.200
2005 Jupiter	Fla.St.	C	2	9	1	2	1	0	0	1	0	.222
2005 Albuquerque	P.C.	C-3B	66	219	56	71	14	3	19	54	5	.324
2005 Florida a	N.L.	C-OF	16	23	3	7	1	0	0	4	0	.304
2006 Carolina	Southern	OF	2	8	0	2	0	0	0	0	0	.250
2006 Florida b	N.L.	OF-C-1B	142	502	62	139	28	2	26	74	2	.277
2007 Florida	N.L.	OF	144	521	75	138	32	4	21	89	8	.265
Major League Totals			4 Yrs.	314	1071	142	289	61	6	48	168	10	.270

a On disabled list from June 30 to September 2, 2005.
b On disabled list from June 7 to June 22, 2006.

WILLITS, REGGIE GENE

Born, Chickasha, Oklahoma, May 30, 1981.
Bats Both. Throws Right. Height, 5 feet, 11 inches. Weight, 185 pounds.

Year	Club	Lea	Pos	G	AB	R	H	2B	3B	HR	RBI	SB	Avg
2003 Provo	Pioneer	OF	59	230	53	69	14	4	4	27	14	.300
2004 Rancho Cucamonga	Calif.	OF	135	526	99	150	17	5	5	52	45	.285
2005 Arkansas	Texas	OF	123	487	75	148	23	6	2	46	40	.304
2006 Salt Lake	P.C.	OF	97	352	85	115	18	4	3	39	31	.327
2006 Los Angeles	A.L.	OF	28	45	12	12	1	0	0	2	4	.267
2007 Los Angeles	A.L.	OF	136	430	74	126	20	1	0	34	27	.293
Major League Totals			2 Yrs.	164	475	86	138	21	1	0	36	31	.291
Division Series													
2007 Los Angeles	A.L.	OF	3	4	0	0	0	0	0	0	1	.000

WILSON, JACK EUGENE
Born, Westlake Village, California, December 29, 1977.
Bats Right. Throws Right. Height, 6 feet. Weight, 185 pounds.

Year	Club	Lea	Pos	G	AB	R	H	2B	3B	HR	RBI	SB	Avg
1998 Johnson Cty	Appal.		SS	61	241	50	90	18	4	4	29	22	.373
1999 Potomac	Carolina		SS	64	257	44	76	10	1	2	18	7	.296
1999 Peoria	Midwest		SS	64	251	47	86	22	4	3	28	11	.343
2000 Potomac	Carolina		SS	13	47	7	13	0	1	2	7	2	.277
2000 Altoona	Eastern		SS	33	139	17	35	7	2	1	16	1	.252
2000 Arkansas a	Texas		SS	88	343	65	101	20	8	6	34	2	.294
2001 Nashville	P.C.		SS	27	103	20	38	6	1	1	6	2	.369
2001 Pittsburgh	N.L.		SS	108	390	44	87	17	1	3	25	1	.223
2002 Pittsburgh	N.L.		SS	147	527	77	133	22	4	4	47	5	.252
2003 Pittsburgh	N.L.		SS	150	558	58	143	21	3	9	62	5	.256
2004 Pittsburgh	N.L.		SS	157	652	82	201	41	*12	11	59	8	.308
2005 Pittsburgh	N.L.		SS	158	587	60	151	24	7	8	52	7	.257
2006 Pittsburgh	N.L.		SS	142	543	70	148	27	1	8	35	4	.273
2007 Pittsburgh	N.L.		SS	135	477	67	141	29	2	12	56	2	.296
Major League Totals		7 Yrs.		997	3734	458	1004	181	30	55	336	32	.269

a Traded by St. Louis Cardinals to Pittsburgh Pirates for pitcher Jason Christiansen, July 30, 2000.

WILSON, JOSHUA AARON (JOSH)
Born, Pittsburgh, Pennsylvania, March 26, 1981.
Bats Right. Throws Right. Height, 6 feet, 1 inch. Weight, 180 pounds.

Year	Club	Lea	Pos	G	AB	R	H	2B	3B	HR	RBI	SB	Avg
1999 Marlins	Gulf Coast		SS	53	203	29	54	9	4	0	27	14	.266
2000 Kane County	Midwest		SS-2B-3B	13	52	2	14	3	1	1	6	0	.269
2000 Utica	N.Y.-Penn.		SS	66	259	43	89	13	6	3	43	9	.344
2001 Kane County	Midwest		2B-SS-3B	123	506	65	144	28	5	4	61	17	.285
2002 Portland	Eastern		SS	12	41	5	14	3	0	2	5	0	.341
2002 Jupiter	Fla.St.		SS-2B-3B	111	398	51	102	17	1	11	50	7	.256
2003 Carolina	Southern		SS-2B	118	434	53	110	30	6	3	58	6	.253
2004 Albuquerque	P.C.		SS	56	240	32	67	12	2	5	23	6	.279
2004 Carolina	Southern		SS	81	311	63	98	21	1	10	41	8	.315
2005 Albuquerque	P.C.		SS-2B	143	526	88	135	31	6	17	82	17	.257
2005 Florida	N.L.		SS-2B	11	10	2	1	1	0	0	0	0	.100
2006 Colorado Springs a-b-c	P.C.		SS-3B-2B	89	335	61	103	18	4	10	45	15	.307
2007 Washington	N.L.		SS	15	19	3	1	0	0	0	0	0	.053
2007 Tampa Bay d-e	A.L.		SS-2B-3B-P	90	263	25	66	15	3	2	24	6	.251
Major League Totals		2 Yrs.		116	292	30	68	16	3	2	24	6	.233

a Traded to Colorado Rockies for player to be named later, January 6, 2006.
b On disabled list from March 28 to June 7, 2006.
c Filed for free agency, November 1, 2006. Signed with Washington Nationals, November 6, 2006.
d Claimed on waivers by Tampa Bay Devil Rays, May 10, 2007.
e Claimed on waivers by Pittsburgh Pirates, December 3, 2007.

WILSON, PRESTON JAMES RICHARD
Born, Bamberg, South Carolina, July 19, 1974.
Bats Right. Throws Right. Height, 6 feet, 2 inches. Weight, 193 pounds.

Year	Club	Lea	Pos	G	AB	R	H	2B	3B	HR	RBI	SB	Avg
1993 Kingsport	Appal.		3B	66	259	44	60	10	0	16	48	6	.232
1993 Pittsfield	N.Y.-Penn.		3B	8	29	6	16	5	1	1	12	1	.552
1994 Columbia	So.Atl.		3B	131	474	55	108	17	4	14	58	13	.228
1995 Columbia	So.Atl.		OF	111	442	70	119	26	5	20	61	20	.269
1996 St. Lucie a	Fla.St.		OF	23	85	6	15	3	0	1	7	1	.176
1997 St. Lucie	Fla.St.		OF	63	245	32	60	12	1	11	48	3	.245
1997 Binghamton	Eastern		OF-3B	70	259	37	74	12	1	19	47	7	.286
1998 Norfolk	Int.		OF	18	73	9	18	5	1	1	9	1	.247
1998 Charlotte	Int.		OF	94	356	71	99	25	3	25	77	14	.278
1998 New York-Florida b	N.L.		OF	22	51	7	8	2	0	1	3	1	.157
1999 Florida	N.L.		OF	149	482	67	135	21	4	26	71	11	.280
2000 Florida	N.L.		OF	161	605	94	160	35	3	31	121	36	.264
2001 Calgary	P.C.		OF	4	10	3	5	2	0	0	1	2	.500
2001 Florida c	N.L.		OF	123	468	70	128	30	2	23	71	20	.274
2002 Florida d	N.L.		OF	141	510	80	124	22	2	23	65	20	.243
2003 Colorado	N.L.		OF	155	600	94	169	43	1	36	*141	14	.282
2004 Tulsa	Texas		OF	6	17	4	7	1	0	1	2	1	.412

Year	Club	Lea	Pos	G	AB	R	H	2B	3B	HR	RBI	SB	Avg
2004 Colorado e	N.L.	OF	58	202	24	50	11	0	6	29	2	.248
2005 Colorado-Washington f-g	N.L.	OF	139	520	73	135	29	2	25	90	6	.260
2006 Houston-St. Louis h-i..	N.L.	OF	135	501	58	132	25	2	17	72	12	.263
2007 St. Louis j-k	N.L.	OF	25	64	6	14	3	0	1	5	2	.219
Major League Totals	10 Yrs.		1108	4003	573	1055	221	16	189	668	124	.264

Division Series

Year	Club	Lea	Pos	G	AB	R	H	2B	3B	HR	RBI	SB	Avg
2006 St. Louis.............	N.L.	OF	2	8	2	2	1	0	0	0	0	.250

Championship Series

Year	Club	Lea	Pos	G	AB	R	H	2B	3B	HR	RBI	SB	Avg
2006 St. Louis.............	N.L.	OF	6	17	2	3	1	0	0	1	0	.176

World Series Record

Year	Club	Lea	Pos	G	AB	R	H	2B	3B	HR	RBI	SB	Avg
2006 St. Louis.............	N.L.	OF	5	10	1	2	0	0	0	1	0	.200

a On disabled list from April 4 to April 29 and May 21 to July 13 and July 29 to September 8, 1996.

b Traded to Florida Marlins with pitcher Ed Yarnall and player to be named later for catcher Mike Piazza, May 22, 1998. Florida Marlins received pitcher Geoff Goetz to complete trade, July 3, 1998.

c On disabled list from July 2 to August 10, 2001.

d Traded to Colorado Rockies with catcher Charles Johnson, pitcher Vic Darensbourg and infielder Pablo Ozuna for pitcher Mike Hampton and outfielder Juan Pierre, November 16, 2002.

e On disabled list from April 13 to June 18 and from August 21 to November 3, 2004.

f Traded to Washington Nationals with cash for pitcher Zach Day, outfielder J.J. Davis and player to be named later, July 13, 2005.

g Filed for free agency, October 27, 2005. Signed with Houston Astros, January 3, 2006.

h Released by Houston Astros, August 15, 2006. Signed with St. Louis Cardinals, August 18, 2006.

i Filed for free agency, November 3, 2006, re-signed with St. Louis Cardinals, January 29, 2007.

j On disabled list from May 6 to November 2, 2007.

k Filed for free agency, November 8, 2007.

WINN, DWIGHT RANDOLPH (RANDY)

Born, Los Angeles, California, June 9, 1974.
Bats Both. Throws Right. Height, 6 feet, 2 inches. Weight, 195 pounds.

Year	Club	Lea	Pos	G	AB	R	H	2B	3B	HR	RBI	SB	Avg
1995 Elmira a	N.Y.-Penn.	OF	51	213	38	67	7	4	0	22	19	.315
1996 Kane County.......	Midwest	OF	130	514	90	139	16	3	0	35	30	.270
1997 Brevard Cty	Fla.St.	OF	36	143	26	45	8	2	0	15	16	.315
1997 Portland b	Eastern	OF	96	384	66	112	15	6	8	36	35	.292
1998 Durham	Int.	OF	29	123	25	35	5	2	1	16	10	.285
1998 Tampa Bay	A.L.	OF	109	338	51	94	9	9	1	17	26	.278
1999 Tampa Bay	A.L.	OF	79	303	44	81	16	4	2	24	9	.267
1999 Durham	Int.	OF	46	207	38	73	20	3	3	30	9	.353
2000 Durham	Int.	OF	79	303	67	100	24	5	7	40	18	.330
2000 Tampa Bay	A.L.	OF	51	159	28	40	5	0	1	16	6	.252
2001 Tampa Bay	A.L.	OF	128	429	54	117	25	6	6	50	12	.273
2002 Tampa Bay c.........	A.L.	OF	152	607	87	181	39	9	14	75	27	.298
2003 Seattle	A.L.	OF	157	600	103	177	37	4	11	75	23	.295
2004 Seattle	A.L.	OF	157	626	84	179	34	6	14	81	21	.286
2005 Seattle	A.L.	OF	102	386	46	106	25	1	6	37	12	.275
2005 San Francisco d.......	N.L.	OF	58	231	39	83	22	5	14	26	7	.359
2006 San Francisco	N.L.	OF	149	573	82	150	34	5	11	56	10	.262
2007 San Francisco	N.L.	OF-3B	155	593	73	178	42	1	14	65	15	.300
Major League Totals	10 Yrs.		1297	4845	691	1386	288	50	94	522	168	.286

a On disabled list from August 22 to September 11, 1995.

b Selected in expansion draft by Tampa Bay Devil Rays, November 18, 1997.

c Traded to Seattle Mariners for infielder Antonio Perez and manager Lou Piniella, October 28, 2002.

d Traded to San Francisco Giants for pitcher Jesse Foppert and catcher Yorvit Torrealba, July 31, 2005.

WOOD, JASON WILLIAM

Born, San Bernardino, California, December 16, 1969.
Bats Right. Throws Right. Height, 6 feet, 1 inch. Weight, 170 pounds.

Year	Club	Lea	Pos	G	AB	R	H	2B	3B	HR	RBI	SB	Avg
1991 Sou Oregon ..	Northwest	SS-2B	44	142	30	44	3	4	3	23	5	.310
1992 Modesto	Calif.	SS	128	454	66	105	28	3	6	49	5	.231
1993 Huntsville.....	Southern	SS	103	370	44	85	21	2	3	36	2	.230
1994 Huntsville.....	Southern	SS	134	468	54	128	29	2	6	84	3	.274
1995 Edmonton	P.C.	3B-2B-SS	127	421	49	99	20	5	2	50	1	.235
1996 Huntsville.....	Southern	3B-1B-SS-P	133	491	77	128	21	1	20	84	2	.261
1996 Edmonton	P.C.	1B-P	3	12	0	0	0	0	0	0	0	.000
1997 Edmonton	P.C.	3B-SS	130	505	83	162	35	7	19	87	2	.321
1998 Edmonton	P.C.	3B-2B-OF-SS	80	307	52	86	20	0	18	73	1	.280

Year Club	Lea	Pos	G	AB	R	H	2B	3B	HR	RBI	SB	Avg
1998 Toledo .... Int.		3B-1B-SS	46	169	24	47	9	0	7	29	0	.278
1998 Oakland-Detroit a ... A.L.		1B-SS-3B	13	24	6	8	2	0	1	1	0	.333
1999 Lakeland .... Fla.St.		SS-1B-2B-3B	5	17	0	4	0	0	0	1	0	.235
1999 Detroit .... A.L.		3B-SS-1B-2B	27	44	5	7	1	0	1	8	0	.159
1999 Toledo b-c .... Int.		3B-1B-SS-2B	48	185	34	53	11	0	6	24	0	.286
2000 Nashville .... P.C.		3B-SS-2B-1B	88	316	40	75	18	0	7	45	2	.237
2001 Nashville .... P.C.		3B-SS-2B-1B	113	379	46	92	19	1	8	38	0	.243
2002 Calgary d .... P.C.		3B-SS-1B	121	457	78	144	37	2	15	70	3	.315
2003 Albuquerque....... P.C.		3B-1B-SS	128	473	80	140	26	4	16	83	5	.296
2004 Albuquerque....... P.C.		3B-1B-2B	102	375	44	92	21	2	8	49	2	.245
2005 Albuquerque....... P.C.		3B-1B-2B-SS	129	452	75	136	18	3	21	77	5	.301
2006 Albuquerque....... P.C.		3B-2B-1B-SS	123	441	64	127	23	3	11	77	1	.288
2006 Florida e .... N.L.		1B-2B	12	13	3	6	2	0	0	1	1	.462
2007 Florida f .... N.L.		1B-3B-2B-OF	98	117	11	28	6	0	3	26	0	.239
Major League Totals	4 Yrs.		150	198	25	49	11	0	5	36	1	.247

a Sent to Detroit Tigers as player to be named later for outfielder Bip Roberts, July 18, 1998.
b On disabled list from March 29 to May 11, 1999.
c Filed for free agency, October 15, 1999. Signed with Pittsburgh Pirates organization, November 17, 1999.
d Filed for free agency, October 15, 2001. Signed with Florida Marlins organization, March 8, 2002.
e Filed for free agency, October 4, 2006, re-signed with Florida Marlins organization, December 1, 2006.
f Filed for free agency, October 16, 2007, re-signed with Florida Marlins organization, January 4, 2008.

WOODWARD, CHRISTOPHER (CHRIS)
Born, Covina, California, June 27, 1976.
Bats Right. Throws Right. Height, 6 feet. Weight, 190 pounds.

Year Club	Lea	Pos	G	AB	R	H	2B	3B	HR	RBI	SB	Avg
1995 Medcine Hat.... Pioneer		SS	72	241	44	56	8	0	3	21	9	.232
1996 Hagerstown ..... So.Atl.		SS	123	424	41	95	24	2	1	48	11	.224
1997 Dunedin .... Fla.St.		SS	91	314	38	92	13	4	1	38	4	.293
1998 Knoxville ..... Southern		SS	73	253	36	62	12	0	3	27	3	.245
1998 Syracuse .... Int.		SS	25	85	9	17	6	0	2	6	1	.200
1999 Syracuse .... Int.		SS	75	281	46	82	20	3	1	20	4	.292
1999 Toronto a .... A.L.		SS-3B	14	26	1	6	1	0	0	2	0	.231
2000 Syracuse .... Int.		2B-3B-SS	37	143	23	46	13	2	5	25	2	.322
2000 Toronto .... A.L.		SS-3B-1B-2B	37	104	16	19	7	0	3	14	1	.183
2001 Syracuse .... Int.		3B-SS-1B-2B	51	193	29	59	14	3	11	31	0	.306
2001 Toronto b .... A.L.		2B-3B-SS-1B	37	63	9	12	3	2	2	5	0	.190
2002 Dunedin .... Fla.St.		SS	2	6	1	2	0	0	0	0	0	.333
2002 Toronto c .... A.L.		SS-2B-1B-3B	90	312	48	86	13	4	13	45	3	.276
2003 Toronto .... A.L.		SS	104	349	49	91	22	2	7	45	1	.261
2004 Dunedin .... Fla.St.		SS	6	16	2	5	2	0	1	3	0	.313
2004 Toronto d-e ...... A.L.		SS	69	213	21	50	13	4	1	24	1	.235
2005 New York .... N.L.		1B-OF-SS-3B	81	173	16	49	10	0	3	18	0	.283
2006 New York f .... N.L.		2B-SS-3B-OF	83	222	25	48	10	1	3	25	1	.216
2007 Atlanta g .... N.L.		3B-SS-2B-1B	92	136	16	27	6	1	1	8	1	.199
Major League Totals	9 Yrs.		607	1598	201	388	85	14	33	186	8	.243
Division Series												
2006 New York .... N.L.		PH	1	1	1	1	1	0	0	0	0	1.000

a On disabled list from May 2 to 17 and May 21 to June 6, 1999.
b On disabled list from June 30 to July 26, 2001.
c On disabled list from June 21 to July 11, 2002.
d On disabled list from May 12 to June 8, 2004.
e Filed for free agency, October 15, 2004. Signed with New York Mets organization, December 28, 2004.
f Filed for free agency, October 28, 2006. Signed with Atlanta Braves, December 20, 2006.
g Filed for free agency, October 30, 2007.

WRIGHT, DAVID ALLEN
Born, Norfolk, Virginia, December 20, 1982.
Bats Right. Throws Right. Height, 6 feet. Weight, 200 pounds.

Year Club	Lea	Pos	G	AB	R	H	2B	3B	HR	RBI	SB	Avg
2001 Kingsport .... Appal.		3B	36	116	27	35	7	0	4	16	9	.302
2002 Columbia .... So.Atl.		3B	135	496	85	132	30	2	11	93	21	.266
2003 St. Lucie........... Fla.St.		3B	133	466	69	126	39	2	15	75	19	.270
2004 Binghamton .... Eastern		3B	60	223	44	81	27	0	10	40	20	.363
2004 Norfolk............... Int.		3B	31	114	18	34	8	0	8	17	2	.298
2004 New York .... N.L.		3B	69	263	41	77	17	1	14	40	6	.293
2005 New York .... N.L.		3B	160	575	99	176	42	1	27	102	17	.306
2006 New York .... N.L.		3B	154	582	96	181	40	5	26	116	20	.311

Year	Club	Lea	Pos	G	AB	R	H	2B	3B	HR	RBI	SB	Avg
2007 New York	N.L.	3B	160	604	113	196	42	1	30	107	34	.325
Major League Totals		4 Yrs.	543	2024	349	630	141	8	97	365	77	.311
Division Series												
2006 New York	N.L.	3B	3	12	1	4	2	0	0	4	0	.333
Championship Series												
2006 New York	N.L.	3B	7	25	2	4	1	0	1	2	0	.160

YOUKILIS, KEVIN EDMUND

Born, Cincinnati, Ohio, March 15, 1979.
Bats Right. Throws Right. Height, 6 feet, 1 inch. Weight, 220 pounds.

Year	Club	Lea	Pos	G	AB	R	H	2B	3B	HR	RBI	SB	Avg
2001 Lowell	N.Y.-Penn.	3B	59	183	52	58	14	2	3	28	4	.317
2001 Augusta	So.Atl.	3B	5	12	0	2	0	0	0	0	0	.167
2002 Augusta	So.Atl.	3B	15	53	5	15	5	0	0	6	0	.283
2002 Sarasota	Fla.St.	1B-3B	76	268	45	79	16	0	3	48	0	.295
2002 Trenton	Eastern	3B	44	160	34	55	10	0	5	26	5	.344
2003 Portland	Eastern	3B	94	312	74	102	23	1	6	37	7	.327
2003 Pawtucket	Int.	3B	32	109	9	18	3	0	2	15	0	.165
2004 Lowell	N.Y.-Penn.	3B	2	4	1	3	1	1	0	0	0	.750
2004 Pawtucket	Int.	3B-1B	38	154	25	41	12	0	3	18	2	.266
2004 Boston a	A.L.	3B	72	208	38	54	11	0	7	35	0	.260
2005 Pawtucket	Int.	3B-1B-2B	43	152	30	49	15	1	8	27	1	.322
2005 Boston	A.L.	3B-1B-2B	44	79	11	22	7	0	1	9	0	.278
2006 Boston	A.L.	1B-OF-3B	147	569	100	159	42	2	13	72	5	.279
2007 Boston	A.L.	1B-3B	145	528	85	152	35	2	16	83	4	.288
Major League Totals		4 Yrs.	408	1384	234	387	95	4	37	199	9	.280
Division Series												
2004 Boston	A.L.	3B	1	2	0	0	0	0	0	0	0	.000
2007 Boston	A.L.	1B	3	12	3	3	1	0	1	2	0	.250
Division Series Totals			4	14	3	3	1	0	1	2	0	.214
Championship Series												
2007 Boston	A.L.	1B	7	28	10	14	1	1	3	7	0	.500
World Series Record												
2007 Boston	A.L.	1B	4	9	3	2	2	0	0	1	0	.222

a On disabled list from August 16 to September 1, 2004.

YOUNG, CHRISTOPHER BRANDON (CHRIS)

Born, Houston, Texas, September 5, 1983.
Bats Right. Throws Right. Height, 6 feet, 2 inches. Weight, 180 pounds.

Year	Club	Lea	Pos	G	AB	R	H	2B	3B	HR	RBI	SB	Avg
2002 White Sox	Arizona	OF	55	184	26	40	13	1	5	17	7	.217
2003 Bristol	Appal.	OF	64	238	47	69	18	3	7	28	21	.290
2003 Great Falls	Pioneer	OF	10	34	5	6	3	0	0	0	0	.176
2004 Kannapolis	So.Atl.	OF	136	467	83	122	31	5	24	56	31	.261
2005 Birmingham a	Southern	OF	126	466	100	129	41	3	26	77	32	.277
2006 Tucson	P.C.	OF	100	402	78	111	32	4	21	77	17	.276
2006 Arizona	N.L.	OF	30	70	10	17	4	0	2	10	2	.243
2007 Arizona	N.L.	OF	148	569	85	135	29	3	32	68	27	.237
Major League Totals		2 Yrs.	178	639	95	152	33	3	34	78	29	.238
Division Series												
2007 Arizona	N.L.	OF	3	11	3	3	0	0	2	4	1	.273
Championship Series												
2007 Arizona	N.L.	OF	4	14	1	4	1	0	0	1	0	.286

a Traded to Arizona Diamondbacks by Chicago White Sox with pitcher Orlando Hernandez and pitcher Luis Vizcaino for pitcher Javier Vazquez, December 20, 2005.

YOUNG, DELMON DAMARCUS

Born, Birmingham, Alabama, September 14, 1985.
Bats Right. Throws Right. Height, 6 feet, 3 inches. Weight, 205 pounds.

Year	Club	Lea	Pos	G	AB	R	H	2B	3B	HR	RBI	SB	Avg
2004 Charleston	So.Atl.	OF	131	513	95	165	26	5	25	116	21	.322
2005 Durham	Int.	OF	52	228	33	65	13	3	6	28	7	.285
2005 Montgomery	Southern	OF	84	330	59	111	13	4	20	71	25	.336
2006 Durham	Int.	OF	86	342	50	108	22	4	8	59	22	.316
2006 Tampa Bay	A.L.	OF	30	126	16	40	9	1	3	10	2	.317

Year	Club	Lea	Pos	G	AB	R	H	2B	3B	HR	RBI	SB	Avg
2007 Tampa Bay a.		A.L.	OF	*162	645	65	186	38	0	13	93	10	.288
Major League Totals		2 Yrs.	192	771	81	226	47	1	16	103	12	.293	

a Traded to Minnesota Twins with infielder Brendan Harris and outfielder Jason Pridie for infielder Jason Bartlett, pitcher Matt Garza and pitcher Eduardo Morlan, November 28, 2007.

YOUNG, DMITRI DELL

Born, Vicksburg, Mississippi, October 11, 1973.
Bats Both. Throws Right. Height, 6 feet, 2 inches. Weight, 235 pounds.

Year	Club	Lea	Pos	G	AB	R	H	2B	3B	HR	RBI	SB	Avg
1991 Johnson Cty	Appal.		3B	37	129	22	33	10	0	2	22	2	.256
1992 Springfield	Midwest		3B	135	493	74	153	36	6	14	72	14	.310
1993 St.Pete	Fla.St.		3B-1B	69	270	31	85	13	3	5	43	3	.315
1993 Arkansas	Texas		1B-3B	45	166	13	41	11	2	3	21	4	.247
1994 Arkansas	Texas		OF-1B	125	453	53	123	33	2	8	54	0	.272
1995 Arkansas	Texas		OF	97	367	54	107	18	6	10	62	2	.292
1995 Louisville	A.A.		OF	2	7	3	2	0	0	0	0	0	.286
1996 Louisville	A.A.		1B	122	459	90	153	31	8	15	64	16	.333
1996 St. Louis.	N.L.		1B	16	29	3	7	0	0	0	2	0	.241
1997 Louisville	A.A.		OF-1B	24	84	10	23	7	0	4	14	1	.274
1997 St. Louis a-b-c	N.L.		1B-OF	110	333	38	86	14	3	5	34	6	.258
1998 Cincinnati	N.L.		OF-1B	144	536	81	166	48	1	14	83	2	.310
1999 Cincinnati	N.L.		OF-1B	127	373	63	112	30	2	14	56	3	.300
2000 Cincinnati	N.L.		OF-1B	152	548	68	166	37	6	18	88	0	.303
2001 Cincinnati d	N.L.		OF-1B-3B	142	540	68	163	28	3	21	69	8	.302
2002 Detroit e	A.L.		DH-1B-3B-OF	54	201	25	57	14	0	7	27	2	.284
2003 Detroit	A.L.		DH-OF-3B-1B	155	562	78	167	34	7	29	85	2	.297
2004 Toledo	Int.		DH	2	10	1	5	1	1	1	5	0	.500
2004 Detroit f	A.L.		DH-1B-OF-3B	104	389	72	106	23	2	18	60	0	.272
2005 Detroit	A.L.		DH-1B-OF	126	469	61	127	25	3	21	72	1	.271
2006 Lakeland	Fla.St.		DH	2	5	1	2	1	0	0	0	0	.400
2006 Erie.	Eastern		1B-OF	6	20	2	3	1	0	0	1	0	.150
2006 Toledo	Int.		1B	8	31	4	14	3	0	1	6	0	.452
2006 Detroit g	A.L.		DH-1B	48	172	19	43	4	1	7	23	1	.250
2007 Washington h	N.L.		1B	136	460	57	147	38	1	13	74	0	.320
Major League Totals		12 Yrs.	1314	4612	633	1347	295	29	167	673	25	.292	
Championship Series													
1996 St. Louis.	N.L.		1B	4	7	1	2	0	1	0	2	0	.286

a Traded to Cincinnati Reds for pitcher Jeff Brantley, November 10, 1997.
b Selected in expansion draft by Tampa Bay Devil Rays, November 18, 1997.
c Sent to Cincinnati Reds as player to be named later for outfielder Mike Kelly, November 18, 1997.
d Traded to Detroit Tigers for outfielder Juan Encarnacion and pitcher Luis Pineda, December 11, 2001.
e On disabled list from April 23 to May 14 and July 6 to November 18, 2002.
f On disabled list from April 7 to May 31, 2004.
g On disabled list from April 15 to May 5 and May 22 to July 21, 2006.
h Released by Detroit Tigers, September 6, 2006. Signed with Washington Nationals organization, February 14, 2007.

YOUNG, MICHAEL BRIAN

Born, Covina, California, October 19, 1976.
Bats Right. Throws Right. Height, 6 feet, 1 inch. Weight, 200 pounds.

Year	Club	Lea	Pos	G	AB	R	H	2B	3B	HR	RBI	SB	Avg
1997 St.Catherines	N.Y.-Penn.		SS-2B	74	276	49	85	18	3	9	48	9	.308
1998 Hagerstown	So.Atl.		2B-SS-OF	140	522	86	147	33	5	16	87	16	.282
1999 Dunedin	Fla.St.		2B	129	495	86	155	36	3	5	83	30	.313
2000 Tennessee	Southern		2B-SS	91	345	51	95	24	5	6	47	16	.275
2000 Tulsa	Texas		SS	43	188	30	60	13	5	1	32	9	.319
2000 Texas a	A.L.		2B	2	2	0	0	0	0	0	0	0	.000
2001 Oklahoma	P.C.		2B-SS	47	189	28	55	8	0	8	28	3	.291
2001 Texas	A.L.		2B	106	386	57	96	18	4	11	49	3	.249
2002 Texas	A.L.	2B-SS-3B	156	573	77	150	26	8	9	62	6	.262
2003 Texas	A.L.	2B-SS	160	666	106	204	33	9	14	72	13	.306
2004 Texas	A.L.		SS	160	690	114	216	33	9	22	99	12	.313
2005 Texas	A.L.		SS	159	668	114*	*221	40	5	24	91	5	*.331
2006 Texas	A.L.		SS	*162	691	93	.217	52	3	14	103	7	.314
2007 Texas	A.L.		SS	156	639	80	201	37	1	9	94	13	.315
Major League Totals		8 Yrs.	1061	4315	641	1305	239	39	103	570	59	.302	

a Traded by Toronto Blue Jays to Texas Rangers with pitcher Darwin Cubillan for pitcher Esteban Loaiza, July 19, 2000.

ZAUN, GREGORY OWEN (GREGG)

Born, Glendale, California, April 14, 1971.
Bats Both. Throws Right. Height, 5 feet, 10 inches. Weight, 190 pounds.

Year	Club	Lea	Pos	G	AB	R	H	2B	3B	HR	RBI	SB	Avg
1990 Wausau	Midwest	C	37	100	3	13	0	1	1	7	0	.130
1990 Bluefield	Appal.	C-3B-SS-P	61	184	29	55	5	2	2	21	5	.299
1991 Kane County	Midwest	C	113	409	67	112	17	5	4	51	4	.274
1992 Frederick	Carolina	C-2B	108	383	54	96	18	6	6	52	3	.251
1993 Bowie	Eastern	C-2B-3B	79	258	25	79	10	0	3	38	4	.306
1993 Rochester a	Int.	C	21	78	10	20	4	2	1	11	0	.256
1994 Rochester	Int.	C	123	388	61	92	16	4	7	43	4	.237
1995 Rochester	Int.	C	42	140	26	41	13	1	6	18	0	.293
1995 Baltimore	A.L.	C	40	104	18	27	5	0	3	14	1	.260
1996 Baltimore	A.L.	C	50	108	16	25	8	1	1	13	0	.231
1996 Rochester	Int.	C	14	47	11	15	2	0	0	4	0	.319
1996 Florida b	N.L.	C	10	31	4	9	1	0	1	2	1	.290
1997 Florida	N.L.	C-1B	58	143	21	43	10	2	2	20	1	.301
1998 Florida c	N.L.	C-2B	106	298	19	56	12	2	5	29	5	.188
1999 Texas d-e	A.L.	C	43	93	12	23	2	1	1	12	1	.247
2000 Omaha	P.C.	DH	9	25	7	7	3	0	0	3	1	.280
2000 Kansas City f-g	A.L.	C-1B-2B	83	234	36	64	11	0	7	33	7	.274
2001 Royals	Gulf Coast	C	6	18	3	1	0	0	0	1	0	.056
2001 Omaha	P.C.	C	11	43	5	12	4	0	1	8	0	.279
2001 Kansas City h-i	A.L.	C	39	125	15	40	9	0	6	18	1	.320
2002 Houston	N.L.	C	76	185	18	41	7	1	3	24	1	.222
2003 Houston-Colorado k-l	N.L.	C	74	166	15	38	8	0	4	21	1	.229
2004 Syracuse	Int.	C	7	23	4	7	1	0	0	2	1	.304
2004 Toronto m-n	A.L.	C	107	338	46	91	24	0	6	36	0	.269
2005 New Hampshire	Eastern	C	2	6	-1	2	1	0	0	0	0	.333
2005 Toronto o	A.L.	C	133	434	61	109	18	1	11	61	2	.251
2006 Dunedin	Fla.St.	C	1	4	0	0	0	0	0	0	0	.000
2006 Toronto p-q	A.L.	C	99	290	39	79	19	0	12	40	0	.272
2007 Syracuse	Int.	C	3	11	1	1	0	0	0	0	0	.091
2007 Toronto r	A.L.	C	110	331	43	80	24	1	10	52	0	.242
Major League Totals		13 Yrs.	1028	2880	363	725	158	9	72	375	21	.252

Championship Series

Year	Club	Lea	Pos	G	AB	R	H	2B	3B	HR	RBI	SB	Avg
1997 Florida	N.L.	C	1	0	0	0	0	0	0	0	0	.000

World Series Record

Year	Club	Lea	Pos	G	AB	R	H	2B	3B	HR	RBI	SB	Avg
1997 Florida	N.L.	C	2	2	0	0	0	0	0	0	0	.000

a On disabled list from June 17 to July 15, 1993.
b Sent to Florida Marlins to complete trade for pitcher Terry Mathews, August 23, 1996.
c Traded to Texas Rangers for player to be named later, November 23, 1998.
d Florida Marlins received cash to complete trade, April 15, 1999.
e Traded to Detroit Tigers with outfielder Juan Gonzalez and pitcher Danny Patterson for pitcher Justin Thompson, pitcher Francisco Cordero, pitcher Alan Webb, outfielder Gabe Kapler, catcher Bill Haselman and infielder Frank Catalanotto, November 2, 1999.
f Traded to Kansas City Royals for player to be named later, March 7, 2000.
g On disabled list from April 15 to May 28, 2000.
h On disabled list from March 31 to July 23, 2001.
i Filed for free agency, November 5, 2001. Signed with Houston Astros, December 8, 2001.
k Released by Houston Astros, August 20, 2003. Signed with Colorado Rockies, August 26, 2003.
l Filed for free agency, October 27, 2003. Signed with Montreal Expos organization January 13, 2004.
m Released by Montreal Expos, April 4, 2004. Signed with Toronto Blue Jays organization, April 9, 2004.
n Filed for free agency, November 1, 2004, re-signed with Toronto Blue Jays, January 5, 2005.
o On disabled list from May 9 to May 24, 2005.
p On disabled list from March 24 to April 8, 2006.
q Filed for free agency, October 30, 2006, re-signed with Toronto Blue Jays, November 28, 2006.
r On disabled list from April 25 to June 8, 2007.

ZIMMERMAN, RYAN WALLACE

Born, Washington, North Carolina, September 28, 1984.
Bats Right. Throws Right. Height, 6 feet, 3 inches. Weight, 210 pounds.

Year	Club	Lea	Pos	G	AB	R	H	2B	3B	HR	RBI	SB	Avg
2005 Savannah	So.Atl.	1B-SS	4	17	5	8	2	1	2	6	0	.471
2005 Harrisburg	Eastern	3B-SS	63	233	40	76	20	0	9	32	1	.326
2005 Washington	N.L.	3B-SS	20	58	6	23	10	0	0	6	0	.397
2006 Washington	N.L.	3B	157	614	84	176	47	3	20	110	11	.287
2007 Washington	N.L.	3B	*162	653	99	174	43	5	24	91	4	.266
Major League Totals		3 Yrs.	339	1325	189	373	100	8	44	207	15	.282

ACCARDO, JEREMY LEE
Born, Phoenix, Arizona, December 18, 1981.
Bats Right. Throws Right. Height, 6 feet, 2 inches. Weight, 190 pounds.

Year	Club	Lea	G	IP	W	L	Pct	SO	BB	H	ERA	SAVES
2004	San Jose	Calif.	50	55	1	2	.333	43	15	57	4.25	27
2004	Norwich	Eastern	7	8^1/$_3$	2	1	.667	5	2	9	5.40	1
2005	Norwich	Eastern	8	9^2/$_3$	1	0	1.000	15	1	8	0.93	4
2005	San Jose	Calif.	2	2	0	0	.000	3	1	1	0.00	1
2005	Fresno	P.C.	25	32^1/$_3$	2	0	1.000	30	10	25	1.95	3
2005	San Francisco	N.L.	28	29^2/$_3$	1	5	.167	16	9	26	3.94	0
2006	Fresno	P.C.	3	5	0	0	.000	8	1	5	1.80	0
2006	San Francisco	N.L.	38	40^1/$_3$	1	3	.250	40	11	38	4.91	3
2006	Toronto a	A.L.	27	28^2/$_3$	1	1	.500	14	9	38	5.97	0
2007	Toronto	A.L.	64	67^1/$_3$	4	4	.500	57	24	51	2.14	30
Major League Totals		3 Yrs.	157	166	7	13	.350	127	53	153	3.80	33

a Traded to Toronto Blue Jays for infielder Shea Hillenbrand and pitcher Vinnie Chulk, July 21, 2006.

AFFELDT, JEREMY DAVID
Born, Phoenix, Arizona, June 6, 1979.
Bats Left. Throws Left. Height, 6 feet, 4 inches. Weight, 225 pounds.

Year	Club	Lea	G	IP	W	L	Pct	SO	BB	H	ERA	SAVES
1997	Royals	Gulf Coast	10	40	2	0	1.000	36	21	34	4.50	0
1998	Royals	Gulf Coast	12	56	4	3	.571	67	24	50	2.89	0
1998	Lansing	Midwest	6	17	0	3	.000	8	12	27	9.53	0
1999	Charleston-Wv	So.Atl.	27	143^1/$_3$	7	7	.500	111	80	140	3.83	0
2000	Wilmington	Carolina	27	147^1/$_3$	5	15	.250	92	59	158	4.09	0
2001	Wichita	Texas	25	145^1/$_3$	10	6	.625	128	46	153	3.90	0
2002	Wichita	Texas	3	6	0	0	.000	3	3	1	1.50	0
2002	Kansas City a	A.L.	34	77^2/$_3$	3	4	.429	67	37	85	4.64	0
2003	Kansas City b	A.L.	36	126	7	6	.538	98	38	126	3.93	4
2004	Omaha	P.C.	4	4	0	0	.000	5	0	2	0.00	3
2004	Kansas City c	A.L.	38	76^1/$_3$	3	4	.429	49	32	91	4.95	13
2005	Omaha	P.C.	9	8^1/$_3$	0	1	.000	9	6	9	6.48	0
2005	Kansas City d	A.L.	49	49^2/$_3$	0	2	.000	39	29	56	5.26	0
2006	Kansas City	A.L.	27	70	4	6	.400	28	42	71	5.91	0
2006	Colorado e	N.L.	27	27^1/$_3$	4	2	.667	20	13	30	6.91	1
2007	Colorado f	N.L.	75	59	4	3	.571	46	33	47	3.51	0
Major League Totals		6 Yrs.	286	486	25	27	.481	347	224	507	4.74	18
Division Series												
2007	Colorado	N.L.	1	1	0	0	.000	2	0	1	9.00	0
Championship Series												
2007	Colorado	N.L.	2	1^1/$_3$	0	0	.000	0	0	0	0.00	0
World Series Record												
2007	Colorado	N.L.	4	3	0	0	.000	2	1	2	0.00	0

a On disabled list from June 9 to August 1, 2002.
b On disabled list from April 20 to May 6, 2003.
c On disabled list from June 27 to August 21, 2004.
d On disabled list from April 16 to June 4 and June 19 to July 7, 2005.
e Traded to Colorado Rockies with pitcher Denny Bautista for infielder Ryan Shealy and pitcher Scott Dohmann, July 31, 2006.
f Filed for free agency, October 29, 2007.

ALBERS, MATTHEW JAMES (MATT)
Born, Houston, Texas, January 20, 1983.
Bats Left. Throws Right. Height, 6 feet. Weight, 205 pounds.

Year	Club	Lea	G	IP	W	L	Pct	SO	BB	H	ERA	SAVES
2002	Martinsville	Appal.	13	59^2/$_3$	2	3	.400	72	38	61	5.13	0
2003	Tri-City	N.Y.-Penn.	15	86^1/$_3$	5	4	.556	94	25	69	2.92	0
2004	Lexington	So.Atl.	22	111^1/$_3$	8	3	.727	140	57	95	3.31	0
2005	Salem	Carolina	28	148^2/$_3$	8	12	.400	146	62	161	4.66	0
2006	Corpus Christi	Texas	19	116	10	2	.833	95	47	96	2.17	0
2006	Round Rock	P.C.	4	25	2	1	.667	26	10	24	3.96	0
2006	Houston	N.L.	4	15	0	2	.000	11	7	17	6.00	0

Year Club	Lea	G	IP	W	L	Pct	SO	BB	H	ERA	SAVES
2007 Round Rock..........P.C.	P.C.	9	53	2	3	.400	43	22	50	3.74	0
2007 Houston a .............N.L.	N.L.	31	110²/₃	4	11	.267	71	50	127	5.86	0
Major League Totals ....2 Yrs.		35	125²/₃	4	13	.235	82	57	144	5.87	0

a Traded to Baltimore Orioles with pitcher Troy Patton, outfielder Luke Scott, pitcher Dennis Sarfate and infielder Michael Costanzo for infielder Miguel Tejada, December 12, 2007.

ALFONSECA, ANTONIO

Born, LaRomana, Dominican Republic, April 16, 1972.
Bats Right. Throws Right. Height, 6 feet, 5 inches. Weight, 250 pounds.

Year Club	Lea	G	IP	W	L	Pct	SO	BB	H	ERA	SAVES
1990 Montreal.........Dominican	Dominican	13	59²/₃	3	5	.375	19	32	60	3.62	0
1991 Expos...........Gulf Coast	Gulf Coast	11	51	3	3	.500	38	25	46	3.88	0
1992 Expos...........Gulf Coast	Gulf Coast	12	66	3	4	.429	62	35	55	3.68	0
1993 Jamestown a .....N.Y.-Penn.	N.Y.-Penn.	15	33²/₃	2	2	.500	29	22	31	6.15	1
1994 Kane County.......Midwest	Midwest	32	86¹/₃	6	5	.545	74	21	78	4.07	0
1995 Portland ....Eastern	Eastern	19	96¹/₃	9	3	.750	75	42	81	3.64	0
1996 Charlotte ....Int.	Int.	14	71²/₃	4	4	.500	51	22	86	5.53	1
1997 Charlotte ....Int.	Int.	46	58¹/₃	7	2	.778	45	20	58	4.32	7
1997 Florida ..............N.L.	N.L.	17	25²/₃	1	3	.250	19	10	36	4.91	0
1998 Florida b.............N.L.	N.L.	58	70²/₃	4	6	.400	46	33	75	4.08	8
1999 Florida ..............N.L.	N.L.	73	77²/₃	4	5	.444	46	29	79	3.24	21
2000 Florida ..............N.L.	N.L.	68	70	5	6	.455	47	24	82	4.24	45
2001 Florida ..............N.L.	N.L.	58	61²/₃	4	4	.500	40	15	68	3.06	28
2002 Chicago c.............N.L.	N.L.	66	74¹/₃	2	5	.286	61	36	73	4.00	19
2003 Iowa ................P.C.	P.C.	3	3²/₃	0	1	.000	5	1	6	4.91	0
2003 Chicago d-e ..........N.L.	N.L.	60	66¹/₃	3	1	.750	51	27	76	5.83	0
2004 Atlanta f.............N.L.	N.L.	79	73²/₃	6	4	.600	45	28	71	2.57	0
2005 Jupiter ....Fla.St.	Fla.St.	3	3	0	0	.000	4	0	3	3.00	0
2005 Florida g.............N.L.	N.L.	33	27¹/₃	1	1	.500	16	14	29	4.94	0
2006 Frisco...............Texas	Texas	1	1	0	0	.000	0	0	0	0.00	0
2006 Oklahoma............P.C.	P.C.	3	3	0	1	.000	1	1	4	6.00	0
2006 Texas h-i.............A.L.	A.L.	19	16	0	0	.000	5	7	23	5.63	0
2007 Philadelphia j-k ........N.L.	N.L.	61	49²/₃	5	2	.714	24	27	65	5.44	8
Major League Totals ....11 Yrs.		592	613	35	37	.486	400	250	677	4.11	129
Division Series											
2003 Chicago ..............N.L.	N.L.	1	1	0	0	.000	0	0	1	0.00	0
2004 Atlanta ..............N.L.	N.L.	4	3²/₃	1	0	1.000	0	2	2	4.91	0
2007 Philadelphia .........N.L.	N.L.	1	1	0	0	.000	0	0	1	0.00	0
Division Series Totals		6	5²/₃	1	0	1.000	0	2	4	3.18	0
Championship Series											
2003 Chicago ..............N.L.	N.L.	3	2¹/₃	0	0	.000	0	0	2	0.00	0
World Series Record											
1997 Florida ..............N.L.	N.L.	3	6¹/₃	0	0	.000	5	1	6	0.00	0

a Selected by Florida Marlins from Montreal Expos in Rule V draft, December 13, 1993.
b On disabled list from May 14 to May 31, 1998.
c Traded to Chicago Cubs with pitcher Matt Clement for pitcher Julian Tavarez, pitcher Jose Cueto, pitcher Dontrelle Willis and catcher Ryan Jorgensen, March 27, 2002.
d On disabled list from March 21 to May 5, 2003.
e Filed for free agency, October 28, 2003. Signed with Atlanta Braves, December 19, 2003.
f Filed for free agency, November 2, 2004. Signed with Florida Marlins, December 17, 2004.
g On disabled list from April 22 to July 26, 2005.
h Filed for free agency, November 2, 2005. Signed with Texas Rangers organization, January 26, 2006.
i On disabled list from May 19 to June 6, 2006.
j Released by Texas Rangers, June 19, 2006. Signed with Philadelphia Phillies, January 23, 2007.
k Filed for free agency, October 30, 2007.

ARMAS, ANTONIO JOSE (TONY)

Born, Puerto Piritu, Venezuela, April 29, 1978.
Bats Right. Throws Right. Height, 6 feet, 3 inches. Weight, 225 pounds.

Year Club	Lea	G	IP	W	L	Pct	SO	BB	H	ERA	SAVES
1995 Yankees ....Gulf Coast	Gulf Coast	5	14	0	1	.000	13	6	12	0.64	0
1996 Oneonta .........N.Y.-Penn.	N.Y.-Penn.	3	15²/₃	1	1	.500	14	11	14	5.74	0
1996 Yankees ....Gulf Coast	Gulf Coast	8	45²/₃	4	1	.800	45	13	41	3.15	1
1997 Greensboro ....So.Atl.	So.Atl.	9	51²/₃	5	2	.714	64	13	36	1.05	0
1997 Tampa ....Fla.St.	Fla.St.	9	46	3	1	.750	26	16	43	3.33	0
1997 Sarasota a-b.........Fla.St.	Fla.St.	3	17²/₃	2	1	.667	9	12	18	6.62	0
1998 Jupiter ....Fla.St.	Fla.St.	27	153¹/₃	12	8	.600	136	59	140	2.88	0
1999 Montreal.............N.L.	N.L.	1	6	0	1	.000	2	2	8	1.50	0

Year Club	Lea	G	IP	W	L	Pct	SO	BB	H	ERA	SAVES
1999 Harrisburg .... Eastern	Eastern	24	149²/₃	9	7	.563	106	55	123	2.89	0
2000 Jupiter .... Fla.St.	Fla.St.	1	4²/₃	0	0	.000	8	0	4	0.00	0
2000 Ottawa .... Int.	Int.	4	19	1	2	.333	12	4	22	3.79	0
2000 Montreal c .... N.L.	N.L.	17	95	7	9	.438	59	50	74	4.36	0
2001 Montreal.............. N.L.	N.L.	34	196²/₃	9	14	.391	176	91	180	4.03	0
2002 Montreal d .... N.L.	N.L.	29	164¹/₃	12	12	.500	131	78	149	4.44	0
2003 Montreal e .... N.L.	N.L.	5	31	2	1	.667	23	8	25	2.61	0
2004 Brevard County ...... Fla.St.	Fla.St.	3	9¹/₃	0	1	.000	7	7	5	6.75	0
2004 Edmonton .... P.C.	P.C.	2	10	0	0	.000	8	1	11	1.80	0
2004 Montreal f .... N.L.	N.L.	16	72	2	4	.333	54	45	66	4.88	0
2005 New Orleans.......... P.C.	P.C.	5	24²/₃	1	2	.333	21	10	26	4.38	0
2005 Washington g-h .... N.L.	N.L.	19	101¹/₃	7	7	.500	59	54	100	4.97	0
2006 Nationals .... Gulf Coast	Gulf Coast	1	5	0	1	.000	7	1	8	5.40	0
2006 Harrisburg .... Eastern	Eastern	1	2¹/₃	0	0	.000	4	1	3	7.71	0
2006 Washington i-j .... N.L.	N.L.	30	154	9	12	.429	97	64	167	5.03	0
2007 Pittsburgh k.......... N.L.	N.L.	31	97	4	5	.444	73	38	111	6.03	0
Major League Totals .... 9 Yrs.		182	917¹/₃	52	65	.444	674	430	880	4.62	0

a Traded to Boston Red Sox by New York Yankees with player to be named later for designated hitter Mike Stanley and infielder Randy Brown, August 13, 1997. Boston Red Sox received pitcher Jim Mecir to complete trade, September 29, 1997.

b Sent to Montreal Expos as player to be named to complete trade for pitcher Pedro J. Martinez, December 18, 1997.

c On disabled list from March 31 to April 27 and July 18 to September 3, 2000.

d On disabled list from July 27 to August 19, 2002.

e On disabled list from April 21 to October 27, 2003.

f On disabled list from March 26 to May 31, 2004.

g On disabled list from March 28 to May 9 and September 17 to October 28, 2005.

h Filed for free agency, October 28, 2005, re-signed with Washington Nationals, December 29, 2005.

i On disabled list from June 20 to July 17, 2006.

j Filed for free agency, October 29, 2006. Signed with Pittsburgh Pirates, February 1, 2007.

k Filed for free agency, October 29, 2007.

ARROYO, BRONSON ANTHONY
Born, Key West, Florida, February 24, 1977.
Bats Right. Throws Right. Height, 6 feet, 5 inches. Weight, 190 pounds.

Year Club	Lea	G	IP	W	L	Pct	SO	BB	H	ERA	SAVES
1995 Pirates .... Gulf Coast	Gulf Coast	13	61¹/₃	5	4	.556	48	9	72	4.26	1
1996 Augusta .... So.Atl.	So.Atl.	26	135²/₃	8	6	.571	107	36	123	3.52	0
1997 Lynchburg .... Carolina	Carolina	24	160¹/₃	12	4	.750	121	33	154	3.31	0
1998 Carolina a........... Southern	Southern	23	127	9	8	.529	90	51	158	5.46	0
1999 Altoona.............. Eastern	Eastern	25	153	15	4	.789	100	58	167	3.65	0
1999 Nashville .... P.C.	P.C.	3	13	0	2	.000	11	10	22	10.38	0
2000 Nashville .... P.C.	P.C.	13	88²/₃	8	2	.800	52	25	82	3.65	0
2000 Pittsburgh .... N.L.	N.L.	20	71²/₃	2	6	.250	50	36	88	6.40	0
2000 Lynchburg .... Carolina	Carolina	1	7	0	0	.000	3	2	8	3.86	0
2001 Pittsburgh .... N.L.	N.L.	24	88¹/₃	5	7	.417	39	34	99	5.09	0
2001 Nashville .... P.C.	P.C.	9	66¹/₃	6	2	.750	49	15	63	3.93	0
2002 Nashville .... P.C.	P.C.	22	143	8	6	.571	116	28	126	2.96	0
2002 Pittsburgh .... N.L.	N.L.	9	27	2	1	.667	22	15	30	4.00	0
2003 Pawtucket .... Int.	Int.	24	149²/₃	12	6	.667	155	23	148	3.43	0
2003 Boston b .... A.L.	A.L.	6	17¹/₃	0	0	.000	14	4	10	2.08	1
2004 Boston .... A.L.	A.L.	32	178²/₃	10	9	.526	142	47	171	4.03	0
2005 Boston .... A.L.	A.L.	35	205¹/₃	14	10	.583	100	54	213	4.51	0
2006 Cincinnati c .... N.L.	N.L.	35	240²/₃	14	11	.560	184	64	222	3.29	0
2007 Cincinnati............. N.L.	N.L.	34	210²/₃	9	15	.375	156	63	232	4.23	0
Major League Totals .... 8 Yrs.		195	1039²/₃	56	59	.487	707	317	1065	4.22	1
Division Series											
2004 Boston .... A.L.	A.L.	1	6	0	0	.000	7	2	3	3.00	0
2005 Boston .... A.L.	A.L.	1	1	0	0	.000	1	2	2	18.00	0
Division Series Totals		2	7	0	0	.000	8	4	5	5.14	0
Championship Series											
2003 Boston .... A.L.	A.L.	3	3¹/₃	0	0	.000	5	2	2	2.70	0
2004 Boston .... A.L.	A.L.	3	4	0	0	.000	3	2	8	15.75	0
Championship Series Totals		6	7¹/₃	0	0	.000	8	4	10	9.82	0
World Series Record											
2004 Boston .... A.L.	A.L.	2	2²/₃	0	0	.000	4	1	4	6.75	0

a On minor league disabled list from May 18 to June 7 and June 18 to July 4, 1998.

b Claimed on waivers by Boston Red Sox, February 4, 2003.

c Traded to Cincinnati Reds for outfielder Wily Mo Pena, March 20, 2006.

ATCHISON, SCOTT BARHAM

Born, Denton, Texas, March 29, 1976.
Bats Right. Throws Right. Height, 6 feet, 2 inches. Weight, 200 pounds.

Year	Club	Lea	G	IP	W	L	Pct	SO	BB	H	ERA	SAVES
1999	Wisconsin	Midwest	15	81²/₃	4	5	.444	85	25	67	3.42	0
2000	Lancaster	Calif.	19	97²/₃	5	5	.500	77	21	117	3.69	0
2000	Tacoma	P.C.	5	26	1	1	.500	18	6	22	3.81	0
2001	San Antonio	Texas	24	136	9	10	.474	83	28	171	4.24	0
2002	Tacoma	P.C.	27	124¹/₃	5	10	.333	112	31	123	4.63	2
2003	Tacoma	P.C.	39	108²/₃	6	9	.400	83	37	114	4.31	1
2004	Tacoma	P.C.	40	69¹/₃	5	3	.625	76	26	71	4.15	7
2004	Seattle	A.L.	25	30²/₃	2	3	.400	36	14	29	3.52	0
2005	Mariners	Arizona	4	5	0	0	.000	9	1	7	5.40	0
2005	San Antonio	Texas	5	6	0	0	.000	8	2	3	0.00	0
2005	Tacoma	P.C.	10	13	0	0	.000	17	5	13	4.15	0
2005	Seattle	A.L.	6	6²/₃	0	0	.000	9	1	7	6.75	0
2006	Tacoma a	P.C.	30	50	4	0	1.000	39	15	49	2.34	1
2007	Fresno	P.C.	38	53²/₃	3	2	.600	51	8	44	2.01	4
2007	San Francisco b	N.L.	22	30²/₃	0	0	.000	25	10	32	4.11	0
Major League Totals		3 Yrs.	53	68	2	3	.400	70	25	68	4.10	0

a Filed for free agency, October 15, 2006. Signed with San Francisco Giants organization, November 13, 2006.
b Filed for free agency, November 28, 2007. Signed with Boston Red Sox organization, December 12, 2007.

AYALA, LUIS IGNACIO

Born, Los Mochis, Mexico, January 12, 1978.
Bats Right. Throws Right. Height, 6 feet, 2 inches. Weight, 175 pounds.

Year	Club	Lea	G	IP	W	L	Pct	SO	BB	H	ERA	SAVES
1997	Saltillo	Mexican	37	62	7	5	.583	30	21	76	4.62	0
1998	Saltillo	Mexican	47	83	7	8	.467	29	45	105	5.62	7
1999	Saltillo a	Mexican	61	79	7	3	.700	28	22	54	1.71	41
2000	Saltillo	Mexican	55	65	5	3	.625	38	13	69	2.76	25
2001	Salem	Carolina	13	13¹/₃	0	1	.000	10	5	19	4.05	7
2001	Saltillo b	Mexican	33	40	1	2	.333	34	11	34	2.03	21
2002	Saltillo	Mexican	49	54	3	5	.375	43	15	43	1.68	23
2002	Ottawa c-d-e	Int.	6	7²/₃	0	0	.000	6	4	7	3.52	0
2003	Expos	Gulf Coast	2	3²/₃	0	0	.000	2	2	2	0.00	0
2003	Montreal f	N.L.	65	71	10	3	.769	46	13	65	2.92	5
2004	Montreal	N.L.	81	90¹/₃	6	12	.333	63	15	92	2.69	2
2005	Washington	N.L.	68	71	8	7	.533	40	14	75	2.66	1
2006	Washington g	N.L.					INJURED—Did Not Play					
2007	Potomac	Carolina	3	2²/₃	0	0	.000	1	1	1	0.00	0
2007	Columbus	Int.	5	7	0	0	.000	5	2	4	1.29	0
2007	Washington h	N.L.	44	42¹/₃	2	2	.500	28	12	43	3.19	1
Major League Totals		4 Yrs.	258	274²/₃	26	24	.520	177	54	275	2.82	9

a Sold to Colorado Rockies by Saltillo (Mexican), October 14, 1999.
b Sold to Saltillo (Mexican), May 15, 2001.
c Sold to Montreal Expos, August 18, 2002.
d Filed for free agency, October 15, 2002. Signed with Arizona Diamondbacks organization, October 23, 2002.
e Selected by Montreal Expos organization in Rule V draft, December 16, 2002.
f On disabled list from June 22 to July 21, 2003.
g On disabled list from March 24 to October 9, 2006.
h On disabled list from March 28 to June 20, 2007.

BACSIK, MICHAEL JOSEPH (MIKE)

Born, Dallas, Texas, November 11, 1977.
Bats Left. Throws Left. Height, 6 feet, 3 inches. Weight, 190 pounds.

Year	Club	Lea	G	IP	W	L	Pct	SO	BB	H	ERA	SAVES
1996	Burlington	Appal.	13	69²/₃	4	2	.667	61	14	49	2.20	0
1997	Columbus	So.Atl.	28	139	4	14	.222	100	47	163	5.44	0
1998	Kinston	Carolina	27	165²/₃	10	9	.526	128	37	147	2.88	0
1999	Akron	Eastern	26	149¹/₃	11	11	.500	84	47	164	4.64	0
2000	Kinston	Carolina	11	65	3	6	.333	56	8	72	4.57	0
2000	Akron	Eastern	11	71¹/₃	7	1	.875	44	15	61	2.78	0
2000	Buffalo	Int.	5	29	0	3	.000	9	7	31	5.59	0
2001	Buffalo	Int.	21	121¹/₃	12	5	.706	81	25	115	3.26	0
2001	Akron	Eastern	4	27¹/₃	1	1	.500	19	3	21	1.98	0
2001	Cleveland a-b	A.L.	3	9	0	0	.000	4	3	13	9.00	0
2002	Norfolk	Int.	25	108¹/₃	5	5	.500	75	25	134	3.74	0

Year Club	Lea	G	IP	W	L	Pct	SO	BB	H	ERA	SAVES
2002 New York . . . . .N.L.	11	55²/₃	3	2	.600	30	19	63	4.37	0	
2003 Norfolk. . . . . .Int.	22	117²/₃	2	9	.182	62	34	129	4.97	0	
2003 New York c. . . . . .N.L.	5	17²/₃	1	2	.333	12	8	28	10.19	0	
2004 Oklahoma. . . . . .P.C.	34	95	8	6	.571	50	23	106	4.55	0	
2004 Texas d. . . . . .A.L.	3	15²/₃	1	1	.500	6	1	16	4.60	0	
2005 Scranton-WB . . . . .Int.	30	160¹/₃	7	10	.412	112	41	184	4.55	0	
2006 Tucson e-f-g. . . . . .P.C.	28	87	11	0	1.000	57	19	81	2.79	0	
2007 Columbus. . . . . .Int.	9	36	1	3	.250	28	6	40	4.00	0	
2007 Washington h . . . . .N.L.	29	118	5	8	.385	45	29	141	5.11	0	
Major League Totals . . . . . . .5 Yrs.	51	216	10	13	.435	97	60	261	5.46	0	

a Traded to New York Mets with infielder Roberto Alomar and outfielder Danny Peoples for outfielder Matt Lawton, outfielder Alex Escobar, pitcher Jerrod Riggan, pitcher Billy Traber and player to be named later, December 11, 2001.

b Cleveland Indians received infielder Earl Snyder to complete trade, December 13, 2001.

c Filed for free agency, October 15, 2003. Signed with Texas Rangers organization, December 22, 2003.

d Filed for free agency, October 5, 2004. Signed with Philadelphia Phillies organization, December 6, 2004.

e Filed for free agency, October 15, 2005. Signed with Washington Nationals organization, February 9, 2006.

f Released by Washington Nationals, March 31, 2006. Signed with Arizona Diamondbacks organization, April 13, 2006.

g Filed for free agency, October 15, 2006. Signed with Washington Nationals organization, November 6, 2006.

h Filed for free agency, October 16, 2007, re-signed with Washington Nationals, November 27, 2007.

BAEK, CHA SEUNG (CHA SEUNG)
Born, Pusan, South Korea, May 29, 1980.
Bats Right. Throws Right. Height, 6 feet, 4 inches. Weight, 220 pounds.

Year Club	Lea	G	IP	W	L	Pct	SO	BB	H	ERA	SAVES
1999 Mariners . . . . Arizona	8	27	3	0	1.000	25	6	30	3.67	0	
2000 Wisconsin . . . . .Midwest	24	127²/₃	8	5	.615	99	36	137	3.95	0	
2001 San Bernardino . . . . . . .Calif.	5	21	1	0	1.000	16	2	17	3.43	0	
2002	INJURED—Did Not Play										
2003 Inland Empire . . . . .Calif.	13	56²/₃	5	1	.833	50	9	55	3.65	1	
2003 San Antonio . . . . .Texas	9	56	3	3	.500	46	17	49	2.57	0	
2004 Tacoma . . . . .P.C.	14	72²/₃	5	4	.556	56	24	85	4.21	0	
2004 Mariners. . . . . Arizona	2	7	0	0	.000	5	1	3	1.29	0	
2004 San Antonio . . . . .Texas	1	5	0	0	.000	5	0	2	0.00	0	
2004 Seattle . . . . .A.L.	7	31	2	4	.333	20	11	35	5.52	0	
2005 Tacoma . . . . .P.C.	25	113²/₃	8	8	.500	73	36	147	6.41	0	
2006 Tacoma . . . . .P.C.	24	147	12	4	.750	103	37	133	3.00	0	
2006 Seattle a. . . . . .A.L.	6	34¹/₃	4	1	.800	23	13	26	3.67	0	
2007 Azl Mariners. . . . . . . Arizona	1	3	0	0	.000	6	0	1	0.00	0	
2007 Wisconsin . . . . .Midwest	1	3²/₃	0	0	.000	6	0	5	4.91	0	
2007 Tacoma . . . . .P.C.	6	31	1	1	.500	18	10	33	3.19	0	
2007 Seattle b. . . . . .A.L.	14	73¹/₃	4	3	.571	49	14	87	5.15	0	
Major League Totals . . . . .3 Yrs.	27	138²/₃	10	-8	.556	92	38	148	4.87	0	

a On disabled list from September 25 to November 2, 2006.
b On disabled list from June 17 to September 17, 2007.

BAILEY, DAVID DEWITT (HOMER)
Born, Lagrange, Texas, May 3, 1986.
Bats Right. Throws Right. Height, 6 feet, 4 inches. Weight, 205 pounds.

Year Club	Lea	G	IP	W	L	Pct	SO	BB	H	ERA	SAVES
2004 Reds. . . . . Gulf Coast	6	12¹/₃	0	1	.000	9	3	14	4.38	0	
2005 Daython . . . . .Midwest	28	103²/₃	8	4	.667	125	62	89	4.43	0	
2006 Sarasota . . . . .Fla.St.	13	70²/₃	3	5	.375	79	22	49	3.31	0	
2006 Chattanooga. . . . . . .Southern	13	68	7	1	.875	77	28	50	1.59	0	
2007 Sarasota. . . . . .Fla.St.	2	8	0	1	.000	7	5	15	10.13	0	
2007 Louisville . . . . .Int.	12	67¹/₃	6	3	.667	59	32	49	3.07	0	
2007 Cincinnati. . . . . .N.L.	9	45¹/₃	4	2	.667	28	28	43	5.76	0	

BAKER, TIMOTHY SCOTT (SCOTT)
Born, Shreveport, Louisiana, September 19, 1981.
Bats Right. Throws Right. Height, 6 feet, 4 inches. Weight, 210 pounds.

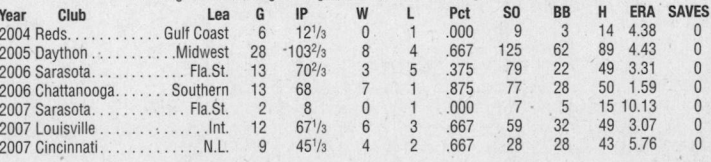

Year Club	Lea	G	IP	W	L	Pct	SO	BB	H	ERA	SAVES
2003 Quad Cities. . . . . . . .Midwest	11	50²/₃	3	1	.750	47	8	45	2.49	0	
2004 New Britain . . . . Eastern	10	70¹/₃	5	3	.625	72	13	44	2.43	0	
2004 Fort Myers . . . . .Fla.St.	7	45	4	2	.667	37	6	40	2.40	0	
2004 Rochester. . . . . .Int.	9	54¹/₃	1	3	.250	36	15	65	4.97	0	

Year	Club	Lea	G	IP	W	L	Pct	SO	BB	H	ERA	SAVES
2005	Rochester	Int.	22	134 2/3	5	8	.385	107	26	123	3.01	0
2005	Minnesota	A.L.	10	53 2/3	3	3	.500	32	14	48	3.35	0
2006	Rochester	Int.	12	84 1/3	5	4	.556	68	25	77	2.67	0
2006	Minnesota	A.L.	16	83 1/3	5	8	.385	62	16	114	6.37	0
2007	Rochester	Int.	7	42 2/3	3	2	.600	41	4	34	3.16	1
2007	Minnesota	A.L.	24	143 2/3	9	9	.500	102	29	162	4.26	0
Major League Totals	3 Yrs.		50	280 2/3	17	20	.459	196	59	324	4.71	0

BANNISTER, BRIAN P.

Born, Scottsdale, Arizona, February 28, 1981.
Bats Right. Throws Right. Height, 6 feet, 2 inches. Weight, 210 pounds.

Year	Club	Lea	G	IP	W	L	Pct	SO	BB	H	ERA	SAVES
2003	Brooklyn	N.Y.-Penn.	12	46	4	1	.800	42	19	27	2.15	1
2004	Binghamton	Eastern	8	44 1/3	3	3	.500	28	17	45	4.06	0
2004	St. Lucie	Fla.St.	20	110 1/3	5	7	.417	106	27	111	4.32	0
2005	Binghamton	Eastern	18	109	9	4	.692	94	27	91	2.56	0
2005	Norfolk	Int.	8	45 1/3	4	1	.800	48	13	48	3.18	0
2006	St. Lucie	Fla.St.	2	12	1	0	1.000	9	4	10	1.50	0
2006	Norfolk	Int.	6	30 1/3	3	3	.500	24	5	34	3.86	0
2006	New York a-b	N.L.	8	38	2	1	.667	19	22	34	4.26	0
2007	Omaha	P.C.	4	20 2/3	1	1	.500	14	4	16	2.61	0
2007	Kansas City	A.L.	27	165	12	9	.571	77	44	156	3.87	0
Major League Totals	2 Yrs.		35	203	14	10	.583	96	66	190	3.95	0

a On disabled list from April 27 to August 25, 2006.
b Traded to Kansas City Royals for pitcher Ambiorix Burgos, December 6, 2006.

BATISTA, MIGUEL JEREZ

Born, Santo Domingo, Dominican Republic, February 19, 1971.
Bats Right. Throws Right. Height, 6 feet, 1 Inch. Weight, 195 pounds.

Year	Club	Lea	G	IP	W	L	Pct	SO	BB	H	ERA	SAVES
1990	Expos	Gulf Coast	9	39 1/3	4	3	.571	21	17	33	2.06	0
1990	Rockford	Midwest	3	12 1/3	0	1	.000	7	5	16	8.76	0
1991	Rockford	Midwest	23	133 2/3	11	5	.688	90	57	126	4.04	0
1992	Pittsburgh b	N.L.	1	2	0	0	.000	1	3	4	9.00	0
1992	Wst Plm Bch	Fla. St.	24	135 1/3	7	7	.500	92	54	130	3.79	0
1993	Harrisburg	Eastern	26	141	13	5	.722	91	86	139	4.34	0
1994	Harrisburg c-d-e	Eastern	3	11 1/3	0	1	.000	5	9	8	2.38	0
1995	Charlotte	Int.	34	116 1/3	6	12	.333	58	60	118	4.80	0
1996	Charlotte	Int.	47	77	4	3	.571	56	39	93	5.38	4
1996	Florida f	N.L.	9	11 1/3	0	0	.000	6	7	9	5.56	0
1997	Iowa	A.A.	31	122	9	4	.692	95	38	117	4.20	0
1997	Chicago g	N.L.	11	36 1/3	0	5	.000	27	24	36	5.70	0
1998	Montreal	N.L.	56	135	3	5	.375	92	65	141	3.80	0
1999	Ottawa h	Int.	3	8	0	1	.000	7	4	3	2.25	0
2000	Montreal i	N.L.	4	8 1/3	0	1	.000	7	3	19	14.04	0
2000	Omaha	P.C.	18	28 1/3	2	2	.500	27	7	35	6.04	3
2000	Kansas City j	A.L.	14	57	2	6	.250	30	34	66	7.74	0
2001	Arizona	N.L.	48	139 1/3	11	8	.579	90	60	113	3.36	0
2002	Arizona	N.L.	36	184 2/3	8	9	.471	112	70	172	4.29	0
2003	Arizona k	N.L.	36	193 1/3	10	9	.526	142	60	197	3.54	0
2004	Toronto	A.L.	38	198 2/3	10	13	.435	104	*96	206	4.80	5
2005	Toronto l	A.L.	71	74 2/3	5	8	.385	54	27	80	4.10	31
2006	Arizona m	N.L.	34	206 1/3	11	8	.579	110	84	231	4.58	0
2007	Seattle	A.L.	33	193	16	11	.593	133	85	209	4.29	0
Major League Totals	13 Yrs.		430	1574 2/3	84	90	.483	1003	676	1629	4.44	37
Division Series												
2001	Arizona	N.L.	2	6 2/3	1	0	1.000	4	1	3	2.70	0
2002	Arizona	N.L.	1	3 2/3	0	1	.000	1	3	5	9.82	0
Division Series Totals			3	10 1/3	1	1	.500	5	4	8	5.23	0
Championship Series												
2001	Arizona	N.L.	2	7	0	1	.000	3	2	5	5.14	0
World Series Record												
2001	Arizona	N.L.	2	8	0	0	.000	6	5	5	0.00	0

a Selected by Pittsburgh Pirates from Montreal Expos in Rule V draft, December 9, 1991.
b Returned to Montreal Expos by Pittsburgh Pirates, April 23, 1992.
c On disabled list April 14 to 30 and May 7 to September 26, 1994.
d Released by Montreal Expos, November 18, 1994.

e Signed as free agent by Florida Marlins organization, December 9, 1994.
f Claimed on waivers by Chicago Cubs, December 10, 1996.
g Traded to Montreal Expos for outfielder Henry Rodriguez, December 12, 1997.
h On disabled list from July 16 to August 10, 1999.
i Traded to Kansas City Royals for pitcher Brad Rigby, April 25, 2000.
j Filed for free agency, October 2, 2000. Signed with Arizona Diamondbacks, November 15, 2000.
k Filed for free agency, November 7, 2003. Signed with Toronto Blue Jays, December 12, 2003.
l Traded to Arizona Diamondbacks with infielder Orlando Hudson for infielder Troy Glaus and infielder Sergio
Santos, December 27, 2005.
m Filed for free agency, October 30, 2006. Signed with Seattle Mariners, December 14, 2006.

BECKETT, JOSHUA PATRICK (JOSH)
Born, Spring, Texas, May 15, 1980.
Bats Right. Throws Right. Height, 6 feet, 5 inches. Weight, 220 pounds.

Year	Club	Lea	G	IP	W	L	Pct	SO	BB	H	ERA	SAVES
2000 Kane County	Midwest		13	59¹/₃	2	3	.400	61	15	45	2.12	0
2001 Brevard County	Fla.St.		13	65²/₃	6	0	1.000	101	15	32	1.23	0
2001 Portland	Eastern		13	74¹/₃	8	1	.889	102	19	50	1.82	0
2001 Florida	N.L.		4	24	2	2	.500	24	11	14	1.50	0
2002 Marlins	Gulf Coast		1	4	0	0	.000	7	1	5	4.50	0
2002 Jupiter	Fla.St.		1	6	1	0	1.000	12	1	4	0.00	0
2002 Florida a	N.L.		23	107²/₃	6	7	.462	113	44	93	4.10	0
2003 Carolina	Southern		1	4	0	0	.000	7	0	4	4.50	0
2003 Jupiter	Fla.St.		1	3	0	0	.000	5	0	2	0.00	0
2003 Florida b	N.L.		24	142	9	8	.529	152	56	132	3.04	0
2004 Florida c-d	N.L.		26	156²/₃	9	9	.500	152	54	137	3.79	0
2005 Florida d-e	N.L.		29	178²/₃	15	8	.652	166	58	153	3.38	0
2006 Boston	A.L.		33	204²/₃	16	11	.593	158	74	191	5.01	0
2007 Boston f	A.L.		30	200²/₃	*20	7	.741	194	40	189	3.27	0
Major League Totals	7 Yrs.		169	1014¹/₃	77	52	.597	959	337	909	3.74	0
Division Series												
2003 Florida	N.L.		1	7	0	1	.000	9	5	2	1.29	0
2007 Boston	A.L.		1	9	1	0	1.000	8	0	4	0.00	0
Division Series Totals			2	16	1	1	.500	17	5	6	0.56	0
Championship Series												
2003 Florida	N.L.		3	19¹/₃	1	0	1.000	19	2	11	3.26	0
2007 Boston	A.L.		2	14	2	0	1.000	18	1	9	1.93	0
Championship Series Totals			5	33¹/₃	3	0	1.000	37	3	20	2.70	0
World Series Record												
2003 Florida	N.L.		2	16¹/₃	1	1	.500	19	5	8	1.10	0
2007 Boston	A.L.		1	7	1	0	1.000	9	1	6	1.29	0
World Series Totals			3	23¹/₃	2	1	.667	28	6	14	1.16	0

a On disabled list from April 29 to May 14 and June 5 to July 16 and August 23 to September 11, 2002.
b On disabled list from May 8 to July 1, 2003.
c On disabled list from May 31 to June 17 and from June 18 to July 5 and July 6 to July 30, 2004.
d On disabled list from June 15 to June 30 and July 6 to July 23, 2005.
e Traded to Boston Red Sox with infielder Mike Lowell and pitcher Guillermo Mota for infielder Hanley Ramirez,
pitcher Anibal Sanchez and pitcher Jesus Delgado, November 24, 2005.
f On disabled list from May 14 to May 29, 2007.

BEDARD, ERIK JOSEPH
Born, Navan, Ontario, Canada, March 5, 1979.
Bats Left. Throws Left. Height, 6 feet, 1 inch. Weight, 190 pounds.

Year	Club	Lea	G	IP	W	L	Pct	SO	BB	H	ERA	SAVES
1999 Orioles	Gulf Coast		8	29	2	1	.667	41	13	20	1.86	0
2000 Delmarva	So.Atl.		29	111	9	4	.692	131	35	98	3.57	2
2001 Frederick	Carolina		17	96¹/₃	9	2	.818	130	26	68	2.15	0
2001 Orioles	Gulf Coast		2	6	0	1	.000	7	3	4	3.00	0
2002 Bowie	Eastern		13	68²/₃	6	3	.667	66	30	43	1.97	0
2002 Baltimore	A.L.		2	0²/₃	0	0	.000	1	0	2	13.50	0
2003 Orioles	Gulf Coast		3	8	0	0	.000	11	2	4	1.13	0
2003 Aberdeen	N.Y.-Penn.		2	7²/₃	0	0	.000	13	1	7	2.35	0
2003 Frederick a	Carolina		1	3²/₃	0	1	.000	2	1	5	7.36	0
2004 Ottawa	Int.		2	5	0	1	.000	3	3	8	7.20	0
2004 Baltimore	A.L.		27	137¹/₃	6	10	.375	121	71	149	4.59	0
2005 Delmarva	So.Atl.		1	5	1	0	1.000	9	1	3	0.00	0
2005 Bowie	Eastern		1	2	0	1	.000	4	1	2	9.00	0

Year Club	Lea	G	IP	W	L	Pct	SO	BB	H	ERA	SAVES
2005 Baltimore b	A.L.	24	141²/₃	6	8	.429	125	57	139	4.00	0
2006 Baltimore	A.L.	33	196¹/₃	15	11	.577	171	69	196	3.76	0
2007 Baltimore c	A.L.	28	182	13	5	.722	221	57	141	3.16	0
Major League Totals .... 5 Yrs.		114	658	40	34	.541	639	254	627	3.83	0

a On disabled list from March 28 to September 29, 2003.
b On disabled list from May 22 to July 18, 2005.
c On disabled list from September 9 to October 23, 2007.

BEIMEL, JOSEPH RONALD (JOE)
Born, St.Marys, Pennsylvania, April 19, 1977.
Bats Left. Throws Left. Height, 6 feet, 2 inches. Weight, 215 pounds.

Year Club	Lea	G	IP	W	L	Pct	SO	BB	H	ERA	SAVES
1998 Erie.............	N.Y.-Penn.	17	47	1	4	.200	37	22	56	6.32	0
1999 Hickory.............	So.Atl.	29	130	5	11	.313	102	43	146	4.43	0
2000 Lynchburg....	Carolina	18	120²/₃	10	6	.625	82	44	111	3.36	0
2000 Altoona...........	Eastern	10	62²/₃	1	6	.143	28	21	72	4.16	0
2001 Pittsburgh	N.L.	42	115¹/₃	7	11	.389	58	49	131	5.23	0
2002 Pittsburgh	N.L.	53	85¹/₃	2	5	.286	53	45	88	4.64	0
2003 Pittsburgh	N.L.	69	62¹/₃	1	3	.250	42	33	69	5.05	0
2004 Rochester..............	Int.	49	62	2	4	.333	44	24	83	6.97	2
2004 Minnesota a	A.L.	3	1²/₃	0	0	.000	2	2	8	43.20	0
2005 Durham	Int.	48	52²/₃	1	2	.333	36	21	58	3.93	0
2005 Tampa Bay b-c	A.L.	7	11	0	0	.000	3	4	15	3.27	0
2006 Las Vegas...........	P.C.	10	13	3	0	1.000	9	4	9	1.38	0
2006 Los Angeles	N.L.	62	70	2	1	.667	30	21	70	2.96	2
2007 Los Angeles	N.L.	83	67¹/₃	4	2	.667	39	24	63	3.88	1
Major League Totals .... 7 Yrs.		319	413	16	22	.421	227	178	444	4.58	3

a Released by Pittsburgh Pirates, March 31, 2004. Signed with Minnesota Twins organization, April 11, 2004.
b Filed for free agency, October 9, 2004. Signed with Tampa Bay Devil Rays organization, November 21, 2005.
c Released by Tampa Bay Devil Rays, November 22, 2005. Signed with Los Angeles Dodgers organization, January 23, 2006.

BELISLE, MATTHEW THOMAS (MATT)
Born, Austin, Texas, June 6, 1980.
Bats Right. Throws Right. Height, 6 feet, 3 inches. Weight, 195 pounds.

Year Club	Lea	G	IP	W	L	Pct	SO	BB	H	ERA	SAVES
1999 Danville	Appal.	14	71¹/₃	2	5	.286	60	23	86	4.67	0
2000 Myrtle Beach	Carolina	12	78²/₃	3	4	.429	71	11	72	3.43	0
2000 Macon	So.Atl.	15	102¹/₃	9	5	.643	97	18	79	2.37	0
2001 Greenville a	Southern					INJURED—Did Not Play					
2002 Greenville.........	Southern	26	159¹/₃	5	9	.357	123	39	162	4.35	0
2003 Greenville.........	Southern	21	125¹/₃	6	8	.429	94	42	128	3.52	0
2003 Richmond	Int.	3	20	1	1	.500	10	0	17	2.25	0
2003 Louisville...........	Int.	4	26	1	3	.250	15	5	31	3.81	0
2003 Cincinnati b	N.L.	6	8²/₃	1	1	.500	6	2	10	5.19	0
2004 Louisville.............	Int.	28	162²/₃	9	11	.450	106	51	192	5.26	0
2005 Cincinnati	N.L.	60	85²/₃	4	8	.333	59	26	101	4.41	1
2006 Dayton	Midwest	2	4	1	0	1.000	3	0	3	0.00	1
2006 Chattanooga..........	Southern	2	3¹/₃	0	0	.000	4	0	3	0.00	0
2006 Louisville.............	Int.	8	9	1	0	1.000	9	1	4	0.00	0
2006 Cincinnati c	N.L.	30	40	2	0	1.000	26	19	43	3.60	0
2007 Louisville.............	Int.	1	6	0	1	.000	7	2	7	3.00	0
2007 Cincinnati	N.L.	30	177²/₃	8	9	.471	125	43	212	5.32	0
Major League Totals .... 4 Yrs.		126	312	15	18	.455	216	90	366	4.85	1

a On minor league disabled list from April 6 to September 18, 2001.
b Sent by Atlanta Braves to Cincinnati Reds as player to be named later for pitcher Kent Mercker, August 14, 2003.
c On disabled list from May 28 to June 27 and July 10 to August 20, 2006.

BELL, HEATH JUSTIN
Born, Oceanside, California, September 29, 1977.
Bats Right. Throws Right. Height, 6 feet, 3 inches. Weight, 225 pounds.

Year Club	Lea	G	IP	W	L	Pct	SO	BB	H	ERA	SAVES
1998 Kingsport...........	Appal.	22	46	1	0	1.000	61	11	40	2.54	8
1999 Columbia	So.Atl.	55	62¹/₃	1	7	.125	68	17	47	2.60	25
2000 St. Lucie.............	Fla.St.	48	60	5	1	.833	75	21	43	2.55	23
2001 Binghamton	Eastern	43	61¹/₃	3	1	.750	55	19	82	6.02	4

Year	Club	Lea	G	IP	W	L	Pct	SO	BB	H	ERA	SAVES
2002	Binghamton........	Eastern	24	38	1	0	1.000	49	6	22	1.18	6
2002	Norfolk..............	.Int.	22	31²/₃	3	4	.429	28	9	38	4.26	5
2003	Norfolk..............	.Int.	40	49²/₃	2	3	.400	54	8	54	4.71	3
2004	Binghamton........	Eastern	1	2	0	0	.000	0	0	2	0.00	0
2004	Norfolk..............	.Int.	45	55²/₃	3	1	.750	68	24	42	3.23	16
2004	New York...........	.N.L.	17	24¹/₃	0	2	.000	27	6	22	3.33	0
2005	Norfolk..............	.Int.	13	26²/₃	1	0	1.000	29	5	15	1.69	6
2005	New York...........	.N.L.	42	46²/₃	1	3	.250	43	13	56	5.59	0
2006	Norfolk..............	.Int.	30	35	3	3	.500	56	8	27	1.29	12
2006	New York a.........	.N.L.	22	37	0	0	.000	35	11	51	5.11	0
2007	San Diego..........	.N.L.	81	93²/₃	6	4	.600	102	30	60	2.02	2
Major League Totals........4 Yrs.			162	201²/₃	7	9	.438	207	60	189	3.57	2

a Traded to San Diego Padres with pitcher Royce Ring for pitcher Jon Adkins and outfielder Ben Johnson, November 15, 2006.

BENITEZ, ARMANDO GERMAN

Born, Ramon Santana, Dominican Republic, November 3, 1972.
Bats Right. Throws Right. Height, 6 feet, 4 inches. Weight, 260 pounds.

Year	Club	Lea	G	IP	W	L	Pct	SO	BB	H	ERA	SAVES
1991	Sarasota Orioles......	Gulf C.	14	36¹/₃	3	2	.600	33	11	35	2.72	0
1992	Bluefield............	Appal.	25	31¹/₃	1	2	.333	37	23	35	4.31	5
1993	Albany............	So. Atl.	40	53¹/₃	5	1	.833	83	19	31	1.52	14
1993	Frederick..........	Carolina	12	13²/₃	3	0	1.000	29	4	7	0.66	4
1994	Bowie............	Eastern	53	71²/₃	8	4	.667	106	39	41	3.14	16
1994	Baltimore.............	A.L.	3	10	0	0	.000	14	4	8	0.90	0
1995	Rochester.............	.Int.	17	21²/₃	2	2	.500	37	7	10	1.25	8
1995	Baltimore............	A.L.	44	47²/₃	1	5	.167	56	37	37	5.66	2
1996	Orioles..........	Gulf Coast	1	2	1	0	1.000	5	0	1	0.00	0
1996	Bowie.............	Eastern	4	6	0	0	.000	8	0	7	4.50	0
1996	Rochester...........	.Int.	2	4	0	0	.000	5	1	3	2.25	0
1996	Baltimore a...........	A.L.	18	14¹/₃	1	0	1.000	20	6	7	3.77	4
1997	Baltimore.............	A.L.	71	73¹/₃	4	5	.444	106	43	49	2.45	9
1998	Baltimore b..........	A.L.	71	68¹/₃	5	6	.455	87	39	48	3.82	22
1999	New York...........	.N.L.	77	78	4	3	.571	128	41	40	1.85	22
2000	New York...........	.N.L.	76	76	4	4	.500	106	38	39	2.61	41
2001	New York...........	.N.L.	73	76¹/₃	6	4	.600	93	40	59	3.77	43
2002	New York...........	.N.L.	62	67¹/₃	1	0	1.000	79	25	46	2.27	33
2003	New York...........	.N.L.	45	49¹/₃	3	3	.500	50	24	41	3.10	21
2003	New York-Seattle c-d-e	.A.L.	24	23²/₃	1	1	.500	25	17	18	2.66	0
2004	Florida f-g	.N.L.	64	69²/₃	2	2	.500	62	21	36	1.29	*47
2005	San Jose........	California	2	2	0	0	.000	0	1	0	0.00	0
2005	San Francisco h........	.N.L.	30	30	2	3	.400	23	16	25	4.50	19
2006	San Francisco i........	.N.L.	41	38¹/₃	4	2	.667	31	21	39	3.52	17
2007	San Francisco-Florida j-k	N.L.	55	50¹/₃	2	8	.200	57	29	49	5.36	9
Major League Totals.......14 Yrs.			754	772²/₃	40	46	.465	937	401	541	3.11	289

Division Series

Year	Club	Lea	G	IP	W	L	Pct	SO	BB	H	ERA	SAVES
1996	Baltimore.............	A.L.	3	4	2	0	1.000	6	2	1	2.25	0
1997	Baltimore.............	A.L.	3	3	0	0	.000	4	2	3	3.00	0
1999	New York...........	.N.L.	2	2¹/₃	0	0	.000	2	1	2	0.00	0
2000	New York...........	.N.L.	2	3	1	0	1.000	3	1	4	6.00	0
Division Series Totals...........			10	12¹/₃	3	0	1.000	15	6	10	2.92	0

Championship Series

Year	Club	Lea	G	IP	W	L	Pct	SO	BB	H	ERA	SAVES
1996	Baltimore.............	A.L.	3	2¹/₃	0	0	.000	2	3	3	7.71	1
1997	Baltimore.............	A.L.	4	3	0	2	.000	6	4	3	12.00	0
1999	New York...........	.N.L.	5	6²/₃	0	0	.000	9	2	3	1.35	1
2000	New York...........	.N.L.	3	3	0	0	.000	2	2	3	0.00	1
Championship Series Totals......			15	15	0	2	.000	19	11	12	4.20	3

World Series Record

Year	Club	Lea	G	IP	W	L	Pct	SO	BB	H	ERA	SAVES
2000	New York.............	.N.L.	3	3	0	0	.000	2	2	3	3.00	1

a On disabled list from April 20 to August 26, 1996.

b Traded to New York Mets for catcher Charles Johnson, December 1, 1998.

c Traded to New York Yankees for pitcher Jason Anderson, pitcher Anderson Garcia and pitcher Ryan Bicondoa, July 16, 2003.

d Traded to Seattle Mariners with cash for pitcher Jeff Nelson, August 6, 2003.

e Filed for free agency, October 27, 2003. Signed with Florida Marlins, December 20, 2003.

f On disabled list from July 23 to August 12, 2004.

g Filed for free agency, October 28, 2004. Signed with San Francisco Giants, November 30, 2004.

h On disabled list from April 27 to August 15, 2005.
i On disabled list from April 2 to April 20 and September 14 to November 1, 2006.
j Traded to Florida Marlins for pitcher Randy Messenger, May 31, 2007.
k Filed for free agency, October 29, 2007.

BENOIT, JOAQUIN ANTONIO

Born, Santiago, Dominican Republic, July 26, 1977.
Bats Right. Throws Right. Height, 6 feet, 3 inches. Weight, 220 pounds.

Year	Club	Lea	G	IP	W	L	Pct	SO	BB	H	ERA	SAVES
1996 Texas	Dominican	14	75	6	5	.545	63	23	63	2.28	0
1997 Rangers	Gulf Coast	10	44	3	3	.500	38	11	40	2.05	0
1998 Savannah	So.Atl.	15	80	4	3	.571	68	18	79	3.83	0
1999 Charlotte	Fla.St.	22	105	7	4	.636	83	50	117	5.31	0
2000 Tulsa a	Texas	16	82$\frac{1}{3}$	4	4	.500	72	30	73	3.83	0
2001 Oklahoma	P.C.	24	131	9	5	.643	142	73	113	4.19	0
2001 Tulsa	Texas	4	21$\frac{2}{3}$	1	0	1.000	23	6	23	3.32	0
2001 Texas	A.L.	1	5	0	0	.000	4	3	8	10.80	0
2002 Charlotte	Fla.St.	1	5	0	0	.000	8	3	1	0.00	0
2002 Oklahoma	P.C.	16	98$\frac{2}{3}$	8	4	.667	103	37	74	3.56	0
2002 Texas	A.L.	17	84$\frac{2}{3}$	4	5	.444	59	58	91	5.31	1
2003 Oklahoma	P.C.	6	33	2	1	.667	31	11	28	3.82	0
2003 Texas b	A.L.	25	105	8	5	.615	87	51	99	5.49	0
2004 Frisco	Texas	1	2	0	0	.000	6	0	0	0.00	0
2004 Texas c	A.L.	28	103	3	5	.375	95	31	113	5.68	0
2005 Rangers	Arizona	1	2	0	0	.000	4	1	0	0.00	0
2005 Oklahoma	P.C.	3	5	0	1	.000	2	4	4	5.40	0
2005 Texas d	A.L.	32	87	4	4	.500	78	38	69	3.72	0
2006 Texas	A.L.	56	79$\frac{2}{3}$	1	1	.500	85	38	68	4.86	0
2007 Texas	A.L.	70	82	7	4	.636	87	28	68	2.85	6
Major League Totals	7 Yrs.	229	546$\frac{1}{3}$	27	24	.529	495	247	516	4.78	7

a On disabled list from May 2 to June 21, 2000.
b On disabled list from June 1 to June 22, 2003.
c On disabled list from August 23 to September 7, 2004.
d On disabled list from March 25 to May 2 and June 9 to June 28, 2005.

BERGMANN, JASON CHRIS

Born, Neptune, New Jersey, September 25, 1981.
Bats Right. Throws Right. Height, 6 feet, 4 inches. Weight, 190 pounds.

Year	Club	Lea	G	IP	W	L	Pct	SO	BB	H	ERA	SAVES
2002 Vermont	N.Y.-Penn.	14	71$\frac{2}{3}$	7	4	.636	57	33	48	2.89	0
2003 Savannah	So.Atl.	23	109	6	11	.353	82	53	108	4.29	0
2004 Harrisburg	Eastern	2	4	0	2	.000	3	2	7	9.00	0
2004 Brevard County	Fla.St.	24	31$\frac{2}{3}$	3	2	.600	28	18	20	1.14	8
2004 Savannah	So.Atl.	13	65	3	7	.300	58	34	67	4.85	0
2005 Harrisburg	Eastern	21	37	2	0	1.000	37	16	27	1.22	5
2005 New Orleans	P.C.	20	37	3	2	.600	39	13	26	3.16	2
2005 Washington	N.L.	15	19$\frac{2}{3}$	2	0	1.000	21	11	14	2.75	0
2006 New Orleans	P.C.	26	60$\frac{1}{3}$	8	2	.800	62	20	54	3.28	4
2006 Washington	N.L.	29	64$\frac{2}{3}$	0	2	.000	54	27	81	6.68	0
2007 Nationals	Gulf Coast	1	3	0	0	.000	4	2	2	0.00	0
2007 Columbus	Int.	5	24	2	1	.667	22	6	20	1.50	0
2007 Washington a	N.L.	21	115$\frac{1}{3}$	6	6	.500	86	42	99	4.45	0
Major League Totals	3 Yrs.	65	199$\frac{2}{3}$	8	8	.500	161	80	194	5.00	0

a On disabled list from May 15 to June 25 and July 25 to August 26, 2007.

BETANCOURT, RAFAEL JOSE

Born, Cumana, Venezuela, April 29, 1975.
Bats Right. Throws Right. Height, 6 feet, 2 inches. Weight, 200 pounds.

Year	Club	Lea	G	IP	W	L	Pct	SO	BB	H	ERA	SAVES
1997 Michigan	Midwest	27	32$\frac{1}{3}$	0	3	.000	52	2	26	1.95	11
1998 Red Sox	Gulf Coast	4	5	0	2	.000	4	1	6	7.20	0
1998 Sarasota	Fla.St.	20	28	3	1	.750	33	6	22	3.54	2
1998 Trenton	Eastern	7	9$\frac{1}{3}$	0	0	.000	9	3	9	6.75	0
1999 Sarasota	Fla.St.	6	7	0	0	.000	6	1	5	0.00	4
1999 Trenton a	Eastern	39	54$\frac{2}{3}$	6	2	.750	57	10	50	3.62	13
2000 Yokohama	Japan Cen.	11	29	1	2	.333	16	11	30	4.08	0
2000 Searex b	Japan East	20	23	1	0	1.000	29	6	17	1.17	6

Year	Club	Lea	G	IP	W	L	Pct	SO	BB	H	ERA	SAVES
2001 Trenton............	Eastern	16	24	0	1	.000	27	3	28	5.63	4
2002 Trenton............	Eastern		INJURED—Did Not Play								
2003 Akron.............	Eastern	31	45⅓	0	0	.000	75	13	33	1.39	16
2003 Buffalo...............	.Int.	4	6⅔	0	0	.000	6	2	6	4.05	1
2003 Cleveland c..........	A.L.	33	38	2	2	.500	36	13	27	2.13	1
2004 Akron.............	Eastern	1	1	0	0	.000	2	1	0	0.00	0
2004 Cleveland d..........	A.L.	68	66⅔	5	6	.455	76	18	71	3.92	4
2005 Cleveland e...........	A.L.	54	67⅔	4	3	.571	73	17	57	2.79	1
2006 Akron f............	Eastern	1	1	0	0	.000	2	1	0	0.00	0
2007 Cleveland............	A.L.	68	79⅓	5	1	.833	80	9	51	1.47	3
Major League Totals........5 Yrs.	273	308⅓	19	16	.543	313	68	258	2.80	12	
Division Series											
2007 Cleveland.............	A.L.	2	2	0	0	.000	3	0	1	0.00	0
Championship Series											
2007 Cleveland.............	A.L.	5	8	0	0	.000	6	1	6	6.75	0
Major League Totals........4 Yrs.	205	229	14	15	.483	233	59	207	3.26	9	

a Sold by Boston Red Sox to Yokohama, November 18,1999.
b Sold to Boston Red Sox, December 13, 2000.
c Filed for free agency, October 15, 2001. Signed with Cleveland Indians organization, January 20, 2003.
d On disabled list from June 26 to July 11, 2004.
e On disabled list from June 30 to July 18, 2005.
f On disabled list from April 20 to May 16, 2006.

BILLINGSLEY, CHAD RYAN

Born, Defiance, Ohio, July 29, 1984.
Bats Right. Throws Right. Height, 6 feet. Weight, 245 pounds.

Year	Club	Lea	G	IP	W	L	Pct	SO	BB	H	ERA	SAVES
2003 Ogden............	Pioneer	11	54	5	4	.556	62	15	49	2.83	0
2004 Vero Beach..........	Fla.St.	18	92	7	4	.636	111	49	68	2.35	0
2004 Jacksonville........	Southern	8	42⅓	4	0	1.000	47	22	32	2.98	0
2005 Jacksonville........	Southern	28	146	13	6	.684	162	50	116	3.51	0
2006 Las Vegas.............	P.C.	13	70⅔	6	3	.667	78	32	57	3.95	0
2006 Los Angeles...........	N.L.	18	90	7	4	.636	59	58	92	3.80	0
2007 Los Angeles...........	N.L.	43	147	12	5	.706	141	64	131	3.31	0
Major League Totals........2 Yrs.	61	237	19	9	.679	200	122	223	3.49	0	
Division Series											
2006 Los Angeles...........	N.L.	2	2	0	0	.000	3	0	1	0.00	0

BLANTON, JOSEPH MATTHEW (JOE)

Born, Bowling Green, Kentucky, December 11, 1980.
Bats Right. Throws Right. Height, 6 feet, 3 inches. Weight, 225 pounds.

Year	Club	Lea	G	IP	W	L	Pct	SO	BB	H	ERA	SAVES
2002 Modesto..........	California	2	6	0	1	.000	6	6	8	7.50	0
2002 Vancouver........	Northwest	4	14⅓	1	1	.500	15	2	11	3.14	0
2003 Kane County........	Midwest	21	133	8	7	.533	144	19	110	2.57	0
2003 Midland..............	Texas	7	35⅔	3	1	.750	30	7	21	1.26	1
2004 Sacramento...........	P.C.	28	176⅓	11	8	.579	143	34	199	4.19	0
2004 Oakland..............	A.L.	3	8	0	0	.000	6	2	6	5.63	0
2005 Oakland..............	A.L.	33	201⅓	12	12	.500	116	67	178	3.53	0
2006 Oakland..............	A.L.	32	194⅓	16	12	.571	107	58	241	4.82	0
2007 Oakland..............	A.L.	34	230	14	10	.583	140	40	*240	3.95	0
Major League Totals........4 Yrs.	102	633⅔	42	34	.553	369	167	665	4.10	0	
Championship Series											
2006 Oakland..............	A.L.	1	2	0	0	.000	2	2	0	0.00	0

BONDERMAN, JEREMY ALLEN

Born, Kennewick, Washington, October 28, 1982.
Bats Right. Throws Right. Height, 6 feet, 2 inches. Weight, 220 pounds.

Year	Club	Lea	G	IP	W	L	Pct	SO	BB	H	ERA	SAVES
2002 Modesto..........	California	25	144⅔	9	8	.529	160	55	129	3.61	0
2002 Lakeland a..........	Fla.St.	2	12	0	1	.000	10	4	11	6.00	0
2003 Detroit..............	A.L.	33	162	6	19	.240	108	58	193	5.56	0
2004 Detroit.............	A.L.	33	184	11	13	.458	168	73	168	4.89	0
2005 Detroit..............	A.L.	29	189	14	13	.519	145	57	199	4.57	0

Year Club	Lea	G	IP	W	L	Pct	SO	BB	H	ERA	SAVES
2006 Detroit	A.L.	34	214	14	8	.636	202	64	214	4.08	0
2007 Detroit b.............	A.L.	28	174¹/₃	11	9	.550	145	48	193	5.01	0
Major League Totals ....5 Yrs.		157	923¹/₃	56	62	.475	768	300	967	4.78	0
Division Series											
2006 Detroit	A.L.	1	8¹/₃	1	0	1.000	4	1	5	2.16	0
Championship Series											
2006 Detroit	A.L.	1	6²/₃	0	0	.000	3	2	6	4.05	0
World Series Record											
2006 Detroit	A.L.	1	5¹/₃	0	0	.000	4	4	6	3.38	0

a Sent by Oakland Athletics to Detroit Tigers to complete trade involving Jeff Weaver, Carlos Pena and Ted Lilly, August 22, 2002.

b On disabled list from May 9 to May 24, 2007.

BONSER, BOOF
Born, St.Petersburg, Florida, October 14, 1981.
Bats Right. Throws Right. Height, 6 feet, 4 inches. Weight, 260 pounds.

Year Club	Lea	G	IP	W	L	Pct	SO	BB	H	ERA	SAVES
2000 Salem-Keizer	Northwest	10	33	1	4	.200	41	29	21	6.00	0
2001 Hagerstown	So.Atl.	27	134	16	4	.800	178	61	91	2.49	0
2002 San Jose	Calif.	23	128¹/₃	8	6	.571	139	70	89	2.88	0
2002 Shreveport...........	Texas	5	24¹/₃	1	2	.333	23	14	30	5.55	0
2003 Norwich	Eastern	24	135	7	10	.412	103	67	122	4.00	0
2003 Fresno a............	P.C.	4	23	1	2	.333	28	8	17	3.13	0
2004 New Britain	Eastern	27	154¹/₃	12	9	.571	146	56	160	4.37	0
2004 Rochester.............	Int.	1	7	1	0	1.000	7	1	5	1.29	0
2005 Rochester.............	Int.	28	160¹/₃	11	9	.550	168	57	153	3.99	0
2006 Rochester............	Int.	14	86¹/₃	6	4	.600	83	35	68	2.81	0
2006 Minnesota	A.L.	18	100¹/₃	7	6	.538	84	24	104	4.22	0
2007 Minnesota	A.L.	31	173	8	12	.400	136	65	199	5.10	0
Major League Totals ....2 Yrs.		49	273¹/₃	15	18	.455	220	89	303	4.77	0
Division Series											
2006 Minnesota	A.L.	1	6	0	0	.000	3	1	7	3.00	0

a Traded by San Francisco Giants to Minnesota Twins with pitcher Joe Nathan and pitcher Francisco Liriano for catcher A.J. Pierzynski and player to be named later, November 14, 2003.

BOOTCHECK, CHRISTOPHER BRANDON (CHRIS)
Born, Laporte, Indiana, October 24, 1978.
Bats Right. Throws Right. Height, 6 feet, 5 inches. Weight, 200 pounds.

Year Club	Lea	G	IP	W	L	Pct	SO	BB	H	ERA	SAVES
2001 Rancho Cucamonga....	Calif.	15	87	8	4	.667	86	23	84	3.93	0
2001 Arkansas	Texas	6	36¹/₃	3	3	.500	22	11	39	5.45	0
2002 Salt Lake	P.C.	9	58	4	3	.571	38	16	64	3.88	0
2002 Arkansas	Texas	19	116	8	7	.533	90	35	130	4.81	0
2003 Salt Lake	P.C.	28	171¹/₃	8	9	.471	82	43	194	4.25	0
2003 Anaheim...............	A.L.	4	10¹/₃	0	1	.000	7	6	16	9.58	0
2004 Salt Lake	P.C.	28	163¹/₃	11	9	.550	105	60	202	5.12	0
2005 Los Angeles	A.L.	5	18²/₃	0	1	.000	8	4	19	3.38	1
2005 Salt Lake	P.C.	21	116¹/₃	7	4	.636	90	50	144	5.42	0
2006 Salt Lake	P.C.	40	65²/₃	4	3	.571	43	34	84	6.72	1
2006 Los Angeles a...........	A.L.	7	10¹/₃	0	1	.000	7	9	16	10.45	0
2007 Los Angeles	A.L.	51	77¹/₃	3	3	.500	56	24	81	4.77	0
Major League Totals ....4 Yrs.		67	116²/₃	3	6	.333	78	43	132	5.48	1

a On disabled list from May 3 to May 22, 2006.

BORKOWSKI, DAVID RICHARD (DAVE)
Born, Detroit, Michigan, February 7, 1977.
Bats Right. Throws Right. Height, 6 feet, 1 inch. Weight, 230 pounds.

Year Club	Lea	G	IP	W	L	Pct	SO	BB	H	ERA	SAVES
1995 Tigers..........	Gulf Coast	10	51²/₃	3	2	.600	36	8	45	2.96	0
1995 Lakeland............	Fla.St.	1	5	1	0	1.000	3	1	2	0.00	0
1996 Fayetteville	So.Atl.	27	178¹/₃	10	10	.500	117	54	158	3.33	0
1997 W Michigan	Midwest	25	164	15	3	.833	104	31	143	3.46	0
1998 Jacksnville	Southern	28	178²/₃	16	7	.696	97	54	204	4.63	0
1999 Toledo	Int.	19	126	6	8	.429	94	43	119	3.50	0
1999 Detroit	A.L.	17	76²/₃	2	6	.250	50	40	86	6.10	0

Year	Club	Lea	G	IP	W	L	Pct	SO	BB	H	ERA	SAVES
2000	Toledo	Int.	8	47	3	1	.750	29	14	44	4.40	0
2000	Detroit	A.L.	2	5⅓	0	1	.000	1	7	11	21.94	0
2000	Tigers	Gulf Coast	3	8	0	0	.000	6	0	7	2.25	0
2000	Lakeland	Fla.St.	2	7⅓	0	1	.000	5	4	11	8.59	0
2001	Toledo	Int.	18	28	1	2	.333	22	9	22	3.54	1
2001	Detroit a-b	A.L.	15	29⅔	0	2	.000	30	15	30	6.37	0
2002	Erie	Eastern	2	8⅓	0	2	.000	6	2	12	7.56	0
2002	Tigers	Gulf Coast	3	5⅓	0	0	.000	4	0	9	8.44	0
2003	Bowie	Eastern	24	120⅓	6	7	.462	66	22	126	3.29	0
2003	Erie c-d	Eastern	6	8	0	1	.000	4	2	10	3.38	0
2004	Ottawa	Int.	16	85⅓	6	9	.400	56	26	99	4.85	0
2004	Baltimore	A.L.	17	56	3	4	.429	45	15	65	5.14	0
2005	Ottawa e	Int.	29	182⅔	10	10	.500	104	38	217	4.34	0
2006	Round Rock	P.C.	6	7	0	1	.000	6	2	6	2.57	3
2006	Houston	N.L.	40	71	3	2	.600	52	23	70	4.69	0
2007	Houston	N.L.	64	71⅔	5	3	.625	63	34	76	5.15	1
Major League Totals	6 Yrs.		155	310⅓	13	18	.419	241	134	338	5.68	1

a On disabled list from July 7 to October 11, 2001.
b Released by Detroit Tigers, November 5 2001, re-signed with Detroit Tigers organization, November 14, 2001.
c Released by Detroit Tigers, April 25, 2003. Signed with Baltimore Orioles organization, May 2, 2003.
d Filed for free agency, October 15, 2003, re-signed with Baltimore Orioles organization, November 24, 2003.
e Filed for free agency, October 15, 2005. Signed with Houston Astros organization, December 22, 2005.

BOROWSKI, JOSEPH THOMAS (JOE)

Born, Bayonne, New Jersey, May 4, 1971.
Bats Right. Throws Right. Height, 6 feet, 2 inches. Weight, 225 pounds.

Year	Club	Lea	G	IP	W	L	Pct	SO	BB	H	ERA	SAVES
1990	White Sox	Gulf Coast	12	61⅓	2	8	.200	67	25	74	5.58	0
1991	Kane County a	Midwest	49	81	7	2	.778	76	43	60	2.56	13
1992	Frederick	Carolina	48	80⅓	5	6	.455	85	50	71	3.70	10
1993	Frederick	Carolina	42	62⅓	1	1	.500	70	37	61	3.61	11
1993	Bowie	Eastern	9	17⅔	3	0	1.000	17	11	11	0.00	0
1994	Bowie	Eastern	49	66	3	4	.429	73	28	52	1.91	14
1995	Bowie	Eastern	16	20⅔	2	2	.500	32	7	16	3.92	7
1995	Rochester	Int.	28	35⅔	1	3	.250	32	18	32	4.04	6
1995	Baltimore b	A.L.	6	7⅓	0	0	.000	3	4	5	1.23	0
1996	Atlanta	N.L.	22	26	2	4	.333	15	13	33	4.85	0
1996	Richmond	Int.	34	53⅓	1	5	.167	40	30	42	3.71	7
1997	Atlanta	N.L.	20	24	2	2	.500	6	16	27	3.75	0
1997	Richmond	Int.	21	37⅔	1	2	.333	34	19	32	3.58	2
1997	New York c	A.L.	1	2	0	1	.000	2	4	2	9.00	0
1998	Columbus	Int.	45	73⅔	3	3	.500	67	39	66	2.93	4
1998	New York d-e	A.L.	8	9⅔	1	0	1.000	7	4	11	6.52	0
1999	Louisville f	Int.	58	89	6	2	.750	70	44	94	5.46	4
2000	Newark	Atlantic	28	37⅔	6	3	.667	39	17	44	5.50	0
2000	Monterrey g-h-i	Mexican	12	42⅓	4	2	.667	44	18	31	3.19	1
2001	Iowa	P.C.	39	110	8	7	.533	131	26	87	2.62	1
2001	Chicago j	N.L.	1	1⅔	0	1	.000	1	3	6	32.40	0
2002	Chicago	N.L.	73	95⅔	4	4	.500	97	29	84	2.73	2
2003	Chicago	N.L.	68	68⅓	2	2	.500	66	19	53	2.63	33
2004	Iowa	P.C.	7	7⅔	0	3	.000	2	4	9	8.22	0
2004	Chicago k	N.L.	22	21⅓	2	4	.333	17	15	27	8.02	9
2005	Iowa	P.C.	7	8	0	0	.000	4	3	3	2.25	0
2005	Chicago l	N.L.	11	11	0	0	.000	11	1	12	6.55	0
2005	Tampa Bay m-n-o	A.L.	32	35⅓	1	5	.167	16	11	26	3.82	0
2006	Florida o	N.L.	72	69⅔	3	3	.500	64	33	63	3.75	36
2007	Cleveland	A.L.	69	65⅔	4	5	.444	58	17	77	5.07	*45
Major League Totals	11 Yrs.		405	437⅔	21	31	.404	363	169	426	4.05	125
Division Series												
2003	Chicago	N.L.	2	2	0	0	.000	5	0	1	0.00	1
2007	Cleveland	A.L.	2	2	0	0	.000	1	2	1	4.50	1
Division Series Totals			4	4	0	0	.000	6	2	2	2.25	2
Championship Series												
2003	Chicago	N.L.	3	5⅔	1	0	1.000	1	3	5	1.59	0
2007	Cleveland	A.L.	4	4	0	0	.000	1	3	6	4.50	1
Championship Series Totals			7	9⅔	1	0	1.000	2	6	11	2.79	1

a Traded by Chicago White Sox to Baltimore Orioles for infielder Pete Rose, Jr., March 21, 1991.
b Traded to Atlanta Braves with pitcher Rachaad Stewart for pitcher Kent Mercker, December 17, 1995.

c Claimed on waivers by New York Yankees, September 15, 1997.
d On disabled list from August 24 to September 8, 1998.
e Claimed on waivers by Milwaukee Brewers, December 4, 1998.
f Filed for free agency, October 15, 1999. Signed with Cincinnati Reds organization, November 9, 1999.
g Released by Cincinnati Reds, April 14, 2000. Signed with Newark for 2000.
h Signed with Monterrey for 2000.
i Signed with Chicago Cubs organization, December 11, 2000.
j Filed for free agency, October 10, 2001, re-signed with Chicago Cubs organization, March 1, 2002.
k On disabled list from June 5 to November 2, 2004.
l On disabled list from March 25 to May 20, 2005.
m Released by Chicago Cubs, July 7, 2005. Signed with Tampa Bay Devil Rays, July 11, 2005.
n Not offered contract, December 21, 2005. Signed with Florida Marlins, December 29, 2005.
o Filed for free agency, October 29, 2006. Signed with Cleveland Indians, December 12, 2006.

BRADFORD, CHADWICK LEE (CHAD)

Born, Jackson, Mississippi, September 14, 1974.
Bats Right. Throws Right. Height, 6 feet, 5 inches. Weight, 205 pounds.

Year	Club	Lea	G	IP	W	L	Pct	SO	BB	H	ERA	SAVES
1996 Hickory		So.Atl.	28	30	0	2	.000	27	7	21	0.90	18
1997 Winston-Sal		Carolina	46	54²/₃	3	7	.300	43	25	51	3.95	15
1998 Birmingham		Southern	10	17¹/₃	1	1	.500	14	8	13	2.60	1
1998 Calgary		P.C.	29	51	4	1	.800	27	11	50	1.94	0
1998 Chicago		A.L.	29	30²/₃	2	1	.667	11	7	27	3.23	1
1999 Charlotte		Int.	47	74¹/₃	9	3	.750	56	15	63	1.94	5
1999 Chicago		A.L.	3	3²/₃	0	0	.000	0	5	9	19.64	0
2000 Charlotte		Int.	55	53²/₃	2	4	.333	42	12	38	1.51	10
2000 Chicago a-b-c		A.L.	12	13²/₃	1	0	1.000	9	1	13	1.98	0
2001 Sacramento		P.C.	12	23²/₃	0	0	.000	24	2	15	0.38	2
2001 Oakland		A.L.	35	36²/₃	2	1	.667	34	6	41	2.70	1
2002 Oakland		A.L.	75	75¹/₃	4	2	.667	56	14	73	3.11	2
2003 Oakland		A.L.	72	77	7	4	.636	62	30	67	3.04	2
2004 Sacramento		P.C.	2	2	0	0	.000	3	0	1	0.00	0
2004 Oakland d		A.L.	68	59	5	7	.417	34	24	51	4.42	1
2005 Athletics		Arizona	3	3	0	0	.000	2	0	3	0.00	0
2005 Sacramento		P.C.	3	3	0	0	.000	1	0	4	6.00	0
2005 Stockton		Calif.	3	2¹/₃	0	0	.000	1	1	3	3.86	0
2005 Boston e-f-g		A.L.	31	23¹/₃	2	1	.667	10	4	29	3.86	0
2006 New York h		N.L.	70	62	4	2	.667	45	13	59	2.90	2
2007 Baltimore		A.L.	78	64²/₃	4	7	.364	29	16	77	3.34	2
Major League Totals	10 Yrs.		473	446	31	25	.554	290	120	446	3.39	11
Division Series												
2000 Chicago		A.L.	1	0²/₃	0	0	.000	0	0	2	0.00	0
2001 Oakland		A.L.	1	1	0	0	.000	1	0	0	0.00	0
2002 Oakland		A.L.	2	3	0	0	.000	1	0	1	0.00	0
2003 Oakland		A.L.	4	3²/₃	0	0	.000	5	2	4	0.00	0
2005 Boston		A.L.	2	1¹/₃	0	0	.000	1	0	1	0.00	0
2006 New York		N.L.	2	0¹/₃	0	0	.000	0	1	1	0.00	0
Division Series Totals			12	10	0	0	.000	8	3	9	0.00	0
Championship Series												
2006 New York		N.L.	5	5¹/₃	0	0	.000	2	0	3	0.00	0

a On disabled list from June 18 to July 5, 2000.
b Traded to Oakland Athletics for player to be named later, December 7, 2000.
c Chicago White Sox received catcher Miguel Olivo to complete trade, December 13, 2000.
d On disabled list from August 8 to August 23, 2004.
e On disabled list from March 30 to July 13, 2005.
f Traded to Boston Red Sox for outfielder Jay Payton, July 13, 2005.
g Not offered contract, December 21, 2005. Signed with New York Mets, December 28, 2005.
h Filed for free agency, October 30, 2006. Signed with Baltimore Orioles, November 30, 2006.

BROCAIL, DOUGLAS KEITH (DOUG)

Born, Clearfield, Pennsylvania, May 16, 1967.
Bats Left. Throws Right. Height, 6 feet, 5 inches. Weight, 250 pounds.

Year	Club	Lea	G	IP	W	L	Pct	SO	BB	H	ERA	SAVES
1986 Spokane		Northwest	16	85	5	4	.556	77	53	85	3.81	0
1987 Chston-SC		So.Atl.	19	92¹/₃	2	6	.250	68	28	94	4.09	0
1988 Chston-SC		So.Atl.	22	107	8	6	.571	107	25	107	2.69	2
1989 Wichita		Texas	23	134²/₃	5	9	.357	95	50	158	5.21	0
1990 Wichita		Texas	12	52	2	2	.500	27	24	53	4.33	0

Year	Club	Lea	G	IP	W	L	Pct	SO	BB	H	ERA	SAVES
1991	Wichita.............	Texas	34	146⅓	10	7	.588	108	43	147	3.87	6
1992	Las Vegas...........	P.C.	29	172⅓	10	10	.500	103	63	187	3.97	0
1992	San Diego	N.L.	3	14	0	0	.000	15	5	17	6.43	0
1993	Las Vegas...........	P.C.	10	51⅓	4	2	.667	32	14	51	3.68	1
1993	San Diego	N.L.	24	128⅓	4	13	.235	70	42	143	4.56	0
1994	Wichita.............	Texas	2	4	0	0	.000	2	1	3	0.00	0
1994	Las Vegas...........	P.C.	7	12⅔	0	0	.000	8	2	21	7.11	0
1994	San Diego a	N.L.	12	17	0	0	.000	11	5	21	5.82	0
1995	Tucson..............	P.C.	3	16⅓	1	0	1.000	16	4	18	3.86	0
1995	Houston b	N.L.	36	77⅓	6	4	.600	39	22	87	4.19	1
1996	Jackson.............	Texas	2	4	0	0	.000	5	1	1	0.00	0
1996	Tucson..............	P.C.	5	7⅓	0	1	.000	4	1	12	7.36	0
1996	Houston c-d..........	N.L.	23	53	1	5	.167	34	23	58	4.58	0
1997	Detroit	A.L.	61	78	3	4	.429	60	36	74	3.23	2
1998	Detroit e.............	A.L.	60	62⅔	5	2	.714	55	18	47	2.73	0
1999	Detroit	A.L.	70	82	4	4	.500	78	25	60	2.52	2
2000	Detroit f-g	A.L.	49	50⅔	5	4	.556	41	14	57	4.09	0
2001	New Orleans..........	P.C.	2	2⅓	0	0	.000	2	1	2	0.00	0
2001	Round Rock h-i	Texas	1	1	0	0	.000	1	0	0	0.00	0
2002	Houston j.............	N.L.				INJURED—Did Not Play						
2003	....					INJURED—Did Not Play						
2004	Oklahoma............	P.C.	12	19⅓	2	0	1.000	19	2	20	4.19	0
2004	Texas...............	A.L.	43	52⅓	4	1	.800	43	20	54	4.13	1
2004	Frisco k-l-m	Texas	1	4⅓	0	0	.000	6	0	2	2.08	0
2005	Texas n..............	A.L.	61	73⅓	5	3	.625	61	34	90	5.52	1
2006	Lake Elsinore	Calif.	6	6⅓	0	0	.000	12	2	3	0.00	0
2006	San Diego o-p	N.L.	25	28⅓	2	2	.500	19	8	27	4.76	0
2007	Lake Elsinore	Calif.	1	2	0	0	.000	3	0	2	0.00	0
2007	San Diego q-r........	N.L.	67	76⅔	5	1	.833	43	24	66	3.05	0
Major League Totals ....13 Yrs.			534	793⅔	44	43	.506	569	276	801	3.99	7

a Traded to Houston Astros with outfielder Derek Bell, outfielder Phil Plantier, pitcher Pedro A. Martinez, infielder Craig Shipley and infielder Ricky Gutierrez for infielder Ken Caminiti, infielder Andujar Cedeno, pitcher Brian Williams, infielder Roberto Petagine and player to be named later, December 28, 1994.

b San Diego received pitcher Sean Fesh to complete trade, May 1, 1995.

c On disabled list from May 11 to August 15, 1996.

d Traded to Detroit Tigers with outfielder Brian Hunter, infielder Orlando Miller and pitcher Todd Jones for catcher Brad Ausmus, pitcher C.J. Nitkowski, pitcher Jose Lima, pitcher Trever Miller and infielder Daryle Ward, December 10, 1996.

e On disabled list from August 9 to August 24, 1998.

f On disabled list from August 14 to August 31 and September 29 to November 6, 2000.

g Traded to Houston Astros with catcher Brad Ausmus and pitcher Nelson Cruz for pitcher Chris Holt, outfielder Roger Cedeno and catcher Mitch Meluskey, December 11, 2000.

h On disabled list from March 22 to October 30, 2001.

i Filed for free agency, November 8, 2001, re-signed with Houston Astros, December 4, 2001.

j On disabled list from March 22 to November 11, 2002.

k Filed for free agency, October 15, 2003. Signed with Texas Rangers organization, February 17, 2004.

l On disabled list from May 9 to June 7 and July 25 to August 9, 2004.

m Filed for free agency, October 29, 2004, re-signed with Texas Rangers, November 12, 2004.

n Filed for free agency, October 31, 2005. Signed with San Diego Padres, December 16, 2005.

o On disabled list from March 24 to July 13 and September 20 to October 30, 2006.

p Filed for free agency, October 30, 2006, re-signed with San Diego Padres, December 20, 2006.

q On disabled list from June 21 to July 7, 2007.

r Filed for free agency, October 30, 2007. Signed with Houston Astros, November 27, 2007.

BROXTON, JONATHAN ROY
Born, Augusta, Georgia, June 16, 1984.
Bats Right. Throws Right. Height, 6 feet, 4 inches. Weight, 275 pounds.

Year	Club	Lea	G	IP	W	L	Pct	SO	BB	H	ERA	SAVES
2002	Great Falls	Pioneer	11	29⅓	2	0	1.000	33	16	22	2.76	2
2003	South Bend	So.Atl.	9	37⅓	4	2	.667	30	22	27	3.13	0
2004	Vero Beach..........	Fla.St.	23	128⅓	11	6	.647	144	43	110	3.23	0
2005	Jacksonville	Southern	33	96⅔	5	3	.625	107	31	79	3.17	5
2005	Los Angeles	N.L.	14	13⅔	1	0	1.000	22	12	13	5.93	0
2006	Las Vegas...........	P.C.	11	11⅓	1	0	1.000	18	3	6	0.00	5
2006	Los Angeles	N.L.	68	76⅓	4	1	.800	97	33	61	2.59	3
2007	Los Angeles	N.L.	83	82	4	4	.500	99	25	69	2.85	2
Major League Totals ....3 Yrs.			165	172	9	5	.643	218	70	143	2.98	5
Division Series												
2006	Los Angeles	N.L.	2	2	0	1	.000	3	2	5	13.50	0

206

BRUNEY, BRIAN ANTHONY

Born, Astoria, Oregon, February 17, 1982.
Bats Right. Throws Right. Height, 6 feet, 3 inches. Weight, 245 pounds.

Year	Club	Lea	G	IP	W	L	Pct	SO	BB	H	ERA	SAVES
2000 Diamondbacks	Arizona		20	25	4	1	.800	24	29	21	6.48	2
2001 South Bend	Midwest		26	32²/₃	1	4	.200	40	19	24	4.13	8
2001 Yakima	Northwest		15	21	1	2	.333	28	11	19	5.14	2
2002 South Bend	Midwest		37	48¹/₃	4	3	.571	54	17	37	1.68	10
2002 El Paso	Texas		10	12¹/₃	0	2	.000	14	4	11	2.92	0
2003 Tucson	P.C.		32	32	3	1	.750	32	18	24	2.81	12
2003 El Paso	Texas		28	31¹/₃	0	2	.000	28	13	29	2.59	14
2004 Tucson	P.C.		31	38	2	0	1.000	42	20	18	1.42	5
2004 Arizona a	N.L.		30	31¹/₃	3	4	.429	34	27	20	4.31	0
2005 Tucson	P.C.		4	4²/₃	1	0	1.000	3	5	3	1.93	0
2005 Arizona	N.L.		47	46	1	3	.250	51	35	56	7.43	12
2006 Tucson	P.C.		4	2²/₃	0	1	.000	4	4	10	33.75	0
2006 Yankees	Gulf Coast		3	3²/₃	0	0	.000	5	3	1	4.91	0
2006 Columbus	Int.		11	14¹/₃	1	1	.500	22	8	10	3.14	3
2006 New York b	A.L.		19	20²/₃	1	1	.500	25	15	14	0.87	0
2007 Scranton-WB	Int.		4	6	2	0	1.000	5	2	5	6.00	1
2007 New York	A.L.		58	50	3	2	.600	39	37	44	4.68	0
Major League Totals	4 Yrs.		154	148	8	10	.444	149	114	134	4.93	12
Division Series												
2006 New York	A.L.		3	2²/₃	0	0	.000	4	0	1	3.38	0

a On disabled list from May 27 to July 6, 2004.
b Released by Arizona Diamondbacks, May 22, 2006. Signed with New York Yankees organization, July 19, 2006.

BUCHHOLZ, CLAY DANIEL

Born, Nederland, Texas, August 14, 1984.
Bats Left. Throws Right. Height, 6 feet, 3 inches. Weight, 190 pounds.

Year	Club	Lea	G	IP	W	L	Pct	SO	BB	H	ERA	SAVES
2005 Lowell	N.Y.-Penn.		15	41¹/₃	0	1	.000	45	9	34	2.61	0
2006 Wilmington	Carolina		3	16	2	0	1.000	23	4	10	1.13	0
2006 Greenville	So.Atl.		21	103	9	4	.692	117	29	78	2.62	0
2007 Portland	Eastern		16	86²/₃	7	2	.778	116	22	55	1.77	0
2007 Pawtucket	Int.		8	38²/₃	1	3	.250	55	13	32	3.96	0
2007 Boston a	A.L.		4	22²/₃	3	1	.750	22	10	14	1.59	0

a Pitched no-hit, no-run game against Baltimore Orioles, September 1, 2007.

BUCHHOLZ, TAYLOR

Born, Lower Merion Twsp., Pennsylvania, October 13, 1981.
Bats Right. Throws Right. Height, 6 feet, 4 inches. Weight, 220 pounds.

Year	Club	Lea	G	IP	W	L	Pct	SO	BB	H	ERA	SAVES
2000 Phillies	Gulf Coast		12	44	2	3	.400	41	14	46	2.25	0
2001 Lakewood	So.Atl.		28	176²/₃	9	14	.391	136	57	165	3.36	0
2002 Reading	Eastern		23	23	0	2	.000	17	6	29	7.43	0
2002 Clearwater	Fla.St.		23	158²/₃	10	6	.625	129	51	140	3.29	0
2003 Reading a	Eastern		25	144²/₃	9	11	.450	114	33	136	3.55	0
2004 New Orleans	P.C.		20	98	6	7	.462	74	29	107	5.23	0
2005 Round Rock	P.C.		20	76²/₃	6	0	1.000	45	27	79	4.81	0
2006 Round Rock	P.C.		7	44	1	3	.250	37	17	47	4.91	0
2006 Houston b	N.L.		22	113	6	10	.375	77	34	107	5.89	0
2007 Colorado	N.L.		41	93²/₃	6	5	.545	61	20	105	4.23	0
Major League Totals	2 Yrs.		63	206²/₃	12	15	.444	138	54	212	5.14	0

a Traded by Philadelphia Phillies to Houston Astros with pitcher Brandon Duckworth and pitcher Ezequiel Astacio for pitcher Billy Wagner, November 3, 2003.
b Traded to Colorado Rockies with outfielder Willy Taveras and pitcher Jason Hirsh for pitcher Jason Jennings and pitcher Miguel Asencio, December 12, 2006.

BUCKNER, WILLIAM JENNINGS (BILLY)

Born, Decatur, Georgia, August 27, 1983.
Bats Right. Throws Right. Height, 6 feet, 2 inches. Weight, 215 pounds.

Year	Club	Lea	G	IP	W	L	Pct	SO	BB	H	ERA	SAVES
2004 Idaho Falls	Pioneer		8	34¹/₃	2	1	.667	37	4	36	2.88	0
2005 Burlington	Midwest		11	60¹/₃	3	7	.300	60	17	66	3.88	0
2005 High Desert	Calif.		17	94	5	6	.455	92	46	105	5.36	0

Year	Club	Lea	G	IP	W	L	Pct	SO	BB	H	ERA	SAVES
2006 High Desert	Calif.	16	90	7	1	.875	85	47	92	3.90	0
2006 Wichita	Texas	13	75²/₃	5	3	.625	63	39	78	4.64	0
2007 Wichita	Texas	4	19¹/₃	1	3	.250	13	6	20	4.66	0
2007 Omaha	P.C.	27	104²/₃	9	7	.563	83	26	108	3.78	0
2007 Kansas City	A.L.	7	34	1	2	.333	17	16	37	5.29	0

a Traded to Arizona Diamondbacks for infielder Alberto Callaspo, December 14, 2007.

BUEHRLE, MARK ANTHONY
Born, St.Charles, Missouri, March 23, 1979.
Bats Left. Throws Left. Height, 6 feet, 2 inches. Weight, 225 pounds.

Year	Club	Lea	G	IP	W	L	Pct	SO	BB	H	ERA	SAVES
1999 Burlington	Midwest	20	98²/₃	7	4	.636	91	16	105	4.10	3
2000 Birmingham	Southern	16	118²/₃	8	4	.667	68	17	95	2.28	0
2000 Chicago	A.L.	28	51¹/₃	4	1	.800	37	19	55	4.21	0
2001 Chicago	A.L.	32	221¹/₃	16	8	.667	126	48	188	3.29	0
2002 Chicago	A.L.	34	239	19	12	.613	134	61	236	3.58	0
2003 Chicago	A.L.	35	230¹/₃	14	14	.500	119	61	250	4.14	0
2004 Chicago	A.L.	35	*245¹/₃	16	10	.615	165	51	257	3.89	0
2005 Chicago	A.L.	33	*236²/₃	16	8	.667	149	40	*240	3.12	0
2006 Chicago	A.L.	32	204	12	13	.480	98	48	*247	4.99	0
2007 Chicago a	A.L.	30	201	10	9	.526	115	45	208	3.63	0
Major League Totals	8 Yrs.	259	1629	107	75	.588	943	373	1681	3.80	0
Division Series											
2000 Chicago	A.L.	1	0¹/₃	0	0	.000	1	0	2	0.00	0
2005 Chicago	A.L.	1	7	1	0	1.000	2	1	8	5.14	0
Division Series Totals		2	7¹/₃	1	0	1.000	3	1	10	4.91	0
Championship Series											
2005 Chicago	A.L.	1	9	1	0	1.000	4	0	5	1.00	0
World Series Record											
2005 Chicago	A.L.	2	7¹/₃	0	0	.000	6	0	7	4.91	1

a Pitched no-hit, no-run game against Texas Rangers, April 18, 2007.

BULLINGTON, BRYAN PAUL
Born, Indianapolis, Indiana, September 30, 1980.
Bats Right. Throws Right. Height, 6 feet, 4 inches. Weight, 220 pounds.

Year	Club	Lea	G	IP	W	L	Pct	SO	BB	H	ERA	SAVES
2003 Lynchburg	Carolina	17	97¹/₃	8	4	.667	67	27	101	3.05	0
2003 Hickory	So.Atl.	8	45¹/₃	5	1	.833	46	11	25	1.39	0
2004 Altoona	Eastern	26	145	12	7	.632	100	47	160	4.10	0
2005 Indianapolis	Int.	18	109¹/₃	9	5	.643	82	26	104	3.38	0
2005 Pittsburgh	N.L.	1	1¹/₃	0	0	.000	1	1	1	13.50	0
2006 Pittsburgh	N.L.		INJURED—Did Not Play								
2007 Indianapolis	Int.	26	150²/₃	11	9	.550	89	59	146	4.00	0
2007 Pittsburgh	N.L.	5	17	0	3	.000	7	5	24	5.29	0
Major League Totals	2 Yrs.	6	18¹/₃	0	3	.000	8	6	25	5.89	0

BURNETT, ALLAN JAMES (A.J.)
Born, North Little Rock, Arkansas, January 3, 1977.
Bats Right. Throws Right. Height, 6 feet, 4 inches. Weight, 230 pounds.

Year	Club	Lea	G	IP	W	L	Pct	SO	BB	H	ERA	SAVES
1995 Mets	Gulf Coast	9	33²/₃	2	3	.400	26	23	27	4.28	0
1996 Kingsport	Appal.	12	58	4	0	1.000	68	54	31	3.88	0
1997 Mets	Gulf Coast	3	11¹/₃	0	1	.000	15	8	8	3.18	0
1997 Pittsfield	N.Y.-Penn.	9	44	3	1	.750	48	35	28	4.70	0
1998 Kane County a	Midwest	20	119	10	4	.714	186	45	74	1.97	0
1999 Portland	Eastern	26	120²/₃	6	12	.333	121	71	132	5.52	0
1999 Florida	N.L.	7	41¹/₃	4	2	.667	33	25	37	3.48	0
2000 Brevard County	Fla.St.	2	7¹/₃	0	0	.000	6	6	4	3.68	0
2000 Calgary	P.C.	1	5	0	0	.000	6	3	0	0.00	0
2000 Florida b	N.L.	13	82²/₃	3	7	.300	57	44	80	4.79	0
2001 Brevard County	Fla.St.	2	9¹/₃	0	0	.000	10	4	4	1.93	0
2001 Florida c-d	N.L.	27	173¹/₃	11	12	.478	128	83	145	4.05	0
2002 Florida e	N.L.	31	204¹/₃	12	9	.571	203	90	153	3.30	0
2003 Florida f	N.L.	4	23	0	2	.000	21	18	14	4.70	0
2004 Jupiter	Fla.St.	1	4	0	0	.000	4	2	2	0.00	0

Year	Club	Lea	G	IP	W	L	Pct	SO	BB	H	ERA	SAVES
2004 Albuquerque...........	P.C.	1	$3\frac{1}{3}$	0	0	.000	6	2	7	10.80	0
2004 Florida g..............	N.L.	20	120	7	6	.538	113	38	102	3.68	0
2005 Florida h..............	N.L.	32	209	12	12	.500	198	79	184	3.44	0
2006 Dunedin...........	Fla.St.	2	8	0	0	.000	6	2	9	3.38	0
2006 New Hampshire.....	Eastern	1	6	1	0	1.000	9	3	2	1.50	0
2006 Syracuse.............	.Int.	1	5	1	0	1.000	7	1	0	0.00	0
2006 Toronto i.............	A.L.	21	$135\frac{2}{3}$	10	8	.556	118	39	138	3.98	0
2007 Syracuse.............	.Int.	1	5	0	0	.000	7	1	3	1.80	0
2007 Toronto j.............	A.L.	25	$165\frac{2}{3}$	10	8	.556	176	66	131	3.75	0
Major League Totals........9 Yrs.		180	1155	69	66	.511	1047	482	988	3.76	

a Traded to Florida Marlins by New York Mets with pitcher Jesus Sanchez and outfielder Robert Stratton for pitcher Al Leiter and infielder Ralph Milliard, February 6, 1998.
b On disabled list from March 17 to July 19, 2000.
c On disabled list from March 23 to May 7, 2001.
d Pitched no-hit, no-run game against San Diego Padres, May 12, 2001.
e On disabled list from August 19 to September 14, 2002.
f On disabled list from March 21 to April 9 and April 26 to September 29, 2003.
g On disabled list from March 26 to June 3, 2004.
h Filed for free agency, October 27, 2005. Signed with Toronto Blue Jays, December 6, 2005.
i On disabled list from March 24 to April 15 and April 22 to June 22, 2006.
j On disabled list from June 13 to June 28 and June 29 to August 12, 2007.

BURRES, BRIAN JAMES
Born, Oregon City, Oregon, April 8, 1981.
Bats Left. Throws Left. Height, 6 feet, 1 inch. Weight, 180 pounds.

Year	Club	Lea	G	IP	W	L	Pct	SO	BB	H	ERA	SAVES
2001 Salem-Keizer.....	Northwest	14	$40\frac{2}{3}$	3	1	.750	38	11	43	3.10	1
2002 Hagerstown.......	So.Atl.	32	$119\frac{1}{3}$	5	10	.333	119	53	114	4.75	1
2003 San Jose..........	Calif.	39	$60\frac{2}{3}$	3	3	.500	64	36	55	3.86	1
2004 San Jose..........	Calif.	36	$123\frac{2}{3}$	12	1	.923	114	30	115	2.84	0
2005 Norwich..........	Eastern	26	$128\frac{2}{3}$	9	6	.600	105	57	130	4.20	0
2006 Ottawa.............	.Int.	26	139	10	6	.625	110	57	133	3.76	0
2006 Baltimore a.......	A.L.	11	8	0	0	.000	6	1	6	2.25	0
2007 Norfolk.............	.Int.	2	4	1	0	1.000	5	1	2	2.25	0
2007 Baltimore.........	A.L.	37	121	6	8	.429	96	66	140	5.95	0
Major League Totals........2 Yrs.		48	129	6	8	.429	102	67	146	5.72	0

a Claimed on waivers by Baltimore Orioles from San Francisco Giants, January 6, 2006.

BURTON, LEVI JARED (JARED)
Born, Westminster, South Carolina, June 2, 1981.
Bats Right. Throws Right. Height, 6 feet, 5 inches. Weight, 225 pounds.

Year	Club	Lea	G	IP	W	L	Pct	SO	BB	H	ERA	SAVES
2002 Vancouver.......	Northwest	13	$37\frac{2}{3}$	0	4	.000	38	14	32	3.58	1
2003 Kane County.......	.Midwest	15	$31\frac{2}{3}$	2	1	.667	33	7	19	2.27	1
2004 Athletics...........	Arizona	5	$21\frac{2}{3}$	1	0	1.000	15	4	21	4.15	0
2004 Modesto.............	Calif.	10	32	3	2	.600	25	20	34	4.78	0
2005 Stockton...........	Calif.	52	$55\frac{1}{3}$	4	4	.500	67	20	44	2.60	24
2006 Midland a...........	Texas	53	74	6	5	.545	66	27	71	4.14	1
2007 Chattanooga.......	Southern	4	$5\frac{1}{3}$	0	1	.000	3	5	10	11.81	0
2007 Louisville...........	.Int.	10	14	1	0	1.000	13	4	11	0.64	1
2007 Cincinnati b...........	N.L.	47	43	4	2	.667	36	22	28	2.51	0

a Selected by Cincinnati Reds from Oakland Athletics in Rule V draft, December 7, 2006.
b On disabled list from April 8 to May 9 and June 11 to July 7, 2007.

BUSH, DAVID THOMAS (DAVE)
Born, Pittsburgh, Pennsylvania, November 9, 1979.
Bats Right. Throws Right. Height, 6 feet, 2 inches. Weight, 210 pounds.

Year	Club	Lea	G	IP	W	L	Pct	SO	BB	H	ERA	SAVES
2002 Auburn...........	N.Y.-Penn.	18	$22\frac{1}{3}$	1	1	.500	39	7	13	2.82	10
2002 Dunedin.............	Fla.St.	7	$13\frac{1}{3}$	0	1	.000	9	2	10	2.03	0
2003 Dunedin...........	Fla.St.	14	77	7	3	.700	75	9	64	2.81	0
2003 New Haven...........	Eastern	14	81	7	3	.700	73	19	73	2.78	0
2004 Syracuse...........	.Int.	16	$99\frac{2}{3}$	6	6	.500	88	20	108	4.06	0
2004 Toronto.............	A.L.	16	$97\frac{2}{3}$	5	4	.556	64	25	95	3.69	0
2005 Syracuse...........	.Int.	9	55	2	2	.500	40	9	65	4.42	0
2005 Toronto a.............	A.L.	25	$136\frac{1}{3}$	5	11	.313	75	29	142	4.49	0

Year	Club	Lea	G	IP	W	L	Pct	SO	BB	H	ERA	SAVES
2006 Milwaukee	....	N.L.	34	210	12	11	.522	166	38	201	4.41	0
2007 Milwaukee	....	N.L.	33	186⅓	12	10	.545	134	44	217	5.12	0
Major League Totals	....	4 Yrs.	108	630⅓	34	36	.486	439	136	655	4.53	0

a Traded to Milwaukee Brewers with outfielder Gabe Gross and pitcher Zach Jackson for infielder Lyle Overbay and pitcher Ty Taubenheim, December 7, 2005.

BYRD, PAUL GREGORY

Born, Louisville, Kentucky, December 3, 1970.
Bats Right. Throws Right. Height, 6 feet, 1 inches. Weight, 190 pounds.

Year	Club	Lea	G	IP	W	L	Pct	SO	BB	H	ERA	SAVES
1991 Kinston	....	Carolina	14	62⅔	4	3	.571	62	36	40	3.16	0
1992 Canton-Akron	....	Eastern	24	152⅓	14	6	.700	118	75	122	3.01	0
1993 Canton-Akron	....	Eastern	2	10	0	0	.000	8	3	7	3.60	0
1993 Charlotte	....	Int.	14	81	7	4	.636	54	30	80	3.89	0
1994 Canton-Akron a	.....	Eastern	21	139⅓	5	9	.357	106	52	135	3.81	0
1994 Charlotte	....	Int.	9	36⅔	2	2	.500	15	11	33	3.93	1
1995 Norfolk	....	Int.	22	87	3	5	.375	61	21	71	2.79	6
1995 New York	....	N.L.	17	22	2	0	1.000	26	7	18	2.05	0
1996 Norfolk	....	Int.	5	7⅔	2	0	1.000	8	4	4	3.52	1
1996 New York b-c	....	N.L.	38	46⅔	1	2	.333	31	21	48	4.24	0
1997 Richmond	....	Int.	3	17	2	1	.667	14	1	14	3.18	0
1997 Atlanta	....	N.L.	31	53	4	4	.500	37	28	47	5.26	0
1998 Richmond	....	Int.	17	102⅓	5	5	.500	84	36	92	3.69	0
1998 Atlanta-Philadelphia d	...	N.L.	9	57	5	2	.714	39	18	45	2.68	0
1999 Philadelphia	....	N.L.	32	199⅔	15	11	.577	106	70	205	4.60	0
2000 Scranton-WB	....	Int.	3	26	2	0	1.000	10	6	20	1.73	0
2000 Philadelphia e-f	....	N.L.	17	83	2	9	.182	53	35	89	6.51	0
2001 Clearwater	....	Fla.St.	4	23⅔	0	3	.000	17	5	24	3.42	0
2001 Scranton-WB	....	Int.	5	37	1	3	.250	35	7	34	3.65	0
2001 Philadelphia	....	N.L.	3	10	0	1	.000	3	4	10	8.10	0
2001 Kansas City g-h	....	A.L.	16	93⅓	6	6	.500	49	22	110	4.05	0
2002 Kansas City i-j	....	A.L.	33	228⅓	17	11	.607	129	38	224	3.90	0
2003 Atlanta	....	N.L.					INJURED—Did Not Play					
2004 Greenville	....	Southern	3	12⅔	1	1	.500	8	5	13	7.11	0
2004 Richmond	....	Int.	1	4⅔	0	1	.000	5	2	3	7.71	0
2004 Atlanta k-l	....	N.L.	19	114⅓	8	7	.533	79	19	123	3.94	0
2005 Los Angeles m	....	A.L.	31	204⅓	12	11	.522	102	28	216	3.74	0
2006 Cleveland	....	A.L.	31	179	10	9	.526	88	38	232	4.88	0
2007 Cleveland	....	A.L.	31	192⅓	15	8	.652	88	28	239	4.59	0
Major League Totals	....	12 Yrs.	308	1483	97	81	.545	830	356	1606	4.35	0
Division Series												
2004 Atlanta	....	N.L.	2	5⅔	0	1	.000	3	3	8	6.35	0
2005 Los Angeles	....	A.L.	1	3⅔	0	0	.000	2	2	7	9.82	0
2007 Cleveland	....	A.L.	1	5	1	0	1.000	2	2	8	3.60	0
Division Series Totals	....		4	14⅓	1	1	.500	7	7	23	6.28	0
Championship Series												
2005 Los Angeles	....	A.L.	2	10⅔	1	0	1.000	2	2	10	3.38	0
2007 Cleveland	....	A.L.	1	5	1	0	1.000	4	0	6	3.60	0
Championship Series Totals	......		3	15⅔	2	0	1.000	6	2	16	3.45	0

a Traded to New York Mets by Cleveland Indians with pitcher Dave Mlicki and pitcher Jerry DiPoto and player to be named later for outfielder Jeromy Burnitz and pitcher Joe Roa, November 18, 1994. New York Mets received infielder Jesus Azujae to complete trade, December 6, 1994.

b On disabled list from April 1 to June 9, 1996.

c Traded to Atlanta Braves with player to be named later for pitcher Greg McMichael, November 25, 1996. Atlanta Braves received pitcher Andy Zwirchitz to complete trade, June 1, 1997.

d Claimed on waivers by Philadelphia Phillies, August 10, 1998.

e On disabled list from July 27 to October 5, 2000.

f Filed for free agency, October 12, 2000, re-signed with Philadelphia Phillies organization, January 29, 2001.

g Traded to Kansas City Royals for pitcher Jose Santiago, June 5, 2001.

h On disabled list from September 22 to November 8, 2001.

i Not offered 2002 contract, December 21, 2001, re-signed with Kansas City Royals, January 10, 2002.

j Filed for free agency, October 28, 2002. Signed with Atlanta Braves, December 17, 2002.

k On disabled list from March 26 to June 19, 2004. On disabled list from March 21 to November 7, 2003.

l Filed for free agency, October 28, 2004. Signed with Anaheim Angels, December 14, 2004.

m Filed for free agency, October 27, 2005. Signed with Cleveland Indians, December 5, 2005.

BYRDAK, TIMOTHY CHRISTOPHER (TIM)
Born, Oak Lawn, Illinois, October 31, 1973.
Bats Left. Throws Left. Height, 5 feet, 11 inches. Weight, 195 pounds.

Year	Club	Lea	G	IP	W	L	Pct	SO	BB	H	ERA	SAVES
1994 Eugene	Northwest	15	73⅓	4	5	.444	77	20	60	3.07	0
1995 Wilmington	Carolina	27	166⅓	11	5	.688	127	45	118	2.16	0
1996 Wichita	Texas	15	84⅔	5	7	.417	47	44	112	6.91	0
1997 Wilmington	Carolina	22	41	4	3	.571	47	12	34	3.51	3
1998 Wichita	Texas	34	52	3	5	.375	37	28	58	4.15	2
1998 Kansas City	A.L.	3	1⅔	0	0	.000	1	0	5	5.40	0
1998 Omaha	P.C.	26	36⅔	2	1	.667	32	20	31	2.45	1
1999 Omaha	P.C.	33	49⅔	3	1	.750	51	28	39	1.81	4
1999 Kansas City	A.L.	33	24⅔	0	3	.000	17	20	32	7.66	1
2000 Omaha	P.C.	34	52⅔	6	2	.750	47	29	59	4.44	4
2000 Kansas City	A.L.	12	6⅓	0	1	.000	8	4	11	11.37	0
2000 Wichita a	Texas	4	6⅔	0	0	.000	1	3	9	5.40	0
2001 Buffalo	Int.	4	17⅓	2	0	1.000	17	5	18	4.67	0
2002 Kinston	Carolina	2	4	1	0	1.000	3	4	3	4.50	0
2002 Akron	Eastern	9	13	0	0	.000	8	11	16	6.23	1
2003 Joliet	Northern	5	34	2	1	.667	18	10	31	2.67	0
2003 Gary	Northern	10	66	2	4	.333	58	25	60	4.34	0
2004 Ottawa	Int.	33	34⅓	2	1	.667	43	12	46	4.19	2
2004 Portland b-c-d	P.C.	20	38	3	0	1.000	25	17	47	5.45	0
2005 Ottawa	Int.	37	38⅔	3	2	.600	44	15	23	2.09	11
2005 Baltimore	A.L.	41	26⅔	0	1	.000	31	21	27	4.05	1
2006 Aberdeen	N.Y.-Penn.	1	1	0	0	.000	3	0	2	9.00	0
2006 Frederick	Carolina	1	1⅓	0	0	.000	0	1	4	13.50	0
2006 Bowie	Eastern	3	4	0	0	.000	7	2	4	2.25	0
2006 Baltimore e-f	A.L.	16	7	1	0	1.000	2	8	14	12.86	0
2007 Toledo	Int.	17	24⅓	1	0	1.000	30	8	22	2.59	0
2007 Detroit g	A.L.	39	45	3	0	1.000	49	26	38	3.20	1
Major League Totals	6 Yrs.	144	111⅓	4	5	.444	108	79	127	5.50	3

a Not offered contract, December 1, 2000. Signed with Cleveland Indians organization, December 24, 2000.
b Released by Cleveland Indians, June 28, 2001. Signed with San Diego Padres organization, January 30, 2004.
c Traded to Baltimore Orioles for player to be named later, June 22, 2004.
d Filed for free agency, October 15, 2004, re-signed with Baltimore Orioles organization, November 16, 2004.
e On disabled list from April 19 to July 30, 2006.
f Filed for free agency, October 15, 2006. Signed with Detroit Tigers organization, November 18, 2006.
g On disabled list from June 27 to July 25, 2007.

CABRERA, DANIEL ALBERTO
Born, San Pedro de Macoris, Dominican Republic, May 28, 1981.
Bats Right. Throws Right. Height, 6 feet, 7 inches. Weight, 260 pounds.

Year	Club	Lea	G	IP	W	L	Pct	SO	BB	H	ERA	SAVES
2001 Orioles	Gulf Coast	12	40⅔	2	3	.400	36	39	31	5.53	0
2002 Bluefield	Appal.	12	60⅓	5	2	.714	69	25	52	3.28	0
2003 Delmarva	So.Atl.	26	125⅓	5	9	.357	120	78	105	4.24	0
2004 Bowie	Eastern	5	27⅓	0	1	.000	35	12	11	2.63	0
2004 Baltimore	A.L.	28	147⅔	12	8	.600	76	89	145	5.00	1
2005 Bowie	Eastern	1	6	1	0	1.000	7	2	8	3.00	0
2005 Baltimore a	A.L.	29	161⅓	10	13	.435	157	87	144	4.52	0
2006 Bowie	Eastern	1	4	0	0	.000	7	1	0	0.00	0
2006 Ottawa	Int.	4	24⅓	3	1	.750	27	9	20	4.07	0
2006 Baltimore b	A.L.	26	148	9	10	.474	157	*104	130	4.74	0
2007 Baltimore	A.L.	34	204⅓	9	*18	.333	166	*108	207	5.55	0
Major League Totals	4 Yrs.	117	661⅓	40	49	.449	556	388	626	4.99	1

a On disabled list from August 17 to September 6, 2005.
b On disabled list from May 15 to June 5, 2006.

CAIN, MATTHEW THOMAS (MATT)
Born, Dothan, Alabama, October 1, 1984.
Bats Right. Throws Right. Height, 6 feet, 3 inches. Weight, 235 pounds.

Year	Club	Lea	G	IP	W	L	Pct	SO	BB	H	ERA	SAVES
2002 Giants	Arizona	8	19⅓	0	1	.000	20	11	13	3.72	0
2003 Hagerstown	So.Atl.	14	74	4	4	.500	90	24	57	2.55	0
2004 San Jose	Calif.	13	72⅔	7	1	.875	89	17	58	1.86	0
2004 Norwich	Eastern	15	86	6	4	.600	72	40	73	3.35	0
2005 Fresno	P.C.	26	145⅔	10	5	.667	176	73	118	4.39	0
2005 San Francisco	N.L.	7	46⅓	2	1	.667	30	19	24	2.33	0

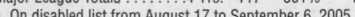

Year	Club	Lea	G	IP	W	L	Pct	SO	BB	H	ERA	SAVES
2006 San Francisco	N.L.	32	190²/₃	13	12	.520	179	87	157	4.15	0
2007 San Francisco	N.L.	32	200	7	16	.304	163	79	173	3.65	0
Major League Totals	3 Yrs.	71	437	22	29	.431	372	185	354	3.73	0

CALERO, ENRIQUE NOMAR (KIKO)
Born, Santurce, Puerto Rico, January 9, 1975.
Bats Right. Throws Right. Height, 6 feet, 1 inch. Weight, 200 pounds.

Year	Club	Lea	G	IP	W	L	Pct	SO	BB	H	ERA	SAVES
1996 Spokane	Northwest	17	75	4	2	.667	61	18	77	2.52	1
1997 Wichita	Texas	23	127²/₃	11	9	.550	100	44	120	4.44	0
1998 Lansing	Midwest	4	16²/₃	1	0	1.000	10	7	19	3.78	0
1998 Wichita	Texas	3	14	1	0	1.000	5	6	23	9.64	0
1998 Wilmington	Carolina	17	97²/₃	7	3	.700	90	51	74	2.86	0
1999 Wichita	Texas	26	129¹/₃	9	3	.750	92	57	143	4.11	1
2000 Wichita	Texas	28	153²/₃	10	7	.588	130	66	141	3.63	0
2001 Wichita	Texas	27	124¹/₃	14	5	.737	94	51	110	3.33	0
2002 Wichita	Texas	5	16	1	0	1.000	15	5	10	2.25	0
2002 Omaha a-b	P.C.	20	125²/₃	7	7	.500	109	35	112	3.44	0
2003 St. Louis c	N.L.	26	38¹/₃	1	1	.500	51	20	29	2.82	0
2004 Memphis	P.C.	12	25¹/₃	0	0	.000	33	11	20	2.49	1
2004 St. Louis d-e	N.L.	41	45¹/₃	3	1	.750	47	10	27	2.78	2
2005 Sacramento	P.C.	2	2	0	0	.000	2	0	4	9.00	0
2005 Oakland f	A.L.	58	55²/₃	4	1	.800	52	18	45	3.23	1
2006 Oakland	A.L.	70	58	3	2	.600	67	24	50	3.41	2
2007 Oakland g-h	A.L.	46	40²/₃	1	5	.167	31	21	46	5.75	1
Major League Totals	5 Yrs.	241	238	12	10	.545	248	93	197	3.55	7
Division Series											
2004 St. Louis	N.L.	1	1	0	0	.000	2	0	0	0.00	0
2006 Oakland	A.L.	1	1	1	0	1.000	1	1	0	0.00	0
Division Series Totals		2	2	1	0	1.000	3	1	0	0.00	0
Championship Series											
2004 St. Louis	N.L.	5	7	0	0	.000	7	1	8	3.86	0
2006 Oakland	A.L.	3	2	0	0	.000	1	1	3	0.00	0
Championship Series Totals		8	9	0	0	.000	8	2	11	3.00	0
World Series Record											
2004 St. Louis	N.L.	2	1¹/₃	0	0	.000	0	4	2	13.50	0

a Traded by Kansas City Royals to Philadelphia Phillies for infielder Brian Harris, March 20, 2002. Returned to Royals, March 22, 2002.
b Filed for free agency, October 15, 2002. Signed with St. Louis Cardinals organization, November 21, 2002.
c On disabled list from June 29 to September 30, 2003.
d On disabled list from August 7 to September 4, 2004.
e Traded to Oakland Athletics with pitcher Danny Haren and catcher Daric Barton for pitcher Mark Mulder, December 18, 2004.
f On disabled list from May 9 to June 5, 2005.
g On disabled list from June 19 to July 6, 2007.
h Not offered contract, December 12, 2007, re-signed with Oakland Athletics, December 13, 2007.

CAMERON, KEVIN JOHN
Born, Joliet, Illinois, December 15, 1979.
Bats Right. Throws Right. Height, 6 feet, 2 inches. Weight, 180 pounds.

Year	Club	Lea	G	IP	W	L	Pct	SO	BB	H	ERA	SAVES
2001 Elizabethton	Appal.	22	23	1	1	.500	30	5	16	1.57	13
2003 Quad Cities	Midwest	39	62	1	5	.167	58	33	57	3.92	2
2004 New Britain	Eastern	26	46¹/₃	1	3	.250	47	21	47	2.33	3
2004 Fort Myers	Fla.St.	22	31²/₃	2	3	.400	22	13	23	3.13	1
2005 New Britain	Eastern	43	79¹/₃	6	2	.750	60	27	76	2.72	6
2006 Rochester a	Int.	40	66¹/₃	6	4	.600	65	26	53	2.98	9
2007 San Diego	N.L.	48	58	2	0	1.000	50	36	55	2.79	0

a Selected by San Diego Padres from Minnesota Twins in Rule V draft, December 7, 2006.

CAPPS, MATTHEW DICUS (MATT)
Born, Douglasville, Georgia, September 3, 1983.
Bats Right. Throws Right. Height, 6 feet, 2 inches. Weight, 240 pounds.

Year	Club	Lea	G	IP	W	L	Pct	SO	BB	H	ERA	SAVES
2002 Pirates	Gulf Coast	7	13	1	0	1.000	8	6	13	0.69	1
2003 Lynchburg	Carolina	1	5	0	0	.000	5	4	3	5.40	0

Year	Club	Lea	G	IP	W	L	Pct	SO	BB	H	ERA	SAVES
2003 Pirates	Gulf Coast		10	62²/₃	5	1	.833	54	9	40	1.87	0
2004 Williamsport	N.Y.-Penn.		11	65	3	5	.375	33	4	84	4.85	0
2004 Hickory	So.Atl.		12	42	2	3	.400	27	16	82	10.07	0
2005 Hickory	So.Atl.		35	53²/₃	3	4	.429	39	5	47	2.52	14
2005 Altoona	Eastern		17	20	0	2	.000	26	1	21	2.70	7
2005 Pittsburgh	N.L.		4	4	0	0	.000	3	0	5	4.50	0
2006 Pittsburgh	N.L.		85	80²/₃	9	1	.900	56	12	81	3.79	1
2007 Pittsburgh	N.L.		76	79	4	7	.364	64	16	64	2.28	18
Major League Totals	3 Yrs.		165	163²/₃	13	8	.619	123	28	150	3.08	19

CAPUANO, CHRISTOPHER (CHRIS)
Born, Springfield, Massachusetts, August 19, 1978.
Bats Left. Throws Left. Height, 6 feet, 2 inches. Weight, 220 pounds.

Year	Club	Lea	G	IP	W	L	Pct	SO	BB	H	ERA	SAVES
2000 South Bend	Midwest		18	101²/₃	10	4	.714	105	45	68	2.21	0
2001 El Paso	Texas		28	159¹/₃	10	11	.476	167	75	184	5.31	0
2002 Tucson a	P.C.		6	36¹/₃	4	1	.800	29	11	30	2.72	0
2003 Tucson	P.C.		23	142²/₃	9	5	.643	108	43	133	3.34	0
2003 Arizona b	N.L.		9	33	2	4	.333	23	11	27	4.64	0
2004 Beloit	Midwest		1	2²/₃	0	0	.000	4	1	3	3.38	0
2004 High Desert	California		1	2	0	1	.000	2	3	6	27.00	0
2004 Indianapolis	Int.		2	8²/₃	0	1	.000	9	5	10	8.31	0
2004 Milwaukee c	N.L.		17	88¹/₃	6	8	.429	80	37	91	4.99	0
2005 Milwaukee	N.L.		35	219	18	12	.600	176	91	212	3.99	0
2006 Milwaukee	N.L.		34	221¹/₃	11	12	.478	174	47	229	4.03	0
2007 Milwaukee d	N.L.		29	150	5	12	.294	132	54	170	5.10	0
Major League Totals	5 Yrs.		124	711²/₃	42	48	.467	585	240	729	4.39	0

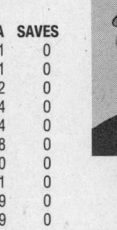

a On minor league disabled list from May 6 through September 10, 2002.
b Traded to Milwaukee Brewers with infielder Junior Spivey, infielder Craig Counsell, infielder Lyle Overbay, catcher Chad Moeller and pitcher Jorge DeRosa for infielder Richie Sexson, pitcher Shane Nance and player to be named later, December 1, 2003. Arizona Diamondbacks received outfielder Noochie Varner to complete trade, December 15, 2003.
c On disabled list from April 19 to May 26 and May 27 to June 12 and August 25 to October 6, 2004.
d On disabled list from June 9 to July 1, 2007.

CARLYLE, EARL L. (BUDDY)
Born, Omaha, Nebraska, December 21, 1977.
Bats Left. Throws Right. Height, 6 feet, 3 inches. Weight, 185 pounds.

Year	Club	Lea	G	IP	W	L	Pct	SO	BB	H	ERA	SAVES
1996 Princeton	Appal.		10	46¹/₃	2	4	.333	42	16	47	4.66	0
1997 Chston-WV	So.Atl.		23	143	14	5	.737	111	27	130	2.77	0
1998 Chattanooga	Southern		1	5	0	1	.000	3	0	6	5.40	0
1998 Mobile a	Southern		24	183²/₃	14	6	.700	97	46	179	3.38	0
1999 Las Vegas	P.C.		25	160	11	8	.579	138	42	180	4.89	0
1999 San Diego	N.L.		7	37²/₃	1	3	.250	29	17	36	5.97	0
2000 San Diego	N.L.		4	3	0	0	.000	2	3	6	21.00	0
2000 Las Vegas b	P.C.		27	151	8	6	.571	127	44	165	4.29	0
2001 Hanshin	Japan Pac.		28	153¹/₃	7	10	.412	111	65	151	3.87	0
2002 Hanshin c	Japan Pac.		3	14¹/₃	0	2	.000	13	5	17	7.53	0
2003 Omaha	P.C.		2	5	0	1	.000	4	1	5	5.40	0
2003 Wichita d	Texas		15	27¹/₃	3	2	.600	41	7	19	1.98	3
2004 Trenton	Eastern		8	37¹/₃	4	0	1.000	48	4	23	0.72	0
2004 Columbus e	Int.		19	104	8	5	.615	92	21	113	4.15	0
2005 Los Angeles	N.L.		10	14	0	0	.000	13	4	16	8.36	0
2005 Dodgers	Gulf Coast		1	3	0	0	.000	1	0	3	3.00	0
2005 Las Vegas f	P.C.		20	48	1	2	.333	53	21	51	4.88	2
2006 Albuquerque g	P.C.		13	28	3	1	.750	22	7	17	1.93	0
2007 Richmond	Int.		9	48²/₃	5	2	.714	56	9	40	2.59	0
2007 Atlanta	N.L.		22	107	8	7	.533	74	32	117	5.21	0
Major League Totals	4 Yrs.		43	161²/₃	9	10	.474	118	56	175	5.96	0

a Traded to San Diego Padres by Cincinnati Reds for pitcher Marc Kroon, April 8, 1998.
b Sold to Hanshin Tigers, November 3, 2000.
c Signed with Kansas City Royals organization, December 18, 2002.
d Filed for free agency, October 15, 2003. Signed with New York Yankees organization, December 23, 2003.
e Filed for free agency, October 15, 2004. Signed with Los Angeles Dodgers organization, November 18, 2004.
f Filed for free agency, October 3, 2005. Signed with Florida Marlins organization, December 15, 2005.
g Released by Florida Marlins, May 18, 2006. Signed with Atlanta Braves organization, December 4, 2006.

CARMONA, FAUSTO C.
Born, Santo Domingo, Dominican Republic, December 7, 1983.
Bats Right. Throws Right. Height, 6 feet, 4 inches. Weight, 220 pounds.

Year	Club	Lea	G	IP	W	L	Pct	SO	BB	H	ERA	SAVES
2002 Burlington	Appal.	13	76⅓	2	4	.333	42	10	89	3.30	1
2002 Mahoning Valley	N.Y.-Penn.	3	4	0	0	.000	0	1	2	0.00	0
2003 Akron	Eastern	1	6	0	0	.000	3	0	8	4.50	0
2003 Lake County	So.Atl.	24	148⅓	17	4	.810	83	14	117	2.06	0
2004 Kinston	Carolina	13	70	5	2	.714	57	20	68	2.83	0
2004 Akron	Eastern	15	87	4	8	.333	63	21	114	4.97	0
2004 Buffalo	Int.	1	6	1	0	1.000	2	3	6	6.00	0
2005 Akron	Eastern	14	90⅔	6	5	.545	57	20	100	4.07	0
2005 Buffalo	Int.	13	83	7	4	.636	49	15	76	3.25	0
2006 Buffalo	Int.	6	27⅔	1	3	.250	28	8	28	5.53	0
2006 Cleveland	A.L.	38	74⅔	1	10	.091	58	31	88	5.42	0
2007 Cleveland	A.L.	32	215	19	8	.704	137	61	199	3.06	0
Major League Totals	2 Yrs.	70	289⅔	20	18	.526	195	92	287	3.67	0
Division Series											
2007 Cleveland	A.L.	1	9	0	0	.000	5	2	3	1.00	0
Championship Series											
2007 Cleveland	A.L.	2	6	0	1	.000	7	9	10	16.50	0

CARPENTER, CHRISTOPHER JOHN (CHRIS)
Born, Exeter, New Hampshire, April 27, 1975.
Bats Right. Throws Right. Height, 6 feet, 6 inches. Weight, 230 pounds.

Year	Club	Lea	G	IP	W	L	Pct	SO	BB	H	ERA	SAVES
1994 Medcine Hat	Pioneer	15	84⅔	6	3	.667	80	39	76	2.76	0
1995 Dunedin	Fla.St.	15	99⅓	3	5	.375	56	50	83	2.17	0
1995 Knoxville	Southern	12	64⅓	3	7	.300	53	31	71	5.18	0
1996 Knoxville	Southern	28	171⅓	7	9	.438	150	91	161	3.94	0
1997 Syracuse	Int.	19	120	4	9	.308	97	53	113	4.50	0
1997 Toronto	A.L.	14	81⅓	3	7	.300	55	37	108	5.09	0
1998 Toronto	A.L.	33	175	12	7	.632	136	61	177	4.37	0
1999 Toronto	A.L.	24	150	9	8	.529	106	48	177	4.38	0
1999 St. Catharines a	N.Y.-Penn.	1	4	0	0	.000	6	1	5	4.50	0
2000 Toronto	A.L.	34	175⅓	10	12	.455	113	83	204	6.26	0
2001 Toronto	A.L.	34	215⅔	11	11	.500	157	75	229	4.09	0
2002 Toronto	A.L.	13	73⅓	4	5	.444	45	27	89	5.28	0
2002 Tennessee	Southern	5	18⅔	0	1	.000	9	8	26	8.20	0
2002 Syracuse b-c	Int.	1	6	0	1	.000	6	2	8	4.50	0
2003 Palm Beach	Fla.St.	4	7	0	1	.000	6	1	6	1.29	0
2003 Memphis	P.C.	3	8⅓	0	0	.000	4	2	11	5.40	0
2003 Tennessee d-e	Southern	1	3⅓	0	1	.000	2	2	7	13.50	0
2004 St. Louis	N.L.	28	182	15	5	.750	152	38	169	3.46	0
2005 St. Louis f	N.L.	33	241⅔	21	5	*.808	213	51	204	2.83	0
2006 St. Louis g	N.L.	32	221⅔	15	8	.652	184	43	194	3.09	0
2007 Palm Beach	Fla.St.	2	4⅓	0	1	.000	4	1	7	6.23	0
2007 St. Louis h	N.L.	1	6	0	1	.000	3	1	9	7.50	0
Major League Totals	10 Yrs.	246	1522	100	69	.592	1164	464	1560	4.10	0
Division Series											
2005 St. Louis	N.L.	1	6	1	0	1.000	3	3	3	0.00	0
2006 St. Louis	N.L.	2	13⅓	2	0	1.000	12	4	12	2.03	0
Division Series Totals		3	19⅓	3	0	1.000	15	7	15	1.40	0
Championship Series											
2005 St. Louis	N.L.	2	15	1	0	1.000	9	4	14	3.00	0
2006 St. Louis	N.L.	2	11	0	1	.000	5	4	13	5.73	0
Championship Series Totals		4	26	1	1	.500	14	8	27	4.15	0
World Series Record											
2006 St. Louis	N.L.	1	8	1	0	1.000	6	0	3	0.00	0

a On disabled list from June 3 to June 28, 1999.
b On disabled list from April 2 to April 20 and April 22 to June 21 and August 14 to October 7, 2002.
c Filed for free agency, October 9, 2002. Signed with St. Louis Cardinals, December 15, 2002.
d On disabled list from March 27 to September 30, 2003.
e Filed for free agency, November 3, 2003, re-signed with St. Louis Cardinals, December 1, 2003.
f Selected Cy Young Award Winner in National League for 2005.
g On disabled list from May 22 to June 6, 2006.
h On disabled list from April 2 to November 2, 2007.

CASILLA, SANTIAGO

Born, Don Gregorio, Dominican Republic, June 25, 1980.
Bats Right. Throws Right. Height, 6 feet. Weight, 165 pounds.

Year	Club	Lea	G	IP	W	L	Pct	SO	BB	H	ERA	SAVES
2001	Athletics	Arizona	12	47¹/₃	4	2	.667	50	6	37	2.85	0
2002	Athletics	Arizona	13	59	2	1	.667	66	17	56	2.44	1
2002	Vancouver	Northwest	3	12¹/₃	0	3	.000	16	7	15	7.30	0
2003	Kane County	Midwest	14	42¹/₃	0	1	.000	28	19	40	2.55	0
2004	Kane County	Midwest	25	30	1	0	1.000	49	6	16	0.30	16
2004	Midland	Texas	13	18	2	0	1.000	32	15	10	1.50	2
2004	Sacramento	P.C.	11	13²/₃	1	2	.333	21	9	10	3.95	1
2004	Oakland	A.L.	4	5²/₃	0	0	.000	5	9	5	12.71	0
2005	Midland	Texas	10	16²/₃	0	0	.000	30	9	9	1.08	6
2005	Sacramento	P.C.	44	48¹/₃	3	6	.333	73	20	45	4.47	20
2005	Oakland	A.L.	3	3	0	0	.000	1	1	2	3.00	0
2006	Oakland	A.L.	2	2¹/₃	0	0	.000	2	2	2	11.57	0
2006	Sacramento	P.C.	25	33	2	0	1.000	32	10	25	3.27	4
2007	Sacramento	P.C.	22	24	2	1	.667	29	14	18	4.13	3
2007	Oakland	A.L.	46	50²/₃	3	1	.750	52	23	43	4.44	2
Major League Totals		4 Yrs.	55	61²/₃	3	1	.750	60	35	52	5.40	2

a Played under name of Jairo Garcia 2001-2005

CHACIN (ADOLFO), GUSTAVO

Born, Maracaibo, Venezuela, December 4, 1980.
Bats Left. Throws Left. Height, 5 feet, 11 inches. Weight, 195 pounds.

Year	Club	Lea	G	IP	W	L	Pct	SO	BB	H	ERA	SAVES
1998	Blue Jays	Dominican	9	36²/₃	3	2	.600	56	15	28	2.70	0
1999	Medicine Hat	Pioneer	15	64	4	3	.571	50	23	68	3.09	1
2000	Dunedin	Fla.St.	25	127²/₃	9	5	.643	77	64	138	4.02	0
2000	Tennessee	Southern	2	5	0	2	.000	5	6	10	12.60	0
2001	Tennessee	Southern	25	140¹/₃	11	8	.579	86	39	138	3.98	0
2002	Tennessee	Southern	35	119²/₃	6	5	.545	68	59	131	4.66	1
2003	New Haven	Eastern	46	69¹/₃	3	4	.429	55	29	78	4.15	2
2004	New Hampshire	Eastern	25	141²/₃	16	2	.889	109	49	113	2.92	0
2004	Syracuse	Int.	2	11²/₃	2	0	1.000	14	3	16	2.31	0
2004	Toronto	A.L.	2	14	1	1	.500	6	3	8	2.57	0
2005	Toronto	A.L.	34	203	13	9	.591	121	70	213	3.72	0
2006	Dunedin	Fla.St.	1	4²/₃	0	0	.000	5	4	6	9.64	0
2006	Syracuse	Int.	4	10²/₃	0	3	.000	11	3	22	10.13	0
2006	Toronto a	A.L.	17	87¹/₃	9	4	.692	47	38	90	5.05	0
2007	Syracuse	Int.	3	9²/₃	0	2	.000	5	3	13	7.45	0
2007	Toronto b	A.L.	5	27¹/₃	2	1	.667	11	7	29	5.60	0
Major League Totals		4 Yrs.	58	331²/₃	25	15	.625	185	118	340	4.18	0

a On disabled list from May 11 to May 30 and June 10 to August 23, 2006.
b On disabled list from April 29 to November 13, 2007.

CHACON, SHAWN ANTHONY

Born, Anchorage, Alaska, December 23, 1977.
Bats Right. Throws Right. Height, 6 feet, 3 inches. Weight, 220 pounds.

Year	Club	Lea	G	IP	W	L	Pct	SO	BB	H	ERA	SAVES
1996	Rockies	Arizona	11	56¹/₃	1	2	.333	64	15	46	1.60	0
1996	Portland	Northwest	4	19²/₃	0	2	.000	17	9	24	6.86	0
1997	Asheville	So.Atl.	28	162	11	7	.611	149	63	155	3.89	0
1998	Salem	Carolina	12	56	0	4	.000	54	31	53	5.30	0
1999	Salem	Carolina	12	72	5	5	.500	66	34	69	4.13	0
2000	Carolina	Southern	27	173²/₃	10	10	.500	172	85	151	3.16	0
2001	Colo Sprngs	P.C.	4	24	2	0	1.000	28	7	18	2.25	0
2001	Colorado	N.L.	27	160	6	10	.375	134	87	157	5.06	0
2002	Colorado a	N.L.	21	119¹/₃	5	11	.313	67	60	122	5.73	0
2002	Colorado Springs	P.C.	4	20²/₃	2	0	1.000	15	10	23	4.79	0
2003	Colorado Springs	P.C.	1	3	0	0	.000	2	0	5	6.00	0
2003	Colorado b	N.L.	23	137	11	8	.579	93	58	124	4.60	0
2004	Colorado	N.L.	66	63¹/₃	1	9	.100	52	52	71	7.11	35
2005	Colorado Springs	P.C.	3	12²/₃	0	2	.000	11	4	19	9.95	0
2005	Colorado	N.L.	13	72²/₃	1	7	.125	39	36	69	4.09	0
2005	New York c-d	A.L.	14	79	7	3	.700	40	30	66	2.85	0
2006	Trenton	Eastern	1	5	0	0	.000	3	2	4	5.40	0
2006	New York e	A.L.	17	63	5	3	.625	35	36	77	7.00	0

Year	Club	Lea	G	IP	W	L	Pct	SO	BB	H	ERA	SAVES
2006 Pittsburgh f		N.L.	9	46	2	3	.400	27	27	47	5.48	0
2007 Pittsburgh g		N.L.	64	96	5	4	.556	79	48	95	3.94	1
Major League Totals	7 Yrs.		254	836⅓	43	58	.426	566	434	828	4.98	36
Division Series												
2005 New York		A.L.	1	6⅓	0	0	.000	5	1	4	2.84	0

a On disabled list from May 9 to June 6, 2002.
b On disabled list from June 30 to July 19 and August 17 to October 8, 2003.
c On disabled list from June 3 to July 6, 2005.
d Traded to New York Yankees for outfielder Ramon Ramirez and pitcher Eduardo Sierra, July 28, 2005.
e On disabled list from May 17 to June 11, 2006.
f Traded to Pittsburgh Pirates for outfielder Craig Wilson, July 31, 2006.
g Filed for free agency, October 30, 2007.

CHAMBERLAIN, JUSTIN L. (JOBA)
Born, Lincoln, Nebraska, September 23, 1985.
Bats Right. Throws Right. Height, 6 feet, 2 inches. Weight, 230 pounds.

Year	Club	Lea	G	IP	W	L	Pct	SO	BB	H	ERA	SAVES
2007 Tampa		Fla.St.	7	40	4	0	1.000	51	11	25	2.03	0
2007 Trenton		Eastern	8	40⅓	4	2	.667	66	15	32	3.35	0
2007 Scranton-WB		Int.	3	8	1	0	1.000	18	1	5	0.00	0
2007 New York		A.L.	19	24	2	0	1.000	34	6	12	0.38	1
Division Series												
2007 New York		A.L.	2	3⅔	0	0	.000	4	3	3	4.91	0

CHICO, MATTHEW BRYAN (MATT)
Born, Fullerton, California, June 10, 1983.
Bats Left. Throws Left. Height, 6 feet. Weight, 205 pounds.

Year	Club	Lea	G	IP	W	L	Pct	SO	BB	H	ERA	SAVES
2003 Yakima		Northwest	17	71⅓	7	4	.636	71	25	75	3.53	0
2004 South Bend		Midwest	14	87⅔	8	5	.615	89	27	59	2.57	0
2004 El Paso		Texas	14	62⅓	3	7	.300	59	36	82	5.78	0
2005 Lancaster		Calif.	18	110	7	2	.778	102	39	101	3.76	0
2005 Tennessee		Southern	10	52⅔	1	7	.125	35	15	75	5.98	0
2006 Lancaster		Calif.	10	50⅓	3	4	.429	49	11	48	3.75	0
2006 Harrisburg		Eastern	4	22	2	0	1.000	13	8	28	3.27	0
2006 Tennessee a		Southern	13	81	7	2	.778	63	21	62	2.22	0
2007 Columbus		Int.	2	11	1	1	.500	7	5	9	3.27	0
2007 Washington		N.L.	31	167	7	9	.438	94	74	183	4.63	0

a Traded to Washington Nationals by Arizona Diamondbacks with pitcher Garrett Mock for pitcher Livan Hernandez and cash, August 7, 2006.

CHULK, CHARLES VINCENT (VINNIE)
Born, Miami, Florida, December 19, 1978.
Bats Right. Throws Right. Height, 6 feet, 1 inch. Weight, 195 pounds.

Year	Club	Lea	G	IP	W	L	Pct	SO	BB	H	ERA	SAVES
2000 Medicine Hat		Pioneer	14	68⅔	2	4	.333	51	20	75	3.80	0
2001 Dunedin		Fla.St.	16	34⅔	1	2	.333	50	13	38	3.12	1
2001 Syracuse		Int.	5	6	1	0	1.000	3	4	5	1.50	0
2001 Tennessee		Southern	24	43	2	5	.286	43	8	34	3.14	2
2002 Tennessee		Southern	25	152	13	5	.722	108	53	133	2.96	1
2002 Syracuse		Int.	2	4⅔	0	1	.000	2	6	6	5.79	0
2003 Syracuse		Int.	23	119⅓	8	10	.444	90	46	118	4.22	0
2003 Toronto		A.L.	3	5⅓	0	0	.000	2	4	6	5.06	0
2004 Syracuse		Int.	18	28⅔	4	2	.667	26	11	27	2.83	3
2004 Toronto		A.L.	47	56	1	3	.250	44	27	59	4.66	2
2005 Toronto		A.L.	62	72	0	1	.000	39	26	68	3.88	0
2006 Syracuse		Int.	19	32	3	2	.600	43	14	20	2.25	1
2006 Toronto		A.L.	20	24	1	0	1.000	18	5	29	5.25	0
2006 San Francisco a		N.L.	28	22⅓	0	3	.000	25	15	17	5.24	0
2007 San Francisco b		N.L.	57	53	5	4	.556	41	14	53	3.57	0
Major League Totals	5 Yrs.		217	232⅔	7	11	.389	169	90	232	4.29	2

a Traded to San Francisco Giants with infielder Shea Hillenbrand for pitcher Jeremy Accardo, July 21, 2006.
b On disabled list from August 26 to October 30, 2007.

CLEMENS, WILLIAM ROGER
Born, Dayton, Ohio, August 4, 1962.
Bats Right. Throws Right. Height, 6 feet, 4 inches. Weight, 235 pounds.

Year	Club	Lea	G	IP	W	L	Pct	SO	BB	H	ERA	SAVES
1983	Winter Haven	Fla. St.	4	29	3	1	.750	36	0	22	1.24	0
1983	New Britain	Eastern	7	52	4	1	.800	59	12	31	1.38	0
1984	Pawtucket	Eastern	7	46²/₃	2	3	.400	50	14	39	1.93	0
1984	Boston	A.L.	21	133¹/₃	9	4	.692	126	29	146	4.32	0
1985	Boston a	A.L.	15	98¹/₃	7	5	.583	74	37	83	3.29	0
1986	Boston b	A.L.	33	254	*24	4	*.857	238	67	179	*2.48	0
1987	Boston c	A.L.	36	281²/₃	*20	9	.690	256	83	248	2.97	0
1988	Boston	A.L.	35	264	18	12	.600	*291	62	217	2.93	0
1989	Boston	A.L.	35	253¹/₃	17	11	.607	230	93	215	3.13	0
1990	Boston d	A.L.	31	228¹/₃	21	6	.778	209	54	193	*1.93	0
1991	Boston e	A.L.	35	*271¹/₃	18	10	.643	*241	65	219	*2.62	0
1992	Boston	A.L.	32	246²/₃	18	11	.621	208	62	203	*2.41	0
1993	Pawtucket	Int.	1	3²/₃	0	0	.000	8	4	1	0.00	0
1993	Boston f	A.L.	29	191²/₃	11	14	.440	160	67	175	4.46	0
1994	Boston	A.L.	24	170²/₃	9	7	.563	168	71	124	2.85	0
1995	Sarasota	Fla. St.	1	4	0	0	.000	7	2	0	0.00	0
1995	Pawtucket	Int.	1	5	0	0	.000	5	3	1	0.00	0
1995	Boston g	A.L.	23	140	10	5	.667	132	60	141	4.18	0
1996	Boston h-i	A.L.	34	242²/₃	10	13	.435	*257	106	216	3.63	0
1997	Toronto j	A.L.	34	*264	*21	7	.750	*292	68	204	*2.05	0
1998	Toronto k	A.L.	33	234²/₃	*20	6	.769	*271	88	169	*2.65	0
1999	New York l-m	A.L.	30	187²/₃	14	10	.583	163	90	185	4.60	0
2000	New York n	A.L.	32	204¹/₃	13	8	.619	188	84	184	3.70	0
2001	New York o	A.L.	33	220¹/₃	20	3	*.870	213	72	205	3.51	0
2002	Tampa	Fla. St.	1	5	1	0	1.000	6	2	5	5.40	0
2002	Norwich	Eastern	1	7	0	1	.000	7	0	5	1.29	0
2002	New York p-q	A.L.	29	180	13	6	.684	192	63	172	4.35	0
2003	New York r-s	A.L.	33	211²/₃	17	9	.654	190	58	199	3.91	0
2004	Houston t	N.L.	33	214¹/₃	18	4	*.818	218	79	169	2.98	0
2005	Houston u	N.L.	32	211¹/₃	13	8	.619	185	62	151	*1.87	0
2006	Lexington	So.Atl.	1	3	0	0	.000	6	0	3	3.00	0
2006	Corpus Christi	Texas	1	6	1	0	1.000	11	0	2	0.00	0
2006	Round Rock	P.C.	1	5²/₃	1	0	1.000	5	3	5	4.76	0
2006	Houston v	N.L.	19	113¹/₃	7	6	.538	102	29	89	2.30	0
2007	Tampa	Fla.St.	1	4	0	0	.000	2	0	3	2.25	0
2007	Trenton	Eastern	1	5¹/₃	0	0	.000	5	4	6	5.06	0
2007	Scranton-WB	Int.	1	6	1	0	1.000	6	2	2	0.00	0
2007	New York w	A.L.	18	99	6	6	.500	68	31	99	4.18	0
Major League Totals	24 Yrs.		709	4916²/₃	354	184	.658	4672	1580	4185	3.12	0

Division Series

Year	Club	Lea	G	IP	W	L	Pct	SO	BB	H	ERA	SAVES
1995	Boston	A.L.	1	7	0	0	.000	5	1	5	3.86	0
1999	New York	A.L.	1	7	1	0	1.000	2	2	3	0.00	0
2000	New York	A.L.	2	11	0	2	.000	10	8	13	8.18	0
2001	New York	A.L.	2	8¹/₃	0	1	.000	6	4	9	5.40	0
2002	New York	A.L.	1	5²/₃	0	0	.000	5	3	8	6.35	0
2003	New York	A.L.	1	7	1	0	1.000	6	1	5	1.29	0
2004	Houston	N.L.	2	12	1	0	1.000	12	8	12	3.00	0
2005	Houston	N.L.	2	8	1	1	.500	6	3	7	5.63	0
2007	New York	A.L.	1	2¹/₃	0	0	.000	1	2	4	11.57	0
Division Series Totals			13	68¹/₃	4	4	.500	53	32	66	4.61	0

Championship Series

Year	Club	Lea	G	IP	W	L	Pct	SO	BB	H	ERA	SAVES
1986	Boston	A.L.	3	22²/₃	1	1	.500	17	7	22	4.37	0
1988	Boston	A.L.	1	7	0	0	.000	8	0	6	3.86	0
1990	Boston	A.L.	2	7²/₃	0	1	.000	4	5	7	3.52	0
1999	New York	A.L.	1	2	0	1	.000	2	2	6	22.50	0
2000	New York	A.L.	1	9	1	0	1.000	15	2	1	0.00	0
2001	New York	A.L.	1	5	0	0	.000	7	4	1	0.00	0
2003	New York	A.L.	2	9	1	0	1.000	8	2	11	5.00	0
2004	Houston	N.L.	2	13	1	1	.500	9	2	10	4.15	0
2005	Houston	N.L.	1	6	1	0	1.000	1	2	6	3.00	0
Championship Series Totals			14	81¹/₃	5	4	.556	71	26	70	3.87	0

World Series Record

Year	Club	Lea	G	IP	W	L	Pct	SO	BB	H	ERA	SAVES
1986	Boston	A.L.	2	11¹/₃	0	0	.000	11	6	9	3.18	0
1999	New York	A.L.	1	7²/₃	1	0	1.000	4	2	4	1.17	0
2000	New York	A.L.	1	8	1	0	1.000	9	0	2	0.00	0
2001	New York	A.L.	2	13¹/₃	1	0	1.000	19	4	10	1.35	0
2003	New York	A.L.	1	7	0	0	.000	5	0	8	3.86	0

Year	Club	Lea	G	IP	W	L	Pct	SO	BB	H	ERA	SAVES
2005 Houston	N.L.	1	2	0	0	.000	1	0	4	13.50	0	
World Series Totals		8	49⅓	3	0	1.000	49	12	37	2.37	0	

a On disabled list from July 8 to August 3 and August 21 to end of 1985 season.
b Selected Most Valuable Player and Cy Young Award winner in American League for 1986.
c Selected Cy Young Award winner in American League for 1987.
d Suspended five games by American League for bumping and threatening umpire and refusing to leave dugout after ejection during Game Four, 1990 American League Championship Series, from April 26 to May 1, 1991.
e Selected Cy Young Award winner in American League for 1991.
f On disabled list from June 19 to July 16, 1993.
g On disabled list from April 16 to June 2, 1995.
h Filed for free agency, November 5, 1996.
i Signed with Toronto Blue Jays, December 13, 1996.
j Selected Cy Young Award Winner in American League for 1997.
k Selected Cy Young Award Winner in American League for 1998.
l Traded to New York Yankees for pitcher David Wells, pitcher Graeme Lloyd and infielder Homer Bush, February 18, 1999.
m On disabled list from April 28 to May 21, 1999.
n On disabled list from June 15 to July 1, 2000.
o Selected Cy Young Award Winner in American League for 2001.
p On disabled list from July 13 to August 7, 2002.
q Filed for free agency, November 7, 2002, re-signed with New York Yankees, December 30, 2002.
r Announced retirement at end of season, March 2003.
s Filed for free agency, November 6, 2003. Decided not to retire and signed with Houston Astros, January 12, 2004.
t Filed for free agency, November 11, 2004, re-signed with Houston Astros, December 19, 2004.
u Filed for free agency, November 10, 2005, re-signed with Houston Astros organization, June 1, 2006.
v Filed for free agency, November 6, 2006. Signed with New York Yankees organization, May 5, 2007.
w Filed for free agency, November 9, 2007.

COFFEY, JUSTIN TODD (TODD)
Born, Shelby, North Carolina, September 9, 1980.
Bats Right. Throws Right. Height, 6 feet, 5 inches. Weight, 230 pounds.

Year	Club	Lea	G	IP	W	L	Pct	SO	BB	H	ERA	SAVES
1998 Billings	Pioneer	3	12	0	0	.000	8	1	13	3.00	0	
1999 Reds	Gulf Coast	5	16	1	1	.500	14	14	9	3.38	0	
2000 Reds a	Gulf Coast					INJURED—Did Not Play						
2001 Reds	Gulf Coast	3	12⅔	0	1	.000	15	5	11	4.26	0	
2001 Billings	Pioneer	14	33⅓	2	2	.500	33	15	34	3.51	1	
2002 Dayton	Midwest	38	80⅓	6	4	.600	62	25	78	3.59	2	
2003 Potomac	Carolina	11	23	0	2	.000	21	3	16	1.96	2	
2003 Dayton	Midwest	39	56	3	3	.500	53	14	61	2.25	9	
2004 Louisville	Int.	15	13⅔	1	0	1.000	11	2	15	5.27	4	
2004 Chattanooga	Southern	40	45⅓	4	1	.800	53	4	36	2.38	20	
2005 Louisville	Int.	8	8⅔	0	0	.000	5	2	8	5.19	3	
2005 Cincinnati............	N.L.	57	58	4	1	.800	26	11	84	4.50	1	
2006 Cincinnati............	N.L.	81	78	6	7	.462	60	27	85	3.58	8	
2007 Louisville	Int.	19	27	2	0	1.000	25	5	17	1.33	1	
2007 Cincinnati............	N.L.	58	51	2	1	.667	43	19	70	5.82	0	
Major League Totals .... 3 Yrs.		196	187	12	9	.571	129	57	239	4.48	9	

a On minor league disabled list from June 19 to September 27, 2000.

COLOME (DE LA CRUZ), JESUS
Born, San Pedro de Macoris, Dominican Republic, December 23, 1977.
Bats Right. Throws Right. Height, 6 feet, 2 inches. Weight, 205 pounds.

Year	Club	Lea	G	IP	W	L	Pct	SO	BB	H	ERA	SAVES
1997 Oaklnd-West	Dominican	18	89⅔	9	3	.750	55	22	73	2.71	0	
1998 Athletics	Arizona	12	56⅔	2	5	.286	62	16	47	3.18	0	
1999 Modesto	Calif.	31	128⅔	8	4	.667	127	60	125	3.36	1	
2000 Orlando	Southern	3	14⅔	1	2	.333	9	7	18	6.75	0	
2000 Midland a	Texas	20	110⅓	9	4	.692	95	50	99	3.59	0	
2001 Durham	Int.	13	17⅓	0	3	.000	18	6	22	6.23	0	
2001 Tampa Bay	A.L.	30	48⅔	2	3	.400	31	25	37	3.33	0	
2002 Tampa Bay	A.L.	32	41⅓	2	7	.222	33	33	56	8.27	0	
2002 Durham	Int.	18	29	2	2	.500	30	13	18	2.17	1	
2003 Tampa Bay	A.L.	54	74	3	7	.300	69	46	69	4.50	2	
2004 Durham	Int.	18	30⅔	2	1	.667	17	16	27	3.52	0	
2004 Tampa Bay b	A.L.	33	41⅓	2	2	.500	40	18	28	3.27	3	
2005 Montgomery	Southern	3	4	0	0	.000	3	0	2	0.00	0	

Year	Club	Lea	G	IP	W	L	Pct	SO	BB	H	ERA	SAVES
2005 Tampa Bay c	A.L.	36	45⅓	2	3	.400	28	18	54	4.57	0
2006 Tampa Bay	A.L.	1	0⅓	0	0	.000	0	1	0	27.00	0
2006 Trenton	Eastern	3	4⅔	2	0	1.000	2	3	2	1.93	0
2006 Columbus d-e	Int.	25	33⅓	1	1	.500	25	15	35	3.78	0
2007 Nationals	Gulf Coast	2	3	1	0	1.000	2	0	2	0.00	0
2007 Columbus	Int.	1	1	0	0	.000	2	0	0	0.00	0
2007 Washington f	N.L.	61	66	5	1	.833	43	27	64	3.82	1
Major League Totals ...... 7 Yrs.		247	317	16	23	.410	244	168	308	4.54	6

a Traded to Tampa Bay Devil Rays by Oakland Athletics with player to be named later for pitcher Jim Mecir and pitcher Todd Belitz, July 27, 2002.
b On disabled list from September 14 to October 29, 2004.
c On disabled list from April 14 to May 10 and June 10 to July 22, 2005.
d Released by Tampa Bay Devil Rays, April 6, 2006. Signed with New York Yankees organization, April 15, 2006.
e Filed for free agency, October 15, 2006. Signed with Washington Nationals organization, November 8, 2006.
f On disabled list from June 25 to August 18, 2007.

COLON, BARTOLO

Born, Altamira, Dominican Republic, May 24, 1973.
Bats Right. Throws Right. Height, 5 feet, 11 inches. Weight, 250 pounds.

Year	Club	Lea	G	IP	W	L	Pct	SO	BB	H	ERA	SAVES
1994 Burlington	Appal.	12	66	7	4	.636	84	44	46	3.14	0
1995 Kinston	Carolina	21	128⅔	13	3	.813	152	39	91	1.96	0
1996 Canton-Akron	Eastern	13	62	2	2	.500	56	25	44	1.74	0
1996 Buffalo	A.A.	8	15	0	0	.000	19	8	16	6.00	0
1997 Buffalo	A.A.	10	56⅔	7	1	.875	58	23	45	2.22	0
1997 Cleveland	A.L.	19	94	4	7	.364	66	45	107	5.65	0
1998 Cleveland	A.L.	31	204	14	9	.609	158	79	205	3.71	0
1999 Cleveland	A.L.	32	205	18	5	.783	161	76	185	3.95	0
2000 Buffalo	Int.	1	5	1	0	1.000	4	0	6	1.80	0
2000 Cleveland a	A.L.	30	188	15	8	.652	212	98	163	3.88	0
2001 Cleveland	A.L.	34	222⅓	14	12	.538	201	90	220	4.09	0
2002 Cleveland	A.L.	16	116⅓	10	4	.714	75	31	104	2.55	0
2002 Montreal b-c-d	N.L.	17	117	10	4	.714	74	39	115	3.31	0
2003 Chicago e	A.L.	34	242	15	13	.536	173	67	223	3.87	0
2004 Anaheim	A.L.	34	208⅓	18	12	.600	158	71	215	5.01	0
2005 Los Angeles f	A.L.	33	222⅔	*21	8	.724	157	43	215	3.48	0
2006 Rancho Cucamonga	Calif.	1	4	0	0	.000	3	1	2	0.00	0
2006 Salt Lake	P.C.	2	11⅔	0	1	.000	3	2	14	6.17	0
2006 Los Angeles g	A.L.	10	56⅓	1	5	.167	31	11	71	5.11	0
2007 Rancho Cucamonga	Calif.	2	9⅔	1	0	1.000	10	1	6	1.86	0
2007 Salt Lake	P.C.	3	15	2	0	1.000	8	3	12	2.40	0
2007 Los Angeles h-i	A.L.	19	99⅓	6	8	.429	76	29	132	6.34	0
Major League Totals ...... 11 Yrs.		309	1975⅓	146	95	.606	1542	679	1955	4.10	0
Division Series											
1998 Cleveland	A.L.	1	5⅔	0	0	.000	3	3	5	1.59	0
1999 Cleveland	A.L.	2	9	0	1	.000	12	4	11	9.00	0
2001 Cleveland	A.L.	2	14⅔	1	1	.500	13	6	12	1.84	0
2004 Anaheim	A.L.	1	6	0	0	.000	3	3	7	4.50	0
2005 Los Angeles	A.L.	2	8	0	1	.000	7	1	10	4.50	0
Division Series Totals		8	43⅓	1	3	.250	38	17	45	4.15	0
Championship Series											
1998 Cleveland	A.L.	1	9	1	0	1.000	3	4	4	1.00	0

a On disabled list from April 16 to May 11, 2000.
b Traded to Montreal Expos with player to be named later for infielder Lee Stevens, infielder Brandon Phillips, outfielder Grady Sizemore and pitcher Cliff Lee, June 27, 2002.
c Montreal Expos received pitcher Tim Drew to complete trade, June 28, 2002.
d Traded to Chicago White Sox with infielder Jorge Nunez for pitcher Orlando Hernandez, pitcher Rocky Biddle, outfielder Jeff Liefer and cash, January 15, 2003.
e Filed for free agency, October 27, 2003. Signed with Anaheim Angels, December 9, 2003.
f Selected Cy Young Award Winner in American League for 2005.
g On disabled list from April 16 to June 18 and July 30 to October 2, 2006.
h On disabled list from March 23 to April 21 and July 24 to September 9, 2007.
i Filed for free agency, October 29, 2007.

CONTRERAS, JOSE ARIEL

Born, Las Martinas, Cuba, December 6, 1971.
Bats Right. Throws Right. Height, 6 feet, 4 inches. Weight, 245 pounds.

Year	Club	Lea	G	IP	W	L	Pct	SO	BB	H	ERA	SAVES
2003 Staten Island	N.Y.-Penn.		1	7	0	0	.000	15	0	2	0.00	0
2003 Tampa	Fla.St.		1	4	0	0	.000	5	3	4	4.50	0
2003 Trenton	Eastern		1	1²/₃	0	0	.000	3	2	1	0.00	0
2003 Columbus	Int.		3	15	2	0	1.000	18	2	10	1.20	0
2003 New York a-b-c	A.L.		18	71	7	2	.778	72	30	52	3.30	0
2004 New York-Chicago d	A.L.		31	170¹/₃	13	9	.591	150	84	166	5.50	0
2005 Chicago	A.L.		32	204²/₃	15	7	.682	154	75	177	3.61	0
2006 Chicago e	A.L.		30	196	13	9	.591	134	55	194	4.27	0
2007 Chicago	A.L.		32	189	10	17	.370	113	62	232	5.57	0
Major League Totals 5 Yrs.			143	831	58	44	.569	623	306	821	4.57	0
Division Series												
2005 Chicago	A.L.		1	7²/₃	1	0	1.000	6	0	8	2.35	0
Championship Series												
2003 New York	A.L.		4	4²/₃	0	1	.000	7	2	6	5.79	0
2005 Chicago	A.L.		2	17¹/₃	1	1	.500	6	2	12	3.12	0
Championship Series Totals			6	22	1	2	.333	13	4	18	3.68	0
World Series Record												
2003 New York	A.L.		4	6¹/₃	0	1	.000	10	5	5	5.68	0
2005 Chicago	A.L.		1	7	1	0	1.000	2	0	6	3.86	0
World Series Totals			5	13¹/₃	1	1	.500	12	5	11	4.72	0

a Played in Cuba 1996 through 2002.
b Signed as free agent by New York Yankees, February 6, 2003.
c On disabled list from June 7 to August 24, 2003.
d Traded to Chicago White Sox for pitcher Esteban Loaiza, July 31, 2004.
e On disabled list from May 5 to May 21, 2006.

COOK, AARON LANE

Born, Fort Campbell, Kentucky, February 8, 1979.
Bats Right. Throws Right. Height, 6 feet, 3 inches. Weight, 215 pounds.

Year	Club	Lea	G	IP	W	L	Pct	SO	BB	H	ERA	SAVES
1997 Rockies	Arizona		9	46	1	3	.250	35	17	48	3.13	0
1998 Portland	Northwest		15	79¹/₃	5	8	.385	38	39	87	4.88	0
1999 Asheville	So.Atl.		25	121²/₃	4	12	.250	73	42	157	6.44	0
2000 Salem	Carolina		7	43	1	6	.143	37	12	52	5.44	0
2000 Asheville	So.Atl.		21	142²/₃	10	7	.588	118	23	130	2.96	0
2001 Salem	Carolina		27	155	11	11	.500	122	38	157	3.08	0
2002 Carolina	Southern		14	95	7	2	.778	58	19	73	1.42	0
2002 Colorado Springs	P.C.		10	64¹/₃	4	4	.500	32	18	67	3.78	0
2002 Colorado	N.L.		9	35²/₃	2	1	.667	14	13	41	4.54	0
2003 Colorado Springs	P.C.		2	16	1	1	.500	12	4	10	2.25	0
2003 Colorado	N.L.		43	124	4	6	.400	43	57	160	6.02	0
2004 Colorado Springs	P.C.		7	46	3	1	.750	25	8	34	2.74	0
2004 Colorado a	N.L.		16	96²/₃	6	4	.600	40	39	112	4.28	0
2005 Tri-City	Northwest		2	7	0	0	.000	0	0	1	0.00	0
2005 Modesto	California		1	5	1	0	1.000	5	0	5	1.80	0
2005 Tulsa	Texas		1	3²/₃	0	1	.000	1	1	10	17.18	0
2005 Colorado Springs	P.C.		3	16¹/₃	1	0	1.000	11	7	18	5.51	0
2005 Colorado b	N.L.		13	83¹/₃	7	2	.778	24	16	101	3.67	0
2006 Colorado	N.L.		32	212²/₃	9	15	.375	92	55	242	4.23	0
2007 Colorado Springs	P.C.		1	1	0	1	.000	0	1	4	27.00	0
2007 Colorado c	N.L.		25	166	8	7	.533	61	44	178	4.12	0
Major League Totals 6 Yrs.			138	718¹/₃	36	35	.507	274	224	834	4.47	0
World Series Record												
2007 Colorado	N.L.		1	6	0	1	.000	2	0	6	4.50	0

a On disabled list from August 8 to November 3, 2004.
b On disabled list from March 25 to July 30, 2005.
c On disabled list from August 16 to October 10, 2007.

CORDERO, CHAD PATRICK

Born, Upland, California, April 18, 1982.
Bats Right. Throws Right. Height, 6 feet. Weight, 200 pounds.

Year	Club	Lea	G	IP	W	L	Pct	SO	BB	H	ERA	SAVES
2003	Brevard County	Fla.St.	19	26$^{1}/_{3}$	1	1	.500	17	10	17	2.05	6
2003	Montreal...............	N.L.	12	11	1	0	1.000	12	3	4	1.64	1
2004	Montreal...............	N.L.	69	82$^{2}/_{3}$	7	3	.700	83	43	68	2.94	14
2005	Washington	N.L.	74	74$^{1}/_{3}$	2	4	.333	61	17	55	1.82	*47
2006	Washington	N.L.	68	73$^{1}/_{3}$	7	4	.636	69	22	59	3.19	29
2007	Washington	N.L.	76	75	3	3	.500	62	29	75	3.36	37
Major League Totals	5 Yrs.		299	316$^{1}/_{3}$	20	14	.588	287	114	261	2.79	128

CORDERO, FRANCISCO JAVIER

Born, Santo Domingo, Dominican Republic, May 11, 1975.
Bats Right. Throws Right. Height, 6 feet, 2 inches. Weight, 235 pounds.

Year	Club	Lea	G	IP	W	L	Pct	SO	BB	H	ERA	SAVES
1994	Detroit	Dominican	12	60	4	3	.571	36	27	65	3.90	0
1995	Fayettevlle	So.Atl.	4	20	0	3	.000	19	12	26	6.30	0
1995	Jamestown.......	N.Y.-Penn.	15	88	4	7	.364	54	37	96	5.22	0
1996	Fayettevlle	So.Atl.	2	7	0	0	.000	7	6	2	2.57	0
1996	Jamestown a	N.Y.-Penn.	2	11	0	0	.000	10	2	5	0.82	0
1997	W Michigan	Midwest	50	54$^{1}/_{3}$	6	1	.857	67	15	36	0.99	35
1998	Jacksnville	Southern	17	16$^{2}/_{3}$	1	1	.500	18	9	19	4.86	8
1998	Lakeland b	Fla.St.	1	0	0	0	.000	0	0	1	0.00	0
1999	Jacksonville	Southern	47	52$^{1}/_{3}$	4	1	.800	58	22	35	1.38	27
1999	Detroit c.............	A.L.	20	19	2	2	.500	19	18	19	3.32	0
2000	Texas	A.L.	56	77$^{1}/_{3}$	1	2	.333	49	48	87	5.35	0
2000	Oklahoma...........	P.C.	3	4$^{1}/_{3}$	0	0	.000	5	3	7	4.15	1
2001	Oklahoma...........	P.C.	12	15$^{1}/_{3}$	0	1	.000	20	3	8	0.59	6
2001	Texas d.............	A.L.	3	2$^{1}/_{3}$	0	1	.000	1	2	3	3.86	0
2002	Oklahoma...........	P.C.	11	12$^{1}/_{3}$	0	2	.000	21	7	15	5.84	2
2002	Texas e.............	A.L.	39	45$^{1}/_{3}$	2	0	1.000	41	13	33	1.79	10
2003	Texas	A.L.	73	82$^{2}/_{3}$	5	8	.385	90	38	70	2.94	15
2004	Texas	A.L.	67	71$^{2}/_{3}$	3	4	.429	79	32	60	2.13	49
2005	Texas	A.L.	69	69	3	1	.750	79	30	61	3.39	37
2006	Texas	A.L.	49	48$^{2}/_{3}$	7	4	.636	54	16	49	4.81	6
2006	Milwaukee f	N.L.	28	26$^{2}/_{3}$	3	1	.750	30	16	20	1.69	16
2007	Milwaukee g...........	N.L.	66	63$^{1}/_{3}$	0	4	.000	86	18	52	2.98	44
Major League Totals	9 Yrs.		470	506	26	27	.491	528	231	454	3.29	177

a On disabled list from June 28 to September 30, 1996.
b On disabled list from May 22 to June 18 and June 26 to September 30, 1998.
c Traded to Texas Rangers with pitcher Justin Thompson, pitcher Alan Webb, outfielder Gabe Kapler, catcher Bill Haselman and infielder Frank Catalanotto for outfielder Juan Gonzalez, pitcher Danny Patterson and catcher Greg Zaun, November 2, 1999.
d On disabled list from March 23 to June 22 and June 26 to October 11, 2001.
e On disabled list from June 25 to July 27, 2002.
f Traded to Milwaukee Brewers with outfielder Kevin Mench, outfielder Laynce Nix and pitcher Julian Cordero for outfielder Carlos Lee and outfielder Nelson Cruz, July 28, 2006.
g Filed for free agency, October 29, 2007. Signed with Cincinnati Reds, November 28, 2007.

CORPAS, MANUEL (MANNY)

Born, Panama City, Panama, December 3, 1982.
Bats Right. Throws Right. Height, 6 feet, 3 inches. Weight, 170 pounds.

Year	Club	Lea	G	IP	W	L	Pct	SO	BB	H	ERA	SAVES
2002	Casper	Pioneer	29	33	2	4	.333	42	18	37	5.73	2
2003	Tri-Cities.........	Northwest	15	84	5	6	.455	47	22	98	5.79	0
2004	Asheville..........	So.Atl.	43	44$^{1}/_{3}$	2	2	.500	52	13	48	3.05	3
2005	Modesto............	Calif.	47	69	3	2	.600	52	14	83	3.78	2
2006	Tulsa	Texas	34	36$^{2}/_{3}$	2	1	.667	35	4	22	0.98	19
2006	Colorado Springs.......	P.C.	8	8$^{2}/_{3}$	0	0	.000	7	2	5	1.04	0
2006	Colorado	N.L.	35	32$^{1}/_{3}$	1	2	.333	27	8	36	3.62	0
2007	Colorado	N.L.	78	78	4	2	.667	58	20	63	2.08	19
Major League Totals	2 Yrs.		113	110$^{1}/_{3}$	5	4	.556	85	28	99	2.53	19
Division Series												
2007	Colorado	N.L.	3	3$^{1}/_{3}$	0	0	.000	3	0	2	0.00	3
Championship Series												
2007	Colorado	N.L.	4	5$^{1}/_{3}$	1	0	1.000	3	0	3	1.69	2
World Series Record												
2007	Colorado	N.L.	2	1$^{2}/_{3}$	0	0	.000	1	0	1	0.00	0

CORREIA, KEVIN JOHN

Born, San Diego, California, August 24, 1980.
Bats Right. Throws Right. Height, 6 feet, 3 inches. Weight, 200 pounds.

Year	Club	Lea	G	IP	W	L	Pct	SO	BB	H	ERA	SAVES
2002	Salem-Keizer	Northwest	10	37²/₃	2	2	.500	31	14	37	4.54	0
2003	Norwich	Eastern	16	86¹/₃	6	6	.500	73	30	80	3.65	0
2003	San Francisco	N.L.	10	39¹/₃	3	1	.750	28	18	41	3.66	0
2003	Fresno	P.C.	3	19	1	0	1.000	23	2	16	2.84	0
2004	Fresno	P.C.	29	105¹/₃	3	7	.300	70	35	118	4.53	0
2004	San Francisco	N.L.	12	19	0	1	.000	14	10	25	8.05	0
2005	San Jose	California	1	7	0	1	.000	7	5	5	2.57	0
2005	Fresno	P.C.	31	46	3	2	.600	35	23	50	6.07	7
2005	San Francisco	N.L.	16	58¹/₃	2	5	.286	44	31	61	4.63	0
2006	San Francisco	N.L.	48	69²/₃	2	0	1.000	57	22	64	3.49	0
2007	San Francisco	N.L.	59	101²/₃	4	7	.364	80	40	94	3.45	0
Major League Totals	5 Yrs.		145	288	11	14	.440	223	121	285	4.03	0

COUTLANGUS, JONATHAN THOMAS (JON)

Born, Ft.Lauderdale, Florida, October 21, 1980.
Bats Left. Throws Left. Height, 6 feet, 1 inch. Weight, 185 pounds.

Year	Club	Lea	G	IP	W	L	Pct	SO	BB	H	ERA	SAVES
2004	Giants	Arizona	1	1	0	0	.000	0	0	1	0.00	0
2005	San Jose	Calif.	50	77	4	0	1.000	79	29	64	3.04	3
2006	Louisville	Int.	2	2²/₃	0	0	.000	2	1	2	0.00	0
2006	Chattanooga a	Southern	49	63	1	3	.250	56	32	40	2.86	9
2007	Louisville	Int.	9	11¹/₃	2	0	1.000	14	7	14	6.35	0
2007	Cincinnati	N.L.	64	41	4	2	.667	38	27	38	4.39	0

a Claimed on waivers by Cincinnati Reds from San Francisco Giants, March 31, 2006.

CRAIN, JESSE ALAN

Born, Toronto, Ontario, Canada, July 5, 1981.
Bats Right. Throws Right. Height, 6 feet, 1 inch. Weight, 205 pounds.

Year	Club	Lea	G	IP	W	L	Pct	SO	BB	H	ERA	SAVES
2002	Elizabethton	Appal.	9	15²/₃	2	1	.667	18	7	4	0.57	2
2002	Quad Cities	Midwest	9	12	1	1	.500	11	4	6	1.50	1
2003	New Britain	Eastern	22	39	1	1	.500	56	10	13	0.69	9
2003	Fort Myers	Fla.St.	10	19	2	1	.667	25	5	10	2.84	0
2003	Rochester	Int.	23	26	3	1	.750	33	10	24	3.12	10
2004	Rochester	Int.	41	50²/₃	3	2	.600	64	17	38	2.49	19
2004	Minnesota	A.L.	22	27	3	0	1.000	14	12	17	2.00	0
2005	Minnesota	A.L.	75	79²/₃	12	5	.706	25	29	61	2.71	1
2006	Minnesota	A.L.	68	76²/₃	4	5	.444	60	18	79	3.52	1
2007	Minnesota a	A.L.	18	16¹/₃	1	2	.333	10	4	19	5.51	0
Major League Totals	4 Yrs.		183	199²/₃	20	12	.625	109	63	176	3.16	2
Division Series												
2004	Minnesota	A.L.	1	0¹/₃	0	0	.000	0	0	1	0.00	0
2006	Minnesota	A.L.	2	1	0	0	.000	1	1	3	9.00	0
Division Series Totals			3	1¹/₃	0	0	.000	1	1	4	6.75	0

a On disabled list from May 16 to October 10, 2007.

CRUZ, JUAN CARLOS

Born, Bonao, Dominican Republic, October 15, 1978.
Bats Right. Throws Right. Height, 6 feet, 2 inches. Weight, 155 pounds.

Year	Club	Lea	G	IP	W	L	Pct	SO	BB	H	ERA	SAVES
1998	Cubs	Arizona	12	41¹/₃	2	4	.333	36	14	61	6.10	0
1999	Eugene	Northwest	15	80¹/₃	5	6	.455	65	33	97	5.94	0
2000	Daytona	Fla.St.	8	44¹/₃	3	0	1.000	54	18	30	3.25	0
2000	Lansing	Midwest	17	96	5	5	.500	106	60	75	3.28	0
2001	West Tenn	Southern	23	121¹/₃	9	6	.600	137	60	107	4.01	0
2001	Chicago	N.L.	8	44²/₃	3	1	.750	39	17	40	3.22	0
2002	Chicago a	N.L.	45	97¹/₃	3	11	.214	81	59	84	3.98	1
2003	Chicago	N.L.	25	61	2	7	.222	65	28	66	6.05	0
2003	Iowa	P.C.	9	50²/₃	4	0	1.000	47	11	37	1.95	0
2004	Atlanta b-c	N.L.	50	72	6	2	.750	70	30	59	2.75	0
2005	Sacramento	P.C.	13	75	5	1	.833	90	28	51	2.40	0
2005	Oakland	A.L.	28	32²/₃	0	3	.000	34	22	38	7.44	0

Year	Club	Lea	G	IP	W	L	Pct	SO	BB	H	ERA	SAVES
2006 Tucson	P.C.	1	3⅓	0	0	.000	4	1	4	2.70	0
2006 Arizona d-e	N.L.	31	94⅔	5	6	.455	88	47	80	4.18	0
2007 Tucson	P.C.	1	2	0	0	.000	5	0	0	0.00	0
2007 Arizona f	N.L.	53	61	6	1	.857	87	32	45	3.10	0
Major League Totals . . . . .7 Yrs.		240	463⅓	25	31	.446	464	235	412	4.16	1
Division Series											
2003 Chicago	N.L.	1	1	0	0	.000	2	1	0	0.00	0
2004 Atlanta	N.L.	3	3⅔	0	0	.000	4	4	6	9.82	0
2007 Arizona	N.L.	1	0⅓	0	0	.000	1	0	1	0.00	0
Division Series Totals		5	5	0	0	.000	7	5	7	7.20	0
Championship Series											
2007 Arizona	N.L.	3	4	0	0	.000	8	3	0	0.00	0

a On disabled list from August 10 to August 25, 2002.
b Traded to Atlanta Braves with pitcher Steve Smyth for pitcher Andy Pratt and pitcher Richard Lewis, March 25, 2004.
c Traded to Oakland Athletics with pitcher Dan Meyer and outfielder Charles Thomas for pitcher Tim Hudson, December 16, 2004.
d Traded to Arizona Diamondbacks for pitcher Brad Halsey, March 26, 2006.
e On disabled list from June 4 to July 3, 2006.
f On disabled list from April 21 to May 11, 2007.

DANKS, JOHN WILLIAM

Born, Austin, Texas, April 15, 1985.
Bats Left. Throws Left. Height, 6 feet, 1 inch. Weight, 200 pounds.

Year	Club	Lea	G	IP	W	L	Pct	SO	BB	H	ERA	SAVES
2003 Rangers	Arizona	5	13	1	0	1.000	22	4	6	0.69	0
2003 Spokane	Northwest	5	12⅔	0	2	.000	13	7	12	8.53	0
2004 Stockton	Calif.	13	55	1	4	.200	48	26	62	5.24	0
2004 Clinton	Midwest	14	49⅔	3	2	.600	64	14	38	2.17	0
2005 Bakersfield	Calif.	10	57⅔	3	3	.500	53	16	50	2.50	0
2005 Frisco	Texas	18	98⅓	4	10	.286	85	34	117	5.49	0
2006 Oklahoma	P.C.	14	70⅔	4	5	.444	72	34	67	4.33	0
2006 Frisco a	Texas	13	69⅓	5	4	.556	82	22	74	4.15	0
2007 Chicago	A.L.	26	139	6	13	.316	109	54	160	5.50	0

a Traded to Chicago White Sox by Texas Rangers with pitcher Nick Masset and pitcher Jacob Rasner for pitcher Brandon McCarthy and outfielder David Paisano, December 23, 2006.

DAVIES, HIRAM KYLE (KYLE)

Born, Decatur, Georgia, September 9, 1983.
Bats Right. Throws Right. Height, 6 feet, 2 inches. Weight, 205 pounds.

Year	Club	Lea	G	IP	W	L	Pct	SO	BB	H	ERA	SAVES
2001 Braves	Gulf Coast	12	56	4	2	.667	53	8	47	2.25	0
2001 Macon	So.Atl.	1	5⅔	1	0	1.000	7	1	2	0.00	0
2002 Danville	Appal.	14	69⅓	5	3	.625	62	23	73	3.50	0
2002 Macon	So.Atl.	2	6	0	1	.000	4	4	6	6.00	0
2003 Rome	So.Atl.	27	146⅓	8	8	.500	148	53	128	2.89	0
2004 Myrtle Beach	Carolina	14	75⅓	9	2	.818	95	32	55	2.63	0
2004 Richmond	Int.	1	5	0	1	.000	5	3	5	9.00	0
2004 Greenville	Southern	11	62	4	0	1.000	73	22	40	2.32	0
2005 Richmond	Int.	13	73⅓	5	2	.714	62	34	66	3.44	0
2005 Atlanta	N.L.	21	87⅔	7	6	.538	62	49	98	4.93	0
2006 Mississippi	Southern	4	14	1	1	.500	9	5	11	4.50	0
2006 Richmond	Int.	2	15	2	0	1.000	8	3	7	0.60	0
2006 Atlanta a	N.L.	14	63⅓	3	7	.300	51	33	90	8.38	0
2007 Richmond	Int.	2	10	0	1	.000	12	6	11	4.50	0
2007 Atlanta	N.L.	17	86	4	8	.333	59	44	92	5.76	0
2007 Kansas City b	A.L.	11	50	3	7	.300	40	26	63	6.66	0
Major League Totals . . . . .3 Yrs.		63	287	17	28	.378	212	152	343	6.24	

a On disabled list from May 16 to September 1, 2006.
b Traded to Kansas City Royals for pitcher Octavio Dotel, July 31, 2007.

DAVIS, DOUGLAS (DOUG)

Born, Sacramento, California, September 21, 1975.
Bats Right. Throws Left. Height, 6 feet, 4 inches. Weight, 210 pounds.

Year	Club	Lea	G	IP	W	L	Pct	SO	BB	H	ERA	SAVES
1996 Rangers	Gulf Coast	8	42²/₃	3	1	.750	49	26	28	1.90	0
1997 Rangers	Gulf Coast	4	21	3	1	.750	27	15	14	1.71	0
1997 Charlotte	Fla.St.	9	49¹/₃	5	3	.625	52	33	29	3.10	0
1998 Charlotte	Fla.St.	27	155¹/₃	11	7	.611	173	74	129	3.24	0
1999 Oklahoma	P.C.	13	78	7	0	1.000	74	31	77	3.00	0
1999 Tulsa	Texas	12	74¹/₃	4	4	.500	79	25	65	2.42	0
1999 Texas	A.L.	2	2²/₃	0	0	.000	3	0	12	33.75	0
2000 Oklahoma	P.C.	12	69²/₃	8	3	.727	53	34	62	2.84	0
2000 Texas	A.L.	30	98²/₃	7	6	.538	66	58	109	5.38	0
2001 Oklahoma	P.C.	2	15²/₃	2	0	1.000	14	4	10	2.87	0
2001 Texas	A.L.	30	186	11	10	.524	115	69	220	4.45	0
2002 Texas	A.L.	10	59²/₃	3	5	.375	28	22	67	4.98	0
2002 Oklahoma	P.C.	9	61¹/₃	4	3	.571	48	11	70	4.99	0
2003 Oklahoma	P.C.	4	27²/₃	3	0	1.000	18	1	29	3.25	0
2003 Texas-Toronto a	A.L.	13	57	4	6	.400	27	30	74	5.37	0
2003 Indianapolis	Int.	5	34²/₃	1	2	.333	19	10	33	4.15	0
2003 Huntsville	Southern	1	6	1	0	1.000	6	3	5	3.00	0
2003 Milwaukee b	N.L.	8	52¹/₃	3	2	.600	35	21	49	2.58	0
2004 Milwaukee	N.L.	34	207¹/₃	12	12	.500	166	79	192	3.39	0
2005 Milwaukee	N.L.	35	222²/₃	11	11	.500	208	93	196	3.84	0
2006 Milwaukee c	N.L.	34	203¹/₃	11	11	.500	159	102	206	4.91	0
2007 Arizona	N.L.	33	192²/₃	13	12	.520	144	95	211	4.25	0
Major League Totals 9 Yrs.		229	1282¹/₃	75	75	.500	951	569	1336	4.34	0
Division Series											
2007 Arizona	N.L.	1	5²/₃	1	0	1.000	8	4	5	6.35	0
Championship Series											
2007 Arizona	N.L.	1	5	0	0	.000	5	4	5	1.80	0

a Claimed on waivers by Toronto Blue Jays, April 30, 2003.
b Filed for free agency, July 12, 2003. Signed with Milwaukee Brewers organization, July 13, 2003.
c Traded to Arizona Diamondbacks with pitcher Dana Eveland and outfielder David Krynzel for pitcher Greg Aquino, catcher Johnny Estrada and pitcher Claudio Vargas, November 25, 2006.

DE LA ROSA, JORGE ALBERTO

Born, Monterrey, Nuevo Leon, Mexico, April 5, 1981.
Bats Left. Throws Left. Height, 6 feet, 1 inch. Weight, 190 pounds.

Year	Club	Lea	G	IP	W	L	Pct	SO	BB	H	ERA	SAVES
1998 Arizona	Dominican	13	14	1	0	1.000	21	8	8	4.50	1
1999 Diamondbacks	Arizona	8	14	0	0	.000	17	3	12	3.21	2
1999 High Desert	California	2	3	0	0	.000	3	2	1	0.00	0
1999 Missoula	Pioneer	13	14²/₃	0	1	.000	14	9	22	7.98	2
2000 Monterrey a	Mexican	37	39	3	2	.600	50	32	38	6.28	1
2001 Trenton	Eastern	29	37	1	3	.250	27	20	56	5.84	0
2001 Sarasota b	Fla.St.	12	29²/₃	0	1	.000	27	12	13	1.21	2
2002 Trenton	Eastern	4	18	1	2	.333	15	9	17	5.50	0
2002 Sarasota	Fla.St.	23	120²/₃	7	7	.500	95	52	105	3.65	0
2003 Portland	Eastern	22	99²/₃	6	3	.667	102	36	87	2.80	1
2003 Pawtucket c-d	Int.	5	24	1	2	.333	17	12	27	3.75	0
2004 Indianapolis	Int.	20	85²/₃	5	6	.455	86	36	80	4.52	0
2004 Milwaukee	N.L.	5	22²/₃	0	3	.000	5	14	29	6.35	0
2005 Milwaukee	N.L.	38	42¹/₃	2	2	.500	42	38	48	4.46	0
2006 Huntsville	Southern	6	30	3	1	.750	23	3	31	2.40	0
2006 Milwaukee	N.L.	18	30¹/₃	2	2	.500	31	22	32	8.60	0
2006 Kansas City e-f	A.L.	10	48²/₃	3	4	.429	36	32	49	5.18	0
2007 Wichita	Texas	3	5²/₃	0	1	.000	7	4	10	11.12	0
2007 Kansas City g	A.L.	26	130	8	12	.400	82	53	160	5.82	0
Major League Totals 4 Yrs.		97	274	15	23	.395	196	159	318	5.85	0

a Sold by Arizona Diamondbacks to Monterrey, April 2, 2000.
b Sold to Boston Red Sox, February 22, 2001.
c Traded by Boston Red Sox to Arizona Diamondbacks with pitcher Casey Fossum, pitcher Brandon Lyon and outfielder Michael Goss for pitcher Curt Schilling, November 28, 2003.
d Traded to Milwaukee Brewers with infielder Junior Spivey, infielder Craig Counsell, infielder Lyle Overbay, catcher Chad Moeller and pitcher Chris Capuano for infielder Richie Sexson, pitcher Shane Nance and player to be named later, December 1, 2003. Arizona Diamondbacks received outfielder Noochie Varner to complete trade, December 15, 2003.
e Traded to Kansas City Royals for infielder Tony Graffanino, July 25, 2006.
f On disabled list from June 10 to July 25, 2006.
g On disabled list from August 1 to September 11, 2007.

DELCARMEN, MANUEL (MANNY)

Born, Boston, Massachusetts, February 16, 1982.
Bats Right. Throws Right. Height, 6 feet, 2 inches. Weight, 190 pounds.

Year	Club	Lea	G	IP	W	L	Pct	SO	BB	H	ERA	SAVES
2001 Red Sox	Gulf Coast		11	46	4	2	.667	62	19	35	2.54	1
2002 Augusta		So.Atl.	26	136	7	8	.467	136	56	124	4.10	0
2003 Sarasota		Fla.St.	4	23	1	1	.500	16	7	16	3.13	0
2004 Sarasota		Fla.St.	19	73	3	6	.333	76	20	84	4.68	0
2005 Portland		Eastern	31	39	4	4	.500	49	20	31	3.23	3
2005 Pawtucket		Int.	15	21	3	1	.750	23	13	17	1.29	2
2005 Boston		A.L.	10	9	0	0	.000	9	7	8	3.00	0
2006 Pawtucket		Int.	10	17	0	1	.000	19	6	9	2.12	0
2006 Boston		A.L.	50	53⅓	2	0	1.000	45	17	68	5.06	0
2007 Boston		A.L.	44	44	0	0	.000	41	17	28	2.05	1
Major League Totals	3 Yrs.		104	106⅓	2	0	1.000	95	41	104	3.64	1
Division Series												
2007 Boston		A.L.	1	1⅓	0	0	.000	1	0	0	0.00	0
Championship Series												
2007 Boston		A.L.	3	1⅔	0	0	.000	3	2	4	16.20	0
World Series Record												
2007 Boston		A.L.	2	1⅓	0	0	.000	1	1	3	6.75	0

DEMPSTER, RYAN SCOTT

Born, Sechelt, British Columbia, Canada, May 3, 1977.
Bats Right. Throws Right. Height, 6 feet, 2 inches. Weight, 215 pounds.

Year	Club	Lea	G	IP	W	L	Pct	SO	BB	H	ERA	SAVES
1995 Rangers	Gulf Coast		8	34⅓	3	1	.750	37	17	34	2.36	0
1995 Hudson Val.	N.Y.-Penn.		1	5⅔	1	0	1.000	6	1	7	3.18	0
1996 Chston-SC		So.Atl.	23	144⅓	7	11	.389	141	58	120	3.30	0
1996 Kane County a		Midwest	4	26⅓	2	1	.667	16	18	18	2.73	0
1997 Brevard Cty		Fla.St.	28	165⅓	10	9	.528	131	46	190	4.90	0
1998 Portland		Eastern	7	44⅔	4	3	.571	33	15	34	3.22	0
1998 Florida		N.L.	14	54⅔	1	5	.167	35	38	72	7.08	0
1998 Charlotte		Int.	5	33	3	1	.750	24	12	33	3.27	0
1999 Calgary		P.C.	5	30⅔	1	1	.500	29	10	30	4.99	0
1999 Florida		N.L.	25	147	7	8	.467	126	93	146	4.71	0
2000 Florida		N.L.	33	226⅓	14	10	.583	209	97	210	3.66	0
2001 Florida		N.L.	34	211⅓	15	12	.556	171	112	218	4.94	0
2002 Florida-Cincinnati b		N.L.	33	209	10	13	.435	153	93	228	5.38	0
2003 Cincinnati		N.L.	22	115⅔	3	7	.300	84	70	134	6.54	0
2003 Louisville c		Int.	2	13⅔	1	1	.500	9	3	13	3.29	0
2004 Lansing		Midwest	5	18⅓	0	0	.000	21	2	20	1.96	0
2004 Iowa		P.C.	6	21	1	1	.500	20	10	19	3.86	0
2004 Chicago d-e		N.L.	23	20⅔	1	1	.500	18	13	16	3.92	2
2005 Chicago		N.L.	63	92	5	3	.625	89	49	83	3.13	33
2006 Chicago		N.L.	74	75	1	9	.100	67	36	77	4.80	24
2007 Iowa		P.C.	2	2	0	0	.000	4	1	1	0.00	0
2007 Chicago f		N.L.	66	66⅔	2	7	.222	55	30	59	4.72	28
Major League Totals	10 Yrs.		387	1218⅓	59	75	.440	1007	631	1243	4.82	87
Division Series												
2007 Chicago		N.L.	1	1	0	0	.000	2	0	0	0.00	0

a Traded by Texas Rangers to Florida Marlins with player to be named later for pitcher John Burkett, August 8, 1996. Florida Marlins received pitcher Rick Helling to complete trade, September 3, 1996.

b Traded to Cincinnati Reds for outfielder Juan Encarnacion, infielder Wilton Guerrero and pitcher Ryan Snare, July 11, 2002.

c On disabled list from May 23 to June 7 and July 29 to November 3, 2003.

d Waived by Cincinnati Reds, November 4, 2003. Signed with Chicago Cubs, January 21, 2004.

e On disabled list from March 26 to August 1, 2004.

f On disabled list from June 23 to July 20, 2007.

DI NARDO, LEONARD EDWARD (LENNY)

Born, Miami, Florida, September 19, 1979.
Bats Left. Throws Left. Height, 6 feet, 4 inches. Weight, 190 pounds.

Year	Club	Lea	G	IP	W	L	Pct	SO	BB	H	ERA	SAVES
2001 Brooklyn		N.Y.-Penn.	9	36	1	2	.333	40	17	26	2.00	0
2002 Columbia		So.Atl.	24	101⅓	5	5	.500	103	56	106	4.35	1
2003 Binghamton		Eastern	7	40	1	3	.250	36	13	35	3.60	0
2003 St. Lucie a		Fla.St.	19	85	3	8	.273	93	14	64	2.01	1

Year	Club	Lea	G	IP	W	L	Pct	SO	BB	H	ERA	SAVES
2004 Sarasota	Fla.St.	1	3	0	0	.000	2	0	2	0.00	0
2004 Pawtucket	Int.	1	3	0	0	.000	4	0	3	0.00	0
2004 Boston	A.L.	22	27²/₃	0	0	.000	21	12	34	4.23	0
2004 Red Sox	Gulf Coast	2	3	0	0	.000	5	0	3	0.00	0
2004 Portland b	Eastern	3	5²/₃	1	0	1.000	4	1	8	9.53	0
2005 Pawtucket	Int.	23	108²/₃	6	3	.667	93	35	109	3.15	0
2005 Boston	A.L.	8	14²/₃	0	1	.000	15	5	13	1.84	0
2006 Red Sox	Gulf Coast	2	4²/₃	0	0	.000	4	0	2	0.00	0
2006 Portland	Eastern	1	2	0	1	.000	2	2	7	31.50	0
2006 Pawtucket	Int.	2	3	0	0	.000	2	1	5	12.00	0
2006 Boston c	A.L.	13	39	1	2	.333	17	20	61	7.85	0
2007 Oakland d	A.L.	35	131¹/₃	8	10	.444	59	50	136	4.11	0
Major League Totals 4 Yrs.		78	212²/₃	9	13	.409	112	87	244	4.66	0

a Selected by Boston Red Sox from New York Mets in Rule V draft, December 15, 2003.
b On disabled list from April 4 to April 19 and July 5 to September 16, 2004.
c On disabled list from May 22 to August 31, 2006.
d Claimed on waivers by Oakland Athletics, February 14, 2007.

DOHMANN, CHRISTOPHER SCOTT (SCOTT)

Born, New Orleans, Louisiana, February 13, 1978.
Bats Right. Throws Right. Height, 6 feet, 1 inch. Weight, 200 pounds.

Year	Club	Lea	G	IP	W	L	Pct	SO	BB	H	ERA	SAVES
2000 Portland	Northwest	5	23	2	1	.667	23	5	14	0.78	0
2000 Asheville	So.Atl.	7	32²/₃	1	5	.167	36	8	43	6.06	0
2001 Asheville	So.Atl.	28	173	11	13	.458	154	33	165	4.32	0
2002 Salem	Carolina	28	170¹/₃	13	5	.722	131	53	149	4.23	0
2003 Tulsa	Texas	50	93²/₃	9	4	.692	102	29	94	4.13	4
2004 Colorado Springs	P.C.	18	22	1	0	1.000	31	7	22	1.64	2
2004 Colorado	N.L.	41	46	0	3	.000	49	19	41	4.11	0
2005 Colorado Springs	P.C.	34	39	2	1	.667	53	16	41	4.38	1
2005 Colorado	N.L.	32	31	2	1	.667	35	19	33	6.10	0
2006 Modesto	Calif.	3	4	0	1	.000	5	2	2	2.25	0
2006 Colorado	N.L.	27	24²/₃	1	1	.500	22	15	26	6.20	1
2006 Colorado Springs	P.C.	10	10²/₃	0	0	.000	12	1	6	2.53	1
2006 Kansas City a	A.L.	21	23²/₃	1	3	.250	22	18	33	7.99	0
2007 Durham	Int.	37	48²/₃	4	1	.800	48	13	37	2.03	5
2007 Tampa Bay b	A.L.	31	32²/₃	3	0	1.000	26	18	29	3.31	0
Major League Totals 4 Yrs.		152	158	7	8	.467	154	89	162	5.24	1

a Traded to Kansas City Royals with infielder Ryan Shealy for pitcher Jeremy Affeldt and pitcher Denny Bautista, July 31, 2006.
b Not offered contract, December 12, 2006. Signed with Tampa Bay Devil Rays, January 22, 2007.

DOWNS, SCOTT JEREMY

Born, Louisville, Kentucky, March 17, 1976.
Bats Left. Throws Left. Height, 6 feet, 2 inches. Weight, 190 pounds.

Year	Club	Lea	G	IP	W	L	Pct	SO	BB	H	ERA	SAVES
1997 Williamsprt.	N.Y.-Penn.	5	23	0	2	.000	28	7	15	2.74	0
1997 Rockford	Midwest	5	36	3	0	1.000	43	8	17	1.25	0
1998 Daytona a	Fla.St.	27	161²/₃	8	9	.471	117	55	179	3.90	0
1999 New Britain	Eastern	6	19²/₃	0	0	.000	22	10	33	8.69	0
1999 Daytona	Fla.St.	7	48	5	0	1.000	41	11	41	1.88	0
1999 Fort Myers	Fla.St.	2	9²/₃	0	1	.000	9	6	7	0.00	0
1999 West Tenn b	Southern	13	80	8	1	.889	101	28	56	1.35	0
2000 Chicago-Montreal c-d	N.L.	19	97	4	3	.571	63	40	122	5.29	0
2001 Montreal	N.L.			INJURED—Did Not Play								
2002 Brevard County	Fla.St.	7	9	0	0	.000	7	2	7	3.00	1
2002 Ottawa e-f	Int.	17	23¹/₃	2	1	.667	15	3	31	5.79	0
2003 Edmonton	P.C.	21	121²/₃	8	9	.471	54	39	119	4.29	0
2003 Montreal	N.L.	1	3	0	1	.000	4	3	5	15.00	0
2004 Edmonton	P.C.	22	135¹/₃	10	6	.625	67	26	143	3.52	0
2004 Montreal g	N.L.	12	63	3	6	.333	38	23	79	5.14	0
2005 Syracuse	Int.	7	39¹/₃	2	3	.400	35	3	45	4.81	0
2005 Toronto	A.L.	26	94	4	3	.571	75	34	93	4.31	0
2006 Toronto	A.L.	59	77	6	2	.750	61	30	73	4.09	1
2007 Toronto	A.L.	*81	58	4	2	.667	57	24	47	2.17	1
Major League Totals 6 Yrs.		198	392	21	17	.553	298	154	419	4.41	2

a Sent by Chicago Cubs to Minnesota Twins as player to be named later for pitcher Mike Morgan, November 3, 1998.
b Traded to Chicago Cubs with pitcher Rick Aguilera for pitcher Jason Ryan and pitcher Kyle Lohse, May 21, 1999.
c On disabled list from August 9 to October 1, 2000.
d Traded to Montreal Expos for outfielder Rondell White, July 31, 2000.
e On disabled list from March 23 to November 14, 2001.
f On disabled list from March 27 to June 10, 2002.
g Released by Montreal Expos, November 29, 2004. Signed with Toronto Blue Jays organization, December 16, 2004.

DUCHSCHERER, JUSTIN CRAIG

Born, Aberdeen, South Dakota, November 19, 1977.
Bats Right. Throws Right. Height, 6 feet, 3 inches. Weight, 200 pounds.

Year	Club	Lea	G	IP	W	L	Pct	SO	BB	H	ERA	SAVES
1996 Red Sox	Gulf Coast	13	54²/₃	0	2	.000	45	14	52	3.13	1
1997 Red Sox	Gulf Coast	10	44²/₃	2	3	.400	59	17	34	1.81	0
1997 Michigan	Midwest	4	24	1	1	.500	19	10	26	5.63	0
1998 Michigan	Midwest	30	142²/₃	7	12	.368	106	47	166	4.79	0
1999 Augusta	So.Atl.	6	41	4	0	1.000	39	8	21	0.22	0
1999 Sarasota	Fla.St.	21	112¹/₃	7	7	.500	105	30	101	4.49	0
2000 Trenton	Eastern	24	143¹/₃	7	9	.438	126	35	134	3.39	0
2001 Trenton	Eastern	12	73²/₃	6	3	.667	69	14	49	2.44	0
2001 Tulsa	Texas	6	43¹/₃	4	0	1.000	55	10	39	2.08	0
2001 Texas	A.L.	5	14²/₃	1	1	.500	11	4	24	12.27	0
2001 Oklahoma a	P.C.	7	50²/₃	3	3	.500	52	10	48	2.84	0
2002 Sacramento b	P.C.	14	63	2	4	.333	52	17	73	5.57	0
2003 Sacramento	P.C.	24	155	14	2	.875	117	18	151	3.25	0
2003 Oakland	A.L.	4	16¹/₃	1	1	.500	15	3	17	3.31	0
2004 Oakland	A.L.	53	96¹/₃	7	6	.538	59	32	85	3.27	0
2005 Oakland	A.L.	65	85²/₃	7	4	.636	85	19	67	2.21	5
2006 Sacramento	P.C.	2	2	0	0	.000	1	0	2	0.00	0
2006 Oakland c	A.L.	53	55²/₃	2	1	.667	51	9	52	2.91	9
2007 Stockton	Calif.	1	1	0	0	.000	1	0	0	0.00	0
2007 Oakland d	A.L.	17	16¹/₃	3	3	.500	13	8	18	4.96	0
Major League Totals .... 6 Yrs.		197	285	21	16	.568	234	75	263	3.44	14
Division Series											
2006 Oakland	A.L.	2	4	0	0	.000	4	0	1	2.25	0

a Traded by Boston Red Sox to Texas Rangers for catcher Doug Mirabelli, June 12, 2001.
b Traded to Oakland Athletics for pitcher Luis Vizcaino, March 18, 2002.
c On disabled list from May 7 to June 23, 2006.
d On disabled list from May 15 to October 8, 2007.

DUKE, ZACHARY THOMAS (ZACH)

Born, Clifton, Texas, April 19, 1983.
Bats Left. Throws Left. Height, 6 feet, 2 inches. Weight, 220 pounds.

Year	Club	Lea	G	IP	W	L	Pct	SO	BB	H	ERA	SAVES
2002 Pirates	Gulf Coast	11	60	8	1	.889	48	18	38	1.95	0
2003 Hickory	So.Atl.	26	141²/₃	8	7	.533	113	46	124	3.11	0
2004 Lynchburg	Carolina	17	97	10	5	.667	106	20	73	1.39	0
2004 Altoona	Eastern	9	51¹/₃	5	1	.833	36	10	41	1.58	0
2005 Indianapolis	Int.	16	108	12	3	.800	66	23	108	2.92	0
2005 Pittsburgh a	N.L.	14	84²/₃	8	2	.800	58	23	79	1.81	0
2006 Pittsburgh	N.L.	34	215¹/₃	10	15	.400	117	68	*255	4.47	0
2007 Pirates	Gulf Coast	2	6²/₃	0	0	.000	3	2	5	1.35	0
2007 NY-Penn	State College	1	5²/₃	1	0	1.000	3	2	3	1.59	0
2007 Indianapolis	Int.	1	3²/₃	0	1	.000	1	2	7	4.91	0
2007 Pittsburgh b	N.L.	20	107¹/₃	3	8	.273	41	25	161	5.53	0
Major League Totals .... 3 Yrs.		68	407¹/₃	21	25	.457	216	116	495	4.20	0

a On disabled list from August 24 to September 16, 2005.
b On disabled list from June 29 to September 11, 2007.

DURBIN, CHAD GRIFFIN

Born, Spring Valley, Illinois, December 3, 1977.
Bats Both. Throws Right. Height, 6 feet, 2 inches. Weight, 200 pounds.

Year	Club	Lea	G	IP	W	L	Pct	SO	BB	H	ERA	SAVES
1996 Royals	Gulf Coast	11	44¹/₃	3	2	.600	43	25	34	4.26	0
1997 Lansing	Midwest	26	144²/₃	5	8	.385	116	53	157	4.79	0
1998 Wilmington	Carolina	26	147²/₃	10	7	.588	162	59	126	2.93	0

Year	Club	Lea	G	IP	W	L	Pct	SO	BB	H	ERA	SAVES
1999 Wichita.............	Texas	28	157	8	10	.444	122	49	154	4.64	0
1999 Kansas City	A.L.	1	2¹/₃	0	0	.000	3	1	1	0.00	0
2000 Kansas City	A.L.	16	72¹/₃	2	5	.286	37	43	91	8.21	0
2000 Omaha................	P.C.	12	72²/₃	4	4	.500	53	22	75	4.46	0
2001 Omaha................	P.C.	5	27	2	2	.500	35	6	22	3.33	0
2001 Kansas City	A.L.	29	179	9	16	.360	95	58	201	4.93	0
2002 Omaha................	P.C.	1	1²/₃	0	1	.000	2	0	4	10.80	0
2002 Royals	Gulf Coast	3	6	0	0	.000	5	1	4	0.00	0
2002 Wichita.............	Texas	3	5¹/₃	0	0	.000	6	4	5	5.06	0
2002 Kansas City	A.L.	2	8¹/₃	0	1	.000	5	4	13	11.88	0
2003 Mahoning Valley...	N.Y.-Penn.	2	12	1	1	.500	8	3	9	2.25	0
2003 Akron.............	Eastern	3	12	2	0	1.000	11	1	7	1.50	0
2003 Buffalo................	Int.	10	58²/₃	3	6	.333	64	16	51	4.60	0
2003 Cleveland a............	A.L.	3	8²/₃	0	1	.000	8	3	18	7.27	0
2004 Cleveland	A.L.	17	51¹/₃	5	6	.455	38	24	63	6.66	0
2004 Buffalo................	Int.	9	52	3	3	.500	40	16	55	3.46	0
2004 Arizona b-c..	N.L.	7	9¹/₃	1	1	.500	10	11	9	8.68	0
2005 New Orleans..........	P.C.	26	115¹/₃	4	5	.444	99	48	121	5.77	0
2006 Toledo	Int.	28	185	11	8	.579	149	46	169	3.11	0
2006 Detroit d..............	A.L.	3	6	0	0	.000	3	0	6	1.50	0
2007 Detroit e..............	A.L.	36	127²/₃	8	7	.533	66	49	133	4.72	1
Major League Totals ....8 Yrs.		114	465	25	37	.403	265	193	535	5.75	1

a Not offered contract, December 20, 2002. Signed with Cleveland Indians organization, February 17, 2003.
b Claimed on waivers by Arizona Diamondbacks, August 13, 2004.
c Filed for free agency, October 11, 2004. Signed with Washington Nationals organization, December 23, 2004.
d Filed for free agency, October 28, 2005. Signed with Detroit Tigers organization, January 10, 2006.
e Not offered contract, December 12, 2007. Signed with Philadelphia Phillies, December 20, 2007.

EATON, ADAM THOMAS
Born, Seattle, Washington, November 23, 1977.
Bats Right. Throws Right. Height, 6 feet, 2 inches. Weight, 200 pounds.

Year	Club	Lea	G	IP	W	L	Pct	SO	BB	H	ERA	SAVES
1997 Piedmont	So.Atl.	14	71¹/₃	5	6	.455	57	30	81	4.16	0
1998 Clearwater	Fla.St.	24	131²/₃	9	8	.529	89	47	152	4.44	0
1999 Reading	Eastern	12	77	5	4	.556	67	28	60	2.92	0
1999 Clearwater	Fla.St.	13	69	5	5	.500	50	24	81	3.91	0
1999 Scranton-WB a.........	Int.	3	21	1	1	.500	10	6	17	3.00	0
2000 Mobile	Southern	10	57	4	1	.800	58	18	47	2.68	0
2000 San Diego	N.L.	22	135	7	4	.636	90	61	134	4.13	0
2001 San Diego b...........	N.L.	17	116²/₃	8	5	.615	109	40	108	4.32	0
2002 Lake Elsinore	California	3	13¹/₃	0	0	.000	19	3	10	2.70	0
2002 Portland	P.C.	2	12¹/₃	1	1	.500	6	3	9	2.92	0
2002 San Diego c...........	N.L.	6	33¹/₃	1	1	.500	25	17	28	5.40	0
2003 San Diego d...........	N.L.	31	183	9	12	.429	146	68	173	4.08	0
2004 San Diego	N.L.	33	199¹/₃	11	14	.440	153	52	204	4.61	0
2005 Lake Elsinore	California	1	3	0	0	.000	2	2	1	0.00	0
2005 Portland	P.C.	2	8	0	0	.000	4	1	11	5.63	0
2005 San Diego e-f...........	N.L.	24	128²/₃	11	5	.688	100	44	140	4.27	0
2006 Frisco................	Texas	2	6¹/₃	0	0	.000	5	1	7	1.42	0
2006 Oklahoma.............	P.C.	2	6	0	0	.000	8	2	3	1.50	0
2006 Texas g-h...........	A.L.	13	65	7	4	.636	43	24	78	5.12	0
2007 Reading	Eastern	1	2	0	0	.000	1	0	3	9.00	0
2007 Philadelphia i...........	N.L.	30	161²/₃	10	10	.500	97	71	192	6.29	0
Major League Totals ....8 Yrs.		176	1022²/₃	64	55	.538	763	377	1057	4.70	0

a Traded to San Diego Padres by Philadelphia Phillies with pitcher Carlton Loewer and pitcher Steve Montgomery for pitcher Andy Ashby, November 10, 1999.
b On disabled list from July 6 to October 10, 2001.
c On disabled list from March 27 to September 1, 2002.
d On disabled list from May 5 to May 20, 2003.
e On disabled list from June 16 to August 1 and August 5 to August 26, 2005.
f Traded to Texas Rangers with pitcher Akinori Otsuka and catcher Billy Killian for pitcher Chris Young, infielder Adrian Gonzalez and outfielder Terrmel Sledge, January 4, 2006.
g On disabled list from March 30 to July 25, 2006.
h Filed for free agency, October 28, 2006. Signed with Philadelphia Phillies, November 30, 2006.
i On disabled list from August 12 to August 28, 2007.

EMBREE, ALAN DUANE

Born, The Dalles, Oregon, January 23, 1970.
Bats Left. Throws Left. Height, 6 feet, 2 inches. Weight, 190 pounds.

Year	Club	Lea	G	IP	W	L	Pct	SO	BB	H	ERA	SAVES
1990 Burlington	Appal.	15	81²/₃	4	4	.500	58	30	87	2.64	0
1991 Columbus.	So. Atl.	27	155¹/₃	10	8	.556	137	77	126	3.59	0
1992 Kinston.	Carolina	15	101	10	5	.667	115	32	89	3.30	0
1992 Canton-Akron.	Eastern	12	79	7	2	.778	56	28	61	2.28	0
1992 Cleveland	A.L.	4	18	0	2	.000	12	8	19	7.00	0
1993 Canton-Akron.	Eastern	1	5¹/₃	0	0	.000	4	3	3	3.38	0
1994 Canton-Akron.	Eastern	30	157	9	16	.360	81	64	183	5.50	0
1995 Buffalo	A.A.	30	40²/₃	3	4	.429	56	19	31	0.89	5
1995 Cleveland	A.L.	23	24²/₃	3	2	.600	23	16	23	5.11	1
1996 Buffalo	A.A.	20	34¹/₃	4	1	.800	46	14	26	3.93	5
1996 Cleveland a.	A.L.	24	31	1	1	.500	33	21	30	6.39	0
1997 Atlanta b.	N.L.	66	46	3	1	.750	45	20	36	2.54	0
1998 Atlanta-Arizona c-d	N.L.	55	53²/₃	4	2	.667	43	23	56	4.19	1
1999 San Francisco	N.L.	68	58²/₃	3	2	.600	53	26	42	3.38	0
2000 San Francisco	N.L.	63	60	3	5	.375	49	25	62	4.95	2
2001 Fresno	P.C.	7	8	1	0	1.000	6	1	5	1.13	1
2001 San Francisco e	N.L.	22	20	0	2	.000	25	10	34	11.25	0
2001 Chicago f-g	A.L.	39	34	1	2	.333	34	7	31	5.03	0
2002 San Diego	N.L.	36	28²/₃	3	4	.429	38	9	23	0.94	0
2002 Boston h-i	A.L.	32	33¹/₃	1	2	.333	43	11	24	2.97	2
2003 Sarasota	Fla.St.	1	0²/₃	0	0	.000	2	0	2	13.50	0
2003 Boston j	A.L.	65	55	4	1	.800	45	16	49	4.25	1
2004 Boston	A.L.	71	52¹/₃	2	2	.500	37	11	49	4.13	0
2005 Boston-New York k-l	A.L.	67	52	2	5	.286	38	14	62	7.62	1
2006 San Diego m-n.	N.L.	73	52¹/₃	4	3	.571	53	15	50	3.27	0
2007 Oakland	A.L.	68	68	1	2	.333	51	19	67	3.97	17
Major League Totals	14 Yrs.	776	687²/₃	35	38	.479	622	251	657	4.52	25
Division Series											
1996 Cleveland	A.L.	3	1	0	0	.000	1	0	0	9.00	0
2000 San Francisco	N.L.	2	1²/₃	0	0	.000	0	0	0	0.00	0
2003 Boston	A.L.	3	2	0	0	.000	0	0	1	0.00	0
2004 Boston	A.L.	2	1	0	0	.000	0	1	0	0.00	0
2006 San Diego	N.L.	1	0¹/₃	0	0	.000	1	0	0	0.00	0
Division Series Totals		11	6	0	0	.000	2	1	1	1.50	0
Championship Series											
1995 Cleveland	A.L.	1	0¹/₃	0	0	.000	1	0	0	0.00	0
1997 Atlanta	N.L.	1	1	0	0	.000	1	1	0	0.00	0
2003 Boston	A.L.	5	4²/₃	1	0	1.000	1	0	3	0.00	0
2004 Boston	A.L.	6	4²/₃	0	0	.000	2	1	9	3.86	0
Championship Series Totals		13	10²/₃	1	0	1.000	5	2	12	1.69	0
World Series Record											
1995 Cleveland	A.L.	4	3¹/₃	0	0	.000	2	2	2	2.70	0
2004 Boston	A.L.	3	1²/₃	0	0	.000	4	0	1	0.00	0
World Series Totals		7	5	0	0	.000	6	2	3	1.80	0

a On disabled list from August 1 to September 7, 1996.
b Traded to Atlanta Braves with outfielder Kenny Lofton for outfielder Marquis Grissom and outfielder David Justice, March 25, 1997.
c Traded to Arizona Diamondbacks for pitcher Russ Springer, June 22, 1998.
d Traded to San Francisco Giants for outfielder Dante Powell, November 10, 1998.
e On disabled list from May 23 to June 12, 2001.
f Traded to Chicago White Sox with cash for pitcher Derek Hasselhoff, June 29, 2001.
g Filed for free agency, November 6, 2001. Signed with San Diego Padres, December 27, 2001.
h Traded to Boston Red Sox with pitcher Andy Shibilo for pitcher Brad Baker and pitcher Dan Giese, June 23, 2002.
i On disabled list from July 14 to July 29, 2002.
j On disabled list from April 9 to April 29, 2003.
k Released by Boston Red Sox, July 27, 2005. Signed with New York Yankees, July 30, 2005.
l Filed for free agency, November 3, 2005. Signed with San Diego Padres organization, January 12, 2006.
m On disabled list from July 2 to July 17, 2006.
n Filed for free agency, October 29, 2006. Signed with Oakland Athletics, December 6, 2006.

ESCOBAR, KELVIM JOSE
Born, LaGuaira, Venezuela, April 11, 1976.
Bats Right. Throws Right. Height, 6 feet, 1 inch. Weight, 230 pounds.

Year	Club	Lea	G	IP	W	L	Pct	SO	BB	H	ERA	SAVES
1994	Blue Jays	Gulf Coast	11	65	4	4	.500	64	18	56	2.35	0
1995	Medcine Hat	Pioneer	14	69⅓	3	3	.500	75	33	66	5.71	0
1996	Dunedin	Fla. St.	18	110⅓	9	5	.643	113	33	101	2.69	0
1996	Knoxville	Southern	10	54	3	4	.429	44	24	61	5.33	0
1997	Dunedin	Fla. St.	3	12	0	1	.000	16	3	16	3.75	0
1997	Knoxville	Southern	5	24⅓	2	1	.667	31	16	20	3.70	0
1997	Toronto	A.L.	27	31	3	2	.600	36	19	28	2.90	14
1998	Syracuse	Int.	13	59⅔	2	2	.500	64	24	51	3.77	1
1998	Toronto a	A.L.	22	79⅔	7	3	.700	72	35	72	3.73	0
1999	Toronto	A.L.	33	174	14	11	.560	129	81	203	5.69	0
2000	Toronto	A.L.	43	180	10	15	.400	142	85	186	5.35	2
2001	Toronto	A.L.	59	126	6	8	.429	121	52	93	3.50	0
2002	Toronto	A.L.	76	78	5	7	.417	85	44	75	4.27	38
2003	Toronto b	A.L.	41	180⅓	13	9	.591	159	78	189	4.29	4
2004	Anaheim	A.L.	33	208⅓	11	12	.478	191	76	192	3.93	0
2005	Rancho Cucamonga	Calif.	1	3	0	0	.000	7	2	1	0.00	0
2005	Salt Lake	P.C.	4	14⅓	1	0	1.000	22	8	14	2.51	0
2005	Los Angeles c	A.L.	16	59⅔	3	2	.600	63	21	45	3.02	1
2006	Los Angeles d	A.L.	30	189⅓	11	14	.440	147	50	192	3.61	0
2007	Los Angeles e	A.L.	30	195⅔	18	7	.720	160	66	182	3.40	0
Major League Totals	11 Yrs.		410	1502	101	90	.529	1305	607	1457	4.15	59
Division Series												
2004	Anaheim	A.L.	1	3⅓	0	0	.000	4	5	5	8.10	0
2005	Los Angeles	A.L.	4	7	1	0	1.000	5	5	2	1.29	0
2007	Los Angeles	A.L.	1	5	0	0	.000	5	5	4	5.40	0
Division Series Totals			6	15⅓	1	0	1.000	14	15	11	4.11	0
Championship Series												
2005	Los Angeles	A.L.	2	4⅓	0	2	.000	10	2	4	2.08	0

a On disabled list from April 16 to May 6, 1998.
b Filed for free agency, October 26, 2003. Signed with Anaheim Angels, November 24, 2003.
c On disabled list from March 31 to April 24 and May 12 to May 28 and June 9 to September 6, 2005.
d On disabled list from July 7 to July 22, 2006.
e On disabled list from April 9 to April 24, 2007.

EYRE, SCOTT ALAN
Born, Inglewood, California, May 30, 1972.
Bats Left. Throws Left. Height, 6 feet, 1 inch. Weight, 215 pounds.

Year	Club	Lea	G	IP	W	L	Pct	SO	BB	H	ERA	SAVES
1992	Butte	Pioneer	15	80⅔	7	3	.700	94	39	71	2.90	0
1993	Chston-Sc	So.Atl.	26	143⅔	11	7	.611	154	59	115	3.45	0
1994	South Bend a-b	Midwest	19	111⅔	8	4	.667	111	37	108	3.47	0
1995	White Sox c	Gulf Coast	9	27⅓	0	2	.000	40	12	16	2.30	0
1996	Birmingham	Southern	27	158⅓	12	7	.632	137	79	170	4.38	0
1997	Birmingham	Southern	22	126⅔	13	5	.722	127	55	110	3.84	0
1997	Chicago	A.L.	11	60⅔	4	4	.500	36	31	62	5.04	0
1998	Chicago	A.L.	33	107	3	8	.273	73	64	114	5.38	0
1999	Charlotte	Int.	12	68⅓	6	4	.600	63	23	75	3.82	0
1999	Chicago d-e	A.L.	21	25	1	1	.500	17	15	38	7.56	0
2000	Chicago	A.L.	13	19	1	1	.500	16	12	29	6.63	0
2000	Charlotte f	Int.	47	48	3	2	.600	46	20	33	3.00	12
2001	Syracuse	Int.	62	79⅓	4	6	.400	96	26	67	3.18	0
2001	Toronto	A.L.	17	15⅔	1	2	.333	16	7	15	3.45	2
2002	Toronto	A.L.	49	63⅓	2	4	.333	51	29	69	4.97	0
2002	San Francisco g	N.L.	21	11⅓	0	0	.000	7	7	11	1.59	0
2003	San Francisco	N.L.	74	57	2	1	.667	35	26	60	3.32	1
2004	Fresno	P.C.	3	3	0	0	.000	1	2	3	0.00	0
2004	San Francisco h	N.L.	83	52⅔	2	2	.500	49	27	43	4.10	1
2005	San Francisco i	N.L.	*86	68⅓	2	2	.500	65	26	48	2.63	0
2006	Chicago j	N.L.	74	61⅓	1	3	.250	73	30	61	3.38	0
2007	Chicago	N.L.	55	52⅓	2	1	.667	45	35	59	4.13	0
Major League Totals	11 Yrs.		537	593⅔	21	29	.420	483	309	609	4.37	4
Division Series												
2002	San Francisco	N.L.	3	1⅓	0	0	.000	0	0	1	0.00	0
2003	San Francisco	N.L.	1	0⅓	0	0	.000	0	0	0	0.00	0

Year	Club	Lea	G	IP	W	L	Pct	SO	BB	H	ERA	SAVES
2007 Chicago	N.L.	1	0	0	0	.000	0	0	1	INF	0
Division Series Totals		5	1²/₃	0	0	.000	0	0	2	0.00	0
Championship Series											
2002 San Francisco	N.L.	4	1²/₃	0	0	.000	0	0	2	0.00	0
World Series Record											
2002 San Francisco	N.L.	3	3	0	0	.000	2	1	5	0.00	0

a Traded by Texas Rangers to Chicago White Sox for infielder Esteban Beltre, March 28, 1994.
b On disabled list from April 8 to 27, 1994.
c On disabled list from April 6 to September 7, 1995.
d On disabled list from June 2 to 13, 1999.
e On disabled list from August 31 to September 26, 1999.
f Traded to Toronto Blue Jays for pitcher Gary Glover, November 7, 2000.
g Claimed on waivers by San Francisco Giants, August 8, 2002.
h On disabled list from March 27 to April 22, 2004.
i Filed for free agency, October 28, 2005. Signed with Chicago Cubs, November 29, 2005.
j On disabled list from August 16 to September 1, 2006.

EYRE, WILLIAM MAYS (WILLIE)

Born, Fountain Valley, California, July 21, 1978.
Bats Right. Throws Right. Height, 6 feet, 2 inches. Weight, 205 pounds.

Year	Club	Lea	G	IP	W	L	Pct	SO	BB	H	ERA	SAVES
1999 Elizabethton	Appal.	16	57²/₃	6	3	.667	59	34	60	4.53	0
1999 Quad Cities	Midwest	2	12²/₃	1	0	1.000	10	6	8	4.26	0
2000 Quad Cities	Midwest	26	99²/₃	5	7	.417	81	56	104	4.61	0
2001 Fort Myers	Fla.St.	32	64¹/₃	2	5	.286	51	33	54	2.52	1
2001 Quad Cities	Midwest	17	22¹/₃	3	0	1.000	21	2	19	2.42	4
2002 New Britain	Eastern	28	50	6	4	.600	43	21	40	3.24	2
2002 Fort Myers	Fla.St.	19	33²/₃	4	1	.800	25	13	28	2.41	2
2003 New Britain	Eastern	29	96¹/₃	6	5	.545	66	38	93	3.46	0
2003 Rochester............	Int.	6	24	0	2	.000	23	16	30	6.00	0
2004 Rochester............	Int.	36	136	6	7	.462	91	53	131	3.64	4
2005 Rochester............	Int.	56	82²/₃	10	3	.769	74	28	79	2.72	7
2006 Minnesota a...........	A.L.	42	59¹/₃	1	0	1.000	26	22	75	5.31	0
2007 Oklahoma............	P.C.	5	7¹/₃	1	0	1.000	8	1	2	0.00	1
2007 Texas b-c	A.L.	33	68	4	6	.400	42	32	78	5.16	1
Major League Totals	2 Yrs.	75	127¹/₃	5	6	.455	68	54	153	5.23	1

a Not offered contract, December 12, 2006. Signed with Texas Rangers organization, December 28, 2006.
b On disabled list from August 17 to October 15, 2007.
c Filed for free agency, October 20, 2007.

FARNSWORTH, KYLE LYNN

Born, Wichita, Kansas, April 14, 1976.
Bats Right. Throws Right. Height, 6 feet, 4 inches. Weight, 240 pounds.

Year	Club	Lea	G	IP	W	L	Pct	SO	BB	H	ERA	SAVES
1995 Cubs............	Gulf Coast	16	31	3	2	.600	18	11	22	0.87	1
1996 Rockford	Midwest	20	112	9	6	.600	82	35	122	3.70	0
1997 Daytona	Fla.St.	27	156¹/₃	10	10	.500	105	47	178	4.09	0
1998 West Tenn	Southern	13	81¹/₃	8	2	.800	73	21	70	2.77	0
1998 Iowa................	P.C.	18	102²/₃	5	9	.357	79	36	129	6.93	0
1999 Iowa................	P.C.	6	39¹/₃	2	2	.500	29	9	38	3.20	0
1999 Chicago	N.L.	27	130	5	9	.357	70	52	140	5.05	0
2000 Chicago	N.L.	46	77	2	9	.182	74	50	90	6.43	1
2000 Chicago............	P.C.	22	25¹/₃	0	2	.000	22	18	24	3.20	0
2001 Chicago	N.L.	76	82	4	6	.400	107	29	65	2.74	2
2002 Chicago a	N.L.	45	46²/₃	4	6	.400	46	24	53	7.33	1
2002 Iowa............	P.C.	2	3	0	1	.000	2	0	3	6.00	0
2003 Chicago	N.L.	77	76¹/₃	3	2	.600	92	36	53	3.30	0
2004 Chicago b............	N.L.	72	66²/₃	4	5	.444	78	33	67	4.72	0
2005 Detroit	A.L.	46	42²/₃	1	1	.500	55	20	29	2.32	6
2005 Atlanta c-d-e	N.L.	26	27¹/₃	0	0	.000	32	7	15	1.98	10
2006 New York	A.L.	72	66	3	6	.333	75	28	62	4.36	6
2007 New York	A.L.	64	60	2	1	.667	48	27	60	4.80	0
Major League Totals	9 Yrs.	551	674²/₃	28	45	.384	677	306	634	4.47	26
Division Series											
2003 Chicago	N.L.	3	2²/₃	0	0	.000	2	1	1	0.00	0
2005 Atlanta	N.L.	2	3	0	0	.000	4	1	2	9.00	0
2006 New York	A.L.	2	2	0	0	.000	1	1	1	0.00	0

Year Club	Lea	G	IP	W	L	Pct	SO	BB	H	ERA	SAVES
2007 New York	A.L.	1	1	0	0	.000	2	0	1	0.00	0
Division Series Totals		8	8²/₃	0	0	.000	9	3	5	3.12	0
Championship Series											
2003 Chicago	N.L.	5	5¹/₃	0	0	.000	7	2	6	10.13	0

a On disabled list from April 10 to June 4, 2002.

b On disabled list from August 28 to September 12, 2004.

c Traded to Detroit Tigers with player to be named later for pitcher Roberto Novoa, infielder Scott Moore and outfielder Clarence Flowers, February 9, 2005.

d Traded to Atlanta Braves for pitcher Roman Colon and pitcher Zach Miner, July 26, 2005.

e Filed for free agency, October 31, 2005. Signed with New York Yankees, December 5, 2005.

FELICIANO (MOLINA), PEDRO JUAN
Born, Rio Piedras, Puerto Rico, August 25, 1976.
Bats Left. Throws Left. Height, 5 feet, 10 inches. Weight, 185 pounds.

Year Club	Lea	G	IP	W	L	Pct	SO	BB	H	ERA	SAVES
1995 Great Falls	Pioneer	6	6²/₃	0	0	.000	9	7	12	13.50	0
1996 Great Falls	Pioneer	22	41	2	3	.400	39	26	50	5.71	3
1997 Savannah	So.Atl.	36	105²/₃	3	7	.300	94	39	90	2.64	4
1997 Vero Beach.	Fla.St.	1	2	0	0	.000	1	0	3	4.50	0
1998 Vero Beach.	Fla.St.	22	68¹/₃	2	5	.286	51	30	68	4.61	2
1999	INJURED—Did Not Play										
2000 Vero Beach.	Fla.St.	25	61¹/₃	4	5	.444	48	24	76	3.82	0
2000 Albuquerque.	P.C.	1	1	0	0	.000	2	1	3	18.00	0
2000 San Antonio a.	Texas	9	9¹/₃	0	0	.000	11	4	7	1.93	2
2001 Las Vegas.	P.C.	6	8²/₃	0	1	.000	5	5	16	7.27	0
2001 Jacksonville b ....:	Southern	54	60¹/₃	5	4	.556	55	11	41	1.94	17
2002 Chattanooga. ......:	Southern	28	38²/₃	2	1	.667	26	11	33	2.56	4
2002 Louisville	Int.	20	26²/₃	1	1	.500	19	4	35	3.04	0
2002 Norfolk.	Int.	5	9	0	0	.000	11	1	14	7.00	2
2002 New York c-d-e	N.L.	6	6	0	0	.000	4	1	9	7.50	0
2003 Norfolk.	Int.	15	22²/₃	3	2	.600	18	6	20	3.97	1
2003 New York f-g	N.L.	23	48¹/₃	0	0	.000	43	21	52	3.35	0
2004 Norfolk.	Int.	32	35²/₃	4	3	.571	25	15	35	5.30	2
2004 New York	N.L.	22	18¹/₃	1	1	.500	14	12	14	5.40	0
2005 Fukuoka h-i	Japan Pac.	37	37	3	2	.600	36	13	30	3.89	0
2006 Norfolk.	Int.	3	4¹/₃	0	0	.000	5	1	4	6.23	0
2006 New York	N.L.	64	60¹/₃	7	2	.778	54	20	56	2.09	0
2007 New York	N.L.	78	64	2	2	.500	61	31	47	3.09	2
Major League Totals	5 Yrs.	193	197	10	5	.667	176	85	178	3.20	2
Division Series											
2006 New York	N.L.	3	1²/₃	1	0	1.000	2	2	0	0.00	0
Championship Series											
2006 New York	N.L.	3	3	0	0	.000	1	0	2	3.00	0

a On minor league disabled list from April 8 to September 22, 1999.

b Filed for free agency from Los Angeles Dodgers, October 15, 2001. Signed with Cincinnati Reds organization, December 21, 2001.

c Traded to New York Mets with outfielder Elvin Andujar, player to be named later and two players to be named later for pitcher Shawn Estes and cash, August 16, 2002.

d New York Mets received outfielder Raul Gonzalez (August 20, 2002) and Brady Clark to complete trade, September 9, 2002.

e Claimed on waivers by Detroit Tigers, October 11, 2002.

f Released by Detroit Tigers, December 17, 2002. Signed with New York Mets organization, April 3, 2003.

g Not offered contract, December 21, 2003, re-signed with New York Mets organization, December 22, 2003.

h Sold to Fukuoka Daiei Hawks (Japan), January 21, 2005.

i Signed with New York Mets organization, December 19, 2005.

FLORES, RANDY ALAN
Born, Bellflower, California, July 31, 1975.
Bats Left. Throws Left. Height, 6 feet. Weight, 180 pounds.

Year Club	Lea	G	IP	W	L	Pct	SO	BB	H	ERA	SAVES
1997 Oneonta	N.Y.-Penn.	13	74²/₃	4	4	.500	70	23	64	3.25	0
1998 Tampa	Fla.St.	5	23²/₃	1	2	.333	15	16	28	6.46	0
1998 Greensboro	So.Atl.	21	130²/₃	12	7	.632	139	33	119	2.62	0
1999 Norwich	Eastern	4	25	0	1	.000	19	11	32	6.48	0
1999 Tampa	Fla.St.	21	135	11	4	.733	99	38	118	2.87	0
2000 Norwich	Eastern	31	141	10	9	.526	97	58	138	2.94	1
2000 Columbus.	Int.	4	23¹/₃	1	2	.333	16	7	43	7.33	0

Year	Club	Lea	G	IP	W	L	Pct	SO	BB	H	ERA	SAVES
2001 Norwich	Eastern		25	158²/₃	14	6	.700	115	63	156	2.78	0
2001 Columbus a	Int.		3	5²/₃	0	1	.000	4	2	5	4.76	0
2002 Oklahoma	P.C.		15	20¹/₃	1	1	.500	16	5	22	5.75	1
2002 Texas	A.L.		20	12	0	0	.000	7	8	11	4.50	1
2002 Colorado Springs	P.C.		7	35²/₃	2	2	.500	27	18	36	3.28	0
2002 Colorado b	N.L.		8	17	0	2	.000	7	8	29	9.53	0
2003 Colorado Springs c	P.C.		28	142²/₃	10	8	.556	116	67	156	4.98	0
2004 Memphis	P.C.		36	122²/₃	5	7	.417	99	46	115	3.82	2
2004 St. Louis	N.L.		9	14	1	0	1.000	7	3	13	1.93	0
2005 Memphis	P.C.		6	7	1	0	1.000	6	0	8	6.43	0
2005 St. Louis d	N.L.		50	41²/₃	3	1	.750	43	13	37	3.46	1
2006 St. Louis	N.L.		65	41²/₃	1	1	.500	40	22	49	5.62	0
2007 St. Louis	N.L.		70	55	3	0	1.000	47	15	71	4.25	1
Major League Totals	5 Yrs.		222	181¹/₃	8	4	.667	151	69	210	4.72	3
Division Series												
2005 St. Louis	N.L.		3	2	0	0	.000	3	0	2	4.50	0
2006 St. Louis	N.L.		2	1	0	0	.000	1	1	2	0.00	0
Division Series Totals			5	3	0	0	.000	4	1	4	3.00	0
Championship Series												
2005 St. Louis	N.L.		2	1¹/₃	0	0	.000	0	1	0	0.00	0
2006 St. Louis	N.L.		4	3²/₃	1	0	1.000	3	0	2	0.00	0
Championship Series Totals			6	5	1	0	1.000	3	1	2	0.00	0
World Series Record												
2006 St. Louis	N.L.		1	1	0	0	.000	0	0	1	0.00	0

a Sent by New York Yankees to Texas Rangers with pitcher Rosman Garcia to complete trade for Randy Velarde, October 11, 2001.
b Claimed on waivers by Colorado Rockies, July 17, 2002.
c Filed for free agency, October 15, 2003. Signed with St. Louis Cardinals organization, November 20, 2003.
d On disabled list from June 24 to July 9, 2005.

FOGG, JOSHUA SMITH (JOSH)

Born, Lynn, Massachusetts, December 13, 1976.
Bats Right. Throws Right. Height, 6 feet. Weight, 205 pounds.

Year	Club	Lea	G	IP	W	L	Pct	SO	BB	H	ERA	SAVES
1998 White Sox	Arizona		2	4	1	0	1.000	5	1	0	0.00	0
1998 Hickory	So.Atl.		8	41¹/₃	1	3	.250	29	13	36	2.18	0
1998 Winston-Sal	Carolina		1	1	0	1	.000	2	0	2	0.00	0
1999 Winston-Salem	Carolina		17	103¹/₃	10	5	.667	109	33	93	2.96	0
1999 Birmingham	Southern		10	55	3	2	.600	40	18	66	5.89	0
2000 Birmingham	Southern		27	192¹/₃	11	7	.611	136	44	190	2.57	0
2001 Charlotte	Int.		40	114²/₃	4	7	.364	89	30	129	4.79	4
2001 Chicago a	A.L.		11	13¹/₃	0	0	.000	17	3	10	2.03	0
2002 Pittsburgh	N.L.		33	194¹/₃	12	12	.500	113	69	199	4.35	0
2003 Nashville	P.C.		2	10	0	1	.000	7	1	12	5.40	0
2003 Pittsburgh b	N.L.		26	142	10	9	.526	71	40	166	5.26	0
2004 Pittsburgh	N.L.		32	178¹/₃	11	10	.524	82	66	193	4.64	0
2005 Pittsburgh c	N.L.		34	169¹/₃	6	11	.353	85	53	196	5.05	0
2006 Colorado	N.L.		31	172	11	9	.550	93	60	206	5.49	0
2007 Colorado Springs	P.C.		1	5	0	1	.000	3	0	6	3.60	0
2007 Colorado d-e	N.L.		30	165²/₃	10	9	.526	94	59	194	4.94	0
Major League Totals	7 Yrs.		197	1035	60	60	.500	555	350	1164	4.90	0
Division Series												
2007 Colorado	N.L.		1	2	1	0	1.000	1	0	1	0.00	0
Championship Series												
2007 Colorado	N.L.		1	6	1	0	1.000	3	1	7	1.50	0
World Series Record												
2007 Colorado	N.L.		1	2²/₃	0	1	.000	2	2	10	20.25	0

a Traded to Pittsburgh Pirates with pitcher Kip Wells and pitcher Sean Lowe for pitcher Todd Ritchie and catcher Lee Evans, December 13, 2001.
b On disabled list from April 21 to May 26, 2003.
c Not offered contract, December 21, 2005. Signed with Colorado Rockies, February 11, 2006.
d On disabled list from May 23 to June 7, 2007.
e Filed for free agency, November 2, 2007.

FRANCIS, JEFFREY WILLIAM (JEFF)

Born, Vancouver, British Columbia, Canada, January 8, 1981.
Bats Left. Throws Left. Height, 6 feet, 5 inches. Weight, 205 pounds.

Year	Club	Lea	G	IP	W	L	Pct	SO	BB	H	ERA	SAVES
2002	Tri-City	Northwest	4	10²/₃	0	0	.000	16	4	5	0.00	0
2002	Asheville	So.Atl.	4	20	0	0	.000	23	4	16	1.80	0
2003	Visalia	California	27	160²/₃	12	9	.571	153	45	135	3.47	0
2004	Tulsa	Texas	17	113²/₃	13	1	.929	147	22	73	1.98	0
2004	Colorado Springs	P.C.	7	41	3	2	.600	49	7	35	2.85	0
2004	Colorado	N.L.	7	36²/₃	3	2	.600	32	13	42	5.15	0
2005	Colorado	N.L.	33	183²/₃	14	12	.538	128	70	228	5.68	0
2006	Colorado	N.L.	32	199	13	11	.542	117	69	187	4.16	0
2007	Colorado	N.L.	34	215¹/₃	17	9	.654	165	63	234	4.22	0
Major League Totals	4 Yrs.		106	634²/₃	47	34	.580	442	215	691	4.68	0
Division Series												
2007	Colorado	N.L.	1	6	1	0	1.000	8	2	4	3.00	0
Championship Series												
2007	Colorado	N.L.	1	6²/₃	1	0	1.000	4	1	7	1.35	0
World Series Record												
2007	Colorado	N.L.	1	4	0	1	.000	3	3	10	13.50	0

FRANCISCO, FRANKLIN (FRANK)

Born, Santo Domingo, Dominican Republic, September 11, 1979.
Bats Right. Throws Right. Height, 6 feet, 2 inches. Weight, 235 pounds.

Year	Club	Lea	G	IP	W	L	Pct	SO	BB	H	ERA	SAVES
1997						INJURED—Did Not Play						
1998	Co-op	Dominican	16	48	0	5	.000	53	76	44	10.31	0
1999	Red Sox	Gulf Coast	12	53¹/₃	2	4	.333	48	35	58	4.56	0
2000	Red Sox	Gulf Coast	1	1	0	0	.000	1	2	2	18.00	0
2001	Augusta	So.Atl.	37	68	4	3	.571	90	30	40	2.91	2
2002	Winston-Salem	Carolina	6	25²/₃	0	4	.000	25	18	31	8.06	0
2002	Trenton	Eastern	9	16	2	2	.500	18	16	10	5.63	0
2002	Sarasota a	Fla.St.	16	53	1	5	.167	58	27	33	2.55	0
2003	Winston-Salem	Carolina	16	78¹/₃	7	3	.700	67	36	59	3.56	0
2003	Frisco b	Texas	7	35¹/₃	2	3	.400	22	18	43	8.41	0
2004	Frisco	Texas	15	17²/₃	1	3	.250	30	10	7	2.55	6
2004	Texas	A.L.	45	51¹/₃	5	1	.833	60	28	36	3.33	0
2005	Oklahoma	P.C.	2	3	0	0	.000	4	2	2	3.00	1
2005	Frisco c	Texas	4	3¹/₃	0	1	.000	3	2	4	8.10	0
2006	Frisco	Texas	13	14²/₃	0	0	.000	22	4	10	1.84	0
2006	Spokane	Northwest	4	4	0	0	.000	6	0	3	0.00	0
2006	Texas d	A.L.	8	7¹/₃	0	1	.000	6	2	8	4.91	0
2007	Oklahoma	P.C.	5	6	1	0	1.000	14	3	0	0.00	2
2007	Texas	A.L.	59	59¹/₃	1	1	.500	49	38	57	4.55	0
Major League Totals	3 Yrs.		112	118	6	3	.667	115	68	101	4.04	0

a Traded to Chicago White Sox by Boston Red Sox with pitcher Byeong An for pitcher Bob Howry, July 31, 2002.
b Sent to Texas Rangers as one of the players to be named later for outfielder Carl Everett, July 23, 2003.
c On disabled list from March 25 to October 12, 2005.
d On disabled list from March 24 to June 19, 2006.

FRANKLIN, RYAN RAY

Born, Fort Smith, Arkansas, March 5, 1973.
Bats Right. Throws Right. Height, 6 feet, 3 inches. Weight, 190 pounds.

Year	Club	Lea	G	IP	W	L	Pct	SO	BB	H	ERA	SAVES
1993	Bellingham	Northwest	15	74	5	3	.625	55	27	72	2.92	0
1994	Appleton	Midwest	18	118	9	6	.600	102	23	105	3.13	0
1994	Calgary	P.C.	1	5²/₃	0	0	.000	2	1	9	7.94	0
1994	Riverside	California	8	61²/₃	4	2	.667	35	8	61	3.06	0
1995	Port City	Southern	31	146	6	10	.375	102	43	153	4.32	0
1996	Port City	Southern	28	182	6	12	.333	127	37	186	4.01	0
1997	Memphis	Southern	11	59¹/₃	4	2	.667	49	14	45	3.03	0
1997	Tacoma	P.C.	14	90¹/₃	5	5	.500	59	24	97	4.18	0
1998	Tacoma	P.C.	34	127²/₃	5	6	.455	90	32	148	4.51	1
1999	Tacoma	P.C.	29	135²/₃	6	9	.400	94	33	142	4.71	2
1999	Seattle	A.L.	6	11¹/₃	0	0	.000	6	8	10	4.76	0
2000	Tacoma	P.C.	31	164	11	5	.688	142	35	147	3.90	0
2001	Tacoma	P.C.	1	3²/₃	0	0	.000	3	0	2	0.00	0

Year	Club	Lea	G	IP	W	L	Pct	SO	BB	H	ERA	SAVES
2001	Seattle	A.L.	38	78 1/3	5	1	.833	60	24	76	3.56	0
2002	Everett	Northwest	1	2 2/3	0	0	.000	1	0	2	0.00	0
2002	Seattle a	A.L.	41	118 2/3	7	5	.583	65	22	117	4.02	0
2003	Seattle	A.L.	32	212	11	13	.458	99	61	199	3.57	0
2004	Seattle	A.L.	32	200 1/3	4	16	.200	104	61	224	4.90	0
2005	Seattle b	A.L.	32	190 2/3	8	15	.348	93	62	212	5.10	0
2006	Philadelphia-Cincinnati c-d	N.L.	66	77 1/3	6	7	.462	43	33	86	4.54	0
2007	St. Louis	N.L.	69	80	4	4	.500	44	-11	70	3.04	1
Major League Totals	8 Yrs.		316	968 2/3	45	61	.425	514	282	994	4.25	1

a On disabled list from June 28 to July 15, 2002.
b Not offered contract, December 21, 2005. Signed with Philadelphia Phillies, January 5, 2006.
c Traded to Cincinnati Reds for pitcher Zac Scott, August 7, 2006.
d Filed for free agency, October 30, 2006. Signed with St. Louis Cardinals, January 11, 2007.

FRASOR, JASON ANDREW

Born, Chicago, Illinois, August 9, 1977.
Bats Right. Throws Right. Height, 5 feet, 10 inches. Weight, 170 pounds.

Year	Club	Lea	G	IP	W	L	Pct	SO	BB	H	ERA	SAVES
1999	Oneonta	N.Y.-Penn.	12	58 2/3	3	3	.500	69	22	36	1.69	0
1999	West Michigan	Midwest	4	24	2	1	.667	33	9	17	2.63	0
2000	West Michigan	Midwest	14	71 1/3	5	3	.625	65	29	55	3.28	0
2001	West Michigan a	Midwest					INJURED—Did Not Play					
2002	Lakeland b	Fla.St.	24	117	5	6	.455	87	46	112	3.54	0
2003	Vero Beach	Fla.St.	15	24 1/3	1	0	1.000	36	4	16	1.85	6
2003	Jacksonville	Southern	31	36 2/3	1	0	1.000	50	14	33	2.95	17
2004	Syracuse	Int.	3	4	0	0	.000	6	5	1	2.25	0
2004	Toronto c	A.L.	63	68 1/3	4	6	.400	54	36	64	4.08	17
2005	Toronto	A.L.	67	74 2/3	3	5	.375	62	28	67	3.25	1
2006	Syracuse	Int.	18	20 1/3	3	1	.750	33	13	21	3.98	1
2006	Toronto	A.L.	51	50	3	2	.600	51	17	47	4.32	0
2007	Toronto	A.L.	51	57	1	5	.167	59	23	47	4.58	3
Major League Totals	4 Yrs.		232	250	11	18	.379	226	104	225	4.00	21

a On minor league disabled list, April 5 to September 14, 2001.
b Sent by Detroit Tigers to Los Angeles Dodgers as player to be named later for infielder Hiram Bocachica, September 18, 2002.
c Traded to Toronto Blue Jays for outfielder Jayson Werth, March 30, 2004.

FUENTES, BRIAN CHRISTOPHER

Born, Merced, California, August 9, 1975.
Bats Left. Throws Left. Height, 6 feet, 4 inches. Weight, 230 pounds.

Year	Club	Lea	G	IP	W	L	Pct	SO	BB	H	ERA	SAVES
1996	Everett	Northwest	13	26 2/3	0	1	.000	26	13	23	4.39	0
1997	Wisconsin	Midwest	22	118 2/3	6	7	.462	153	59	84	3.56	0
1998	Lancaster a	California	24	118 2/3	7	7	.500	137	81	121	4.17	0
1999	New Haven b	Eastern	15	60	3	3	.500	66	46	53	4.95	0
2000	New Haven	Eastern	26	139 2/3	7	12	.368	152	70	127	4.51	0
2001	Tacoma	P.C.	35	52	3	2	.600	70	25	35	2.94	6
2001	Seattle c-d	A.L.	10	11 2/3	1	1	.500	10	8	6	4.63	0
2002	Colorado Springs	P.C.	41	49 1/3	3	3	.500	62	32	44	3.65	1
2002	Colorado	N.L.	31	26 2/3	2	0	1.000	38	13	25	4.72	0
2003	Colorado	N.L.	75	75 1/3	3	3	.500	82	34	64	2.75	4
2004	Colorado Springs	P.C.	5	5	0	0	.000	6	3	1	0.00	0
2004	Colorado e	N.L.	47	44 2/3	2	4	.333	48	19	46	5.64	0
2005	Colorado	N.L.	78	74 1/3	2	5	.286	91	34	59	2.91	31
2006	Colorado	N.L.	66	65 1/3	3	4	.429	73	26	50	3.44	30
2007	Asheville	So.Atl.	1	1	0	0	.000	2	0	0	0.00	0
2007	Colorado Springs	P.C.	2	2	0	0	.000	2	0	2	0.00	0
2007	Colorado f	N.L.	64	61 1/3	3	5	.375	56	23	46	3.08	20
Major League Totals	7 Yrs.		371	359 1/3	16	22	.421	398	157	296	3.53	85
Division Series												
2007 Colorado	N.L.		3	2 1/3	1	0	1.000	4	3	1	0.00	0
Championship Series												
2007 Colorado	N.L.		4	3 2/3	0	0	.000	6	0	7	7.36	0
World Series Record												
2007 Colorado	N.L.		3	3 2/3	0	0	.000	1	2	6	9.82	0

a On disabled list from April 2 to 20, 1998.
b On disabled list from June 9 to August 22, 1999.

c On disabled list from August 26 to September 29, 2001.
d Traded to Colorado Rockies with pitcher Dennis Stark and pitcher Jose Paniagua for infielder Jeff Cirillo, December 15, 2001.
e On disabled list from June 7 to August 15, 2004.
f On disabled list from July 4 to August 14, 2007.

FULTZ, RICHARD AARON (AARON)
Born, Memphis, Tennessee, September 4, 1973.
Bats Left. Throws Left. Height, 6 feet. Weight, 210 pounds.

Year	Club	Lea	G	IP	W	L	Pct	SO	BB	H	ERA	SAVES
1992 Giants	Arizona		14	67²/₃	3	2	.600	72	33	51	2.13	0
1993 Clinton	Midwest		26	148	14	8	.636	144	64	132	3.41	0
1993 Ft. Wayne a	Midwest		1	4	0	0	.000	3	0	10	9.00	0
1994 Ft. Myers	Fla.St.		28	168¹/₃	9	10	.474	132	60	193	4.33	0
1995 New Britain	Eastern		3	15	0	2	.000	12	9	11	6.60	0
1995 Fort Myers	Fla.St.		21	122	3	6	.333	127	41	115	3.25	0
1996 San Jose b	California		36	104²/₃	9	5	.643	103	54	101	3.96	1
1997 Shreveport	Texas		49	70	6	3	.667	60	19	65	2.83	1
1998 Shreveport	Texas		54	62	5	7	.417	61	29	58	3.77	15
1998 Fresno c	P.C.		10	16	0	0	.000	13	2	22	5.06	0
1999 Fresno	P.C.		37	137¹/₃	9	8	.529	151	51	141	4.98	0
2000 San Francisco	N.L.		58	69¹/₃	5	2	.714	62	28	67	4.67	1
2001 San Francisco	N.L.		66	71	3	1	.750	67	21	70	4.56	1
2002 Fresno	P.C.		17	22²/₃	1	3	.250	22	11	18	3.18	3
2002 San Francisco d	N.L.		43	41¹/₃	2	2	.500	31	19	47	4.79	0
2003 Frisco	Texas		1	1	0	0	.000	0	0	2	9.00	0
2003 Oklahoma	P.C.		1	1	0	0	.000	2	1	2	27.00	0
2003 Texas e-f	A.L.		64	67¹/₃	1	3	.250	53	27	75	5.21	0
2004 Rochester	Int.		7	8¹/₃	0	0	.000	5	5	6	0.00	0
2004 Minnesota g	A.L.		55	50	3	3	.500	37	23	50	5.04	1
2005 Philadelphia	N.L.		62	72¹/₃	4	0	1.000	54	23	47	2.24	0
2006 Philadelphia h	N.L.		66	71¹/₃	3	1	.750	62	28	80	4.54	0
2007 Lake County	So.Atl.		1	1	0	0	.000	1	0	0	0.00	0
2007 Akron	Eastern		1	1	0	0	.000	1	0	0	0.00	0
2007 Cleveland i	A.L.		49	37	4	3	.571	28	18	31	2.92	0
Major League Totals	8 Yrs.		463	479²/₃	25	15	.625	394	187	467	4.26	3
Division Series												
2000 San Francisco	N.L.		1	1¹/₃	0	1	.000	0	0	3	6.75	0
2002 San Francisco	N.L.		2	0	0	0	.000	0	0	2	INF	0
2007 Cleveland	A.L.		1	1	0	0	.000	1	1	2	0.00	0
Division Series Totals			4	2¹/₃	0	1	.000	1	1	7	7.71	0
Championship Series												
2002 San Francisco	N.L.		1	0¹/₃	0	0	.000	0	0	0	0.00	0
2007 Cleveland	A.L.		1	0	0	0	.000	0	2	0	INF	0
Championship Series Totals			2	0¹/₃	0	0	.000	0	2	0	0.00	0
World Series Record												
2002 San Francisco	N.L.		2	2¹/₃	0	0	.000	0	1	4	3.86	0

a Traded by San Francisco Giants to Minnesota Twins with infielder Andres Duncan and pitcher Greg Brummett for pitcher Jim Deshaies, August 28, 1993.
b Released by Minnesota Twins, April 1, 1996. Signed with San Francisco Giants organization, April 4, 1996.
c Filed for free agency, October 16, 1998, re-signed with San Francisco Giants organization, October 23, 1998.
d Not offered contract, December 20, 2002. Signed with Texas Rangers, December 31, 2002.
e On disabled list from June 23 to July 11, 2003.
f Filed for free agency, October 4, 2003. Signed with Minnesota Twins organization, January 8, 2004.
g Claimed on waivers by Philadelphia Phillies, October 15, 2004.
h Filed for free agency, October 28, 2006. Signed with Cleveland Indians, December 2, 2006.
i On disabled list from June 24 to August 1, 2007.

GABBARD, KASON RONALD
Born, Oxford, Ohio, April 8, 1982.
Bats Left. Throws Left. Height, 6 feet, 3 inches. Weight, 205 pounds.

Year	Club	Lea	G	IP	W	L	Pct	SO	BB	H	ERA	SAVES
2001 Red Sox	Gulf Coast		6	14¹/₃	0	1	.000	17	9	11	5.65	0
2002 Augusta	So.Atl.		7	38	0	4	.000	31	7	31	1.89	0
2003 Sarasota	Fla.St.		2	7	0	1	.000	4	3	13	10.29	0
2004 Portland	Eastern		14	53	3	6	.333	35	26	61	6.28	0
2004 Sarasota	Fla.St.		10	43¹/₃	3	2	.600	30	16	43	2.70	1

Year	Club	Lea	G	IP	W	L	Pct	SO	BB	H	ERA	SAVES
2005	Portland	Eastern	27	132$\frac{2}{3}$	9	11	.450	96	65	128	4.61	0
2006	Portland	Eastern	13	73$\frac{2}{3}$	9	2	.818	68	25	51	2.57	0
2006	Pawtucket	Int.	9	51$\frac{2}{3}$	1	7	.125	48	26	51	5.23	0
2006	Boston	A.L.	7	25$\frac{2}{3}$	1	3	.250	15	16	24	3.51	0
2007	Pawtucket	Int.	14	75	7	2	.778	64	25	66	3.24	0
2007	Boston-Texas a	A.L.	15	81$\frac{1}{3}$	6	1	.857	55	41	68	4.65	0
Major League Totals		2 Yrs.	22	107	7	4	.636	70	57	92	4.37	0

a Traded to Texas Rangers with outfielder David Murphy and outfielder Engle Beltre for pitcher Eric Gagne, July 31, 2007.

GAGNE, ERIC SERGE

Born, Montreal, Quebec, Canada, January 7, 1976.
Bats Right. Throws Right. Height, 6 feet, 2 inches. Weight, 245 pounds.

Year	Club	Lea	G	IP	W	L	Pct	SO	BB	H	ERA	SAVES
1996	Savannah	So.Atl.	23	115$\frac{1}{3}$	7	6	.538	131	43	94	3.28	0
1997						INJURED—Did Not Play						
1998	Vero Beach	Fla.St.	25	139$\frac{2}{3}$	9	7	.563	144	48	118	3.74	0
1999	San Antonio	Texas	26	167$\frac{2}{3}$	12	4	.750	185	64	122	2.63	0
1999	Los Angeles	N.L.	5	30	1	1	.500	30	15	18	2.10	0
2000	Albuquerque	P.C.	9	55$\frac{2}{3}$	5	1	.833	59	15	56	3.88	0
2000	Los Angeles	N.L.	20	101$\frac{1}{3}$	4	6	.400	79	60	106	5.15	0
2001	Las Vegas	P.C.	4	23$\frac{2}{3}$	3	0	1.000	31	8	15	1.52	0
2001	Los Angeles	N.L.	33	151$\frac{2}{3}$	6	7	.462	130	46	144	4.75	0
2002	Los Angeles	N.L.	77	82$\frac{1}{3}$	4	1	.800	114	16	55	1.97	52
2003	Los Angeles a	N.L.	77	82$\frac{1}{3}$	2	3	.400	137	20	37	1.20	*55
2004	Los Angeles	N.L.	70	82$\frac{1}{3}$	7	3	.700	114	22	53	2.19	45
2005	Las Vegas b	P.C.	3	4	0	0	.000	7	0	0	0.00	0
2005	Los Angeles b	N.L.	14	13$\frac{1}{3}$	1	0	1.000	22	3	10	2.70	8
2006	Las Vegas	P.C.	2	2	0	0	.000	3	0	1	0.00	2
2006	Los Angeles c-d	N.L.	2	2	0	0	.000	3	1	0	0.00	1
2007	Frisco	Texas	3	2$\frac{2}{3}$	0	1	.000	3	1	2	3.38	0
2007	Texas-Boston e-f-g	A.L.	54	52	4	2	.667	51	21	49	3.81	16
Major League Totals		9 Yrs.	352	597$\frac{1}{3}$	29	23	.558	680	204	472	3.31	177
Division Series												
2004	Los Angeles	N.L.	2	3	0	0	.000	3	1	1	0.00	0
2007	Boston	A.L.	1	1	0	0	.000	1	0	1	9.00	0
Division Series Totals			3	4	0	0	.000	4	1	2	2.25	0
Championship Series												
2007	Boston	A.L.	3	2$\frac{1}{3}$	0	1	.000	4	2	3	7.71	0
World Series Record												
2007	Boston	A.L.	1	1	0	0	.000	1	0	0	0.00	0

a Selected Cy Young Award Winner in National League for 2003.
b On disabled list from April 1 to May 14 and June 13 to November 16, 2005.
c On disabled list from April 1 to May 30 and June 7 to October 26, 2006.
d Filed for free agency, October 31, 2006. Signed with Texas Rangers, December 12, 2006.
e On disabled list from March 28 to April 13 and April 23 to May 8, 2007.
f Traded to Boston Red Sox for pitcher Kason Gabbard, outfielder David Murphy and outfielder Engle Beltre, July 31, 2007.
g Filed for free agency, October 31, 2007. Signed with Milwaukee Brewers, December 10, 2007.

GALLARDO, YOVANI

Born, La Piedad, Mexico, February 27, 1986.
Bats Right. Throws Right. Height, 6 feet, 1 inch. Weight, 210 pounds.

Year	Club	Lea	G	IP	W	L	Pct	SO	BB	H	ERA	SAVES
2004	Brewers	Arizona	6	19$\frac{1}{3}$	0	0	.000	23	4	14	0.47	0
2004	Beloit	Midwest	2	7$\frac{1}{3}$	0	1	.000	8	4	12	12.27	0
2005	West Tenn	So.Atl.	26	121$\frac{1}{3}$	8	3	.727	110	51	100	2.74	1
2006	Brevard County	Fla.St.	13	77$\frac{2}{3}$	6	3	.667	103	23	54	2.09	0
2006	Huntsville	Southern	13	77$\frac{1}{3}$	5	2	.714	85	28	50	1.63	0
2007	Nashville	P.C.	13	77$\frac{2}{3}$	8	3	.727	110	28	53	2.90	0
2007	Milwaukee	N.L.	20	110$\frac{1}{3}$	9	5	.643	101	37	103	3.67	0

GARCIA, FREDDY ANTONIO
Born, Caracas, Venezuela, June 10, 1975.
Bats Right. Throws Right. Height, 6 feet, 4 inches. Weight, 250 pounds.

Year	Club	Lea	G	IP	W	L	Pct	SO	BB	H	ERA	SAVES
1994	Hou/Mil	Dominican	16	85	4	6	.400	68	38	80	5.29	0
1995	Astros	Gulf Coast	11	58 1/3	6	3	.667	58	14	60	4.47	0
1996	Quad City	Midwest	13	60 2/3	5	4	.556	57	57	57	3.12	0
1997	Kissimmee	Fla.St.	27	179	10	8	.556	131	49	165	2.56	0
1998	Jackson	Texas	19	119 1/3	6	7	.462	115	58	94	3.24	0
1998	New Orleans	P.C.	2	14 1/3	1	0	1.000	13	1	14	3.14	0
1998	Tacoma a	P.C.	5	32 2/3	3	1	.750	30	13	30	3.86	0
1999	Seattle	A.L.	33	201 1/3	17	8	.680	170	90	205	4.07	0
2000	Everett	Northwest	2	10	0	0	.000	15	2	11	4.50	0
2000	Tacoma	P.C.	1	7	1	0	1.000	11	2	5	2.57	0
2000	Seattle b	A.L.	21	124 1/3	9	5	.643	79	64	112	3.91	0
2001	Seattle	A.L.	34	*238 2/3	18	6	.750	163	69	199	*3.05	0
2002	Seattle	A.L.	34	223 2/3	16	10	.615	181	63	227	4.39	0
2003	Seattle	A.L.	33	201 1/3	12	14	.462	144	71	196	4.51	0
2004	Seattle-Chicago c	A.L.	31	210	13	11	.542	184	64	192	3.81	0
2005	Chicago	A.L.	33	228	14	8	.636	146	60	225	3.87	0
2006	Chicago d-e	A.L.	33	216 1/3	17	9	.654	135	48	228	4.53	0
2007	Phillies	Gulf Coast	1	2	0	0	.000	2	0	2	4.50	0
2007	Clearwater	Fla.St.	2	6 1/3	0	0	.000	8	1	5	0.00	0
2007	Philadelphia f	N.L.	11	58	1	5	.167	50	19	74	5.90	0
Major League Totals	9 Yrs.		263	1701 2/3	117	76	.606	1252	548	1658	4.07	0

Division Series

Year	Club	Lea	G	IP	W	L	Pct	SO	BB	H	ERA	SAVES
2000	Seattle	A.L.	1	3 1/3	0	0	.000	2	3	6	10.80	0
2001	Seattle	A.L.	2	11 2/3	1	1	.500	13	3	13	3.86	0
2005	Chicago	A.L.	1	5	1	0	1.000	1	4	5	5.40	0
Division Series Totals			4	20	2	1	.667	16	10	24	5.40	0

Championship Series

Year	Club	Lea	G	IP	W	L	Pct	SO	BB	H	ERA	SAVES
2000	Seattle	A.L.	2	11 2/3	2	0	1.000	11	4	10	1.54	0
2001	Seattle	A.L.	1	7 1/3	0	1	.000	6	4	7	3.68	0
2005	Chicago	A.L.	1	9	1	0	1.000	5	1	6	2.00	0
Championship Series Totals			4	28	3	1	.750	22	9	23	2.25	0

World Series Record

Year	Club	Lea	G	IP	W	L	Pct	SO	BB	H	ERA	SAVES
2005	Chicago	A.L.	1	7	1	0	1.000	7	3	4	0.00	0

a Traded by Houston Astros to Seattle Mariners with infielder Carlos Guillen and a player to be named later for pitcher
   Randy Johnson, July 31, 1998. Mariners received pitcher John Halama to complete trade, October 1, 1998.
b On disabled list from April 22 to July 6, 2000.
c Traded to Chicago White Sox with catcher Ben Davis and cash for catcher Miguel Olivo, outfielder Jeremy Reed
   and infielder Michael Morse, June 27, 2004.
d Traded to Philadelphia Phillies for pitcher Gavin Floyd and player to be named later, December 6, 2006.
e Chicago White Sox received pitcher Gio Gonzalez to complete trade, December 7, 2006.
f On disabled list from March 23 to April 16 and June 9 to October 31, 2007.

GARDNER, TERRENCE LEE (LEE)
Born, Hartland, Michigan, January 16, 1975.
Bats Right. Throws Right. Height, 6 feet. Weight, 220 pounds.

Year	Club	Lea	G	IP	W	L	Pct	SO	BB	H	ERA	SAVES
1998	St. Pete	Fla.St.	3	4	0	0	.000	2	1	3	0.00	0
1998	Chston-SC	So.Atl.	28	35 2/3	0	3	.000	55	4	38	4.04	3
1999	St. Petersburg	Fla.St.	20	23	2	0	1.000	22	5	20	1.96	7
1999	Orlando	Southern	1	2	0	0	.000	1	1	3	9.00	0
2000	Durham	Int.	21	18 2/3	1	0	1.000	8	9	12	3.38	5
2000	Orlando	Southern	36	45	3	2	.600	48	14	34	3.40	12
2001	Durham	Int.	56	76	5	2	.714	55	23	76	2.72	2
2001	Orlando	Southern	1	1 2/3	0	0	.000	0	0	0	0.00	0
2002	Durham	Int.	45	49 2/3	2	1	.667	52	15	50	2.36	25
2002	Tampa Bay	A.L.	12	13 1/3	1	1	.500	8	8	12	4.05	0
2003	Durham a	Int.	57	62 2/3	3	7	.300	56	14	68	3.73	30
2004	Fresno	P.C.	57	70 2/3	7	4	.636	42	22	79	4.46	1
2005	Tampa Bay	A.L.	7	7 1/3	0	0	.000	4	2	12	4.91	0
2005	Durham b	Int.	48	52	4	3	.571	35	15	56	3.29	15
2006	Toledo c	Int.	58	61 2/3	5	5	.500	45	17	46	2.92	30
2007	Albuquerque	P.C.	9	13 1/3	0	2	.000	9	2	10	4.72	1
2007	Florida d	N.L.	62	74 1/3	3	4	.429	52	18	72	1.94	2
Major League Totals	3 Yrs.		79	95	4	5	.444	64	28	96	2.46	2

238

a Filed for free agency, September 30, 2003. Signed with San Francisco Giants organization, March 19, 2004.
b Filed for free agency, October 15, 2004. Signed with Tampa Bay Devil Rays organization, February 1, 2005.
c Filed for free agency, October 3, 2005. Signed with Detroit Tigers organization, January 20, 2006.
d Filed for free agency, October 15, 2006. Signed with Florida Marlins organization, January 4, 2007.

GARLAND, JON STEVEN

Born, Valencia, California, September 27, 1979.
Bats Right. Throws Right. Height, 6 feet, 6 inches. Weight, 215 pounds.

Year	Club	Lea	G	IP	W	L	Pct	SO	BB	H	ERA	SAVES
1997 Cubs	Arizona		10	40	3	2	.600	39	10	37	2.70	0
1998 Rockford	Midwest		19	107⅓	4	7	.364	70	45	124	5.03	0
1998 Hickory a	So.Atl.		5	26⅔	1	4	.200	19	13	36	5.40	0
1999 Winston-Salem	Carolina		19	119	5	7	.417	84	39	109	3.33	0
1999 Birmingham	Southern		7	39	3	1	.750	27	18	39	4.38	0
2000 Charlotte	Int.		16	103⅔	9	2	.818	63	32	99	2.26	0
2000 Birmingham	Southern		1	6	0	0	.000	10	1	4	0.00	0
2000 Chicago b	A.L.		15	69⅔	4	8	.333	42	40	82	6.46	0
2001 Charlotte	Int.		5	33	0	3	.000	26	11	31	2.73	0
2001 Chicago	A.L.		35	117	6	7	.462	61	55	123	3.69	1
2002 Chicago	A.L.		33	192⅔	12	12	.500	112	83	188	4.58	0
2003 Chicago	A.L.		32	191⅔	12	13	.480	108	74	188	4.51	0
2004 Chicago	A.L.		34	217	12	11	.522	113	76	223	4.89	0
2005 Chicago	A.L.		32	221	10	10	.643	115	47	212	3.50	0
2006 Chicago	A.L.		33	211⅓	18	7	.720	112	41	*247	4.51	0
2007 Chicago c	A.L.		32	208⅓	10	13	.435	98	57	219	4.23	0
Major League Totals	8 Yrs.		246	1428⅔	92	81	.532	761	473	1482	4.41	1
Championship Series												
2005 Chicago	A.L.		1	9	1	0	1.000	7	1	4	2.00	0
World Series Record												
2005 Chicago	A.L.		1	7	0	0	.000	4	2	7	2.57	0

a Traded by Chicago Cubs to Chicago White Sox for pitcher Matt Karcher, July 29, 1998.
b On disabled list from August 19 to September 2, 2000.
c Traded to Los Angeles Angels for infielder Orlando Cabrera, November 19, 2007.

GARZA, MATTHEW SCOTT (MATT)

Born, Selma, California, November 11, 1983.
Bats Right. Throws Right. Height, 6 feet, 4 inches. Weight, 205 pounds.

Year	Club	Lea	G	IP	W	L	Pct	SO	BB	H	ERA	SAVES
2005 Elizabethton	Appal.		4	19⅔	1	1	.500	25	6	14	3.66	0
2006 Fort Myers	Fla.St.		8	44⅓	5	1	.833	53	11	27	1.42	0
2006 New Britain	Eastern		10	57⅓	6	2	.750	68	14	40	2.51	0
2006 Rochester	Int.		5	34	3	1	.750	33	7	20	1.85	0
2006 Minnesota	A.L.		10	50	3	6	.333	38	23	62	5.76	0
2007 Rochester	Int.		16	92	4	6	.400	95	31	93	3.63	0
2007 Minnesota a	A.L.		16	83	5	7	.417	67	32	96	3.69	0
Major League Totals	2 Yrs.		26	133	8	13	.381	105	55	158	4.47	0

a Traded to Tampa Bay Devil Rays with infielder Jason Bartlett and pitcher Eduardo Morlan for infielder Brendan Harris, outfielder Jason Pridie and outfielder Delmon Young, November 28, 2007.

GAUDIN, CHAD EDWARD

Born, Metairie, Louisiana, March 24, 1983.
Bats Right. Throws Right. Height, 5 feet, 11 inches. Weight, 165 pounds.

Year	Club	Lea	G	IP	W	L	Pct	SO	BB	H	ERA	SAVES
2002 Charleston-SC	So.Atl.		26	119⅓	4	6	.400	106	37	106	2.26	1
2003 Bakersfield	Calif.		14	80⅓	5	3	.625	70	23	63	2.13	0
2003 Orlando	Southern		3	19	2	0	1.000	23	3	8	0.47	0
2003 Tampa Bay	A.L.		15	40	2	0	1.000	23	16	37	3.60	0
2004 Tampa Bay	A.L.		26	42⅔	1	2	.333	30	16	59	4.85	0
2004 Durham a	Int.		17	47⅔	1	3	.250	52	17	48	4.72	2
2005 Toronto	A.L.		5	13	1	3	.250	12	6	31	13.15	0
2005 Syracuse b-c	Int.		23	150⅓	9	8	.529	113	35	140	3.35	0
2006 Sacramento	P.C.		4	24⅓	3	0	1.000	26	8	14	0.37	0
2006 Oakland	A.L.		55	64	4	2	.667	36	42	51	3.09	2
2007 Oakland	A.L.		34	199⅓	11	13	.458	154	100	205	4.42	0
Major League Totals	5 Yrs.		135	359	19	20	.487	255	180	383	4.46	2

Year	Club	Lea	G	IP	W	L	Pct	SO	BB	H	ERA	SAVES
Championship Series												
2006 Oakland . . . . A.L.			3	3¹/₃	0	0	.000	1	3	2	0.00	0

a Traded to Toronto Blue Jays for catcher Kevin Cash, December 13, 2004.
b Traded to Oakland Athletics for player to be named later, December 5, 2005.
c Toronto Blue Jays received outfielder Dustin Majewski to complete trade, December 8, 2005.

GEARY, GEOFFREY MICHAEL (GEOFF)
Born, Buffalo, New York, August 26, 1976.
Bats Right. Throws Right. Height, 6 feet. Weight, 175 pounds.

Year	Club	Lea	G	IP	W	L	Pct	SO	BB	H	ERA	SAVES
1998 Batavia	N.Y.-Penn.	16	95¹/₃	9	1	.900	101	14	78	1.60	0	
1999 Clearwater	Fla.St.	24	139	10	5	.667	77	31	175	3.95	0	
2000 Reading	Eastern	22	129¹/₃	7	6	.538	112	22	141	4.11	0	
2001 Reading	Eastern	29	112¹/₃	9	7	.563	88	21	101	3.61	2	
2001 Scranton-W.B.	Int.	7	22	0	3	.000	21	6	35	6.95	0	
2002 Scranton-W.B.	Int.	38	101	4	2	.667	82	32	108	3.03	1	
2003 Scranton/W.B.	Int.	46	87²/₃	9	4	.692	80	13	73	2.16	5	
2003 Philadelphia	N.L.	5	6	0	0	.000	3	3	8	4.50	0	
2004 Scranton/W.B.	Int.	21	23¹/₃	1	2	.333	23	13	20	2.31	10	
2004 Philadelphia a	N.L.	33	44²/₃	1	0	1.000	30	16	52	5.44	0	
2005 Reading	Eastern	1	2	0	0	.000	2	0	0	0.00	0	
2005 Scranton/W.B.	Int.	10	16²/₃	1	2	.333	14	2	15	2.70	1	
2005 Philadelphia b	N.L.	40	58	2	1	.667	42	21	54	3.72	0	
2006 Philadelphia	N.L.	81	91¹/₃	7	1	.875	60	20	103	2.96	1	
2007 Ottawa	Int.	14	25	2	1	.667	21	1	28	2.52	0	
2007 Philadelphia c	N.L.	57	67¹/₃	3	2	.600	38	25	72	4.41	0	
Major League Totals . . . . 5 Yrs.		216	267¹/₃	13	4	.765	173	85	289	3.94	1	

a Filed for free agency, December 21, 2004, re-signed with Philadelphia Phillies organization, December 21, 2004.
b On disabled list from July 9 to July 24, 2005.
c Traded to Houston Astros with outfielder Michael Bourn and infielder Mike Costanzo for infielder Eric Bruntlett and pitcher Brad Lidge, November 12, 2007.

GERMANO, JUSTIN WILLIAM
Born, Pasadena, California, August 6, 1982.
Bats Right. Throws Right. Height, 6 feet, 1 inch. Weight, 205 pounds.

Year	Club	Lea	G	IP	W	L	Pct	SO	BB	H	ERA	SAVES
2000 Padres	Arizona	17	66²/₃	5	5	.500	67	9	65	4.59	1	
2001 Fort Wayne	Midwest	13	65	2	6	.250	55	16	80	4.98	0	
2001 Eugene	Northwest	13	80	6	5	.545	74	11	77	3.49	0	
2002 Lake Elsinore	Calif.	3	19	2	0	1.000	18	5	12	0.95	0	
2002 Fort Wayne	Midwest	24	155²/₃	12	5	.706	119	19	166	3.18	0	
2003 Lake Elsinore	Calif.	19	110²/₃	9	5	.643	78	25	127	4.23	0	
2003 Mobile	Southern	9	58	2	5	.286	44	13	60	4.34	0	
2004 Mobile	Southern	5	32¹/₃	2	1	.667	20	7	31	2.51	0	
2004 Portland	P.C.	20	122²/₃	9	5	.643	98	25	113	3.38	0	
2004 San Diego	N.L.	7	21¹/₃	1	2	.333	16	14	31	8.86	0	
2005 Louisville	Int.	8	49¹/₃	3	2	.600	38	5	62	4.01	0	
2005 Portland a	P.C.	19	112	7	6	.538	100	32	111	3.70	0	
2006 Louisville	Int.	19	117	8	6	.571	67	22	124	3.69	0	
2006 Cincinnati	N.L.	2	6²/₃	0	0	.000	8	3	8	5.40	0	
2006 Scranton-WB b	Int.	6	38¹/₃	2	0	1.000	25	2	40	2.82	0	
2007 Portland	P.C.	5	32	4	0	1.000	20	3	23	1.69	0	
2007 San Diego c	N.L.	26	133¹/₃	7	10	.412	78	40	133	4.46	0	
Major League Totals . . . . 3 Yrs.		35	161¹/₃	8	13	.381	102	57	172	5.08	0	

a Traded to Cincinnati Reds with pitcher Travis Chick for infielder Joe Randa, July 23, 2005.
b Traded to Philadelphia Phillies for pitcher Rheal Cormier, July 31, 2006.
c Claimed on waivers by San Diego Padres, March 19, 2007.

GLAVINE, THOMAS MICHAEL (TOM)
Born, Concord, Massachusetts, March 25, 1966.
Bats Left. Throws Left. Height, 6 feet. Weight, 185 pounds.

Year	Club	Lea	G	IP	W	L	Pct	SO	BB	H	ERA	SAVES
1984 Bradenton Braves	Gulf C.	8	32¹/₃	2	3	.400	34	13	29	3.34	0
1985 Sumter	So. Atl.	26	168²/₃	9	6	.600	174	73	114	*2.35	0

Year	Club	Lea	G	IP	W	L	Pct	SO	BB	H	ERA	SAVES
1986	Greenville........	Southern	22	145⅓	11	6	.647	114	70	129	3.41	0
1986	Richmond	.Int.	7	40	1	5	.167	12	27	40	5.63	0
1987	Richmond	.Int.	22	150⅓	6	12	.333	91	56	142	3.35	0
1987	Atlanta	N.L.	9	50⅓	2	4	.333	20	33	55	5.54	0
1988	Atlanta	N.L.	34	195⅓	7	*17	.292	84	63	201	4.56	0
1989	Atlanta	N.L.	29	186	14	8	.636	90	40	172	3.68	0
1990	Atlanta a.............	N.L.	33	214⅓	10	12	.455	129	78	232	4.28	0
1991	Atlanta b-c	N.L.	34	246⅔	*20	11	.645	192	69	201	2.55	0
1992	Atlanta d.............	N.L.	33	225	*20	8	.714	129	70	197	2.76	0
1993	Atlanta	N.L.	36	239⅓	*22	6	.786	120	90	236	3.20	0
1994	Atlanta e.............	N.L.	25	165⅓	13	9	.591	140	70	173	3.97	0
1995	Atlanta	N.L.	29	198⅔	16	7	.696	127	66	182	3.08	0
1996	Atlanta	N.L.	36	235⅓	15	10	.600	181	85	222	2.98	0
1997	Atlanta	N.L.	33	240	14	7	.667	152	79	197	2.96	0
1998	Atlanta f	N.L.	33	229⅓	*20	6	.769	157	74	202	2.47	0
1999	Atlanta	N.L.	35	234	14	11	.560	138	83	*259	4.12	0
2000	Atlanta	N.L.	35	241	*21	9	.700	152	65	222	3.40	0
2001	Atlanta	N.L.	35	219⅓	16	7	.696	116	97	213	3.57	0
2002	Atlanta g.............	N.L.	36	224⅔	18	11	.621	127	78	210	2.96	0
2003	New York	N.L.	32	183⅓	9	14	.391	82	66	205	4.52	0
2004	New York	N.L.	33	212⅓	11	14	.440	109	70	204	3.60	0
2005	New York	N.L.	33	211⅓	13	13	.500	105	61	227	3.53	0
2006	New York h..........	N.L.	32	198	15	7	.682	131	62	202	3.82	0
2007	New York I...........	N.L.	34	200⅓	13	8	.619	89	64	219	4.45	0
Major League Totals ....21 Yrs.			669	4350	303	199	.604	2570	1463	4231	3.51	0

Division Series

Year	Club	Lea	G	IP	W	L	Pct	SO	BB	H	ERA	SAVES
1995	Atlanta	N.L.	1	7	0	0	.000	3	1	5	2.57	0
1996	Atlanta	N.L.	1	6⅔	1	0	1.000	7	3	5	1.35	0
1997	Atlanta	N.L.	1	6	1	0	1.000	4	5	5	4.50	0
1998	Atlanta	N.L.	1	7	0	0	.000	8	1	3	1.29	0
1999	Atlanta	N.L.	1	6	0	0	.000	6	3	5	3.00	0
2000	Atlanta	N.L.	1	2⅓	0	1	.000	2	1	6	27.00	0
2001	Atlanta	N.L.	1	8	1	0	1.000	3	2	6	0.00	0
2002	Atlanta	N.L.	2	7⅔	0	2	.000	4	7	17	15.26	0
2006	New York	N.L.	1	6	1	0	1.000	2	2	4	0.00	0
Division Series Totals			10	56⅔	4	3	.571	39	25	56	4.61	0

Championship Series

Year	Club	Lea	G	IP	W	L	Pct	SO	BB	H	ERA	SAVES
1991	Atlanta	N.L.	2	14	0	2	.000	11	6	12	3.21	0
1992	Atlanta	N.L.	2	7⅓	0	2	.000	2	13	12.27		0
1993	Atlanta	N.L.	1	7	1	0	1.000	5	0	6	2.57	0
1995	Atlanta	N.L.	1	7	0	0	.000	5	2	7	1.29	0
1996	Atlanta	N.L.	2	13	1	1	.500	9	0	10	2.08	0
1997	Atlanta	N.L.	2	13⅓	1	1	.500	9	11	13	5.40	0
1998	Atlanta	N.L.	2	11⅓	0	2	.000	8	9	13	2.31	0
1999	Atlanta	N.L.	1	7	1	0	1.000	8	1	7	0.00	0
2001	Atlanta	N.L.	2	12	1	1	.500	5	5	10	1.50	0
2006	New York	N.L.	2	11	1	1	.500	4	5	11	2.45	0
Championship Series Totals			17	103⅓	6	10	.375	66	42	102	3.22	0

World Series Record

Year	Club	Lea	G	IP	W	L	Pct	SO	BB	H	ERA	SAVES
1991	Atlanta	N.L.	2	13⅓	1	1	.500	8	7	8	2.70	0
1992	Atlanta	N.L.	2	17	1	1	.500	8	4	10	1.59	0
1995	Atlanta	N.L.	2	14	2	0	1.000	11	6	4	1.29	0
1996	Atlanta	N.L.	1	7	0	1	.000	8	3	4	1.29	0
1999	Atlanta	N.L.	1	7	0	0	.000	3	0	7	5.14	0
World Series Totals.............			8	58⅓	4	3	.571	38	20	33	2.16	0

a Appeared in one additional game as pinch runner.
b Appeared in one additional game as pinch hitter and one additional game as pinch runner.
c Selected Cy Young Award winner in National League for 1991.
d Appeared in two additional games as pinch hitter.
e Appeared in one additional game as pinch hitter.
f Selected Cy Young Award Winner in National League for 1998.
g Filed for free agency, October 28, 2002. Signed with New York Mets, December 5, 2002.
h Filed for free agency, November 9, 2006, re-signed with New York Mets, December 1, 2006.
i Filed for free agency, October 31, 2007. Signed with Atlanta Braves, November 19, 2007.

GLOVER, JOHN GARY (GARY)

Born, Cleveland, Ohio, December 3, 1976.
Bats Right. Throws Right. Height, 6 feet, 5 inches. Weight, 220 pounds.

Year	Club	Lea	G	IP	W	L	Pct	SO	BB	H	ERA	SAVES
1994	Blue Jays	Gulf Coast	2	1 1/3	0	0	.000	2	4	4	47.25	0
1995	Blue Jays	Gulf Coast	12	62 1/3	3	7	.300	46	26	62	4.91	0
1996	Medicine Hat	Pioneer	15	83 2/3	3	12	.200	54	29	119	7.75	0
1997	Hagerstown	So.Atl.	28	173 2/3	6	17	.261	155	58	165	3.73	0
1998	Knoxville	Southern	8	37 1/3	0	5	.000	14	28	41	6.75	0
1998	Dunedin	Fla.St.	19	109 1/3	7	6	.538	88	36	117	4.28	0
1999	Knoxville	Southern	13	86	8	2	.800	77	27	70	3.56	0
1999	Syracuse	Int.	14	76 1/3	4	6	.400	57	35	93	5.19	0
1999	Toronto	A.L.	1	1	0	0	.000	0	1	0	0.00	0
2000	Syracuse a	Int.	27	166 2/3	9	9	.500	119	62	181	5.02	0
2001	Charlotte	Int.	6	38 1/3	2	1	.667	29	5	21	1.88	0
2001	Chicago	A.L.	46	100 1/3	5	5	.500	63	32	98	4.93	0
2002	Chicago	A.L.	41	138 1/3	7	8	.467	70	52	136	5.20	1
2003	Chicago-Anaheim b-c	A.L.	42	62 2/3	2	0	1.000	37	22	77	4.74	0
2004	Iowa	P.C.	20	30 2/3	3	2	.600	18	14	43	7.92	0
2004	Rochester	Int.	5	16	0	1	.000	8	5	27	8.44	0
2004	Indianapolis	Int.	8	40 2/3	3	3	.500	18	11	47	3.98	0
2004	Milwaukee d-e	N.L.	4	18	2	1	.667	8	8	18	3.50	0
2005	Nashville	P.C.	17	92	6	4	.600	75	29	91	3.03	1
2005	Milwauke f	N.L.	15	64 2/3	5	4	.556	58	20	74	5.57	0
2006	Yomiuri g	Japan Cent.	20	96	5	7	.417	63	23	125	4.97	0
2007	Tampa Bay	A.L.	67	77 1/3	6	5	.545	51	27	87	4.89	2
Major League Totals		7 Yrs.	216	462 1/3	27	23	.540	287	162	490	5.00	3

a Traded to Chicago White Sox for pitcher Scott Eyre, November 7, 2000.
b Traded to Anaheim Angels with pitcher Scott Dunn and pitcher Tim Bittner for pitcher Scott Schoeneweis and pitcher Doug Nickle, July 29, 2003.
c Filed for free agency October 15, 2003. Signed with Chicago Cubs organization, December 18, 2003.
d Released by Chicago Cubs, June 5, 2004. Signed with Minnesota Twins organization, June 7, 2004.
e Released by Minnesota Twins, July 1, 2004. Signed with Milwaukee Brewers organization, July 15, 2004.
f Released by Milwaukee Brewers, November 22, 2005. Signed with Yomuri Giants, November 29, 2005.
g Signed with Tampa Bay Devil Rays organization, December 21, 2006.

GOBBLE, BILLY JAMES (JIMMY)

Born, Bristol, Tennessee, July 19, 1981.
Bats Left. Throws Left. Height, 6 feet, 3 inches. Weight, 205 pounds.

Year	Club	Lea	G	IP	W	L	Pct	SO	BB	H	ERA	SAVES
1999	Royals	Gulf Coast	4	6 2/3	0	0	.000	8	5	6	2.70	0
2000	Charleston-WV	So.Atl.	25	145	12	10	.545	115	34	144	3.66	0
2001	Wilmington	Carolina	27	162 1/3	10	6	.625	154	33	134	2.55	0
2002	Wichita	Texas	13	69 1/3	5	7	.417	52	19	71	3.38	0
2003	Wichita	Texas	22	132 2/3	12	8	.600	100	40	128	3.19	0
2003	Kansas City	A.L.	9	52 2/3	4	5	.444	31	15	56	4.61	0
2004	Omaha	P.C.	4	19 2/3	3	1	.750	15	7	25	4.58	0
2004	Kansas City	A.L.	25	148	9	8	.529	49	43	157	5.35	0
2005	Omaha	P.C.	12	58 1/3	2	7	.222	45	21	76	6.63	0
2005	Kansas City	A.L.	28	53 2/3	1	1	.500	38	30	64	5.70	0
2006	Kansas City	A.L.	60	84	4	6	.400	80	29	95	5.14	2
2007	Kansas City	A.L.	74	53 2/3	4	1	.800	50	23	56	3.02	1
Major League Totals		5 Yrs.	196	392	22	21	.512	248	140	428	4.94	3

GONZALEZ, ENRIQUE CESAR

Born, Ciudad Bolivar, Venezuela, August 6, 1982.
Bats Right. Throws Right. Height, 5 feet, 10 inches. Weight, 210 pounds.

Year	Club	Lea	G	IP	W	L	Pct	SO	BB	H	ERA	SAVES
2000	Diamondbacks	Arizona	11	17 2/3	1	0	1.000	17	12	16	1.53	1
2000	Tucson	P.C.	1	4	1	0	1.000	1	1	1	0.00	0
2001	South Bend	Midwest	26	146	4	12	.250	92	53	142	4.01	0
2002	Lancaster	Calif.	5	18 1/3	1	4	.200	11	14	34	12.27	0
2002	South Bend	Midwest	4	21 2/3	1	2	.333	20	9	23	3.74	0
2002	Yakima	Northwest	11	66	5	2	.714	57	23	53	2.45	0
2003	South Bend	Midwest	55	72	4	3	.571	63	29	58	2.13	3
2004	Lancaster	Calif.	42	142 1/3	13	6	.684	110	44	128	3.22	0
2005	Tennessee	Southern	27	161 1/3	11	8	.579	146	52	160	3.46	0
2006	Tucson	P.C.	10	60 1/3	4	3	.571	35	14	61	2.24	0

Year Club	Lea	G	IP	W	L	Pct	SO	BB	H	ERA	SAVES
2006 Arizona.............N.L.	22	106$\frac{1}{3}$	3	7	.300	66	34	114	5.67	0
2007 Tucson...............P.C.	27	153$\frac{2}{3}$	8	10	.444	118	61	186	5.15	0
2007 Arizona a............N.L.	32	102	8	4	.667	62	28	110	5.03	0
Major League Totals.......2 Yrs.	54	208$\frac{1}{3}$	11	11	.500	128	62	224	5.36	0

a Claimed on waivers by Washington Nationals, September 17, 2007.

GONZALEZ, MICHAEL VELA (MIKE)

Born, Corpus Christi, Texas, May 23, 1978.
Bats Right. Throws Left. Height, 6 feet, 2 inches. Weight, 220 pounds.

Year Club	Lea	G	IP	W	L	Pct	SO	BB	H	ERA	SAVES
1997 Pirates.........Gulf Coast	7	29	2	0	1.000	33	8	21	2.48	0
1997 Augusta............So.Atl.	4	19$\frac{1}{3}$	1	1	.500	22	8	11	1.86	0
1998 Lynchburg........Carolina	7	28$\frac{1}{3}$	0	3	.000	22	13	40	6.67	0
1998 Augusta............So.Atl.	11	50$\frac{2}{3}$	4	2	.667	72	26	43	2.84	0
1999 Lynchburg........Carolina	20	112	10	4	.714	119	63	98	4.02	0
1999 Altoona...........Eastern	7	26$\frac{2}{3}$	2	3	.400	31	19	34	8.10	0
2000 Pirates..........Gulf Coast	2	6	1	0	1.000	7	4	8	4.50	0
2000 Lynchburg........Carolina	12	56	4	3	.571	53	34	57	4.66	0
2001 Lynchburg........Carolina	14	30$\frac{2}{3}$	2	2	.500	32	7	28	2.93	0
2001 Altoona...........Eastern	14	87$\frac{1}{3}$	5	4	.556	66	36	81	3.71	0
2002 Altoona...........Eastern	16	85$\frac{1}{3}$	8	4	.667	82	47	77	3.80	0
2002 Pirates..........Gulf Coast	2	13$\frac{1}{3}$	2	0	1.000	14	3	5	0.00	0
2003 Lynchburg........Carolina	5	7	0	1	.000	9	5	7	5.14	0
2003 Altoona...........Eastern	5	7$\frac{1}{3}$	0	0	.000	10	2	4	1.23	1
2003 Nashville.............P.C.	7	10	0	0	.000	10	4	9	4.50	2
2003 Pawtucket............Int.	2	1$\frac{2}{3}$	0	0	.000	2	1	2	0.00	1
2003 Pittsburgh a-b.........N.L.	16	8$\frac{1}{3}$	0	1	.000	6	6	7	7.56	0
2004 Nashville.............P.C.	20	20	2	0	1.000	35	7	12	0.90	2
2004 Pittsburgh.............N.L.	47	43$\frac{1}{3}$	3	1	.750	55	6	32	1.25	1
2005 Indianapolis..........Int.	2	3$\frac{1}{3}$	0	0	.000	5	0	0	0.00	0
2005 Pittsburgh c..........N.L.	51	50	1	3	.250	58	31	35	2.70	3
2006 Pittsburgh d-e........N.L.	54	54	3	4	.429	64	31	42	2.17	24
2007 Atlanta f.............N.L.	18	17	2	0	1.000	13	8	15	1.59	2
Major League Totals.......5 Yrs.	186	172$\frac{2}{3}$	9	9	.500	196	82	131	2.29	30

a Traded to Boston Red Sox with pitcher Scott Sauerbeck for pitcher Brandon Lyon and pitcher Anastacio Martinez, July 22, 2003.

b Traded to Pittsburgh Pirates with infielder Freddy Sanchez and cash for pitcher Jeff Suppan, pitcher Brandon Lyon and pitcher Anastacio Martinez, July 31, 2003.

c On disabled list from June 23 to August 16, 2005.

d On disabled list from August 25 to October 3, 2006.

e Traded to Atlanta Braves with infielder Brent Lillibridge for infielder Adam LaRoche and outfielder Jamie Romak, January 17, 2007.

f On disabled list from May 16 to November 13, 2007.

GORDON, THOMAS (TOM)

Born, Sebring, Florida, November 18, 1967.
Bats Right. Throws Right. Height, 5 feet, 10 inches. Weight, 195 pounds.

Year Club	Lea	G	IP	W	L	Pct	SO	BB	H	ERA	SAVES
1986 Sarasota Royals....Gulf C.	9	44	3	1	.750	47	23	31	1.02	0
1986 Omaha..............A.A.	1	1$\frac{1}{3}$	0	0	.000	3	2	6	47.25	0
1987 Eugene.........Northwest	15	72$\frac{1}{3}$	*9	0	*1.000	91	47	48	2.86	1
1987 Fort Myers.........Fla. St.	3	13$\frac{2}{3}$	1	0	1.000	11	17	5	2.63	0
1988 Appleton..........Midwest	17	118	7	5	.583	*172	43	69	2.06	0
1988 Memphis.........Southern	6	47$\frac{1}{3}$	6	0	1.000	62	17	16	0.38	0
1988 Omaha..............A.A.	3	20$\frac{1}{3}$	3	0	1.000	29	15	11	1.33	0
1988 Kansas City...........A.L.	5	15$\frac{2}{3}$	0	2	.000	18	7	16	5.17	0
1989 Kansas City...........A.L.	49	163	17	9	.654	153	86	122	3.64	1
1990 Kansas City...........A.L.	32	195$\frac{1}{3}$	12	11	.522	175	99	192	3.73	0
1991 Kansas City...........A.L.	45	158	9	14	.391	167	87	129	3.87	1
1992 Kansas City...........A.L.	40	117$\frac{2}{3}$	6	10	.375	98	55	116	4.59	0
1993 Kansas City...........A.L.	48	155$\frac{2}{3}$	12	6	.667	143	77	125	3.58	1
1994 Kansas City a-b.......A.L.	24	155$\frac{1}{3}$	11	7	.611	126	87	136	4.35	0
1995 Kansas City c-d-e-f....A.L.	31	189	12	12	.500	119	89	204	4.43	0
1996 Boston...............A.L.	34	215$\frac{2}{3}$	12	9	.571	171	105	249	5.59	0
1997 Boston...............A.L.	42	182$\frac{2}{3}$	6	10	.375	159	78	155	3.74	11
1998 Boston...............A.L.	73	79$\frac{1}{3}$	7	4	.636	78	25	55	2.72	*46
1999 Boston g.............A.L.	21	17$\frac{2}{3}$	0	2	.000	24	12	17	5.60	11
2000 Boston h-i...........A.L.				INJURED—Did Not Play						

Year	Club	Lea	G	IP	W	L	Pct	SO	BB	H	ERA	SAVES
2001	Daytona	Fla.St.	2	2	0	0	.000	3	0	0	0.00	0
2001	Iowa	P.C.	2	2	0	0	.000	2	1	1	0.00	0
2001	Chicago j	N.L.	47	$45\frac{1}{3}$	1	2	.333	67	16	32	3.38	27
2002	Daytona	Fla.St.	2	$2\frac{2}{3}$	0	0	.000	3	2	1	3.38	0
2002	Iowa	P.C.	2	$1\frac{2}{3}$	0	0	.000	0	3	1	16.20	1
2002	Chicago-Houston k-l-m-n	N.L.	34	$42\frac{2}{3}$	1	3	.250	48	16	42	3.38	0
2003	Chicago o	A.L.	66	74	7	6	.538	91	31	57	3.16	12
2004	New York	A.L.	80	$89\frac{2}{3}$	9	4	.692	96	23	56	2.21	4
2005	New York p	A.L.	79	$80\frac{2}{3}$	5	4	.556	69	29	59	2.57	2
2006	Clearwater	Fla.St.	2	4	0	0	.000	5	1	1	0.00	0
2006	Philadelphia q	N.L.	59	$59\frac{1}{3}$	3	4	.429	68	22	53	3.34	34
2007	Phillies	Gulf Coast	2	$2\frac{1}{3}$	0	1	.000	3	1	5	19.29	0
2007	Clearwater	Fla.St.	2	$2\frac{2}{3}$	0	0	.000	1	1	1	0.00	0
2007	Philadelphia r	N.L.	44	40	3	2	.600	32	13	40	4.72	6
Major League Totals		19 Yrs.	853	$2076\frac{2}{3}$	133	121	.524	1902	957	1855	3.93	156
	Division Series											
1998	Boston	A.L.	2	3	0	1	.000	1	4	4	9.00	0
1999	Boston	A.L.	2	2	0	0	.000	3	1	1	4.50	0
2004	New York	A.L.	3	$3\frac{2}{3}$	0	0	.000	3	0	2	4.91	0
2005	New York	A.L.	3	$2\frac{1}{3}$	0	0	.000	2	0	2	3.86	0
2007	Philadelphia	N.L.	2	2	0	0	.000	4	1	2	4.50	0
Division Series Totals			12	13	0	1	.000	13	6	11	5.54	0
	Championship Series											
1999	Boston	A.L.	3	2	0	0	.000	3	1	3	13.50	0
2004	New York	A.L.	6	$6\frac{2}{3}$	0	0	.000	3	2	10	8.10	0
Championship Series Totals			9	$8\frac{2}{3}$	0	0	.000	6	3	13	9.35	0

a Filed for free agency, October 17, 1994; ruled ineligible by Player Relations Committee due to insufficient service time.
b Declared restricted free agent under Major League Baseball implemented labor proposal, December 23, 1994.
c Re-signed with Kansas City Royals, April 28, 1995.
d On disabled list from May 8 to May 24, 1995.
e Filed for free agency, November 12, 1995.
f Signed with Boston Red Sox, December 21, 1995.
g On disabled list from April 18 to May 10 and June 12 to September 27, 1999.
h On disabled list from April 2 to October 30, 2000.
i Not offered contract, October 31, 2000. Signed with Chicago Cubs, December 14, 2000.
j On disabled list from March 23 to May 1, 2001.
k On disabled list from March 28 to July 2, 2002.
l Traded to Houston Astros for pitcher Russ Rohlicek and two players to be named later, August 23, 2002.
m Chicago Cubs received pitcher Travis Anderson and pitcher Mike Nannini to complete trade, September 11, 2002.
n Filed for free agency, October 29, 2002. Signed with Chicago White Sox, January 20, 2003.
o Filed for free agency, October 27, 2003. Signed with New York Yankees, December 23, 2003.
p Filed for free agency, October 28, 2005. Signed with Philadelphia Phillies, December 3, 2005.
q On disabled list from August 13 to September 3, 2006.
r On disabled list from May 2 to July 16, 2007.

GORZELANNY, THOMAS STEPHEN (TOM)

Born, Evergreen Park, Illinois, July 12, 1982.
Bats Left. Throws Left. Height, 6 feet, 2 inches. Weight, 210 pounds.

Year	Club	Lea	G	IP	W	L	Pct	SO	BB	H	ERA	SAVES
2003	Williamsport	N.Y.-Penn.	8	$30\frac{1}{3}$	1	2	.333	22	10	23	1.78	0
2004	Lynchburg	Carolina	10	$55\frac{2}{3}$	3	5	.375	61	19	54	4.85	0
2004	Hickory	So.Atl.	16	93	7	2	.778	106	34	63	2.23	0
2005	Altoona	Eastern	23	$129\frac{2}{3}$	8	5	.615	124	46	114	3.26	0
2005	Pittsburgh	N.L.	3	6	0	1	.000	3	3	10	12.00	0
2006	Indianapolis	Int.	16	$99\frac{2}{3}$	6	5	.545	94	27	67	2.35	0
2006	Pittsburgh a	N.L.	11	$61\frac{2}{3}$	2	5	.286	40	31	50	3.79	0
2007	Pittsburgh	N.L.	32	$201\frac{2}{3}$	14	10	.583	135	68	214	3.88	0
Major League Totals		3 Yrs.	46	$269\frac{1}{3}$	16	16	.500	178	102	274	4.04	0

a On disabled list from August 18 to September 16, 2006.

GRABOW, JOHN WILLIAM

Born, Arcadia, California, November 4, 1978.
Bats Left. Throws Left. Height, 6 feet, 2 inches. Weight, 210 pounds.

Year	Club	Lea	G	IP	W	L	Pct	SO	BB	H	ERA	SAVES
1997	Pirates	Gulf Coast	11	$45\frac{1}{3}$	2	7	.222	28	14	57	4.57	0
1998	Augusta	So.Atl.	17	$71\frac{2}{3}$	6	3	.667	67	34	84	5.78	0

Year	Club	Lea	G	IP	W	L	Pct	SO	BB	H	ERA	SAVES
1999 Hickory		So.Atl.	26	156¹/₃	9	10	.474	164	32	152	3.80	0
2000 Altoona		Eastern	24	145¹/₃	8	7	.533	109	65	145	4.33	0
2001 Altoona		Eastern	10	50²/₃	2	5	.286	42	39	30	3.38	0
2001 Pirates		Gulf Coast	6	12	0	1	.000	9	4	11	3.75	0
2001 Lynchburg		Carolina	7	36²/₃	1	3	.250	35	26	42	6.38	0
2002 Altoona		Eastern	28	146¹/₃	8	13	.381	97	47	181	5.47	0
2003 Altoona		Eastern	24	83	6	1	.857	73	19	87	3.36	1
2003 Nashville		P.C.	17	24²/₃	0	2	.000	26	7	31	4.74	0
2003 Pittsburgh		N.L.	5	5	0	0	.000	9	0	6	3.60	0
2004 Pittsburgh		N.L.	68	61²/₃	2	5	.286	64	28	81	5.11	1
2005 Pittsburgh		N.L.	63	52	2	3	.400	42	25	46	4.85	0
2006 Pittsburgh		N.L.	72	69²/₃	4	2	.667	66	30	68	4.13	0
2007 Indianapolis		.Int.	4	4	0	0	.000	4	2	4	2.25	0
2007 Pittsburgh a		N.L.	63	51²/₃	3	2	.600	42	19	56	4.53	1
Major League Totals ....5 Yrs.			271	240	11	12	.478	223	102	257	4.61	2

a On disabled list from March 23 to April 23, 2007.

GREEN, SEAN WILLIAM

Born, Louisville, Kentucky, April 20, 1979.
Bats Right. Throws Right. Height, 6 feet, 6 inches. Weight, 235 pounds.

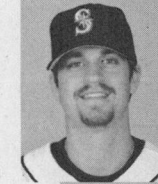

Year	Club	Lea	G	IP	W	L	Pct	SO	BB	H	ERA	SAVES
2000 Portland		Northwest	22	28²/₃	1	4	.200	17	19	45	8.48	0
2001 Asheville		So.Atl.	43	58	3	4	.429	37	28	66	5.90	0
2002 Salem		Carolina	52	67	2	5	.286	26	31	92	3.90	2
2003 Visalia		Calif.	46	80	3	4	.429	56	38	90	4.84	0
2004 Tulsa a		Texas	52	77¹/₃	4	3	.571	50	29	63	3.03	2
2005 Tacoma		P.C.	33	49¹/₃	4	2	.667	44	29	40	3.65	1
2005 San Antonio		Texas	21	24¹/₃	0	1	.000	18	8	17	2.96	14
2006 Tacoma		P.C.	15	24	4	1	.800	12	11	18	2.25	5
2006 Seattle b		A.L.	24	32	0	0	.000	15	13	34	4.50	0
2007 Tacoma		P.C.	10	17²/₃	2	1	.667	10	8	13	2.04	1
2007 Seattle		A.L.	64	68	5	2	.714	53	34	77	3.84	0
Major League Totals ....2 Yrs.			88	100	5	2	.714	68	47	111	4.05	0

a Traded to Seattle Mariners by Colorado Rockies for pitcher Aaron Taylor, December 20, 2004.
b On disabled list from July 3 to July 29 and September 8 to November 2, 2006.

GREGG, KEVIN MARSCHALL

Born, Corvallis, Oregon, June 20, 1978.
Bats Right. Throws Right. Height, 6 feet, 6 inches. Weight, 235 pounds.

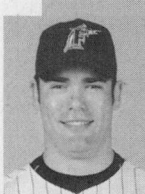

Year	Club	Lea	G	IP	W	L	Pct	SO	BB	H	ERA	SAVES
1996 Athletics		Arizona	11	40²/₃	3	3	.500	48	21	30	3.10	0
1997 Visalia		California	25	115¹/₃	6	8	.429	136	74	116	5.70	0
1998 Modesto		California	30	144	8	7	.533	141	76	139	3.81	1
1999 Visalia		California	13	64	4	4	.500	48	23	60	3.80	1
1999 Midland		Texas	16	91¹/₃	4	7	.364	66	31	75	3.74	0
1999 Vancouver		P.C.	1	5	1	0	1.000	4	2	6	3.60	0
2000 Midland		Texas	28	140²/₃	5	14	.263	97	73	171	6.40	0
2001 Midland		Texas	44	81¹/₃	5	5	.500	72	40	88	4.54	1
2002 Midland		Texas	11	37²/₃	3	3	.500	45	18	31	4.30	0
2002 Sacramento		P.C.	16	58²/₃	2	5	.286	45	23	82	7.52	0
2002 Visalia a		California	3	17¹/₃	2	1	.667	11	9	8	2.08	0
2003 Arkansas		Texas	15	66¹/₃	4	3	.571	60	19	60	3.53	0
2003 Salt Lake		P.C.	15	91²/₃	7	4	.636	75	18	90	4.03	0
2003 Anaheim		A.L.	5	24²/₃	2	0	1.000	14	8	18	3.28	0
2004 Anaheim		A.L.	55	87²/₃	5	2	.714	84	28	86	4.21	1
2005 Salt Lake		P.C.	7	34²/₃	3	1	.750	36	10	36	3.89	0
2005 Los Angeles		A.L.	33	64¹/₃	1	2	.333	52	29	70	5.04	0
2006 Salt Lake		P.C.	3	10	1	0	1.000	8	4	5	0.00	0
2006 Los Angeles b		A.L.	32	78¹/₃	3	4	.429	71	21	88	4.14	0
2007 Florida		N.L.	74	84	0	5	.000	87	40	63	3.54	32
Major League Totals ....5 Yrs.			199	339	11	13	.458	308	126	325	4.12	33
Division Series												
2004 Anaheim		A.L.	1	2	0	0	.000	0	1	3	0.00	0
Championship Series												
2005 Los Angeles		A.L.	1	2	0	0	.000	3	1	1	0.00	0

a Filed for free agency from Oakland Athletics, October 15, 2002. Signed with Anaheim Angels organization, November 20, 2002.
b Traded to Florida Marlins for pitcher Chris Resop, November 20, 2006.

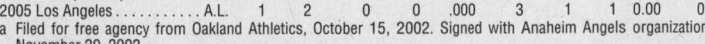

GREINKE, DONALD ZACKARY (ZACK)

Born, Orlando, Florida, October 21, 1983.
Bats Right. Throws Right. Height, 6 feet, 2 inches. Weight, 185 pounds.

Year Club	Lea	G	IP	W	L	Pct	SO	BB	H	ERA	SAVES
2002 Wilmington	Carolina	1	2	0	0	.000	0	0	1	0.00	0
2002 Royals	Gulf Coast	3	4²/₃	0	0	.000	4	3	3	1.93	0
2002 Spokane	Northwest	2	4²/₃	0	0	.000	5	0	9	7.71	0
2003 Wilmington	Carolina	14	87	11	1	.917	78	13	56	1.14	0
2003 Wichita	Texas	9	53	4	3	.571	34	5	58	3.23	0
2004 Omaha	P.C.	6	28²/₃	1	1	.500	23	6	25	2.51	0
2004 Kansas City	A.L.	24	145	8	11	.421	100	26	143	3.97	0
2005 Kansas City	A.L.	33	183	5	17	.227	114	53	233	5.80	0
2006 Wichita	Texas	18	105²/₃	8	3	.727	94	27	96	4.34	0
2006 Kansas City a	A.L.	3	6¹/₃	1	0	1.000	5	3	7	4.26	0
2007 Kansas City	A.L.	52	122	7	7	.500	106	36	122	3.69	1
Major League Totals	4 Yrs.	112	456¹/₃	21	35	.375	325	118	505	4.63	1

a On disabled list from April 1 to June 21, 2006.

GRILLI, JASON MICHAEL

Born, Royal Oak, Michigan, November 11, 1976.
Bats Right. Throws Right. Height, 6 feet, 5 inches. Weight, 225 pounds.

Year Club	Lea	G	IP	W	L	Pct	SO	BB	H	ERA	SAVES
1998 Shreveport	Texas	21	123¹/₃	7	10	.412	100	37	113	3.79	0
1998 Fresno	P.C.	8	42	2	3	.400	37	18	49	5.14	0
1999 Calgary	P.C.	8	41	1	5	.167	27	23	56	7.68	0
1999 Fresno a	P.C.	19	100²/₃	7	5	.583	76	39	124	5.54	0
2000 Calgary	P.C.	8	41¹/₃	1	4	.200	21	23	58	7.19	0
2000 Florida	N.L.	1	6²/₃	1	0	1.000	3	2	11	5.40	0
2001 Florida	N.L.	6	26²/₃	2	2	.500	17	11	30	6.07	0
2001 Calgary	P.C.	8	47	1	2	.333	35	20	46	4.02	0
2001 Marlins	Gulf Coast	2	4	0	0	.000	6	0	2	0.00	0
2001 Brevard County	Fla.St.	3	13²/₃	2	0	1.000	14	5	12	1.98	0
2001 Portland	Eastern	1	4	0	1	.000	3	0	3	2.25	0
2002 Calgary	P.C.	1	5²/₃	0	1	.000	8	3	3	1.59	0
2003 Jupiter	Fla.St.	7	42²/₃	4	2	.667	30	6	38	2.53	0
2003 Albuquerque b	P.C.	12	66²/₃	6	2	.750	38	30	64	3.38	0
2004 Charlotte	Int.	25	152²/₃	9	9	.500	101	58	163	4.83	0
2004 Chicago	A.L.	8	45	2	3	.400	26	20	52	7.40	0
2005 Toledo	Int.	28	167¹/₃	12	9	.571	120	58	170	4.09	0
2005 Detroit c	A.L.	3	16	1	1	.500	5	6	14	3.38	0
2006 Detroit	A.L.	51	62	2	3	.400	31	25	61	4.21	0
2007 Detroit	A.L.	57	79²/₃	5	3	.625	62	32	81	4.74	0
Major League Totals	6 Yrs.	126	236	13	12	.520	144	96	249	5.19	0
Division Series											
2006 Detroit	A.L.	1	0¹/₃	0	0	.000	0	0	0	0.00	0
Championship Series											
2006 Detroit	A.L.	2	1	0	0	.000	1	3	1	0.00	0
World Series Record											
2006 Detroit	A.L.	2	1²/₃	0	0	.000	0	1	0	0.00	0

a Traded by San Francisco Giants to Florida Marlins with pitcher Nathan Bump for pitcher Livan Hernandez, July 24, 1999.

b Selected by Chicago White Sox in Rule V draft, December 15, 2003.

c Released by Chicago White Sox, January 28, 2005. Signed with Detroit Tigers organization, February 10, 2005.

GUERRIER, MATTHEW OLSON (MATT)

Born, Cleveland, Ohio, August 2, 1978.
Bats Right. Throws Right. Height, 6 feet, 3 inches. Weight, 195 pounds.

Year Club	Lea	G	IP	W	L	Pct	SO	BB	H	ERA	SAVES
1999 Bristol	Appal.	21	25²/₃	5	0	1.000	37	14	18	1.05	10
1999 Winston-Salem	Carolina	4	3¹/₃	0	0	.000	5	0	3	5.40	2
2000 Winston-Salem	Carolina	30	34²/₃	0	3	.000	35	12	25	1.30	19
2000 Birmingham	Southern	23	23¹/₃	3	1	.750	19	12	17	2.70	7
2001 Charlotte	Int.	12	81¹/₃	7	1	.875	43	18	75	3.54	0
2001 Birmingham	Southern	15	98²/₃	11	3	.786	75	32	85	3.10	0
2002 Nashville a	P.C.	27	157	7	12	.368	130	47	154	4.59	0
2003 Nashville b	P.C.	20	105¹/₃	4	6	.400	78	18	108	4.53	0
2004 Rochester	Int.	24	144	5	10	.333	97	25	135	3.19	0
2004 Minnesota	A.L.	9	19	0	1	.000	11	6	22	5.68	0

Year Club	Lea	G	IP	W	L	Pct	SO	BB	H	ERA	SAVES
2005 Minnesota .... A.L.		43	71²/₃	0	3	.000	46	24	71	3.39	0
2006 New Britain .... Eastern		4	8²/₃	2	0	1.000	10	3	3	1.04	0
2006 Minnesota c .... A.L.		39	69²/₃	1	0	1.000	37	21	78	3.36	1
2007 Minnesota .... A.L.		73	88	2	4	.333	68	21	71	2.35	1
Major League Totals .... 4 Yrs.		164	248¹/₃	3	8	.273	162	72	242	3.19	2
Division Series											
2006 Minnesota .... A.L.		1	1	0	0	.000	0	0	0	0.00	0

a Traded by Chicago White Sox to Pittsburgh Pirates for pitcher Damaso Marte and infielder Edwin Yan, March 27, 2002.
b Claimed on waivers by Minnesota Twins, November 20, 2003.
c On disabled list from June 9 to August 1, 2006.

GUTHRIE, JEREMY SHANE
Born, Roseburg, Oregon, April 8, 1979.
Bats Right. Throws Right. Height, 6 feet, 1 inch. Weight, 200 pounds.

Year Club	Lea	G	IP	W	L	Pct	SO	BB	H	ERA	SAVES
2003 Akron .... Eastern		10	62²/₃	6	2	.750	35	14	44	1.44	0
2003 Buffalo .... Int.		18	96²/₃	4	9	.308	62	30	129	6.52	0
2004 Buffalo .... Int.		4	19¹/₃	1	2	.333	10	18	23	7.91	0
2004 Akron .... Eastern		23	130¹/₃	8	8	.500	94	42	145	4.21	0
2004 Cleveland .... A.L.		6	11²/₃	0	0	.000	7	6	9	4.63	0
2005 Cleveland .... A.L.		1	6	0	0	.000	3	2	9	6.00	0
2005 Buffalo .... Int.		25	136¹/₃	12	10	.545	100	49	152	5.08	0
2006 Buffalo .... Int.		21	123¹/₃	9	5	.643	88	48	104	3.14	0
2006 Cleveland .... A.L.		9	19¹/₃	0	0	.000	14	15	24	6.98	0
2007 Baltimore a .... A.L.		32	175¹/₃	7	5	.583	123	47	165	3.70	0
Major League Totals .... 4 Yrs.		48	212¹/₃	7	5	.583	147	70	207	4.11	0

a Claimed on waivers by Baltimore Orioles, January 29, 2007.

HALLADAY, HARRY LEROY (ROY)
Born, Denver, Colorado, May 14, 1977.
Bats Right. Throws Right. Height, 6 feet, 6 inches. Weight, 225 pounds.

Year Club	Lea	G	IP	W	L	Pct	SO	BB	H	ERA	SAVES
1995 Blue Jays .... Gulf Coast		10	50¹/₃	3	5	.375	48	16	35	3.40	0
1996 Dunedin .... Fla.St.		27	164²/₃	15	7	.682	109	46	158	2.73	0
1997 Knoxville .... Southern		7	36²/₃	2	3	.400	30	11	46	5.40	0
1997 Syracuse .... Int.		22	125²/₃	7	10	.412	64	53	132	4.58	0
1998 Syracuse .... Int.		21	116¹/₃	9	5	.643	71	53	107	3.79	0
1998 Toronto .... A.L.		2	14	1	0	1.000	13	2	9	1.93	0
1999 Toronto .... A.L.		36	149¹/₃	8	7	.533	82	79	156	3.92	1
2000 Syracuse .... Int.		11	73²/₃	2	3	.400	38	21	85	5.50	0
2000 Toronto .... A.L.		19	67²/₃	4	7	.364	44	42	107	10.64	0
2001 Dunedin .... Fla.St.		13	22²/₃	0	1	.000	15	3	28	3.97	2
2001 Tennessee .... Southern		5	34	2	1	.667	29	6	25	2.12	0
2001 Syracuse .... Int.		2	14	1	0	1.000	13	0	12	3.21	0
2001 Toronto .... A.L.		17	105¹/₃	5	3	.625	96	25	97	3.16	0
2002 Toronto .... A.L.		34	*239¹/₃	19	7	.731	168	62	223	2.93	0
2003 Toronto a .... A.L.		36	*266	*22	7	*.759	204	32	*253	3.25	0
2004 Toronto b .... A.L.		21	133	8	8	.500	95	39	140	4.20	0
2005 Toronto c .... A.L.		19	141²/₃	12	4	.750	108	18	118	2.41	0
2006 Toronto .... A.L.		32	220	16	5	*.762	132	34	208	3.19	0
2007 Toronto d .... A.L.		31	225¹/₃	16	7	.696	139	48	232	3.71	0
Major League Totals .... 10 Yrs.		247	1561²/₃	111	55	.669	1081	381	1543	3.63	1

a Selected Cy Young Award Winner in American League for 2003.
b On disabled list from May 28 to June 12 and from July 17 to September 21, 2004.
c On disabled list from July 9 to October 3, 2005.
d On disabled list from May 11 to May 31, 2007.

HAMELS, COLBERT RICHARD (COLE)
Born, San Diego, California, December 27, 1983.
Bats Left. Throws Left. Height, 6 feet, 4 inches. Weight, 195 pounds.

Year Club	Lea	G	IP	W	L	Pct	SO	BB	H	ERA	SAVES
2003 Clearwater .... Fla.St.		5	26¹/₃	0	2	.000	32	14	29	2.73	0
2003 Lakewood........... So.Atl.		13	74²/₃	6	1	.857	115	25	32	0.84	0
2004 Clearwater .... Fla.St.		4	16	1	0	1.000	24	4	10	1.13	0

Year	Club	Lea	G	IP	W	L	Pct	SO	BB	H	ERA	SAVES
2005	Reading	Eastern	3	19	2	0	1.000	19	12	10	2.37	0
2005	Clearwater	Fla.St.	3	16	2	0	1.000	18	7	7	2.25	0
2006	Lakewood	So.Atl.	1	5²/₃	0	0	.000	3	2	3	1.59	0
2006	Clearwater	Fla.St.	4	20¹/₃	1	1	.500	29	9	16	1.77	0
2006	Scranton/WB	Int.	3	23	2	0	1.000	36	1	10	0.39	0
2006	Philadelphia a	N.L.	23	132¹/₃	9	8	.529	145	48	117	4.08	0
2007	Philadelphia b	N.L.	28	183¹/₃	15	5	.750	177	43	163	3.39	0
Major League Totals	2 Yrs.		51	315²/₃	24	13	.649	322	91	280	3.68	0
Division Series												
2007	Philadelphia	N.L.	1	6²/₃	0	1	.000	7	4	3	4.05	0

a On disabled list from May 19 to June 6, 2006.
b On disabled list from August 17 to September 18, 2007.

HAMMEL, JASON AARON
Born, Greenville, South Carolina, September 2, 1982.
Bats Right. Throws Right. Height, 6 feet, 6 inches. Weight, 220 pounds.

Year	Club	Lea	G	IP	W	L	Pct	SO	BB	H	ERA	SAVES
2002	Princeton	Appal.	2	5¹/₃	0	0	.000	5	0	7	0.00	1
2002	Hudson Valley	N.Y.-Penn.	13	51²/₃	1	5	.167	38	14	71	5.23	1
2003	Charleston	So.Atl.	14	76²/₃	6	2	.750	50	27	70	3.40	0
2004	Bakersfield	Calif.	11	71¹/₃	6	2	.750	65	20	52	1.89	0
2004	Charleston	So.Atl.	18	94²/₃	4	7	.364	88	27	94	3.23	0
2005	Durham	Int.	10	54²/₃	3	2	.600	48	27	57	4.12	0
2005	Montgomery	Southern	12	81¹/₃	8	2	.800	76	19	70	2.66	0
2006	Durham	Int.	24	127²/₃	5	9	.357	117	36	133	4.23	0
2006	Tampa Bay	A.L.	9	44	0	6	.000	32	21	61	7.77	0
2007	Durham	Int.	13	76¹/₃	4	5	.444	75	28	61	3.42	0
2007	Tampa Bay	A.L.	24	85	3	5	.375	64	40	100	6.14	0
Major League Totals	2 Yrs.		33	129	3	11	.214	96	61	161	6.70	0

HAMPSON, JUSTIN MICHAEL
Born, Belleville, Illinois, May 24, 1980.
Bats Left. Throws Left. Height, 6 feet, 1 inch. Weight, 200 pounds.

Year	Club	Lea	G	IP	W	L	Pct	SO	BB	H	ERA	SAVES
2000	Portland	Northwest	14	68²/₃	1	8	.111	44	27	74	3.54	0
2001	Tri-City	Northwest	15	81²/₃	4	6	.400	63	23	84	4.52	0
2002	Asheville	So.Atl.	27	164¹/₃	9	8	.529	123	58	162	3.83	0
2003	Visalia	Calif.	26	159	14	7	.667	150	51	153	3.68	0
2003	Tulsa	Texas	1	4	0	1	.000	0	3	8	13.50	0
2004	Tulsa	Texas	27	170¹/₃	10	9	.526	104	63	176	3.49	0
2005	Colorado Springs	P.C.	27	144¹/₃	5	13	.278	93	71	167	5.99	0
2006	Colorado Springs	P.C.	31	121²/₃	8	4	.667	95	39	121	3.33	0
2006	Colorado a	N.L.	5	12	1	0	1.000	9	5	19	7.50	0
2007	Portland	P.C.	10	12²/₃	1	1	.500	12	8	12	3.55	0
2007	San Diego	N.L.	39	53¹/₃	2	3	.400	34	16	48	2.70	0
Major League Totals	2 Yrs.		44	65¹/₃	3	3	.500	43	21	67	3.58	0

a Claimed on waivers by San Diego Padres, October 12, 2006.

HARANG, AARON MICHAEL
Born, San Diego, California, May 9, 1978.
Bats Right. Throws Right. Height, 6 feet, 7 inches. Weight, 270 pounds.

Year	Club	Lea	G	IP	W	L	Pct	SO	BB	H	ERA	SAVES
1999	Pulaski	Appal.	16	78¹/₃	9	2	.818	87	17	64	2.30	1
2000	Charlotte a	Fla.St.	28	157	13	5	.722	136	50	128	3.32	0
2001	Midland	Texas	27	150	10	8	.556	112	37	173	4.14	0
2002	Midland	Texas	3	16²/₃	2	0	1.000	21	7	12	1.08	0
2002	Sacramento	P.C.	8	38²/₃	3	3	.500	39	9	41	3.26	0
2002	Oakland	A.L.	16	78¹/₃	5	4	.556	64	45	78	4.83	0
2003	Louisville	Int.	1	3	0	1	.000	4	2	5	15.00	0
2003	Sacramento	P.C.	12	69²/₃	8	2	.800	60	17	62	2.71	0
2003	Oakland	A.L.	7	30¹/₃	1	3	.250	16	9	41	5.34	0
2003	Cincinnati b	N.L.	9	46	4	3	.571	26	10	48	5.28	0
2004	Louisville	Int.	1	3	0	1	.000	3	3	9	12.00	0
2004	Cincinnati c	N.L.	28	161	10	9	.526	125	53	177	4.86	0
2005	Cincinnati	N.L.	32	211²/₃	11	13	.458	163	51	217	3.83	0

Year	Club		Lea	G	IP	W	L	Pct	SO	BB	H	ERA	SAVES
2006 Cincinnati	....	N.L.		36	234¹/₃	*16	11	.593	*216	56	242	3.76	0
2007 Cincinnati	....	N.L.		34	231²/₃	16	6	.727	218	52	213	3.73	0
Major League Totals	........6 Yrs.			162	993¹/₃	63	49	.563	828	276	1016	4.15	0

a Traded by Texas Rangers to Oakland Athletics with pitcher Ryan Cullen for infielder Randy Velarde, November 17, 2000.

b Traded to Cincinnati Reds with pitcher Joe Valentine and pitcher Jeff Bruksch for outfielder Jose Guillen, July 30, 2003.

c On disabled list from June 2 to June 26, 2004.

HARDEN, JAMES RICHARD (RICH)
Born, Victoria, British Columbia, Canada, November 30, 1981.
Bats Left. Throws Right. Height, 6 feet, 1 inch. Weight, 195 pounds.

Year	Club		Lea	G	IP	W	L	Pct	SO	BB	H	ERA	SAVES
2001 Vancouver	....	Northwest		18	74¹/₃	2	4	.333	100	38	47	3.39	0
2002 Visalia	....	California		12	68	4	3	.571	85	24	49	2.91	0
2002 Midland	....	Texas		16	85¹/₃	8	3	.727	102	52	67	2.95	0
2003 Midland	....	Texas		2	13	2	0	1.000	17	0	0	0.00	0
2003 Sacramento	....	P.C.		16	88²/₃	9	4	.692	91	35	72	3.15	0
2003 Oakland	....	A.L.		15	74²/₃	5	4	.556	67	40	72	4.46	0
2004 Sacramento	....	P.C.		1	5	0	0	.000	6	3	6	5.40	0
2004 Oakland	....	A.L.		31	189²/₃	11	7	.611	167	81	171	3.99	0
2005 Sacramento	....	P.C.		1	3	0	0	.000	7	0	1	0.00	0
2005 Oakland a	....	A.L.		22	128	10	5	.667	121	43	93	2.53	0
2006 Sacramento	....	P.C.		1	2	0	0	.000	3	0	1	0.00	0
2006 Oakland b	....	A.L.		9	46²/₃	4	0	1.000	49	26	31	4.24	0
2007 Sacramento	....	P.C.		1	1	0	0	.000	1	0	1	0.00	0
2007 Oakland c	....	A.L.		7	25²/₃	1	2	.333	27	11	18	2.45	0
Major League Totals	........5 Yrs.			84	464²/₃	31	18	.633	431	201	385	3.60	0
Division Series													
2003 Oakland	....	A.L.		2	1¹/₃	1	1	.500	1	2	2	13.50	0
Championship Series													
2006 Oakland		A.L.		1	5²/₃	0	1	.000	4	5	5	4.76	0

a On disabled list from May 14 to June 21, 2005.

b On disabled list from April 27 to June 4 and June 5 to September 21, 2006.

c On disabled list from April 16 to June 22 and July 8 to October 8, 2007.

HAREN, DANIEL JOHN (DANNY)
Born, Monterey Park, California, September 17, 1980.
Bats Right. Throws Right. Height, 6 feet, 5 inches. Weight, 220 pounds.

Year	Club		Lea	G	IP	W	L	Pct	SO	BB	H	ERA	SAVES
2001 New Jersey	......	N.Y.-Penn.		12	52¹/₃	3	3	.500	57	8	47	3.10	1
2002 Potomac	....	Carolina		14	92	3	6	.333	82	19	90	3.62	0
2002 Peoria	....	Midwest		14	101²/₃	7	3	.700	89	12	89	1.95	0
2003 Memphis	....	P.C.		8	45²/₃	2	1	.667	35	8	50	4.93	0
2003 Tennessee	....	Southern		8	55	6	0	1.000	49	6	36	0.82	0
2003 St. Louis	....	N.L.		14	72²/₃	3	7	.300	43	22	84	5.08	0
2004 Memphis	....	P.C.		21	128	11	4	.733	150	33	136	4.15	0
2004 St. Louis a	....	N.L.		14	46	3	3	.500	32	17	45	4.50	0
2005 Oakland	....	A.L.		34	217	14	12	.538	163	53	212	3.73	0
2006 Oakland	....	A.L.		34	223	14	13	.519	176	45	224	4.12	0
2007 Oakland b	....	A.L.		34	222²/₃	15	9	.625	192	55	214	3.07	0
Major League Totals	........5 Yrs.			130	781¹/₃	49	44	.527	606	192	779	3.82	0
Division Series													
2004 St. Louis	....	N.L.		1	2	1	0	1.000	3	1	1	0.00	0
2006 Oakland	....	A.L.		1	6	1	0	1.000	2	1	9	3.00	0
Division Series Totals	....			2	8	2	0	1.000	5	2	10	2.25	0
Championship Series													
2004 St. Louis	....	N.L.		2	1²/₃	0	0	.000	2	0	3	10.80	0
2006 Oakland	....	A.L.		1	5	0	0	.000	7	2	7	5.40	0
Championship Series Totals	......			3	6²/₃	0	0	.000	9	2	10	6.75	0
World Series Record													
2004 St. Louis	....	N.L.		2	4²/₃	0	0	.000	2	3	4	0.00	0

a Traded to Oakland Athletics with pitcher Kiko Calero and catcher Daric Barton for pitcher Mark Mulder, December 18, 2004.

b Traded to Arizona Diamondbacks with pitcher Connor Robertson for pitcher Brett Anderson, pitcher Dana Eveland, pitcher Greg Smith, infielder Chris Carter, outfielder Aaron Cunningham and outfielder Carlos Gonzalez, December 14, 2007.

HAWKINS, LA TROY

Born, Gary, Indiana, December 21, 1972.
Bats Right. Throws Right. Height, 6 feet, 5 inches. Weight, 195 pounds.

Year	Club	Lea	G	IP	W	L	Pct	SO	BB	H	ERA	SAVES
1991	Twins	Gulf Coast	11	55	4	3	.571	47	26	62	4.75	0
1992	Twins	Gulf Coast	6	36⅓	3	2	.600	35	10	36	3.22	0
1992	Elizabethton	Appal.	5	26⅔	0	1	.000	36	11	21	3.38	0
1993	Ft. Wayne	Midwest	26	157⅓	15	5	.750	179	41	110	2.06	0
1994	Ft. Myers	Fla. St.	6	38⅔	4	0	1.000	36	6	32	2.33	0
1994	Nashville	Southern	11	73⅓	9	2	.818	53	28	50	2.33	0
1994	Salt Lake	P.C.	12	81⅔	5	4	.556	37	33	92	4.08	0
1995	Salt Lake	P.C.	22	144⅓	9	7	.563	74	40	150	3.55	0
1995	Minnesota	A.L.	6	27	2	3	.400	9	12	39	8.67	0
1996	Minnesota	A.L.	7	26⅓	1	1	.500	24	9	42	8.20	0
1996	Salt Lake	P.C.	20	137⅔	9	8	.529	99	31	138	3.92	0
1997	Salt Lake	P.C.	14	76	9	4	.692	53	16	100	5.45	0
1997	Minnesota	A.L.	20	103⅓	6	12	.333	58	47	134	5.84	0
1998	Minnesota	A.L.	33	190⅓	7	14	.333	105	61	227	5.25	0
1999	Minnesota	A.L.	33	174⅓	10	14	.417	103	60	238	6.66	0
2000	Minnesota	A.L.	66	87⅔	2	5	.286	59	32	85	3.39	14
2001	Minnesota	A.L.	62	51⅓	1	5	.167	36	39	59	5.96	28
2002	Minnesota	A.L.	65	80⅓	6	0	1.000	63	15	63	2.13	0
2003	Minnesota a	A.L.	74	77⅓	9	3	.750	75	15	69	1.86	2
2004	Chicago	N.L.	77	82	5	4	.556	69	14	72	2.63	25
2005	Fresno	P.C.	2	2	0	0	.000	1	0	2	0.00	0
2005	Chicago-San Francisco b-c-d	N.L.	66	56⅓	2	8	.200	43	24	58	3.83	6
2006	Baltimore e	A.L.	60	60⅓	3	2	.600	27	15	73	4.48	0
2007	Colorado Springs	P.C.	4	4	1	0	1.000	5	2	2	2.25	0
2007	Colorado f-g	N.L.	62	55⅓	2	5	.286	29	16	52	3.42	0
Major League Totals	13 Yrs.		631	1072	56	76	.424	700	359	1211	4.68	75
Division Series												
2002	Minnesota	A.L.	3	2⅓	0	0	.000	5	0	0	0.00	0
2003	Minnesota	A.L.	3	3	1	0	1.000	5	0	5	6.00	0
2007	Colorado	N.L.	1	1	0	0	.000	0	1	0	0.00	0
Division Series Totals			7	6⅓	1	0	1.000	10	1	5	2.84	0
Championship Series												
2002	Minnesota	A.L.	4	1⅓	0	0	.000	1	1	4	20.25	0
2007	Colorado	N.L.	2	2	0	0	.000	1	0	1	0.00	0
Championship Series Totals			6	3⅓	0	0	.000	2	1	5	8.10	0
World Series Record												
2007	Colorado	N.L.	2	2	0	0	.000	2	0	1	4.50	0

a Filed for free agency, October 27, 2003. Signed with Chicago Cubs, December 3, 2003.
b Traded to San Francisco Giants for pitcher Jerome Williams and pitcher David Aardsma, May 28, 2005.
c On disabled list from June 10 to July 4, 2005.
d Traded to Baltimore Orioles for pitcher Steve Kline, December 6, 2005.
e Filed for free agency, October 31, 2006. Signed with Colorado Rockies, December 5, 2006.
f On disabled list from April 21 to May 22, 2007.
g Filed for free agency, November 1, 2007. Signed with New York Yankees, December 27, 2007.

HEILMAN, AARON MICHAEL

Born, Logansport, Indiana, November 12, 1978.
Bats Right. Throws Right. Height, 6 feet, 5 inches. Weight, 220 pounds.

Year	Club	Lea	G	IP	W	L	Pct	SO	BB	H	ERA	SAVES
2001	St. Lucie	Fla.St.	7	38⅓	0	1	.000	39	13	26	2.35	0
2002	Binghamton	Eastern	17	96⅔	4	4	.500	97	28	85	3.82	0
2002	Norfolk	Int.	10	49⅓	2	3	.400	35	16	42	3.28	0
2003	Norfolk	Int.	16	94⅓	6	4	.600	71	32	99	3.24	0
2003	New York	N.L.	14	65⅓	2	7	.222	51	41	79	6.75	0
2004	Norfolk	Int.	26	151⅔	7	10	.412	123	66	156	4.33	0
2004	New York	N.L.	5	28	1	3	.250	22	13	27	5.46	0
2005	New York	N.L.	53	108	5	3	.625	106	37	87	3.17	5
2006	New York	N.L.	74	87	4	5	.444	73	28	73	3.62	0
2007	New York	N.L.	81	86	7	7	.500	63	20	72	3.03	1
Major League Totals	5 Yrs.		227	374⅓	19	25	.432	315	139	338	4.04	6
Division Series												
2006	New York	N.L.	3	3	0	0	.000	1	0	3	3.00	0
Championship Series												
2006	New York	N.L.	3	4⅓	0	1	.000	5	1	4	4.15	0

HENDRICKSON, MARK ALLAN

Born, Mount Vernon, Washington, June 23, 1974.
Bats Left. Throws Left. Height, 6 feet, 9 inches. Weight, 230 pounds.

Year	Club	Lea	G	IP	W	L	Pct	SO	BB	H	ERA	SAVES
1998 Dunedin	Fla.St.	16	49¹/₃	4	3	.571	38	26	44	2.37	1
1999 Knoxville	Southern	12	55²/₃	2	7	.222	39	21	73	6.63	0
2000 Dunedin	Fla.St.	12	51¹/₃	2	2	.500	38	29	63	5.61	0
2000 Tennessee	Southern	6	39²/₃	3	1	.750	29	12	32	3.63	0
2001 Syracuse	Int.	38	73¹/₃	2	9	.182	33	18	80	4.66	0
2002 Syracuse	Int.	19	92	7	5	.583	68	22	90	3.52	0
2002 Toronto a	A.L.	16	36²/₃	3	0	1.000	21	12	25	2.45	0
2003 Syracuse	Int.	1	6	0	0	.000	5	1	8	4.50	0
2003 Dunedin	Fla.St.	1	5²/₃	1	0	1.000	3	4	5	1.59	0
2003 Toronto b-c	A.L.	30	158¹/₃	9	9	.500	76	40	207	5.51	0
2004 Tampa Bay	A.L.	32	183¹/₃	10	15	.400	87	46	211	4.81	0
2005 Tampa Bay d	A.L.	31	178¹/₃	11	8	.579	89	49	227	5.90	0
2006 Tampa Bay	A.L.	13	89²/₃	4	8	.333	51	34	81	3.81	0
2006 Los Angeles e-f	N.L.	18	75	2	7	.222	48	28	92	4.68	0
2007 Los Angeles g	N.L.	39	122²/₃	4	8	.333	92	29	142	5.21	0
Major League Totals	6 Yrs.	179	844	43	55	.439	464	238	985	5.01	0

Division Series

Year	Club	Lea	G	IP	W	L	Pct	SO	BB	H	ERA	SAVES
2006 Los Angeles	N.L.	3	2²/₃	0	0	.000	1	1	1	0.00	0

a On disabled list from June 18 to July 12, 2002.
b Traded to Colorado Rockies with player named later for pitcher Justin Speier, December 14, 2003.
c Traded to Tampa Bay Devil Rays for pitcher Joe Kennedy, December 14, 2003.
d On disabled list from April 14 to April 30, 2005.
e On disabled list from April 7 to April 25, 2006.
f Traded to Los Angeles Dodgers with catcher Toby Hall and cash for catcher Dioner Navarro, pitcher Jae Seo and player named later, June 27, 2006.
g Not offered contract, December 12, 2007. Signed with Florida Marlins, January 16, 2008.

HENNESSEY, BRAD MARTIN

Born, Toledo, Ohio, February 7, 1980.
Bats Right. Throws Right. Height, 6 feet, 2 inches. Weight, 195 pounds.

Year	Club	Lea	G	IP	W	L	Pct	SO	BB	H	ERA	SAVES
2001 Salem-Keizer	Northwest	9	34	1	0	1.000	22	11	28	2.38	0
2002 Salem-Keizer a	Northwest		INJURED—Did Not Play								
2003 Hagerstown	So.Atl.	15	79¹/₃	3	9	.250	44	27	81	4.20	0
2004 Norwich	Eastern	18	101	5	5	.500	55	34	106	3.56	0
2004 Fresno	P.C.	5	35²/₃	4	1	.800	16	15	26	2.02	0
2004 San Francisco	N.L.	7	34¹/₃	2	2	.500	25	15	42	4.98	0
2005 Fresno	P.C.	11	67²/₃	4	2	.667	46	22	75	5.19	0
2005 San Francisco	N.L.	21	118¹/₃	5	8	.385	64	52	127	4.64	0
2006 Fresno	P.C.	2	10²/₃	0	1	.000	7	1	11	2.53	0
2006 San Francisco	N.L.	34	99¹/₃	5	6	.455	42	42	92	4.26	1
2007 San Francisco	N.L.	69	68¹/₃	4	5	.444	40	23	66	3.42	19
Major League Totals	4 Yrs.	131	320¹/₃	16	21	.432	171	132	327	4.30	20

a On minor league disabled list from June 22 to September 12, 2002.

HERGES, MATTHEW TYLER (MATT)

Born, Champaign, Illinois, April 1, 1970.
Bats Left. Throws Right. Height, 6 feet. Weight, 210 pounds.

Year	Club	Lea	G	IP	W	L	Pct	SO	BB	H	ERA	SAVES
1992 Yakima	Northwest	27	44²/₃	2	3	.400	57	24	33	3.22	9
1993 Bakersfield	Calif.	51	90¹/₃	2	6	.250	84	56	70	3.69	2
1994 Vero Beach	Fla.St.	48	111	8	9	.471	61	33	115	3.32	3
1995 San Antonio	Texas	19	27²/₃	0	3	.000	18	16	34	4.88	8
1995 San Bernardino	Calif.	22	51²/₃	5	2	.714	35	15	58	3.66	1
1996 San Antonio	Texas	30	83	3	2	.600	45	28	83	2.71	3
1996 Albuquerque	P.C.	10	34²/₃	4	1	.800	15	14	33	2.60	0
1997 Albuquerque	P.C.	31	85	0	8	.000	61	46	120	8.89	0
1997 San Antonio	Texas	4	15¹/₃	0	1	.000	12	10	22	8.80	0
1998 San Antonio	Texas	3	6	0	0	.000	3	2	3	0.00	0
1998 Albuquerque	P.C.	34	88¹/₃	3	5	.375	75	37	115	5.71	0
1999 Albuquerque	P.C.	21	131¹/₃	8	3	.727	88	47	135	4.73	0
1999 Los Angeles a	N.L.	17	24¹/₃	0	2	.000	18	8	24	4.07	0
2000 Los Angeles	N.L.	59	110²/₃	11	3	.786	75	40	100	3.17	1
2001 Los Angeles	N.L.	75	99¹/₃	9	8	.529	76	46	97	3.44	1

Year	Club	Lea	G	IP	W	L	Pct	SO	BB	H	ERA	SAVES
2002 Montreal b-c	N.L.	62	64⅔	2	5	.286	50	26	80	4.04	6
2003 Portland	P.C.	4	5	0	0	.000	5	2	1	1.80	0
2003 San Diego-San Fran. d-e-f	N.L.	67	79	3	2	.600	68	29	68	2.62	3
2004 San Francisco	N.L.	70	65⅓	4	5	.444	39	21	90	5.23	23
2005 Tucson	P.C.	26	28⅔	1	2	.333	29	8	39	3.14	0
2005 San Fran.-Arizona g-h	N.L.	28	29	1	1	.500	9	12	35	7.14	0
2006 Florida i	N.L.	66	71	2	3	.400	36	28	94	4.31	0
2007 Colorado Springs	P.C.	32	35⅓	2	1	.667	33	10	24	1.27	1
2007 Colorado j	N.L.	35	48⅔	5	1	.833	30	15	34	2.96	0
Major League Totals	9 Yrs.	479	592	37	30	.552	401	225	622	3.82	34
Division Series											
2003 San Francisco	N.L.	3	4⅓	0	0	.000	5	2	1	0.00	0
2007 Colorado	N.L.	1	0⅔	0	0	.000	0	0	0	0.00	0
Division Series Totals		4	5	0	0	.000	5	2	1	0.00	0
Championship Series											
2007 Colorado	N.L.	3	3	1	0	1.000	2	1	1	0.00	0
World Series Record											
2007 Colorado	N.L.	3	3⅓	0	0	.000	4	2	1	0.00	0

a Filed for free agency, October 15, 1998, re-signed by Los Angeles Dodgers organization, January 6, 1999.
b Traded to Montreal Expos with infielder Jorge Nunez for pitcher Guillermo Mota and outfielder Wilkin Ruan, March 23, 2002.
c Traded to Pittsburgh Pirates for pitcher Chris Young and pitcher Jon Searles, December 20, 2002.
d Released by Pittsburgh Pirates, March 26, 2003. Signed with San Diego Padres organization, March 30, 2003.
e Traded to San Francisco Giants for pitcher Clay Hensley and player to be named later, July 13, 2003.
f San Diego Padres received pitcher R.D. Spiehs to complete trade, July 27, 2003.
g Traded to Arizona Diamondbacks for outfielder Doug DeVore, June 3, 2005.
h Filed for free agency, October 3, 2005. Signed with Florida Marlins organization, February 1, 2006.
i Filed for free agency, October 28, 2006. Signed with Colorado Rockies organization, February 12, 2007.
j Filed for free agency, November 6, 2007, re-signed with Colorado Rockies, November 30, 2007.

HERNANDEZ, EISLER LIVAN
Born, Villa Clara, Cuba, February 20, 1975.
Bats Right. Throws Right. Height, 6 feet, 2 inches. Weight, 245 pounds.

Year	Club	Lea	G	IP	W	L	Pct	SO	BB	H	ERA	SAVES
1996 Charlotte	Int.	10	49	2	4	.333	45	34	61	5.14	0
1996 Portland	Eastern	15	93⅓	9	2	.818	95	34	81	4.34	0
1996 Florida	N.L.	1	3	0	0	.000	2	2	3	0.00	0
1997 Portland	Eastern	1	4	0	0	.000	2	7	2	2.25	0
1997 Charlotte	Int.	14	81⅓	5	3	.625	58	38	76	3.98	0
1997 Florida	N.L.	17	96⅓	9	3	.750	72	38	81	3.18	0
1998 Florida	N.L.	33	234⅓	10	12	.455	162	104	*265	4.72	0
1999 Florida-San Francisco a	N.L.	30	199⅔	8	12	.400	144	76	227	4.64	0
2000 San Francisco	N.L.	33	240	17	11	.607	165	73	*254	3.75	0
2001 San Francisco	N.L.	34	226⅔	13	15	.464	138	85	*266	5.24	0
2002 San Francisco	N.L.	33	216	12	*16	.429	134	71	233	4.38	0
2003 Montreal b-c	N.L.	33	*233⅓	15	10	.600	178	57	225	3.20	0
2004 Montreal	N.L.	35	*255	11	15	.423	186	83	234	3.60	0
2005 Washington	N.L.	35	*246⅓	15	10	.600	147	84	*268	3.98	0
2006 Washington-Arizona d	N.L.	34	216	13	13	.500	128	78	246	4.83	0
2007 Arizona e	N.L.	33	204⅓	11	11	.500	90	79	*247	4.93	0
Major League Totals	12 Yrs.	351	2371	134	128	.511	1546	830	2549	4.25	0
Division Series											
1997 Florida	N.L.	1	4	0	0	.000	3	0	3	2.25	0
2000 San Francisco	N.L.	1	7⅔	1	0	1.000	5	5	5	1.17	0
2002 San Francisco	N.L.	1	8⅓	1	0	1.000	6	2	8	3.24	0
2007 Arizona	N.L.	1	6	1	0	1.000	2	5	5	1.50	0
Division Series Totals		4	26	3	0	1.000	16	12	21	2.08	0
Championship Series											
1997 Florida	N.L.	2	10⅔	2	0	1.000	16	2	5	0.84	0
2002 San Francisco	N.L.	1	6⅓	0	0	.000	0	1	9	2.84	0
2007 Arizona	N.L.	1	5⅔	0	1	.000	4	2	8	6.35	0
Championship Series Totals		4	22⅔	2	1	.667	20	5	22	2.78	0
World Series Record											
1997 Florida	N.L.	2	13⅔	2	0	1.000	7	10	15	5.27	0
2002 San Francisco	N.L.	2	5⅔	0	2	.000	4	9	9	14.29	0
World Series Totals		4	19⅓	2	2	.500	11	19	24	7.91	0

a Traded to San Francisco Giants for pitcher Jason Grilli and pitcher Nathan Bump, July 24, 1999.

b Traded to Montreal Expos with catcher Edwards Guzman for pitcher Jim Brower and player to be named later, March 24, 2003.
c San Francisco Giants received pitcher Matt Blank to complete trade, April 30, 2003.
d Traded to Arizona Diamondbacks with cash for pitcher Garrett Mock and pitcher Matt Chico, August 7, 2006.
e Filed for free agency, October 29, 2007.

HERNANDEZ, FELIX ABRAHAM
Born, Valencia, Venezuela, April 8, 1986.
Bats Right. Throws Right. Height, 6 feet, 3 inches. Weight, 230 pounds.

Year	Club	Lea	G	IP	W	L	Pct	SO	BB	H	ERA	SAVES
2003	Wisconsin	Midwest	2	14	0	0	.000	18	3	9	1.93	0
2003	Everett	Northwest	11	55	7	2	.778	73	24	43	2.29	0
2004	Inland Empire	California	16	92	9	3	.750	114	26	85	2.74	0
2004	San Antonio	Texas	10	57^{1}/$_{3}$	5	1	.833	58	21	47	3.30	0
2005	Tacoma	P.C.	19	88	9	4	.692	100	48	62	2.25	0
2005	Seattle	A.L.	12	84^{1}/$_{3}$	4	4	.500	77	23	61	2.67	0
2006	Seattle	A.L.	31	191	12	14	.462	176	60	195	4.52	0
2007	Seattle a	A.L.	30	190^{1}/$_{3}$	14	7	.667	165	53	209	3.92	0
Major League Totals		3 Yrs.	73	465^{2}/$_{3}$	30	25	.545	418	136	465	3.94	0

a On disabled list from April 19 to May 15, 2007.

HERNANDEZ, ORLANDO P. (EL DUQUE)
Born, Villa Clara, Cuba, October 11, 1965.
Bats Right. Throws Right. Height, 6 feet, 2 inches. Weight, 220 pounds.

Year	Club	Lea	G	IP	W	L	Pct	SO	BB	H	ERA	SAVES
1998	Tampa	Fla.St.	2	9	1	1	.500	15	3	3	1.00	0
1998	Columbus	Int.	7	42^{1}/$_{3}$	6	0	1.000	59	17	41	3.83	0
1998	New York a	A.L.	21	141	12	4	.750	131	52	113	3.13	0
1999	New York	A.L.	33	214^{1}/$_{3}$	17	9	.654	157	87	187	4.12	0
2000	Tampa	Fla.St.	1	4	0	0	.000	5	1	1	0.00	0
2000	New York b	A.L.	29	195^{2}/$_{3}$	12	13	.480	141	51	186	4.51	0
2001	Tampa	Fla.St.	2	7	0	0	.000	8	1	6	0.00	0
2001	Staten Island	N.Y.-Penn.	1	6	1	0	1.000	11	1	2	0.00	0
2001	New York c	A.L.	17	94^{2}/$_{3}$	4	7	.364	77	42	90	4.85	0
2002	Columbus	Int.	1	5^{2}/$_{3}$	1	0	1.000	5	1	7	1.59	0
2002	New York d-e-f	A.L.	24	146	8	5	.615	113	36	131	3.64	1
2003	Montreal g	N.L.		INJURED—Did Not Play								
2003	Brevard County	Fla.St.	2	5	0	1	.000	7	4	5	10.80	0
2004	Tampa	Fla.St.	3	12	1	0	1.000	11	7	3	1.50	0
2004	Columbus	Int.	3	17^{2}/$_{3}$	2	1	.667	16	3	17	5.60	0
2004	New York h-i	A.L.	15	84^{2}/$_{3}$	8	2	.800	84	36	73	3.30	0
2005	Charlotte	Int.	1	4	0	1	.000	2	0	4	2.25	0
2005	Chicago j-k	A.L.	24	128^{1}/$_{3}$	9	9	.500	91	50	137	5.12	1
2006	Arizona-New York l-m	N.L.	29	162^{1}/$_{3}$	11	11	.500	164	61	155	4.66	0
2007	New York n	N.L.	27	147^{2}/$_{3}$	9	5	.643	128	64	109	3.72	0
Major League Totals		9 Yrs.	219	1314^{2}/$_{3}$	90	65	.581	1086	479	1181	4.13	2

Division Series

1999	New York	A.L.	1	8	1	0	1.000	4	6	2	0.00	0
2000	New York	A.L.	2	7^{1}/$_{3}$	1	0	1.000	5	5	5	2.45	0
2001	New York	A.L.	1	5^{2}/$_{3}$	1	0	1.000	5	2	8	3.18	0
2002	New York	A.L.	2	6^{1}/$_{3}$	0	1	.000	7	0	5	2.84	0
2005	Chicago	A.L.	1	3	0	0	.000	4	0	1	0.00	0
Division Series Totals			7	30^{1}/$_{3}$	3	1	.750	25	13	21	1.78	0

Championship Series

1998	New York	A.L.	1	7	1	0	1.000	6	2	3	0.00	0
1999	New York	A.L.	2	15	1	0	1.000	13	6	12	1.80	0
2000	New York	A.L.	2	15	2	0	1.000	14	8	13	4.20	0
2001	New York	A.L.	1	5	0	1	.000	7	5	5	7.20	0
2004	New York	A.L.	1	5	0	0	.000	6	5	3	5.40	0
Championship Series Totals			7	47	4	1	.800	46	26	36	3.26	0

World Series Record

1998	New York	A.L.	1	7	1	0	1.000	7	3	6	1.29	0
1999	New York	A.L.	1	7	1	0	1.000	10	2	1	1.29	0
2000	New York	A.L.	1	7^{1}/$_{3}$	0	1	.000	12	3	9	4.91	0
2001	New York	A.L.	1	6^{1}/$_{3}$	0	0	.000	5	4	4	1.42	0
2005	Chicago	A.L.	1	1	0	0	.000	2	4	0	0.00	0
World Series Totals			5	28^{2}/$_{3}$	2	1	.667	36	16	20	2.20	0

a Signed with New York Yankees, March 7, 1998.
b On disabled list from July 14 to August 5, 2000.
c On disabled list from May 26 to August 21, 2001.
d On disabled list from May 16 to June 27, 2002.
e Traded to Chicago White Sox with cash for pitcher Antonio Osuna and pitcher Delvis Lantigua, January 15, 2003.
f Traded to Montreal Expos with pitcher Rocky Biddle, outfielder Jeff Liefer and cash for pitcher Bartolo Colon and infielder Jorge Nunez, January 15, 2003. On disabled list from March 21 to October 27, 2003.
g Not offered contract, December 21, 2003. Signed with New York Yankees, March 11, 2004.
h On disabled list from March 19 to July 11, 2004.
i Filed for free agency, November 2, 2004. Signed with Chicago White Sox, December 22, 2004.
j On disabled list from May 17 to June 3 and June 15 to July 18, 2005.
k Traded to Arizona Diamondbacks with pitcher Luis Vizcaino and outfielder Chris Young for pitcher Javier Vazquez, December 20, 2005.
l Traded to New York Mets for pitcher Jorge Julio, May 24, 2006.
m Filed for free agency, October 28, 2006, re-signed with New York Mets, November 15, 2006.
n On disabled list from April 25 to May 25, 2007.

HILL, RICHARD JOSEPH (RICH)

Born, Boston, Massachusetts, March 11, 1980.
Bats Left. Throws Left. Height, 6 feet, 5 inches. Weight, 205 pounds.

Year	Club	Lea	G	IP	W	L	Pct	SO	BB	H	ERA	SAVES
2002 Boise	Northwest	6	14	0	2	.000	12	14	15	8.36	0
2003 Lansing	Midwest	15	29⅓	0	1	.000	50	36	14	2.76	0
2003 Boise	Northwest	14	68⅓	1	6	.143	99	32	57	4.35	0
2004 Daytona	Fla.St.	28	109⅓	7	6	.538	136	72	88	4.03	0
2005 West Tenn	Southern	10	57⅔	4	3	.571	90	21	42	3.28	0
2005 Peoria	Midwest	1	8	1	0	1.000	12	0	5	1.13	0
2005 Iowa	P.C.	11	65	6	1	.857	92	14	53	3.60	0
2005 Chicago	N.L.	10	23⅔	0	2	.000	21	17	25	9.13	0
2006 Iowa	P.C.	15	100	7	1	.875	135	21	62	1.80	0
2006 Chicago	N.L.	17	99⅓	6	7	.462	90	39	83	4.17	0
2007 Chicago	N.L.	32	195	11	8	.579	183	63	170	3.92	0
Major League Totals ....3 Yrs.		59	318	17	17	.500	294	119	278	4.39	0
Division Series											
2007 Chicago	N.L.	1	3	0	1	.000	3	2	6	9.00	0

HILL, SHAWN RICHARD

Born, Mississauga, Ontario, Canada, April 28, 1981.
Bats Right. Throws Right. Height, 6 feet, 2 inches. Weight, 185 pounds.

Year	Club	Lea	G	IP	W	L	Pct	SO	BB	H	ERA	SAVES
2000 Expos	Gulf Coast	7	24⅓	1	3	.250	20	10	25	4.81	0
2001 Vermont	N.Y.-Penn.	7	35⅔	2	2	.500	23	8	22	2.27	0
2002 Clinton	Midwest	25	146⅔	12	7	.632	99	35	149	3.44	0
2003 Harrisburg	Eastern	4	20⅓	3	1	.750	12	11	23	3.54	0
2003 Brevard County	Fla.St.	22	126⅔	9	4	.692	66	26	118	2.56	0
2004 Harrisburg	Eastern	17	87⅔	5	7	.417	53	20	90	3.39	0
2004 Montreal	N.L.	3	9	1	2	.333	10	7	17	16.00	0
2006 New Orleans	P.C.	1	5	0	0	.000	2	2	6	3.60	0
2006 Washington	N.L.	6	36⅔	1	3	.250	16	12	43	4.66	0
2006 Harrisburg a	Eastern	10	50⅓	3	3	.500	32	5	46	2.68	0
2007 Potomac	Carolina	2	7	0	0	.000	4	1	3	1.29	0
2007 Columbus	Int.	1	5	0	1	.000	0	0	4	1.80	0
2007 Washington b	N.L.	16	97⅓	4	5	.444	65	25	86	3.42	0
Major League Totals ....3 Yrs.		25	143	6	10	.375	91	44	146	4.53	0

a On disabled list from June 29 to October 6, 2006.
b On disabled list from May 12 to August 14, 2007.

HIRSH, JASON MICHAEL

Born, Santa Monica, California, February 20, 1982.
Bats Right. Throws Right. Height, 6 feet, 8 inches. Weight, 250 pounds.

Year	Club	Lea	G	IP	W	L	Pct	SO	BB	H	ERA	SAVES
2003 Tri-City	N.Y.-Penn.	10	32⅓	3	1	.750	33	7	22	1.95	0
2004 Salem	Carolina	26	130⅓	11	7	.611	96	57	128	4.01	0
2005 Corpus Christi	Texas	29	172⅓	13	8	.619	165	42	137	2.87	0
2006 Round Rock	P.C.	23	137⅓	13	2	.867	118	51	94	2.10	0

Year	Club	Lea	G	IP	W	L	Pct	SO	BB	H	ERA	SAVES
2006 Houston a	N.L.	9	44⅔	3	4	.429	29	22	48	6.04	0	
2007 Colorado Springs	P.C.	3	13	1	2	.333	7	4	16	4.85	0	
2007 Colorado b	N.L.	19	112⅓	5	7	.417	75	48	103	4.81	0	
Major League Totals ....2 Yrs.		28	157	8	11	.421	104	70	151	5.16	0	

a Traded to Colorado Rockies with outfielder Willy Taveras and pitcher Taylor Buchholz for pitcher Jason Jennings and pitcher Miguel Asencio, December 12, 2006.
b On disabled list from July 3 to August 2 and August 8 to October 30, 2007.

HOCHEVAR, LUKE ANTHONY
Born, Denver, Colorado, September 15, 1983.
Bats Right. Throws Right. Height, 6 feet, 5 inches. Weight, 205 pounds.

Year	Club	Lea	G	IP	W	L	Pct	SO	BB	H	ERA	SAVES
2006 Burlington	Midwest	4	15⅓	0	1	.000	16	2	8	1.17	0	
2007 Wichita	Texas	17	94	3	6	.333	94	26	110	4.69	0	
2007 Omaha	P.C.	10	58	1	3	.250	44	21	53	5.12	0	
2007 Kansas City	A.L.	4	12⅔	0	1	.000	5	4	11	2.13	0	

HOFFMAN, TREVOR WILLIAM
Born, Bellflower, California, October 13, 1967.
Bats Right. Throws Right. Height, 6 feet, 1 inch. Weight, 215 pounds.

Year	Club	Lea	G	IP	W	L	Pct	SO	BB	H	ERA	SAVES
1991 Cedar Rapids	Midwest	27	33⅔	1	1	.500	52	13	22	1.87	12
1991 Chattanooga.......	Southern	14	14	1	0	1.000	23	7	10	1.93	8
1992 Chattanooga.......	Southern	6	29⅔	3	0	1.000	31	11	22	1.52	0
1992 Nashville a	A.A.	42	65⅓	4	6	.400	63	32	57	4.27	6
1993 Florida-San Diego b	N.L.	67	90	4	6	.400	79	39	80	3.90	5
1994 San Diego	N.L.	47	56	4	4	.500	68	20	39	2.57	20
1995 San Diego	N.L.	55	53⅓	7	4	.636	52	14	48	3.88	31
1996 San Diego	N.L.	70	88	9	5	.643	111	31	50	2.25	42
1997 San Diego	N.L.	70	81⅓	6	4	.600	111	24	59	2.66	37
1998 San Diego	N.L.	66	73	4	2	.667	86	21	41	1.48	*53
1999 San Diego	N.L.	64	67⅓	2	3	.400	73	15	48	2.14	40
2000 San Diego	N.L.	70	72⅓	4	7	.364	85	11	61	2.99	43
2001 San Diego	N.L.	62	60⅓	3	4	.429	63	21	48	3.43	43
2002 San Diego	N.L.	61	59⅓	2	5	.286	69	18	52	2.73	38
2003 Lake Elsinore	California	3	3	0	0	.000	4	0	2	0.00	0
2003 San Diego c	N.L.	9	9	0	0	.000	11	3	7	2.00	0
2004 San Diego	N.L.	55	54⅔	3	3	.500	53	8	42	2.30	41
2005 San Diego d	N.L.	60	57⅔	1	6	.143	54	12	52	2.97	43
2006 San Diego	N.L.	65	63	0	2	.000	50	13	48	2.14	*46
2007 San Diego	N.L.	61	57⅓	4	5	.444	44	15	49	2.98	42
Major League Totals ....15 Yrs.		882	942⅔	53	60	.469	1009	265	724	2.73	524

Division Series

Year	Club	Lea	G	IP	W	L	Pct	SO	BB	H	ERA	SAVES
1996 San Diego	N.L.	2	1⅔	0	1	.000	2	1	3	10.80	0
1998 San Diego	N.L.	4	3	0	0	.000	4	1	3	0.00	2
2005 San Diego	N.L.	1	1	0	0	.000	0	0	1	0.00	0
2006 San Diego	N.L.	1	1	0	0	.000	1	0	0	0.00	1
Division Series Totals		8	6⅔	0	1	.000	7	2	7	2.70	3

Championship Series

Year	Club	Lea	G	IP	W	L	Pct	SO	BB	H	ERA	SAVES
1998 San Diego	N.L.	3	4⅓	1	0	1.000	7	2	2	2.08	1

World Series Record

Year	Club	Lea	G	IP	W	L	Pct	SO	BB	H	ERA	SAVES
1998 San Diego	N.L.	1	2	0	1	.000	0	1	2	9.00	0

Record as Position Player

Year	Club	Lea	Pos	G	AB	R	H	2B	3B	HR	RBI	SB	Avg
1989 Bellingham........	Pioneer	SS	61	201	22	50	5	0	1	20	1	.249
1990 Charleston	So. Atl.	SS-3B	103	278	41	59	10	1	2	23	3	.212

a Selected by Florida Marlins from Cincinnati Reds organization in expansion draft, November 17, 1992.
b Traded to San Diego Padres with pitchers Andres Berumen and Jose Martinez for infielder Greg Sheffield and pitcher Rich Rodriguez, June 25, 1993.
c On disabled list from March 25 to September 2, 2003.
d Filed for free agency, October 28, 2005, re-signed with San Diego Padres, December 7, 2005.

HOWRY, BOBBY DEAN (BOB)
Born, Phoenix, Arizona, August 4, 1973.
Bats Left. Throws Right. Height, 6 feet, 5 inches. Weight, 220 pounds.

Year Club	Lea	G	IP	W	L	Pct	SO	BB	H	ERA	SAVES
1994 Everett	Northwest	5	19	0	4	.000	16	10	29	7.11	0
1994 Clinton	.Midwest	9	49^1/$_3$	1	3	.250	22	16	61	4.20	0
1995 San Jose	California	27	165^1/$_3$	12	10	.545	107	54	171	3.54	0
1996 Shreveport	Texas	27	156^2/$_3$	10	8	.556	57	56	163	4.65	0
1997 Shreveport	Texas	48	55	6	3	.667	43	21	58	4.91	22
1997 Birmingham a	Southern	12	12^2/$_3$	0	0	.000	3	3	16	2.84	2
1998 Calgary.............	P.C.	23	31^2/$_3$	1	2	.333	22	10	25	3.41	5
1998 Chicago	A.L.	44	54^1/$_3$	0	3	.000	51	19	37	3.15	9
1999 Chicago	A.L.	69	67^2/$_3$	5	3	.625	80	38	58	3.59	28
2000 Chicago	A.L.	65	71	2	4	.333	60	29	54	3.17	7
2001 Chicago	A.L.	69	78^2/$_3$	4	5	.444	64	30	85	4.69	5
2002 Chicago-Boston b	A.L.	67	68^2/$_3$	3	5	.375	45	21	67	4.19	0
2003 Boston	A.L.	4	4^1/$_3$	0	0	.000	4	3	11	12.46	0
2003 Pawtucket c-d	Int.	13	17	2	0	1.000	10	1	14	1.06	0
2004 Buffalo	Int.	18	26	1	1	.500	24	6	22	5.19	0
2004 Cleveland	A.L.	37	42^2/$_3$	4	2	.667	39	12	37	2.74	0
2005 Cleveland e............	A.L.	79	73	7	4	.636	48	16	49	2.47	3
2006 Chicago	N.L.	84	76^2/$_3$	4	5	.444	71	17	70	3.17	5
2007 Chicago	N.L.	78	81^1/$_3$	6	7	.462	72	19	76	3.32	8
Major League Totals ......10 Yrs.		596	618^1/$_3$	35	38	.479	534	204	544	3.49	65
Division Series											
2000 Chicago	A.L.	2	2^2/$_3$	0	0	.000	4	2	2	3.38	0
2007 Chicago	N.L.	2	3	0	0	.000	6	0	1	0.00	0
Division Series Totals		4	5^2/$_3$	0	0	.000	10	2	3	1.59	0

a Traded by San Francisco Giants to Chicago White Sox with infielder Mike Caruso, outfielder Brian Manning, pitcher Lorenzo Barcelo, pitcher Keith Foulke and pitcher Ken Vining for pitcher Wilson Alvarez, pitcher Danny Darwin and pitcher Roberto Hernandez, July 31, 1997.

b Traded to Boston Red Sox for pitcher Franklin Francisco and pitcher Byeong An, July 31, 2002.

c On disabled list from August 22 to September 29, 2003.

d Released by Boston Red Sox October 24, 2003. Signed with Cleveland Indians organization, December 17, 2003.

e Filed for free agency, October 27, 2005. Signed with Chicago Cubs, November 29, 2005.

HUDSON, TIMOTHY ADAM (TIM)
Born, Columbus, Georgia, July 14, 1975.
Bats Right. Throws Right. Height, 6 feet, I inch. Weight, 170 pounds.

Year Club	Lea	G	IP	W	L	Pct	SO	BB	H	ERA	SAVES
1997 Sou Oregon	Northwest	8	28^2/$_3$	3	1	.750	37	15	12	2.51	0
1998 Modesto	California	8	37^2/$_3$	4	0	1.000	48	18	19	1.67	0
1998 Huntsville.........	Southern	22	134^2/$_3$	10	9	.526	104	71	136	4.54	0
1999 Midland	Texas	3	18	3	0	1.000	18	3	9	0.50	0
1999 Vancouver	P.C.	8	49	4	0	1.000	61	21	38	2.20	0
1999 Oakland	A.L.	21	136^1/$_3$	11	2	.846	132	62	121	3.23	0
2000 Oakland	A.L.	32	202^1/$_3$	*20	6	*.769	169	82	169	4.14	0
2001 Oakland	A.L.	35	235	18	9	.667	181	71	216	3.37	0
2002 Oakland	A.L.	34	238^1/$_3$	15	9	.625	152	62	237	2.98	0
2003 Oakland	A.L.	34	240	16	7	.696	162	61	197	2.70	0
2004 Sacramento	P.C.	1	3	0	0	.000	3	2	2	6.00	0
2004 Oakland a-b	A.L.	27	188^2/$_3$	12	6	.667	103	44	194	3.53	0
2005 Atlanta c............	N.L.	29	192	14	9	.609	115	65	194	3.52	0
2006 Atlanta	N.L.	35	218^1/$_3$	13	12	.520	141	79	235	4.86	0
2007 Atlanta	N.L.	34	224^1/$_3$	16	10	.615	132	53	221	3.33	0
Major League Totals ....9 Yrs.		281	1875^1/$_3$	135	70	.659	1287	579	1784	3.51	0
Division Series											
2000 Oakland	A.L.	1	8	0	1	.000	5	4	6	3.38	0
2001 Oakland	A.L.	2	9^2/$_3$	1	0	1.000	5	1	8	0.93	0
2002 Oakland	A.L.	2	8^2/$_3$	0	1	.000	8	4	13	6.23	0
2003 Oakland	A.L.	2	7^2/$_3$	0	0	.000	6	1	10	3.52	0
2005 Atlanta	N.L.	2	13^2/$_3$	0	1	.000	8	6	13	5.27	0
Division Series Totals		9	47^2/$_3$	1	3	.250	32	16	50	3.97	0

a On disabled list from June 23 to August 7, 2004.

b Traded to Atlanta Braves for pitcher Juan Cruz, pitcher Dan Meyer and outfielder Charles Thomas, December 16, 2004.

c On disabled list from June 14 to July 16, 2005.

HUGHES, PHILIP JOSEPH

Born, Mission Viejo, California, June 24, 1986.
Bats Right. Throws Right. Height, 6 feet, 5 inches. Weight, 220 pounds.

Year	Club	Lea	G	IP	W	L	Pct	SO	BB	H	ERA	SAVES
2004 Yankees	Gulf Coast		3	5	0	0	.000	8	0	4	0.00	0
2005 Tampa	Fla.St.		5	17²/₃	2	0	1.000	21	4	8	3.06	0
2005 Charleston	So.Atl.		12	68²/₃	7	1	.875	72	16	46	1.97	0
2006 Trenton	Eastern		21	116	10	3	.769	138	32	73	2.25	0
2006 Tampa	Fla.St.		5	30	2	3	.400	30	2	19	1.80	0
2007 Tampa	Fla.St.		1	2	0	0	.000	3	2	0	0.00	0
2007 Trenton	Eastern		2	7	0	0	.000	11	2	5	1.29	0
2007 Scranton-WB	Int.		5	28²/₃	4	1	.800	28	8	16	2.20	0
2007 New York	A.L.		13	72²/₃	5	3	.625	58	29	64	4.46	0
Division Series												
2007 New York	A.L.		2	5²/₃	1	0	1.000	6	0	3	1.59	0

a On disabled list from May 2 to August 4, 2007.

IGAWA, KEI

Born: Oarai, Japan, July 13, 1979
Bats Left. Throws Left. Height, 6 feet, 1 inch, Weight, 210 pounds.

Year	Club	Lea	G	IP	W	L	Pct	SO	BB	H	ERA	SAVES
1999 Hanshin	Japan Pac.		7	15¹/₃	1	1	.500	14	13	23	6.46	0
2000 Hanshin	Japan Pac.		9	39¹/₃	1	3	.250	37	19	36	4.35	0
2001 Hanshin	Japan Pac.		29	192	9	13	.409	171	89	174	2.67	0
2002 Hanshin	Japan Pac.		31	209²/₃	14	9	.609	206	53	163	2.49	1
2003 Hanshin	Japan Pac.		29	206	20	5	.800	179	58	184	2.80	0
2004 Hanshin	Japan Pac.		29	200¹/₃	14	11	.560	228	54	190	3.73	0
2005 Hanshin	Japan Pac.		27	172¹/₃	13	9	.591	145	60	199	3.86	0
2006 Hanshin a	Japan Pac.		29	209	14	9	.609	194	49	180	2.97	0
2007 Tampa	Fla.St.		2	9	1	1	.500	6	3	7	2.00	0
2007 Scranton-WB	Int.		11	68¹/₃	5	4	.556	71	15	68	3.69	0
2007 New York	A.L.		14	67²/₃	2	3	.400	53	37	76	6.25	0

a Signed with New York Yankees, December 27, 2006.

ISRINGHAUSEN, JASON DERIK

Born, Brighton, Illinois, September 7, 1972.
Bats Right. Throws Right. Height, 6 feet, 3 inches. Weight, 230 pounds.

Year	Club	Lea	G	IP	W	L	Pct	SO	BB	H	ERA	SAVES
1992 Mets	Gulf Coast		6	29	2	4	.333	25	17	26	4.34	0
1992 Kingsport	Appal.		7	36	4	1	.800	24	12	32	3.25	0
1993 Pittsfield	N.Y.-Penn.		15	90¹/₃	7	4	.636	104	28	68	3.29	0
1994 St. Lucie	Fla.St.		14	101	6	4	.600	59	27	76	2.23	0
1994 Binghamton	Eastern		14	92¹/₃	5	4	.556	69	23	78	3.02	0
1995 Binghamton	Eastern		6	41	2	1	.667	59	12	26	2.85	0
1995 Norfolk	Int.		12	87	9	1	.900	75	24	64	1.55	0
1995 New York	N.L.		14	93	9	2	.818	55	31	88	2.81	0
1996 New York a	N.L.		27	171²/₃	6	14	.300	114	73	190	4.77	0
1997 Mets	Gulf Coast		1	4²/₃	1	0	1.000	7	1	2	1.93	0
1997 St. Lucie	Fla.St.		2	12	1	0	1.000	15	5	8	0.00	0
1997 Norfolk	Int.		3	20	0	2	.000	17	8	20	4.05	0
1997 New York b	N.L.		6	29²/₃	2	2	.500	25	22	40	7.58	0
1998 New York c	N.L.				INJURED—Did Not Play							
1999 New York	N.L.		13	39¹/₃	1	3	.250	31	22	43	6.41	1
1999 Oakland d	A.L.		20	25¹/₃	0	1	.000	20	12	21	2.13	8
2000 Oakland	A.L.		66	69	6	4	.600	57	32	67	3.78	33
2001 Oakland e	A.L.		65	71¹/₃	4	3	.571	74	23	54	2.65	34
2002 St. Louis	N.L.		60	65¹/₃	3	2	.600	68	18	46	2.48	32
2003 Tennessee	Southern		2	2	0	0	.000	3	0	1	0.00	0
2003 St. Louis f	N.L.		40	42	0	1	.000	41	18	31	2.36	22
2004 St. Louis	N.L.		74	75¹/₃	4	2	.667	71	23	55	2.87	*47
2005 St. Louis g	N.L.		63	59	1	2	.333	51	27	43	2.14	39
2006 St. Louis	N.L.		59	58¹/₃	4	8	.333	52	38	47	3.55	33
2007 St. Louis	N.L.		63	65¹/₃	4	0	1.000	54	28	42	2.48	32
Major League Totals	12 Yrs.		570	864²/₃	44	44	.500	713	367	767	3.51	281
Division Series												
2000 Oakland	A.L.		2	2	0	0	.000	3	0	1	0.00	1
2001 Oakland	A.L.		2	2	0	0	.000	3	1	1	0.00	2
2002 St. Louis	N.L.		2	2	0	0	.000	1	0	0	0.00	2

Year	Club	Lea	G	IP	W	L	Pct	SO	BB	H	ERA	SAVES
2004 St. Louis............	N.L.		2	2	0	0	.000	2	2	1	4.50	0
2005 St. Louis............	N.L.		3	3	0	0	.000	4	1	5	3.00	1
Division Series Totals...........			11	11	0	0	.000	13	4	8	1.64	6
Championship Series												
2002 St. Louis.............	N.L.		2	2	0	0	.000	3	3	1	4.50	1
2004 St. Louis.............	N.L.		6	7²/3	0	1	.000	3	4	4	4.70	3
2005 St. Louis.............	N.L.		3	4	1	0	1.000	2	0	3	0.00	1
Championship Series Totals......			11	13²/3	1	1	.500	8	7	8	3.29	5
World Series Record												
2004 St. Louis.............	N.L.		1	2	0	0	.000	2	1	1	0.00	0

a On disabled list from August 13 to September 1, 1996.
b On disabled list from March 24 to August 27, 1997.
c On disabled list from March 21 to September 28, 1998.
d Traded to Oakland Athletics with pitcher Greg McMichael for pitcher Billy Taylor, July 31, 1999.
e Filed for free agency, November 5, 2001. Signed with St. Louis Cardinals, December 10, 2001.
f On disabled list from March 21 to June 10, 2003.
g On disabled list from April 27 to May 13, 2005.

JACKSON, EDWIN

Born, Neu-Ulm, West Germany, September 9, 1983.
Bats Right. Throws Right. Height, 6 feet, 3 inches. Weight, 190 pounds.

Year	Club	Lea	G	IP	W	L	Pct	SO	BB	H	ERA	SAVES
2001 Dodgers........	Gulf Coast		12	22	2	1	.667	23	19	14	2.45	0
2002 South Bend.........	So.Atl.		19	104²/3	5	2	.714	85	33	79	1.98	0
2003 Jacksonville.......	Southern		27	148¹/3	7	7	.500	157	53	121	3.70	0
2003 Los Angeles...........	N.L.		4	22	2	1	.667	19	11	17	2.45	0
2004 Las Vegas.............	P.C.		19	90²/3	6	4	.600	70	55	90	5.86	0
2004 Los Angeles a.........	N.L.		8	24²/3	2	1	.667	16	11	31	7.30	0
2005 Jacksonville.......	Southern		11	62	6	4	.600	44	18	52	3.48	0
2005 Las Vegas.............	P.C.		12	55¹/3	3	7	.300	33	37	76	8.62	0
2005 Los Angeles...........	N.L.		7	28²/3	2	2	.500	13	17	31	6.28	0
2006 Durham...............	Int.		22	73	3	7	.300	66	35	84	5.55	5
2006 Tampa Bay b	A.L.		23	36¹/3	0	0	.000	27	25	42	5.45	0
2007 Tampa Bay...........	A.L.		32	161	5	15	.250	128	88	195	5.76	0
Major League Totals.......5 Yrs.			74	272²/3	11	19	.367	203	152	316	5.64	0

a On disabled list from July 9 to September 7, 2004.
b Traded to Tampa Bay Devil Rays with pitcher Chuck Tiffany for pitcher Danys Baez and pitcher Lance Carter, January 14, 2006.

JAMES, CHARLES HAMILTON (CHUCK)

Born, Atlanta, Georgia, November 9, 1981.
Bats Left. Throws Left. Height, 6 feet. Weight, 190 pounds.

Year	Club	Lea	G	IP	W	L	Pct	SO	BB	H	ERA	SAVES
2003 Danville.............	Appal.		11	50¹/3	2	1	.667	68	19	26	1.25	0
2004 Rome................	So.Atl.		26	132²/3	10	5	.667	156	48	92	2.24	0
2005 Myrtle Beach.......Carolina			7	41²/3	3	3	.500	59	8	20	1.08	0
2005 Mississippi........	Southern		16	86	9	1	.900	104	18	62	2.09	0
2005 Richmond.............	Int.		6	33²/3	1	3	.250	30	10	21	3.48	0
2005 Atlanta...............	N.L.		2	5²/3	0	0	.000	5	3	4	1.59	0
2006 Rome................	So.Atl.		1	1	0	0	.000	1	0	0	0.00	0
2006 Richmond.............	Int.		7	33²/3	1	0	1.000	25	6	30	2.67	0
2006 Atlanta a.............	N.L.		25	119	11	4	.733	91	47	101	3.78	0
2007 Atlanta b.............	N.L.		30	161¹/3	11	10	.524	116	58	164	4.24	0
Major League Totals........3 Yrs.			57	286	22	14	.611	212	108	269	4.00	0

a On disabled list from May 6 to June 7, 2006.
b On disabled list from August 17 to September 1, 2007.

JANSSEN, ROBERT CASEY (CASEY)

Born, Orange, California, September 17, 1981.
Bats Right. Throws Right. Height, 6 feet, 4 inches. Weight, 205 pounds.

Year	Club	Lea	G	IP	W	L	Pct	SO	BB	H	ERA	SAVES
2004 Auburn..........N.Y.-Penn.			10	50	3	1	.750	45	10	47	3.60	0
2005 New Hampshire.....	Eastern		9	43	3	3	.500	47	4	49	2.93	0
2005 Dunedin............	Fla.St.		10	59²/3	6	1	.857	51	12	46	2.26	0
2005 Lansing...........	Midwest		7	46	4	0	1.000	38	4	27	1.37	0

258

Year	Club	Lea	G	IP	W	L	Pct	SO	BB	H	ERA	SAVES
2006 Syracuse	Int.	9	42²/₃	1	5	.167	32	8	47	4.85	0
2006 Toronto	A.L.	19	94	6	10	.375	44	21	103	5.07	0
2007 Toronto	A.L.	70	72²/₃	2	3	.400	39	20	67	2.35	6
Major League Totals .... 2 Yrs.		89	166²/₃	8	13	.381	83	41	170	3.89	6

JENKS, ROBERT SCOTT (BOBBY)
Born, Mission Hills, California, March 14, 1981.
Bats Right. Throws Right. Height, 6 feet, 3 inches. Weight, 280 pounds.

Year	Club	Lea	G	IP	W	L	Pct	SO	BB	H	ERA	SAVES
2000 Butte	Pioneer	14	52²/₃	1	7	.125	42	44	61	7.86	0
2001 Cedar Rapids	Midwest	21	99	3	7	.300	98	64	90	5.27	0
2001 Arkansas	Texas	2	10	1	0	1.000	10	5	8	3.60	0
2002 Rancho Cucamonga	California	11	65¹/₃	3	5	.375	64	46	50	4.82	0
2002 Arkansas	Texas	10	58	3	6	.333	58	44	49	4.66	0
2003 Angels	Arizona	1	4	0	0	.000	5	0	2	0.00	0
2003 Arkansas	Texas	16	83	7	2	.778	103	51	56	2.17	0
2004 Angels	Arizona	1	3¹/₃	0	0	.000	5	3	2	8.10	0
2004 Rancho Cucamonga	California	1	3²/₃	0	1	.000	3	7	5	19.64	0
2004 Salt Lake a	P.C.	3	12¹/₃	0	1	.000	13	6	19	8.76	0
2005 Birmingham	Southern	35	41	1	2	.333	48	20	34	2.85	19
2005 Chicago	A.L.	32	39¹/₃	1	1	.500	50	15	34	2.75	6
2006 Chicago	A.L.	67	69²/₃	3	4	.429	80	31	66	4.00	41
2007 Chicago	A.L.	66	65	3	5	.375	56	13	45	2.77	40
Major League Totals .... 3 Yrs.		165	174	7	10	.412	186	59	145	3.26	87
Division Series											
2005 Chicago	A.L.	2	3	0	0	.000	1	1	1	0.00	2
World Series Record											
2005 Chicago	A.L.	4	5	0	0	.000	7	2	3	3.60	2

a Claimed on waivers by Chicago White Sox from Anaheim Angels, December 17, 2004.

JIMENEZ, UBALDO
Born, Nagua, Dominican Republic, January 22, 1984.
Bats Right. Throws Right. Height, 6 feet, 4 inches. Weight, 200 pounds.

Year	Club	Lea	G	IP	W	L	Pct	SO	BB	H	ERA	SAVES
2002 Casper	Pioneer	14	62	3	5	.375	65	29	72	6.53	0
2003 Visalia	Calif.	1	5	1	0	1.000	7	1	3	0.00	0
2003 Asheville	So.Atl.	27	153²/₃	10	6	.625	138	67	129	3.46	0
2004 Visalia	Calif.	9	44¹/₃	4	1	.800	61	12	29	2.23	0
2005 Modesto	Calif.	14	72¹/₃	5	3	.625	78	40	61	3.98	0
2005 Tulsa	Texas	12	63	2	5	.286	53	31	58	5.43	0
2006 Tulsa	Texas	13	73¹/₃	9	2	.818	86	40	49	2.45	0
2006 Colorado Springs	P.C.	13	78¹/₃	5	2	.714	64	43	74	5.06	0
2006 Colorado	N.L.	2	7²/₃	0	0	.000	3	3	5	3.52	0
2007 Colorado Springs	P.C.	19	103	8	5	.615	89	62	110	5.85	0
2007 Colorado	N.L.	15	82	4	4	.500	68	37	70	4.28	0
Major League Totals .... 2 Yrs.		17	89²/₃	4	4	.500	71	40	75	4.22	0
Division Series											
2007 Colorado	N.L.	1	6¹/₃	0	0	.000	5	4	3	1.42	0
Championship Series											
2007 Colorado	N.L.	1	5	0	0	.000	6	4	5	1.80	0
World Series Record											
2007 Colorado	N.L.	1	4²/₃	0	1	.000	2	5	3	3.86	0

JOHNSON, RANDALL DAVID (RANDY)
Born, Walnut Creek, California, September 10, 1963.
Bats Right. Throws Left. Height, 6 feet, 10 inches. Weight, 230 pounds.

Year	Club	Lea	G	IP	W	L	Pct	SO	BB	H	ERA	SAVES
1985 Jamestown	N.Y.-Penn.	8	27¹/₃	0	3	.000	21	24	29	5.93	0
1986 West Palm Beach	Fla. St.	26	119²/₃	8	7	.533	133	94	89	3.16	0
1987 Jacksonville	Southern	25	140	11	8	.579	*163	128	100	3.73	0
1988 Indianapolis	A.A.	20	113¹/₃	8	7	.533	111	72	85	3.26	0
1988 Montreal	N.L.	4	26	3	0	1.000	25	7	23	2.42	0
1989 Montreal	N.L.	7	29²/₃	0	4	.000	26	26	29	6.67	0
1989 Indianapolis a	A.A.	3	18	1	1	.500	17	9	13	2.00	0
1989 Seattle	A.L.	22	131	7	9	.438	104	70	118	4.40	0

Year	Club	Lea	G	IP	W	L	Pct	SO	BB	H	ERA	SAVES
1990	Seattle b-c	A.L.	33	219²/₃	14	11	.560	194	*120	174	3.65	0
1991	Seattle	A.L.	33	201¹/₃	13	10	.565	228	*152	151	3.98	0
1992	Seattle d	A.L.	31	210¹/₃	12	14	.462	*241	*144	154	3.77	0
1993	Seattle	A.L.	35	255¹/₃	19	8	.704	*308	99	185	3.24	1
1994	Seattle	A.L.	23	172	13	6	.684	*204	72	132	3.19	0
1995	Seattle e	A.L.	30	214¹/₃	18	2	*.900	*294	65	159	*2.48	0
1996	Everett	Northwest	1	2	0	0	.000	5	0	0	0.00	0
1996	Seattle f	A.L.	14	61¹/₃	5	0	1.000	85	25	48	3.67	1
1997	Seattle	A.L.	30	213	20	4	*.833	291	77	147	2.28	0
1998	Seattle	A.L.	23	160	9	10	.474	213	60	146	4.33	0
1998	Houston g-h-i.	N.L.	11	84¹/₃	10	1	.909	116	26	57	1.28	0
1999	Arizona j	N.L.	35	*271²/₃	17	9	.654	364	70	*207	*2.48	0
2000	Arizona k	N.L.	35	248²/₃	19	7	*.731	*347	76	202	2.64	0
2001	Arizona l	N.L.	35	249²/₃	21	6	.778	*372	71	181	*2.49	0
2002	Arizona m	N.L.	35	*260	*24	5	*.828	*334	71	197	*2.32	0
2003	Lancaster	California	1	6	0	1	.000	6	0	11	6.00	0
2003	Tucson	P.C.	1	4	0	0	.000	4	0	0	0.00	0
2003	El Paso	Texas	1	4	0	0	.000	5	1	3	0.00	0
2003	Arizona n	N.L.	18	114	6	8	.429	125	27	125	4.26	0
2004	Arizona o-p	N.L.	35	245²/₃	16	14	.533	*290	44	177	2.60	0
2005	New York	A.L.	34	225²/₃	17	8	.680	211	47	207	3.79	0
2006	New York	A.L.	33	205	17	11	.607	172	60	194	5.00	0
2007	Visalia	Calif.	1	6	0	0	.000	4	0	4	3.00	0
2007	Tucson	P.C.	2	12	1	0	1.000	10	2	15	3.00	0
2007	Arizona r	N.L.	10	56²/₃	4	3	.571	72	13	52	3.81	0
Major League Totals	20 Yrs.		566	3855¹/₃	284	150	.654	4616	1422	3065	3.22	2
Division Series												
1995	Seattle	A.L.	2	10	2	0	1.000	16	6	5	2.70	0
1997	Seattle	A.L.	2	13	0	2	.000	16	6	14	5.54	0
1998	Houston	N.L.	2	14	0	2	.000	17	2	12	1.93	0
1999	Arizona	N.L.	1	8¹/₃	0	1	.000	11	3	8	7.56	0
2001	Arizona	N.L.	1	8	0	1	.000	9	2	6	3.38	0
2002	Arizona	N.L.	1	6	0	1	.000	4	2	10	7.50	0
2005	New York	A.L.	2	7¹/₃	0	0	.000	4	1	12	6.14	0
2006	New York q	A.L.	1	5²/₃	0	1	.000	4	2	8	7.94	0
Division Series Totals			12	72¹/₃	2	8	.200	81	24	75	4.85	0
Championship Series												
1995	Seattle	A.L.	2	15¹/₃	0	1	.000	13	2	12	2.35	0
2001	Arizona	N.L.	2	16	2	0	1.000	19	3	10	1.13	0
Championship Series Totals			4	31¹/₃	2	1	.667	32	5	22	1.72	0
World Series Record												
2001	Arizona	N.L.	3	17¹/₃	3	0	1.000	19	3	9	1.04	0

a Traded by Montreal Expos to Seattle Mariners with pitchers Brian Holman and Gene Harris for pitcher Mark Langston and player to be named, May 25; Montreal acquired pitcher Mike Campbell to complete trade, July 31, 1989.

b Pitched no-hit, no-run game against Detroit Tigers, winning 2-0, June 2, 1990.

c Suspended three games by American League for June 30 fight from July 11 to July 13, 1990.

d On disabled list from June 11 to June 27, 1992.

e Selected Cy Young Award Winner in American League for 1995.

f On disabled list from May 13 to August 6 and August 27 to September 30, 1996.

g Traded to Houston Astros for infielder Carlos Guillen, pitcher Freddy Garcia and player to be named later, July 31, 1998.

h Seattle Mariners received pitcher John Halama to complete trade, October 1, 1998.

i Filed for free agency, October 28, 1998. Signed with Arizona Diamondbacks, November 30, 1998.

j Selected Cy Young Award Winner in National League for 1999.

k Selected Cy Young Award Winner in National League for 2000.

l Selected Cy Young Award Winner in National League for 2001.

m Selected Cy Young Award Winner in National League for 2002.

n On disabled list from April 12 to April 27 and April 28 to July 20, 2003.

o Pitched no-hit, no-run perfect game against Atlanta Braves, May 18, 2004.

p Traded to New York Yankees for pitcher Javier Vazquez, pitcher Brad Halsey, catcher Dioner Navarro and cash, January 11, 2005.

q Traded to Arizona Diamondbacks with cash for pitcher Luis Vizcaino, pitcher Steven Jackson, pitcher Ross Ohlendorf and infielder Alberto Gonzalez, January 9, 2007.

r On disabled list from March 30 to April 24 and June 11 to June 28 and June 29 to November 9, 2007.

JOHNSON, TYLER JAMES

Born, Columbia, Missouri, June 7, 1981.
Bats Both. Throws Left. Height, 6 feet, 2 inches. Weight, 180 pounds.

Year	Club	Lea	G	IP	W	L	Pct	SO	BB	H	ERA	SAVES
2001	Johnson City	Appal.	9	40²/₃	1	1	.500	58	21	26	2.66	0
2001	Peoria	Midwest	3	13²/₃	0	1	.000	15	10	14	3.95	0
2002	Peoria	Midwest	22	121¹/₃	15	3	.833	132	42	96	2.00	0
2003	Palm Beach	Fla.St.	22	79	5	5	.500	81	38	79	3.08	0
2003	Tennessee	Southern	20	27¹/₃	1	0	1.000	39	15	16	1.65	0
2004	Tennessee	Southern	53	56¹/₃	2	2	.500	77	37	48	4.79	4
2005	Memphis	P.C.	57	59	2	1	.667	77	26	51	4.27	7
2005	St. Louis a	N.L.	5	2²/₃	0	0	.000	4	3	3	0.00	0
2006	Memphis	P.C.	8	8¹/₃	0	0	.000	8	4	12	8.64	0
2006	St. Louis	N.L.	56	36¹/₃	2	4	.333	37	23	33	4.95	0
2007	Springfield	Texas	3	3	0	0	.000	3	2	2	3.00	0
2007	Memphis	P.C.	1	1	0	0	.000	1	0	0	0.00	0
2007	St. Louis b	N.L.	55	38	1	1	.500	24	16	31	4.03	0
Major League Totals	3 Yrs.		116	77	3	5	.375	65	42	67	4.32	0
Division Series												
2006	St. Louis	N.L.	4	2²/₃	0	0	.000	6	1	2	0.00	0
Championship Series												
2006	St. Louis	N.L.	4	3²/₃	0	0	.000	5	1	2	2.45	0
World Series Record												
2006	St. Louis	N.L.	2	1	0	0	.000	1	0	0	0.00	0

a Selected by Oakland Athletics from St. Louis Cardinals in Rule V draft, December 13, 2004. Returned to St. Louis Cardinals, March 22, 2005.
b On disabled list from June 19 to August 6, 2007.

JONES, TODD BARTON

Born, Marietta, Georgia, April 24, 1968.
Bats Left. Throws Right. Height, 6 feet, 3 inches. Weight, 230 pounds.

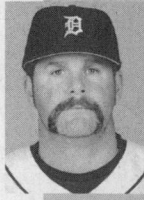

Year	Club	Lea	G	IP	W	L	Pct	SO	BB	H	ERA	SAVES
1989	Auburn	N.Y.-Penn.	11	49²/₃	2	3	.400	71	42	47	5.44	0
1990	Osceola	Fla. St.	27	151¹/₃	12	10	.545	106	109	124	3.51	0
1991	Osceola	Fla. St.	14	72¹/₃	4	4	.500	51	35	69	4.35	0
1991	Jackson	Texas	10	55¹/₃	4	3	.571	37	39	51	4.88	0
1992	Jackson	Texas	61	66	3	7	.300	60	44	52	3.14	25
1992	Tucson	P.C.	3	4	0	1	.000	4	10	1	4.50	0
1993	Tucson	P.C.	41	48²/₃	4	2	.667	45	31	49	4.44	12
1993	Houston	N.L.	27	37¹/₃	1	2	.333	25	15	28	3.13	2
1994	Houston	N.L.	48	72²/₃	5	2	.714	63	26	52	2.72	5
1995	Houston	N.L.	68	99²/₃	6	5	.545	96	52	89	3.07	15
1996	Tucson	P.C.	1	2	0	0	.000	0	2	1	0.00	0
1996	Houston a-b	N.L.	51	57¹/₃	6	3	.667	44	32	61	4.40	17
1997	Detroit	A.L.	68	70	5	4	.556	70	35	60	3.09	31
1998	Detroit	A.L.	65	63¹/₃	1	4	.200	57	36	58	4.97	28
1999	Detroit	A.L.	65	66¹/₃	4	4	.500	64	35	64	3.80	30
2000	Detroit	A.L.	67	64	2	4	.333	67	25	67	3.52	*42
2001	Detroit-Minnesota c-d	A.L.	69	68	5	5	.500	54	29	87	4.24	13
2002	Colorado	N.L.	79	82¹/₃	1	4	.200	73	28	84	4.70	1
2003	Colorado	N.L.	33	39¹/₃	1	4	.200	28	18	61	8.24	0
2003	Boston e-f	A.L.	26	29¹/₃	2	1	.667	31	13	32	5.52	0
2004	Cincinnati-Philadelphia g-h-i	N.L.	78	82¹/₃	11	5	.688	59	33	84	4.15	2
2005	Florida j	N.L.	68	73	1	5	.167	62	14	61	2.10	40
2006	Detroit k	A.L.	62	64	2	6	.250	28	11	70	3.94	37
2007	Detroit l	A.L.	63	61¹/₃	1	4	.200	33	23	64	4.26	38
Major League Totals	15 Yrs.		937	1030¹/₃	54	62	.466	854	425	1022	3.93	301
Division Series												
2006	Detroit	A.L.	2	2	0	0	.000	2	0	1	0.00	1
Championship Series												
2003	Boston	A.L.	1	0¹/₃	0	0	.000	1	1	1	0.00	0
2006	Detroit	A.L.	3	3	0	0	.000	2	1	3	0.00	2
Championship Series Totals			4	3¹/₃	0	0	.000	3	2	4	0.00	2
World Series Record												
2006	Detroit	A.L.	2	1²/₃	0	0	.000	0	0	3	0.00	1

a On disabled list from July 19 to August 12 and August 18 to September 12, 1996.
b Traded to Detroit Tigers with outfielder Brian Hunter, infielder Orlando Miller and pitcher Doug Brocail for catcher Brad Ausmus, pitcher C.J. Nitkowski, pitcher Jose Lima, pitcher Trever Miller and infielder Daryle Ward, December 10, 1996.
c Traded to Minnesota Twins for pitcher Mark Redman, July 28, 2001.

d Filed for free agency, November 5, 2001. Signed with Colorado Rockies, January 11, 2002.
e Released by Colorado Rockies, June 30, 2003. Signed with Boston Red Sox, July 2, 2003.
f Filed for free agency, October 30, 2003. Signed with Tampa Bay Devil Rays organization, January 12, 2004.
g Released by Tampa Bay Devil Rays, March 24, 2004. Signed with Cincinnati Reds organization, March 25, 2004.
h Traded to Philadelphia Phillies with outfielder Brad Correll for pitcher Josh Hancock and infielder Anderson Machado, July 30, 2004.
i Filed for free agency, October 29, 2004. Signed with Florida Marlins, December 13, 2004.
j Filed for free agency, October 28, 2005. Signed with Detroit Tigers, December 8, 2005.
k On disabled list from April 5 to April 21, 2006.
l Filed for free agency, October 29, 2007, re-signed with Detroit Tigers, November 12, 2007.

JULIO, JORGE DANDYS
Born, Caracas, Venezuela, March 3, 1979.
Bats Right. Throws Right. Height, 6 feet, 1 inch. Weight, 235 pounds.

Year Club	Lea	G	IP	W	L	Pct	SO	BB	H	ERA	SAVES
1996 Montreal......... Dominican	10	$16^{1}/_{3}$	1	1	.500	21	11	13	6.06	0
1997 Expos........... Gulf Coast	15	$55^{1}/_{3}$	5	6	.455	42	21	57	3.58	1
1997 Wst Plm Bch .... Fla.St.	1	0	0	0	.000	0	0	2	0.00	0
1998 Vermont......... N.Y.-Penn.	7	42	3	1	.750	52	15	30	2.57	0
1998 Cape Fear........... So.Atl.	6	$31^{2}/_{3}$	2	2	.500	20	12	33	5.68	0
1999 Jupiter .... Fla.St.	23	$114^{2}/_{3}$	4	8	.333	80	34	116	3.92	0
2000 Jupiter a........... Fla.St.	21	$79^{1}/_{3}$	2	10	.167	67	35	93	5.90	1
2001 Bowie............ Eastern	12	$12^{1}/_{3}$	0	0	.000	14	2	5	0.73	7
2001 Rochester............... Int.	34	$43^{1}/_{3}$	1	2	.333	48	19	39	3.74	12
2001 Baltimore............ A.L.	18	$21^{1}/_{3}$	1	1	.500	22	9	25	3.80	0
2002 Baltimore............ A.L.	67	68	5	6	.455	55	27	55	1.99	25
2003 Baltimore............ A.L.	64	$61^{2}/_{3}$	0	7	.000	52	34	60	4.38	36
2004 Baltimore............ A.L.	65	69	2	5	.286	70	39	59	4.57	22
2005 Baltimore............ A.L.	67	$71^{2}/_{3}$	3	5	.375	58	24	76	5.90	0
2006 New York-Arizona b-c ... N.L.	62	66	2	4	.333	88	35	52	4.23	16
2007 Jupiter .... Fla.St.	2	5	0	1	.000	6	1	11	3.60	0
2007 Florida-Colorado d-e-f-g . N.L.	68	62	0	5	.000	56	31	68	5.23	0
Major League Totals ....7 Yrs.	411	$419^{2}/_{3}$	13	33	.283	401	199	395	4.35	99

a Traded by Montreal Expos to Baltimore Orioles for infielder Ryan Minor, December 23, 2000.
b Traded to New York Mets with pitcher John Maine for pitcher Kris Benson, January 21, 2006.
c Traded to Arizona Diamondbacks for pitcher Orlando Hernandez, May 24, 2006.
d Traded to Florida Marlins for pitcher Yusmeiro Petit, March 26, 2007.
e On disabled list from April 18 to May 4, 2007.
f Traded to Colorado Rockies for pitcher Byung-Hyun Kim, May 13, 2007.
g Filed for free agency, October 29, 2007.

KAZMIR, SCOTT EDWARD
Born, Houston, Texas, January 24, 1984.
Bats Left. Throws Left. Height, 6 feet. Weight, 190 pounds.

Year Club	Lea	G	IP	W	L	Pct	SO	BB	H	ERA	SAVES
2002 Brooklyn......... N.Y.-Penn.	5	18	0	1	.000	34	7	5	0.50	0
2003 St. Lucie........... Fla.St.	7	33	1	2	.333	40	16	29	3.27	0
2003 Capital City......... So.Atl.	18	$76^{1}/_{3}$	4	4	.500	105	28	50	2.36	0
2004 St. Lucie........... Fla.St.	11	50	1	2	.333	51	22	49	3.42	0
2004 Binghamton ...... Eastern	4	26	2	1	.667	29	9	16	1.73	0
2004 Montgomery ...... Southern	4	25	1	2	.333	24	11	14	1.44	0
2004 Tampa Bay a........... A.L.	8	$33^{1}/_{3}$	2	3	.400	41	21	33	5.67	0
2005 Tampa Bay .... A.L.	32	186	10	9	.526	174	*100	172	3.77	0
2006 Tampa Bay b .... A.L.	24	$144^{2}/_{3}$	10	8	.556	163	52	132	3.24	0
2007 Tampa Bay............ A.L.	34	$206^{2}/_{3}$	13	9	.591	*239	89	196	3.48	0
Major League Totals ....4 Yrs.	98	$570^{2}/_{3}$	35	29	.547	617	262	533	3.64	0

a Traded by New York Mets to Tampa Bay Devil Rays with pitcher Jose Diaz for pitcher Victor Zambrano and pitcher Bartolome Fortunado, July 30, 2004.
b On disabled list from July 31 to August 8 and August 23 to October 2, 2006.

KENDRICK, KYLE RODNEY
Born, Houston, Texas, August 26, 1984.
Bats Right. Throws Right. Height, 6 feet, 3 inches. Weight, 190 pounds.

Year Club	Lea	G	IP	W	L	Pct	SO	BB	H	ERA	SAVES
2003 Phillies........... Gulf Coast	9	$31^{1}/_{3}$	0	4	.000	26	12	40	5.46	0
2004 Batavia.......... N.Y.-Penn.	13	$70^{2}/_{3}$	2	8	.200	53	18	94	5.48	0

Year	Club	Lea	G	IP	W	L	Pct	SO	BB	H	ERA	SAVES
2004 Lakewood	So.Atl.	15	66²/₃	3	8	.273	36	33	85	6.07	0
2005 Clearwater	Fla.St.	1	4	0	1	.000	1	2	5	0.00	0
2005 Batavia	N.Y.-Penn.	14	91¹/₃	5	4	.556	70	22	94	3.74	0
2005 Lakewood	So.Atl.	5	22²/₃	0	3	.000	11	10	38	9.13	0
2006 Clearwater	Fla.St.	21	130	9	7	.563	79	37	117	3.53	0
2006 Lakewood	So.Atl.	7	46	3	2	.600	54	15	34	2.15	0
2007 Reading	Eastern	12	81¹/₃	4	7	.364	50	18	82	3.21	0
2007 Philadelphia	N.L.	20	121	10	4	.714	49	25	129	3.87	0
Division Series											
2007 Philadelphia	N.L.	1	3²/₃	0	1	.000	2	2	5	12.27	0

KIM, BYUNG-HYUN

Born, Kwangju, South Korea, January 19, 1979.
Bats Right. Throws Right. Height, 5 feet, 9 inches. Weight, 175 pounds.

Year	Club	Lea	G	IP	W	L	Pct	SO	BB	H	ERA	SAVES
1999 El Paso	Texas	10	21¹/₃	2	0	1.000	32	9	6	2.11	0
1999 Tucson	P.C.	11	30	4	0	1.000	40	15	21	2.40	1
1999 Arizona	N.L.	25	27¹/₃	1	2	.333	31	20	20	4.61	1
1999 Diamondbacks a	Arizona	1	2	0	0	.000	2	1	1	0.00	0
2000 Arizona	N.L.	61	70²/₃	6	6	.500	111	46	52	4.46	14
2000 Tucson	P.C.	2	8¹/₃	0	0	.000	13	4	1	0.00	0
2001 Arizona	N.L.	78	98	5	6	.455	113	44	58	2.94	19
2002 Arizona	N.L.	72	84	8	3	.727	92	26	64	2.04	36
2003 Arizona	N.L.	7	43	1	5	.167	33	15	34	3.56	0
2003 Tucson	P.C.	3	17²/₃	1	1	.500	8	1	17	2.55	0
2003 Boston b-c	A.L.	49	79¹/₃	8	5	.615	69	18	70	3.18	16
2004 Sarasota	Fla.St.	1	2	0	0	.000	2	0	0	0.00	0
2004 Pawtucket	Int.	22	60²/₃	2	6	.250	39	12	71	5.34	0
2004 Boston d	A.L.	7	17¹/₃	2	1	.667	6	7	17	6.23	0
2005 Colorado e-f	N.L.	40	148	5	12	.294	115	71	156	4.86	0
2006 Colorado Springs	P.C.	3	13	0	1	.000	11	4	18	6.23	0
2006 Colorado g	N.L.	27	155	8	12	.400	129	61	179	5.57	0
2007 Colorado Springs	P.C.	5	24¹/₃	1	1	.500	31	11	21	2.96	0
2007 Col.-Fl.-Ariz. h-i-j-k-l	N.L.	28	118¹/₃	10	8	.556	107	68	131	6.08	0
Major League Totals	9 Yrs.	394	841	54	60	.474	806	376	781	4.42	86
Division Series											
2001 Arizona	N.L.	1	1¹/₃	0	0	.000	1	2	1	0.00	1
2002 Arizona	N.L.	1	1	0	0	.000	0	3	2	18.00	0
2003 Boston	A.L.	1	0²/₃	0	0	.000	1	1	0	13.50	0
Division Series Totals		3	3	0	0	.000	2	6	3	9.00	1
Championship Series											
2001 Arizona	N.L.	3	5	0	0	.000	3	1	0	0.00	2
World Series Record											
2001 Arizona	N.L.	2	3¹/₃	0	1	.000	6	1	6	13.50	0

a On disabled list from July 28 to September 10, 1999.
b On disabled list from April 30 to May 27, 2003.
c Traded to Boston Red Sox for infielder Shea Hillenbrand, May 29, 2003.
d On disabled list from March 31 to April 29, 2004.
e Traded to Colorado Rockies for catcher Charles Johnson, pitcher Chris Narveson and cash, March 30, 2005.
f Filed for free agency, October 31, 2005, re-signed with Colorado Rockies, January 6, 2006.
g On disabled list from March 29 to April 30, 2006.
h Traded to Florida Marlins for pitcher Jorge Julio, May 13, 2007.
i On disabled list from April 16 to May 17, 2007.
j Claimed on waivers by Arizona Diamondbacks, August 3, 2007.
k Released by Arizona Diamondbacks, August 15, 2007. Signed with Florida Marlins, August 25, 2007.
l Filed for free agency, October 31, 2007.

KING, RAYMOND KEITH (RAY)

Born, Chicago, Illinois, January 15, 1974.
Bats Left. Throws Left. Height, 6 feet, 1 inch. Weight, 240 pounds.

Year	Club	Lea	G	IP	W	L	Pct	SO	BB	H	ERA	SAVES
1995 Billings	Pioneer	28	43	3	0	1.000	43	15	31	1.67	5
1996 Macon	So.Atl.	18	70²/₃	3	5	.375	63	20	63	2.80	0
1996 Durham a-b	Carolina	14	82²/₃	3	6	.333	52	15	104	4.46	0
1997 Greenville	Southern	12	65²/₃	5	5	.500	42	24	85	6.85	0
1997 Durham	Carolina	24	71²/₃	6	9	.400	60	26	89	5.40	3
1998 West Tenn	Southern	25	29²/₃	1	2	.333	26	10	23	2.43	3

Year	Club	Lea	G	IP	W	L	Pct	SO	BB	H	ERA	SAVES
1998	Iowa c	P.C.	37	32⅓	1	3	.250	26	15	36	5.01	2
1999	Iowa	P.C.	37	43	4	4	.500	41	22	31	1.88	2
1999	Chicago	N.L.	10	10⅔	0	0	.000	5	10	11	5.91	0
2000	Iowa	P.C.	1	1⅓	1	0	1.000	1	0	1	0.00	0
2000	Indianapolis	Int.	29	25⅔	0	3	.000	20	12	26	3.51	1
2000	Milwaukee d	N.L.	36	28⅔	3	2	.600	19	10	18	1.26	0
2001	Milwaukee	N.L.	82	55	0	4	.000	49	25	49	3.60	1
2002	Indianapolis	Int.	1	1	0	0	.000	1	1	1	0.00	0
2002	Milwaukee e-f	N.L.	76	65	3	2	.600	50	24	61	3.05	0
2003	Atlanta g	N.L.	80	59	3	4	.429	43	27	46	3.51	0
2004	St. Louis	N.L.	86	62	5	2	.714	40	24	43	2.61	0
2005	St. Louis h	N.L.	77	40	4	4	.500	23	16	46	3.38	0
2006	Colorado i	N.L.	67	44⅔	1	4	.200	23	20	56	4.43	1
2007	Harrisburg	Eastern	1	1⅓	0	0	.000	1	1	0	0.00	0
2007	Washington-Milwaukee j-k-l	N.L.	67	39⅔	1	1	.500	25	21	37	4.76	0
Major League Totals	9 Yrs.		581	404⅔	20	23	.465	277	177	367	3.43	2
Division Series												
2003	Atlanta	N.L.	4	0⅔	0	0	.000	0	1	1	0.00	0
2004	St. Louis	N.L.	3	2⅓	0	0	.000	1	0	0	0.00	0
Division Series Totals			7	3	0	0	.000	1	1	1	0.00	0
Championship Series												
2004	St. Louis	N.L.	4	1⅔	0	0	.000	1	0	4	10.80	0
World Series Record												
2004	St. Louis	N.L.	3	2⅔	0	0	.000	1	1	1	0.00	0

a Cincinnati Reds traded pitcher Chad Fox to Atlanta Braves with player named later for outfielder Mike Kelly, January 9, 1996.
b Sent to Atlanta Braves to complete trade, June 11, 1996.
c Traded to Chicago Cubs for pitcher Jon Ratliff, January 20, 1998.
d Traded to Milwaukee Brewers for pitcher Doug Johnston, April 14, 2000.
e On disabled list from April 4 to April 19, 2002.
f Traded to Atlanta Braves for infielder Wes Helms and pitcher John Foster, December 16, 2002.
g Traded to St. Louis Cardinals with pitcher Jason Marquis and pitcher Adam Wainwright for catcher Eli Marrero and outfielder J.D. Drew, December 13, 2003.
h Traded to Colorado Rockies for infielder Aaron Miles and outfielder Larry Bigbie, December 7, 2005.
i Filed for free agency, October 28, 2006. Signed with Washington Nationals organization, December 18, 2006.
j On disabled list from April 12 to April 29, 2007.
k Traded to Milwaukee Brewers for player to be named later, September 4, 2007. Washington Nationals received pitcher Andrew LeFave to complete trade, September 14, 2007.
l Filed for free agency, October 29, 2007. Signed with Washington Nationals organization, November 30, 2007.

KLINE, STEVEN JAMES (STEVE)

Born, Sunbury, Pennsylvania, August 22, 1972.
Bats Both. Throws Left. Height, 6 feet, 1 inches. Weight, 210 pounds.

Year	Club	Lea	G	IP	W	L	Pct	SO	BB	H	ERA	SAVES
1993	Burlington	Appal.	2	7⅓	1	1	.500	4	2	11	4.91	0
1993	Watertown	N.Y.-Penn.	13	79	5	4	.556	45	12	77	3.19	0
1994	Columbus	So. Atl.	28	185⅔	18	5	.783	174	36	175	3.01	0
1995	Canton-Akrn.	Eastern	14	89⅓	2	3	.400	45	30	86	2.42	0
1996	Canton-Akrn.	Eastern	25	146⅔	8	12	.400	107	55	168	5.46	0
1997	Buffalo	A.A.	20	51⅓	3	3	.500	41	13	53	4.03	1
1997	Cleveland a	A.L.	20	26⅓	3	1	.750	17	13	42	5.81	0
1997	Montreal	N.L.	26	26⅓	1	3	.250	20	10	31	6.15	0
1998	Ottawa	Int.	2	2⅔	0	0	.000	1	0	1	0.00	0
1998	Montreal	N.L.	78	71⅔	3	6	.333	76	41	62	2.76	1
1999	Montreal b	N.L.	*82	69⅔	7	4	.636	69	33	56	3.75	0
2000	Montreal c	N.L.	*83	82⅓	1	5	.167	64	27	88	3.50	14
2001	St. Louis	N.L.	*89	75	3	3	.500	54	29	53	1.80	9
2002	Peoria	Midwest	2	2⅓	0	0	.000	5	1	1	0.00	0
2002	New Haven	Eastern	1	2	0	0	.000	2	1	0	0.00	0
2002	St. Louis d	N.L.	66	58⅓	2	1	.667	41	21	54	3.39	6
2003	St. Louis e	N.L.	78	63⅔	5	5	.500	31	30	56	3.82	3
2004	St. Louis f-g	N.L.	67	50⅓	2	2	.500	35	17	37	1.79	3
2005	Baltimore h	A.L.	67	61	2	4	.333	36	30	59	4.28	0
2006	San Francisco i	N.L.	72	51⅔	4	3	.571	33	26	53	3.66	1
2007	San Francisco	N.L.	68	46	1	2	.333	17	18	58	4.70	2
Major League Totals	11 Yrs.		796	682⅓	34	39	.466	493	295	649	3.51	39
Division Series												
2001	St. Louis	N.L.	4	4⅓	0	1	.000	0	2	4	2.08	2
2002	St. Louis	N.L.	2	1⅓	0	0	.000	0	1	1	0.00	0

Year Club	Lea	G	IP	W	L	Pct	SO	BB	H	ERA	SAVES
2004 St. Louis.............	N.L.	2	$1\frac{1}{3}$	0	0	.000	0	0	0	0.00	0
Division Series Totals...........		8	7	0	1	.000	0	3	5	1.29	2
Championship Series											
2002 St. Louis.............	N.L.	4	$2\frac{1}{3}$	0	0	.000	1	0	2	0.00	0
2004 St. Louis.............	N.L.	1	0	0	0	.000	0	0	2	INF	0
Championship Series Totals......		5	$2\frac{1}{3}$	0	0	.000	1	0	4	0.00	0

a Traded to Montreal Expos with player to be named later for pitcher Jeff Juden, July 31, 1997.
b On disabled list from April 11 to April 27, 1999.
c Traded to St. Louis Cardinals with pitcher Dustin Hermanson for infielder Fernando Tatis and pitcher Britt Reames, December 14, 2000.
d On disabled list from April 29 to May 31, 2002.
e Filed for free agency, October 27, 2003, re-signed with St. Louis Cardinals, December 7, 2003.
f On disabled list from August 28 to September 29, 2004.
g Filed for free agency, November 1, 2004. Signed with Baltimore Orioles, December 20, 2004.
h Traded to San Francisco Giants for pitcher La Troy Hawkins, December 6, 2005.
i Filed for free agency, October 29, 2006, re-signed with San Francisco Giants, December 8, 2006.

KUO, HONG-CHIH

Born, Tainan City, Taiwan, July 23, 1981.
Bats Left. Throws Left. Height, 6 feet. Weight, 235 pounds.

Year Club	Lea	G	IP	W	L	Pct	SO	BB	H	ERA	SAVES
2000 San Bernardino	Calif.	1	3	0	0	.000	7	0	0	0.00	0
2001 Dodgers.........	Gulf Coast	7	$19\frac{1}{3}$	0	0	.000	21	4	13	2.33	0
2002 Vero Beach..........	Fla.St.	4	8	0	1	.000	8	2	11	6.75	0
2002 Dodgers.........	Gulf Coast	3	6	0	0	.000	9	1	4	4.50	0
2003 Columbus a	So.Atl			INJURED—Did Not Play							
2004 Columbus...........	So.Atl	3	6	1	0	1.000	10	4	8	4.50	0
2005 Vero Beach.........	Fla.St.	11	26	1	1	.500	42	10	19	2.08	0
2005 Jacksonville	Southern	17	$28\frac{1}{3}$	1	1	.500	44	11	22	1.91	3
2005 Los Angeles	N.L.	9	$5\frac{1}{3}$	0	1	.000	10	5	5	6.75	0
2006 Las Vegas.............	P.C.	23	53	4	3	.571	63	22	52	3.06	1
2006 Los Angeles	N.L.	28	$59\frac{2}{3}$	1	5	.167	71	33	54	4.22	0
2007 Las Vegas.............	P.C.	7	20	0	1	.000	28	8	18	3.60	0
2007 Los Angeles b	N.L.	8	$30\frac{1}{3}$	1	4	.200	27	14	35	7.42	0
Major League Totals ....3 Yrs.		45	$95\frac{1}{3}$	2	10	.167	108	52	94	5.38	0
Division Series											
2006 Los Angeles	N.L.	1	$4\frac{1}{3}$	0	1	.000	4	2	4	4.15	0

a On minor league disabled list from April 3 to September 8, 2003.
b On disabled list from March 23 to May 3 and June 30 to October 31, 2007.

KURODA, HIROKI

Born, Osaka, Japan, February 10, 1975.
Bats Right. Throws Right. Height, 6 feet, 1 inch. Weight, 175 pounds.

Year Club	Lea	G	IP	W	L	Pct	SO	BB	H	ERA	SAVES
1997 Hiroshima	Japan Cent.	23	135	6	9	.400	64	63	147	4.40	0
1998 Hiroshima	Japan Cent.	18	45	1	4	.200	25	24	53	6.60	0
1999 Hiroshima	Japan Cent.	21	$87\frac{2}{3}$	5	8	.385	55	39	106	6.78	0
2000 Hiroshima	Japan Cent.	29	144	9	6	.600	116	61	147	4.31	0
2001 Hiroshima	Japan Cent.	27	190	12	8	.600	146	45	175	3.03	0
2002 Hiroshima	Japan Cent.	23	$164\frac{1}{3}$	10	10	.500	144	34	166	3.67	0
2003 Hiroshima	Japan Cent.	28	$205\frac{2}{3}$	13	9	.591	137	45	197	3.11	0
2004 Hiroshima	Japan Cent.	21	147	7	9	.438	138	29	187	4.65	0
2005 Hiroshima	Japan Cent.	29	$212\frac{2}{3}$	15	12	.556	165	42	183	3.17	0
2006 Hiroshima	Japan Cent.	26	$189\frac{1}{3}$	13	6	.684	144	21	169	1.85	1
2007 Hiroshima a	Japan Cent.	26	$179\frac{2}{3}$	12	8	.600	123	42	176	3.56	0

a Signed with Los Angeles Dodgers, December 16, 2007.

LACKEY, JOHN DERRAN

Born, Abilene, Texas, October 23, 1978.
Bats Right. Throws Right. Height, 6 feet, 6 inches. Weight, 235 pounds.

Year Club	Lea	G	IP	W	L	Pct	SO	BB	H	ERA	SAVES
1999 Boise	Northwest	15	$81\frac{1}{3}$	6	2	.750	77	50	81	4.98	0
2000 Lake Elsinore	California	15	$100\frac{2}{3}$	6	6	.500	74	42	94	3.40	0
2000 Erie..............	Eastern	8	$57\frac{1}{3}$	6	1	.857	43	9	58	3.30	0
2000 Cedar Rapids	Midwest	5	$30\frac{1}{3}$	3	2	.600	21	5	20	2.08	0

Year	Club	Lea	G	IP	W	L	Pct	SO	BB	H	ERA	SAVES
2001	Salt Lake	P.C.	10	57²/₃	3	4	.429	42	16	75	6.71	0
2001	Arkansas	Texas	18	127¹/₃	9	7	.563	94	29	106	3.46	0
2002	Salt Lake	P.C.	16	101²/₃	8	2	.800	82	28	89	2.57	0
2002	Anaheim	A.L.	18	108¹/₃	9	4	.692	69	33	113	3.66	0
2003	Anaheim	A.L.	33	204	10	16	.385	151	66	223	4.63	0
2004	Anaheim	A.L.	33	198¹/₃	14	13	.519	144	60	215	4.67	0
2005	Los Angeles	A.L.	33	209	14	5	.737	199	71	208	3.44	0
2006	Los Angeles	A.L.	33	217²/₃	13	11	.542	190	72	203	3.56	0
2007	Los Angeles	A.L.	33	224	19	9	.679	179	52	219	*3.01	0
Major League Totals		6 Yrs.	183	1161¹/₃	79	58	.577	932	354	1181	3.82	0
Division Series												
2002	Anaheim	A.L.	1	3	0	0	.000	3	1	3	0.00	0
2005	Los Angeles	A.L.	2	11¹/₃	0	0	.000	9	9	7	2.38	0
2007	Los Angeles	A.L.	1	6	0	1	.000	4	2	9	6.00	0
Division Series Totals			4	20¹/₃	0	1	.000	16	12	19	3.10	0
Championship Series												
2002	Anaheim	A.L.	1	7	1	0	1.000	7	0	3	0.00	0
2005	Los Angeles	A.L.	1	5	0	1	.000	3	1	8	9.00	0
Championship Series Totals			2	12	1	1	.500	10	1	11	3.75	0
World Series Record												
2002	Anaheim	A.L.	3	12¹/₃	1	0	1.000	7	5	15	4.38	0

LAFFEY, AARON STEVEN
Born, Cumberland, Maryland, April 15, 1985.
Bats Left. Throws Left. Height, 6 feet. Weight, 185 pounds.

Year	Club	Lea	G	IP	W	L	Pct	SO	BB	H	ERA	SAVES
2003	Burlington	Appal.	9	34	3	1	.750	46	15	22	2.91	0
2004	Mahoning Valley	N.Y.-Penn.	8	43²/₃	3	1	.750	30	10	38	1.24	0
2004	Lake County	So.Atl.	19	74	3	7	.300	69	44	79	6.45	1
2005	Akron	Eastern	1	5	1	0	1.000	6	2	8	3.60	0
2005	Lake County	So.Atl.	25	142¹/₃	7	7	.500	69	52	123	3.22	1
2006	Kinston	Carolina	10	41¹/₃	4	1	.800	24	6	38	2.18	1
2006	Akron	Eastern	19	112¹/₃	8	3	.727	61	33	121	3.53	0
2007	Akron	Eastern	6	35	4	1	.800	24	7	29	2.31	0
2007	Buffalo	Int.	16	96¹/₃	9	3	.750	75	23	89	3.08	0
2007	Cleveland	A.L.	9	49¹/₃	4	2	.667	25	12	54	4.56	0
Championship Series												
2007	Cleveland	A.L.	1	4²/₃	0	0	.000	3	1	1	0.00	0

LANNAN, JOHN E.
Born, Long Beach, New York, September 27, 1984.
Bats Left. Throws Left. Height, 6 feet, 5 inches. Weight, 200 pounds.

Year	Club	Lea	G	IP	W	L	Pct	SO	BB	H	ERA	SAVES
2005	Vermont	N.Y.-Penn.	14	63¹/₃	3	5	.375	41	31	74	5.26	0
2006	Savannah	So.Atl.	27	138	6	8	.429	114	54	149	4.76	0
2007	Potomac	Carolina	8	50²/₃	6	0	1.000	35	15	31	2.13	0
2007	Harrisburg	Eastern	6	36	3	2	.600	20	15	31	3.25	0
2007	Columbus	Int.	7	38	3	1	.750	19	12	30	1.66	0
2007	Washington	N.L.	6	34²/₃	2	2	.500	10	17	36	4.15	0

LEDEZMA, WILFREDO JOSE
Born, Guarico, Venezuela, January 21, 1981.
Bats Left. Throws Left. Height, 6 feet, 4 inches. Weight, 210 pounds.

Year	Club	Lea	G	IP	W	L	Pct	SO	BB	H	ERA	SAVES
1998	Sp Red Sox	Dominican	11	47	2	4	.333	34	38	38	4.40	0
1999	Red Sox	Gulf Coast	13	57¹/₃	5	1	.833	52	20	51	3.30	1
2000	Augusta	So.Atl.	14	52²/₃	2	4	.333	60	36	51	5.13	0
2001	Augusta a	So.Atl.					INJURED—Did Not Play					
2002	Red Sox	Gulf Coast	1	3	0	0	.000	3	0	4	6.00	0
2002	Augusta b	So.Atl.	5	23²/₃	2	2	.500	38	8	23	3.80	0
2003	Detroit	A.L.	34	84	3	7	.300	49	35	99	5.79	0
2004	Erie	Eastern	17	111²/₃	10	3	.769	98	24	95	2.42	0
2004	Detroit	A.L.	15	53¹/₃	4	3	.571	29	18	55	4.39	0
2005	Detroit	A.L.	10	49²/₃	2	4	.333	30	24	61	7.07	0
2005	Toledo	Int.	11	51	5	3	.625	44	27	52	5.29	0

Year	Club	Lea	G	IP	W	L	Pct	SO	BB	H	ERA	SAVES
2006 Toledo ....Int.			12	71 1/3	4	3	.571	66	23	60	2.52	0
2006 Detroit ................A.L.			24	60 1/3	3	3	.500	39	23	60	3.58	0
2007 Detroit ..............A.L.			23	35 2/3	3	1	.750	24	26	38	4.79	0
2007 Atlanta-San Diego c-d ...N.L.			21	23 2/3	0	2	.000	23	12	32	6.85	0
Major League Totals ....5 Yrs.			127	306 2/3	15	20	.429	194	138	345	5.28	0
Championship Series												
2006 Detroit ...............A.L.			2	2 2/3	1	0	1.000	1	1	2	3.38	0
World Series Record												
2006 Detroit ...............A.L.			2	1 1/3	0	0	.000	1	0	2	0.00	0

a On minor league disabled list from June 19 to September 6, 2001.
b Selected by Detroit Tigers from Boston Red Sox in Rule V draft, December 16, 2002.
c Traded to Atlanta Braves for pitcher Macay McBride, June 20, 2007.
d Traded to San Diego Padres with pitcher Will Startup for pitcher Royce Ring, July 31, 2007.

LEE, CLIFTON PHIFER (CLIFF)

Born, Benton, Arkansas, August 30, 1978.
Bats Left. Throws Left. Height, 6 feet, 3 inches. Weight, 190 pounds.

Year	Club	Lea	G	IP	W	L	Pct	SO	BB	H	ERA	SAVES
2000 Cape Fear...........So.Atl.			11	44 2/3	1	4	.200	63	36	50	5.24	0
2001 Jupiter ....Fla.St.			21	109 2/3	6	7	.462	179	46	78	2.79	0
2002 Harrisburg ....Eastern			15	86 1/3	7	2	.778	105	23	61	3.23	0
2002 Akron ....Eastern			3	16 2/3	2	1	.667	18	10	11	5.40	0
2002 Buffalo ....Int.			8	43	3	2	.600	30	22	36	3.77	0
2002 Cleveland a-b..........A.L.			2	10 1/3	0	1	.000	6	8	6	1.74	0
2003 Buffalo................Int.			11	63 1/3	6	1	.857	61	31	62	3.27	0
2003 Kinston...........Carolina			1	4 1/3	0	0	.000	4	3	0	0:00	0
2003 Akron.............Eastern			2	12	1	0	1.000	13	4	7	1.50	0
2003 Cleveland c..........A.L.			9	52 1/3	3	3	.500	44	20	41	3.61	0
2004 Cleveland .............A.L.			33	179	14	8	.636	161	81	188	5.43	0
2005 Cleveland .............A.L.			32	202	18	5	*.783	143	52	194	3.79	0
2006 Cleveland .............A.L.			33	200 2/3	14	11	.560	129	58	224	4.40	0
2007 Kinston ....Carolina			1	2	0	0	.000	4	0	1	0.00	0
2007 Akron.............Eastern			1	5	1	0	1.000	7	1	2	0.00	0
2007 Buffalo................Int.			8	41	1	3	.250	50	25	32	3.51	0
2007 Cleveland d ..........A.L.			20	97 1/3	5	8	.385	66	36	112	6.29	0
Major League Totals ....6 Yrs.			129	741 2/3	54	36	.600	549	255	765	4.64	0

a Traded to Cleveland Indians with infielder Lee Stevens, infielder Brandon Phillips and outfielder Grady Sizemore for pitcher Bartolo Colon and player to be named later, June 27, 2002.
b Montreal Expos received pitcher Tim Drew to complete trade, June 28, 2002.
c On disabled list from March 29 to May 30, 2003.
d On disabled list from March 23 to May 3, 2007.

LESTER, JONATHAN TYLER (JON)

Born, Tacoma, Washington, January 7, 1984.
Bats Left. Throws Left. Height, 6 feet, 2 inches. Weight, 190 pounds.

Year	Club	Lea	G	IP	W	L	Pct	SO	BB	H	ERA	SAVES
2002 Red Sox ....Gulf Coast			1	0 2/3	0	1	.000	1	1	5	13.50	0
2003 Augusta ....So.Atl.			24	106	6	9	.400	71	44	102	3.65	0
2004 Sarasota ....Fla.St.			21	90 1/3	7	6	.538	97	37	82	4.28	0
2004 Red Sox ....Gulf Coast			1	1	0	0	.000	1	2	0	0.00	0
2005 Portland ....Eastern			26	148 1/3	11	6	.647	163	57	114	2.61	0
2006 Pawtucket ....Int.			11	46 2/3	3	4	.429	43	25	43	2.70	0
2006 Boston a..............A.L.			15	81 1/3	7	2	.778	60	43	91	4.76	0
2007 Greenville...........So.Atl.			3	13	0	0	.000	15	2	11	2.08	0
2007 Portland ....Eastern			1	6	1	0	1.000	4	4	5	1.50	0
2007 Pawtucket ....Int.			14	71 2/3	4	5	.444	51	31	67	3.89	0
2007 Boston b .............A.L.			12	63	4	0	1.000	50	31	61	4.57	0
Major League Totals ....2 Yrs.			27	144 1/3	11	2	.846	110	74	152	4.68	0
Championship Series												
2007 Boston ...............A.L.			2	3 2/3	0	0	.000	5	1	3	4.91	0
World Series Record												
2007 Boston ...............A.L.			1	5 2/3	1	0	1.000	3	3	3	0.00	0

a On disabled list from August 24 to November 6, 2006.
b On disabled list from March 23 to June 11, 2007.

LEWIS, JENSEN DANIEL
Born, Cincinnati, Ohio, May 16, 1984.
Bats Right. Throws Right. Height, 6 feet, 3 inches. Weight, 195 pounds.

Year	Club	Lea	G	IP	W	L	Pct	SO	BB	H	ERA	SAVES
2005	Mahoning Valley	N.Y.-Penn.	13	59	4	2	.667	59	11	58	3.20	0
2006	Kinston	Carolina	21	108⅓	7	6	.538	94	29	110	3.99	0
2006	Akron	Eastern	7	39⅓	1	2	.333	44	12	41	3.89	0
2007	Akron	Eastern	24	39	2	0	1.000	49	13	27	1.85	1
2007	Buffalo	Int.	10	13	1	0	1.000	12	4	5	1.38	1
2007	Cleveland	A.L.	26	29⅓	1	1	.500	34	10	26	2.15	0
	Division Series											
2007	Cleveland	A.L.	2	2	0	0	.000	4	0	0	0.00	0
	Championship Series											
2007	Cleveland	A.L.	5	5⅔	0	0	.000	3	0	6	6.35	0

LIDGE, BRADLEY THOMAS (BRAD)
Born, Sacramento, California, December 23, 1976.
Bats Right. Throws Right. Height, 6 feet, 5 inches. Weight, 210 pounds.

Year	Club	Lea	G	IP	W	L	Pct	SO	BB	H	ERA	SAVES
1998	Quad City a-b	Midwest	4	11	0	1	.000	6	5	10	3.27	0
1999	Kissimmee c	Fla.St.	6	21⅓	0	2	.000	19	11	13	3.38	0
2000	Kissimmee d	Fla.St.	8	41⅔	2	1	.667	46	15	28	2.81	0
2001	Round Rock e	Texas	5	26	2	0	1.000	42	7	21	1.73	0
2002	Round Rock	Texas	5	11	1	1	.500	18	3	9	2.45	0
2002	Houston	N.L.	6	8⅔	1	0	1.000	12	9	12	6.23	0
2002	New Orleans	P.C.	24	111⅔	5	5	.500	110	47	83	3.39	0
2003	Houston	N.L.	78	85	6	3	.667	97	42	60	3.60	1
2004	Houston	N.L.	80	94⅔	6	5	.545	157	30	57	1.90	29
2005	Houston	N.L.	70	70⅔	4	4	.500	103	23	58	2.29	42
2006	Houston	N.L.	78	75	1	5	.167	104	36	69	5.28	32
2007	Corpus Christi	Texas	1	1	0	0	.000	0	0	0	0.00	0
2007	Houston f-g	N.L.	66	67	5	3	.625	88	30	54	3.36	19
Major League Totals	6 Yrs.		378	401	23	20	.535	561	170	310	3.30	123
	Division Series											
2004	Houston	N.L.	3	4⅓	0	0	.000	6	1	4	2.08	1
2005	Houston	N.L.	3	4	0	0	.000	5	4	2	0.00	0
Division Series Totals			6	8⅓	0	0	.000	11	5	6	1.08	1
	Championship Series											
2004	Houston	N.L.	4	8	1	0	1.000	14	2	1	0.00	2
2005	Houston	N.L.	4	5	0	1	.000	7	2	6	7.20	3
Championship Series Totals			8	13	1	1	.500	21	4	7	2.77	5
	World Series Record											
2005	Houston	N.L.	3	3⅔	0	2	.000	6	0	4	4.91	0

a Drafted by Texas Rangers with choice received for Colorado Rockies signing pitcher Darryl Kile, June 2, 1998.
b On disabled list from August 18 to September 29, 1998.
c On disabled list from April 1 to June 1 and July 10 to September 29, 1999.
d On disabled list from April 24 to June 13 and July 1 to September 29, 2000.
e On disabled list from May 5 to September 29, 2001.
f On disabled list from June 16 to July 13, 2007.
g Traded to Philadelphia Phillies with infielder Eric Bruntlett for pitcher Geoff Geary, outfielder Michael Bourn and infielder Mike Costanzo, November 12, 2007.

LIEBER, JONATHAN RAY (JON)
Born, Council Bluffs, Iowa, April 2, 1970.
Bats Left. Throws Right. Height, 6 feet, 2 inches. Weight, 235 pounds.

Year	Club	Lea	G	IP	W	L	Pct	SO	BB	H	ERA	SAVES
1992	Eugene	Northwest	5	31	3	0	1.000	23	2	26	1.16	0
1992	Baseball City	Fla. St.	7	31	3	3	.500	19	8	45	4.65	0
1993	Wilmington	Carolina	17	114⅔	9	3	.750	89	9	125	2.67	0
1993	Memphis-Carol. a	Southern	10	55	6	3	.667	45	16	71	5.07	0
1994	Carolina	Southern	3	21	2	0	1.000	21	2	13	1.29	0
1994	Buffalo	A.A.	3	21⅓	1	1	.500	21	1	16	1.69	0
1994	Pittsburgh	N.L.	17	108⅔	6	7	.462	71	25	116	3.73	0
1995	Calgary	P.C.	14	77	1	5	.167	34	19	122	7.01	0
1995	Pittsburgh	N.L.	21	72⅔	4	7	.364	45	14	103	6.32	0
1996	Pittsburgh	N.L.	51	142	9	5	.643	94	28	156	3.99	1
1997	Pittsburgh	N.L.	33	188⅓	11	14	.440	160	51	193	4.49	0

Year	Club	Lea	G	IP	W	L	Pct	SO	BB	H	ERA	SAVES
1998 Pittsburgh b	N.L.	29	171	8	14	.364	138	40	182	4.11	1	
1999 Chicago c	N.L.	31	203⅓	10	11	.476	186	46	226	4.07	0	
2000 Chicago	N.L.	35	*251	12	11	.522	192	54	248	4.41	0	
2001 Chicago	N.L.	34	232⅓	20	6	.769	148	41	226	3.80	0	
2002 Chicago d	N.L.	21	141	6	8	.429	87	12	153	3.70	0	
2003 New York e	A.L.	INJURED—Did Not Play										
2004 Tampa	Fla.St.	1	7	1	0	1.000	4	0	2	0.00	0	
2004 New York f-g	A.L.	27	176⅔	14	8	.636	102	18	216	4.33	0	
2005 Philadelphia	N.L.	35	218⅓	17	13	.567	149	41	223	4.20	0	
2006 Phillies	Gulf Coast	1	3	0	0	.000	1	0	4	3.00	0	
2006 Clearwater	Fla.St.	2	11⅓	0	2	.000	6	0	19	7.15	0	
2006 Philadelphia h	N.L.	27	168	9	11	.450	100	24	196	4.93	0	
2007 Clearwater	Fla.St.	1	3⅔	0	0	.000	4	0	4	2.45	0	
2007 Philadelphia i-j	N.L.	14	78	3	6	.333	54	22	91	4.73	0	
Major League Totals	13 Yrs.	375	2151⅓	129	121	.516	1526	416	2329	4.28	2	
Division Series												
2004 New York	A.L.	1	6⅔	0	0	.000	4	1	7	4.05	0	
Championship Series												
2004 New York	A.L.	2	14⅓	1	1	.500	5	1	12	3.14	0	

a Traded by Kansas City Royals to Pittsburgh Pirates organization with pitcher Dan Miceli for pitcher Stan Belinda, July 31, 1993.
b On disabled list from August 21 to September 14, 1998.
c On disabled list from April 21 to May 8, 1999.
d On disabled list from August 2 to October 9, 2002.
e Filed for free agency, November 1, 2002. Signed with New York Yankees, January 24, 2003. On disabled list from March 21 to November 13, 2003.
f On disabled list from March 19 to May 1, 2004.
g Filed for free agency, November 5, 2004. Signed with Philadelphia Phillies, December 8, 2004.
h On disabled list from May 30 to July 7, 2006.
i On disabled list from March 23 to April 9 and June 21 to October 29, 2007.
j Filed for free agency, October 29, 2007. Signed with Chicago Cubs, January 16, 2008.

LILLY, THEODORE ROOSEVELT (TED)

Born, Lamita, California, January 4, 1976.
Bats Left. Throws Left. Height, 6 feet, 1 inch. Weight, 190 pounds.

Year	Club	Lea	G	IP	W	L	Pct	SO	BB	H	ERA	SAVES
1996 Yakima	Northwest	13	53⅔	4	0	1.000	75	14	25	0.84	0	
1997 San Bernardino	California	23	134⅔	7	8	.467	158	32	116	2.81	0	
1998 San Antonio	Texas	17	111⅔	8	4	.667	96	37	114	3.30	0	
1998 Albuquerque	P.C.	5	31	1	3	.250	25	9	39	4.94	0	
1998 Ottawa a	Int.	7	39	2	2	.500	49	19	45	4.85	0	
1999 Ottawa	Int.	16	89	8	5	.615	78	23	81	3.84	0	
1999 Montreal b-c	N.L.	9	23⅔	0	1	.000	28	9	30	7.61	0	
2000 Tampa	Fla.St.	1	6⅔	0	0	.000	6	1	5	1.35	0	
2000 Columbus	Int.	22	137⅓	8	11	.421	127	48	157	4.19	0	
2000 New York d-e	A.L.	7	8	0	0	.000	11	5	8	5.63	0	
2001 Columbus	Int.	5	25⅓	0	0	.000	30	8	16	2.84	0	
2001 New York	A.L.	26	120⅔	5	6	.455	112	51	126	5.37	0	
2002 New York-Oakland f-g	A.L.	22	100	5	7	.417	77	31	80	3.69	0	
2003 Oakland h	A.L.	32	178⅓	12	10	.545	147	58	179	4.34	0	
2004 Toronto	A.L.	32	197⅓	12	10	.545	168	89	171	4.06	0	
2005 Syracuse	Int.	2	8⅔	0	1	.000	9	5	5	3.12	0	
2005 Toronto i	A.L.	25	126⅓	10	11	.476	96	58	135	5.56	0	
2006 Toronto j	A.L.	32	181⅔	15	13	.536	160	81	179	4.31	0	
2007 Chicago	N.L.	34	207	15	8	.652	174	55	181	3.83	0	
Major League Totals	9 Yrs.	219	1143	74	66	.529	973	437	1089	4.46	0	
Division Series												
2002 Oakland	A.L.	2	4	0	1	.000	3	1	10	13.50	0	
2003 Oakland	A.L.	2	9	0	0	.000	7	2	2	0.00	0	
2007 Chicago	N.L.	1	3⅓	0	1	.000	4	4	7	16.20	0	
Division Series Totals		5	16⅓	0	2	.000	14	7	19	6.61	0	

a Traded by Los Angeles Dodgers to Montreal Expos with infielder Wilton Guerrero, outfielder Peter Bergeron and infielder Jonathan Tucker for infielder Mark Grudzielanek, outfielder Hiram Bocachica and pitcher Carlos Perez, July 31, 1998.
b Montreal Expos traded pitcher Jake Westbrook and two players to be named later to New York Yankees for pitcher Hideki Irabu, December 22, 1999.
c On disabled list from June 21 to September 30, 1999.
d Sent to New York Yankees, March 17, 2000, Yankees received pitcher Christian Parker to complete trade, March 22, 2000.

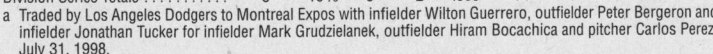

e On disabled list from March 25 to May 22, 2000.
f Traded to Oakland Athletics with pitcher Jason Arnold and outfielder John-Ford Griffin for pitcher Jeff Weaver, July 5, 2002.
g On disabled list from July 23 to September 10, 2002.
h Traded to Toronto Blue Jays for outfielder Bobby Kielty and player to be named later, November 18, 2003.
i On disabled list from March 25 to April 10 and July 25 to September 6, 2005.
j Filed for free agency, October 28, 2006. Signed with Chicago Cubs, December 15, 2006.

LINCECUM, TIMOTHY LEROY (TIM)
Born, Bellevue, Washington, June 15, 1984.
Bats Left. Throws Right. Height, 5 feet, 11 inches. Weight, 160 pounds.

Year	Club	Lea	G	IP	W	L	Pct	SO	BB	H	ERA	SAVES
2006	San Jose	Calif.	6	27²/₃	2	0	1.000	48	12	13	1.95	0
2006	Salem-Keizer	Northwest	2	4	0	0	.000	10	0	1	0.00	0
2007	Fresno	P.C.	5	31	4	0	1.000	46	11	12	0.29	0
2007	San Francisco	N.L.	24	146¹/₃	7	5	.583	150	65	122	4.00	0

LINDSTROM, MATTHEW JAMES (MATT)
Born, Rexburg, Idaho, February 11, 1980.
Bats Right. Throws Right. Height, 6 feet, 4 inches. Weight, 210 pounds.

Year	Club	Lea	G	IP	W	L	Pct	SO	BB	H	ERA	SAVES
2002	Kingsport	Appal.	12	48¹/₃	0	6	.000	39	21	56	4.84	0
2003	Brooklyn	N.Y.-Penn.	14	65¹/₃	7	3	.700	52	27	61	3.44	0
2003	Capital City	So.Atl.	12	56²/₃	2	3	.400	50	33	46	2.86	0
2004	St. Lucie	Fla.St.	14	79²/₃	5	5	.500	50	20	83	3.73	0
2004	Capital City	So.Atl.	12	56	3	2	.600	64	10	47	3.21	0
2005	Binghamton	Eastern	35	73¹/₃	2	5	.286	58	55	90	5.40	0
2006	Binghamton	Eastern	35	40²/₃	2	4	.333	54	14	42	3.76	11
2006	St. Lucie a	Fla.St.	11	18	1	0	1.000	16	7	14	2.50	2
2007	Florida	N.L.	71	67	3	4	.429	62	21	66	3.09	0

a Traded to Florida Marlins by New York Mets with pitcher Henry Owens for pitcher Adam Bostick and pitcher Jason Vargas, November 20, 2006.

LINEBRINK, SCOTT CAMERON
Born, Austin, Texas, August 4, 1976.
Bats Right. Throws Right. Height, 6 feet, 2 inches. Weight, 200 pounds.

Year	Club	Lea	G	IP	W	L	Pct	SO	BB	H	ERA	SAVES
1997	Salem-Keizr	Northwest	3	10	0	0	.000	6	6	7	4.50	0
1997	San Jose	California	6	28¹/₃	2	1	.667	40	10	29	3.18	0
1998	Shreveport	Texas	21	113	10	8	.556	128	58	101	5.02	0
1999	Shreveport	Texas	10	43¹/₃	1	8	.111	33	14	48	6.44	0
2000	Fresno	P.C.	28	62	1	4	.200	49	12	54	5.23	4
2000	San Francisco-Houston	N.L.	11	12	0	0	.000	6	8	18	6.00	0
2000	New Orleans a	P.C.	11	15	2	0	1.000	22	7	15	1.80	1
2001	New Orleans	P.C.	50	72	7	6	.538	72	24	52	3.50	8
2001	Houston	N.L.	9	10¹/₃	0	0	.000	9	6	6	2.61	0
2002	Houston	N.L.	22	24¹/₃	0	0	.000	24	13	31	7.03	0
2002	New Orleans	P.C.	13	15	1	1	.500	16	11	17	6.00	0
2002	Round Rock b	Texas	2	2	0	0	.000	1	2	2	0.00	0
2003	New Orleans	P.C.	2	10	0	2	.000	6	5	8	2.70	0
2003	Houston-San Diego c-d	N.L.	52	92¹/₃	3	2	.600	68	36	93	3.31	0
2004	San Diego	N.L.	73	84	7	3	.700	83	26	61	2.14	0
2005	San Diego	N.L.	73	73²/₃	8	1	.889	70	23	55	1.83	1
2006	San Diego	N.L.	73	75²/₃	7	4	.636	68	22	70	3.57	2
2007	San Diego-Milwaukee e-f	N.L.	71	70¹/₃	5	6	.455	50	25	68	3.71	1
Major League Totals	8 Yrs.		384	442²/₃	30	16	.652	378	159	402	3.21	4
Division Series												
2005	San Diego	N.L.	1	1	0	0	.000	1	0	2	0.00	0
2006	San Diego	N.L.	2	1¹/₃	0	0	.000	0	1	1	6.75	0
Division Series Totals			3	2¹/₃	0	0	.000	1	1	3	3.86	0

a Traded to Houston Astros for pitcher Doug Henry, July 30, 2000.
b On disabled list from May 20 to June 17, 2002.
c Signed with Houston Astros organization, January 31, 2003.
d Claimed on waivers by San Diego Padres, May 29, 2003.
e Traded to Milwaukee Brewers for pitcher Will Inman, pitcher Joe Thatcher and pitcher Steve Garrison, July 25, 2007.
f Filed for free agency, October 29, 2007. Signed with Chicago White Sox, November 28, 2007.

LIRIANO, FRANCISCO CASILLAS

Born, San Cristobal, Dominican Republic, October 26, 1983.
Bats Left. Throws Left. Height, 6 feet, 2 inches. Weight, 185 pounds.

Year	Club	Lea	G	IP	W	L	Pct	SO	BB	H	ERA	SAVES
2001 Giants.............	Arizona	13	62	5	4	.556	67	24	51	3.63	0
2001 Salem-Keizer.....	Northwest	2	9	0	0	.000	12	1	7	5.00	0
2002 Hagerstown.........	So.Atl.	16	80	3	6	.333	85	31	61	3.49	0
2003 Giants.............	Arizona	4	8¹/₃	0	1	.000	9	6	5	4.32	0
2003 San Jose a..........	Calif.	1	0²/₃	0	1	.000	0	2	5	54.00	0
2004 New Britain........	Eastern	7	39²/₃	3	2	.600	49	17	45	3.18	0
2004 Fort Myers.........	Fla.St.	21	117	6	7	.462	125	43	118	4.00	0
2005 New Britain........	Eastern	13	76²/₃	3	5	.375	92	26	70	3.64	0
2005 Rochester.............	Int.	14	91	9	2	.818	112	24	56	1.78	0
2005 Minnesota...........	A.L.	6	23²/₃	1	2	.333	33	7	19	5.70	0
2006 Minnesota b...........	A.L.	28	121	12	3	.800	144	32	89	2.16	1
2007 Minnesota c...........	A.L.	INJURED—Did Not Play									
Major League Totals........2 Yrs.		34	144²/₃	13	5	.722	177	39	108	2.74	1

a Traded by San Francisco Giants to Minnesota Twins with pitcher Joe Nathan and pitcher Boof Bonser for catcher A.J. Pierzynski and player to be named later, November 14, 2003.
b On disabled list from August 8 to September 11, 2006.
c On disabled list from March 24 to October 10, 2007.

LITSCH, JESSE ALLEN

Born, Pinellas Park, Florida, March 9, 1985.
Bats Right. Throws Right. Height, 6 feet, 1 inch. Weight, 205 pounds.

Year	Club	Lea	G	IP	W	L	Pct	SO	BB	H	ERA	SAVES
2005 Pulaski..............	Appal.	11	65²/₃	5	1	.833	67	10	51	2.74	0
2005 Auburn..........	N.Y.-Penn.	4	10	0	1	.000	7	6	11	3.60	0
2006 New Hampshire.....	Eastern	12	69¹/₃	3	4	.429	54	13	85	5.06	0
2006 Dunedin.............	Fla.St.	16	89¹/₃	6	6	.500	81	8	94	3.53	0
2007 New Hampshire.....	Eastern	10	61¹/₃	7	2	.778	46	14	51	2.35	0
2007 Syracuse..............Int.		2	15	1	0	1.000	10	3	12	1.80	0
2007 Toronto..............	A.L.	20	111	7	9	.438	50	36	116	3.81	0

LOE, KAMERON DAVID

Born, Simi Valley, California, September 10, 1981.
Bats Right. Throws Right. Height, 6 feet, 7 inches. Weight, 240 pounds.

Year	Club	Lea	G	IP	W	L	Pct	SO	BB	H	ERA	SAVES
2002 Pulaski.............	Appal.	14	58¹/₃	4	4	.500	55	17	64	4.47	1
2003 Stockton...........California		9	37²/₃	3	0	1.000	31	6	26	0.96	1
2003 Clinton...........Midwest		23	97	4	3	.571	94	19	78	1.95	2
2004 Frisco...............Texas		19	113¹/₃	7	7	.500	97	29	122	3.10	0
2004 Oklahoma.............	P.C.	8	52¹/₃	5	2	.714	42	13	52	3.27	0
2004 Texas................	A.L.	2	6²/₃	0	0	.000	3	6	6	5.40	0
2005 Oklahoma.............	P.C.	7	28¹/₃	2	1	.667	23	10	32	5.08	0
2005 Texas................	A.L.	48	92	9	6	.600	45	31	89	3.42	1
2006 Frisco...............Texas		2	7	0	1	.000	4	4	8	5.14	0
2006 Oklahoma.............	P.C.	13	22²/₃	1	2	.333	21	13	32	9.13	1
2006 Texas a..............	A.L.	15	78¹/₃	3	6	.333	34	22	105	5.86	0
2007 Frisco...............Texas		1	3	0	0	.000	1	5	1	6.00	0
2007 Texas b..............	A.L.	28	136	6	11	.353	78	56	162	5.36	0
Major League Totals........4 Yrs.		93	313	18	23	.439	160	115	362	4.92	1

a On disabled list from June 19 to August 3, 2006.
b On disabled list from July 30 to August 18, 2007.

LOEWEN, ADAM A.

Born, Surrey, British Columbia, Canada, April 9, 1984.
Bats Left. Throws Left. Height, 6 feet, 5 inches. Weight, 235 pounds.

Year	Club	Lea	G	IP	W	L	Pct	SO	BB	H	ERA	SAVES
2003 Aberdeen.........N.Y.-Penn.		7	23¹/₃	0	2	.000	25	9	13	2.70	0
2004 Frederick.........Carolina		2	8	0	2	.000	3	9	7	6.75	0
2004 Delmarva...........So.Atl.		20	85¹/₃	4	5	.444	82	58	77	4.11	0
2005 Frederick.........Carolina		28	142	10	8	.556	146	86	130	4.12	0
2006 Bowie.............	Eastern	9	49²/₃	4	2	.667	55	26	46	2.72	0
2006 Ottawa................Int.		3	21¹/₃	2	0	1.000	21	3	10	1.27	0
2006 Baltimore.............	A.L.	22	112¹/₃	6	6	.500	98	62	111	5.37	0

Year	Club	Lea	G	IP	W	L	Pct	SO	BB	H	ERA	SAVES
2007 Baltimore a		A.L.	6	30⅓	2	0	1.000	22	26	27	3.56	0
Major League Totals	2 Yrs.		28	142⅔	8	6	.571	120	88	138	4.98	0

a On disabled list from May 2 to October 23, 2007.

LOGAN, BOONE

Born, San Antonio, Texas, August 13, 1984.
Bats Right. Throws Left. Height, 6 feet, 5 inches. Weight, 200 pounds.

Year	Club	Lea	G	IP	W	L	Pct	SO	BB	H	ERA	SAVES
2003 Great Falls		Pioneer	16	67	3	3	.500	48	31	76	6.58	0
2004 Great Falls		Pioneer	18	64⅓	3	7	.300	48	31	74	5.60	1
2005 Winston-Salem		Carolina	4	5⅓	0	0	.000	5	4	7	5.06	0
2005 Great Falls		Pioneer	21	35⅓	1	1	.500	29	4	34	3.31	2
2006 Charlotte		Int.	38	42⅔	3	1	.750	57	12	35	3.38	11
2006 Chicago		A.L.	21	17⅓	0	0	.000	15	15	21	8.31	1
2007 Charlotte		Int.	4	8⅓	0	1	.000	11	4	8	2.16	1
2007 Chicago		A.L.	68	50⅔	2	1	.667	35	20	59	4.97	0
Major League Totals	2 Yrs.		89	68	2	1	.667	50	35	80	5.82	1

LOHSE, KYLE MATTHEW

Born, Chico, California, October 4, 1978.
Bats Right. Throws Right. Height, 6 feet, 2 inches. Weight, 210 pounds.

Year	Club	Lea	G	IP	W	L	Pxt	SO	BB	H	ERA	SAVES
1997 Cubs		Arizona	12	47⅔	2	2	.500	49	22	46	3.02	0
1998 Rockford		Midwest	28	170⅔	13	8	.619	121	45	158	3.22	0
1999 New Britain		Eastern	11	70⅓	3	4	.429	41	23	87	5.89	0
1999 Daytona		Fla.St.	9	53	5	3	.625	41	16	48	2.89	0
1999 Fort Myers a		Fla.St.	7	41⅔	2	3	.400	33	9	47	5.18	0
2000 New Britain		Eastern	28	167	3	18	.143	124	55	196	6.04	0
2001 New Britain		Eastern	6	38	3	1	.750	32	4	32	2.37	0
2001 Edmonton		P.C.	8	49	4	2	.667	48	13	50	3.12	0
2001 Minnesota		A.L.	19	90⅓	4	7	.364	64	29	102	5.68	0
2002 Minnesota		A.L.	32	180⅔	13	8	.619	124	70	181	4.23	0
2003 Minnesota		A.L.	33	201	14	11	.560	130	45	211	4.61	0
2004 Minnesota		A.L.	35	194	9	13	.409	111	76	240	5.34	0
2005 Minnesota		A.L.	31	178⅔	9	13	.409	86	44	211	4.18	0
2006 Rochester		Int.	4	24	2	1	.667	12	6	15	1.50	0
2006 Minnesota		A.L.	22	63⅔	2	5	.286	46	25	80	7.07	0
2006 Cincinnati b		N.L.	12	63	3	5	.375	51	19	70	4.57	0
2007 Cincinnati-Philadelphia c-d		N.L.	34	192⅔	9	12	.429	122	57	207	4.62	0
Major League Totals	7 Yrs.		218	1164	63	74	.460	734	365	1302	4.82	0
Division Series												
2002 Minnesota		A.L.	2	4	0	0	.000	5	0	2	0.00	0
2003 Minnesota		A.L.	1	5	0	1	.000	5	2	6	5.40	0
2004 Minnesota		A.L.	1	2	0	1	.000	3	0	1	4.50	0
2007 Philadelphia		N.L.	1	1⅔	0	0	.000	1	0	1	6.75	0
Division Series Totals			5	12⅔	0	2	.000	14	2	10	3.65	0
Championship Series												
2002 Minnesota		A.L.	1	1	0	0	.000	1	0	0	0.00	0

a Traded by Chicago Cubs to Minnesota Twins with pitcher Jason Ryan for pitcher Rick Aguilera and pitcher Scott Downs, May 21, 1999.
b Traded to Cincinnati Reds for pitcher Zach Ward, July 31, 2006.
c Traded to Philadelphia Phillies for pitcher Matt Maloney, July 30, 2007.
d Filed for free agency, October 31, 2007.

LOOPER, BRADEN LA VERN

Born, Weatherford, Oklahoma, October 28, 1974.
Bats Right. Throws Right. Height, 6 feet, 3 inches. Weight, 220 pounds.

Year	Club	Lea	G	IP	W	L	Pct	SO	BB	H	ERA	SAVES
1997 Pr William		Carolina	12	64⅓	3	6	.333	58	25	71	4.48	0
1997 Arkansas		Texas	19	21⅓	1	4	.200	20	7	24	5.91	5
1998 Memphis		P.C.	40	40⅔	2	3	.400	43	13	43	3.10	20
1998 St. Louis a		N.L.	4	3⅓	0	1	.000	4	1	5	5.40	0
1999 Florida		N.L.	72	83	3	3	.500	50	31	96	3.80	0
2000 Florida		N.L.	73	67⅓	5	1	.833	29	36	71	4.41	2
2001 Florida		N.L.	71	71	3	3	.500	52	30	63	3.55	3

Year Club	Lea	G	IP	W	L	Pct	SO	BB	H	ERA	SAVES
2002 Florida .... N.L.		78	86	2	5	.286	55	28	73	3.14	13
2003 Florida b............. N.L.		74	80²/₃	6	4	.600	56	29	82	3.68	28
2004 New York .... N.L.		71	83¹/₃	2	5	.286	60	16	·86	2.70	29
2005 New York c........... N.L.		60	59¹/₃	4	7	.364	27	22	65	3.94	28
2006 St. Louis............. N.L.		69	73¹/₃	9	3	.750	41	20	76	3.56	0
2007 St. Louis d........... N.L.		31	175	12	12	.500	87	51	183	4.94	0
Major League Total ....10 Yrs.		603	782¹/₃	46	44	.511	461	264	800	3.88	103
Division Series											
2003 Florida .... N.L.		2	1²/₃	1	0	1.000	0	2	1	0.00	0
2006 St. Louis............. N.L.		1	1²/₃	0	0	.000	0	0	1	0.00	0
Division Series Totals		3	3¹/₃	1	0	1.000	0	2	2	0.00	0
Championship Series											
2003 Florida .... N.L.		2	1²/₃	0	0	.000	1	1	1	0.00	1
2006 St. Louis............. N.L.		3	4²/₃	0	0	.000	1	0	7	5.79	0
Championship Series Totals		5	6¹/₃	0	0	.000	2	1	8	4.26	1
World Series Record											
2003 Florida .... N.L.		4	3²/₃	1	0	1.000	4	0	6	9.82	0
2006 St. Louis............. N.L.		3	2¹/₃	0	0	.000	1	0	· 1	3.86	0
World Series Totals............		7	6	1	0	1.000	5	0	7	7.50	0

a Traded to Florida Marlins with pitcher Armando Almanza and infielder Pablo Ozuna for infielder Edgar Renteria, December 14, 1998.
b Not offered contract, December 21, 2003. Signed with New York Mets, January 6, 2004.
c Filed for free agency, November 4, 2005. Signed with St. Louis Cardinals, December 15, 2005.
d On disabled list from June 16 to July 2, 2007.

LOPEZ, JAVIER ALFONSO
Born, San Juan, Puerto Rico, June 11, 1977.
Bats Left. Throws Left. Height, 6 feet, 4 inches. Weight, 220 pounds.

Year Club	Lea	G	IP	W	L	Pct	SO	BB	H	ERA	SAVES
1998 South Bend ....Midwest		16	44	2	4	.333	31	30	60	6.55	0
1999 South Bend ....Midwest		20	99	4	6	.400	70	43	122	6.00	0
2000 High Desert ...... Calif.		30	136¹/₃	4	8	.333	98	57	152	5.22	2
2001 Lancaster........... Calif.		17	24	1	3	.250	18	5	30	2.63	1
2001 El Paso.............. Texas		22	40	1	0	1.000	21	14	64	7.43	0
2002 El Paso a........... Texas		61	46¹/₃	2	2	.500	47	16	34	2.72	6
2003 Colorado b............ N.L.		75	58¹/₃	4	1	.800	40	12	58	3.70	1
2004 Colorado Springs....... P.C.		8	9	0	1	.000	9	2	10	4.00	0
2004 Colorado .... N.L.		64	40²/₃	1	2	.333	20	26	45	7.52	0
2005 Tucson .... P.C.		27	24¹/₃	0	1	.000	16	12	17	2.22	2
2005 Arizona-Colorado c ..... N.L.		32	16¹/₃	1	1	.500	12	11	26	11.02	2
2006 Charlotte ....Int.		26	33	2	1	.667	26	6	28	0.55	12
2006 Pawtucket ....Int.		13	16²/₃	0	0	.000	12	8	20	4.86	4
2006 Boston d-e............ A.L.		27	16²/₃	1	0	1.000	11	10	13	2.70	1
2007 Pawtucket ....Int.		17	16²/₃	2	1	.667	15	8	19	3.78	0
2007 Boston .... A.L.		61	40²/₃	2	1	.667	26	18	36	3.10	0
Major League Totals ....5 Yrs.		259	172²/₃	9	5	.643	109	77	178	5.06	4
Division Series											
2007 Boston .... A.L.		1	0¹/₃	0	0	.000	0	0	0	0.00	0
Championship Series											
2007 Boston .... A.L.		3	2	0	0	.000	0	2	3	18.00	0
World Series Record											
2007 Boston .... A.L.		1	0	0	0	.000	0	0	2	INF	0

a Selected by Boston Red Sox from Arizona Diamondbacks in Rule V draft, December 16, 2002.
b Traded to Colorado Rockies for player to be named later, March 28, 2003. Boston Red Sox received pitcher Ryan Cameron to complete trade, March 29, 2003.
c Claimed on waivers by Arizona Diamondbacks, April 14, 2005.
d Filed for free agency, October 14, 2005. Signed with Chicago White Sox organization, January 19, 2006.
e Traded to Boston Red Sox for pitcher David Riske, June 15, 2006.

LOPEZ, RODRIGO
Born, Tlalnepantla, Mexico, December 14, 1975.
Bats Right. Throws Right. Height, 6 feet, 1 inch. Weight, 185 pounds.

Year Club	Lea	G	IP	W	L	Pct	SO	BB	H	ERA	SAVES
1993 Veracruz.......... Mexican		2	1	0	0	.000	0	3	3	36.00	0
1994 Aguila............. Mexican		10	12²/₃	0	0	.000	5	3	15	4.97	0
1995 Padres a.......... Arizona		11	34²/₃	1	1	.500	33	14	41	5.45	1

Year Club	Lea	G	IP	W	L	Pct	SO	BB	H	ERA	SAVES
1996 Poza Rica.........Mexican		7	20$^{1/3}$	1	1	.500	22	16	15	3.54	1
1996 Idaho Falls.........Pioneer		15	71	4	4	.500	72	34	76	5.70	1
1997 Clinton.......Midwest		37	121$^{2/3}$	6	8	.429	123	42	103	3.18	9
1998 Mexico City Reds....Mexican		26	163$^{2/3}$	10	6	.625	95	79	165	3.35	0
1998 Mobile..........Southern		4	25$^{2/3}$	3	0	1.000	20	4	21	1.40	0
1999 Mobile...........Southern		28	169$^{1/3}$	10	8	.556	138	58	187	4.41	0
2000 Las Vegas............P.C.		20	109$^{1/3}$	8	7	.533	100	45	123	4.69	0
2000 San Diego............N.L.		6	24$^{2/3}$	0	3	.000	17	13	40	8.76	0
2001 Lake Elsinore......California		9	13	0	1	.000	9	4	15	0.69	0
2001 Portland b...........P.C.		11	52$^{1/3}$	2	2	.500	37	15	45	3.44	0
2002 Baltimore...........A.L.		33	196$^{2/3}$	15	9	.625	136	62	172	3.57	0
2003 Bowie............Eastern		1	6$^{1/3}$	1	0	1.000	13	0	3	0.00	0
2003 Baltimore c...........A.L.		26	147	7	10	.412	103	43	188	5.82	0
2004 Baltimore...........A.L.		37	170$^{2/3}$	14	9	.609	121	54	164	3.59	0
2005 Baltimore...........A.L.		35	209$^{1/3}$	15	12	.556	118	63	232	4.90	0
2006 Baltimore d..........A.L.		36	189	9	*18	.333	136	59	234	5.90	0
2007 Colorado Springs......P.C.		2	11$^{1/3}$	1	0	1.000	4	3	4	2.38	0
2007 Colorado e-f.........N.L.		14	79$^{1/3}$	5	4	.556	43	21	83	4.42	0
Major League Totals........7 Yrs.		187	1016$^{2/3}$	65	65	.500	674	315	1113	4.80	0

a Sold to San Diego Padres organization, March 21, 1995.
b Filed for free agency, October 15, 2001. Signed with Baltimore Orioles organization, November 23, 2001.
c On disabled list from May 2 to June 15, 2003.
d Traded to Colorado Rockies for pitcher Jim Miller and pitcher Jason Burch, January 12, 2007.
e On disabled list from April 19 to May 29 and July 27 to October 31, 2007.
f Filed for free agency, October 31, 2007.

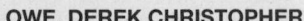

LOWE, DEREK CHRISTOPHER

Born, Dearborn, Michigan, June 1, 1973.
Bats Right. Throws Right. Height, 6 feet, 6 inches. Weight, 230 pounds.

Year Club	Lea	G	IP	W	L	Pct	SO	BB	H	ERA	SAVES
1991 Mariners..........Arizona		12	71	5	3	.625	60	21	58	2.41	0
1992 Bellingham.......Northwest		14	85$^{2/3}$	7	3	.700	66	22	69	2.42	0
1993 Riverside.......California		27	154	12	9	.571	80	60	189	5.26	0
1994 Jacksnville.......Southern		26	151$^{1/3}$	7	10	.412	75	50	177	4.94	0
1995 Mariners..........Arizona		2	9$^{2/3}$	1	0	1.000	11	2	5	0.93	0
1995 Port City.........Southern		10	53$^{1/3}$	1	6	.143	30	22	70	6.07	0
1996 Port City.........Southern		10	65	5	3	.625	33	17	56	3.05	0
1996 Tacoma..............P.C.		17	105	6	9	.400	54	37	118	4.54	0
1997 Tacoma..............P.C.		10	57$^{1/3}$	3	4	.429	49	20	53	3.45	0
1997 Pawtucket............Int.		6	30$^{1/3}$	4	0	1.000	21	11	23	2.37	0
1997 Seattle-Boston a.......A.L.		20	69	2	6	.250	52	23	74	6.13	0
1998 Boston...............A.L.		63	123	3	9	.250	77	42	126	4.02	4
1999 Boston...............A.L.		74	109$^{1/3}$	6	3	.667	80	25	84	2.63	15
2000 Boston...............N.L.		74	91$^{1/3}$	4	4	.500	79	22	90	2.56	*42
2001 Boston...............A.L.		67	91$^{2/3}$	5	10	.333	82	29	103	3.53	24
2002 Boston b.............A.L.		32	219$^{2/3}$	21	8	.724	127	48	166	2.58	0
2003 Boston...............A.L.		33	203$^{1/3}$	17	7	.708	110	72	216	4.47	0
2004 Boston c.............A.L.		33	182$^{2/3}$	14	12	.538	105	71	224	5.42	0
2005 Los Angeles...........N.L.		35	222	12	15	.444	146	55	223	3.61	0
2006 Los Angeles...........N.L.		35	218	*16	8	.667	123	55	221	3.63	0
2007 Los Angeles...........N.L.		33	199$^{1/3}$	12	14	.462	147	59	194	3.88	0
Major League Totals.......11 Yrs.		499	1729$^{1/3}$	112	96	.538	1128	501	1721	3.81	85
Division Series											
1998 Boston...............A.L.		2	4$^{1/3}$	0	0	.000	2	1	3	2.08	0
1999 Boston...............A.L.		3	8$^{1/3}$	1	1	.500	7	1	6	4.32	0
2003 Boston...............A.L.		3	9$^{2/3}$	0	1	.000	6	7	7	0.93	1
2004 Boston...............A.L.		1	1	1	0	1.000	0	1	1	0.00	0
2006 Los Angeles...........N.L.		1	5$^{1/3}$	0	0	.000	6	2	6	6.75	0
Division Series Totals...........		10	28$^{2/3}$	2	2	.500	21	12	23	3.14	1
Championship Series											
1999 Boston...............A.L.		3	6$^{1/3}$	0	0	.000	7	2	6	1.42	0
2003 Boston...............A.L.		2	14	0	2	.000	5	7	14	6.43	0
2004 Boston...............A.L.		2	11$^{1/3}$	1	0	1.000	6	1	7	3.18	0
Championship Series Totals......		7	31$^{2/3}$	1	2	.333	18	10	27	4.26	0
World Series Record											
2004 Boston...............A.L.		1	7	1	0	1.000	4	1	3	0.00	0

a Traded to Boston Red Sox with catcher Jason Varitek for pitcher Heathcliff Slocumb, July 31, 1997.
b Pitched no-hit, no-run game against Tampa Bay Devil Rays, April 27, 2002.
c Filed for free agency, November 1, 2004. Signed with Los Angeles Dodgers, January 11, 2005.

LOWRY, NOAH RYAN

Born, Ventura, California, October 10, 1980.
Bats Right. Throws Left. Height, 6 feet, 2 inches. Weight, 200 pounds.

Year	Club	Lea	G	IP	W	L	Pct	SO	BB	H	ERA	SAVES
2001	Salem-Keizer	Northwest	8	25	1	1	.500	28	8	26	3.60	0
2002	San Jose	California	15	58²/₃	6	5	.545	62	20	38	2.15	0
2003	Norwich	Eastern	23	118¹/₃	9	6	.600	97	47	127	4.72	0
2003	Fresno	P.C.	4	19	1	0	1.000	13	6	15	2.37	0
2003	San Francisco	N.L.	4	6¹/₃	0	0	.000	5	2	1	0.00	0
2004	Fresno	P.C.	17	89¹/₃	7	5	.583	73	28	98	4.13	0
2004	San Francisco	N.L.	16	92	6	0	1.000	72	28	91	3.82	0
2005	San Francisco	N.L.	33	204²/₃	13	13	.500	172	76	193	3.78	0
2006	San Jose	Calif.	1	4²/₃	0	0	.000	9	1	5	0.00	0
2006	Fresno	P.C.	1	6	0	0	.000	6	1	5	4.50	0
2006	San Francisco a	N.L.	27	159¹/₃	7	10	.412	84	56	166	4.74	0
2007	San Francisco	N.L.	26	156	14	8	.636	87	87	155	3.92	0
Major League Totals	5 Yrs.		106	618¹/₃	40	31	.563	420	249	606	4.03	0

a On disabled list from April 7 to May 8, 2006.

LUGO, RUDDY JORAIDER

Born, Barahona, Dominican Republic, May 22, 1980.
Bats Right. Throws Right. Height, 6 feet. Weight, 190 pounds.

Year	Club	Lea	G	IP	W	L	Pct	SO	BB	H	ERA	SAVES
1999	Ogden	Pioneer	6	24	1	2	.333	26	12	35	7.87	0
2000	Ogden	Pioneer	16	91²/₃	5	5	.500	88	52	82	3.44	0
2001	Beloit	Midwest	10	15	1	0	1.000	20	6	10	0.60	5
2001	Wilmington a	So.Atl.	16	31	0	2	.000	23	13	29	3.77	2
2002	Vero Beach	Fla.St.	22	87	8	2	.800	77	26	68	2.38	1
2002	Jacksonville	Southern	11	33¹/₃	3	1	.750	23	13	34	4.05	1
2003	Round Rock b	Texas	41	118¹/₃	4	15	.211	112	53	133	6.01	1
2004	Jupiter	Fla.St.	31	39¹/₃	1	7	.125	33	15	42	5.26	11
2004	Carolina	Southern	8	14²/₃	0	1	.000	6	9	16	4.91	0
2005	Visalia	Calif.	1	2	0	0	.000	0	1	7	13.50	0
2005	Montgomery c-d	Southern	26	40¹/₃	1	1	.500	48	23	25	1.12	2
2006	Visalia	Calif.	4	4	0	0	.000	5	2	6	6.75	1
2006	Tampa Bay e	A.L.	64	85	2	4	.333	48	37	75	3.81	0
2007	Sacramento	P.C.	17	20	3	0	1.000	22	7	5	0.45	10
2007	Durham	Int.	11	14²/₃	2	1	.667	7	12	12	1.84	0
2007	Tampa Bay-Oakland f	A.L.	38	48¹/₃	6	0	1.000	34	37	48	5.40	0
Major League Totals	2 Yrs.		102	133¹/₃	8	4	.667	82	74	123	4.39	0

a Sent by Milwaukee Brewers to Los Angeles Dodgers as player to be named later for outfielder Devon White, June 1, 2001.
b Traded to Houston Astros for outfielder Daryle Ward, January 28, 2003.
c Released by Houston Astros, March 30, 2005. Signed with Tampa Bay Devil Rays organization, April 20, 2005.
d Filed for free agency, October 15, 2005, re-signed with Tampa Bay Devil Rays organization, November 3, 2005.
e On disabled list from June 21 to July 14, 2006.
f Claimed on waivers by Oakland Athletics, June 14, 2007.

LYON, BRANDON JAMES

Born, Salt Lake City, Utah, August 10, 1979.
Bats Right. Throws Right. Height, 6 feet, 1 inch. Weight, 195 pounds.

Year	Club	Lea	G	IP	W	L	Pct	SO	BB	H	ERA	SAVES
2000	Queens	N.Y.-Penn.	15	60¹/₃	5	3	.625	55	6	43	2.39	0
2001	Tennessee	Southern	9	58²/₃	5	0	1.000	45	9	57	3.68	0
2001	Syracuse	Int.	11	68¹/₃	5	3	.625	53	10	68	3.69	0
2001	Toronto	A.L.	11	63	5	4	.556	35	15	63	4.29	0
2002	Toronto	A.L.	15	62	1	4	.200	30	19	78	6.53	0
2002	Syracuse a	Int.	14	75²/₃	4	9	.308	35	19	99	5.11	0
2003	Boston	A.L.	49	59	4	6	.400	50	19	73	4.12	9
2003	Pawtucket b-c-d-e	Int.	5	8¹/₃	0	0	.000	7	2	7	3.24	0
2004	Tucson f	P.C.	6	8¹/₃	2	3	.400	4	4	15	15.12	0
2005	Tucson	P.C.	5	5	0	1	.000	4	0	5	5.40	0
2005	Arizona g	N.L.	32	29¹/₃	0	2	.000	17	10	44	6.44	14
2006	Arizona	N.L.	68	69¹/₃	2	4	.333	46	22	68	3.89	0
2007	Arizona	N.L.	73	74	6	4	.600	40	22	70	2.68	2
Major League Totals	6 Yrs.		248	356²/₃	18	24	.429	218	107	396	4.42	25

Division Series

Year	Club	Lea	G	IP	W	L	Pct	SO	BB	H	ERA	SAVES
2007	Arizona	N.L.	3	3	0	0	.000	1	1	1	0.00	0

Year	Club	Lea	G	IP	W	L	Pct	SO	BB	H	ERA	SAVES
	Championship Series											
2007	Arizona................	N.L.	2	3	0	0	.000	4	0	0	0.00	0

a Claimed on waivers by Boston Red Sox, October 9, 2002.
b Traded to Pittsburgh Pirates with pitcher Anastacio Martinez for pitcher Scott Sauerbeck and pitcher Mike Gonzalez, July 22, 2003.
c On disabled list from July 24 to September 1, 2003.
d Traded to Boston Red Sox with pitcher Jeff Suppan and pitcher Anastacio Martinez for infielder Freddy Sanchez, pitcher Mike Gonzalez and cash, July 31, 2003.
e Traded to Arizona Diamondbacks with pitcher Casey Fossum, pitcher Jorge DeRosa and outfielder Michael Goss for pitcher Curt Schilling, November 28, 2003.
f On disabled list from April 3 to October 4, 2004.
g On disabled list from May 13 to August 13, 2005.

MADDUX, GREGORY ALAN
Born, San Angelo, Texas, April 14, 1966.
Bats Right. Throws Right. Height, 6 feet. Weight, 180 pounds.

Year	Club	Lea	G	IP	W	L	Pct	SO	BB	H	ERA	SAVES
1984	Pikeville........	Appalachian	14	85²/₃	6	2	.750	62	41	63	2.63	0
1985	Peoria............	Midland	27	186	13	9	.591	125	52	176	3.19	0
1986	Pittsfield..........	Eastern	8	62²/₃	4	3	.571	35	15	49	2.69	0
1986	Iowa................	A.A.	18	128¹/₃	10	1	*.909	65	30	127	3.02	0
1986	Chicago	N.L.	6	31	2	4	.333	20	11	44	5.52	0
1987	Iowa................	A.A.	4	27²/₃	3	0	1.000	22	12	17	0.98	0
1987	Chicago a..........	N.L.	30	155²/₃	6	14	.300	101	74	181	5.61	0
1988	Chicago	N.L.	34	249	18	8	.692	140	81	230	3.18	0
1989	Chicago	N.L.	35	238¹/₃	19	12	.613	135	82	222	2.95	0
1990	Chicago	N.L.	35	237	15	15	.500	144	71	*242	3.46	0
1991	Chicago	N.L.	39	*263	15	11	.577	198	66	232	3.35	0
1992	Chicago b-c......	N.L.	35	*268	*20	11	.645	199	70	201	2.18	0
1993	Atlanta d..........	N.L.	36	*267	20	10	.667	197	52	228	*2.36	0
1994	Atlanta e..........	N.L.	25	*202	*16	6	.727	156	31	150	*1.56	0
1995	Atlanta f..........	N.L.	28	*209²/₃	*19	2	*.905	181	23	147	*1.63	0
1996	Atlanta	N.L.	35	245	15	11	.577	172	28	225	2.72	0
1997	Atlanta	N.L.	33	232²/₃	19	4	*.826	177	20	200	2.20	0
1998	Atlanta	N.L.	34	251	18	9	.667	204	45	201	*2.22	0
1999	Atlanta	N.L.	33	219¹/₃	19	9	.679	136	37	258	3.57	0
2000	Atlanta	N.L.	35	249¹/₃	19	9	.679	190	42	225	3.00	0
2001	Atlanta	N.L.	34	233	17	11	.607	173	27	220	3.05	0
2002	Atlanta g-h......	N.L.	34	199¹/₃	16	6	.727	118	45	194	2.62	0
2003	Atlanta i..........	N.L.	36	218¹/₃	16	11	.593	124	33	225	3.96	0
2004	Chicago	N.L.	33	212²/₃	16	11	.593	151	33	218	4.02	0
2005	Chicago	N.L.	35	225	13	15	.464	136	36	239	4.24	0
2006	Chicago-Los Angeles j-k .	N.L.	34	210	15	14	.517	117	37	219	4.20	0
2007	San Diego	N.L.	34	198	14	11	.560	104	25	221	4.14	0
Major League Totals .... 22 Yrs.			711	4814¹/₃	347	214	.619	3273	969	4522	3.11	0
	Division Series											
1995	Atlanta	N.L.	2	14	1	0	1.000	7	2	19	4.50	0
1996	Atlanta	N.L.	1	7	1	0	1.000	7	0	3	0.00	0
1997	Atlanta	N.L.	1	9	1	0	1.000	6	1	7	1.00	0
1998	Atlanta	N.L.	1	7	1	0	1.000	4	0	7	2.57	0
1999	Atlanta	N.L.	2	7	0	1	.000	5	5	10	2.57	0
2000	Atlanta	N.L.	1	4	0	1	.000	2	3	9	11.25	0
2001	Atlanta	N.L.	1	6	0	0	.000	5	3	4	3.00	0
2002	Atlanta	N.L.	1	6	1	0	1.000	3	1	5	3.00	0
2003	Atlanta	N.L.	1	6	0	1	.000	1	1	6	3.00	0
2006	Los Angeles	N.L.	1	4	0	0	.000	0	2	7	9.00	0
Division Series Totals			12	70	5	3	.625	40	18	77	3.47	0
	Championship Series											
1989	Chicago	N.L.	2	7¹/₃	0	1	.000	5	4	13	13.50	0
1993	Atlanta	N.L.	2	12²/₃	1	1	.500	11	7	11	4.97	0
1995	Atlanta	N.L.	1	8	1	0	1.000	4	2	7	1.13	0
1996	Atlanta	N.L.	2	14¹/₃	1	1	.500	10	2	15	2.51	0
1997	Atlanta	N.L.	2	13	0	2	.000	16	4	9	1.38	0
1998	Atlanta	N.L.	2	6	0	1	.000	4	3	5	3.00	0
1999	Atlanta	N.L.	2	14	1	0	1.000	7	1	12	1.93	0
2001	Atlanta	N.L.	2	10	0	2	.000	7	2	14	5.40	0
Championship Series Totals			15	85¹/₃	4	8	.333	64	25	86	3.80	1
	World Series Record											
1995	Atlanta	N.L.	2	16	1	1	.500	8	3	9	2.25	0

Year Club	Lea	G	IP	W	L	Pct	SO	BB	H	ERA	SAVES
1996 Atlanta	N.L.	2	15²/₃	1	1	.500	5	1	14	1.72	0
1999 Atlanta	N.L.	1	7	0	1	.000	5	3	5	2.57	0
World Series Totals.............		5	38²/₃	2	3	.400	18	7	28	2.09	0

a Appeared in two games as pinch hitter.
b Selected Cy Young Award winner in National League for 1992.
c Filed for free agency, October 26; signed with Atlanta Braves, December 9, 1992.
d Selected Cy Young Award winner in National League for 1993.
e Selected Cy Young Award winner in National League for 1994.
f Selected Cy Young Award Winner in National League for 1995.
g On disabled list from March 26 to April 12, 2002.
h Filed for free agency, October 29, 2002, re-signed with Atlanta Braves, December 19, 2002.
i Filed for free agency, October 29, 2003. Signed with Chicago Cubs, February 18, 2004.
j Traded to Los Angeles Dodgers for infielder Cesar Izturis, July 31, 2006.
k Filed for free agency, October 31, 2006. Signed with San Diego Padres, December 13, 2006.

MADSON, RYAN MICHAEL
Born, Long Beach, California, August 28, 1980.
Bats Left. Throws Right. Height, 6 feet, 6 inches. Weight, 195 pounds.

Year Club	Lea	G	IP	W	L	Pct	SO	BB	H	ERA	SAVES
1998 Martinsvlle	Appal.	12	54	3	3	.500	52	20	57	4.83	0
1999 Batavia	N.Y.-Penn.	15	87²/₃	5	5	.500	75	43	80	4.72	0
2000 Piedmont	So.Atl.	21	135²/₃	14	5	.737	123	45	113	2.59	0
2001 Clearwater	Fla.St.	22	117²/₃	9	9	.500	101	49	137	3.90	0
2002 Reading	Eastern	26	171¹/₃	16	4	.800	132	53	150	3.20	0
2003 Clearwater	Fla.St.	2	8	0	0	.000	9	2	11	5.63	0
2003 Scranton/WB	Int.	26	157	12	8	.600	138	42	157	3.50	0
2003 Philadelphia	N.L.	1	2	0	0	.000	0	0	0	0.00	0
2004 Reading	Eastern	2	2	0	0	.000	1	2	3	4.50	0
2004 Philadelphia a	N.L.	52	77	9	3	.750	55	19	68	2.34	1
2005 Philadelphia	N.L.	78	87	6	5	.545	79	25	84	4.14	0
2006 Philadelphia	N.L.	50	134¹/₃	11	9	.550	99	50	176	5.69	2
2007 Reading	Eastern	2	3	0	0	.000	4	0	3	0.00	0
2007 Philadelphia a.........	N.L.	38	56	2	2	.500	43	23	48	3.05	1
Major League Totals	5 Yrs.	219	356¹/₃	28	19	.596	276	117	376	4.14	4

a On disabled list from May 4 to May 22 and July 30 to November 2, 2007.

MAHAY, RONALD MATTHEW (RON)
Born, Crestwood, Illinois, June 28, 1971.
Bats Left. Throws Left. Height, 6 feet, 2 inches. Weight, 190 pounds.

Year Club	Lea	G	IP	W	L	Pct	SO	BB	H	ERA	SAVES
1996 Sarasota...........	Fla.St.	31	70²/₃	2	2	.500	68	35	61	3.82	2
1996 Trenton...........	Eastern	1	3²/₃	0	1	.000	0	6	12	29.45	0
1997 Trenton...........	Eastern	17	40²/₃	3	3	.500	47	13	29	3.10	5
1997 Pawtucket	Int.	2	4²/₃	1	0	1.000	6	1	3	0.00	0
1997 Boston...............	A.L.	28	25	3	0	1.000	22	11	19	2.52	0
1998 Pawtucket	Int.	23	41	3	1	.750	41	19	37	4.17	3
1998 Boston...............	A.L.	29	26	1	1	.500	14	15	26	3.46	1
1999 Vancouver.............	P.C.	32	107	7	2	.778	73	45	116	4.29	0
1999 Oakland a.............	A.L.	6	19¹/₃	2	0	1.000	15	3	8	1.86	1
2000 Oakland	A.L.	5	16	0	1	.000	5	9	26	9.00	0
2000 Florida	N.L.	18	25¹/₃	1	0	1.000	27	16	31	6.04	0
2000 Calgary b-c............	P.C.	8	13	0	1	.000	15	7	7	4.85	0
2001 Portland	P.C.	14	16²/₃	1	2	.333	18	5	13	3.78	0
2001 Iowa.................	P.C.	36	46²/₃	3	1	.750	52	10	29	2.31	14
2001 Chicago d.............	N.L.	17	20²/₃	0	0	.000	24	15	14	2.61	0
2002 Iowa.................	P.C.	39	46²/₃	0	1	.000	50	15	32	1.93	2
2002 Chicago e-f...........	N.L.	11	14²/₃	2	0	1.000	14	8	13	8.59	0
2003 Oklahoma...........	P.C.	26	42²/₃	4	2	.667	51	10	36	4.22	3
2003 Texas	A.L.	35	45¹/₃	3	3	.500	38	20	33	3.18	0
2004 Texas	A.L.	60	67	3	0	1.000	54	29	60	2.55	0
2005 Oklahoma...........	P.C.	3	3²/₃	0	0	.000	5	1	2	0.00	0
2005 Texas	A.L.	30	35²/₃	0	2	.000	30	16	47	6.81	1
2005 Frisco g	Texas	5	19²/₃	1	3	.250	20	9	24	7.78	0
2006 Oklahoma...........	P.C.	5	6¹/₃	0	1	.000	11	0	5	1.42	2
2006 Texas	A.L.	62	57	1	3	.250	56	28	54	3.95	0
2007 Frisco...............	Texas	3	4²/₃	0	0	.000	4	1	5	0.00	0
2007 Oklahoma...........	P.C.	4	5²/₃	0	1	.000	5	4	10	11.12	0
2007 Texas h...............	A.L.	28	39	2	0	1.000	32	21	33	2.77	1

Year	Club	Lea	G	IP	W	L	Pct	SO	BB	H	ERA	SAVES
2007 Atlanta i-j	....	N.L.	30	28	1	0	1.000	23	16	19	2.25	0
Major League Totals	.......11 Yrs.		359	419	19	10	.655	354	207	383	3.87	4

a Claimed on waivers by Oakland Athletics, March 30, 1999.
b Sold to Florida Marlins, May 11, 2000.
c Filed for free agency, October 2, 2000. Signed with San Diego Padres organization, November 20, 2000.
d Released by San Diego Padres, May 15, 2001. Signed with Chicago Cubs organization, May 19, 2001.
e On disabled list from May 24 to June 13, 2002.
f Filed for free agency, September 30, 2002. Signed with Texas Rangers organization, November 13, 2002.
g On disabled list from June 8 to June 24, 2005.
h On disabled list from May 12 to June 15, 2007.
i Traded to Atlanta Braves with infielder Mark Teixeira for catcher Jarrod Saltalamacchia, infielder Elvis Andrews, pitcher Neftali Feliz, pitcher Matt Harrison and pitcher Beau James, July 31, 2007.
j Filed for free agency, October 29, 2007. Signed with Kansas City Royals, December 20, 2007.

MAHOLM, PAUL GURNER
Born, Greenwood, Mississippi, June 25, 1982.
Bats Left. Throws Left. Height, 6 feet, 2 inches. Weight, 230 pounds.

Year	Club	Lea	G	IP	W	L	Pct	SO	BB	H	ERA	SAVES
2003 Williamsport	......	N.Y.-Penn.	8	34⅓	2	1	.667	32	10	25	1.83	0
2004 Lynchburg	....	Carolina	8	44	1	3	.250	28	15	39	1.84	0
2004 Pirates	....	Gulf Coast	1	4	0	0	.000	2	1	5	2.25	0
2004 Hickory	......	So.Atl.	3	12⅓	0	2	.000	12	10	17	9.49	0
2005 Altoona	....	Eastern	16	81⅔	6	2	.750	75	26	73	3.20	0
2005 Indianapolis	....	Int.	6	35⅔	1	1	.500	21	12	40	3.53	0
2005 Pittsburgh	....	N.L.	6	41⅓	3	1	.750	26	17	31	2.18	0
2006 Pittsburgh	....	N.L.	30	176	8	10	.444	117	81	202	4.76	0
2007 Pittsburgh	....	N.L.	29	177⅔	10	15	.400	105	49	204	5.02	0
Major League Totals	.......3 Yrs.		65	395	21	26	.447	248	147	437	4.60	0

MAINE, JOHN KEVIN
Born, Fredericksburg, Virginia, May 8, 1981.
Bats Right. Throws Right. Height, 6 feet, 4 inches. Weight, 205 pounds.

Year	Club	Lea	G	IP	W	L	Pct	SO	BB	H	ERA	SAVES
2002 Aberdeen	....	N.Y.-Penn.	4	10⅓	1	1	.500	21	3	6	1.74	0
2002 Delmarva	....	So.Atl.	6	33	1	1	.500	39	4	21	1.36	0
2003 Frederick	....	Carolina	12	70⅓	6	1	.857	77	20	48	3.07	0
2003 Delmarva	....	So.Atl.	14	76⅓	7	3	.700	108	18	43	1.53	0
2004 Bowie	....	Eastern	5	28	4	0	1.000	34	7	16	2.25	0
2004 Ottawa	....	Int.	22	119⅔	5	7	.417	105	52	123	3.91	0
2004 Baltimore	....	A.L.	1	3⅔	0	1	.000	1	3	7	9.82	0
2005 Ottawa	....	Int.	23	128⅓	6	11	.353	111	42	128	4.56	0
2005 Baltimore	....	A.L.	10	40	2	3	.400	24	24	39	6.30	0
2006 St. Lucie	....	Fla.St.	1	5	1	0	1.000	7	2	3	0.00	0
2006 Norfolk	....	Int.	10	56⅔	3	5	.375	48	20	55	3.49	0
2006 New York a-b	....	N.L.	16	90	6	5	.545	71	33	69	3.60	0
2007 New York	....	N.L.	32	191	15	10	.600	180	75	168	3.91	0
Major League Totals	........4 Yrs.		59	324⅔	23	19	.548	276	135	283	4.19	0
Division Series												
2006 New York	....	N.L.	1	4⅓	0	0	.000	5	2	6	2.08	0
Championship Series												
2006 New York	....	N.L.	2	9⅓	1	0	1.000	8	9	4	2.89	0

a Traded to New York Mets with pitcher Jorge Julio for pitcher Kris Benson, January 21, 2006.
b On disabled list from May 3 to June 12, 2006.
a On disabled list from July 26 to September 3, 2004.

MARCUM, SHAUN MICHAL
Born, Kansas City, Missouri, December 14, 1981.
Bats Right. Throws Right. Height, 6 feet. Weight, 190 pounds.

Year	Club	Lea	G	IP	W	L	Pct	SO	BB	H	ERA	SAVES
2003 Auburn	....	N.Y.-Penn.	21	34	1	0	1.000	47	7	15	1.32	8
2004 Dunedin	....	Fla.St.	12	69⅓	3	2	.600	72	4	74	3.12	0
2004 Charleston	....	So.Atl.	13	79	7	4	.636	83	16	64	3.19	0
2005 New Hampshire	.....	Eastern	9	53⅓	7	1	.875	40	10	44	2.53	0
2005 Syracuse	....	Int.	18	103⅔	6	4	.600	90	18	112	4.95	0
2005 Toronto	....	A.L.	5	8	0	0	.000	4	4	6	0.00	0

Year	Club	Lea	G	IP	W	L	Pct	SO	BB	H	ERA	SAVES
2006 Syracuse	Int.		18	52²/₃	4	0	1.000	60	9	48	3.42	0
2006 Toronto	A.L.		21	78¹/₃	3	4	.429	65	38	87	5.06	0
2007 Toronto	A.L.		38	159	12	6	.667	122	49	149	4.13	1
Major League Totals ....3 Yrs.			64	245¹/₃	15	10	.600	191	91	242	4.29	1

MARMOL, CARLOS AGUSTIN
Born, Bonao, Dominican Republic, October 14, 1982.
Bats Right. Throws Right. Height, 6 feet, 2 inches. Weight, 180 pounds.

Year	Club	Lea	G	IP	W	L	Pct	SO	BB	H	ERA	SAVES
2002 Cubs.............	Arizona		1	1	0	0	.000	1	1	1	0.00	0
2003 Cubs.............	Arizona		15	64¹/₃	3	5	.375	74	37	59	4.76	0
2004 Lansing	Midwest		26	154²/₃	14	8	.636	154	53	131	3.20	0
2005 Daytona	Fla.St.		13	72¹/₃	6	2	.750	71	37	60	2.99	0
2005 West Tenn	Southern		14	81¹/₃	3	4	.429	70	40	70	3.65	0
2006 West Tenn	Southern		11	58	3	2	.600	67	25	42	2.33	0
2006 Iowa.................	P.C.		2	3	0	0	.000	1	1	4	9.00	0
2006 Chicago a............	N.L.		19	77	5	7	.417	59	59	71	6.08	0
2007 Iowa.................	P.C.		8	41	4	1	.800	48	12	30	3.95	0
2007 Chicago	N.L.		59	69¹/₃	5	1	.833	96	35	41	1.43	1
Major League Totals ....2 Yrs.			78	146¹/₃	10	8	.556	155	94	112	3.87	1
Division Series												
2007 Chicago	N.L.		2	3	0	1	.000	6	3	3	9.00	0

a On disabled list from August 19 to September 4, 2006.

MARQUIS, JASON SCOTT
Born, Manhasset, New York, August 21, 1978.
Bats Left. Throws Right. Height, 6 feet, 1 inch. Weight, 210 pounds.

Year	Club	Lea	G	IP	W	L	Pct	SO	BB	H	ERA	SAVES
1996 Danville	Appal.		7	23¹/₃	1	1	.500	24	7	30	4.63	0
1997 Macon	So.Atl.		28	141²/₃	14	10	.583	121	55	156	4.38	0
1998 Danville	Carolina		22	114²/₃	2	12	.143	135	41	120	4.87	0
1999 Myrtle Beach	Carolina		6	32	3	0	1.000	41	17	22	0.28	0
1999 Greenville a	Southern		12	55	3	4	.429	35	29	52	4.58	0
2000 Greenville.........	Southern		11	68	4	2	.667	49	23	68	3.57	0
2000 Atlanta	N.L.		15	23¹/₃	1	0	1.000	17	12	23	5.01	0
2000 Richmond	Int.		6	20	0	3	.000	18	13	26	9.00	0
2001 Atlanta	N.L.		38	129¹/₃	5	6	.455	98	59	113	3.48	0
2002 Richmond	Int.		1	5	0	1	.000	6	1	5	3.60	0
2002 Atlanta b.............	N.L.		22	114¹/₃	8	9	.471	84	49	127	5.04	0
2003 Richmond	Int.		15	94	8	4	.667	75	34	93	3.35	0
2003 Atlanta c.............	N.L.		21	40²/₃	0	0	.000	19	18	43	5.53	1
2004 St. Louis.............	N.L.		32	201¹/₃	15	7	.682	138	70	215	3.71	0
2005 St. Louis.............	N.L.		33	207	13	14	.481	100	69	206	4.13	0
2006 St. Louis d............	N.L.		33	194¹/₃	14	*16	.467	96	75	221	6.02	0
2007 Chicago	N.L.		34	191²/₃	12	9	.571	109	76	190	4.60	0
Major League Totals ....8 Yrs.			228	1102	68	61	.527	661	428	1138	4.56	1
Division Series												
2004 St. Louis.............	N.L.		1	3¹/₃	0	0	.000	0	4	4	8.10	0
Championship Series												
2001 Atlanta	N.L.		2	2	0	0	.000	3	2	2	0.00	0
2004 St. Louis.............	N.L.		1	4	0	0	.000	2	2	5	6.75	0
2005 St. Louis.............	N.L.		3	5¹/₃	0	1	.000	4	3	6	3.38	0
Championship Series Totals			6	11¹/₃	0	1	.000	9	7	13	3.97	0
World Series Record												
2004 St. Louis.............	N.L.		7		0	1	.000	4	7	6	3.86	0

a On disabled list from July 5 to 31, 1999.
b On disabled list from April 15 to May 11, 2002.
c Traded to St. Louis Cardinals with pitcher Ray King and pitcher Adam Wainwright for catcher Eli Marrero and outfielder J.D. Drew, December 13, 2003.
d Filed for free agency, October 30, 2006. Signed with Chicago Cubs, December 19, 2006.

MARSHALL, SEAN CHRISTOPHER
Born, Richmond, Virginia, August 30, 1982.
Bats Left. Throws Left. Height, 6 feet, 7 inches. Weight, 205 pounds.

Year	Club	Lea	G	IP	W	L	Pct	SO	BB	H	ERA	SAVES
2003 Lansing	Midwest	1	7	1	0	1.000	11	0	5	0.00	0
2003 Boise	Northwest	14	73²/₃	5	6	.455	88	23	66	2.57	0
2004 Lansing	Midwest	7	48²/₃	2	0	1.000	51	4	29	1.11	0
2004 West Tenn	Southern	6	29	2	2	.500	23	12	36	5.90	0
2005 Daytona	Fla.St.	12	69	4	4	.500	61	26	63	2.74	0
2005 West Tenn	Southern	4	25	0	1	.000	24	5	16	2.52	0
2006 Iowa	P.C.	4	21²/₃	0	2	.000	21	14	17	3.32	0
2006 Chicago a	N.L.	24	125²/₃	6	9	.400	77	59	132	5.59	0
2007 Daytona	Fla.St.	1	6	1	0	1.000	4	1	7	3.00	0
2007 Iowa	P.C.	4	24²/₃	2	0	1.000	15	8	17	1.82	0
2007 Chicago	N.L.	21	103¹/₃	7	8	.467	67	35	107	3.92	0
Major League Totals	2 Yrs.	45	229	13	17	.433	144	94	239	4.83	0

a On disabled list from July 23 to September 1, 2006.

MARTE, DAMASO
Born, Santo Domingo, Dominican Republic, February 14, 1975.
Bats Left. Throws Left. Height, 6 feet, 2 inches. Weight, 210 pounds.

Year	Club	Lea	G	IP	W	L	Pct	SO	BB	H	ERA	SAVES
1993 Seattle	Dominican	17	56¹/₃	2	5	.286	29	50	62	6.55	0
1994 Seattle	Dominican	17	65¹/₃	7	0	1.000	80	48	53	3.86	0
1995 Everett	Northwest	11	36²/₃	2	2	.500	39	10	25	2.21	0
1996 Wisconsin	Midwest	26	142¹/₃	8	6	.571	115	75	134	4.49	0
1997 Lancaster	California	25	139¹/₃	8	8	.500	127	62	144	4.13	0
1998 Orlando	Southern	22	121¹/₃	7	6	.538	99	47	136	5.27	0
1999 Tacoma	P.C.	31	73²/₃	3	3	.500	59	40	79	5.13	0
1999 Seattle	A.L.	5	8²/₃	0	1	.000	3	6	16	9.35	0
2000 Mariners	Arizona	2	5	0	0	.000	6	0	1	0.00	0
2000 New Haven a	Eastern	4	5²/₃	0	0	.000	4	2	6	1.59	0
2001 Norwich	Eastern	23	36	3	1	.750	36	7	29	3.50	1
2001 Nashville	P.C.	4	5¹/₃	0	0	.000	4	0	3	3.38	0
2001 Pittsburgh b	N.L.	23	36¹/₃	0	1	.000	39	12	34	4.71	0
2002 Chicago c	A.L.	68	60¹/₃	1	1	.500	72	18	44	2.83	10
2003 Chicago	A.L.	71	79²/₃	4	2	.667	87	34	50	1.58	11
2004 Chicago	A.L.	74	73²/₃	6	5	.545	68	34	56	3.42	6
2005 Charlotte	Int.	1	1²/₃	0	0	.000	2	1	4	5.40	0
2005 Chicago d-e	A.L.	66	45¹/₃	3	4	.429	54	33	45	3.77	4
2006 Pittsburgh	N.L.	75	58¹/₃	1	7	.125	63	31	51	3.70	0
2007 Pittsburgh	N.L.	65	45¹/₃	2	0	1.000	51	18	32	2.38	0
Major League Totals	8 Yrs.	447	407²/₃	17	21	.447	437	186	328	3.18	31
Division Series											
2005 Chicago	A.L.	1	0	0	0	.000	0	2	1	INF	0
World Series Record											
2005 Chicago	A.L.	1	1²/₃	1	0	1.000	3	2	0	0.00	0

a Filed for free agency, October 15, 2000. Signed with New York Yankees organization, November 21, 2000.
b Traded to Pittsburgh Pirates for infielder Enrique Wilson, June 13, 2001.
c Traded to Chicago White Sox with infielder Edwin Yan for pitcher Matt Guerrier, March 27, 2002.
d On disabled list from June 27 to July 14, 2005.
e Traded to Pittsburgh Pirates for outfielder Rob Mackowiak, December 13, 2005.

MARTINEZ, PEDRO JAMIE
Born, Manoguyabo, Dominican Republic, October 25, 1971.
Bats Right. Throws Right. Height, 5 feet, 11 inches. Weight, 195 pounds.

Year	Club	Lea	G	IP	W	L	Pct	SO	BB	H	ERA	SAVES
1988 Santo Domingo	Domin. Sum.	8	49¹/₃	5	1	.833	28	16	45	3.12	0
1989 Santo Domingo	Domin. Sum.	13	85²/₃	7	2	.778	63	25	59	2.75	1
1990 Great Falls	Pioneer	14	77	8	3	.727	82	40	74	3.62	0
1991 Bakersfield	California	10	61¹/₃	8	0	1.000	83	19	41	2.05	0
1991 San Antonio	Texas	12	76²/₃	7	5	.583	74	31	57	1.76	0
1991 Albuquerque	P.C.	6	39¹/₃	3	3	.500	35	16	28	3.66	0
1992 Albuquerque	P.C.	20	125¹/₃	7	6	.538	124	57	104	3.81	0
1992 Los Angeles	N.L.	2	8	0	1	.000	8	1	6	2.25	0
1993 Albuquerque	P.C.	1	3	0	0	.000	4	1	1	3.00	0
1993 Los Angeles a	N.L.	65	107	10	5	.667	119	57	76	2.61	2
1994 Montreal	N.L.	24	144²/₃	11	5	.688	142	45	115	3.42	1

Year	Club	Lea	G	IP	W	L	Pct	SO	BB	H	ERA	SAVES
1995 Montreal		N.L.	30	194²/₃	14	10	.583	174	66	158	3.51	0
1996 Montreal		N.L.	33	216²/₃	13	10	.565	222	70	189	3.70	0
1997 Montreal b-c		N.L.	31	241¹/₃	17	8	.680	305	67	158	*1.90	0
1998 Boston		A.L.	33	233²/₃	19	7	.731	251	67	188	2.89	0
1999 Boston d-e		A.L.	31	213¹/₃	*23	4	*.852	*313	37	160	*2.07	0
2000 Boston f-g		A.L.	29	217	18	6	.750	*284	32	128	*1.74	0
2001 Boston h		A.L.	18	116²/₃	7	3	.700	163	25	84	2.39	0
2002 Boston		A.L.	30	199¹/₃	20	4	*.833	*239	40	144	*2.26	0
2003 Boston i		A.L.	29	186²/₃	14	4	.778	206	47	147	*2.22	0
2004 Boston j		A.L.	33	217	16	9	.640	227	61	193	3.90	0
2005 New York		N.L.	31	217	15	8	.652	208	47	159	2.82	0
2006 New York k		N.L.	23	132²/₃	9	8	.529	137	39	108	4.48	0
2007 Mets		Gulf Coast	1	4	0	0	.000	4	1	3	6.75	0
2007 St. Lucie		Fla.St.	3	14	1	1	.500	13	3	13	3.21	0
2007 New York l		N.L.	5	28	3	1	.750	32	7	33	2.57	0
Major League Totals	16 Yrs.		447	2673²/₃	209	93	.692	3030	708	2046	2.80	3
Division Series												
1998 Boston		A.L.	1	7	1	0	1.000	8	0	6	3.86	0
1999 Boston		A.L.	2	10	1	0	1.000	11	4	3	0.00	0
2003 Boston		A.L.	2	14	1	0	1.000	9	5	13	3.86	0
2004 Boston		A.L.	1	7	1	0	1.000	6	2	6	3.86	0
Division Series Totals			6	38	4	0	1.000	34	11	28	2.84	0
Championship Series												
1999 Boston		A.L.	1	7	1	0	1.000	12	2	2	0.00	0
2003 Boston		A.L.	2	14¹/₃	0	1	.000	14	2	16	5.65	0
2004 Boston		A.L.	3	13	0	1	.000	14	9	14	6.23	0
Championship Series Totals			6	34¹/₃	1	2	.333	40	13	32	4.72	0
World Series Record												
2004 Boston		A.L.	1	7	1	0	1.000	6	2	3	0.00	0

a Traded to Montreal Expos for second baseman Delino DeShields, November 19, 1993.
b Traded to Boston Red Sox for pitcher Carl Pavano and player to be named later, November 18, 1997. Montreal Expos received pitcher Tony Armas to complete trade, December 18, 1997.
c Selected Cy Young Award Winner in National League for 1997.
d On disabled list from July 19 to August 3, 1999.
e Selected Cy Young Award Winner in American League for 1999.
f On disabled list from June 26 to July 12, 2000.
g Selected Cy Young Award Winner in American League for 2000.
h On disabled list from June 27 to August 26 and September 8 to November 7, 2001.
i On disabled list from May 16 to June 11, 2003.
j Filed for free agency, November 2, 2004. Signed with New York Mets, December 16, 2004.
k On disabled list from June 29 to July 28 and August 15 to September 15, 2006.
l On disabled list from March 23 to September 3, 2007.

MASTNY, THOMAS RAYMOND (TOM)
Born, East Bontang, Indonesia, February 4, 1981.
Bats Right. Throws Right. Height, 6 feet, 6 inches. Weight, 220 pounds.

Year	Club	Lea	G	IP	W	L	Pct	SO	BB	H	ERA	SAVES
2003 Auburn		N.Y.-Penn.	14	63²/₃	8	0	1.000	68	12	56	2.26	0
2004 Charleston a		So.Atl.	27	149	10	3	.769	143	41	123	2.17	0
2005 Kinston		Carolina	29	88	7	3	.700	94	26	78	2.35	2
2005 Akron		Eastern	5	20²/₃	1	1	.500	18	5	18	2.18	0
2006 Akron		Eastern	12	24²/₃	0	1	.000	30	8	15	1.09	1
2006 Buffalo		Int.	24	38	2	1	.667	46	16	25	2.61	0
2006 Cleveland		A.L.	15	16¹/₃	0	1	.000	14	8	17	5.51	5
2007 Cleveland		A.L.	51	57²/₃	7	2	.778	52	32	63	4.68	0
Major League Totals	2 Yrs.		66	74	7	3	.700	66	40	80	4.86	5
Championship Series												
2007 Cleveland		A.L.	3	4²/₃	1	0	1.000	3	2	2	0.00	0

a Sent to Cleveland Indians by Toronto Blue Jays as player to be named later for John McDonald, December 13, 2004.

MATSUZAKA, DAISUKE
Born, Tokoyo, Japan, September 13, 1980.
Bats Right. Throws Right. Height, 6 feet. Weight, 185 pounds.

Year	Club	Lea	G	IP	W	L	Pct	SO	BB	H	ERA	SAVES
1999 Seibu		Japan Pac.	25	180	16	5	.762	151	87	124	2.60	0
2000 Seibu		Japan Pac.	27	167²/₃	14	7	.667	144	95	132	3.97	1

Year	Club	Lea	G	IP	W	L	Pct	SO	BB	H	ERA	SAVES
2001 Seibu . . . . .Japan Pac.			33	240$^{1}/_{3}$	15	15	.500	214	117	184	3.60	0
2002 Seibu . . . . .Japan Pac.			14	73$^{2}/_{3}$	6	2	.750	78	15	60	3.68	0
2003 Seibu . . . . .Japan Pac.			29	.194	16	7	.696	215	63	165	2.83	0
2004 Seibu . . . . .Japan Pac.			23	146	10	6	.625	127	42	127	2.90	0
2005 Seibu . . . . .Japan Pac.			28	215	14	13	.519	226	49	172	2.30	0
2006 Seibu a-b . . . . . . .Japan Pac.			25	186$^{1}/_{3}$	17	5	.773	200	34	138	2.13	0
2007 Boston . . . . .A.L.			32	204$^{2}/_{3}$	15	12	.556	201	80	191	4.40	0
Division Series												
2007 Boston . . . . .A.L.			1	4$^{2}/_{3}$	0	0	.000	3	3	7	5.79	0
Championship Series												
2007 Boston . . . . .A.L.			2	9$^{2}/_{3}$	1	1	.500	9	2	12	5.59	0
World Series Record												
2007 Boston . . . . .A.L.			1	5$^{1}/_{3}$	1	0	1.000	5	3	3	3.38	0

a Signed with Boston Red Sox, December 14, 2006.
b World Baseball Classic most valuable player.

MC CARTHY, BRANDON PATRICK
Born, Glendale, California, July 7, 1983.
Bats Right. Throws Right. Height, 6 feet, 7 inches. Weight, 190 pounds.

Year	Club	Lea	G	IP	W	L	Pct	SO	BB	H	ERA	SAVES
2002 White Sox	Arizona		14	78$^{1}/_{3}$	4	4	.500	79	15	78	2.76	0
2003 Great Falls	Pioneer		16	101	9	4	.692	125	15	105	3.65	0
2004 Kannapolis	So.Atl.		15	94	8	5	.615	113	21	80	3.64	0
2004 Winston-Salem	Carolina		8	52	6	0	1.000	60	3	31	2.08	0
2004 Birmingham	Southern		4	26	3	1	.750	29	6	23	3.46	0
2005 Charlotte	Int.		20	119$^{1}/_{3}$	7	7	.500	130	32	104	3.92	0
2005 Chicago	A.L.		12	67	3	2	.600	48	17	62	4.03	0
2006 Chicago a	A.L.		53	84$^{2}/_{3}$	4	7	.364	69	33	77	4.68	0
2007 Oklahoma	P.C.		1	4$^{1}/_{3}$	0	0	.000	6	0	3	0.00	0
2007 Texas b	A.L.		23	101$^{2}/_{3}$	5	10	.333	59	48	111	4.87	0

| Major League Totals . . . . .3 Yrs. | | | 88 | 253$^{1}/_{3}$ | 12 | 19 | .387 | 176 | 98 | 250 | 4.58 | 0 |

a Traded to Texas Rangers with outfielder David Paisano for pitcher John Danks, pitcher Nick Masset and pitcher Jacob Rasner, December 23, 2006.
b On disabled list from June 10 to July 2 and August 11 to September 11, 2007.

MC GOWAN, DUSTIN MICHAEL
Born, Savannah, Georgia, March 24, 1982.
Bats Right. Throws Right. Height, 6 feet, 3 inches. Weight, 220 pounds.

Year	Club	Lea	G	IP	W	L	Pct	SO	BB	H	ERA	SAVES
2000 Medicine Hat	Pioneer		8	25	0	3	.000	19	25	26	6.48	0
2001 Auburn	N.Y.-Penn.		15	67	3	6	.333	80	49	57	3.76	0
2002 Charleston-WV	So.Atl.		28	148$^{1}/_{3}$	11	10	.524	163	59	143	4.19	0
2003 New Haven	Eastern		14	76$^{2}/_{3}$	7	0	1.000	72	19	78	3.17	0
2003 Dunedin	Fla.St.		14	75$^{2}/_{3}$	5	6	.455	66	25	62	2.85	0
2004 New Hampshire	Eastern		6	31	2	0	1.000	29	15	24	4.06	0
2005 Dunedin	Fla.St.		5	21	0	1	.000	20	5	21	4.29	0
2005 New Hampshire	Eastern		6	35	0	2	.000	33	10	35	3.34	0
2005 Toronto	A.L.		13	45$^{1}/_{3}$	1	3	.250	34	17	49	6.35	0
2006 Syracuse	Int.		23	84	4	5	.444	86	39	77	4.39	1
2006 Toronto	A.L.		16	27$^{1}/_{3}$	1	2	.333	22	25	35	7.24	0
2007 Syracuse	Int.		5	22	0	2	.000	29	9	16	1.64	0
2007 Toronto	A.L.		27	169$^{2}/_{3}$	12	10	.545	144	61	146	4.08	0

| Major League Totals . . . . .3 Yrs. | | | 56 | 242$^{1}/_{3}$ | 14 | 15 | .483 | 200 | 103 | 230 | 4.87 | 0 |

MC LEMORE, MARK STEVEN
Born, Sacramento, California, October 9, 1980.
Bats Left. Throws Left. Height, 6 feet, 2 inches. Weight, 220 pounds.

Year	Club	Lea	G	IP	W	L	Pct	SO	BB	H	ERA	SAVES
2002 Martinsville	Appal.		4	10	0	1	.000	11	5	9	1.80	0
2002 Tri-City	N.Y.-Penn.		9	23	1	5	.167	16	17	42	14.09	0
2003 Lexington	So.Atl.		36	92$^{1}/_{3}$	2	11	.154	100	55	84	4.58	0
2004 Salem.	Carolina		37	93$^{1}/_{3}$	7	7	.500	79	44	80	3.66	6
2005 Corpus Christi	Texas		15	73$^{2}/_{3}$	5	6	.455	65	34	59	2.81	0
2006 Round Rock	P.C.		21	57$^{2}/_{3}$	2	3	.400	52	38	48	2.81	0
2007 Round Rock	P.C.		21	52	0	1	.000	52	35	34	2.77	0
2007 Houston	N.L.		29	35	3	0	1.000	35	18	38	3.86	0

MECHE, GILBERT ALLEN (GIL)

Born, Lafayette, Louisiana, September 8, 1978.
Bats Right. Throws Right. Height, 6 feet, 3 inches. Weight, 220 pounds.

Year	Club	Lea	G	IP	W	L	Pct	SO	BB	H	ERA	SAVES
1996	Mariners	Arizona	2	3	0	1	.000	4	1	4	6.00	0
1997	Everett	Northwest	12	74²/₃	3	4	.429	62	24	75	3.98	0
1997	Wisconsin	Midwest	2	12	0	2	.000	14	4	12	3.00	0
1998	Wisconsin	Midwest	26	149	8	7	.533	168	63	136	3.44	0
1999	New Haven	Eastern	10	59	3	4	.429	56	26	51	3.05	0
1999	Tacoma	P.C.	6	31	2	2	.500	24	13	31	3.19	0
1999	Seattle	A.L.	16	85²/₃	8	4	.667	47	57	73	4.73	0
2000	Seattle	A.L.	15	85²/₃	4	4	.500	60	40	75	3.78	0
2000	Tacoma	P.C.	3	14	1	1	.500	15	10	10	3.86	0
2000	Wisconsin	Midwest	1	5	0	0	.000	6	2	1	0.00	0
2000	Everett a	Northwest	1	1	0	1	.000	0	0	3	9.00	0
2001	Seattle b	A.L.				INJURED—Did Not Play						
2002	San Antonio	Texas	25	65	4	6	.400	56	32	68	6.51	0
2003	Seattle	A.L.	32	186¹/₃	15	13	.536	130	63	187	4.59	0
2004	Tacoma	P.C.	10	57	1	3	.250	45	27	55	5.05	0
2004	Seattle	A.L.	23	127²/₃	7	7	.500	99	47	139	5.01	0
2005	Seattle c	A.L.	29	143¹/₃	10	8	.556	83	72	153	5.09	0
2006	Seattle d	A.L.	32	186²/₃	11	8	.579	156	84	183	4.48	0
2007	Kansas City	A.L.	34	216	9	13	.409	156	62	218	3.67	0
Major League Totals	7 Yrs.		181	1031¹/₃	64	57	.529	731	425	1028	4.44	0

a On disabled list from May 29 to June 12 and July 31 to October 1, 2000.
b On disabled list from March 31 to November 6, 2001.
c On disabled list from August 20 to September 16, 2005.
d Filed for free agency, October 28, 2006. Signed with Kansas City Royals, December 7, 2006.

MEREDITH, OLISE CLA (CLA)

Born, Richmond, Virginia, June 4, 1983.
Bats Right. Throws Right. Height, 6 feet. Weight, 180 pounds.

Year	Club	Lea	G	IP	W	L	Pct	SO	BB	H	ERA	SAVES
2004	Sarasota	Fla.St.	16	16¹/₃	0	2	.000	16	3	15	2.20	12
2004	Augusta	So.Atl.	13	15¹/₃	1	0	1.000	18	3	8	0.00	6
2005	Portland	Eastern	12	15	1	0	1.000	12	3	5	0.00	9
2005	Boston	A.L.	3	2¹/₃	0	0	.000	0	4	6	27.00	0
2005	Wilmington	Carolina	1	1	0	0	.000	2	0	1	0.00	0
2005	Pawtucket	Int.	40	48¹/₃	2	5	.286	42	12	63	5.59	10
2006	Portland	P.C.	24	32¹/₃	3	0	1.000	24	4	26	1.39	2
2006	Pawtucket	Int.	8	13²/₃	0	0	.000	14	5	16	5.27	0
2006	San Diego a	N.L.	45	50²/₃	5	1	.833	37	6	30	1.07	0
2007	San Diego	N.L.	80	79²/₃	5	6	.455	59	17	94	3.50	0
Major League Totals	3 Yrs.		128	132²/₃	10	7	.588	96	27	130	2.98	0
Division Series												
2006	San Diego	N.L.	2	3²/₃	0	0	.000	3	0	3	0.00	0

a Traded to San Diego Padres with catcher Josh Bard for catcher Doug Mirabelli, May 1, 2006.

MESSENGER, RANDALL (RANDY)

Born, Reno, Nevada, August 13, 1981.
Bats Right. Throws Right. Height, 6 feet, 6 inches. Weight, 240 pounds.

Year	Club	Lea	G	IP	W	L	Pct	SO	BB	H	ERA	SAVES
1999	Marlins	Gulf Coast	13	26¹/₃	0	3	.000	23	19	28	7.52	2
2000	Marlins	Gulf Coast	12	59²/₃	2	2	.500	29	22	66	4.83	0
2001	Brevard County	Fla.St.	18	92²/₃	7	4	.636	42	35	99	4.08	0
2001	Kane County	Midwest	14	18¹/₃	2	1	.667	14	5	22	3.93	0
2002	Jupiter	Fla.St.	28	156²/₃	11	8	.579	96	58	178	4.37	0
2003	Carolina	Southern	29	113²/₃	5	7	.417	78	51	137	5.46	0
2004	Carolina	Southern	58	69²/₃	6	3	.667	71	29	67	2.58	21
2005	Albuquerque	P.C.	39	48²/₃	4	2	.667	35	17	46	3.88	7
2005	Florida	N.L.	29	37	0	0	.000	29	30	39	5.35	0
2006	Jupiter	Fla.St.	1	1	0	0	.000	1	0	1	0.00	0
2006	Albuquerque	P.C.	4	3	0	0	.000	1	3	1	9.00	0
2006	Florida	N.L.	59	60¹/₃	2	7	.222	45	24	72	5.67	0
2007	Florida-San Francisco a-b	N.L.	60	64¹/₃	2	4	.333	34	21	85	4.20	1
Major League Totals	3 Yrs.		148	161²/₃	4	11	.267	108	75	196	5.01	1

a Traded to San Francisco Giants for pitcher Armando Benitez, May 31, 2007.
b On disabled list from August 15 to September 14, 2007.

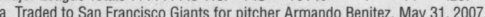

MILLER, ANDREW MARK

Born, Gainesville, Florida, May 21, 1985.
Bats Left. Throws Left. Height, 6 feet, 6 inches. Weight, 210 pounds.

Year Club	Lea	G	IP	W	L	Pct	SO	BB	H	ERA	SAVES
2006 Bluefield............	Appal.	16	42⅓	0	4	.000	27	19	50	6.59	0
2006 Detroit...............	A.L.	8	10⅓	0	1	.000	6	10	8	6.10	0
2007 Aberdeen........	N.Y.-Penn.	16	55	3	5	.375	40	17	66	4.91	0
2007 Lakeland...........	Fla.St.	7	41⅓	1	4	.200	28	15	43	3.48	0
2007 Erie...............	Eastern	4	30⅔	2	0	1.000	24	5	22	0.59	0
2007 Toledo...............	Int.	2	6	0	0	.000	9	5	6	9.00	0
2007 Detroit a-b............	A.L.	13	64	5	5	.500	56	39	73	5.63	0
Major League Totals........2 Yrs.		21	74⅓	5	6	.455	62	49	81	5.69	0

a On disabled list from August 4 to August 24, 2007.
b Traded to Florida Marlins with pitcher Burke Badenhop, pitcher Eulogio De La Cruz, catcher Mike Rabelo and outfielder Cameron Maybin for pitcher Dontrelle Willis and infielder Miguel Cabrera, December 5, 2007.

MILLER, JUSTIN MARK

Born, Torrance, California, August 27, 1977.
Bats Right. Throws Right. Height, 6 feet, 2 inches. Weight, 200 pounds.

Year Club	Lea	G	IP	W	L	Pct	SO	BB	H	ERA	SAVES
1997 Portland.........	Northwest	14	67⅓	4	2	.667	54	20	68	2.14	0
1998 Asheville........	So.Atl.	27	163⅓	13	8	.619	142	40	177	3.69	0
1999 Salem a-b.........	Carolina	8	37	1	2	.333	35	11	35	4.14	0
2000 Sacramento...........	P.C.	9	54⅔	4	1	.800	34	13	42	2.47	0
2000 Midland.............	Texas	18	87	5	4	.556	82	41	74	4.55	0
2001 Sacramento c.........	P.C.	29	165	7	10	.412	134	64	174	4.75	0
2002 Syracuse..............	Int.	8	44⅔	3	2	.600	29	16	34	1.61	0
2002 Toronto..............	A.L.	25	102⅓	9	5	.643	68	66	103	5.54	0
2003 Dunedin............	Fla.St.	1	6	0	1	.000	5	2	3	4.50	0
2004 Syracuse..............	Int.	3	16⅔	1	1	.500	21	4	16	2.16	0
2004 Toronto d.............	A.L.	19	81⅔	3	4	.429	47	42	101	6.06	0
2005 Toronto..............	A.L.	1	2⅓	0	0	.000	2	0	5	15.43	0
2005 Syracuse..............	Int.	28	50⅓	3	1	.750	56	14	39	2.32	2
2006 Durham e.............	Int.	5	7	2	0	1.000	11	2	5	3.86	1
2007 Albuquerque...........	P.C.	11	12	0	0	.000	20	4	9	1.50	6
2007 Ottawa................	Int.	3	2⅓	0	0	.000	2	3	4	3.86	0
2007 Florida f-g...........	N.L.	62	61⅔	5	0	1.000	74	24	53	3.65	0
Major League Totals........4 Yrs.		107	248	17	9	.654	191	132	262	5.33	0

a Traded to Milwaukee Brewers by Colorado Rockies with catcher Henry Blanco and pitcher Jamey Wright for infielder Jeff Cirillo and pitcher Scott Karl, December 13, 1999.
b Traded to Oakland A's for pitcher Jimmy Haynes, December 13, 1999.
c Traded to Toronto Blue Jays with infielder Eric Hinske for pitcher Billy Koch, December 7, 2001.
d On disabled list from May 31 to August 4, 2004.
e Filed for free agency, October 3, 2005. Signed with Tampa Bay Devil Rays, January 11, 2006.
f Released by Tampa Bay Devil Rays, March 31, 2007. Signed with Philadelphia Phillies organization, April 1, 2007.
g Released by Philadelphia Phillies, April 19, 2007. Signed with Florida Marlins organization, April 24, 2007.

MILLER, TREVER DOUGLAS

Born, Louisville, Kentucky, May 29, 1973.
Bats Right. Throws Left. Height, 6 feet, 3 inches. Weight, 200 pounds.

Year Club	Lea	G	IP	W	L	Pct	SO	BB	H	ERA	SAVES
1991 Bristol.............	Appal.	13	54	2	7	.222	46	29	60	5.67	0
1992 Bristol.............	Appal.	12	69⅓	3	8	.273	64	27	75	4.93	0
1993 Fayettevlle..........	So.Atl.	28	161	8	13	.381	116	67	151	4.19	0
1994 Trenton...........	Eastern	26	174⅓	7	16	.304	73	51	198	4.39	0
1995 Jacksnville........	Southern	31	122⅓	8	2	.800	77	34	122	2.72	0
1996 Toledo...............	Int.	27	165⅓	13	6	.684	115	65	167	4.90	0
1996 Detroit a.............	A.L.	5	16⅔	0	4	.000	8	9	28	9.18	0
1997 New Orleans...........	A.A.	29	163⅔	6	7	.462	99	54	177	3.30	0
1998 Houston..............	N.L.	37	53⅓	2	0	1.000	30	20	57	3.04	1
1999 Houston..............	N.L.	47	49⅔	3	2	.600	37	29	58	5.07	1
2000 Phil.-Los Angeles b-c....	N.L.	16	16⅓	0	0	.000	11	12	27	10.47	0
2000 Albuquerque...........	P.C.	12	58	4	2	.667	39	20	60	3.41	0
2001 Sarasota.............	Fla.St.	3	8	0	0	.000	6	1	3	2.25	0
2001 Pawtucket d-e.........	Int.	33	116	3	11	.214	93	34	142	5.20	0
2002 Louisville f...........	Int.	65	82	9	5	.643	80	23	76	3.18	0
2003 Toronto g.............	A.L.	*79	52⅔	2	2	.500	44	28	46	4.61	4

Year	Club	Lea	G	IP	W	L	Pct	SO	BB	H	ERA	SAVES
2004 Tampa Bay	A.L.	60	49	1	1	.500	43	15	48	3.12	1
2005 Tampa Bay h-i	A.L.	61	44⅓	2	2	.500	35	29	45	4.06	0
2006 Round Rock	P.C.	2	2	0	0	.000	3	0	0	0.00	0
2006 Houston j	N.L.	70	50⅔	2	3	.400	56	13	42	3.02	1
2007 Houston k	N.L.	76	46⅓	0	0	.000	46	23	45	4.86	1
Major League Totals	9 Yrs.	451	379	12	14	.462	310	178	396	4.46	8
Division Series											
1998 Houston	N.L.	1	0	0	0	.000	0	1	0	INF	0
1999 Houston	N.L.	2	1⅓	0	0	.000	2	0	1	0.00	0
Division Series Totals		3	1⅓	0	0	.000	2	1	1	0.00	0

a Traded to Houston Astros with catcher Brad Ausmus, pitcher C.J. Nitkowski, pitcher Jose Lima and infielder Daryle Ward for outfielder Brian Hunter, infielder Orlando Miller, pitcher Todd Jones and pitcher Doug Brocail, December 10, 1996.
b Traded to Philadelphia Phillies for pitcher Yorkis Perez, March 29, 2000.
c Claimed on waivers by Los Angeles Dodgers, May 19, 2000.
d Filed for free agency, October 15, 2000. Signed with Boston Red Sox organization, January 22, 2001.
e Filed for free agency, October 15, 2001. Signed with Cincinnati Reds organization, November 8, 2001.
f Released by Cincinnati Reds, September 4, 2002. Signed with Toronto Blue Jays, November 13, 2002.
g Not offered contract, December 21, 2003. Signed with Tampa Bay Devil Rays, January 6, 2004.
h On disabled list from June 13 to June 28, 2005.
i Not offered contract, December 21, 2005. Signed with Houston Astros, January 9, 2006.
j On disabled list from April 19 to May 12, 2006.
k Filed for free agency, October 29, 2007.

MILLWOOD, KEVIN AUSTIN

Born, Gastonia, North Carolina, December 24, 1974.
Bats Right. Throws Right. Height, 6 feet, 4 inches. Weight, 230 pounds.

Year	Club	Lea	G	IP	W	L	Pct	SO	BB	H	ERA	SAVES
1993 Braves	Gulf Coast	12	50	3	3	.500	49	28	36	3.06	0
1994 Macon	So. Atl.	12	32⅔	0	5	.000	24	32	31	5.79	1
1994 Danville	Appal.	13	46	3	3	.500	56	34	42	3.72	1
1995 Macon	So. Atl.	29	103	5	6	.455	89	57	86	4.63	0
1996 Durham	Carolina	33	149⅓	6	9	.400	139	58	138	4.28	1
1997 Greenville	Southern	11	61⅓	3	5	.375	61	24	59	4.11	0
1997 Richmond	Int.	9	60⅔	7	0	1.000	46	16	38	1.93	0
1997 Atlanta	N.L.	12	51⅓	5	3	.625	42	21	55	4.03	0
1998 Atlanta	N.L.	31	174⅓	17	8	.680	163	56	175	4.08	0
1999 Atlanta	N.L.	33	228	18	7	.720	205	59	168	2.68	0
2000 Atlanta	N.L.	36	212⅔	10	13	.435	168	62	213	4.66	0
2001 Macon	So.Atl.	1	3	0	0	.000	5	0	0	0.00	0
2001 Greenville	Southern	2	10	0	1	.000	10	3	9	4.50	0
2001 Atlanta a	N.L.	21	121	7	7	.500	84	40	121	4.31	0
2002 Atlanta b	N.L.	35	217	18	8	.692	178	65	186	3.24	0
2003 Philadelphia c-d	N.L.	35	222	14	12	.538	169	68	210	4.01	0
2004 Philadelphia e-f	N.L.	25	141	9	6	.600	125	51	155	4.85	0
2005 Cleveland g-h	A.L.	30	192	9	11	.450	146	52	182	*2.86	0
2006 Texas	A.L.	34	215	16	12	.571	157	53	228	4.52	0
2007 Frisco	Texas	1	5	0	0	.000	3	1	1	0.00	0
2007 Texas i	A.L.	31	172⅔	10	14	.417	123	67	213	5.16	0
Major League Totals	11 Yrs.	323	1947	133	101	.568	1560	594	1906	3.97	0
Division Series											
1999 Atlanta	N.L.	2	10	1	0	1.000	9	0	1	0.90	1
2000 Atlanta	N.L.	1	4⅔	0	1	.000	3	3	4	7.71	0
2002 Atlanta	N.L.	2	11	1	1	.500	14	0	7	3.27	0
Division Series Totals		5	25⅔	2	2	.500	26	3	12	3.16	1
Championship Series											
1999 Atlanta	N.L.	2	12⅔	1	0	1.000	9	1	13	3.55	0
2001 Atlanta	N.L.	1	1	0	0	.000	1	0	0	0.00	0
Championship Series Totals		3	13⅔	1	0	1.000	10	1	13	3.29	0
World Series											
1999 Atlanta	N.L.	1	2	0	1	.000	2	2	8	18.00	0

a On disabled list from May 7 to July 20, 2001.
b Traded to Philadelphia Phillies for catcher Johnny Estrada, December 20, 2002.
c Pitched no-hit, no-run game against San Francisco Giants, April 27, 2003.
d Filed for free agency, October 29, 2003, re-signed with Philadelphia Phillies, December 19, 2003.
e On disabled list from August 6 to September 12, 2004.
f Filed for free agency, October 28, 2004. Signed with Cleveland Indians, January 7, 2005.

g On disabled list from May 26 to June 16, 2005.
h Filed for free agency, October 28, 2005. Signed with Texas Rangers, December 29, 2005.
i On disabled list from April 29 to May 14 and May 15 to June 1, 2007.

MINER, ZACHARY CHARLES (ZACH)
Born, St.Louis, Missouri, March 12, 1982.
Bats Right. Throws Right. Height, 6 feet, 3 inches. Weight, 200 pounds.

Year	Club	Lea	G	IP	W	L	Pct	SO	BB	H	ERA	SAVES
2001	Jamestown	N.Y.-Penn.	15	90²/₃	3	4	.429	68	16	76	1.89	0
2002	Macon	So.Atl.	29	159	8	9	.471	131	51	143	3.28	0
2003	Myrtle Beach	Carolina	27	153²/₃	6	10	.375	88	61	150	3.69	0
2004	Greenville	Southern	27	129¹/₃	6	10	.375	111	55	132	5.22	0
2005	Richmond	Int.	17	89¹/₃	2	7	.222	63	45	97	4.23	0
2005	Toledo	Int.	6	34¹/₃	3	1	.750	20	20	28	2.36	0
2005	Mississippi a	Southern	4	16²/₃	0	1	.000	18	5	21	4.32	1
2006	Toledo	Int.	9	51	6	0	1.000	40	21	43	2.82	0
2006	Detroit	A.L.	27	93	7	6	.538	59	32	100	4.84	0
2007	Erie	Eastern	2	2	0	0	.000	2	1	4	4.50	0
2007	Toledo	Int.	11	51²/₃	1	4	.200	33	22	43	4.88	0
2007	Detroit b	A.L.	34	53²/₃	3	4	.429	34	22	56	3.02	0
Major League Totals	2 Yrs.		61	146²/₃	10	10	.500	93	54	156	4.17	0
World Series Record												
2006	Detroit	A.L.	1	0²/₃	0	0	.000	0	0	0	0.00	0

a Traded by Atlanta Braves to Detroit Tigers with pitcher Roman Colon for pitcher Kyle Farnsworth, July 26, 2005.
b On disabled list from June 6 to June 29, 2007.

MITRE, SERGIO ARMANDO
Born, Los Angeles, California, February 16, 1981.
Bats Right. Throws Right. Height, 6 feet, 4 inches. Weight, 210 pounds.

Year	Club	Lea	G	IP	W	L	Pct	SO	BB	H	ERA	SAVES
2001	Boise	Northwest	15	91	8	4	.667	71	18	85	3.07	0
2002	Lansing	Midwest	27	168²/₃	8	10	.444	96	27	166	2.83	0
2003	West Tenn	Southern	25	145²/₃	7	9	.438	128	41	162	3.34	0
2003	Chicago	N.L.	3	8²/₃	0	1	.000	3	4	15	8.31	0
2004	Iowa	P.C.	18	102²/₃	6	3	.667	95	39	97	2.98	1
2004	Chicago	N.L.	12	51²/₃	2	4	.333	37	20	71	6.62	0
2005	Iowa	P.C.	13	70²/₃	5	6	.455	55	22	72	4.33	0
2005	Chicago a	N.L.	21	60¹/₃	2	5	.286	37	23	62	5.37	0
2006	Marlins	Gulf Coast	1	1	0	0	.000	0	1	0	0.00	0
2006	Florida b	N.L.	15	41	1	5	.167	31	20	44	5.71	0
2007	Jupiter	Fla.St.	2	9	2	0	1.000	4	0	5	1.00	0
2007	Florida c	N.L.	27	149	5	8	.385	80	41	180	4.65	0
Major League Totals	5 Yrs.		78	310²/₃	10	23	.303	188	108	372	5.36	0

a Traded to Florida Marlins with pitcher Ricky Nolasco and pitcher Renyel Pinto for outfielder Juan Pierre, December 7, 2005.
b On disabled list from May 13 to August 9, 2006.
c On disabled list from April 18 to May 5, 2007.

MOEHLER, BRIAN MERRITT
Born, Rockingham, North Carolina, December 31, 1971.
Bats Right. Throws Right. Height, 6 feet, 3 inches. Weight, 235 pounds.

Year	Club	Lea	G	IP	W	L	Pct	SO	BB	H	ERA	SAVES
1993	Niagara Fls	N.Y.-Penn.	12	58²/₃	6	5	.545	38	27	51	3.22	0
1994	Lakeland	Fla.St.	26	164²/₃	12	12	.500	92	65	153	3.01	0
1995	Jacksonville	Southern	28	162¹/₃	8	10	.444	89	52	176	4.82	0
1996	Jacksnville	Southern	28	173¹/₃	15	6	.714	120	50	186	3.48	0
1996	Detroit	A.L.	2	10¹/₃	0	1	.000	2	8	11	4.35	0
1997	Detroit a	A.L.	31	175¹/₃	11	12	.478	97	61	198	4.67	0
1998	Detroit	A.L.	33	221¹/₃	14	13	.519	123	56	220	3.90	0
1999	Detroit	A.L.	32	196¹/₃	10	*16	.385	106	59	229	5.04	0
2000	Detroit	A.L.	29	178	12	9	.571	103	40	222	4.50	0
2000	West Michigan b	Midwest	1	6¹/₃	0	1	.000	4	1	5	4.26	0
2001	Detroit	A.L.	1	8	0	0	.000	2	1	6	3.38	0
2001	Toledo c	Int.	2	10¹/₃	0	2	.000	6	2	12	4.35	0
2002	Lakeland	Fla.St.	2	12¹/₃	1	1	.500	7	1	10	2.92	0

Year	Club	Lea	G	IP	W	L	Pct	SO	BB	H	ERA	SAVES
2002 Toledo	Int.		4	24	2	1	.667	7	3	28	4.88	0
2002 Detroit	A.L.		3	19²/₃	1	1	.500	13	2	17	2.29	0
2002 Cincinnati d-e-f	N.L.		10	43¹/₃	2	4	.333	18	11	61	6.02	0
2003 Houston.............	N.L.		3	13²/₃	0	0	.000	5	6	22	7.90	0
2003 New Orleans g-h	P.C.		1	2	0	0	.000	3	0	3	4.50	0
2004 Greenville i-j.......	Southern		20	108	3	9	.250	57	27	113	4.17	0
2005 Florida k..............	N.L.		37	158¹/₃	6	12	.333	95	42	198	4.55	0
2006 Marlins..........	Gulf Coast		1	5	0	1	.000	4	0	8	3.60	0
2006 Florida l-m...........	N.L.		29	122	7	11	.389	58	38	164	6.57	0
2007 Houston n	N.L.		42	59²/₃	1	4	.200	36	17	67	4.07	1
Major League Totals ....11 Yrs.			252	1206	64	83	.435	658	341	1415	4.75	1

a On disabled list from August 7 to August 22, 1997.
b On disabled list from April 17 to May 18, 2000.
c On disabled list from April 6 to November 14, 2001.
d On disabled list from August 28 to September 13, 2002.
e On disabled list from March 22 to July 3, 2002.
f Traded to Cincinnati Reds with infielder Matt Boone for infielder David Espinosa, two players to be named later, July 23, 2002. Detroit Tigers received outfielder Gary Varner to complete trade, August 30, 2002.
g Filed for free agency, October 28, 2002. Signed with Houston Astros, January 17, 2003.
h On disabled list from April 17 to September 29, 2003.
i Filed for free agency, October 27, 2003. Signed with Atlanta Braves organization, February 17, 2004.
j Filed for free agency, October 15, 2004. Signed with Florida Marlins organization, December 14, 2004.
k Filed for free agency, October 27, 2005, re-signed with Florida Marlins, December 7, 2005.
l On disabled list from July 2 to July 30, 2006.
m Filed for free agency, October 28, 2006. Signed with Houston Astros organization, January 19, 2007.
n Filed for free agency, October 29, 2007.

MORRIS, MATTHEW CHRISTIAN (MATT)

Born, Middletown, New York, August 9, 1994.
Bats Right. Throws Right. Height, 6 feet, 5 inches. Weight, 220 pounds.

Year	Club	Lea	G	IP	W	L	Pct	SO	BB	H	ERA	SAVES
1995 New Jersey	N.Y.-Penn.		2	11	2	0	1.000	13	3	12	1.64	0
1995 St. Petersburg	Fla. St.		6	34	3	2	.600	31	11	22	2.38	0
1996 Arkansas	Texas		27	167	12	12	.500	120	48	178	3.88	0
1996 Louisville	A.A.		1	8	0	1	.00	9	1	8	3.38	0
1997 St. Louis.............	N.L.		33	217	12	9	.571	149	69	208	3.19	0
1998 Arkansas	Texas		1	4	0	0	.000	2	0	4	0.00	1
1998 Memphis	P.C.		4	14	1	0	1.000	21	4	16	4.50	0
1998 St. Louis a	N.L.		17	113²/₃	7	5	.583	79	42	101	2.53	0
1999 St. Louis b..........	N.L.				INJURED—Did Not Play							
2000 Arkansas	Texas		2	7	0	0	.000	7	4	8	6.43	0
2000 Memphis	P.C.		3	14²/₃	1	2	.333	8	6	20	7.98	0
2000 St. Louis c	N.L.		31	53	3	3	.500	34	17	53	3.57	4
2001 St. Louis.............	N.L.		34	216¹/₃	*22	8	.733	185	54	218	3.16	0
2002 St. Louis d...........	N.L.		32	210¹/₃	17	9	.654	171	64	210	3.42	0
2003 St. Louis e...........	N.L.		27	172¹/₃	11	8	.579	120	39	164	3.76	0
2004 St. Louis f...........	N.L.		32	202	15	10	.600	131	56	205	4.72	0
2005 Palm Beach	Fla. St.		2	9²/₃	0	1	.000	15	2	12	6.52	0
2005 St. Louis g-h	N.L.		31	192²/₃	14	10	.583	117	37	209	4.11	0
2006 San Francisco	N.L.		33	207²/₃	10	15	.400	117	63	218	4.98	0
2007 San Francisco-Pittsburgh i-j	N.L.		32	198²/₃	10	11	.476	102	61	240	4.89	0
Major League Totals ....10 Yrs.			302	1783²/₃	121	88	.579	1205	502	1826	3.91	4
Division Series												
2000 St. Louis.............	N.L.		2	2	0	0	.000	0	1	0	0.00	0
2001 St. Louis.............	N.L.		2	15	0	1	.000	12	5	13	1.20	0
2002 St. Louis.............	N.L.		1	7	1	0	1.000	3	2	7	1.29	0
2004 St. Louis.............	N.L.		1	7	0	1	.000	5	2	6	5.14	0
2005 St. Louis.............	N.L.		1	6	1	0	1.000	4	3	5	3.00	0
Division Series Totals			7	37	7	2	.500	24	13	31	2.19	0
Championship Series												
2000 St. Louis.............	N.L.		2	3²/₃	0	0	.000	2	2	3	4.91	0
2002 St. Louis.............	N.L.		1	13	0	2	.000	6	6	16	6.23	0
2004 St. Louis.............	N.L.		2	10	0	0	.000	6	8	11	5.40	0
2005 St. Louis.............	N.L.		1	5¹/₃	0	0	.000	3	1	8	5.06	0
Championship Series Totals			7	32	0	3	.000	17	17	38	5.63	0
World Series Record												
2004 St. Louis.............	N.L.		1	4¹/₃	0	1	.000	3	4	4	8.31	0

a On disabled list from March 31 to April 11 and April 12 to July 10, 1998.
b On disabled list from March 26 to November 8, 1999.
c On disabled list from March 25 to May 27, 2000.
d On disabled list from August 24 to September 10, 2002.
e On disabled list from July 22 to August 23, 2003.
f Filed for free agency, November 1, 2004, re-signed with St. Louis Cardinals, December 7, 2004.
g On disabled list from April 3 to April 19, 2005.
h Filed for free agency, October 28, 2005. Signed with San Francisco Giants, December 12, 2005.
i Traded to Pittsburgh Pirates for outfielder Rajai Davis and player to be named later, July 31, 2007.
j San Francisco Giants received pitcher Steve MacFarland to complete trade, August 27, 2007.

MORROW, BRANDON JOHN
Born, Santa Rosa, California, July 26, 1984.
Bats Right. Throws Right. Height, 6 feet, 3 inches. Weight, 190 pounds.

Year Club	Lea	G	IP	W	L	Pct	SO	BB	H	ERA	SAVES
2006 Mariners........... Arizona		7	13	0	2	.000	13	9	10	2.77	0
2006 Inland Empire......... Calif.		1	3	0	0	.000	4	0	0	0.00	0
2007 Seattle .... A.L.		60	63⅓	3	4	.429	66	50	56	4.12	0

MOSELEY, DUSTIN AARON
Born, Texarkana, Texas, December 26, 1981.
Bats Right. Throws Right. Height, 6 feet, 4 inches. Weight, 190 pounds.

Year Club	Lea	G	IP	W	L	Pct	SO	BB	H	ERA	SAVES
2001 Dayton .... Midwest		25	148	10	8	.556	108	42	158	4.20	0
2002 Stockton. .... Calif.		14	88⅔	6	3	.667	80	21	60	2.74	0
2002 Chattanooga....... Southern		13	80⅔	5	6	.455	52	37	91	4.13	0
2003 Louisville .... Int.		8	50	2	3	.400	27	14	46	2.70	0
2003 Chattanooga....... Southern		18	112⅔	5	6	.455	73	28	116	3.83	0
2004 Louisville .... Int.		12	71⅔	2	4	.333	48	34	78	4.65	0
2004 Chattanooga a ..... Southern		8	47⅓	3	2	.600	40	10	33	2.66	0
2005 Salt Lake .... P.C.		17	82⅓	4	6	.400	38	30	102	5.03	0
2006 Salt Lake .... P.C.		26	149⅔	13	8	.619	114	51	164	4.69	0
2006 Los Angeles........... A.L.		3	11	1	0	1.000	3	2	22	9.00	0
2007 Los Angeles........... A.L.		46	92	4	3	.571	50	27	97	4.40	0
Major League Totals .... 2 Yrs.		49	103	5	3	.625	53	29	119	4.89	0
Division Series											
2007 Los Angeles........... A.L.		1	1	0	0	.000	1	0	1	0.00	0

a Traded to Anaheim Angels by Cincinnati Reds for pitcher Ramon Ortiz, December 14, 2004.

MOTA, GUILLERMO
Born, San Pedro de Macoris, Dominican Republic, July 25, 1973.
Bats Right. Throws Right. Height, 6 feet, 6 inches. Weight, 210 pounds.

Year Club	Lea	G	IP	W	L	Pct	SO	BB	H	ERA	SAVES
1997 Cape Fear a-b........ So.Atl.		25	126	5	10	.333	112	33	135	4.36	0
1998 Jupiter .... Fla.St.		20	41	3	2	.600	27	6	18	0.66	2
1998 Harrisburg .... Eastern		12	17	2	0	1.000	19	2	10	1.06	4
1999 Ottawa .... Int.		14	19	2	0	1.000	17	5	16	1.89	5
1999 Montreal............... N.L.		51	55⅓	2	4	.333	27	25	54	2.93	0
2000 Ottawa .... Int.		35	63	4	5	.444	35	31	49	2.29	7
2000 Montreal............... N.L.		29	30	1	1	.500	24	12	27	6.00	0
2001 Ottawa .... Int.		4	4	0	0	.000	4	0	1	2.25	0
2001 Montreal c .... N.L.		53	49⅔	1	3	.250	31	18	51	5.26	0
2002 Las Vegas............. P.C.		20	36⅔	1	3	.250	38	8	34	2.95	1
2002 Los Angeles d .... N.L.		43	60⅔	1	3	.250	49	27	45	4.15	0
2003 Los Angeles........... N.L.		76	105	6	3	.667	99	26	78	1.97	1
2004 Los Angeles-Florida e... N.L.		78	96⅔	9	8	.529	85	37	75	3.07	4
2005 Jupiter .... Fla.St.		2	2⅔	0	0	.000	4	0	3	0.00	0
2005 Florida f-g .... N.L.		56	67	2	2	.500	60	32	65	4.70	2
2006 Cleveland h .... A.L.		34	37⅔	1	3	.250	27	19	45	6.21	0
2006 New York i-j........... N.L.		18	18	3	0	1.000	19	5	10	1.00	0
2007 New Orleans........... P.C.		7	7⅔	0	1	.000	7	5	11	7.04	0
2007 New York k........... N.L.		52	59⅓	2	2	.500	47	18	63	5.76	0
Major League Totals .... 9 Yrs.		490	579⅓	28	29	.491	468	219	513	3.91	7
Division Series											
2006 New York............. N.L.		2	4	1	0	1.000	5	0	6	6.75	0
Championship Series											
2006 New York............. N.L.		5	4⅓	0	0	.000	2	2	4	4.15	0

a Played infield, starting in the Dominican Summer League and finishing in the Florida State League, from 1991 to 1996.
b Selected by Montreal Expos from New York Mets in Rule V draft, December 9, 1996.
c On disabled list from July 13 to September 1, 2001.
d Traded to Los Angeles Dodgers with outfielder Wilkin Ruan for pitcher Matt Herges and infielder Jorge Nunez, March 23, 2002.
e Traded to Florida Marlins with catcher Paul LoDuca and outfielder Juan Encarnacion for pitcher Brad Penny, pitcher Bill Murphy and infielder Hee Seop Choi, July 30, 2004.
f On disabled list from May 1 to May 27, 2005.
g Traded to Boston Red Sox with pitcher Josh Beckett and infielder Mike Lowell for infielder Hanley Ramirez, pitcher Anibal Sanchez and pitcher Jesus Delgado, November 24, 2005.
h Traded to Cleveland Indians with infielder Andy Marte and catcher Kelly Shoppach for outfielder Coco Crisp, pitcher David Riske and catcher Josh Bard, January 27, 2006.
i Traded to New York Mets for player to be named later, August 20, 2006.
j Filed for free agency, October 30, 2006, re-signed with New York Mets, December 7, 2006.
k Traded to Milwaukee Brewers for catcher Johnny Estrada, November 20, 2007.

MOYER, JAMIE

Born, Sellersville, Pennsylvania, November 18, 1962.
Bats Left. Throws Left. Height, 6 feet. Weight, 180 pounds.

Year Club	Lea	G	IP	W	L	Pct	SO	BB	H	ERA	SAVES
1984 Geneva	N.Y.-Penn.	14	*104²/3	*9	3	.750	*120	31	59	1.89	0
1985 Winston-Salem	Carolina	12	94	8	2	.800	94	22	82	2.30	0
1985 Pittsfield	Eastern	15	96²/3	7	6	.538	51	32	99	3.72	0
1986 Pittsfield	Eastern	6	41	3	1	.750	42	16	27	0.88	0
1986 Iowa	A.A.	6	42¹/3	3	2	.600	25	11	25	2.55	0
1986 Chicago	N.L.	16	87¹/3	7	4	.636	45	42	107	5.05	0
1987 Chicago	N.L.	35	201	12	15	.444	147	97	210	5.10	0
1988 Chicago a	N.L.	34	202	9	15	.375	121	55	212	3.48	0
1989 Charlotte Rangers	Gulf C.	3	11	1	0	1.000	18	1	8	1.64	0
1989 Tulsa	Texas	2	12¹/3	1	1	.500	9	3	16	5.11	0
1989 Texas b	A.L.	15	76	4	9	.308	44	33	84	4.86	0
1990 Texas c	A.L.	33	102¹/3	2	6	.250	58	39	115	4.66	0
1991 Louisville	A.A.	20	125²/3	5	10	.333	43	45	125	3.80	0
1991 St. Louis d-e	N.L.	8	31¹/3	0	5	.000	20	16	38	5.74	0
1992 Toledo f	Int.	21	138²/3	10	8	.556	80	37	128	2.86	0
1993 Rochester	Int.	8	54	6	0	1.000	41	13	42	1.67	0
1993 Baltimore	A.L.	25	152	12	9	.571	90	38	154	3.43	0
1994 Baltimore	A.L.	23	149	5	7	.417	87	38	158	4.77	0
1995 Baltimore g-h	A.L.	27	115²/3	8	6	.571	65	30	117	5.21	0
1996 Boston-Seattle i-j-k	A.L.	34	160²/3	13	3	*.813	79	46	177	3.98	0
1997 Tacoma	P.C.	1	5	1	0	1.000	6	0	1	0.00	0
1997 Seattle l	A.L.	30	188²/3	17	5	.773	113	43	187	3.86	0
1998 Seattle	A.L.	34	234¹/3	15	9	.625	158	42	234	3.53	0
1999 Seattle	A.L.	32	228	14	8	.636	137	48	235	3.87	0
2000 Seattle m	A.L.	26	154	13	10	.565	98	53	173	5.49	0
2001 Seattle	A.L.	33	209²/3	20	6	.769	119	44	187	3.43	0
2002 Seattle n	A.L.	34	230²/3	13	8	.619	147	50	198	3.32	0
2003 Seattle	A.L.	33	215	21	7	.750	129	66	199	3.27	0
2004 Seattle	A.L.	34	202	7	13	.350	125	63	217	5.21	0
2005 Seattle o	A.L.	32	200	13	7	.650	102	52	225	4.28	0
2006 Seattle	A.L.	25	160	6	12	.333	82	44	179	4.39	0
2006 Philadelphia p	N.L.	8	51¹/3	5	2	.714	26	7	49	4.03	0
2007 Philadelphia	N.L.	33	199¹/3	14	12	.538	133	66	222	5.01	0
Major League Totals	21 Yrs.	604	3550¹/3	230	178	.564	2125	1012	3677	4.21	0
Divisional Series											
1997 Seattle	A.L.	1	4²/3	0	1	.000	2	1	5	5.79	0
2001 Seattle	A.L.	2	12	2	0	1.000	10	2	8	1.50	0
2007 Philadelphia	N.L.	1	6	0	0	.000	2	2	5	1.50	0
Division Series Totals		4	22²/3	2	1	.667	14	5	18	2.38	0
Championship Series											
2001 Seattle	A.L.	1	7	1	0	1.000	5	1	4	2.57	0

a Traded to Texas Rangers with outfielder Rafael Palmeiro and pitcher Drew Hall for infielders Curtis Wilkerson and Luis Benitez, pitchers Mitch Williams, Paul Kilgus and Steve Wilson, and outfielder Pablo Delgado, December 5, 1988.
b On disabled list from May 31 to September 1, 1989.
c Released, November 13, 1990. Signed with St. Louis Cardinals organization, January 10, 1991.
d Became free agent, October 15, 1991. Signed with Chicago Cubs organization, January 8, 1992.
e Released by Chicago Cubs, March 30. Signed with Detroit Tigers organization, March 30, 1992.
f Became free agent, October 15. Signed with Baltimore Orioles organization, December 19, 1992.
g Filed for free agency, November 12, 1995.

h   Signed with Signed with Boston Red Sox, January 2, 1996.
i   Traded to Seattle Mariners for outfielder Darren Bragg, July 30, 1996.
j   Filed for free agency, October 29, 1996.
k   Re-signed with Seattle Mariners, November 20, 1996.
l   On disabled list from April 1 to April 29, 1997.
m On disabled list from April 15 to June 1, 2000.
n   Filed for free agency, October 28, 2002, re-signed with Seattle Mariners, December 7, 2002.
o   Filed for free agency, November 7, 2005, re-signed with Seattle Mariners, December 7, 2005.
p   Traded to Philadelphia Phillies for pitcher Andrew Baldwin and pitcher Andrew Barb, August 19, 2006.

MOYLAN, PETER MICHAEL

Born, Attadale, Western Australia,Australia, December 2, 1978.
Bats Right. Throws Right. Height, 6 feet, 2 inches. Weight, 220 pounds.

Year	Club	Lea	G	IP	W	L	Pct	SO	BB	H	ERA	SAVES
1996 Twins	Gulf Coast	13	28²/₃	1	1	.500	16	9	34	4.08	1
1997 Twins	Gulf Coast	12	40	4	2	.667	40	10	46	4.05	0
2006 Richmond	Int.	35	56²/₃	1	7	.125	54	38	61	6.35	1
2006 Atlanta	N.L.	15	15	0	0	.000	14	5	18	4.80	0
2007 Richmond	Int.	2	2	0	0	.000	3	1	0	0.00	1
2007 Atlanta	N.L.	80	90	5	3	.625	63	31	65	1.80	1
Major League Totals	2 Yrs.	95	105	5	3	.625	77	36	83	2.23	1

MULDER, MARK ALAN

Born, South Holland, Illinois, August 5, 1977.
Bats Left. Throws Left. Height, 6 feet, 6 inches. Weight, 215 pounds.

Year	Club	Lea	G	IP	W	L	Pct	SO	BB	H	ERA	SAVES
1999 Vancouver	P.C.	22	128²/₃	6	7	.462	81	31	152	4.06	0
2000 Sacramento	P.C.	2	8¹/₃	1	1	.500	6	4	15	5.40	0
2000 Oakland	A.L.	27	154	9	10	.474	88	69	191	5.44	0
2001 Oakland	A.L.	34	229¹/₃	*21	8	.724	153	51	214	3.45	0
2002 Oakland a	A.L.	30	207¹/₃	19	7	.731	159	55	182	3.47	0
2003 Oakland b	A.L.	26	186²/₃	15	9	.625	128	40	180	3.13	0
2004 Oakland c	A.L.	33	225²/₃	17	8	.680	140	83	223	4.43	0
2005 St. Louis	N.L.	32	205	16	8	.667	111	70	212	3.64	0
2006 Quad Cities	Midwest	1	5	0	0	.000	1	2	2	1.80	0
2006 Memphis	P.C.	2	8	0	1	.000	5	9	11	9.00	0
2006 St. Louis d-e	N.L.	17	93¹/₃	6	7	.462	50	35	124	7.14	0
2007 Palm Beach	Fla.St.	3	9¹/₃	0	2	.000	5	3	7	1.93	0
2007 Memphis	P.C.	1	5	0	0	.000	4	2	5	3.60	0
2007 St. Louis f	N.L.	3	11	0	3	.000	3	7	22	12.27	0
Major League Totals	8 Yrs.	202	1312¹/₃	103	60	.632	832	410	1348	4.18	0
Division Series											
2001 Oakland	A.L.	2	11	1	1	.500	7	2	14	2.45	0
2002 Oakland	A.L.	2	13	1	1	.500	12	3	14	2.08	0
2005 St. Louis	N.L.	1	6²/₃	1	0	1.000	2	1	8	1.35	0
Division Series Totals		5	30²/₃	3	2	.600	21	6	36	2.05	0
Championship Series											
2005 St. Louis	N.L.	2	11²/₃	0	2	.000	8	3	14	3.09	0

a   On disabled list from April 12 to May 10, 2002.
b   On disabled list from August 20 to October 7, 2003.
c   Traded to St. Louis Cardinals for pitcher Danny Haren, pitcher Kiko Calero and catcher Daric Barton, December 18, 2004.
d   On disabled list from June 21 to August 23 and August 30 to November 2, 2006.
e   Filed for free agency, November 2, 2006, re-signed with St. Louis Cardinals, January 11, 2007.
f   On disabled list from March 23 to September 5, 2007.

MUSSINA, MICHAEL COLE (MIKE)

Born, Williamsport, Pennsylvania, December 8, 1968.
Bats Right. Throws Right. Height, 6 feet, 2 inches. Weight, 190 pounds.

Year	Club	Lea	G	IP	W	L	Pct	SO	BB	H	ERA	SAVES
1990 Hagerstown	Eastern	7	42¹/₃	3	0	1.000	40	7	34	1.49	0
1990 Rochester	Int.	2	13¹/₃	0	0	.000	15	4	8	1.35	0
1991 Rochester a	Int.	19	122¹/₃	10	4	.714	107	31	108	2.87	0
1991 Baltimore	A.L.	12	87²/₃	4	5	.444	52	21	77	2.87	0
1992 Baltimore	A.L.	32	241	18	5	*.783	130	48	212	2.54	0
1993 Bowie	Eastern	2	8	1	0	1.000	10	1	5	2.25	0

290

Year	Club	Lea	G	IP	W	L	Pct	SO	BB	H	ERA	SAVES
1993	Baltimore b	A.L.	25	167²/₃	14	6	.700	117	44	163	4.46	0
1994	Baltimore	A.L.	24	176¹/₃	16	5	.762	99	42	163	3.06	0
1995	Baltimore	A.L.	32	221²/₃	*19	9	.679	158	50	187	3.29	0
1996	Baltimore	A.L.	36	243¹/₃	19	11	.633	204	69	264	4.81	0
1997	Baltimore	A.L.	33	224²/₃	15	8	.652	218	54	197	3.20	0
1998	Baltimore c	A.L.	29	206¹/₃	13	10	.565	175	41	189	3.49	0
1999	Baltimore	A.L.	31	203¹/₃	18	7	.720	172	52	207	3.50	0
2000	Baltimore d	A.L.	34	*237²/₃	11	15	.423	210	46	236	3.79	0
2001	New York	A.L.	34	228²/₃	17	11	.607	214	42	202	3.15	0
2002	New York	A.L.	33	215²/₃	18	10	.643	182	48	208	4.05	0
2003	New York	A.L.	31	214²/₃	17	8	.680	195	40	192	3.40	0
2004	Columbus	Int.	1	3	0	0	.000	5	0	2	0.00	0
2004	New York e	A.L.	27	164²/₃	12	9	.571	132	40	178	4.59	0
2005	New York	A.L.	30	179²/₃	13	8	.619	142	47	199	4.41	0
2006	New York f-g	A.L.	32	197¹/₃	15	7	.682	172	35	184	3.51	0
2007	New York h	A.L.	28	152	11	10	.524	91	35	188	5.15	0
Major League Totals	17 Yrs.		503	3362¹/₃	250	144	.635	2663	754	3246	3.70	0
Division Series												
1996	Baltimore	A.L.	1	6	0	0	.000	6	2	7	4.50	0
1997	Baltimore	A.L.	2	14	2	0	1.000	16	3	7	1.93	0
2001	New York	A.L.	1	7	1	0	1.000	4	1	4	0.00	0
2002	New York	A.L.	1	4	0	0	.000	2	0	6	9.00	0
2003	New York	A.L.	1	7	0	1	.000	6	3	7	3.86	0
2004	New York	A.L.	1	7	0	1	.000	7	1	7	2.57	0
2005	New York	A.L.	2	8¹/₃	1	1	.500	7	1	11	5.40	0
2006	New York	A.L.	1	7	0	1	.000	5	0	8	5.14	0
2007	New York	Fla.St.	1	4²/₃	0	0	.000	3	4	4	3.86	0
Division Series Totals			11	65	4	4	.500	56	15	61	3.60	0
Championship Series												
1996	Baltimore	A.L.	1	7²/₃	0	1	.000	6	2	8	5.87	0
1997	Baltimore	A.L.	2	15	0	0	.000	25	4	4	0.60	0
2001	New York	A.L.	1	6	1	0	1.000	3	1	4	3.00	0
2003	New York	A.L.	3	15¹/₃	0	2	.000	17	4	16	4.11	0
2004	New York	A.L.	2	12²/₃	1	0	1.000	15	2	10	4.26	0
Championship Series Totals			9	56²/₃	2	3	.400	66	13	42	3.34	0
World Series Record												
2001	New York	A.L.	2	11	0	1	.000	14	4	11	4.09	0
2003	New York	A.L.	1	7	1	0	1.000	9	1	7	1.29	0
World Series Totals			3	18	1	1	.500	23	5	18	3.00	0

a On disabled list from May 5 to May 12, 1991.
b On disabled list from July 22 to August 20, 1993.
c On disabled list from April 17 to May 3 and May 15 to June 6, 1998.
d Filed for free agency, October 27, 2000. Signed with New York Yankees, November 30, 2000.
e On disabled list from July 7 to August 18, 2004.
f On disabled list from August 23 to September 5, 2006.
g Filed for free agency, November 11, 2006, re-signed with New York Yankees, November 27, 2006.
h On disabled list from April 12 to May 3, 2007.

MYERS, BRETT ALLEN
Born, Jacksonville, Florida, August 17, 1980.
Bats Right. Throws Right. Height, 6 feet, 4 inches. Weight, 220 pounds.

Year	Club	Lea	G	IP	W	L	Pct	SO	BB	H	ERA	SAVES
1999	Phillies	Gulf Coast	7	27	2	1	.667	30	7	17	2.33	0
2000	Piedmont	So.Atl.	27	175¹/₃	13	7	.650	140	69	165	3.18	0
2001	Reading	Eastern	26	156	13	4	.765	130	43	156	3.87	0
2002	Scranton-WB	Int.	19	128	9	6	.600	97	20	121	3.59	0
2002	Philadelphia	N.L.	12	72	4	5	.444	34	29	73	4.25	0
2003	Philadelphia	N.L.	32	193	14	9	.609	143	76	205	4.43	0
2004	Philadelphia	N.L.	32	176	11	11	.500	116	62	196	5.52	0
2005	Philadelphia	N.L.	34	215¹/₃	13	8	.619	208	68	193	3.72	0
2006	Philadelphia	N.L.	31	198	12	7	.632	189	63	194	3.91	0
2007	Clearwater	Fla.St.	3	3¹/₃	0	0	.000	4	1	2	0.00	0
2007	Philadelphia a	N.L.	51	68²/₃	5	7	.417	83	27	61	4.33	21
Major League Totals	6 Yrs.		192	923	59	47	.557	773	325	922	4.34	21
Division Series												
2007	Philadelphia	N.L.	2	1¹/₃	0	0	.000	3	0	2	0.00	0

a On disabled list from May 24 to July 27, 2007.

MYERS, MICHAEL STANLEY (MIKE)

Born, Arlington Heights, Illinois, June 26, 1969.
Bats Left. Throws Left. Height, 6 feet, 3 inches. Weight, 225 pounds.

Year	Club	Lea	G	IP	W	L	Pct	SO	BB	H	ERA	SAVES
1990 Everett	Northwest	15	85⅓	4	5	.444	73	30	91	3.90	0
1991 Clinton	Midwest	11	65⅓	5	3	.625	59	18	61	2.62	0
1991 Giants	Arizona	1	3	0	1	.000	2	2	5	12.00	0
1992 Clinton	Midwest	7	37⅔	1	2	.333	32	8	28	1.19	0
1992 San Jose a	California	8	54⅔	5	1	.833	40	17	43	2.30	0
1993 Edmonton	P.C.	27	161⅔	7	14	.333	112	52	195	5.18	0
1994 Brevard County	Fla. St.	3	11⅓	0	0	.000	15	4	7	0.79	0
1994 Edmonton	P.C.	12	60	1	5	.167	55	21	78	5.55	0
1995 Charlotte	Int.	37	36⅔	0	5	.000	24	15	41	5.65	0
1995 Toledo	Int.	6	8⅓	0	0	.000	8	3	6	4.32	0
1995 Florida	N.L.	2	2	0	0	.000	0	3	1	0.00	0
1995 Detroit b-c	A.L.	11	6⅓	1	0	1.000	4	4	10	9.95	0
1996 Detroit	A.L.	*83	64⅔	1	5	.167	69	34	70	5.01	6
1997 Detroit d	A.L.	*88	53⅔	0	4	.000	50	25	58	5.70	2
1998 Milwaukee	N.L.	70	50	2	2	.500	40	22	44	2.70	1
1999 Milwaukee f	N.L.	71	41⅓	2	1	.667	35	13	46	5.23	0
2000 Colorado	N.L.	78	45⅓	0	1	.000	41	24	24	1.99	1
2001 Colorado g	N.L.	73	40	2	3	.400	36	24	32	3.60	0
2002 Arizona	N.L.	69	37	4	3	.571	31	17	39	4.38	4
2003 Arizona h	N.L.	64	36⅓	0	1	.000	21	21	38	5.70	0
2004 Seattle-Boston i-j	A.L.	75	42⅔	5	1	.833	32	23	45	4.64	0
2005 Boston k-l	A.L.	65	37⅓	3	1	.750	21	13	30	3.13	0
2006 New York	A.L.	62	30⅔	1	2	.333	22	10	29	3.23	0
2007 New York-Chicago m-n	A.L.	72	54⅓	4	0	1.000	27	23	59	4.80	0
Major League Totals	13 Yrs.	883	541⅔	25	24	.510	429	256	525	4.29	14
Division Series											
2002 Arizona	N.L.	2	1⅔	0	0	.000	1	0	2	0.00	0
2004 Boston	A.L.	2	0⅓	0	0	.000	1	1	0	27.00	0
2005 Boston	A.L.	1	0	0	0	.000	0	1	0	INF	0
2006 New York	A.L.	1	0	0	0	.000	0	0	1	INF	0
Division Series Totals		6	2	0	0	.000	2	2	3	9.00	0
Championship Series											
2004 Boston	A.L.	3	2⅓	0	0	.000	4	1	5	7.71	0

a Selected by Florida Marlins from San Francisco Giants in Rule V draft, December 7, 1992.
b Buddy Groom was traded to Florida Marlins for player to be named later, August 7, 1995.
c Detroit Tigers received pitcher Mike Myers to complete trade, August 9, 1995.
d Traded to Milwaukee Brewers with pitcher Rick Greene and infielder Santiago Perez for pitcher Bryce Florie and player to be named later, November 21, 1997.
f Traded to Colorado Rockies for pitcher Curtis Leskanic, November 17, 1999.
g Traded to Arizona Diamondbacks for outfielder Jack Cust and catcher J.D. Closser, January 7, 2002.
h Filed for free agency, October 26, 2003. Signed with Seattle Mariners organization, January 16, 2004.
i Claimed on waivers by Boston Red Sox, August 6, 2004.
j Filed for free agency, November 1, 2004. Signed with St. Louis Cardinals, December 22, 2004.
k Traded to Boston Red Sox for outfielder Carlos de la Cruz, March 29, 2005.
l Filed for free agency, October 31, 2005. Signed with New York Yankees, December 15, 2005.
m Released by New York Yankees, August 14, 2007. Signed with Chicago White Sox, August 19, 2007.
n Filed for free agency, October 30, 2007.

NATHAN, JOSEPH MICHAEL (JOE)

Born, Houston, Texas, November 22, 1974.
Bats Right. Throws Right. Height, 6 feet, 4 inches. Weight, 220 pounds.

Year	Club	Lea	G	IP	W	L	Pct	SO	BB	H	ERA	SAVES
1995 San Francisco a	N.L.					Did Not Play					
1996						Did Not Play					
1997 Salem-Keizer	Northwest	18	62	2	1	.667	44	26	53	2.47	2
1998 Shreveport	Texas	4	15⅓	1	3	.250	10	9	20	8.80	0
1998 San Jose	California	22	122	8	6	.571	118	48	100	3.32	0
1999 Shreveport	Texas	2	8⅔	0	1	.000	7	7	5	3.12	0
1999 San Francisco	N.L.	19	90⅓	7	4	.636	54	46	84	4.18	1
1999 Fresno	P.C.	13	74⅔	6	4	.600	82	36	68	4.46	0
2000 San Francisco	N.L.	20	93⅓	5	2	.714	61	63	89	5.21	0
2000 San Jose	California	1	5	0	1	.000	2	1	4	3.60	0
2000 Bakersfield	California	1	5⅓	1	0	1.000	6	7	2	5.06	0
2000 Fresno b	P.C.	3	14⅓	0	2	.000	9	7	15	4.40	0
2001 Fresno	P.C.	10	46⅓	0	5	.000	21	33	63	7.77	0
2001 Shreveport	Texas	21	62⅓	3	6	.333	33	37	73	6.93	0

Year Club	Lea	G	IP	W	L	Pct	SO	BB	H	ERA	SAVES
2002 Fresno .... P.C.		31	146$\frac{1}{3}$	6	12	.333	117	74	167	5.60	0
2002 San Francisco .... N.L.		4	3$\frac{2}{3}$	0	0	.000	2	0	1	0.00	0
2003 San Francisco c .... N.L.		78	79	12	4	.750	83	33	51	2.96	0
2004 Minnesota .... A.L.		73	72$\frac{1}{3}$	1	2	.333	89	23	48	1.62	44
2005 Minnesota .... A.L.		69	70	7	4	.636	94	22	46	2.70	43
2006 Minnesota .... A.L.		64	68$\frac{1}{3}$	7	0	1.000	95	16	38	1.58	36
2007 Minnesota .... A.L.		68	71$\frac{2}{3}$	4	2	.667	77	19	54	1.88	37
Major League Totals ....8 Yrs.		395	548$\frac{2}{3}$	43	18	.705	555	222	411	3.00	161
Division Series											
2003 San Francisco .... N.L.		2	0$\frac{1}{3}$	0	1	.000	1	1	4	81.00	0
2004 Minnesota .... A.L.		3	5	0	1	.000	6	5	2	3.60	1
2006 Minnesota .... A.L.		1	0$\frac{2}{3}$	0	0	.000	1	0	1	0.00	0
Division Series Totals		6	6	0	2	.000	8	6	7	7.50	1

a Drafted by San Francisco Giants, June 1, 1995.
b On disabled list from May 13 to June 5 and July 14 to August 18, 2000.
c Traded to Minnesota Twins with pitcher Boof Bonser and pitcher Francisco Liriano for catcher A.J. Pierzynski and player to be named later, November 14, 2003.

NESHEK, PATRICK J. (PAT)

Born, Madison, Wisconsin, September 4, 1980.
Bats Both. Throws Right. Height, 6 feet, 3 inches. Weight, 205 pounds.

Year Club	Lea	G	IP	W	L	Pct	SO	BB	H	ERA	SAVES
2002 Elizabethton .... Appal.		23	27$\frac{1}{3}$	0	2	.000	41	6	13	0.99	15
2003 New Britain .... Eastern		5	7$\frac{2}{3}$	1	1	.500	5	3	7	5.87	1
2003 Fort Myers .... Fla.St.		20	29$\frac{1}{3}$	4	1	.800	29	6	22	2.15	2
2003 Quad Cities........ Midwest		28	34$\frac{1}{3}$	3	2	.600	53	11	20	0.52	14
2004 New Britain .... Eastern		26	35$\frac{1}{3}$	2	1	.667	38	18	34	3.82	2
2004 Fort Myers .... Fla.St.		16	18$\frac{1}{3}$	0	1	.000	19	2	16	2.95	10
2005 New Britain .... Eastern		55	82$\frac{1}{3}$	6	4	.600	95	21	69	2.19	24
2006 Rochester............. Int.		33	60	6	2	.750	87	14	41	1.95	14
2006 Minnesota .... A.L.		32	37	4	2	.667	53	6	23	2.19	0
2007 Minnesota .... A.L.		74	70$\frac{1}{3}$	7	2	.778	74	27	44	2.94	0
Major League Totals ....2 Yrs.		106	107$\frac{1}{3}$	11	4	.733	127	33	67	2.68	0
Division Series											
2006 Minnesota .... A.L.		2	1	0	1	.000	1	0	1	9.00	0

NUNEZ (MORALES), LEONEL (LEO)

Born, Jamao Norte, Dominican Republic, August 14, 1983.
Bats Right. Throws Right. Height, 6 feet, 1 inch. Weight, 165 pounds.

Year Club	Lea	G	IP	W	L	Pct	SO	BB	H	ERA	SAVES
2001 Pirates .... Gulf Coast		10	53$\frac{1}{3}$	2	2	.500	34	9	62	4.39	0
2002 Pirates .... Gulf Coast		11	60$\frac{1}{3}$	4	2	.667	52	5	54	3.43	0
2002 Hickory............. So.Atl.		1	4	0	0	.000	1	3	5	0.00	0
2003 Williamsport...... N.Y.-Penn.		8	38$\frac{1}{3}$	4	3	.571	41	12	31	3.05	0
2003 Hickory............. So.Atl.		13	48$\frac{1}{3}$	2	1	.667	37	14	59	5.59	0
2004 Hickory a .... So.Atl.		27	144	10	4	.714	140	46	121	3.13	1
2005 High Desert .... Calif.		8	13	0	0	.000	15	3	23	9.00	0
2005 Wichita............... Texas		12	13	1	0	1.000	14	2	8	0.69	4
2005 Kansas City .... A.L.		41	53$\frac{2}{3}$	3	2	.600	32	18	73	7.55	0
2006 Wichita............... Texas		15	21	1	2	.333	22	12	18	4.29	3
2006 Kansas City .... A.L.		7	13$\frac{1}{3}$	0	0	.000	7	5	15	4.72	0
2006 Omaha............... P.C.		23	38	2	2	.500	33	13	37	2.13	5
2007 Omaha............... Texas		6	20$\frac{2}{3}$	1	0	1.000	13	6	10	0.87	0
2007 Omaha............... P.C.		5	23	1	2	.333	19	4	16	2.74	0
2007 Kansas City b .... A.L.		13	43$\frac{2}{3}$	2	4	.333	37	10	44	3.92	0
Major League Totals ....3 Yrs.		61	110$\frac{2}{3}$	5	6	.455	76	33	132	5.77	0

a Traded to Kansas City Royals by Pittsburgh Pirates for catcher Benito Santiago, December 16, 2004.
b On disabled list from April 1 to June 10, 2007.

O'FLAHERTY, ERIC GEORGE

Born, Walla Walla, Washington, February 5, 1985.
Bats Left. Throws Left. Height, 6 feet, 2 inches. Weight, 195 pounds.

Year Club	Lea	G	IP	W	L	Pct	SO	BB	H	ERA	SAVES
2003 Mariners.......... Arizona		13	27$\frac{2}{3}$	3	0	1.000	20	7	17	1.95	0
2003 Everett .... Northwest		3	10$\frac{2}{3}$	1	0	1.000	7	3	8	3.38	0

Year	Club	Lea	G	IP	W	L	Pct	SO	BB	H	ERA	SAVES
2004 Wisconsin	Midwest	12	$57\frac{1}{3}$	3	3	.500	38	23	83	6.12	0
2005 Wisconsin	Midwest	45	$69\frac{2}{3}$	4	4	.500	51	30	73	3.75	13
2006 Inland Empire	Calif.	16	$28\frac{2}{3}$	0	1	.000	33	6	31	3.45	1
2006 San Antonio	Texas	25	$39\frac{1}{3}$	2	2	.500	36	15	45	1.14	7
2006 Tacoma	P.C.	2	$3\frac{2}{3}$	1	0	1.000	4	1	3	0.00	0
2006 Seattle	A.L.	15	11	0	0	.000	6	6	18	4.09	0
2007 Tacoma	P.C.	6	8	0	0	.000	8	4	5	1.13	3
2007 Seattle	A.L.	56	$52\frac{1}{3}$	7	1	.875	36	20	45	4.47	0
Major League Totals ....2 Yrs.		71	$63\frac{1}{3}$	7	1	.875	42	26	63	4.41	0

OHMAN, WILLIAM MC DANIEL (WILL)
Born, Frankfurt, West Germany, August 13, 1977.
Bats Left. Throws Left. Height, 6 feet, 2 inches. Weight, 195 pounds.

Year	Club	Lea	G	IP	W	L	Pct	SO	BB	H	ERA	SAVES
1998 Williamsprt.	N.Y.-Penn.	10	39	4	4	.500	35	13	39	6.46	0
1998 Rockford	Midwest	4	$24\frac{1}{3}$	1	1	.500	21	7	25	4.44	0
1999 Daytona	Fla.St.	31	$106\frac{2}{3}$	4	7	.364	97	41	102	3.46	5
2000 West Tenn	Southern	59	$71\frac{1}{3}$	6	4	.600	85	36	53	1.89	3
2000 Chicago	N.L.	6	$3\frac{1}{3}$	1	0	1.000	2	4	4	8.10	0
2001 Iowa	P.C.	40	51	5	2	.714	66	18	51	4.06	4
2001 Chicago	N.L.	11	$11\frac{2}{3}$	0	1	.000	12	6	14	7.71	0
2002 Chicago a	N.L.		INJURED—Did Not Play								
2003 Chicago b	N.L.		INJURED—Did Not Play								
2004 Iowa c	P.C.	45	$52\frac{1}{3}$	3	3	.500	75	29	53	4.30	0
2005 Iowa	P.C.	8	$8\frac{2}{3}$	1	0	1.000	12	2	4	4.15	1
2005 Chicago	N.L.	69	$43\frac{1}{3}$	2	2	.500	45	24	32	2.91	0
2006 Chicago	N.L.	78	$65\frac{1}{3}$	1	1	.500	74	34	51	4.13	0
2007 Iowa	P.C.	9	$6\frac{2}{3}$	0	0	.000	9	5	7	2.70	0
2007 Chicago d	N.L.	56	$36\frac{1}{3}$	2	4	.333	33	16	42	4.95	1
Major League Totals ....5 Yrs.		220	160	6	8	.429	166	84	143	4.33	1

a On disabled list from March 15 to October 9, 2002.
b On disabled list from March 28 to September 29, 2003.
c Released by Chicago Cubs, October 20, 2003, re-signed with Chicago Cubs organization, February 11, 2004.
d Traded to Atlanta Braves with infielder Omar Infante for pitcher Jose Ascanio, December 4, 2007.

OKAJIMA, HIDEKI (HIDEKI)
Born, Kyoto, Japan, December 25, 1975.
Bats Left. Throws Left. Height, 6 feet, 1 inch. Weight, 195 pounds.

Year	Club	Lea	G	IP	W	L	Pct	SO	BB	H	ERA	SAVES
1995 Yomiuri	Japan Cent.	1	5	0	0	.000	9	2	5	1.80	0
1996 Yomiuri	Japan Cent.	5	$12\frac{2}{3}$	1	0	1.000	8	9	13	0.71	0
1997 Yomiuri	Japan Cent.	25	$109\frac{1}{3}$	4	9	.308	102	59	92	3.46	0
1998 Yomiuri	Japan Cent.	14	$62\frac{1}{3}$	3	6	.333	54	32	61	4.33	0
1999 Yomiuri	Japan Cent.	37	$69\frac{2}{3}$	4	1	.800	77	28	42	2.97	0
2000 Yomiuri	Japan Cent.	56	$72\frac{1}{3}$	5	4	.556	102	31	53	3.11	7
2001 Yomiuri	Japan Cent.	58	62	2	1	.667	70	39	62	2.76	25
2002 Yomiuri	Japan Cent.	52	$55\frac{2}{3}$	6	3	.667	58	33	42	3.40	0
2003 Yomiuri	Japan Cent.	41	$38\frac{2}{3}$	2	3	.400	29	20	45	4.89	0
2004 Yomiuri	Japan Cent.	53	$46\frac{2}{3}$	4	3	.571	53	20	33	3.09	5
2005 Yomiuri	Japan Cent.	42	53	1	0	1.000	56	19	55	4.75	0
2006 Hokkaido a	Japan Pac.	55	$54\frac{2}{3}$	2	2	.500	63	14	46	2.14	4
2007 Boston	A.L.	66	69	3	2	.600	63	17	50	2.22	5
Division Series												
2007 Boston	A.L.	2	$2\frac{1}{3}$	0	0	.000	2	1	1	0.00	0
Championship Series												
2007 Boston	A.L.	3	5	0	0	.000	3	2	4	0.00	0
World Series Record												
2007 Boston	A.L.	3	$3\frac{2}{3}$	0	0	.000	6	0	4	7.36	0

a Signed with Boston Red Sox, November 30, 2006.

OLIVER, DARREN CHRISTOPHER
Born, Rio Linda, California, October 6, 1970.
Bats Right. Throws Left. Height, 6 feet, 2 inches. Weight, 220 pounds.

Year	Club	Lea	G	IP	W	L	Pct	SO	BB	H	ERA	SAVES
1988 Rangers	Gulf Coast	12	$54\frac{1}{3}$	5	1	.833	59	18	39	2.15	0
1989 Gastonia	So.Atl.	24	$122\frac{1}{3}$	8	7	.533	108	82	86	3.16	0

Year	Club	Lea	G	IP	W	L	Pct	SO	BB	H	ERA	SAVES
1990	Rangers	Gulf Coast	3	6	0	0	.000	7	1	1	0.00	0
1990	Gastonia	So.Atl.	1	2	0	0	.000	2	4	1	13.50	0
1991	Charlotte	Fla.St.	2	8	0	1	.000	12	3	6	4.50	0
1992	Charlotte	Fla.St.	8	25	1	0	1.000	33	10	11	0.72	2
1992	Tulsa	Texas	3	14^1/$_3$	0	1	.000	14	4	15	3.14	0
1993	Tulsa	Texas	46	73^1/$_3$	7	5	.583	77	41	51	1.96	6
1993	Texas	A.L.	2	3^1/$_3$	0	0	.000	4	1	2	2.70	0
1994	Okla City	A.A.	6	7^1/$_3$	0	0	.000	6	3	1	0.00	1
1994	Texas	A.L.	43	50	4	0	1.000	50	35	40	3.42	2
1995	Texas	A.L.	17	49	4	2	.667	39	32	47	4.22	0
1996	Charlotte	Fla.St.	2	12	0	1	.000	9	3	8	3.00	0
1996	Texas	A.L.	30	173^2/$_3$	14	6	.700	112	76	190	4.66	0
1997	Texas	A.L.	32	201^1/$_3$	13	12	.520	104	82	213	4.20	0
1998	Oklahoma	P.C.	1	5	0	0	.000	1	1	2	0.00	0
1998	Texas a	A.L.	19	103^1/$_3$	6	7	.462	58	43	140	6.53	0
1998	St. Louis b-c	N.L.	10	57	4	4	.500	29	23	64	4.26	0
1999	St. Louis	N.L.	30	196^1/$_3$	9	9	.500	119	74	197	4.26	0
2000	Texas	A.L.	21	108	2	9	.182	49	42	151	7.42	0
2000	Oklahoma	P.C.	7	32	2	1	.667	28	14	22	1.97	0
2000	Tulsa d-e	Texas	1	4^2/$_3$	0	1	.000	5	2	10	11.57	0
2001	Texas	A.L.	28	154	11	11	.500	104	65	189	6.02	0
2001	Oklahoma	P.C.	1	3	0	0	.000	3	0	3	0.00	0
2001	Tulsa f-g	Texas	1	5	0	1	.000	5	2	4	5.40	0
2002	Memphis	P.C.	5	16	0	2	.000	9	17	17	7.87	0
2002	Boston h	A.L.	14	58	4	5	.444	32	27	70	4.66	0
2003	Colorado i	N.L.	33	180^1/$_3$	13	11	.542	88	61	201	5.04	0
2004	Florida-Houston j-k-l	N.L.	27	72^2/$_3$	3	3	.500	46	21	87	5.94	0
2005	Iowa	P.C.	3	13^1/$_3$	0	3	.000	10	5	28	13.50	0
2005	Tucson m-n-o-p	P.C.	4	18^1/$_3$	1	0	1.000	8	3	33	6.38	0
2006	New York q	A.L.	45	81	4	1	.800	60	21	70	3.44	0
2007	Los Angeles	A.L.	61	64^1/$_3$	3	1	.750	51	23	58	3.78	0
Major League Totals		14 Yrs.	412	1552^1/$_3$	94	81	.537	945	626	1719	4.93	2
Division Series												
1996	Texas	A.L.	1	8	0	1	.000	3	2	6	3.38	0
2006	New York	N.L.	1	1^1/$_3$	0	0	.000	0	0	3	20.25	0
2007	Los Angeles	A.L.	1	0^2/$_3$	0	0	.000	0	0	2	27.00	0
Division Series Totals			3	10	0	1	.000	3	2	11	7.20	0
Championship Series												
2006	New York	N.L.	1	6	0	0	.000	3	1	3	0.00	0

a On disabled list from June 11 to June 26, 1998.
b Traded to St. Louis Cardinals with infielder Fernando Tatis and player to be named later for infielder Royce Clayton and pitcher Todd Stottlemyre, July 31, 1998.
c St. Louis Cardinals received infielder Mark Little to complete trade, August 9, 1998.
d Filed for free agency, October 29, 1999. Signed with Texas Rangers, January 27, 2000.
e On disabled list from June 17 to July 19 and July 31 to August 31, 2000.
f On disabled list from May 8 to June 6, 2001.
g Traded to Boston Red Sox for outfielder Carl Everett, December 12, 2001.
h Released by Boston Red Sox, July 2, 2002. Signed with St. Louis Cardinals organization, July 20, 2002.
i Released by St. Louis Cardinals, August 13, 2002. Signed with Colorado Rockies organization, January 29, 2003.
j Filed for free agency, October 26, 2003. Signed with Florida Marlins, January 28, 2004.
k Sold to Houston Astros, July 22, 2004.
l On disabled list from August 6 to September 6, 2004.
m Filed for free agency, November 8, 2004. Signed with Colorado Rockies organization, January 22, 2005.
n Released by Colorado Rockies, March 31, 2005. Signed with Arizona Diamondbacks organization, April 12, 2005.
o Released by Arizona Diamondbacks, May 3, 2005. Signed with Chicago Cubs organization, May 7, 2005.
p Released by Chicago Cubs, May 20, 2005. Signed with New York Mets organization, December 16, 2005.
q Filed for free agency, October 31, 2006. Signed with Los Angeles Angels, December 11, 2006.

OLSEN, SCOTT MATTHEW

Born, Kalamazoo, Michigan, January 12, 1984.
Bats Left. Throws Left. Height, 6 feet, 4 inches. Weight, 200 pounds.

Year	Club	Lea	G	IP	W	L	Pct	SO	BB	H	ERA	SAVES
2002	Marlins	Gulf Coast	13	51^2/$_3$	2	3	.400	50	17	39	2.96	0
2003	Greensboro	So.Atl.	25	128^1/$_3$	7	9	.438	129	59	101	2.81	0
2004	Jupiter	Fla.St.	25	136^1/$_3$	7	6	.538	158	53	127	2.97	0
2005	Carolina	Southern	14	80^1/$_3$	6	4	.600	94	27	75	3.92	0
2005	Florida	N.L.	5	20^1/$_3$	1	1	.500	21	10	21	3.98	0
2006	Albuquerque	P.C.	1	6^1/$_3$	0	0	.000	5	3	5	0.00	0
2006	Florida	N.L.	31	180^2/$_3$	12	10	.545	166	75	160	4.04	0

Year Club	Lea	G	IP	W	L	Pct	SO	BB	H	ERA	SAVES
2007 Florida	N.L.	33	176²/₃	10	15	.400	133	85	226	5.81	0
Major League Totals ....3 Yrs.		69	377²/₃	23	26	.469	320	170	407	4.86	0

ORTIZ, DIOGENES RAMON

Born, Cotui, Dominican Republic, March 23, 1973.
Bats Right. Throws Left. Height, 6 feet. Weight, 175 pounds.

Year Club	Lea	G	IP	W	L	Pct	SO	BB	H	ERA	SAVES
1995 California	Dominican	16	97	8	6	.571	100	54	79	2.23	0
1996 Angels	Arizona	16	68	5	4	.556	78	27	55	2.12	1
1996 Boise	Northwest	3	19²/₃	1	1	.500	18	6	21	3.66	0
1997 Cedar Rapids	Midwest	27	181	11	10	.524	225	53	156	3.58	0
1998 Midland ..... .̇.....	Texas	7	47	2	1	.667	53	16	50	5.55	0
1999 Erie.	Eastern	15	102	9	4	.692	86	40	88	2.82	0
1999 Edmonton	P.C.	9	53¹/₃	5	3	.625	64	19	46	4.05	0
1999 Anaheim	A.L.	9	48¹/₃	2	3	.400	44	25	50	6.52	0
2000 Lake Elsinore	California	1	6	1	0	1.000	7	2	8	3.00	0
2000 Edmonton	P.C.	15	89	6	6	.500	76	37	74	4.55	0
2000 Anaheim a	A.L.	18	111¹/₃	8	6	.571	73	55	96	5.09	0
2001 Anaheim..............	A.L.	32	208²/₃	13	11	.542	135	76	223	4.36	0
2002 Anaheim	A.L.	32	217¹/₃	15	9	.625	162	68	188	3.77	0
2003 Anaheim	A.L.	32	180	16	13	.552	94	63	209	5.20	0
2004 Anaheim b	A.L.	34	128	5	7	.417	82	38	139	4.43	0
2005 Sarasota............	Fla.St.	1	3	0	1	.000	3	0	7	9.00	0
2005 Cincinnati c-d.......	N.L.	30	171¹/₃	9	11	.450	96	51	206	5.36	0
2006 Washington e........	N.L.	33	190²/₃	11	*16	.407	104	64	230	5.57	0
2007 Minnesota	A.L.	28	91	4	4	.500	44	15	112	5.14	0
2007 Colorado f-g..........	N.L.	10	13	1	0	1.000	7	7	15	7.62	0
Major League Totals ....9 Yrs.		258	1359²/₃	84	80	.512	841	462	1468	4.90	0
Division Series											
2002 Anaheim...............	A.L.	1	2²/₃	0	0	.000	1	4	3	20.25	0
2004 Anaheim...............	A.L.	1	2	0	0	.000	0	1	2	4.50	0
Division Series Totals		2	4²/₃	0	0	.000	1	5	5	13.50	0
Championship Series											
2002 Anaheim...............	A.L.	1	5¹/₃	1	0	1.000	3	1	10	5.06	0
World Series Record											
2002 Anaheim...............	A.L.	1	5	1	0	1.000	3	4	5	7.20	0

a On disabled list from March 25 to April 10, 2000.
b Traded to Cincinnati Reds for pitcher Dustin Moseley, December 14, 2004.
c On disabled list from April 9 to May 1, 2005.
d Not offered contract, October 28, 2005. Signed with Washington Nationals, December 29, 2005.
e Filed for free agency, November 1, 2006. Signed with Minnesota Twins, January 22, 2007.
f Traded to Colorado Rockies for infielder Matt Macri, August 15, 2007.
g Filed for free agency, October 11, 2007.

OSWALT, ROY EDWARD

Born, Kosciusko, Mississippi, August 29, 1977.
Bats Right. Throws Right. Height, 6 feet. Weight, 185 pounds.

Year Club	Lea	G	IP	W	L	Pct	SO	BB	H	ERA	SAVES
1997 Astros	Gulf Coast	5	28¹/₃	1	1	.500	28	7	25	0.64	0
1997 Auburn...........	N.Y.-Penn.	9	51²/₃	2	4	.333	44	15	50	4.53	0
1998 Astros	Gulf Coast	4	16	1	1	.500	27	1	10	2.25	0
1998 Auburn...........	N.Y.-Penn.	11	70¹/₃	4	5	.444	67	31	49	2.18	0
1999 Michigan	Midwest	22	151¹/₃	13	4	.765	143	54	144	4.46	0
2000 Kissimmee..........	Fla.St.	8	45¹/₃	4	3	.571	47	11	52	2.98	0
2000 Round Rock..........	Texas	19	129²/₃	11	4	.733	141	22	106	1.94	2
2001 New Orleans..........	P.C.	5	31	2	3	.400	34	6	32	4.35	0
2001 Houston	N.L.	28	141²/₃	14	3	.824	144	24	126	2.73	0
2002 Houston..............	N.L.	35	233	19	9	.679	208	62	215	3.01	0
2003 New Orleans..........	P.C.	1	3	0	0	.000	2	0	3	3.00	0
2003 Houston a	N.L.	21	127¹/₃	10	5	.667	108	29	116	2.97	0
2004 Houston..............	N.L.	36	237	*20	10	.667	206	62	233	3.49	0
2005 Houston..............	N.L.	35	241²/₃	20	12	.625	184	48	243	2.94	0
2006 Houston b	N.L.	33	220²/₃	15	8	.652	166	38	220	*2.98	0
2007 Houston..............	N.L.	33	212	14	7	.667	154	60	221	3.18	0
Major League Totals ....7 Yrs.		221	1413¹/₃	112	54	.675	1170	323	1374	3.07	0

Year	Club	Lea	G	IP	W	L	Pct	SO	BB	H	ERA	SAVES
	Division Series											
2004 Houston		N.L.	2	11⅓	1	0	1.000	8	4	15	2.38	0
2005 Houston		N.L.	1	7⅓	1	0	1.000	7	2	6	3.68	0
Division Series Totals			3	18⅔	2	0	1.000	15	6	21	2.89	0
	Championship Series											
2004 Houston		N.L.	2	8	0	0	.000	2	4	11	6.75	0
2005 Houston		N.L.	2	14	2	0	1.000	12	4	8	1.29	0
Championship Series Totals			4	22	2	0	1.000	14	8	19	3.27	0
	World Series Record											
2005 Houston		N.L.	1	6	0	0	.000	3	5	8	7.50	0

a On disabled list from May 16 to May 31 and June 19 to July 7 and July 30 to September 8, 2003.
b On disabled list from May 30 to June 14, 2006.

OTSUKA, AKINORI

Born, Chiba, Japan, January 13, 1972.
Bats Right. Throws Right. Height, 6 feet. Weight, 210 pounds.

Year	Club	Lea	G	IP	W	L	Pct	SO	BB	H	ERA	SAVES
1997 Kintetsu	Japan Pac.	52	82⅔	4	5	.444	127	46	44	2.07	7
1998 Kintetsu	Japan Pac.	49	55⅓	3	2	.600	74	25	43	2.11	35
1999 Kintetsu	Japan Pac.	25	29⅔	1	4	.200	32	10	24	2.73	6
2000 Kintetsu	Japan Pac.	39	41⅔	1	3	.250	49	13	31	2.38	24
2001 Kintetsu	Japan Pac.	48	56	2	5	.286	82	15	42	4.02	26
2002 Kintetsu	Japan Pac.	41	42⅓	2	1	.667	54	3	22	1.28	22
2003 Chunichi a	Japan Cent.	51	43	1	3	.250	56	5	31	2.09	17
2004 San Diego	N.L.	73	77⅓	7	2	.778	87	26	56	1.75	2
2005 San Diego b	N.L.	60	62⅔	2	8	.200	60	34	55	3.59	1
2006 Texas	A.L.	63	59⅔	2	4	.333	47	11	53	2.11	32
2007 Texas c-d	A.L.	34	32⅓	2	1	.667	23	9	26	2.51	4
Major League Totals 4 Yrs.		236	232	13	15	.464	217	80	190	2.44	39
	Division Series										
2005 San Diego	N.L.	3	3	0	0	.000	0	1	1	0.00	0

a Signed with San Diego Padres, December 9, 2003.
b Traded to Texas Rangers with pitcher Adam Eaton and catcher Billy Killian for pitcher Chris Young, infielder Adrian Gonzalez and outfielder Terrmel Sledge, January 4, 2006.
c On disabled list from July 9 to October 15, 2007.
d Not offered contract, December 12, 2007.

OWINGS, MICAH BURTON

Born, Gainesville, Georgia, September 28, 1982.
Bats Right. Throws Right. Height, 6 feet, 5 inches. Weight, 225 pounds.

Year	Club	Lea	G	IP	W	L	Pct	SO	BB	H	ERA	SAVES
2006 Tucson	P.C.	15	87⅔	10	0	1.000	61	34	96	3.70	0
2006 Tennessee	Southern	12	74⅓	6	2	.750	69	17	66	2.91	0
2007 Tucson	P.C.	1	5	0	0	.000	7	1	4	0.00	0
2007 Arizona a	N.L.	29	152⅔	8	8	.500	106	50	146	4.30	0
	Championship Series										
2007 Arizona	N.L.		3⅔	0	1	.000	2	2	6	4.91	0

a On disabled list from April 18 to May 3, 2007.

PADILLA, VICENTE DE LA CRUZ

Born, Chinandega, Nicaraqua, September 27, 1977.
Bats Right. Throws Right. Height, 6 feet, 2 inches. Weight, 220 pounds.

Year	Club	Lea	G	IP	W	L	Pct	SO	BB	H	ERA	SAVES
1999 High Desert	California	9	50⅔	4	1	.800	55	17	50	3.73	0
1999 Tucson	P.C.	18	93⅔	7	4	.636	58	24	107	3.75	0
1999 Arizona	N.L.	5	2⅔	0	1	.000	0	3	7	16.88	0
2000 Tucson	P.C.	12	18⅓	0	1	.000	22	8	22	4.42	1
2000 Arizona-Philadelphia a	N.L.	55	65⅓	4	7	.364	51	28	72	3.72	2
2001 Scranton-WB	Int.	16	81⅔	7	0	1.000	75	11	64	2.42	0
2001 Philadelphia b	N.L.	23	34	3	1	.750	29	12	36	4.24	0
2002 Philadelphia	N.L.	32	206	14	11	.560	128	53	198	3.28	0
2003 Philadelphia	N.L.	32	208⅔	14	12	.538	133	62	196	3.62	0
2004 Clearwater	Fla.St.	1	2	0	1	.000	1	1	3	9.00	0
2004 Scranton/WB	Int.	2	4⅔	0	0	.000	6	5	6	13.50	0
2004 Philadelphia c	N.L.	20	115⅓	7	7	.500	82	36	119	4.53	0

Year	Club	Lea	G	IP	W	L	Pct	SO	BB	H	ERA	SAVES
2005	Clearwater	Fla.St.	1	5	0	1	.000	3	1	4	1.80	0
2005	Scranton/WB	Int.	1	5	1	0	1.000	4	2	6	3.60	0
2005	Philadelphia d-e	N.L.	27	147	9	12	.429	103	74	146	4.71	0
2006	Texas f	A.L.	33	200	15	10	.600	156	70	206	4.50	0
2007	Frisco..............	Texas	6	12	0	1	.000	12	9	14	8.25	0
2007	Texas g..............	A.L.	23	120⅓	6	10	.375	71	50	146	5.76	0
Major League Totals ....9 Yrs.			250	1099⅓	72	71	.503	753	388	1126	4.25	2

a Traded to Philadelphia Phillies with infielder Travis Lee, pitcher Omar Daal and pitcher Nelson Figueroa for pitcher Curt Schilling, July 26, 2000.
b On disabled list from May 4 to May 30, 2001.
c On disabled list from May 30 to August 10, 2004.
d On disabled list from March 25 to April 19, 2005.
e Traded to Texas Rangers for player to be named later, December 12, 2005. Philadelphia Phillies received pitcher Ricardo Rodriguez to complete trade, December 19, 2005.
f Filed for free agency, October 30, 2006, re-signed with Texas Rangers, December 9, 2006.
g On disabled list from June 22 to August 15, 2007.

PAPELBON, JONATHAN ROBERT

Born, Baton Rouge, Louisiana, November 23, 1980.
Bats Right. Throws Right. Height, 6 feet, 4 inches. Weight, 230 pounds.

Year	Club	Lea	G	IP	W	L	Pct	SO	BB	H	ERA	SAVES
2003	Lowell	N.Y.-Penn.	13	32⅔	1	2	.333	36	9	43	6.34	0
2004	Sarasota...........	Fla.St.	24	129⅔	12	7	.632	153	43	97	2.64	0
2005	Portland...........	Eastern	14	87	5	2	.714	83	23	59	2.48	0
2005	Pawtucket	Int.	7	27⅓	1	2	.333	27	3	21	2.93	1
2005	Boston................	A.L.	17	34	3	1	.750	34	17	33	2.65	0
2006	Boston................	A.L.	59	68⅓	4	2	.667	75	13	40	0.92	35
2007	Boston................	A.L.	59	58⅓	1	3	.250	84	15	30	1.85	37
Major League Totals ....3 Yrs.			135	160⅔	8	6	.571	193	45	103	1.62	72
Division Series												
2005	Boston................	A.L.	2	4	0	0	.000	2	0	2	0.00	0
2007	Boston................	A.L.	1	1⅓	1	0	1.000	1	2	0	0.00	0
Division Series Totals			3	5⅓	1	0	1.000	3	2	2	0.00	0
Championship Series												
2007	Boston..............	A.L.	3	5	0	0	.000	3	2	3	0.00	1
World Series Record												
2007	Boston..............	A.L.	3	4⅓	0	0	.000	3	0	2	0.00	3

PARONTO, CHAD MICHAEL

Born, Woodsville, New Hampshire, July 28, 1975.
Bats Right. Throws Right. Height, 6 feet, 5 inches. Weight, 250 pounds.

Year	Club	Lea	G	IP	W	L	Pct	SO	BB	H	ERA	SAVES
1996	Frederick	Carolina	8	15	0	1	.000	6	8	11	4.80	0
1996	Bluefield............	Appal.	9	21⅓	1	1	.500	24	5	16	1.69	1
1997	Delmarva	So.Atl.	28	127⅓	6	9	.400	93	56	133	4.74	0
1998	Frederick	Carolina	18	103⅔	7	6	.538	87	39	116	3.13	0
1998	Bowie..............	Eastern	8	35⅔	1	3	.250	28	23	38	5.80	1
1999	Frederick	Carolina	13	72⅓	3	5	.375	55	26	81	4.73	0
1999	Bowie..............	Eastern	15	41	0	4	.000	27	32	59	8.12	0
2000	Bowie..............	Eastern	8	47	4	2	.667	31	16	29	2.87	0
2000	Rochester............	Int.	12	36	1	1	.500	18	15	40	5.75	0
2001	Rochester............	Int.	33	43⅓	3	3	.500	39	24	44	4.57	1
2001	Baltimore a...........	A.L.	24	27	1	3	.250	16	11	33	5.00	0
2002	Buffalo................	Int.	8	13	0	0	.000	7	1	10	0.00	1
2002	Cleveland	A.L.	29	35⅔	0	2	.000	23	11	34	4.04	0
2002	Akron b	Eastern	1	0⅓	0	0	.000	0	1	1	27.00	0
2003	Cleveland	A.L.	6	6⅔	0	2	.000	6	3	7	9.45	0
2003	Buffalo c...........	Int.	49	56	3	5	.375	48	22	64	4.34	18
2004	Memphis d..........	P.C.	47	55	5	3	.625	38	25	46	2.13	4
2005	Richmond	Int.	26	41	3	1	.750	28	17	43	3.95	0
2005	Nashville e-f..........	P.C.	27	39⅓	3	1	.750	38	19	40	2.75	4
2006	Richmond	Int.	12	17⅔	1	1	.500	15	3	17	1.02	4
2006	Atlanta..............	N.L.	65	56⅔	2	3	.400	41	19	53	3.18	0
2007	Richmond	Int.	11	16⅔	0	0	.000	11	4	18	3.78	2
2007	Atlanta g-h..............	N.L.	41	40⅓	3	1	.750	14	19	47	3.57	1
Major League Totals ....5 Yrs.			165	166⅓	6	11	.353	100	63	174	4.00	1

a Claimed on waivers by Cleveland Indians, November 19, 2001.
b On disabled list from July 29 to November 4, 2002.
c Filed for free agency, October 15, 2003. Signed with St. Louis Cardinals organization, November 24, 2003.
d Filed for free agency, October 15, 2004. Signed with Milwaukee Brewers organization, December 21, 2004.
e Released by Milwaukee Brewers, June 17, 2005. Signed with Atlanta Braves organization, June 21, 2005.
f Filed for free agency, October 15, 2005, re-signed with Atlanta Braves organization, November 22, 2005.
g On disabled list from April 14 to April 30, 2007.
h Filed for free agency, October 29, 2007. Signed with Houston Astros, December 18, 2007.

PARRISH, JOHN HENRY

Born, Lancaster, Pennsylvania, November 26, 1977.
Bats Left. Throws Left. Height, 5 feet, 11 inches. Weight, 210 pounds.

Year	Club	Lea	G	IP	W	L	Pct	SO	BB	H	ERA	SAVES
1996	Orioles	Gulf Coast	11	19^1/$_3$	2	0	1.000	33	11	13	1.86	2
1996	Bluefield	Appal.	8	13^1/$_3$	2	1	.667	18	9	11	2.70	1
1997	Bowie	Eastern	1	5	1	0	1.000	3	2	3	1.80	0
1997	Frederick	Carolina	5	22^1/$_3$	1	3	.250	17	16	23	6.04	0
1997	Delmarva	So.Atl.	23	72^2/$_3$	3	3	.500	76	32	69	3.84	1
1998	Frederick	Carolina	16	82^2/$_3$	4	4	.500	81	27	77	3.27	0
1999	Frederick	Carolina	6	36^2/$_3$	2	2	.500	44	12	34	4.17	0
1999	Bowie	Eastern	12	55^2/$_3$	0	2	.000	42	43	49	4.04	0
1999	Delmarva	So.Atl.	4	10	0	1	.000	10	6	9	7.20	0
2000	Bowie	Eastern	3	16	2	0	1.000	16	7	12	1.69	0
2000	Rochester	Int.	18	104	6	7	.462	87	56	85	4.24	0
2000	Baltimore	A.L.	8	36^1/$_3$	2	4	.333	28	35	40	7.18	0
2001	Rochester	Int.	26	133	7	7	.500	126	51	115	3.52	0
2001	Baltimore	A.L.	16	22	1	2	.333	20	17	22	6.14	0
2002	Baltimore a	A.L.					INJURED—Did Not Play					
2003	Bowie	Eastern	49	76^1/$_3$	3	3	.500	85	33	58	2.00	6
2003	Baltimore	A.L.	14	23^2/$_3$	0	1	.000	15	8	17	1.90	0
2004	Baltimore	A.L.	56	78	6	3	.667	71	55	68	3.46	1
2005	Baltimore	A.L.	14	17^1/$_3$	1	0	1.000	25	17	19	3.12	0
2005	Bowie b	Eastern	5	9^1/$_3$	0	0	.000	13	6	7	2.89	0
2006	Baltimore c	A.L.					INJURED—Did Not Play					
2007	Tacoma	P.C.	3	4^1/$_3$	1	0	1.000	4	4	8	14.54	0
2007	Baltimore-Seattle d-e	A.L.	53	52	2	2	.500	41	37	63	5.71	0
Major League Totals		6 Yrs.	161	229^1/$_3$	12	12	.500	200	169	229	4.63	1

a On disabled list from March 30 to October 21, 2002.
b On disabled list from September 6 to October 27, 2005.
c On disabled list from March 15 to October 30, 2006.
d Traded to Seattle Mariners for outfielder Sebastien Boucher, August 9, 2007.
e Not offered contract, December 12, 2007. Signed with Toronto Blue Jays organization, January 2, 2008.

PATTERSON, JOHN HOLLIS

Born, Orange, Texas, January 30, 1978.
Bats Right. Throws Right. Height, 6 feet, 5 inches. Weight, 210 pounds.

Year	Club	Lea	G	IP	W	L	Pct	SO	BB	H	ERA	SAVES
1997	South Bend a	Midwest	18	78	1	9	.100	95	34	63	3.23	0
1998	High Desert	California	25	127	8	7	.533	148	42	102	2.83	0
1999	Tucson	P.C.	7	30^2/$_3$	1	5	.167	29	18	43	7.04	0
1999	El Paso	Texas	18	100	8	6	.571	117	42	98	4.77	0
2000	Tucson b	P.C.	3	15	0	2	.000	10	9	21	7.80	0
2001	Lancaster	California	2	9^1/$_3$	0	0	.000	9	3	9	5.79	0
2001	Tucson	P.C.	13	67^2/$_3$	2	7	.222	40	31	82	5.85	0
2001	El Paso c	Texas	5	25^1/$_3$	1	2	.333	19	9	30	4.26	0
2002	Tucson d	P.C.	19	112^2/$_3$	10	5	.667	104	45	117	4.23	0
2002	Arizona d	N.L.	7	30^2/$_3$	2	0	1.000	31	7	27	3.23	0
2003	Tucson	P.C.	18	109^1/$_3$	10	5	.667	74	43	100	2.63	0
2003	Arizona	N.L.	16	55	1	4	.200	43	30	61	6.05	1
2004	Brevard County	Fla.St.	2	7^2/$_3$	0	0	.000	7	1	3	0.00	0
2004	Harrisburg	Eastern	1	4	0	0	.000	9	2	0	0.00	0
2004	Montreal e-f	N.L.	19	98^1/$_3$	4	7	.364	99	46	100	5.03	0
2005	Washington g	N.L.	31	198^1/$_3$	9	7	.563	185	65	172	3.13	0
2006	Potomac	Carolina	2	8^2/$_3$	0	1	.000	11	2	12	5.19	0
2006	New Orleans	P.C.	1	4^2/$_3$	0	0	.000	3	2	4	1.93	0
2006	Washington h	N.L.	8	40^2/$_3$	1	2	.333	42	9	36	4.43	0
2007	Potomac	Carolina	2	5^1/$_3$	0	0	.000	2	5	6	6.75	0

Year Club	Lea	G	IP	W	L	Pct	SO	BB	H	ERA	SAVES
2007 Washington i .... N.L.		7	31⅓	1	5	.167	15	22	39	7.47	0
Major League Totals ....6 Yrs.		88	454⅓	18	25	.419	415	179	435	4.32	1

a Released by Montreal Expos, October 24, 1995 (did not play). Signed with Arizona Diamondbacks organization, November 7, 1996.
b On minor league disabled list from April 6 to 24 and May 6 to September 8, 2000.
c On minor league disabled list from April 5 to 19 and April 25 to May 13, 2001.
d On minor league disabled list from April 4 to May 5, 2002.
e Traded to Montreal Expos for pitcher Randy Choate, March 25, 2004.
f On disabled list from April 28 to July 15, 2004.
g On disabled list from May 16 to May 31, 2005.
h On disabled list from April 22 to June 23 and July 10 to October 6, 2006.
i On disabled list from May 6 to October 1, 2007.

PEAVY, JACOB EDWARD (JAKE)
Born, Mobile, Alabama, May 3, 1981.
Bats Right. Throws Right. Height, 6 feet, 1 inch. Weight, 180 pounds.

Year Club	Lea	G	IP	W	L	Pct	SO	BB	H	ERA	SAVES
1999 Padres .... Arizona		13	73⅔	7	1	.875	90	23	52	1.34	0
1999 Idaho Falls .... Pioneer		2	11	2	0	1.000	13	1	5	0.00	0
2000 Fort Wayne........ .Midwest		26	133⅔	13	8	.619	164	53	107	2.90	0
2001 Mobile .... Southern		5	28	2	1	.667	44	12	19	2.57	0
2002 Mobile .... Southern		14	80⅓	4	5	.444	89	30	65	2.80	0
2002 San Diego .... N.L.		17	97⅔	6	7	.462	90	33	106	4.52	0
2003 San Diego .... N.L.		32	194⅔	12	11	.522	156	82	173	4.11	0
2004 Mobile .... Southern		1	4⅔	0	1	.000	4	2	7	5.79	0
2004 San Diego a .... N.L.		27	166⅓	15	6	.714	173	53	146	*2.27	0
2005 San Diego .... N.L.		30	203	13	7	.650	*216	50	162	2.88	0
2006 San Diego .... N.L.		32	202⅓	11	14	.440	215	62	187	4.09	0
2007 San Diego b .... N.L.		34	223⅓	*19	6	.760	*240	68	169	*2.54	0
Major League Totals ....6 Yrs.		172	1087⅓	76	51	.598	1090	348	943	3.31	0
Division Series											
2005 San Diego .... N.L.		1	4⅓	0	1	.000	3	3	8	16.62	0
2006 San Diego .... N.L.		1	5⅓	0	1	.000	2	1	11	8.44	0
Division Series Totals		2	9⅔	0	2	.000	5	4	19	12.10	0

a On disabled list from May 20 to July 2, 2004.
b Selected Cy Young Award Winner in National League for 2007.

PELFREY, MICHAEL ALAN (MIKE)
Born, Wright-Patterson AFB, Ohio, January 14, 1984.
Bats Right. Throws Right. Height, 6 feet, 7 inches. Weight, 210 pounds.

Year Club	Lea	G	IP	W	L	Pct	SO	BB	H	ERA	SAVES
2006 St. Lucie........... Fla.St.		4	22	2	1	.667	26	2	17	1.64	0
2006 Binghamton .... Eastern		12	66⅓	4	2	.667	77	26	60	2.71	0
2006 New York............ N.L.		4	21⅓	2	1	.667	13	12	25	5.48	0
2006 Norfolk............... Int.		2	8	1	0	1.000	6	5	4	2.25	0
2007 St. Lucie........... Fla.St.		1	6	0	0	.000	2	3	5	3.00	0
2007 New Orleans.......... P.C.		14	74	3	6	.333	56	26	74	4.01	0
2007 New York............ N.L.		15	72⅔	3	8	.273	45	39	85	5.57	0
Major League Totals ....2 Yrs.		19	94	5	9	.357	58	51	110	5.55	0

PENA, RAMON ANTONIO (TONY)
Born, Santo Domingo, Dominican Republic, January 9, 1982.
Bats Right. Throws Right. Height, 6 feet, 1 inch. Weight, 220 pounds.

Year Club	Lea	G	IP	W	L	Pct	SO	BB	H	ERA	SAVES
2005 Tennessee .... Southern		25	148⅓	7	13	.350	95	40	165	4.43	0
2006 Tennessee .... Southern		17	20⅓	2	0	1.000	17	5	18	0.89	6
2006 Tucson............... P.C.		24	26⅓	3	1	.750	21	2	17	1.71	7
2006 Arizona............... N.L.		25	30⅔	3	4	.429	21	8	36	5.58	1
2007 Arizona............... N.L.		75	85⅓	5	4	.556	63	31	63	3.27	2
Major League Totals ....2 Yrs.		100	116	8	8	.500	84	39	99	3.88	3
Division Series											
2007 Arizona............... N.L.		2	2	0	0	.000	0	0	2	0.00	0
Championship Series											
2007 Arizona............... N.L.		3	3⅓	0	0	.000	7	0	1	0.00	0

PENNY, BRADLEY WAYNE (BRAD)
Born, Broken Arrow, Oklahoma, May 24, 1978.
Bats Right. Throws Right. Height, 6 feet, 4 inches. Weight, 260 pounds.

Year	Club	Lea	G	IP	W	L	Pct	SO	BB	H	ERA	SAVES
1996	Diamondbcks	Arizona	11	49²/₃	2	2	.500	52	14	36	2.36	0
1997	South Bend	Midwest	25	118²/₃	10	5	.667	116	43	91	2.73	0
1998	High Desert	California	28	164	14	5	.737	207	35	138	2.96	0
1999	El Paso a-b-c	Texas	17	90	2	7	.222	100	25	109	4.80	0
1999	Portland	Eastern	6	32¹/₃	1	0	1.000	35	14	28	3.90	0
2000	Brevard County	Fla.St.	2	8	0	1	.000	11	4	5	1.13	0
2000	Calgary	P.C.	3	15	2	0	1.000	16	10	8	1.80	0
2000	Florida d	N.L.	23	119²/₃	8	7	.533	80	60	120	4.81	0
2001	Florida	N.L.	31	205	10	10	.500	154	54	183	3.69	0
2002	Jupiter	Fla.St.	2	7²/₃	0	0	.000	9	0	5	0.00	0
2002	Florida e	N.L.	24	129¹/₃	8	7	.533	93	50	148	4.66	0
2003	Florida	N.L.	32	196¹/₃	14	10	.583	138	56	195	4.13	0
2004	Florida-Los Angeles f-g	N.L.	24	143	9	10	.474	111	45	130	3.15	0
2005	Vero Beach	Fla.St.	1	5	1	0	1.000	3	1	2	1.80	0
2005	Las Vegas	P.C.	1	6	1	0	1.000	9	2	5	3.00	0
2005	Los Angeles h	N.L.	29	175¹/₃	7	9	.438	122	41	185	3.90	0
2006	Los Angeles	N.L.	34	189	*16	9	.640	148	54	206	4.33	0
2007	Los Angeles	N.L.	33	208	16	4	*.800	135	73	199	3.03	0
Major League Totals	8 Yrs.		230	1365²/₃	88	66	.571	981	433	1366	3.90	0
Division Series												
2003	Florida	N.L.	2	5²/₃	0	0	.000	6	1	5	6.35	0
2006	Los Angeles	N.L.	1	1	0	1	.000	1	2	2	18.00	0
Division Series Totals			3	6²/₃	0	1	.000	7	3	7	8.10	0
Championship Series												
2003	Florida	N.L.	3	4	1	1	.500	0	3	9	15.75	0
World Series Record												
2003	Florida	N.L.	2	12¹/₃	2	0	1.000	7	5	15	2.19	0

a On disabled list from April 20 to 30, 1999.
b Traded by Arizona Diamondbacks to Florida Marlins with pitcher Vladimir Nunez and player to be named later for pitcher Matt Mantei, July 9, 1999.
c Florida Marlins received outfielder Abraham Nunez to complete trade, December 13, 1999.
d On disabled list from July 20 to September 1, 2000.
e On disabled list from May 19 to July 2, 2002.
f Traded to Los Angeles Dodgers with pitcher Bill Murphy and infielder Hee Seop Choi for catcher Paul LoDuca, outfielder Juan Encarnacion and pitcher Guillermo Mota, July 30, 2004.
g On disabled list from August 9 to September 22, 2004.
h On disabled list from March 25 to April 24, 2005.

PERALTA (GUTIERREZ), JOEL
Born, Bonao, Dominican Republic, March 23, 1976.
Bats Right. Throws Right. Height, 5 feet, 11 inches. Weight, 180 pounds.

Year	Club	Lea	G	IP	W	L	Pct	SO	BB	H	ERA	SAVES
2000	Boise	Northwest	4	8¹/₃	0	0	.000	9	5	12	6.48	0
2000	Butte	Pioneer	10	19	2	1	.667	17	10	24	6.63	1
2001	Cedar Rapids	Midwest	41	42¹/₃	0	0	.000	53	5	27	2.13	23
2001	Arkansas	Texas	9	10	0	1	.000	14	5	15	6.30	2
2002	Cedar Rapids	Midwest	41	47¹/₃	5	0	1.000	53	11	28	0.95	21
2002	Arkansas	Texas	12	17²/₃	0	0	.000	11	10	25	6.62	0
2003	Salt Lake	P.C.	1	0	0	0	.000	0	1	0	0.00	0
2003	Arkansas	Texas	47	52¹/₃	5	4	.556	48	12	39	2.24	20
2004	Angels	Arizona	2	4¹/₃	0	0	.000	9	0	1	2.08	0
2004	Rancho Cucamonga	Calif.	1	2	0	0	.000	1	1	5	9.00	0
2004	Salt Lake	P.C.	39	56	4	2	.667	68	18	64	4.98	1
2005	Los Angeles	A.L.	28	34²/₃	1	0	1.000	30	14	28	3.89	0
2005	Salt Lake a	P.C.	19	20	4	1	.800	18	6	11	2.70	10
2006	Omaha	P.C.	6	7²/₃	1	0	1.000	8	3	8	2.35	2
2006	Kansas City	A.L.	64	73²/₃	1	3	.250	57	17	74	4.40	1
2007	Kansas City	A.L.	62	87²/₃	1	3	.250	66	19	93	3.80	1
Major League Totals	3 Yrs.		154	196	3	6	.333	153	50	195	4.04	2

a Claimed on waivers by Kansas City Royals, October 7, 2005.

PERCIVAL, TROY EUGENE
Born, Fontana, California, August 9, 1969.
Bats Right. Throws Right. Height, 6 feet, 3 inches. Weight, 240 pounds.

Year Club	Lea	G	IP	W	L	Pct	SO	BB	H	ERA	SAVES
1991 Boise	Northwest	28	38^1/$_3$	2	0	1.000	63	18	23	1.41	12
1992 Palm Sprngs	Calif.	11	10^2/$_3$	1	1	.500	16	8	6	5.06	2
1992 Midland	Texas	20	19	3	0	1.000	21	11	18	2.37	5
1993 Vancouver	P.C.	18	18^2/$_3$	0	1	.000	19	13	24	6.27	4
1994 Vancouver	P.C.	49	61	2	6	.250	73	29	63	4.13	15
1995 California	A.L.	62	74	3	2	.600	94	26	37	1.95	3
1996 California	A.L.	62	74	0	2	.000	100	31	38	2.31	36
1997 Lake Elsinore	Calif.	2	2	0	0	.000	3	0	1	0.00	0
1997 Anaheim a	A.L.	55	52	5	5	.500	72	22	40	3.46	27
1998 Anaheim..............	A.L.	67	66^2/$_3$	2	7	.222	87	37	45	3.65	42
1999 Anaheim..............	A.L.	60	57	4	6	.400	58	22	38	3.79	31
2000 Anaheim..............	A.L.	54	50	5	5	.500	49	30	42	4.50	32
2000 Lake Elsinore b........	Calif.	2	2	0	0	.000	1	1	1	4.50	0
2001 Anaheim..............	A.L.	57	57^2/$_3$	4	2	.667	71	18	39	2.65	39
2002 Anaheim c	A.L.	58	56^1/$_3$	4	1	.800	68	25	38	1.92	40
2003 Anaheim d	A.L.	52	49^1/$_3$	0	5	.000	48	23	33	3.47	33
2004 Anaheim e-f	A.L.	52	49^2/$_3$	2	3	.400	33	19	43	2.90	33
2005 Detroit g..............	A.L.	26	25	1	3	.250	20	11	19	5.76	8
2006 Detroit h..............	A.L.					INJURED—Did Not Play					
2007 Memphis	P.C.	6	6^2/$_3$	0	0	.000	9	5	4	1.35	0
2007 St. Louis h-i-j-k-l	N.L.	34	40	3	0	1.000	36	10	24	1.80	0
Major League Totals ....12 Yrs.		639	651^2/$_3$	33	41	.446	736	274	436	3.02	324
Division Series											
2002 Anaheim..............	A.L.	3	3^1/$_3$	0	0	.000	4	0	6	5.40	2
Championship Series											
2002 Anaheim..............	A.L.	3	3^1/$_3$	0	0	.000	3	0	0	0.00	2
World Series Record											
2002 Anaheim..............	A.L.	3	3^1/$_3$	0	0	.000	3	1	2	3.00	3

a On disabled list from April 7 to May 16, 1997.
b On disabled list from August 5 to August 25, 2000.
c On disabled list from April 3 to April 18 and July 12 to July 27, 2002.
d On disabled list from May 23 to June 7, 2003.
e On disabled list from June 2 to June 27, 2004.
f Filed for free agency, October 28, 2004. Signed with Detroit Tigers, November 17, 2004.
g On disabled list from May 8 to June 5 and July 10 to October 31, 2005.
h On disabled list from April 1 to November 1, 2006.
i Filed for free agency, November 2, 2006.
j Signed with Los Angeles Angels organization, April 2, 2007.
k Announced retirement, April 2, 2007. Signed with St. Louis Cardinals organization, June 8, 2007.
l Filed for free agency, October 29, 2007. Signed with Tampa Bay Devil Rays, November 30, 2007.

PEREZ, ODALIS AMADOL
Born, Las Matas de Farfan, Dominican Republic, June 11, 1977.
Bats Left. Throws Left. Height, 6 feet. Weight, 220 pounds.

Year Club	Lea	G	IP	W	L	Pct	SO	BB	H	ERA	SAVES
1995 Braves	Gulf Coast	12	65	3	5	.375	62	18	48	2.22	0
1996 Eugene	Northwest	10	23^2/$_3$	2	1	.667	38	11	26	3.80	0
1997 Macon	So.Atl.	36	87^1/$_3$	4	5	.444	100	27	67	1.65	5
1998 Greenville.........	Southern	23	132	6	5	.545	143	53	127	4.02	0
1998 Richmond	Int.	13	24^1/$_3$	1	2	.333	22	7	26	2.96	3
1998 Atlanta	N.L.	10	10^2/$_3$	0	1	.000	5	4	10	4.22	0
1999 Atlanta a.............	N.L.	18	93	4	6	.400	82	53	100	6.00	0
2000 Atlanta b.............	N.L.					INJURED—Did Not Play					
2001 Richmond	Int.	5	23	1	0	1.000	22	2	23	2.74	0
2001 Atlanta c-d...........	N.L.	24	95^1/$_3$	7	8	.467	71	39	108	4.91	0
2002 Los Angeles	N.L.	32	222^1/$_3$	15	10	.600	155	38	182	3.00	0
2003 Los Angeles	N.L.	30	185^1/$_3$	12	12	.500	141	46	191	4.52	0
2004 Los Angeles e-f......	N.L.	31	196^1/$_3$	7	6	.538	128	44	180	3.25	0
2005 Las Vegas........	P.C.	4	14^2/$_3$	1	0	1.000	11	4	14	4.30	0
2005 Los Angeles g	N.L.	19	108^2/$_3$	7	8	.467	74	28	109	4.56	0
2006 Los Angeles	N.L.	20	59^1/$_3$	4	4	.500	33	13	89	6.83	0
2006 Kansas City h.........	A.L.	12	67	2	4	.333	48	18	80	5.64	0
2007 Kansas City i-j.......	A.L.	26	137^1/$_3$	8	11	.421	64	50	178	5.57	0
Major League Totals ....9 Yrs.		222	1175^1/$_3$	66	70	.485	801	333	1227	4.47	0
Division Series											
1998 Atlanta	N.L.	1	0^2/$_3$	1	0	1.000	1	0	0	0.00	0

302

Year	Club	Lea	G	IP	W	L	Pct	SO	BB	H	ERA	SAVES
2004 Los Angeles	N.L.	2	5	0	1	.000	3	7	8	14.40	0
Division Series Totals		3	5²/₃	1	1	.500	4	7	8	12.71	0
Championship Series											
1998 Atlanta	N.L.	2	0¹/₃	0	0	.000	0	2	5	54.00	0

a On disabled list from July 23 to November 1, 1999.
b On disabled list from April 2 to October 30, 2000.
c On disabled list from July 22 to September 1, 2001.
d Traded to Los Angeles Dodgers with outfielder Brian Jordan and pitcher Andy Brown for outfielder Gary Sheffield, January 15, 2002.
e On disabled list from June 27 to July 17, 2004.
f Filed for free agency, November 1, 2004, re-signed with Los Angeles Dodgers, January 7, 2005.
g On disabled list from May 15 to July 5 and August 18 to September 24, 2005.
h Traded to Kansas City Royals with pitcher Blake Johnson, pitcher Julio Pimental and cash for pitcher Elmer Dessens, July 25, 2006.
i On disabled list from August 19 to October 31, 2007.
j Filed for free agency, October 31, 2007.

PEREZ, OLIVER

Born, Culiacan, Mexico, August 15, 1981.
Bats Left. Throws Left. Height, 6 feet, 3 inches. Weight, 210 pounds.

Year	Club	Lea	G	IP	W	L	Pct	SO	BB	H	ERA	SAVES
1999 Padres	Arizona	15	28¹/₃	1	2	.333	37	16	28	5.08	3
2000 Yucatan	Mexican	11	43	3	2	.600	37	17	39	4.36	1
2000 Idaho Falls a	Pioneer	5	24¹/₃	3	1	.750	27	9	24	4.07	0
2001 Lake Elsinore	California	9	53	2	4	.333	62	25	45	2.72	0
2001 Fort Wayne	Midwest	19	101¹/₃	8	5	.615	98	43	84	3.46	0
2002 Lake Elsinore	California	9	48²/₃	3	3	.500	66	24	36	1.85	0
2002 Mobile	Southern	4	23	1	0	1.000	34	16	11	1.17	0
2002 San Diego b	N.L.	16	90	4	5	.444	94	48	71	3.50	0
2003 Portland	P.C.	8	47²/₃	3	3	.500	48	12	44	3.02	0
2003 San Diego-Pittsburgh c-d	N.L.	24	126²/₃	4	10	.286	141	77	129	5.47	0
2004 Pittsburgh	N.L.	30	196	12	10	.545	239	81	145	2.98	0
2005 Indianapolis	Int.	3	10	0	1	.000	4	12	14	9.90	0
2005 Pittsburgh e	N.L.	20	103	7	5	.583	97	70	102	5.85	0
2006 Indianapolis	Int.	6	32	1	3	.250	34	11	28	5.63	0
2006 Norfolk	Int.	4	19¹/₃	1	2	.333	26	12	18	6.05	0
2006 Pittsburgh-New York f	N.L.	22	112²/₃	3	13	.188	102	68	129	6.55	0
2007 Mets	Gulf Coast	1	4	0	0	.000	7	0	2	0.00	0
2007 New York g	N.L.	29	177	15	10	.600	174	79	153	3.56	0
Major League Totals	6 Yrs.	141	805¹/₃	45	53	.459	847	423	729	4.43	0
Championship Series											
2006 New York	N.L.	2	11²/₃	1	0	1.000	7	3	13	4.63	0

a Loaned to Yucatan by San Diego Padres, June 2 to 22 and July 18 to September 6, 2000.
b On disabled list from August 7 to September 2, 2002.
c Traded to Pittsburgh Pirates with outfielder Jason Bay and player to be named later for outfielder Brian Giles, August 26, 2003.
d Pittsburgh Pirates received pitcher Cory Stewart to complete trade, October 2, 2003.
e On disabled list from June 27 to September 3, 2005.
f Traded to New York Mets with pitcher Roberto Hernandez for outfielder Xavier Nady, July 31, 2006.
g On disabled list from June 27 to July 15, 2007.

PEREZ, RAFAEL JEROME

Born, Santo Domingo, Dominican Republic, May 15, 1982.
Bats Left. Throws Left. Height, 6 feet, 3 inches. Weight, 185 pounds.

Year	Club	Lea	G	IP	W	L	Pct	SO	BB	H	ERA	SAVES
2003 Burlington	Appal.	13	69	9	3	.750	63	16	56	1.70	0
2004 Kinston	Carolina	1	4²/₃	0	0	.000	3	2	10	11.57	0
2004 Lake County	So.Atl.	23	115	7	6	.538	99	47	121	4.85	0
2005 Kinston	Carolina	14	77²/₃	8	5	.615	48	32	54	3.36	0
2005 Akron	Eastern	15	66²/₃	4	3	.571	46	12	53	1.75	1
2006 Akron	Eastern	12	67¹/₃	4	5	.444	53	22	53	2.81	0
2006 Buffalo	Int.	13	27¹/₃	0	3	.000	33	8	20	2.63	0
2006 Cleveland	A.L.	18	12¹/₃	0	0	.000	15	6	10	4.38	0
2007 Buffalo	Int.	8	46²/₃	3	3	.500	31	11	53	3.66	0
2007 Cleveland	A.L.	44	60²/₃	1	2	.333	62	15	41	1.78	1
Major League Totals	2 Yrs.	62	73	1	2	.333	77	21	51	2.22	1

Year	Club	Lea	G	IP	W	L	Pct	SO	BB	H	ERA	SAVES
	Division Series											
2007	Cleveland	A.L.	3	6	1	0	1.000	6	1	3	1.50	0
	Championship Series											
2007	Cleveland	A.L.	3	1	0	0	.000	0	2	7	45.00	0

PETTITTE, ANDREW EUGENE (ANDY)

Born, Baton Rouge, Louisiana, June 15, 1972.
Bats Left. Throws Left. Height, 6 feet, 5 inches. Weight, 225 pounds.

Year	Club	Lea	G	IP	W	L	Pct	SO	BB	H	ERA	SAVES
1991	Yankees	Gulf Coast	6	36²/₃	4	1	.800	51	8	16	0.98	0
1991	Oneonta	N.Y.-Penn.	6	33	2	2	.500	32	16	33	2.18	0
1992	Greensboro	So. Atl.	27	168	10	4	.714	130	55	141	2.20	0
1993	Prince William	Carolina	26	159²/₃	11	9	.550	129	47	146	3.04	0
1993	Albany	Eastern	1	5	1	0	1.000	6	2	5	3.60	0
1994	Albany	Eastern	11	73	7	2	.778	50	18	60	2.71	0
1994	Columbus	Int.	16	96²/₃	7	2	.778	61	21	101	2.98	0
1995	Columbus	Int.	2	11²/₃	0	0	.000	8	0	7	0.00	0
1995	New York	A.L.	31	175	12	9	.571	114	63	183	4.17	0
1996	New York	A.L.	35	221	*21	8	.724	162	72	229	3.87	0
1997	New York	A.L.	35	240¹/₃	18	7	.720	166	65	233	2.88	0
1998	New York	A.L.	33	216¹/₃	16	11	.593	146	87	226	4.24	0
1999	Tampa	Fla.St.	1	5	1	0	1.000	8	2	4	0.00	0
1999	New York a	A.L.	31	191²/₃	14	11	.560	121	89	216	4.70	0
2000	New York b	A.L.	32	204²/₃	19	9	.679	125	80	219	4.35	0
2001	New York c	A.L.	31	200²/₃	15	10	.600	164	41	224	3.99	0
2002	Tampa	Fla.St.	2	5	0	0	.000	4	0	3	0.00	0
2002	Norwich	Eastern	1	6¹/₃	0	0	.000	5	0	2	1.42	0
2002	New York d	A.L.	22	134²/₃	13	5	.722	97	32	144	3.27	0
2003	New York e	A.L.	33	208¹/₃	21	8	.724	180	50	227	4.02	0
2004	Round Rock	Texas	2	8	0	0	.000	9	2	4	2.25	0
2004	Houston f	N.L.	15	83	6	4	.600	79	31	71	3.90	0
2005	Houston	N.L.	33	222¹/₃	17	9	.654	171	41	188	2.39	0
2006	Houston g	N.L.	36	214¹/₃	14	13	.519	178	70	238	4.20	0
2007	New York h	A.L.	36	215¹/₃	15	9	.625	141	69	238	4.05	0
Major League Totals	13 Yrs.		403	2527²/₃	201	113	.640	1844	790	2636	3.83	0
	Division Series											
1995	New York	A.L.	1	7	0	0	.000	0	3	9	5.14	0
1996	New York	A.L.	1	6¹/₃	0	0	.000	3	6	4	5.68	0
1997	New York	A.L.	2	11²/₃	0	2	.000	5	1	15	8.49	0
1998	New York	A.L.	1	7	1	0	1.000	8	0	3	1.29	0
1999	New York	A.L.	1	7¹/₃	1	0	1.000	5	0	7	1.23	0
2000	New York	A.L.	2	11¹/₃	1	0	1.000	7	3	15	3.97	0
2001	New York	A.L.	1	6¹/₃	0	1	.000	4	2	7	1.42	0
2002	New York	A.L.	1	3	0	0	.000	1	0	8	12.00	0
2003	New York	A.L.	1	7	1	0	1.000	10	3	4	1.29	0
2005	Houston	N.L.	1	7	1	0	1.000	6	2	4	3.86	0
2007	New York	A.L.	1	6¹/₃	0	0	.000	5	2	7	0.00	0
Division Series Totals			13	80¹/₃	5	3	.625	54	22	83	3.92	0
	Championship Series											
1996	New York	A.L.	2	15	1	0	1.000	7	5	10	3.60	0
1998	New York	A.L.	1	4²/₃	0	1	.000	1	3	8	11.57	0
1999	New York	A.L.	1	7¹/₃	1	0	1.000	5	1	8	2.45	0
2000	New York	A.L.	1	6²/₃	1	0	1.000	2	1	9	2.70	0
2001	New York	A.L.	2	14¹/₃	2	0	1.000	8	2	11	2.51	0
2003	New York	A.L.	2	11²/₃	1	0	1.000	10	4	17	4.63	0
2005	Houston	N.L.	2	12¹/₃	0	1	.000	6	4	15	5.11	0
Championship Series Totals			11	72	6	2	.750	39	20	78	4.13	0
	World Series Record											
1996	New York	A.L.	2	10²/₃	1	1	.500	5	4	11	5.91	0
1998	New York	A.L.	1	7¹/₃	1	0	1.000	4	3	5	0.00	0
1999	New York	A.L.	1	3²/₃	0	0	.000	1	1	10	12.27	0
2000	New York	A.L.	2	13²/₃	0	0	.000	9	4	16	1.98	0
2001	New York	A.L.	2	9	0	2	.000	9	2	12	10.00	0
2003	New York	A.L.	2	15²/₃	1	1	.500	14	4	12	0.57	0
2005	Houston	N.L.	1	6	0	0	.000	4	0	8	3.00	0
World Series Totals			11	66	3	4	.429	46	18	74	3.82	0

a On disabled list from March 26 to April 17, 1999.

b On disabled list from April 8 to April 25, 2000.
c On disabled list from June 16 to July 1, 2001.
d On disabled list from April 16 to June 14, 2002.
e Filed for free agency, November 6, 2003. Signed with Houston Astros, December 11, 2003.
f On disabled list from April 7 to April 29 and from May 27 to June 29 and from August 18 to October 28, 2004.
g Filed for free agency, November 6, 2006. Signed with New York Yankees, December 8, 2006.
h Filed for free agency, November 12, 2007, re-signed with New York Yankees, December 12, 2007.

PINEIRO, JOEL ALBERTO

Born, Rio Piedras, Puerto Rico, September 25, 1978.
Bats Right. Throws Right. Height, 6 feet, 1 inch. Weight, 200 pounds.

Year	Club	Lea	G	IP	W	L	Pct	SO	BB	H	ERA	SAVES
1997 Mariners	. . . . Arizona		1	3	1	0	1.000	4	0	1	0.00	0
1997 Everett	. . . . Northwest		18	49	4	2	.667	59	18	54	5.33	2
1998 Wisconsin	. . . . .Midwest		16	96	8	4	.667	84	28	92	3.19	0
1998 Lancaster	. . . . .California		9	45	2	0	1.000	48	22	58	7.80	0
1998 Orlando	. . . . Southern		1	5	1	0	1.000	2	2	7	5.40	0
1999 New Haven	. . . . Eastern		28	166	10	15	.400	116	52	190	4.72	0
2000 New Haven	. . . . Eastern		9	52 1/3	2	1	.667	43	12	42	4.13	0
2000 Tacoma	. . . . P.C.		10	61	7	1	.875	41	22	53	2.80	0
2000 Seattle	. . . . A.L.		8	19 1/3	1	0	1.000	10	13	25	5.59	0
2001 Tacoma	. . . . P.C.		18	77	6	3	.667	64	33	68	3.62	0
2001 Seattle	. . . . A.L.		17	75 1/3	6	2	.750	56	21	50	2.03	0
2002 Seattle	. . . . A.L.		37	194 1/3	14	7	.667	136	54	189	3.24	0
2003 Seattle	. . . . A.L.		32	211 2/3	16	11	.593	151	76	192	3.78	0
2004 Seattle a	. . . . A.L.		21	140 2/3	6	11	.353	111	43	144	4.67	0
2005 Tacoma	. . . . P.C.		1	7	0	0	.000	6	0	5	1.29	0
2005 Seattle b	. . . . A.L.		30	189	7	11	.389	107	56	224	5.62	0
2006 Seattle c	. . . . A.L.		40	165 2/3	8	13	.381	87	64	209	6.36	1
2007 Lowell	. . . . N.Y.-Penn.		1	1	0	0	.000	2	0	0	0.00	0
2007 Pawtucket	. . . . .Int.		2	8	0	0	.000	3	4	3	2.25	0
2007 Boston	. . . . A.L.		31	34	1	1	.500	20	14	41	5.03	0
2007 St. Louis d-e-f	. . . . N.L.		11	63 2/3	6	4	.600	40	12	69	3.96	0
Major League Totals	. . . . . . .8 Yrs.		227	1093 2/3	65	60	.520	718	353	1143	4.47	1
Championship Series												
2001 Seattle	. . . . A.L.		1	2	0	0	.000	5	2	4	4.50	0

a On disabled list from July 26 to November 1, 2004.
b On disabled list from March 27 to April 15, 2005.
c Not offered contract, December 12, 2006. Signed with Boston Red Sox, January 4, 2007.
d On disabled list from June 28 to July 13, 2007.
e Traded to St. Louis Cardinals for player to be named later, July 31, 2007.
f Boston Red Sox received outfielder Sean Danielson to complete trade, November 2, 2007.

PINTO, RENYEL ELIGIO

Born, Cupira, Venezuela, July 8, 1982.
Bats Left. Throws Left. Height, 6 feet, 4 inches. Weight, 195 pounds.

Year	Club	Lea	G	IP	W	L	Pct	SO	BB	H	ERA	SAVES
2000 Cubs	. . . . Arizona		9	30	0	2	.000	23	16	42	6.30	0
2001 Lansing	. . . . .Midwest		20	88	4	8	.333	69	44	94	5.22	0
2002 Daytona	. . . . Fla.St.		7	32 2/3	3	3	.500	24	11	45	5.51	0
2002 Lansing	. . . . .Midwest		17	98	7	5	.583	92	28	80	3.31	0
2003 Daytona	. . . . Fla.St.		23	114 2/3	3	8	.273	104	45	91	3.22	0
2004 Iowa	. . . . P.C.		2	9 1/3	1	1	.500	9	8	9	7.71	0
2004 West Tenn	. . . . Southern		25	141 2/3	11	8	.579	179	72	107	2.92	0
2005 Iowa	. . . . P.C.		6	22 2/3	1	2	.333	24	24	31	9.53	0
2005 West Tenn a	. . . . Southern		22	129 2/3	10	3	.769	123	58	101	2.71	0
2006 Albuquerque	. . . . P.C.		18	95 1/3	8	2	.800	96	47	82	3.40	0
2006 Florida	. . . . N.L.		27	29 2/3	0	0	.000	36	27	20	3.03	1
2007 Florida b	. . . . N.L.		57	58 2/3	2	4	.333	56	32	45	3.68	1
Major League Totals	. . . . .2 Yrs.		84	88 1/3	2	4	.333	92	59	65	3.46	2

a Traded to Florida Marlins by Chicago Cubs with pitcher Sergio Mitre and pitcher Ricky Nolasco for outfielder Juan Pierre, December 7, 2005.
b On disabled list from August 3 to September 14, 2007.

PROCTOR, SCOTT CHRISTOPHER

Born, Stuart, Florida, January 2, 1977.
Bats Right. Throws Right. Height, 6 feet, 1 inch. Weight, 195 pounds.

Year	Club	Lea	G	IP	W	L	Pct	SO	BB	H	ERA	SAVES
1998 Yakima	Northwest	3	5	0	1	.000	4	1	9	10.80	2
1999 Yakima	Northwest	16	50	4	2	.667	41	26	57	7.20	0
2000 Vero Beach	Fla.St.	35	89	3	7	.300	70	54	93	5.16	1
2001 Vero Beach	Fla.St.	15	90 2/3	6	4	.600	79	30	73	2.48	0
2001 Jacksonville	Southern	10	49 2/3	4	3	.571	48	31	39	4.17	0
2002 Jacksonville	Southern	26	133 1/3	7	9	.438	131	85	111	3.51	0
2003 Columbus	Int.	10	19	2	0	1.000	26	3	13	1.42	0
2003 Las Vegas	P.C.	24	39 1/3	4	2	.667	35	13	35	3.66	1
2003 Jacksonville a	Southern	17	27	1	2	.333	24	7	20	1.00	0
2004 Columbus	Int.	35	44	2	3	.400	42	18	37	2.86	4
2004 New York	A.L.	26	25	2	1	.667	21	14	29	5.40	0
2005 Columbus	Int.	35	42 2/3	6	1	.857	54	11	47	4.22	14
2005 New York	A.L.	29	44 2/3	1	0	1.000	36	17	46	6.04	0
2006 New York	A.L.	*83	102 1/3	6	4	.600	89	33	89	3.52	1
2007 New York	A.L.	52	54 1/3	2	5	.286	37	29	53	3.81	0
2007 Los Angeles b	N.L.	31	32	3	0	1.000	27	15	25	3.38	0
Major League Totals	4 Yrs.	221	258 1/3	14	10	.583	210	108	242	4.18	1
Division Series											
2005 New York	A.L.	2	2	0	0	.000	1	0	3	0.00	0
2006 New York	A.L.	3	4	0	0	.000	1	1	5	2.25	0
Division Series Totals		5	6	0	0	.000	2	1	8	1.50	0

a Traded by Los Angeles Dodgers to New York Yankees with outfielder Bubba Crosby for infielder Robin Ventura, July 31, 2003.
b Traded to Los Angeles Dodgers for infielder Wilson Betemit, July 31, 2007.

PUTZ, JOSEPH JASON (J.J.)

Born, Trenton, Michigan, February 2, 1977.
Bats Right. Throws Right. Height, 6 feet, 5 inches. Weight, 250 pounds.

Year	Club	Lea	G	IP	W	L	Pct	SO	BB	H	ERA	SAVES
1999 Everett	Northwest	10	22 1/3	0	0	.000	17	11	23	4.84	2
2000 Wisconsin	Midwest	26	142 2/3	12	6	.667	105	63	130	3.15	0
2001 San Antonio	Texas	27	148	7	9	.438	135	59	145	3.83	0
2002 San Antonio	Texas	15	84	3	10	.231	60	28	84	3.64	0
2002 Tacoma	P.C.	9	54	2	4	.333	39	21	51	3.83	0
2003 Tacoma	P.C.	41	86	0	3	.000	60	34	69	2.51	11
2003 Seattle	A.L.	3	3 2/3	0	0	.000	3	3	4	4.91	0
2004 Tacoma	P.C.	7	8 1/3	0	0	.000	13	3	10	4.32	3
2004 Seattle	A.L.	54	63	0	3	.000	47	24	66	4.71	9
2005 Seattle	A.L.	64	60	6	5	.545	45	23	58	3.60	1
2006 Seattle	A.L.	72	78 1/3	4	1	.800	104	13	59	2.30	36
2007 Seattle	A.L.	68	71 2/3	6	1	.857	82	13	37	1.38	40
Major League Totals	5 Yrs.	261	276 2/3	16	10	.615	281	76	224	2.93	86

QUALLS, CHAD MICHAEL

Born, Lomita, California, August 17, 1978.
Bats Right. Throws Right. Height, 6 feet, 5 inches. Weight, 220 pounds.

Year	Club	Lea	G	IP	W	L	Pct	SO	BB	H	ERA	SAVES
2001 Michigan	Midwest	26	162	15	6	.714	125	31	149	3.72	0
2002 Round Rock	Texas	29	163	6	13	.316	142	67	174	4.36	0
2003 Round Rock	Texas	28	175 1/3	8	11	.421	132	61	174	3.85	0
2004 New Orleans	P.C.	32	106 2/3	3	6	.333	72	30	134	5.57	1
2004 Houston	N.L.	25	33	4	0	1.000	24	8	34	3.55	1
2005 Houston	N.L.	77	79 2/3	6	4	.600	60	23	73	3.28	0
2006 Houston	N.L.	81	88 2/3	7	3	.700	56	28	76	3.76	0
2007 Houston a	N.L.	79	82 2/3	6	5	.545	78	25	84	3.05	5
Major League Totals	4 Yrs.	262	284	23	12	.657	218	84	267	3.39	6
Division Series											
2004 Houston	N.L.	4	4	0	0	.000	3	1	4	6.75	0
2005 Houston	N.L.	2	3	0	0	.000	1	2	5	6.00	0
Division Series Totals		6	7	0	0	.000	4	3	9	6.43	0
Championship Series											
2004 Houston	N.L.	2	4	0	1	.000	4	2	8	11.25	0

Year	Club	Lea	G	IP	W	L	Pct	SO	BB	H	ERA	SAVES
2005 Houston		N.L.	4	4²/₃	1	0	1.000	4	0	0	0.00	0
Championship Series Totals			6	8²/₃	1	1	.500	8	2	8	5.19	0
World Series Record												
2005 Houston		N.L.	3	5¹/₃	0	0	.000	5	2	3	1.69	0

a Traded to Arizona Diamondbacks with pitcher Juan Gutierrez and outfielder Chris Burke for pitcher Jose Valverde, December 14, 2007.

RAUCH, JON ERICH
Born, Louisville, Kentucky, September 27, 1978.
Bats Right. Throws Right. Height, 6 feet, 11 inches. Weight, 260 pounds.

Year	Club	Lea	G	IP	W	L	Pct	SO	BB	H	ERA	SAVES
1999 Bristol		Appal.	14	56²/₃	4	4	.500	66	16	65	4.45	2
1999 Winston-Salem		Carolina	1	6	0	0	.000	7	3	4	3.00	0
2000 Winston-Salem		Carolina	18	110	11	3	.786	124	33	102	2.86	0
2000 Birmingham		Southern	8	56	5	1	.833	63	16	36	2.25	0
2001 Charlotte		Int.	6	28	1	3	.250	27	7	28	5.79	0
2002 Chicago		A.L.	8	28²/₃	2	1	.667	19	14	28	6.59	0
2002 Charlotte		Int.	19	109¹/₃	7	8	.467	97	42	91	4.28	0
2003 Charlotte		Int.	24	124²/₃	7	1	.875	94	35	121	4.11	0
2004 Charlotte		Int.	14	72¹/₃	6	3	.667	61	25	57	3.11	0
2004 Chicago		A.L.	2	8²/₃	1	1	.500	4	4	16	6.23	0
2004 Edmonton		P.C.	3	18	1	1	.500	13	2	17	4.50	0
2004 Montreal a-b		N.L.	9	23¹/₃	3	0	1.000	18	7	14	1.54	0
2005 New Orleans		P.C.	7	21¹/₃	1	1	.500	25	2	19	2.53	0
2005 Washington c		N.L.	15	30	2	4	.333	23	11	24	3.60	0
2006 Washington		N.L.	85	91¹/₃	4	5	.444	86	36	78	3.35	2
2007 Washington		N.L.	*88	87¹/₃	8	4	.667	71	21	75	3.61	4

Major League Totals ....5 Yrs. 207 269¹/₃ 20 15 .571 221 93 235 3.74 6

a Traded to Montreal Expos with pitcher Gary Majewski for outfielder Carl Everett, July 18, 2004.
b On disabled list from August 14 to September 14, 2004.
c On disabled list from May 26 to September 6, 2005.

RAY, CHRISTOPHER THOMAS (CHRIS)
Born, Tampa, Florida, January 12, 1982.
Bats Right. Throws Right. Height, 6 feet, 3 inches. Weight, 225 pounds.

Year	Club	Lea	G	IP	W	L	Pct	SO	BB	H	ERA	SAVES
2003 Aberdeen		N.Y.-Penn.	9	38¹/₆	2	0	1.000	44	10	32	2.82	0
2004 Frederick		Carolina	14	73¹/₃	6	3	.667	71	20	82	3.80	0
2004 Delmarva		So.Atl.	10	50	2	3	.400	48	17	43	3.42	0
2005 Bowie		Eastern	31	37¹/₃	1	2	.333	40	7	17	0.96	18
2005 Baltimore		A.L.	41	40²/₃	1	3	.250	43	18	34	2.66	0
2006 Baltimore		A.L.	61	66	4	4	.500	51	27	45	2.73	33
2007 Baltimore a		A.L.	43	42²/₃	5	6	.455	44	18	35	4.43	16

Major League Totals ....3 Yrs. 145 149¹/₃ 10 13 .435 138 63 114 3.19 49

a On disabled list from July 21 to October 23, 2007.

REDDING, TIMOTHY JAMES (TIM)
Born, Rochester, New York, February 12, 1978.
Bats Right. Throws Right. Height, 6 feet. Weight, 195 pounds.

Year	Club	Lea	G	IP	W	L	Pct	SO	BB	H	ERA	SAVES
1998 Auburn		N.Y.-Penn.	16	73²/₃	7	3	.700	98	50	49	4.52	1
1999 Michigan		Midwest	43	105	8	6	.571	141	76	84	4.97	14
2000 Kissimmee		Fla.St.	24	154²/₃	12	5	.706	170	57	125	2.68	0
2000 Round Rock		Texas	5	26	2	0	1.000	22	22	14	3.46	0
2001 Round Rock		Texas	14	90²/₃	10	2	.833	113	25	64	2.18	0
2001 New Orleans		P.C.	6	37²/₃	4	1	.800	42	19	22	4.54	0
2001 Houston		N.L.	13	55²/₃	3	1	.750	55	24	62	5.50	0
2002 New Orleans		P.C.	11	38	3	3	.500	50	13	32	5.21	0
2002 Houston		N.L.	18	73¹/₃	3	6	.333	63	35	78	5.40	0
2003 Houston		N.L.	33	176	10	14	.417	116	65	179	3.68	0
2004 Houston		N.L.	27	100²/₃	5	7	.417	56	43	125	5.72	0
2004 New Orleans		P.C.	5	28¹/₃	1	3	.250	26	12	30	6.04	0
2005 Portland		P.C.	2	10	0	0	.000	5	2	7	0.90	0
2005 San Diego		N.L.	9	29²/₃	0	5	.000	17	13	40	9.10	0
2005 New York		A.L.	1	1	0	1	.000	2	4	4	54.00	0
2005 Columbus a-b-c		Int.	10	51¹/₃	3	4	.429	47	13	62	5.08	0

307

Year	Club	Lea	G	IP	W	L	Pct	SO	BB	H	ERA	SAVES
2006 Charlotte d-e	Int.	29	187²/₃	12	10	.545	148	56	168	3.40	0
2007 Columbus.	Int.	17	89²/₃	9	5	.643	63	24	110	5.32	0
2007 Washington	N.L.	15	84	3	6	.333	47	38	84	3.64	0
Major League Totals ....:..6 Yrs.		116	520¹/₃	24	40	.375	356	222	572	4.91	0

a Traded to San Diego Padres with cash for catcher Humberto Quintero, March 28, 2005.
b On disabled list from May 9 to June 22, 2005.
c Traded to New York Yankees with pitcher Darrell May and cash for pitcher Paul Quantrill, July 2, 2005.
d Filed for free agency, October 6, 2005. Signed with Chicago White Sox, January 19, 2006.
e Filed for free agency, October 15, 2006. Signed with Washington Nationals, November 6, 2006.

REYES, ANTHONY LOZA

Born, Downey, California, October 16, 1981.
Bats Right. Throws Right. Height, 6 feet, 2 inches. Weight, 215 pounds.

Year	Club	Lea	G	IP	W	L	Pct	SO	BB	H	ERA	SAVES
2004 Palm Beach	Fla.St.	6	30²/₃	3	0	1.000	38	7	41	5.58	0
2004 Tennessee	Southern	12	74¹/₃	6	2	.750	102	13	62	2.91	0
2005 Memphis	P.C.	23	128²/₃	7	6	.538	136	34	105	3.64	0
2005 St. Louis.	N.L.	4	13¹/₃	1	1	.500	12	4	6	2.70	0
2006 Memphis	P.C.	13	84	6	1	.857	82	11	70	2.57	0
2006 St. Louis.	N.L.	17	85¹/₃	5	8	.385	72	34	84	5.06	0
2007 Memphis	P.C.	6	38²/₃	1	1	.500	33	11	27	2.79	0
2007 St. Louis.	N.L.	22	107¹/₃	2	14	.125	74	43	108	6.04	0
Major League Totals ....3 Yrs.		43	206	8	23	.258	158	81	198	5.42	0
Championship Series											
2006 St. Louis.	N.L.	1	4	0	0	.000	4	4	3	4.50	0
World Series Record											
2006 St. Louis.	N.L.	1	8	1	0	1.000	4	1	4	2.25	0

REYES (VALARDE), DENNYS

Born, Higuera de Zaragoza, Mexico, April 19, 1977.
Bats Left. Throws Left. Height, 6 feet, 3 inches. Weight, 246 pounds.

Year	Club	Lea	G	IP	W	L	Pct	SO	BB	H	ERA	SAVES
1993 Mexico City Reds a ..	Mexican	7	5¹/₃	0	1	.000	5	9	4	5.06	0
1994 Vero Beach..........	Fla.St.	9	41²/₃	2	4	.333	25	18	58	6.70	0
1994 Great Falls	Pioneer	14	66²/₃	7	1	.875	70	25	71	3.78	0
1995 Mexico	Mexican	17	58²/₃	5	5	.500	44	41	76	6.60	0
1995 Vero Beach..........	Fla.St.	3	10	1	0	1.000	9	6	8	1.80	0
1996 San Bernardino	Calif.	29	166	11	12	.478	176	77	166	4.17	0
1997 San Antonio	Texas	12	80¹/₃	8	1	.889	66	28	79	3.02	0
1997 Albuquerque..........	P.C.	10	57¹/₃	6	3	.667	45	33	70	5.65	0
1997 Los Angeles	N.L.	14	47	2	3	.400	36	18	51	3.83	0
1998 Albuquerque..........	P.C.	7	43²/₃	1	4	.200	58	18	31	1.44	0
1998 Indianapolis	Int.	4	24	2	0	1.000	27	14	20	3.00	0
1998 Los Angeles-Cincinnati b	N.L.	19	67¹/₃	3	5	.375	77	47	62	4.54	0
1999 Cincinnati	N.L.	65	61²/₃	2	2	.500	72	39	53	3.79	2
2000 Cincinnati	N.L.	62	43²/₃	2	1	.667	36	29	43	4.53	0
2001 Cincinnati	N.L.	35	53	2	6	.250	52	35	51	4.92	0
2001 Louisville c-d	Int.	7	34¹/₃	4	2	.667	34	16	34	3.67	0
2002 Colorado	N.L.	43	40¹/₃	0	1	.000	30	24	43	4.24	0
2002 Texas e.	A.L.	15	42¹/₃	4	3	.571	29	21	55	6.38	0
2003 Tucson	P.C.	33	31²/₃	2	1	.667	30	22	24	2.84	2
2003 Pittsburgh-Arizona f-g-h	N.L.	15	12²/₃	0	0	.000	16	10	15	10.66	0
2004 Kansas City i	A.L.	40	108	4	8	.333	91	50	114	4.75	0
2005 San Diego j.	N.L.	36	43²/₃	3	2	.600	35	32	57	5.15	0
2006 Rochester.	Int.	4	18	1	0	1.000	13	3	11	0.50	0
2006 Minnesota	A.L.	66	50²/₃	5	0	1.000	49	15	35	0.89	0
2007 Minnesota k	A.L.	50	29¹/₃	2	1	.667	21	21	34	3.99	0
Major League Totals ....11 Yrs.		460	599²/₃	29	32	.475	544	341	613	4.43	2
Division Series											
2006 Minnesota	A.L.	2	1	0	0	.000	0	2	1	9.00	0

a Sold to Los Angeles Dodgers, July 5, 1993.
b Traded to Cincinnati Reds with infielder Paul Konerko for pitcher Jeff Shaw, July 4, 1998.
c On disabled list from May 30 to July 2, 2001.
d Traded to Colorado Rockies with infielder Pokey Reese for pitcher Gabe White and pitcher Luke Hudson, December 18, 2001.
e Traded to Texas Rangers with outfielder Todd Hollandsworth for outfielder Gabe Kapler, outfielder Jason Romano and cash, July 31, 2002.

f Not offered contract, December 20, 2002. Signed with Pittsburgh Pirates organization, February 7, 2003.
g Filed for free agency, May 19, 2003. Signed with Arizona Diamondbacks organization, June 11, 2003.
h Filed for free agency, October 3, 2003. Signed with Kansas City Royals organization, November 6, 2003.
i Filed for free agency, October 29, 2004. Signed with San Diego Padres, November 29, 2004.
j Released by San Diego Padres, July 18, 2005. Signed with Minnesota Twins organization, December 23, 2005.
k On disabled list from May 21 to June 14 and August 22 to October 10, 2007.

REYES, RAFAEL ALBERTO (AL)

Born, San Cristobal, Dominican Republic, April 10, 1971.
Bats Right. Throws Right. Height, 6 feet, 1 inch. Weight, 210 pounds.

Year	Club	Lea	G	IP	W	L	Pct	SO	BB	H	ERA	SAVES
1989	Expos	Dominican	12	71	3	4	.429	49	33	68	2.79	0
1990	Wst Plm Bch	Fla.St.	16	57	5	4	.556	47	32	58	4.74	1
1991	Rockford	Midwest	3	11¹/₃	0	1	.000	10	2	14	5.56	0
1992	Albany	So.Atl.	27	27¹/₃	0	2	.000	29	13	24	3.95	4
1993	Burlington	Midwest	53	74	7	6	.538	80	26	52	2.68	11
1994	Harrisburg a	Eastern	60	69¹/₃	2	2	.500	60	13	68	3.25	35
1995	Milwaukee	A.L.	27	33¹/₃	1	1	.500	29	18	19	2.43	1
1996	Beloit	Midwest	13	19²/₃	1	0	1.000	22	6	17	1.83	0
1996	Milwaukee	A.L.	5	5²/₃	1	0	1.000	2	2	8	7.94	0
1997	Tucson	P.C.	38	57¹/₃	2	4	.333	70	34	52	5.02	7
1997	Milwaukee	A.L.	19	29²/₃	1	2	.333	28	9	32	5.46	1
1998	Louisville	Int.	3	4¹/₃	0	1	.000	5	2	5	8.31	0
1998	Milwaukee b	N.L.	50	57	5	1	.833	58	31	55	3.95	0
1999	Louisville	Int.	6	9²/₃	0	2	.000	8	7	12	8.38	0
1999	Milwaukee	N.L.	26	36	2	0	1.000	39	25	27	4.25	0
1999	Baltimore c	A.L.	27	29²/₃	2	3	.400	28	16	23	4.85	0
2000	Baltimore	A.L.	13	13	1	0	1.000	10	11	13	6.92	0
2000	Rochester	Int.	9	11²/₃	0	1	.000	17	9	13	7.71	2
2000	Albuquerque	P.C.	30	38²/₃	3	2	.600	39	21	33	3.72	8
2000	Los Angeles d	N.L.	6	6²/₃	0	0	.000	8	1	2	0.00	0
2001	Las Vegas	P.C.	19	29¹/₃	0	1	.000	37	10	24	3.38	0
2001	Los Angeles	N.L.	19	25²/₃	2	1	.667	23	13	28	3.86	1
2002	Nashville e	P.C.	43	66²/₃	7	3	.700	90	22	40	2.70	1
2002	Pittsburgh e	N.L.	15	17	0	0	.000	21	7	9	2.65	0
2003	Columbus	Int.	15	17	1	1	.500	21	5	16	3.71	2
2003	New York f	A.L.	13	17	0	0	.000	9	9	13	3.18	0
2004	Durham	Int.	20	22	2	1	.667	22	6	22	2.45	10
2004	Memphis	P.C.	37	39²/₃	2	2	.500	47	14	32	2.95	23
2004	St. Louis g-h	N.L.	12	12	0	0	.000	11	2	3	0.75	0
2005	St. Louis	N.L.	65	62²/₃	4	2	.667	67	20	38	2.15	3
2006	Durham i	Int.	2	3	0	0	.000	3	0	3	3.00	0
2007	Vero Beach	Fla.St.	1	1	0	0	.000	1	0	2	9.00	0
2007	Tampa Bay j	A.L.	61	60²/₃	2	4	.333	70	21	49	4.90	26
Major League Totals	12 Yrs.		358	406	21	14	.600	403	185	319	3.79	32
World Series Record												
2004	St. Louis	N.L.	2	1¹/₃	0	0	.000	0	0	0	0.00	0

a Selected by Milwaukee Brewers from Montreal Expos in Rule V draft, December 5, 1994.
b On disabled list from July 25 to September 8, 1998.
c Sent to Baltimore Orioles as player to be named later for pitcher Rocky Coppinger, July 21, 1999.
d Traded to Los Angeles Dodgers for pitcher Alan Mills and cash, June 13, 2000.
e Filed for free agency, October 17, 2001. Signed with Pittsburgh Pirates, January 25, 2002.
f Released by Pittsburgh Pirates, March 10, 2003. Signed with New York Yankees organization, March 25, 2003.
g Released by New York Yankees, July 25, 2003. Signed with Tampa Bay Devil Rays organization, January 12, 2004.
h Released by Tampa Bay Devil Rays, June 1, 2004. Signed with St. Louis Cardinals organization, June 6, 2004.
i Filed for free agency, November 1, 2005. Signed with Tampa Bay Devil Rays organization, March 19, 2006.
j On disabled list from July 3 to July 18, 2007.

RINCON, JUAN MANUEL

Born, Maracaibo, Venezuela, January 23, 1979.
Bats Right. Throws Right. Height, 5 feet, 11 inches. Weight, 205 pounds.

Year	Club	Lea	G	IP	W	L	Pct	SO	BB	H	ERA	SAVES
1997	Twins	Gulf Coast	11	58	3	3	.500	46	24	55	2.95	0
1997	Elizabethtown	Appal.	2	9¹/₃	0	1	.000	7	3	11	3.86	0
1998	Fort Wayne	Midwest	37	96¹/₃	6	4	.600	74	54	84	3.83	6
1999	Quad City	Midwest	28	163¹/₃	14	8	.636	153	66	146	2.92	0
2000	New Britain	Eastern	15	89	3	9	.250	79	39	96	4.65	0
2000	Fort Myers	Fla.St.	13	76¹/₃	5	3	.625	55	23	67	2.12	0

Year Club	Lea	G	IP	W	L	Pct	SO	BB	H	ERA	SAVES
2001 New Britain .... Eastern		29	153⅓	14	6	.700	133	57	130	2.88	0
2001 Minnesota .... A.L.		4	5⅔	0	0	.000	4	5	7	6.35	0
2002 Edmonton .... P.C.		19	101⅔	7	4	.636	75	35	111	4.78	0
2002 Minnesota .... A.L.		10	28⅔	0	2	.000	21	9	44	6.28	0
2003 Rochester............ Int.		2	8⅓	0	2	.000	8	5	12	7.56	0
2003 Minnesota .... A.L.		58	85⅔	5	6	.455	63	38	74	3.68	0
2004 Minnesota .... A.L.		77	82	11	6	.647	106	32	52	2.63	2
2005 Minnesota .... A.L.		75	77	6	6	.500	84	30	63	2.45	0
2006 Minnesota .... A.L.		75	74⅓	3	1	.750	65	24	76	2.91	1
2007 Minnesota .... A.L.		63	59⅔	3	3	.500	49	28	65	5.13	0
Major League Totals ....7 Yrs.		362	413	28	24	.538	392	166	381	3.53	3
Division Series											
2003 Minnesota .... A.L.		3	2⅓	0	0	.000	1	4	1	0.00	0
2004 Minnesota .... A.L.		3	3⅓	0	0	.000	5	2	4	10.80	0
2006 Minnesota .... A.L.		2	3	0	0	.000	3	0	1	3.00	0
Division Series Totals		8	8⅔	0	0	.000	9	6	6	5.19	0

RISKE, DAVID RICHARD
Born, Renton, Washington, October 23, 1976.
Bats Right. Throws Right. Height, 6 feet, 2 inches. Weight, 180 pounds.

Year Club	Lea	G	IP	W	L	Pct	SO	BB	H	ERA	SAVES
1997 Kinston............Carolina		39	72	4	4	.500	90	33	58	2.25	2
1998 Kinston............Carolina		53	54	1	1	.500	67	15	48	2.33	33
1998 Akron..........:.. Eastern		2	3	0	0	.000	5	1	1	0.00	1
1999 Akron............ Eastern		23	23⅔	0	0	.000	33	13	5	1.90	12
1999 Buffalo..............Int.		23	27⅔	3	0	1.000	22	7	14	0.65	6
1999 Cleveland .... A.L.		12	14	1	1	.500	16	6	20	8.36	0
2000 Akron............ Eastern		3	4	0	0	.000	4	0	2	0.00	1
2000 Buffalo a..............Int.		2	3	0	0	.000	2	2	2	3.00	0
2001 Buffalo .._...........Int.		38	53⅓	1	2	.333	72	17	45	2.36	15
2001 Cleveland .... A.L.		26	27⅓	2	0	1.000	29	18	20	1.98	1
2002 Akron............ Eastern		4	6	0	0	.000	10	1	5	3.00	0
2002 Buffalo..............Int.		9	9⅔	0	1	1.000	17	4	6	3.72	3
2002 Cleveland b .... A.L.		51	51⅓	2	2	.500	65	35	49	5.26	1
2003 Cleveland .... A.L.		68	74⅔	2	2	.500	82	20	52	2.29	0
2004 Cleveland .... A.L.		72	77⅓	7	3	.700	78	41	69	3.72	5
2005 Cleveland ....:. A.L.		58	72⅔	3	4	.429	48	15	55	3.10	1
2006 Pawtucket ....Int.		5	5	0	1	.000	8	5	5	5.40	0
2006 Boston-Chicago c-d-e-f .. A.L.		41	44	1	2	.333	28	17	40	3.89	0
2007 Kansas City g .... A.L.		65	69⅔	1	4	.200	52	27	61	2.45	4
Major League Totals ....8 Yrs.		393	431	19	18	.514	398	179	366	3.40	20
Division Series											
2001 Cleveland .... A.L.		3	3⅔	0	0	.000	5	1	2	0.00	0

a On disabled list from March 25 to April 25 and April 30 to September 3 and September 14 to October 31, 2000.

b On disabled list from June 19 to July 17, 2002.

c Traded to Boston Red Sox with outfielder Coco Crisp and catcher Josh Bard for infielder Andy Marte, catcher Kelly Shoppach and pitcher Guillermo Mota, January 27, 2006.

d On disabled list from April 5 to May 22, 2006.

e Traded to Chicago White Sox for pitcher Javier Lopez, June 15, 2006.

f Filed for free agency, October 28, 2006. Signed with Kansas City Royals, December 20, 2006.

g Filed for free agency, October 30, 2007. Signed with Milwaukee Brewers, December 5, 2007.

RIVERA, MARIANO
Born, Panama City, Panama, November 29, 1969.
Bats Right. Throws Right. Height, 6 feet, 2 inches. Weight, 195 pounds.

Year Club	Lea	G	IP	W	L	Pct	SO	BB	H	ERA	SAVES
1990 Yankees .... Gulf Coast		22	52	5	1	.833	58	7	17	0.17	1
1991 Greensboro .... So. Atl.		29	114⅔	4	9	.308	123	36	103	2.75	0
1992 Ft. Lauderdale ....Fla. St.		10	59⅓	5	3	.625	42	5	40	2.28	0
1993 Yankees .... Gulf Coast		2	4	0	1	.000	6	1	2	2.25	0
1993 Greensboro .... So. Atl.		10	39⅓	1	0	1.000	32	15	31	2.06	0
1994 Tampa ....Fla. St.		7	36⅔	3	0	1.000	27	12	34	2.21	0
1994 Albany .... Eastern		9	63⅓	3	0	1.000	39	8	58	2.27	0
1994 Columbus..............Int.		6	31	4	2	.667	23	10	34	5.81	0
1995 Columbus..............Int.		7	30	2	2	.500	30	3	25	2.10	0
1995 New York .... A.L.		19	67	5	3	.625	51	30	71	5.51	0
1996 New York .... A.L.		61	107⅔	8	3	.727	130	34	73	2.09	5

Year	Club	Lea	G	IP	W	L	Pct	SO	BB	H	ERA	SAVES
1997	New York	A.L.	66	71²/₃	6	4	.600	68	20	65	1.88	43
1998	New York a	A.L.	54	61¹/₃	3	0	1.000	36	17	48	1.91	36
1999	New York	A.L.	66	69	4	3	.571	52	18	43	1.83	*45
2000	New York	A.L.	66	75²/₃	7	4	.636	58	25	58	2.85	36
2001	New York	A.L.	71	80²/₃	4	6	.400	83	12	61	2.34	*50
2002	Yankees	Gulf Coast	1	2	0	0	.000	2	1	2	0.00	0
2002	New York b	A.L.	45	46	1	4	.200	41	11	35	2.74	28
2003	New York c	A.L.	64	70²/₃	5	2	.714	63	10	61	1.66	40
2004	New York	A.L.	74	78²/₃	4	2	.667	66	20	65	1.94	*53
2005	New York	A.L.	71	78¹/₃	7	4	.636	80	18	50	1.38	43
2006	New York	A.L.	63	75	5	5	.500	55	11	61	1.80	34
2007	New York d	A.L.	67	71¹/₃	3	4	.429	74	12	68	3.15	30
Major League Totals	13 Yrs.		787	953	62	44	.585	857	238	759	2.35	443

Division Series

Year	Club	Lea	G	IP	W	L	Pct	SO	BB	H	ERA	SAVES
1995	New York	A.L.	3	5¹/₃	1	0	1.000	8	1	3	0.00	0
1996	New York	A.L.	2	4²/₃	0	0	.000	1	1	0	0.00	0
1997	New York	A.L.	2	2	0	0	.000	1	0	2	4.50	1
1998	New York	A.L.	3	3¹/₃	0	0	.000	2	1	1	0.00	2
1999	New York	A.L.	2	3	0	0	.000	3	0	1	0.00	2
2000	New York	A.L.	3	5	0	0	.000	2	0	2	0.00	3
2001	New York	A.L.	3	5	0	0	.000	4	0	4	0.00	2
2002	New York	A.L.	1	1	0	0	.000	0	0	1	0.00	1
2003	New York	A.L.	2	4	0	0	.000	4	0	0	0.00	2
2004	New York	A.L.	4	5²/₃	1	0	1.000	2	0	2	0.00	0
2005	New York	A.L.	2	3	0	0	.000	2	1	1	3.00	2
2006	New York	A.L.	1	1	0	0	.000	0	0	1	0.00	0
2007	New York	A.L.	3	4²/₃	0	0	.000	6	1	2	0.00	0
Division Series Totals			31	47²/₃	2	0	1.000	35	5	20	0.38	15

Championship Series

Year	Club	Lea	G	IP	W	L	Pct	SO	BB	H	ERA	SAVES
1996	New York	A.L.	2	4	1	0	1.000	5	1	6	0.00	0
1998	New York	A.L.	4	5²/₃	0	0	.000	5	1	0	0.00	1
1999	New York	A.L.	3	4²/₃	1	0	1.000	3	0	5	0.00	2
2000	New York	A.L.	3	4²/₃	0	0	.000	1	0	4	1.93	1
2001	New York	A.L.	4	4²/₃	1	0	1.000	3	1	2	1.93	2
2003	New York	A.L.	4	8	1	0	1.000	6	0	5	1.13	2
2004	New York	A.L.	5	7	0	0	.000	6	2	6	1.29	2
Championship Series Totals			25	38²/₃	4	0	1.000	29	5	28	0.93	10

World Series Record

Year	Club	Lea	G	IP	W	L	Pct	SO	BB	H	ERA	SAVES
1996	New York	A.I.	4	5²/₃	0	0	.000	4	3	4	1.59	0
1998	New York	A.I.	3	4¹/₃	0	0	.000	4	0	5	0.00	3
1999	New York	A.L.	3	4²/₃	1	0	1.000	3	1	3	0.00	2
2000	New York	A.L.	4	6	0	0	.000	7	1	4	3.00	2
2001	New York	A.L.	4	6¹/₃	1	1	.500	7	1	6	1.42	0
2003	New York	A.L.	2	4	0	0	.000	4	0	2	0.00	1
World Series Totals			20	31	2	1	.667	29	6	24	1.16	9

a On disabled list from April 6 to April 24, 1998.
b On disabled list from June 9 to June 25 and July 21 to August 8 and August 18 to September 20, 2002.
c On disabled list from March 25 to April 29, 2003.
d Filed for free agency, October 30, 2007, re-signed with New York Yankees, December 17, 2007.

RIVERA, RABELL SAUL (SAUL)
Born, San Juan, Puerto Rico, December 7, 1977.
Bats Both. Throws Right. Height, 5 feet, 11 inches. Weight, 150 pounds.

Year	Club	Lea	G	IP	W	L	Pct	SO	BB	H	ERA	SAVES
1998	Elizabethtown	Appal.	23	36	3	3	.500	65	19	19	2.25	7
1999	Quad Cities	Midwest	60	69²/₃	4	1	.800	102	36	42	1.42	23
2000	New Britain	Eastern	22	37	1	0	1.000	47	22	28	3.89	0
2000	Fort Myers	Fla.St.	29	37²/₃	8	1	.889	45	19	34	3.58	5
2001	New Britain	Eastern	33	42²/₃	5	2	.714	55	18	35	3.16	13
2001	Twins a	Gulf Coast	3	3	0	0	.000	4	1	2	0.00	0
2002	Binghamton	Eastern	30	38²/₃	2	3	.400	32	23	25	3.03	13
2002	Harrisburg b	Eastern	15	19	0	2	.000	15	9	21	3.32	3
2003					INJURED—Did Not Play								
2004	Harrisburg	Eastern	18	20²/₃	0	2	.000	15	12	27	7.84	3
2004	Huntsville c-d	Southern	26	33¹/₃	2	1	.667	25	16	30	1.62	1
2005	Harrisburg e	Eastern	40	76²/₃	3	3	.500	70	20	72	2.47	9
2006	New Orleans	P.C.	12	28¹/₃	1	1	.500	25	12	25	1.59	1
2006	Washington	N.L.	54	60¹/₃	3	0	1.000	41	32	59	3.43	1

Year	Club	Lea	G	IP	W	L	Pct	SO	BB	H	ERA	SAVES
2007	Columbus	Int.	1	$0\frac{2}{3}$	0	1	.000	0	0	2	13.50	0
2007	Washington	N.L.	85	93	4	6	.400	64	42	88	3.68	3
Major League Totals		2 Yrs.	139	$153\frac{1}{3}$	7	6	.538	105	74	147	3.58	4

a Claimed on waivers by New York Mets from Minnesota Twins, November 20, 2001.

b Sent to Montreal Expos by New York Mets to complete trade for pitcher Scott Strickland, July 14, 2002.

c Traded to Milwaukee Brewers with outfielder Peter Bergeron for outfielder Jason Belcher and pitcher Jason Childers, June 6, 2004.

d Filed for free agency, October 15, 2004. Signed with Montreal Expos, November 16, 2004.

e Filed for free agency, October 15, 2005, re-signed with Washington Nationals, November 21, 2005.

ROBERTSON, NATHAN DANIEL (NATE)

Born, Wichita, Kansas, September 3, 1977.

Bats Right. Throws Left. Height, 6 feet, 2 inches. Weight, 225 pounds.

Year	Club	Lea	G	IP	W	L	Pct	SO	BB	H	ERA	SAVES
1999	Utica	N.Y.-Penn.	5	26	2	0	1.000	26	8	22	2.77	0
1999	Kane County	Midwest	8	51	6	1	.857	33	12	42	2.29	0
2000	Kane County	Midwest	6	$17\frac{2}{3}$	0	2	.000	15	6	24	5.09	0
2001	Brevard County	Fla.St.	19	$106\frac{1}{3}$	11	4	.733	67	43	95	2.88	0
2002	Portland	Eastern	27	163	10	9	.526	109	50	156	3.42	0
2002	Florida	N.L.	6	$8\frac{1}{3}$	0	1	.000	3	4	15	11.88	0
2003	Toledo	Int.	24	155	9	7	.563	102	47	145	3.14	0
2003	Detroit a	A.L.	8	$44\frac{2}{3}$	1	2	.333	33	23	55	5.44	0
2004	Detroit	A.L.	34	$196\frac{2}{3}$	12	10	.545	155	66	210	4.90	1
2005	Detroit	A.L.	32	$196\frac{2}{3}$	7	16	.304	122	65	202	4.48	0
2006	Detroit	A.L.	32	$208\frac{2}{3}$	13	13	.500	137	67	206	3.84	0
2007	Erie	Eastern	1	6	1	0	1.000	6	1	0	0.00	0
2007	Detroit b	A.L.	30	$177\frac{2}{3}$	9	13	.409	119	63	199	4.76	0
Major League Totals		6 Yrs.	142	$832\frac{2}{3}$	42	55	.433	569	288	887	4.60	1
	Division Series											
2006	Detroit	A.L.	1	$5\frac{2}{3}$	0	1	.000	1	0	12	11.12	0
	Championship Series											
2006	Detroit	A.L.	1	5	1	0	1.000	4	3	6	0.00	0
	World Series Record											
2006	Detroit	A.L.	1	5	0	1	.000	3	3	5	3.60	0

a Traded to Detroit Tigers with pitcher Gary Knotts and pitcher Rob Henkel for pitcher Mark Redman and pitcher Jerrod Fuell, January 11, 2003.

b On disabled list from June 6 to June 26, 2007.

RODNEY, FERNANDO

Born, Samana, Dominican Republic, March 17, 1977.

Bats Right. Throws Right. Height, 5 feet, 11 inches. Weight, 220 pounds.

Year	Club	Lea	G	IP	W	L	Pct	SO	BB	H	ERA	SAVES
1998	Detroit	Dominican	11	32	1	3	.250	37	19	25	3.38	1
1999	Lakeland	Fla.St.	4	$6\frac{1}{3}$	1	0	1.000	5	1	7	1.42	2
1999	Tigers	Gulf Coast	22	30	3	3	.500	39	21	20	2.40	9
2000	West Michigan	Midwest	22	$82\frac{2}{3}$	6	4	.600	56	35	74	2.94	0
2001	Erie	Eastern	4	$6\frac{1}{3}$	0	0	.000	8	3	7	4.26	1
2001	Lakeland	Fla.St.	16	$55\frac{1}{3}$	4	2	.667	44	19	53	3.42	0
2001	Tigers	Gulf Coast	1	1	0	0	.000	1	1	0	0.00	0
2002	Erie	Eastern	21	$20\frac{1}{3}$	1	0	1.000	18	5	14	1.33	11
2002	Detroit	A.L.	20	18	1	3	.250	10	10	25	6.00	0
2002	Toledo	Int.	20	$22\frac{1}{3}$	1	1	.500	25	9	13	0.81	4
2003	Toledo	Int.	38	$40\frac{2}{3}$	1	1	.500	58	13	22	1.33	23
2003	Detroit	A.L.	27	$29\frac{2}{3}$	1	3	.250	33	17	35	6.07	3
2004	Detroit a	A.L.	INJURED—Did Not Play									
2005	Toledo	Int.	3	3	0	0	.000	4	1	2	3.00	0
2005	Detroit b	A.L.	39	44	2	3	.400	42	17	39	2.86	9
2006	Detroit	A.L.	63	$71\frac{2}{3}$	7	4	.636	65	34	51	3.52	7
2007	Toledo	Int.	4	3	0	0	.000	4	2	4	0.00	0
2007	Detroit c	A.L.	48	$50\frac{2}{3}$	2	6	.250	54	21	46	4.26	1
Major League Totals		5 Yrs.	197	214	13	19	.406	204	99	196	4.12	20
	Championship Series											
2006	Detroit	A.L.	3	$3\frac{2}{3}$	0	0	.000	4	1	1	0.00	0
	World Series Record											
2006	Detroit	A.L.	4	4	0	0	.000	5	4	5	4.50	0

a On disabled list from March 26 to October 4, 2004.

b On disabled list from March 29 to June 9, 2005.

c On disabled list from May 21 to June 5 and June 24 to August 4, 2007.

RODRIGUEZ, FRANCISCO JOSE

Born, Caracas, Venezuela, January 7, 1982.
Bats Right. Throws Right. Height, 6 feet. Weight, 165 pounds.

Year	Club	Lea	G	IP	W	L	Pct	SO	BB	H	ERA	SAVES
1999 Boise	Northwest		1	5	1	0	1.000	6	1	3	5.40	0
1999 Butte	Pioneer		12	51²/₃	1	1	.500	69	21	33	3.31	0
2000 Lake Elsinore	California		13	64	4	4	.500	79	32	43	2.81	0
2001 Rancho Cucamonga	California		20	113²/₃	5	7	* .417	147	55	127	5.38	0
2002 Arkansas	Texas		23	41¹/₃	3	3	.500	61	15	32	1.96	9
2002 Salt Lake	P.C.		27	42	2	3	.400	59	13	30	2.57	6
2002 Anaheim	A.L.		5	5²/₃	0	0	.000	13	2	3	0.00	0
2003 Anaheim	A.L.		59	86	8	3	.727	95	35	50	3.03	2
2004 Anaheim	A.L.		69	84	4	1	.800	123	33	51	1.82	12
2005 Los Angeles a	A.L.		66	67¹/₃	2	5	.286	91	32	45	2.67	*45
2006 Los Angeles	A.L.		69	73	2	3	.400	98	28	52	1.73	*47
2007 Los Angeles	A.L.		64	67¹/₃	5	2	.714	90	34	50	2.81	40
Major League Totals	6 Yrs.		332	383¹/₃	21	14	.600	510	164	251	2.37	146
Division Series												
2002 Anaheim	A.L.		3	5²/₃	2	0	1.000	8	2	2	3.18	0
2004 Anaheim	A.L.		2	4²/₃	0	2	.000	5	3	4	3.86	0
2005 Los Angeles	A.L.		3	3¹/₃	0	0	.000	2	0	5	2.70	2
2007 Los Angeles	A.L.		1	0¹/₃	0	0	.000	1	1	1	54.00	0
Division Series Totals			9	14	2	2	.500	16	6	12	4.50	2
Championship Series												
2002 Anaheim	A.L.		4	4¹/₃	2	0	1.000	7	2	2	0.00	0
2005 Los Angeles	A.L.		2	2¹/₃	0	0	.000	3	3	2	0.00	1
Championship Series Totals			6	6²/₃	2	0	1.000	10	5	4	0.00	1
World Series Record												
2002 Anaheim	A.L.		4	8²/₃	1	1	.500	13	1	6	2.08	0

a On disabled list from May 15 to June 1, 2005.

RODRIGUEZ, WANDY FULTON

Born, Santiago Rodriguez, Dominican Republic, January 18, 1979.
Bats Both. Throws Left. Height, 5 feet, 11 inches. Weight, 160 pounds.

Year	Club	Lea	G	IP	W	L	Pct	SO	BB	H	ERA	SAVES
2001 Martinsville	Appal.		12	74	4	3	.571	67	20	54	1.58	0
2002 Lexington	So.Atl.		28	159¹/₃	11	4	.733	137	44	167	3.78	0
2003 Salem	Carolina		20	111	8	7	.533	72	41	102	3.49	0
2004 Round Rock	Texas		26	142²/₃	11	6	.647	115	57	159	4.48	0
2005 Corpus Christi	Texas		1	3¹/₃	0	0	.000	3	2	3	2.70	0
2005 Round Rock	P.C.		8	46¹/₃	4	2	.667	48	16	43	3.69	0
2005 Houston	N.L.		25	128²/₃	10	10	.500	80	53	135	5.53	0
2006 Round Rock	P.C.		5	26	2	2	.500	13	13	32	6.92	0
2006 Houston	N.L.		30	135²/₃	9	10	.474	98	63	154	5.64	0
2007 Houston	N.L.		31	182²/₃	9	13	.409	158	62	179	4.58	0
Major League Totals	3 Yrs.		86	447	28	33	.459	336	178	468	5.17	0
Division Series												
2005 Houston	N.L.		1	1	0	0	.000	2	0	1	9.00	0
World Series Record												
2005 Houston	N.L.		2	3²/₃	0	1	.000	2	5	4	2.45	0

ROGERS, KENNETH SCOTT (KENNY)

Born, Savannah, Georgia, November 10, 1964.
Bats Left. Throws Left. Height, 6 feet, 1 inch. Weight, 190 pounds.

Year	Club	Lea	G	IP	W	L	Pct	SO	BB	H	ERA	SAVES
1982 Sarasota Rangers	Gulf C.		2	3	0	0	.000	4	0	0	0.00	0
1983 Sarasota Rangers	Gulf C.		15	53¹/₃	4	1	.800	36	20	40	2.36	1
1984 Burlington	Midwest		39	92²/₃	4	7	.364	93	33	87	3.98	3
1985 Daytona Beach	Fla. St.		6	10	0	1	.000	9	11	12	7.20	0
1985 Burlington	Midwest		33	95	2	5	.286	96	61	67	2.84	4
1986 Tulsa a	Texas		10	26¹/₃	0	3	.000	23	18	39	9.91	0
1986 Salem	Carolina		12	66	2	7	.222	46	26	75	6.27	0
1987 Charlotte b	Fla. St.		5	17	0	3	.000	14	8	17	4.76	0
1987 Tulsa	Texas		28	69	1	5	.167	59	35	80	5.35	2
1988 Charlotte c	Fla. St.		8	35¹/₃	2	0	1.000	26	11	22	1.27	1
1988 Tulsa	Texas		13	83¹/₃	4	6	.400	76	34	73	4.00	0
1989 Texas	A.L.		73	73²/₃	3	4	.429	63	42	60	2.93	2

Year	Club	Lea	G	IP	W	L	Pct	SO	BB	H	ERA	SAVES
1990 Texas	A.L.	69	97²/₃	10	6	.625	74	42	93	3.13	15
1991 Texas	A.L.	63	109²/₃	10	10	.500	73	61	121	5.42	5
1992 Texas	A.L.	*81	78²/₃	3	6	.333	70	26	80	3.09	6
1993 Texas	A.L.	35	208¹/₃	16	10	.615	140	71	210	4.10	0
1994 Texas d-e-f	A.L.	24	167¹/₃	11	8	.579	120	52	169	4.46	0
1995 Texas g-h	A.L.	31	208	17	7	.708	140	76	192	3.38	0
1996 New York	A.L.	30	179	12	8	.600	92	83	179	4.68	0
1997 New York i	A.L.	31	145	6	7	.462	78	62	161	5.65	0
1998 Oakland	A.L.	34	238²/₃	16	8	.667	138	67	215	3.17	0
1999 Oakland j	A.L.	19	119¹/₃	5	3	.625	68	41	135	4.30	0
1999 New York k	N.L.	12	76	5	1	.833	58	28	71	4.03	0
2000 Texas	A.L.	34	227¹/₃	13	13	.500	127	78	257	4.55	0
2001 Texas	A.L.	20	120²/₃	5	7	.417	74	49	150	6.19	0
2002 Texas l	A.L.	33	210²/₃	13	8	.619	107	70	212	3.84	0
2003 Minnesota m	A.L.	33	195	13	8	.619	116	50	227	4.57	0
2004 Texas	A.L.	35	211²/₃	18	9	.667	126	66	248	4.76	0
2005 Texas n	A.L.	30	195¹/₃	14	8	.636	87	53	205	3.46	0
2006 Detroit	A.L.	34	204	17	8	.680	99	62	195	3.84	0
2007 West Michigan	Midwest	1	5	0	1	.000	4	2	7	1.80	0
2007 Toledo	Int.	1	3²/₃	0	0	.000	2	0	3	0.00	0
2007 Detroit o-p	A.L.	11	63	3	4	.429	36	25	65	4.43	0
Major League Totals ...... 19 Yrs.		732	3129	210	143	.595	1886	1104	3245	4.19	28
Division Series											
1996 New York	A.L.	2	2	0	0	.000	1	2	5	9.00	0
1999 New York	N.L.	1	4¹/₃	0	1	.000	6	2	5	8.31	0
2003 Minnesota	A.L.	1	1¹/₃	0	0	.000	3	1	1	0.00	0
2006 Detroit	A.L.	1	7²/₃	1	0	1.000	8	2	5	0.00	0
Division Series Totals		5	15¹/₃	1	1	.500	18	7	16	3.52	0
Championship Series											
1996 New York	A.L.	1	3	0	0	.000	3	2	5	12.00	0
1999 New York	N.L.	3	7²/₃	0	2	.000	2	7	11	5.87	0
2006 Detroit	A.L.	1	7¹/₃	1	0	1.000	6	2	2	0.00	0
Championship Series Totals		5	18	1	2	.333	11	11	18	4.50	0
World Series Record											
1996 New York	A.L.	1	2	0	0	.000	0	2	5	22.50	0
2006 Detroit	A.L.	1	8	1	0	1.000	5	3	2	0.00	0
World Series Totals		2	10	1	0	1.000	5	5	7	4.50	0

a On disabled list from April 12 to April 30, 1986.
b On disabled list from March 28 to April 30, 1987.
c On disabled list from March 20 to May 15, 1988.
d Pitched perfect no-hit, no-run game against California Angels, winning 4-0, July 28, 1994.
e Filed for free agency, October 19, 1994; ruled ineligible by Player Relations Committee due to insufficient service time.
f Declared restricted free agent under Major League Baseball implemented labor proposal, December 23, 1994.
g Re-signed with Texas Rangers, April 7, 1995.
h Filed for free agency, November 12, 1995. Signed with New York Yankees, December 30, 1995.
i Traded to Oakland Athletics for player to be named later, November 7, 1997. New York Yankees received infielder Scott Brosius to complete trade, November 18, 1997.
j Traded to New York Mets for outfielder Terrence Long and pitcher Leoner Vasquez, July 23, 1999.
k Filed for free agency, October 29, 1999. Signed with Texas Rangers, December 29, 1999.
l Filed for free agency, October 29, 2002. Signed with Minnesota Twins, March 12, 2003.
m Filed for free agency, October 29, 2003. Signed with Texas Rangers, January 13, 2004.
n Filed for free agency, October 28, 2005. Signed with Detroit Tigers, December 12, 2005.
o On disabled list from March 25 to June 22 and July 26 to September 5, 2007.
p Filed for free agency, October 31, 2007, re-signed with Detroit Tigers, November 30, 2007.

ROMERO, JUAN CARLOS (J.C.)
Born, Rio Piedras, Puerto Rico, June 4, 1976.
Bats Both. Throws Left. Height, 5 feet, 11 inches. Weight, 205 pounds.

Year	Club	Lea	G	IP	W	L	Pct	SO	BB	H	ERA	SAVES
1997 Elizabethtown	Appal.	18	24	3	2	.600	29	7	27	4.88	3
1997 Ft. Myers	Fla.St.	7	12¹/₃	1	1	.500	9	4	11	4.38	0
1998 New Britain	Eastern	51	78	6	3	.667	79	43	48	2.19	2
1999 New Britain	Eastern	36	53	4	4	.500	53	34	51	3.40	7
1999 Salt Lake	P.C.	15	19²/₃	4	1	.800	20	14	18	3.20	1
1999 Minnesota	A.L.	5	9²/₃	0	0	.000	4	0	13	3.72	0
2000 Fort Myers	Fla.St.	2	4²/₃	0	0	.000	3	1	4	1.93	0
2000 Salt Lake	P.C.	17	65¹/₃	4	2	.667	38	25	60	3.44	4

Year Club	Lea	G	IP	W	L	Pct	SO	BB	H	ERA	SAVES
2000 Minnesota a	A.L.	12	57²/₃	2	7	.222	50	30	72	7.02	0
2001 Edmonton	P.C.	12	63²/₃	3	3	.500	55	24	67	3.68	0
2001 Minnesota	A.L.	14	65	1	4	.200	39	24	71	6.23	0
2002 Minnesota	A.L.	81	81	9	2	.818	76	36	62	1.89	1
2003 Minnesota	A.L.	73	63	2	0	1.000	50	42	66	5.00	0
2004 Rochester............	Int.	3	8	0	0	.000	11	5	4	2.25	0
2004 Minnesota	A.L.	74	74¹/₃	7	4	.636	69	38	61	3.51	1
2005 Minnesota b	A.L.	68	57	4	3	.571	48	39	50	3.47	0
2006 Los Angeles c	A.L.	65	48¹/₃	1	2	.333	31	28	57	6.70	0
2007 Boston	A.L.	23	20	1	0	1.000	11	15	24	3.15	1
2007 Philadelphia d-e	N.L.	51	36¹/₃	1	2	.333	31	25	15	1.24	0
Major League Totals ....9 Yrs.		466	512¹/₃	28	24	.538	409	277	491	4.30	3
Division Series											
2002 Minnesota	A.L.	3	3¹/₃	0	0	.000	2	1	3	0.00	0
2003 Minnesota	A.L.	3	3¹/₃	0	0	.000	1	2	3	0.00	0
2004 Minnesota	A.L.	2	1	0	0	.000	1	1	0	9.00	0
2007 Philadelphia	N.L.	3	2	0	1	.000	1	0	3	4.50	0
Division Series Totals........		11	9²/₃	0	1	.000	5	4	9	1.86	0
Championship Series											
2002 Minnesota	A.L.	4	2	0	1	.000	3	2	4	22.50	0

a On disabled list from March 25 to May 9, 2000.
b Traded to Los Angeles Angels for infielder Alexi Casilla, December 9, 2005.
c Filed for free agency, October 28, 2006. Signed with Boston Red Sox, December 15, 2006.
d Released by Boston Red Sox, June 18, 2007. Signed with Philadelphia Phillies organization, June 22, 2007.
e Filed for free agency, October 30, 2007, re-signed with Philadelphia Phillies, November 10, 2007.

RYAN, ROBERT VICTOR (B.J.)

Born, Bossier City, Louisiana, December 28, 1975.
Bats Left. Throws Left. Height, 6 feet, 6 inches. Weight, 260 pounds.

Year Club	Lea	G	IP	W	L	Pct	SO	BB	H	ERA	SAVES
1998 Billings............	Pioneer	14	18²/₃	2	1	.667	25	5	15	1.93	4
1998 Chstn-Wv...........	So.Atl.	3	4¹/₃	0	0	.000	5	1	1	2.08	2
1998 Chattanooga	Southern	16	16¹/₃	1	0	1.000	21	6	13	2.20	4
1999 Rochester..............	Int.	11	14¹/₃	0	0	.000	20	4	8	2.51	1
1999 Chattanooga.......	Southern	35	41²/₃	2	1	.667	46	17	33	2.59	6
1999 Indianapolis.........	Int.	11	9	1	0	1.000	12	3	9	4.00	0
1999 Cincinnati.............	N.L.	1	2	0	0	.000	1	1	4	4.50	0
1999 Baltimore a............	A.L.	13	18¹/₃	1	0	1.000	28	12	9	2.95	0
2000 Rochester.............	Int.	14	24²/₃	0	1	.000	28	9	23	4.74	1
2000 Baltimore	A.L.	42	42²/₃	2	3	.400	41	31	36	5.91	0
2001 Baltimore	A.L.	61	53	2	4	.333	54	30	47	4.25	2
2002 Baltimore	A.L.	67	57²/₃	2	1	.667	56	33	51	4.68	1
2003 Baltimore	A.L.	76	50¹/₃	4	1	.800	63	27	42	3.40	0
2004 Baltimore	A.L.	76	87	4	6	.400	122	35	64	2.28	3
2005 Baltimore b	A.L.	69	70¹/₃	1	4	.200	100	26	54	2.43	36
2006 Toronto	A.L.	65	72¹/₃	2	2	.500	86	20	42	1.37	38
2007 Toronto c	A.L.	5	4¹/₃	0	2	.000	3	4	7	12.46	3
Major League Totals ....9 Yrs.		475	458	18	23	.439	554	219	356	3.28	83

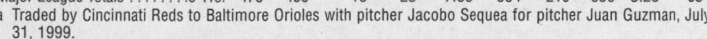

a Traded by Cincinnati Reds to Baltimore Orioles with pitcher Jacobo Sequea for pitcher Juan Guzman, July 31, 1999.
b Filed for free agency, October 28, 2005. Signed with Toronto Blue Jays, November 28, 2005.
c On disabled list from April 15 to November 13, 2007.

SABATHIA, CARSTEN CHARLES (C.C.)

Born, Vallejo, California, July 21, 1980.
Bats Left. Throws Left. Height, 6 feet, 7 inches. Weight, 290 pounds.

Year Club	Lea	G	IP	W	L	Pct	SO	BB	H	ERA	SAVES
1998 Burlington	Appal.	5	18	1	0	1.000	35	8	20	4.50	0
1999 Kinston...........	Carolina	7	32	3	3	.500	29	19	30	5.34	0
1999 Mahoning Valley...	N.Y.-Penn.	6	19²/₃	0	0	.000	27	12	9	1.83	0
1999 Columbus a	So.Atl.	3	16²/₃	2	0	1.000	20	5	8	1.08	0
2000 Kinston...........	Carolina	10	56	3	2	.600	69	24	48	3.54	0
2000 Akron.............	Eastern	17	90¹/₃	3	7	.300	90	48	75	3.59	0
2001 Cleveland	A.L.	33	180¹/₃	17	5	.773	171	95	149	4.39	0
2002 Cleveland	A.L.	33	210	13	11	.542	149	88	198	4.37	0
2003 Cleveland	A.L.	30	197²/₃	13	9	.591	141	66	190	3.60	0
2004 Cleveland	A.L.	30	188	11	10	.524	139	72	176	4.12	0

Year	Club	Lea	G	IP	W	L	Pct	SO	BB	H	ERA	SAVES
2005 Akron	....	Eastern	2	9	0	1	.000	9	2	4	1.00	0
2005 Cleveland b	....	A.L.	31	196²/₃	15	10	.600	161	62	185	4.03	0
2006 Buffalo	....	Int.	1	5	1	0	1.000	5	1	6	1.80	0
2006 Cleveland c	....	A.L.	28	192²/₃	12	11	.522	172	44	182	3.22	0
2007 Cleveland d	....	A.L.	34	*241	19	7	.731	209	37	238	3.21	0
Major League Totals	.... 7 Yrs.		219	1406¹/₃	100	63	.613	1142	464	1318	3.83	0
Division Series												
2001 Cleveland	....	A.L.	1	6	1	0	1.000	5	5	6	3.00	0
2007 Cleveland	....	A.L.	1	5	1	0	1.000	5	6	4	5.40	0
Division Series Totals	....		2	11	2	0	1.000	10	11	10	4.09	0
Championship Series												
2007 Cleveland	....	A.L.	2	10¹/₃	0	2	.000	9	7	17	10.45	0

a On disabled list from April 1 through June 20, 1999.
b On disabled list from March 25 to April 17, 2005.
c On disabled list from April 3 to May 2, 2006.
d Selected Cy Young Award Winner in American League for 2007.

SAITO, TAKASHI

Born, Miyagi, Japan, February 14, 1970.
Bats Left. Throws Right. Height, 6 feet, 2 inch. Weight, 200 pounds.

Year	Club	Lea	G	IP	W	L	Pct	SO	BB	H	ERA	SAVES
1992 Yokohama	......	Japan Cent.	6	16	0	2	.000	21	10	18	8.44	0
1993 Yokohama	......	Japan Cent.	29	149	8	10	.444	125	61	127	3.81	0
1994 Yokohama	......	Japan Cent.	28	181	9	12	.429	169	69	175	3.13	0
1995 Yokohama	......	Japan Cent.	26	162	8	9	.471	132	45	166	3.94	0
1996 Yokohama	......	Japan Cent.	28	196²/₃	10	10	.500	206	63	157	3.29	0
1997	....						INJURED—Did Not Play					
1998 Yokohama	......	Japan Cent.	34	143²/₃	13	5	.722	101	23	131	2.94	1
1999 Yokohama	......	Japan Cent.	26	184²/₃	14	3	.824	125	31	178	3.95	0
2000 Yokohama	......	Japan Cent.	19	115²/₃	6	10	.375	97	36	123	5.52	0
2001 Yokohama	......	Japan Cent.	50	64²/₃	7	1	.857	60	14	51	1.67	27
2002 Yokohama	......	Japan Cent.	39	47²/₃	1	2	.333	46	15	37	2.45	20
2003 Yokohama	......	Japan Cent.	17	103¹/₃	6	7	.462	72	22	103	4.18	0
2004 Yokohama	......	Japan Cent.	16	44	2	5	.286	37	13	64	7.71	0
2005 Yokohama	......	Japan Cent.	21	106	3	4	.429	93	29	111	3.82	0
2006 Los Angeles a	....	N.L.	72	78¹/₃	6	2	.750	107	23	48	2.07	24
2007 Los Angeles	....	N.L.	63	64¹/₃	2	1	.667	78	13	33	1.40	39
Major League Totals	.... 2 Yrs.		135	142²/₃	8	3	.727	185	36	81	1.77	63
Division Series												
2006 Los Angeles	....	N.L.	2	2²/₃	0	0	.000	4	0	0	0.00	0

a Signed with Los Angeles Dodgers organization, February 7, 2006.

SAMPSON, CHRISTOPHER KEITH (CHRIS)

Born, Pasadena, Texas, May 23, 1978.
Bats Right. Throws Right. Height, 6 feet, 1 inch. Weight, 190 pounds.

Year	Club	Lea	G	IP	W	L	Pct	SO	BB	H	ERA	SAVES
2003 Salem	....	Carolina	9	10²/₃	1	1	.500	6	5	14	5.91	1
2003 Lexington	....	So.Atl.	22	84	4	3	.571	66	14	66	1.39	1
2004 Salem	....	Carolina	27	151²/₃	7	11	.389	101	26	170	3.80	0
2004 Round Rock	....	Texas	1	2	0	0	.000	1	0	3	0.00	0
2005 Corpus Christi	....	Texas	32	150	4	12	.250	92	19	147	3.12	4
2006 Round Rock	....	P.C.	27	125²/₃	12	3	.800	68	14	110	2.51	4
2006 Houston	....	N.L.	12	34	2	1	.667	15	5	25	2.12	0
2007 Round Rock	....	P.C.	2	3	1	0	1.000	0	2	3	0.00	0
2007 Houston a	....	N.L.	24	121²/₃	7	8	.467	51	30	138	4.59	0
Major League Totals	.... 2 Yrs.		36	155²/₃	9	9	.500	66	35	163	4.05	0

a On disabled list from August 1 to August 31, 2007.

SANCHEZ, ANIBAL ALEJANDRO

Born, Maracay, Venezuela, February 27, 1984.
Bats Right. Throws Right. Height, 6 feet. Weight, 180 pounds.

Year	Club	Lea	G	IP	W	L	Pct	SO	BB	H	ERA	SAVES
2003 Lowell a	....	N.Y.-Penn.					INJURED—Did Not Play					
2004 Lowell	....	N.Y.-Penn.	15	76¹/₃	4	4	.500	101	29	43	1.77	0
2005 Wilmington	....	Carolina	14	78²/₃	6	1	.857	95	24	53	2.40	0

Year	Club	Lea	G	IP	W	L	Pct	SO	BB	H	ERA	SAVES
2005 Portland b	Eastern	11	57⅓	3	5	.375	63	16	53	3.45	0
2006 Carolina	Southern	15	85⅔	3	6	.333	92	27	82	3.15	0
2006 Florida c	N.L.	18	114⅓	10	3	.769	72	46	90	2.83	0
2007 Florida d	N.L.	6	30	2	1	.667	14	19	43	4.80	0
Major League Totals ....2 Yrs.		24	144⅓	12	4	.750	86	65	133	3.24	0

a On minor league disabled list July 1 to September 16, 2003.

b Traded by Boston Red Sox to Florida Marlins with infielder Hanley Ramirez and pitcher Jesus Delgado for pitcher Josh Beckett, infielder Mike Lowell and pitcher Guillermo Mota, November 24, 2005.

c Pitched no-hit, no-run game against Arizona Diamondbacks, September 6, 2006.

d On minor league disabled list from May 8 to September 1, 2007.

SANTANA, ERVIN RAMON
Born, LaRomana, Dominican Republic, January 10, 1983.
Bats Right. Throws Right. Height, 6 feet, 2 inches. Weight, 160 pounds.

Year	Club	Lea	G	IP	W	L	Pct	SO	BB	H	ERA	SAVES
2001 Angels	Arizona	10	58⅔	3	2	.600	69	35	40	3.22	0
2001 Provo	Pioneer	4	18⅔	2	1	.667	22	12	19	7.71	0
2002 Cedar Rapids	Midwest	27	147	14	8	.636	146	48	133	4.16	0
2003 Rancho Cucamonga	California	20	124⅔	10	2	.833	130	36	98	2.53	0
2003 Arkansas	Texas	6	29⅔	1	1	.500	23	12	23	3.94	0
2004 Arkansas	Texas	8	43⅔	2	1	.667	48	18	41	3.30	0
2005 Arkansas	Texas	7	39	5	1	.833	32	15	34	2.31	0
2005 Salt Lake	P.C.	3	19⅓	1	0	1.000	17	2	19	4.19	0
2005 Los Angeles	A.L.	23	133⅔	12	8	.600	99	47	139	4.65	0
2006 Los Angeles	A.L.	33	204	16	8	.667	141	70	181	4.28	0
2007 Salt Lake	P.C.	5	32⅓	2	1	.667	32	10	39	5.01	0
2007 Los Angeles	A.L.	28	150	7	14	.333	126	58	174	5.76	0
Major League Totals ....3 Yrs.		84	487⅔	35	30	.538	366	175	494	4.84	0
Division Series											
2005 Los Angeles	A.L.	1	5⅓	1	0	1.000	2	3	5	5.06	0
2007 Los Angeles	A.L.	1	2	0	0	.000	2	0	0	0.00	0
Division Series Totals		2	7⅓	1	0	1.000	4	3	5	3.68	0
Championship Series											
2005 Los Angeles	A.L.	1	4⅓	0	1	.000	2	3	3	10.38	0

SANTANA, JOHAN ALEXANDER
Born, Tovar, Venezuela, March 13, 1979.
Bats Left. Throws Left. Height, 6 feet. Weight, 210 pounds.

Year	Club	Lea	G	IP	W	L	Pct	SO	BB	H	ERA	SAVES
1996 Houston/Bos	Dominican	23	40	4	3	.571	51	22	26	2.70	3
1997 Auburn	N.Y.-Penn.	1	4	0	0	.000	5	6	1	2.25	0
1997 Astros	Gulf Coast	9	36⅓	0	4	.000	25	18	49	7.93	0
1998 Quad City	Midwest	2	6⅔	0	1	.000	6	3	14	9.45	0
1998 Auburn	N.Y.-Penn.	15	86⅔	7	5	.583	88	21	81	4.36	0
1999 Michigan a-b	Midwest	27	160⅓	8	8	.500	150	55	162	4.66	0
2000 Minnesota	A.L.	30	86	2	3	.400	64	54	102	6.49	0
2001 Minnesota	A.L.	15	43⅔	1	0	1.000	28	16	50	4.74	0
2002 Edmonton	P.C.	11	48⅔	5	2	.714	75	27	37	3.14	0
2002 Minnesota	A.L.	27	108⅓	8	6	.571	137	49	84	2.99	1
2003 Minnesota	A.L.	45	158⅓	12	3	.800	169	47	127	3.07	0
2004 Minnesota c	A.L.	34	228	20	6	.769	*265	54	156	*2.61	0
2005 Minnesota	A.L.	33	231⅔	16	7	.696	*238	45	180	2.87	0
2006 Minnesota d	A.L.	34	*233⅔	*19	6	.760	*245	47	186	*2.77	0
2007 Minnesota	A.L.	33	219	15	13	.536	235	52	183	3.33	0
Major League Totals ....8 Yrs.		251	1308⅔	93	44	.679	1381	364	1068	3.22	1
Division Series											
2002 Minnesota	A.L.	2	3	0	0	.000	2	2	3	6.00	0
2003 Minnesota	A.L.	2	7⅔	0	1	.000	6	3	9	7.04	0
2004 Minnesota	A.L.	2	12	1	0	1.000	12	4	14	0.75	0
2006 Minnesota	A.L.	1	8	0	1	.000	8	1	5	2.25	0
Division Series Totals		7	30⅔	1	2	.333	28	10	31	3.23	0
Championship Series											
2002 Minnesota	A.L.	4	3⅓	0	1	.000	4	0	4	10.80	0

a Selected by Florida Marlins from Houston Astros in Rule V draft, December 13, 1999.

b Traded to Minnesota Twins with cash for pitcher Jared Camp, December 13, 1999.

c Selected Cy Young Award Winner in American League for 2004.

d Selected Cy Young Award Winner in American League for 2006.

SAUNDERS, JOSEPH FRANCIS (JOE)

Born, Falls Church, Virginia, June 16, 1981.
Bats Left. Throws Left. Height, 6 feet, 3 inches. Weight, 210 pounds.

Year	Club	Lea	G	IP	W	L	Pct	SO	BB	H	ERA	SAVES
2002	Cedar Rapids	Midwest	5	28⅔	3	1	.750	27	9	16	1.88	0
2002	Provo	Pioneer	8	32⅓	2	1	.667	21	11	40	3.62	0
2003	Provo a	Pioneer			INJURED—Did Not Play							
2004	Rancho Cucamonga	Calif.	19	105⅔	9	7	.563	76	23	106	3.41	0
2004	Arkansas	Texas	8	39	4	3	.571	25	14	51	5.77	0
2005	Arkansas	Texas	18	105⅔	7	4	.636	80	32	107	3.49	0
2005	Salt Lake	P.C.	9	55	3	3	.500	29	21	65	4.58	0
2005	Los Angeles	A.L.	2	9⅓	0	0	.000	4	4	10	7.71	0
2006	Salt Lake	P.C.	21	135	10	4	.714	97	38	117	2.67	0
2006	Los Angeles	A.L.	13	70⅔	7	3	.700	51	29	71	4.71	0
2007	Salt Lake	P.C.	14	86⅓	4	7	.364	84	20	89	5.11	0
2007	Los Angeles	A.L.	18	107⅓	8	5	.615	69	34	129	4.44	0
Major League Totals	3 Yrs.		33	187⅓	15	8	.652	124	67	210	4.71	0

a On minor league disabled list from April 3 to September 18, 2003.

SCHILLING, CURTIS MONTAGUE (CURT)

Born, Anchorage, Alaska, November 14, 1966.
Bats Right. Throws Right. Height, 6 feet, 5 inches. Weight, 235 pounds.

Year	Club	Lea	G	IP	W	L	Pct	SO	BB	H	ERA	SAVES
1986	Elmira	N.Y.-Penn.	16	93⅔	7	3	.700	75	31	92	2.59	0
1987	Greensboro	So. Atl.	29	184	8	*15	.348	*189	65	179	3.82	0
1988	New Britain a	Eastern	21	106	8	5	.615	62	40	91	2.97	1
1988	Charlotte	Southern	7	45⅓	5	2	.714	32	23	36	3.18	0
1988	Baltimore	A.L.	4	14⅔	0	3	.000	4	10	22	9.82	0
1989	Rochester	Int.	27	*185⅓	*13	11	.542	109	59	176	3.21	0
1989	Baltimore	A.L.	5	8⅔	0	1	.000	6	3	10	6.23	0
1990	Rochester	Int.	15	87⅓	4	4	.500	83	25	95	3.92	0
1990	Baltimore b	A.L.	35	46	1	2	.333	32	19	38	2.54	3
1991	Tucson	P.C.	13	23⅔	0	1	.000	21	12	16	3.42	3
1991	Houston c	N.L.	56	75⅔	3	5	.375	71	39	79	3.81	8
1992	Philadelphia	N.L.	42	226⅓	14	11	.560	147	59	165	2.35	2
1993	Philadelphia	N.L.	34	235⅓	16	7	.696	186	57	234	4.02	0
1994	Reading	Eastern	1	4	0	0	.000	4	1	6	0.00	0
1994	Scranton	Int.	2	10	0	0	.000	6	5	6	1.80	0
1994	Philadelphia d	N.L.	13	82⅓	2	8	.200	58	28	87	4.48	0
1995	Philadelphia e	N.L.	17	116	7	5	.583	114	26	96	3.57	0
1996	Clearwater	Fla. St.	2	14	2	0	1.000	17	1	9	1.29	0
1996	Scranton-W.B.	Int.	2	13	1	0	1.000	10	5	9	1.38	0
1996	Philadelphia f	N.L.	26	183⅓	9	10	.474	182	50	149	3.19	0
1997	Philadelphia	N.L.	35	254⅓	17	11	.607	*319	58	208	2.97	0
1998	Philadelphia	N.L.	35	*268⅔	15	14	.517	*300	61	236	3.25	0
1999	Philadelphia g	N.L.	24	180⅓	15	6	.714	152	44	159	3.54	0
2000	Clearwater	Fla.St.	4	20⅔	1	0	1.000	23	2	10	1.31	0
2000	Scranton-WB	Int.	1	5	0	0	.000	7	1	9	3.60	0
2000	Philadelphia-Arizona h-i	N.L.	29	210⅓	11	12	.478	168	45	204	3.81	0
2001	Arizona	N.L.	35	*256⅔	*22	6	*.786	293	39	237	2.98	0
2002	Arizona	N.L.	36	259⅓	23	7	.767	316	33	218	3.23	0
2003	Tucson	P.C.	2	10	1	0	1.000	15	3	10	4.50	0
2003	Arizona j-k	N.L.	24	168	8	9	.471	194	32	144	2.95	0
2004	Boston	A.L.	32	226⅔	*21	6	*.778	203	35	206	3.26	0
2005	Pawtucket	Int.	6	19	0	2	.000	21	3	27	6.63	0
2005	Boston l	A.L.	32	93⅓	8	8	.500	87	22	121	5.69	9
2006	Boston	A.L.	31	204	15	7	.682	183	28	220	3.97	0
2007	Pawtucket	Int.	3	15	0	0	.000	18	0	8	0.00	0
2007	Boston m-n	A.L.	24	151	9	8	.529	101	23	165	3.87	0
Major League Totals	20 Yrs.		569	3261	216	146	.597	3116	711	2998	3.46	22
Division Series												
2001	Arizona	N.L.	2	18	2	0	1.000	18	2	9	0.50	0
2002	Arizona	N.L.	1	7	0	0	.000	7	1	7	1.29	0
2004	Boston	A.L.	1	6⅔	1	0	1.000	4	2	9	2.70	0
2007	Boston	A.L.	1	7	1	0	1.000	4	1	6	0.00	0
Division Series Totals			5	38⅔	4	0	1.000	33	6	31	0.93	0
Championship Series												
1993	Philadelphia	N.L.	2	16	0	0	.000	19	5	11	1.69	0
2001	Arizona	N.L.	1	9	1	0	1.000	12	2	4	1.00	0

Year	Club	Lea	G	IP	W	L	Pct	SO	BB	H	ERA	SAVES
2004 Boston	A.L.		2	10	1	1	.500	5	2	10	6.30	0
2007 Boston	A.L.		2	11²/₃	1	0	1.000	8	0	15	5.40	0
Championship Series Totals			7	46²/₃	3	1	.750	*44	9	40	3.47	0
World Series Record												
1993 Philadelphia	N.L.		2	15¹/₃	1	1	.500	9	5	13	3.52	0
2001 Arizona	N.L.		3	21¹/₃	1	0	1.000	26	2	12	1.69	0
2004 Boston	A.L.		1	6	1	0	1.000	4	1	4	0.00	0
2007 Boston	A.L.		1	5¹/₃	1	0	1.000	4	2	4	1.69	0
World Series Totals			7	48	4	1	.800	43	10	33	2.06	0

a Traded by Boston Red Sox to Baltimore Orioles organization with outfielder Brady Anderson for pitcher Mike Boddicker, July 29, 1988.
b Traded to Houston Astros with pitcher Pete Harnisch and outfielder Steve Finley for first baseman Glenn Davis, January 10, 1991.
c Traded to Philadelphia Phillies for pitcher Jason Grimsley, April 2, 1992.
d On disabled list from May 17 to July 25, 1994.
e On disabled list from July 19 to October 2, 1995.
f On disabled list from April 1 to May 14, 1996.
g On disabled list from August 8 to September 3, 1999.
h On disabled list from March 25 to April 29, 2000.
i Traded to Arizona Diamondbacks for infielder Travis Lee, pitcher Omar Daal, pitcher Vicente Padilla and pitcher Nelson Figueroa, July 26, 2000.
j On disabled list from April 18 to May 3 and May 31 to July 12, 2003.
k Traded to Boston Red Sox for pitcher Casey Fossum, pitcher Brandon Lyon, pitcher Jorge DeRosa and outfielder Michael Goss, November 28, 2003.
l On disabled list from March 26 to April 13 and April 24 to July 13, 2005.
m On disabled list from June 19 to August 6, 2007.
n Filed for free agency, October 30, 2007, re-signed with Boston Red Sox, November 6, 2007.

SCHMIDT, JASON DAVID
Born, Lewiston, Idaho, January 29, 1973.
Bats Right. Throws Right. Height, 6 feet, 5 inches. Weight, 210 pounds.

Year	Club	Lea	G	IP	W	L	Pct	SO	BB	H	ERA	SAVES
1991 Braves	Gulf Coast		11	45¹/₃	3	4	.429	44	23	32	2.38	0
1992 Macon	So. Atl.		7	24²/₃	0	3	.000	33	19	31	4.01	0
1992 Pulaski	Appal.		11	58¹/₃	3	4	.429	56	31	55	4.01	0
1993 Durham	Carolina		22	116²/₃	7	11	.389	110	47	128	4.94	0
1994 Greenville	Southern		24	140²/₃	8	7	.533	131	54	135	3.65	0
1995 Richmond	Int.		19	116	8	6	.571	95	48	97	2.25	0
1995 Atlanta	N.L.		9	25	2	2	.500	19	18	27	5.76	0
1996 Greenville	Southern		1	2	0	0	.000	2	0	4	9.00	0
1996 Richmond	Int.		7	45²/₃	3	0	1.000	41	19	36	2.56	0
1996 Atlanta-Pittsburgh a-b	N.L.		19	96¹/₃	5	6	.455	74	53	108	5.70	0
1997 Pittsburgh	N.L.		32	187²/₃	10	9	.526	136	76	193	4.60	0
1998 Pittsburgh	N.L.		33	214¹/₃	11	14	.440	158	71	228	4.07	0
1999 Pittsburgh	N.L.		33	212²/₃	13	11	.542	148	85	219	4.19	0
2000 GC Pirates	Gulf Coast		1	4	0	0	.000	1	1	4	2.25	0
2000 Pittsburgh c	N.L.		11	63¹/₃	2	5	.286	51	41	71	5.40	0
2001 Altoona	Eastern		3	9¹/₃	0	1	.000	17	1	7	0.96	0
2001 Nashville	P.C.		1	7	1	0	1.000	6	0	4	0.00	0
2001 Pittsburgh-San Fran. d-e-f	N.L.		25	150¹/₃	13	7	.650	142	61	138	4.07	0
2002 Fresno	P.C.		2	12	2	0	1.000	12	2	11	3.00	0
2002 San Francisco g	N.L.		29	185¹/₃	13	8	.619	196	73	148	3.45	0
2003 San Francisco	N.L.		29	207²/₃	17	5	*.773	208	46	152	*2.34	0
2004 San Jose	California		1	5	1	0	1.000	7	1	2	0.00	0
2004 San Francisco h	N.L.		32	225	18	7	.720	251	77	165	3.20	0
2005 San Francisco i	N.L.		29	172	12	7	.632	165	85	160	4.40	0
2006 San Francisco j	N.L.		32	213¹/₃	11	9	.550	180	80	189	3.59	0
2007 Inland Empire.	Calif.		1	6	0	0	.000	7	1	2	0.00	0
2007 Los Angeles k	N.L.		6	25²/₃	1	4	.200	22	14	32	6.31	0
Major League Totals	13 Yrs.		319	1978²/₃	128	94	.577	1750	780	1830	3.94	0
Division Series												
2002 San Francisco	N.L.		1	5¹/₃	0	1	.000	5	4	3	6.75	0
2003 San Francisco	N.L.		1	9	1	0	1.000	5	0	3	0.00	0
Division Series Totals			2	14¹/₃	1	1	.500	10	4	6	2.51	0
Championship Series												
2002 San Francisco	N.L.		1	7²/₃	1	0	1.000	8	1	4	1.17	0
World Series Record												
2002 San Francisco	N.L.		2	10¹/₃	1	0	1.000	14	4	16	5.23	0

a Traded to Pittsburgh Pirates with infielder Ron Wright and outfielder Corey Pointer for pitcher Denny Neagle, August 29, 1996.
b On disabled list from July 15 to August 28, 1996.
c On disabled list from April 15 to May 1 and June 10 to November 17, 2000.
d On disabled list from March 22 to May 11, 2001.
e Traded to San Francisco Giants with outfielder John Vander Wal for outfielder Armando Rios and pitcher Ryan Vogelsong, July 30, 2001.
f Filed for free agency, November 5, 2001, re-signed with San Francisco Giants, December 14, 2001.
g On disabled list from March 21 to April 24, 2002.
h On disabled list from March 26 to April 16, 2004.
i On disabled list from May 8 to May 24, 2005.
j Filed for free agency October 29, 2006. Signed with Los Angeles Dodgers, December 8, 2006.
k On disabled list from April 15 to June 5 and June 17 to October 31, 2007.

SCHOENEWEIS, SCOTT DAVID
Born, Long Branch, New Jersey, October 2, 1973.
Bats Left. Throws Left. Height, 6 feet. Weight, 190 pounds.

Year	Club	Lea	G	IP	W	L	Pct	SO	BB	H	ERA	SAVES
1996	Lake Elsinore	California	14	93²/₃	8	3	.727	83	27	86	3.94	0
1997	Midland	Texas	20	113¹/₃	7	5	.583	94	39	145	5.96	0
1998	Vancouver	P.C.	27	180	11	8	.579	133	59	188	4.50	0
1999	Anaheim	A.L.	31	39¹/₃	1	1	.500	22	14	47	5.49	0
1999	Edmonton	P.C.	9	35¹/₃	2	4	.333	29	12	58	7.64	0
2000	Lake Elsinore	California	1	4²/₃	0	0	.000	3	3	3	1.93	0
2000	Edmonton	P.C.	1	7	0	0	.000	6	1	2	0.00	0
2000	Anaheim a	A.L.	27	170	7	10	.412	78	67	183	5.45	0
2001	Anaheim	A.L.	32	205¹/₃	10	11	.476	104	77	227	5.08	0
2002	Anaheim	A.L.	54	118	9	8	.529	65	49	119	4.88	1
2003	Anaheim-Chicago b	A.L.	59	64²/₃	3	2	.600	56	19	63	4.18	0
2004	Chicago c-d	A.L.	20	112²/₃	6	9	.400	69	49	129	5.59	0
2005	Toronto	A.L.	80	57	3	4	.429	43	25	54	3.32	1
2006	Toronto	A.L.	55	37¹/₃	2	2	.500	18	16	39	6.51	1
2006	Cincinnati e-f-g	N.L.	16	14¹/₃	2	0	1.000	11	8	9	0.63	3
2007	New York	N.L.	70	59	0	2	.000	41	28	62	5.03	2
Major League Totals		9 Yrs.	444	877²/₃	43	49	.467	507	352	932	5.01	8
Division Series												
2002	Anaheim	A.L.	3	0¹/₃	0	0	.000	0	0	2	27.00	0
Championship Series												
2002	Anaheim	A.L.	1	0²/₃	0	0	.000	0	0	0	0.00	0
World Series Record												
2002	Anaheim	A.L.	2	2	0	0	.000	2	1	1	0.00	0

a On disabled list from June 17 to July 25, 2000.
b Traded to Chicago White Sox with pitcher Doug Nickle for pitcher Gary Glover, pitcher Scott Dunn and pitcher Tim Bittner, July 29, 2003.
c On disabled list from June 22 to July 7 and from August 5 to September 30, 2004.
d Not offered contract, December 20, 2004. Signed with Toronto Blue Jays, January 11, 2005.
e Traded to Cincinnati Reds for player to be named later, August 16, 2006.
f Toronto Blue Jays received infielder Trevor Lawhorn to complete trade, October 13, 2006.
g Filed for free agency, October 31, 2006. Signed with New York Mets, January 16, 2007.

SCHRODER, CHRISTOPHER KEITH (CHRIS)
Born, Okarche, Oklahoma, August 20, 1978.
Bats Right. Throws Right. Height, 6 feet, 3 inches. Weight, 210 pounds.

Year	Club	Lea	G	IP	W	L	Pct	SO	BB	H	ERA	SAVES
2001	Jupiter	Fla.St.	10	15²/₃	1	0	1.000	20	4	12	2.30	0
2001	Vermont	N.Y.-Penn.	11	12	0	0	.000	18	5	8	1.50	2
2002	Brevard County	Fla.St.	23	29²/₃	2	2	.500	36	19	13	1.52	6
2002	Clinton	Midwest	22	27¹/₃	1	3	.250	42	14	15	1.65	10
2003	Harrisburg	Eastern	49	82¹/₃	9	2	.818	81	47	68	2.84	4
2004	Harrisburg	Eastern	32	48¹/₃	2	2	.500	51	17	39	2.42	11
2004	Edmonton	P.C.	17	26²/₃	2	1	.667	32	15	24	4.39	0
2005	Potomac	Carolina	5	7	0	0	.000	10	2	7	0.00	1
2005	Harrisburg	Eastern	16	23	2	3	.400	28	11	20	4.70	0
2005	Nationals	Gulf Coast	1	1	0	0	.000	3	0	2	9.00	0
2005	New Orleans	P.C.	19	23	2	0	1.000	29	15	21	7.83	1
2006	Harrisburg	Eastern	9	14¹/₃	2	0	1.000	13	6	18	5.02	1
2006	New Orleans	P.C.	28	47¹/₃	2	1	.667	60	16	25	1.52	1
2006	Washington	N.L.	21	28¹/₃	0	2	.000	39	15	23	6.35	0
2007	Columbus	Int.	26	33	2	2	.500	45	18	23	1.64	1

Year	Club	Lea	G	IP	W	L	Pct	SO	BB	H	ERA	SAVES
2007	Washington	N.L.	37	45^1/$_3$	2	3	.400	43	15	36	3.18	0
Major League Totals ....2 Yrs.			58	73^2/$_3$	2	5	.286	82	30	59	4.40	0

SEANEZ, RUDY CABALLERO
Born, Brawley, California, October 20, 1968.
Bats Right. Throws Right. Height, 5 feet, 11 inches. Weight, 200 pounds.

Year	Club	Lea	G	IP	W	L	Pct	SO	BB	H	ERA	SAVES
1986	Burlington	Appal.	13	76	5	2	.714	56	32	59	3.20	0
1987	Waterloo a	Midwest	10	34^2/$_3$	0	4	.000	23	23	35	6.75	0
1988	Waterloo	Midwest	22	113^1/$_3$	6	6	.500	93	68	98	4.69	0
1989	Kinston...........	Carolina	25	113	8	10	.444	149	111	94	4.14	0
1989	Colo Sprngs..........	P.C.	1	1	0	0	.000	0	0	1	0.00	0
1989	Cleveland	A.L.	5	5	0	0	.000	7	4	1	3.60	0
1990	Canton-Akrn.......	Eastern	15	16^2/$_3$	1	0	1.000	27	12	9	2.16	5
1990	Cleveland	A.L.	24	27^1/$_3$	2	1	.667	24	25	22	5.60	0
1990	Colo Sprngs..........	P.C.	12	12	1	4	.200	7	10	15	6.75	1
1991	Canton-Akrn.......	Eastern	25	38^1/$_3$	4	2	.667	73	30	17	2.58	7
1991	Colo Sprngs..........	P.C.	16	17^1/$_3$	0	0	.000	19	22	17	7.27	0
1991	Cleveland b-c..........	A.L.	5	5	0	0	.000	7	7	10	16.20	0
1992	Los Angeles d-e	N.L.			INJURED—Did Not Play							
1993	Central Val	California	5	8^1/$_3$	0	2	.000	7	11	9	9.72	0
1993	Colo Sprngs...........	P.C.	3	3	0	0	.000	5	1	3	9.00	0
1993	Las Vegas...........	P.C.	14	19^2/$_3$	0	1	.000	14	11	24	6.41	0
1993	San Diego f-g.........	N.L.	3	3^1/$_3$	0	0	.000	1	2	8	13.50	0
1994	Albuquerque..........	P.C.	20	22	2	1	.667	26	13	28	5.32	9
1994	Los Angeles h	N.L.	17	23^2/$_3$	1	1	.500	18	9	24	2.66	0
1995	San Berndno	California	4	6	2	0	1.000	5	3	2	0.00	1
1995	Los Angeles i	N.L.	37	34^2/$_3$	1	3	.250	29	18	39	6.75	3
1996	Albuquerque j.........	P.C.	20	19^1/$_3$	0	2	.000	20	11	27	6.52	6
1997	Omaha	A.A.	28	47	2	5	.286	46	25	53	6.51	0
1997	Norfolk k-l-m..........	Int.	9	13^1/$_3$	1	0	1.000	17	11	12	4.05	0
1998	Richmond	Int.	16	21	2	0	1.000	33	7	13	1.29	7
1998	Atlanta	N.L.	34	36	4	1	.800	50	16	25	2.75	2
1999	Atlanta n-o	N.L.	56	53^2/$_3$	6	1	.857	41	21	47	3.35	3
2000	Greenville.........	Southern	2	2	0	0	.000	3	0	2	0.00	0
2000	Atlanta p............	N.L.	23	21	2	4	.333	20	9	15	4.29	2
2001	Lake Elsinore	California	7	8^2/$_3$	2	0	1.000	8	2	7	2.08	0
2001	San Diego-Atlanta q-r-s-t	N.L.	38	36	0	2	.000	41	19	23	2.75	1
2002	Texas	A.L.	33	33	1	3	.250	40	24	28	5.73	0
2002	Oklahoma u-v-w.......	P.C.	4	4	0	0	.000	3	0	4	4.50	0
2003	Oklahoma............	P.C.	5	4^1/$_3$	0	1	.000	7	5	3	2.08	0
2003	Pawtucket	Int.	17	20^2/$_3$	2	2	.500	24	10	20	6.10	3
2003	Boston	A.L.	9	8^2/$_3$	0	1	.000	9	6	11	6.23	0
2003	Iowa x-y	P.C.	13	13	1	2	.333	13	9	12	3.46	2
2004	Omaha	P.C.	24	34^1/$_3$	2	1	.667	41	12	19	1.57	3
2004	Kansas City z	A.L.	16	23	0	1	.000	21	11	21	3.91	0
2004	Florida aa-bb	N.L.	23	23	3	1	.750	25	8	18	2.74	0
2005	Lake Elsinore	California	1	1	0	1	.000	0	1	3	36.00	0
2005	San Diego cc-dd........	N.L.	57	60^1/$_3$	7	1	.875	84	22	49	2.69	0
2006	Boston	A.L.	41	46^2/$_3$	2	1	.667	48	26	51	4.82	0
2006	San Diego ee-ff	N.L.	8	6^1/$_3$	1	2	.333	6	6	7	5.68	0
2007	Los Angeles gg	N.L.	73	76	6	3	.667	73	27	78	3.79	1
Major League Totals ....16 Yrs.			502	522^2/$_3$	36	26	.581	544	260	477	4.15	12

Division Series

Year	Club	Lea	G	IP	W	L	Pct	SO	BB	H	ERA	SAVES
1998	Atlanta	N.L.	1	1	0	0	.000	0	0	0	0.00	0
2001	Atlanta	N.L.	1	1	1	0	1.000	0	1	0	0.00	0
2005	San Diego	N.L.	2	3	0	0	.000	4	1	3	6.00	0
2006	San Diego	N.L.	1	1^2/$_3$	0	0	.000	2	0	0	0.00	0
Division Series Totals			5	6^2/$_3$	1	0	1.000	6	2	3	2.70	0

Championship Series

Year	Club	Lea	G	IP	W	L	Pct	SO	BB	H	ERA	SAVES
1998	Atlanta	N.L.	4	3	0	0	.000	4	1	2	6.00	0
2001	Atlanta	N.L.	2	2	0	0	.000	3	3	1	0.00	0
Championship Series Totals			6	5	0	0	.000	7	4	3	3.60	0

a On minor league disabled list from May 4 to July 11 and August 9 to August 29, 1987.
b On disabled list from April 1 to 16 and July 30 to September 2, 1991.
c Traded to Los Angeles Dodgers for pitcher Dennis Cook and pitcher Mike Christopher, December 10, 1991.
d On disabled list from March 29 to September 30, 1992.
e Traded to Colorado Rockies for infielder Jody Reed, November 17, 1992.

f   On disabled list from April 4 to July 16, 1993.
g   Filed for free agency, July 16, 1993, signed with San Diego Padres organization, July 22, 1993.
h   Released by San Diego Padres, November 18, 1993, signed with Los Angeles Dodgers, January 12, 1994.
i   On disabled list from May 28 to June 16, 1995.
j   On minor league disabled list from May 25 to August 30, 1996.
k   Filed for free agency October 15, 1996, signed with New York Mets organization, January 15, 1997.
l   Traded to Kansas City Royals for pitcher Mike Fyhrie, May 30, 1997.
m   Filed for free agency October 15 1997, signed with Atlanta Braves organization, December 15, 1997.
n   On disabled list from August 21 to November 1, 1999.
o   Filed for free agency, November 2, 1999, re-signed with Atlanta Braves, December 12, 1999.
p   On disabled list from March 23 to April 26 and June 14 to October 29, 2000.
q   Filed for free agency, October 30, 2000. Signed with San Diego Padres organization, Fenruary 14, 2001.
r   On minor league disabled list from April 5 to May 6, 2001.
s   On disabled list from June 6 to June 21, 2001.
t   Traded to Atlanta Braves for player to be named later, August 31, 2001. San Diego Padres received pitcher Winston Abreu to complete trade, September 6, 2001.
u   Filed for free agency, November 5, 2001. Signed with Texas Rangers organization, January 28, 2002.
v   On disabled list from May 30 to September 2, 2002.
w   Filed for free agency, October 28, 2002, re-signed with Texas Rangers organization, December 6, 2002.
x   Released by Texas Rangers, May 3, 2003. Signed with Boston Red Sox organization, May 9, 2003.
y   Released by Boston Red Sox, June 29, 2003. Signed with Chicago Cubs organization, August 2, 2003.
z   Filed for free agency, October 15, 2003. Signed with Kansas City Royals organization, February 12, 2004.
aa   Traded to Florida Marlins for outfielder Abraham Nunez, July 31, 2004.
bb   Filed for free agency, October 28, 2004. Signed with San Diego Padres, November 23, 2004.
cc   On disabled list from July 8 to August 12, 2005.
dd   Filed for free agency, October 27, 2005. Signed with Boston Red Sox, December 20, 2005.
ee   Released by Boston Red Sox, August 28, 2006. Signed with San Diego Padres, August 31, 2006.
ff   Filed for free agency, October 28, 2006. Signed with Los Angeles Dodgers organization, January 22, 2007.
gg   Filed for free agency, October 30, 2007.

SEAY, ROBERT MICHAEL (BOBBY)

Born, Sarasota, Florida, June 20, 1978.
Bats Left. Throws Left. Height, 6 feet, 2 inches. Weight, 235 pounds.

Year	Club	Lea	G	IP	W	L	Pct	SO	BB	H	ERA	SAVES
1997 Chston-SC	So.Atl.	13	61$\frac{1}{3}$	3	4	.429	64	37	56	4.55	0
1998 Chston-SC	So.Atl.	15	69	1	7	.125	74	29	59	4.30	0
1999 St. Petersburg	Fla.St.	12	57	2	6	.250	45	23	56	3.00	0
1999 Orlando	Southern	6	17	1	2	.333	16	15	22	7.94	0
2000 Orlando	Southern	24	132$\frac{1}{3}$	8	7	.533	106	53	132	3.88	0
2001 Orlando	Southern	15	64$\frac{2}{3}$	2	5	.286	49	26	81	5.98	0
2001 Tampa Bay	A.L.	12	13	1	1	.500	12	5	13	6.23	0
2002 Durham	Int.	10	15	0	0	.000	14	2	15	6.00	0
2002 Orlando a	Southern	15	35$\frac{2}{3}$	2	0	1.000	24	15	31	3.28	0
2003 Tampa Bay	A.L.	12	9	0	0	.000	5	6	7	3.00	0
2003 Durham b	Int.	25	30	3	0	1.000	29	15	23	2.10	0
2004 Durham	Int.	29	36$\frac{2}{3}$	2	1	.667	35	9	26	1.72	1
2004 Tampa Bay	A.L.	21	22$\frac{2}{3}$	0	0	.000	17	5	21	2.38	0
2005 Tulsa	Texas	4	5	1	0	1.000	3	0	3	1.80	1
2005 Colorado	N.L.	17	11$\frac{2}{3}$	0	0	.000	11	8	18	8.49	0
2005 Colorado Springs c-d-e	P.C.	17	22$\frac{2}{3}$	1	0	1.000	24	10	23	2.38	3
2006 Detroit	A.L.	14	15$\frac{1}{3}$	0	0	.000	12	9	14	6.46	0
2006 Toledo	Int.	24	24$\frac{2}{3}$	1	2	.333	14	6	25	4.74	0
2007 Detroit f	A.L.	58	46$\frac{1}{3}$	3	0	1.000	38	15	38	2.33	1
Major League Totals	6 Yrs.	134	118	4	1	.800	95	48	111	3.97	1

a   On disabled list from March 22 to June 3, 2002.
b   On disabled list from April 24 to June 3, 2003.
c   On disabled list from April 17 to June 5, 2005.
d   Traded to Colorado Rockies for outfielder Reggie Taylor, April 8, 2005.
e   Filed for free agency, October 3, 2005. Signed with Detroit Tigers organization, November 30, 2005.
f   Filed for free agency, October 2, 2006, re-signed with Detroit Tigers organization, January 9, 2007.

SHEETS, BEN M.

Born, Baton Rouge, Louisiana, July 18, 1978.
Bats Right. Throws Right. Height, 6 feet, 1 inch. Weight, 220 pounds.

Year	Club	Lea	G	IP	W	L	Pct	SO	BB	H	ERA	SAVES
1999 Stockton	California	5	27$\frac{2}{3}$	1	0	1.000	28	14	23	3.58	0
1999 Ogden	Pioneer	2	8	0	1	.000	12	2	8	5.63	0
2000 Indianapolis	Int.	14	81$\frac{2}{3}$	3	5	.375	59	31	77	2.87	0
2000 Huntsville	Southern	13	72	5	3	.625	60	25	55	1.88	0

Year	Club	Lea	G	IP	W	L	Pct	SO	BB	H	ERA	SAVES
2001	Indianapolis . . . . .Int.		2	10²/₃	1	1	.500	6	3	14	3.38	0
2001	Milwaukee a	N.L.	25	151¹/₃	11	10	.524	94	48	166	4.76	0
2002	Milwaukee . . . . , ...	N.L.	34	216²/₃	11	*16	.407	170	70	237	4.15	0
2003	Milwaukee	N.L.	34	220²/₃	11	13	.458	157	43	232	4.45	0
2004	Milwaukee	N.L.	34	237	12	14	.462	264	32	201	2.70	0
2005	Milwaukee b	N.L.	22	156²/₃	10	9	.526	141	25	142	3.33	0
2006	Brewers	Arizona	1	4¹/₃	0	0	.000	8	2	5	10.38	0
2006	Huntsville	Southern	1	2²/₃	0	0	.000	5	0	4	3.38	0
2006	Nashville	P.C.	3	15	2	1	.667	15	5	9	2.40	0
2006	Milwaukee c	N.L.	17	106	6	7	.462	116	11	105	3.82	0
2007	Milwaukee d	N.L.	24	141¹/₃	12	5	.706	106	37	138	3.82	0
Major League Totals . . . . .7 Yrs.			190	1229²/₃	73	74	.497	1048	266	1221	3.83	0

a On disabled list from August 6 to September 21, 2001.
b On disabled list from April 21 to May 28 and August 27 to October 10, 2005.
c On disabled list from March 24 to April 16 and May 3 to July 25, 2006.
d On disabled list from July 15 to August 29, 2007.

SHERRILL, GEORGE FRIEDERICH

Born, Memphis, Tennessee, April 19, 1977.
Bats Left. Throws Left. Height, 6 feet. Weight, 225 pounds.

Year	Club	Lea	G	IP	W	L	Pct	SO	BB	H	ERA	SAVES
1999	Evansville (Ind)	Frontier	22	40	2	4	.333	33	18	40	3.15	2
2000	Evansville (Ind)	Frontier	13	75¹/₃	3	5	.375	61	35	71	4.66	2
2001	Sioux Falls (Ind)	Northern	48	58²/₃	4	4	.500	45	14	53	2.45	2
2002	Winnipeg (Ind)	Northern	38	41	3	5	.375	61	13	35	3.07	2
2003	Winnipeg (Ind)	Northern	16	16	1	0	1.000	30	4	8	1.13	2
2003	San Antonio a	Texas	16	27¹/₃	3	0	1.000	31	12	19	0.33	0
2004	Tacoma	P.C.	36	50¹/₃	4	2	.667	62	9	42	2.32	13
2004	Seattle	A.L.	21	23²/₃	2	1	.667	16	9	24	3.80	0
2005	Mariners	Arizona	3	4	0	0	.000	5	0	0	0.00	0
2005	Tacoma	P.C.	22	23²/₃	1	3	.250	38	6	19	2.28	7
2005	Seattle	A.L.	29	19	4	3	.571	24	7	13	5.21	0
2006	Seattle	A.L.	72	40	2	4	.333	42	27	30	4.28	1
2007	Seattle	A.L.	73	45²/₃	2	0	1.000	56	17	28	2.36	3
Major League Totals . . . . .4 Yrs.			195	128¹/₃	10	8	.556	138	60	95	3.65	4

a Sold to Seattle Mariners, July 2, 2003.

SHIELDS, JAMES ANTHONY (JAMIE)

Born, Newhall, California, December 20, 1981.
Bats Right. Throws Right. Height, 6 feet, 4 inches. Weight, 215 pounds.

Year	Club	Lea	G	IP	W	L	Pct	SO	BB	H	ERA	SAVES
2001	Hudson Valley	N.Y.-Penn.	5	27¹/₃	2	1	.667	25	5	27	2.30	0
2001	Charleston-SC	So.Atl.	10	71¹/₃	4	5	.444	60	10	63	2.65	0
2002	Charleston-SC a			INJURED—Did Not Play								
2003	Bakersfield	Calif.	26	143²/₃	10	10	.500	119	38	161	4.45	1
2004	Bakersfield	Calif.	20	117	8	5	.615	92	33	119	4.23	0
2004	Montgomery	Southern	4	18¹/₃	0	3	.000	14	8	24	7.85	0
2005	Durham	Int.	1	6	1	0	1.000	6	3	9	6.00	0
2005	Montgomery	Southern	17	109¹/₃	7	5	.583	104	31	95	2.80	0
2006	Durham	Int.	10	61¹/₃	3	2	.600	64	6	60	2.64	0
2006	Tampa Bay	A.L.	21	124²/₃	6	8	.429	104	38	141	4.84	0
2007	Tampa Bay	A.L.	31	215	12	8	.600	184	36	202	3.85	0
Major League Totals . . . . .2 Yrs.			52	339²/₃	18	16	.529	288	74	343	4.21	0

a On minor league disabled list April 4 to September 10, 2002.

SHIELDS, ROBERT SCOT (SCOT)

Born, Fort Lauderdale, Florida, July 22, 1975.
Bats Right. Throws Right. Height, 6 feet, 1 inch. Weight, 170 pounds.

Year	Club	Lea	G	IP	W	L	Pct	SO	BB	H	ERA	SAVES
1997	Boise	Northwest	30	52	7	2	.778	61	24	45	2.94	2
1998	Cedar Rapids	Midwest	58	74	6	5	.545	81	29	62	3.65	7
1999	Lake Elsinore	California	24	107¹/₃	10	3	.769	113	39	91	2.52	1
1999	Erie	Eastern	10	74²/₃	4	4	.500	81	26	57	2.89	0
2000	Edmonton	P.C.	27	163	7	13	.350	156	82	158	5.41	0
2001	Salt Lake	P.C.	21	137²/₃	6	11	.353	104	31	141	4.97	0

Year	Club	Lea	G	IP	W	L	Pct	SO	BB	H	ERA	SAVES
2001 Anaheim	A.L.	8	11	0	0	.000	7	7	8	0.00	0
2002 Salt Lake	P.C.	28	47	2	2	.500	50	6	39	3.06	1
2002 Anaheim	A.L.	29	49	5	3	.625	30	21	31	2.20	0
2003 Anaheim	A.L.	44	148^{1}/$_{3}$	5	6	.455	111	38	138	2.85	1
2004 Anaheim	A.L.	60	105^{1}/$_{3}$	8	2	.800	109	40	97	3.33	4
2005 Los Angeles	A.L.	78	91^{2}/$_{3}$	10	11	.476	98	37	66	2.75	7
2006 Los Angeles	A.L.	74	87^{2}/$_{3}$	7	7	.500	84	24	70	2.87	2
2007 Los Angeles	A.L.	71	77	4	5	.444	77	33	62	3.86	2
Major League Totals ....7 Yrs.		364	570	39	34	.534	516	200	472	2.95	16
Division Series											
2004 Anaheim	A.L.	2	3	0	0	.000	3	2	5	6.00	0
2005 Los Angeles	A.L.	4	5	1	1	.500	5	3	4	3.60	0
2007 Los Angeles	A.L.	2	4	0	0	.000	4	4	0	2.25	0
Division Series Totals		8	12	1	1	.500	12	9	9	3.75	0
Championship Series											
2005 Los Angeles	A.L.	4	6	0	0	.000	5	1	4	0.00	0
World Series Record											
2002 Anaheim	A.L.	1	1^{2}/$_{3}$	0	0	.000	1	0	5	5.40	0

SHOUSE, BRIAN DOUGLAS

Born, Effingham, Illinois, September 26, 1968.
Bats Left. Throws Left. Height, 5 feet, 11 inches. Weight, 190 pounds.

Year	Club	Lea	G	IP	W	L	Pct	SO	BB	H	ERA	SAVES
1990 Welland	N.Y.-Penn.	17	39^{2}/$_{3}$	4	3	.571	39	7	50	5.22	2
1991 Augusta	So.Atl.	26	31	2	3	.400	32	9	22	3.19	8
1991 Salem	Carolina	17	33^{2}/$_{3}$	2	1	.667	25	15	35	2.94	3
1992 Carolina	Southern	59	77^{1}/$_{3}$	5	6	.455	79	28	71	2.44	4
1993 Pittsburgh	N.L.	6	4	0	0	.000	3	2	7	9.00	0
1993 Buffalo	A.A.	48	51^{2}/$_{3}$	1	0	1.000	25	17	54	3.83	2
1994 Buffalo	A.A.	43	52	3	4	.429	31	15	44	3.63	0
1995 Calgary	P.C.	8	39^{1}/$_{3}$	4	4	.500	17	7	62	6.18	0
1995 Carolina	Southern	21	114^{2}/$_{3}$	7	6	.538	76	19	126	4.47	0
1996 Calgary	P.C.	12	12^{2}/$_{3}$	1	0	1.000	12	4	22	10.66	0
1996 Rochester a	Int.	32	50	1	2	.333	45	16	53	4.50	2
1997 Rochester	Int.	54	71^{1}/$_{3}$	6	2	.750	81	21	48	2.27	9
1998 Kintetsu	Pacific	13	26	0	2	.000	20	13	40	0.00	0
1998 Boston	A.L.	7	8	0	1	.000	5	4	9	5.63	0
1998 Pawtucket b-c-d	Int.	22	31	2	0	1.000	25	7	21	2.90	6
1999 Tucson e-f	P.C.	30	44^{2}/$_{3}$	3	4	.429	32	18	63	6.25	0
2000 Norfolk	Int.	4	3^{1}/$_{3}$	0	1	.000	1	2	6	13.50	0
2000 Rochester g-h	Int.	43	57^{2}/$_{3}$	4	4	.500	52	14	63	2.81	2
2001 New Orleans i	P.C.	56	53	2	2	.500	56	15	51	2.89	1
2002 Kansas City	A.L.	23	14^{2}/$_{3}$	0	0	.000	11	9	15	6.14	0
2002 Omaha j	P.C.	5	2^{1}/$_{3}$	0	0	.000	2	1	7	11.57	0
2002 New Orleans k-l	P.C.	19	21	1	0	1.000	20	3	17	3.43	0
2003 Oklahoma	P.C.	6	7^{1}/$_{3}$	0	1	.000	2	3	8	3.68	1
2003 Texas	A.L.	62	61	0	1	.000	40	14	62	3.10	1
2004 Oklahoma	P.C.	9	7^{1}/$_{3}$	0	0	.000	3	4	12	6.14	0
2004 Texas m	A.L.	53	44^{1}/$_{3}$	2	0	1.000	34	18	36	2.23	0
2005 Texas	A.L.	64	53^{1}/$_{3}$	3	2	.600	35	18	55	5.23	0
2006 Frisco	Texas	2	2	0	0	.000	1	1	2	0.00	0
2006 Oklahoma	P.C.	5	5	0	1	.000	3	4	7	5.40	0
2006 Texas n-o	A.L.	6	4^{1}/$_{3}$	0	0	.000	3	1	6	4.15	0
2006 Milwaukee	N.L.	59	34	1	3	.250	20	17	34	3.97	2
2007 Milwaukee	N.L.	73	47^{2}/$_{3}$	1	1	.500	32	14	46	3.02	1
Major League Totals ....8 Yrs.		353	271^{1}/$_{3}$	7	8	.467	183	97	270	3.81	4

a Released by Pittsburgh Pirates, May 16, 1996. Signed with Baltimore Orioles organization, May 22, 1996.
b Filed for free agency October 17, 1997. Signed with Boston Red Sox organization, April 6, 1998.
c Sold to Kintetsu (Japan), June 25, 1998.
d Signed by Arizona Diamondbacks organization, November 11, 1998.
e On disabled list from September 18 to October 5, 1999.
f Filed for free agency, October 15, 1999. Signed with New York Mets organization, November 16, 1999.
g Released by New York Mets, April 14, 2000. Signed with Baltimore Orioles organization, May 13, 2000.
h Filed for free agency, October 15, 2000. Signed with Houston Astros organization, December 22, 2000.
i Filed for free agency, October 15, 2001. Signed with Kansas City Royals organization, December 8, 2001.
j On disabled list from April 28 to May 13, 2002.
k Released by Kansas City Royals, June 27, 2002. Signed with Houston Astros organization, July 16, 2002.
l Filed for free agency, October 15, 2002. Signed with Texas Rangers organization, November 13, 2002.

m On disabled list from March 27 to May 13, 2004.
n On disabled list from April 22 to May 8, 2006.
o Traded to Milwaukee Brewers for infielder Enrique Cruz and cash, May 13, 2006.

SILVA, CARLOS

Born, Bolivar, Venezuela, April 23, 1979.
Bats Right. Throws Right. Height, 6 feet, 4 inches. Weight, 245 pounds.

Year	Club	Lea	G	IP	W	L	Pct	SO	BB	H	ERA	SAVES
1996 Martinsvlle	Appal.	7	18	0	0	.000	16	5	20	4.00	0
1997 Martinsvlle	Appal.	11	57²/₃	2	2	.500	31	14	66	5.15	0
1998 Martinsvlle	Appal.	7	41	1	4	.200	21	4	48	5.05	0
1998 Batavia	N.Y.-Penn.	9	45¹/₃	2	3	.400	27	9	61	6.35	0
1999 Piedmont	So.Atl.	26	164¹/₃	11	8	.579	99	41	176	3.12	0
2000 Clearwater	Fla.St.	26	176¹/₃	8	13	.381	82	26	229	3.57	0
2001 Reading	Eastern	28	180	15	8	.652	100	27	197	3.90	0
2002 Reading	Eastern	2	3	0	0	.000	1	0	0	0.00	1
2002 Philadelphia a	N.L.	68	84	5	0	1.000	41	22	88	3.21	1
2003 Philadelphia b	N.L.	62	87¹/₃	3	1	.750	48	37	92	4.43	1
2004 Minnesota	A.L.	33	203	14	8	.636	76	35	255	4.21	0
2005 Minnesota c	A.L.	27	188¹/₃	9	8	.529	71	9	212	3.44	0
2006 Minnesota	A.L.	36	180¹/₃	11	15	.423	70	32	246	5.94	0
2007 Minnesota	A.L.	33	202	13	14	.481	89	36	229	4.19	0
Major League Totals	6 Yrs.	259	945	55	46	.545	395	171	1122	4.31	2
Division Series											
2004 Minnesota	A.L.	1	5	0	1	.000	1	0	10	10.80	0

a On disabled list from May 27 to June 14, 2002.
b Traded to Minnesota Twins with infielder Nick Punto and player to be named later for pitcher Eric Milton, December 3, 2003.
c On disabled list from April 7 to April 22, 2005.

SLATEN, DOUGLAS (DOUG)

Born, Venice, California, February 4, 1980.
Bats Left. Throws Left. Height, 6 feet, 5 inches. Weight, 200 pounds.

Year	Club	Lea	G	IP	W	L	Pct	SO	BB	H	ERA	SAVES
2000 Diamondbacks	Arizona	9	9¹/₃	0	0	.000	7	3	7	0.96	0
2001 Lancaster	Calif.	28	157²/₃	9	8	.529	110	45	207	4.79	0
2002 Lancaster	Calif.	8	35	1	6	.143	23	12	59	9.00	0
2002 South Bend	Midwest	7	14¹/₃	0	0	.000	5	4	18	4.40	0
2003 Lancaster	Calif.	32	119¹/₃	6	7	.462	78	47	156	6.03	0
2004 South Bend	Midwest	36	44	5	2	.714	40	13	44	2.25	5
2004 El Paso	Texas	11	9	0	1	.000	6	10	16	10.00	0
2005 Tennessee	Southern	58	61¹/₃	2	2	.500	72	26	61	4.26	1
2006 Tennessee	Southern	40	43	2	3	.400	59	15	31	1.88	8
2006 Tucson	P.C.	18	20	2	1	.667	21	7	10	0.45	2
2006 Arizona	N.L.	9	5²/₃	0	0	.000	3	2	3	0.00	0
2007 Arizona	N.L.	61	36¹/₃	3	2	.600	28	14	41	2.72	0
Major League Totals	2 Yrs.	70	42	3	2	.600	31	16	44	2.36	0
Championship Series											
2007 Arizona	N.L.	3	1¹/₃	0	0	.000	1	2	1	0.00	0

SLOWEY, KEVIN MICHAEL

Born, Conroe, Texas, May 4, 1984.
Bats Right. Throws Right. Height, 6 feet, 3 inches. Weight, 195 pounds.

Year	Club	Lea	G	IP	W	L	Pct	SO	BB	H	ERA	SAVES
2005 Elizabethton	Appal.	4	7²/₃	0	0	.000	15	0	2	1.17	1
2006 New Britain	Eastern	9	59¹/₃	4	3	.571	52	13	50	3.19	0
2006 Fort Myers	Fla.St.	14	89¹/₃	4	2	.667	99	9	52	1.01	0
2007 Rochester	Int.	20	133²/₃	10	5	.667	107	18	110	1.89	0
2007 Minnesota	A.L.	13	66²/₃	4	1	.800	47	11	82	4.72	0

SMITH, JOSEPH MICHAEL (JOE)

Born, Cincinnati, Ohio, March 22, 1984.
Bats Right. Throws Right. Height, 6 feet, 2 inches. Weight, 215 pounds.

Year	Club	Lea	G	IP	W	L	Pct	SO	BB	H	ERA	SAVES
2006 Binghamton	Eastern	10	12²/₃	0	2	.000	12	11	12	5.68	0
2006 Brooklyn	N.Y.-Penn.	17	20	0	1	.000	28	3	10	0.45	9

Year	Club	Lea	G	IP	W	L	Pct	SO	BB	H	ERA	SAVES
2007 New Orleans	P.C.	8	9	0	0	.000	5	4	7	2.00	2	
2007 New York	N.L.	54	44¹/₃	3	2	.600	45	21	48	3.45	0	

SMOLTZ, JOHN ANDREW
Born, Detroit, Michigan, May 15, 1967.
Bats Right. Throws Right. Height, 6 feet, 3 inches. Weight, 220 pounds.

Year	Club	Lea	G	IP	W	L	Pct	SO	BB	H	ERA	SAVES
1986 Lakeland	Fla. St.	17	96	7	8	.467	47	31	86	3.56	0
1987 Glens Falls a	Eastern	21	130	4	10	.286	86	81	131	5.68	0
1987 Richmond	Int.	3	16	0	1	.000	5	11	17	6.19	0
1988 Richmond	Int.	20	135¹/₃	10	5	.667	115	37	118	2.79	0
1988 Atlanta	N.L.	12	64	2	7	.222	37	33	74	5.48	0
1989 Atlanta	N.L.	29	208	12	11	.522	168	72	160	2.94	0
1990 Atlanta b	N.L.	34	231¹/₃	14	11	.560	170	*90	206	3.85	0
1991 Atlanta c	N.L.	36	229²/₃	14	13	.519	148	77	206	3.80	0
1992 Atlanta d	N.L.	35	246²/₃	15	12	.556	*215	80	206	2.85	0
1993 Atlanta	N.L.	35	243²/₃	15	11	.577	208	100	208	3.62	0
1994 Atlanta e	N.L.	21	134²/₃	6	10	.375	113	48	120	4.14	0
1995 Atlanta f	N.L.	29	192²/₃	12	7	.632	193	72	166	3.18	0
1996 Atlanta g-h	N.L.	35	*253²/₃	*24	8	*.750	*276	55	199	2.94	0
1997 Atlanta	N.L.	35	*256	15	12	.556	241	63	*234	3.02	0
1998 Greenville	Southern	3	14	0	1	.000	16	3	11	2.57	0
1998 Macon	So.Atl.	2	10	0	0	.000	14	1	7	3.60	0
1998 Atlanta i	N.L.	26	167²/₃	17	3	*.850	173	44	145	2.90	0
1999 Greenville	Southern	2	4	0	0	.000	7	1	5	4.50	0
1999 Atlanta j	N.L.	29	186¹/₃	11	8	.579	156	40	168	3.19	0
2000 Atlanta k	N.L.			INJURED—Did Not Play							
2001 Macon	So.Atl.	1	5	0	0	.000	5	0	4	1.80	0
2001 Greenville	Southern	3	6	0	0	.000	6	0	3	0.00	0
2001 Atlanta l-m	N.L.	36	59	3	3	.500	57	10	53	3.36	10
2002 Atlanta	N.L.	75	80¹/₃	3	2	.600	85	24	59	3.25	*55
2003 Atlanta n	N.L.	62	64¹/₃	0	2	.000	73	8	48	1.12	45
2004 Atlanta	N.L.	73	81²/₃	0	1	.000	85	13	75	2.76	44
2005 Atlanta	N.L.	33	229²/₃	14	7	.667	169	53	210	3.06	0
2006 Atlanta	N.L.	35	232	*16	9	.640	211	55	221	3.49	0
2007 Atlanta o	N.L.	32	205²/₃	14	8	.636	197	47	196	3.11	0
Major League Totals 19 Yrs.		702	3367	207	145	.588	2975	984	2954	3.26	154
Division Series											
1995 Atlanta	N.L.	1	5²/₃	0	0	.000	6	1	5	7.94	0
1996 Atlanta	N.L.	1	9	1	0	1.000	7	2	4	1.00	0
1997 Atlanta	N.L.	1	9	1	0	1.000	11	1	3	1.00	0
1998 Atlanta	N.L.	1	7²/₃	1	0	1.000	6	0	5	1.17	0
1999 Atlanta	N.L.	1	7	1	0	1.000	3	3	6	5.14	0
2001 Atlanta	N.L.	3	4	0	0	.000	3	0	3	2.25	2
2002 Atlanta	N.L.	2	3¹/₃	0	0	.000	7	2	2	2.70	0
2003 Atlanta	N.L.	2	3	1	0	1.000	1	0	4	6.00	1
2004 Atlanta	N.L.	2	5	1	0	1.000	4	2	4	0.00	0
2005 Atlanta	N.L.	1	7	1	0	1.000	5	1	7	1.29	0
Division Series Totals		15	60²/₃	7	0	1.000	53	12	43	2.52	3
Championship Series											
1991 Atlanta	N.L.	2	15¹/₃	2	0	1.000	15	3	14	1.76	0
1992 Atlanta	N.L.	3	20¹/₃	2	0	1.000	19	10	14	2.66	0
1993 Atlanta	N.L.	1	6¹/₃	0	1	.000	10	5	8	0.00	0
1995 Atlanta	N.L.	1	7	0	0	.000	2	2	7	2.57	0
1996 Atlanta e	N.L.	2	15	2	0	1.000	12	3	12	1.20	0
1997 Atlanta	N.L.	1	6	0	1	.000	9	5	5	7.50	0
1998 Atlanta	N.L.	2	13²/₃	0	0	.000	13	6	13	3.95	0
1999 Atlanta	N.L.	3	8²/₃	0	0	.000	8	0	8	6.23	1
2001 Atlanta	N.L.	2	3	0	0	.000	1	0	0	0.00	0
Championship Series Totals		17	95¹/₃	6	2	.750	89	34	81	2.83	1
World Series Record											
1991 Atlanta	N.L.	2	14¹/₃	0	0	.000	11	1	13	1.26	0
1992 Atlanta	N.L.	2	13¹/₃	1	0	1.000	12	7	13	2.70	0
1995 Atlanta	N.L.	1	2¹/₃	0	0	.000	4	2	6	15.43	0
1996 Atlanta	N.L.	2	14	1	1	.500	14	8	6	0.64	0
1999 Atlanta	N.L.	1	7	0	1	.000	11	3	6	3.86	0
World Series Totals		8	51	2	2	.500	52	21	44	2.47	0

a Traded by Detroit Tigers to Atlanta Braves organization for pitcher Doyle Alexander, August 12, 1987.
b Appeared in four additional games as pinch runner.

c Appeared in two additional games as pinch runner.
d Appeared in one additional game as pinch hitter.
e Suspended eight games by National League for May 14 hitting batter with pitch, June 20 to June 28, 1994.
f Selected Cy Young Award Winner in National League for 1996.
g Filed for free agency, October 31, 1996.
h Re-signed with Atlanta Braves, November 20, 1996.
i On disabled list from March 31 to April 15 and May 24 to June 20, 1998.
j On disabled list from May 17 to June 1 and July 5 to July 24, 1999.
k On disabled list from April 2 to October 30, 2000.
l On disabled list from March 23 to May 17 and June 10 to July 22, 2001.
m Filed for free agency, November 5, 2001, re-signed with Atlanta Braves, December 2, 2001.
n On disabled list from August 24 to September 20, 2003.
o On disabled list from July 3 to July 18, 2007.

SNELL, IAN DANTE

Born, Dover, Delaware, October 30, 1981.
Bats Right. Throws Right. Height, 5 feet, 11 inches. Weight, 190 pounds.

Year	Club	Lea	G	IP	W	L	Pct	SO	BB	H	ERA	SAVES
2000 Pirates	Gulf Coast		4	7²/₃	1	0	1.000	8	1	5	2.35	0
2001 Pirates	Gulf Coast		3	19	3	0	1.000	13	5	12	0.47	0
2001 Williamsport	N.Y.-Penn.		10	64²/₃	7	0	1.000	56	10	55	1.39	0
2002 Hickory	So.Atl.		24	139²/₃	11	6	.647	149	45	127	2.71	0
2003 Lynchburg	Carolina		20	116¹/₃	10	3	.769	122	33	105	3.33	0
2003 Altoona	Eastern		6	36²/₃	4	0	1.000	23	10	36	1.96	0
2004 Altoona	Eastern		26	151	11	7	.611	142	40	147	3.16	0
2004 Pittsburgh	N.L.		3	12	0	1	.000	9	9	14	7.50	0
2005 Pittsburgh	N.L.		15	42	1	2	.333	34	24	43	5.14	0
2005 Indianapolis	Int.		18	112	11	3	.786	104	23	90	3.70	0
2006 Pittsburgh	N.L.		32	186	14	11	.560	169	74	198	4.74	0
2007 Pittsburgh	N.L.		32	208	9	12	.429	177	68	209	3.76	0
Major League Totals	4 Yrs.		82	448	24	26	.480	389	175	464	4.40	0

SNYDER, KYLE EHREN

Born, Houston, Texas, September 9, 1977.
Bats Both. Throws Right. Height, 6 feet, 8 inches. Weight, 215 pounds.

Year	Club	Lea	G	IP	W	L	Pct	SO	BB	H	ERA	SAVES
1999 Spokane	Northwest		7	24	1	0	1.000	25	7	20	4.13	0
2000 Wilmington	Carolina		1	0	0	0	.000	0	1	0	0.00	0
2000 Royals	Gulf Coast		1	2	0	0	.000	4	0	1	0.00	0
2001				INJURED—Did Not Play								
2002 Wilmington	Carolina		15	48¹/₃	0	2	.000	48	11	49	2.98	0
2002 Wichita	Texas		5	25²/₃	2	2	.500	18	7	21	4.21	0
2003 Omaha	P.C.		5	29	3	0	1.000	15	6	28	2.79	0
2003 Kansas City	A.L.		15	85¹/₃	1	6	.143	39	21	94	5.17	0
2003 Royals 1	Arizona		1	2	0	0	.000	1	0	3	4.50	0
2003 Wichita a	Texas		1	5	0	0	.000	2	0	2	0.00	0
2004 Kansas City b	A.L.			INJURED—Did Not Play								
2005 Wichita	Texas		1	5	1	0	1.000	1	1	5	5.40	0
2005 Omaha	P.C.		15	66	2	3	.400	48	22	61	3.55	0
2005 Kansas City c	A.L.		13	36	1	3	.250	19	10	55	6.75	0
2006 Omaha	P.C.		10	60¹/₃	0	4	.000	43	9	63	3.88	1
2006 Pawtucket	Int.		3	20¹/₃	1	1	.500	7	2	24	3.54	0
2006 Kansas City-Boston d	A.L.		17	60¹/₃	4	5	.444	57	20	87	6.56	0
2007 Boston	A.L.		46	54¹/₃	2	3	.400	41	32	45	3.81	0
Major League Totals	4 Yrs.		91	236	8	17	.320	156	83	281	5.45	0

a On disabled list from July 1 to July 21 and from August 6 to November 7, 2003.
b On disabled list from March 26 to November 1, 2004.
c On disabled list from May 10 to July 13, 2005.
d Claimed on waivers by Boston Red Sox, June 16, 2006.

SONNANSTINE, ANDREW MICHAEL (ANDY)

Born, Barberton, Ohio, March 18, 1983.
Bats Left. Throws Right. Height, 6 feet, 3 inches. Weight, 185 pounds.

Year	Club	Lea	G	IP	W	L	Pct	SO	BB	H	ERA	SAVES
2004 Hudson Valley	N.Y.-Penn.		9	27	3	1	.750	24	3	18	1.00	1
2004 Charleston	So.Atl.		8	30²/₃	2	0	1.000	42	7	18	0.59	0

Year	Club	Lea	G	IP	W	L	Pct	SO	BB	H	ERA	SAVES
2005 Visalia	Calif.	10	64	4	1	.800	75	7	71	3.80	0
2005 Southwest	Midwest	18	116²/₃	10	4	.714	103	11	103	2.55	0
2006 Montgomery	Southern	28	185²/₃	15	8	.652	153	34	151	2.67	0
2007 Durham	Int.	11	71	6	4	.600	66	13	60	2.66	0
2007 Tampa Bay	A.L.	22	130²/₃	6	10	.375	97	26	151	5.85	0

SORIA, JOAKIM AGUSTIN (RAMOS)
Born, Monclova, Mexico, May 18, 1984.
Bats Right. Throws Right. Height, 6 feet, 3 inches. Weight, 185 pounds.

Year	Club	Lea	G	IP	W	L	Pct	SO	BB	H	ERA	SAVES
2002 Dodgers	Gulf Coast	4	5	0	0	.000	6	0	6	3.60	0
2003				INJURED—Did Not Play							
2004 Dodgers	Dominican	4	5¹/₃	0	0	.000	4	5	3	1.69	1
2005 Mexico City a	Mexican	30	66¹/₃	5	0	1.000	60	31	75	4.48	0
2006 Mexico City	Mexican	39	37	0	0	.000	30	11	37	3.89	15
2006 Fort Wayne b	Midwest	7	11²/₃	1	0	1.000	11	2	5	2.31	0
2007 Kansas City c	A.L.	62	69	2	3	.400	75	19	46	2.48	17

a Released by Los Angeles Dodgers, October 12, 2004. Signed with San Diego Padres organization, December 20, 2005.

b Selected by Kansas City Royals from San Diego Padres in Rule V draft, December 7, 2006.

c On disabled list from May 23 to June 7, 2007.

SORIANO, RAFAEL
Born, San Jose, Dominican Republic, December 19, 1979.
Bats Right. Throws Right. Height, 6 feet, 1 inch. Weight, 220 pounds.

Year	Club	Lea	G	IP	W	L	Pct	SO	BB	H	ERA	SAVES
1999 Everett	Northwest	14	75¹/₃	5	4	.556	83	49	56	3.11	0
2000 Wisconsin	Midwest	21	122¹/₃	8	4	.667	90	50	97	2.87	0
2001 San Bernardino	Calif.	15	89	6	3	.667	98	39	49	2.53	0
2001 San Antonio	Texas	8	48¹/₃	2	2	.500	53	14	34	3.35	0
2002 San Antonio	Texas	10	46²/₃	2	3	.400	52	15	32	2.31	0
2002 Seattle a	A.L.	10	47¹/₃	0	3	.000	32	16	45	4.56	1
2003 Tacoma	P.C.	11	62	4	3	.571	63	12	43	3.19	0
2003 Seattle	A.L.	40	53	3	0	1.000	68	12	30	1.53	1
2004 Seattle	A.L.	6	3¹/₃	0	3	.000	3	3	9	13.50	0
2004 Inland Empire	Calif.	2	8	0	0	.000	9	1	7	2.25	0
2004 San Antonio	Texas	2	8	1	0	1.000	10	0	4	1.13	0
2004 Tacoma b	P.C.	3	3²/₃	0	0	.000	5	2	2	2.45	0
2005 Inland Empire	Calif.	3	4	0	0	.000	5	0	2	0.00	0
2005 San Antonio	Texas	1	1	0	0	.000	0	0	0	0.00	0
2005 Everett	Northwest	4	6	0	0	.000	8	2	6	3.00	0
2005 Tacoma	P.C.	5	5¹/₃	1	0	1.000	11	1	3	0.00	0
2005 Seattle c	A.L.	7	7¹/₃	0	0	.000	9	1	6	2.45	0
2006 Seattle d-e	A.L.	53	60	1	2	.333	65	21	44	2.25	2
2007 Atlanta	N.L.	71	72	3	3	.500	70	15	47	3.00	9

Major League Totals .... 6 Yrs. 187 243 7 11 .389 247 68 181 2.93 13

a On disabled list from July 3 to August 2, 2002.

b On disabled list from May 10 to November 1, 2004.

c On disabled list from April 1 to September 5, 2005.

d On disabled list from July 20 to August 4, 2006.

e Traded to Atlanta Braves for pitcher Horacio Ramirez, December 7, 2006.

SOSA, JORGE BOLIVAR
Born, Santo Domingo, Dominican Republic, April 28, 1978.
Bats Both. Throws Right. Height, 6 feet, 2 inches. Weight, 175 pounds.

Year	Club	Lea	G	IP	W	L	Pct	SO	BB	H	ERA	SAVES
2001 Everett	Northwest	21	58²/₃	3	1	.750	57	19	45	1.69	7
2001 Wisconsin a-b-c	Midwest	2	2	0	0	.000	4	0	3	9.00	0
2002 Orlando	Southern	2	7	0	0	.000	3	1	4	0.00	0
2002 Tampa Bay d	A.L.	31	99¹/₃	2	7	.222	48	54	88	5.53	0
2003 Durham	Int.	4	24²/₃	1	1	.500	17	9	32	5.47	0
2003 Tampa Bay	A.L.	29	128²/₃	5	12	.294	72	60	137	4.62	0
2004 Durham	Int.	3	13	1	2	.333	23	0	11	2.77	0
2004 Tampa Bay	A.L.	43	99¹/₃	4	7	.364	94	54	100	5.53	1
2005 Atlanta e	N.L.	44	134	13	3	.813	85	64	122	2.55	0
2006 Atlanta-St. Louis f-g	N.L.	45	118	3	11	.214	75	40	138	5.42	4

Year	Club	Lea	G	IP	W	L	Pct	SO	BB	H	ERA	SAVES
2007 New Orleans..........	P.C.	5	32	4	0	1.000	29	4	29	1.13	0	
2007 New York h............	N.L.	42	112^{2}/$_{3}$	9	8	.529	69	41	109	4.47	0	
Major League Totals ....6 Yrs.		234	692	36	48	.429	443	313	694	4.59	5	
Division Series												
2005 Atlanta	N.L.	1	6	0	1	.000	3	2	7	4.50	0	

a Played infield and outfield in Colorado Rockies organization from 1995 through 2000.
b Selected by Seattle Mariners from Colorado Rockies in Rule V draft, December 11, 2000.
c Selected by Tampa Bay Devil Rays in Rule V draft, December 13, 2001.
d On disabled list from May 26 to June 25, 2002.
e Traded to Atlanta Braves for infielder Nick Green, March 31, 2005.
f Traded to St. Louis Cardinals for pitcher Rich Scalamandre, July 31, 2006.
g Not offered contract, December 12, 2006. Signed with New York Mets, January 16, 2007.
h On disabled list from July 1 to July 16, 2007.

SPEIER, JUSTIN JAMES

Born, Daly City, California, November 6, 1973.
Bats Right. Throws Right. Height, 6 feet, 4 inches. Weight, 205 pounds.

Year	Club	Lea	G	IP	W	L	Pct	SO	BB	H	ERA	SAVES
1995 Williamsport......	N.Y.-Penn.	30	36^{1}/$_{3}$	2	1	.667	39	4	27	1.49	12
1996 Daytona	Fla.St.	33	38^{1}/$_{3}$	2	4	.333	34	19	32	3.76	13
1996 Orlando	Southern	24	26^{1}/$_{3}$	4	1	.800	14	5	23	2.05	6
1997 Orlando	Southern	50	78^{1}/$_{3}$	6	5	.545	63	23	77	4.48	6
1997 Iowa.................	A.A.	8	12^{1}/$_{3}$	2	0	1.000	9	1	5	0.00	1
1998 Iowa.................	P.C.	45	51^{2}/$_{3}$	3	3	.500	49	19	52	5.05	12
1998 Chicago-Florida a.......	N.L.	19	20^{2}/$_{3}$	0	3	.000	17	13	27	8.71	0
1999 Richmond.............	Int.	27	41^{2}/$_{3}$	2	4	.333	39	22	51	5.62	3
1999 Atlanta b-c	N.L.	19	28^{2}/$_{3}$	0	0	.000	22	13	28	5.65	0
2000 Buffalo...............	Int.	13	13	0	0	.000	12	3	13	4.15	9
2000 Cleveland	A.L.	47	68^{1}/$_{3}$	5	2	.714	69	28	57	3.29	0
2001 Cleveland	A.L.	12	20^{2}/$_{3}$	2	0	1.000	15	8	24	6.97	0
2001 Colo Sprngs..........	P.C.	11	12^{1}/$_{3}$	1	0	1.000	16	7	10	1.46	2
2001 Colorado d-e-f	N.L.	42	56	4	3	.571	47	12	47	3.70	0
2002 Colorado Springs.......	P.C.	12	14	2	0	1.000	14	3	20	3.86	2
2002 Colorado g............	N.L.	63	62^{1}/$_{3}$	5	1	.833	47	19	51	4.33	1
2003 Colorado h............	N.L.	72	73^{1}/$_{3}$	3	1	.750	66	23	73	4.05	9
2004 Dunedin	Fla.St.	2	2	0	0	.000	2	0	3	4.50	0
2004 Toronto i..............	A.L.	62	69	3	8	.273	52	25	61	3.91	7
2005 Toronto..............	A.L.	65	66^{2}/$_{3}$	3	2	.600	56	15	48	2.57	0
2006 Toronto j-k............	A.L.	58	51^{1}/$_{3}$	2	0	1.000	55	21	47	2.98	0
2007 Azl Angels	Arizona	2	3	0	0	.000	3	0	1	0.00	0
2007 Rancho Cucamonga....	Calif.	8	9	1	0	1.000	7	5	10	3.00	0
2007 Los Angeles l..........	A.L.	51	50	2	3	.400	47	12	36	2.88	0
Major League Totals ....10 Yrs.		510	567	29	23	.558	493	189	499	3.92	17
Division Series												
2007 Los Angeles...........	A.L.	2	1^{2}/$_{3}$	0	1	.000	0	1	4	27.00	0

a Traded to Florida Marlins with infielder Kevin Orie and pitcher Todd Noel for pitcher Felix Heredia and infielder Steve Hoff, July 31, 1998.
b Traded to Atlanta Braves for player to be named later, April 1, 1999. Atlanta Braves received pitcher Matt Targac to complete trade, June 11, 1999.
c Claimed on waivers by Cleveland Indians, November 23, 1999.
d Traded to New York Mets for player to be named later, May 19, 2001.
e Cleveland Indians received pitcher Brian Jenkins to complete trade, May 21, 2001.
f Claimed on waivers by Colorado Rockies, May 29, 2001.
g On disabled list from March 31 to May 6, 2002.
h Traded to Toronto Blue Jays for pitcher Joe Kennedy and player to be named later, December 14, 2003. Colorado Rockies received pitcher Sandy Nin to complete trade, December 15, 2003.
i On disabled list from May 11 to June 8, 2004.
j On disabled list from August 9 to September 10, 2006.
k Filed for free agency, October 28, 2006. Signed with Los Angeles Angels, November 19, 2006.
l On disabled list from May 1 to July 13, 2007.

SPRINGER, RUSSELL PAUL (RUSS)

Born, Alexandria, Louisiana, November 7, 1968.
Bats Right. Throws Right. Height, 6 feet, 4 inches. Weight, 215 pounds.

Year	Club	Lea	G	IP	W	L	Pct	SO	BB	H	ERA	SAVES
1989 Yankees	Gulf Coast	6	24	3	0	1.000	34	10	14	1.50	0
1990 Yankees	Gulf Coast	4	15	0	2	.000	17	4	10	1.20	0

329

Year	Club	Lea	G	IP	W	L	Pct	SO	BB	H	ERA	SAVES
1990	Greensboro	So.Atl.	10	56$^{1}/_{3}$	2	3	.400	51	31	51	3.67	0
1991	Ft.Lauderdale	Fla.St.	25	152$^{1}/_{3}$	5	9	.357	139	62	118	3.49	0
1991	Albany	Eastern	2	15	1	0	1.000	16	6	9	1.80	0
1992	Columbus	Int.	20	123$^{2}/_{3}$	8	5	.615	95	54	89	2.69	0
1992	New York a	A.L.	14	16	0	0	.000	12	10	18	6.19	0
1993	Vancouver	P.C.	11	59	5	4	.556	40	33	58	4.27	0
1993	California	A.L.	14	60	1	6	.143	31	32	73	7.20	0
1994	Vancouver	P.C.	12	83	7	4	.636	58	19	77	3.04	0
1994	California	A.L.	18	45$^{2}/_{3}$	2	2	.500	28	14	53	5.52	2
1995	California	A.L.	19	51$^{2}/_{3}$	1	2	.333	38	25	60	6.10	1
1995	Vancouver	P.C.	6	34	2	0	1.000	23	23	24	3.44	0
1995	Philadelphia b-c	N.L.	14	26$^{2}/_{3}$	0	0	.000	32	10	22	3.71	0
1996	Philadelphia	N.L.	51	96$^{2}/_{3}$	3	10	.231	94	38	106	4.66	0
1997	Jackson	Texas	1	1	0	0	.000	2	0	2	9.00	0
1997	Houston d-e	N.L.	54	55$^{1}/_{3}$	3	3	.500	74	27	48	4.23	3
1998	Arizona-Atlanta f-g	N.L.	48	52$^{2}/_{3}$	5	4	.556	56	30	51	4.10	0
1999	Richmond	Int.	11	15$^{1}/_{3}$	1	0	1.000	13	1	9	1.17	2
1999	Atlanta h-i	N.L.	49	47$^{1}/_{3}$	2	1	.667	49	22	31	3.42	1
2000	Arizona	N.L.	52	62	2	4	.333	59	34	63	5.08	0
2001	Arizona	N.L.	18	17$^{2}/_{3}$	0	0	.000	12	4	20	7.13	1
2001	Tucson j	P.C.	7	7$^{1}/_{3}$	0	0	.000	6	3	7	4.91	0
2002							Did Not Play					
2003	St. Louis	N.L.	17	17$^{1}/_{3}$	1	1	.500	11	6	19	8.31	0
2003	Memphis k-l	P.C.	7	6$^{1}/_{3}$	0	0	.000	5	4	2	1.42	0
2004	New Orleans	P.C.	26	31	1	2	.333	33	14	31	3.48	6
2004	Houston m-n	N.L.	16	13$^{2}/_{3}$	0	1	.000	9	6	15	2.63	0
2005	Houston o	N.L.	62	59	4	4	.500	54	21	49	4.73	0
2006	Houston p	N.L.	72	59$^{2}/_{3}$	1	1	.500	46	16	46	3.47	0
2007	St. Louis	N.L.	76	66	8	1	.889	66	19	41	2.18	0
Major League Totals		15 Yrs.	594	747$^{1}/_{3}$	33	40	.452	671	314	715	4.70	8
Division Series												
1997	Houston	N.L.	2	1$^{2}/_{3}$	0	0	.000	3	1	2	5.40	0
1999	Atlanta	N.L.	1	1	0	0	.000	1	1	2	0.00	0
2004	Houston	N.L.	2	2	0	1	.000	5	1	3	18.00	0
2005	Houston	N.L.	2	2$^{1}/_{3}$	0	0	.000	1	1	5	3.86	0
Division Series Totals			7	7	0	1	.000	10	4	12	7.71	0
Championship Series												
1999	Atlanta	N.L.	2	2	1	0	1.000	1	1	0	0.00	0
2005	Houston	N.L.	1	1	0	0	.000	1	1	0	0.00	0
Championship Series Totals			3	3	1	0	1.000	2	2	0	0.00	0
World Series Record												
1999	Atlanta	N.L.	2	2$^{1}/_{3}$	0	0	.000	1	0	1	0.00	0
2005	Houston	N.L.	2	2	0	0	.000	1	0	2	4.50	0
World Series Totals			4	4$^{1}/_{3}$	0	0	.000	2	0	3	2.08	0

a Traded to California Angels with infielder J.T. Snow and pitcher Jerry Neilsen for pitcher Jim Abbott, December 6, 1992.

b Kevin Flora was traded to Philadelphia Phillies with player to be named later for outfielder Dave Gallagher, August 9, 1995. Philadelphia Phillies received pitcher Russ Springer to complete trade, August 15, 1995.

c Released by Philadelphia Phillies, December 20, 1996. Signed with Houston Astros, December 30, 1996.

d On disabled list from June 17 to July 10, 1997.

e Selected in expansion draft by Arizona Diamondbacks, November 18, 1997.

f On disabled list from August 6 to August 21, 1998.

g Traded to Atlanta Braves for pitcher Alan Embree, June 22, 1998.

h On disabled list from April 3 to May 17, 1999.

i Filed for free agency, November 2, 1999. Signed with Arizona Diamondbacks, November 23, 1999.

j On disabled list from May 23 to November 7, 2001.

k Filed for free agency, November 7, 2001. Signed with St. Louis Cardinals organization, January 3, 2003.

l On disabled list from May 1 to August 30, 2003.

m Filed for free agency, October 28, 2003. Signed with Houston Astros organization, June 29, 2004.

n Filed for free agency, November 4, 2004. Re-signed with Houston Astros organization, December 7, 2004.

o Filed for free agency, November 10, 2005, re-signed with Houston Astros, December 2, 2005.

p Filed for free agency, October 30, 2006. Signed with St. Louis Cardinals, December 8, 2006.

SPURLING, CHRISTOPHER MICHAEL (CHRIS)

Born, Dayton, Ohio, June 28, 1977.
Bats Right. Throws Right. Height, 6 feet, 5 inches. Weight, 240 pounds.

Year	Club	Lea	G	IP	W	L	Pct	SO	BB	H	ERA	SAVES
1998	Yankees	Gulf Coast	13	51¹/₃	2	1	.667	44	11	57	2.28	1
1998	Greensboro	So.Atl.	1	6	1	0	1.000	5	1	7	3.00	0
1999	Greensboro	So.Atl.	49	76¹/₃	4	6	.400	68	23	78	3.66	4
2000	Lynchburg	Carolina	9	18¹/₃	1	0	1.000	17	3	8	0.98	5
2000	Tampa a	Fla.St.	34	57	4	6	.400	55	22	50	3.79	1
2001	Altoona.	Eastern	34	121²/₃	5	7	.417	63	28	133	3.11	1
2002	Altoona b	Eastern	51	70	4	3	.571	60	12	54	2.19	20
2003	Detroit c	A.L.	66	77	1	3	.250	38	22	78	4.68	3
2005	Toledo	Int.	12	19²/₃	2	1	.667	15	3	18	4.12	1
2005	Detroit	A.L.	56	70²/₃	3	4	.429	26	22	58	3.44	0
2004	Detroit d	A.L.				INJURED—Did Not Play						
2006	Detroit	A.L.	9	11¹/₃	0	0	.000	4	4	13	3.18	0
2006	Toledo	Int.	49	66	1	4	.200	34	10	61	2.05	5
2006	Milwaukee e-f.	N.L.	7	10	0	0	.000	3	4	12	7.20	0
2007	Nashville	P.C.	10	16	2	0	1.000	9	2	19	1.69	0
2007	Milwaukee g	N.L.	49	50	2	1	.667	28	14	63	4.68	0
Major League Totals	4 Yrs.		187	219	6	8	.429	99	66	224	4.32	3

a Traded to Pittsburgh Pirates by New York Yankees for infielder Luis Sojo, August 7, 2000.
b Selected by Atlanta Braves in Rule V minor league draft, December 16, 2002.
c Traded to Detroit Tigers for pitcher Matt Coenen, March 25, 2003.
d On disabled list from April 2 to October 4, 2004.
e Claimed on waivers by Milwaukee Brewers, September 8, 2006.
f Filed for free agency, October 9, 2006, re-signed with Milwaukee Brewers organization, October 11, 2006.
g Filed for free agency, October 5, 2007.

STANTON, WILLIAM MICHAEL (MIKE)

Born, Houston, Texas, June 2, 1967.
Bats Left. Throws Left. Height, 6 feet, 1 inch. Weight, 215 pounds.

Year	Club	Lea	G	IP	W	L	Pct	SO	BB	H	ERA	SAVES
1987	Pulaski	Appal.	15	83¹/₃	4	8	.333	82	42	64	3.24	0
1988	Burlington	Midwest	30	154	11	5	.688	160	69	154	3.62	0
1988	Durham	Carolina	2	12¹/₃	1	0	1.000	14	5	14	1.46	0
1989	Greenville	Southern	47	51¹/₃	4	1	.800	54	31	32	1.58	19
1989	Richmond	Int.	13	20	2	0	1.000	20	13	6	0.00	8
1989	Atlanta	N.L.	20	24	0	1	.000	27	8	17	1.50	7
1990	Atlanta a	N.L.	7	7	0	3	.000	7	4	16	18.00	2
1990	Greenville	Southern	4	5²/₃	0	1	.000	5	3	7	1.59	0
1991	Atlanta	N.L.	74	78	5	5	.500	54	21	62	2.88	7
1992	Atlanta	N.L.	65	63²/₃	5	4	.556	44	20	59	4.10	8
1993	Atlanta	N.L.	63	52	4	6	.400	43	29	51	4.67	27
1994	Atlanta b	N.L.	49	45²/₃	3	1	.750	35	26	41	3.55	3
1995	Atlanta	N.L.	26	19¹/₃	1	1	.500	13	6	31	5.59	1
1995	Boston c-d-e	A.L.	22	21	1	0	1.000	10	8	17	3.00	0
1996	Boston-Texas f-g	A.L.	81	78²/₃	4	4	.500	60	27	78	3.66	1
1997	New York	A.L.	64	66²/₃	6	1	.857	70	34	50	2.57	3
1998	New York	A.L.	67	79	4	1	.800	69	26	71	5.47	6
1999	New York h.	A.L.	73	62¹/₃	2	2	.500	59	18	71	4.33	0
2000	New York	A.L.	69	68	2	3	.400	75	24	80	4.10	0
2001	New York	A.L.	76	80¹/₃	9	4	.692	78	29	80	2.58	0
2002	New York i	A.L.	79	78	7	1	.875	44	28	73	3.00	6
2003	Brooklyn	N.Y.-Penn.	1	2	0	0	.000	1	0	1	0.00	0
2003	Binghamton	Eastern	1	1	0	0	.000	1	0	6	9.00	0
2003	New York j	N.L.	50	45¹/₃	2	7	.222	34	19	37	4.57	5
2004	New York k.	N.L.	83	77	2	6	.250	58	33	70	3.16	0
2005	Washington	N.L.	30	27²/₃	2	1	.667	14	9	31	3.58	0
2005	New York-Boston l-m-n .	A.L.	29	15	1	2	.333	13	6	18	6.60	0
2006	Washington-San Fran. o-p.	N.L.	82	67²/₃	7	7	.500	48	27	70	3.99	8
2007	Dayton	Midwest	1	1	0	0	.000	2	0	1	9.00	0
2007	Cincinnati q	N.L.	69	57²/₃	1	3	.250	40	18	75	5.93	0
Major League Totals	19 Yrs.		1178	1114	68	63	.519	895	420	1086	3.92	84
Division Series												
1995	Boston	A.L.	1	2¹/₃	0	0	.000	4	0	1	0.00	0
1996	Texas	A.L.	3	3¹/₃	0	1	.000	3	3	2	2.70	0
1997	New York	A.L.	3	1	0	0	.000	3	1	1	0.00	0
2000	New York	A.L.	3	4¹/₃	1	0	1.000	3	1	5	2.08	0
2001	New York	A.L.	3	4²/₃	1	0	1.000	1	0	3	0.00	0

Year Club	Lea	G	IP	W	L	Pct	SO	BB	H	ERA	SAVES
2002 New York	A.L.	3	2⅔	0	1	.000	1	1	6	10.13	0
Division Series Totals		16	18⅓	2	2	.500	15	6	18	2.45	0
Championship Series											
1991 Atlanta	N.L.	3	3⅔	0	0	.000	3	3	4	2.45	0
1992 Atlanta	N.L.	5	4⅓	0	0	.000	5	2	2	0.00	0
1993 Atlanta	N.L.	1	1	0	0	.000	0	1	1	0.00	0
1998 New York	A.L.	3	3⅔	0	0	.000	4	1	2	0.00	0
1999 New York	A.L.	3	0⅓	0	0	.000	0	1	1	0.00	0
2001 New York	A.L.	2	1	0	0	.000	0	2	1	27.00	0
Championship Series Totals		17	14	0	0	.000	12	10	11	2.57	0
World Series Record											
1991 Atlanta	N.L.	5	7⅓	1	0	1.000	7	2	5	0.00	0
1992 Atlanta	N.L.	4	5	0	0	.000	1	2	3	0.00	1
1998 New York	A.L.	1	0⅔	0	0	.000	1	0	3	27.00	0
1999 New York	A.L.	1	0⅓	0	0	.000	1	0	0	0.00	0
2000 New York	A.L.	4	4⅓	2	0	1.000	7	0	0	0.00	0
2001 New York	A.L.	5	5⅔	0	0	.000	3	1	3	3.18	0
World Series Totals		20	23⅓	3	0	1.000	20	5	14	1.54	1

a On disabled list from April 27 to November 13, 1990.
b Not offered contract, December 23, 1994.
c Re-signed with Atlanta Braves, April 12, 1995.
d Traded to Boston Red Sox for two players to be named later, July 31, 1995.
e Boston Red Sox received pitcher Matt Murray and Atlanta Braves received pitcher Michael Jacobs and outfielder Marc Lewis to complete trade, August 31, 1995.
f Traded to Texas Rangers with player to be named later for pitcher Mark Brandenberg and pitcher Kerry Lacy, July 31, 1996. Texas Rangers received outfielder Dwyane Hosey to complete trade, November 4, 1996.
g Filed for free agency, October 27, 1996. Signed with New York Yankees, December 11, 1996.
h Filed for free agency, November 5, 1999, re-signed with New York Yankees, November 29, 1999.
i Filed for free agency, October 30, 2002. Signed with New York Mets, December 16, 2002.
j On disabled list from May 22 to June 6 and from June 11 to July 12, 2003.
k Traded to New York Yankees with cash for pitcher Felix Heredia, December 3, 2004.
l Released by New York Yankees, July 11, 2005. Signed with Washington Nationals, July 13, 2005.
m Traded to Boston Red Sox for pitcher Rhys Taylor and pitcher Yader Peralta, September 29, 2005.
n Filed for free agency, October 12, 2005. Signed with Washington Nationals, December 24, 2005.
o Traded to San Francisco Giants for pitcher Shairon Martis, July 28, 2006.
p Filed for free agency, October 28, 2006. Signed with Cincinnati Reds, November 20, 2006.
q On disabled list from June 17 to July 5, 2007.

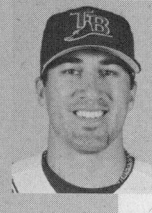

STOKES, BRIAN ALEXANDER
Born, Pomona, California, September 7, 1979.
Bats Right. Throws Right. Height, 6 feet, 1 inch. Weight, 205 pounds.

Year Club	Lea	G	IP	W	L	Pct	SO	BB	H	ERA	SAVES
1999 Princeton	Appal.	33	37	2	3	.400	39	21	33	3.89	9
2000 Charleston-SC	So.Atl.	46	70⅓	5	6	.455	66	34	45	2.56	5
2001 Bakersfield	Calif.	32	128⅔	8	6	.571	92	64	118	3.92	1
2002 Bakersfield	Calif.	28	165⅔	10	7	.588	152	57	156	3.26	0
2003 Orlando	Southern	10	50⅔	2	5	.286	33	13	55	3.20	0
2004				INJURED—Did Not Play							
2005 Visalia	Calif.	4	17	1	2	.333	21	5	15	4.24	0
2005 Montgomery	Southern	16	93⅓	4	6	.400	70	28	82	3.47	0
2006 Durham	Int.	29	133⅔	7	7	.500	103	49	134	4.11	0
2006 Tampa Bay	A.L.	5	24	1	0	1.000	15	9	31	4.88	0
2007 Tampa Bay a..........	A.L.	59	62⅓	2	7	.222	35	25	90	7.07	0
Major League Totals .... 2 Yrs.		64	86⅓	3	7	.300	50	34	121	6.46	0

a Sold to New York Mets, November 27, 2007.

STREET, HUSTON LOWELL
Born, Austin, Texas, August 2, 1983.
Bats Right. Throws Right. Height, 6 feet. Weight, 190 pounds.

Year Club	Lea	G	IP	W	L	Pct	SO	BB	H	ERA	SAVES
2004 Kane County........	Midwest	9	10⅔	0	1	.000	14	5	9	1.69	4
2004 Sacramento	P.C.	2	2	0	0	.000	2	0	2	0.00	1
2004 Midland	Texas	10	13⅓	1	0	1.000	14	3	10	1.35	3
2005 Oakland a.............	A.L.	67	78⅓	5	1	.833	72	26	53	1.72	23
2006 Oakland b.............	A.L.	69	70⅔	4	4	.500	67	13	64	3.31	37
2007 Sacramento	P.C.	1	1	0	0	.000	2	0	1	0.00	0

Year	Club	Lea	G	IP	W	L	Pct	SO	BB	H	ERA	SAVES
2007 Oakland c............	A.L.	48	50	5	2	.714	63	12	35	2.88	16
Major League Totals ....3 Yrs.	184	199	14	7	.667	202	51	152	2.58	76
Division Series												
2006 Oakland	A.L.	3	3	0	0	.000	1	1	4	3.00	2
Championship Series												
2006 Oakland	A.L.	2	3⅓	0	1	.000	3	0	4	10.80	0

a Selected Rookie of the Year in American League for 2005.
b On disabled list from August 19 to September 8, 2006.
c On disabled list from May 13 to July 23, 2007.

SUPPAN, JEFFREY SCOT (JEFF)

Born, Oklahoma City, Oklahoma, January 2, 1975.
Bats Right. Throws Right. Height, 6 feet, 2 inch. Weight, 220 pounds.

Year	Club	Lea	G	IP	W	L	Pct	SO	BB	H	ERA	SAVES
1993 Red Sox.........	Gulf Coast	10	57⅔	4	3	.571	64	16	52	2.18	0
1994 Sarasota............	Fla. St.	27	174	13	7	.650	173	50	153	3.26	0
1995 Trenton...........	Eastern	15	99	6	2	.750	88	26	86	2.36	0
1995 Pawtucket	Int.	7	45⅔	2	3	.400	32	9	50	5.32	0
1995 Boston...............	A.L.	8	22⅓	1	2	.333	19	5	29	5.96	0
1996 Pawtucket	Int.	22	145⅓	10	6	.625	142	25	130	3.22	0
1996 Boston a..............	A.L.	8	22⅔	1	1	.500	13	13	29	7.54	0
1997 Pawtucket	Int.	9	60⅔	5	1	.833	40	15	51	3.71	0
1997 Boston b.............	A.L.	23	112⅓	7	3	.700	67	36	140	5.69	0
1998 Arizona...............	N.L.	13	66	1	7	.125	39	21	82	6.68	0
1998 Tucson c..............	P.C.	13	67	4	3	.571	62	17	75	3.63	0
1998 Kansas City	A.L.	4	12⅔	0	0	.000	12	1	9	0.71	0
1999 Kansas City	A.L.	32	208⅔	10	12	.455	103	62	222	4.53	0
2000 Kansas City	A.L.	35	217	10	9	.526	128	84	240	4.94	0
2001 Kansas City	A.L.	34	218⅓	10	14	.417	120	74	227	4.37	0
2002 Kansas City d.........	A.L.	33	208	9	16	.360	109	68	229	5.32	0
2003 Pittsburgh	N.L.	21	141	10	7	.588	78	31	147	3.57	0
2003 Boston e-f............	A.L.	11	63	3	4	.429	32	20	70	5.57	0
2004 St. Louis.............	N.L.	31	188	16	9	.640	110	65	192	4.16	0
2005 St. Louis.............	N.L.	32	194⅓	16	10	.615	114	63	206	3.57	0
2006 St. Louis g..........	N.L.	32	190	12	7	.632	104	69	207	4.12	0
2007 Milwaukee	N.L.	34	206⅔	12	12	.500	114	68	243	4.62	0
Major League Totals ....13 Yrs.	351	2071⅓	118	113	.511	1162	680	2272	4.61	0
Division Series												
2004 St. Louis.............	N.L.	1	7	1	0	1.000	2	3	2	2.57	0
2006 St. Louis.............	N.L.	1	4⅓	0	1	.000	3	3	6	6.23	0
Division Series Totals	2	11⅓	1	1	.500	5	6	8	3.97	0
Championship Series												
2004 St. Louis.............	N.L.	2	12	1	1	.500	9	4	8	3.00	0
2005 St. Louis.............	N.L.	1	5	0	0	.000	5	3	3	1.80	0
2006 St. Louis.............	N.L.	2	15	1	0	1.000	6	6	5	0.60	0
Championship Series Totals	5	32	2	1	.667	20	13	16	1.69	0
World Series Record												
2004 St. Louis.............	N.L.	1	4⅔	0	1	.000	4	1	8	7.71	0
2006 St. Louis.............	N.L.	1	6	0	0	.000	4	2	8	4.50	0
World Series Totals.............	2	10⅔	0	1	.000	8	3	16	5.91	0

a On disabled list from August 25 to September 30, 1996.
b Selected in expansion draft by Arizona Diamondbacks, November 18, 1997.
c Sold to Kansas City Royals, September 3, 1998.
d Not offered contract, December 20, 2002. Signed with Pittsburgh Pirates, January 29, 2003.
e Traded to Boston Red Sox with pitcher Brandon Lyon and pitcher Anastacio Martinez for infielder Freddy Sanchez, pitcher Mike Gonzalez and cash, July 31, 2003.
f Filed for free agency, October 27, 2003. Signed with St. Louis Cardinals, December 16, 2003.
g Filed for free agency, November 1, 2006. Signed with Milwaukee Brewers, December 24, 2006.

TALLET, BRIAN CURTIS

Born, Midwest City, Oklahoma, September 21, 1977.
Bats Left. Throws Left. Height, 6 feet, 7 inches. Weight, 220 pounds.

Year	Club	Lea	G	IP	W	L	Pct	SO	BB	H	ERA	SAVES
2000 Mahoning Valley...	N.Y.-Penn.	6	15⅔	0	0	.000	20	3	10	1.15	0
2001 Kinston...........	Carolina	27	160	9	7	.563	164	38	134	3.04	0
2002 Akron.............	Eastern	18	102⅓	10	1	.909	73	32	93	3.08	0

Year	Club	Lea	G	IP	W	L	Pct	SO	BB	H	ERA	SAVES
2002 Buffalo	Int.	8	44	2	3	.400	25	16	47	3.07	0
2002 Cleveland	A.L.	2	12	1	0	1.000	5	4	9	1.50	0
2003 Buffalo	Int.	15	84	4	4	.500	67	34	89	5.14	0
2003 Cleveland	A.L.	5	19	0	2	.000	9	8	23	4.74	0
2004 Akron	Eastern	14	22⅔	1	1	.500	24	13	26	5.56	1
2004 Buffalo	Int.	5	8⅔	0	0	.000	7	3	7	4.15	0
2004 Mahoning Valley	N.Y.-Penn.	2	2⅔	0	0	.000	2	0	3	0.00	0
2004 Lake County a	So.Atl.	2	2	0	0	.000	1	0	1	0.00	0
2005 Cleveland	A.L.	2	4⅔	0	0	.000	2	3	6	7.71	0
2005 Buffalo	Int.	22	97⅔	6	5	.545	61	25	98	4.05	0
2006 Syracuse	Int.	20	25⅓	1	2	.333	21	10	32	5.68	3
2006 Toronto b	A.L.	44	54⅓	3	0	1.000	37	31	45	3.81	0
2007 Syracuse	Int.	7	6⅔	0	0	.000	11	3	4	1.35	0
2007 Toronto	A.L.	48	62⅓	2	4	.333	54	28	49	3.47	0
Major League Totals	5 Yrs.	101	152⅓	6	6	.500	107	74	132	3.72	0

a On disabled list from April 1 to July 26, 2004.
b Traded to Toronto Blue Jays for pitcher Bubbie Buzachero, January 17, 2006.

TANKERSLEY, TAYLOR MARK
Born, Missoula, Montana, March 7, 1983.
Bats Left. Throws Left. Height, 6 feet, 1 inch. Weight, 220 pounds.

Year	Club	Lea	G	IP	W	L	Pct	SO	BB	H	ERA	SAVES
2004 Jamestown	N.Y.-Penn.	6	26⅔	1	1	.500	32	8	21	3.38	0
2005 Jupiter	Fla.St.	4	24	1	0	1.000	19	9	21	3.38	0
2005 Greensboro	So.Atl.	12	66	2	7	.222	63	25	74	5.18	0
2006 Carolina	Southern	22	28⅓	4	1	.800	40	14	11	0.95	6
2006 Florida	N.L.	49	41	2	1	.667	46	26	33	2.85	3
2007 Jupiter	Fla.St.	4	4	1	0	1.000	5	0	4	6.75	0
2007 Albuquerque	P.C.	7	5⅔	0	1	.000	5	2	3	4.76	0
2007 Florida a	N.L.	67	47⅓	6	1	.857	49	29	42	3.99	1
Major League Totals	2 Yrs.	116	88⅓	8	2	.800	95	55	75	3.46	4

a On disabled list from March 23 to April 13, 2007.

TASCHNER, JACK GERARD
Born, Milwaukee, Wisconsin, April 21, 1978.
Bats Left. Throws Left. Height, 6 feet, 3 inches. Weight, 210 pounds.

Year	Club	Lea	G	IP	W	L	Pct	SO	BB	H	ERA	SAVES
1999 Salem-Keizer	Northwest	7	28⅔	3	2	.600	36	10	26	2.51	0
2000 San Jose	Calif.	10	26⅓	2	2	.500	22	17	23	4.10	1
2001 San Jose	Calif.	14	65⅔	4	4	.500	72	29	62	4.11	0
2002			INJURED—Did Not Play									
2003 Norwich	Eastern	34	75⅔	0	6	.000	46	45	78	5.71	0
2004 Norwich	Eastern	14	58	3	1	.750	55	16	47	2.48	0
2004 Fresno	P.C.	18	53⅓	4	7	.364	44	32	71	9.28	0
2005 Fresno	P.C.	44	49⅓	3	0	1.000	62	24	30	1.64	10
2005 San Francisco	N.L.	24	22⅔	2	0	1.000	19	13	15	1.59	0
2006 Fresno	P.C.	45	49⅓	6	7	.462	68	17	49	3.65	14
2006 San Francisco	N.L.	24	19⅓	0	1	.000	15	7	31	8.38	0
2007 San Francisco	N.L.	63	50	3	1	.750	51	29	44	5.40	0
Major League Totals	3 Yrs.	111	92	5	2	.714	85	49	90	5.09	0

TAVAREZ (CARMEN), JULIAN
Born, Santiago, Dominican Republic, May 22, 1973.
Bats Left. Throws Right. Height, 6 feet, 2 inches. Weight, 195 pounds.

Year	Club	Lea	G	IP	W	L	Pct	SO	BB	H	ERA	SAVES
1990 Cleveland	Dominican	2	4⅔	0	1	.000	1	7	6	11.57	0
1991 Cleveland	Dominican	19	121⅓	8	2	.800	75	28	95	2.67	0
1992 Burlington	Appal.	14	87⅓	6	3	.667	69	12	86	2.68	0
1993 Kinston	Carolina	18	119	11	5	.688	107	28	102	2.42	0
1993 Canton-Akron	Eastern	3	19	2	1	.667	11	1	14	0.95	0
1993 Cleveland	A.L.	8	37	2	2	.500	19	13	53	6.57	0
1994 Cleveland	A.L.	1	1⅔	0	1	.000	0	1	6	21.60	0
1994 Charlotte	Int.	26	176	15	6	.714	102	43	167	3.48	0
1995 Cleveland	A.L.	57	85	10	2	.833	68	21	76	2.44	0
1996 Buffalo	A.A.	2	14	1	0	1.000	10	3	10	1.29	0
1996 Cleveland a-b	A.L.	51	80⅔	4	7	.364	46	22	101	5.36	0

Year	Club	Lea	G	IP	W	L	Pct	SO	BB	H	ERA	SAVES
1997 San Francisco	N.L.	89	88¹/₃	6	4	.600	38	34	91	3.87	0
1998 Fresno	P.C.	1	2¹/₃	0	0	.000	1	0	6	19.29	0
1998 San Francisco c	N.L.	60	85¹/₃	5	3	.625	52	36	96	3.80	1
1999 Fresno	P.C.	4	8	0	0	.000	9	3	3	2.25	0
1999 San Jose	California	1	4	0	0	.000	3	1	1	0.00	0
1999 San Francisco d-e	N.L.	47	54²/₃	2	0	1.000	33	25	65	5.93	0
2000 Colorado f	N.L.	51	120	11	5	.688	62	53	124	4.42	1
2001 Chicago	N.L.	34	161¹/₃	10	9	.526	107	69	172	4.52	0
2002 Florida g-h-i	N.L.	29	153²/₃	10	12	.455	67	74	188	5.39	0
2003 Pittsburgh j	N.L.	64	83²/₃	3	3	.500	39	27	75	3.66	11
2004 St. Louis	N.L.	77	64¹/₃	7	4	.636	48	19	57	2.38	4
2005 St. Louis k	N.L.	74	65²/₃	2	3	.400	47	19	68	3.43	4
2006 Boston	A.L.	58	98²/₃	5	4	.556	56	44	110	4.47	1
2007 Boston	A.L.	34	134²/₃	7	11	.389	77	51	151	5.15	0
Major League Totals 15 Yrs.		734	1314²/₃	84	70	.545	759	508	1433	4.42	22
Division Series											
1995 Cleveland	A.L.	3	2²/₃	0	0	.000	3	0	5	6.75	0
1996 Cleveland	A.L.	2	1¹/₃	0	0	.000	1	2	1	0.00	0
1997 San Francisco	N.L.	3	4	0	1	.000	0	2	4	4.50	0
2004 St. Louis	N.L.	2	2¹/₃	0	0	.000	3	0	2	0.00	0
2005 St. Louis	N.L.	2	1¹/₃	0	0	.000	0	1	4	13.50	0
Division Series Totals		12	11²/₃	0	1	.000	7	5	16	4.63	0
Championship Series											
1995 Cleveland	A.L.	4	3¹/₃	0	1	.000	2	1	3	2.70	0
2004 St. Louis	N.L.	5	6	2	1	.667	3	2	3	3.00	0
2005 St. Louis	N.L.	3	3¹/₃	0	0	.000	2	0	5	5.40	0
Championship Series Totals		12	12²/₃	2	2	.500	7	3	11	3.55	0
World Series Record											
1995 Cleveland	A.L.	5	4¹/₃	0	0	.000	1	2	3	0.00	0
2004 St. Louis	N.L.	2	2	0	1	.000	1	0	1	4.50	0
World Series Totals		7	6¹/₃	0	1	.000	2	2	4	1.42	0

a Traded to San Francisco Giants with infielder Jeff Kent, infielder Jose Vizcaino and player to be named later for infielder Matt Williams and player to be named later, November 13, 1996.

b Cleveland Indians received outfielder Trenidad Hubbard and San Francisco Giants received pitcher Joe Roa to complete trade, December 16, 1996.

c On disabled list from July 13 to August 7, 1998.

d On disabled list from May 1 to June 1, 1999.

e Claimed on waivers by Colorado Rockies, November 16, 1999.

f Filed for free agency, October 31, 2000. Signed with Chicago Cubs, November 16, 2000.

g Traded to Florida Marlins with pitcher Jose Cueto, pitcher Dontrelle Willis and catcher Ryan Jorgensen for pitcher Antonio Alfonseca and pitcher Matt Clement, March 27, 2002.

h On disabled list from April 17 to May 11, 2002.

i Filed for free agency, October 28, 2002. Signed with Pittsburgh Pirates organization, January 28, 2003.

j Filed for free agency, November 2, 2003. Signed with St. Louis Cardinals, January 9, 2004.

k Filed for free agency, October 28, 2005. Signed with Boston Red Sox, January 18, 2006.

THOMPSON, BRADLEY JOSEPH (BRAD)

Born, Las Vegas, Nevada, January 31, 1982.
Bats Right. Throws Right. Height, 6 feet, 1 inch. Weight, 190 pounds.

Year	Club	Lea	G	IP	W	L	Pct	SO	BB	H	ERA	SAVES
2003 Palm Beach	Fla.St.	2	6	1	0	1.000	4	0	3	0.00	0
2003 Peoria	Midwest	30	65	5	3	.625	43	10	70	2.91	0
2004 Memphis	P.C.	3	14²/₃	1	0	1.000	10	3	20	5.52	0
2004 Tennessee	Southern	13	72¹/₃	8	2	.800	57	11	56	2.36	0
2005 Memphis	P.C.	9	13²/₃	2	1	.667	11	7	12	3.29	0
2005 St. Louis	N.L.	40	55	4	0	1.000	29	15	46	2.95	1
2006 Memphis	P.C.	14	42²/₃	2	0	1.000	33	6	36	2.11	0
2006 St. Louis	N.L.	43	56²/₃	1	2	.333	32	20	58	3.34	0
2007 Memphis	P.C.	2	8¹/₃	0	0	.000	2	1	8	4.32	0
2007 St. Louis	N.L.	44	129¹/₃	8	6	.571	53	40	157	4.73	0
Major League Totals 3 Yrs.		127	241	13	8	.619	114	75	261	4.00	1
Division Series											
2005 St. Louis	N.L.	2	1¹/₃	0	0	.000	1	0	3	13.50	0
2006 St. Louis	N.L.	1	0²/₃	0	0	.000	1	1	0	0.00	0
Division Series Totals		3	2	0	0	.000	2	1	3	9.00	0
Championship Series											
2005 St. Louis	N.L.	2	1	0	0	.000	0	0	2	0.00	0

Year	Club	Lea	G	IP	W	L	Pct	SO	BB	H	ERA	SAVES
2006 St. Louis..............	N.L.	2	0²/₃	0	1	.000	1	0	3	27.00	0
Championship Series Totals		4	1²/₃	0	1	.000	1	0	5	10.80	0
World Series Record											
2006 St. Louis..............	N.L.	1	0²/₃	0	0	.000	1	0	0	0.00	0

THORNTON, MATTHEW J. (MATT)
Born, Three Rivers, Michigan, September 15, 1976.
Bats Left. Throws Left. Height, 6 feet, 6 inches. Weight, 235 pounds.

Year	Club	Lea	G	IP	W	L	Pct	SO	BB	H	ERA	SAVES
1998 Everett	Northwest	2	1¹/₃	0	0	.000	0	3	1	27.00	0
1999 Wisconsin	.Midwest	25	29¹/₃	0	0	.000	34	25	39	4.91	1
2000 Wisconsin	.Midwest	26	103¹/₃	6	9	.400	88	72	94	4.01	0
2001 San Bernardino	California	27	157	14	7	.667	192	60	126	2.52	0
2002 San Antonio	Texas	12	62	1	5	.167	44	29	52	3.63	0
2003 Inland Empire......	California	2	9	0	0	.000	14	4	9	4.00	0
2003 Tacoma	P.C.	2	9	0	2	.000	5	3	14	8.00	0
2003 San Antonio	Texas	4	25¹/₃	3	0	1.000	18	9	8	0.36	0
2004 Tacoma	P.C.	16	83	7	5	.583	74	63	85	5.20	0
2004 Seattle	A.L.	19	32²/₃	1	2	.333	30	25	30	4.13	0
2005 Seattle	A.L.	55	57	0	4	.000	57	42	54	5.21	0
2006 Chicago a.............	A.L.	63	54	5	3	.625	49	21	46	3.33	2
2007 Chicago	A.L.	68	56¹/₃	4	4	.500	55	26	59	4.79	2
Major League Totals .... 4 Yrs.		205	200	10	13	.435	191	114	189	4.41	4

a Traded to Chicago White Sox for outfielder Joe Borchard, March 20, 2006.

TIMLIN, MICHAEL AUGUST (MIKE)
Born, Midland, Texas, March 10, 1966.
Bats Right. Throws Right. Height, 6 feet, 4 inches. Weight, 210 pounds.

Year	Club	Lea	G	IP	W	L	Pct	SO	BB	H	ERA	SAVES
1987 Medicine Hat	Pioneer	13	75¹/₃	4	8	.333	66	26	79	5.14	0
1988 Myrtle Beach	So. Atl.	35	151	10	6	.625	106	77	119	2.86	0
1989 Dunedin	Fla. St.	33	88²/₃	5	8	.385	64	36	90	3.25	7
1990 Dunedin	Fla. St.	42	50¹/₃	7	2	.778	46	16	36	1.43	22
1990 Knoxville	Southern	17	26	1	2	.333	21	7	20	1.73	8
1991 Toronto a.............	A.L.	63	108¹/₃	11	6	.647	85	50	94	3.16	3
1992 Dunedin	Fla. St.	6	10	0	0	.000	7	2	9	0.90	1
1992 Syracuse	Int.	7	11¹/₃	0	1	.000	7	5	15	8.74	3
1992 Toronto b.............	A.L.	26	43²/₃	0	2	.000	35	20	45	4.12	1
1993 Dunedin	Fla. St.	4	9	0	0	.000	8	0	4	1.00	1
1993 Toronto	A.L.	54	55²/₃	4	2	.667	49	27	63	4.69	1
1994 Toronto c.............	A.L.	34	40	0	1	.000	38	20	41	5.17	2
1995 Syracuse	Int.	8	17¹/₃	1	1	.500	13	4	13	1.04	0
1995 Toronto d.............	A.L.	31	42	4	3	.571	36	17	38	2.14	5
1996 Toronto	A.L.	59	56²/₃	1	6	.143	52	18	47	3.65	31
1997 Toronto-Seattle e	A.L.	64	72²/₃	6	4	.600	45	20	69	3.22	10
1998 Seattle f..............	A.L.	70	79¹/₃	3	3	.500	60	16	78	2.95	19
1999 Baltimore	A.L.	62	63	3	9	.250	50	23	51	3.57	27
2000 Baltimore g	A.L.	37	35	2	3	.400	26	15	37	4.89	11
2000 St. Louis h...........	N.L.	25	29²/₃	3	1	.750	26	20	30	3.34	1
2001 St. Louis i.............	N.L.	67	72²/₃	4	5	.444	47	19	78	4.09	3
2002 St. Louis-Philadelphia j-k	N.L.	72	96²/₃	4	6	.400	50	14	75	2.98	0
2003 Boston I..............	A.L.	72	83²/₃	6	4	.600	65	9	77	3.55	2
2004 Boston	A.L.	76	76¹/₃	5	4	.556	56	19	75	4.13	1
2005 Boston	A.L.	*81	80¹/₃	7	3	.700	59	20	86	2.24	13
2006 Boston m..............	.A.L.	68	64	6	6	.500	30	16	78	4.36	9
2007 Pawtucket	.Int.	8	8²/₃	0	0	.000	3	3	9	4.15	0
2007 Boston n-o............	A.L.	50	55¹/₃	2	1	.667	31	14	46	3.42	1
Major League Totals ....17 Yrs.		1011	1155	71	69	.507	840	357	1108	3.55	140
Division Series											
1997 Seattle	A.L.	1	0²/₃	0	0	.000	1	1	3	54.00	0
2000 St. Louis..............	N.L.	2	1²/₃	0	0	.000	2	1	5	10.80	0
2001 St. Louis..............	N.L.	1	1¹/₃	0	0	.000	0	0	1	0.00	0
2003 Boston	A.L.	3	4¹/₃	0	0	.000	5	0	0	0.00	0
2004 Boston	A.L.	3	3	0	0	.000	5	1	3	9.00	0
2005 Boston	A.L.	1	1	0	0	.000	1	0	1	9.00	0
Division Series Totals		11	12	0	0	.000	14	3	13	7.50	0

Year	Club	Lea	G	IP	W	L	Pct	SO	BB	H	ERA	SAVES
	Championship Series											
1991	Toronto	A.L.	4	5²/₃	0	1	.000	5	2	5	3.18	0
1992	Toronto	A.L.	2	1¹/₃	0	0	.000	1	0	4	6.75	0
1993	Toronto	A.L.	1	2¹/₃	0	0	.000	2	0	3	3.86	0
2000	St. Louis..............	N.L.	3	3¹/₃	0	1	.000	0	2	1	0.00	0
2003	Boston	A.L.	5	5¹/₃	0	0	.000	6	2	1	0.00	0
2004	Boston	A.L.	5	5²/₃	0	0	.000	2	5	10	4.76	0
2007	Boston	A.L.	3	3¹/₃	0	0	.000	3	0	1	0.00	0
Championship Series Totals			23	27	0	2	.000	19	11	25	2.33	0
	World Series Record											
1992	Toronto	A.L.	2	1¹/₃	0	0	.000	0	0	0	0.00	1
1993	Toronto	A.L.	2	2¹/₃	0	0	.000	4	0	2	0.00	0
2004	Boston	A.L.	3	3	0	0	.000	0	1	2	6.00	0
2007	Boston	A.L.	3	2¹/₃	0	0	.000	4	0	2	7.71	0
World Series Totals.............			10	9	0	0	.000	8	1	6	4.00	1

a On disabled list from August 1 to August 15, 1991.
b On disabled list from March 27 to June 12, 1992.
c On disabled list from May 25 to June 9, 1994.
d On disabled list from June 22 to August 18, 1995.
e Traded to Seattle Mariners with pitcher Paul Spoljaric for outfielder Jose Cruz Jr., July 31, 1997.
f Filed for free agency, October 22, 1998. Signed with Baltimore Orioles, November 13, 1998.
g On disabled list from April 2 to April 16, 2000.
h Traded to St. Louis Cardinals for outfielder Chris Richard and pitcher Mark Nussbeck, July 29, 2000.
i On disabled list from July 26 to August 17, 2001.
j Traded to Philadelphia Phillies with infielder Placido Polanco and pitcher Bud Smith for infielder Scott Rolen and pitcher Doug Nickle, July 29, 2002.
k Filed for free agency, October 28, 2002. Signed with Boston Red Sox, December 24, 2002.
l Filed for free agency, October 28, 2003, re-signed with Boston Red Sox, November 17, 2003.
m On disabled list from May 26 to June 13, 2006.
n On disabled list from March 23 to April 10 and May 3 to June 9, 2007.
o Filed for free agency, November 6, 2007, re-signed with Boston Red Sox, December 7, 2007.

TOMKO, BRETT DANIEL

Born, Cleveland, Ohio, April 7, 1973.
Bats Right. Throws Right. Height, 6 feet, 4 inches. Weight, 225 pounds.

Year	Club	Lea	G	IP	W	L	Pct	SO	BB	H	ERA	SAVES
1995	Charleston-WV.	So.Atl.	9	49	4	2	.667	46	9	41	1.84	0
1996	Chattanooga.......	Southern	27	157²/₃	11	7	.611	164	54	131	3.88	0
1997	Indianapolis	A.A.	10	61	6	3	.667	60	9	53	2.95	0
1997	Cincinnati..............	N.L.	22	126	11	7	.611	95	47	106	3.43	0
1998	Cincinnati..............	N.L.	34	210²/₃	13	12	.520	162	64	198	4.44	0
1999	Cincinnati..............	N.L.	33	172	5	7	.417	132	60	175	4.92	0
1999	Indianapolis	Int.	2	12²/₃	2	0	1.000	9	1	15	4.97	0
2000	Tacoma	P.C.	2	12²/₃	1	0	1.000	8	5	13	2.84	0
2000	Seattle a-b	A.L.	32	92¹/₃	7	5	.583	59	40	92	4.68	1
2001	Tacoma	P.C.	19	127	10	6	.625	117	25	124	4.04	0
2001	Seattle c	A.L.	11	34²/₃	3	1	.750	22	15	42	5.19	0
2002	San Diego d	N.L.	32	204¹/₃	10	10	.500	126	60	212	4.49	0
2003	St. Louis e	N.L.	33	202²/₃	13	9	.591	114	57	*252	5.28	0
2004	Fresno	P.C.	1	5	0	0	.000	4	2	4	5.40	0
2004	San Francisco f	N.L.	32	194	11	7	.611	108	64	196	4.04	0
2005	San Francisco g	N.L.	33	190²/₃	8	15	.348	114	57	205	4.48	1
2006	Las Vegas.............	P.C.	2	2	0	0	.000	3	1	3	0.00	0
2006	Los Angeles h	N.L.	44	112¹/₃	8	7	.533	76	29	123	4.73	0
2007	Los Angeles-San Diego i-j	N.L.	40	131¹/₃	4	12	.250	105	48	149	5.55	0
Major League Totals ....11 Yrs.			346	1671	93	92	.503	1113	541	1750	4.62	2
	Division Series											
2000	Seattle	A.L.	1	2²/₃	0	0	.000	0	1	1	0.00	0
2006	Los Angeles	N.L.	2	1	0	0	.000	0	2	4	9.00	0
Division Series Totals			3	3²/₃	0	0	.000	0	3	5	2.45	0
	Championship Series											
2000	Seattle	A.L.	2	5	0	0	.000	4	4	3	7.20	0

a Traded to Seattle Mariners with outfielder Mike Cameron, infielder Antonio Perez and pitcher Jake Meyer for outfielder Ken Griffey, February 10, 2000.
b On disabled list from June 7 to June 23, 2000.
c Traded to San Diego Padres with catcher Tom Lampkin and infielder Ramon Vazquez for catcher Ben Davis, pitcher Wascar Serrano and infielder Alex Arias, December 11, 2001.
d Traded to St. Louis Cardinals for pitcher Luther Hackman and pitcher Mike Wodnicki, December 15, 2002.

e Filed for free agency, October 26, 2003. Signed with San Francisco Giants, January 9, 2004.
f On disabled list from June 8 to June 24, 2004.
g Filed for free agency, November 2, 2005. Signed with Los Angeles Dodgers, December 22, 2005.
h On disabled list from June 25 to July 28, 2006.
i Released by Los Angeles Dodgers, August 31, 2007. Signed with San Diego Padres, September 4, 2007.
j Filed for free agency, November 2, 2007. Signed with Kansas City Royals, January 21, 2008.

TORRES, SALOMON (RAMIREZ)

Born, San Pedro de Macoris, Dominican Republic, March 11, 1972.
Bats Right. Throws Right. Height, 5 feet, 11 inches. Weight, 210 pounds.

Year	Club	Lea	G	IP	W	L	Pct	SO	BB	H	ERA	SAVES
1990 San Fran.	Dominican		13	90	11	1	.917	101	27	44	0.50	0
1991 Clinton	Midwest		28	210¹/₃	16	5	.762	214	47	148	1.41	0
1992 Shreveport	Texas		25	162¹/₃	6	10	.375	151	34	167	4.21	0
1993 Shreveport	Texas		12	83¹/₃	7	4	.636	67	.12	67	2.70	0
1993 Phoenix	P.C.		14	105¹/₃	7	4	.636	99	27	105	3.50	0
1993 San Francisco	N.L.		8	44²/₃	3	5	.375	23	27	37	4.03	0
1994 San Francisco	N.L.		16	84¹/₃	2	8	.200	42	34	95	5.44	0
1994 Phoenix	P.C.		13	79	5	6	.455	64	31	85	4.22	0
1995 San Francisco	N.L.		4	8	0	1	.000	2	7	13	9.00	0
1995 Phoenix	P.C.		1	2	0	0	.000	5	0	2	0.00	0
1995 Tacoma	P.C.		5	28	1	1	.500	19	13	20	3.21	0
1995 Seattle a	A.L.		16	72	3	8	.273	45	42	87	6.00	0
1996 Tacoma	P.C.		22	134¹/₃	7	10	.412	121	52	150	5.29	0
1996 Seattle	A.L.		10	49	3	3	.500	36	23	44	4.59	0
1997 Seattle	A.L.		2	3¹/₃	0	0	.000	0	3	7	27.00	0
1997 Montreal.	N.L.		12	22¹/₃	0	0	.000	11	12	25	7.25	0
1997 Ottawa b.	Int.		2	5	0	0	.000	2	2	7	5.40	0
1998-2000				Voluntarily Retired								
2001 Samsung c-d-e	Kore		2	5¹/₃	0	2	.000	5	10	8	20.25	0
2002 Nashville	P.C.		26	162¹/₃	8	5	.615	136	39	169	3.83	0
2002 Pittsburgh f	N.L.		5	30	2	1	.667	12	13	28	2.70	0
2003 Nashville	P.C.		1	5	1	0	1.000	4	1	2	1.80	0
2003 Pittsburgh g	N.L.		41	121	7	5	.583	84	42	128	4.76	2
2004 Pittsburgh	N.L.		84	92	7	7	.500	62	22	87	2.64	0
2005 Pittsburgh	N.L.		78	94²/₃	5	5	.500	55	36	76	2.76	3
2006 Pittsburgh	N.L.		*94	93¹/₃	3	6	.333	72	38	98	3.28	12
2007 Pirates	Gulf Coast		2	3	0	0	.000	4	0	2	0.00	0
2007 Indianapolis	Int.		1	1¹/₃	0	0	.000	3	0	1	0.00	0
2007 Pittsburgh h-i.	N.L.		56	52²/₃	2	4	.333	45	17	57	5.47	12

| Major League Totals | 11 Yrs. | | 426 | 767¹/₃ | 37 | 53 | .411 | 489 | 316 | 782 | 4.40 | 29 |

a Traded to Seattle Mariners for pitcher Shawn Estes and infielder Wilson Delgado, May 20, 1995.
b Claimed on waivers by Montreal Expos, April 18, 1997.
c Voluntarily retired, August 1, 1997 though January 29, 2001.
d Released by Montreal Expos, January 29, 2001. Signed with Samsung (Korea) for 2001.
e Signed with Pittsburgh Pirates organization, December 30, 2001.
f On disabled list from July 2 to 15, 2002.
g On disabled list from August 6 to August 29, 2003.
h On disabled list from June 9 to July 15 and August 22 to September 11, 2007.
i Traded to Milwaukee Brewers for pitcher Marino Salas and pitcher Kevin Roberts, December 7, 2007.

TOWERS, JOSHUA ERIC (JOSH)

Born, Port Hueneme, California, February 26, 1977.
Bats Right. Throws Right. Height, 6 feet, 1 inch. Weight, 180 pounds.

Year	Club	Lea	G	IP	W	L	Pct	SO	BB	H	ERA	SAVES
1996 Bluefield.	Appal.		14	55	4	1	.800	61	6	63	5.24	0
1997 Delmarva	So.Atl.		9	18¹/₃	0	0	.000	16	2	18	3.44	1
1997 Frederick	Carolina		25	53²/₃	6	2	.750	64	18	74	4.86	1
1998 Frederick	Carolina		25	145¹/₃	8	7	.533	122	9	137	3.34	1
1998 Bowie	Eastern		5	18	2	1	.667	7	4	20	3.50	0
1999 Bowie	Eastern		29	189	12	7	.632	106	26	204	3.76	0
2000 Rochester	Int.		24	148	8	6	.571	102	21	157	3.47	0
2001 Rochester.	Int.		6	41	3	1	.750	27	8	40	3.51	0
2001 Baltimore	A.L.		24	140¹/₃	8	10	.444	58	16	165	4.49	0
2002 Rochester.	Int.		15	69	0	9	.000	43	14	109	7.57	0
2002 Baltimore a	A.L.		5	27¹/₃	0	3	.000	13	5	42	7.90	0
2003 Syracuse	Int.		21	132²/₃	5	7	.417	76	20	133	3.32	0
2003 Toronto	A.L.		14	64¹/₃	8	1	.889	42	7	67	4.48	1
2004 Syracuse	Int.		6	36	3	1	.750	25	7	33	2.50	0

Year	Club	Lea	G	IP	W	L	Pct	SO	BB	H	ERA	SAVES
2004 Toronto	A.L.	21	116^{1}/$_{3}$	9	9	.500	51	26	148	5.11	0
2005 Toronto	A.L.	33	208^{2}/$_{3}$	13	12	.520	112	29	237	3.71	0
2006 Syracuse	Int.	15	101^{1}/$_{3}$	5	5	.500	76	11	121	4.00	0
2006 Toronto	A.L.	15	62	2	10	.167	35	17	93	8.42	0
2007 Toronto b	A.L.	25	107	5	10	.333	76	22	129	5.38	0
Major League Totals ...... 7 Yrs.		137	726	45	55	.450	387	122	881	4.96	1

a Filed for free agency, October 15, 2002. Signed with Toronto Blue Jays organization, November 8, 2002.
b Not offered contract, December 12, 2007. Signed with Colorado Rockies, January 7, 2008.

TRACHSEL, STEPHEN (STEVE)

Born, Oxnard, California, October 31, 1970.
Bats Right. Throws Right. Height, 6 feet, 4 inches. Weight, 205 pounds.

Year	Club	Lea	G	IP	W	L	Pct	SO	BB	H	ERA	SAVES
1991 Geneva	N.Y.-Penn.	2	14^{1}/$_{3}$	1	0	1.000	7	6	10	1.26	0
1991 Winston-Salem	Carolina	12	73^{2}/$_{3}$	4	4	.500	69	19	70	3.67	0
1992 Charlotte	Southern	29	191	13	8	.619	135	35	180	3.06	0
1993 Iowa	A.A.	27	170^{2}/$_{3}$	13	6	.684	135	45	170	3.96	0
1993 Chicago	N.L.	3	19^{2}/$_{3}$	0	2	.000	14	3	16	4.58	0
1994 Chicago	N.L.	22	146	9	7	.563	108	54	133	3.21	0
1994 Iowa	A.A.	2	9	0	2	.000	8	7	11	10.00	0
1995 Chicago	N.L.	30	160^{2}/$_{3}$	7	13	.350	117	76	174	5.15	0
1996 Orlando	Southern	2	13	0	1	.000	12	0	11	2.77	0
1996 Chicago	N.L.	31	205	13	9	.591	132	62	181	3.03	0
1997 Chicago	N.L.	34	201^{1}/$_{3}$	8	12	.400	160	69	225	4.51	0
1998 Chicago	N.L.	33	208	15	8	.652	149	84	204	4.46	0
1999 Chicago	N.L.	34	205^{2}/$_{3}$	8	18	.308	149	64	226	5.56	0
2000 Tampa Bay-Toronto a-b-c	A.L.	34	200^{2}/$_{3}$	8	15	.348	110	74	232	4.80	0
2001 Norfolk	Int.	3	19^{1}/$_{3}$	2	0	1.000	12	6	13	2.79	0
2001 New York	N.L.	28	173^{2}/$_{3}$	11	13	.458	144	47	168	4.46	0
2002 Binghamton	Eastern	1	5^{2}/$_{3}$	1	0	1.000	5	4	3	0.00	0
2002 New York d-e	N.L.	30	173^{2}/$_{3}$	11	11	.500	105	69	170	3.37	0
2003 New York	N.L.	33	204^{2}/$_{3}$	16	10	.615	111	65	204	3.78	0
2004 New York	N.L.	33	202^{2}/$_{3}$	12	13	.480	117	83	203	4.00	0
2005 St. Lucie	Fla.St.	2	6^{2}/$_{3}$	0	1	.000	5	1	5	1.35	0
2005 Binghamton	Eastern	2	1^{2}/$_{3}$	1	0	1.000	7	4	8	3.00	0
2005 Norfolk	Int.	2	14	0	1	.000	12	2	10	2.57	0
2005 New York f	N.L.	6	37	1	4	.200	24	12	37	4.14	0
2006 New York g	N.L.	30	164^{2}/$_{3}$	15	8	.652	79	78	185	4.97	0
2007 Frederick	Carolina	1	7	0	1	.000	4	1	7	2.57	0
2007 Baltimore	A.L.	25	140^{2}/$_{3}$	6	8	.429	45	69	151	4.48	0
2007 Chicago h-i-j	N.L.	4	17^{1}/$_{3}$	1	3	.250	11	7	25	8.31	0
Major League Totals .... 15 Yrs.		410	2461^{1}/$_{3}$	141	154	.478	1575	916	2534	4.32	0
Division Series											
2006 New York	N.L.	1	3^{1}/$_{3}$	0	0	.000	2	1	6	5.40	0
Championship Series											
2006 New York	N.L.	1	1	0	1	.000	1	5	5	45.00	0

a Filed for free agency, October 28, 1999. Signed with Tampa Bay Devil Rays, January 28, 2000.
b Traded to Toronto Blue Jays with pitcher Mark Guthrie for infielder Brent Abernathy and player to be named later, July 21, 2000.
c Filed for free agency, October 31, 2000. Signed with New York Mets, December 11, 2000.
d On disabled list from July 1 to July 22, 2002.
e Filed for free agency, October 28, 2002, re-signed with New York Mets, December 7, 2002.
f On disabled list from March 30 to August 23, 2005.
g Filed for free agency, October 28, 2006. Signed with Baltimore Orioles, February 14, 2007.
h On disabled list from June 30 to July 20, 2007.
i Traded to Chicago Cubs for pitcher Rocky Cherry and infielder Scott Moore, August 31, 2007.
j Filed for free agency, October 31, 2007.

TURNBOW, THOMAS DERRICK

Born, Union City, Tennessee, January 25, 1978.
Bats Right. Throws Right. Height, 6 feet, 3 inches. Weight, 210 pounds.

Year	Club	Lea	G	IP	W	L	Pct	SO	BB	H	ERA	SAVES
1997 Martinsvlle	Appal.	7	24^{1}/$_{3}$	1	3	.250	7	16	34	7.40	0
1998 Martinsvlle	Appal.	13	70	2	6	.250	45	66	66	5.01	0
1999 Piedmont a	So.Atl.	26	161	12	8	.600	149	53	130	3.35	0
2000 Anaheim	A.L.	24	38	0	0	.000	25	36	36	4.74	0
2001 Arkansas	Texas	3	14	0	0	.000	11	5	12	2.57	0

Year	Club	Lea	G	IP	W	L	Pct	SO	BB	H	ERA	SAVES
2002	Angels	Arizona	3	8	0	1	.000	12	3	5	4.50	0
2002	Rancho Cucamonga	California	13	12	0	0	.000	14	9	16	5.25	0
2003	Arkansas	Texas	7	14	1	0	1.000	19	5	4	0.00	3
2003	Anaheim	A.L.	11	15⅓	2	0	1.000	15	3	7	0.59	0
2003	Salt Lake	P.C.	35	55	1	2	.333	63	24	68	5.73	2
2004	Salt Lake	P.C.	46	74⅔	2	6	.250	56	42	75	5.06	6
2004	Anaheim b	A.L.	4	6⅓	0	0	.000	3	7	2	0.00	0
2005	Milwaukee	N.L.	69	67⅓	7	1	.875	64	24	49	1.74	39
2006	Milwaukee	N.L.	64	56⅓	4	9	.308	69	39	56	6.87	24
2007	Milwaukee	N.L.	77	68	4	5	.444	84	46	44	4.63	1
Major League Totals	6 Yrs.		249	251⅓	17	15	.531	260	155	194	4.01	64

a Selected by Anaheim Angels from Philadelphia Phillies in Rule V draft, December 13, 1999.
b Claimed on waivers by Milwaukee Brewers, October 15, 2004.

VALVERDE, JOSE RAFAEL
Born, San Pedro de Macoris, Dominican Republic, July 24, 1979.
Bats Right. Throws Right. Height, 6 feet, 4 inches. Weight, 255 pounds.

Year	Club	Lea	G	IP	W	L	Pct	SO	BB	H	ERA	SAVES
1997	Arizona	Dominican	14	18⅔	0	0	.000	19	13	20	5.30	0
1998	Arizona	Dominican	23	51⅓	1	3	.250	56	22	31	1.75	7
1999	Diamondbacks	Arizona	20	28⅔	1	2	.333	47	10	34	4.08	8
1999	South Bend	Midwest	2	2⅔	0	0	.000	3	2	2	0.00	0
2000	South Bend	Midwest	31	31⅔	0	5	.000	39	25	31	5.40	14
2000	Missoula	Pioneer	12	11⅔	1	0	1.000	24	4	3	0.00	4
2001	El Paso	Texas	39	41⅓	2	2	.500	72	27	36	3.92	13
2002	Tucson	P.C.	49	47⅔	2	4	.333	65	23	45	5.85	5
2003	Tucson	P.C.	22	29	1	1	.500	26	14	26	3.10	5
2003	Arizona	N.L.	54	50⅓	2	1	.667	71	26	24	2.15	10
2004	Arizona	N.L.	29	29⅔	1	2	.333	38	17	23	4.25	8
2004	Tucson a	P.C.	10	10⅔	1	1	.500	5	5	9	4.22	3
2005	Tucson	P.C.	2	2	0	0	.000	3	1	1	0.00	0
2005	Arizona b	N.L.	61	66⅓	3	4	.429	75	20	51	2.44	15
2006	Tucson	P.C.	15	17⅔	1	0	1.000	18	10	13	3.06	3
2006	Arizona	N.L.	44	49⅓	2	3	.400	69	22	50	5.84	18
2007	Arizona c	N.L.	65	64⅓	1	4	.200	78	26	46	2.66	*47
Major League Totals	5 Yrs.		253	260	9	14	.391	331	111	194	3.29	98
Division Series												
2007	Arizona	N.L.	3	3	0	0	.000	6	1	1	0.00	1
Championship Series												
2007	Arizona	N.L.	1	1⅔	0	1	.000	2	3	1	5.40	0

a On disabled list from June 14 to October 4, 2004.
b On disabled list from March 25 to May 2, 2005.
c Traded to Houston Astros for pitcher Chad Qualls, pitcher Juan Gutierrez and outfielder Chris Burke, December 14, 2007.

VANDENHURK, HENRICUS NICOLAS (RICK)
Born, Eindhoven, Netherlands, May 22, 1985.
Bats Right. Throws Right. Height, 6 feet, 5 inches. Weight, 195 pounds.

Year	Club	Lea	G	IP	W	L	Pct	SO	BB	H	ERA	SAVES
2003	Marlins	Gulf Coast	11	38⅔	2	6	.250	30	20	49	5.35	0
2004	Jupiter	Fla.St.	14	58	2	3	.400	43	31	54	3.26	0
2005	Jupiter	Fla.St.	2	6⅔	0	1	.000	6	0	7	4.05	0
2005	Greensboro	So.Atl.	4	22	1	2	.333	26	11	17	2.45	0
2006	Jupiter	Fla.St.	3	10	0	0	.000	15	6	5	2.70	0
2006	Marlins	Gulf Coast	5	15	0	0	.000	26	8	4	1.20	0
2007	Carolina	Southern	9	53⅔	2	2	.500	61	21	42	3.52	0
2007	Albuquerque	P.C.	2	12	2	0	1.000	14	4	6	2.25	0
2007	Florida	N.L.	18	81⅔	4	6	.400	82	48	94	6.83	0

VARGAS, CLAUDIO (ALMONTE)
Born, Mao, Dominican Republic, May 19, 1979.
Bats Right. Throws Right. Height, 6 feet, 3 inches. Weight, 230 pounds.

Year	Club	Lea	G	IP	W	L	Pct	SO	BB	H	ERA	SAVES
1996	Florida	Dominican	15	46⅔	2	3	.400	37	26	41	3.09	0
1997	Florida	Dominican	13	72	6	2	.750	81	31	62	2.50	0
1998	Brevard County	Fla.St.	2	9⅔	0	1	.000	9	4	15	4.66	0

Year	Club	Lea	G	IP	W	L	Pct	SO	BB	H	ERA	SAVES
1998	Marlins.........	Gulf Coast	5	28²/₃	0	4	.000	27	7	24	4.08	0
1999	Kane County.......	Midwest	19	99²/₃	5	5	.500	88	41	97	3.88	0
2000	Portland..........	Eastern	3	15	1	1	.500	13	6	16	3.60	0
2000	Brevard County	Fla.St.	24	145¹/₃	10	5	.667	143	44	126	3.28	0
2001	Portland..........	Eastern	27	159	8	9	.471	151	67	122	4.19	0
2002	Calgary.............	P.C.	17	76¹/₃	4	11	.267	61	35	88	6.72	0
2002	Harrisburg a-b	Eastern	8	33	2	2	.500	34	9	38	4.64	0
2003	Edmonton	P.C.	2	9²/₃	0	0	.000	12	5	7	2.79	0
2003	Harrisburg	Eastern	2	12	1	0	1.000	13	3	7	0.75	0
2003	Montreal c	N.L.	23	114	6	8	.429	62	41	111	4.34	0
2004	Montreal.............	N.L.	45	118¹/₃	5	5	.500	89	64	120	5.25	0
2005	New Orleans..........	P.C.	5	28	2	2	.500	35	12	24	4.18	0
2005	Washington-Arizona d-e..	N.L.	25	132¹/₃	9	9	.500	95	47	146	5.24	0
2006	Arizona f.............	N.L.	31	167²/₃	12	10	.545	123	52	185	4.83	0
2007	Milwaukee g..........	N.L.	29	134¹/₃	11	6	.647	107	54	153	5.09	1
Major League Totals ....5 Yrs.			153	666²/₃	43	38	.531	476	258	715	4.95	1

a Traded to Montreal Expos by Florida Marlins with outfielder Cliff Floyd, infielder Wilton Guerrero and cash for pitcher Carl Pavano, pitcher Graeme Lloyd, infielder Mike Mordecai, pitcher Justin Wayne and player to be named later, July 11, 2002.
b Florida Marlins received pitcher Don Levinski to complete trade, August 5, 2002.
c On disabled list from August 6 to September 15, 2003.
d On disabled list from March 16 to May 11, 2005.
e Claimed on waivers by Arizona Diamondbacks, June 3, 2005.
f Traded to Milwaukee Brewers with pitcher Greg Aquino and catcher Johnny Estrada for pitcher Doug Davis, pitcher Dana Eveland and outfielder David Krynzel, November 25, 2006.
g On disabled list from August 25 to September 9, 2007.

VAZQUEZ, JAVIER CARLOS
Born, Ponce, Puerto Rico, June 25, 1976.
Bats Right. Throws Right. Height, 6 feet, 2 inches. Weight, 215 pounds.

Year	Club	Lea	G	IP	W	L	Pct	SO	BB	H	ERA	SAVES
1994	Expos...........	Gulf Coast	15	67²/₃	5	2	.714	56	15	37	2.53	0
1995	Albany	So.Atl.	21	102²/₃	6	6	.500	87	47	109	5.08	0
1996	Delmarva	So.Atl.	27	164¹/₃	14	3	.824	173	57	138	2.68	0
1997	Wst Plm Bch	Fla.St.	19	112²/₃	6	3	.667	100	28	98	2.16	0
1997	Harrisburg	Eastern	6	42	4	0	1.000	47	12	15	1.07	0
1998	Montreal.............	N.L.	33	172¹/₃	5	15	.250	139	68	196	6.06	0
1999	Ottawa	Int.	7	42²/₃	4	2	.667	46	16	45	4.85	0
1999	Montreal.............	N.L.	26	154²/₃	9	8	.529	113	52	154	5.00	0
2000	Montreal.............	N.L.	33	217²/₃	11	9	.550	196	61	247	4.05	0
2001	Montreal.............	N.L.	32	223²/₃	16	11	.593	208	44	197	3.42	0
2002	Montreal.............	N.L.	34	230¹/₃	10	13	.435	179	49	*243	3.91	0
2003	Montreal a	N.L.	34	230²/₃	13	12	.520	241	57	198	3.24	0
2004	New York b...........	A.L.	32	198	14	10	.583	150	60	195	4.91	0
2005	Arizona c	N.L.	33	215²/₃	11	15	.423	192	46	223	4.42	0
2006	Chicago	A.L.	33	202²/₃	11	12	.478	184	56	206	4.84	0
2007	Chicago	A.L.	32	216²/₃	15	8	.652	213	50	197	3.74	0
Major League Totals ....10 Yrs.			322	2062¹/₃	115	113	.504	1815	543	2056	4.28	0
Division Series												
2004	New York.............	A.L.	1	5	0	0	.000	6	2	7	9.00	0
Championship Series												
2004	New York.............	A.L.	2	6¹/₃	1	0	1.000	6	7	9	9.95	0

a Traded to New York Yankees for infielder Nick Johnson, outfielder Juan Rivera and pitcher Randy Choate, December 4, 2003.
b Traded to Arizona Diamondbacks with pitcher Brad Halsey, catcher Dioner Navarro and cash for pitcher Randy Johnson, January 11, 2005.
c Traded to Chicago White Sox for pitcher Orlando Hernandez, pitcher Luis Vizcaino and outfielder Chris Young, December 20, 2005.

VERLANDER, JUSTIN BROOKS
Born, Manakin Sabot, Virginia, February 20, 1983.
Bats Right. Throws Right. Height, 6 feet, 5 inches. Weight, 200 pounds.

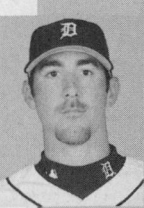

Year	Club	Lea	G	IP	W	L	Pct	SO	BB	H	ERA	SAVES
2005	Lakeland...........	Fla.St.	13	86	9	2	.818	104	19	70	1.67	0
2005	Erie..............	Eastern	7	32²/₃	2	0	1.000	32	7	11	0.28	0
2005	Detroit	A.L.	2	11¹/₃	0	2	.000	7	5	15	7.15	0
2006	Detroit a.............	A.L.	30	186	17	9	.654	124	60	187	3.63	0

Year	Club	Lea	G	IP	W	L	Pct	SO	BB	H	ERA	SAVES
2007 Detroit b.............	A.L.	32	201²/₃	18	6	*.750	183	67	181	3.66	0
Major League Totals ....3 Yrs.		64	399	35	17	.673	314	132	383	3.74	0
Division Series											
2006 Detroit...............	A.L.	1	5¹/₃	0	0	.000	5	4	7	5.06	0
Championship Series											
2006 Detroit...............	A.L.	1	5¹/₃	1	0	1.000	6	1	7	6.75	0
World Series Record											
2006 Detroit...............	A.L.	2	11	0	2	.000	12	5	12	5.73	0

a Selected Rookie of the Year in American League for 2006.

b Pitched no-hit, no-run game against Milwaukee Brewers, June 12, 2007.

VILLANUEVA, CARLOS MANUEL
Born, Santiago, Dominican Republic, November 28, 1983.
Bats Right. Throws Right. Height, 6 feet, 2 inches. Weight, 190 pounds.

Year	Club	Lea	G	IP	W	L	Pct	SO	BB	H	ERA	SAVES
2002 Giants.............	Arizona	19	30¹/₃	4	0	1.000	23	3	24	0.59	3
2003 Giants.............	Arizona	12	59	3	6	.333	67	13	64	3.97	0
2004 Beloit a...........	Midwest	25	114²/₃	8	8	.500	113	30	102	3.77	1
2005 Brevard County	Fla.St.	21	112¹/₃	8	1	.889	124	32	78	2.32	0
2005 Huntsville.........	Southern	4	20²/₃	1	3	.250	14	9	21	7.40	0
2006 Huntsville.........	Southern	11	62¹/₃	4	5	.444	59	14	60	3.75	0
2006 Nashville.........	P.C.	11	66¹/₃	7	1	.875	61	26	42	2.71	0
2006 Milwaukee	N.L.	10	53²/₃	2	2	.500	39	11	43	3.69	0
2007 Nashville	P.C.	2	8¹/₃	0	0	.000	9	1	3	3.24	0
2007 Milwaukee	N.L.	59	114¹/₃	8	5	.615	99	53	101	3.94	1
Major League Totals ....2 Yrs.		69	168	10	7	.588	138	64	144	3.86	1

a Traded to Milwaukee Brewers by San Francisco Giants with pitcher Glenn Woolard for pitcher Wayne Franklin and pitcher Leo Estrella, March 30, 2004.

VILLARREAL, OSCAR EDUARDO
Born, San Nicolas de Los Garza, Mexico, November 22, 1981.
Bats Left. Throws Right. Height, 6 feet. Weight, 215 pounds.

Year	Club	Lea	G	IP	W	L	Pct	SO	BB	H	ERA	SAVES
1999 Diamondbacks......	Arizona	14	64¹/₃	1	5	.167	51	25	64	3.78	0
2000 Diamondbacks......	Arizona	1	1	0	0	.000	1	0	2	9.00	0
2000 High Desert	Calif.	9	24²/₃	0	2	.000	18	14	24	3.65	0
2000 South Bend	Midwest	13	32²/₃	1	3	.250	30	17	37	4.41	0
2000 Tucson..............	P.C.	2	4¹/₃	1	0	1.000	4	2	6	2.08	0
2001 El Paso.............	Texas	27	140²/₃	6	9	.400	108	63	154	4.41	0
2002 Tucson..............	P.C.	10	64	3	3	.500	40	22	68	4.36	0
2002 El Paso.............	Texas	14	84¹/₃	6	3	.667	85	26	73	3.74	0
2003 Arizona..............	N.L.	86	98	10	7	.588	80	46	80	2.57	0
2004 Arizona..............	N.L.	17	18	0	2	.000	17	7	25	7.00	0
2004 Tucson a............	P.C.	6	10²/₃	0	2	.000	12	4	20	14.34	0
2005 Tucson..............	P.C.	12	17¹/₃	0	3	.000	8	4	19	5.19	0
2005 Arizona b-c...........	N.L.	11	13²/₃	2	0	1.000	5	6	11	5.27	0
2006 Atlanta..............	N.L.	58	92¹/₃	9	1	.900	55	27	93	3.61	0
2007 Atlanta d.............	N.L.	51	76¹/₃	2	2	.500	58	32	75	4.24	1
Major League Totals ....5 Yrs.		223	298¹/₃	23	12	.657	215	118	284	3.71	1

a On disabled list from May 10 to October 4, 2004.

b On disabled list from April 11 to September 2, 2005.

c Traded to Atlanta Braves with pitcher Lance Cormier for catcher Johnny Estrada, December 7, 2005.

d Traded to Houston Astros for outfielder Josh Anderson, November 16, 2007.

VILLONE, RONALD THOMAS (RON)
Born, Englewood, New Jersey, January 16, 1970.
Bats Left. Throws Left. Height, 6 feet, 3 inches. Weight, 245 pounds.

Year	Club	Lea	G	IP	W	L	Pct	SO	BB	H	ERA	SAVES
1993 Riverside	California	16	83¹/₃	7	4	.636	82	62	74	4.21	0
1993 Jacksonville	Southern	11	63²/₃	3	4	.429	66	41	49	4.38	0
1994 Jacksonville	Southern	41	79¹/₃	6	7	.462	94	68	56	3.86	8
1995 Seattle	A.L.	19	19¹/₃	0	2	.000	26	23	20	7.91	0
1995 Tacoma	P.C.	22	29²/₃	1	0	1.000	43	19	9	0.61	13
1995 San Diego a...........	N.L.	19	25²/₃	2	1	.667	37	11	24	4.21	1
1996 Las Vegas............	P.C.	23	22	2	1	.667	29	9	13	1.64	3
1996 San Diego	N.L.	21	18¹/₃	1	1	.500	19	7	17	2.95	0

Year Club	Lea	G	IP	W	L	Pct	SO	BB	H	ERA	SAVES
1996 Milwaukee b	A.L.	23	24 2/3	0	0	.000	19	18	14	3.28	2
1997 Milwaukee c	A.L.	50	52 2/3	1	0	1.000	40	36	54	3.42	0
1998 Buffalo	Int.	23	22 1/3	2	2	.500	28	11	20	2.01	7
1998 Cleveland d	A.L.	25	27	0	0	.000	15	22	30	6.00	0
1999 Indianapolis	Int.	18	19	2	0	1.000	23	13	9	1.42	1
1999 Cincinnati	N.L.	29	142 2/3	9	7	.563	97	73	114	4.23	2
2000 Cincinnati e	N.L.	35	141	10	10	.500	77	78	154	5.43	0
2001 Colorado-Houston f-g	N.L.	53	114 2/3	6	10	.375	113	53	133	5.89	0
2002 Pittsburgh h-i	N.L.	45	93	4	6	.400	55	34	95	5.81	0
2003 Tucson	P.C.	15	25 1/3	1	1	.500	22	12	20	3.55	1
2003 New Orleans	P.C.	5	29 1/3	3	1	.750	18	10	24	1.23	0
2003 Houston j-k	N.L.	19	106 2/3	6	6	.500	91	48	91	4.13	0
2004 Seattle l	A.L.	56	117	8	6	.571	86	64	102	4.08	0
2005 Seattle	A.L.	52	40 1/3	2	3	.400	41	23	33	2.45	1
2005 Florida k-l	N.L.	27	23 2/3	3	2	.600	29	12	24	6.85	0
2006 New York m	A.L.	70	80 1/3	3	3	.500	72	51	75	5.04	0
2007 Scranton-WB	Int.	17	23 2/3	0	1	.000	27	10	21	1.90	1
2007 New York n-o	A.L.	37	42 1/3	0	0	.000	25	18	36	4.25	0
Major League Totals .... 13 Yrs.		580	1069 1/3	55	57	.491	842	571	1016	4.76	6
Division Series											
2001 Houston	N.L.	1	0 2/3	0	0	.000	0	0	0	0.00	0
2006 New York	A.L.	1	1	0	0	.000	1	1	1	0.00	0
2007 New York	A.L.	1	0 1/3	0	0	.000	0	0	0	0.00	0
Division Series Totals		3	2	0	0	.000	1	1	1	0.00	0

a Traded to San Diego Padres with outfielder Marc Newfield for pitcher Andy Benes and a player to be named later, July 31, 1995. Mariners received pitcher Greg Keagle to complete trade, September 16, 1995.

b Traded to Milwaukee Brewers with pitcher Bryce Florie and outfielder Marc Newfield for outfielder Greg Vaughn and a player to be named later, July 31, 1996. Padres received outfielder Jerry Parent to complete trade, September 16, 1996.

c Traded to Cleveland Indians with pitcher Mike Fetters and pitcher Ben McDonald for pitcher Jeff Juden and outfielder Marquis Grissom, December 8, 1997.

d Released by Cleveland Indians, April 2, 1999. Signed with Cincinnati Reds organization, April 5, 1999.

e Traded to Colorado Rockies for two players to be named later, November 8, 2000. Cincinnati Reds received pitcher Jeff Tahlienti and pitcher Justin Carter to complete trade, December 20, 2000.

f Traded to Houston Astros with cash for pitcher Jay Powell, June 27, 2001.

g Filed for free agency, November 5, 2001. Signed with Pittsburgh Pirates organization, February 12, 2002.

h On disabled list from August 15 to September 1, 2002.

i Filed for free agency, October 29, 2002. Signed with Arizona Diamondbacks organization, January 29, 2003.

j Released by Arizona Diamondbacks, May 15, 2003. Signed with Houston Astros organization, May 18, 2003.

k Filed for free agency, November 2, 2003, re-signed with Seattle Mariners, December 19, 2004.

l Filed for free agency, October 28, 2004.

k Traded to Florida Marlins for pitcher Yorman Bazardo and pitcher Michael Flannery, July 31, 2005.

l Traded to New York Yankees for pitcher Ben Julianel, December 16, 2005.

m Filed for free agency, October 31, 2006. Signed with New York Yankees organization, February 13, 2007.

n On disabled list from August 22 to September 6, 2007.

o Filed for free agency, October 31, 2007.

VIZCAINO, LUIS
Born, Bani, Dominican Republic, August 6, 1974
Bats Right. Throws Right. Height, 5 feet, 11 inches. Weight, 185 pounds.

Year Club	Lea	G	IP	W	L	Pct	SO	BB	H	ERA	SAVES
1995 Oakland	Dominican	16	115	10	2	.833	89	29	93	2.27	0
1996 Athletics	Arizona	15	59 2/3	6	3	.667	52	24	58	4.07	1
1997 Modesto	California	7	14 1/3	0	3	.000	15	13	24	13.19	0
1997 Sou Oregon	Northwest	22	47 2/3	1	6	.143	42	27	62	7.93	0
1998 Modesto	California	23	102	6	3	.667	108	43	72	2.74	0
1998 Huntsville	Southern	7	38 2/3	3	2	.600	26	22	43	4.66	0
1999 Midland	Texas	25	104 2/3	8	7	.533	88	48	120	5.85	0
1999 Vancouver	P.C.	7	13	0	1	.000	7	6	13	1.38	0
1999 Oakland	A.L.	1	3 1/3	0	0	.000	2	3	3	5.40	0
2000 Oakland	A.L.	12	19 1/3	0	1	.000	18	11	25	7.45	0
2000 Sacramento	P.C.	33	48 1/3	6	2	.750	41	21	48	5.03	5
2001 Sacramento	P.C.	27	42	2	2	.500	56	10	35	2.14	7
2001 Oakland	A.L.	36	36 2/3	2	1	.667	31	12	38	4.66	1
2002 Milwaukee a-b	N.L.	76	81 1/3	5	3	.625	79	30	55	2.99	5
2003 Milwaukee	N.L.	75	62	4	3	.571	61	25	64	6.39	0
2004 Milwaukee c	N.L.	73	72	4	4	.500	63	24	61	3.75	1
2005 Chicago d	A.L.	65	70	6	5	.545	43	29	74	3.73	0
2006 Arizona e	N.L.	70	65 1/3	4	4	.400	72	29	51	3.58	0

Year Club	Lea	G	IP	W	L	Pct	SO	BB	H	ERA	SAVES
2007 New York f . . . . .A.L.		77	75⅓	8	2	.800	62	43	66	4.30	0
Major League Totals . . . . .9 Yrs.		485	485⅓	33	25	.569	431	206	437	4.25	7
Division Series											
2007 New York . . . . A.L.		1	0⅔	0	1	.000	0	2	2	13.50	0

a Traded to Texas Rangers for pitcher Justin Duchscherer, March 18, 2002.
b Traded to Milwaukee Brewers for pitcher Jesus Pena, March 23, 2002.
c Traded to Chicago White Sox with outfielder Scott Podsednik and player to be named later for outfielder Carlos Lee, December 13, 2004. Chicago White Sox received infielder Travis Hinton to complete trade, January 10, 2005.
d Traded to Arizona Diamondbacks with pitcher Orlando Hernandez and outfielder Chris Young for pitcher Javier Vazquez, December 20, 2005.
e Traded to New York Yankees with pitcher Steven Jackson, pitcher Ross Ohlendorf and infielder Alberto Gonzalez for pitcher Randy Johnson and cash, January 9, 2007.
f Filed for free agency, October 29, 2007. Signed with Colorado Rockies, December 21, 2007.

WAGNER, WILLIAM EDWARD (BILLY)

Born, Tannersville, Virginia, July 25, 1971.
Bats Left. Throws Left. Height, 5 feet, 11 inches. Weight, 205 pounds.

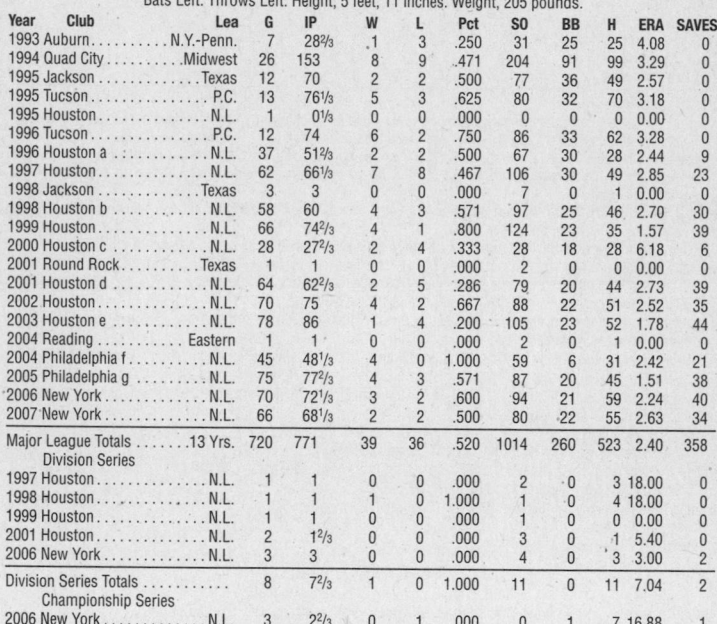

Year Club	Lea	G	IP	W	L	Pct	SO	BB	H	ERA	SAVES
1993 Auburn . . . . N.Y.-Penn.		7	28⅔	1	3	.250	31	25	25	4.08	0
1994 Quad City . . . . .Midwest		26	153	8	9	.471	204	91	99	3.29	0
1995 Jackson . . . . Texas		12	70	2	2	.500	77	36	49	2.57	0
1995 Tucson . . . . P.C.		13	76⅓	5	3	.625	80	32	70	3.18	0
1995 Houston . . . . N.L.		1	0⅓	0	0	.000	0	0	0	0.00	0
1996 Tucson . . . . P.C.		12	74	6	2	.750	86	33	62	3.28	0
1996 Houston a . . . . N.L.		37	51⅔	2	2	.500	67	30	28	2.44	9
1997 Houston . . . . N.L.		62	66⅓	7	8	.467	106	30	49	2.85	23
1998 Jackson . . . . Texas		3	3	0	0	.000	7	0	1	0.00	0
1998 Houston b . . . . N.L.		58	60	4	3	.571	97	25	46	2.70	30
1999 Houston . . . . N.L.		66	74⅔	4	1	.800	124	23	35	1.57	39
2000 Houston c . . . . N.L.		28	27⅔	2	4	.333	28	18	28	6.18	6
2001 Round Rock . . . . Texas		1	1	0	0	.000	2	0	0	0.00	0
2001 Houston d . . . . N.L.		64	62⅔	2	5	.286	79	20	44	2.73	39
2002 Houston . . . . N.L.		70	75	4	2	.667	88	22	51	2.52	35
2003 Houston e . . . . N.L.		78	86	1	4	.200	105	23	52	1.78	44
2004 Reading . . . . Eastern		1	1	0	0	.000	2	0	1	0.00	0
2004 Philadelphia f . . . . N.L.		45	48⅓	4	0	1.000	59	6	31	2.42	21
2005 Philadelphia g . . . . .N.L.		75	77⅔	4	3	.571	87	20	45	1.51	38
2006 New York . . . . N.L.		70	72⅓	3	2	.600	94	21	59	2.24	40
2007 New York . . . . N.L.		66	68⅓	2	2	.500	80	22	55	2.63	34
Major League Totals . . . . . . .13 Yrs.		720	771	39	36	.520	1014	260	523	2.40	358
Division Series											
1997 Houston . . . . N.L.		1	1	0	0	.000	2	0	3	18.00	0
1998 Houston . . . . N.L.		1	1	1	0	1.000	1	0	4	18.00	0
1999 Houston . . . . N.L.		1	1	0	0	.000	1	0	0	0.00	0
2001 Houston . . . . N.L.		2	1⅔	0	0	.000	3	0	1	5.40	0
2006 New York . . . . N.L.		3	3	0	0	.000	4	0	3	3.00	2
Division Series Totals		8	7⅔	1	0	1.000	11	0	11	7.04	2
Championship Series											
2006 New York . . . . N.L.		3	2⅔	0	1	.000	0	1	7	16.88	1

a On disabled list from August 23 to September 7, 1996.
b On disabled list from July 16 to August 7, 1998.
c On disabled list from June 18 to November 5, 2000.
d On disabled list from June 4 to June 19, 2001.
e Traded to Philadelphia Phillies for pitcher Brandon Duckworth, pitcher Taylor Buchholz and pitcher Ezequiel Astacio, November 3, 2003.
f On disabled list from May 8 to June 8 and from July 22 to September 4, 2004.
g Filed for free agency, October 27, 2005. Signed with New York Mets, November 29, 2005.

WAINWRIGHT, ADAM PARRISH

Born, Brunswick, Georgia, August 30, 1981.
Bats Right. Throws Right. Height, 6 feet, 7 inches. Weight, 205 pounds.

Year Club	Lea	G	IP	W	L	Pct	SO	BB	H	ERA	SAVES
2000 Danville . . . . Appal.		6	29⅓	2	2	.500	39	2	28	3.68	0
2000 Braves . . . . Gulf Coast		7	32	4	0	1.000	42	10	15	1.13	0
2001 Macon . . . . So.Atl.		28	164⅔	10	10	.500	184	48	144	3.77	0
2002 Myrtle Beach . . . . . . .Carolina		28	163⅓	9	6	.600	167	66	149	3.31	0

Year	Club	Lea	G	IP	W	L	Pct	SO	BB	H	ERA	SAVES
2003 Greenville a	Southern		27	149²/₃	10	8	.556	128	37	133	3.37	0
2004 Memphis		P.C.	12	63²/₃	4	4	.500	64	28	68	5.37	0
2005 Memphis		P.C.	29	182	10	10	.500	147	51	204	4.40	0
2005 St. Louis		N.L.	2	2	0	0	.000	0	1	2	13.50	0
2006 St. Louis		N.L.	61	75	2	1	.667	72	22	64	3.12	3
2007 St. Louis		N.L.	32	202	14	12	.538	136	70	212	3.70	0
Major League Totals	3 Yrs.		95	279	16	13	.552	208	93	278	3.61	3
Division Series												
2006 St. Louis		N.L.	3	3²/₃	0	0	.000	6	0	3	0.00	1
Championship Series												
2006 St. Louis		N.L.	3	3	0	0	.000	4	1	2	0.00	2
World Series Record												
2006 St. Louis		N.L.	3	3	1	0	1.000	5	1	2	0.00	1

a Traded by Atlanta Braves to St. Louis Cardinals with pitcher Jason Marquis and pitcher Ray King for catcher Eli Marrero and outfielder J.D. Drew, December 13, 2003.

WAKEFIELD, TIMOTHY STEPHEN (TIM)

Born, Melborne, Florida, August 2, 1966.
Bats Right. Throws Right. Height, 6 feet, 2 inches. Weight, 210 pounds.

Year	Club	Lea	G	IP	W	L	Pct	SO	BB	H	ERA	SAVES
1989 Welland	N.Y.-Penn.		18	39²/₃	1	1	.500	42	21	30	3.40	2
1990 Salem	Carolina		20	190¹/₃	10	14	.417	127	85	187	4.73	0
1991 Buffalo		A.A.	1	4²/₃	0	1	.000	4	1	8	11.57	0
1991 Carolina	Southern		26	183	15	8	.652	123	51	155	2.90	0
1992 Buffalo		A.A.	20	135¹/₃	10	3	.769	71	51	122	3.06	0
1992 Pittsburgh		N.L.	13	92	8	1	.889	51	35	76	2.15	0
1993 Carolina	Southern		9	56²/₃	3	5	.375	36	22	68	6.99	0
1993 Pittsburgh		N.L.	24	128¹/₃	6	11	.353	59	75	145	5.61	0
1994 Buffalo		A.A.	30	175²/₃	5	15	.250	83	98	197	5.84	0
1995 Pawtucket		Int.	4	25	2	1	.667	14	9	23	2.52	0
1995 Boston a-b		A.L.	27	195¹/₃	16	8	.667	119	68	163	2.95	0
1996 Boston		A.L.	32	211²/₃	14	13	.519	140	90	238	5.14	0
1997 Boston c		A.L.	35	201¹/₃	12	*15	.444	151	87	193	4.25	0
1998 Boston		A.L.	36	216	17	8	.680	146	79	211	4.58	0
1999 Boston		A.L.	49	140	6	11	.353	104	72	146	5.08	15
2000 Boston d		A.L.	51	159¹/₃	6	10	.375	102	65	170	5.48	0
2001 Boston		A.L.	45	168²/₃	9	12	.429	148	73	156	3.90	3
2002 Boston		A.L.	45	163¹/₃	11	5	.688	134	51	121	2.81	3
2003 Boston		A.L.	35	202¹/₃	11	7	.611	169	71	193	4.09	1
2004 Boston		A.L.	32	188¹/₃	12	10	.545	116	63	197	4.87	0
2005 Boston		A.L.	33	225¹/₃	16	12	.571	151	68	210	4.15	0
2006 Boston e		A.L.	23	140	7	11	.389	90	51	135	4.63	0
2007 Boston		A.L.	31	189	17	12	.586	110	64	191	4.76	0
Major League Totals	15 Yrs.		511	2621	168	146	.535	1790	1012	2545	4.33	22
Division Series												
1995 Boston		A.L.	1	5¹/₃	0	1	.000	4	5	5	11.81	0
1998 Boston		A.L.	1	1¹/₃	0	1	.000	1	2	3	33.75	0
1999 Boston		A.L.	2	2	0	0	.000	4	4	3	13.50	0
2003 Boston		A.L.	2	7²/₃	0	1	.000	7	3	6	3.52	0
2005 Boston		A.L.	1	5¹/₃	0	1	.000	4	1	6	6.75	0
Division Series Totals			7	21²/₃	0	4	.000	20	15	23	9.14	0
Championship Series												
1992 Pittsburgh		N.L.	2	18	2	0	1.000	7	5	14	3.00	0
2003 Boston		A.L.	3	14	2	1	.667	10	6	8	2.57	0
2004 Boston		A.L.	3	7¹/₃	1	0	1.000	6	3	9	8.59	0
2007 Boston		A.L.	1	4²/₃	0	1	.000	7	2	5	9.64	0
Championship Series Totals			9	44	5	2	.714	30	16	36	4.50	0
World Series Record												
2004 Boston		A.L.	1	3²/₃	0	0	.000	2	5	3	12.27	0

a Released by Pittsburgh Pirates, April 20, 1995.
b Signed by Boston Red Sox, April 27, 1995.
c On disabled list from April 15 to May 6, 1997.
d Filed for free agency, October 31, 2000, re-signed with Boston Red Sox, December 7, 2000.
e On disabled list from July 18 to September 13, 2006.

WALKER, JAMES ROSS (JAMIE)

Born, McMinnville, Tennessee, July 1, 1971.
Bats Left. Throws Left. Height, 6 feet, 2 inches. Weight, 185 pounds.

Year	Club	Lea	G	IP	W	L	Pct	SO	BB	H	ERA	SAVES
1992	Auburn	N.Y.-Penn.	15	83 1/3	4	6	.400	67	21	75	3.13	0
1993	Quad City	Midwest	25	131 2/3	3	11	.214	121	48	140	5.13	0
1994	Quad City	Midwest	32	125	8	10	.444	104	42	133	4.18	1
1995	Jackson	Texas	50	58	4	2	.667	38	24	59	4.50	2
1996	Jackson a	Texas	45	101	5	1	.833	79	35	94	2.50	2
1997	Wichita	Texas	5	6 2/3	0	1	.000	6	5	6	9.45	0
1997	Kansas City b	A.L.	50	43	3	3	.500	24	20	46	5.44	0
1998	Omaha	P.C.	7	46 2/3	5	1	.833	21	11	57	2.70	0
1998	Kansas City	A.L.	6	17 1/3	0	1	.000	15	3	30	9.87	0
1999	Royals	Gulf Coast	2	8	1	0	1.000	9	0	10	3.38	0
1999	Omaha c	P.C.	4	17 1/3	0	1	.000	11	4	22	4.67	0
2000	Omaha	P.C.	24	101 2/3	3	10	.231	52	25	138	5.22	0
2001	Buffalo d	Int.	38	93	7	2	.778	51	27	104	3.87	2
2002	Toledo	Int.	10	13 2/3	0	1	.000	9	3	7	1.98	1
2002	Detroit	A.L.	57	43 2/3	1	1	.500	40	9	32	3.71	1
2003	Detroit	A.L.	78	65	4	3	.571	45	17	61	3.32	3
2004	Detroit	A.L.	70	64 2/3	3	4	.429	53	12	69	3.20	1
2005	Detroit	A.L.	66	48 2/3	4	3	.571	30	13	49	3.70	0
2006	Detroit e	A.L.	56	48	0	1	.000	37	8	47	2.81	0
2007	Baltimore	A.L.	*81	61 1/3	3	2	.600	41	17	57	3.23	7
Major League Totals	8 Yrs.		464	391 2/3	18	18	.500	285	99	391	3.84	12

Division Series

Year	Club	Lea	G	IP	W	L	Pct	SO	BB	H	ERA	SAVES
2006	Detroit	A.L.	3	3 2/3	1	0	1.000	1	1	3	4.91	0

Championship Series

Year	Club	Lea	G	IP	W	L	Pct	SO	BB	H	ERA	SAVES
2006	Detroit	A.L.	1	0 1/3	0	0	.000	1	0	0	0.00	0

World Series Record

Year	Club	Lea	G	IP	W	L	Pct	SO	BB	H	ERA	SAVES
2006	Detroit	A.L.	1	0 1/3	0	0	.000	1	0	0	0.00	0

a Selected by Atlanta Braves from Houston Astros in Rule V draft, December 9, 1996.
b Traded to Kansas City Royals with outfielder Jermaine Dye for infielder Keith Lockhart and outfielder Michael Tucker, March 27, 1997.
c Filed for free agency, December 19, 1998, re-signed with Kansas City Royals, January 28, 1999.
d Filed for free agency, October 15, 2001. Signed with Detroit Tigers organization, November 6, 2001.
e Filed for free agency, October 30, 2006. Signed with Baltimore Orioles, November 21, 2006.

WANG, CHIEN-MING

Born, Tainan City, Taiwan, March 31, 1980.
Bats Right. Throws Right. Height, 6 feet, 3 inches. Weight, 220 pounds.

Year	Club	Lea	G	IP	W	L	Pct	SO	BB	H	ERA	SAVES
2000	Staten Island	N.Y.-Penn.	14	87	4	4	.500	75	21	77	2.48	0
2001	Staten Island a	N.Y.-Penn.				INJURED—Did Not Play						
2002	Staten Island	N.Y.-Penn.	13	78 1/3	6	1	.857	64	14	63	1.72	0
2003	Trenton	Eastern	21	122	7	6	.538	84	32	143	4.65	0
2003	Yankees	Gulf Coast	1	3	0	0	.000	2	0	2	0.00	0
2004	Trenton	Eastern	18	109	6	5	.545	90	26	112	4.05	0
2004	Columbus	Int.	6	40 1/3	5	1	.833	35	8	31	2.01	0
2005	Columbus	Int.	6	34	2	1	.667	21	6	40	4.24	0
2005	New York b	A.L.	18	116 1/3	8	5	.615	47	32	113	4.02	0
2006	New York	A.L.	34	218	*19	6	.760	76	52	233	3.63	1
2007	Tampa	Fla.St.	1	5	0	0	.000	4	1	5	5.40	0
2007	New York c	A.L.	30	199 1/3	19	7	.731	104	59	199	3.70	0
Major League Totals	3 Yrs.		82	533 2/3	46	18	.719	227	143	545	3.74	1

Division Series

Year	Club	Lea	G	IP	W	L	Pct	SO	BB	H	ERA	SAVES
2005	New York	A.L.	1	6 2/3	0	1	.000	1	0	6	1.35	0
2006	New York	A.L.	1	6 2/3	1	0	1.000	4	1	8	4.05	0
2007	New York	A.L.	2	5 2/3	0	2	.000	2	4	14	19.06	0
Division Series Totals			4	19	1	3	.250	7	5	28	7.58	0

a On minor league disabled list from April 5 to September 15, 2001.
b On disabled list from July 9 to September 6, 2005.
c On disabled list from March 23 to April 24, 2007.

WASHBURN, JARROD MICHAEL

Born, LaCrosse, Wisconsin, August 13, 1974.
Bats Left. Throws Left. Height, 6 feet, 1 inch. Weight, 190 pounds.

Year	Club	Lea	G	IP	W	L	Pct	SO	BB	H	ERA	SAVES
1995 Boise	Northwest	8	46	3	2	.600	54	14	35	3.33	0
1995 Cedar Rapids	Midwest	3	18¹/₃	0	1	.000	20	7	17	3.44	0
1996 Lake Elsinore	California	14	92²/₃	6	3	.667	93	33	79	3.30	0
1996 Vancouver	P.C.	2	8¹/₃	0	2	.000	5	12	12	10.80	0
1996 Midland	Texas	13	88	5	6	.455	58	25	77	4.40	0
1997 Midland	Texas	29	189¹/₃	15	12	.556	146	65	211	4.80	0
1997 Vancouver	P.C.	1	5	0	0	.000	6	2	4	3.60	0
1998 Midland	Texas	1	8²/₃	0	1	.000	8	2	13	6.23	0
1998 Vancouver	P.C.	14	91²/₃	4	5	.444	66	43	91	4.32	0
1998 Anaheim	A.L.	15	74	6	3	.667	48	27	70	4.62	0
1999 Edmonton	P.C.	11	59	1	5	.167	55	17	50	4.73	0
1999 Anaheim	A.L.	16	61²/₃	4	5	.444	39	26	61	5.25	0
2000 Lake Elsinore	California	1	3	0	0	.000	7	2	3	6.00	0
2000 Edmonton	P.C.	5	30²/₃	3	0	1.000	20	13	35	3.52	0
2000 Anaheim a	A.L.	14	84¹/₃	7	2	.778	49	37	64	3.74	0
2001 Salt Lake	P.C.	1	7²/₃	0	1	.000	5	1	9	5.87	0
2001 Anaheim b	A.L.	30	193¹/₃	11	10	.524	126	54	196	3.77	0
2002 Anaheim	A.L.	32	206	18	6	.750	139	59	183	3.15	0
2003 Anaheim	A.L.	32	207¹/₃	10	15	.400	118	54	205	4.43	0
2004 Rancho Cucamonga	California	1	4	0	0	.000	5	3	4	2.25	0
2004 Anaheim c	A.L.	25	149¹/₃	11	8	.579	86	40	159	4.64	0
2005 Los Angeles d-e	A.L.	29	177¹/₃	8	8	.500	94	51	184	3.20	0
2006 Seattle	A.L.	31	187	8	14	.364	103	55	198	4.67	0
2007 Seattle	A.L.	32	193²/₃	10	15	.400	114	67	201	4.32	0
Major League Totals ....10 Yrs.		256	1534	93	86	.520	916	470	1521	4.07	0

Division Series

Year	Club	Lea	G	IP	W	L	Pct	SO	BB	H	ERA	SAVES
2002 Anaheim	A.L.	2	12	1	0	1.000	4	3	12	3.75	0
2004 Anaheim	A.L.	2	3¹/₃	0	1	.000	3	3	6	10.80	0
Division Series Totals		4	15¹/₃	1	1	.500	7	6	18	5.28	0

Championship Series

Year	Club	Lea	G	IP	W	L	Pct	SO	BB	H	ERA	SAVES
2002 Anaheim	A.L.	1	7	0	0	.000	7	0	6	1.29	0
2005 Los Angeles	A.L.	1	4²/₃	0	0	.000	1	1	4	0.00	0
Championship Series Totals		2	11²/₃	0	0	.000	8	1	10	0.77	0

World Series Record

Year	Club	Lea	G	IP	W	L	Pct	SO	BB	H	ERA	SAVES
2002 Anaheim	A.L.	2	9²/₃	0	2	.000	6	7	12	9.31	0

a On disabled list from March 25 to April 8 and July 22 to August 6 and August 8 to October 1, 2000.
b On disabled list from March 23 to April 16, 2001.
c On disabled list from July 21 to September 2, 2004.
d On disabled list from July 25 to August 12, 2005.
e Filed for free agency, October 28, 2005. Signed with Seattle Mariners, December 22, 2005.

WASSERMAN, EHREN JOSEF

Born, Sylacauga, Alabama, December 6, 1980.
Bats Both. Throws Right. Height, 6 feet. Weight, 185 pounds.

Year	Club	Lea	G	IP	W	L	Pct	SO	BB	H	ERA	SAVES
2003 Bristol	Appal.	4	3²/₃	0	1	.000	4	3	9	14.73	0
2003 Kannapolis	So.Atl.	6	9	1	1	.500	10	3	8	1.00	0
2004 Winston-Salem	Carolina	10	10	1	0	1.000	5	5	11	2.70	1
2004 Kannapolis	So.Atl.	51	56¹/₃	2	3	.400	42	16	44	2.56	30
2005 Winston-Salem	Carolina	42	46	4	2	.667	37	9	41	1.37	20
2005 Birmingham	Southern	14	21	2	0	1.000	18	7	23	2.14	0
2006 Birmingham	Southern	61	63¹/₃	4	8	.333	47	25	60	2.56	22
2007 Charlotte	Int.	38	42²/₃	2	4	.333	33	18	34	2.11	5
2007 Chicago	A.L.	33	23	1	1	.500	14	7	20	2.74	0

WEATHERS, JOHN DAVID

Born, Lawrenceburg, Tennessee, September 25, 1969.
Bats Right. Throws Right. Height, 6 feet, 3 inches. Weight, 230 pounds.

Year	Club	Lea	G	IP	W	L	Pct	SO	BB	H	ERA	SAVES
1988 St. Catharines	N.Y.-Penn.	15	62²/₃	4	4	.500	36	26	58	3.02	0
1989 Myrtle Beach	So. Atl.	31	172²/₃	11	*13	.458	111	86	163	3.86	0
1990 Dunedin	Fla. St.	27	158	10	7	.588	96	59	158	3.70	0
1991 Knoxville	Southern	24	139¹/₃	10	7	.588	114	49	121	2.45	0

Year	Club	Lea	G	IP	W	L	Pct	SO	BB	H	ERA	SAVES
1991	Toronto	A.L.	15	14⅔	1	0	1.000	13	17	15	4.91	0
1992	Syracuse a	Int.	12	48⅓	1	4	.200	30	21	48	4.66	0
1992	Toronto b	A.L.	2	3⅓	0	0	.000	3	2	5	8.10	0
1993	Edmonton	P.C.	22	141	11	4	.733	117	47	150	3.83	0
1993	Florida	N.L.	14	45⅔	2	3	.400	34	13	57	5.12	0
1994	Florida c	N.L.	24	135	8	12	.400	72	59	166	5.27	0
1995	Brevard City	Fla. St.	1	4	0	0	.000	3	1	4	0.00	0
1995	Charlotte	Int.	1	5	0	1	.000	0	5	10	9.00	0
1995	Florida d	N.L.	28	90⅓	4	5	.444	60	52	104	5.98	0
1996	Charlotte	Int.	1	2⅓	0	0	.000	0	3	5	7.71	0
1996	Florida e	N.L.	31	71⅓	2	2	.500	40	28	85	4.54	0
1996	Columbus	Int.	3	16⅔	0	2	.000	7	5	20	5.40	0
1996	New York	A.L.	11	17⅓	0	2	.000	13	14	23	9.35	0
1997	Columbus	Int.	5	36⅔	2	2	.500	35	7	35	3.19	0
1997	Buffalo f-g	A.A.	11	68⅔	4	3	.571	51	17	71	3.15	0
1997	New York-Cleveland h ...	A.L.	19	25⅔	1	3	.250	18	15	38	8.42	0
1998	Cincinnati-Milwaukee i ...	N.L.	44	110	6	5	.545	94	41	130	4.91	0
1999	Milwaukee j	N.L.	63	93	7	4	.636	74	38	102	4.65	2
2000	Milwaukee k	N.L.	69	76⅓	3	5	.375	50	32	73	3.07	1
2001	Milwaukee-Chicago l-m	N.L.	80	86	4	5	.444	66	34	65	2.41	4
2002	New York	N.L.	71	77⅓	6	3	.667	61	36	69	2.91	0
2003	New York	N.L.	77	87⅔	1	6	.143	75	40	87	3.08	7
2004	N.Y.-Houston-Florida n-o-p	N.L.	66	82⅓	7	7	.500	61	35	85	4.15	0
2005	Cincinnati	N.L.	73	77⅔	7	4	.636	61	29	71	3.94	15
2006	Cincinnati q	N.L.	67	73⅔	4	4	.500	50	34	61	3.54	12
2007	Cincinnati	N.L.	70	77⅔	2	6	.250	48	27	67	3.59	33
Major League Totals .... 17 Yrs.			824	1245	65	76	.461	893	546	1303	4.32	74
Division Series												
1996	New York	A.L.	2	5	1	0	1.000	5	0	1	0.00	0
Championship Series												
1996	New York	A.L.	2	3	1	0	1.000	0	0	3	0.00	0
World Series Record												
1996	New York	A.L.	3	3	0	0	.000	3	3	2	3.00	0

a On disabled list from May 11 to July 31, 1992.
b Selected by Florida Marlins in expansion draft, November 17, 1992.
c Appeared in two additional games as pinch runner.
d On disabled list from June 26 to July 13, 1995.
e Traded to New York Yankees for pitcher Mark Hutton, July 31, 1996.
f Traded to Cleveland Indians for outfielder Chad Curtis, June 9, 1997.
g Released by Cleveland Indians, December 15, 1997.
h Signed as free agent with Cincinnati Reds, December 19, 1997.
i Claimed on waivers by Milwaukee Brewers, June 24, 1998.
j Filed for free agency, October 29, 1999, re-signed with Milwaukee Brewers, December 2, 1999.
k On disabled list from August 2 to August 21, 2000.
l Traded to Chicago Cubs with pitcher Roberto Miniel for pitcher Ruben Quevedo and outfielder Peter Zoccolillo, July 30, 2001.
m Filed for free agency, November 5, 2001. Signed with New York Mets, December 13, 2001.
n Traded to Houston Astros with pitcher Jeremy Griffiths for outfielder Richard Hidalgo, June 17, 2004.
o Waived by Houston Astros, September 7, 2004. Signed with Florida Marlins, September 8, 2004.
p Filed for free agency, November 1, 2004. Signed with Cincinnati Reds, December 15, 2004.
q Filed for free agency, October 28, 2006, re-signed with Cincinnati Reds, December 12, 2006.

WEAVER, JEFFREY CHARLES (JEFF)

Born, Northridge, California, August 22, 1976.
Bats Right. Throws Right. Height, 6 feet, 5 inches. Weight, 200 pounds.

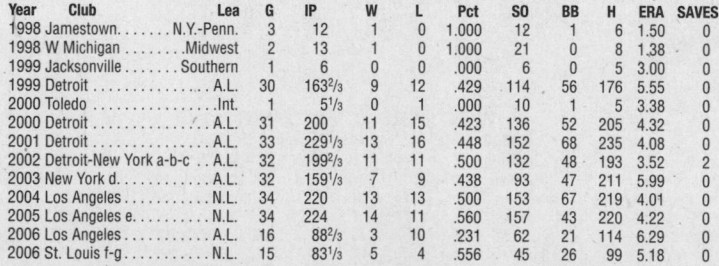

Year	Club	Lea	G	IP	W	L	Pct	SO	BB	H	ERA	SAVES
1998	Jamestown	N.Y.-Penn.	3	12	1	0	1.000	12	1	6	1.50	0
1998	W Michigan	Midwest	2	13	1	0	1.000	21	0	8	1.38	0
1999	Jacksonville	Southern	1	6	0	0	.000	6	0	5	3.00	0
1999	Detroit	A.L.	30	163⅔	9	12	.429	114	56	176	5.55	0
2000	Toledo	Int.	1	5⅓	0	1	.000	10	1	5	3.38	0
2000	Detroit	A.L.	31	200	11	15	.423	136	52	205	4.32	0
2001	Detroit	A.L.	33	229⅓	13	16	.448	152	68	235	4.08	0
2002	Detroit-New York a-b-c	A.L.	32	199⅔	11	11	.500	132	48	193	3.52	2
2003	New York d	A.L.	32	159⅓	7	9	.438	93	47	211	5.99	0
2004	Los Angeles	N.L.	34	220	13	13	.500	153	67	219	4.01	0
2005	Los Angeles e	N.L.	34	224	14	11	.560	157	43	220	4.22	0
2006	Los Angeles	N.L.	16	88⅔	3	10	.231	62	21	114	6.29	0
2006	St. Louis f-g	N.L.	15	83⅓	5	4	.556	45	26	99	5.18	0

Year	Club	Lea	G	IP	W	L	Pct	SO	BB	H	ERA	SAVES
2007 Seattle h-i	A.L.	27	146²/₃	7	13	.350	80	35	190	6.20	0
Major League Totals	9 Yrs.	284	1714²/₃	93	114	.449	1124	463	1862	4.72	2
Division Series											
2002 New York	A.L.	2	2²/₃	0	0	.000	1	3	4	6.75	0
2004 Los Angeles	N.L.	1	4²/₃	0	1	.000	4	2	8	11.57	0
2006 St. Louis	N.L.	1	5	1	0	1.000	3	3	2	0.00	0
Division Series Totals		4	12¹/₃	1	1	.500	8	8	14	5.84	0
Championship Series											
2006 St. Louis	N.L.	2	11²/₃	1	1	.500	2	4	10	3.09	0
World Series Record											
2003 New York	A.L.	1	1	0	1	.000	0	0	1	9.00	0
2006 St. Louis	N.L.	2	13	1	1	.500	14	2	13	2.77	0
World Series Totals		3	14	1	2	.333	14	2	14	3.21	0

a Traded to Oakland Athletics for infielder Carlos Pena, pitcher Franklyn German and player to be named later, July 5, 2002.
b Traded to New York Yankees for pitcher Ted Lilly, pitcher Jason Arnold and outfielder John-Ford Griffin, July 5, 2002.
c Detroit Tigers received pitcher Jeremy Bonderman to complete trade, August 22, 2002.
d Traded to Los Angeles Dodgers with pitcher Yhency Brazoban, player to be named later and cash for pitcher Kevin Brown, December 13, 2003. Los Angeles Dodgers received pitcher Brandon Weeden to complete trade, December 15, 2003.
e Filed for free agency, October 28, 2005. Signed with Los Angeles Angels, February 15, 2006.
f Traded to St. Louis Cardinals for outfielder Terry Evans, July 5, 2006.
g Filed for free agency, October 31, 2006. Signed with Seattle Mariners, January 29, 2007.
h On disabled list from May 11 to June 9, 2007.
i Filed for free agency, October 31, 2007.

WEAVER, JERED DAVID

Born, Northridge, California, October 4, 1982.
Bats Right. Throws Right. Height, 6 feet, 7 inches. Weight, 205 pounds.

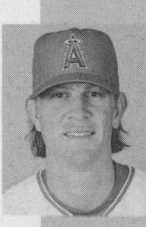

Year	Club	Lea	G	IP	W	L	Pct	SO	BB	H	ERA	SAVES
2005 Arkansas	Texas	8	43	3	3	.500	46	19	43	3.98	0
2006 Salt Lake	P.C.	12	77	6	1	.857	93	10	63	2.10	0
2006 Los Angeles	A.L.	19	123	11	2	.846	105	33	94	2.56	0
2007 Rancho Cucamonga	Calif.	2	11	1	0	1.000	12	3	5	0.82	0
2007 Los Angeles a	A.L.	28	161	13	7	.650	115	45	178	3.91	0
Major League Totals	2 Yrs.	47	284	24	9	.727	220	78	272	3.33	0
Division Series											
2007 Los Angeles	A.L.	1	5	0	1	.000	5	3	4	3.60	0

a On disabled list from March 23 to April 17, 2007.

WEBB, BRANDON TYLER

Born, Ashland, Kentucky, May 9, 1979.
Bats Right. Throws Right. Height, 6 feet, 3 inches. Weight, 230 pounds.

Year	Club	Lea	G	IP	W	L	Pct	SO	BB	H	ERA	SAVES
2000 Diamondbacks	Arizona	1	1	0	0	.000	3	0	2	9.00	0
2000 South Bend	Midwest	12	16²/₃	0	0	.000	18	9	10	3.24	2
2001 Lancaster	California	29	162¹/₃	6	10	.375	158	44	174	3.99	0
2002 El Paso	Texas	26	152	10	6	.625	122	59	141	3.14	0
2002 Tucson	P.C.	1	7	0	1	.000	5	4	5	3.86	0
2003 Tucson	P.C.	3	18	1	1	.500	17	9	18	6.00	0
2003 Arizona a	N.L.	29	180²/₃	10	9	.526	172	68	140	2.84	0
2004 Arizona	N.L.	35	208	7	*16	.304	164	*119	194	3.59	0
2005 Arizona	N.L.	33	229	14	12	.538	172	59	229	3.54	0
2006 Arizona b	N.L.	33	235	*16	8	.667	178	50	216	3.10	0
2007 Arizona	N.L.	34	*236¹/₃	18	10	.643	194	72	209	3.01	0
Major League Totals	5 Yrs.	164	1089	65	55	.542	880	368	988	3.22	0
Division Series											
2007 Arizona	N.L.	1	7	1	0	1.000	9	3	4	1.29	0
Championship Series											
2007 Arizona	N.L.	1	6	0	1	.000	4	2	7	6.00	0

a On disabled list from May 24 to June 8, 2003.
b Selected Cy Young Award Winner in National League for 2006.

WELLEMEYER, TODD ALLEN

Born, Louisville, Kentucky, August 30, 1978.
Bats Right. Throws Right. Height, 6 feet, 3 inches. Weight, 225 pounds.

Year	Club	Lea	G	IP	W	L	Pct	SO	BB	H	ERA	SAVES
2000 Eugene	Northwest	15	76	4	4	.500	85	33	62	3.67	0	
2001 Lansing	Midwest	27	147	13	9	.591	167	74	165	4.16	0	
2002 Daytona	Fla.St.	14	73²⁄₃	2	4	.333	87	19	63	3.79	0	
2002 West Tenn	Southern	8	46	3	3	.500	37	18	33	4.70	0	
2003 West Tenn	Southern	4	21¹⁄₃	1	1	.500	34	10	19	5.48	0	
2003 Iowa	P.C.	13	66	5	5	.500	56	33	68	5.18	0	
2003 Chicago	N.L.	15	27²⁄₃	1	1	.500	30	19	25	6.51	1	
2004 Chicago	N.L.	20	24¹⁄₃	2	1	.667	30	20	27	5.92	0	
2004 Iowa a	P.C.	14	23	1	1	.500	22	11	23	3.91	0	
2005 Iowa	P.C.	12	53²⁄₃	3	2	.600	48	25	47	3.02	0	
2005 Chicago	N.L.	22	32¹⁄₃	2	1	.667	32	22	32	6.12	1	
2006 Florida b	N.L.	18	21¹⁄₃	0	2	.000	17	13	20	5.48	0	
2006 Kansas City c	A.L.	28	57	1	2	.333	37	37	48	3.63	1	
2007 Springfield	Texas	1	1	0	0	.000	2	1	3	0.00	0	
2007 Kansas City	A.L.	12	15²⁄₃	0	1	.000	9	11	25	10.34	0	
2007 St. Louis d-e	N.L.	20	63²⁄₃	3	2	.600	51	29	52	3.11	0	
Major League Totals	5 Yrs.	135	242	9	10	.474	206	151	229	4.98	3	

a On disabled list from May 22 to July 16, 2004.
b Traded to Florida Marlins for pitcher Lincoln Holdzkom and pitcher Zach McCormack, March 28, 2006.
c Claimed on waivers by Kansas City Royals, June 9, 2006.
d Claimed on waivers by St. Louis Cardinals, May 15, 2007.
e On disabled list from July 9 to August 24, 2007.

WELLS, DAVID LEE

Born, Torrance, California, May 20, 1963.
Bats Left. Throws Left. Height, 6 feet, 3 inches. Weight, 250 pounds.

Year	Club	Lea	G	IP	W	L	Pct	SO	BB	H	ERA	SAVES
1982 Medicine Hat	Pioneer	12	64¹⁄₃	4	3	.571	53	32	71	5.18	0	
1983 Kinston	Carolina	25	157	6	5	.545	115	71	141	3.73	0	
1984 Kinston	Carolina	7	42	1	6	.143	44	19	51	4.71	0	
1984 Knoxville a	Southern	8	59	3	2	.600	34	17	58	2.59	0	
1985 Knoxville b	Southern		INJURED—Did Not Play									
1986 Florence	So. Atl.	4	12²⁄₃	0	0	.000	14	9	7	3.55	0	
1986 Ventura	California	5	19	2	1	.667	26	4	13	1.89	0	
1986 Knoxville c	Southern	10	40	1	3	.250	32	18	42	4.05	0	
1986 Syracuse	Int.	3	3²⁄₃	0	1	.000	2	1	6	9.82	0	
1987 Syracuse	Int.	43	109¹⁄₃	4	6	.400	106	32	102	3.87	6	
1987 Toronto	A.L.	18	29¹⁄₃	4	3	.571	32	12	37	3.99	1	
1988 Syracuse	Int.	6	5²⁄₃	0	0	.000	8	2	7	0.00	3	
1988 Toronto	A.L.	41	64¹⁄₃	3	5	.375	56	31	65	4.62	4	
1989 Toronto	A.L.	54	86¹⁄₃	7	4	.636	78	28	66	2.40	2	
1990 Toronto	A.L.	43	189	11	6	.647	115	45	165	3.14	3	
1991 Toronto	A.L.	40	198¹⁄₃	15	10	.600	106	49	188	3.72	1	
1992 Toronto d	A.L.	41	120	7	9	.438	62	36	138	5.40	2	
1993 Detroit e-f	A.L.	32	187	11	9	.550	139	42	183	4.19	0	
1994 Lakeland	Fla. St.	2	6	0	0	.000	3	0	5	0.00	0	
1994 Detroit g	A.L.	16	111¹⁄₃	5	7	.417	71	24	113	3.96	0	
1995 Detroit	A.L.	18	130¹⁄₃	10	3	.769	83	37	120	3.04	0	
1995 Cincinnati h-i	N.L.	11	72²⁄₃	6	5	.545	50	16	74	3.59	0	
1996 Baltimore j-k	A.L.	34	224¹⁄₃	11	14	.440	130	51	247	5.14	0	
1997 New York	A.L.	32	218	16	10	.615	156	45	239	4.21	0	
1998 New York l	A.L.	30	214¹⁄₃	18	4	*.818	163	29	195	3.49	0	
1999 Toronto m	A.L.	34	*231²⁄₃	17	10	.630	169	62	*246	4.82	0	
2000 Toronto n	A.L.	35	229²⁄₃	*20	8	.714	166	31	*266	4.11	0	
2001 Chicago o-p	A.L.	16	100²⁄₃	5	7	.417	59	21	120	4.47	0	
2002 New York	A.L.	31	206¹⁄₃	19	7	.731	137	45	210	3.75	0	
2003 New York q	A.L.	31	213	15	7	.682	101	20	242	4.14	0	
2004 San Diego r-s	N.L.	31	195²⁄₃	12	8	.600	101	20	203	3.73	0	
2005 Boston t	A.L.	30	184	15	7	.682	107	21	220	4.45	0	
2006 Pawtucket	Int.	2	10	1	1	.500	4	4	10	8.10	0	
2006 Boston u	A.L.	8	47	2	3	.400	24	8	64	4.98	0	
2006 San Diego v-w	N.L.	5	28¹⁄₃	1	2	.333	14	4	33	3.49	0	
2007 San Diego-Los Angeles x-y	N.L.	29	157¹⁄₃	9	9	.500	82	42	201	5.43	0	
Major League Totals	21 Yrs.	660	3439	239	157	.604	2201	719	3635	4.13	13	

Year	Club	Lea	G	IP	W	L	Pct	SO	BB	H	ERA	SAVES
	Division Series											
1995 Cincinnati		N.L.	1	6⅓	1	0	1.000	8	1	6	0.00	0
1996 Baltimore		A.L.	2	13⅔	1	0	1.000	6	4	15	4.61	0
1997 New York		A.L.	1	9	1	0	1.000	1	0	5	1.00	0
1998 New York		A.L.	1	8	1	0	1.000	9	1	5	0.00	0
2002 New York		A.L.	1	4⅔	0	1	.000	0	0	10	15.43	0
2003 New York		A.L.	1	7⅔	1	0	1.000	5	0	8	1.17	0
2005 Boston		A.L.	1	6⅔	0	1	.000	2	0	7	2.70	0
2006 San Diego		N.L.	1	5	0	1	.000	2	0	7	3.60	0
Division Series Totals			9	61	5	3	.625	33	6	63	3.10	0
	Championship Series											
1989 Toronto		A.L.	1	1	0	0	.000	1	2	0	0.00	0
1991 Toronto		A.L.	4	7⅔	0	0	.000	9	2	6	2.35	0
1995 Cincinnati		N.L.	1	6	0	1	.000	3	2	8	4.50	0
1996 Baltimore		A.L.	6	6⅔	1	0	1.000	6	3	8	4.05	0
1998 New York		A.L.	2	15⅔	2	0	1.000	18	2	12	2.87	0
2003 New York		A.L.	2	7⅔	1	0	1.000	5	2	5	2.35	0
Championship Series Totals			11	44⅔	4	1	.800	42	13	39	3.02	0
	World Series Record											
1992 Toronto		A.L.	4	4⅓	0	0	.000	3	2	1	0.00	0
1998 New York		A.L.	1	7	1	0	1.000	4	2	7	6.43	0
2003 New York		A.L.	2	8	0	1	.000	1	2	6	3.38	0
World Series Totals			7	19⅓	1	1	.500	8	6	14	3.72	0

a On disabled list from June 24 to end of 1984 season.
b On disabled list from April 10 to end of 1985 season.
c On disabled list from July 7 to August 20, 1986.
d Released, March 30. Signed with Detroit Tigers, April 3, 1993.
e On disabled list from August 1 to August 20, 1993.
f Filed for free agency, October 28, re-signed with Detroit Tigers, December 14, 1993.
g On disabled list from April 16 to June 4, 1994.
h Traded to Cincinnati Reds for pitcher C.J. Nitkowski, pitcher Dave Tuttle and player to be named later, July 31, 1995. Detroit Tigers received infielder Mark Lewis to complete trade, November 16, 1995.
i Traded to Baltimore Orioles for outfielder Curtis Goodwin and outfielder Trovin Valdez, December 26, 1995.
j Filed for free agency, October 29, 1996.
k Signed with New York Yankees, December 17, 1996.
l Pitched perfect no-hit, no-run game against Minnesota Twins, May 17, 1998, winning 4-0
m Traded to Toronto Blue Jays with pitcher Graeme Lloyd and infielder Homer Bush for pitcher Roger Clemens, February 18, 1999.
n Traded to Chicago White Sox with pitcher Matt DeWitt for pitcher Mike Sirotka, pitcher Kevin Beirne, pitcher Mike Williams and outfielder Brian Simmons, January 14, 2001.
o On disabled list from June 29 to October 12, 2001.
p Filed for free agency, November 5, 2001. Signed with New York Yankees, January 10, 2002.
q Filed for free agency, November 2, 2003. Signed with San Diego Padres, December 31, 2003.
r On disabled list from May 17 to June 7, 2004.
s Filed for free agency, November 2, 2004. Signed with Boston Red Sox, December 14, 2004.
t On disabled list from April 26 to May 18, 2005.
u On disabled list from March 28 to April 12 and April 13 to May 26 and May 27 to July 31, 2006.
v Traded to San Diego Padres for player to be named later, August 31, 2006. Red Sox received catcher George Kottaras to complete trade, September 5, 2006.
w Filed for free agency, November 9, 2006, re-signed with San Diego Padres, January 19, 2007.
x Released by San Diego Padres, August 13, 2007. Signed with Los Angeles Dodgers, August 24, 2007.
y Filed for free agency, October 30, 2007.

WELLS, ROBERT (KIP)
Born, Houston, Texas, April 21, 1977.
Bats Right. Throws Right. Height, 6 feet, 3 inches. Weight, 205 pounds.

Year	Club	Lea	G	IP	W	L	Pct	SO	BB	H	ERA	SAVES
1999 Winston-Salem	Carolina		14	85⅔	5	6	.455	95	34	78	3.57	0
1999 Birmingham	Southern		11	70⅓	8	2	.800	44	31	49	2.94	0
1999 Chicago		A.L.	7	35⅔	4	1	.800	29	15	33	4.04	0
2000 Chicago		A.L.	20	98⅔	6	9	.400	71	58	126	6.02	0
2000 Charlotte		Int.	12	62	5	3	.625	38	27	67	5.37	0
2001 Charlotte		Int.	4	25⅓	2	1	.667	24	8	26	3.55	0
2001 Chicago a		A.L.	40	133⅓	10	11	.476	99	61	145	4.79	0
2002 Pittsburgh		N.L.	33	198⅓	12	14	.462	134	71	197	3.58	0
2003 Pittsburgh b		N.L.	31	197⅓	10	9	.526	147	76	171	3.28	0
2004 Pittsburgh		N.L.	24	138⅓	5	7	.417	116	66	145	4.55	0
2005 Pittsburgh		N.L.	33	182	8	*18	.308	132	99	186	5.09	0

Year	Club	Lea	G	IP	W	L	Pct	SO	BB	H	ERA	SAVES
2006 Lynchburg	Carolina		1	6	1	0	1.000	5	2	3	0.00	0
2006 Altoona	Eastern		1	7⅓	1	0	1.000	4	1	6	3.68	0
2006 Pittsburgh	N.L.		7	36⅓	0	5	.167	16	18	46	6.69	0
2006 Texas c-d-e	A.L.		2	8	1	0	1.000	4	3	15	5.63	0
2007 St. Louis f	N.L.		34	162⅔	7	*17	.292	122	78	186	5.70	0
Major League Totals	9 Yrs.		231	1190⅔	64	91	.413	870	545	1250	4.63	0

a Traded to Pittsburgh Pirates with pitcher Sean Lowe and pitcher Josh Fogg for pitcher Todd Ritchie and catcher Lee Evans, December 13, 2001.
b On disabled list from August 14 to September 5, 2004.
c On disabled list from March 24 to June 18 and August 12 to October 11, 2006.
d Traded to Texas Rangers for pitcher Jesse Chavez, July 31, 2006.
e Filed for free agency, November 6, 2006. Signed with St. Louis Cardinals, November 28, 2006.
f Filed for free agency, October 29, 2007. Signed with Colorado Rockies, December 19, 2007.

WESTBROOK, JACOB CAUTHEN (JAKE)

Born, Athens, Georgia, September 29, 1977.
Bats Right. Throws Right. Height, 6 feet, 3 inches. Weight, 200 pounds.

Year	Club	Lea	G	IP	W	L	Pct	SO	BB	H	ERA	SAVES
1996 Rockies	Arizona		11	62⅔	4	2	.667	57	14	66	2.87	0
1996 Portland	Northwest		4	24⅔	1	1	.500	19	5	22	2.55	0
1997 Asheville a	So.Atl.		28	170	14	11	.560	92	55	176	4.29	0
1998 Jupiter	Fla.St.		27	171	11	6	.647	79	60	169	3.26	0
1999 Harrisburg b	Eastern		27	174⅔	11	5	.688	90	63	180	3.92	0
2000 Columbus	Int.		16	89	5	7	.417	61	38	94	4.65	0
2000 New York c-d-e-f	A.L.		3	6⅔	0	2	.000	1	4	15	13.50	0
2001 Buffalo	Int.		12	64⅔	8	1	.889	45	23	60	3.20	0
2001 Cleveland	A.L.		23	64⅔	4	4	.500	48	22	79	5.85	0
2002 Akron	Eastern		3	15	0	1	.000	8	1	13	4.80	0
2002 Buffalo	Int.		1	6	1	0	1.000	2	0	8	6.00	0
2002 Cleveland g	A.L.		11	41⅔	1	3	.250	20	12	50	5.83	0
2003 Buffalo	Int.		2	10	1	0	1.000	7	4	0	0.00	0
2003 Cleveland	A.L.		34	133	7	10	.412	58	56	142	4.33	0
2004 Cleveland	A.L.		33	215⅔	14	9	.609	116	61	208	3.38	0
2005 Cleveland	A.L.		34	210⅔	15	15	.500	119	56	218	4.49	0
2006 Cleveland	A.L.		32	211⅓	15	10	.600	109	55	*247	4.17	0
2007 Lake County	So.Atl.		1	5	0	1	.000	5	0	6	7.20	0
2007 Akron	Eastern		1	2⅓	0	1	.000	1	3	5	15.43	0
2007 Buffalo	Int.		2	5⅓	0	1	.000	5	5	9	8.44	0
2007 Cleveland h	A.L.		25	152	6	9	.400	93	55	159	4.32	0
Major League Totals	8 Yrs.		195	1035⅔	62	62	.500	564	321	1118	4.35	0
Division Series												
2007 Cleveland	A.L.		1	5	0	1	.000	1	0	9	10.80	0
Championship Series												
2007 Cleveland	A.L.		2	12⅔	1	1	.500	7	4	16	3.55	0

a Traded to Montreal Expos by Colorado Rockies with pitcher John Nicholson and outfielder Mike Hamlin for infielder Mike Lansing, November 18, 1997.
b Traded to New York Yankees with player to be named later and player to be named later for pitcher Hideki Irabu, December 22, 1999.
c On disabled list from May 5 to 23, 2000.
d Sent to Cleveland Indians by New York Yankees with pitcher Zach Day to complete trade for outfielder David Justice, July 24, 2000.
e On disabled list from July 25 to September 1, 2000.
f On disabled list from September 1 to October 31, 2000.
g On disabled list from March 30 to July 11 and August 26 to November 4, 2002.
h On disabled list from May 3 to June 24, 2007.

WHEELER, DANIEL MICHAEL (DAN)

Born, Providence, Rhode Island, December 10, 1977.
Bats Right. Throws Right. Height, 6 feet, 3 inches. Weight, 220 pounds.

Year	Club	Lea	G	IP	W	L	Pct	SO	BB	H	ERA	SAVES
1997 Hudson Valley	N.Y.-Penn.		15	84	6	7	.462	81	17	75	3.00	0
1998 Chston-Sc	So.Atl.		29	181	12	14	.462	136	29	206	4.43	0
1999 Orlando	Southern		9	58	3	0	1.000	53	8	56	3.26	0
1999 Durham	Int.		14	82⅓	7	5	.583	58	25	103	4.92	0
1999 Tampa Bay	A.L.		6	30⅔	0	4	.000	32	13	35	5.87	0
2000 Tampa Bay	A.L.		11	23	1	1	.500	17	11	29	5.48	0
2000 Durham	Int.		26	150⅓	5	11	.313	91	42	183	5.63	0

Year	Club	Lea	G	IP	W	L	Pct	SO	BB	H	ERA	SAVES
2001	Durham	Int.	18	65⅓	3	5	.375	39	11	72	5.23	0
2001	Tampa Bay	A.L.	13	17⅔	1	0	1.000	12	5	30	8.66	0
2001	Orlando	Southern	3	16	0	2	.000	12	6	15	2.81	0
2002	Richmond a	Int.	27	155	9	6	.600	110	42	163	4.65	0
2003	Norfolk b	Int.	22	45⅔	4	2	.667	44	16	48	3.94	4
2003	New York	N.L.	35	51	1	3	.250	35	17	49	3.71	2
2004	Norfolk	Int.	5	7⅓	1	0	1.000	10	2	8	2.45	0
2004	New York-Houston c	N.L.	46	65	3	1	.750	55	20	76	4.29	0
2005	Houston	N.L.	71	73⅓	2	3	.400	69	19	53	2.21	3
2006	Houston	N.L.	75	71⅓	3	5	.375	68	24	58	2.52	9
2007	Houston	N.L.	45	49⅔	1	4	.200	56	13	46	5.07	11
2007	Tampa Bay d	A.L.	25	25	0	5	.000	26	10	28	5.76	0
Major League Totals		8 Yrs.	327	406⅔	12	26	.316	370	132	404	4.09	25
Division Series												
2004	Houston	N.L.	1	1	0	0	.000	0	0	0	0.00	0
2005	Houston	N.L.	3	4⅓	0	0	.000	5	3	4	2.08	0
Division Series Totals			4	5⅓	0	0	.000	5	3	4	1.69	0
Championship Series												
2004	Houston	N.L.	4	7	1	0	1.000	9	0	4	0.00	0
2005	Houston	N.L.	3	2⅔	0	0	.000	2	0	2	0.00	0
Championship Series Totals			7	9⅔	1	0	1.000	11	0	6	0.00	0
World Series Record												
2005	Houston	N.L.	2	2	0	0	.000	1	1	2	13.50	0

a Released by Tampa Bay Devil Rays, December 13, 2001. Signed with Atlanta Braves organization, January 20, 2002.
b Filed for free agency, October 15, 2002. Signed with New York Mets organization, January 27, 2003.
c Traded to Houston Astros for outfielder Adam Seuss, August 27, 2004.
d Traded to Tampa Bay Devil Rays for infielder Ty Wigginton, July 28, 2007.

WICKMAN, ROBERT JOE (BOB)

Born, Green Bay, Wisconsin, February 6, 1969.
Bats Right. Throws Right. Height, 6 feet, 1 inch. Weight, 240 pounds.

Year	Club	Lea	G	IP	W	L	Pct	SO	BB	H	ERA	SAVES
1990	White Sox	Gulf Coast	2	11	2	0	1.000	15	1	7	2.45	0
1990	Sarasota	Fla.St.	2	13⅔	0	1	.000	8	4	17	1.98	0
1990	South Bend	Midwest	9	65⅓	7	2	.778	50	16	50	1.38	0
1991	Sarasota	Fla.St.	7	44	5	1	.833	32	11	43	2.05	0
1991	Birmingham a	Southern	20	131⅓	6	10	.375	81	50	127	3.56	0
1992	Columbus	Int.	23	157	12	5	.706	108	55	131	2.92	0
1992	New York	A.L.	8	50⅓	6	1	.857	21	20	51	4.11	0
1993	New York	A.L.	41	140	14	4	.778	70	69	156	4.63	4
1994	New York	A.L.	53	70	5	4	.556	56	27	54	3.09	6
1995	New York	A.L.	63	80	2	4	.333	51	33	77	4.05	1
1996	New York-Milwaukee b	A.L.	70	95⅔	7	1	.875	75	44	106	4.42	0
1997	Milwaukee	A.L.	74	95⅔	7	6	.538	78	41	89	2.73	1
1998	Milwaukee	N.L.	72	82⅓	6	9	.400	71	39	79	3.72	25
1999	Milwaukee	N.L.	71	74⅓	3	8	.273	66	14	75	3.39	37
2000	Milwaukee	N.L.	43	46	2	2	.500	44	20	37	2.93	16
2000	Cleveland c-d	A.L.	26	26⅔	1	3	.250	11	12	27	3.38	14
2001	Cleveland	A.L.	70	67⅔	5	0	1.000	66	14	61	2.39	32
2002	Cleveland	A.L.	36	34⅓	1	3	.250	36	10	42	4.46	20
2003	Akron e	Eastern	2	1⅔	0	0	.000	2	1	3	16.20	0
2003	Lake County	So.Atl.	2	2	0	0	.000	4	0	1	0.00	0
2004	Akron	Eastern	1	1	0	0	.000	1	2	0	0.00	0
2004	Buffalo	Int.	6	5⅓	1	0	1.000	4	4	4	10.13	0
2004	Cleveland f-g	A.L.	30	29⅔	0	2	.000	26	10	33	4.25	13
2005	Cleveland h	A.L.	64	62	0	4	.000	41	21	57	2.47	*45
2006	Cleveland	A.L.	29	28	1	4	.200	17	11	29	4.18	15
2006	Atlanta i	N.L.	28	26	0	2	.000	25	2	24	1.04	18
2007	Atlanta-Arizona j-k-l	N.L.	57	50⅓	3	4	.429	37	21	54	3.58	20
Major League Totals		15 Yrs.	835	1059	63	61	.508	785	432	1051	3.57	267
Division Series												
1995	New York	A.L.	3	3	0	0	.000	3	0	5	0.00	0
2001	Cleveland	A.L.	1	1	0	0	.000	2	0	0	0.00	0
Division Series Totals			4	4	0	0	.000	5	0	5	0.00	0

a Traded by Chicago White Sox to New York Yankees organization with pitchers Melido Perez and Domingo Jean for infielder Steve Sax and cash, January 10, 1992.

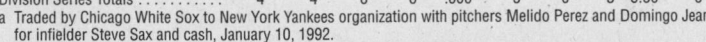

b Traded to Milwaukee Brewers with outfielder Gerald Williams for pitcher Graeme Lloyd, pitcher Ricky Bones and player to be named later, August 23, 1996. New York Yankees received infielder Gabby Martinez to complete trade, November 5, 1996.
c Traded to Cleveland Indians with pitcher Steve Woodard and pitcher Jason Bere for infielder Richie Sexson, pitcher Paul Rigdon, pitcher Kane Davis and player to be named later, July 28, 2000.
d Milwaukee Brewers received infielder Marcus Scutaro to complete trade, August 30, 2000.
e On disabled list from July 22 to August 10 and August 10 to November 4, 2002.
f On disabled list from April 2 to July 6, 2004.
g Filed for free agency, October 29, 2004, re-signed with Cleveland Indians, November 24, 2004.
h Filed for free agency, October 27, 2005, re-signed with Cleveland Indians, December 7, 2005.
i Traded to Atlanta Braves for catcher Max Ramirez, July 20, 2006.
j On disabled list from April 30 to May 15, 2007.
k Released by Atlanta Braves, August 24, 2007. Signed with Arizona Diamondbacks, September 7, 2007.
l Filed for free agency, October 29, 2007.

WILLIAMS, GREGORY SCOTT (WOODY)
Born, Houston, Texas, August 19, 1966.
Bats Right. Throws Right. Height, 6 feet. Weight, 200 pounds.

Year Club	Lea	G	IP	W	L	Pct	SO	BB	H	ERA	SAVES
1988 St. Catharines..... N.Y.-Penn.		12	76	8	2	.800	58	21	48	1.54	0
1988 Knoxville .... Southern		6	28⅓	2	2	.500	25	12	27	3.81	0
1989 Dunedin .... Fla. St.		20	81⅓	3	5	.375	60	27	63	2.32	3
1989 Knoxville .... Southern		14	71	3	5	.375	51	33	61	3.55	1
1990 Syracuse .... Int.		3	9	0	1	.000	8	4	15	10.00	0
1990 Knoxville .... Southern		42	126	7	9	.438	74	39	111	3.14	5
1991 Knoxville .... Southern		18	42⅔	3	2	.600	37	14	42	3.59	3
1991 Syracuse .... Int.		31	54⅔	4	3	.429	37	27	52	4.12	6
1992 Syracuse .... Int.		25	120⅔	6	8	.429	81	41	115	3.13	1
1993 Syracuse .... Int.		12	16⅓	1	1	.500	16	5	15	2.20	3
1993 Dunedin .... Fla. St.		2	4	0	0	.000	2	2	0	0.00	0
1993 Toronto .... A.L.		30	37	3	1	.750	24	22	40	4.38	0
1994 Syracuse .... Int.		1	1⅔	0	0	.000	1	0	0	0.00	1
1994 Toronto .... A.L.		38	59⅓	1	3	.250	56	33	44	3.64	0
1995 Toronto .... A.L.		23	53⅔	1	2	.333	41	28	44	3.69	0
1995 Syracuse .... Int.		5	7⅔	0	0	.000	13	5	5	3.52	1
1996 Dunedin .... Fla. St.		2	7⅔	0	2	.000	11	2	9	8.22	0
1996 St. Catharines..... N.Y.-Penn.		2	7⅓	0	0	.000	12	4	7	3.68	0
1996 Syracuse .... Int.		7	32	3	1	.750	33	7	22	1.41	0
1996 Toronto a .... A.L.		12	59	4	5	.444	43	21	64	4.73	0
1997 Toronto .... A.L.		31	194⅔	9	14	.391	124	66	201	4.35	0
1998 Toronto b .... A.L.		32	209⅔	10	9	.526	151	81	196	4.46	0
1999 San Diego .... N.L.		33	208⅓	12	12	.500	137	73	213	4.41	0
2000 Rancho Cucamonga California		1	5	0	0	.000	10	0	3	0.00	0
2000 Las Vegas............. P.C.		1	6	0	0	.000	5	0	7	1.50	0
2000 San Diego c .... N.L.		23	168	10	8	.556	111	54	152	3.75	0
2001 San Diego-St. Louis d ... N.L.		34	220	15	9	.625	154	56	224	4.05	0
2002 Memphis .... P.C.		1	5	1	0	1.000	7	1	1	1.80	0
2002 St. Louis e-f .... N.L.		17	103⅓	9	4	.692	76	25	84	2.53	0
2003 St. Louis............. N.L.		34	220⅔	18	9	.667	153	55	220	3.87	0
2004 St. Louis g .... N.L.		31	189⅔	11	8	.579	131	58	193	4.18	0
2005 San Diego h .... N.L.		28	159⅔	9	12	.429	106	51	174	4.85	0
2006 Lake Elsinore .... Calif.		1	3	0	0	.000	5	1	0	0.00	0
2006 Portland............. P.C.		1	2⅔	0	1	.000	2	2	8	20.25	0
2006 San Diego i-j .... N.L.		25	145⅓	12	5	.706	72	35	152	3.65	0
2007 Houston .... N.L.		33	188	8	15	.348	101	53	216	5.27	0
Major League Totals .... 15 Yrs.		424	2216⅓	132	116	.532	1480	711	2217	4.19	0
Division Series											
2001 St. Louis.............. N.L.		1	7	1	0	1.000	9	1	4	1.29	0
2004 St. Louis.............. N.L.		1	6	1	0	1.000	2	1	8	3.00	0
2005 San Diego .... N.L.		1	1⅔	0	1	.000	2	2	6	27.00	0
2006 San Diego .... N.L.		1	5⅓	0	1	.000	1	2	5	6.75	0
Division Series Totals		4	20	2	2	.500	14	6	23	5.40	0
Championship Series											
2002 St. Louis.............. N.L.		1	6	0	1	.000	7	1	6	4.50	0
2004 St. Louis.............. N.L.		2	13	1	0	1.000	9	3	5	2.77	0
Championship Series Totals		3	19	1	1	.500	16	4	11	3.32	0
World Series Record											
2004 St. Louis.............. N.L.		1	2⅓	0	0	.000	1	3	8	27.00	0

a On disabled list from April 1 to May 31 and June 7 to July 26, 1996.

b Traded to San Diego Padres with pitcher Carlos Almanzar and outfielder Peter Tucci for pitcher Joey Hamilton, December 13, 1998.
c On disabled list from May 6 to July 1, 2000.
d Traded to St. Louis Cardinals for outfielder Ray Lankford, August 2, 2001.
e On disabled list from April 6 to May 15 and July 7 to August 29, 2002.
f Filed for free agency, October 30, 2002, re-signed with St. Louis Cardinals, November 25, 2002.
g Filed for free agency, November 4, 2004. Signed with San Diego Padres, December 8, 2004.
h On disabled list from May 2 to June 5, 2005.
i On disabled list from May 13 to July 1, 2006.
j Filed for free agency, October 30, 2006. Signed with Houston Astros, November 24, 2006.

WILLIS, DONTRELLE WAYNE

Born, Oakland, California, January 12, 1982.
Bats Left. Throws Left. Height, 6 feet, 4 inches. Weight, 240 pounds.

Year	Club	Lea	G	IP	W	L	Pct	SO	BB	H	ERA	SAVES
2000	Cubs............	Arizona	9	28	3	1	.750	22	8	26	3.86	0
2001	Boise...........	Northwest	15	93²/₃	8	2	.800	77	19	76	2.98	0
2002	Kane County.......	.Midwest	19	127²/₃	10	2	.833	101	21	91	1.83	0
2002	Jupiter a...........	Fla.St.	5	30	2	0	1.000	27	3	24	1.80	0
2003	Carolina........	Southern	6	36¹/₃	4	0	1.000	32	9	24	1.49	0
2003	Florida b.............	N.L.	27	160²/₃	14	6	.700	142	58	148	3.30	0
2004	Florida..............	N.L.	32	197	10	11	.476	139	61	210	4.02	0
2005	Florida..............	N.L.	34	236¹/₃	*22	10	.688	·170	55	213	2.63	0
2006	Florida..............	N.L.	34	223¹/₃	12	12	.500	160	83	234	3.87	0
2007	Florida c.............	N.L.	35	205¹/₃	10	15	.400	146	87	241	5.17	0
Major League Totals........	.5 Yrs.		162	1022²/₃	68	54	.557	757	344	1046	3.78	0
Division Series												
2003	Florida..............	N.L.	2	5²/₃	0	0	.000	3	2	7	7.94	0
Championship Series												
2003	Florida..............	N.L.	2	3¹/₃	0	1	.000	4	6	4	18.90	0
World Series Record												
2003	Florida..............	N.L.	3	3²/₃	0	0	.000	3	2	4	0.00	0

a Traded by Chicago Cubs to Florida Marlins with pitcher Julian Tavarez, pitcher Jose Cueto and catcher Ryan Jorgensen for pitcher Antonio Alfonseca and pitcher Matt Clement, March 27, 2002.
b Selected Rookie of the Year in National League for 2003.
c Traded to Detroit Tigers with infielder Miguel Cabrera for pitcher Burke Badenhop, pitcher Eulogio De La Cruz, pitcher Andrew Miller, catcher Mike Rabelo and outfielder Cameron Maybin, December 5, 2007.

WILSON, BRIAN PATRICK

Born, Londonderry, New Hampshire, March 16, 1982.
Bats Right. Throws Right. Height, 6 feet, 1 inch. Weight, 205 pounds.

Year	Club	Lea	G	IP	W	L	Pct	SO	BB	H	ERA	SAVES
2004	Hagerstown.........	So.Atl.	23	57¹/₃	2	5	.286	41	22	63	5.34	3
2005	Norwich...........	Eastern	15	15²/₃	0	0	.000	22	5	6	0.57	8
2005	Fresno..............	P.C.	9	11¹/₃	1	1	.500	13	8	8	3.97	0
2005	Augusta............	So.Atl.	26	33	5	1	.833	30	7	23	0.82	13
2006	San Jose...........	Calif.	1	1	0	0	.000	1	1	1	9.00	0
2006	Fresno..............	P.C.	24	28	1	3	.250	30	14	20	2.89	7
2006	San Francisco.........	N.L.	31	30	2	3	.400	23	21	32	5.40	1
2007	San Jose...........	Calif.	3	3	0	0	.000	6	0	1	0.00	2
2007	Fresno..............	P.C.	31	34¹/₃	1	2	.333	37	24	24	2.10	11
2007	San Francisco.........	N.L.	24	23²/₃	1	2	.333	18	7	16	2.28	6
Major League Totals........	.2 Yrs.		55	53²/₃	3	5	.375	41	28	48	4.02	7

WILSON, CHRISTOPHER JOHN (C.J.)

Born, Newport Beach, California, November 18, 1980.
Bats Left. Throws Left. Height, 6 feet, 2 inches. Weight, 215 pounds.

Year	Club	Lea	G	IP	W	L	Pct	SO	BB	H	ERA	SAVES
2001	Pulaski.............	Appal.	8	37²/₃	1	0	1.000	49	9	24	0.96	0
2001	Savannah...........	So.Atl.	15	34	1	2	.333	26	9	30	3.18	0
2002	Charlotte...........	Fla.St.	26	106	10	2	.833	76	41	86	3.06	1
2002	Tulsa..............	Texas	5	30	1	0	1.000	17	12	23	1.80	0
2003	Frisco..............	Texas	22	123	6	9	.400	89	38	135	5.05	0
2004					INJURED—Did Not Play							
2005	Bakersfield..........	Calif.	4	13²/₃	0	1	.000	14	4	10	3.29	0
2005	Frisco..............	Texas	12	44²/₃	0	4	.000	43	14	51	4.43	0
2005	Texas..............	A.L.	24	48	1	7	.125	30	18	63	6.94	1

Year	Club	Lea	G	IP	W	L	Pct	SO	BB	H	ERA	SAVES
2006 Frisco	Texas	4	3⅓	0	0	.000	6	2	3	2.70	0
2006 Oklahoma	P.C.	9	11	1	0	1.000	17	5	10	2.45	2
2006 Texas a	A.L.	44	44⅓	2	4	.333	43	18	39	4.06	1
2007 Texas	A.L.	66	68⅓	2	1	.667	63	33	50	3.03	12
Major League Totals	3 Yrs.	134	160⅔	5	12	.294	136	69	152	4.48	14

a On disabled list from March 24 to April 14, 2006.

WOLF, RANDALL CHRISTOPHER (RANDY)

Born, Canoga Park, California, August 22, 1976.
Bats Left. Throws Left. Height, 6 feet. Weight, 205 pounds.

Year	Club	Lea	G	IP	W	L	Pct	SO	BB	H	ERA	SAVES
1997 Batavia	N.Y.-Penn.	7	40	4	0	1.000	53	8	29	1.58	0
1998 Reading	Eastern	4	25	2	0	1.000	33	4	15	1.44	0
1998 Scranton-WB	Int.	24	148	9	7	.563	118	48	167	4.62	0
1999 Scranton-WB	Int.	12	77⅓	4	5	.444	72	29	73	3.61	0
1999 Philadelphia	N.L.	22	121⅔	6	9	.400	116	67	126	5.55	0
2000 Philadelphia	N.L.	32	206⅓	11	9	.550	160	83	210	4.36	0
2001 Scranton-WB	Int.	2	9	0	1	.000	7	5	10	5.00	0
2001 Reading	Eastern	1	6	0	0	.000	7	2	5	4.50	0
2001 Philadelphia a	N.L.	28	163	10	11	.476	152	51	150	3.70	0
2002 Clearwater	Fla.St.	1	5	0	0	.000	8	1	1	0.00	0
2002 Philadelphia b	N.L.	31	210⅔	11	9	.550	172	63	172	3.20	0
2003 Philadelphia	N.L.	33	200	16	10	.615	177	78	176	4.23	0
2004 Reading	Eastern	1	4	0	0	.000	4	0	5	2.25	0
2004 Philadelphia c	N.L.	23	136⅔	5	8	.385	89	36	145	4.28	0
2005 Philadelphia d	N.L.	13	80	6	4	.600	61	26	87	4.39	0
2006 Clearwater	Fla.St.	2	5⅔	0	0	.000	4	4	6	0.00	0
2006 Reading	Eastern	3	12	1	1	.500	11	7	15	6.75	0
2006 Lakewood	So.Atl.	2	8	0	0	.000	7	3	2	1.13	0
2006 Philadelphia e-f	N.L.	12	56⅔	4	0	1.000	44	33	63	5.56	0
2007 Inland Empire	Calif.	1	4	0	0	.000	4	1	6	6.75	0
2007 Los Angeles g-h	N.L.	18	102⅔	9	6	.600	94	39	110	4.73	0
Major League Totals	9 Yrs.	212	1277⅔	78	66	.542	1065	476	1239	4.25	0

a On disabled list from August 2 to September 1, 2001.
b On disabled list from March 25 to April 12, 2002.
c On disabled list from June 3 to June 26 and August 29 to October 8, 2004.
d On disabled list from June 12 to November 1, 2005.
e On disabled list from March 24 to July 30, 2006.
f Filed for free agency, October 28, 2006. Signed with Los Angeles Dodgers, November 28, 2006.
g On disabled list from July 4 to October 31, 2007.
h Filed for free agency, November 9, 2007. Signed with San Diego Padres, December 10, 2007.

WOLFE, BRIAN THOMAS

Born, Fullerton, California, November 29, 1980.
Bats Right. Throws Right. Height, 6 feet, 3 inches. Weight, 220 pounds.

Year	Club	Lea	G	IP	W	L	Pct	SO	BB	H	ERA	SAVES
1999 Twins	Gulf Coast	9	38	4	0	1.000	40	9	33	2.84	0
2000 Quad Cities	Midwest	31	123⅓	5	9	.357	91	34	148	4.74	0
2001 Quad Cities	Midwest	28	160	13	8	.619	128	32	128	2.81	0
2002 Fort Myers	Fla.St.	25	132	6	9	.400	85	34	160	4.64	0
2003 New Britain	Eastern	30	82⅔	5	7	.417	42	24	111	6.42	0
2003 Fort Myers	Fla.St.	7	46⅓	2	1	.667	22	6	41	2.53	0
2004 New Britain	Eastern	7	11	1	1	.500	6	3	16	8.18	0
2005 New Britain	Eastern	5	7⅔	1	0	1.000	4	7	10	7.04	0
2005 Brevard County	Fla.St.	18	22⅔	1	1	.500	22	8	19	0.79	8
2005 Rochester	Int.	3	6⅓	0	2	.000	5	2	10	8.53	0
2005 Huntsville a	Southern	16	24	3	1	.750	19	8	32	3.38	0
2006 New Hampshire	Eastern	24	42⅓	1	3	.250	34	15	54	5.74	0
2006 Dunedin b-c	Fla.St.	5	24	1	4	.200	17	3	33	6.00	0
2007 Syracuse	Int.	17	26	2	0	1.000	23	6	18	1.04	0
2007 Toronto	A.L.	38	45⅓	3	1	.750	22	9	36	2.98	0

a Released by Minnesota Twins, May 13, 2005. Signed with Milwaukee Brewers organization, May 23, 2005.
b Traded to Toronto Blue Jays for infielder Corey Koskie, January 6, 2006.
c Filed for free agency, October 15, 2006, re-signed with Toronto Blue Jays organization, November 10, 2006.

WOOD, KERRY LEE

Born, Irving, Texas, June 16, 1977.
Bats Right. Throws Right. Height, 6 feet, 5 inches. Weight, 225 pounds.

Year	Club	Lea	G	IP	W	L	Pct	SO	BB	H	ERA	SAVES
1995 Cubs............	Gulf Coast	1	3	0	0	.000	2	1	0	0.00	0
1995 Williamsport......	N.Y.-Penn.	2	4⅓	0	0	.000	5	5	5	10.38	0
1996 Daytona a..........	Fla.St.	22	114⅓	10	2	.833	136	70	72	2.91	0
1997 Orlando	Southern	19	94	6	7	.462	106	79	58	4.50	0
1997 Iowa.................	A.A.	10	57⅔	4	2	.667	80	52	35	4.68	0
1998 Iowa................	P.C.	1	5	1	0	1.000	11	2	1	0.00	0
1998 Chicago b.............	N.L.	26	166⅔	13	6	.684	233	85	117	3.40	0
1999 Chicago c............	N.L.			INJURED—Did Not Play								
2000 Daytona	Fla.St.	2	12	2	0	1.000	17	5	3	1.50	0
2000 Iowa................	P.C.	1	7	0	0	.000	7	4	4	2.57	0
2000 Chicago d.............	N.L.	23	137	8	7	.533	132	87	112	4.80	0
2001 Chicago e.............	N.L.	28	174⅓	12	6	.667	217	92	127	3.36	0
2002 Chicago	N.L.	33	213⅔	12	11	.522	217	97	169	3.66	0
2003 Chicago	N.L.	32	211	14	11	.560	*266	100	152	3.20	0
2004 Iowa................	P.C.	1	5	1	0	1.000	4	1	2	0.00	0
2004 Chicago f.............	N.L.	22	140⅓	8	9	.471	144	51	127	3.72	0
2005 Peoria...........	Midwest	2	2⅓	0	0	.000	5	0	1	0.00	0
2005 Iowa...............	P.C.	3	12⅔	0	0	.000	18	6	11	2.84	0
2005 Chicago g.............	N.L.	21	66	3	4	.429	77	26	52	4.23	0
2006 Peoria...........	Midwest	1	5	0	0	.000	12	1	1	0.00	0
2006 Iowa...............	P.C.	1	5	0	1	.000	3	2	5	1.80	0
2006 Chicago h-i............	N.L.	4	19⅔	1	2	.333	13	8	19	4.12	0
2007 Azl Cubs...........	Arizona	4	4	0	1	.000	5	1	4	2.25	0
2007 Peoria............	Midwest	3	3	1	0	1.000	3	1	1	0.00	0
2007 Tennessee	Southern	1	1⅔	0	0	.000	1	1	0	0.00	0
2007 Chicago j-k............	N.L.	22	24⅓	1	1	.500	24	13	18	3.33	0
Major League Totals	9 Yrs.	211	1153	72	57	.558	1323	559	893	3.67	0
Division Series												
1998 Chicago	N.L.	1	5	0	1	.000	5	4	3	1.80	0
2003 Chicago	N.L.	2	15⅓	2	0	1.000	18	7	7	1.76	0
2007 Chicago	N.L.	2	3	0	0	.000	2	0	3	3.00	0
Division Series Totals		5	23⅓	2	1	.667	25	11	13	1.93	0
Championship Series												
2003 Chicago	N.L.	2	12⅓	0	1	.000	13	7	14	7.30	0

a On disabled list from May 24 to June 19, 1996.
b Selected Rookie of the Year in National League for 1998.
c On disabled list from March 31 to November 2, 1999.
d On disabled list from March 25 to May 1 and July 30 to August 21, 2000.
e On disabled list from August 4 to September 7, 2001.
f On disabled list from May 12 to July 11, 2004.
g On disabled list from May 1 to June 29 and July 21 to August 5 and August 30 to October 31, 2005.
h On disabled list from March 27 to May 18 and June 7 to October 29, 2006.
i Filed for free agency, October 29, 2006, re-signed with Chicago Cubs, November 15, 2006.
j On disabled list from March 29 to August 3, 2007.
k Filed for free agency, October 29, 2007, re-signed with Chicago Cubs, November 28, 2007.

WRIGHT, JAMEY ALAN

Born, Oklahoma City, Oklahoma, December 24, 1974.
Bats Right. Throws Right. Height, 6 feet, 6 inches. Weight, 235 pounds.

Year	Club	Lea	G	IP	W	L	Pct	SO	BB	H	ERA	SAVES
1993 Rockies	Arizona	8	36	1	3	.250	26	9	35	4.00	0
1994 Asheville............	So.Atl.	28	143⅓	7	14	.333	103	59	188	5.97	0
1995 Salem............	Carolina	26	171	10	8	.556	95	72	160	2.47	0
1995 New Haven.........	Eastern	1	3	0	1	.000	0	3	6	9.00	0
1996 New Haven.........	Eastern	7	44⅔	5	1	.833	54	12	27	0.81	0
1996 Colorado Springs.......	P.C.	9	59⅔	4	2	.667	40	22	53	2.72	0
1996 Colorado	N.L.	16	91⅓	4	4	.500	45	41	105	4.93	0
1997 Salem............	Carolina	1	1	0	1	.000	1	1	1	9.00	0
1997 Colorado Springs.......	P.C.	2	11	1	0	1.000	11	5	9	1.64	0
1997 Colorado a	N.L.	26	149⅔	8	12	.400	59	71	198	6.25	0
1998 Colorado	N.L.	34	206⅓	9	14	.391	86	95	235	5.67	0
1999 Colorado	N.L.	16	94⅓	4	3	.571	49	54	110	4.87	0
1999 Colorado Springs b	P.C.	17	100⅓	5	7	.417	75	38	133	6.46	0
2000 Huntsville..........	Southern	2	12⅓	2	0	1.000	10	5	7	0.00	0
2000 Indianapolis............	Int.	1	5	0	0	.000	7	3	8	1.80	0
2000 Milwaukee c...........	N.L.	26	164⅔	7	9	.438	96	88	157	4.10	0

Year	Club	Lea	G	IP	W	L	Pct	SO	BB	H	ERA	SAVES
2001	Milwaukee d	N.L.	33	194²/₃	11	12	.478	129	98	201	4.90	0
2002	Indianapolis	Int.	3	15¹/₃	1	1	.500	13	5	16	4.11	0
2002	Milwaukee-St. Louis e-f-g	N.L.	23	129¹/₃	7	13	.350	77	75	130	5.29	0
2003	Indianapolis	Int.	7	22	1	3	.250	17	10	32	7.36	0
2003	Oklahoma	P.C.	7	39¹/₃	2	1	.667	40	21	38	4.12	0
2003	Omaha	P.C.	13	76²/₃	3	5	.375	65	38	70	3.64	0
2003	Kansas City h-i-j-k-l	A.L.	4	25¹/₃	1	2	.333	19	11	23	4.26	0
2004	Omaha	P.C.	18	104²/₃	8	6	.571	70	35	111	4.21	0
2004	Colorado m	N.L.	14	78²/₃	2	3	.400	41	45	82	4.12	0
2005	Colorado n	N.L.	34	171¹/₃	8	16	.333	101	81	201	5.46	0
2006	San Francisco o	N.L.	34	156	6	10	.375	79	64	167	5.19	0
2007	Frisco	Texas	1	4	0	0	.000	2	0	6	4.50	0
2007	Oklahoma	P.C.	3	16¹/₃	2	1	.667	11	3	21	4.41	0
2007	Texas p-q	A.L.	20	77	4	5	.444	39	41	72	3.62	0
Major League Totals	12 Yrs.		280	1538²/₃	71	103	.408	820	764	1681	5.06	0

a   On disabled list from May 15 to June 8, 1997.
b   Traded to Milwaukee Brewers with catcher Henry Blanco and pitcher Justin Miller for infielder Jeff Cirillo and pitcher Scott Karl, December 13, 1999.
c   On disabled list from March 28 to May 22, 2000.
d   On disabled list from May 21 to June 10, 2001.
e   On disabled list from April 5 to May 24, 2002.
f   Traded to St. Louis Cardinals with cash for outfielder Chris Morris and player to be named later, August 29, 2002.
g   Milwaukee Brewers received pitcher Mike Matthews to complete trade, September 11, 2002.
h   Filed for free agency, November 1, 2002. Signed with Seattle Mariners organization, January 24, 2003.
i   Released by Seattle Mariners, March 18, 2003. Signed with Milwaukee Brewers organization, March 23, 2003.
j   Released by Milwaukee Brewers, April 28, 2003. Signed with Texas Rangers organization, May 5, 2003.
k   Released by Texas Rangers, June 16, 2003. Signed with Kansas City Royals organization, June 24, 2003.
l   Filed for free agency, October 30, 2003. Signed with Chicago Cubs organization, December 18, 2003. Released by Chicago Cubs March 26, 2004. Signed with Kansas City Royals organization, March 29, 2004.
m   Filed for free agency, November 1, 2004, re-signed with Colorado Rockies, December 21, 2004.
n   Filed for free agency, November 2, 2005. Signed with San Francisco Giants organization, January 17, 2006.
o   Filed for free agency, November 2, 2006. Signed with Texas Rangers organization, January 25, 2007.
p   On disabled list from April 11 to June 16, 2007.
q   Filed for free agency, November 12, 2007. Signed with Texas Rangers organization, January 11, 2008.

WUERTZ, MICHAEL JAMES

Born, Austin, Minnesota, December 15, 1978.
Bats Right. Throws Right. Height, 6 feet, 3 inches. Weight, 205 pounds.

Year	Club	Lea	G	IP	W	L	Pct	SO	BB	H	ERA	SAVES
1998	Williamsport	N.Y.-Penn.	14	86¹/₃	7	5	.583	59	19	79	3.44	0
1999	Lansing	Midwest	28	161¹/₃	11	12	.478	127	44	191	4.80	0
2000	Daytona	Fla.St.	28	171¹/₃	12	7	.632	142	64	166	3.78	0
2001	West Tenn	Southern	27	160	4	9	.308	135	58	160	3.99	0
2002	Iowa	P.C.	28	154	9	5	.643	131	69	185	5.55	0
2003	Iowa	P.C.	43	124	3	9	.250	92	35	140	4.57	1
2004	Chicago	N.L.	31	29	1	0	1.000	30	17	22	4.34	1
2004	Iowa	P.C.	37	44²/₃	1	1	.500	59	15	30	2.42	19
2005	Chicago	N.L.	75	75²/₃	6	2	.750	89	40	60	3.81	0
2006	Iowa	P.C.	30	41²/₃	6	0	1.000	67	9	30	1.73	10
2006	Chicago	N.L.	41	40²/₃	3	1	.750	42	16	35	2.66	0
2007	Chicago	N.L.	73	72¹/₃	2	3	.400	79	35	64	3.48	0
Major League Totals	4 Yrs.		220	217²/₃	12	6	.667	240	108	181	3.56	1
Division Series												
2007	Chicago	N.L.	2	1²/₃	0	0	.000	2	1	0	0.00	0

YOUNG, CHRISTOPHER RYAN (CHRIS)

Born, Dallas, Texas, May 25, 1979.
Bats Right. Throws Right. Height, 6 feet, 10 inches. Weight, 260 pounds.

Year	Club	Lea	G	IP	W	L	Pct	SO	BB	H	ERA	SAVES
2001	Hickory	So.Atl.	12	74¹/₃	5	3	.625	72	20	79	4.12	0
2002	Hickory a	So.Atl.	26	144²/₃	11	9	.550	136	34	127	3.11	0
2003	Harrisburg	Eastern	15	83	4	4	.500	64	22	83	4.01	0
2003	Brevard County	Fla.St.	8	50	5	2	.714	39	5	26	1.62	0
2004	Frisco	Texas	18	88¹/₃	6	5	.545	75	31	94	4.48	0
2004	Oklahoma	P.C.	5	30¹/₃	3	0	1.000	34	9	20	1.48	0
2004	Texas b	A.L.	7	36¹/₃	3	2	.600	27	10	36	4.71	0
2005	Lynchburg	Carolina	10	15	0	1	.000	14	5	9	3.00	2

Year Club	Lea	G	IP	W	L	Pct	SO	BB	H	ERA	SAVES
2005 Tulsa	Texas	35	53	3	2	.600	35	17	53	4.75	1
2005 Texas c-d	A.L.	31	164²/₃	12	7	.632	137	45	162	4.26	0
2006 San Diego	N.L.	31	179¹/₃	11	5	.688	164	69	134	3.46	0
2007 San Diego e	N.L.	30	173	9	8	.529	167	72	118	3.12	0
Major League Totals ....4 Yrs.		99	553¹/₃	35	22	.614	495	196	450	3.68	0
Division Series											
2006 San Diego	N.L.	1	6²/₃	1	0	1.000	9	2	4	0.00	0

a Traded by Pittsburgh Pirates to Montreal Expos with pitcher Jon Searles for pitcher Matt Herges, December 20, 2002.

b Traded to Texas Rangers with catcher Josh McKinley for catcher Einar Diaz, April 3, 2004.

c Traded to Arizona Diamondbacks with pitcher Orlando Hernandez and pitcher Luis Vizcaino for pitcher Javier Vazquez, December 20, 2005.

d Traded to San Diego Padres with infielder Adrian Gonzalez and outfielder Terrmel Sledge for pitcher Adam Eaton, pitcher Akinori Otsuka and catcher Billy Killian, January 4, 2006.

e On disabled list from July 25 to August 9, 2007.

ZAMBRANO, CARLOS ALBERTO

Born, Puerto Cabello, Venezuela, June 1, 1981.
Bats Both. Throws Right. Height, 6 feet, 5 inches. Weight, 255 pounds.

Year Club	Lea	G	IP	W	L	Pct	SO	BB	H	ERA	SAVES
1998 Cubs...............	Arizona	14	40	0	1	.000	36	25	39	3.15	1
1999 Lansing	Midwest	27	153¹/₃	13	7	.650	98	62	150	4.17	0
2000 Iowa................	P.C.	34	56²/₃	2	5	.286	46	40	54	3.97	6
2000 West Tenn	Southern	9	60¹/₃	3	1	.750	43	21	39	1.34	0
2001 Iowa................	P.C.	26	150²/₃	10	5	.667	155	68	124	3.88	0
2001 Chicago	N.L.	6	7²/₃	1	2	.333	4	8	11	15.26	0
2002 Iowa...............	P.C.	3	9	0	0	.000	11	6	2	0.00	0
2002 Chicago a	N.L.	32	108¹/₃	4	8	.333	93	63	94	3.66	0
2003 Chicago	N.L.	32	214	13	11	.542	168	94	188	3.11	0
2004 Chicago	N.L.	31	209²/₃	16	8	.667	188	81	174	2.75	0
2005 Chicago	N.L.	33	223¹/₃	14	6	.700	202	86	170	3.26	0
2006 Chicago	N.L.	33	214	*16	7	*.696	210	*115	162	3.41	0
2007 Chicago	N.L.	34	216¹/₃	18	13	.581	177	*101	187	3.95	0
Major League Totals ....7 Yrs.		201	1193¹/₃	82	55	.599	1042	548	986	3.41	0
Division Series											
2003 Chicago	N.L.	1	5²/₃	0	0	.000	4	0	11	4.76	0
2007 Chicago	N.L.	1	6	0	0	.000	8	1	4	1.50	0
Division Series Totals		2	11²/₃	0	0	.000	12	1	15	3.09	0
Championship Series											
2003 Chicago	N.L.	2	11	0	1	.000	8	5	14	5.73	0

a On disabled list from May 10 to June 7, 2002.

ZITO, BARRY WILLIAM

Born, Las Vegas, Nevada, May 13, 1978.
Bats Left. Throws Left. Height, 6 feet, 4 inches. Weight, 210 pounds.

Year Club	Lea	G	IP	W	L	Pct	SO	BB	H	ERA	SAVES
1999 Vancouver	P.C.	1	6	1	0	1.000	6	2	5	1.50	0
1999 Midland	Texas	4	22	2	1	.667	29	11	22	4.91	0
1999 Visalia	California	8	40¹/₃	3	0	1.000	62	22	21	2.45	0
2000 Sacramento	P.C.	18	101²/₃	8	5	.615	91	45	88	3.19	0
2000 Oakland	A.L.	14	92²/₃	7	4	.636	78	45	64	2.72	0
2001 Oakland	A.L.	35	214¹/₃	17	8	.680	205	80	184	3.49	0
2002 Oakland a	A.L.	35	229¹/₃	*23	5	.821	182	78	182	2.75	0
2003 Oakland	A.L.	35	231²/₃	14	12	.538	146	88	186	3.30	0
2004 Oakland	A.L.	34	213	11	11	.500	163	81	216	4.48	0
2005 Oakland	A.L.	35	228¹/₃	14	13	.519	171	89	185	3.86	0
2006 Oakland b	A.L.	34	221	16	10	.615	151	99	211	3.83	0
2007 San Francisco	N.L.	34	196²/₃	11	13	.458	131	83	182	4.53	0
Major League Totals ....8 Yrs.		256	1627	113	76	.598	1227	643	1410	3.67	0
Division Series											
2000 Oakland	A.L.	1	5²/₃	1	0	1.000	5	2	7	1.59	0
2001 Oakland	A.L.	1	8	0	1	.000	6	1	2	1.13	0
2002 Oakland	A.L.	1	6	1	0	1.000	8	4	5	4.50	0
2003 Oakland	A.L.	2	13	1	1	.500	13	4	9	3.46	0
2006 Oakland	A.L.	1	8	1	0	1.000	1	3	4	1.13	0
Division Series Totals		6	40²/₃	4	2	.667	33	14	27	2.43	0

Year	Club		Lea	G	IP	W	L	Pct	SO	BB	H	ERA	SAVES
Championship Series													
2006 Oakland	. . . .		A.L.	1	3²/₃	0	1	.000	0	3	7	12.27	0

a Selected Cy Young Award Winner in American League for 2002.

b Filed for free agency, October 31, 2006. Signed with San Francisco Giants, December 29, 2006.

ZUMAYA, JOEL MARTIN
Born, Chula Vista, California, November 9, 1984.
Bats Right. Throws Right. Height, 6 feet, 3 inches. Weight, 210 pounds.

Year	Club	Lea	G	IP	W	L	Pct	SO	BB	H	ERA	SAVES
2002 Tigers	. . . .	Gulf Coast	9	37¹/₃	2	1	.667	46	11	21	1.93	0
2003 West Michigan	. . . . . .	Midwest	19	90¹/₃	7	5	.583	126	38	69	2.79	0
2004 Erie	. . . .	Eastern	4	20	2	2	.500	29	10	19	6.30	0
2004 Lakeland	. . . .	Fla.St.	16	94	6	4	.600	92	43	65	3.54	0
2005 Erie	. . . .	Eastern	18	107¹/₃	8	3	.727	143	52	71	2.77	0
2005 Toledo	. . . .	Int.	8	44	1	2	.333	56	24	30	2.66	0
2006 Detroit	. . . .	A.L.	62	83¹/₃	6	3	.667	97	42	56	1.94	1
2007 Toledo	. . . .	Int.	3	2²/₃	0	0	.000	2	2	3	6.75	0
2007 Detroit a	. . . .	A.L.	28	33²/₃	2	3	.400	27	17	23	4.28	1
Major League Totals	. . . .	2 Yrs.	90	117	8	6	.571	124	59	79	2.62	2
Division Series												
2006 Detroit	. . . .	A.L.	2	2	0	0	.000	3	0	0	0.00	0
Championship Series												
2006 Detroit	. . . .	A.L.	1	1	0	0	.000	0	0	1	9.00	0
World Series Record												
2006 Detroit	. . . .	A.L.	3	3	0	1	.000	3	3	1	3.00	0

a On disabled list from May 3 to August 21, 2007.

COLLECTOR'S EDITIONS AVAILABLE

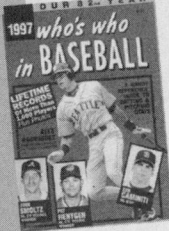